T0183094

Lecture Notes in Computer Science 9257

Commenced Publication in 1973
Founding and Former Series Editors:
Gerhard Goos, Juris Hartmanis, and Jan van Leeuwen

Editorial Board

More information about this series at http://www.springer.com/series/7412

George Azzopardi · Nicolai Petkov (Eds.)

Computer Analysis of Images and Patterns

16th International Conference, CAIP 2015
Valletta, Malta, September 2–4, 2015
Proceedings, Part II

 Springer

Editors
George Azzopardi
University of Malta
Msida
Malta

Nicolai Petkov
University of Groningen
Groningen
The Netherlands

ISSN 0302-9743 ISSN 1611-3349 (electronic)
Lecture Notes in Computer Science
ISBN 978-3-319-23116-7 ISBN 978-3-319-23117-4 (eBook)
DOI 10.1007/978-3-319-23117-4

Library of Congress Control Number: 2015946746

LNCS Sublibrary: SL6 – Image Processing, Computer Vision, Pattern Recognition, and Graphics

Springer Cham Heidelberg New York Dordrecht London

Springer International Publishing AG Switzerland is part of Springer Science+Business Media
(www.springer.com)

Preface

This book constitutes one part of the two-part volume of proceedings of the 16th International Conference on Computer Analysis of Images and Patterns, CAIP 2015, held in Valletta, Malta, during September 2–4, 2015.

CAIP is a series of biennial international conferences devoted to all aspects of computer vision, image analysis and processing, pattern recognition and related fields. Previous conferences were held in York, Seville, Münster, Vienna, Paris, Groningen, Warsaw, Ljubljana, Kiel, Prague, Budapest, Dresden, Leipzig, Wismar, and Berlin.

CAIP 2015 featured three plenary lectures by the invited speakers Patrizio Campisi from the Università degli Studi Roma Tre, Bart ter Haar Romenij from the Eindhoven University of Technology, and Mario Vento from the University of Salerno. CAIP 2015 aimed to extend the scope of the series by allowing also submissions in pattern recognition of non-image data, machine learning and brain-inspired computing. Each submission was reviewed by at least three members of the international Program Committee and only high-quality papers were selected for inclusion in these proceedings.

We thank the Steering Committee of CAIP for giving us the honor of organizing this reputable conference in Malta. We also thank the Maltese Ministry of Finance, the Malta Council for Science and Technology, the Malta Tourism Authority, Springer, and the Jülich Supercomputing Center for sponsorships. Last but not least, we thank Charles Theuma, principal of Saint Martin's Institute of Higher Education (Malta), for coordinating the local arrangements.

September 2015

George Azzopardi
Nicolai Petkov

Organization

Program Committee

Enrique Alegre	University of Leon, Spain
Muhammad Raza Ali	Vision Research Division, InfoTech, Rawalpindi, Pakistan
Furqan Aziz	Institute of Management Sciences, Pakistan
George Azzopardi	University of Malta, Malta
Andrew Bagdanov	Computer Vision Center, Barcelona, Spain
Donald Bailey	Massey University, New Zealand
Antonio Bandera	University of Malaga, Spain
Ardhendu Behera	Edge Hill University, UK
Gyan Bhanot	Rutgers University, USA
Michael Biehl	University of Groningen, The Netherlands
Adrian Bors	University of York, UK
Henri Bouma	TNO, The Netherlands
Kerstin Bunte	University of Birmingham, UK
Ceyhun Burak Akgül	Boğaziçi University, Turkey
Kenneth Camilleri	University of Malta, Malta
Patrizio Campisi	University of Rome Tre, Italy
Mateu Sbert Casasayas	University of Girona, Spain
Andrea Cerri	University of Bologna, Italy
Kwok-Ping Chan	The University of Hong Kong, Hong Kong, SAR China
Rama Chellappa	University of Maryland, USA
Dmitry Chetverikov	Hungarian Academy of Sciences, Hungary
Marco Cristani	Università degli Studi di Verona, Italy
Gabriel Cristobal	Instituto de Optica (CSIC), Spain
Guillaume Damiand	LIRIS/Université de Lyon, France
Carl James Debono	University of Malta, Malta
Joachim Denzler	University of Jena, Germany
Mariella Dimiccoli	Universitat Politècnica de Catalunya, Spain
Junyu Dong	Ocean University of China, China
Pieter Eendebak	TNO, The Netherlands
Hakan Erdogan	Sabanci University, Turkey
Francisco Escolano	University of Alicante, Spain
Taner Eskil	IŞIK University, Turkey
Alexandre Falcao	University of Campinas, Brazil
Giovanni Maria Farinella	University of Catania, Italy
Reuben Farrugia	University of Malta, Malta
Gernot Fink	Dortmund University of Technology, Germany

Patrizio Frosini	University of Bologna, Italy
Laurent Fuchs	Université de Poitiers, France
Edel García	Advanced Technologies Applications Center (CENATAV), Cuba
Eduardo Garea	Advanced Technologies Applications Center (CENATAV), Cuba
Daniela Giorgi	ISTI-CNR, Pisa, Italy
Javier Gonzalez	University of Malaga, Spain
Rocio Gonzalez-Diaz	University of Seville, Spain
Cosmin Grigorescu	European Patent Office, The Netherlands
Miguel Gutiérrez-Naranjo	University of Seville, Spain
Michal Haindl	Institute of Information Theory and Automation, Czech Republic
Edwin Hancock	University of York, UK
Yo-Ping Huang	National Taipei University of Technology, Taiwan
Atsushi Imiya	IMIT Chiba University, Japan
Xiaoyi Jiang	Universität Münster, Germany
Maria-Jose Jimenez	University of Seville, Spain
Martin Kampel	Vienna University of Technology, Austria
Vivek Kaul	Facebook, USA
Nahum Kiryati	Tel Aviv University, Israel
Reinhard Klette	Auckland University of Technology, New Zealand
Gisela Klette	Auckland University of Technology, New Zealand
Andreas Koschan	University of Tennessee Knoxville, USA
Walter Kropatsch	Vienna University of Technology, Austria
Pascal Lienhardt	Université de Poitiers, France
Guo-Shiang Lin	Da-Yeh University, Taiwan
Agnieszka Lisowska	University of Silesia, Poland
Josep Llados	Computer Vision Center, Universitat Autonoma de Barcelona, Spain
Rebeca Marfil	University of Malaga, Spain
Manuel Marin	Universidad de Córdoba, Spain
Thomas Martinetz	University of Lübeck, Germany
Phayung Meesad	King Mongkuts University of Technology North Bangkok, Thailand
Heydi Mendez	Advanced Technologies Applications Center (CENATAV), Cuba
Eckart Michaelsen	Fraunhofer IOSB, Germany
Mariofanna Milanova	University of Arkansas at Little Rock, USA
Majid Mirmehdi	University of Bristol, UK
Matthew Montebello	University of Malta, Malta
Rafael Muñoz Salinas	University of Córdoba, Spain
Adrian Muscat	University of Malta, Malta
Radu Nicolescu	Auckland University of Technology, New Zealand
Mark Nixon	University of Southampton, UK

Laurens van der Maaten	Delft University of Technology, The Netherlands
Mario Vento	University of Salerno, Italy
Thomas Villman	University of Applied Sciences Mittweida, Germany
Michael Wilkinson	University of Groningen, The Netherlands
Richard Wilson	University of York, UK
David Windridge	University of Surrey, UK
Christian Wolf	Université de Lyon, France
Xianghua Xie	Swansea University, UK
Wei Qi Yan	Auckland University of Technology, New Zealand
Hongbin Zha	Peking University, China
Zhao Zhang	Soochow University, China

Local Organizing Committee

Charles Theuma	Saint Martin's Institute of Higher Education, Malta

Steering Committee

Edwin Hancock	University of York, UK
Reinhard Klette	Auckland University of Technology, New Zealand
Xiaoyi Jiang	Universität Münster, Germany
Nicolai Petkov	University of Groningen, The Netherlands
George Azzopardi	University of Malta, Malta

Contents – Part II

Contents – Part I

Texture and Mathematical Morphology for Hot-Spot Detection in Whole Slide Images of Meningiomas and Oligodendrogliomas

Zaneta Swiderska[1(✉)], Tomasz Markiewicz[1,2], Bartlomiej Grala[2], and Wojciech Kozlowski[2]

[1] Warsaw University of Technology, 1 Politechniki Sq., 00-661 Warsaw, Poland
Zaneta.Swiderska@gmail.com, markiewt@iem.pw.edu.pl
[2] Military Institute of Medicine, 128 Szaserow Str., 04-141 Warsaw, Poland
{bgrala,wkozlowski}@wim.mil.pl

Abstract. The paper presents a combined method for an automatic hot-spot areas selection in the whole slide images to support the pathomorphological diagnostic procedure. The studied slides represent the meningiomas and oligodendrogliomas tumour stained with the Ki-67/MIB-1 immunohistochemical reaction. The presented method based on mathematical morphology and texture analysis helps to determine the tumour proliferation index complementing medical information for prognosis and treatment. The major functions of the algorithm include detection of immunopositive cells in the tumour area and the identification and elimination of hemorrhages areas from the specimen map. The results of the numerical experiments confirm high efficiency of the proposed solutions.

Keywords: Image processing · Mathematical morphology · Texture

1 Introduction

Histopathological examination of tissues using immunostaining tests is a basic method of identifying tumours. It often serves as a tool supporting the choice of optimal therapy and defines the prognostic indicators. Tumour proliferation in central nervous system tumours can be characterised with the widely used Ki-67/MIB-1 marker. The immunopositive (proliferated) cell nuclei are marked with brown whereas ther cell nuclei are marked with blue, and their raitio gives the proliferation index. In meningiomas and oligodendrogliomas (the most frequent primary intracranial tumours) this index is used for classification of tumours into meningothelial (WHO I), atypical (WHO II), anaplastic (WHO III), and oligodendrogliomas (WHO II and III), and to it correlates with tumour recurrences. Thus, the automatic quantitative evaluation of the specimen can offers a very useful tool for the pathologists.

The several solutions to this problem have been proposed in literature [1,4,9]. Most approaches are based on the quantitative evaluation of the percentage of

G. Azzopardi and N. Petkov (Eds.): CAIP 2015, Part II, LNCS 9257, pp. 1–12, 2015.
DOI: 10.1007/978-3-319-23117-4_1

immunopositive cells in the areas of greatest tumour proliferation. The areas with a high immunopositive reactions are called hot-spots. In the paper [8] is proposed a method for the increasing of visibility of the positive nuclei at low resolution image in manual examination. In [7] the author presented the automated selection method of hot spots algorithm. This method is based on adaptive step finding techniques for the increasing the computational efficiency and performance of hot spot detection. A problem of the spatial distribution of the selected hot spot fields was not taken into account in this paper. To the best of our knowledge, algorithm containing hotspot selection and problem of the hot spot spatial distribution, for whole slide image, not yet been presented in the literature. For objective evaluation, some scattering of selected fields is also recommended. For example, one of the schemes is the choice of fields of view of the highest levels of Ki-67 and then choosing several adjacent regions with positive reaction in short distance from this field, followed by the search for other areas of specimen. The major problem in the tested formulations are hemorrhages, which are stained with brown creating false-positive results. This paper presents a computational method for improved identification of tumour proliferation and areas of hemorrhages.

A lot of algorithms for medical image processing are based on mathematical morphology and texture analysis. In many cases these methods are successfully used to analyze single microscopic images. Recently, texture analysis and classification have been applied to processing and context analysis of large images covering the whole specimen [2,11]. The whole histological specimen acquired on a microscopic glass scanner is called a whole slide image (WSI). The size of this slide is usually very large (for example 100000×80000 pixels). The contextual analysis of such images requires matching the image resolution to the task and also developing new methods of image analysis and classification.

The example part of WSI of tumour, blood and background stained with Ki-67 is presented in Fig. 1. To perform the proper quantitative evaluation of the proliferative Ki-67 index, a hot-spot regions must be identified. One of them is outlined in Fig. 1 as a part of tumour with increased Ki-67 proliferation index, compared to such index for the neighbourhood tumour area. Normally WSI may include a lot of hot-spot regions. However, in the specimen exist also the dense brown areas indicated by the arrows. There are the touching blood neutrophils. So, correct classification of tumour and hemorrhages areas allow to accurate identification of hot-spot areas and may help improve sample analysis.

In spite of some progress in this field there is still a need for an extensive study aimed at supporting clinical decisions [6]. In this work we propose a new method for an identification of the hot-spot areas in brain tumour images. The textural and classification methods are applied to differentiate the tumour areas against the hemorrhage areas. At the same time we apply the mathematical morphology based analysis to estimate the number of immunopositive cells. Also, we introduce a penalty criterion for the selection of the hot-spot areas. The quantification results of an automatic selection of tumour proliferation is compared with standard visual selection performed by the expert.

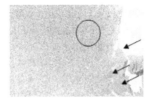

Fig. 1. An example of a part of the whole slide image representing the brain tumour with the outlined hot-spot area. The hemorrhages are marked by the arrows.

2   Material and Methods

Fifteen cases of meningiomas and oligodendrogliomas subject to Ki-67/MIB-1 immunohistochemical staining were obtained from the archives of Department of Pathomorphology from the Military Institute of Medicine in Warsaw, Poland. Acquisition of WSI was performed on the Aperio ScanScope scanner. The images were acquired under magnification 400x with a resolution 0.279 μm per pixels. Due to a very large size of images in the contextual analysis of the specimen it was necessary to reduce the resolution to enable direct examination and visualisation. We have chosen eight-fold reduction of the resolution to enable the evaluation performed both manually and by a computer.

The proposed scheme of the image processing is organized in the following stages: a) defining a map of specimen, b) elimination of the areas containing blood cells (hemorrhages), c) selection of sequential fields of the hot-spots based on stained cells segmentation. This stage requires defining the punishment function preventing from identifying hot-spot areas located in close proximity.

The map of specimen is produced by using the thresholding procedure and morphological filtering [12]. The differentiation of the tumour with hemorrhage areas is solved using the texture analysis [14] and classification. The key step of the identification of the high immunopositive cell concentration (hot-spots) is implemented in two different ways. One of them is based on the colour representation, whilst the second on the mathematical morphology operations. The final analysis of Ki-67 index in manually and automatically selected hot-spot areas is performed on the full resolution images. The proposed computational approach is validated by the quantitative comparison of both methods.

2.1   Detection of Specimen Map

The first stage of image processing is to define a map of specimen, and possible view field localizations, encompassing the complete tumour. To start with, an image produced by the morphological operation of opening is subjected to brightness equalization. It is performed using a structuring element shaped as a disc with a large beam (100 pixels). The operation expressed in the form [12]

$$f = f / \Theta_{SE}^{f} \tag{1}$$

is performed independently for every RGB colour components. Afterwards, differencing image B and R components is processed with Otsu thresholding method. Developed algorithm is based on advantage in the brown color component (negative values in the differencing image are set to zero). Morphological operations such as: erosion, dilatation, fill holes are conducted on the resulting image. Small areas are eliminated from final specimen map in order to remove the unnecessary part of image. This reduces the number of operations and shorten the time of image processing.

2.2   Texture Analysis and Classification for Hemorrhage Exclusion

The next step of image processing is detecting the areas with hemorrhage and then excluding them from the quantitative analysis. This is an important task because the proliferative Ki-67 index can be significantly overestimated if the hemorrhage areas are processed like hot-spot areas. Thus, the whole tissue structures must be analysed using the description of a texture in the local fields.

Our approach to texture analysis is based on the normalized probability applied to the pixel intensity of the image. In defining texture descriptors we apply the histograms of the sum (s) and difference (d) of images [13,14], where N_Ω is count of pixels in the analyzed neighborhood area for selected texture descriptor, and μ_Ω is mean intensity of the neighborhood. These images are formed from the original image by applying the relative translation (it is the sum or difference of the original image and his translation of 3 pixels in the horizontal axis). We use the modified formulas of Unser features [13] to a local definition, which can be expressed in the following form for e.g. homogeneity (sixth feature):

$$f_6 = \sum_{\mathbf{x} \in \Omega} \frac{1}{1+d(\mathbf{x})^2} / N_\Omega \tag{2}$$

An important step is to determine the image resolution and radius resulting in the best characterization of the local structures in specimens. Also, the resolution of the objects should enable to represent nuclei of the tumour cells by at least a few pixels. Too small radius causes a little ambient impact on the properties for a given pixel and a strong heterogeneity. On the other side, too large radius causes excessive generalization. We decided to use Unser method due to their easy implementation in the Matlab environment. In the future research we want try to use different methods of quantifying texture.

Another challenge is the choice of colour components for best differentiation between tumour and hemorrhage. An original colour representation of the analyzed images is the RGB. However, as a result of the immunohistochemical reaction, one may observe the occurrence of the chromogen not only in immunopositive cells, but also of changeable quantity in blood cells. This may lead to similar values in the RGB components. Also, we aim to establish the texture description of the tumour areas uniformly, irrespective of the percentage of immunopositive cells. Using RGB components we observed a significant variability in values of texture characteristics. So, it is desirable to propose such an image colour representation in which the used descriptors will be independent

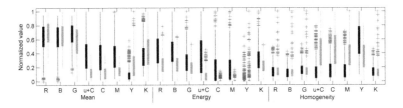

Fig. 2. The box-and-wiskers plot for areas of tumour (left black boxes) and hemorrhages (right grey boxes), for colour componments and three features: mean, energy, and homogeneity.

on percentage of the immunopositive cells. At the same time they should allow for differentiation of the blood from the tumour areas. We achieved an image colour representation, independent on percentage of the immunopositive cells by introducing the additional colour representation in the form of a sum of u (from CIE Luv colour space) multiplied by 512 and C (CMYK colour space) components. The defined textures were determined for each of the components in the RGB, CMYK colour spaces, and for the combined u and C representation. The latter representation unifies the image description in the areas of tumour, and at the same time assumes lower values in the areas of blood. The box-and-wiskers plot presented in the Fig. 2 contains the comparison of feature ranges for areas of tumour (left black boxes) with for hemorrhages (right grey boxes), for colour componments and three features: mean, energy, and homogeneity. It can be observed that the proposed u and C representation has not worse or better ability to differentiate the studied areas of tissue that the other (single) colour components. In this way we have determined 64 features as descriptors of the defined patterns. To assess the suitability of individual features in the differentiation of tumour and hemorrhage, the Fishers linear discriminant for the feature f assessment was applied [3]. It is defined for recognition of two classes as follows

$$F_{12}(f) = \left| \frac{\mu_1 - \mu_2}{\sigma_1 + \sigma_2} \right| \tag{3}$$

where μ_1, μ_2 are the average values and σ_1, σ_2 are the standard deviations of the feature f, for the first and second class, respectively. The features of high values of Fisher measure represent good input attributes for the classifier. To classify the data into the tumour area and hemorrhage, the Support Vector Machine (SVM) with Gaussian kernel function was selected. The primary advantage of this classifier is its good generalization ability resulting from the maximizing the separation margin between classes during learning.

2.3 Recognition and Counting Immunopositive Cells for Hot-Spot Localization

The accurate detection of immunopositive cells within the tumour area is a key step in the algorithm of hot-spot area localization. These fields correspond to areas with dense immunopositive reactions, so it is important to distinguish between immunopositive and immunonegative cells. We assume the higher concentration of immunopositive cells is directly related to the higher value of Ki-67 index.

The first approach presented in this peper is based on thresholding of differential image of B and G colour components. In order to obtain the most adequate map of immunopositive cell nuclei, values of G component were multiplied by 0.85 factor before subtracting both components. Through this operation, only the brownish areas of the image receive value greater than zero. The resulting image is multiplied by the previously obtained specimen mask. The next step is to threshold this image using the threshold value obtained by the Otsu method [10]. The purpose is to remove the components other than immunopositive cells, for example areas representing the colouration of stromal.

The second method is based on the evaluation of the spatial relation of the stained brown objects to their neighboring environment. It is carried out by morphological operations performed on the component u of CIE Luv representation of colours after image transformation. This component is strictly associated with the red colour and it is the best for differentiating the immunopositive cells from the remaining part of the image. In order to detect objects with pixel intensity standing out significantly from the environmental components, the extended regional minima transformation was applied. The regional minima connecting pixels with a constant intensity value and whose external boundary pixels have a higher value, are detected. The key parameter of the extended regional minima transformation is the choice of h value, representing the criterion for the minimum difference between the intensity of the point in a local minimum and its close environment. This value was determined in an experimental way and was set on the level of 45. It should be noted that this method is more independent of colour intensity of immunohistochemical staining. Finally, for the isolated areas representing the tumour cells, a binary mask locating the centers of tumour cells/areas is created. The final image map contains the spatial distribution of centers representing the immunopositive tumour cells.

2.4   Localization of Hot-Spot Areas

The localization of areas representing hot-spots is based on finding the local maxima with the highest density of immunopositive cell nuclei. The image of density distribution can be obtained, inter alia, by counting the number of objects in each window (field of view) or by averaging the filtration performed on the binary mask. In practice, it may happen that only one area of considerable dominance proliferative Ki-67 index occurs within the analyzed specimen. In such case an automatic quantitative analysis can lead to the selection of the hot-spot areas only in this particular region. However, one of the guidelines for quantitative assessment of tumour scan is to identify the fields for the analysis within multiple areas of tumour proliferation. In order to force the selection of the hot-spots in the entire scanned image, the penalty function is proposed and applied. It associates the distance between the designated areas and position of another candidate for hot-spot. Now, the positions of the hot-spots depend on the value of the local maxima and their localization in the scan. This operation is realized by the multiplication of the received mask of specimen by the mask of distances. The penalty term for the candidate centre placed in (x,y) position takes the value defined by the following formula

$$penalty = 1 - \rho \sum \frac{1}{\sqrt[4]{(x-x_i)^2+(y-y_i)^2}} \qquad (4)$$

in which x_i, y_i represent the coordinates of the neighbouring (existing) centres. The value of ρ was chosen experimentally and equals 0.2. The increase of ρ value results in enforcing greater scattering of the designated areas. In the case where one hot-spot area is dominating, the penalty term allows to determine the hot-spot positions in different localizations of the tumour. As a result, the algorithm determines a set of hot-spot localizations representing high immunopositive reaction in diverse locations. The final analysis of Ki-67 index in these selections is performed on full resolution images with the help of the algorithm described in[5].

In order to compare and verify the proposed procedure of an automatic selection of hot-spot fields, we introduce the procedure marking the area of tumour proliferation. To identify the areas of tumour proliferation, the regional maxima were extended by neighborhood areas only if these areas meet the following criterion:

$$\eta \geq \alpha \eta_{max} \qquad (5)$$

where η_{max} is the local maxima of Ki-67 index, and α is the scaling coefficient determined experimentally and equal 0.7 in our experiments. Reduction of α value results in an increase of the neighbourhood areas connected to the maxima. This analysis allows determining to what extent the manually and automatically selected hot-spot fields represent different regions of tumour proliferation in the specimen.

3 Results

Fifteen cases of meningiomas and oligodendrogliomas were subject to a quantitative analysis. Using the presented algorithm we determined ten hot-spot fields in each scan and made their diagnostic evaluation by the quantitative analysis. The aim of this quantitative analysis was to determine the number of immunopositive and immunonegative cells, and then to determine the percentage of the immunopositive cells for each of the areas (Ki-67 index).

In the first step of a WSI processing, a specimen map is determined. The exemplary result is presented in Fig. 3 with three well outlined tissue scraps. Next, a texture description was calculated for each specimen pixel and its surroundings. The applied radius of the neighborhood region Ω was 12 pixels in the learning process and 11 pixels for the testing purposes (these values gave the best results in the classification step). The number of features forming the input vector to the classifier was reduced to 25, each corresponding to Fisher discriminant value higher than 0.5. There were 4 features from RGB space, 15 from CMYK and 6 from combined u and C space. The most of the chosen features represented the energy, homogeneity and contrast. In learning SVM classifier we have chosen the regularization coefficient C=150 and sigma of Gaussian kernel function equal 4.5. Data used for the learning process were selected by the expert from different images. It was 18 areas representing hemorrhages, and 32 areas representing cells (areas with tumour and areas with normal cells). For each of area, 20 locations of Ω were randomly selected . This gives a collection of 1080 learning data. Data used to the test process originated from different formulations.

a)   b)

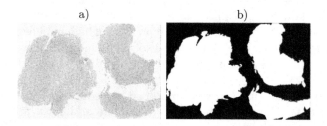

Fig. 3. Specimen area identification in the whole slide image for unprocessed sample (a) and as a binary mask (b).

The aim of the classification process is to determine if the pixel belongs to the normal tissue structure, or to the area with hemorrhages. In this way we obtain a map of areas containing hemorrhages. An example is presented in Fig. 4 with identified specimen map and hemorrhages (Fig. 4b and c). Imposing the maps of hemorrhage and specimen results in the map of specimen area that can be quantitatively analysed.

In the following step, the tumour proliferation areas were identified in WSI by applying the thresholding (algorithm I) or extended regional minima (algorithm II) approaches. Both methods were associated with the region growing for demonstrate which areas are focus of interest (Fig. 5). Significant differences of the results there are visible. Nevertheless, all selected regions are located in

a)   b)   c)

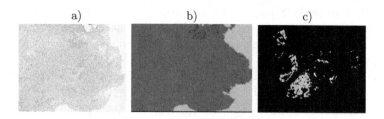

Fig. 4. Hemorrhage area detection in original image (a) marked on dark grey on light grey specimen map (b) and focused on the detected hemorrhage(c).

a)   b)

Fig. 5. Identification of the proliferation areas based on the algorithm I (a) and algorithm II (b).

the higher proliteration areas of the specimens. The detailed quantitative analysis better explain the significance of these selections on the assessment of the analyzed material.

Finally, the selection of 10 hot-spot fields of view was performed. In order to assess the variability and reproducibility of the obtained results, we asked an independent expert, to perform twice the manual selection of the hot-spot areas for each of the preparations (Series I and Series II) within an interval of 6 months. Figure 6 shows the virtual slide with 10 hot-spots marked by an expert in Series I (marked as ∗), 10 hot-spot areas in Series II (marked as □), 10 hot-spot areas identified by the algorithm I (marked as ○) and 10 hot-spot areas designated by the algorithm II (marked as △).

Although there are some differences in locations in each pair of selections, most of them are in the same areas of specimen. In the next step the values of Ki-67 index were calculated in the areas designated by the program, and then compared with the average values of two results given by an expert. The recognition and cell counting was carried out at the resolution of selected areas, compatible with that used in the algorithm presented in the paper [5]. The quantitative results served

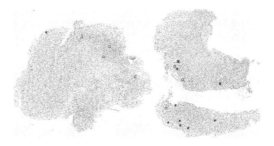

Fig. 6. Virtual slide with the hot-spot areas marked by an expert (Series I-∗, Series II-□) and the hot-spots designated by the algorithm I (○) and algorithm II (△).

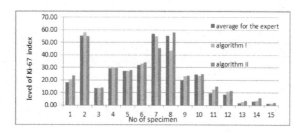

Fig. 7. The comparative results of analysis of 15 specimens for which areas of interest were determined by the medical expert and by the developed algorithms.

to assess the effectiveness of the hot-spot localizations made by our automatic system. Quantitative analysis also showed the differences in the numerical results of image analysis between two implemented algorithms.

Figure 7 presents the comparison of the average values of the Ki-67 index for the fields of view selected by an expert (the mean values for Series I and Series II) and by the developed algorithms I and II. The comparison was done for fifteen WSI. In three specimens, it was necessary to manually remove some fields selected by developed algorithms due to artifacts (specimen damage). The detailed results are included in Table 1. We have observed that:

Table 1. The quantitative analysis of Ki-67 index in the designated fields of view for the hot-spot areas selected by the expert (average for series I and II), and by the developed algorithms (algorithm I and algorithm II).

Case	Expert			Automatic	
	Series I	Series II	Average	Algorithm I	Algorithm II
1	18.39	17.69	18.04	20.45	23.64
2	56.11	54.54	55.32	57.96	55.03
3	13.61	13.43	13.52	13.58	14.07
4	28.47	30.30	29.39	29.56	29.67
5	27.28	26.91	27.10	27.23	27.99
6	29.41	34.31	31.86	33.13	34.02
7	54.71	59.35	57.03	55.03	45.39
8	60.12	50.48	55.30	43.60	58.18
9	21.11	19.40	20.26	23.21	23.64
10	24.63	24.06	24.35	23.51	24.71
11	9.82	9.43	9.62	12.64	14.88
12	8.28	9.05	8.66	10.96	11.73
13	1.72	1.75	1.74	2.73	3.83
14	2.95	3.06	3.01	3.68	5.85
15	1.61	1.39	1.50	1.63	2.19
Mean:			23.78	23.93	24.99

- in fourteen cases the values of the Ki-67 index for the fields determined automatically by algorithm I were comparable (the maximum difference was less than 3%) with the expert results,
- in one case the automatic result of algorithm I was 11.7% lower than the expert results,
- in ten cases the values of the Ki-67 index for the fields determined automatically by algorithm II were comparable (the maximum difference was less than 3%) with the expert results,
- in four cases the automatic results of algorithm II were 3-6% higher than the expert results,
- in one case the automatic result of algorithm II was 11.6% lower than the expert results.

There are some differences between the average values of Ki-67 index for the areas selected by expert (two series) and by the developed algorithms I and II. The algorithm I appears to give results closer to expert opinion, compared to algorithm II. However, the algorithm II can more accurately recognize the hot-spot areas with the higher Ki-67 index. The Wilcoxon matched pairs test confirms that no significant differences exist between the mean of experts results and Algorithm I (Z=1.7, p=0.088), but there is a significant difference when compared with Algorithm II (Z=2.44, p=0.014). Also, it should be noted that in the case of the analysis of low reaction specimens, fields selected by developed algorithms had similar or higher reaction than the reaction in fields selected by the expert. It is clear that in the low reaction specimen, finding hot-spot areas manually is much more difficult compared to the high reaction cases. Our results confirm the advantage of automatic evaluation over the manual assessment.

4 Conclusions

We have presented the effective method for an automatic localization of the hot-spot areas in meningioma and oligodendrogliomas tumours. Two different approaches have been suggested. The algorithm II has shown the advantage over the algorithm I in accurate detection of hot-spot areas in the presence of staining artifacts. The use of maps of specimen and the elimination of hemorrhage areas have reduced the size of an image under analysis and also the computational time. The presented methods have good reproducibility (characterized by the repeatability of results) which gives them an advantage over the traditional, manual way of identification of hot-spot areas in meningioma and oligodendrogliomas. Future research will be include: study different methods of quantifying texture, determine dependence between penalty factor and localization of hot spot areas; detection and elimination artefacts on slide.

Acknowledgements. This work has been supported by the National Centre for Research and Development (PBS2/A9/21/2013 grant), Poland.

References

1. Colman, H., Giannini, C., Huang, L., Gonzalez, J., Hess, K., Bruner, J., Fuller, G., Langford, L., Pelloski, C., Aaron, J., Burger, P., Aldape, K.: Assessment and prognostic significance of mitotic index using the mitosis marker phospho-histone h3 in low and intermediate-grade infiltrating astrocytomas. Am. J. Surg. Pathol. **30**(5), 657–664 (2006)
2. Cruz-Roa, A., Gonzalez, F., Galaro, J., Judkins, A., Ellison, D., Baccon, J., Madabhushi, A., Romero, E.: A visual latent semantic approach for automatic analysis and interpretation of anaplastic medulloblastoma virtual slides. Med. Image Comput. Comput. Assist. Interv. **15**(Pt 1), 157–164 (2012)
3. Duda, R., Hart, P., Stork, P.: Pattern classification and scene analysis. Wiley, New York (2003)
4. Gavrielides, M.A., Conway, C., OFlaherty, N., Gallas, B.D., Hewitt, S.M.: Observer performance in the use of digital and optical microscopy for the interpretation of tissue-based biomarkers. Anal. Cell. Pathol. **2014**, ID 157308 (2014)
5. Grala, B., Markiewicz, T., Kozlowski, W., Osowski, S., Slodkowska, J., Papierz, W.: New automated image analysis method for the assessment of ki-67 labeling index in meningiomas. Folia Histo. Cyto. **47**(4), 587–592 (2009)
6. Kothari, S., Phan, J., Stokes, T., Wang, M.: Pathology imaging informatics for quan-titative analysis of whole-slide images. J. Am. Med. Inform. Assoc. **20**(6), 1099–1108 (2013)
7. Lu, H., Papathomas, T.G., van Zessen, D., Palli, I., de Krijger, R.R., van der Spek, P.J., Dinjens, W.N.M., Stubbs, A.P.: Automated selection of hotspots (ash): enhanced automated segmentation and adaptive step finding for ki67 hotspot detection in adrenal cortical cancer. Diagn. Pathol. **9**, 216 (2014)
8. Molin, J., Devan, K.S., Wardell, K., Lundstrom, C.: Feature-enhancing zoom to facilitate ki-67 hot spot detection. In: Proc. SPIE 9041, Medical Imaging 2014: Digital Pathology, San Diego, USA, February 15, 2014 (2014)
9. Nakasu, S., Li, D.H., Okabe, H., Nakajima, M., Matsuda, M.: Significance of mib-1 staining indices in meningiomas. comparison of two counting methods. Am. J. Surg. Pathol. **25**(4), 472–478 (2001)
10. Otsu, N.: A threshold selection method from gray-level histograms. IEEE Trans. Sys. Man. Cyber. **9**(1), 62–66 (1979)
11. Roullier, V., Lezoray, O., Ta, V., Elmoataz, A.: A visual latent semantic approach for automatic analysis and interpretation of anaplastic medulloblastoma virtual slides. Comput. Med. Imaging Graph. **35**(7–8), 603–615 (2011)
12. Soille, P.: Morphological Image Analysis, Principles and Applications, 2nd edn. Springer, Berlin (2003)
13. Unser, M.: Sum and difference histograms for texture classification. IEEE Trans. Pattern Anal. Mach. Intell. **8**(1), 118–125 (2013)
14. Wagner, P.: Texture analysis. In: Jahne, B., Haussecker, H., Geissler, P. (Eds.) Handbook of Computer Vision and Applications, vol. 2, chapter 12. Academic Press, San Diego (1999)

Scale Estimation in Multiple Models Fitting via Consensus Clustering

Luca Magri[1]([✉]) and Andrea Fusiello[2]([✉])

[1] Department of Mathematics, University of Milan,
Via Saldini, 50, 20133 Milan, Italy
luca.magri@unimi.it
[2] DIEGM, University of Udine, Via Delle Scienze, 208,
33100 Udine, Italy
andrea.fusiello@unimi.it

Abstract. This paper presents a new procedure for fitting multiple geometric structures without having a priori knowledge of scale. Our method leverages on Consensus Clustering, a single-term model selection strategy relying on the principle of stability, thereby avoiding the explicit tradeoff between data fidelity (i.e., modeling error) and model complexity. In particular we tailored this model selection to the estimate of the inlier threshold of T-linkage, a fitting algorithm based on random sampling and preference analysis. A potential clustering is evaluated based on a consensus measure. The crucial inlier scale ϵ is estimated using an interval search. Experiments on synthetic and real data show that this method succeeds in finding the correct scale.

Keywords: Multi-model fitting · Segmentation · Scale estimation

1 Introduction

An ubiquitous issue in Pattern Recognition is the robust fitting of geometric structures to noisy data corrupted by outliers. This task becomes demanding when the data have arisen from multiple instances of the same structure, since it is necessary to cope with the so called *pseudo*-outlier (i.e. "outliers to the structure of interest but inliers to a different structure" [15]) straining robust estimation. If in addition the number of structures is not known in advance the problem of multiple fitting turns into a challenging model selection problem as we have to choose, among all the possible interpretation of the data, the most appropriate one. In general there is not a canonical way to judge the appropriateness of a model, which may have been proposed in order to resolve the problem of multiple fitting, most of which rely on the well known model selection principle based on the balance between model complexity and data fidelity.

In this paper we develop a novel technique for fitting multiple geometric structures avoiding the classical model selection trade-off of two terms in favor

© Springer International Publishing Switzerland 2015
G. Azzopardi and N. Petkov (Eds.): CAIP 2015, Part II, LNCS 9257, pp. 13–25, 2015.
DOI: 10.1007/978-3-319-23117-4_2

of a single term criterion. In particular we borrow from the *Consensus Clustering* technique [9] the idea that the stability of the clustering suffices in disambiguating the correct estimate of models. The rationale behind this method is that the "best" partition of the data is the one more stable with respect to input randomization. We translate this principle in the context of geometric fitting, tailoring the Consensus Clustering strategy to T-Linkage, a clustering-based algorithm for fitting multiple instances of a model to noisy data possibly corrupted by outliers [7]. This gives rise to an automatic method for multiple fitting that will be shown to perform favorably on some simulated data and on some publicly available real dataset.

1.1   Related Works

Two main approaches can be recognized that aim at fitting multiple models: non parametric methods and parametric ones. Among the non parametric Randomize Hough Transform [22], Multi-RANSAC [25] and FLoSS [6] rely on the inspecting of consensus sets of models. An alternative approach is represented by the so called *preference* analysis. Originally introduced by RHA [24], these preference-oriented methods reverse the role of data points and model typical of consensus analysis, examining the residuals of individual data points with respect to the models, in order to work in a conceptual space. J-Linkage [16], T-Linkage [7], in which points are represented as *preference functions*, [1] and QP-MF [23], where points are represented by the permutation that arrange the models in order of ascending residuals, belong to this category. Parametric methods commonly achieve better performances than non parametric ones and have a more general applicability. However their success depends critically onto the correct specification of the inlier threshold ϵ (also called scale), which is usually manually tuned.

Since in many real applications selecting the correct scale is a hard problem, several solutions for automatic scale selection have been proposed. For example this problem is addressed in [2,12] as regard the case of one model (i.e. in the case of RANSAC), whereas [4,8,20] treat the case of inlier noise estimation for multiple models exploiting elaborated robust statistic. Probably the approach of StaRSaC is the most closely related prior work; In [2] Choi and Medioni demonstrate that choosing the correct ϵ enforces the stability of the parameter of the solution in the case of a single structure. We extend this result to the multiple structures scenario, reasoning on segmentation rather than on models parameters.

Multiple model fitting is usually dealt with using criteria of model selection. The classical model selection strategies consist in striking a good balance between fidelity to the data and model complexity (see e.g. [18]). Following the spirit of Occam's razor, all these methods result in minimizing an appropriate cost function composed by two terms: a modelling error and a penalty term for model complexity. This approach is taken also in [3,5,10,11,13] where sophisticated and effective minimization techniques such as SA-RCM [11], ARJMC [10] have been proposed.

Several alternatives have been explored for encoding model complexity. PEaRL [5] for example, optimizes a global energy function that balances geometric errors and regularity of inlier clusters, also exploiting spatial coherence. In [17], an iterative strategy for estimating the inlier-threshold, the score function, named J-Silhouette, is composed by a looseness term, dealing with fidelity, and a separation one, controlling complexity.

The idea of exploiting stability appears in the context of clustering validation. In particular in [9] the authors propose Consensus Clustering, a strategy that succeeds in estimating the number of clusters in the data with a single term model selection criterion based on stability. The next section is devoted to present the Consensus Stability approach and to summarize the T-linkage.

2 Background Material

2.1 Stability and Consensus Clustering

In some cases the thorny problem of correctly tradeoff data fidelity for model complexity (a.k.a. bias-variance dilemma) can be bypassed introducing a different model selection principle based exclusively on the *stability* of models. The key idea of this method is that good models should be found among the ones that are stable with respect to small perturbations of the data. This very general principle with the necessary specifications can be applied in many contexts, and can be exploited also in the classical segmentation problem.

In [9] the authors develop this idea and present the Consensus Clustering approach to determine the correct number of clusters by maximizing the *consensus*, i.e., the agreement of clustering after perturbation of the data.

More in detail, the Consensus Clustering approach consists in assuming a clustering algorithm, for example k-means, and a resampling scheme (e.g. bootstrapping) in order to perturb the data. Then for each possible clusters number $k = 2, 3, \ldots, k_{\max}$ the data are subsampled several times and processed by the clustering algorithm. The corresponding results are described for each k by means of a *consensus matrix* M_k which is intended to capture the mutual consensus of attained clusters. The consensus matrix M_k is defined as follows: the element $(M_k)_{ij}$ stores the number of times points i and j are assigned to the same cluster divided by the total number of times both items are selected by the resampling scheme. In other words, the consensus matrix records the proportion of clustering runs in which the two points i, j have been clustered together. For this reason $(M_k)_{ij} \in [0, 1]$ and perfect consensus corresponds to a clean consensus matrix with all the entries equal to either 0 or 1[1], whereas a deviation from this case should be explained with lack of stability of the estimated clusters. Exploiting this observation, the k that yields the cleanest consensus matrices according to an ad hoc measure, is selected as the optimal estimate of number of model.

---

[1] If the data points were arranged so that points belonging to the same model are adjacent to each other, perfect consensus would translate into a block-diagonal matrix.

2.2   T-Linkage

T-Linkage [7] is a clustering-based algorithm for fitting multiple instances of a model to noisy data (possibly) corrupted by outliers. The method is based on random sampling, and, along the same line of J-Linkage [16], follows a preference oriented approach: fixed an inlier threshold ϵ, rather than taking models and see which points match them, T-Linkage uses the model hypotheses each point "likes better" to determine which points belong to the same cluster.

Choosing the Scale in T-Linkage: A Model Selection Problem.   Since T-linkage does not have any scale selection strategy, the inlier threshold ϵ has to be manually specified by the user (as in RANSAC). If some prior knowledge of the noise in the data is available, ϵ can be easily tuned, otherwise the scale turns out to be a free parameter onto which T-Linkage depends critically.

It is important to observe that ϵ plays a crucial role in both the two steps of T-Linkage. At first, in conceptual representation step, the inlier threshold ϵ explicitly defines which points belong to which model (a point belongs to a model if its distance is less than ϵ). If the scale is underestimated the models do not fit all their inliers; on the contrary, if the scale is overestimated, the models are affected by outliers or pseudo outliers. As regards the clustering step, points are linked together by T-Linkage until their vectorial representations are orthogonal. Here again, since ϵ controls the orthogonality between these vectors, also the final number of models depends on this parameter.

In other words the tuning of ϵ is a typical model selection problem: If ϵ is too small, we are stuck in under-segmentation: multiple similar structures explain the same model in a redundant way. On the contrary, if ϵ is too large, we run into the problem of over-segmentation obtaining fewer structures than necessary that poorly describe the data.

For these reasons by tuning the single free parameter ϵ we are able at the same time to implicitly balance between both the complexity of the obtained models and their fidelity to the data.

In the next Sections we will show how stability can be fruitfully exploited for automatically selecting a reasonable scale.

Refinement Step and Outlier Rejection.   T-Linkage, as any hierarchical clustering method, is a greedy algorithm that fits models to all the data points, outliers included. In this section we propose some adjustment on T-Linkage in order to alleviate its greediness and introduce an outlier rejection criterion necessary, if outliers are present, to filter out bad models.

The problem of multiple fitting can be regarded from two alternative points of view usually coexisting: we want to faithfully segment the data and at the same time to obtain an accurate estimate of the underlying models. Each of these two tasks can not be undertaken without the other. T-Linkage concentrates on the first task segmenting the data in the conceptual space and extracting model only at the end via least-squares fitting. Once models have been obtained, we propose to perform an additional *refinement* step: points are reassigned to

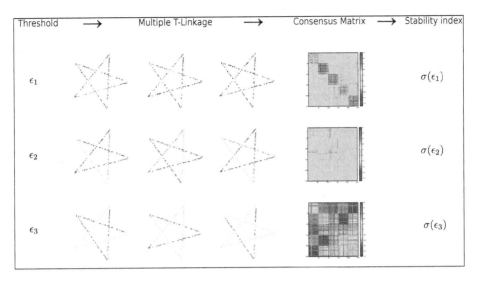

Fig. 1. The proposed method in a nutshell. Different ϵ values are used for running multiple times T-Linkage on the perturbed data. The corresponding consensus matrices measure the mutual consensus between the attained segmentations and are used in order to define the stability index. The more stable clustering, corresponding to ϵ_2, is selected. (Best viewed in color)

their nearest model – if it has distance smaller than ϵ – and finally models are re-estimated according to this new segmentation. In this way not only the segmentation and the model estimation step can take advantages from each other, but we also gain the benefit of mitigating the greedy behavior of T-Linkage since the final clustering depends less critically on the order in which points were merged together.

As outliers are concerned, T-Linkage is agnostic about the strategy for dichotomizing inliers and outliers and an outlier rejection criterion has to be specified at the end of the algorithm. In [7] a simple strategy has been proposed, which we refine here by proposing the following criterion. The procedure starts rejecting all those clusters that have less than $|h| + 1$ elements where $|h|$ denotes the cardinality of a minimal sample set. Then we aim at recognizing and discarding those models that "happen by chance" and do not reflect an authentic structure in the data. More precisely, under the assumption that outliers are independently distributed [14], it is possible to estimate how much it is likely that a cluster is entirely composed by outliers according to its cardinality and the model it defines. Consequently we retain only the groups with high confidence of being inliers and discard the others.

In practice at first the probability p that an outlier belongs to a specific model is estimated with Monte-Carlo simulation. Then the probability that k points belong to the same given model is computed as $\alpha(k) = 1 - \mathcal{F}(k, n, p)$, where n is the total number of data points, and $\mathcal{F}$ is the binomial cumulative distribution function. For each model we compute $k_{\min} = \alpha^{-1}(0.01)$ the minimum cardinality necessary to be not considered mere coincidence, if the considered model is supported by less than $k_{\min}$ points is rejected as outlier.

This outlier rejection criterion differs from the one adopted in [7], since here we compute the values of p (and consequently $k_{\min}$) for every specific model attained by T-Linkage at the end of the clustering, instead of estimating in advance a single probability value for a generic model. In this way our approach takes into account the fact that in general models are not all equiprobable and avoids to consider a fixed minimum cardinality and to reason about cardinality drop of clusters.

3   Method

In this Section we shall concentrate on a method (henceforth referred to as TLCC) for automatically fitting multiple models tailoring Consensus Clustering to T-Linkage algorithm without having a priori knowledge of the scale ϵ conceiving a single term model selection criterion based on consensus stability.

In the case of T-Linkage we do not have to select the number of clusters (that is automatically determined by T-Linkage clustering) but we shall concentrate on the scale ϵ which, as explained in Section 2.2, is a sensitive input parameter that implicitly tunes the balance between the complexity of the obtained clusters and their fidelity to the data.

The outline of our approach is sketched in Figure 1. The estimation of ϵ is iteratively laid out as follows. At first the interval search $[\epsilon_L, \epsilon_R]$ has to be defined, ensuring that the correct ϵ belongs to the interval. For this reason a sound choice of ϵ_L is a small scale value that surely over-segments the data, whereas ϵ_R has to give rise to under-segmentation (for example it can be estimated fitting a single model to all the data point and taking the maximum of their residuals). For each ϵ value belonging to the interval search, T-Linkage is run t times $t = 1, \ldots, t_{\max}$ on the data properly perturbed.

Rather than bootstrapping in advance the raw data as in [9], we perturb their representation in the conceptual space inside T-Linkage by bootstrapping the generated hypothesis. After the data have been processed we obtain $t_{\max}$ clustering outputs for each ϵ value. The intuition is that, at the correct scale, there will be consistency between the partitions produced by T-linkage. For each scale the consistency of the partitions is hence tabulated via the consensus clustering matrix M_ϵ introduced in Section 2.1.

Now we measure the consensus stability of each matrix boiling down each M_ϵ to a single consensus stability value σ per scale. If we were to plot a histogram of the entries of $(M_\epsilon)_{ij}$, perfect consensus would translate into two bins centered at 0 and 1 and, in general, a histogram skewed toward 0 and 1 indicates good clustering. With this idea in mind, consider the following change of variable:

$$F(x) = \begin{cases} x & \text{if } x < 0.5 \\ x - 1 & \text{if } x \geq 0.5. \end{cases} \tag{1}$$

F redistributes the entries of M_ϵ from the $[0,1]$ range to the interval $[-0.5, 0.5]$. The effect is to rearrange the histogram symmetrically around the origin. In this way stable entries are concentrated around 0 whereas unstable ones are accumulated at the tails of the histogram. For this reason measuring how far the entries of $F(M_\epsilon)$ are spread out accounts for the consensus stability of a given scale ϵ. For this purpose we propose to employ the variance[2] of the vectorized upper triangular part of $F(M_\epsilon)$ and define a *consensus stability index* as

$$\sigma(\epsilon) = \mathrm{Var}(\mathrm{vech}(F(M_\epsilon))), \tag{2}$$

where vech returns the vectorization of the upper triangular matrix it receives in input. Then, assuming to deal with authentic multiple structures, the scale is selected between the tested ϵ that segment the data in almost two clusters. Within these ϵ we retain as correct the smallest one obtaining the lower score of σ:

$$\epsilon^* = \min \left(\underset{\epsilon: \,\#\,\mathrm{cluster}>1}{\mathrm{argmin}} \;\; \sigma(\epsilon) \right). \tag{3}$$

The most stable solution (the one obtained with ϵ^*) is then returned.

The procedure can be summarized in Algorithm 1.

Algorithm 1. TLCC

Input: the set of data points X;
    an interval search $[\epsilon_L, \epsilon_H]$;
Output: scale ϵ^*;
    clusters of point belonging to the same model.

Generate hypotheses H;
for $\epsilon \in [\epsilon_L, \epsilon_H]$ **do**
    for $t = 1, \ldots, t_{\max}$ **do**
        $\tilde{H} = \mathrm{Bootstrapping}(H)$;
    end for
    $C_t = \mathrm{T\text{-}Linkage}(X, \epsilon, \tilde{H})$;
    $M_\epsilon = \mathrm{Consensus\ Matrix}(C_1, \ldots, C_{t_{\max}})$;
    Compute $\sigma(\epsilon)$;
end for
$\epsilon^* = \min(\mathrm{argmin}_{\epsilon: \,\#\,\mathrm{cluster}>1} \sigma)$;
$C^* = \mathrm{T\text{-}Linkage}(X, \epsilon^*, H)$;

As regards the computational complexity of this method, if c is the execution time of T-linkage, k_1 the threshold values tested and k_2 the number of bootstrapping trials, the total execution time of TLCC is $k_1 k_2 c$ to which the time needed for computing the consensus matrices has to be added. Even if the number of bootstrap iterations is small ($k_2 = 4$ in our experiments suffices in providing good results), there is space for improvement for example by replacing exhaustive search on the interval $[\epsilon_L, \epsilon_R]$ with a suitable (direct) minimization strategy reducing the number of scale values that are evaluated.

---

[2] We also tested the entropy and other dispersion indices with comparable results.

4   Experimental Results

This section is devoted to evaluating the proposed method on both simulated and real data, proving that consensus stability σ can be exploited as a single term model selection criterion for automatically fit multiple structures. The *misclassification error* (ME) is employed for assessing clustering results, defined as the percentage of misclassified points, where a point is misclassified when it is assigned to the wrong model, according to the ground-truth.

First we compare TLCC with T-linkage + "oracle", where the "oracle" guesses always the optimal scale according to the ME, in the interval search:

$$\epsilon_{opt} = \operatorname*{argmin}_{\epsilon \in [\epsilon_L, \epsilon_R]} \mathrm{ME}(\epsilon), \tag{4}$$

in other words ϵ_{opt} is the global minimum of ME. For each experiments we compare the $\mathrm{ME}(\epsilon^\star)$ achieved by the scale $\epsilon^\star$ estimated by TLCC with the $\mathrm{ME}(\epsilon_{opt})$ of the *optimal* scale.

Finally we also compare indirectly TLCC with several other methods on some real datasets that have been used in the literature [19,21].

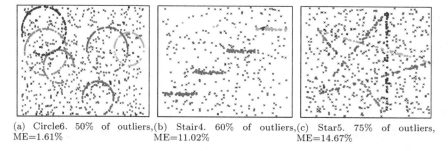

(a) Circle6. 50% of outliers, ME=1.61%   (b) Stair4. 60% of outliers, ME=11.02%   (c) Star5. 75% of outliers, ME=14.67%

Fig. 2. *Synthetic examples*: models returned by TLCC are color coded, black crosses are outliers.

4.1   Experiments with Simulated Data

Some synthetic experiments are carried on in order to asses the proposed approach. In particular, as shown in Fig. 2, we address the problem of fitting circles (Fig. 2a) and lines (Fig. 2b, 2c) to noisy data contaminated by gross outlier. The scale selected by TLCC always corresponds to the optimal one; the outlier rejection criterion works properly filtering out bad models with different percentage of outliers.

4.2   Experiments with Real Data

In this section we deal with three applications of geometric multi model fitting on real data: video motion segmentation, two views motion segmentation and two views plane segmentation.

Table 1. ME (%) for video **motion segmentation**.

Sequence	TLCC	Optimal
cars10	3.07	3.07
cars2B	0	0
cars2_06	0	0
cars2_07	0	0
cars3	0	0
cars5	0	0
cars9	0	0

Table 2. Sample results of TLCC in video **motion segmentation** (point membership is color coded)

(a) Cars10

(b) Cars9

Video Motion Segmentation. In video motion segmentation the input data consist in a set of features trajectories across a video taken by a moving camera, the goal consists in recovering the multiple rigid-body motions contained in the dynamic scene.

Segmentation of motion in a video can be seen as a subspace segmentation problem under the modeling assumption of affine cameras as explained in [19]. We evaluate TLCC on the seven Traffic sequence (Tab. 2) with three motion of the Hopkins 155 motion dataset [19]. All the trajectories are inherently corrupted by noise, but no outliers are present. Our algorithm succeeds for all the sequences in estimating optimal segmentations as shown in Tab. 1, for the estimated scale always achieves the same ME as the optimal one.

Two-Views Segmentation. In two views segmentation experiments, given two images of the same scene composed by several objects moving independently, the aim is to recognize and segment the motions by fitting fundamental matrices. The datasets used in these experiments consist of matching points in two uncalibrated images corrupted by gross outliers.

We tested our method on image pairs correspondences taken from the AdelaideRMF dataset[21].

According to Tab. 3 TLCC succeeds in estimating the optimal ϵ in six cases (marked in bold) and misses the global optimum in two cases, for which we plot

(a) breadcartoychips

(b) breadtoycar

(c) dinobooks

Fig. 3. Sample results of TLCC in two-view **motion segmentation** (point membership is color coded, red dots are points rejected as outliers)

(a) ladysymon   (b) oldclassicswing   (c) johnsonb

Fig. 4. Sample results of TLCC in two-view **plane segmentation** (point membership is color coded, outliers are colored in red)

the ME and the stability index in Figures 5a and 5b. It can be appreciated that the profile of the ME is fairly flat near the optimum, and that the minimum of the stability index is fairly close to the optimum of ME anyway.

Our conjecture for such a behavior is that the models have mutual intersections (or close to), and the ME does not measure properly the quality of a clustering.

Using the data reported in [11] we are able to compare indirectly TLCC with other state of the art algorithms inspired to the classical model selection approach, results are presented in Tab. 4.

In all but two cases TLCC achieves the best result, and it is the best algorithm if the mean ME is considered. These two cases are reported in Fig. 3 where it can be appreciated that the resulting segmentation is reasonable anyway.

Plane Segmentation. In the third case (*plane segmentation*) the setup is similar to the previous one: given two uncalibrated views of a scene, the aim is to recover robustly the multiplanar structures fitting homography to points correspondences. Results on the dataset taken from the AdelaideRMF dataset [21], are collected in Tab. 5.

In five cases (marked in bold) the proposed method estimate an optimal scale according to ME.

Table 3. ME (%) for two-view **motion segmentation**.

Sequence	TLCC	Optimal
biscuitbookbox	2.71	0.39
breadcartoychips	5.19	5.19
breadcubechips	2.17	2.17
breadtoycar	4.27	4.27
carchipscube	1.22	1.22
cubebreadtoychips	4.46	3.50
dinobooks	13.86	13.86
toycubecar	3.03	3.03

Table 4. ME (%) comparison for two views **motion segmentation**.

	PEARL	QP-MF	FLOSS	ARJMC	SA-RCM	TLCC
biscuitbookbox	4.25	9.27	8.88	8.49	7.04	**2.71**
breadcartoychips	5.91	10.55	11.81	10.97	**4.81**	5.19
breadcubechips	4.78	9.13	10.00	7.83	7.85	**2.17**
breadtoycar	6.63	11.45	10.84	9.64	**3.82**	4.27
carchipscube	11.82	7.58	11.52	11.82	11.75	**1.22**
cubebreadtoychips	4.89	9.79	11.47	6.42	5.93	**4.46**
dinobooks	14.72	19.44	17.64	18.61	**8.03**	13.86
toycubecar	9.5	12.5	11.25	15.5	7.32	**3.03**
Mean	7.81	11.21	11.68	11.16	7.07	**4.62**

Table 5. ME (%) for **plane segmentation**.

Sequence	TLCC	Optimal
johnsona	3.12	3.12
johnsonb	8.33	8.81
ladysymon	6.17	6.17
neem	4.78	4.78
oldclassicswing	1.65	1.65
sene	0.42	0.42

Table 6. ME (%) comparison for **plane segmentation**.

	PEARL	QP-MF	FLOSS	ARJMC	SA-RCM	TLCC
johnsona	4.02	18.5	4.16	6.88	5.9	**3.12**
johnsonb	18.18	24.65	18.18	21.49	17.95	**8.33**
ladysymon	**5.49**	18.14	5.91	5.91	7.17	6.17
neem	5.39	31.95	5.39	8.81	5.81	**4.78**
oldclassicswing	**1.58**	13.72	1.85	1.85	2.11	**1.65**
sene	0.80	14	**0.80**	**0.80**	**0.80**	0.42
Mean	5.91	20.16	6.05	7.62	6.62	**4.08**

For the *johnsonb* image pairs the attained segmentation by TLCC is slightly less accurate than the optimal one, however from Fig. 5c, where the ME and the stability index are shown, it can be appreciated that the value achieved by TLCC correspond to a plateau of ME. The segmentation produced by TLCC is presented in Fig. 4. Notice that the actual global optimum of ME can be conditioned by arbitrary tie-breaking of disputed points between models.

Tab. 6 compares TLCC with state of the art methods (results for all the methods but TLCC are taken from [11]). Our method achieves in all cases, but one, the best ME and a reasonable segmentation and it scores first on the average.

In summary, results show that TLCC places in the same range as the state of the art competing algorithm adopting a classical two-term model selection strategy, with a free balancing parameter. Experiments show that this method succeeds in estimating the scale parameter of T-linkage and more importantly provide evidence that stability has a minimum in the "right" spot, ideally the same spot where the misclassification error (ME) achieves its minimum. The study of a suitable direct optimization strategy for minimizing consensus stability is in focus for future work.

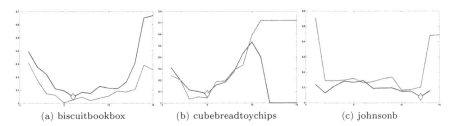

(a) biscuitbookbox   (b) cubebreadtoychips   (c) johnsonb

Fig. 5. Stability index σ (blue) and ME (red) as a function of the scale ϵ parameter for some image pairs of the **motion segmentation** (5a, 5b) and **plane segmentation** experiments (5c). The estimated scale is marked with a diamond on the σ curve.

5 Conclusion

In this paper we presented an automatic approach aimed at estimating the scale in the context of multiple structure geometric fitting. Our method exploits a single term model selection strategy relying on the principle of stability, thereby avoiding the tricky trade-off between data fidelity and model complexity. Experimental evaluation on both simulated and real data provides evidence that consensus stability succeeds in producing accurate and reliable multiple models.

Acknowledgments. The use of the AdelaideRMF dataset[3] and the Hopkins 155 motion dataset[4] is here acknowledged.

References

1. Chin, T., Wang, H., Suter, D.: Robust fitting of multiple structures: the statistical learning approach. In: Proc. Int. Conf. Comp. Vis., pp. 413–420 (2009)
2. Choi, J., Medioni, G.G.: Starsac: stable random sample consensus for parameter estimation. In: Proc. Conf. on Comp. Vis. and Patt. Rec. IEEE (2009)
3. Delong, A., Veksler, O., Boykov, Y.: Fast fusion moves for multi-model estimation. In: Fitzgibbon, A., Lazebnik, S., Perona, P., Sato, Y., Schmid, C. (eds.) ECCV 2012, Part I. LNCS, vol. 7572, pp. 370–384. Springer, Heidelberg (2012)
4. Fan, L., Pylvänäinen, T.: Robust scale estimation from ensemble inlier sets for random sample consensus methods. In: Forsyth, D., Torr, P., Zisserman, A. (eds.) ECCV 2008, Part III. LNCS, vol. 5304, pp. 182–195. Springer, Heidelberg (2008)
5. Isack, H., Boykov, Y.: Enegy-based geometric multi-model fitting. Int. J. Comp. Vis. **97**(2), 123–147 (2012)
6. Lazic, N., Givoni, I.E., Frey, B.J., Aarabi, P.: FLoSS: facility location for subspace segmentation. In: Proc. Int. Conf. Comp. Vis., pp. 825–832 (2009)
7. Magri, L., Fusiello, A.: T-linkage: a continuous relaxation of J-linkage for multi-model fitting. In: Proc. Conf. on Comp. Vis. and Patt. Rec., June 2014
8. Mittal, S., Anand, S., Meer, P.: Generalized projection based m-estimator: theory and applications. In: Proc. Conf. on Comp. Vis. and Patt. Rec. (2011)
9. Monti, S., Tamayo, P., Mesirov, J., Golub, T.: Consensus clustering: A resampling-based method for class discovery and visualization of gene expression microarray data. Machine Learning **52**(1–2), 91–118 (2003)
10. Pham, T.T., Chin, T.J., Yu, J., Suter, D.: Simultaneous sampling and multi-structure fitting with adaptive reversible jump mcmc. In: Neural Information Processing Systems, pp. 540–548 (2011)
11. Pham, T.T., Chin, T.J., Yu, J., Suter, D.: The random cluster model for robust geometric fitting. In: Proc. Conf. on Comp. Vis. and Patt. Rec. (2012)
12. Raguram, R., Frahm, J.M.: Recon: scale-adaptive robust estimation via residual consensus. In: International Conference on Computer Vision, pp. 1299–1306 (2011)
13. Schindler, K., Suter, D., Wang, H.: A model-selection framework for multibody structure-and-motion of image sequences. Int. J. Comp. Vis. **79**(2), 159–177 (2008)
14. Stewart, C.V.: MINPRAN: A new robust estimator for computer vision. IEEE Trans. on Patt. Anal. and Mach. Intell. **17**(10), 925–938 (1995)

---

[3] Available online at http://cs.adelaide.edu.au/~hwong/doku.php?id=data

[4] Available online at http://www.vision.jhu.edu/data/hopkins155

15. Stewart, C.V.: Bias in robust estimation caused by discontinuities and multiple structures. IEEE Trans. on Patt. Anal. and Mach. Intell. **19**(8), 818–833 (1997)
16. Toldo, R., Fusiello, A.: Robust multiple structures estimation with J-linkage. In: Forsyth, D., Torr, P., Zisserman, A. (eds.) ECCV 2008, Part I. LNCS, vol. 5302, pp. 537–547. Springer, Heidelberg (2008)
17. Toldo, R., Fusiello, A.: Automatic estimation of the inlier threshold in robust multiple structures fitting. In: Proc. Int. Conf. Image An. Proc., pp. 123–131 (2009)
18. Torr, P.H.S.: An assessment of information criteria for motion model selection. In: Proc. Conf. on Comp. Vis. and Patt. Rec., pp. 47–53 (1997)
19. Tron, R., Vidal, R.: A benchmark for the comparison of 3d motion segmentation algorithms. In: Proc. Conf. on Comp. Vis. and Patt. Rec. (2007)
20. Wang, H., Suter, D.: Robust adaptive-scale parametric model estimation for computer vision. IEEE Trans. on Patt. Anal. and Mach. Intell., 1459–1474 (2004)
21. Wong, H.S., Chin, T.J., Yu, J., Suter, D.: Dynamic and hierarchical multi-structure geometric model fitting. In: Proc. Int. Conf. Comp. Vis. (2011)
22. Xu, L., Oja, E., Kultanen, P.: A new curve detection method: randomized Hough transform (RHT). Patt. Rec. Lett. **11**(5), 331–338 (1990)
23. Yu, J., Chin, T., Suter, D.: A global optimization approach to robust multi-model fitting. In: Proc. Conf. on Comp. Vis. and Patt. Rec. (2011)
24. Zhang, W., Kosecká, J.: Nonparametric estimation of multiple structures with outliers. In: Vidal, R., Heyden, A., Ma, Y. (eds.) WDV 2005/2006. LNCS, vol. 4358, pp. 60–74. Springer, Heidelberg (2007)
25. Zuliani, M., Kenney, C.S., Manjunath, B.S.: The multiRANSAC algorithm and its application to detect planar homographies. In: Proc. Int. Conf. Image Proc. (2005)

Writer Identification and Retrieval Using a Convolutional Neural Network

Stefan Fiel$^{(\boxtimes)}$ and Robert Sablatnig$^{(\boxtimes)}$

Computer Vision Lab, TU Wien, Vienna, Austria
{fiel,sab}@caa.tuwien.ac.at

Abstract. In this paper a novel method for writer identification and retrieval is presented. Writer identification is the process of finding the author of a specific document by comparing it to documents in a database where writers are known, whereas retrieval is the task of finding similar handwritings or all documents of a specific writer. The method presented is using Convolutional Neural Networks (CNN) to generate a feature vector for each writer, which is then compared with the precalculated feature vectors stored in the database. For the generation of this vector the CNN is trained on a database with known writers and after training the classification layer is cut off and the output of the second last fully connected layer is used as feature vector. For the identification a nearest neighbor classification is used. The evaluation is performed on the *ICDAR2013 Competition on Writer Identification, ICDAR 2011 Writer Identification Contest*, and the *CVL-Database* datasets. Experiments show, that this novel approach achieves better results to previously presented writer identification approaches.

Keywords: Writer identification · Writer retrieval · Convolutional neural networks

1 Introduction

Writer identification is the task of identifying an author of a handwritten document by comparing the writing with the ones stored in a database. The authors of the documents in the database have to be known in advance for identification. For writer retrieval the documents with the most similar handwriting are searched, generally these are the documents which are written by the same writer. For this task a feature vector is generated, which describes the handwriting of the reference document and the distance to the precalculated features vectors of all documents in the dataset is calculated. For retrieval the documents are sorted according to the distance and for identification the writer of the document with the highest similarity (resp. the smallest distance) is then assigned as author to the document. Writer identification can be used for tasks in forensics like for threat letters, where the writing has to be compared with older ones so that connections between different letters can be established. Also for historical

© Springer International Publishing Switzerland 2015
G. Azzopardi and N. Petkov (Eds.): CAIP 2015, Part II, LNCS 9257, pp. 26–37, 2015.
DOI: 10.1007/978-3-319-23117-4_3

document analysis writer identification ca be used to trace the routes of medieval scribes along the different monasteries and scriptorias, or to identify the writer of books or pages where the author is not known. Since often a database of known writers is not available for such tasks, the main goal of this approach is to perform writer retrieval. Thus, only a nearest neighbor classification is carried out which allows for searching of documents which have a similar handwriting as a reference document. Especially for the two tasks mentioned the last decision will be made by human experts, but automated methods can be used to reduce the possible handwritings which have to be examined.

The challenges for writer identification and writer retrieval include the use of different pens, which changes a person's writing style, the physical condition of the writer, distractions like multitasking and noise, and also that the writing style changes with age. The changing of the style with increasing age is not covered by any available dataset and cannot be examined, but makes the identification or retrieval harder for real life data. Fig. 1 shows a sample image of the CVL dataset in which the handwriting changes due to distraction of the writer. Fig. 2 shows a part of an image of the CVL dataset, where the writer used two different pens.

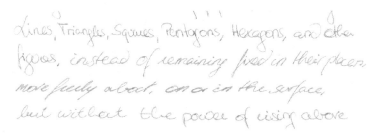

Fig. 1. Part of a sample image of the CVL dataset, which shows the changing of the handwriting when the writer is distracted (Writer Id: 191 Page: 1).

Current state-of-the-art methods either analyze the characters itself by describing their characteristics and properties which are then integrated into a feature vector. Since a binarization and segmentation of the text is necessary, the methods are dependent on these preprocessing steps. To overcome these problems other approaches consider the handwriting as texture and thus use texture analysis methods for the generation of a feature vector. Recent approaches[2][4][5][9] use local features for the task of writer identification which originate in the field of object recognition.

This paper presents an approach that uses Convolutional Neural Networks (CNN) for writer identification and retrieval. CNNs are feed-forward artificial neural networks and are used by currently top ranked methods for object recognition [18], recognition of digits (MNIST dataset[1]), and speech recognition [19]. They have been brought to the field of text recognition by Wang et al.[20] and are also used for text recognition in natural scenes[16]. To the best of our knowledge,

---

[1] http://yann.lecun.com/exdb/mnist/ - accessed March 2015.

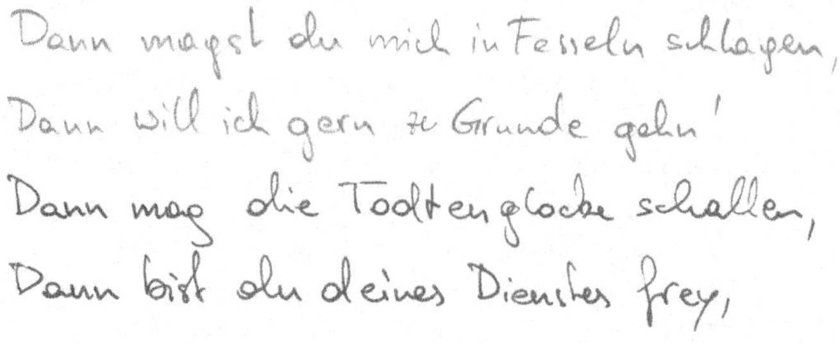

Fig. 2. Part of a sample image of the CVL dataset, on which the writer changed the pen (Writer Id: 369 Page: 6).

this is the first attempt to bring this method to the field of writer identification and writer retrieval. CNN consists of multiple layers which apply various combinations of convolutions and fully connected neural networks. Since a feature vector is needed for the tasks of identification and retrieval, the last layer of the CNN, which basically does the labeling of the input data, is cut off and the output of the neurons of the second last fully connected layer are used as feature vector. This vector is then used for the distance measurement between two different document images to describe the similarity of the handwriting.

The work is organized as follows: Section 2 gives a brief overview of the current state-of-the-art of writer identification. Section 3 describes the methodology used. The experiments and results are presented in Section 4. Finally, a short conclusion is given in Section 5.

2   Related Work

A writer identification method which is based on features extracted from text lines or characters is proposed by Marti et al. [15]. Features like slant, width, and three heights of the writing zone (descender, x-height, and ascender height) are used for the identification of the writer. Using a neural network classifier, a recognition rate of 90% on 20 writers of the IAM Database is achieved. New features which are calculated on character level are introduced by Bulacu et al. [1]. They calculate the contour-hinge, which describes various angles of the written character. Furthermore they use a writer-specific grapheme emission and the run-length. With a nearest neighbor classifier they achieve a recognition rate of 89% on the Firemaker dataset, which contains of 250 writers. Another approach is the "Grid Microstructure Features" which are introduced by Li and Ding [11]. For each border pixel of the edge of a writing the neighborhood is described by means of three simple rules. These rules describe the characteristics of the edge on the connected component within a small window. The probability density distribution of different pixel pairs which fullfill these rules is regarded as feature representing the writing style. With this method they were able to win the *ICDAR 2011 Writer Identification Contest*[13] with an identification rate of 99.5% on the complete pages and 90.9% on cropped pages, each of the datasets

are written by 26 writers. Jain and Doermann [7] propose an offline writer identification method by using K-adjacent segment features in a bag-of-features framework. It represents the relationship between sets of neighboring edges in an image
which are then used to form a codebook and classify new handwritings using the
nearest neighbors. A recognition rate of 93.3% is achieved on 300 writers of the
IAM Dataset. The same authors propose the usage of an alphabet of contour
gradient descriptors for writer identification [8]. By analyzing the contour gradients of the characters in a sliding window, they form a pseudo-alphabet for each
writing sample and calculate the distance between these alphabets as similarity
measurement. With this method they were able to win the *ICDAR 2013 Competition on Writer Identification*[12] with an identification rate of 95.1%. The
dataset was written by 250 writers.

Hiremath et al. [6] assume the writing as texture image and are proposing to
use the wavelet transform to compute co-occurrence matrices for 8 directions.
When dealing with 30 writers at a time the identification rate is 88%. Our previous approaches [4] [5] use SIFT features for classification. With a bag-of-words
approach respectively using the Fisher information of Gaussian Mixture Models
an identification rate of 90.8% and 99.5% is achieved on the CVL Dataset with
310 writers. On the same dataset Christlein et al. [2] achieve an accuracy of up
to 99.2% by using RootSIFT and GMM supervectors for their identification system. Jain and Doermann [9] propose a combination of local features. They use a
linear combination of their k-adjacent segments, their alphabet of contour gradient descriptors, and SURF for identification. With a nearest neighbor approach
they achieve a recognition rate of 99.4% on the CVL Dataset.

The evaluation of all methods has been carried out on various databases with
different properties and thus the results cannot be compared with another.

3   Methodology

Our approach uses CNN for the task of writer identification and writer retrieval.
Since a feature vector is needed for every document image to allow for a comparison with precalculated features in a dataset to identify a specific writer or to
search for the most similar handwriting style, the output of the second last fully
connected layer is used. CNNs require as input an image with fixed size, thus
preprocessing of the document images is necessary. The preprocessing includes
binarization, text line segmentation, and sliding windows. The next step is the
generation of the feature vector using the CNN. These vectors are then used for
the identification of a writer or the retrieval of similar writers using a nearest
neighbor approach.

3.1   Preprocessing

The first step is, if the input images are grayscale like in the CVL-Dataset [10],
a binarization. For this work the method of Otsu [17] is used since the dataset
contains only scanned pages without any noise and thus a global threshold will

give a nearly optimal binarization. Second, the words respectively the lines have to be segmented. The CVL-Database [10] and the IAM-Dataset [14] already provide a segmentation of the words, thus these images are used for evaluation and training. For the *ICDAR 2011 Writer Identification Contest*[13] and *ICDAR 2013 Competition on Writer Identification* [12] datasets the lines are segmented using the method of Diem et al.[3], which uses Local Projection Profiles for grouping the characters to words. The text lines are then detected by globally minimizing the distances of all words. Since the CNNs require an image of fixed size as input, the word images respectively the line images are split up using a sliding window approach with a step size of 20 pixels. But first these images are size normalized to ensure that the height of the writing does not have an influence on the feature vector generation. Thus, the x-height of the words or lines are calculated by fitting a line through the upper and lower points of the text line and the image is resized that the x-height of the words cover half of the result image, to ensure that ascenders and descenders have sufficient space to be also present in the image. Additionally, since some lines in the ICDAR datasets are slightly skewed, the lines are also deskewed with the mean angle of the upper and lower profile of the x-height. The upper image in Fig. 3 shows the original line from the ICDAR 2011 dataset with the profiles of the x-height as new line. The lower image shows the deskewed line, which was also size normalized. Note that not the slant of the font is corrected since it is a discriminative feature of the writer, only the orientation of the text line is processed which cannot be used as feature for identification since it is highly depended on the paper the text is written on, e.g. if it is a lined or blank paper.

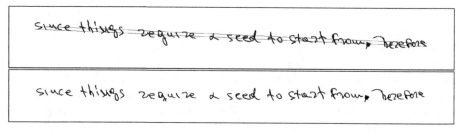

Fig. 3. Sample line extracted from the ICDAR 2011 dataset. The upper image shows the original line with the upper and lower profile. The lower images shows the size normalized and deskewed line.

3.2 Generation of the Feature Vector

For the generation of the feature vector a CNN is used. For this work a well-known model for CNN is used, namely "caffenet" which is part of the "Caffe - Deep learning framework"[2]. The design of the network is presented in Fig. 4 . It consists of five convolution layers which are using kernel sizes of 11-3 and three fully connected layers. Like the original network it is trained using a softmax

---

[2] http://caffe.berkeleyvision.org - accessed March 2015.

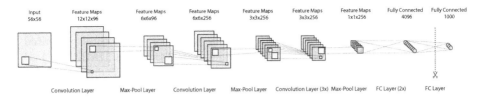

Fig. 4. Design of the CNN, the "caffenet" of the "Caffe - Deep learning framwork"

loss function. The last layer of the CNN is used for labeling the input data and consists of 1000 neurons, which is more than the actual number of writers in the IAM dataset but leads to better results. The reason for this behavior will be examined in more detail as future work. Since a classification is not intended, this layer is cut off and the output values of the second last fully connected layer is used as feature vector for further processing. The classification layer could have been also used as feature vector for the writer identification but lead to worse results since the outputs of this layer focuses rather on one class whereas when using the last fully connected layer all neurons are activated and thus giving a more discriminative feature vector.

The CNN has to be trained beforehand. To ensure independence between the training images and the ones used for evaluation, the CNN has been trained on the word images of the IAM dataset. The IAM Dataset consists of 1539 document images written by 657 different writers. The document images are not equally distributed among the writers, most of the writers only contributed one document whereas one writer has written 60 pages. Since CNNs have to be trained on a large amount of data to achieve a good performance (e.g. for ILSVCRC 2014 the training set contained 1.2 Mio images), the trainings set has been enlarged artificially by rotating each image of a sliding window from -25 to $+25$ degrees using a step size of 5 degrees. These values are found empirically and are a good trade-off between the performance of the method and training time. The rotation of the images may also have a positive effect for handwritings with a certain slant, these images are no longer assigned to the same writer in the training dataset using a similar slant. This property has to be confirmed in future work. With the rotation of the image the training set consists of more than 2.3 Mio image patches, which are not equally distributed among the 657 writers of the dataset due to their properties. Each writer has at most 7700 patches (700 for each direction) in the trainings set.

To generate a feature vector for a complete page, all image patches of this page are fed into the CNN without any rotation since experiments have shown that the performance is not improved. As mentioned above, the last layer is cut off for the generation of the feature vector. Thus, we receive the normalized output of the last 4096 neurons of the second last fully connected layer. The mean values of the vectors of all image patches of one page is then taken as feature vector for the identification respectively the retrieval. These feature vectors are compared with each other using the χ^2-distance, which has been found out empirically to give the best results.

4   Experiments and Results

This section will give an overview of the performance of the method presented on various databases. For the evaluation the datasets of the ICDAR 2011 and ICDAR 2013 Writer identification contests, as well as the CVL database have been used. The ICDAR 2011 dataset consists of 26 writers, where each has contributed 8 different documents (two in English, French, German, and Greek). The second dataset of this contest contains the same pages, but only the first two text lines from each document are taken. Fig. 5a show two small parts of images of this dataset. The ICDAR 2013 dataset contains the document images from 50 writers, one in English and one in Greek. From each image two pieces were cropped, each containing four text line, thus resulting in four parts of text per writer. Two parts of sample images are shown in Fig. 5b. The CVL dataset is the largest dataset in this evaluation. It consists of 1545 pages written by 309 writers. Each writer has written 5 different texts (four in English, one in German). Sample images have already been presented in Section 1. As mentioned in Section 3.2 the CNN has been trained on the IAM database to ensure independence of the trainings set and the evaluation sets. One CNN has been trained for all experiments although different designs of the CNN slightly improved the performances for some experiments. The results of the CNN which has the best overall performance are presented.

The evaluation has been carried out in the same way as in the ICDAR 2011 and ICDAR 2013 contest. For each document a ranking of the other documents according to the similarity is generated. There the top N documents are examined whether they are from the same writer or not. Two criteria have been defined: for the soft criteria, if one of the documents in the top N is from the same writer like the reference document it is considered as a correct hit. For the

(a) ICDAR 11, WriterId: 2, Text 2 and Text 3

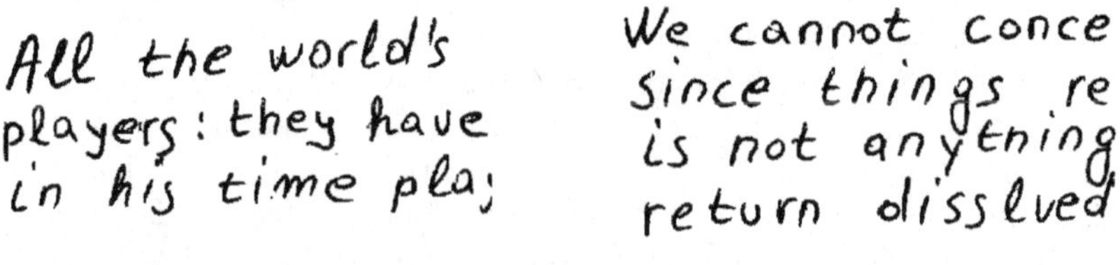

(b) ICDAR 13, Writer: 29, Text 1 and Text 2

Fig. 5. Parts of sample images of the ICDAR 2011 and the ICDAR 2013 dataset.

hard criterion all N documents have to be from the same writer to be considered as correct hit. The value of N is varying for all the datasets, since the number of documents from one writer is also varying. For the ICDAR 2011 contest the values of N are: 1, 2, 5, and 7, whereas the values for the hard criterion are 2, 5, and 7. For the ICDAR 2013 dataset the values for the soft criterion are 1, 2, 5, and 10 and for the hard criterion 2 and 3. The CVL dataset uses the same numbers for the soft criterion and for the hard criterion 2, 3, and 4 are used, since the dataset contains 5 documents of each writer. Furthermore the CVL dataset has a retrieval criterion, which is defined as the percentage of the documents of the corresponding writer in the first N documents. For this criterion the values of N are the same as for the hard criterion.

The first evaluation is carried out on the ICDAR 2011 datasets. The results for the soft criterion of both datasets are presented in Table 1 in comparison with the three best ranked methods of the contest. It can be seen that for the soft criterion all methods have a good performance, our method has one misclassified page in the "Top 1" task. On the cropped dataset the performance of all methods are dropping, since there is less written text in the image. Still our method has the best performance for the "Top 1", which is the exact identification of the writer.

Table 1. The soft criterion evaluation results on the ICDAR 2011 dataset (in %)

complete dataset				
	Top 1	Top 2	Top 5	Top 7
Tsinghua	98.6	100.0	100.0	100.0
MCS-NUST	99.0	99.5	99.5	99.5
Tebessa C	98.6	100.0	100.0	100.0
proposed method	**99.5**	100.0	100.0	100.0
cropped dataset				
	Top 1	Top 2	Top 5	Top 7
Tsinghua	90.9	93.8	**98.6**	**99.5**
MCS-NUST	82.2	91.8	96.6	97.6
Tebessa C	87.5	92.8	97.6	**99.5**
proposed method	**94.7**	**97.6**	98.1	**99.5**

The evaluation of the hard criterion of the ICDAR 2011 datasets are shown in Table 2. For the hard criterion similar results can be seen like for the soft criterion. The proposed method outperforms the other methods for all but one task. For the "Top 2" task on the cropped dataset, the improvement is 4.8%. Only the results of the "Top 7" task on the cropped dataset, which is finding all other 7 pages of the same writer, the proposed method provides slightly worse results than the other methods.

The next experiments have been carried out on the ICDAR 2013 dataset. The results of both criteria compared to the top ranked methods of the contests are presented in Table 3. It can be seen that the proposed method performs

Table 2. The hard criterion evaluation results on the ICDAR 2011 dataset (in %)

complete dataset			
	Top 2	Top 5	Top 7
Tsinghua	95.2	84.1	41.4
MCS-NUST	93.3	78.9	39.9
Tebessa C	97.1	81.3	50.0
proposed method	**98.6**	**87.0**	**52.4**
cropped dataset			
	Top 2	Top 5	Top 7
Tsinghua	79.8	48.6	12.5
MCS-NUST	71.6	35.6	11.1
Tebessa C	76.0	34.1	**14.4**
proposed method	**84.6**	**53.8**	10.1

Table 3. Evaluation of the soft and hard criteria on the ICDAR 2013 dataset (in %)

	soft criterion				hard criterion	
	Top 1	Top 2	Top 5	Top 10	Top 2	Top 3
CS-UMD-a	**95.1**	**97.7**	98.6	99.1	19.6	7.1
CS-UMD-b	95.0	97.2	**98.6**	**99.2**	20.2	8.4
HIT-ICG	94.8	96.7	98.0	98.3	**63.2**	**36.5**
proposed method	88.5	92.2	96.0	98.3	40.5	15.8

worse than the best three participants of the competition. This has two reasons: the line segmentation used has problems on this dataset and often the ascenders and descenders of characters are cut off and thus these characteristic parts for different writers are missing in the classification. Second, like the "CS-UMD" methods, the proposed method has difficulties in finding the corresponding Greek text for an English input text and vice versa since the training data does not contain any Greek text. This can be seen in the hard criterion, where at least one document image written in the other language has to be found.

The last evaluation has been carried out on the CVL dataset. The results of the soft and hard criterion are shown in Table 4, whereas results of the retrieval criterion are shown in Table 5. The proposed method has the best performance on each task except for the "Top 3" of the hard criterion compared to the top ranked methods in [10]. Remarkable is the improvement of performance for "Top 4" hard criterion, which is 6.9%. For this task all other 4 pages of one writer has to be retrieved. These results can also be seen in the retrieval criterion, where the proposed method achieves higher results as the other methods.

Table 4. Evaluation results of the soft and hard criteria on the CVL-Database (in %)

	soft criterion				hard criterion		
	Top 1	Top 2	Top 5	Top 10	Top 2	Top 3	Top 4
Tsinghua	97.7	98.3	99.0	99.1	95.3	**94.5**	73.0
Tebessa C	97.6	97.9	98.3	98.5	94.3	88.2	73.0
proposed method	**98.9**	**99.0**	**99.3**	**99.5**	**97.6**	93.3	**79.9**

Table 5. The retrieval criterion evaluation results on the CVL-Database (in %)

	Top 2	Top 3	Top 4
Tsinghua	96.8	94.5	90.2
Tebessa C	96.1	94.2	90.0
proposed method	**98.3**	**96.9**	**93.3**

5 Conclusion

A novel method for writer identification and writer retrieval has been presented. The method uses CNN for generating a feature vector which are then compared using the χ^2-distance. As preprocessing steps the images need to be binarized, normalized, and the skew of the text line needs to be corrected. The method proposed has been evaluated on three different datasets, namely the datasets of the ICDAR 2011 and 2013 writer identification contests and the CVL dataset. Experiments show that the proposed method achieves slightly better results on two of three datasets, but worse results on the remaining dataset which originates mainly from the preprocessing steps.

Future work includes the design of a new CNN customized to the input data and which is capable of achieving better performance on various datasets. Furthermore the preprocessing step will be improved by using a better normalization of the image patches and a post processing step with a voting strategy on the complete page and the rejection of not significant image patches will be introduced. Also some image patches may be skipped already in the preprocessing step if they show no relevant information for a successful writer identification and writer retrieval.

References

1. Bulacu, M., Schomaker, L., Vuurpijl, L.: Writer identification using edge-based directional features. In: Proceedings. Seventh International Conference on Document Analysis and Recognition, 2003, pp. 937–941, August 2003
2. Christlein, V., Bernecker, D., Hönig, F., Angelopoulou, E.: Writer identification and verification using GMM supervectors. In: Proceedings of the 2014 IEEE Winter Conference on Applications of Computer Vision (2014)

3. Diem, M., Kleber, F., Sablatnig, R.: Text line detection for heterogeneous documents. In: 2013 12th International Conference on Document Analysis and Recognition (ICDAR), pp. 743–747 (2013)
4. Fiel, S., Sablatnig, R.: Writer retrieval and writer identification using local features. In: 2012 10th IAPR International Workshop on Document Analysis Systems (DAS), pp. 145–149. IEEE, March 2012
5. Fiel, S., Sablatnig, R.: Writer identification and writer retrieval using the fisher vector on visual vocabularies. In: 2013 12th International Conference on Document Analysis and Recognition (ICDAR), pp. 545–549 (2013)
6. Hiremath, P., Shivashankar, S., Pujari, J., Kartik, R.: Writer identification in a handwritten document image using texture features. In: International Conference on Signal and Image Processing (ICSIP), pp. 139–142, December 2010
7. Jain, R., Doermann, D.: Offline writer identification using K-adjacent segments. In: 2011 International Conference on Document Analysis and Recognition (ICDAR), pp. 769–773, September 2011
8. Jain, R., Doermann, D.: Writer identification using an alphabet of contour gradient descriptors. In: 2013 12th International Conference on Document Analysis and Recognition (ICDAR), pp. 550–554, August 2013
9. Jain, R., Doermann, D.: Combining local features for offline writer identification. In: 2014 14th International Conference on Frontiers in Handwriting Recognition (ICFHR), pp. 583–588, September 2014
10. Kleber, F., Fiel, S., Diem, M., Sablatnig, R.: CVL-database: an off-line database for writer retrieval, writer identification and word spotting. In: 2013 12th International Conference on Document Analysis and Recognition (ICDAR), pp. 560–564 (2013)
11. Li, X., Ding, X.: Writer identification of chinese handwriting using grid microstructure feature. In: Tistarelli, M., Nixon, M.S. (eds.) ICB 2009. LNCS, vol. 5558, pp. 1230–1239. Springer, Heidelberg (2009)
12. Louloudis, G., Gatos, B., Stamatopoulos, N., Papandreou, A.: ICDAR 2013 competition on writer identification. In: 2013 12th International Conference on Document Analysis and Recognition (ICDAR), pp. 1397–1401, August 2013
13. Louloudis, G., Stamatopoulos, N., Gatos, B.: ICDAR 2011 writer identification contest. In: 2011 11th International Conference on Document Analysis and Recognition (ICDAR), pp. 1475–1479 (2011)
14. Marti, U.V., Bunke, H.: The IAM-database: an English sentence database for offline handwriting recognition. International Journal on Document Analysis and Recognition 5(1), 39–46 (2002)
15. Marti, U.V., Messerli, R., Bunke, H.: Writer identification using text line based features. In: Proceedings. Sixth International Conference on Document Analysis and Recognition, pp. 101–105 (2001)
16. Opitz, M., Diem, M., Fiel, S., Kleber, F., Sablatnig, R.: End-to-End text recognition with local ternary patterns, MSER and deep convolutional nets. In: Proceedings of the 11th International Workshop on Document Analysis Systems, pp. 186–190 (2014)
17. Otsu, N.: A Threshold Selection Method from Gray-Level Histograms. IEEE Transactions on Systems, Man and Cybernetics 9(1), 62–66 (1979)

18. Russakovsky, O., Deng, J., Su, H., Krause, J., Satheesh, S., Ma, S., Huang, Z., Karpathy, A., Khosla, A., Bernstein, M.S., Berg, A.C., Fei-Fei, L.: ImageNet Large Scale Visual Recognition Challenge. CoRR abs/1409.0575 (2014). http://arxiv.org/abs/1409.0575
19. Sainath, T., Mohamed, A.R., Kingsbury, B., Ramabhadran, B.: Deep convolutional neural networks for LVCSR. In: 2013 IEEE International Conference on Acoustics, Speech and Signal Processing (ICASSP), pp. 8614–8618, May 2013
20. Wang, T., Wu, D., Coates, A., Ng, A.: End-to-end text recognition with convolutional neural networks. In: 2012 21st International Conference on Pattern Recognition (ICPR), pp. 3304–3308, November 2012

Optical Truck Tracking
for Autonomous Platooning

Christian Winkens[(⊠)], Christian Fuchs, Frank Neuhaus, and Dietrich Paulus

Active Vision Group, Institute for Computational Visualistics,
University of Koblenz-Landau, Universitätsstraße 1, 56070 Koblenz, Germany
{cwinkens,fuchsc,fneuhaus,paulus}@uni-koblenz.de

Abstract. Platooning applications require precise knowledge about position and orientation (pose) of the leading vehicle. We present an optical solution for a robust pose estimation using artificial markers and a camera as the only sensor. Temporal coherence of image sequences is used in a Kalman filter to obtain precise estimates. The system is designed for and tested in off-road scenarios. A pose evaluation is performed in a simulation testbed.

Keywords: Off-road platooning · Optical tracking · Kalman filter · Autonomous vehicles

1 Introduction and Motivation

Modern transportation scenarios require efficient handling of huge loads, high capacities, and flexible scheduling. Especially on long distance routes, scenarios in which subsequent vehicles autonomously follow a leading vehicle operated by a human driver become more and more important to match the needs of the increasing amount of transportation goods. The knowledge about the exact position and orientation of the leading vehicle is a vital prerequisite for the development of so-called *platooning* scenarios.

Several approaches in literature use sensors like stereo cameras, laser/radar sensors or communication between vehicles or vehicle and infrastructure to solve this problem. Since vehicles will usually drive on roads, an assumption of the ground to be a plane can be used to simplify the problem. The majority of published platooning approaches rely on special infrastructure and are limited to structured environments.

The goal of our approach is to allow convoys to move off-roads on rough terrain, enabling precise position and orientation estimation without requiring communication systems or complex cost-intensive sensors. Applications are in forest or agricultural environments, for example. Dealing with off-road scenarios, the ground plane assumption no longer holds, making it necessary to compute a full *6-D* position and orientation state for the leading vehicle in real time. As the system is planned to work while driving at relatively high velocities, it has to maintain a long range position and orientation estimate. In order to solve these

© Springer International Publishing Switzerland 2015
G. Azzopardi and N. Petkov (Eds.): CAIP 2015, Part II, LNCS 9257, pp. 38–48, 2015.
DOI: 10.1007/978-3-319-23117-4_4

problems, we use a mono-camera setup with a high image resolution and artificial markers on the leading vehicle that allow an accurate pose reconstruction in real-time.

We propose an algorithm that makes use of temporal coherence in order to robustly track the leading vehicle with high precision in this publication.

This work is structured as follows: Section 2 gives an overview of related work and the pre-requisites for the work presented. Our approach is then introduced (Section 3) and explained (Section 4). Test results and evaluation of the position and orientation quality are shown in Section 5 and discussed in Section 6.

2 Related Work

Several research topics have to be taken into account when developing an extended pose estimation system that utilizes tracking mechanisms. In the following paragraphs, the relevant state-of-the-art techniques are briefly discussed.

2.1 Platooning

The matter of platooning has already been discussed in various publications. An overview of some active projects is given by Bergenheim et al. [4]. A lot of already published approaches utilize *Vehicle-To-Infrastructure Communication* (V2I) or *Vehicle-To-Vehicle Communication* (V2V) such as [11,21].

Benhimane et al. [3] use a camera and compute homographies to estimate the pose of a leading vehicle. Franke et al. [8] use triangulation to address the matter, whereas Manz et al. [17] utilize a particle filter.

2.2 Tracking

As the camera provides image sequences as input for our algorithm, it makes sense to use the temporal coherence between single image frames. Kalman [15] introduced a probabilistically sound way to fuse measurements appropriate motion models. Measurements in our case are the individual image frames. They can be fused to the the motion of the leading vehicle. The Kalman filter is of common use in tracking applications. For example, Barth and Franke [1,2] proposed a method for image-based tracking of oncoming vehicles from a moving platform using stereo-data and an extended Kalman filter. They used images with a resolution of 640 px by 480 px. Dellaert [6] presented a method to track vehicles using Bayesian templates and a Kalman filter. A lot of vehicle tracking approaches like Broggi et al. [5] rely on the "flat world" assumption. While this simplifcation works well for urban environments, it is not suitable for off-road scenarios, as the geometry assumption of the terrain is violated.

Tracking dynamic system states that contain non-Euclidean spaces – such as unit quaternions – can be problematic for a Kalman filter. In order to avoid the involved issues, the Kalman filter was extended to work on manifolds by Hertzberg et al. [13] and Wagner et al. [22]. We adapt the underlying methodology for our approach by implementing an extended Kalman filter that obeys the topological structure of rotational spaces.

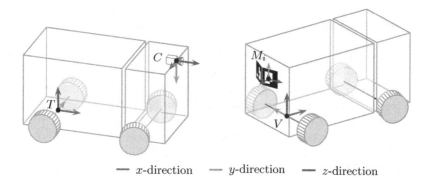

— x-direction   — y-direction   — z-direction

Fig. 1. Defined coordinate systems and orientation of the orthonormal bases

2.3   Artificial Markers

Artificial markers are of common use, especially in augmented reality (AR) and tracking applications. Various different libraries have been developed and are available free for use [7,16,18,20]. We decided to use *AprilTags* [18] in our system.

3   Optical Tracking Approach

In our setup we use a high resolution camera, which is mounted on a vehicle that follows a leading vehicle. Two static artificial markers are mounted at the back of the leading vehicle. The marker setup is observed by a camera mounted on the following vehicle.

Fig. 1 illustrates the geometric setup of the camera and the markers and defines the coordinate systems used in our system:

Symbol	Coordinate System	Symbol	Coordinate System
C	Camera	T	Following Vehicle
M_i	Marker M_i	V	Leading Vehicle

The position and orientation of an object in *3-D* space can be combined to the so-called *pose* of an object. It is defined as a tuple $p = \langle s, q \rangle$ with $s \in \mathbb{R}^3$ the position of the object relative to the origin of the coordinate system and $q \in \mathbb{R}^4$ the vector representation of a unit quaternion for the rotation relative to the coordinate system's orthonormal bases.

The system can be configured for various marker setups. At least one marker is required for our method to work, but the higher the number of (visible) markers get, the more precise the pose estimate for the vehicle will be.

With $M = \{M_i \mid i \in \mathbb{N}^+\}$ the set of markers mounted at the leading vehicle, a transformation from $\mathcal{T}_{V \to M_i}$ is defined for each marker, thus modelling the transformation from vehicle to marker coordinate system and the position and orientation relative to the vehicle at the same time. The corners of a marker M_i

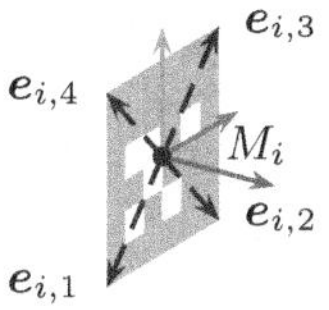

$$e_{i,1} = 0.5 \cdot (-m_i, -m_i, 0)^{\mathrm{T}} \qquad e_{i,3} = 0.5 \cdot (m_i, m_i, 0)^{\mathrm{T}}$$

$$e_{i,2} = 0.5 \cdot (m_i, -m_i, 0)^{\mathrm{T}} \qquad e_{i,4} = 0.5 \cdot (-m_i, m_i, 0)^{\mathrm{T}}$$

with $m_i \in \mathrm{I\!R}^+$ the side length of marker M_i

Fig. 2. Marker corner definition for M_i in the local marker coordinate system

are described using constant vectors $e_{i,j}, e_{i,j} \in \mathrm{I\!R}^3, j \in \{1, 2, 3, 4\}$ in the marker coordinate system (see Fig. 2).

In the proposed setup, two artificial markers are placed on the leading vehicle. They are slightly rotated in order to be viewable from the side as well (see Fig. 3).

3.1 Dynamic Kalman State

As the estimation of the pose of the leading vehicle is prone to uncertainties, a Kalman filter [15] is be utilized to improve the pose estimate. The dynamic Kalman state of the vehicle pose is represented by a vector:

$$x = \left(s^{\mathrm{T}}, q^{\mathrm{T}}, v^{\mathrm{T}}, \omega^{\mathrm{T}}\right)^{\mathrm{T}} \in \mathrm{I\!R}^{13}.$$

Where $s = (s_x, s_y, s_z)^{\mathrm{T}}$ the position and $q \in \mathrm{I\!R}^4, q = (q_w, q_x, q_y, q_z)^{\mathrm{T}}$, the vector representation of a unit quaternion, define the position and orientation of the leading vehicle relative to the following vehicle. The vectors $v \in \mathrm{I\!R}^3$ and $\omega \in \mathrm{I\!R}^3$ describe the system's linear and angular velocity.

4 Kalman Motion Model

The real dynamics of the system are characterized by a superposition of the two Ackermann motion models of the involved vehicles. Since it is very complex to directly model this behavior, we instead use a simple linear motion model, which is reasonable assumption for many motion models. The motion model is defined as follows:

$$x_t = f(x_{t-1}) + a_{t-1}$$
$$= \begin{pmatrix} s_{t-1} + \Delta_t v_{t-1} \\ q_{t-1} \mathcal{Q}(\Delta_t \omega_{t-1}) \\ v_{t-1} \\ \omega_{t-1} \end{pmatrix} + a_{t-1}$$

Where $t \in \mathrm{I\!N}^+$ is the time step, $\Delta_t \in \mathrm{I\!R}^+$ defines the time since the last prediction in seconds and the function $\mathcal{Q}$ computes a unit quaternion, describing the rotation since the last time step. The random variable $a_{t-1} \sim \mathcal{N}(0, Q_{t-1})$ models the additive Gaussian noise ($\mathcal{N}$) of the system, including inaccuracies of the model and in particular all dynamic movements of the system, as no odometry or inertial sensors are available. Matrix $\boldsymbol{Q}$ is the covariance matrix of the additive noise.

4.1 Kalman Observation Model

The corners of the detected markers $\boldsymbol{e}_{i,j}$ on the leading vehicle are used as the raw measurements (see Fig. 3) for the optimization process using the Kalman filter. The observation model is calculated for each marker's corners and is formulated as:

$$\boldsymbol{z}_t = \boldsymbol{h}(\boldsymbol{x}_t) + \boldsymbol{g}_t = \mathcal{P}(\mathcal{T}_{T \to C} \cdot \mathcal{T}_{V \to T}(\boldsymbol{p}_t) \cdot \mathcal{T}_{M_i \to V} \cdot \boldsymbol{e}_{i,j}) + \boldsymbol{g}_t$$

with $\boldsymbol{g}_t \in \mathbb{R}^2, \boldsymbol{g}_t \sim \mathcal{N}(\boldsymbol{0}, \mathbf{R}_t)$. $\boldsymbol{R}_t$ is the covariance matrix of the additive noise of the measurement model. Functions $\mathcal{T}$ describe the transformations between the coordinate systems.

Function $\boldsymbol{h}$ transforms a corner $\boldsymbol{e}_{i,j}$ of an observed marker M_i to the anticipated position in image coordinates, using the known stationary marker setup. The pose $\boldsymbol{p}_t = \langle \boldsymbol{s}_t, \boldsymbol{q}_t \rangle$ of the current dynamic system state $\boldsymbol{x}_t$ is used to transform the point to the coordinate system V of the following vehicle. Using the known position of the camera relative to the vehicle, the point is transformed into the camera coordinate system C. Finally the known intrinsic parameters desired for calibration [23] are used in the imaging function $\mathcal{P}$ to project the point onto the image plane (pixel coordinates) (see Fig. 3).

This Kalman update step is performed exactly once for all vertices of the detected markers. The use of this model leads to a minimization of the square reprojection error of all detected marker corners.

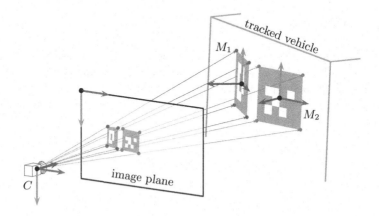

Fig. 3. Imaging process $\mathcal{P}$ and measurements used for pose estimation

4.2 Kalman Filter

Since there are non-Euclidean components in the system state (q and $\boldsymbol{\omega}$), the conventional extended Kalman filter cannot be applied directly. Because of this, our implementation follows an extension of the Kalman filter to work on manifolds [13,22]. We briefly introduce the idea, details on manifolds can be found in the original publications.

In the following notation the operators $\boxplus$ and $\boxminus$ correspond to the Euclidean $+$ and $-$ operators, except for the rotational component which we treat as a locally Euclidean space by implementing $\boxplus$ and $\boxminus$ using the quaternion logarithm and exponential [13,22].

Given a Gaussian estimate of the system state with mean $\hat{\boldsymbol{x}}_{t-1}$ and covariance $\boldsymbol{P}_{t-1}$ at time $t-1$, the prediction of the system state at time step t is computed using:

$$\hat{\boldsymbol{x}}_{t|t-1} = f(\hat{\boldsymbol{x}}_{t-1}) \qquad \boldsymbol{P}_{t|t-1} = \boldsymbol{F}_{t-1}\boldsymbol{P}_{t-1}\boldsymbol{F}_{t-1}^{\mathrm{T}} + \boldsymbol{Q}_{t-1}.$$

The matrix $\boldsymbol{F}$ represents the Jacobian matrix of the motion model f:

$$\boldsymbol{F}_{t-1} = \left.\frac{\partial(f(\hat{\boldsymbol{x}}_{t-1} \boxplus \boldsymbol{d}) \boxminus f(\hat{\boldsymbol{x}}_{t-1}))}{\partial \boldsymbol{d}}\right|_{\boldsymbol{d}=0}.$$

After the prediction, the correction of the estimation $t|t-1$ is done using the measurement $\boldsymbol{z}_t$ and the measurement model $\boldsymbol{h}$ by using:

$$\tilde{\boldsymbol{y}}_t = -(\boldsymbol{z}_t \boxminus \boldsymbol{h}(\hat{\boldsymbol{x}}_{t|t-1}))$$
$$\boldsymbol{S}_t = \boldsymbol{H}_t\boldsymbol{P}_{t|t-1}\boldsymbol{H}_t^{\mathrm{T}} + \boldsymbol{R}_t \qquad \hat{\boldsymbol{x}}_t = \hat{\boldsymbol{x}}_{t|t-1} \boxplus \boldsymbol{G}_t\tilde{\boldsymbol{y}}_t$$
$$\boldsymbol{G}_t = \boldsymbol{P}_{t|t-1}\boldsymbol{H}_t^{\mathrm{T}}\boldsymbol{S}_t^{-1} \qquad \boldsymbol{P}_t = (\boldsymbol{I} - \boldsymbol{G}_t\boldsymbol{H}_t)\boldsymbol{P}_{t|t-1}.$$

Thereby $\boldsymbol{H}_t$, the Jacobian matrix of the measurement model $\boldsymbol{h}$, is defined as:

$$\boldsymbol{H}_t = \left.\frac{\partial(\boldsymbol{g}_t \boxminus \boldsymbol{h}(\hat{\boldsymbol{x}}_{t|t-1} \boxplus \boldsymbol{d}))}{\partial \boldsymbol{d}}\right|_{\boldsymbol{d}=0}.$$

5 Evaluation

The system is designed to work at high velocities and in off-road scenarios. Capturing ground truth data for evaluation is a difficult issue, as a high precision in the pose of both the following and the leading vehicle is mandatory. External position tracking systems do not suit the demands as the needed off-road track is too long and it is therefore too cost- and time-intense to equip with appropriate hardware. Radio based position systems such as GPS or Galileo do not offer an adequate pose quality. Equipping one of the vehicles with hardware like *3-D* LIDAR sensors does not present a solution as well, because the sensors themselves have uncertainties. To make things worse, we consider an off-road scenario where a full *6-D* pose is required as a ground truth.

5.1 Evaluation Using Synthetic Camera Images

Our first approach for evaluation is based on a virtual testbed. A simulation environment is utilized for the generation of synthetic camera images: The simulation environment used is derived from previously published approaches for pose estimate evaluations [9,10]. Its adaptive architecture allows an easy integration for the presented evaluation. The camera in the simulation environment can be configured to match various resolutions and opening angles to test the impact on the pose quality. The intrinsic camera parameters needed for the pose tracking can easily be derived from the simulation configuration following the method described by Fuchs et al. [10]. A 3×3 camera matrix $\boldsymbol{K} \in \mathbb{P}^{2 \times 2}$ [12] is defined using $c_w \times c_h$ the camera resolution and α the horizontal opening angle of the camera (camera constant $f_x = f_y = 1$):

$$\boldsymbol{K} = \begin{bmatrix} k_x & 0 & c_x \\ 0 & k_y & c_y \\ 0 & 0 & 1 \end{bmatrix} \qquad \begin{aligned} c_x &= 0.5 \cdot c_w \\ c_y &= 0.5 \cdot c_h \end{aligned} \qquad k_x = k_y = (2 \cdot c_w^{-1} \cdot \tan{(0.5 \cdot \alpha)})^{-1}$$

The modeling of the (relative) movement between the leading and following vehicle is described using the relative pose $\boldsymbol{p} = \langle \boldsymbol{s}, \boldsymbol{q} \rangle$ between the coordinate system of the following vehicle T and coordinate system of the leading vehicle V. A virtual track is configured using an interpolated spline generated from a GPS log file recorded during outdoor tests (see Fig. 5). The poses of both the following and the leading vehicle are sampled along the generated spline in order to create a realistic movement. Additional torsion in both roll and pitch direction is used to model rough terrain. Of course, sudden pose and direction changes (as caused by potholes for example) are included to test the robustness of the proposed algorithm.

This way, a movement sequence as on a real vehicle setup is generated. The poses are sampled over time at a frame rate of 25 Hz so that the configuration data for the simulation environment is computed. The renderer is configured with a resolution of 640 px by 640 px and the length of the sequence used is 300 s. The side length of the markers is $m_1 = m_2 = 37.5$ cm, as in the real-world test scenario. The rendered image frames are then used as the input for the tracking mechanism proposed. For each time frame, the configured ground truth pose $\boldsymbol{p}$ and the estimated pose $\boldsymbol{p}' = \langle \boldsymbol{s}', \boldsymbol{q}' \rangle$ are recorded and used for analysis. As a pose consists of both translation and rotation, it is mandatory to use appropriate distance measures. The difference Δ between translations $\boldsymbol{s}$ and $\boldsymbol{s}'$ is defined as:

$$\Delta(\boldsymbol{s}, \boldsymbol{s}') = \|\boldsymbol{s} - \boldsymbol{s}'\| \qquad \Delta_\xi(\boldsymbol{s}, \boldsymbol{s}') = |s_\xi - s'_\xi| \qquad \xi \in \{x, y, z\}$$

Deviations between the rotations $\boldsymbol{q}$ and $\boldsymbol{q}'$ cannot be quantified using measurements of Euclidean space. Therefore, a distance measurement defined by Park [19] and discussed by Huynh [14] is used (function $\Phi : \mathbb{R}^4 \to \mathbb{R}^{3 \times 3}$ converts a quaternion to a rotation matrix):

$$\Gamma(\boldsymbol{q}, \boldsymbol{q}') = \|\log(\Phi(\boldsymbol{q}), \Phi(\boldsymbol{q}')^{\mathrm{T}})\|$$

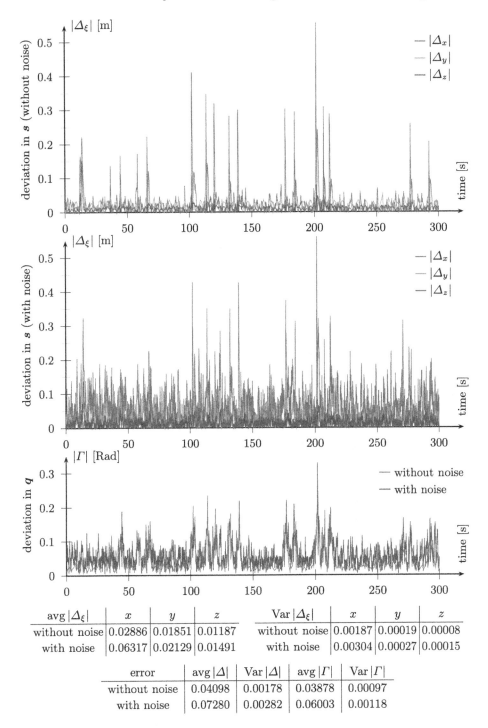

Fig. 4. Evaluation results using the simulation environment

In a first evaluation, the rendered image sequences have directly been processed the Kalman tracking as proposed above. In a second pass, Gaussian noise $\mathcal{N}(\mathbf{0}, \boldsymbol{I}_{2\times 2})$ was added to the raw marker detections extracted from the image. This way, the robustness of our method is quantified. The results of the evaluation are shown in Fig. 4.

5.2   Off-Road Testing Scenario

The pose estimation system as proposed in this publication has been tested using datasets specifically recorded for this purpose with velocities up to 60 km/h. A truck with a marker system mounted on its back was followed by another vehicle equipped with a camera. The estimated pose is reprojected to the camera image, facilitating a visual examination of the results (see Fig. 5). The examination showed that the system provided robust poses up to a range of 25 m while processing at 20 Hz. However, a quantitative analysis of the system cannot be done in this scenario, because no reliable ground truth pose information is available.

sample frame #1

sample frame #2

magnified estimated pose #1

magnified estimated pose #2

Fig. 5. Example detections from recorded test data. The camera has a resolution of 2046 px by 2046 px. The wireframe box visualizes the estimated pose of the vehicle, the rectangle highlights the region of interest for marker extraction used for detection speed-up

6 Conclusion

We proposed an optical tracking mechanism that only uses one camera and artificial markers. A Kalman filter is utilized to include the advantages of temporal coherence. Our system is able of estimating the relative pose between two vehicles very robustly in real-time. The results of the evaluation (see Fig. 4) show the precision of our approach. At an average distance of 8 m, the average absolute error in the translation (avg $|\Delta|$) is about 7.3 cm when artificial noise is added. The average error in the orientation (avg $|\Gamma|$) is 0.06 Rad $\approx$ 3.4 Deg.

High peaks in the precision data (see Fig. 4) are caused by single frames after a rapid position change (pothole-problem), but are compensated quickly. In x-direction, the average absolute error and corresponding variance show larger values, as the depth perception (see Fig. 1) with a single camera is prone to uncertainties. Nevertheless, the overall precision of the system is promising.

With the pose estimation proposed, we introduced an algorithm capable of tracking leading vehicles in off-road platooning scenarios, without the need for communication and/or infrastructure. The leading vehicle could therefore be a regular truck equipped with a marker pattern. This saves time and reduces costs significantly, as no complex setup is necessary. The system works independently from any external services and infrastructure.

For future work it is planned to extend the approach by adding dynamic features to the Kalman tracking. The idea is to learn features detected on the leading vehicle at runtime, so that the pose of the vehicle can still be estimated even when the leading vehicle gets too far away to detect artificial markers. In closer range scenarios, dynamic features can improve the accuracy of the estimated pose. Another possible extension is the integration of the pose tracking for articulated vehicles (truck-trailer-combinations) which have certain degrees of freedom within [9,10].

References

1. Barth, A., Franke, U.: Where will the oncoming vehicle be the next second? In: IEEE Intelligent Vehicles Symposium, pp. 1068–1073, June 2008
2. Barth, A., Franke, U.: Estimating the driving state of oncoming vehicles from a moving platform using stereo vision. IEEE Transactions on Intelligent Transportation Systems 10(4), 560–571 (2009)
3. Benhimane, S., Malis, E., Rives, P., Azinheira, J.: Vision-based control for car platooning using homography decomposition. In: IEEE International Conference on Robotics and Automation, pp. 2161–2166, April 2005
4. Bergenhem, C., Shladover, S., Coelingh, E., Englund, C., Tsugawa, S.: Overview of platooning systems. In: Proceedings of the 19th ITS World Congress, Vienna (2012)
5. Broggi, A., Bertozzi, M., Fascioli, A., Bianco, C., Piazzi, A.: Visual perception of obstacles and vehicles for platooning. IEEE Transactions on Intelligent Transportation Systems 1(3), 164–176 (2000)

6. Dellaert, F., Thorpe, C.E.: Robust car tracking using kalman filtering and bayesian templates. In: Intelligent Transportation Systems (Proc. SPIE), vol. 3207, pp. 72–83 (1998)
7. Fiala, M.: Artag, a fiducial marker system using digital techniques. In: IEEE Computer Society Conference on Computer Vision and Pattern Recognition, vol. 2, pp. 590–596. IEEE (2005)
8. Franke, U., Bottiger, F., Zomotor, Z., Seeberger, D.: Truck platooning in mixed traffic. In: IEEE Intelligent Vehicles Symposium, pp. 1–6, September 1995
9. Fuchs, C., Eggert, S., Knopp, B., Zöbel, D.: Pose detection in truck and trailer combinations for advanced driver assistance systems. In: IEEE Intelligent Vehicles Symposium Proceedings, pp. 1175–1180. IEEE (2014)
10. Fuchs, C., Zöbel, D., Paulus, D.: 3-d pose detection for articulated vehicles. In: 13th International Conference on Intelligent Autonomous Systems (IAS) (2014)
11. Gehring, O., Fritz, H.: Practical results of a longitudinal control concept for truck platooning with vehicle to vehicle communication. In: IEEE Conference on Intelligent Transportation System (ITSC), pp. 117–122, November 1997
12. Hartley, R., Zisserman, A.: Multiple View Geometry in Computer Vision, 2nd edn. Cambridge University Press, New York (2003)
13. Hertzberg, C., Wagner, R., Frese, U., Schröder, L.: Integrating generic sensor fusion algorithms with sound state representations through encapsulation of manifolds. Information Fusion **14**(1), 57–77 (2013)
14. Huynh, D.: Metrics for 3d rotations: Comparison and analysis. Journal of Mathematical Imaging and Vision **35**(2), 155–164 (2009)
15. Kalman, R.E.: A new approach to linear filtering and prediction problems. Journal of Fluids Engineering **82**(1), 35–45 (1960)
16. Kato, H., Billinghurst, M.: Marker tracking and hmd calibration for a video-based augmented reality conferencing system. In: Proceedings of the 2nd IEEE and ACM International Workshop on Augmented Reality (IWAR 1999), pp. 85–94. IEEE (1999)
17. Manz, M., Luettel, T., von Hundelshausen, F., Wuensche, H.J.: Monocular model-based 3d vehicle tracking for autonomous vehicles in unstructured environment. In: IEEE International Conference on Robotics and Automation (ICRA), pp. 2465–2471, May 2011
18. Olson, E.: AprilTag: A robust and flexible visual fiducial system. In: 2011 IEEE International Conference on Robotics and Automation (ICRA), pp. 3400–3407. IEEE (2011)
19. Park, F.C.: Distance metrics on the rigid-body motions with applications to mechanism design. Journal of Mechanical Design **117**(1), 48–54 (1995)
20. Schmalstieg, D., Fuhrmann, A., Hesina, G., Szalavári, Z., Encarnaçao, L.M., Gervautz, M., Purgathofer, W.: The Studierstube augmented reality project. Presence: Teleoperators and Virtual Environments **11**(1), 33–54 (2002)
21. Tank, T., Linnartz, J.P.: Vehicle-to-vehicle communications for avcs platooning. IEEE Transactions on Vehicular Technology **46**(2), 528–536 (1997)
22. Wagner, R., Birbach, O., Frese, U.: Rapid development of manifold-based graph optimization systems for multi-sensor calibration and slam. In: IEEE/RSJ International Conference on Intelligent Robots and Systems (IROS), pp. 3305–3312. IEEE (2011)
23. Zhang, Z.: A flexible new technique for camera calibration. IEEE Trans. Pattern Anal. Mach. Intell. **22**(11), 1330–1334 (2000)

Combination of Air- and Water-Calibration for a Fringe Projection Based Underwater 3D-Scanner

Christian Bräuer-Burchardt[1]([✉]), Peter Kühmstedt[1], and Gunther Notni[1,2]

[1] Fraunhofer Institute Applied Optics and Precision Engineering Jena,
Jena, Germany
{christian.braeuer-burchardt,peter.kuehmstedt}@iof.fraunhofer.de
[2] Technical University Ilmenau, Ilmenau, Germany
gunther.notni@iof.fraunhofer.de

Abstract. A new calibration methodology for photogrammetric underwater stereo scanners is presented. By combination with a complete air calibration, the water part of the calibration can be performed with low expenditure. This leads to an easy handling of the whole procedure. In this paper an underwater camera model is described which considers the refraction effects at the interfaces of the different media air, glass, and water, leading to a ray based presentation. In order to facilitate the calibration procedure and to increase robustness, some simplifications concerning the sensor geometry were made. First results obtained with a new fringe projection based underwater 3D scanner are presented which show the effectiveness of the new calibration strategy.

Keywords: Underwater camera calibration · Underwater 3D-scanner · Fringe projection technique · Photogrammetry

1 Introduction

Underwater photogrammetry is already performed for more than 40 years [1,2] and has been strongly developed in the last few decades. There are applications concerning documentation of ship wrecks [3], exploration of archaeological sites [4,5], or for underwater navigation [6]. Measurements are desired in a growing manner for underwater applications such as fish size measurements [7,8] or coral reef size measurement [9]. The precision of underwater measurements strongly depends on the calibration quality, because the geometric conditions are different from camera mapping in air. Under water, the refraction of the vision rays at the interfaces between the media air, glass, and water must be considered [10]. Consequently, for precise measurements, calibration strategies are necessary different from the pinhole model based common photogrammetric calibration techniques.

Some publications concerning underwater calibration considering the refraction effects are available [10–14]. However, although there occur considerable systematic errors, the pinhole model is also used for underwater calibration [6,8,15–18].

© Springer International Publishing Switzerland 2015
G. Azzopardi and N. Petkov (Eds.): CAIP 2015, Part II, LNCS 9257, pp. 49–60, 2015.
DOI: 10.1007/978-3-319-23117-4_5

The use of fringe projection for a structured illumination of the underwater scene is quite new. However, new works concerning structured light projection techniques for underwater use have been recently published [19–22].

In this paper a new, but simple method for underwater stereo sensor calibration is introduced. It is suitable for plane port glasses and perpendicular camera orientation in relation to the glasses and considers refraction effects.

The outline of the paper is as follows. First, a motivation for our development of our underwater 3D scanner based on fringe projection technique is given. Then the camera and 3D reconstruction modelling in the underwater case is treated. The combined air- and water-calibration method is described. The new scanner will be introduced, and first experiments and the results are presented.

2   Motivation and Approaches

2.1   Fringe Projection Technique

Fringe projection technique is typically used in applications of industrial quality control, medicine, archaeology, arts and cultural heritage preservation, and also in the forensics. Typically, high measurement accuracy (see [23]) can be achieved.

Although it is not to be expected to obtain comparable accuracy results in underwater measurements, there are some benefits of structured light illumination under water concerning measurability and accuracy in opposite to the common photogrammetric 3D measurements. Additionally, complete automation of the whole measurement is easier to obtain by the use of the structured light technique. On the other hand, structured illumination requires a powerful projection system.

Improved measurement precision can only obtained if the sensor calibration is accurate. A correct underwater sensor calibration should be achieved using an appropriate camera model and a suitable calibration procedure which will be described in this work.

2.2   Air- and Water-Calibration

As it was already described by several authors, e.g. [10, 14, 24], underwater stereo camera calibration usually means considerable effort. Additionally, a decreased precision has to be expected. Hence Lavest et al. [17] propose a dry camera calibration for underwater applications. However, his method is restricted to the intrinsic camera parameters.

Air calibration of a stereo camera system is a quite typical task in photogrammetry [23] or fringe projection profilometry [25]. Hence sufficient methods are available. The question is now: can we find a simple calibration in order to get the underwater description of the system by the a-priori use of the air calibration? We believe so, because the camera properties do not really change if we put it into water. What does actually change is the direction of the rays. Hence our task should be the determination of the ray directions of the rays under water corresponding to the image points and an appropriate modeling of the two cameras.

2.3 Approach for 3D Measurements

The 3D measurement for our underwater stereo sensor should be performed analogously to air sensors by ray triangulation. Our aim is to find as few parameters as possible which determine the correct description of the rays under water. In order to find these parameters, as few as possible underwater images should be necessary. As we will see in the next section, these parameters are the refraction indices of air, glass, and water, the thickness of the glasses, the normal angle of the camera concerning the glass surface, and the distance between the projection centre of the camera and the glass interface.

In order to find a suitable modelling of the ray we use the ray based camera model [26] in an own notation (see next section) derived from the pinhole model. Briefly spoken, every image point corresponds to a ray in the 3D space given by any representation (typically one 3D point and one 3D direction vector) describing the ray (only) in the water which corresponds to a certain image point.

2.4 Approach for Calibration

In order to get a most accurate calibration result with a most simple calibration procedure we suggest a three-step procedure for the underwater stereo-sensor calibration based on the use of the ray based camera model (RM):

- first step: air calibration of the sensor outside the underwater housing using the pinhole model, transformation of this model into the ray based model
- second step: determination of the glass thickness, obtain a ray based model of the sensor inside the housing for air measurements
- third step: water calibration in order to determine the camera-interface-distance using the ray based model

3 Underwater Camera Model

3.1 Modelling of Refraction

In principle, two different modelling approaches are used for photogrammetric underwater systems. First, the pinhole camera model is used and the calibration parameters are adapted to the underwater situation as best as possible (see e.g. [15,17]). This includes the acceptance of systematic errors which should be minimized. The second way is to consider the refraction effects at the interfaces between the different media (air, glass, water) in some manner. This may be the use of the ray based camera model or the consideration of the caustics (see [10]) as a deviation from the pinhole model.

As described by Sedlazeck and Koch [10] the simple adaptation of the pinhole model leads to measurement errors of the 3D reconstruction, which would be inacceptable for certain measurements. Hence, this model will not be used here, except for comparison of the measurement errors (see section 5).

First, let us consider the two (usual) different cases of housing glass realization as the interface between the stereo camera system and the water medium. We distinguish planar and dome port glasses (see Fig. 1). If we use spherical dome ports it would be useful to place the projection centre of the camera into the centre point of the sphere. Then no refraction would occur and the pinhole model would stay valid also in the underwater case. However, deviation from the centre point placement of the cameras would lead to errors in the 3D measurements which should be estimated and compensated somehow.

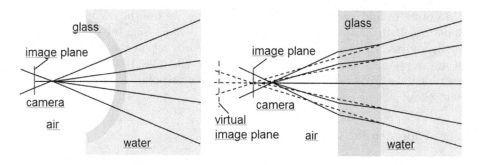

Fig. 1. Ray geometry in the case of spherical dome ports (left) and plane glasses (right)

In the case of a plane glass interface we distinguish between orthogonal and tilted orientation of the cameras concerning the glass surface. For both these cases Korduan et al. [3] suggest the use of the pinhole model and an additional distortion correction function which is dependent on the glass thickness th, the refraction indizes n_a, n_w, n_g, the interface distance d, the normal angle γ, and the object distance D. Equation (1) describes the distortion function $\triangle r$ in the general case for image points with radial distance r from the principal point.

$$\triangle r = \frac{c}{D} \left[\frac{d \cdot \tan(\gamma + \varepsilon_1)}{(1 + \tan(\alpha) \cdot \tan(\gamma))} + \frac{th \cdot \cos(\gamma + \varepsilon_2) \cdot \tan(\gamma + \varepsilon_2)}{\cos(\varepsilon_2)} + \right. \tag{1}$$
$$\left. \left(D - \frac{d}{(1 + \tan(\alpha) \cdot \tan(\gamma))} - \frac{th \cdot \cos(\gamma + \varepsilon_2)}{\cos(\varepsilon_2)} \right) \cdot \tan(\gamma + \varepsilon_3) \right]$$

with $\alpha = \arctan\left(\frac{r}{c}\right)$, the tilt angle γ concerning glass surface, $\varepsilon_1 = \alpha - \gamma$, $\varepsilon_2 = \arcsin\left(\sin\left(\varepsilon_1 \cdot \frac{n_a}{n_g}\right)\right)$, and $\varepsilon_3 = \arcsin\left(\sin\left(\varepsilon_1 \cdot \frac{n_a}{n_w}\right)\right)$. Because of the unknown (and for various image points also different) values of D, equation (1) should be applied iteratively. However, it is expected to be time consuming and error sensitive, even if we assume no tilt ($\gamma = 0$).

3.2   Camera Model for Plane Glasses and Orthogonal Orientation

In our modelling we use the following simplifications. We assume a constant glass thickness, homogeneous optical glass properties and a perpendicular orientation of the cameras concerning the image plane and the glass surfaces.

Let us first consider the course of the rays corresponding to the image points. For illustration see Fig. 2. The refraction is assumed according to Snells law. If we want to describe the rays in water which correspond to the image points, we extend the water-rays and consider the intersection with the optical axis x. This yields a certain shift l of the projection centre on x depending on the radial distance r of the image point from the principal point. Additionally, we obtain an extended principal distance c also depending on r (or α, respectively).

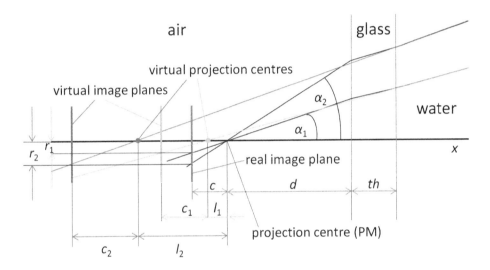

Fig. 2. Ray geometry in the case of plane glasses for two image points with radial distances r_1 and r_2

If we now assume to know the parameters of the air calibration and the refraction indices, our task is to determine the parameters l and c' which will be realized by the following equations:

$$l = \frac{\frac{d \cdot r}{c} + th \cdot \left(\tan \left(\arcsin \left(\frac{\sin\left(\arctan\left(\frac{r}{c}\right)\right)}{n_g} \right) \right) \right)}{\tan \left(\arcsin \left(\frac{\sin\left(\arctan\left(\frac{r}{c}\right)\right)}{n_w} \right) \right)} - th - d, \qquad (2)$$

$$c' = \frac{r}{\tan \left(\arcsin \left(\frac{\sin\left(\arctan\left(\frac{r}{c}\right)\right)}{n_w} \right) \right)}. \qquad (3)$$

In order to solve these equations we have to determine the glass thickness th_i and the interface distance d_i for both cameras C_i (i=1, 2).

If we consider the case of the sensor use in air within the housing, we obtain for the shift l and the principal distance c':

$$l = th \left(\frac{c}{r} \tan \left(\arcsin \left(\frac{\arctan \left(\frac{r}{c} \right)}{n_g} \right) \right) - 1 \right), \tag{4}$$

$$c' = c. \tag{5}$$

Hence, if we'd like to use the sensor within the housing for air measurements, e.g. for outdoor measurements under bad weather conditions such as rain, snow, or wind, the shift of the projection centre according to (4) should be considered, whereas the principal distance is kept.

With equations (2) and (3) we can uniquely describe the rays corresponding to the image points $q = (x, y)$ according to the RM by the two 3D points $O_i(x, y)$ and $Q_i(x, y)$.

$$O_i(x, y) = O_i - l(r) \cdot \mathbf{R} \cdot \mathbf{e}, \tag{6}$$

$$Q_i(x, y) = O_i(x, y) - c'(r) \cdot \mathbf{R} \cdot \begin{pmatrix} x \\ y \\ -c'(r) \end{pmatrix}, \tag{7}$$

where $\mathbf{R}$ is the rotation matrix of the air calibration and $\mathbf{e}$ is the unit vector.

For simplification we assume w.l.o.g. no distortion here.

4 The Calibration Procedure

4.1 Air Calibration

The sensor can be calibrated in the laboratory using a common calibration method (see e.g. [23]) for stereo scanners. We used a self-calibration methodology using an additional calibration camera and producing the calibration points by phase values generated by projected fringe sequences [25].

4.2 Determination of the Glass Thickness

For the determination of the glass thickness we have several possibilities. The most elegant solution is the exact thickness measurement before the housing assembly using any arbitrary method. If the glass thickness measurement is not possible before the mounting of the sensor into the housing, we can estimate th using equation (4) and an air measurement of known geometries with the sensor inside the housing equivalently to the procedure of getting the interface distance. This will be described in the next section.

4.3   Calibration of the Interface Distance

The determination of the interface distances of the two cameras will be realized using few underwater measurements of a plane and a calibrated length and the minimization of a certain test quantity. Alternatively, other approaches could be applied. Chen and Yang propose a method for simultaneous determination of the interface thickness and distance [27].

The analogous measurement of the interface distance may be difficult and erroneous because the location of the camera projection centres is not trivial. However, if the position of the projection centre can be determined exactly according to the lens front and the mechanical adjustment of the sensor into the housing is perfect, one could omit the determination of the interface distances and use the distances obtained from construction. Finally, the correctness should be checked by measurements.

Because we are not able to determine the interface distances by construction as exact as necessary, we performed the interface distance calibration using the following methodology. Considering equations (2) to (7) it seems to be quite complicate to find an analytical solution for the determination of the interface distance. However, we can fairly restrict the interval for the possible values of d_1 and d_2. If we now perform a systematic search for d_1 and d_2 in the range $[d_{min}, d_{max}]$ with a certain step width $\triangle d$ and apply the potential values for 3D point calculation, we obtain certain 3D measurement results. These results should be characterized using a test quantity T such, that a minimal value for T denotes the best 3D reconstruction result. Finding the minimal T we obtain the values d_1 and d_2 as the searched interface distances. Iterative application may refine the result by making the step with $\triangle d$ smaller.

For the characterization of the 3D reconstruction quality we used the quantities relative length deviation rld and relative planarity rpd according to [28]:

$$rld = \left| \frac{dist_{meas} - dist_{calib}}{dist_{calib}} \right| \; ; rpd = 2 \cdot \frac{md}{len_{ref}} \tag{8}$$

where $dist_{calib}$ is the known and $dist_{meas}$ is the measured sphere distance. The maximal Euclidean deviation of a measured 3D point from a fitted plane is denoted by md. A maximum of 0.3% outliers can be removed. We selected four underwater measurements (M_i):

- M_1: plane surface (see Fig. 3), approximately orthogonal to the main sensor direction, most close position in the measurement volume (MV)
- M_2: plane surface (see Fig. 3), approximately orthogonal to the main sensor direction, most far position in the MV
- M_3: calibrated sphere bed (see Fig. 3) with two spheres with known distance between the centre-points, most close position in the MV
- M_4: calibrated sphere bed (see Fig. 3) with two spheres with known distance between the centre-points, most far position in the MV

The test quantity T was defined as

$$T(d_1, d_2) = rpd_{M_1}^2 + rpd_{M_2}^2 + rpd_{M_3}^2 + rpd_{M_4}^2. \tag{9}$$

Fig. 3. Plane from ceramics 245 mm x 254 mm (left) and sphere bed (right)

5   The New Underwater Scanner

At the development of our new underwater 3D scanner we started from the "kolibri Cordless" device [29]. For the underwater use some functional groups had to be constructed completely new. This concerned a more robust mechanics and the camera and projection technique used. The desired system parameters are collected by Table 1. A complete new concept we followed by the insertion

Table 1. Intended system parameters.

Parameter	Intended values
Measurement volume (MV)	$250 \times 200 \times 150 \ mm^3$
Working distance	500 mm
Camera pixel resolution	1600×1200 Pixel
Lateral resolution in the MV	150 m
Frame rate	60 Hz
Time for recording one scan	350 ms
Maximal water depth	40 m
Sensor weight without housing	appr. 2 kg
Sensor weight with housing	appr. 10 kg

of the PC and the display into the housing. So no additional cable connection between the sensor and an external PC is necessary which improved the handling under water. On the other hand, the sensor becomes a bit heavier.

The development of the underwater housing was realized by the 4h Jena engineering GmbH [30]. It can be used in both fresh and salt water. Photographs of the sensor and the housing are shown in Figs. 4 and 5.

In order to realize a sufficient heat removal from the system there were constructed suitable cooling elements and a housing base plate with cooling ribs. This is necessary because of the strong heating of the projection unit. See Fig. 5 for two views.

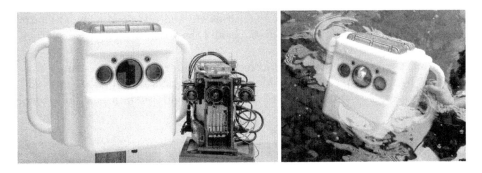

Fig. 4. Sensor unit and housing separated (left), complete scanner in water basin (right)

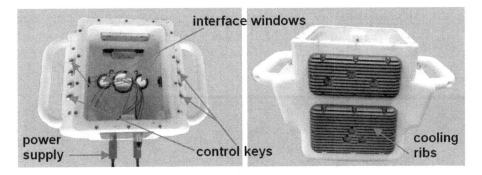

Fig. 5. Housing with power supply cables (left), view from above with heatsink (right)

6   Experiments and Results

First experiments were performed after air calibration in order to evaluate the scanners measurement accuracy. The plane and the sphere bed were measured in different position in the measurement volume, and the quantities rld and rpd according to equations (8) were determined. A further measurement object was a pyramid stump with known length measures of the covering surface (see Fig. 6). Additionally, the noise of the measured 3D points was determined as the standard deviation of the measured points from a fitted plane surface in a small local environment. The results are documented in Table 2.

The same procedure was performed using the scanner within the underwater housing but for air measurements in order to estimate the influence of the housing glasses on the measurement accuracy. The results are also given in Table 2.

The third part of our evaluation experiments was performed under water. The three reference measurement objects were put into a rain barrel (see Fig. 6) which was filled with fresh water. The same measurements as in air were performed. The results of the underwater measurements are also collected in Table 2. For illustration of the insufficiency of the pinhole model (PM) for underwater measurements the same data were used to calculate the 3D points using the best fitted pinhole calibration. The quantities ald and apd denote the absolute length deviation $ald = |dist_{meas} - dist_{calib}|$ and the absolute planarity deviation $apd = 2md$, respectively.

The next experiments were performed in a water basin. The scanner was handheld by a diver (see Fig. 6). Measurement objects were besides the calibration bodies plane and sphere bed and the pyramid stump a pipe and stone structures.

Table 2. Results for the calibration evaluation measurements.

Location/model	ald [mm]	rld [%]	apd [mm]	rpd [%]	noise [mm]
Air, PM	0.1	0.05	0.2	0.1	0.02
Air in housing, PM	0.2	0.1	0.3	0.15	0.02
Water, PM	2.0	1.0	3.4	1.7	0.05
Water, RM	0.8	0.4	1.3	0.65	0.05

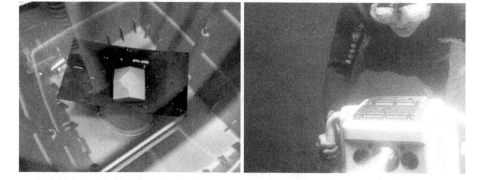

Fig. 6. Pyramid stump in the rain barrel (left), underwater use of the scanner (right)

7   Summary, Discussion, and Outlook

We presented a simple new methodology for the calibration of photogrammetric underwater stereo scanners with plane ports. The technique combines a common air calibration using the pinhole camera model with few underwater measurements for the calibration of the interface distance. The glass thickness was determined by a tactile measurement. Additionally, it was assumed for simplification that the camera orientations are perpendicular to the plane interface glass surface. Hence, it is only applicable, if the camera orientation is really nearly perpendicular. Measurement accuracy has the same magnitude as those reported by Bruno et al. [19], Bianco et al. [20], and Zhang et al [21].

The case of non-perpendicular orientation concerning the glass surfaces is, however, not yet considered and should be one of the next steps of our work.

This should also include a comparison to the method proposed by Chen and Yang [27].

Future work will be furthermore addressed on the analysis of the measurement conditions on the accuracy. This includes water quality (clear water, dirty water) and possible difference concerning fresh or salt water.

Another part of our future activities should be the development of improved underwater 3D scanners. One of the goals will be a significant enlargement of the measurement volume in order to make the structured light projection technique more suitable for underwater 3D measurement applications such as inspection of underwater industrial plants or pipeline systems. This means above all the improvement of the illumination power of the structured light projector and the solution of the upcoming cooling problem which corresponds to a higher illumination power.

Acknowledgements. This work was supported by the state Thuringia and the European Union (EFRE) under grant label TNA VIII-1/2012.

References

1. Höhle, J.: Zur theorie und praxis der unterwasser-photogrammetrie. In: Deutsche Geodätische Kommission, Reihe C, Dissertationen, Bayerische Akademie der Wissenschaften in Kommission bei der C.H.Beckschen Verlagsbuchhandlung München (1971)
2. Moore, E.J.: Underwater photogrammetry. Photogrammetric Record **8**(48), 748–763 (1976)
3. Korduan, P., Förster, T., Obst, R.: Unterwasser-Photogrammetrie zur 3D-Rekonstruktion des Schiffswracks "Darsser Kogge". Photogrammetrie Fernerkundung Geoinformation **5**, 373–381 (2003)
4. Drap, P.: Underwater photogrammetry for archaeology. In: Carneiro Da Silva, D. (Ed.): Special Applications of Photogrammetry, pp. 111–136. InTech publ. (2012). ISBN: 978-953-51-0548-0
5. Roman, C., Inglis, G., Rutter, J.: Application of structured light imaging for high resolution mapping of underwater archaeological sites. In: OCEANS 2010, pp. 1–9. IEEE, Sydney (2010)
6. Gracias, N., Santos-Victor, J.: Underwater video mosaics as visual navigation maps. CVIU **79**, 66–91 (2000)
7. Dunbrack, R.L.: In situ measurement of fish body length using perspective-based remote stereo-video. Fisheries Research **82**, 327–331 (2006)
8. Costa, C., Loy, A., Cataudella, S., Davis, D., Scardi, M.: Extracting fish size using dual underwater cameras. Aquacultural Engineering **35**, 218–227 (2006)
9. Bythell, J.C., Pan, P., Lee, J.: Three-dimensional morphometric measurements of reef corals using underwater photogrammetry techniques. Springer Coral Reefs **20**, 193–199 (2001)
10. Sedlazeck, A., Koch, R.: Perspective and non-perspective camera models in underwater imaging – overview and error analysis. In: Dellaert, F., Frahm, J.-M., Pollefeys, M., Leal-Taixé, L., Rosenhahn, B. (eds.) Real-World Scene Analysis 2011. LNCS, vol. 7474, pp. 212–242. Springer, Heidelberg (2012)

11. Li, R., Tao, C., Curran, T., Smith, R.: Digital underwater photogrammetric system for large scale underwater spatial information acquisition. Marine Geodesy **20**, 163–173 (1996)
12. Maas, H.G.: New developments in multimedia photogrammetry. In: Grün, A., Kahmen, H. (eds.) Optical 3-D Measurement Techniques III. Wichmann Verlag, Karlsruhe (1995)
13. Kwon, Y.H., Casebolt, J.B.: Effects of light refraction on the accuracy of camera ca-libration and reconstruction in underwater motion analysis. Sports Biom. **5**, 315–340 (2006)
14. Telem, G., Filin, S.: Photogrammetric modeling of underwater environments. ISPRS Journal of Photogrammetry and Remote Sensing **65**(5), 433 (2010)
15. Fryer, J.G., Fraser, C.S.: On the calibration of underwater cameras. The Photogrammetric Record **12**(67), 73–85 (1986)
16. Lavest, J.-M., Rives, G., Lapresté, J.T.: Underwater camera calibration. In: Vernon, D. (ed.) ECCV 2000. LNCS, vol. 1843, pp. 654–668. Springer, Heidelberg (2000)
17. Lavest, J.M., Rives, G., Lapreste, J.T.: Dry camera calibration for underwater applications. Machine Vision and Applications **2003**(13), 245–253 (2003)
18. Bryant, M., Wettergreen, D., Abdallah, S., Zelinsky, A.: Robust camera calibration for an autonomous underwater vehicle. In: Australian Conference on Robotics and Automation, ACRA 2000 (2000)
19. Bruno, F., Bianco, G., Muzzupappa, M., Barone, S., Razionale, A.V.: Experimentation of structured light and stereo vision for underwater 3D reconstruction. ISPRS Journal of Photogrammetry and Remote Sensing **66**, 508–518 (2011)
20. Bianco, G., Gallo, A., Bruno, F., Muzzupappa, M.: A comparative analysis between active and passive techniques for underwater 3D reconstruction of close-range objects. Sensors **2013**(13), 11007–11031 (2013)
21. Zhang, Q., Wang, Q., Hou, Z., Liu, Y., Su, X.: Three-dimensional shape measurement for an underwater object based on two-dimensional grating pattern projection. Optics & Laser Technology **43**, 801–805 (2011)
22. Massot-Campos, M., Oliver-Codina, G.: Underwater laser-based structured light system for one-shot 3D reconstruction. In: 5th Int Workshop on Marine Technology, Girona (2014)
23. Luhmann, T., Robson, S., Kyle, S., Harley, I.: Close range photogrammetry. Wiley Whittles Publishing (2006)
24. Shortis, M.R., Miller, S., Harvey, E.S., Robson, S.: An analysis of the calibration stability and measurement accuracy of an underwater stereo-video system used for shellfish surveys. Geomatics Research Australasia **73**, 1–24 (2000)
25. Schreiber, W., Notni, G.: Theory and arrangements of self-calibrating whole-body three-dimensional measurement systems using fringe projection techniques. Opt. Eng. **39**, 159–169 (2000)
26. Bothe, T., Li, W., Schulte, M., von Kopylow, C., Bergmann, R.B., Jüptner, W.: Vision ray calibration for the quantitative geometric description of general imaging and projection optics in metrology. Applied Optics **49**(30), 5851–5860 (2010)
27. Chen X., Yang, Y.H.: Two view camera housing parameters calibration for multi-layer flat refractive interface. In: CVPR (2014)
28. VDI/VDE 2634. Optical 3D-measuring systems. VDI/VDE guidelines, Parts 1–3 (2008)
29. Munkelt, C., Bräuer-Burchardt, C., Kühmstedt, P., Schmidt, I., Notni, G.: Cordless hand-held optical 3D sensor. In: Proc. SPIE, vol. 6618, pp. 66180D-1-8 (2007)
30. 4h Jena (2015). http://www.4h-jena.de/

Calibration of Stereo 3D Scanners with Minimal Number of Views Using Plane Targets and Vanishing Points

Christian Bräuer-Burchardt[1]([⊠]), Peter Kühmstedt[1], and Gunther Notni[1,2]

[1] Fraunhofer Institute Applied Optics and Precision Engineering Jena,
Jena, Germany
{christian.braeuer-burchardt,peter.kuehmstedt}@iof.fraunhofer.de
[2] Technical University Ilmenau, Ilmenau, Germany
gunther.notni@iof.fraunhofer.de

Abstract. A new calibration methodology of photogrammetric stereo scanners using minimal number of views of plane targets is introduced which can be applied with small effort in equipment and time. It is especially interesting for the fast re-calibration of measurement systems which should be frequently adjusted (changing focus distances, variable focal lengths) or can be easily disturbed. A novel technique is introduced for the determination of the intrinsic camera parameters using only two images of a plane pattern or one image showing two planes. The determination of the extrinsic parameters is obtained using a two-step algorithm. Results of the accuracy of the calibration parameter determination are given as well as examples of 3D reconstruction errors.

Keywords: Camera calibration · 3D reconstruction · Photogrammetry · Single view method · Vanishing points

1 Introduction

Modern trends in optical 3D measurement techniques move to either high-accuracy systems or high-speed applications for the acquisition of even moving measurement objects. Deeply specialized developments realize these requirements. Photogrammetric 3D scanners are used in a various field of application such as industrial quality control, rapid prototyping, medicine, arts and cultural heritage preservation, archaeology and palaeontology, and also underwater applications.

High precision 3D measurement systems are typically designed for one special application in order to obtain most accurate measurement results. These systems cover a certain measurement field. Calibration takes usually high effort in time and handling.

However, sometimes also measurement systems are desired, which can be used in a variable field of applications including different measurement object sizes. In this field not so many systems are available. There are some systems with several sets of lenses in order to realize measurement fields of different size.

G. Azzopardi and N. Petkov (Eds.): CAIP 2015, Part II, LNCS 9257, pp. 61–72, 2015.
DOI: 10.1007/978-3-319-23117-4_6

However, using more than one lens for each camera makes the device bigger and heavier. Additionally, changing the lenses means more technical effort. Re-calibration is also necessary.

An alternative to the change-the-lenses solution would be systems using zoom lenses. However, using zoom lenses in a photogrammetric stereo system requires a complete calibration after every adjustment either of focal length or focus. Here, fast and effortless calibration methods are necessary.

An effortless calibration method is also interesting, if a re-calibration after a re-adjustment or mechanical disturbances (hit or fall) is necessary, and highest measurement precision is not demanded.

Fast calibration methods are requested at the place of measurement. Hence, complicate, large, and sensitive calibration targets may be unpractical. A use of the environment of the application site for the calibration would be perfect. However, suitable calibration targets may help to perform an effortless and accurate calibration. Plane calibration targets such as chessboard patterns are widely used in practice for many calibration tasks. They are typically easy to transport, and a lot of software solutions is available for edge and corner detection and even for the complete calibration task.

The methodology which will be described in the following provides a fast, robust, and medium accurate calibration technique for photogrammetric stereo scanners using a minimum of image recordings for the calibration procedure. After a brief survey of the state of the art, the geometric basics of the proposed calibration technique are explained. Then the particular steps of the calibration procedure for both intrinsic and extrinsic parameters based on a plane grid calibration target will be described.

After presentation of several experiments, the results will be discussed and compared to those obtained by a more effortful calibration technique. Finally, an outlook will be given to future work.

2   State of the Art

Single shot algorithms have been proposed for different purposes by several authors. One of the application fields is the photogrammetric use of images without calibration information concerning the camera (e.g. lost data, only images available, measurement objects eventually no more present as in the case of destroyed buildings, see e.g. [1–3]). Single view metrology has been developed to an own field of computer vision [4] including special single view calibration algorithms. Here, typically additional a-priori information concerning the measurement objects is used. A typical field of application is the generation of architectural models [5,6]. Single views are also used for calibration in robotics [7].

Calibration of the intrinsic camera parameters using single images are proposed by several authors. Caprile and Torre [8] first used three vanishing points from mutually orthogonal directions for the calibration of the intrinsic and extrinsic camera parameters. They showed that the principal point is the intersection of the heights of the triangle with the three vanishing points as corners.

Based on this knowledge several methodologies have been proposed (see e.g. [9,10]). Some methods are restricted to the determination of only the intrinsic parameters [11–14]. Beardsley and Murray [15] propose a method for the determination of the intrinsic parameters from vanishing points of planes using only two images which is similar to our approach.

Recently, many authors prefer the use of plenty images of planar patterns such as grid patterns, point patterns, chessboard-patterns, and even man-made structures from the environment with geometric properties such as parallelism and perpendicularity (e.g. [16,17]). However it has to be analysed, whether many recordings improve the calibration quality or only reduce the random error by averaging.

Another approach to the calibration of stereo cameras is the determination of the fundamental matrix, which has been described e.g. by Faugeras [18], Lourakis [19], or Hartley and Zisserman [20]. Here, typically at least seven pairs of corresponding points, which are not coplanar, are used to determine the fundamental matrix, from which the extrinsic camera parameters can be derived.

3   Modelling and Approach

3.1   Camera and 3D Reconstruction Model

As usual in photogrammetric applications the common pinhole camera model is used extended by lens distortion. The distortion function will be modelled as a sum of radial symmetric, decentering, and additional distortion, expressed by a third order polynomial. The use of more distortion parameters seems not meaningful because of the relative few input data coming from a single image.

We consider the intrinsic camera parameters principal point $p_0 = (x_0, y_0)$ and principal distance c. Distortion functions

$$\triangle x = \triangle x_r + \triangle x_d + \triangle x_p$$

$$\triangle y = \triangle y_r + \triangle y_d + \triangle y_p \tag{1}$$

can e.g. consider radial symmetric $(\triangle x_r, \triangle y_r)$ and decentering $(\triangle x_d, \triangle y_d)$ distortion, and contain a remaining distortion part $(\triangle x_p, \triangle y_p)$ which may described by a polynomial as expressed by equation (2):

$$\triangle x_p = a_1 x^3 + a_2 x^2 y + a_3 x y^2 + a_4 y^3 + a_5 x^2 + a_6 xy + a_7 y^2 + a_8 x + a_9 y + a_{10}$$

$$\triangle y_p = b_1 x^3 + b_2 x^2 y + b_3 x y^2 + b_4 y^3 + b_5 x^2 + b_6 xy + b_7 y^2 + b_8 x + b_9 y + b_{10} \tag{2}$$

with coefficients a_i and b_i. Note that we have here already 20 distortion parameters for each camera. The relative orientation of the two cameras is expressed by the extrinsic camera parameters of both cameras. Typically, a rotation matrix **R** describes the orientation in the world co-ordinate system and a 3D vector

$v_O = (x_O, y_O, z_O)^T$ the position of the projection centre O of the camera. The rotation matrix $\mathbf{R}$ is determined by the three angles ϕ, ω, and κ.

The calculation of the 3D points will be performed by triangulation between corresponding image points using the intrinsic and extrinsic camera parameters. For a more detailed description see e.g. [21].

3.2   Calibration Approach

Calibration (for both cameras C_1 and C_2) will be obtained by the consecutive performance of the following three steps:

- Distortion determination
- Determination of the intrinsic camera parameters
- Determination of the relative orientation between the two cameras (extrinsic camera parameters)

For all calibration tasks either a planar target (chessboard, point pattern, grid pattern) or a calibration target is used, where line segments of three mutually perpendicular directions as shown in Fig. 1 can be extracted.

For the determination of the intrinsic parameters, first, the well-known method using three vanishing points of mutually orthogonal directions (see [8]) is suggested. This requires e.g. a calibration target as shown in Fig. 1.

The determination of the relative orientation between the two cameras may be obtained using one of the known methods from the literature, e.g. the determination of the fundamental matrix using the seven or eight corresponding point algorithm ([18–20]), the method proposed by Caprile and Torre [8], or any other suitable algorithm [9,10,22]. Alternatively, a simple method will be proposed in section 4.3 using point correspondences and known distances [23].

The selection of the calibration pattern depends on the size of the measurement field and the available targets. The larger the field of view (FOV) of the

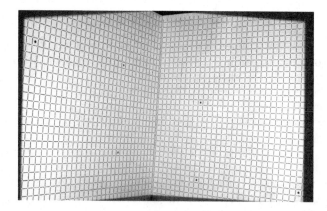

Fig. 1. Calibration grid pattern representing three mutually perpendicular directions

camera the larger the target should be. This may be problematic in the case of large FOVs. Here, eventually urban man-made objects may be used such as house facades (see [4–6]).

4 Calibration Realization

4.1 Distortion Determination

Distortion determination from a single image requires a consistent distribution of calibration points over the whole image or a confirmed knowledge concerning the effective distortion function. We suggest using a plane pattern (part of the target shown in Fig. 1), determination of reference point co-ordinates in the image, and fitting a projective transform of the known 3D positions (in a plane) to the reference points. The differences of the measured points to the ideal fitted points yield a set of 2D distortion vectors DVS in the image plane (see Fig. 2). If these points are quite dense and well distributed, a so called distortion matrix can be produced by averaging (see also [24]). Alternatively, a distortion function can be fitted to DVS, and the parameters of this function can be obtained by linear optimization.

For the description of the distortion of our scanner we used the distortion functions (1) and (2). If the distortion parameters were not significant, the next lower distortion level of the function was used. Figure 2 shows an example of the distortion vector fields.

4.2 Intrinsic Parameter Determination

For the determination of the intrinsic camera parameters principal point p_0 and principal distance c, the distortion should be already corrected. This can be realized either by dewarping the complete images or by correction of the reference points co-ordinates.

A very suitable model for the determination of the intrinsic parameters from a single view is the processing of the vanishing points of three mutually perpendicular directions which can be extracted from the image. As shown by Caprile and Torre [8] and used by other authors, the intersection point of the heights of the vanishing point triangle is the principal point of the image. Because this model is well known, we use it only for experimental evaluation and comparison and do not describe the theory, which can be found e.g. in [8,9,25,26].

Here, we will describe a new technique for determination of principal distance and principal point using only two vanishing points of orthogonal directions from at least two images or from two planes in one single image. Comparable algorithms from literature assume the principal point in the image centre [10,12]. Our algorithm determines the principal point explicitly.

The outline of the algorithm is the following. We compute two vanishing points vp_1 and vp_2 of orthogonal directions and assume the principal point p_0 in a certain area in the image plane. This area is typically a square with centre point

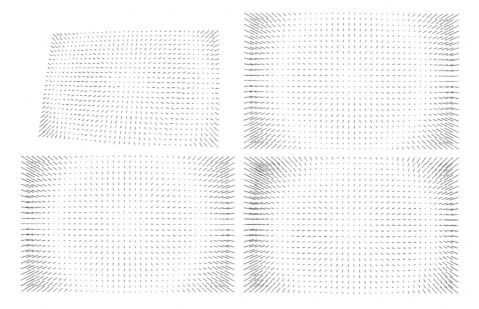

Fig. 2. Example for distortion vector fields: measured (left upper), calculated radial (right upper), radial and decentering (left lower), and complete inclusive polynomial (right lower)

in the image centre and an edge length of about a fifth of the image diagonal. We chose consistently distributed sampling points in that square and consider them as potential principal points p_i. This allows computing a potential principal distance c_i and, additionally, a third virtual vanishing point vp_3 representing the third orthogonal direction (which is the normal direction to the plane defined by vp_1 and vp_2). Then we use the standard projection $\mathbf{K}$ proposed by Kanatani [27] for the transformation of vp_3 onto p_i obtaining a similarity mapping of the plane defined by vp_1 and vp_2. $\mathbf{K}$ will be applied to all image points.

The correctness of $\mathbf{K}$ is checked by the aspect ratio of our calibration grid squares (or, alternatively known aspect ratios). If the aspect ratios are true, p_i is a candidate for p_0. This procedure yields a set of principal point candidates lying on a straight line g_1, which should be called pp-line and is perpendicular to the vanishing line. The vanishing line is the straight line though vp_1 and vp_2. Considering the sampling points, g_1 can be obtained by linear regression. If we repeat this procedure using a second image (of the same camera), we obtain a second straight line g_2. The angle between g_1 and g_2 should be not too small, which can be controlled by the image recording. The intersection of g_1 and g_2 yields the principal point. With the obtained principal point $p_0 = (x_0, y_0)$ the principal distance c can be calculated using the two vanishing points $vp_1 = (x_1, y_1)$ and $vp_2 = (x_2, y_2)$ according to:

$$c = \sqrt{- \left[(x_0 - x_1)(x_0 - x_2) + (y_0 - y_1)(y_0 - y_2) \right]}. \qquad (3)$$

4.3 Extrinsic Parameter Determination

For the determination of the extrinsic camera parameters one can use any of the algorithms proposed in the literature. Using vanishing points, one can implement the methods proposed by Caprile and Torre [8] or Orghidan [10]. An interesting method is also proposed by Chen [22] using two coplanar circles in a single view. A common single view calibration method for stereo systems is the determination of the fundamental matrix [18–20].

Here, we propose a two-step algorithm for the extrinsic camera parameters. The first step may be an arbitrary method for the rough estimation of the relative orientation of the two cameras. We suggest the use of a calibration pattern with spatial extension and three vanishing points from orthogonal directions (as shown in Fig. 1). Then the algorithm of Caprile and Torre [8] can be applied or the fundamental matrix method. Alternatively, if it is known that the sensor is realized close to the geometric design, an initial extrinsic calibration can be derived from the design parameters.

The second step should be the refinement of the current calibration parameters using a single or double view including well distributed corresponding points and at least one known measure of length in the approximate direction of the epipolar lines. This has been described in detail by the authors [23], and should be outlined here briefly.

The idea of the method is a systematic search in the parameter space of the relative orientation (six parameters) and the assumption, that no local minima of the evaluation function occur. The intrinsic of both and the extrinsic parameters of one camera are set fix. The remaining six extrinsic parameters of the second camera are changed systematically. The evaluation error function which should be minimized, includes the error $\triangle L$ of the known length and the residual error which correspond to the epipolar line error $\triangle E$ [23]. The weighting of the length error and the residual error is one parameter of freedom. Finishing criterion may be the amount of the change of the test quantity or of the change of the parameters.

The test quantity T can be defined as

$$T = w_E \cdot \triangle E + w_L \cdot \triangle L = w_E \left(\frac{1}{n} \sum_{i=1}^{n} err_{pos}\,(p,q)_i \right) + w_L \left(len_{meas} - len_{ref} \right) \quad (4)$$

with epipolar line position error $err_{pos}(p,q)_i$, defined as the perpendicular distance of the correct corresponding point q_i to the epipolar line (in the image of camera C_2) defined by a point p_i (in the image of camera C_1) and weights w_E and w_L. For a more detailed description see [23].

5 Experiments and Results

5.1 The 3D Scanner System

For our experiments we used a handheld stereo scanner consisting of two cameras and a projection unit for structured illumination, which was developed at our department. For the calibration procedure the projection unit was not used. However, in order to evaluate the quality of the 3D measurements, the projector was used for structured illumination generation with the goal of high precision measurements of lengths and flatness with a small random error ($< 10 \ \mu m$).

The camera resolution is 2048 x 1280 pixels, the pixel size is 5.5 μm, and the focal length is 16 mm. See an image of the scanner shown by Fig. 3.

Fig. 3. Handheld stereo scanner used for the experiments

5.2   Distortion Determination Experiments

In order to evaluate the methodology described above, several experiments were performed. The first series of measurements concerned distortion determination using one single image. We used a plane grid pattern and the method described in section 4.1. Using a semi-automatic algorithm we found as many as possible grid points and set them to the (known) corresponding original 3D co-ordinates (in a plane, i.e. z = 0). The grid point co-ordinates were found by detection of the four line segments in the environment of the grid point and intersection of the two straight lines obtained by linear regression.

By fitting a projective 2D-2D-transform **T** and application of **T** to the original points we obtain the estimated undistorted image points. The differences to the measured image points lead to distortion vectors DVS in dependence on either the distorted or undistorted points. In our experiments we realized the further processing of the DVS as follows. First we fitted a pure radial symmetric distortion function of the form

$$\triangle x_r = x' - x = x_s + (x - x_s) \cdot \left(1 + k_0 + k_2 r'^2 + k_4 r'^4\right)$$

$$\triangle y_r = y' - y = y_s + (y - y_s) \cdot \left(1 + k_0 + k_2 r'^2 + k_4 r'^4\right)$$

(5)

where $p_s = (x_s, y_s)$ is the symmetry point of the radial distortion and k_0, k_2, and k_4 are three distortion coefficients. The fitting can be realized using linear optimization, e.g. by the method proposed in [24]. Next, we additionally fitted decentering distortion of the form

$$\triangle x_d = d_1 \cdot \left(r'^2 + 2x'^2\right) + 2d_2 \cdot x'y'$$

$$\triangle x_d = d_2 \cdot \left(r'^2 + 2y'^2\right) + 2d_1 \cdot x'y' \qquad (6)$$

with distortion coefficients d_1 and d_2. Finally, additional distortion can be estimated by fitting the polynomial coefficients a_i and b_i ($i=1,...,10$) according to
equation (2). The quality of the distortion determination will be described by
the variation of the estimated distortion between the images. This variation
(between the different n measurements) should be described as the maximal difference $\triangle l_{max}$ of any of the distortion vectors over the image. Table 1 documents
the results for the described three levels of distortion determination.

Table 1. Variation of the distortion determination from single images ($n = 10$). Mean
distortion vector length is denoted by dvl_{mean}.

Distortion level	dvl_{mean} [pixel]	$\triangle l_{max}$ [pixel]
Radial	2.53	0.79
Radial + decentering	2.54	0.80
Radial + decentering + polynomial	2.98	1.47

5.3 Experiments for Evaluation of the Intrinsic Parameter Determination

For the evaluation of the intrinsic camera parameter estimation we performed
the determination according to the method proposed in section 4.2 ($2x2vp$) and
the method based on the determination of three vanishing points ($3vp$) using the
calibration target with three orthogonal directions (see Fig. 1). For comparison
we performed a classical scanner calibration based on self-calibration [21] and
denoted it by Ref.

We used ten images in order to determine the three vanishing points. The
results of the principal point $p_0 = (x_0, y_0)$ and principal distance c determination are shown in Table 2. There are given averaged values (mn) and standard
deviations (sd).

Next, we performed principal point and principal distance determination
using the proposed algorithm with pairs of images of the planar grid pattern

Table 2. Variation of the intrinsic parameter calculation ($mean \pm sd$) for cameras C_1
and C_2 using one ($3vp$) or two ($2x2vp$) images, respectively, compared with refreence
calibration Ref. Unit is always mm.

Parameter	$C_1|3vp$	$C_1|2x2vp$	$C_1|Ref$	$C_2|3vp$	$C_2|2x2vp$	$C_2|Ref$
x_0	-0.28 ± 0.28	0.05 ± 0.03	-0.03 ± 0	-0.32 ± 0.19	-0.23 ± 0.04	-0.23 ± 0
y_0	0.19 ± 0.23	0.09 ± 0.02	0.13 ± 0	0.07 ± 0.40	0.07 ± 0.03	0.20 ± 0
C	16.11 ± 0.12	16.42 ± 0.13	16.30 ± 0	16.11 ± 0.07	16.70 ± 0.30	16.25 ± 0

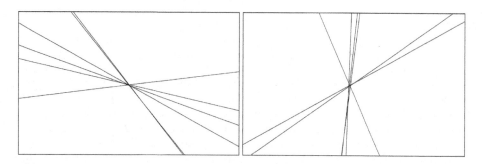

Fig. 4. Calculated pp-lines of six images of camera C_1 (left) and camera C_2 (right)

(see section 4.2). We used six images for both cameras, respectively. If the angle α between the intersection lines was too small ($\alpha < 10$), this pair was excluded from the calculation. Figure 4 shows the pp-lines of the two cameras.

It must be ascertained systematic deviations of the parameters between the three methods and the two cameras. The $3vp$ method leads to a higher variation of the principal point co-ordinates and a lower for the principal distance than the $2x2vp$ method. The reason may be the imperfect calibration target.

5.4   Experiments for Evaluation of the Extrinsic Parameter Determination

For the evaluation of the extrinsic camera parameter estimation we performed the determination according to the method proposed in section 4.3 using either one image (3D Target - $3vp$) or two images (plane target - $2x2vp$). The complete obtained set of calibration parameters was used to perform measurements of a calibrated plane surface (stone slab) in different measurement distances and length measurements using a calibrated ball bar.

In order to compare the results, the same set of intrinsic parameters was used for all different extrinsic parameter sets. The quality of the extrinsic parameters should be characterized by the quantities length measurement deviation ld and flatness deviation fd defined as

$$ld = max \left\{ dist_i^{meas} - dist_i^{calib} \right\} \tag{7}$$

$$fd = max \left\{ fd_j \right\} \tag{8}$$

where $dist_i^{meas}$ is the measured length and $dist_i^{calib}$ the calibrated length at measurement i, and fd_j is the double maximal deviation of the measured stone slab from a fitted plane at measurement j. Maximal 0.3% outliers may be removed. At least seven measurements were performed in both cases ($i, j = 1, ..., 7$). This definition is supposed by [28]. The results of the determination of ld and fd are shown in Table 3 (averaged values mn and standard deviations sd).

Table 3. Calibration quality results concerning 3D reconstruction errors. The reference of the length measurement was 200 mm as well as the diameter of the reference plane

Method	$mn_{ld} \pm sd_{ld}[mm]$	$mn_{fd} \pm sd_{fd}[mm]$
$3vp$	1.02 ± 0.45	0.98 ± 0.56
$2 \times 2vp$	0.85 ± 0.34	1.12 ± 0.72
Ref	0.19 ± 0.05	0.09 ± 0.02

6   Summary, Discussion, and Outlook

A new methodology for stereo scanner calibration was introduced based on data obtained from one image mapping at least two planes or two images showing one plane. It was shown that calibration results of medium accuracy can be obtained. The procedure can be performed easily in a short time and is therefore suitable for the calibration of scanners which must often be adjusted.

The obtained measurement results are not as accurate as results achieved by a calibration performed with considerable more effort. However, certain improvements of the proposed method may lead to increased measurement accuracy. Compared to the method of Beardley and Murray [15] we obtained a little better localization of the principal points, whereas the principle distance values had a little higher standard deviation. Distortion determination should be rather performed using more than one single image, e.g. by averaging some ten views. The reproducibility of the intrinsic parameters should be improved, e.g. by finding ideal recording angles concerning the planes and improvement of the vanishing point determination as part of the future tasks concerning this technique.

Additionally, the proposed method should be compared to similar calibration methods known from the literature using identic data material. Another task for future activities is the complete automation of the calibration procedure by an appropriate software development. An interesting question concerning this kind of calibration procedures is, whether there is an optimal pattern for the calibration target. Here, different planar patterns such as grids, point patterns, and chessboards can be analysed concerning robustness and noise sensitivity, and also compared to alternative patterns such as circles or other objects.

References

1. Hemmleb, M.: Digital rectification of historical images. In: CIPA Int. Symposium, IAPRS 1999, vol. XXXII (1999)
2. van den Heuvel, F.: 3D reconstruction from a single image using geometric constraints. ISPRS Journ of Photogramm and Remote Sensing **53**, 354–368 (1998)
3. Bräuer-Burchardt, C., Voss, K.: Facade reconstruction of destroyed buildings using historical photographs. In: Proc. 18th Int. Symp. CIPA, pp. 543–550 (2001)
4. Criminisi, A., Reid, I., Zisserman, A.: Single View Metrology. International Journal of Computer Vision **40**(2), 123–148 (2000)
5. Liebowitz, D., Criminisi, A., Zisserman, A.: Creating architectural models from Images. In: Proc. EuroGraphics, pp. 39–50 (1999)

6. van den Heuvel, F.: Object reconstruction from a single architectural image taken with an uncalibrated camera. Photogrammetrie Fernerkundung Geoinf. **4**, 247–260 (2001)
7. Mei, C., Rives, P.: Single view point omnidirectional camera calibration from planar grids. In: IEEE Int. Conf. on Robotics and Automation, pp. 3945–3950 (2007)
8. Caprile, B., Torre, V.: Using vanishing points for camera calibration. Int. Journal for Computer Vision, 127–140 (1990)
9. Wang, G., Tsui, H.T., Wu, Q.M.J.: What can we learn about the scene structure from three orthogonal vanishing points in images. Pattern Recognition Letters **30**, 192–202 (2009)
10. Orghidan, R, Salvi, J., Gordanm, M., Orza, B.: Camera calibration using two or three vanishing points. In: Proc. Fed. Conf. Computer Science and Information Systems, pp. 123–130 (2012)
11. Danilidis, K., Ernst, J.: Active intrinsic calibration using vanishing points. Pattern Recognition Letters **17**, 1179–1189 (1996)
12. Grammatikopoulos, L., Karras, G., Petsa, E.: An automatic approach for camera calibration from vanishing points. ISPRS Journ Photogrammetry Remote Sensing **62**, 64–76 (2007)
13. Heikkinen, J., Inkil, K.: The comparison of single view calibration methods. In: Proc. of SPIE, vol. 8085, p. 80850Q1-Q9 (2011)
14. Lourakis, M.I.A., Argyros, A.A.: Refining Single View Calibration With the Aid of Metric Scene Properties. Journal of WSCG **15**(1–3), 129–134 (2007)
15. Beardsley, P., Murray, D.: Camera calibration using vanishing points. In: The British Machine Vision Conference (BMVC), pp. 416–425 (1992)
16. Zhang, Z.: A Flexible New Technique for Camera Calibration. IEEE Trans. PAMI **22**(11), 1330–1334 (2000)
17. Strobl, K.H., Hirzinger, G.: More accurate pinhole camera calibration with imperfect planar target. In: IEEE ICCV Workshops, pp. 1068–1075 (2011)
18. Faugeras, O.: Three Dimensional Computer Vision. MIT Press (1993)
19. Lourakis M.I.A., Deriche, R.: Camera self-calibration using the singular value decomposition of the fundamental matrix. In: Proc ACCV 2000, pp. 402–408 (1999)
20. Hartley, R., Zisserman, A.: Multiple view geometry. Cambridge University Press (2003)
21. Luhmann, T., Robson, S., Kyle, S., Harley, I.: Close range photogrammetry. Wiley Whittles Publishing (2006)
22. Chen, Y., Ip, H., Huang, Z., Wang, G.: Full camera calibration from a single view of planar scene. In: Bebis, G., et al. (eds.) ISVC 2008, Part I. LNCS, vol. 5358, pp. 815–824. Springer, Heidelberg (2008)
23. Bräuer-Burchardt, C., Kühmstedt, P., Notni, G.: Error compensation by sensor re-calibration in fringe projection based optical 3D stereo scanners. In: Maino, G., Foresti, G.L. (eds.) ICIAP 2011, Part II. LNCS, vol. 6979, pp. 363–373. Springer, Heidelberg (2011)
24. Bräuer-Burchardt, C., Kühmstedt, P., Notni, G.: Lens distortion determination with plane calibration targets. In: Proc. ISPA 2013, pp. 199–204 (2013)
25. Cipolla, R., Drummond T., Robertson, D.: Camera calibration from vanishing points in images of architectural scenes. In: BMVC, pp. 382–391 (1999)
26. He, B.W., Li, Y.F.: Camera calibration from vanishing points in a vision system. Optics & Laser Technology **40**, 555–561 (2008)
27. Kanatani, K.: Constraints on length and angle. Computer Vision and Graphics for Images and Patterns **41**, 28–42 (1988)
28. VDI/VDE 2634. Optical 3D-measuring systems. VDI/VDE guidelines, Parts 1–3 (2008)

Spatially Aware Enhancement of BoVW-Based Image Retrieval Exploiting a Saliency Map

Zijun Zou and Hisashi Koga[(✉)]

Graduate School of Information Systems,
University of Electro-Communications, Tokyo, Japan
koga@is.uec.ac.jp

Abstract. The Bag-of-Visual-Words (BoVW) scheme is the most popular approach to similar image retrieval. The conventional BoVW models an image as a histogram of local features in which all of the features are uniformly weighed. Recently, researchers have focused on the similarity between the foregrounds of two images, because the foreground properly expresses the semantics of the image. Given an image, these methods approximate the likelihood that a local feature belongs to the foreground with its saliency value derived from the saliency map. The foreground histogram is then constructed in such a way that each local feature is accumulated to the histogram in proportion to its saliency value. Finally, the similarity between images is measured by comparing the foreground histograms of the images. However, the above strategy discounts local features with small saliency values, even if they lie on the genuine foreground. This paper proposes a new technique that does not disregard such local features and examines their spatial surroundings. In particular, a high weight is assigned to a local feature with a low saliency value when the spatial surrounding has a high saliency value, because this local feature is also likely to be a part of the foreground.

1 Introduction

Similar image retrieval has always been a challenging task in computer vision. Given a query image, the purpose of similar image retrieval is to retrieve images having similar semantics from a large image database. The Bag-of-Visual-Words (BoVW) scheme [1] is the most popular approach to similar image retrieval. The conventional BoVW simply models an image as an unordered set of local features. The BoVW scheme is used in various vision applications such as object discovery [2]. In the context of similar image retrieval, this scheme represents images as histograms of local features (i.e., visual words) and measures the similarity between two images as the similarity between their histograms.

This paper studies the improvement of BoVW-based similar image retrieval. In literatures, this has been accomplished through two approaches. The first approach incorporates the spatial relation between local features into the BoVW model [3] [4] [5] [6] [7], which is ignored in the standard BoVW model.

The second approach isolates the foreground from the background in an image and concentrates on the foreground similarity because the semantics of

© Springer International Publishing Switzerland 2015
G. Azzopardi and N. Petkov (Eds.): CAIP 2015, Part II, LNCS 9257, pp. 73–84, 2015.
DOI: 10.1007/978-3-319-23117-4_7

(a)   (b)   (c)   (d)

Fig. 1. Non-salient Foreground Components

an image is well represented by the foreground. This approach usually uses a salient region detection algorithm to find the foreground in an unsupervised manner. Typically, local features are regarded as the foreground with stronger confidence and are given more votes in constructing the foreground histogram, as they take higher saliency values [8][9].

The second approach implicitly assumes that the saliency values of local features decrease monotonically as the features become more distant from the core center of the foreground. However, in many images, this is not the case in practice and the saliency map is dappled. Namely, the foreground contains some non-salient components (i.e., local features). For example, see Fig. 1. This figure shows two pairs of the original images and the corresponding saliency map generated by the algorithm in [11], in which brighter pixels have larger saliency values. For the image of the sunflower, the center of the sunflower becomes a non-salient foreground component in the saliency map. For the image of the metronome, the white line running through the center of the metronome is completely non-salient. This phenomenon is natural because the saliency map is produced from raw image features irrespective of the image semantics.

Considering the inconsistency between the saliency map and the genuine foreground, we herein develop a unique technique to place such non-salient local features inside the foreground object in the foreground histogram. Experimentally, we show that the proposed approach improves the retrieval accuracy as compared with the saliency-based approach proposed in [8].

This paper is organized as follows. Section 2 introduces the known BoVW-based similar image retrieval. Section 3 introduces the proposed approach and explains how to determine the foreground region, so that non-salient local features in the foreground object may be included in the foreground region. This foreground region is used to calculate the foreground similarity measure. In Section 4, the property of the foreground similarity is analyzed, based on which Section 5 describes our ultimate similarity which combines the foreground similarity and the global similarity computed from all of the local features in the entire image. Section 6 describes the results of the experimental evaluation. Our conclusions are presented in Section 7.

2   BoVW-Based Image Retrieval

In the following, we introduce the standard BoVW-based similar image retrieval. Let I_q be a query image, and let S be the image collection. The goal of similar image retrieval is to choose images from S that are semantically similar to I_q.

The BoVW scheme gathers all of the local feature points in each image $I \in S$. In this paper, the SIFT feature is used as the local feature. Each local feature point is described with a 128-dimensional SIFT descriptor [10]. By clustering all of the local feature points in S with the k-means, k clusters of local feature points are generated. The center vectors of these k clusters become k visual words. A visual word is also referred to as a *codebook*, and k is referred to as the codebook size. Once the visual words are fixed, any image I can be represented as an unordered set of visual words by associating each local feature f in I with the visual word nearest to f. Then, I is expressed with the histogram h_I of visual words for which the bin number is equal to the codebook size. The height of the j-th bin, denoted $h_I[j]$ $(1 \leq j \leq k)$, is proportional to the frequency of the j-th visual word in I. Usually, h_I is normalized so that $\sum_{j=1}^{k} h_I[j] = 1$. The similarity between the two images I_1 and I_2 is defined as the intersection similarity between h_{I_1} and h_{I_2}, which is represented as $\mathrm{sim}(h_{I_1}, h_{I_2}) = \sum_{j=1}^{k} \min(h_{I_1}[j], h_{I_2}[j])$. As a result of the retrieval, the BoVW scheme outputs the images in S that have the highest similarity values to I_q.

However, the BoVW has a drawback such that it discards the spatial information between local features. Several studies have recently attempted to overcome this drawback. Spatial pyramid matching [3] segments an image into subimages referred to as *tile* and generates one histogram per tile. The similarity between the two images is calculated by comparing multiple histograms. Viitaniemi *et al.* [4] extended [3] and developed a soft tiling technique that allows one local feature to be assigned to several tiles with varying degrees. Another approach to expressing the spatial relation between local features is to construct the histograms by counting visual phrases, i.e., a set of visual words, so as to model the co-occurrences of visual words in local neighborhoods [5][6][7].

On the other hand, other studies have focused on the similarity of the foreground. These studies rely on a salient region detection algorithm to find the foreground. Then, local features with higher saliency values are treated as the foreground with stronger confidence, and these features have more votes to construct the foreground histogram [8][9]. Soares *et al.* [8] collected the local features with the SIFT keypoint detector [10] and built the histograms for both the foreground and the background. After normalizing the maximum saliency value to 1, one local feature contributes to the histograms in a fuzzy manner, such that its saliency value is voted to the foreground histogram, while $(1 - \text{saliency value})$ is voted to the background histogram. Then, for a pair of images I_1 and I_2, their similarity measure is defined by summing the similarity between their foreground histograms and the similarity between their background histograms, as shown in Eq. (1). Here, α denotes the mixture weight of the background similarity.

$$(1 - \alpha) \times \text{the foreground similarity} + \alpha \times \text{the background similarity}. \quad (1)$$

Biagio *et al.* [9] also used a similar approach. They extracted the SIFT local features by dense grid sampling. The local features were then assigned weights according to the saliency values of the associated local grids. Both of the above studies neglect non-salient foreground components because they estimate the likelihood that a local feature belongs to the foreground region based solely on the local saliency value.

3   Proposed Approach

Our method is similar to the previous methods [8][9] described in Section 2 in that we pay much attention to the foreground. However, our method is unique with regard to the following two points:

- Foreground components with low saliency values can still be identified correctly as belonging to the foreground when they are spatially surrounded by salient foreground components.
- All of the local features have an equal weight in the foreground histogram, once they are judged to be a part of the foreground.

Our algorithm executes the following steps. The SIFT features are extracted from images using the keypoint detector.

Step 1: Given an image I, we compute a saliency map of I in order to roughly grasp the location of the foreground in an unsupervised manner.

Step 2: I is divided into the foreground region f_I and the background region B_I. We first derive the intermediate foreground region wf_I by inspecting only the saliency values of pixels, without considering their spatial context. Next, wf_I is modified to yield the (final) foreground region f_I. In this modification process, the spatial context for local features is used. In particular, we regard non-salient regions spatially surrounded by the intermediate foreground region as non-salient foreground components and add these regions to f_I. After f_I is fixed, the foreground histogram fh_I is constructed with the local features in f_I.

Step 3: The foreground similarity between two images I_1 and I_2 is measured by the histogram intersection similarity between fh_{I_1} and fh_{I_2}.

Section 3.1 describes the salient region detection algorithm [11] used to compute the saliency map of I in Step 1. Then, Section 3.2 describes how to determine the foreground region in Step 2, given the saliency map.

3.1   Saliency Map Generation

Regions in an image are referred to as salient regions if they attract a great deal of human attention. Visual saliency is closely related to how we perceive and process visual stimuli and has been studied for use in several areas, including computer vision [12][14]. Salient region detection is a task to identify salient regions from image I based on image features such as color, gradient, and edges. Among the various salient-region detection algorithms, we use the region-based

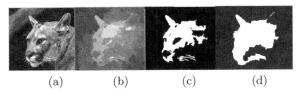

(a)   (b)   (c)   (d)

Fig. 2. Modification Method

contrast (RC) algorithm [11], which provided the best performance at the time this research was undertaken.

The RC first segments I into n regions $r_1, r_2, \cdots, r_n$. The saliency value of r_k is then decided according to the color contrast with respect to the other regions, as shown in Eq. (2):

$$S(r_k) = \sum_{r_k \neq r_i} \exp(-\frac{D_s(r_k, r_i)}{\sigma_s^2}) w(r_i) D_r(r_k, r_i) \qquad (2)$$

where $D_r(r_k, r_i)$ and $D_s(r_k, r_i)$ are the color distance and the spatial distance between r_i and r_k, respectively. $w(r_i)$ denotes the number of pixels in r_i and makes the color contrast with large regions more important. Roughly speaking, the saliency value $S(r_k)$ increases as the color of r_k becomes more distant from nearby large regions. Examples of saliency maps for images are presented in Fig. 2. Fig. 2(a) shows the original image, and Fig. 2(b) shows the saliency map of this image, where brighter pixels have larger saliency values.

3.2 Extraction of the Foreground Region

This subsection describes the procedure that receives the saliency map as the input and outputs the foreground region f_I.

First, the saliency map represented as a gray-scale image is binarized into a binary image by Otsu's thresholding method [15]. In the binary image, pixels with large salient values are painted in white, whereas those with small salient values are painted in black. Though the developer of the RC algorithm [11] proposed an algorithm called Saliency Cut to binarize the saliency map, this paper does not use this, because Saliency Cut repeats the slow graphcut procedure. The white regions in the binary image form the intermediate foreground region wf_I.

Next, wf_I is modified to the foreground region f_I as follows. Our basic idea is to search small non-salient regions spatially surrounded by wf_I and let them join the foreground region f_I. In designing this modification procedure, we take into account the following feature of the RC method. As shown in Eq. (2), $S(r_k)$ is dominated by the color contrast with other large regions. Therefore, the foreground components that are similar in color to the background can take low saliency values and can be classified as belonging to the background, i.e., the black region, in the binary image. On one hand, if such a foreground component lies strictly inside the foreground contour, the component forms a black hole surrounded by a white region. On the other hand, if such a foreground component borders between the foreground and the background, the boundary information is lost and the white region becomes concave at this location. See Fig. 2 as an illustration. In the binarized saliency map shown in Fig. 2(c), the left eye and the nose of the leopard make the white region concave, because they are adjacent to the boundary and their colors are similar to the background. In the same manner, the right eye becomes a black hole in Fig. 2(c).

In order to treat the above two cases in a unified manner, our modification method first dilates the intermediate foreground region α times. This dilation effectively transforms a concave white region into a white region surrounding a black hole. Then, we regard black holes surrounded by a white region as non-salient foreground components, when they are small and occupy less than 10% of the image area. Then, we add the local features in such non-salient foreground components to the foreground region simply by filling the associated black holes with white. Finally, we erode the white region α times to restore the boundary before the dilation except the filled holes. At this time, the white region is identified as the foreground region f_I. Empirically, we set $\alpha = 4$. Fig. 2(d) shows the results of the modification. The foreground components whose color are similar to the background now belong to the foreground region.

We believe that local features inside the (ground-truth) foreground should not be discriminated, even if their saliency values are different. By contrast, in the previous saliency-based approach, they are assigned different weights in proportion to their saliency values. Our method treats the features inside the foreground equally as follows. First, by binarizing the saliency map adaptively, the local features whose saliency values are greater than the threshold are assigned the same weight. At this time, however, the local features whose saliency values are less than the threshold are ignored completely, even if they originate in the ground-truth foreground. Then, the modification to wf_I moves the ignored local features into the foreground histogram and assigns them the same weight.

4   Feature of Foreground Similarity

This section investigates the foreground similarity (FS) by comparing it to the standard BoVW in an experiment to retrieve similar images. Hereafter, the similarity used in the standard BoVW is referred to as the global similarity (GS) because the standard BoVW constructs the histogram from all of the local features in the image.

For the dataset, we choose 40 classes from the Caltech-101 image database at random. The chosen classes are as follows: ant, bonsai, butterfly, car, crab, Dalmatian, dolphin, faces, fan, ferry, Garfield, hawksbill, hedgehog, helicopter, llama, lobster, mandolin, metronome, minaret, motorbike, nautilus, pagoda, panda, piano, pizza, revolver, saxophone, schooner, scorpion, seahorse, skate, snoopy, soccerball, starfish, stop_sign, sunflower, trilobite, waterlily, wheelchair, and Windsor chair. For each class, we randomly select 25 images. Thus, the dataset consists of 40×25=1000 images.

Table 1. Retrieval Accuracy Rate for the Four Classes of Images

Class name	BoVW	FS
soccerball	0.28	0.72
fan	0.32	0.48
butterfly	0.44	0.24
dolphin	0.64	0.48

We evaluate the FS and GS using the leave-one-out method such that the similar images to a query image I_q are searched from the remaining 999 images, where the codebook size is set to 4096. For each I_q, we extract the 24 most similar images to I_q. Here, the figure 24=(25-1) denotes the number of images in the same class as I_q in the dataset. We then classify I_q using the K-NN method with these 24 images. If I_q is recognized as the ground-truth class, the image retrieval for I_q is deemed to be successful. Let N_c be the number of images in class C for which the image retrieval is successful. Then, the accuracy rate for C is defined as $\frac{N_c}{25}$.

Our FS achieves a higher accuracy rate than the BoVW (i.e., the GS). More concretely, the results indicate that the FS defeats the BoVW for 22 of the 40 classes, whereas the BoVW achieves a better result for 13 classes. The remaining five classes result in a tie. Table 1 shows the accuracy rate for specific four classes. Here, the FS is superior to the BoVW for the top two classes and inferior to the BoVW for the bottom two classes. Next, we discuss the reason for the difference between the FS and GS for these four classes.

The soccerball is an artificial object. Therefore, most instances of a soccerball in different images have a fixed structure and shape, although the images are taken from different visual angles. On the other hand, the background of a soccerball image, which may include roads, weeds, or sky, varies greatly for each image. Therefore, the FS, which places great significance on the foreground, successfully identifies the soccerball object. The same discussion also holds for the fan.

In contrast, many images that contain a butterfly share a similar background, i.e., plants, whereas the butterflies themselves may have different texture patterns and postures. See Fig. 3. Thus, the FS deteriorates for images containing a butterfly. In addition, when a poor saliency map is generated for a query image, which is too different from the genuine foreground location, the similar image retrieval for this query can fail under the FS measure. This often occurs for the dolphin class of images because the color of dolphins is similar to the color of the sea, i.e., the background. Thus, the accuracy of the FS is lower than that of the BoVW for this class. Therefore, it is desirable for the FS measure that the quality of the saliency map is high.

Fig. 3. Images of Butterflies

5   Combination of the FS and the Background Similarity

Section 4 mentions two defects of the FS: (1) the performance of the FS may be poor for object classes in which the foreground is diverse, while the background is invariant, and (2) when a poor saliency map is generated for an image I, the FS cannot adequately retrieve similar images to I.

In order to supplement the FS, we propose incorporating background similarity into similar image retrieval. An immediate embodiment of this conception is to make the background histogram from the local features existing in the background region defined as the complement of the foreground region in the image and to compute the weighted sum of the foreground similarity and the background similarity. This approach was adopted by Soares *et al.* [8].

However, this solution is vulnerable to the imperfection of the saliency map. This is because, as the foreground region becomes less accurate, the background region also becomes less accurate. Therefore, we suggest combining the FS with the GS. Note that the GS is not affected by the inaccuracy of the foreground region. Let $FS(I_1, I_2)$ $(GS(I_1, I_2))$ be the foreground (global) similarity between I_1 and I_2. Then, we take their weighted sum, as shown in Eq. (3), where α denotes the mixture weight to mix $GS(I_1, I_2)$ with $FS(I_1, I_2)$. We refer to this similarity measure as the Front-Global Similarity (FGS) measure.

$$FGS(I_1, I_2) = (1 - \alpha)FS(I_1, I_2) + \alpha GS(I_1, I_2). \tag{3}$$

We recommend setting α to 0.5 as the default value. Eq. (3) emphasizes the similarity between the foreground without ignoring the background. Moreover, even when an irrelevant saliency map is generated, the GS suppresses the adverse effect.

6   Experimental Evaluation

This section reports the experimental evaluation. We use the same experimental dataset and the evaluation measure described in Section 4.

6.1   Effect of Spatially Aware Enhancement

First, we investigate the effectiveness of the proposed spatially aware enhancement of BoVW, as explained in Sections 3 and 5. We implement the following four similarity measures: (1) the FGS proposed in Section 5, (2) the FS proposed

Table 2. Average Accuracy Rate

Similarity	FGS	FS	FS_NOM	BoVW
Retrieval Accuracy Rate	0.564	0.541	0.519	0.507

in Section 3, (3) the foreground similarity measure for which the foreground histogram is computed for the intermediate foreground region wf_I in Section 3.2, and (4) the standard BoVW. We refer to the third measure as the FS measure with no modification (FS_NOM). Here, let us summarize the difference between the three similarity measures introduced herein. While the FGS considers both the foreground similarity and the global similarity in order to incorporate the background similarity, the FS deals with only the foreground similarity. Although FS_NOM also measures the foreground similarity, it identifies the local features in the foreground region based only on their saliency values without considering their spatial surroundings. For the FGS, the mixture weight α is set to 0.5.

Table 2 summarizes the average accuracy rate taken over the 40 classes for the above four similarity measures. From Table 2, we have the following:

- The FS is superior to FS_NOM, which demonstrates the validity of our strategy for treating non-salient regions that are spatially surrounded by the salient regions as part of the foreground region.
- The FGS performs better than the FS, which indicates that the defects of the FS are mitigated by compounding the global similarity with the FS.

The performance gain relative to the standard BoVW reaches 11.1% and 6.7% for the FGS and the FS, respectively.

6.2   Performance Comparison with the Fuzzy Approach

We also implement the Fuzzy approach in [8], which we refer to as FUZZ, so as to compare our method with another recent image retrieval algorithm supported by salient region detection. Our implementation of FUZZ differs slightly from the original implementation in [8], as follows. While [8] measures the cosine similarity between two histograms, this paper uses the histogram intersection similarity. We faithfully implement two instances of FUZZ with the same two salient region detection algorithms as in the original paper [8]. The first instance uses the graph-based salient region detection by Harel [13] and so is referred to as FUZZ_Harel. The second instance is based on that devised by Itti [12] and is referred to as FUZZ_Itti. We compare our FGS with the similarity measure of FUZZ shown in Eq. (1) that combines the foreground similarity with the background similarity. In particular, we investigate the average accuracy rate over the 40 classes, as the mixture weight α increases from 0 to 1. Note that the FGS coincides with the FS when $\alpha = 0$ and is reduced to the standard BoVW when $\alpha = 1$. Fig. 4 shows the experimental results.

FUZZ_Harel and FUZZ_Itti achieve the highest accuracy rates of 0.539 and 0.529 respectively, when $\alpha = 0$. As α increases, they become less accurate.

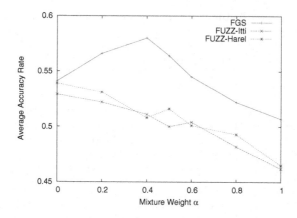

Fig. 4. Average Accuracy Rate for Various α Values

Importantly, this result shows that FUZZ never benefits by the introduction of the background similarity. We confirm that FUZZ_Harel slightly surpasses FUZZ_Itti, which was also reported in [8] previously.

Remarkably, the average accuracy rate of the FGS becomes higher than the accuracies of the two instances of FUZZ for any α. The FGS achieves the highest average accuracy rate of 0.580 when $\alpha = 0.4$. Thus, the performance of the FGS is improved by coupling the FS and GS. This result indicates that our strategy of combining the foreground similarity with the global similarity is more efficient than the strategy of pairing the foreground similarity and the background similarity, which was introduced in some previous researches. Recall that the FGS is reduced to the standard BoVW when $\alpha = 1$. Since the accuracy of FGS takes the minimum value when $\alpha = 1$, the FGS achieves a higher accuracy rate than the standard BoVW for any α except 1. If we pay attention to the case in which $\alpha = 0$, we can say that the FS, our foreground similarity, works better than the foreground similarity of FUZZ.

Let us consider the reason why the background similarity of FUZZ does not help the retrieval accuracy. FUZZ places non-salient foreground components into the background histogram. As an example, see Fig. 5, in which the middle image shows Itti's saliency map for the original image on the left side. Since some components of the hawksbill are dark, they belong to the background histogram for FUZZ_Itti. Moreover, non-salient foreground components are variant and different depending on images, even if the images display instances of the same object class. Thus, different images of the same object class place different non-salient foreground components in the background histogram, so that the background similarity becomes less reliable in FUZZ. Our method prevents such a phenomenon by including non-salient foreground components surrounded by salient foreground components in the foreground histogram. The right image in Fig. 5 presents the foreground region generated by our method. At least,

Original Image   FUZZ   FS

Fig. 5. Saliency Map

regarding to this example, our method obviously stops non-salient foreground components from contributing to the background histogram.

7   Conclusion

This paper proposes a new direction for enhancing BoVW-based similar image retrieval supported by a saliency map. Motivated by the observation that the foreground contains non-salient components with low saliency values, our method uniquely recognizes these components correctly as the foreground, when the components are spatially surrounded by salient foreground components. Then, the foreground histogram is generated from all of the local features recognized as the foreground and is used to compute the foreground similarity (FS) between images. Finally, we couple the global similarity with the FS in order to consider the background similarity for the similar image retrieval.

We demonstrate experimentally that the retrieval accuracy is improved by considering non-salient regions that are spatially surrounded by salient regions as part of the foreground. We also demonstrate that the combination of the FS and the ground similarity realizes more accurate similar image retrieval than the FS itself by mitigating the drawbacks of the FS. Moreover, our similarity measure is shown to be superior to another recent similarity measure, FUZZ, which requires a salient region detection technique.

Acknowledgments. This work is supported by the Ministry of Education, Culture, Sports, Science and Technology, Grant-in-Aid for Scientific Research (C) 24500111, 2015.

References

1. Sivic, J., Zisserman, A.: Video google: a text retrieval approach to object matching in videos. In: Proc. of 9th ICCV, pp. 1470–1477 (2003)
2. Pineda, G.F., Koga, H., Watanabe, T.: Scalable Object Discovery: A Hash-Based Approach to Clustering Co-occurring Visual Words. IEICE Transactions on Information and Systems **E94–D**(10), 2024–2035 (2011)
3. Lazebnik, S., Schmid, C., Ponce, J.: Beyond bags of features: spatial pyramid matching for recognizing natural scene categories. In: Proc. of CVPR, pp. 2169–2178 (2006)
4. Viitaniemi, V., Laaksonen, J.: Spatial extensions to bag of visual words. In: Proc. of CIVR, Article No. 37 (2009)

5. Yuan, J., Wu, Y., Yang, M.: Discovery of collocation patterns: from visual words to visual phrases. In: Proc. of CVPR 2007
6. Zhang, Y., Jia, Z., Chen, T.: Image retrieval with geometry-preserving visual phrases. In: Proc. of CVPR, pp. 809–816 (2011)
7. Yang, Y., Newsam, S.: Spatial pyramid co-occurrence for image classification. In: Proc. of ICCV, pp. 1465–1472 (2011)
8. de Carvalho Soares, R., da Silva, I.R., Guliato, D.: Spatial locality weighting of features using saliency map with a bag-of-visual-words approach. In: Proc. of IEEE ICTAI, pp. 1070–1075 (2012)
9. Biagio, S., Bazzani, L., Cristani, M., Murino, V.: Weighted bag of visual words for object recognition. In: Proc. of ICIP, pp. 2734–2738 (2014)
10. Lowe, D.: Distinctive image features from scale invariant keypoints. IJCV, 91–110 (2004)
11. Cheng, M.: Global contrast based salient region detection. In: Proc. of CVPR, pp. 409–416 (2011)
12. Itti, L., Koch, C., Niebur, E.: A model of saliency-based visual attention for rapid scene analysis. IEEE Transactions on PAMI **20**, 1254–1259 (1998)
13. Harel, J., Koch, C., Perona, P.: Graph-based visual saliency. In: Advances in Neural Information Processing Systems, pp. 545–552. MIT Press (2007)
14. Achanta, R., Hemami, S., Estrada, F., Susstrunk, S.: Frequency-tuned salient region detection. In: Proc. of CVPR, pp. 1597–1604 (2009)
15. Otsu, N.: A Threshold Selection Method from Gray-Level Histograms. IEEE Transactions on Systems, Man and Cybernetics **9**(1), 62–66 (1979)

An Edge-Based Matching Kernel for Graphs Through the Directed Line Graphs

Lu Bai[1], Zhihong Zhang[2], Chaoyan Wang[3], and Edwin R. Hancock[4]

[1] School of Information, Central University of Finance and Economics, Beijing, China
[2] Software School, Xiamen University, Xiamen, Fujian, China
[3] School of Contemporary Chinese Studies, University of Nottingham, Nottingham, UK
[4] Department of Computer Science, University of York, York, UK

Abstract. In this paper, we propose a new edge-based matching kernel for graphs. We commence by transforming a graph into a directed line graph. The reasons of using the line graph structure are twofold. First, for a graph, its directed line graph is a dual representation and each vertex of the line graph represents a corresponding edge in the original graph. As a result, we can develop an edge-based matching kernel for graphs by aligning the vertices in their directed line graphs. Second, the directed line graph may expose richer graph characteristics than the original graph. For a pair of graphs, we compute the h-layer depth-based representations rooted at the vertices of their directed line graphs, i.e., we compute the depth-based representations for edges of the original graphs through their directed line graphs. Based on the new representations, we define an edge-based matching method for the pair of graphs by aligning the h-layer depth-based representations computed through the directed line graphs. The new edge-based matching kernel is thus computed by counting the number of matched vertices identified by the matching method on the directed line graphs. Experiments on standard graph datasets demonstrate the effectiveness of our new edge-based matching kernel.

1 Introduction

Graph-based representations are powerful tools for structural analysis in pattern recognition and machine learning [1]. One problem of classifying graphs is how to convert the discrete graph structures into numeric features. One way to achieve this is to use graph kernels. The main advantage of using graph kernels is that they characterize graph features in a high dimensional space and thus better preserve graph structures.

Generally speaking, a graph kernel is a similarity measure between a pair of graphs [1]. To extend the large spectrum of kernel methods from the general machine learning domain to the graph domain, Haussler [2] has proposed a generic way, namely the R-convolution, to define a graph kernel. For a pair of graphs, an R-convolution kernel is computed by decomposing each graph

© Springer International Publishing Switzerland 2015
G. Azzopardi and N. Petkov (Eds.): CAIP 2015, Part II, LNCS 9257, pp. 85–95, 2015.
DOI: 10.1007/978-3-319-23117-4_8

into smaller subgraphs and counting the number of isomorphic subgraph pairs between the two original graphs. Thus, a new type of decomposition of a graph usually results in a new graph kernel. Following this scenario, Kashima et al. [3] introduced the random walk kernel, which is based on the enumeration of common random walks between two graphs. Borgwardt et al. [4], on the other hand, proposed a shortest path kernel by counting the numbers of matching shortest paths over the graphs. Aziz et al. [5] introduced a backtrackless kernel using the cycles identified by the Ihara zeta function [6] in a pair of graphs. Shervashidze et al. [7] developed a fast subtree kernel by comparing pairs of subtrees identified by the Weisfeiler-Lehman (WL) algorithm. Some other alternative R-convolution kernels include a) the segmentation graph kernel developed by Harchaoui and Bach [8], b) the point cloud kernel developed by Bach [9], and c) the (hyper)graph kernel based on directed subtree isomorphism tests [10].

Unfortunately, R-convolution kernels tend to neglect the relative locations of substructures. This is because R-convolution kernels add an unit value to the kernel function by roughly identifying a pair of isomorphic substructures, i.e., any pair of isomorphic substructures will contribute an unit kernel value. As a result, the R-convolution kernels cannot establish reliable structural correspondences between the substructures. This drawback limits the precise kernel-based similarity measure for graphs.

To overcome the problem arising in existing R-convolution kernels, in our previous work [11,12], we have developed a new depth-based matching kernel for graphs. The depth-based matching kernel is based on aligning the h-layer depth-based representations around vertices of graphs (i.e., aligning the vertices of the graphs), and is computed by counting the number of matched vertex pairs. In [11], the depth-based matching kernel can be seen as an aligned subgraph kernel that encapsulates location correspondence information between pairwise inexact isomorphic h-layer expansion subgraphs. As a result, the depth-based matching kernel overcomes the shortcoming of neglecting location correspondences between substructures arising in R-convolution kernels.

In this work, we aim to develop our previous work in [11,12] one step further. We develop a new edge-based matching kernel for graphs. For a graph, we commence by transforming the graph into a directed line graph [6]. The reason of using the directed line graph is that the line graph is a dual representation of the original graph [6], i.e., the vertex of the directed line graph represents a corresponding edge of the original graph. As a result, the directed line graph provides a way of developing new edge-based matching kernels. For a pair of graphs, we compute the h-layer depth-based representations rooted at the vertices of their directed line graphs, i.e., we compute the depth-based representations for edges of the original graphs through their directed line graphs. Based on the new representations, we define a new edge-based matching method for the pair of graphs by aligning the h-layer depth-based representations computed through the directed line graphs. The new edge-based matching kernel is thus computed by counting the number of matched vertices identified by the matching method on the directed line graphs. Experiments on standard graph datasets demonstrate the effectiveness of our new edge-based matching kernel.

2 Depth-Based Representations from Directed Line Graphs

We aim to develop the edge-based matching kernel of graphs from their directed line graphs. To this end, in this section we commence by introducing the concept of directed line graphs. The reasons of using the line graph structures are twofold. First, for an original graph, the directed line graph is its dual representation, i.e., the edge of the original graph is represented as a new vertex in the directed line graph. As a result, we can develop a new edge-based matching kernel for graphs by aligning the vertices of their directed line graphs. Second, comparing to the original graph, the directed line graph may expose richer graph characteristics. This is because the cardinality of the vertex set for the directed line graph is much greater than, or at least equal to, that of the original graph. Thus, the adjacency matrix (i.e., the Perron-Frobenius operator) of the directed line graph is described in a high dimensional space than the original graph. Furthermore, we show how to compute the required depth-based representations on the line graphs, through the definition in our previous work [12,13].

2.1 Directed Line Graphs

Based on the definition of Ren et al. in [6], for a sample graph $G(V, E)$, the directed line graph $OLG(V_L, E_{dL})$ is a dual representation of $G(V, E)$. To obtain $OLG(V_L, E_{dL})$, we first construct the associated symmetric digraph $SDG(V, E_d)$ of $G(V, E)$, by replacing every edge $e(u, w) \in E(G)$ by a pair of reverse arcs, i.e., directed edges $e_d(u, w) \in E_d(G)$ and $e_d(w, u) \in E_d(G)$ for $u, w \in V$. The directed line graph $OLG(V_L, E_{dL})$ is the directed graph with vertex set V_L and arc set E_{dL} defined as

$$
\begin{aligned}
V_L &= E_d(SDG), \\
E_{dL} &= \{(e_d(u, v), e_d(v, w)) \in E_d(SDG) \times E_d(SDG) \mid u, v, w \in V, u \neq w\}.
\end{aligned} \tag{1}
$$

The Perron-Frobenius operator $\boldsymbol{T} = [T_{i,j}]_{|V_L| \times |V_L|}$ of $G(V, E)$ is the adjacency matrix of the associated directed line graph $OLG(V_L, E_{dL})$.

2.2 Depth-Based Representations of Edges Through Directed Line Graphs

In this subsection, we compute the h-layer depth-based representation for an edge of an original graph through the directed line graph transformed from the original graph, i.e., we compute the representation around a corresponding vertex of the line graph.

The h-Layer Undirected Depth-Based Representation. For a graph $G(V, E)$ and its directed line graphs $G_D(V_D, \overrightarrow{E}_D))$, we commence by computing the h-layer undirected depth-based representation on the undirected line graph $G_U(V_U, E_U)$ by replacing each unidirectional edge of G_D in to a bidirectional edge. For $G_U(V_U, E_U)$ and a vertex $v_U \in V_U$, let a vertex set $N_{v_U}^K$ be defined as $N_{v_U}^K = \{u_U \in V_U \mid S_G(v_U, u_U) \leq K\}$, where S_G is the shortest path matrix of G_U and $S_G(v_U, u_U)$ is the shortest path length between v_U and u_U. For G_U, the K-layer expansion subgraph $\mathcal{G}_{v_U}^K(\mathcal{V}_{v_U}^K; \mathcal{E}_{v_U}^K)$ around v_U is

$$\begin{cases} \mathcal{V}_{v_U}^K = \{u_U \in N_{v_U}^K\}; \\ \mathcal{E}_{v_U}^K = \{u_U, w_U \in N_{v_U}^K, \ (u_U, w_U) \in E_U\}. \end{cases} \tag{2}$$

For G_U, the h-layer undirected depth-based representation around $v_U \in V_U$ is

$$DB_{G_U}^h(v_U) = [H_S(\mathcal{G}_{v_U}^1), \cdots, H_S(\mathcal{G}_{v_U}^K), \cdots, H_S(\mathcal{G}_{v_U}^h)]^\top, \tag{3}$$

where $(K \leq h)$. $H_S(\mathcal{G}_{v_U}^K)$ is the Shannon entropy of $\mathcal{G}_{v_U}^K$ associated with the steady state random walk (SSRW) [14] defined as

$$H_S(\mathcal{G}_{v_U}^K) = - \sum_{u_U \in \mathcal{V}_{v_U}^K} P(u_U) \log P(u_U), \tag{4}$$

where $P(u_U) = D_{\mathcal{G}_{v_U}^K}(u_U, u_U) / \sum_{w_U \in \mathcal{V}_{v_U}^K} D_{\mathcal{G}_{v_U}^K}(w_U, w_U)$ is the probability of the SSRW visiting $u_U \in \mathcal{V}_{v_U}^K$, and $D_{\mathcal{G}_{v_U}^K}$ is the diagonal degree matrix of $\mathcal{G}_{v_U}^K$. □

We can observe that the h-layer undirected depth-based representation $DB_{G_U}^h(v_u)$ can reflect the entropy-based information content flow rooted at each vertex on the undirected line graph G_U in terms of the topological information. However, this representation ignores the directed information residing on the edges of the directed line graph G_D. To capture the directed information, we also compute the directed depth-based representations on the directed line graph G_D.

The h-Layer Directed Depth-Based Representation. For $G(V, E)$ and its directed line graph $G_D(V_D, \overrightarrow{E}_D)$, we first establish the K-layer directed expansion subgraph of G_D through the undirected line graph $G_U(V_U, E_U)$ and the K-layer expansion subgraph $\mathcal{G}_{v_U}^K(\mathcal{V}_{v_U}^K; \mathcal{E}_{v_U}^K)$ on G_U. The K-layer directed expansion subgraph $\mathcal{G}_{v_D}^K(\mathcal{V}_{v_D}^K; \overrightarrow{\mathcal{E}}_{v_D}^K)$ around $v_D \in V_D$ is

$$\begin{cases} \mathcal{V}_{v_D}^K = \{u_U \mid u_U \in \mathcal{V}_{v_U}^K\}; \\ \overrightarrow{\mathcal{E}}_{v_D}^K = \{\overrightarrow{(u_U, w_U)} \in \overrightarrow{E}_D \mid (u_U, w_U) \in \mathcal{E}_{v_U}^K\}. \end{cases} \tag{5}$$

where $v_D \in V_D$, $v_U \in V_U$, and $v_D = v_U$. In other words, the K-layer directed expansion subgraph $\mathcal{G}_{v_U}^K$ can be seen as a transformed graph of the K-layer expansion subgraph $\mathcal{G}_{v_U}^K(\mathcal{V}_{v_U}^K; \mathcal{E}_{v_U}^K)$ of G_U associated with the directed edges in

G_D. For G_D, the h-layer directed DB representation around $v_D \in V_D$ is defined as

$$\overrightarrow{DB}^h_{G_D}(v_D) = [H_F(\mathcal{G}^1_{v_D}), \cdots, H_F(\mathcal{G}^K_{v_D}), \cdots, H_F(\mathcal{G}^h_{v_D})]^\top, \tag{6}$$

where $H_F(\mathcal{G}^K_{v_D})$ is the directed heat flow complexity measure of $\mathcal{G}^K_{v_D}$ [15], when the time t for computing the directed heat flow complexity H_F is infinity. H_F is defined as

$$H_F(\mathcal{G}^K_{v_D}) = F(\infty) = \frac{\overrightarrow{\mathcal{E}}^K_{v_D}}{\mathcal{V}^K_{v_D}}. \tag{7}$$

where $F(\infty)$ indicates that the time t for computing $H_F(\mathcal{G}^K_{v_D})$ is infinity.   □

The h-Layer Depth-Based Representations of Directed Line Graphs.
As we have stated in Section 2.1, for the directed line graph $G_D(V_D, E_D)$ transformed from the original graph $G(V, E)$, each vertex represents a corresponding edge of $G(V, E)$. As a result, either the h-layer undirected depth-based representation of a vertex in $G_U(V_U, E_U)$ or the h-layer directed depth-based representation of a vertex in $G_D(V_D, \overrightarrow{E}_D)$ can be seen as a depth-based representation or a vectorial representation of a corresponding edge in $G(V, E)$. Thus, for the graph $G(V, E)$ and its directed line graph $G_D(V_D, \overrightarrow{E}_D)$, the h-layer depth-based representation of an edge $e \in E$ corresponded by a vertex $v_D \in V_D$ can be computed by a new h-layer depth-based representation around v_D

$$DB^h(v_D) = DB^h_{G_U}(v_U) + \overrightarrow{DB}^h_{G_D}(v_D), \tag{8}$$

where $v_U \in V_U$, $v_D \in V_D$, $v_U = v_D$ and $V_U = V_D$. $DB^h(v_D)$ can be seen as a mixed h-layer depth-based representation by summing both the h-layer undirected depth-based representation defined in Eq.(3) and the h-layer directed depth-based representation defined in Eq.(6).   □

Clearly, based on the above description, we can develop an edge-based matching method for a pair of graphs by aligning the h-layer depth-based representations around vertices in their directed line graphs.

3   An Edge-Based Matching Kernel Through Directed Line Graphs

In this section, we commence by developing a new edge-based matching method for graphs through their directed line graphs. Moreover, based on the new matching method, we define a new edge-based matching kernel.

3.1   Edge-Based Matching Through Directed Line Graphs

As we have stated in Section 2.2, we can develop an edge-based matching method for graphs by aligning the vertices of their directed line graphs. Because, for an original graph and its directed line graph, each vertex of the line graph represents a corresponding edge in the original graph. For a pair of graphs $G_p(V_p, E_p)$ and $G_q(V_q, E_q)$, $G_{D;p}(V_{D;p}, \overrightarrow{E}_{D;p})$ and $G_{D;q}(V_{D;q}, \overrightarrow{E}_{D;q})$ are their directed line graphs. For each directed line graph, we compute the h-layer depth-based representation around each vertex as the vectorial representation of the vertex. We compute the Euclidean distance between the depth-based representations $DB^h(v_i)$ and $DB^h(v_j)$ as the distance measure of the pairwise vertices v_i and u_j of the directed line graphs $G_{D;p}$ and $G_{D;q}$, respectively. The affinity matrix element $R(i,j)$ is defined as

$$R(i,j) = \sqrt{[DB^h(v_i) - DB^h(u_j)]^T [DB^h(v_i) - DB^h(u_j)]}. \qquad (9)$$

where R is a $|V_{D;p}| \times |V_{D;q}|$ matrix. The element $R(i,j)$ represents the dissimilarity between the vertex v_i in $G_{D;p}$ and the vertex u_j in $G_{D;q}$. The rows of $R(i,j)$ index the vertices of $G_{D;p}$, and the columns index the vertices of $G_{D;q}$. If $R(i,j)$ is the smallest element both in row i and in column j, there should be a one-to-one correspondence between the vertex v_i of $G_{D;p}$ and the vertex u_j of $G_{D;q}$. We record the state of correspondence using the correspondence matrix $C \in \{0,1\}^{|V_{D;p}||V_{D;q}|}$ satisfying

$$C(i,j) = \begin{cases} 1 \text{ if } R(i,j) \text{ is the smallest element} \\ \quad \text{both in row } i \text{ and in column } j; \\ 0 \text{ otherwise.} \end{cases} \qquad (10)$$

Eq.(10) implies that if $C(i,j) = 1$, the vertices v_i and v_j are matched. Note that, like the depth-based matching previously introduced in our previous work [12], for a pair of directed line graphs a vertex from a line graph may have more than one matched vertex in the other line graph. In our work, we assign each vertex from a line graph at most one vertex in the other line graph. One way to achieve this is to update the matrix C by means of the Hungarian algorithm [16], following the strategy proposed in [12]. Unfortunately, the Hungarian algorithm usually requires expensive computation and thus may lead to computational inefficiency for the new edge-based matching method. To address the inefficiency, an alternative strategy is to randomly assign each vertex an unique matched vertex through the correspondence matrix C. In other words, for C, from the first row and the first column, we will set each evaluating element of C as 0 if there has been an existing element that is 1 either in the same row or the same column. We find that this strategy will not influence the effectiveness of the resulting kernel in Section 3.2, and the kernel will be more efficient.

3.2   An Edge-Based Depth-Based Matching Kernel

Based on the graph matching strategy in Section 3.1, we define a new graph kernel.

Definition 3.1 (The edge-based matching kernel). Consider G_p and G_q as a pair of sample graphs, $G_{D;p}(V_{D;p}, \vec{E}_{D;p})$ and $G_{D;q}(V_{D;q}, \vec{E}_{D;q})$ are their directed line graphs transformed from their directed line graphs. Based on the definitions in Eq.(3), Eq.(9) and Eq.(10), we compute the correspondence matrix C. The edge-based matching kernel $k_{EB}^{(h)}$ using the h-layer depth-based representations of the directed line graphs is

$$k_{EB}^{(h)}(G_p, G_q) = k_{EB}^{(h)}(G_{D;p}, G_{D;q}) = \sum_{i=1}^{|V_{D;p}|} \sum_{j=1}^{|V_{D;q}|} C(i, j). \tag{11}$$

which counts the number of matched vertex pairs between $G_{D;p}$ and $G_{D;q}$. Intuitively, the edge-based matching kernel k_{EB}^h is positive definite. This is because k_{EB}^h counts pairs of matched vertices over the correspondence matrix C. $\square$

Discussions. Clearly, like our previous depth-based matching kernel [12], the edge-based matching kernel is also related to the depth-based representation defined in [13]. However, there are three significant differences. First, the depth-based representations in [13] are computed on original graphs. By contrast, the h-layer depth-based representations for graphs required in this work are computed through directed line graphs transformed from original graphs. Second, in [13], we only compute the depth-based representation rooted at a centroid vertex of an original graph which is identified by evaluating the variance of the shortest path lengths between vertices. By contrast, in this work, we compute the h-layer depth-based representation rooted at each vertex of the directed line graph. Third, the depth-based representation from the centroid vertex is a vectorial signature of an original graph, i.e., it is an embedding vector for the graph. Embedding a graph into a vector tends to approximate the structural correlations in a low dimensional space, and thus leads to information loss. By contrast, the edge-based matching kernel aligning the h-layer depth-based representation represents directed line graphs (transformed from original graphs) in a high dimensional space and thus better preserves graph structures.

Moreover, as we have stated, the directed line graph may expose richer graph characteristics. Because the cardinality of the vertex set for the directed line graph is much greater than, or at least equal to, that of the original graph. As a result, the new edge-based matching kernel can not only encapsulate the correspondence information between edges of original graphs, but also reflect richer graph characteristics through directed line graphs.

Finally, like our previous depth-based matching kernel [11], the new edge-based matching kernel can also be seen as an aligned subgraph kernel (details of the discussion can be found in [11]). Differently, the edge-based matching kernel identifies the locational correspondence between pairwise h-layer expansion subgraphs of the directed line graphs transformed from the original graphs. By contrast, our previous depth-based matching kernel identifies the locational correspondence between pairwise h-layer expansion subgraphs of the original graphs. The expansion subgraphs from the directed line graphs may encapsulate more information that those from the original graphs, thus our new edge-based matching kernel can preserve more structural information than the depth-based matching kernel.

4 Experimental Results

In this section, we empirically compare our new edge-based matching kernel with several state-of-the-art graph kernels on several standard graph datasets from both computer vision and bioinformatics databases.

4.1 Graph Datasets

We demonstrate the performance of our new kernel on five standard graph datasets from computer vision and bioinformatics databases. These datasets include BAR31, BSPHERE31, GEOD31, SHOCK' and ENZYMES. Details of these datasets can be found as follows.

BAR31, BSPHERE31 and GEOD31. The SHREC 3D Shape database consists of 15 classes and 20 individuals per class, that is 300 shapes [17]. This is an usual benchmark in 3D shape recognition. From the SHREC 3D Shape database, we establish three graph datasets named BAR31, BSPHERE31 and GEOD31 datasets through three mapping functions. These functions are a) ERG barycenter: distance from the center of mass/barycenter, b) ERG bsphere: distance from the center of the sphere that circumscribes the object, and c) ERG integral geodesic: the average of the geodesic distances to the all other points. The number of maximum, minimum and average vertices for the three datasets are a) 220, 41 and 95.42 (for BAR31), b) 227, 43 and 99.83 (for BSPHERE31), and c) 380, 29 and 57.42 (for GEOD31), respectively.

Shock. The Shock dataset consists of graphs from the Shock 2D shape database. Each graph is a skeletal-based representation of the differential structure of the boundary of a 2D shape. There are 150 graphs divided into 10 classes. Each class contains 15 graphs. The number of maximum, minimum and average vertices for the dataset are 33, 4 and 13.16 respectively.

ENZYMES. The ENZYMES dataset consists of graphs representing protein tertiary structures consisting of 600 enzymes from the BRENDA enzyme. The task is to correctly assign each enzyme to one of the 6 EC top-level. The number of maximum, minimum and average vertices for the dataset are 126, 2 and 32.63 respectively.

4.2   Experiments on Graph Datasets

Experimental Setup: We evaluate the performance of our new edge-based matching kernel (EBMK), on graph classification problems. We also compare our kernel with several alternative state-of-the-art graph kernels. These graph kernels include 1) the depth-based matching kernel (DBMK) [11,12], 2) the Weisfeiler-Lehman subtree kernel (WLSK) [7], 3) the shortest path graph kernel (SPGK) [4], 4) the graphlet count graph kernel [18] with graphlet of size 4 (GCGK) [18], 5) the un-aligned quantum Jensen-Shannon kernel (UQJS) [19], and 6) the Jensen-Shannon graph kernel (JSGK) [14]. For the WLSK kernel, we set the highest dimension (i.e., the highest height of subtrees) of the Weisfeiler-Lehman isomorphism (for the WLSK kernel) as 10. For the EBMK kernel and the DBMK kernel, we set the highest layer of the required depth-based representation as 10. The reason for this is that the 10-layer expansion subgraph rooted at a vertex of an original graph (for the DBMK kernel) or a directed line graph (for the EBMK kernel) usually encapsulates most vertices of the original graph or the line graph. Moreover, note that, some kernels (i.e., the WLSK kernel and the SPGK kernel) can accommodate vertex labels, in this paper we use the degree of a vertex as the label of the vertex. For each kernel, we compute the kernel matrix on each graph dataset. We perform 10-fold cross-validation using the C-Support Vector Machine (C-SVM) Classification to compute the classification accuracy, using LIBSVM [20]. We use nine samples for training and one for testing. All the C-SVMs were performed along with their parameters optimized on each dataset. We report the average classification accuracy (± standard error) and the runtime for each kernel in Table 1 and Table 2, respectively. The runtime is measured under Matlab R2011a running on a 2.5GHz Intel 2-Core processor (i.e. i5-3210m).

Table 1. Classification Accuracy (In % ± Standard Error) Using C-SVM.

Datasets	EBMK	DBMK	WLSK	SPGK	GCGK	UQJS	JSGK
BAR31	67.06 ± .64	**69.40 ± .56**	58.53 ± .53	55.73 ± .44	23.40 ± .60	30.80 ± .61	24.10 ± .86
BSPHERE31	51.20 ± .73	**56.43 ± .69**	42.10 ± .68	48.20 ± .76	18.80 ± .50	24.80 ± .61	21.76 ± .53
GEOD31	**43.33 ± .79**	42.83 ± .50	38.20 ± .68	38.40 ± .65	22.36 ± .55	23.73 ± .66	18.93 ± .50
Shock	**42.06 ± .85**	30.80 ± .93	36.40 ± .99	37.88 ± .93	27.06 ± .99	40.60 ± .92	21.73 ± .76
ENZYMES	**40.53 ± .29**	35.23 ± .52	38.41 ± .45	32.57 ± .45	24.87 ± .22	33.93 ± .61	20.81 ± .29

Table 2. Runtime of Computing the Kernel Matrix.

Datasets	EBMK	DBMK	WLSK	SPGK	GCGK	UQJS	JSGK
BAR31	302"	682"	30"	11"	1"	630"	1"
BSPHERE31	268"	720"	25"	14"	1"	828"	1"
GEOD31	163"	649"	15"	11"	1"	519"	1"
Shock	8"	7"	3"	1"	1"	14"	1"
ENZYMES	529"	349"	21"	2"	2"	627"	1"

Experimental Results: In terms of the classification accuracy from the C-SVM, we observe that our EBMK kernel can easily outperform all the alternative graph kernels excluding the DBMK kernel, on any dataset. The reasons for the effectiveness are threefold. First, the EBMK kernel can be seen as a vertex matching kernel through directed line graphs transformed from original graphs. By contrast, other kernels are defined on original graphs. As we have stated in Section 2, the directed line graph transformed from an original graph can reflect richer characteristics than the original graph. As a result, the EBMK kernel defined on line graphs can encapsulate more information than other kernels defined on original graphs. Second, compared to the WLSK, SPGK and GCGK kernels that require decomposing graphs into substructures, our EBMK kernel can establish the substructure location correspondences in directed line graphs transformed from original graphs. By contrast, the WLSK, SPGK and GCGK kernels do not consider the location correspondence between pairwise substructures in the original graphs. Third, compared to the JSGK and UQJS kernels that rely on the similarity measure between original global graphs in terms of the classical or quantum JSD, our EBMK kernel can identify the correspondence information between both the vertices and the substructures of directed line graphs, and can thus reflect richer interior topological characteristics. By contrast, the JSGK and QJSK kernels only reflect the global graph similarity information of original graphs.

Finally, our EBMK kernel outperforms the DBMK kernel on the ENZYMES, Shock and GEOD31 datasets. Especially, the classification accuracies of our new EBMK kernel on the ENZYMES and Shock datasets are much more better than those of the DBMK kernel. On the BSPHERE31 and BAR31 datasets, the classification accuracies of our EBMK kernel are a little lower than those of the DBMK kernel. Overall, our EBMK kernel outperforms or is competitive to the DBMK kernel. The effectiveness for this is that both our EBMK kernel and the DBMK kernel can identify the location correspondence between substructures. However, the EBMK kernel defined through directed line graphs can reflect richer characteristics than the DBMK kernel defined on original graphs.

5   Conclusion

In this paper, we have developed a new edge-based matching kernel for graphs. For a pair of graphs, the new kernel is based on the directed line graphs which are dual representations of the pair of graphs, i.e., for an original graph the vertex of its directed line graph represent a corresponding edge in the original graph. We compute the depth-based representations for edges of the original graphs through their directed line graphs. Based on the new representations, we define the new edge-based matching by counting the number of matched vertices identified by the matching method on the directed line graphs. Experiments on standard graph datasets demonstrate the effectiveness of our new edge-based matching kernel.

Acknowledgments. This work is supported by program for innovation research in Central University of Finance and Economics, and National Natural Science Foundation of China (Grant No. 61402389 and 61272398). Edwin R. Hancock is supported by a Royal Society Wolfson Research Merit Award.

References

1. Bai, L., Rossi, L., Bunke, H., Hancock, E.R.: Attributed graph kernels using the Jensen-Tsallis q-differences. In: Calders, T., Esposito, F., Hüllermeier, E., Meo, R. (eds.) ECML PKDD 2014, Part I. LNCS, vol. 8724, pp. 99–114. Springer, Heidelberg (2014)

2. Haussler, D.: Convolution kernels on discrete structures. Technical Report UCS-CRL-99-10, UC Santa Cruz (1999)

3. Kashima, H., Tsuda, K., Inokuchi, A.: Marginalized kernels between labeled graphs. In: ICML, pp. 321–328 (2003)

4. Borgwardt, K.M., Kriegel, H.: Shortest-path kernels on graphs. In: Proceedings of ICDM, pp. 74–81 (2005)

5. Aziz, F., Wilson, R.C., Hancock, E.R.: Backtrackless walks on a graph. IEEE Trans. Neural Netw. Learning Syst. **24**, 977–989 (2013)

6. Ren, P., Wilson, R.C., Hancock, E.R.: Graph characterization via ihara coefficients. IEEE Transactions on Neural Networks **22**, 233–245 (2011)

7. Shervashidze, N., Schweitzer, P., van Leeuwen, E.J., Mehlhorn, K., Borgwardt, K.M.: Weisfeiler-lehman graph kernels. Journal of Machine Learning Research **12**, 2539–2561 (2011)

8. Harchaoui, Z., Bach, F.: Image classification with segmentation graph kernels. In: Proceedings of CVPR (2007)

9. Bach, F.R.: Graph kernels between point clouds. In: Proceedings of ICML, pp. 25–32 (2008)

10. Bai, L., Ren, P., Hancock, E.R.: A hypergraph kernel from isomorphism tests. In: 22nd International Conference on Pattern Recognition, ICPR 2014, Stockholm, Sweden, August 24–28, 2014, pp. 3880–3885 (2014)

11. Bai, L.: Information Theoretic Graph Kernels. University of York, UK (2014)

12. Bai, L., Ren, P., Bai, X., Hancock, E.R.: A graph kernel from the depth-based representation. In: Fränti, P., Brown, G., Loog, M., Escolano, F., Pelillo, M. (eds.) S+SSPR 2014. LNCS, vol. 8621, pp. 1–11. Springer, Heidelberg (2014)

13. Bai, L., Hancock, E.R.: Depth-based complexity traces of graphs. Pattern Recognition **47**, 1172–1186 (2014)

14. Bai, L., Hancock, E.R.: Graph kernels from the jensen-shannon divergence. Journal of Mathematical Imaging and Vision **47**, 60–69 (2013)

15. Escolano, F., Hancock, E., Lozano, M.: Heat diffusion: Thermodynamic depth complexity of networks. Physical Review E **85**, 206236 (2012)

16. Munkres, J.: Algorithms for the assignment and transportation problems. Journal of the Society for Industrial and Applied Mathematics **5** (1957)

17. Biasotti, S., Marini, S., Mortara, M., Patané, G., Spagnuolo, M., Falcidieno, B.: 3D shape matching through topological structures. In: Nyström, I., Sanniti di Baja, G., Svensson, S. (eds.) DGCI 2003. LNCS, vol. 2886, pp. 194–203. Springer, Heidelberg (2003)

18. Shervashidze, N., Vishwanathan, S., Petri, T., Mehlhorn, K., Borgwardt, K.: Efficient graphlet kernels for large graph comparison. Journal of Machine Learning Research **5**, 488–495 (2009)

19. Bai, L., Rossi, L., Torsello, A., Hancock, E.R.: A quantum jensen-shannon graph kernel for unattributed graphs. Pattern Recognition **48**, 344–355 (2015)

20. Chang, C.C., Lin, C.J.: Libsvm: A library for support vector machines (2011). Software available at http://www.csie.ntu.edu.tw/cjlin/libsvm

The Virtues of Peer Pressure: A Simple Method for Discovering High-Value Mistakes

Shumeet Baluja[✉], Michele Covell, and Rahul Sukthankar

Google Research, Mountain View, USA
shumeet@google.com

Abstract. Much of the recent success of neural networks can be attributed to the deeper architectures that have become prevalent. However, the deeper architectures often yield unintelligible solutions, require enormous amounts of labeled data, and still remain brittle and easily broken. In this paper, we present a method to efficiently and intuitively discover input instances that are misclassified by well-trained neural networks. As in previous studies, we can identify instances that are so similar to previously seen examples such that the transformation is visually imperceptible. Additionally, unlike in previous studies, we can also generate mistakes that are significantly different from any training sample, while, importantly, still remaining in the space of samples that the network should be able to classify correctly. This is achieved by training a basket of N "peer networks" rather than a single network. These are similarly trained networks that serve to provide consistency pressure on each other. When an example is found for which a single network, S, disagrees with all of the other $N - 1$ networks, which are consistent in their prediction, that example is a potential mistake for S. We present a simple method to find such examples and demonstrate it on two visual tasks. The examples discovered yield realistic images that clearly illuminate the weaknesses of the trained models, as well as provide a source of numerous, diverse, labeled-training samples.

1 Introduction

The recent rapid resurgence of interest in deep neural networks has been spurred by state of the art performance on vision and speech tasks. However, despite their impressive performance, the deeper architectures require enormous amounts of labeled data and are surprisingly fragile. Additionally, because the training is done through following derivatives in high-dimensional spaces and often through ad-hoc architectures and input groupings, the results can be unintelligible with surprising error modes [9,13,16].

The three problems of needing vast amounts of training data, being brittle, and being unintelligible are interrelated. In this paper, we address them by finding *high-value* mistakes that the network makes. A high-value mistake is one where the network is expected to perform correctly and does not – e.g., the input lies in the space of realistic inputs for the task and yet is misclassified. Finding where these mistakes are likely to occur yields insight into the computation of

© Springer International Publishing Switzerland 2015
G. Azzopardi and N. Petkov (Eds.): CAIP 2015, Part II, LNCS 9257, pp. 96–108, 2015.
DOI: 10.1007/978-3-319-23117-4_9

Fig. 1. (Left) 49 digits that the network classified correctly. (Middle) Examples of *high-value* mistakes generated by our method. They are digits that should be classified correctly, since the images are of the same type as the training images. (Right) Examples of *low-value* mistakes. They all contain individual pixel-based noise which, though small, is not representative of the types of images the network was designed to recognize.

the network. These mistakes can also be used to further augment the training set to mitigate the brittle decision boundaries that may have been created with only the original training examples. Figure 1 provides a visual example of high-value and low-value mistakes for the familiar MNIST dataset. It shows examples that are classified perfectly by a trained network, examples that are misclassified, but should be classified well (high-value mistakes), and examples that are not classified well, but are outside the set of examples the network is trained on (low-value mistakes). If too many low-value mistakes are used for retraining the networks, or any machine learning classification tools, they face the problem of artificial concept drift [15]; the training examples no longer become representative of the actual problem.

Through the last three decades, a variety of approaches have been explored to understand the performance of neural networks and to generate new examples based on their encoded computations. In a broad sense, the approach taken here is *behaviorist* in nature. We do not look at the internal states of the network to determine how it will perform; instead, we observe how the network responds to different inputs. Similar approaches were described in [1,7]. Alternative approaches interpret the internal states of a neural network by discovering what the hidden units and layers encode [3,13,14].

The remainder of the paper is structured as follows. Section 2 details the proposed method for finding high-value mistakes; a simple, two-dimensional, example is provided to concretely demonstrate the algorithms. Section 3 describes experiments on the 10-digit MNIST database. Section 4 describes experiments with state-of-the-art networks trained to classify real-world images into 1,000 categories. Section 5 presents further experiments to illuminate limitations of the approach. Finally, Section 6 concludes the paper and presents directions for future work.

2   Using Peer Networks to Find Inconsistencies in Training

The underlying decision boundaries inferred by well trained classification models depend on a number of factors: the training examples used, the learning algorithms employed, the exact architecture and form of the trained models, and the proper use of validation sets and hold-out sets, to name a few. With neural networks, further unpredictability in the decision boundaries arises because the training is sensitive to the order in which the examples are presented, the initial weights, and the numerous hyper-parameters associated with typical training algorithms such a backpropagation.

With this in mind, consider the simple two-class problem of classifying points on a checkerboard: does a given point fall on a red of black square? This is a version of the X-OR problem often used with neural networks; see Figure 2.

Fig. 2. (Left) A toy two-dimensional, two-class, classification problem. (Right) 200 randomly selected samples used for training a network (100 from each class).

To concretely show the different learning boundaries created, five neural networks with 10, 12, 14, 16 & 18 units per hidden-layer were trained on 200 sample points. Each network had two inputs (x and y coordinates), 2 fully-connected hidden layers, and 1 output classification node. The inferred classification boundaries are shown in Figure 3.

Fig. 3. Decision boundaries of the five networks trained on the toy task in Figure 2. Close inspection reveals many differences.

Though this variability may be initially considered a limitation in training, an enormous amount of research has already shown the benefits of using these individual networks as members of an *ensemble classifier* (e.g., [4]). In ensemble methods, the outputs of multiple networks are combined through any number of voting schemes to output the final classification. In contrast to typical ensemble methods, this study uses the variability in networks to find potential mistakes.

Fig. 4. Sample points where each network disagrees with *all* of its peers. Note that each falls near the decision boundaries shown in Figure 3.

In this simple example, for any target network, A, we scan through valid values of x & y to find points where A disagrees with all of its peers (the other 4 networks). Such points are good candidates for new training examples for network A because all of the other similarly trained networks were able to classify them correctly (see Figure 4). The labels for these points can either be provided as a supervisory signal (analogous to an active learning approach where the learner requests labels for selected instances [2]) or can be supplied by the consistent labeling generated by the peers.[1]

The toy 2-D example allows complete exploration of the input space. However, for more realistic problems, such as image classification one cannot consider the set of all potential input images. Not only is the space of possible images too large, but the set of all images is vastly dominated by unrealistic pixel combinations (e.g., white noise) that will not appear either during training or inference.

Instead, to find high-value-examples, we must either have a set of promising candidates (e.g., a repository of unlabeled data) or we can synthesize extra instances from known good images. With both of these approaches, we use the consistent classification of the peer networks as a filter to select images. For the MNIST task, we take the latter approach: we search the space of transformations on image X for an input image X' where for a given network A and $\forall$ networks $p_i, p_j, p_k \in$ peer networks $\{B, C, D, E\}$, we attempt to find examples X' that simultaneously:

$$\min\{\text{DIST}(p_i(X'), p_j(X'))\} \quad \text{and} \quad \max\{\text{DIST}(A(X'), p_k(X')\},$$

where $\text{DIST}(p_i(X'), p_j(X'))$ is the magnitude of the difference in classifier outputs between networks p_i and p_j when applied to X' (this is minimized to ensure consistency between peers). $\text{DIST}(A(X'), p_k(X'))$ is the magnitude of the difference between the target network, A, and its peers (maximized to ensure A and its peers are different).

How do we find this image? Naively sampling random images to find one that maximizes/minimizes these two objectives simultaneously would be prohibitively slow. Instead, we search through the space of potential images by stochastically perturbing an example digit to satisfy the above constraints. The algorithm in its simplest form is described in the procedure below.

---

[1] This raises the question: The worst performing network in the set will likely see improvement using this method, but will *all* the networks? This is an immediate area for future research.

- Start with seed image, X. If X is not classified in the same class, C, for all of the networks, find a different seed.
- done = False
- while (not done):
  - Generate a candidate, X', with a stochastically chosen constrained image transform on X.
  - If X' is not classified in the same class, C, by all the peers, reject X'. *(this ensures consistency of peers).*
  - Else: Measure network-A activation w/input X' for class C: $A(X')_C$.
    If $(A(X')_C < A(X)_C)$ then accept X' ; $X \leftarrow X'$
    Else: Reject X'.
  - done = network-A classifies X' sufficiently differently than peers do. e.g., minimize $A(X')_C$ where $\forall P \in$ Peers, $P(X') = C$.

Note for labeled data: In the cases where we know the label L of initial image X, we simply ensure that $C = L$ throughout the run.

Illustrating using the MNIST example, we start by randomly selecting a digit image from the training set (seed). We also randomly generate a small affine transformation (e.g., small rotation, translation, stretch). If applying this transform to the seed increases the difference between the output activation of the target network and its peers (with the peers still agreeing on their prediction), then we keep the transformed image and use it as the seed for the next iteration. We compose transforms in this manner until we either find a sequence of transforms that causes a misclassification by the target network (with peers still classifying correctly) or until we try too many transforms for the given seed — in which case we restart with a new seed image drawn from the training set.

Alternatives to next-ascent hillclimbing include more sophisticated search heuristics. Evolutionary algorithms such as genetic algorithms, population-based incremental hillclimbing or other evolutionary strategies may be used to search the space of image transforms; see [10]. Like hillclimbing, these quickly search discrete spaces without the need for derivatives [1,7].

In the next section, we apply the proposed algorithm to networks trained to recognize MNIST digits. To keep our experiments reproducible, we use simple hillclimbing as the search mechanism. Because of space restrictions, we only note there that we have also successfully applied several other evolutionary algorithms on this task with similar qualitative results, although the efficiency varied greatly depending on the specific algorithm and search heuristics.

3   Result Set I: The MNIST Digit Database

For the experiments with MNIST [8], 60,000 digit images were used for training five different networks. Other than the number of hidden units in the networks (10, 20, 30, 40 & 50), the networks were identical and trained identically. Samples from the MNIST database are shown in Figure 1.

Fig. 5. A typical hillclimbing session. The leftmost of the bars in each group (blue) is the output activation of the target network. The four other bars (green) show the peers' activations. Top row: the '9' is correctly and confidently classified by all networks (all activations are close to 1.0). Bottom row: within five operations, the target network misclassifies the '9' as a '3', but its peers continue classifying it correctly with high confidence.

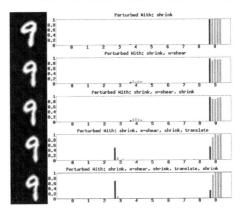

Figure 5 shows a typical hillclimbing session to obtain mistake images. Within five transformations (starting from the top), the target network misclassifies the digit '9' as a '3' with high confidence, yet its peer networks confidently predict the correct class for all transformations. Note that the sequence of constrained transforms results in an image that is still unambiguously a '9' for humans.

This image is a high-value mistake because the target network strongly misclassifies it while its four peers are confident in the correct prediction. Based on the sequence of transforms that generated this mistake, it appears as though the target network may be susceptible to small amounts of shrinking, to which its peers are robust. Adding this mistake to the target network's training set may help to make it more robust to such transforms. Additional examples are shown in Figure 6.

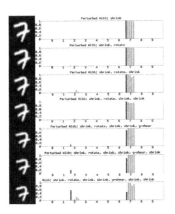

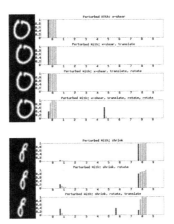

Fig. 6. Three hillclimbing sessions. Left: '7' mistaken as '2' in 7 image transformations. Right-Top: '0' mistaken as '5' in 4 moves. Right-Bottom: '8' mistaken as both '1' and '6' within only 3 moves. Note that in all of these examples, the peers still correctly identified the digit, while the target network did not.

Table 1. Inferences and moves required to find a high-value mistake per network

Target network	Hidden Nodes	% Successful Trials	# moves	# forward inferences
				(average over successful trials)
A	10	63%	5	507
B	20	25%	5	640
C	30	9%	6	852
D	40	5%	6	801
E	50	7%	6	819

On average, only five small transforms were required to change a training image into one that is incorrectly classified. However, many more candidate images were evaluated by the networks in the process of finding this sequence of five moves. This is typical with stochastic search; the other candidates were rejected because they did not improve the objective function.

To give an indication of how much effort it takes to find a potential mistake, in Table 1, the results with over 1,000 trials per network are shown. In the first row, network A was chosen as the one for which errors were found, and networks B, C, D, and E were chosen as its peers. For each of the 1,000 trials, a random digit was selected as a seed and next-ascent-stochastic hillclimbing was used to search the space of affine image transformation. 63% of the trials resulted in a mistaken classification (Figure 5, Figure 6). These 630 sequences are labeled successful. Trials in which 250 consecutive transformations were tested without improvement were marked as *un*successful.

The last column shows the number of forward inferences needed on the successful trials through the five networks. On average, 507 forward inferences were required per successful trial. As there are a total of five networks, this is approximately 101 forward inferences through each. This means that, for the successful trials, on average, 101 image transformations were also created and tested through the hillclimbing procedure before the transformation sequence that led to a high-value mistake was found.

The next rows in Table 1 repeat the same process for each of the other networks. For example, in the last row network E is considered the primary network and its peers are networks A, B, C, and D. This is the largest network of the ones tried, with 50 hidden units. Note that the procedure has a lower success rate in terms of mistakes found and requires more forward inferences. In general, the more robust the target network, the harder it is to find errors that other, worse performing, networks do not also make. Interestingly, although the hillclimbing procedure had to search longer, the average length of the transform sequence needed to generate a high-value mistake only rose to six.

4   Results Set II: Deep Vision Networks

We present some early results on applying peer pressure on the ImageNet [11] dataset. We trained five convolutional neural networks on the ImageNet training

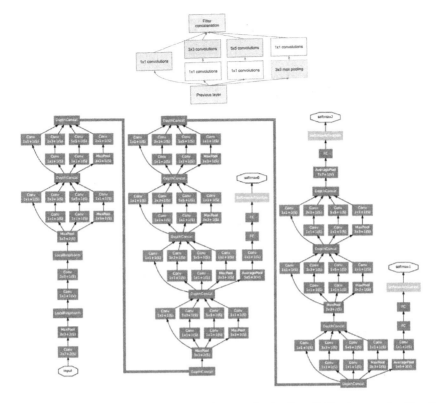

Fig. 7. (Top) A single Inception module. (Bottom) The GoogLeNet image classification network is built from many such modules. In this diagram, the pairs of "DepthConcat" units that are connected by heavy green lines are shown as pairs to make the diagram easier to fold — there is a single "DepthConcat" unit at each of these fold locations. Diagrams adapted from [12] with permission.

set to classify a given image into one of 1000 categories (synsets). Unlike in the MNIST experiments in Section 3, where the peers had slightly different architectures, all of the GoogLeNet networks employed the same GoogLeNet architecture [12]. GoogLeNet consists of a series of *Inception modules* shown in Figure 7 (Top) connected in the very deep structure, illustrated in Figure 7 (Bottom).

The input layer was a 224 × 224 RGB image. The inputs automatically subtracted the mean from the image as the first normalization. All units, including those in the Inception modules used rectified linear units (ReLU) as the nonlinearity. Given the challenge of propagating gradients through its significant depth (27 layers), GoogLeNet employs auxiliary classifiers, shown as side branches ending in "SoftMax" units in Figure 7, that connect to intermediate layers and boost the loss signal to provide data-driven regularization. For additional details about GoogLeNet, see [12].

104   S. Baluja et al.

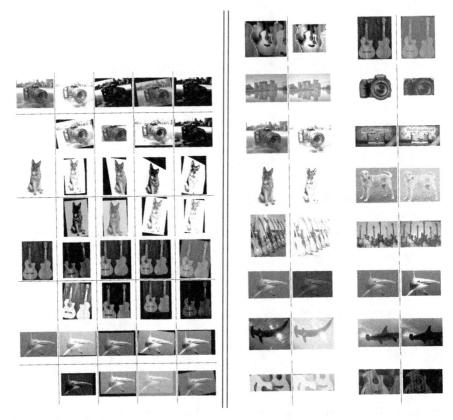

Fig. 8. (LEFT) All five networks are successfully trained to be robust to many severe transformations. The original image and the 8 transformed images are all classified correctly by all five networks. Note the variations in rotation, lighting, crop, the presence of black borders, etc. (RIGHT) For each column - left: original image, right: transformed image that the hillclimbing procedure found that caused an error for the target network. In this case, Network 1 (shown) was very sensitive to lighting conditions especially when coupled with small rotations or crops. Note that all the peers *correctly* classified these samples; thereby making these high-value mistakes for Network 1.

The networks were explicitly trained to be robust to common image transformations, such as cropping and rotation by sampling crops from the original image at various sizes (8%–100%), aspect ratios (3/4–4/3) and photometric distortions [6]. Some of the transforms that can be handled are shown in Figure 8 (LEFT). Note the severe shearing, large black borders, rotation and color and intensity variations.

With such robust training, we initially believed that it would be difficult to find images that cause a single network to fail without also impacting the accuracy of its peers. However, in practice, this proved to not be the case. See Figure 8 (RIGHT). Each network had unique failure modes despite the observed resistance to numerous image transformations. Network 1 (shown) was often sensitive to lighting cues. Other networks' failures sometimes exhibited differences to individual classes; for example, varying degrees of robustness were exhibited with camera images than with hammerhead sharks. Because of space restrictions, we only show the failure modes for a single network; however, all networks proved susceptible to the this mistake generation method, enabling us to quickly generate high-value training images for each network.

5   Limitations, Discussion and Further Experiments

In this section, we present two extra experiments conducted in the design of the algorithm. They are included to elucidate both the limitations and potential of our work.

One of the implicit assumptions throughout this paper has been that whatever is done for a network A with peers B, C, D, and E can be equivalently done for network B with peers A, C, D, and E. Thus, each network can serve as a peer for the other networks. In the next example, we seek a seed image from the training set, X, that can be transformed such that every network, in turn, will make a mistake on it while its peers maintain the correct classification. Of course, the sequence of transforms required will be different to drive each network to an error. Two such input images and their transformations are shown in Figure 9. Note, in general, we do not need to use the same image as a seed for different networks; however, this demonstrates that it is possible.

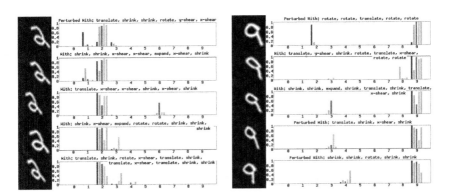

Fig. 9. (Left) The number '2' is mistaken by network A as a '1', by network B as '1', network C as '6', network D as '3' and network E as '3'. To find an error for each network, different transform sequences are found. (Right) Similar results for '9'.

Finally, it is important to explore the limitations of the proposed approach. In the experiments described above, we used small affine image transforms as the perturbation operator. These generate images that look reasonable by using the peer networks to ensure that radical transforms are suppressed (e.g., successively rotating a '6' until it becomes a '9'). This suggests a natural question: can peer pressure ensure that we only generate realistic images as mistakes?

We replaced the affine transforms in the proposed method with simple pixel swaps. Applying a sequence of pixel swaps to a seed image quickly yields noisy images that fall outside the domain of realistic inputs for this task. Nguyen et al. [9] examined similar effects (without the use of peers) in the extreme: white noise images that were classified incorrectly by trained networks. Unlike our study which attempts to find images that the network may encounter in practice, [9] showed that images far outside the training sets may be classified incorrectly with high confidence. We wanted to see whether peer pressure alone would suppress such images from being generated as valuable mistakes.

Unfortunately, as shown in Figure 1 (right), given the pixel swap operator, our method is able to find unrealistic images that are correctly classified by peers and misclassified by the target network. If the underlying image transformations are small, it is possible to "poke holes" in the target network's training in the precise locations where they have little effect on the peers. Naively adding such images to the training set would be inadvisable as they are unlikely to help on the original task.

The benefit of peers is not lost, however. Peers make it more difficult to create such a mistake. We can examine the effect of peers by attempting to find a mistake in the network A with no peers, with 1 peer, etc., up to 4 peers. See Table 2.

Table 2. Effects of peers on difficulty of finding unrealistic mistakes

Number of peers	Successes (of 300)	#number of transforms
0	299	36
1	145	37
2	96	39
3	72	40
4	57	41

As can be seen in the table, without peers, 299/300 hillclimbing attempts transformed the seed image into a low-value mistake. This means that almost every run generated an unrealistic instance. The average number of pixel swaps it took to find the mistake was 36. For comparison, recall that the average number of affine transforms with 4 peers for MNIST was 5–6 moves. When peers are added, the number of successful trials drops sharply. With 4 peers, only 57 of 300 trials were successful in finding a mistake, and the average number of swaps increased to 41. This indicates what we hoped: having peers decreases the likelihood of escaping a reasonable input space.

6   Conclusions and Future Work

The successes of neural networks in real-world tasks has increased the need for finding ever increasing amounts of training data as well as finding insights into what the network has learned, and importantly, where it will fail. In this paper, we have shown that by training multiple "peer" networks to solve the same task, the inherent, unique, biases that are learned in the networks can be used to find mistakes that each network should have classified correctly. The mistakes lie within the space of examples that can be reasonably expected to be seen; thereby yielding valuable insights into the limitations of the trained models.

There are five immediate directions for future work. The most pressing is extending this work by augmenting the training of the networks with the generated high-value mistakes. To accomplish this, many decisions need to be made; for example, how are the new images weighted, and how frequently should they be introduced into training? Second, the effect of increasing the number of peers should be studied. Does adding more peers increase reliability at the expense of mistake coverage? Third, if all the networks were trained by using each others as peers, would they eventually reach a steady state and how soon would this happen? Does this then mimic the effects of using the ensemble for voting, and does this effectively become a technique for ensemble compression [5]. Fourth, instead of using stochastic search, if appropriate derivatives can be created for an input transformation layer, that will yield an alternate way to find meaningful mistakes. Finally, only the simplest search algorithm was employed here; other multi-point search algorithms should also be evaluated for increased efficiency.

Acknowledgments. The authors gratefully acknowledge Christian Szegedy, George Toderici, and Jon Shlens for their discussions, code and help with GoogLeNet experiments.

References

1. Baluja, S.: Finding regions of uncertainty in learned models: an application to face detection. In: Eiben, A.E., Bäck, T., Schoenauer, M., Schwefel, H.-P. (eds.) PPSN 1998. LNCS, vol. 1498, p. 461. Springer, Heidelberg (1998)
2. Cohn, D.A., Ghahramani, Z., Jordan, M.I.: Active learning with statistical models. Journal of Artificial Intelligence Research 4 (1996)
3. Erhan, D., Bengio, Y., Courville, A., Vincent, P.: Visualizing higher-layer features of a deep network. Tech. Rep. 1341, Université de Montréal (2009)
4. Hansen, L.K., Salamon, P.: Neural network ensembles. IEEE Transactions on Pattern Analysis and Machine Intelligence **12**(10) (1990)
5. Hinton, G.E., Vinyals, O., Dean, J.: Distilling the knowledge in a neural network. In: NIPS Deep Learning Workshop (2014)
6. Howard, A.G.: Some improvements on deep convolutional neural network based image classification (2013). arXiv:1312.5402
7. Kindermann, J., Linden, A.: Inversion of neural networks by gradient descent. Parallel Computing **14**(3) (1990)

8. LeCun, Y., Cortes, C., Burges, C.: The MNIST database of handwritten images (1998), http://yann.lecun.com/exdb/mnist/

9. Nguyen, A., Yosinksi, J., Clune, J.: Deep neural networks are easily fooled: High confidence predictions for unrecognizable images. In: Computer Vision and Pattern Recognition (2015)

10. Pelikan, M., Sastry, K., Cantú-Paz, E.: Scalable optimization via probabilistic modeling: From algorithms to applications, vol. 33. Springer Science & Business Media (2006)

11. Russakovsky, O., Deng, J., Su, H., Krause, J., Satheesh, S., Ma, S., Huang, Z., Karpathy, A., Khosla, A., Bernstein, M., Berg, A.C., Fei-Fei, L.: ImageNet large scale visual recognition challenge (2014). arXiv:1409.0575

12. Szegedy, C., Liu, W., Jia, Y., Sermanet, P., Reed, S., Anguelov, D., Erhan, D., Vanhoucke, V., Rabinovich, A.: Going deeper with convolutions (2014). arXiv:1409.4842

13. Szegedy, C., Zaremba, W., Sutskever, I., Bruna, J., Erhan, D., Goodfellow, I., Fergus, R.: Intriguing properties of neural networks (2013). arXiv:1312.6199

14. Touretzky, D.S., Pomerleau, D.A.: What's hidden in the hidden layers. Byte (1989)

15. Tsymbal, A.: The problem of concept drift: Definitions and related work. Tech. Rep. 106, Computer Science Department, Trinity College Dublin (2004)

16. Zeiler, M.D., Fergus, R.: Visualizing and understanding convolutional networks. In: Fleet, D., Pajdla, T., Schiele, B., Tuytelaars, T. (eds.) ECCV 2014, Part I. LNCS, vol. 8689, pp. 818–833. Springer, Heidelberg (2014)

Binarization of MultiSpectral Document Images

Fabian Hollaus[(⊠)] , Markus Diem, and Robert Sablatnig

Computer Vision Lab, TU Wien, Vienna, Austria
{holl,diem,sab}@caa.tuwien.ac.at

Abstract. This work is concerned with the binarization of document images caputured by MultiSpectral Imaging (MSI) systems. The documents imaged are historical manuscripts and MSI is used to gather more information compared to traditional RGB photographs or scans. The binarization method proposed makes use of a state-of-the-art binarization algorithm, which is applied on a single image taken from the stack of multispectral images. This output is then combined with the output of a target detection algorithm. The target detection method is named Adaptive Coherence Estimator (ACE) and it is used to improve the binarization performance. Numerical results show that the combination of both algorithms leads to a performance increase. Additionally, the results exhibit that the method performs partially better than other binarization methods designed for grayscale and multispectral images.

1 Introduction

This work deals with document image binarization of historical documents that have been captured by MultiSpectral Imaging (MSI) systems. MSI is a non-invasive investigation technique that is capable of revealing information which is not visible for the human eye [9]. MSI has proven to be a valuable investigation tool for such historical documents, since it can be used to increase the legibility of faded out or erased writings [9] or to differentiate between different ink types [16].

Several works have shown that post-processing methods can be applied on multispectral images in order to increase the legibility of faded out text. For this purpose researchers have applied for instance Principal Component Analysis, Independent Component Analysis (ICA) [16] or Linear Discriminant Analysis [7] onto multispectral images of historical writings. Recently, Hedjam et al. proposed another enhancement method for documents that have been captured with a MSI system [6]. The authors suggest to consider the problem of increasing the contrast of faded-out ink as detecting a target, which is defined by the spectral signature of the ink. In order to enhance the image regions containing this target signature, Hedjam et al. make use of a target detection approach stemming from the field of remote sensing. The approach used is named Constrained Energy Minimization (CEM) [4]: CEM aims at maximizing an energy function while suppressing the remaining document background. Therefore, a linear filter is designed that is applied on the multispectral scan. Contrary to the original CEM algorithm, which makes use of an external target reference, the authors propose to find the

G. Azzopardi and N. Petkov (Eds.): CAIP 2015, Part II, LNCS 9257, pp. 109–120, 2015.
DOI: 10.1007/978-3-319-23117-4_10

target reference in the image itself. Therefore, the visible bands belonging to the multispectral scan are binarized and the mask found is used to determine the mean spectral signature of the writing.

The works mentioned above are dedicated to the enhancement of multispectral images of ancient manuscripts, which are partially in a poor condition. Therefore, the enhancement techniques are used to increase the legibility of the writings but a binarization of the images is error-prone due to the low foreground to background contrast and background variation. Contrary, the documents considered in this work, are in a better condition, and hence image binarization methods can be successfully applied onto the images. Image binarization is typically performed in a preprocessing step of a document analysis system in order to make subsequent analysis techniques, such as optical character recognition, applicable or more efficient [18]. The overall aim of document image binarization is to classify pixels of an input image as belonging to the foreground or background. Historical documents are partially degraded, including faded out characters or background variation [18]. In order to deal with these degradations, binarization techniques have been developed, which are especially designed for ancient documents. For instance in [8] a binarization method is proposed that makes use of an edge detection and a graph cut algorithm. In [3] an adaptive binarization method is proposed that makes use of a background model in order to deal with background variation.

While the majority of the binarization techniques is designed for grayscale images [9], recently several techniques have been introduced that aim at binarizing multispectral images of historical documents. For instance, Mitianoudis and Papamarkos [10] propose an algorithm that makes use of image fusion, ICA and a K-harmonic means classifier to binarize a stack of multispectral images. In [9] a higher order Markov Random Field (MRF) is used to combine the spatial and spectral information contained in the multispectral images and to subsequently classify the pixels as belonging to the foreground or background. Farrahi Moghaddam and Cheriet [13] proposed recently a binarization framework for multispectral images, which is based on subspace selection and makes use of state-of-the-art binarization methods that have been developed for gray value images.

Similar to [13] our binarization method makes also use of a state-of-the-art binarization method suggested in [18] for the binarization of grayscale images: This method is applied on a single image taken from the multispectral scan and the output is used for the analysis of the spectral information. Inspired by the enhancement method suggested in [6], we apply also a target detection method in order to detect pixels, whose spectra is similar to the spectra of the foreground regions found. Contrary to [6] we apply a nonlinear target detector, named Adaptive Coherence Estimator (ACE) [17]. The output of the ACE target detector is then combined with the output of the initially used binarization method. It is shown in the following that the combination of both techniques leads to an accuracy increase.

The work is structured as follows. In Section 2 the binarization method suggested is introduced. Afterwards, the method is evaluated in Section 3 and a conclusion is finally drawn at the end of this work.

2   Methodology

The binarization method proposed is designed for historical handwritings that are visible under normal white light and also under UltraViolet (UV) light[1]. One example for the images investigated is given in Figure 1. The images shown have been captured at 500nm (Figure 1 (left)) and at the NearInfraRed (NIR) range of 900nm (Figure 1 (right)). These and the other multispectral images used in this work are belonging to a data-set kindly provided by Hedjam and Cheriet [5]. It can be seen that the writing is visible under 500nm and is vanishing at the NIR range, which is typical for writings written with iron gall ink [5]. In the images considered, the writing is often best visible under 500nm. Therefore, the initial binarization step is applied onto images acquired under this spectral range. This step is introduced in the following.

2.1   Initial Binarization

The first stage is named 'Initial Binarization' stage. At this stage, the selected image acquired at 500nm is binarized with the method suggested by Su et al. [18]. This algorithm makes use of a contrast image, which encodes local gray value differences. The contrast image is defined by:

$$D(i,j) = \frac{f_{max}(i,j) - f_{min}(i,j)}{f_{max}(i,j) + f_{min}(i,j)}, \tag{1}$$

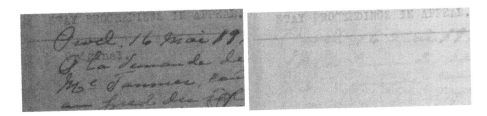

Fig. 1. Two images belonging to one multispectral stack. Image acquired at a spectral range of 500nm (left) and image acquired at 900nm (right).

---

[1] It should be noted that the handwritings investigated are in a relatively good condition compared to the multispectral images that are for instance investigated in [7] and [16]. In the latter mentioned documents the entire writing is only visible in the UV range.

where $f_{max}(i,j)$ and $f_{min}(i,j)$ encode the maximum and minimum intensity values within a local neighborhood. The local neighborhood window size is 3×3 pixels. The denominator consists of a normalization term, which makes the binarization robust against local degradations, such as background variation. The algorithm proceeds with the detection of so-called high contrast pixels, which are typically located at stroke boundaries. These high-contrast pixels are found by applying a global Otsu [14] threshold on the contrast image. Afterwards, a pixel is classified as a foreground pixel, if the following two conditions are met: (1) At least a certain number of high contrast pixels must be in its local neighborhood. (2) The intensity of the pixel must be smaller than the mean intensity of its neighboring pixels that have been identified as high contrast pixels. The overall output of the 'Initial Binarization' step is then used in the next stage of the algorithm in order to determine the spectral signature of the writing.

2.2 Target Detection

The overall aim of target detection algorithms is to estimate the likelihood that a test pixel signature contains a target signature. Therefore, each pixel of the input image is compared with an target signature and a decision is made whether the pixel contains the target signature or not. In order to make this decision, a spectral target detector is applied:

$$y = T(\mathbf{x}, \mathbf{s}), \tag{2}$$

where y is the detector output, $\mathbf{x}$ is the spectral signature of the test pixel, $\mathbf{s}$ is the spectral signature of the target and T is a transformation defined by a specific target detector. A test pixel is then classified as a target pixel if y exceeds a selected threshold. Otherwise the test pixel is declared as a background pixel.

ACE Target Detector. Several target detectors have been developed, including for instance CEM and adaptive matched filters (AMF). These target detectors apply linear transformations that make use of first and second order statistics of selected background pixels [20]. Similar the ACE algorithm makes also use of these statistics, but the transformation found is nonlinear. Several works conducted in the field of remote sensing, found that the performance of ACE is partially superior to CEM [1] and AMF [19]. Due to these findings, we use the ACE algorithm for the detection of image regions that contain the target signature, which is in our case the ink. The detector is formally defined by:

$$y_{ACE}(x) = \frac{sign\left[(\mathbf{s}-\boldsymbol{\mu})^T \Sigma^{-1}(\mathbf{x}-\boldsymbol{\mu})\right]\left[(\mathbf{s}-\boldsymbol{\mu})^T \Sigma^{-1}(\mathbf{x}-\boldsymbol{\mu})\right]^2}{\left[(\mathbf{s}-\boldsymbol{\mu})^T \Sigma^{-1}(\mathbf{s}-\boldsymbol{\mu})\right]\left[(\mathbf{x}-\boldsymbol{\mu})^T \Sigma^{-1}(\mathbf{x}-\boldsymbol{\mu})\right]}, \tag{3}$$

where $\mathbf{x}$ is the pixel signature investigated, Σ is the covariance matrix of the background and $\boldsymbol{\mu}$ is the mean spectral signature [2]. The target signature is depicted by $\mathbf{s}$ and is in our case the mean signature of the foreground regions.

The works cited above are concerned with target detection in the field of remote sensing and are using so called external target signatures, which are signatures that are defined in a training database. Contrary, in our work the target signature is directly estimated from the multispectral scan investigated.

Target Signature Estimation. In order to determine the target signature s, the output of the 'Initial Binarization' stage is used. Since it cannot be assumed that the foreground regions found contain no false positives, a simple procedure is used to sort out outliers, which are falsely labeled as foreground pixels. For this outlier detection, the distance between the spectral signature $\mathbf{x}$ of a foreground pixel and the median value $\tilde{\mathbf{x}}$ of the spectral signatures of all foreground pixels is calculated:

$$D(x_i) = |x_i - \tilde{x}_i| \quad \forall i = 1, ..., n \qquad (4)$$

whereby n is the number of channels, e.g. the third dimension of the multispectral image set. Thus, for each foreground pixel a n-dimensional distance vector to the median value is calculated. The pixel is then labeled as an outlier if 50% or more of the elements in the distance vector $D(\mathbf{x})$ are exceeding the following threshold:

$$t_{\sigma_i} = \sigma(x_i)/k \quad \forall i = 1, ..., n \qquad (5)$$

whereby $\sigma(x_i)$ is the standard deviation of the foreground elements in the ith channel and k is a user-defined scalar value. In the current implementation a value of $k = 3$ is used. The outlier detection is based on the assumption that the majority of the foreground pixels is correctly labeled and the median $\tilde{\mathbf{x}}$ is close to the real target signature of the handwriting. In the cases considered in this work, this assumption is valid. The foreground regions, which are not labeled as outliers are then used to calculate the average spectral signature of the target, which is in our case the writing. The pixels, which are classified as being background pixels are used for the calculation of Σ, which is the covariance matrix of the background.

One example for the target signature estimation is given in Figure 2. The image in Figure 2 (top row, left) has been gained by applying the 'Initial Binarization' step on the image shown in Figure 1 (left) and contains false positives arising from the machine-written text in the upper image region. In Figure 2 (bottom row, left) the output of the outlier detection step is given. It can be seen that the false positives in the upper image region are completely removed. Additionally, several true positives are also removed by the outlier detection, but the output of the target detection algorithm is not drastically worsened by the removal of these true positives. This can be seen in Figure 2 (right column), where the corresponding target detection outputs are given. The machine-written text and the horizontal line in the upper image region are slightly less visible in the resulting image shown at the bottom row, compared to the image shown at the upper row.

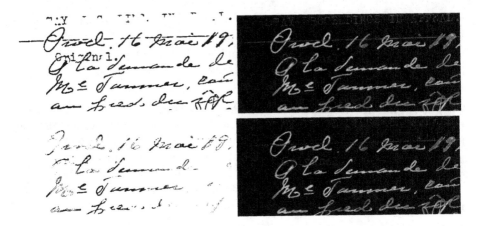

Fig. 2. Effect of the outlier removal step. Top row: Original binarization output (left) and corresponding target detection result (right). Bottom row: Result of the outlier removal step (left) and the resulting target detection image (right).

2.3 False Positive Elimination

The output of the target detection step serves as the basis for the elimination of false positives found by the binarization algorithm. This stage is hereafter denoted as 'False Positive Elimination' step. In this step, true positives are first identified by applying a global Otsu threshold onto the target detection result. By applying the Otsu threshold only pixels that possess a relatively high likelihood of containing the target signature are labeled as foreground pixels. These pixels have a high probability of being true positives and are hereafter denoted as true positive candidates. The true positive candidates are then used to eliminate false positives found in the 'Initial Binarization' stage: A foreground pixel is assumed to be wrongly labeled if the number of true positive candidates within its local neighborhood is smaller than a predefined number of true positive candidates. In the current implementation at least one true positive candidate must be in a local neighborhood with a size of 21×21 pixels. An example for the 'False Positive Elimination' step is given in Figure 3 (top, left).

2.4 Refinement

The output the target detection step is also used for the identification of false negatives. This step is denoted as 'Refinement' step. It was found that such a false negative is partially occurring at a stroke that is considerably thinner or brighter than the majority of the remaining strokes. Such thin and bright strokes are partially not classified as high contrast pixels and are therefore subsequently often classified as background pixels. In order to resolve this drawback, the binarization algorithm in [18] is again applied and the same image as in the first stage is used. Contrary to the 'Initial Binarization' stage, the contrast image $D(i,j)$ is not used. Instead, the output of the target detection step is used to

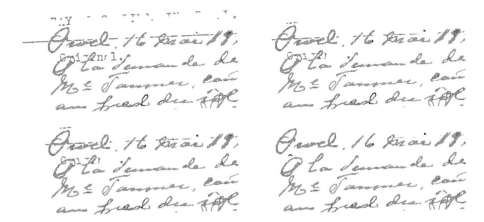

Fig. 3. Stages of the binarization method. The binarization output of each stage is color coded: Red depicts false positives, black depicts false negatives and green depicts true positives. Top row: Result of the 'Initial Binarization' stage (left) and result of the 'False Positive Elimination' stage (right). Bottom row: Result of the 'Refinement' stage (left) and result of the final 'Thresholding' stage.

determine the high contrast pixels. Therefore, simply the gradient magnitude image of the target detection image is calculated and Otsu thresholded. This binary image is slightly dilated - by 2 pixels - and the foreground pixels in the resulting image are classified as high contrast pixels. The ensuing binarization method is the same as described in Section 2.1. By using the gradient magnitude image of the target detection algorithm, pixels that are enhanced by the target detector are more likely to get labeled as high contrast pixels. Thus, foreground pixels, which have been misclassified in the initial binarization step, can be correctly labeled as foreground pixels in the 'Refinement' step.

The outcome of the second binarization is then combined with the output of the 'False Positive Elimination' stage: Therefore, the connected components found in the second binarization step are only added to the resulting image if they are connected to the foreground regions found in the 'False Positive Elimination' stage. The entire output of the 'False Positive Elimination' is added to the resulting image. Thus, strokes (or connected components) are only extended in the 'Refinement' step. One example for the 'Refinement' step is shown in Figure 3 (bottom, left).

2.5 Thresholding

In the last step of the algorithm - denoted as 'Thresholding' stage -, the resulting image of the target detection step is again analyzed: If the ACE algorithm assigned a high likelihood to a certain pixel that the target signature is present or absent, the pixel is assumed to be correctly labeled. Thus, the corresponding pixel in the resulting image of the 'Refinement' step is labeled accordingly. In the current implementation a pixel is definitely classified as belonging to the foreground class if $y_{ACE}(x) > 0.9$. If $y_{ACE}(x) < 0.1$ the pixel is classified as background pixel. Figure 3 (bottom, right) shows the final output gained on the input data shown in Figure 1.

3   Results

In this section, the method proposed is evaluated. For this purpose, two data sets kindly provided by Hedjam and Cheriet [5] are used. The first data set[2], hereafter denoted as HISTODOC1 consists of 9 different sets of multispectral images. This data set is used in [5] and [10] for image restoration and binarization. The data set is very similar to the second data set[3], since the images in the first data set are portions of images that are contained in the second data set. The second data set, hereafter denoted as MSI-HISTODOC, contains 21 sets of multispectral images. Each multispectral stack consists of 8 grayscale images, which have been imaged in narrow-band spectral ranges, ranging from 340 nm until 1100 nm. The performance is quantified with Precision, Recall and F-Measure as defined in [3].

3.1   HISTODOC1

The overall performance in terms of F-Measure is shown in Figure 4, whereby the cyan bar depicts the average F-Measure gained by approach proposed. Additionally, the results gained in [10] are depicted by the yellow bar and the remaining bars denote the 5 best results gained by Hedjam and Cheriet in [5]. The algorithm in [5] is concerned with image restoration and the evaluation of this task is performed with binarization. Therefore, the authors applied in total 9 different binarization algorithm on the resulting images of their work. The results of [5] that are shown in Figure 4 have all been gained by applying the binarization algorithms onto restoration results. The corresponding bars are labeled with the binarization method in squared brackets and additionally with 'Hedjam' to indicate that the result was gained by combining the restoration method in [5] with a particular binarization technique.

    The algorithm proposed in this work gains an average F-Measure of 84.40%, which is a significant performance increase compared to the output of the 'Initial Binarization' stage in which an average F-Measure of 78.54% is achieved. The performance gained by method proposed is similar to the F-Measure of 84.37% that Hedjam and Cheriet gained by applying the binarization method in [18] on their restoration result. The results also show that the performance of the algorithm proposed is worse than the two best binarization results gained in [5]: The AdOtsu [12] method performed best, resulting in an average performance increase of 1.71%, compared to our method. It has to be mentioned that this is a significant performance increase, which is eventually arising from the inpainting step performed in [5]: This inpainting step is dedicated to restoration of broken

---

[2] http://www.synchromedia.ca/databases/HISTODOC1
[3] http://www.synchromedia.ca/databases/msi-histodoc

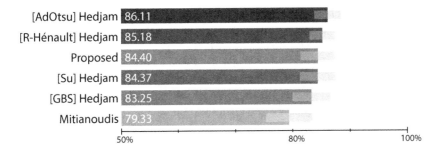

Fig. 4. Average F-Measures gained on the HISTODOC1 dataset. The semi-transparent gray bars depict the standard deviation. The method proposed is shown by the cyan bar. The green bar shows the performance gained by Mitianoudis and Papamarkos [10]. The remaining results have been gained in [5] by applying the following binarization methods onto restoration results: AdOtsu - [12], R-Hénault - [15], Su - [18], GBS - [11].

strokes. Such a restoration step is not performed in our current method, but the algorithm proposed gains still an average F-Measure, which is higher than the F-Measure gained by 7 of the algorithms used in [5] and it also outperforms the binarization method for multispectral images that is proposed by Mitianoudis and Papamarkos [10], depicted by the yellow bar in Figure 4.

3.2   MSI-HISTODOC

The MSI-HISTODOC database was introduced recently and hence, the methods mentioned in the previous section have not been evaluated on this data set. Instead, the data set is only used in the recent work of Farrahi Moghaddam and Cheriet [13]. The performance of their method is shown in Figure 5, whereby the bar at the bottom depicts a baseline result, defined by Farrahi Moghaddam and Cheriet [13]. Their best result is an F-Measure of 80.81, which is 4.99% less than the F-Measure gained by our algorithm. By applying solely the 'Initial Binarization' method, we achieved an average F-Measure of 82.6%.

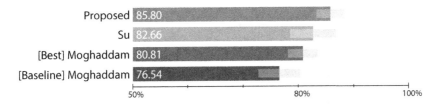

Fig. 5. Average F-Measures gained on the MSI-HISTODOC dataset. The semi-transparent gray bars depict the standard deviation. The method proposed is shown by the cyan bar and the performance of the 'Initial Binarization' is depicted by the yellow bar. The remaining bars show results gained in [13].

Since the MSI-HISTODOC database is larger than the HISTODOC1 database and the results are therefore more significant, the diverse steps of our algorithm are evaluated on the former mentioned. The results gained by the four sub steps of the algorithms are provided in Table 1. It can be seen that the average F-Measure gained by the 'Initial Binarization' is 82.66%. The ensuing 'False Positive Elimination' results in the highest performance increase (2.37%) compared to the remaining steps. In the ensuing refinement step, the F-Measure is increased by 0.46%. This increase is a result of the recovering of false negatives that are mainly located at thin and faded-out strokes. However, this reduction of false negatives leads also to an increased number of false positives, which is also reflected by the reduction of the average Precision value by 0,65%. In the last step of the algorithm the Precision is again raised, while the Recall is slightly reduced, resulting in an average F-Measure of 85.80%.

Table 1. Precision (P.), Recall (R.) and F-Measure (F.) gained on the MSI-HISTODOC dataset.

Steps	Mean P.	Std P.	Mean R.	Std R.	Mean F.	Std F.
1: Initial Binarization	82.10	10.94	84.38	8.22	82.66	8.06
2: False Positive Elimination	86.50	7.09	84.22	7.03	85.03	4.92
3: Refinement	85.85	7.80	85.69	5.73	85.49	4.99
4: Thresholding (Final Result)	87.65	7.62	84.48	5.18	85.80	4.87
Otsu ACE	76.35	22.54	84.50	4.86	77.73	16.09
Otsu CEM	69.66	24.71	92.24	3.09	76.10	20.94

The last two rows in Table 1 contain results that are provided in order to get a glance of the performance of the ACE target detector and additionally of the CEM target detector. Therefore, the target signatures and background models estimated, have been used as an input for both target detectors. The resulting images have been binarized by applying a global Otsu threshold and the binarized images have been evaluated. The results show that the ACE algorithm produces a smaller number of false positives but also a higher number of false negatives, compared to the CEM detector. The ACE gains also a higher performance in terms of F-Measure. One example output of both algorithms is given in Figure 6. It can be seen that the resulting image of the CEM detector contains more background variation, which is better suppressed by the ACE algorithm. However, the latter mentioned produces an image, in which the foreground has a lower contrast to the remaining background. This circumstance is also shown by the numerical results. Therefore, it can be concluded that the target detector can be used for the binarization of the handwritings considered, but it is not appropriate for the enhancement of barely visible handwritings. The average F-Measure gained by the ACE algorithm is 77.73% which is considerably smaller than the F-Measure of 82.66% that is gained by applying solely the 'Initial Binarization'. This result shows that using solely the target detector is error-prone. Nevertheless, the overall performance of 85.80% shows that the incorporation of the spectral information leads to a performance increase. This performance increase can be attributed to the fact that the ACE method is capable of identifying pixels that contain the target signature or contain spectral signatures stemming from other sources.

Fig. 6. Comparison of CEM and ACE target detectors. (Left) Input image acquired at 500nm. (Middle) CEM output. (Right) ACE output.

4   Conclusion

In this work a binarization method for multispectral document images is proposed. The method applies a state-of-the-art binarization method on a single image. The binarization output is used to estimate the spectral signature of the ink. This signature is used to train an ACE target detector and its resulting image is then used to improve the overall binarization performance. By combining spatial information and the spectral information, the overall performance is increased. The algorithm is compared to other binarization techniques that are designed for multispectral images. On one database, the algorithm outperforms the state-of-the-art methods, but on another database the algorithm is at least partially outperformed. In the future, we are planning to use image restoration techniques - such as inpainting - as preprocessing steps in order to increase the binarization performance. Additionally, we will evaluate if local thresholding methods can be successfully applied directly on the output of the ACE algorithm.

Acknowledgement. The research was funded by the Austrian Federal Ministry of Science, Research and Economy. The authors whish to thank Rachid Hedjam and Mohamed Cheriet for providing their data set to the public.

References

1. Cisz, A.P., Schott, J.R.: Performance comparison of hyperspectral target detection algorithms in altitude varying scenes. In: SPIE Conference on Algorithms and Technologies for Multispectral, Hyperspectral, and Ultraspectral Imagery XI, vol. 5806 (2005)
2. Cohen, Y., August, Y., Blumberg, D.G., Rotman, S.R.: Evaluating subpixel target detection algorithms in hyperspectral imagery. J. Electrical and Computer Engineering 2012 (2012)
3. Gatos, B., Pratikakis, I., Perantonis, S.J.: Adaptive degraded document image binarization. Pattern Recognition **39**(3), 317–327 (2006)

4. Harsanyi, J.C.: Detection and classification of subpixel spectral signatures in hyperspectral image sequences. Ph.D. thesis, Dept. Elect. Eng. University of Maryland, Baltimore County (1993)
5. Hedjam, R., Cheriet, M.: Historical document image restoration using multispectral imaging system. Pattern Recognition **46**(8), 2297–2312 (2013)
6. Hedjam, R., Cheriet, M., Kalacska, M.: Constrained energy maximization and self-referencing method for invisible ink detection from multispectral historical document images. In: ICPR, pp. 3026–3031 (2014)
7. Hollaus, F., Gau, M., Sablatnig, R.: Enhancement of multispectral images of degraded documents by employing spatial information. In: ICDAR, pp. 145–149 (2013)
8. Howe, N.R.: A laplacian energy for document binarization. In: ICDAR, pp. 6–10 (2011)
9. Lettner, M., Sablatnig, R.: Higher order mrf for foreground-background separation in multi-spectral images of historical manuscripts. In: Document Analysis Systems, pp. 317–324 (2010)
10. Mitianoudis, N., Papamarkos, N.: Multi-spectral document image binarization using image fusion and background subtraction techniques. In: ICIP, pp. 5172–5176 (2014)
11. Moghaddam, R.F., Cheriet, M.: A multi-scale framework for adaptive binarization of degraded document images. Pattern Recognition **43**(6), 2186–2198 (2010)
12. Moghaddam, R.F., Cheriet, M.: Adotsu: An adaptive and parameterless generalization of otsu's method for document image binarization. Pattern Recognition **45**(6), 2419–2431 (2012)
13. Moghaddam, R.F., Cheriet, M.: A multiple-expert binarization framework for multispectral images. CoRR abs/1502.01199 (2015)
14. Otsu, N.: A Threshold Selection Method from Gray-level Histograms. IEEE Transactions on Systems, Man and Cybernetics **9**(1), 62–66 (1979)
15. Rivest-Hénault, D., Moghaddam, R.F., Cheriet, M.: A local linear level set method for the binarization of degraded historical document images. IJDAR **15**(2), 101–124 (2012)
16. Salerno, E., Tonazzini, A., Bedini, L.: Digital image analysis to enhance underwritten text in the archimedes palimpsest. IJDAR **9**(2–4), 79–87 (2007)
17. Scharf, L., McWhorter, L.: Adaptive matched subspace detectors and adaptive coherence estimators. In: Conference Record of the Thirtieth Asilomar Conference on Signals, Systems and Computers, vol. 2, pp. 1114–1117 (1996)
18. Su, B., Lu, S., Tan, C.L.: Binarization of historical document images using the local maximum and minimum. In: DAS, pp. 159–166 (2010)
19. Theiler, J., Foy, B.R., Fraser, A.M.: Beyond the adaptive matched filter: nonlinear detectors for weak signals in high-dimensional clutter. In: SPIE Conference on Algorithms and Technologies for Multispectral, Hyperspectral, and Ultraspectral Imagery XIII, vol. 6565, pp. 656503–656503-12 (2007)
20. West, J.E., Messinger, D.W., Ientilucci, E.J., Kerekes, J.P., Schott, J.R.: Matched filter stochastic background characterization for hyperspectral target detection. In: SPIE Conference on Algorithms and Technologies for Multispectral, Hyperspectral, and Ultraspectral Imagery XI, vol. 5806, pp. 1–12 (2005)

Parallel 2D Local Pattern Spectra of Invariant Moments for Galaxy Classification

Ugo Moschini[1]([✉]), Paul Teeninga[1],
Scott C. Trager[2], and Michael H.F. Wilkinson[1]

[1] Johann Bernoulli Institute, University of Groningen,
P.O. Box 407, 9700 AK Groningen, The Netherlands
[2] Kapteyn Astronomical Institute, University of Groningen,
P.O. Box 407, 9700 AK Groningen, The Netherlands
{u.moschini,s.c.trager,m.h.f.wilkinson}@rug.nl, p.teeninga@home.nl

Abstract. In this paper, we explore the possibility to use 2D pattern spectra as suitable feature vectors in galaxy classification tasks. The focus is on separating mergers from projected galaxies in a data set extracted from the Sloan Digital Sky Survey Data Release 7. Local pattern spectra are built in parallel and are based on an object segmentation obtained by filtering a max-tree structure that preserves faint structures. A set of pattern spectra using size and Hu's and Flusser's image invariant moments information is computed for every segmented galaxy. The C4.5 tree classifier with bagging gives the best classification result. Mergers and projected galaxies are classified with a precision of about 80%.

Keywords: Classification · Astronomy · Pattern spectra · Parallel computing

1 Introduction

Nowadays, astronomy, as well as many other scientific disciplines, has to face the problem of analysing the burden of data that are produced by modern instrumentation and tools. In particular, sky surveys like the Sloan Digital Sky Survey [1] (SDSS) contain hundreds of millions of objects. Finding and classifying the relevant objects, mostly stars or galaxies, cannot be done manually. The classification of the morphologies of galaxies is not a trivial task. Parametrized models [14], non-parametric approaches [11] and crowd-sourcing projects such as GalaxyZoo [10] are used for galaxy classification. Commonly used morphological classes are elliptical, spirals and *mergers*. The galaxies of the latter type are irregular and asymmetrical galaxies often connected by faint filaments of dust or gases, whose length and shape varies according to the stage of the merging. Parametrized models assume that the galaxies show a predefined light distribution and they are not irregular. Crowd-sourcing takes time and if a different classification class arise, users must be asked again to give their feedback.

M.H.F. Wilkinson—This work was funded by the Netherlands Organisation for Scientific Research (NWO) under project number 612.001.110.

G. Azzopardi and N. Petkov (Eds.): CAIP 2015, Part II, LNCS 9257, pp. 121–133, 2015.
DOI: 10.1007/978-3-319-23117-4_11

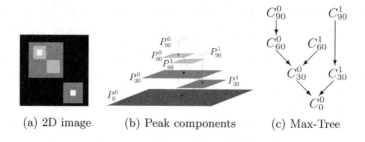

(a) 2D image   (b) Peak components   (c) Max-Tree

Fig. 1. A grey-scale 2D image with intensities from 0 to 90, its peak components P_h^k at intensity h and the corresponding max-tree nodes C_h^k.

Non-parametric approaches are independent of any assumption and are often effectively combined with machine learning techniques [2,11].

In our work, we want to distinguish mergers from other galaxies that could look close to each other due to a projection effect but are not interacting. They are referred to as *projected* or overlapping galaxies. We apply a non-parametric approach and investigate if a tool from mathematical morphology can be used for classifying galaxies: the pattern spectrum. Pattern spectra were introduced by Maragos in [12]. A pattern spectrum can be defined as an aggregated feature space that shows how much image content is present in the image components that satisfy certain classes of attributes. It represents the distribution of image details over those classes. Experiments with 2D pattern spectra using size and shape classes showed that they work effectively in pattern recognition and classification tasks on popular data sets [21]. Image invariant moments from Hu [9] and Flusser [7] have also been applied successfully to many pattern recognition tasks, ranging from satellite imagery to character recognition. The term *local* pattern spectra is used when pattern spectra are computed for every segmented object and not on the image as a whole. In this paper, we selected a dataset from SDSS Data Release 7 containing 196 merging and overlapping galaxies. The method in [20] is used to segment the galaxies and retain the faint tidal structures typical of mergers. Local pattern spectra of size and image moment invariants are created for each galaxy. Sets of 2D local pattern spectra are computed in parallel, modifying a parallel algorithm presented in [15]. Such collection of pattern spectra is used as feature vector in C4.5, a decision tree classifier. Section 2 reviews the segmentation method, Section 3 and Section 4 describe the moment invariants used and define the local pattern spectrum. In Section 5 and Section 6 show the experiments performed with different pattern spectra and the speed performance of the parallel algorithm. Mergers and projected galaxies in the dataset are correctly classified in about 80% of the cases.

2   Max-Tree Object Segmentation

Any grey-scale image can be represented as a set of connected components, that are groups of pixels path-wise connected and with the same intensity, according to the classical definition of connectivity [18]. There being an ordering in the image intensities, the connected components can be nested in a hierarchical tree structure, namely a max-tree [17]. Every node in the tree corresponds to a peak component, which is a connected component at a given intensity level in the image. The leaves of the tree represent the local maxima of the image. Fig. 1b illustrates the hierarchy of peak components at different intensities h for the image in Fig. 1a. The arrows in Fig 1c represent parent-child relationships that link the nested peak components. Useful measures related to the components can be computed efficiently while the max-tree is being built. The node structure is augmented with the attributes that can be used to identify the nodes that would possibly belong to objects of interest. In the specific case of astronomical images, in [20] we proposed a novel method that performs astronomical object detection using the max-tree structure. It starts with estimating the background in the image looking for tiles devoid of objects. After the background is subtracted, a max-tree is built. A statistical attribute filtering [5] is used. It is based on the expected noise distribution in the image compared with the distribution of the power attribute, as a function of its area. It selects which nodes of the tree are likely to belong to objects and which nodes are due to noise. The method showed an improved segmentation with respect to Source Extractor [3] (SExtractor), especially on faint extended sources, as in Fig. 2. The background estimate of SExtractor often correlates with astronomical objects. This is an issue in the case of structure close to the background level. If such structures are considered background, there is no threshold value able to identify them. On top of that, a fixed threshold above its background estimate is used to identify objects on a highly quantized version of the image, without considering noise and object properties. We refer to [20] for more examples and a detailed explanation of the differences between SExtractor and our solution.

(a) Original image (log scaled) (b) Segmentation by SExtractor (c) Max-Tree segmentation

Fig. 2. (a) original image with a galaxy whose protruding filament and outer boundary are segmented better in by our method [20] in (c) than by SExtractor in (b).

3 Moments

Moment invariants are properties used to characterise images, for classification and pattern recognition tasks. In this paper, moment invariants are computed through geometric (raw) moments, for each connected component rather on the image as a whole. Let us define a component at a given intensity level as a binary image $f(x, y)$, where the background is made of the pixels that do not belong to the component. The moment of order $p + q$ of f is defined as:

$$m_{pq}(f) = \sum_{(x,y) \in f} x^p y^q f(x, y). \tag{1}$$

Raw moments can be transformed in *central* moments by using the coordinates of the component centroids $\bar{x} = m_{10}/m_{00}$ and $\bar{y} = m_{01}/m_{00}$ as follows:

$$\mu_{pq} = \sum_{(x,y) \in f} (x - \bar{x})^p (y - \bar{y})^q f(x, y). \tag{2}$$

Central moments are translation invariant. *Normalised central* moments are scale invariant moments derived from central moments, defined as $\eta_{pq} = \mu_{pq}/\mu_{00}^{\alpha}$, with $\alpha = p + q/2 + 1$. Hu [9] derived seven two dimensional descriptors suitable for 2D images (or components). The seven invariant moments were demonstrated to be translation, scale and rotation invariant. They are defined in terms of normalised central moments below:

$\phi_1 = \eta_{20} + \eta_{02}$
$\phi_2 = (\eta_{20} - \eta_{02})^2 + 4\eta_{11}^2$
$\phi_3 = (\eta_{30} - 3\eta_{12})^2 + (3\eta_{21} - \eta_{03})^2$
$\phi_4 = (\eta_{30} + \eta_{12})^2 + (\eta_{21} + \eta_{03})$
$\phi_5 = (\eta_{30} - 3\eta_{12})(\eta_{30} + \eta_{12}))(\eta_{30} + \eta_{12})^2 - 3(\eta_{21} + \eta_{03})^2) + (3\eta_{21} - \eta_{03})(\eta_{21} + \eta_{03})(3(\eta_{30} + \eta_{12})^2 - (\eta_{21} + \eta_{03})^2)$
$\phi_6 = (\eta_{20} - \eta_{02})((\eta_{30} + \eta_{12})^2 - (\eta_{21} + \eta_{03})^2) + 4\eta_{11}(\eta_{30} + \eta_{12})(\eta_{21} + \eta_{03})$
$\phi_7 = (3\eta_{21} - \eta_{03})(\eta_{30} + \eta_{12})((\eta_{30} + \eta_{12})^2 - 3(\eta_{21} + \eta_{03})^2) + (3\eta_{12} - \eta_{30}(\eta_{21} + \eta_{03})(3(\eta_{30} + \eta_{12})^2) - (\eta_{21} + \eta_{03})^2)$

Flusser in [7] and Flusser and Suk in [6] showed that Hu's moment invariants are dependent and incomplete. It was pointed out that in pattern recognition problems, it is important to work with independent descriptors because they grant the same discriminative effect at the lowest computational cost, especially in high dimensional feature spaces. There are six Flusser's invariant moments that form a complete and independent set. They correspond to a subset of five Hu's moments ($\psi_1 = \phi_1$, $\psi_2 = \phi_4$, $\psi_3 = \phi_6$, $\psi_5 = \phi_5$, $\psi_6 = \phi_7$) with the addition of ψ_4:

$$\psi_4 = \eta_{11}((\eta_{30} + \eta_{12})^2 - (\eta_{03} + \eta_{21}^2)) - (\eta_{20} - \eta_{02})(\eta_{30} + \eta_{12})(\eta_{03} + \eta_{21})$$

The six Flusser invariants used are of the second and third order. The first moment invariant ψ_1 is know also as the normalized moment of inertia and it can be used as a measure of the elongation of a component. We recall here that the moments

ψ_4 and ψ_6 are skew invariant in the sense that they can separate between mirrored components, that it is not always desirable. As in [21], we modified the segmentation algorithm to compute raw moments for every node. The moment invariants can be easily computed from raw moments when the spectra are created. In such way, it is possible convey in the pattern spectrum of an object the information coming from the moment invariants for all the components that a galaxy is made of. Hu's and Flusser's moment invariants are used in the computation of the pattern spectrum of every galaxy, previously segmented with the algorithm illustrated in Section 2.

4 Parallel Local Pattern Spectra

Without a hierarchical image representation like the max-tree, pattern spectra are computed using a number of morphological openings, with structuring elements of increasing sizes. The difference between two consecutive openings is an image that contains the structures (connected components) having a size in the range given by the areas of the two structuring elements. The sum of the pixel intensities in the difference image, gives the amount of image detail for those components. In this case, the pattern spectrum is a 1D histogram where each bin corresponds to a range of areas, called *size* pattern spectrum. Max-trees can be used to compute the pattern spectra efficiently and independently of the structuring element used to sample the image. The nodes of the tree contain the exact area of every component without explicitly computing morphological openings. On top of that, they keep track of useful attributes such as moments, for all the components. Multidimensional pattern spectra can be obtained by binning the connected components not only according to their area but also to some other attribute. For example, a measure of the elongation of a component given by the first Hu's invariant moment was used in [21] was used to generate a 2D *shape-size* pattern spectra. A pattern spectrum is called *local* when it is computed on a segmented object and not on the whole image. After the max-tree is built, for each node visited in arbitrary order, the bin of the spectrum in which a given attribute value falls is chosen. Once the correct bins are identified, the product between the area of the component and the intensity difference with its parent node in the tree is added at that location. The computation of the pattern spectra can be parallelized applying a technique similar to the one presented in [15], tested on high resolution remote sensing images. When the pixels are partitioned among the threads of the parallel program, each thread handles the nodes of the tree falling under its partition corresponding to those pixels. The difference is that now a pattern spectrum for every object must be stored, whereas in [15] a single pattern spectrum was used for the whole image. Every thread stores now a number of pattern spectra equals to the number of objects found. The pattern spectra values are computed in every thread and the partial results are merged at the end. The output is a list of pattern spectra, one for every object in the image.

5   Classifying Galaxies: The Experiment

We investigate if 2D local pattern spectra that use invariant moments show statistically significant differences to distinguish merging from projected galaxies. The images used are obtained from the SDSS Data Release 7 [1]. The data set used consists of 98 monochrome $r-$band images containing a pair of close-by galaxies each for a total of 98 mergers and 98 overlapping galaxies. The image resolution is 2048x1489 pixels. Galaxies classified as interacting were selected from the Arp's Atlas of Peculiar Galaxies, whereas the projected galaxies were obtained from the classification of GalaxyZoo. The Weka 3.6.12 software package [8] and its implementation of the C4.5 decision tree classifier algorithm [16] were used to perform the experiments. The feature vector used as input by the C4.5 algorithm is a collection of 2D pattern spectra: one for each moment invariant. For every local 2D pattern spectrum, a dimension shows the bins for the area values of the components. The area is normalized dividing by the total size of the segmented galaxy. For every galaxy, the node of the tree that corresponds to its component of lowest intensity is normalised to have area equal 1. It represents the perimeter of the galaxy. Early tests showed that a logarithmic binning of area gives better results: it is desirable to have finer bins for lower values of area. The other dimension of the pattern spectrum refers to the bins for the moment invariant values. A 2D pattern spectrum is created for every moment invariant. For example, in the case of Hu's invariants, a set of seven 2D pattern spectra will be used as feature vector. The moment invariants tested are summarised in the first two columns of Table 1 and reported below.

Hu: The seven Hu's moment invariants.
Flusser: The six Flusser's moment invariants of the second and third order.
Flusser*: A non-skew invariant subset of the Flusser's invariants.

The value of such invariants was computed for all the components belonging to the 196 objects in the dataset. In total, there are about $2.5 \cdot 10^6$ components for all the 196 objects. As reported in the third column in Table 1, tests were also performed discarding the components smaller than 4 pixels: about $2.0 \cdot 10^6$ nodes were left. Binning of moment values was chosen so that the same number of components falls in each bin. Moment invariant and area values were binned in 7, 14 and 30 intervals, as reported in the last column of Table 1. The feature

Table 1. Pattern spectra with different settings are used. The first two columns illustrate three sets of moments considered; the third column shows that components with area larger than or equals to 1 and 4 pixels were used for different pattern spectra; the fourth column shows the number of bins used for area and moment invariant values.

Type of Moments	Invariants	Area of components	Dimension of PS
Hu	$\phi_1, \phi_2, \phi_3, \phi_4, \phi_5, \phi_6, \phi_7$	$>= 1$	7x7
Flusser	$\psi_1, \psi_2, \psi_3, \psi_4, \psi_5, \psi_6$	$>= 4$	14x14
Flusser*	$\psi_1, \psi_2, \psi_3, \psi_5$		30x30

vector of every galaxy is made of a number 2D pattern spectra equal to the number of moment invariants used. For example, in the case of Hu's moment invariants, seven pattern spectra are calculated, each one with dimension, for example, 7x7 or 30x30. In this case, every galaxy is described by a 7x49 or 30x210 feature vector. As mentioned in Section 4, once the correct location in the pattern spectrum is identified given an area and a moment invariant value, the area of the component is multiplied by the intensity difference with its parent node: such product is added at that location in the spectrum. As a further test, a normalised version of the pattern spectra is computed: the product of area of a component and intensity difference is normalized by dividing for the total area of the galaxy. In short, a total of 36 different kinds of feature vectors were tested by composing three types of moment invariants, components with area larger than or equal to 1 and 4 pixels, three different binnings and lastly enabling or not normalization of the pattern spectra values.

6   Classification Results and Speed Performance

The C4.5 classifier in Weka software package was tested in three variants: standard, with adaptive boosting (AdaBoost) and with bagging, commonly used techniques to improve decision tree classifiers. The results are shown from Table 2 to Table 5. The last three columns of every table show the percentage of correctly classified instances (galaxies) for the three variants. Every value is the average result got over 10 repetitions of 10-fold cross validation, for a total of 100 folds. The tables refer to the four cases that originate from the analysis of components larger than or equal to 1 or 4 pixels and normalizing or not the pattern spectra values. The average standard deviation of all the runs is 9.92 for the standard C4.5 and 8.90 for the C4.5 with bagging. The best results are achieved with bagging enabled in Table 2, Table 3 and Table 5 and with boosting in Table 4. In every table, the three highest percent values are underlined. We notice that there is no big difference among the correct predictions over the tables. The two highest percentages of correct classification of objects as merging and overlapping galaxies are 81.00% in Table 2 for the Flusser set normalized, and 80.89% with the Flusser set not normalized in Table 4, using 7x7 pattern spectra. In general, better results are got when a smaller number of bins is chosen and when all the components are considered, not only those larger than 3 pixels. This could be explained by the fact that merging galaxies often show faint structures made of small dust-like particles, that result in an increased number of small components. Smaller components might convey a kind of information that is absent in projected galaxies. Normalizing the pattern spectra values seems to bring little benefit. The main differences are due to the smaller feature space having a lower number of bins and to the area of the components considered. A larger decrease of correct classifications was expected with the normalization of the pattern spectra than the one observed. In principle, normalization would make the method to account less for the existing size differences present in some images of the dataset between mergers and overlapping galaxies. However, using scale-invariant moment invariants can have counteracted this effect.

Table 2. Percentages of correctly classified instances. Pattern spectra were normalized and components with area >=1 were processed.

Moments	Dim. of PS	C4.5 (%)	Boosting (%)	Bagging (%)
Hu	7x7	71.41	76.34	<u>79.64</u>
Hu	14x 14	71.88	73.65	78.11
Hu	30x30	64.71	67.80	72.80
Flusser	7x7	72.48	78.05	<u>81.00</u>
Flusser	14x14	72.00	72.51	76.54
Flusser	30x30	67.83	68.41	70.53
Flusser*	7x7	74.93	78.17	<u>79.87</u>
Flusser*	14x14	71.87	72.61	75.56
Flusser*	30x30	67.70	67.24	70.50

Table 3. Percentages of correctly classified instances. Pattern spectra were normalized and components with area >=4 were processed.

Moments	Dim. of PS	C4.5 (%)	Boosting (%)	Bagging (%)
Hu	7x7	74.52	78.33	<u>78.88</u>
Hu	14x 14	70.67	73.86	77.33
Hu	30x30	66.83	66.15	71.44
Flusser	7x7	71.36	77.21	<u>79.60</u>
Flusser	14x14	71.17	73.23	77.92
Flusser	30x30	66.91	67.72	72.04
Flusser*	7x7	73.62	77.26	<u>79.54</u>
Flusser*	14x14	72.51	72.41	77.46
Flusser*	30x30	66.58	65.72	71.82

Table 4. Percentages of correctly classified instances. Pattern spectra were not normalized and components with area >=1 were processed.

Moments	Dim. of PS	C4.5 (%)	Boosting (%)	Bagging (%)
Hu	7x7	71.64	<u>80.08</u>	79.11
Hu	14x 14	71.88	73.65	78.11
Hu	30x30	70.61	70.06	76.63
Flusser	7x7	73.15	<u>80.89</u>	79.79
Flusser	14x14	72.00	72.51	76.54
Flusser	30x30	70.56	69.21	73.17
Flusser*	7x7	74.42	<u>80.13</u>	78.70
Flusser*	14x14	71.87	72.61	75.56
Flusser*	30x30	69.00	68.38	72.61

Table 5. Percentages of correctly classified instances. Pattern spectra were not normalized and components with area $>=4$ were processed.

Moments	Dim. of PS	C4.5 (%)	Boosting (%)	Bagging (%)
Hu	7x7	74.52	78.33	<u>78.88</u>
Hu	14x 14	70.67	73.86	77.33
Hu	30x30	65.67	68.96	74.41
Flusser	7x7	71.36	77.21	<u>79.60</u>
Flusser	14x14	71.17	73.23	77.92
Flusser	30x30	67.02	66.58	73.66
Flusser*	7x7	73.62	77.26	<u>79.54</u>
Flusser*	14x14	72.51	72.41	77.46
Flusser*	30x30	67.16	67.31	74.68

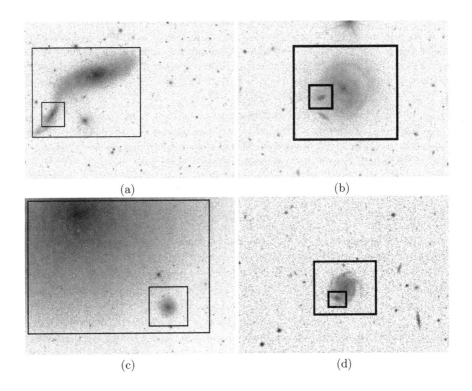

Fig. 3. (a) and (b) show correctly classified merging and projected galaxies, respectively; in (c) the small galaxy is correctly classified as overlapping; in (d) the two galaxies are overlapping but they are classified as mergers. Separate objects are segmented in different colours. The black rectangles highlight which objects we are referring to.

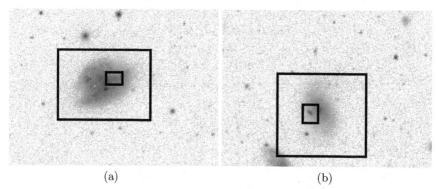

(a)   (b)

Fig. 4. (a) last stage of a merging phase with small segmented structures and (b) a small projected galaxy made of a few pixels. In both cases, classification is a difficult task. Separate objects are segmented in different colours. The black rectangles highlight which objects we are referring to.

Fig. 3a and Fig. 3b show two cases of correctly classified mergers and projected galaxies, respectively. Fig. 3c shows the large merger Messier 49. Its companion galaxy is a dwarf irregular galaxy, cropped out of the picture. In this figure, it is interesting to notice that the smaller galaxy is correctly classified as overlapping, in spite of being also visually linked to the wide halo. Fig. 3d shows instead two misclassified galaxies: both the galaxies are classified as mergers, but they are actually overlapping. Surely, the small area of the objects in Fig. 3d does not help the classification. Fig. 4a shows two (or more) merging galaxies at a very late stage. It is very difficult to define the boundaries of the galaxies involved and the image looks like over-segmented. The larger galaxy is correctly classified as a merger, but the companion is not clearly defined. The same happens for the overlapping galaxies in Fig. 4b. The large one is correctly classified, the smaller one is not. In general, it is of course difficult to classify objects that span a few pixels. The classification could be possibly improved with a better separation among close-by objects. We noticed that, during the segmentation, it can happen that too many pixels are assigned to the larger objects, thus reducing the amount of available information for the smaller galaxies. In a previous thesis work [19] compiled at the Kapteyn Astronomical Institute of Groningen, multiscale connectivity [4] was used to create feature vectors made of collection of 1D *size* pattern spectra at several scales. Such pattern spectra were not local: a single pattern spectrum was produced from every image and object segmentation was not performed. Running the same algorithm of [19] on our dataset gave a percentage of correctly classified objects of 77.81% with C4.5 tree classifier with bagging. The main issue with this solution was that several (hundreds) astronomical objects are present in every image: it is not very clear what is being classified if objects are not segmented and global pattern spectra are used. On the contrary, classification based on segmented objects guarantees a more reliable and truthful outcome and evaluation of the results. We are not aware of other approaches that try to distinguish mergers from overlapping

Table 6. Execution times (in seconds) and speed-up values obtained after computing in parallel 2D local pattern spectra, for the 98 SDSS images and the WSRT cube, with 30x30 pattern spectra for each object in the images.

Test / Threads:	1	2	4	8	16	32	64
Run-time SDSS (s)	421.47	227.09	130.32	91.53	104.05	136.62	258.28
Run-time WSRT (s)	242.13	156.91	100.01	46.15	40.63	34.81	46.18
Speed-up SDSS	1.00	1.86	3.23	4.60	4.05	3.08	1.63
Speed-up WSRT	1.00	1.54	2.42	5.25	5.96	6.96	5.24

galaxies, since the focus of most of the papers is rather on classifying the different morphologies.

The parallel algorithm to compute local pattern spectra was tested for speed performance. It was implemented in C language with POSIX Threads. A shared-memory Dell R815 Rack Server with four 16-core AMD Opteron processors and RAM memory of 512GB was used in the tests. Table 6 at row 1 and 3 shows the run-time and the speed-up value to compute the pattern spectra of hundreds of stars and galaxies in each of the 98 images, with 30x30 pattern spectra. Flusser's and Hu's moments were used. Run-time decreases from almost 7 minutes to 1 minute and a half on 8 threads. In general, the images in the SDSS are small, about 3Mpx resolution and the performance is affected more by the time spent merging the results of the different threads than by the time spent in the actual computation of moments and pattern spectra. Moreover, load balance is not optimal: in case the partition assigned to a thread contains a small number of components or any object at all, the thread will have a small computational work. We decided then to test the parallel computation of 2D local pattern spectra on a large radio cube with 360x360x1464 resolution, named WSRT (Westerbork Synthesis Radio Telescope, courtesy of P. Serra). It contains radio emission values from galactic sources. The results are shown in Table 6, at row 2 and 4. The time to compute the pattern spectra for the objects identified (about five hundred) goes from 4 minutes on a single threads to 34 seconds on 32 threads. Load balance issues are still evident in the speed-up computation, though. We recall here that an important step of the pipeline that leads to object classification is also the segmentation of astronomical objects. In the case of the WSRT cube, segmentation was done in parallel, as in [13]: run-times went from 11 minutes on single thread to 2 minutes and 10 seconds on 16 threads, on the same Dell machine.

7   Conclusions and Future Work

The use of collections of local 2D pattern spectra as feature vectors suitable for classification of astronomical object looks promising. Experiments were made on a dataset of 196 galaxies from the SDSS Data Release 7. The goal was to classify if two close-by galaxies present in each image were either merging or overlapping.

The galaxies were automatically segmented by our own segmentation algorithm. A set of local 2D pattern spectra, binned using the size of the components in the segmented galaxies and image moment invariant information is computed in parallel. The Weka C4.5 tree classifier with bagging gave the best classification results: the percentage of correctly classified instances is about 80%. In future work, other attributes could be investigated, for example shape measures derived from moments. Other classifiers should also be tested. Neural networks approaches as in [2] look promising. Further improvements to object segmentation following more accurately the brightness profiles could possibly enrich the quality of the pattern spectra and improve classification.

References

1. Abazajian, K.N., Adelman-McCarthy, J.K., Agüeros, M.A., Allam, S.S., Allende Prieto, C., An, D., Anderson, K.S.J., Anderson, S.F., Annis, J., Bahcall, N.A.: The Seventh Data Release of the Sloan Digital Sky Survey. The Astrophysical Journal Supplement Series **182**, 543 (2009)
2. Banerji, M., Lahav, O., Lintott, C.J., Abdalla, F.B., Schawinski, K., Bamford, S.P., Andreescu, D., Murray, P., Raddick, M.J., Slosar, A., Szalay, A., Thomas, D., Vandenberg, J.: Galaxy zoo: reproducing galaxy morphologies via machine learning. Monthly Notices of the Royal Astronomical Society **406**(1), 342–353 (2010)
3. Bertin, E., Arnouts, B.: Sextractor: software for source extraction. Astronomy and Astrophysics **117**(Suppl. Ser.), 393–404 (1996)
4. Braga-Neto, U., Goutsias, J.: A multiscale approach to connectivity. Comp. Vis. Image Understand. **89**, 70–107 (2003)
5. Breen, E.J., Jones, R.: Attribute openings, thinnings and granulometries. Comp. Vis. Image Understand. **64**(3), 377–389 (1996)
6. Flusser, J., Suk, T.: Construction of complete and independent systems of rotation moment invariants. In: Petkov, N., Westenberg, M.A. (eds.) CAIP 2003. LNCS, vol. 2756, pp. 41–48. Springer, Heidelberg (2003)
7. Flusser, J.: On the independence of rotation moment invariants. Pattern Recognition (PR) **33**(9), 1405–1410 (2000)
8. Hall, M., Frank, E., Holmes, G., Pfahringer, B., Reutemann, P., Witten, I.H.: The weka data mining software: An update. SIGKDD Explor. Newsl. **11**(1), 10–18 (2009). http://doi.acm.org/10.1145/1656274.1656278
9. Hu, M.K.: Visual pattern recognition by moment invariants. IRE Transactions on Information Theory **8**(2), 179–187 (1962)
10. Lintott, C.J., Schawinski, K., Slosar, A., Land, K., Bamford, S., Thomas, D., Raddick, M.J., Nichol, R.C., Szalay, A., Andreescu, D., Murray, P., Vandenberg, J.: Galaxy Zoo: morphologies derived from visual inspection of galaxies from the Sloan Digital Sky Survey. Monthly Notices of the Royal Astronomical Society **389**(3), 1179–1189 (2008)
11. Lotz, J.M., Primack, J., Madau, P.: A new nonparametric approach to galaxy morphological classification. The Astronomical Journal **128**(1), 163 (2004)
12. Maragos, P.: Pattern spectrum and multiscale shape representation. IEEE Trans. Pattern Anal. Mach. Intell. **11**, 701–715 (1989)

13. Moschini, U., Teeninga, P., Wilkinson, M.H.F., Giese, N., Punzo, D., van der Hulst, J.M., Trager, S.C.: Towards better segmentation of large floating point 3D astronomical data sets: first results. In: Proceedings of the 2014 Conference on Big Data from Space (BiDS 2014), pp. 232–235. Publications Office of the European Union (2014)

14. Peng, C.Y., Ho, L.C., Impey, C.D., Rix, H.W.: Detailed structural decomposition of galaxy images. The Astronomical Journal **124**(1), 266 (2002). http://stacks.iop.org/1538-3881/124/i=1/a=266

15. Pesaresi, M., Wilkinson, M.H.F., Moschini, U., Ouzounis, G.K.: Concurrent computation of connected pattern spectra for very large image information mining. In: ESA-EUSC-JRC 8th Conference on Image Information Mining, pp. 21–25. Publications Office of the European Union (2012)

16. Quinlan, J.R.: C4.5: Programs for Machine Learning. Morgan Kaufmann Publishers Inc., San Francisco (1993)

17. Salembier, P., Oliveras, A., Garrido, L.: Anti-extensive connected operators for image and sequence processing. IEEE Trans. Image Proc. **7**, 555–570 (1998)

18. Serra, J.: Image Analysis and Mathematical Morphology. II: Theoretical Advances. Academic Press, London (1988)

19. Starkenburg, T.: Classifying galaxies with mathematical morphology (2009). https://www.mysciencework.com/publication/read/7470103/classifying-galaxies-with-mathematical-morphology

20. Teeninga, P., Moschini, U., Trager, S.C., Wilkinson, M.H.F.: Improved detection of faint extended astronomical objects through statistical attribute filtering. In: Benediktsson, J.A., Chanussot, J., Najman, L., Talbot, H. (eds.) ISMM 2015. LNCS, vol. 9082, pp. 157–168. Springer, Heidelberg (2015)

21. Urbach, E.R., Roerdink, J.B.T.M., Wilkinson, M.H.F.: Connected shape-size pattern spectra for rotation and scale-invariant classification of gray-scale images. IEEE Trans. Pattern Anal. Mach. Intell. **29**(2), 272–285 (2007)

Automatic Detection of Nodules in Legumes by Imagery in a Phenotyping Context

Simeng Han[1,2](✉), Frédéric Cointault[1,2],
Christophe Salon[2], and Jean-Claude Simon[1,2]

[1] AgroSup Dijon, 26 Boulevard Docteur Petitjean, 21000 Dijon, France
{simeng.han,frederic.cointault,jean-claude.simon}@agrosupdijon.fr
[2] UMR Agroécologie, INRA Dijon, 17 Rue Sully, 21000 Dijon, France
christophe.salon@dijon.inra.fr

Abstract. Plant Phenotyping consists in characterizing their morphometric pa-rameters which allows correlating them to genotype expression, modulated by their environment. Particularly, nutrition and environment of plants impact significantly roots and symbiotic nodules growths. Under conditions of low mineral nitrogen in soil, legumes have the ability to fix atmospheric nitrogen symbiotically in nodules which are organs formed on the roots of the host plant. The observation of nodules and the evaluation of their characteristics are quite difficult manually, and commercial software provide currently time consuming and no accurate results. This paper proposes a fast and automated image processing technique using the skeletonization technique to determine very accurately nodule parameters, such as their number, location and size on the primary root. The results obtained will be used for the determination of other root parameters including dynamic follow of root architecture.

Keywords: Phenotyping · Nodules detection · Skeletonization · Imagery · Automatic

1 Introduction

Nowadays, agriculture is facing the dual challenge of feeding an evergrowing world population while having to preserve resources (biodiversity, soil, water, climate...), in a changing environment (climate change, scarcity of resources...). In this context where agricultural production has to be combined with less reliance on fossil fuels and inputs, crucial objectives are 1) to select plants with more efficient root system for the collection of terrestrial resources (water, minerals) and 2) to refine the understanding of the regulation of root system architecture and functions in response to environmental stresses (abiotic but also including interaction with rhizosphere microorganisms).

To reach the first previous objective, legumes are most interesting candidates for innovative cropping systems [1]. Pea (Pisum sativum L.) is the predominant legume seed of European agricultural systems. This culture has many advantages

G. Azzopardi and N. Petkov (Eds.): CAIP 2015, Part II, LNCS 9257, pp. 134–145, 2015.
DOI: 10.1007/978-3-319-23117-4_12

that make it an essential component of strategies for diversification of agricultural systems, with the objective of food security and agroecological behaviour's environmentally acceptable [2].

However, up to now a limited number of studies have been done on plant root architecture because accessing easily to the root system directly in the soil is tedious. Different tools for root system visualizations have been developed [3,4] and resulting images are generally processed using commercial software.

Despite this and for the second objective, up to now a limited number of studies tackled plant root architecture because accessing easily to the root system in the soil is tedious. Different root systems visualizations have been developed and images are generally processed using commercial software.

Although several commercial tools or software are available today to process rhizotron images, none is completely automatic, accurate and less time consuming. Moreover, they cannot provide the detection of all the root phenotypic traits, and especially the nodules.

Thus this paper presents a set of methods and a flow chart for the analysis of root images and the characterization of nodules on the primary root. Images are acquired using a new and patented rhizotron system, and image processing combines the optimization of the skeletonization technique and local processing according to root architecture.

2   Materials and Methods

2.1   Rhizotron Images

The patented system installed on the High Throughput Phenotyping Platform of the INRA Dijon, called rhizotron system [5], allows the visualization of the development of plant root system without any destruction. Rhizotron images are acquired by an optical scanner in 2D (Fig. 1).

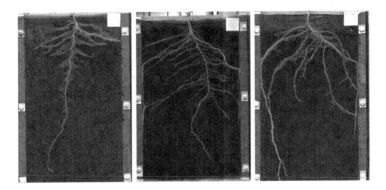

Fig. 1. Examples of images acquired with an optical scanner and the rhizotron system of the high throughput phenotyping platform of INRA Dijon, at different growth stages.

The rhizotron system allows observing in situ the root system and its interactions with pathogenic or mutualistic micro-organisms contained in the soil. These interactions had never been studied previously due to difficulty of access, but are now considered to be a major determinant of the adaptation of plants to various environments, such as drought stress conditions or low soil mineral availability.

2.2   Existing Imaging Methods and Software

Detection of nodules on the primary root needs to first detect the whole root system. Root architecture appears as very similar to other objects such as retinal vascular network or cracks on pavement surface.

Detection in retinal vasculature implies to find the connected pixels belonging to a vascular network, the vessels direction, or the arteriovenous circulation of the retina [6]. It may give us clues for the pre-processing of our root images, such as segmentation processing or extraction of ROI (Region of Interest), but is of no help for further detection of phenotypic traits of roots, especially for nodules.

For detection of cracks on pavement surface, the authors [7] used wavelet transform method, which cannot be used in our application because such method takes into account factors such as the variation of the reflection coefficient, moisture or the texture of the coating..., which are not known for our root images.

In phenotyping domain, several commercial software have been developed for the biologists, such as Smart Root [8], WinRhizo [9] or Dart Root [10], with however more or less unacceptable drawbacks due to cost, computation time, no detection of a large range of morphological traits, manual setup needed and no automation.

2.3   Image Processing

The first plants which have been studied are the legumes, composed of a taproot system during their growth (Fig. 2(a)).

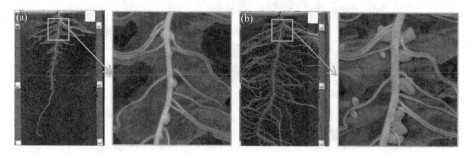

Fig. 2. Legumes plant with taproot system and nodules at different growth stages: (a) Young nodules. (b) Old nodules.

According to biologist and agronomic researchers, among the parameter traits which may constitute genetic parameters to be extracted to characterize the whole root system, nodules are the most important , since they allow the circulation of carbon and nitrogen inside the plants (Fig. 2(b)).

A new fast and automatic image processing technique for nodule characterization are thus proposed in this paper, which allows to determine accurately the location, number and size of the nodules on the primary root.

Hybrid Spaces

First, to detect the nodules, it seemed promising to use a method of image analysis combining colour and texture information. A "Color - Texture Hybrid Spaces" method has been applicated here.

This method is based on the determination of a hybrid space of the representation of images combining color and texture information; it was developed in the context of a feasibility study of a system designed to count ears of wheat [11]. After determining different classes of points to find, the image is represented in a three-dimensional space: each dimension being a pair of parameters [texture parameter, color parameter].

Images tested here give some interesting results (Fig. 3), especially in the stage that the nodules are well developed: each nodule was detected and located, that gives the possibility to continue the refined detection. But this method has great limits to detect young nodules, because the nodules in an early stage have almost the same colour and texture as the main root. For this problem,

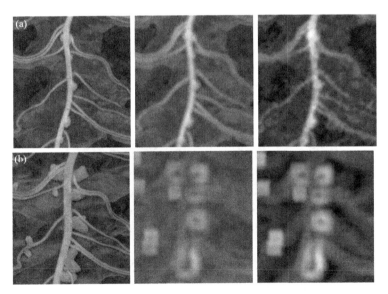

Fig. 3. Hybrid space method for nodule detection: (a) Early stage nodules detection shown in false colour and in black and white. (b) Late stage nodules detected in false colour and in black and white.

we propose here our own image processing method explained in the following paragraphs.

2.4   Rhizotron Image Detection Method Proposed

The first steps of image processing are based on image calibration and image segmentation to provide a binary image. Among several standard segmentation techniques such as Edge detection, Region-growing methods, Watershed segmentation, a simple thresholding by gray-level histograms [12] is finally used here for image segmentation with some morphological operations like opening and closing, to extract the root from the noisy background (Fig. 4).

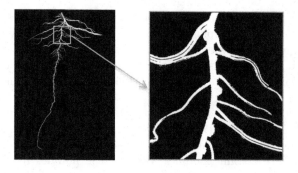

Fig. 4. Binary image by Thresholding and zoom on a ROI.

Extracting nodules from the binary image implies to determine the primary root first. Standard Skeletonization Technique [13] is used to obtain the skeleton of each root (Fig. 5). This method consists to remove pixels on the boundaries of objects without allowing objects to break apart. It is widely used in the detection of end items, such as the fingerprint recognition, or the letter recognition in vehicle number plate detection.

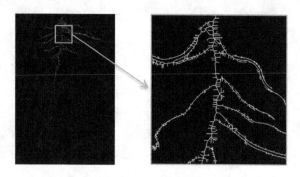

Fig. 5. Example of Skeletonization result.

The skeleton image is after treated by our original image processing method [14] to separate the primary root from the other elements on the whole image, which means to eliminate the little artefacts of the skeleton due to nodules, lateral roots and absorbent hairs on the primary root.

The final skeleton of the primary root is shown on Fig. 6(a). The Fig. 6(b) provides part of the binary image with superimposition of the skeleton found with our method on the primary root.

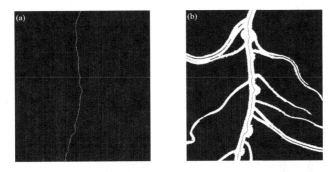

Fig. 6. (a) Skeleton of the primary root. (b) Superimposition of the skeleton on the binary image.

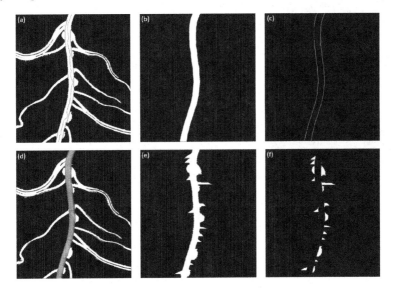

Fig. 7. (a) Elimination of lateral roots and nodules. (b) Reconstructed primary root. (c) Boundary of primary root. (d) Superimposition of the primary root on the binary image. (e) Laterals eliminated. (f) Nodules and laterals information on the primary root.

The primary root can thus be reconstructed (Fig. 7(b)) by searching crossovers between the primary and the lateral roots on their boundary, in order to eliminate both all of lateral roots and nodules which are located nearby the primary root (Fig. 7(a)). This allows to find the boundary of the primary root (Fig. 7(c)).

Then, from the primary root, increasing towards each side until reached the boundary between the roots (white part) and the background (black part) gives an image contains the beginnings of nodules or laterals (Fig. 7(c)). From this image, after removing the primary root, an image is obtained as shown in (Fig. 7(e)).

This method provides us just the main part of the primary root and volume images of lateral roots and nodules. Histogram images show us the differences between the two last (Fig. 8).

For each "spectrum", maxima are extracted which correspond to the presence of nodules or lateral roots. Each peak has a rising side with an acceleration rate (noted by Rate 1), and a falling side (noted by Rate 2) (Fig. 9). Nodules' bottom width, height, projected area and location can be calculated thus.

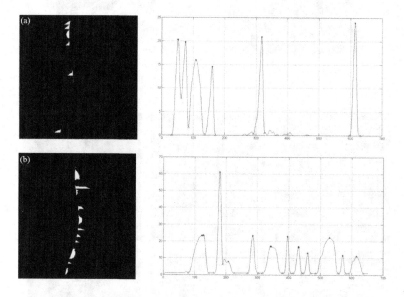

Fig. 8. Crossing image and Histogram: (a) Left side. (c) Right side.

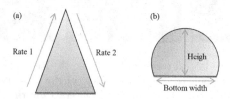

Fig. 9. : (a) Acceleration rate of nodule or lateral root. (b) Phenotyping traits.

Nodules can be distinguished from lateral roots by calculating Rate 1 and Rate 2, because nodule's acceleration rates (rising or falling) are both lower than lateral root. Nodule detection can be done by combining the bottom width (nodule's bottom width is wider than lateral root) and projected area information.

3   Results and Discussion

Primary Root Reconstruction

Fig. 10 present some results of the reconstructed primary root of images in the Fig. 1. Reconstruction of the primary root is important step for our next work.

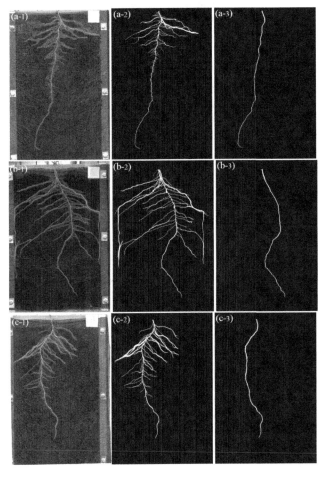

Fig. 10. Primary root reconstruction.

Nodule Detection

The the Fig. 11 shows some nodule detection for part of the image of the Fig. 10(a). The Table 1 show that these nodules have been followed and characterized in terms of location, size, width and height. The results are given in pixels but a target in each image provides us the correspondence between pixel and cm.

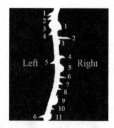

Fig. 11. Nodules or Lateral roots located

Table 1. Some results of nodules and lateral roots detection.

Nodule or Lateral root		Rate 1	Rate 2	Average rate	Width	Height	Area
Left part	1	0.978	1.584	1.281	35	19.8	477
	2	0.862	1.86	1.360	20	13.6	264
	3	0.597	0.514	0.556	52	14.3	441
	4	0.662	1.390	1.026	31	13.9	178
	5	0.881	1.762	1.321	30	17.6	209
	6	1.152	1.408	1.280	40	25.3	323
Right part	1	0.450	1.559	1.005	67	23	1008
	2	3.091	5.246	4.168	29	55.6	673
	3	0.095	0.389	0.242	36	4	241
	4	1.702	1.344	1.523	36	27.1	430
	5	0.838	0.586	0.712	64	22	849
	6	1.756	1.748	1.752	28	24.5	256
	7	0.797	1.405	1.101	33	16.8	253
	8	0.828	1.324	1.076	26	13.2	158
	9	0.498	0.812	0.655	71	22	989
	10	0.801	1.068	0.935	21	9.616	102
	11	0.402	0.498	0.450	47	10	328

The method also allows us to monitor the growth of a nodule. Table 2 provides examples of monitoring of the nodules 'Left 1', 'Right 5' and 'Right 9' indicated in the image of Fig 11. Several parameters of this nodule are evaluated for 4 continuous days, nodule location is calculated from the (0,0) point of the image.

Same results have been obtained on more than 100 images of nodulated plant, with more than 95% of precision, compared to manual measurements done by agronomical researchers, considered as experts. Moreover the follow of the dynamic growth of nodules (Area or Location (Fig. 12)) during the time provides a model, for the biologists.

Table 2. Monitoring of 3 nodules in 4 days

	Left 3				Right 5				Right 9			
	Day1	Day2	Day3	Day4	Day1	Day2	Day3	Day4	Day1	Day2	Day3	Day4
Width	52	58	77	124	64	67	71	78	71	77	79	87
Height	14	24	45	67	22	29	34	38	22	28	35	36
Area	441	1319	1901	2162	849	1234	1673	2028	989	1396	1920	2412
Location(x)	1353	1363	1367	1361	1605	1603	1605	1611	1779	1784	1788	1781
Location(y)	3249	3272	3262	3254	3373	3370	3369	3374	3339	3335	3333	3334

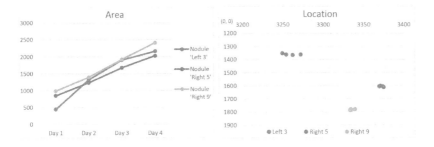

Fig. 12. Monitoring of a nodule in 4 days.

Inchoate Early Nodule Detection

The Fig. 13 shows three images of the same legume took at three different growth stages. On the right the nodules appear clearly on the primary root with a big size and specific colour, contrary to the image on the left, on which the nodules are not developed. Location of the nodules have been proved by image processing not to vary during the time. This is visually confirmed by the images of the Fig. 13.

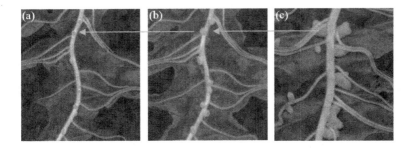

Fig. 13. Young nodule detection: (a) Day n+1. (b) Day n+4. (c) Day n+16.

When the nodules are old, the change of their colour can be a means to detect them easily. For example the color/texture hybrid space as we previously presented. However it dosen't work when the nodules are too young. Moreover, learning process of this method is not suitable with the development of an automatic imaging technique. Even if our technique is completely automatic and works well, it is not appropriated for the detection of nodules at all the growth stages.

We have developed a methodology and software to measure the morphological and phenotypic traits of root, especially the nodule detection. Compared with several commercial tools or software available on the market to process rhizotron images, our method is totally automatic and accurate compared to manual results.

One of our other advantages deals with the computation time: our system is 60 times faster than Smart Root, and 13 times faster (1 min. 30 sec. for a 144 Mega-pixel image) than other image processing method [15].

This program allows us to create a nodule growth model, which currently does not exist in biology. Improvements must however be done for the segmentation part.

4   Conclusion

In this paper, we presented an application based on skeletonization technique for nodule detection in legume images. This research is incorporated through the High-Throughput Phenotyping Platform (PPHD) of the INRA Centre of Dijon in France.

Identification of primary root's skeleton helps us to reconstruct the whole primary root. The boundary detection allows separating nodules and lateral root from roots, and the spectrum method gives finally the possibility of nodule identification.

With this technique, the program allows the extraction of the number of nodules on the primary root, their area information and their locations, automatically. It also provides the number of lateral roots on the primary root, the second important parameter for biologists.

Our method helps us to avoid the wrong detection in the identification of nodule in different states. With the same principle and idea, we can apply this method for the detection of several other morphological traits such as the primary root length, primary root diameter, total length of root, total number of nodules on roots and number of nodules on the lateral root etc.

Spatial analysis of nodulated roots provides the possibility to relate phenotypes to their genetic basis for legume species. This approach can also be used to analyze non taproots system and even several other species than legume species.

References

1. Postgate, J.: Nitrogen Fixation, 3rd edn. Cambridge University Press, Cambridge (1998)
2. Voisin, A.S., Cazenave, A.B., Duc, G., Salon, C.: Pea nodule gradients explain C nutrition and depressed growth phenotype of hypernodulating mutants. Agron. Sustain. Dev. **33**, 829–838 (2013)

3. Hoover, B.: Manual method: using a knife or a gouge, shovel the root, clean soil and measure by hand. Cal Poly (2010–2011)
4. CID: CI-600 In-Situ Root Imager: Install acrylic tubes within the study area prior to the growing season, when the plant begins to build a network of roots, slide the scanner head within the tube at the desired depth and download images. Bio-Science (2005)
5. Salon, C.: PPHD: a platform for high-speed phenotyping. Biofutur **338**, 61–64 (2012)
6. Calvo, D., Ortega, M., Penedo, M.G., Rouco, J.: Automatic detection and characterisation of retinal vessel tree bifurcations and crossovers in eye fundus images. Comput Methods Programs Biomed. **103**(1), 28–38 (2011)
7. Subirats, P., Fabre, O., Dumoulin, J., Legeay V., Barba, D.: A combined wavelet-based image processing method for emergent crack detection on pavement surface images. In: 12th European Signal Processing Conference (EUSIPCO), Vienna, Austria, pp. 257–260, September 6–10, 2004
8. Lobet, G., Pagés, L., Draye, X.: A Novel Image Analysis Toolbox Enabling Quantitative Analysis of Root System Architecture. Plant Physiology **157**, 29–39 (2011)
9. Arsenault, J.-L., Pouleur, S., Messier, C., Guay, R.: WinRHIZO, a root-measuring system with a unique overlap correction method. HortScience **30**, 906 (1995)
10. Le Bot, J.: DART: a software to analyse root system architecture and development from captured images. Plant and Soil **326**(1–2), 261–273 (2010)
11. Cointault, F., Guérin, D., Guillemin, J.P., Chopinet, B.: In-Field Wheat ears Counting Using Color-Texture Image Analysis. New Zealand Journal of Crop and Horticultural Science **36**, 117–130 (2008)
12. Otsu, N.: A threshold selection method from gray-level histograms. IEEE Trans. Sys., Man., Cyber **9**, 62–66 (1979)
13. Lam, L., Lee, S.-W., Ching, Y.: Thinning Methodologies-A Comprehensive Survey. IEEE TrPAMI **14**(9), 869–885 (1992)
14. Han, S., Cointault, F.: Imagery for Phenotypic Trait Detection. IAMPS, Aberystwyth (2014)
15. Remmler, L., et al.: Standardized mapping of nodulation patterns in legume roots. New Phytologist. **202**(3), 1083–1094 (2014)

Human Skin Segmentation
Improved by Saliency Detection

Anderson Santos[(✉)] and Helio Pedrini

Institute of Computing, University of Campinas,
Campinas, SP 13083-852, Brazil
acarlos@liv.ic.unicamp.br

Abstract. Several applications demand the segmentation of images in skin and non-skin regions, such as face recognition, hand gesture detection, nudity recognition, among others. Human skin detection is still a challenging task since it depends on inumerous factors, for instance, illumination conditions, ethnicity variation and image resolution. This work proposes and analyzes a skin segmentation method improved by saliency detection. Experimental results on public data sets demonstrate significant improvement of the proposed skin segmentation method over state-of-the-art approaches.

Keywords: Skin segmentation · Saliency detection · Probability map

1 Introduction

Several applications require the detection of human skin regions in digital images, such as gesture analysis, face detection, content-based image retrieval, nudity detection. Skin detection can be considered as a binary classification problem, where pixels are assigned to belong to skin or non-skin class.

Human skin detection is challenging since it is sensitive to camera properties, illumination conditions, individual appearance such as age, gender and ethnicity, among other factors.

In this work, we propose the use of saliency to reduce false positives found in probability maps. The objective of the saliency detection process here is to exclude background from the images. Skin probability information is combined with saliency to generate the final skin probability map. Experiments conducted on large and challenging data sets demonstrate that the proposed method is capable of improving other skin segmentation approaches available in the literature.

The text is organized as follows. Section 2 briefly reviews some works related to skin detection. Section 3 presents the proposed skin segmentation method based on saliency detection. Experiments conducted on public data sets are discussed in Section 4. Finally, Section 5 concludes the paper with final remarks and some directions for future work.

G. Azzopardi and N. Petkov (Eds.): CAIP 2015, Part II, LNCS 9257, pp. 146–157, 2015.
DOI: 10.1007/978-3-319-23117-4_13

2   Background

This section briefly describes some relevant concepts and works related to the skin segmentation problem in digital images.

2.1   Skin Segmentation

The problem of skin segmentation is object of many researches [11,14,17,19,20, 25]. The approaches found in the literature can be categorized into two main groups: pixel-based and region-based.

In pixel-based strategies, the pixel skin color is modeled in a certain color space. Various works [2,21,23] use fixed rules and thresholds to define a pixel as skin or not skin. Sobottka et al. [21] limit the skin to a subsection of the HSV color space. Soriano et al. [23] propose a rule based on two quadratic functions for the normalized RGB space. Kovac et al. [15] opt for the RGB space, however, with rules concerning the minimum and maximum values of the channel and their differences. Cheddad et al. [2] propose to work with a 1-dimensional error signal, where simple low and high threshold values define the skin.

Another approach is to fit a parametric model for the distribution of skin and non-skin color. The most common is to use a single Gaussian [24] or a Gaussian Mixture Model [28]. Jones et al. [10] propose to model both skin ($P(c|skin)$) and non-skin ($P(c|\neg skin)$) in order to define the probability of a pixel as skin given its color (c) to be

$$P(skin|c) = \frac{P(c|skin)P(skin)}{P(c|skin)P(skin) + P(c|\neg skin)P(\neg skin)} \tag{1}$$

as stated by the Bayes' rule.

For a Gaussian Mixture Model, the skin or non-skin prior probability is established as

$$P(c|class) = \sum_{i=1}^{N} w_i \frac{1}{(2\pi)^{\frac{3}{2}}|\Sigma_i|^{\frac{1}{2}}} e^{-\frac{1}{2}(x-\mu_i)^{\tau}\Sigma_i^{-1}(x-\mu_i)} \tag{2}$$

where c is an RGB color vector, *class* can be skin or non-skin and the contribution of the i-th Gaussian is determined by a scalar weight w_i, mean vector μ_i, and diagonal covariance matrix Σ_i.

The model can also be achieved in a non-parametric way by histogram density [10], where the prior probabilities are calculated as

$$P(c|class) = \frac{H_{class}(c)}{\sum_{i=1}^{N}(H_{class}(i))} \tag{3}$$

Although these models retrieve a significant amount of skin, they also incorporate many false positives, which is inevitable if the skin and non-skin colors overlap to each other. Thus, region-based methods can be employed as a second step, where some of them use texture [9,16], whereas others investigate the spatial analysis in the form of interactive segmentation [12,13,22]. Many approaches improve pixel-based methods by adapting the model to particular characteristics of the image through the analysis of the entire image [15,18] or just a part of it, such as detecting a face [4] or precise skin blobs [19].

2.2   Saliency Detection

The goal of saliency detection methods is to find the content in images which attracts human attention. There are two approaches toward this issue: estimation of the eye fixation points or determination of the saliency object. Here, we will discuss the second approach in more details since it is coherent with our background elimination purpose.

The methods that perform figure-ground separation – a term to define the separation between object and background content – can be further classified based on the its domain: spatial frequency or color space.

The first relies on the signal within an image transform. Hou et al. [8] propose the use of spectral residual – the difference between the log amplitude signal obtained with Fourier Transform (FT) and its smoothed version. Later, Guo et at. [6] show that the image phase spectrum of the FT can generate the saliency map. More recently, Hou et al. [7] describe an image signature based on Discrete Cosine Transform (DCT), which is used to obtain a saliency map that was proved to concentrate the energy of spatially sparse foreground. This method is simple and provides good accuracy in terms of biological principles, however, we found that the produced map is too blurry, which affects segmentation precision and also tends to work well only for small centered objects.

The methods that rely on color spatial domain can be further divided into using local or global contrast. They deal with the rarity of the foreground in relation to the vicinity of the pixel/region [1] or the entire image, respectively [3]. The local one is more sensitive to edges and noise, whereas the global exploits the overall structure and relations, making it more suitable for segmentation. A combination of both [5] can also be beneficial.

The intuitive strategy in global methods is to calculate the contrast of each region to the entire image. Nevertheless, this produces unsatisfied results and often classifies background regions as salient. Recent works have introduced boundary priors with the assumption that the image boundaries belong to the background [27] or the regions that most easily connect with the boundary to form the background [26].

The drawback of these methods is that they fail if the foreground object touches the boundary. In order to overcome this, Zhu et al. [30] propose a measure of boundary connectivity, *BndCon*, defined as

$$BndCon(R) = \frac{|\{p|p \in R, p \in Bnd\}|}{\sqrt{|\{p|p \in R\}|}} \tag{4}$$

where R is an image region, Bnd is the set of image boundary patches and p is an image patch. Regions that are heavily connected to the boundary, in other words, regions that have more patches belonging to the boundary set in relation to the total patches will produce larger values of boundary connectivity. For effective computation, they extend this notion through superpixels. Zhu et al. [30] also propose to determine the saliency with the minimization of a cost function that considers a background weight, a foreground weight and a smoothness term.

3   Proposed Method

We propose a method for reducing the false positive rate in skin segmentation with the use of a saliency detection method. This is based on the premise that the skin is not always salient in the image, but that the background will be not salient. Therefore, saliency detection methods that operate by finding the background to achieve the salient region are preferable, for instance, methods with boundary priors.

Since the skin regions will not be always classified as salient, we need to provide skin information for the considered saliency detector. We deal with skin probability information, however, binary output methods would also be suitable just by considering then having only probability 0 and 1. The main steps of our skin detection framework are illustrated in the diagram of Figure 1.

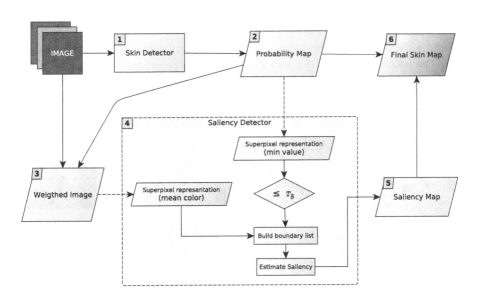

Fig. 1. Main stages of the proposed skin detection framework.

First, the skin detector (Stage 1) is applied to the image, creating a probability map (P_{map}) (Stage 2). This is used to build a weighted image (Stage 3), as shown in Equation 5

$$W_I(i,j,k) = P_{map}(i,j) * I(i,j,k) \tag{5}$$

where $W_I(i,j,k)$ represents the weighted image pixel in channel k and $I(i,j,k)$ the original image pixel in channel k.

The weighted image serves as input for the saliency detector (Stage 4), whereas the probability map is also used to exclude probable skin from the boundary list. This is done with a threshold (T_β) applied to the map and aims to prevent that skin pixels adjacent to the boundary will be discarded. Since many saliency implementations use superpixels, in that case the probability map needs to be modeled with the same superpixel structure, however the representative value of each superpixel will be the minimum value of the region instead of the usual mean value. This is done such that only regions containing all probability values larger than T_β will be excluded as background.

The output saliency map (S_{map}) (Stage 5) is again combined with P_{map}, as shown in Equation 6

$$F_{map}(i) = \gamma P_{map}(i) + (1 - \gamma)S_{map}(i) \tag{6}$$

where F_{map} is the final skin map (Stage 6) and γ defines the weight of the probability map in the mean combination in the range between 0 and 1.

At the final stage, the framework outputs a map for the skin, even for binary skin detectors. Thus, the final segmentation can be performed by a simple threshold or a more sophisticated strategy.

Figure 2 illustrates the application of the proposed method to an input image, where the probability map, the weighted image, the saliency map, the final map and the resulting segmentation are shown.

Original   Probability map   Weighted image   Saliency map   Final map   Segmentation

Fig. 2. Examples of images obtained by applying each stage of our method to an input image.

4   Experiments

Experiments were conducted on different data sets to evaluate the proposed methodology. For training, we used 8963 non-skin images and 4666 skin images from the Compaq database [10], which contains images acquired from the Internet in a diverse variety of settings. Its approximately 1 billion pixels make the data set sufficiently large for estimation of skin color distribution.

For evaluation and comparison purposes, we used two publicly available skin databases. The ECU database [17] was divided into 1000 images for validation and 3000 images for test, and the IBTD database [29] is composed of 555 images all used for test. The first ensures a diversity in terms of background scenes, lighting conditions and skin types (whitish, pinkish, yellowish, light brownish, reddish, darkish, dark brownish), whereas the second was collected from a larger database through a filtering tool for objectionable images, where the suspicious images were retained in the data set, such that these images present more skin-like pixels what constitute a harder database.

All data sets provide a ground-truth that makes it possible to identify the pixel class (skin or non-skin) for the training and quantitatively evaluate the detection output.

The performance of the skin detection was measured through a number of metrics: true positive rate (η_{tp} - percentage of skin correctly classified as skin); false positive rate (δ_{fp} - percentage of non-skin classified as skin); F_{score} (harmonic mean between η_{prec} and η_{tp}) and detection error ($\delta_{min} = (1 - \eta_{tp}) + \delta_{fp}$). Additionally for non-binary classification, the ROC (receiver operating characteristics) and the respective area under curve (AUC) are applied.

In order to evaluate the proposed framework, we selected three widely used skin detectors with different approaches: Cheddad's rule [2] (rule based), Gaussian Mixture Model (GMM) [10] (parametric) and Histogram Model [10] (non-parametric). For the Gaussian Mixture, we used the 16 kernels trained in the original paper for skin and non-skin samples. The Histogram Model was built with 64 bins per channel in the RGB space. It is important to highlight that both GMM and Histogram share the same training set.

As the saliency detector, we chose the saliency optimization method from Zhu et al. [30] since it can cope with the wild scenario of the skin images. In other words, it can work with no centralized foreground and with images of different sizes, preserving the scale and producing less false saliencies. We maintained its original parameters changing only the boundary list as stated in Section 3.

Besides the parameters of the chosen skin detectors and saliency detector, our framework adds only two new parameters: the threshold T_β and the weight γ. In the validation stage, we performed a grid search and found that 0.5 is a proper value for both.

Figure 3 and 4 shows comparative ROC curves between the original skin detector and our combination with saliency detector. It can be seen that the proposed method always achieves superior results on both tested data sets.

Tables 1 and 2 show the result values when considering the closest point to the optimum point (0, 100%) in the ROC curve. For Cheddad's rule, which is a binary method, the tables present isolated point values. A noticeable aspect in Table 1 is that the methods which holds worst results, becomes better than all others without saliency when they are combined by our method with saliency detection.

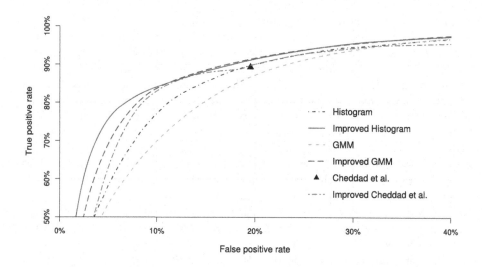

Fig. 3. ROC curves showing the results on ECU data set for the original method and the improvement with the framework.

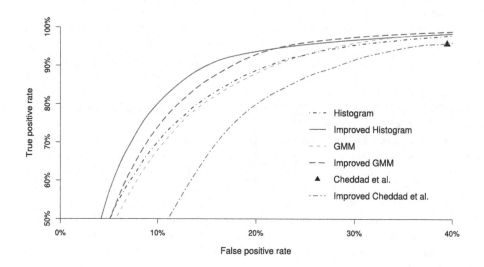

Fig. 4. ROC curves showing the results on IBTD data set for the original method and the improvement with the framework.

For a better view of the differences in performance with and without our proposed methodology, Figure 5 shows a graph bar for F-score metric for the original method and its improved version.

Table 1. Detection results for different methods (ECU data set).

Method	Original				+ Saliency			
	η_{tp} (%)	δ_{fp} (%)	F_{score} (%)	δ_{min} (%)	η_{tp} (%)	δ_{fp} (%)	F_{score} (%)	δ_{min} (%)
Cheddad et al. [2]	89.33	19.51	64.78	30.18	85.81	12.10	71.67	26.29
Gaussian Mixture [10]	87.55	20.30	63.09	32.76	85.91	11.84	72.08	25.93
Histogram Model [10]	87.21	16.54	66.95	29.33	84.10	10.00	**73.63**	**25.91**

Table 2. Detection results for different methods (IBTD data set).

Method	Original				+ Saliency			
	η_{tp} (%)	δ_{fp} (%)	F_{score} (%)	δ_{min} (%)	η_{tp} (%)	δ_{fp} (%)	F_{score} (%)	δ_{min} (%)
Cheddad et al. [2]	95.74	39.98	53.96	44.24	88.12	26.10	60.36	37.98
Gaussian Mixture [10]	90.83	22.59	64.71	31.76	92.69	19.78	68.30	27.09
Histogram Model [10]	89.70	20.91	65.74	31.21	91.37	16.19	**71.44**	**24.82**

For a more detailed comparison, we provide true positive rate values for a 10% false positive rate in Tables 3 and 4. In other words, this represents how much of

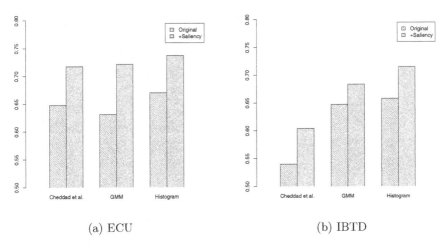

(a) ECU   (b) IBTD

Fig. 5. Comparative F_{score} results for original methods and our approach both in (a) ECU and (b) IBTD data sets.

Table 3. True positive rates for a fixed value of false positive rate (ECU data set).

Method	$\eta_{tp}(\%)$, $\delta_{fp} = 10\%$	
	Original	+ Saliency
Cheddad et al. [2]	46	**83**
Gaussian Mixture [10]	70	**83**
Histogram Model [10]	77	**84**

Table 4. True positive rates for a fixed value of false positive rate (IBTD data set).

Method	$\eta_{tp}(\%)$, $\delta_{fp} = 10\%$	
	Original	+ Saliency
Cheddad et al. [2]	24	**48**
Gaussian Mixture [10]	67	**74**
Histogram Model [10]	70	**80**

true skin is possible to detect since there is only 10% tolerance for skin-like. In case of the original method by Cheddad et al. [2], we perform a linear approximation preserving the same ratio between η_{tp} and δ_{fp}.

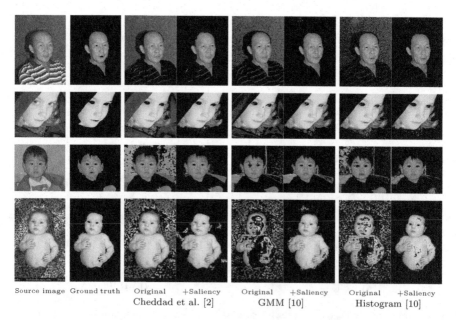

Source image Ground truth   Original   +Saliency   Original   +Saliency   Original   +Saliency
                              Cheddad et al. [2]   GMM [10]   Histogram [10]

Fig. 6. Examples of skin regions detected through different methods.

It is worth mentioning that our method always results in higher true positive rates with a considerable advantage over the original approaches.

Figure 6 shows some examples of final segmentation in the two tested data sets. The first column presents the original image, the second one shows the ground-truth, whereas the remaining columns show the segmentation result for each original method on the left and its correspondent improved segmentation results on the right.

It can be observed that the segmentation results of the methods improved by our framework are clearer and have much less non-skin background. From the last row, it is noticeable that our method not only removes false skin, but also is capable of recovering false negatives.

5   Conclusions

This work described and analyzed a new general framework for improving skin segmentation using saliency detection. It supports any skin segmentation technique and can be adapted to any saliency detection method based on background priors.

Experiments conducted on two public data sets, a well-known large test set and a more challenging data set, demonstrated that the proposed technique can provide a significant improvement on the results for different skin detection approaches. Nevertheless, additional refinements can be incorporated into the framework, for instance, in cases where skin covers most of the image, avoiding that true skin is discarded due to its classification as background.

As future directions, we intend to expand the framework to address the false positives that inevitably belong to a salient region by removing not only non-skin background, but also non skin in the foreground.

Acknowledgements. The authors are grateful to FAPESP, CNPq and CAPES for the financial support.

References

1. Achanta, R., Estrada, F.J., Wils, P., Süsstrunk, S.: Salient region detection and segmentation. In: Gasteratos, A., Vincze, M., Tsotsos, J.K. (eds.) ICVS 2008. LNCS, vol. 5008, pp. 66–75. Springer, Heidelberg (2008)
2. Cheddad, A., Condell, J., Curran, K., Mc Kevitt, P.: A Skin Tone Detection Algorithm for an Adaptive Approach to Steganography. Signal Processing **89**(12), 2465–2478 (2009)
3. Cheng, M.M., Zhang, G.X., Mitra, N.J., Huang, X., Hu, S.M.: Global contrast based salient region detection. In: IEEE Conference on Computer Vision and Pattern Recognition, pp. 409–416. IEEE (2011)
4. Fritsch, J., Lang, S., Kleinehagenbrock, M., Fink, G.A., Sagerer, G.: Improving adaptive skin color segmentation by incorporating results from face detection. In: 11th IEEE International Workshop on Robot and Human Interactive Communication, pp. 337–343 (2002)

5. Goferman, S., Zelnik-Manor, L., Tal, A.: Context-Aware Saliency Detection. IEEE Transactions on Pattern Analysis and Machine Intelligence **34**(10), 1915–1926 (2012)
6. Guo, C., Ma, Q., Zhang, L.: Spatio-temporal saliency detection using phase spectrum of quaternion fourier transform. In: IEEE Conference on Computer Vision and Pattern Recognition, pp. 1–8. IEEE (2008)
7. Hou, X., Harel, J., Koch, C.: Image Signature: Highlighting Sparse Salient Regions. IEEE Transactions on Pattern Analysis and Machine Intelligence **34**(1), 194–201 (2012)
8. Hou, X., Zhang, L.: Saliency detection: a spectral residual approach. In: IEEE Conference on Computer Vision and Pattern Recognition, pp. 1–8. IEEE (2007)
9. Jiang, Z., Yao, M., Jiang, W.: Skin detection using color, texture and space information. In: Fourth International Conference on Fuzzy Systems and Knowledge Discovery, vol. 3, pp. 366–370 (2007)
10. Jones, M.J., Rehg, J.M.: Statistical Color Models with Application to Skin Detection. International Journal of Computer Vision **46**(1), 81–96 (2002)
11. Kakumanu, P., Makrogiannis, S., Bourbakis, N.: A Survey of Skin-Color Modeling and Detection Methods. Pattern Recognition **40**(3), 1106–1122 (2007)
12. Kawulok, M.: Energy-based Blob Analysis for Improving Precision of Skin Segmentation. Multimedia Tools and Applications **49**(3), 463–481 (2010)
13. Kawulok, M.: Fast propagation-based skin regions segmentation in color images. In: 10th IEEE International Conference and Workshops on Automatic Face and Gesture Recognition, pp. 1–7 (2013)
14. Kawulok, M., Nalepa, J., Kawulok, J.: Skin detection and segmentation in color images. In: Advances in Low-Level Color Image Processing, pp. 329–366. Springer (2014)
15. Kovac, J., Peer, P., Solina, F.: Human skin color clustering for face detection. In: International Conference on Computer as a Tool (Eurocon), vol. 2, pp. 144–148, September 2003. IEEE
16. Ng, P., Pun, C.M.: Skin color segmentation by texture feature extraction and K-mean clustering. In: Third International Conference on Computational Intelligence, Communication Systems and Networks, pp. 213–218. IEEE (2011)
17. Phung, S.L., Bouzerdoum, A., Chai Sr, D.: Skin Segmentation using Color Pixel Classification: Analysis and Comparison. IEEE Transactions on Pattern Analysis and Machine Intelligence **27**(1), 148–154 (2005)
18. Phung, S.L., Chai, D., Bouzerdoum, A.: Adaptive skin segmentation in color images. In: International Conference on Multimedia and Expo, vol. 3, pp. III-173 (2003)
19. Santos, A., Pedrini, H.: A self-adaptation method for human skin segmentation based on seed growing. In: 10th International Conference on Computer Vision Theory and Applications, pp. 455–462. Berlin, Germany (March 2015)
20. Saxen, F., Al-Hamadi, A.: Color-based skin segmentation: an evaluation of the state of the art. In: IEEE International Conference on Image Processing, pp. 4467–4471. IEEE (2014)
21. Sobottka, K., Pitas, I.: A Novel Method for Automatic Face Segmentation, Facial Feature Sxtraction and Tracking. Signal Processing: Image Communication **12**(3), 263–281 (1998)
22. Ruiz-del Solar, J., Verschae, R.: Skin detection using neighborhood information. In: Sixth IEEE International Conference on Automatic Face and Gesture Recognition, pp. 463–468. IEEE (2004)

23. Soriano, M., Martinkauppi, B., Huovinen, S., Laaksonen, M.: Skin detection in video under changing illumination conditions. In: 15th International Conference on Pattern Recognition, vol. 1, pp. 839–842. IEEE (2000)

24. Subban, R., Mishra, R.: Human skin segmentation in color images using gaussian color model. In: Thampi, S.M., Abraham, A., Pal, S.K., Rodriguez, J.M.C. (eds.) Recent Advances in Intelligent Informatics. AISC, vol. 235, pp. 13–21. Springer, Heidelberg (2014)

25. Vezhnevets, V., Sazonov, V., Andreeva, A.: A survey on pixel-based skin color detection techniques. In: Graphicon, vol. 3, pp. 85–92. Moscow, Russia (2003)

26. Wei, Y., Wen, F., Zhu, W., Sun, J.: Geodesic saliency using background priors. In: Fitzgibbon, A., Lazebnik, S., Perona, P., Sato, Y., Schmid, C. (eds.) ECCV 2012, Part III. LNCS, vol. 7574, pp. 29–42. Springer, Heidelberg (2012)

27. Yang, C., Zhang, L., Lu, H., Ruan, X., Yang, M.H.: Saliency detection via graph-based manifold ranking. In: IEEE Conference on Computer Vision and Pattern Recognition, pp. 3166–3173. IEEE (2013)

28. Yang, M.H., Ahuja, N.: Gaussian mixture model for human skin color and its application in image and video databases. In: SPIE: Storage and Retrieval for Image and Video Databases VII, vol. 3656, pp. 458–466 (1999)

29. Zhu, Q., Wu, C.T., Cheng, K.T., Wu, Y.L.: An adaptive skin model and its application to objectionable image filtering. In: 12th annual ACM International Conference on Multimedia, pp. 56–63. ACM (2004)

30. Zhu, W., Liang, S., Wei, Y., Sun, J.: Saliency optimization from robust background detection. In: IEEE Conference on Computer Vision and Pattern Recognition, pp. 2814–2821. IEEE (2014)

Disparity Estimation for Image Fusion in a Multi-aperture Camera

Janne Mustaniemi$^{(\boxtimes)}$, Juho Kannala, and Janne Heikkilä

Center for Machine Vision Research, University of Oulu, Oulu, Finland
{janne.mustaniemi,jkannala,jth}@ee.oulu.fi

Abstract. In this paper, an image fusion algorithm is proposed for a multi-aperture camera. Such camera is a worthy alternative to traditional Bayer filter camera in terms of image quality, camera size and camera features. The camera consists of several camera units, each having dedicated optics and color filter. The main challenge of a multi-aperture camera arises from the fact that each camera unit has a slightly different viewpoint. Our image fusion algorithm corrects the parallax error between the sub-images using a disparity map, which is estimated from the multi-spectral images. We improve the disparity estimation by combining matching costs over multiple views with help of trifocal tensors. Images are matched using two alternative matching costs, mutual information and Census transform. We also compare two different disparity estimation methods, graph cuts and semi-global matching. The results show that the overall quality of the fused images is near the reference images.

Keywords: Mutual information · Census transform · Trifocal tensor

1 Introduction

Multi-aperture camera refers to an imaging device that comprises more than one camera unit. The camera produces several sub-images, which are combined into a single image. The main challenge of the multi-aperture camera arises from the fact that each camera unit has a slightly different viewpoint. This results to misalignment of images that needs to be corrected before images can be properly combined. In practice, the problem is solved by finding the corresponding pixels from each image.

Multi-aperture cameras can improve the image quality, camera size and camera features over the traditional single-aperture cameras. There already exist patents of such systems [1,2]. Some of the largest mobile phone companies have also patented their versions of the multi-aperture cameras [3–5]. Probably the most complete implementations of multi-aperture camera modules come from LinX Imaging [6] and Pelican Imaging [7].

LinX Imaging has successfully developed small-sized multi-aperture cameras for mobile devices. Camera modules have two, three or four cameras and they come in various configurations and sizes. Modules use different combination of

© Springer International Publishing Switzerland 2015
G. Azzopardi and N. Petkov (Eds.): CAIP 2015, Part II, LNCS 9257, pp. 158–170, 2015.
DOI: 10.1007/978-3-319-23117-4_14

color and monochrome cameras. Based on technology presentation in [6], captured images have higher dynamic range, lower noise levels and better color accuracy over the traditional mobile phone cameras. The height of the camera module is nearly half of a typical mobile phone camera module.

PiCam (Pelican Imaging Camera-Array) is another example of working multi-aperture camera. PiCam module consists of 4 × 4 array of cameras, each having dedicated optics and color filter. The final image is constructed from the low-resolution images using superresolution techniques. The image quality is comparable to existing smartphone cameras and the thickness of the camera module is less than 3 mm. [7]

An example of multi-aperture camera is shown in Figure 1. In this case, three of the lenses are equipped with red, green and blue filters. The fourth camera captures the luminance information of the scene. It may be used to increase the light sensitivity of the camera and to increase the robustness of disparity estimation. The final image is formed by combining the sub-images into a single RGB image.

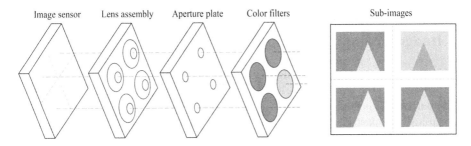

Fig. 1. Image sensing arrangement of the four-aperture camera

The thickness of the camera is closely related to the image quality the camera produces. Cameras equipped with larger image sensors typically produce better images. However, the increase in sensor size will also increase the height of the optics. Multi-aperture camera solves this problem by using a combination of smaller sensors, each having dedicated optics with reduced optical height. [3]

In Bayer filter cameras, the adjacent pixels capture the light intensity of different color bands. Consequently, the neighboring pixels may interact with each other. This phenomenon is known as crosstalk and it typically causes desaturation of color. The camera in Figure 1 does not suffer from crosstalk since each sensor is only measuring a single spectral color. [7]

Chromatic aberration is a type of distortion in which a lens failures to focus different colors to the same point on the image sensor. This occurs because lens material refracts different wavelengths of light at different angles. The effect can be seen as colored and blurred edges especially along boundaries that separate dark and bright parts of the image. The lenses in the multi-aperture camera can be much simpler since chromatic aberration does not complicate the optics design. Besides the improved image quality, a simpler design usually means lower manufacturing costs. [7]

One of the disadvantages of the current camera phones is that they cannot produce images with shallow depth of field. Mobile phone applications such as Google Lens Blur [8] aim to address this weakness. Lens Blur captures the scene depth from the camera movement and then uses the information for post-capture refocusing. Multi-aperture camera can acquire depth information via stereo matching. Depth information is also useful in various other applications such as background removal and replacement, resizing of objects, depth based color effects and 3D scanning of objects. [6,7]

In this paper, we propose an image fusion algorithm for a four aperture camera in Figure 1. In contrast to PiCam, we cannot match images that are captured with similar color filters. This complicates the disparity estimation since corresponding pixels may have completely different intensities in each image. Therefore, we use a robust matching cost such as mutual information or Census transform. We improve the robustness of disparity estimation over traditional two-view stereo methods such as [9,10] by combining matching costs over four-views. We further improve the estimation by adding a luminance constraint to the cost function.

2   Image Fusion Algorithm

In this Section, an image fusion algorithm is proposed for a four-aperture camera. The processing steps of the algorithm are shown in Figure 2. Algorithm is based on disparity estimation, in which the aim is to find corresponding pixels from each image. Disparities are estimated from the multi-spectral images captured by the four-aperture camera. Parallax error between the images is then corrected using the disparity map.

2.1   Offline Calibration

For this implementation, it was chosen that I_1 is the reference image and it corresponds the image captured with green color filter. Images I_2 and I_3 correspond

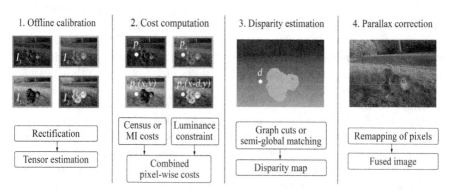

Fig. 2. Processing steps of the image fusion algorithm

to red and blue filtered images, respectively. The fourth image is used as a luminance image. The algorithm assumes that the camera movement between the first and second view is purely horizontal. This is difficult to ensure in practise, which is why image pair I_1 and I_2 is rectified. Other images are not rectified because algorithm utilizes trifocal tensors.

Trifocal Tensor. Image fusion can be performed by matching each image pair independently. However, such approach would not utilize the full potential of multiple views. Robustness of matching increases when matching costs from different views are combined. This will lead to a more accurate disparity map as will be demonstrated in Section 3. Consequently, the fused image will have better quality as well.

In the case of two views, a fundamental matrix is often defined to relate the geometry of a stereo pair. For three views, this role is played by the trifocal tensor. Trifocal tensor encapsulates all the geometric relations among three views. It only depends on the motion between the views and internal parameters of the cameras. Trifocal tensor is expressed by a set of three 3×3 matrices defined uniquely by the camera matrices of the views. Tensor can be constructed from the camera matrices or from the point correspondences. We used the latter approach because the camera system was uncalibrated. [11]

In practice, one can use the tensor to transfer point from a correspondence in two views to the corresponding point in a third view. This is known as point transfer. We define two trifocal tensors for each test scene. First tensor T_1 is computed for the images I_1, I_2 and I_3. Similarly, a second tensor T_2 is defined for the images I_1, I_2, and I_4. Let assume that there is a point $p_1 = (x, y)$ in the first image and its disparity d in relation to second image is known $p_2 = (x-d, y)$. Then, the corresponding points in third and fourth image can be computed using the tensors T_1 and T_2 respectively.

2.2 Matching Cost Computation

In order to find the corresponding pixels from each image, one needs a way to measure the similarity of image locations. It is common to presume that corresponding pixels have similar intensities in all views. This assumption is often violated, in the presence of radiometric differences such as noise, specularities and reflections. Similar problems arise when cameras are equipped with different color filters. This work utilizes mutual information and Census transform similarity measures. They both are known to be robust against radiometric differences [12,13].

To further improve the robustness of disparity estimation we use a luminance cost C_L, which is combined with mutual information or Census transform costs. Matching cost is computed at each pixel for all candidate disparities in a given disparity range. Disparity value that minimizes the cost represents the best match. The cost of assigning disparity d for pixel p is defined as follows:

$$C(p, d) = C_{MI/census} + K \cdot C_L, \tag{1}$$

where K is a constant, which controls the influence of the luminance cost C_L.

Mutual Information (MI) has been used as a similarity measure with local [13] and global [9, 10] stereo matching methods. The main advantage of MI is its ability to handle complex radiometric relationships between images. For example, MI handles matching image I_1 with the negative of image I_2 as easily as simply matching I_1 and I_2. Mutual information of images I_1 and I_2 is defined using entropies:

$$MI_{I_1,I_2} = H_{I_1} + H_{I_2} - H_{I_1,I_2}, \tag{2}$$

where H_{I_1} and H_{I_2} are the entropies of individual images and H_{I_1,I_2} is their joint entropy. The idea of using mutual information for stereo matching comes from the observation that joint entropy is low when images are well-aligned. It can be seen from previous equation that mutual information increases when joint entropy is low.

In order to calculate the entropies, one needs to estimate the marginal and joint probability distributions of underlying images. This can be done by using a simple histogram of corresponding image parts. Joint distribution is formed by binning the corresponding intensity pairs into a two-dimensional array. The marginal distributions are then obtained from the joint distribution by summing the corresponding rows and columns.

It is possible to apply mutual information to fixed-sized windows [13]. Window-based approach suffers from the common limitations of fixed-sized windows, such as poor performance at discontinuities and in textureless regions. To overcome the difficulties of window-based approach, Kim [9] used mutual information as a pixel-wise matching cost. The computation of joint entropy H_{I_1,I_2} was transformed into a cost matrix $h_{I_1,I_2}(i_1, i_2)$, which contains costs for each combination of pixel intensities $I_1(p) = i_1$ and $I_2(p) = i_2$. In the case of two views, the cost matrix is calculated with formula:

$$h_{I_1,I_2}(i_1, i_2) = -\frac{1}{n} log((P_{I_1,I_2}(i_1, i_2) * g(i_1, i_2)) * g(i_1, i_2), \tag{3}$$

where $g(i_1, i_2)$ is Gaussian kernel, which is convolved with the joint distribution $P_{I_1,I_2}(i_1, i_2)$. Number of all combinations of intensities is n. Details of the derivation can be found in [9].

Cost computation is illustrated in Figure 3. The cost matrix is calculated iteratively using the disparity map from the previous iteration. At each iteration, a new disparity map is estimated based on the current cost matrix. Usually only a few number of iterations (e.g. 3 iterations) are needed until the disparity map no longer improves. First, pixels in the image I_2 are remapped based on the current disparity map. The joint distribution P_{I_1,I_2} of corresponding intensities is then calculated between the image I_1 and remapped version of the image I_2. First iteration can use a random disparity map since even wrong disparities allow a good estimation of the joint distribution due to high number of pixels.

In our case, there are four images. We perform similar computations for other images, resulting to three different cost matrices h_{I_1,I_2}, h_{I_1,I_3} and h_{I_1,I_4}. Trifocal

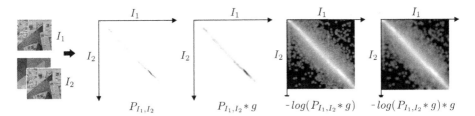

Fig. 3. Computation of mutual information cost matrix h_{I_1,I_2}

tensors are needed in order to remap images I_3 and I_4. The matching cost of assigning disparity d for pixel p is defined as follows:

$$C_{MI}(p,d) = h_{I_1,I_2}(i_1,i_2) + h_{I_1,I_3}(i_1,i_3) + h_{I_1,I_4}(i_1,i_4). \tag{4}$$

where i_1 is the intensity of the pixel p in the first image. Intensities i_2, i_3 and i_4 in other images depend on the disparity d.

Census Transform is based on the relative ordering of local intensity values. It can tolerate all radiometric distortions that preserve this ordering [14]. Census transform maps the local neighborhood of pixel into a bit string. Pixel's intensity is compared against the neighboring pixels and the bit is set if the neighboring pixel has lower intensity than the pixel of interest. Census transform for a pixel p can be defined as follows:

$$R_p = \mathop{\otimes}_{[x,y]\in D} \xi(p, p + [x,y]), \tag{5}$$

where symbol $\otimes$ denotes concatenation and D is the window around pixel p. The comparison operation $\xi(p, p + [x,y])$ is 1 if the neighboring pixel has lower intensity than the pixel p and otherwise 0. In this work, we use a window of 9 x 7 pixels. Each pixel in the window is compared to the center pixel. This will result to a bit string that consists of 62 bits. Computation is repeated for each of the four images.

The actual pixel-wise matching cost depends on the Hamming distance between the corresponding bit strings. Hamming distance is defined by counting the number of bits that differ in the two bit strings. For instance, the Hamming distance between two identical bit strings is zero since all bits are the same. Disparity value that minimizes the distance represents the best match. Let $H(R_{p,1}, R_{p,2})$ denote the Hamming distance between the corresponding bit strings in images I_1 and I_2. Since there are four images in this implementation, the pixel-wise cost is a sum of Hamming distances:

$$C_{census}(p,d) = H(R_{p,1}, R_{p,2}) + H(R_{p,1}, R_{p,3}) + H(R_{p,1}, R_{p,4}). \tag{6}$$

Luminance Constraint. There is an additional constraint related to the fourth image, which can be combined with mutual information or Census transform costs. Let us assume that there are four corresponding points p_1, p_2, p_3 and p_4 in each image. Because the fourth image represents the luminance, the corresponding points should satisfy the following equation:

$$\hat{I}_4(p_4) = G \cdot I_1(p_1) + R \cdot I_2(p_2) + B \cdot I_3(p_3), \tag{7}$$

where point's intensity is denoted by $I(p)$. Coefficients G, R and B in the previous equation depend on the color filters of the cameras. In case there is a large difference between the left and right side of the equation, it is likely that points are not correspondences. Based on this assumption, the luminance cost can be written as:

$$C_L = |I_4(p_4) - \hat{I}_4(p_4)|. \tag{8}$$

2.3 Disparity Estimation

We evaluate two different disparity estimation methods, graph cuts and semi-global matching. These methods aim to find correct disparities for every pixel in the image by using matching costs and smoothness assumptions. The idea is to favor disparity configurations in which disparity varies smoothly among neighbouring pixels.

Graph cuts method performs a global optimization process over the whole image. We employ the multi-label optimization library developed by Veksler et al. [15]. Global energy is minimized with an expansion move algorithm using the truncated absolute difference as a smoothness cost. Truncated absolute difference gave the best overall performance over Potts model.

Semi-global Matching (SGM) approximates the global energy by pathwise optimization from all directions through the image. It approximates 2D smoothness constraint by combining many 1D constraints. This work implements the semi-global block matching algorithm that is part of the OpenCV library. It is a variation of the original SGM algorithm in [10]. In contrast to graph cuts, the SGM performs post-processing steps such as subpixel interpolation, left-right consistency check and speckle filtering.

2.4 Parallax Correction

After the disparity estimation, the parallax error between the images can be corrected. In practise, pixels in the red filtered image I_2 and blue filtered image I_3 are remapped using the calculated disparity map. The green filtered image I_1 is used as a reference so there is no need to remap the image. Whereas image I_2 can be directly remapped using the disparity map, trifocal tensor is needed to remap image I_3. After remapping, the corresponding pixels will have the same image coordinates. In case the point does not correspond to any particular pixel, the pixels intensity is computed from neighboring pixels using bilinear interpolation.

An RGB image is then constructed by simply combining images I_1, I_2 and I_3. In this implementation, the luminance image I_4 is not used when forming the final image. Pixels that are located near the borders of the image may not be visible in all the images. These areas are removed from the final image based on maximum disparity parameter.

3   Experiments

The performance of the image fusion algorithm was evaluated using a test camera system. The evaluation aims to find the best combination of similarity measures and disparity estimation methods for the image fusion. Input images were captured with a traditional Bayer matrix camera, which was moved between the shots. In order to simulate the presence of different color filters, the original 24-bit RGB images were split to separate color channels. Luminance image was created from the original RGB image by weighting each color component by different amounts.

Test scenes are shown in Figure 4. Tea, Flowers and Grass datasets were captured using the same camera arrangement as illustrated in Figure 1. The baseline was approximately 12 mm for each pair of horizontal and vertical camera positions. We also used the standard Middlebury stereo datasets Teddy, Cones and Venus in which cameras are parallel to each other [16,17]. Ground truth disparity maps were available for the images 2 and 6 in each dataset. In order to perform comparison to ground truth, we used images 2 and 6 as a first and second input image. Improved fused image could have be obtained if adjacent images were used. Image sizes and disparity ranges are listed in Table 1.

Fig. 4. Reference views for the Teddy, Cones, Venus, Tea, Flowers and Grass datasets

Table 1. Image sizes and disparity ranges in pixels

	Tea	Flowers	Grass	Teddy	Cones	Venus
Image size	1000x745	1150x860	1024x783	450x375	450x375	434x383
Disparity range	64	32	32	64	64	32

Fused images were compared against the original RGB images captured by the camera system. We also measured the similarity of the images using the peak signal-to-noise ratio (PSNR) and structural similarity (SSIM). SSIM values are computed for each channel of the image. Value of 1 represents the perfect match. The accuracy of the disparity estimation was evaluated by counting the number of invalid disparities in the disparity map. Disparities were not evaluated in occluded areas since occlusion handling was not implemented. Disparity was classified as invalid if its value differs more than 1 pixel from the ground truth. Smoothness parameters of the semi-global matching and graph cuts methods were manually tuned for the mutual information and Census transform costs. Parameters were kept constant for Tea, Flowers and Grass datasets. Different, although constant parameters were used for Middlebury datasets.

Table 2 shows the statistics for both similarity measures when graph cuts method is used. Census transform outperforms the mutual information in all test cases if error percentages are considered. There are no significant differences in PSNR and SSIM scores.

Table 2. Results of graph cuts method

	Mutual Information			Census		
	Errors	PSNR	SSIM (rgb)	Errors	PSNR	SSIM (rgb)
Teddy	11.01	37.97	0.86; 1.00; 0.81	7.60	37.57	0.87; 1.00; 0.81
Cones	7.11	33.97	0.83; 1.00; 0.79	4.92	34.42	0.85; 1.00; 0.79
Venus	2.80	39.56	0.89; 1.00; 0.83	1.49	39.26	0.89; 1.00; 0.83
Tea	–	39.47	0.95; 1.00; 0.88	–	39.58	0.95; 1.00; 0.88
Flowers	–	39.44	0.94; 1.00; 0.86	–	39.36	0.94; 1.00; 0.86
Grass	–	33.97	0.82; 1.00; 0.84	–	34.12	0.83; 1.00; 0.85

The results of semi-global matching are shown in Table 3. As with graph cuts, the Census transform performs better than the mutual information. SGM further improves the accuracy of disparity estimation over graph cuts. PSNR and SSIM scores are also better. The main improvements come from the sub-pixel accurate disparity estimation and left-right consistency check. The resulting disparity map and fused image for the Teddy dataset is shown in Figure 5.

Table 3. Results of semi-global matching

	Mutual Information			Census		
	Errors	PSNR	SSIM (rgb)	Errors	PSNR	SSIM (rgb)
Teddy	10.92	38.43	0.88; 1.00; 0.81	6.81	38.32	0.89; 1.00; 0.81
Cones	6.84	34.95	0.86; 1.00; 0.79	4.67	35.10	0.87; 1.00; 0.79
Venus	2.96	41.22	0.91; 1.00; 0.83	1.30	40.40	0.90; 1.00; 0.83
Tea	–	40.45	0.96; 1.00; 0.89	–	40.36	0.96; 1.00; 0.89
Flowers	–	40.05	0.94; 1.00; 0.87	–	40.12	0.95; 1.00; 0.87
Grass	–	34.19	0.82; 1.00; 0.84	–	35.01	0.86; 1.00; 0.87

The advantages of using trifocal tensor and four different views are best demonstrated with disparity maps. The left most disparity map in Figure 6 is

Disparity map   Error map   Reference image   Fused image

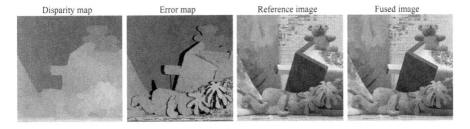

Fig. 5. The result of semi-global matching and Census transform on Teddy dataset. Red areas in the error map represent erroneous disparities and black areas are occlusions.

2-view (err = 13.08 [%])   3-view (err = 10.91 [%])   4-view (err = 8.25 [%])   4-view + lum. (err = 4.67 [%])

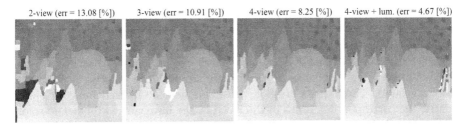

Fig. 6. Disparity maps generated using two, three and four views

generated using only one pair of stereo images, graph cuts and Census transform. In this example, the green filtered image is matched to red filtered image. The second image is matched using green, red and blue filtered images and trifocal tensor. The third image uses all four input images but does not take advantage of the luminance constraint. Adding the luminance constraint to the cost function will further improve the disparity map as shown in the last image. Consequently, the disparity map will also produce the best fused image. Smoothness parameter was tuned for each test so that the disparity map would be as accurate as possible.

Even though the disparity maps, which are computed using Census transform are more accurate, the differences in the fused images are quite imperceptible. Some of the errors in the disparity map are only slightly inaccurate. Moreover, it can be noted that even though the image fusion is based on the disparity map, the errors in the disparity map do not necessarily propagate to the fused image. For example, there are erroneous disparities in the right side of the teddy bear in Figure 5 but there are no color errors in the corresponding areas in the fused image. This is true for many other areas in all of the datasets.

On the other hand, even the ground truth disparity map does not give the perfect output image because occlusions are not considered. In fact, for all Middlebury datasets it holds that the estimated disparity map gives better results than the ground truth map. In the estimated disparity map, the occluded areas are interpolated from the occluder rather than from the occludee. From the viewpoint of the first view, this will result to somewhat incorrect disparity map. However, such disparity map works better for the image fusion.

Fig. 7. Synthetic refocusing on Grass dataset. Details from the reference image (green), fused image (blue), foreground in focus image (yellow) and disparity map (red).

In general, color errors are most noticeable in occluded areas and near discontinuities. This is expected because proper occlusion handling is not implemented. Figure 7a shows a smaller image patch chosen for the closer inspection (blue rectangle). The red flower on the foreground occludes some of the grass on the background. These areas are not visible in the blue filtered image. Consequently, the corresponding areas in the fused image have turned blue. The color error results from the fact that missing color values in the blue filtered image are taken from the pixels that belong to red flower.

All tests were performed with a desktop PC that has Intel Core i5 3.20 GHz CPU and 8 GB of RAM. Computational time highly depends on the chosen disparity estimation method, image size and disparity range. Not surprisingly, the graph cut method is significantly slower than the semi-global matching. For example, the average running time of the graph cuts method with Census transform is 69 seconds for the Tea dataset and 55 seconds for the Grass dataset. The corresponding times for the semi-global matching are 8.4 s and 4.9 s.

The result of synthetic refocusing on Grass dataset is shown in Figure 7(b-c). The underlying disparity map was computed using SGM and Census transform. The overall quality of the depth of field effect is good. The refocusing ability depends on the accuracy of the disparity map. There are small inaccuracies in the disparity map near the edges of the flower (red rectangle). As a result, some of these areas are unrealistically blurred in the refocused image (yellow rectangle). Errors are most visible in the middle of the image where foreground is in focus.

4   Conclusion

An image fusion algorithm was designed and implemented for a four-aperture camera. According to experiments, the semi-global matching with Census transform gave the best overall performance. The quality of the fused images is near the reference images. Closer inspection of the fused images reveals small color errors, typically found near the object borders. Future improvements, such as occlusion handling would significantly increase the quality of fused images.

It was also demonstrated that the robustness of disparity estimation increases when matching costs from multiple views are combined. Event though this work is focused on image fusion, similar approach could be used in other multi-spectral matching problems. One could also add more cameras to the system without significantly increasing the computation time. Disparity estimation would stay the same, only the matching costs would be different. Moreover, there are no limitation on how cameras are arranged since algorithm utilizes trifocal tensors. Our test setup did not show all the advantages of the actual four-aperture camera because test images were captured with a Bayer filter camera. However, the promising test results imply that further research and development of the algorithm is desirable. The four-aperture camera has potential to become a serious competitor to the traditional Bayer matrix cameras in portable devices.

References

1. Suda, Y.: Image sensing apparatus and its control method, control program, and storage medium for correcting position deviation of images. US Patent No. 7847843 (2010)
2. Yu, Y., Zhang, Z.: Digital cameras using multiple sensors with multiple lenses. US Patent No. 6611289 (2003)
3. Kolehmainen, T., Rytivaara, M., Tokkonen, T., Mäkelä, J., Ojala, K.: Imaging device. US Patent No. 7453510 (2008)
4. Gere, D., S.: Image capture using luminance and chrominance sensors. US Patent No. 8497897 (2013)
5. Sung, G.-Y., Park, D.-S., Lee, H.-Y., Kim, S.-S., Kim, C.-Y.:Camera module. European Patent No. 1871091 (2007)
6. LinX Imaging: Technology presentation (2014). http://linximaging.com/imaging/
7. Venkataraman, K., Lelescu, D., Duparre, J., McMahon, A., Molina, G., Chatterjee, P., Mullis, R., Nayar, S.: PiCam: An ultra-thin high performance monolithic camera array. ACM Transactions on Graphics $32(6)$, 13 (2013)
8. Hernández, C.: Lens blur in the new google camera app (2014). googleresearch.blogspot.com/2014/04/lens-blur-in-new-google-camera-app.html
9. Kim, J., Kolmogorov, V., Zabih, R.: Visual correspondence using energy minimization and mutual information. In: The Proceedings of the 9th IEEE International Conference on Computer Vision, vol. 2, pp. 1033–1040 (2003)
10. Hirschmüller, H.: Stereo processing by semiglobal matching and mutual information. IEEE Transactions on Pattern Analysis and Machine Intelligence $30(2)$, 328–341 (2008)
11. Hartley, R., Zisserman, A.: Multiple view geometry in computer vision, 2nd edn. Cambridge University Press, United States of America, 655 p. (2003)
12. Hirschmüller, H., Scharstein, D.: Evaluation of stereo matching costs on images with radiometric differences. IEEE Transactions on Pattern Analysis and Machine Intelligence $31(9)$, 1582–1599 (2008)
13. Egnal, G.: Mutual information as a stereo correspondence measure. University of Pennsylvania, Department of Computer and Information Science, Technical Report No. MS-CIS-00-20 (2000)
14. Zabih, R., Woodfill, J.: Non-parametric local transforms for computing visual correspondence. In: Eklundh, J.-O. (ed.) ECCV 1994. LNCS, vol. 801, pp. 151–158. Springer, Heidelberg (1994)

15. Boykov, Y., Veksler, O., Zabih, R.: Fast approximate energy minimization via graph cuts. IEEE Transactions on Pattern Analysis and Machine Intelligence **23**(11), 1222–1239 (2001)
16. Scharstein, D., Szeliski, R.: A taxonomy and evaluation of dense two-frame stereo correspondence algorithms. International Journal of Computer Vision **47**(1–3), 7–42 (2002)
17. Scharstein, D., Szeliski, R.: High-accuracy stereo depth maps using structured light. IEEE Computer Society Conference on Computer Vision and Pattern Recognition **1**, 195–202 (2003)

Optimizing the Accuracy and Compactness of Multi-view Reconstructions

Markus Ylimäki$^{(\boxtimes)}$, Juho Kannala, and Janne Heikkilä

Center for Machine Vision Research, University of Oulu,
P.O.Box 4500, 90014 Oulu, Finland
{markus.ylimaki,juho.kannala,janne.heikkila}@ee.oulu.fi

Abstract. Current evaluation metrics and benchmarks for multi-view stereo reconstruction methods mainly focus on measuring the accuracy and completeness and they do not explicitly measure the compactness, and especially the compactness-accuracy trade-off of the reconstructed models. To answer this issue, we present an evaluation method that completes and improves the existing benchmarks. The proposed method is capable of jointly evaluating the accuracy, completeness and compactness of a three-dimensional reconstruction which is represented as a triangle mesh. The evaluation enables the optimization of both the whole reconstruction pipeline from multi-view stereo data to a compact mesh and the mesh simplification. The method takes the ground truth model and the reconstruction as input and outputs an accuracy and completeness value as well as the compactness measure for the reconstructed model. The values of the evaluation measures are independent of the scale of the scene, and therefore easy to interpret.

Keywords: Multi-view stereo evaluation · Compactness-accuracy trade-off · Mesh optimization

1 Introduction

Multi-view stereo reconstruction methods, which create three-dimensional scene models solely from photographs, have improved a lot during the recent years [15,17]. The focus of research has been shifting from basic algorithms to system aspects and large-scale models [1,16,18]. Currently there are automatic reconstruction pipelines which are able to produce compact mesh models of both outdoor and indoor environments from images [2–4,11,12,19]. In addition, several companies, such as Google, Nokia HERE, and Acute3D, have shown interest and efforts towards city-scale models.

The compactness of mesh models is essential for storing and rendering large-scale reconstructions. In particular, for mobile device applications, the models should be light-weight and streamable, yet realistic and accurate. Thus, in order to advance the development of image-based modeling techniques further, there is a need for evaluation metrics and benchmarks that enable quantitative evaluation of trade-offs between the compactness and accuracy of the reconstructed models.

© Springer International Publishing Switzerland 2015
G. Azzopardi and N. Petkov (Eds.): CAIP 2015, Part II, LNCS 9257, pp. 171–183, 2015.
DOI: 10.1007/978-3-319-23117-4_15

In fact, the recent progress of multi-view stereo has been largely driven by benchmark datasets, which have enabled quantitative comparisons of different methods. The Middlebury [14] and EPFL [15] datasets have been widely used, and recently a similar dataset with more scenes was proposed in [8]. However, the evaluation metrics used in these standard benchmarks have solely focused on measuring the reconstruction quality, i.e. accuracy and completeness, and do not explicitly measure the compactness of the models. Therefore the previous evaluation metrics can not be used for evaluating compactness-accuracy trade-off and are hence not suitable for jointly optimizing the accuracy and compactness of the results of the reconstruction pipeline.

The problem related to the lack of suitable evaluation metrics is reflected by the fact that most of the recent papers studying compactness aspects of reconstructions (e.g. [2,4,11,12]) do not perform quantitative evaluations of the compactness or compactness-accuracy trade-off. In fact, in the papers [2,4] the results are evaluated only visually.

In this paper, we address the aforementioned problem by proposing an evaluation method which is able to illustrate both the accuracy, completeness and compactness of the reconstructions with respect to the ground truth model. The method measures the accuracy and completeness jointly with the Jaccard index between the voxel representations of the ground truth model and the reconstruction. The compactness of the reconstruction is measured with a compression ratio representing the ratio of the number of vertices in the ground truth and the reconstruction. The relation between earlier evaluations and the proposed one is illustrated in Figure 1.

The proposed method is particularly suitable for evaluating the full reconstruction pipeline from images to a compact mesh but it can also be used to evaluate the following sub-tasks separately: (a) point cloud generation from a set of photographs, (b) surface mesh generation from a point cloud, and (c) surface mesh simplification. Further, the proposed evaluation metrics are not scale dependent and therefore the results are easy to interpret for different ground truth models. The proposed method is also versatile and flexible because both the ground truth model and evaluated reconstructions can be either point clouds or triangle meshes.

The rest of the paper is organized as follows. First, Section 2 presents the most essential related work. Then the evaluation method is descibed in more detail in Section 3. Evaluation results are presented and discussed in Section 4 and Section 5 concludes the paper.

2   Related Work

The first widely used benchmark dataset for evaluating MVS algorithms was the Middlebury Multi-View Stereo Data [14]. The data consists of two different scenes, both having three sets with a varying number of low-resolution images. The evaluation is available in the Internet[1] where anyone can submit their own

---

[1] http://vision.middlebury.edu/mview/eval/

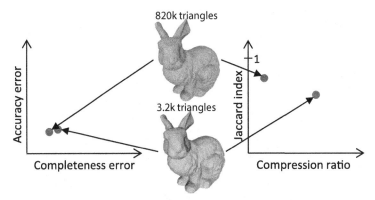

Fig. 1. Two mesh evaluations plotted with the current evaluation metric [8] (left) and with the proposed one. The Jaccard index joins the accuracy and completeness of the current metric and that enables the compression ratio, illustrating the compactness, to be shown in the same graph. According to the current evaluation metric the meshes are almost equal even though the latter mesh has over 250 times less triangles.

result for evaluation and compare the performance of their method with dozens of other MVS algorithms. Later, Strecha et al published the EPFL evaluation benchmark [15] consisting of more scenes with higher resolution[2]. The evaluation is no longer available, but the laser scanned ground truth models for two scenes are still downloadable on the web page. The recently published DTU dataset [8] further improved the existing benchmarks with totally 80 datasets covering a wider range of 3D scenes.

The current evaluation benchmarks evaluate the accuracy and completeness of the reconstructions. In [8], accuracy is measured as the distance from the reconstruction to the ground truth, and the completeness is measured from the ground truth to the reconstruction. Therefore, changes in the compactness of the reconstruction cannot be explicitly observed. The proposed method focuses on the compactness evaluation but still measures the accuracy and completeness jointly with the Jaccard index. As far as we know, this evaluation is the first of its kind, and thus, brings a new aspect for reconstruction evaluation in the future research challenges.

The main parts of a typical reconstruction pipeline from MVS data to a compact mesh, that need to be evaluated, are the point cloud creation and the meshing. In the pipeline, the consistency data of photographs is first converted into a three-dimensional point cloud using e.g. PMVS [6]. Then the point cloud is transformed into a surface mesh using methods like Poisson Surface Reconstruction (PSR) [9] or energy minimization approach [10]. Thus, both phases affect the compactness of the final reconstruction and can be optimized separately by the proposed evaluation metric.

The meshing process, if not already optimised, could be followed by mesh simplification [5] which tries to optimize the mesh by converting several

---

[2] http://cvlabwww.epfl.ch/data/multiview/

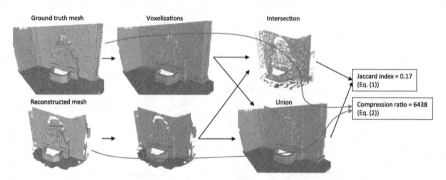

Fig. 2. An overview of the proposed evaluation pipeline with an example data. The ground truth and the reconstruction are converted to voxel representations. The Jaccard index is the ratio of intersection and union of the voxelizations. The compression ratio represents the ratio of the number of vertices in the ground truth and the reconstruction.

triangles into one which follow the original surface as well as possible. One simple approach, presented in [13], clusters the vertices of the triangle mesh and then triangulates the cluster centres to form a new mesh with fewer faces. On the other hand, one of the top performing decimation methods, presented in [7], simplify the surface mesh by iterative contraction of vertex pairs (edges) so that the geometric error approximation, represented using quadric matrices, is maintained. However, although widely used, the method in [7] is almost twenty years old. With the proposed method, the mesh decimation algorithms can be quantitatively evaluated, which facilitates further developments.

3   Evaluation Method

3.1   Overview

The proposed evaluation method takes the ground truth and the reconstruction as input and outputs two evaluation values: the Jaccard index J and the compression ratio R. The evaluation pipeline with an example data is presented in Figure 2. The input data can be meshes or point clouds. The Jaccard index illustrates the accuracy and completeness of the reconstruction, indicating the proportion of the ground truth mesh which is covered by the reconstruction within a certain threshold. The index is calculated using the voxel representations of the ground truth and the reconstruction and the threshold is the width of a voxel. The compression ratio illustrates the compactness of the reconstruction representing the ratio of the number of vertices in the ground truth and the reconstruction.

The proposed evaluation method consists of three phases: (1) the initialization of the voxel grids of the ground truth and the reconstruction, (2) transforming the ground truth and the reconstruction into voxel representations and (3) the actual calculation of the evaluation values. The following sections give more detailed descriptions of the phases.

3.2   Voxel Grid Initialization

The resolution of the voxel grids is defined by the width of a voxel and the size of the bounding box covering both the reconstruction and the ground truth. The width of a voxel is defined by the average distance between the ground truth vertices. That is, the width is twice as long as the median distance between a point and its k:th nearest neighbor. The value of k defines the sensitivity of the evaluation. Thus, too large voxel width smooths the details of the reconstruction and too small width causes holes in the voxelization of the ground truth. However, we found a value that can be kept as a default width for datasets for which the ground truth has a uniform vertex/point density. In all our experiments, the value of k was fixed to 10.

The bounding box is turned into a grid of voxels by dividing its dimensions with the defined voxel width. The grid is presented in an integer coordinate frame where every voxel has integer index coordinates. This grid is used in the voxel representations of the ground truth and the reconstruction.

3.3   Converting a Mesh to a Voxel Representation

At first, both the ground truth and the reconstruction are converted to point clouds. The vertices of the ground truth mesh form the ground truth point cloud which is assumed to be dense, so that the average distance between points is below the voxel width. The mesh reconstruction is converted to a point cloud by sampling points on the triangles so that the density of the points matches the density of the ground truth vertices. Then, the point clouds are mapped into the integer coordinate frame of the voxel grid. The voxels are labelled as occupied if at least one point is inside the voxel or as unoccupied otherwise.

3.4   Calculation of Evaluation Values

The Jaccard index is calculated by comparing the voxel representations of the ground truth and the reconstruction. Lets denote the voxel grids of the ground truth and the reconstruction with $\mathbf{V_g}$ and $\mathbf{V_r}$, respectively. Now, the Jaccard index J is defined with the equation:

$$J = \frac{|\mathbf{V_g} \cap \mathbf{V_r}|}{|\mathbf{V_g} \cup \mathbf{V_r}|}, \tag{1}$$

where $|\cdot|$ means the number of voxels. Thus, the value of $|\mathbf{V_g} \cap \mathbf{V_r}|$ is the number of voxels which are occupied both in $\mathbf{V_g}$ and $\mathbf{V_r}$ and $|\mathbf{V_g} \cup \mathbf{V_r}|$ is the total number of occupied voxels in both grids. The Jaccard index is in the interval [0,1].

The compression ratio R is defined with the equation:

$$R = \frac{N_{GT}}{N_{REC}}, \tag{2}$$

where N_{GT} is the number of vertices/points in the ground truth model and N_{REC} is the number of vertices/points in the evaluated point cloud or mesh. Thus, the compression ratio illustrates the ratio of memory usage of the compared models.

4   Experiments

4.1   Overview

The experiments were carried out in three phases. First, the proposed evaluation method was tested with the range scanned data from the Stanford 3D Scanning Repository[3]. Then the results of the proposed method were compared with those of the DTU benchmark dataset in [8] and finally, a couple of evaluations were made with the EPFL dataset in [15]. The experiments are described in the following sections.

4.2   Stanford Range Scan Dataset

In the first phase, the proposed method was tested with the range scanned data of the Stanford bunny. Notice that this kind of data does not contain the computer vision aspect but can still be used for benchmarking meshing and mesh simplification methods. The bunny data consists of ten scans which were transformed into the same coordinate frame to form a single point cloud. Then, the point cloud was turned into a triangular mesh using the Poisson Surface Reconstruction [9] (PSR) and our implementation of [10] (LAB). PSR was used with the default parameters except the Octree Depth which was set to 14. The parameters for LAB were $\alpha_{vis} = 32$, $\lambda_{qual} = 5$ and $\sigma = 0.001$. The meshes were then gradually decimated in Meshlab[4] using the Quadric Edge Collapse Decimation [7] (QECD) by halving the amount of triangles in every step. Meshes were also decimated with the Clustering Decimation [13] (CD) so that the step sizes were roughly the same as in QECD. All the meshes were evaluated with the proposed method. The results are presented in Figure 3. The x-axis illustrates the compactness as the compression ratio which represents the ratio of the number of vertices in the ground truth and the reconstruction (see Eq. 2). Notice the logarithmic scale on the x-axis. The y-axis is the Jaccard index calculated with Equation 1. In addition to the meshes, also the point cloud, from which the meshes were created, was evaluated. That is presented as a single dot (PC) in the figure.

The figure clearly shows the difference between the decimation methods. That is, with CD the Jaccard indices of the meshes drops much earlier than with QECD. Also, when looking at a few left most meshes, i.e. the most complex ones, the LAB meshes have somewhat better Jaccard index and compression ratio in comparison with the PSR meshes.

The main reason for the Jaccard index difference between the evaluated point cloud and the mesh reconstruction is the fact that the evaluated point cloud is the ground truth model. In addition, the ground truth has some holes which do not appear in the reconstructions, and therefore, they also drop the index a bit. PSR tends to round the sharp edges of the reconstruction, and therefore, the LAB meshes have a somewhat better Jaccard index.

---

[3] http://graphics.stanford.edu/data/3Dscanrep/
[4] http://meshlab.sourceforge.net/

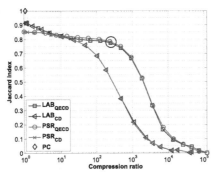

Fig. 3. Evaluation result of the Stanford Bunny. LAB and PSR refer to the mesh creation methods, i.e. [10] and [9], respectively. Subscripts QECD and CD refer to the used decimation methods, that is [7] and [13], respectively. PC is the point cloud which was used to create the meshes. The black circle indicate the decimated mesh presented in Figure 4.

Fig. 4. Bunny voxelizations and mesh reconstructions. Top: the ground truth point cloud (left) and voxel representations of the ground truth and the LAB mesh reconstruction. Bottom: The triangle mesh of the reconstruction created with PSR [9] (left) and LAB [10] and the triangle mesh decimated from the LAB mesh by QECD.

Figure 4 shows the ground truth point cloud, the voxel presentation of it, the voxel presentation of the LAB mesh, the PSR and LAB meshes and a simplified

version of the LAB mesh decimated with QECD. The voxel presentations of the
ground truth and the reconstruction look very similar, because the reconstruction
was created from the ground truth data. The voxelization of the ground truth
is dense enough to preserve the details of the model but still sparse enough to
make the voxelization uniform regardless of the minor misalignment issues of
the scans. The decimated mesh has lost some details but has still relatively high
Jaccard index as indicated with the black circle in Figure 3.

4.3   DTU Multi-view Dataset

In the second experiment, we illustrate the difference between the results of the
proposed evaluation method and those of DTU benchmark [8]. We took the point
cloud and mesh reconstructions (created with PMVS [6] and PSR [9], respectively) from the DTU package (House, scan no. 025) and did the decimations for
the mesh with QECD [7] and CD [13], like with the range data in Section 4.2, and
evaluated the meshes both with the proposed method and DTU method. The
meshes were evaluated against the structured light reference (STL) provided by
DTU. The results are presented in Figure 5. In DTU evaluations the accuracy
and completeness are illustrated with mean distances in millimetres from the
reconstruction to STL and from STL to the reconstruction, respectively.

   As the results show, both evaluations are able to illustrate the difference
between the decimation methods, but DTU does not explicitly show the com-

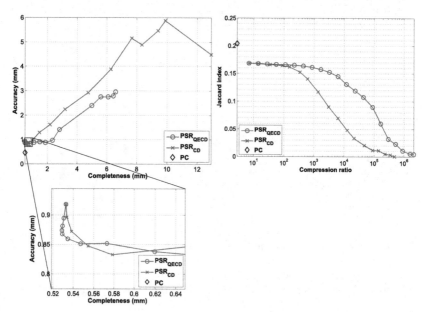

Fig. 5. Comparison of DTU evaluation (left) [8] and the proposed one (right). The
original mesh provided in DTU dataset is created with [9] (PSR) and the decimations
were made with [7] (QECD) and [13] (CD). PC is the point cloud which was used to
generate the original mesh.

Fig. 6. Voxel presentations of the House. Top: Voxelization of the ground truth (left) and the PMVS point cloud. Bottom: the PSR triangle mesh of the reconstruction (left) and its voxelization. Ellipses highlight the areas which contain surfaces that are incorrectly (black) or correctly (white) reconstructed in the mesh (bottom) but do not appear either in the ground truth or the point cloud (top).

pactness of the reconstructions. Also notice that DTU values are in millimeters, and thus, scale dependent and more difficult to interpret. In addition, due to the distance differences between the values, the interpretation of DTU result is not possible without a closer look of the first values.

Both methods give better accuracy or Jaccard index for the point cloud (PC) than the meshes. That happens because the mesh reconstructions contain both correct and incorrect surfaces that exist neither in the structured light reference nor the point cloud, as illustrated in Figure 6. In other words, the ground truth scans are incomplete. Due to PSR meshing, the incorrectly reconstructed areas are mainly located at the outer boudaries of the reconstruction (black ellipses). However, PSR can also fill holes correctly (white ellipses).

The metric used in DTU benchmark is not able to detect pure compactness change. For example, regardless of the number of triangles (if at least two), the accuracy and the completeness of a rectangular wall do not change. That is, the more planar surfaces in the scene the less the compactness affects the evaluation results of DTU benchmark.

4.4   EPFL Multi-view Dataset

In the third phase, we performed evaluations using the two publicly available models from EPFL dataset [15]; Fountain-P11 and Herz-Jesu-P8. Point cloud reconstructions were first created using the PMVS program [6]. The number of points in the point clouds were then reduced to about 500k points in order to run our implementation of [10] in reasonable time. The same reduced point cloud was used in all mesh constructions and evaluations. Now, the evaluation results were obtained like with the range data in Section 4.2. The parameters for PSR and LAB were the same as in Section 4.2 except σ in LAB which was now fixed to 0.01. The point cloud (PC) which was used to create the meshes was also evaluated. The results are presented in Figure 7 (right).

In addition to the reconstruction evaluations, we performed the same decimations and evaluations for the ground truth meshes. Also, the point clouds containing only those vertices of the ground truths which are in the field of view of at least two or three cameras were evaluated. These point clouds illustrate the theoretical maximum part of the ground truth model which could be reconstructed using MVS methods. The results are presented in Figure 7 (left). Like the range data results, the results clearly show the difference between the

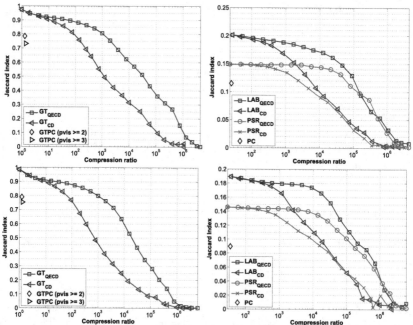

Fig. 7. Evaluations of Fountain-P11 (top) and Herz-Jesu-P8 (bottom) datasets. Left: The evaluations of the ground truth meshes (GT) decimated with [7] (QECD) and [13] (CD) and the evaluations of the ground truth vertices lying in the field of view of at least two or three cameras. Right: The evaluations of the LAB [10] and PSR [9] reconstructions decimated with QECD and CD and the evaluations of the point clouds which were used to generate the corresponding meshes.

decimation methods (QECD vs CD) as well as mesh creation methods (LAB vs PSR). The difference between the mesh and point cloud reconstructions is explained mainly by the sparsity of the point cloud. In addition to the sparsity, the difference between the point cloud reconstruction and the ground truth point cloud where points are in the field of view of three cameras (GTPC, pvis>=3), is explained by the noise, holes and missing regions in the PMVS point cloud (bottom left vs bottom right in Figure 8). The holes and missing regions result from self occlusions and certain textureless areas. Also, a possible misalignment between the ground truth model and images may cause errors in the PMVS point cloud and thus also in the mesh reconstruction.

Fig. 8. Voxel presentations of the Fountain-P11. Top: Voxelization of the ground truth (left) and the reconstruction. Bottom: Voxelization of the ground truth vertices which are in the field of view of at least three cameras (left) and the voxelization of the PMVS point cloud. Notice the sparsity, noise, holes and missing regions on the right voxelizations compared with voxelizations on the left.

5   Conclusion

In this paper, we presented a method for the evaluation of multi-view stereo algorithms and triangle mesh decimations. The method enables the evaluation of the compactness-accuracy trade-off of the reconstructed models and thus completes and improves the existing evaluation benchmarks from Middlebury [14], by Strecha et al. [15] and Jensen et al. [8]. The proposed method facilitates optimization of both the reconstruction pipeline from MVS data to a compact triangle mesh and the mesh simplification. The method takes the ground truth model and the reconstruction as input and outputs the accuracy and the completeness of the model, presented with the Jaccard index, and the compactness measure. As presented in the experiments, the method can clearly illustrate the accuracy and compactness differences of certain meshes created with different meshing and decimation algorithms. In addition, the values of evaluation measures are independent of the scale of scene and can be used for any dataset with a ground truth model.

References

1. Agarwal, S., Furukawa, Y., Snavely, N., Simon, I., Curless, B., Seitz, S.M., Szeliski, R.: Building Rome in a day. Communications of the ACM (2011)
2. Bodis-Szomoru, A., Riemenschneider, H., Van Gool, L.: Fast, approximate piecewise-planar modeling based on sparse structure-from-motion and superpixels. In: IEEE Conference on Computer Vision and Pattern Recognition (CVPR) (2014)
3. Cabral, R., Furukawa, Y.: Piecewise planar and compact floorplan reconstruction from images. In: IEEE Conference on Computer Vision and Pattern Recognition (CVPR), pp. 628–635, June 2014
4. Chauve, A.L., Labatut, P., Pons, J.P.: Robust piecewise-planar 3D reconstruction and completion from large-scale unstructured point data. In: IEEE Conference on Computer Vision and Pattern Recognition (CVPR) (2010)
5. Cignoni, P., Montani, C., Scopigno, R.: A comparison of mesh simplification algorithms. Computers & Graphics **22**, 37–54 (1997)
6. Furukawa, Y., Ponce, J.: Accurate, dense, and robust multi-view stereopsis. IEEE Transactions on Pattern Analysis and Machine Intelligence (TPAMI) **32**(8), 1362–1376 (2010)
7. Garland, M., Heckbert, P.S.: Surface simplification using quadric error metrics. In: 24th Annual Conference on Computer Graphics and Interactive Techniques (1997)
8. Jensen, R., Dahl, A., Vogiatzis, G., Tola, E., Aanaes, H.: Large scale multi-view stereopsis evaluation. In: IEEE Conference on Computer Vision and Pattern Recognition (CVPR) (2014)
9. Kazhdan, M., Bolitho, M., Hoppe, H.: Poisson surface reconstruction. In: Eurographics Symposium on Geometry Processing (2006)
10. Labatut, P., Pons, J.P., Keriven, R.: Robust and efficient surface reconstruction from range data. Computer Graphics Forum (CGF) **28**(8), 2275–2290 (2009)
11. Lafarge, F., Alliez, P.: Surface Reconstruction through Point Set Structuring. Research Report RR-8174, INRIA, December 2012
12. Lafarge, F., Keriven, R., Bredif, M., Vu, H.H.: A hybrid multi-view stereo algorithm for modeling urban scenes. IEEE Transactions on Pattern Analysis and Machine Intelligence (TPAMI) **35**(1), 5–17 (2013)
13. Rossignac, J., Borrel, P.: Multi-resolution 3d approximations for rendering complex scenes. In: Falcidieno, B., Kunii, T. (eds.) Methods and Applications. IFIP, pp. 455–465. Springer, Heidelberg (1993)
14. Seitz, S., Curless, B., Diebel, J., Scharstein, D., Szeliski, R.: A comparison and evaluation of multi-view stereo reconstruction algorithms. In: IEEE Conference on Computer Vision and Pattern Recognition (CVPR), pp. 519–528 (2006)
15. Strecha, C., von Hansen, W., Van Gool, L., Fua, P., Thoennessen, U.: On benchmarking camera calibration and multi-view stereo for high resolution imagery. In: IEEE Conference on Computer Vision and Pattern Recognition (CVPR) (2008)

16. Tola, E., Strecha, C., Fua, P.: Efficient large-scale multi-view stereo for ultra high-resolution image sets. Machine Vision and Applications **23**(5), 903–920 (2012)
17. Vu, H.H., Labatut, P., Pons, J.P., Keriven, R.: High accuracy and visibility-consistent dense multiview stereo. IEEE Transactions on Pattern Analysis and Machine Intelligence (TPAMI) **34**(5), 889–901 (2012)
18. Wu, C.: Towards linear-time incremental structure from motion. In: International Conference on 3D Vision (3DV), pp. 127–134, June 2013
19. Wu, C., Agarwal, S., Curless, B., Seitz, S.: Schematic surface reconstruction. In: IEEE Conference on Computer Vision and Pattern Recognition (CVPR), pp. 1498–1505, June 2012

Multiframe Super-Resolution
for Flickering Objects

Atsushi Fukushima and Takahiro Okabe[✉]

Department of Artificial Intelligence, Kyushu Institute of Technology,
680-4 Kawazu, Iizuka, Fukuoka 820-8502, Japan
okabe@ai.kyutech.ac.jp

Abstract. In this paper, we propose a MAP-based multiframe super-resolution method for flickering objects such as LED electronic message boards. Since LED message boards often flicker at low refresh rates, missing areas where LEDs are off during the exposure time of a camera by chance are observed. To suppress unexpected artifacts due to those missing areas, our proposed method detects outlier pixels on the basis of the spatio-temporal analysis of pixel values, and removes them from the MAP estimation by incorporating the weights of pixels into the likelihood term. We conducted a number of experiments using both real and synthetic images, and qualitatively and quantitatively confirmed that our method works better than the existing methods.

Keywords: Image/video enhancement · Multiframe super-resolution · Maximum a posteriori estimation · Outlier removal · Electronic message board

1 Introduction

Electronic message boards are used for displaying various important and/or useful information such as news, weather forecasts, road traffic information and signs, arrival and departure information of flights and trains, and advertisements. Along with the popularization of mobile phones with cameras and car-mounted cameras, we have greater opportunities to capture the image sequences of electronic message boards. Since those image sequences are often low resolution, improving their image quality makes it easier for both us and computers to understand the messages displayed on them.

Most electronic message boards consist of LED arrays. In a similar manner to CRT displays, LED message boards often flicker at low refresh rates. When we capture an image sequence of such a flickering object with a long exposure time, flickering is not observed, but the high-frequency components of the images are lost due to motion blur. Recovering the high-frequency components of blurred images is still a challenging problem to be addressed. On the other hand, when capturing with a short exposure time, motion blur is reduced, but flickering is observed. For example, band-like dark areas, *i.e.* missing areas are observed in

© Springer International Publishing Switzerland 2015
G. Azzopardi and N. Petkov (Eds.): CAIP 2015, Part II, LNCS 9257, pp. 184–194, 2015.
DOI: 10.1007/978-3-319-23117-4_16

Fig. 1. Real images of an electronic message board: band-like dark areas are observed due to flickering.

Fig. 1; the LEDs in those areas are off during the exposure time of a camera by chance. In this paper, we address a novel super-resolution problem; super-resolution for flickering objects when missing areas are observed.

In general, super-resolution techniques are classified into two approaches; a learning-based one and a reconstruction-based one. The learning-based approach makes use of a set of example images, and is able to enhance image quality even from a single input image. However, when missing areas are observed in the single image, it is difficult, if not impossible, to detect and restore missing areas. Therefore, we address a reconstruction-based approach, which makes use of multiple input images of the same object, to super-resolution for flickering objects. In particular, we consider multiframe super-resolution based on MAP (Maximum-A-Posteriori) estimation[4].

Conventionally, multiframe super-resolution assumes that the brightness of an object of interest is time-invariant. However, the brightness of a flickering object such as an electronic message board changes temporally, and as a result the performance of the conventional multiframe super-resolution is significantly degraded when missing areas are observed. Accordingly, our proposed method detects those missing areas, *i.e.* outlier pixels on the basis of the spatio-temporal analysis of pixel values, and then removes those outlier pixels from the MAP estimation by incorporating the weights of pixels into the likelihood term. We conducted a number of experiments by using both real and synthetic images, and qualitatively and quantitatively confirmed that the proposed method works well for flickering objects.

Robust super-resolution is one of the most important research topics in image/video enhancement[1,2,7,8]. It has already been reported that outlier removal is effective for suppressing unexpected artifacts due to registration errors[7] and video compression[2]. The main contribution of this study is twofold; we experimentally demonstrate that (i) the framework of outlier removal is effective also for suppressing unexpected artifacts due to flickering objects such as electronic message boards, and that (ii) the spatio-temporal analysis of pixel values works well for detecting outliers caused by flickering.

The rest of this paper is organized as follows. We briefly summarize related work in Section 2. A MAP-based multiframe super-resolution method for flickering objects such as LED electronic message boards is proposed in Section 3. We report the experimental results in Section 4 and present concluding remarks in Section 5.

2   Related Work

Existing methods for robust super-resolution can be classified into two categories; one is based on robust estimator and the other is based on outlier removal. In this section, we briefly explain the existing methods in each category, and then describe the relationship to our proposed method.

The former approach makes use of robust estimator, which is insensitive to outliers. In order to reduce the effects of noises and errors in motion model and blur model, Farsiu *et al.*[1] propose a robust super-resolution method by using the L1-norm likelihood term and the edge-preserving regularization term. Zomet *et al.*[8] incorporate median estimator into the optimization of super-resolution reconstruction. Those methods can reduce unexpected artifacts due to outlier pixels without explicitly detecting them. However, it is difficult to remove the effects of outlier pixels throughly.

The latter approach explicitly detects outlier pixels and removes them from super-resolution reconstruction. Zhao and Sawhney[7] propose an optical flow based super-resolution method, and make use of outlier removal in order to get rid of registration errors. The framework of outlier removal is used also for dealing with multiple motions in a scene[6]. Ivanovski *et al.*[2] propose a super-resolution method robust to noises due to video compression.

Ivanovski's method is most closely related to ours, because it detects outliers pixel-wisely on the basis of the temporal analysis of pixel values. Specifically, they compute the median of pixel values at corresponding pixels in the observed image sequence, and then consider a pixel in a certain frame as outlier if the difference between its pixel value and the median is larger than a threshold. Unfortunately, however, their method is not suited for flickering objects, because the median can be outlier when missing areas are observed in more than half of the frames. In addition, we need to tune the threshold for detecting outliers manually.

3   Proposed Method

In this section, we propose multiframe super-resolution for flickering objects such as electronic message boards when missing areas are observed. We describe how the framework of outlier removal is used for dealing with missing areas due to flickering, and then describe how to detect outliers on the basis of the spatio-temporal analysis of pixel values.

3.1   Multiframe Super-Resolution with Outlier Removal

The relationship between a desired high-resolution image and observed low-resolution images is described by the observation model;

$$\boldsymbol{y}_f = \boldsymbol{D}\boldsymbol{B}_f\boldsymbol{M}_f\boldsymbol{x} + \boldsymbol{n}_f. \tag{1}$$

Fig. 2. Pixels in an observed low-resolution image are classified into three categories; true foreground, false background, and true background.

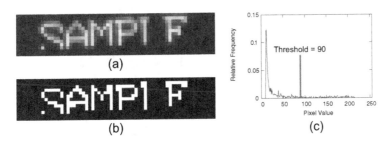

Fig. 3. True foreground detection based on spatial analysis: an observed image (a) is binarized by thresholding (b). The threshold is automatically determined from the histogram of pixel values (c) in the observed image on the basis of discriminant criterion. White pixels stand for true foreground.

Here, x and y_f ($f = 1, 2, 3, ..., F$) are the vectors representing the desired high-resolution image and observed low-resolution images, and F is the number of frames, *i.e.* the number of the observed images. M_f, B_f, and D are matrices representing the (camera) motion of the f-th frame, the point spread function (PSF) of the f-th frame, and the down sampling respectively. n_f is a vector representing noises in the f-th observed image. Hereafter, we describe the observation model as

$$y_f = A_f x + n_f, \tag{2}$$

where $A_f = D B_f M_f$ for the sake of simplicity.

Assuming that the noises obey the zero-mean Gaussian distribution, the cost function for multiframe super-resolution based on MAP estimation is given by

$$c(x) = \sum_{f=1}^{F} ||y_f - A_f x||_2^2 + \lambda ||H x||_2^2, \tag{3}$$

and the high-resolution image is estimated by minimizing the cost function $c(x)$ with respect to x. Here, the first and second terms represent the likelihood and prior knowledge of the high-resolution image, and λ is the parameter that balances those two terms. In order to obtain a smooth high-resolution image, high-pass filters are often used for H.

We assume that an object of interest is static except for flickering. Specifically, our proposed method assumes that characters and/or symbols themselves displayed on an electronic message board are fixed during capturing an image

188   A. Fukushima and T. Okabe

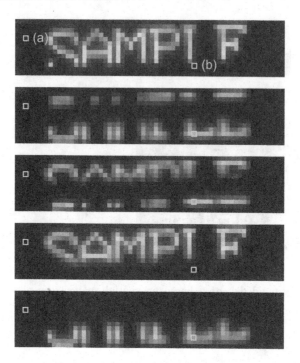

Fig. 4. Classification of true background and false background based on temporal analysis: we consider a dark pixel in a certain frame as (a) true background if all of the corresponding pixels in the different frames are also dark or (b) false background if at least one of the corresponding pixel in the different frame is bright.

sequence[1]. The objective of our method is to improve the image quality of those characters and symbols, *i.e.* to estimate the high-resolution image x without missing areas.

As shown in Fig. 2, the pixels in the observed low-resolution image are classified into three categories; *true foreground, false background,* and *true background.* The true foreground pixels correspond to the LEDs composing characters and symbols, and those LEDs are on during the exposure time of a camera. The false background pixels also correspond to the LEDs composing characters and symbols, but those LEDs are off during the exposure time by chance. The true background pixels correspond to the remaining LEDs, and those LEDs are always off. The true foreground pixels and true background pixels are considered to satisfy the observation model with the zero-mean Gaussian noises in eq.(2). On the other hand, the false background pixels significantly deviate from the observation model.

Accordingly, our proposed method makes use of the framework of outlier removal[2,7]. Specifically, the proposed method removes outlier pixels from the MAP estimation by incorporating the weights of pixels into the likelihood term as

---

[1] If necessary, segmentation via image subtraction could be used for dynamic messages.

$$c'(\boldsymbol{x}) = \sum_{f=1}^{F}(\boldsymbol{y}_f - \boldsymbol{A}_f\boldsymbol{x})^{\top}\mathrm{diag}(\boldsymbol{w}_f)(\boldsymbol{y}_f - \boldsymbol{A}_f\boldsymbol{x}) + \lambda\|\boldsymbol{H}\boldsymbol{x}\|_2^2. \qquad (4)$$

Here, $\mathrm{diag}(\boldsymbol{w}_f)$ is the diagonal matrix whose diagonal elements are the elements of $\boldsymbol{w}_f$. If the p-th pixel ($p = 1, 2, 3, ..., P$) in the f-th frame is an inlier (outlier), $w_{f,p} = 1$ ($w_{f,p} = 0$). Our method considers the true foreground pixels and true background pixels as inliers, and considers the false background pixels as outliers, and then estimates the high-resolution image by minimizing the cost function $c'(\boldsymbol{x})$ with respect to $\boldsymbol{x}$.

3.2 Outlier Detection Based on Spatio-Temporal Analysis

We assume that a region of interest (ROI), *i.e.* the region corresponding to an electronic message board is cropped in advance. Then, we detect outliers on the basis of the spatio-temporal analysis of pixel values. In other words, we classify the pixels in the ROI into true foreground, false background, and true background.

First, we detect true foreground pixels on the basis of the spatial analysis of pixel values. Specifically, we consider bright pixels, whose pixel values are larger than a certain threshold, as true foreground as shown in Fig. 3. According to Otsu's method [3], the threshold is automatically determined from the histogram of pixel values in the ROI of each observed image on the basis of discriminant criterion. Note that dark pixels, whose pixel values are smaller than the threshold, can be either false background or true background.

Second, we classify the remaining pixels into false background and true background on the basis of the temporal analysis of pixel values. Specifically, we consider a dark pixel in a certain frame as true background, if all of the corresponding pixels in the different frames are also dark as shown in Fig. 4 (a). On the other hand, we consider a dark pixel in a certain frame as false background, if at least one of the corresponding pixel in the different frame is bright as shown in Fig. 4 (b).

4 Experiments

To demonstrate the effectiveness of our proposed method, we conducted a number of experiments using both real and synthetic images. We compared the performance of our method with those of existing methods; Pickup *et al.*[5] and Ivanovski *et al.*[2].

We used Pickup *et al.*[5] as a conventional method without outlier removal, and used Ivanovski *et al.*[2] as a robust method with outlier removal because it is the most closely related work to ours. Ivanovski *et al.* detect outlier pixels on the basis of the temporal analysis of pixel values. Specifically, they compute the median of pixel values at corresponding pixels in the observed image sequence, and then consider a pixel in a certain frame as outlier if the difference between

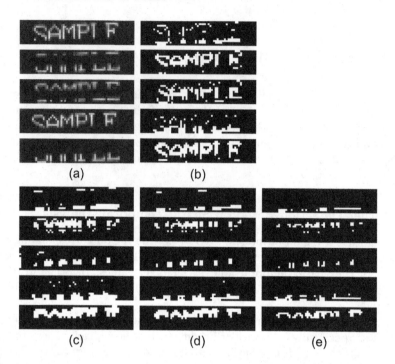

Fig. 5. The observed low-resolution images (a), the weights of pixels given by our proposed method based on the spatio-temporal analysis and automatic thresholding (b), and those given by the existing method based on the median and manual thresholding: (c) $t = 0.05$, (d) $t = 0.1$, and (e) $t = 0.2$. White pixels stand for outliers with $w = 0$.

its pixel value and the median is larger than a threshold t. Here, the threshold for detecting outliers is empirically determined.

Both our proposed method and Ivanovski et al.[2] were implemented by incorporating the outlier detection and removal into the implementation of Pickup et al.[5] for fair comparison. Note that they could be combined with other existing methods for multiframe super-resolution based on MAP estimation.

4.1 Experiments Using Real Images

We conducted experiments using the real images of two different LED electronic message boards. Those images were captured by using a Point Grey Chameleon camera with a global shutter. The exposure time was 5.3[ms]. The number of frames in each image sequence was 5 (P=5). We assumed planar homography estimated by using markers and achieved the registration of those images[2].

In Fig. 5, we show the observed low-resolution images (a), the weights of pixels given by our proposed method based on the spatio-temporal analysis and

---

[2] In natural scenes, time-invariant feature points such as the corners of an electronic message board could be used for registration.

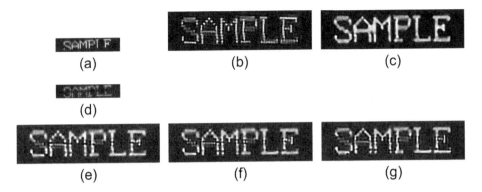

Fig. 6. Super-resolution reconstruction (SAMPLE): an input image (a), the conventional method without outlier removal (b), our proposed method (c), the median image (d), and the median-based method with (e) $t = 0.05$, (f) $t = 0.1$, and (g) $t = 0.2$.

automatic thresholding (b), and those given by the existing method based on the median and manual thresholding: (c) $t = 0.05$, (d) $t = 0.1$, and (e) $t = 0.2$[3]. Here, white pixels stand for outliers with $w = 0$. We can see that our method works well although slightly excessive amount of outliers are detected. On the other hand, we can see that the amount of outliers detected by the median-based method significantly depends on the empirically-determined threshold. More importantly, some of false background pixels are misclassified into inliers, because the median image is wrong, *i.e.* missing areas are observed in the median image shown in Fig. 6 (d).

In Fig. 6, we show an input image from the observed image sequence (a), the super-resolution reconstruction by using the conventional method without outlier removal (b), and our proposed method (c). In addition, we show the median image (d), and the super-resolution reconstruction by using the median-based method with (e) $t = 0.05$, (f) $t = 0.1$, and (g) $t = 0.2$. We can see that our method works better than the conventional method without outlier removal. Specifically, the conventional method tries to explain the temporal brightness variations due to flickering as the degradation of high-frequency grained patterns, and as a result annoying artifacts due to flickering are visible. We can also see that the median-based method does not work well, in particular where missing areas are observed in the median image. In addition, the performance of the median-based method depends on the empirically-determined threshold.

Fig. 7 and Fig. 8 show the results for other image sequences; different LED message boards, different characters and symbols, and different imaging conditions. We can see that our proposed method outperforms the conventional method without outlier removal[5] and the median-based method with an empirically-determined threshold[2]. Therefore, we can conclude that those experimental results qualitatively demonstrate the effectiveness of our method.

---

[3] 8-bit pixel values are normalized to $[0, 1]$.

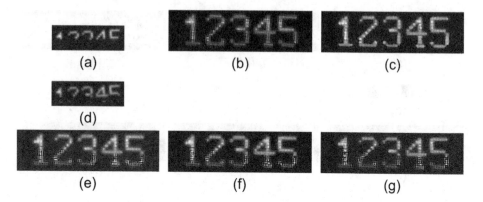

Fig. 7. Super-resolution reconstruction (12345): an input image (a), the conventional method without outlier removal (b), our proposed method (c), the median image (d), and the median-based method with (e) $t = 0.05$, (f) $t = 0.1$, and (g) $t = 0.2$.

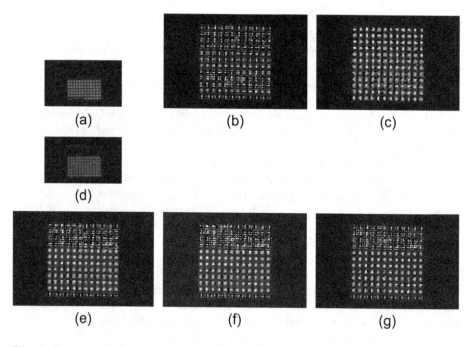

Fig. 8. Super-resolution reconstruction (square): an input image (a), the conventional method without outlier removal (b), our proposed method (c), the median image (d), and the median-based method with (e) $t = 0.05$, (f) $t = 0.1$, and (g) $t = 0.2$.

4.2 Experiments Using Synthetic Images

In order to quantitatively demonstrate the effectiveness of our proposed method, we conducted experiments using synthetic images under the condition that the

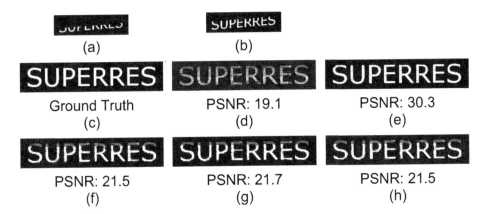

Fig. 9. Super-resolution reconstruction (synthetic): an input image (a), the median image (b), the ground truth of a high-resolution image (c), the conventional method without outlier removal (d), our proposed method (e), and the median-based method with (f) $t = 0.05$, (g) $t = 0.1$, and (h) $t = 0.2$.

ground truth of a high-resolution image is known. The number of frames was 5 (P=5). We assumed that planar homography is also known.

In Fig. 9, we show an input image from the synthetic image sequence (a), the median image (b), the ground truth of a high-resolution image (c), the super-resolution reconstruction by using the conventional method without outlier removal (d), our proposed method (e), and the median-based method with (f) $t = 0.05$, (g) $t = 0.1$, and (h) $t = 0.2$. We also show the PSNR (Peak Signal-to-Noise Ratio) of each reconstructed image. Similar to the results on the real images, we can see that our method works better than the conventional method without outlier removal[5] and the median-based method with an empirically-determined threshold[2]. Those results quantitatively demonstrate the effectiveness of our method.

5   Conclusion and Future Work

In this paper, we proposed a multiframe super-resolution method for flickering objects such as electronic message boards. Specifically, our proposed method detects outlier pixels due to flickering on the basis of the spatio-temporal analysis of pixel values, and then removes them from the MAP estimation by incorporating the weights of pixels into the likelihood term. We conducted a number of experiments using both real and synthetic images, and demonstrated that our method works better than the existing methods. The future work of this study includes the extension to dynamic messages and the extension to image sequences in which not only flickering but also motion blur are observed.

Acknowledgments. We would like to thank Prof. Tsukasa Noma for his valuable comments and suggestions early in this project.

References

1. Farsiu, S., Robinson, M., Elad, M., Milanfar, P.: Fast and robust multiframe super resolution. IEEE Trans. Image Processing **13**(10), 1327–1344 (2004)
2. Ivanovski, Z., Panovski, L., Karam, L.: Robust super-resolution based on pixel-level selectivity. In: Proc. SPIE 6077, Visual Communications and Image Processing 2006, 607707 (2006)
3. Otsu, N.: A threshold selection method from gray-level histograms. IEEE Trans. Systems, Man, and Cybernetics **SMC–9**(1), 62–66 (1979)
4. Park, S., Park, M., Kang, M.: Super-resolution image reconstruction: a technical overview. IEEE Signal Processing Magazine **20**(3), 21–36 (2003)
5. Pickup, L., Roberts, S., Zisserman, A.: A sampled texture prior for image super-resolution. In: Proc. NIPS 2003, pp. 1587–1594 (2003)
6. Tanaka, M., Yaguchi, Y., Okutomi, M.: Robust and accurate estimation of multiple motions for whole-image super-resolution. In: Proc. IEEE ICIP 2008, pp. 649–652 (2008)
7. Zhao, W., Sawhney, H.S.: Is super-resolution with optical flow feasible? In: Heyden, A., Sparr, G., Nielsen, M., Johansen, P. (eds.) ECCV 2002, Part I. LNCS, vol. 2350, pp. 599–613. Springer, Heidelberg (2002)
8. Zomet, A., Rav-Acha, A., Peleg, S.: Robust super-resolution. In: Proc. IEEE CVPR 2001, pp. I-640–I-650 (2001)

Entropy-Based Automatic Segmentation and Extraction of Tumors from Brain MRI Images

Maria De Marsico[1(✉)], Michele Nappi[2], and Daniel Riccio[3]

[1] Sapienza University of Rome, Rome, Italy
demarsico@di.uniroma1.it
[2] University of Salerno, Fisciano, Italy
mnappi@unisa.it
[3] University of Naples Federico II, Naples, Italy
daniel.riccio@unina.it

Abstract. We present a method for automatic segmentation and tumor extraction for brain MRI images. The method does not require preliminary training, and uses an extended concept of image entropy. The latter is computed over gray levels (which are in fixed number) instead of single pixels. The obtained measure can be assumed as a measure of homogeneity/similarity of regions, and therefore be the base for image segmentation. Being independent from the number of pixels in the image, its computation is highly scalable with respect to image resolution. As a matter of fact, it is always carried out over the fixed number of 256 gray levels. Moreover, being region-based rather than pixel-based, the measure is also more robust to slight differences in orientation.

Keywords: Entropy · MRI segmentation · Tumor extraction

1 Introduction

This work proposes an automatic approach to brain tumor segmentation in Magnetic Resonance Images (MRI). Most present methods require supervised training. An example can be found in [12] which exploits SVM approach. On the contrary, we propose an unsupervised technique, along the same line of [9]. The lack of a training phase can be considered as an advantage: methods with this characteristic are generally robust to some extent to changes in capture technologies, possibly causing consequent changes in score distributions. Of course, medical imaging can be an aid, but cannot substitute in any case the human-in-the-loop approach . What can be reasonably avoided is to engage physicians with cases which are negative with very high confidence. Luckily enough, these are the majority of cases. This relieves humans from the most burden of work, allowing one to concentrate on cases marked as ambiguous as well as positive by the automatic system, therefore increasing the overall efficiency.

Among brain tumors, gliomas are the most widespread kind of primary malignant brain tumor (not deriving from a metastasis process) among adults (about

G. Azzopardi and N. Petkov (Eds.): CAIP 2015, Part II, LNCS 9257, pp. 195–206, 2015.
DOI: 10.1007/978-3-319-23117-4_17

70%). They can be classified in four World Health Organization (WHO) grades. Grades I and II (Low-Grade) can be considered semi-malignant tumors that carry a better prognosis, whereas grades III and IV tumors (High-Grade) are malignant tumors that almost certainly lead to a death of the subject [4].

We have two possible classes for input images: with a possible tumor, and with no tumor. The first one also includes images with multi-focal tumors, i.e., tumors located in two or more different regions in the image. The properties to take into account for a binary classification are those clearly distinguishing the two classes under consideration. In the case of brain, we can distinguish two main sources for prior knowledge. The first accredited one is the so called probability brain atlas, reporting the computed probability of tissues locations. The goal of such an atlas is to detect and quantify distributed patterns of deviation from normal anatomy, in a 3-D brain image from any given subject. Related algorithms analyze a sufficiently large reference population of normal scans and automatically generate color-coded probability maps of the anatomy of new subjects. A first work dealing with the design and implementation of a technique for creating a comprehensive probabilistic atlas of the human brain can be found in [16]. A version especially devoted to the lobe region is created in [10]. Examples of works using this source for prior knowledge can be found in [13] and [3]. The second widely used information is related the general sagittal symmetry of healthy brain. The underlying assumption of methods using this kind of information is that areas that break this symmetry are highly suspect as they are most likely parts of a tumor or represent anyway a kind of pathology. Examples of works based on this assumption can be found in [15], [2], and [9]. Our work develops following this approach. It is worth underlining that shape analysis is not a feasible choice in this problem, since tumors can get different shapes according to the way they spread along the fibers of the white matter. The contribution of this work is to propose the use of a revisited notion of entropy to compute a measure of the homogeneity of set of objects. This measure can underlie unsupervised clustering, and in particular, when either pixels or image regions are the objects of interest, it can provide accurate image segmentation.

2   MRI Brain Images

A very short presentation of the different MRI modes seems worth, since we will see that images captured with different techniques provide different information. MRI scanners use strong magnetic fields and radio waves to form images of the body. Contrast in MR imaging can be manipulated to a much greater extent than in other imaging techniques, by varying the amount of excitation exercised by the magnetic field and the number of repetitions. Nevertheless, certain diagnostic questions require even sharper regions and this can be obtained by the application of contrast agents, each achieving a specific result. A separate sequence is obtained from each of them, and often more sequences are captured for better diagnosis accuracy (multi-contrast MRI). Present clinical practice deals with T1-weighted (T1 for short), T1-weighted contrast enhanced

(T1c for short), T2-weighted (T2 for short), and a kind of T2-weighted denoted as Fluid-attenuated inversion recovery (FLAIR), where T1 stands for the longitudinal relaxation time, and T2 for transverse relaxation time. Obtaining T1-weighted contrast enhanced images requires the contrast agent (usually gadolinium) to be injected into the patient blood, making this kind of magnetic resonance quite invasive, while the others just require oral administration. Further details on the use of contrast agents are out of the scope of this paper, but the interested reader can find them in [14]. BRATS [11] is a very popular public database for experiments with 3D volumes, with a complete series of images captured by such contrast agents for each slice. For our experiments, we used BRATS-1 dataset with ground truth from the 2012 edition (available at http://challenge.kitware.com/midas/folder/102). Figure 4(a) shows examples of images for a single slice of a single volume from BRATS with variations obtained with different contrast agents. More details on the database can be found in the Section 6.1 below. T1 is the most commonly used sequence for structural analysis and for annotation of healthy tissues. In T1c, tumor edges appear lighter because the contrast agent concentrates there due to the perturbations of barriers of encephalic blood in the proliferation of tumor region. In this sequence, it is easy to distinguish a necrotic region and the active part of the tumor. In T2, the edema region around the tumor appears as lighter. FLAIR helps separating the edema region from the cerebro-spinal fluid (CSF). The regions identified by the different techniques are those relevant to the determination of the tumor approximate size and position. These characteristics explain why more sequences are used. It is to notice that BRATS sequences are quite well aligned, and in any case our approach is region-based rather than pixel-based, and therefore it is more robust to slight differences in orientation.

3   Entropy as a Homogeneity Measure

The classical way to exploit entropy for image analysis is to evaluate the degree of randomness of image pixels. Each pixel x in an image I is considered as a symbol in the alphabet emitted by a source S. In the case of a gray scale image, the alphabet is represented by the set of 8-bit integers in the range $[0 - 255]$. The image histogram represents the frequency table of all such symbols. Once its values have been normalized in the range $[0, 1]$, and according to the total number of pixels in the image, each of them represents the probability of occurrence of the corresponding symbol in I. Entropy H(I) can be therefore defined as:

$$H(I) = -\sum_{k=0}^{255} p(k) log_2 p(k) \qquad (1)$$

It is trivial to notice that Equation 1 can be generalized to express in general the amount of homogeneity in a set of any kind of objects, given that the suited abstractions are devised. From this we can implement an accurate clustering algorithm which, when the objects of interest are image regions, underlies image segmentation. For readers' sake, we first summarize the appropriate notation.

More details associated with a number of possible applications of the same concepts to different problems can be found in [5], [6].

We consider a gallery G of objects/elements/observations (for short, objects from here on), and any similarity measure d, which associates a real scalar value to any pair of feature vectors (template) extracted from the objects of interest according to the chosen set of discriminating characteristics. In order to get preliminary definitions, we assume to compare a probe template v (extracted from a new object to classify) with a gallery template g_i. We get $s(v, g_i)$ and denote it as s_i. In particular, after a possible score normalization, s_i is a real value in the interval $[0,1]$. We can then assume a probability distribution over the gallery G such that the score s_i can be interpreted as the probability that template v conforms to g_i that is:

$$s_{i,v} = p(v \approx g_i) \qquad (2)$$

In order to compute a value for the entropy of the gallery we can take each element of the class in turn to play the role of v, and compute all intra-class similarities. After denoting as Q the number of pairs $\langle q_i, q_j \rangle$ in G such that $s_{i,j} > 0$ we can write:

$$H(G) = -\frac{1}{log_2(|Q|)} \sum\nolimits_{q_{i,j} \in Q} s_{i,j} log_2(s_{i,j}) \qquad (3)$$

The above equations can be used for clustering unclassified objects of interest, either as in [6] or as in [7]. We report here the approach essentials, while further details can be found in the cited paper. The value of $H(G)$ represents a measure of heterogeneity for a set of objects G. As such, it can be used to order all the objects in the overall gallery according to their informative power. Given G, the proposed procedure computes an all-against-all similarity matrix M and, using its elements, the value for $H(G)$. For each object $g_i \in G$, M is then used to compute the value of $H(G\, g_i)$ that would be obtained by ignoring g_i. The object g_i, achieving the minimum difference $f(G, g_i) = H(G) - H(G\, g_i)$, is selected; the matrix M is updated by deleting the $i-th$ row and column, and the process is repeated, until all elements of G have been selected. In practice, we first select the most representative samples, i.e. those causing the lower entropy decrease. This approach progressively reduces the inhomogeneity of a set of samples. In this work we perform clustering using the ordering of objects induced by the iterative application of $f(\cdot, \cdot)$, in a way similar to the method proposed in [7]. We describe it in the following section.

4   Entropy-Based Clustering to Segment MRI Images

In the specific context of this work, namely the segmentation of MRI images of the brain district with possible presence of a tumor, we use the above specification of entropy to obtain a smart and adaptive quantization of gray tones in a gray scale image. In other words, given a picture where gray levels occur, we want to identify representative subsets of these, so as to facilitate the partitioning of the image into regions, i.e., clusters of gray levels with similar information content. As a consequence, the objects we are dealing with are the single image pixels and their gray levels in the range [0, ..., 255]. It is important to preliminarily notice that a similarity measure achieving our goal, once defined, must be computed on a per image basis. In other words, to serve as a firm basis for clustering, the difference of any two gray levels cannot be fixed once and for all, but depends on the content of the single image I at hand. This is to be taken into consideration to interpret the following discussion.

As a first option, we might trivially consider a similarity measure s inversely proportional to the absolute difference between two different gray levels. However, in our tests this produced one single cluster. The main reason is that this measure does not take into account the actual presence in the image I at hand of pixels with a certain gray level. This can be obtained by weighting each pixel with the probability that it is present in I, before computing the difference. The latter can be easily derived from the normalized histogram computed on I. However, even this solution produces anomalies (black and white with respective probabilities larger than 0 and 0 go in the same cluster). This is because now the actual difference between levels has been smoothed too much. Therefore, both difference and weighted difference must be considered in some way. A last factor to take into account is the actual topological distribution, or *sparsity*, of pixels with the same gray level in I. This measure can be identified as the standard deviation $\sigma(g)$ of the coordinates of the pixels with a certain gray level g. Since we are computing a similarity between two gray levels, we have to derive a kind of *joint sparsity index*, which, given two gray levels g_i and g_j, can be defined as:

$$\sigma(g_i, g_j) = \frac{min\{\sigma(g_i), \sigma(g_j)\}}{max\{\sigma(g_i), \sigma(g_j)\}} \tag{4}$$

The final similarity can be computed as:

$$s(g_i, g_j) = 1 - \psi(|p(g_i)g_i - p(g_j)g_j|) + log(|g_i - g_j| + 1) + \sigma(g_i, g_j) \tag{5}$$

where ψ is a normalization function to have the weighted difference in the range [0,1], the logarithm balances the contribution of the difference, and the addition of 1 avoids the presence of a term $log(0)$. Notice that for simplicity of notation the mention of the single image I is omitted from all equations, but it is implicit.

Applying the similarity measure $s(g_i, g_j)$ to a gray scale MRI image, the plot of function $f(G, g_i)$ assumes a typical pattern where the values associated to the gray tones, in the order they are selected by the function, are arranged along a curve with a typical coarse parabolic behavior, and where at a finer detail we can identify peaks and downslopes. We can observe that gray tones with the same degree of representativeness for image I tend to arrange themselves along a descending portion of the curve, while the peaks can be considered as the starting element of a new cluster. Figure 1 shows the iteration of the function on the x axis, and the value of f on the y axis. Each point in the plot can be labeled with the gray level that achieves the maximum of f (value on y) at the iteration

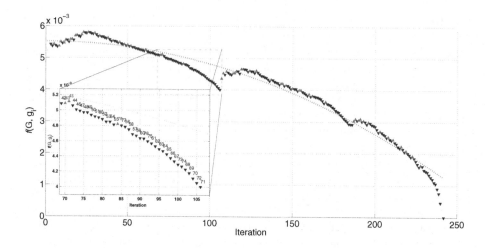

Fig. 1. The curve obtained by computing function $f(G, g_i)$ and plotting the obtained values in different iterations

(on the x). The Figure displays a zoomed portion to show labels. The clustering algorithm then proceeds as follows: a) create the first cluster and enter the first element; b) if the current element is on a descending portion of the curve, include it in the current cluster, otherwise create a new cluster and add that element; c) if there are more elements to cluster, return to b). After clustering procedure is complete, we compute the centroid for each cluster, and substitute it for all the cluster elements, to produce an image I_c. In certain cases, the algorithm produces a over-segmentation, for which there are clusters that could be possibly fused together. For this reason, after the clustering process, we perform a merging of clusters by taking into account consistency among neighbors. Given a cluster, we check if there are other clusters within a certain threshold t, with which to carry out a merge operation. For a cluster whose representative is the gray level g_k, the algorithm tries to merge it with the clusters represented by gray levels in the interval $[g_{k+1}, g_{k+t}]$. If this is done for gray level g_{k+h}, the latter becomes the starting point for the search of other clusters that can be melted, checking the interval $[g_{k+h+1}, g_{k+h+t}]$. For this work, we experimentally set $t = 4$. When two clusters respectively represented by gray levels g_i and g_j are merged, all the gray levels in the image I represented by g_j are replaced with g_i. We denote the final image as I_{cm}. The procedure ends when no cluster can be further fused. Notice that, though the similarity measure we adopt takes topology into account, clusters are created over gray levels, and not over regions. This entails that groups of pixels of the same cluster may be located in different regions of the image. Figure 2 shows an histogram with representative gray levels after clustering step (blu/dark lines) and final levels after merging (red/light lines). Figure 3 shows in pseudo-colors an example of a MRI slice and of the obtained clustering of gray levels. Our clustering algorithm has several advantages:

- With the use of entropy it is not necessary to specify in advance the number of clusters (as in a normal algorithm based on fuzzy techniques).

- In fuzzy clustering, assignment of elements to individual clusters is made pixel by pixel, while by the method based on entropy it is made on the basis of gray levels, which are in a fixed number. The higher the resolution of the image, the more significant the saving we obtain in terms of computational cost.

It is worth noticing that no knowledge about the training data is hard engineered in the final algorithm and its associated parameters. Even if the concrete instantiation of the similarity measure and the obtained values depend on the content of each single image, its definition holds in general and is is automatically derived from the image. As usual, some parameters may depend on the kind of images, but not on the specific dataset. The most important consequence is that the method can be used without major changes for the segmentation of any other kind of gray scale images.

A different approach to entropy-based segmentation, applied to satellite images, can be found in [1]. However, since entropy is computed on single-pixels basis, it is not equally scalable to resolution.

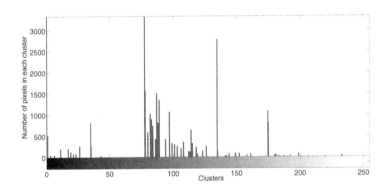

Fig. 2. An histogram with representative gray levels after clustering step (blu/dark lines) and final levels after merging (red/light lines)

5   MRI Image Segmentation and Extraction of Tumor Region

In general, a tumor may not be evident in all MRI slices. As an example, in Figure 4(a) it is only visible in T1c, T2 and FLAIR images. The tumor mass is composed of a nucleus, which in most MRI images tends to the white color, and an edema region around, which instead in most MRI images tends to a gray color with lighter shade than the mass of the healthy brain. In the extraction phase of the tumor mass, the algorithm we propose checks if the original gray level image I image contains pixels with light gray level; if this is the case, it analyzes

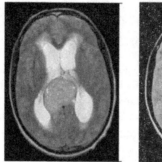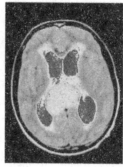

Fig. 3. A brain MRI slice with the result of entropy-based clustering of gray levels

the possibly different clusters in I_{cm} obtained in the previous step that contains those gray levels: for each such cluster the algorithm checks if it is dense (its pixels are concentrated in a small space) or scattered (its pixels are distributed in a large space). Since groups of pixels of the same cluster can be far from each other in the image, one can exploit the variance of pixel coordinates to determine if a cluster is dense (small variance) or scattered (high variance). The search for the nucleus is carried out by analyzing the FLAIR, T1c and T2 images. In particular, the algorithm performs a product pixel by pixel between FLAIR and T1c images, the result of which is is compared to a threshold. Similarly we proceed with the pair of images FLAIR and T2. The results of these two products undergo a logical AND operation. As for edema, we analyze the FLAIR image, from which we extracted the whitish gray levels . From this set we eliminate all the pixels previously classified as as nucleus. The full mass is given by the union of the nucleus and edema. Figure 4 (c) shows the ground truth of a slice (left) and the result of the algorithm for the extraction of the tumor mass (right). The time needed for the segmentation of a single slice is in the order of milliseconds.

6   Experimental Results

In this section we report the achieved results, after introducing the dataset used for the experiments.

6.1   BRATS-1 Dataset

The first step of the experimentation was to choose a dataset of MRI volumes that is representative of the problem and widely accepted, so as to make comparisons with the results obtained by other methods in literature. We decided to use the MRI volumes provided by Kitware / MIDAS, available at http://challenge.kitware.com/midas/folder/102. The dataset contains multi-contrast MRI images from 30 patients with gliomas (both low-grade, and high-grade, and both with or without resection). In addition, the images were manually annotated by experts, to provide a ground truth (or gold standard) for three different classes of targets: core, edema and complete mass . For each patient, images are available with different contrast types, namely T1, T2, FLAIR and post-gadolinium T1 (T1c). All volumes were co-registered to the T1 contrast image and interpolated to 1 mm isotropic resolution. On the contrary, the images have not been co-registered in order to place the volumes of all patients in a single reference space. The manual segmentations (file names ending in "_truth.mha") have only three levels of intensity: 1 for edema, two for active tumor, and 0 for the rest. The dataset contains also images in which the tumor mass was simulated for 25 low-grade and 25 high-grade tumors. These simulated images faithfully follow the conventions used for real data.

6.2   Compared Method

As for comparison, we chose one of the few methods in literature that does not require a training phase, namely the one proposed by Dvorak and Bartusek [9], which uses the detection of asymmetries in MRI images and is one of the latest proposals in literature. A further set of candidates would include the methods presented at MICCAI 2012 Challenge, whose results are reported in [11]. However, the challenge was focused on segmentation of tumor and edema separately, so that the results reported in this paper cannot be compared to those described in [11]. Furthermore, our work is fully automatic and does not require any training phase, as all methods proposed in the proceedings. Training causes a twofold limitation. On the one hand, if it is run on the overall dataset at hand, it requires some inter-volume normalization that may introduce inaccuracies if the conditions are not perfectly similar. On the other hand, if it is patient-specific it introduces a further complication in the diagnostic process and makes it longer.

   In the method proposed in [9], the mid-sagittal plane must be detected first, to correctly align the head. Assuming that the head has been already aligned and the skull is approximately symmetric, the symmetry plane divides the volume of the detected brain into left and right halves of the same size. In the aligned volume, the method locates the asymmetric parts. The algorithm scans both halves symmetrically by a cubic block, whose size is computed from the size of the image. Normalized histograms with the same range are computed for corresponding cubic regions, left and right, and they are compared by Bhattacharya coefficient. Since this coefficient expresses similarity, its complement is used to evaluate asymmetry. Since regions overlap during block sliding, the average asymmetry is computed for each pixel. The whole cycle is repeated at different resolutions. Each cycle outputs an asymmetry map. The product of values corresponding to a particular pixel in the different maps creates a multi-resolution asymmetry map. This computation is performed for each contrast volume separately. For each multi-resolution asymmetry map a threshold is set to extract pathological (asymmetric) regions. As it can be noticed, though being region-based, this method relies on a number of computations which depend on the number of pixels in the image and on its original resolution. Therefore, it might not scale well with respect to high resolution settings.

6.3   Evaluation of the Algorithm Based on Gray Level Entropy

The accuracy of results of segmentation and tumor extraction is measured using Dice coefficient [8]:

$$DC = \frac{2|A \cap B|}{|A| + |B|} \tag{6}$$

where A and B denote the ground truth and the result from the tested method respectively. DC is in the range $[0, 1]$, with 1 identifying a perfect segmentation and 0 a completely wrong one.

From the dataset described in the previous section, we report here an example of processing steps of a slice from the first volume BRATS_HG0001, namely slice 100: Figure 4 shows the original multi-contrast images, the images after entropy-based quantization, and the comparison between extracted tumor mass and ground truth. The achieved DC values for nucleus, edema and total tumor mass were respectively 0.94, 0.82, and 0.86. We ran the method on the complete dataset (all volumes and all images, both real and simulated data). Table 1 reports the cumulative results, compared with those achieved by the approach by Dvorak and Bartusek discussed above. In the table, Symmetry denotes the method in [9] and Entropy denotes our method. Moreover, HG stands for high-grade and LG for low-grade cases, while cells report the average DC achieved.

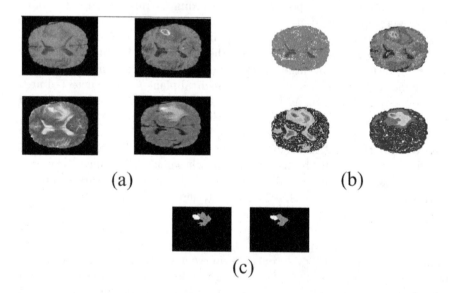

(a)   (b)

(c)

Fig. 4. Slice 100 from BRATS_HG0001: (a) (b) from left to right and top to bottom original images and quantized ones for respectively T1, T1c, T2, and FLAIR; (c) ground truth on the left and algorithm results on the right for tumor extraction

Table 1. Comparison with results achieved by [9]

	Simmetry HG	Simmetry LG	Entropy HG	Entropy LG
Real Data	0.67 ± 0.22	0.78 ± 0.10	0.68 ± 0.17	0.63 ± 0.17
Simulated data	0.80 ± 0.10	0.72 ± 0.05	0.73 ± 0.18	0.71 ± 0.19

According to [17], a value of $DC > 0.7$ indicates an excellent similarity. This statement was met for both high and low grade gliomas in both real and simulated data. Even if the results achieved by our method are sometimes lower than the compared one, though comparable, we want to underline some points. The first consideration is that our method can be further improved. As an example, we obtained some very preliminary results suggesting that a smarter merging strategy can improve the final quantization of image gray levels, e.g., when the merging phase after clustering takes into account the topology of clusters in image space to decide their fusion. The second consideration is that our method is independent from the image resolution, i.e., from the number of pixels, since clustering is performed on a gray level basis, and these are in a fixed number. Last but not least, since we do not rely on any kind of specific geometric feature of the analyzed region, e.g., symmetry, our method might be effective with other anatomical districts as well, where symmetry cannot be assumed. The authors of [9] state that their method would not work for highly rotated volumes, even though the perfect alignment is not necessary. Our method is robust to rotations, since it does not assume any reference axis.

7 Conclusions and Future Work

In this work we presented a completely automatic method for tumor mass extraction from brain MRI images. It exploits a revised concept of entropy to perform gray level quantization. The advantages of this method are manifold. It is completely automatic and does not require any kind of training. The main component of its cost is related with the number of gray levels (fixed at 256) in the image rather than to the number of pixels (dramatically increasing with resolution). It is region-based, therefore it is robust to orientation. It does rely on any pre-defined anatomical feature, e.g., symmetry, therefore can be quite straightforwardly extended to any anatomical district. Further improvements are planned in the near future to make the merging process, following the gray level clustering operation, more accurate, by taking into account topological features of the regions that are going to be merged. Finally, the similarity measure between gray levels will be further investigated.

References

1. Barbieri, A.L., De Arruda, G.F., Rodrigues, F.A., Bruno, O.M., da Fontoura Costa, L.: An entropy-based approach to automatic image segmentation of satellite images. Physica A: Statistical Mechanics and its Applications **390**(3), 512–518 (2011)

2. Cap, M., Gescheidtova, E., Marcon, P., Bartusek, K.: Automatic detection and segmentation of the tumor tissue. In: Progress in Electromagnetics Research Symposium, pp. 53–56 (2013)
3. Cuadra, M.B., Pollo, C., Bardera, A., Cuisenaire, O., Villemure, J.G., Thiran, J.P.: Atlas-based segmentation of pathological MR brain images using a model of lesion growth. IEEE Trans. Med. Imaging **23**(1), 1301–1314 (2004)
4. von Deimling, A. (ed.): Gliomas. Recent Results in Cancer Research, vol. 171. Springer, Berlin (2009)
5. De Marsico, M., Nappi, M., Riccio, D., Tortora, G.: Entropy Based Template Analysis in Face Biometric Identification Systems. Journal of Signal, Image and Video Processing **7**(3), 493–505 (2013)
6. De Marsico, M., Nappi, M., Riccio, D.: Entropy based biometric template clustering. In: Proceedings of International Conference on Pattern Recognition Applications and Methods - ICPRAM 2013, pp. 560–563 (2013)
7. De Marsico, M., Riccio, D., Plasencia-Calana, Y., Mendez-Vazquez, H.: GETSEL: gallery entropy for template selection on large datasets. In: Proceedings of International Joint Conference on Biometrics, IJCB 2014, pp. 1–8 (2014)
8. Dice, L.R.: Measures of the amount of ecologic association between species. Ecology **26**(3), 297–302 (1945)
9. Dvorak, P., Bartusek, K.: Fully automatic 3D glioma extraction in multi-contrast MRI. In: Campilho, A., Kamel, M. (eds.) ICIAR 2014, Part II. LNCS, vol. 8815, pp. 239–246. Springer, Heidelberg (2014)
10. Hammers, A., Allom, R., Koepp, M.J., Free, S.L., Myers, R., Lemieux, L., Mitchell, T.N., Brooks, D.J., Duncan, J.S.: Three-dimensional maximum probability atlas of the human brain, with particular reference to the temporal lobe. Human brain mapping **19**(4), 224–247 (2003)
11. Menze, B., Reyes, M., Van Leemput, K.: The Multimodal Brain Tumor Image Segmentation Benchmark (BRATS). IEEE Transactions on Medical Imaging **PP**(99), 1 (2014). doi:10.1109/TMI.2014.2377694. Published online December at http://ieeexplore.ieee.org/stamp/stamp.jsp?tp=&arnumber=6975210&isnumber=4359023
12. Mikulka, J., Gescheidtova, E.: An improved segmentation of brain tumor, edema and necrosis. In: Progress in Electromagnetics Research Symposium, pp. 25–28 (2013)
13. Prastawa, M., Bullitt, E., Moon, N., Van Leemput, K., Gerig, G.: Automatic brain tumor segmentation by subject specific modification of atlas priors. Academic Radiology **10**(12), 1341–1348 (2003)
14. Rinck P.: Magnetic Resonance in Medicine. The Basic Textbook of the European Magnetic Resonance Forum, 8th edn. (2014). Electronic version 8.2, published January 1, 2015. http://www.trtf.eu
15. Saha, B.N., Ray, N., Greiner, R., Murtha, A., Zhang, H.: Quick detection of brain tumors and edemas: A bounding box method using symmetry. Computerized Medical Imaging and Graphics **36**(2), 95–107 (2012)
16. Thompson, P.M., Toga, A.W.: Detection, visualization and animation of abnormal anatomic structure with a deformable probabilistic brain atlas based on random vector field transformations. Medical image analysis **1**(4), 271–294 (1997)
17. Zijdenbos, A., Dawant, B.: Brain segmentation and white matter lesion detection in mr images. Critical Reviews in Biomedical Engineering **22**, 401–465 (1994)

Multiple Hypothesis Tracking with Sign Language Hand Motion Constraints

Mark Borg[(✉)] and Kenneth P. Camilleri

Systems and Control Engineering, Faculty of Engineering,
University of Malta, Msida, Malta
mborg2005@gmail.com

Abstract. In this paper, we propose to incorporate *prior* knowledge from sign language linguistic models about the motion of the hands within a multiple hypothesis tracking framework. A critical component for automated visual sign language recognition is the tracking of the signer's hands, especially when faced with frequent and persistent occlusions and complex hand interactions. Hand motion constraints identified by sign language phonological models, such as the hand symmetry condition, are used as part of the data association process. Initial experimental results show the validity of the proposed approach.

Keywords: Sign langage recognition · MHT · Tracking

1 Introduction

Hand tracking is a critical component of vision-based automated sign language recognition (ASLR) systems [1], as the hands constitute the main articulators for signing. The position of the hands, their motion, and the shapes that the hands take, all are discriminative linguistic features that contribute to the semantic meaning in sign recognition.

Object tracking is a very challenging problem, mostly due to the noisy, compressed nature of videos, the presence of motion blur, the loss of depth information, and the high variability in illumination and scene conditions. In multi-object tracking, the interaction between objects and occlusion events, make consistent labelling of objects across video frames an especially hard problem.

For ASLR in particular, tracking faces problems of frequent and persistent hand and face occlusions, and complex hand motions and interactions (like crossovers and bounce-back events), since signing occurs within a small volume of space centred on the signer. The non-rigid and articulated nature of the hands gives rise to large variations in pose and appearance, as well as issues of self-occlusion and self-shadowing. Keeping track of both (unadorned) hands over long video sequences is a very challenging problem, often fraught with the loss of hand identity and mismatch errors, which can severely degrade the performance of subsequent sign recognition modules. Thus, the core issue in multi-object tracking, like ASLR, is *data association*, i.e., determining which acquired observation corresponds to which of the objects being tracked [13].

© Springer International Publishing Switzerland 2015
G. Azzopardi and N. Petkov (Eds.): CAIP 2015, Part II, LNCS 9257, pp. 207–219, 2015.
DOI: 10.1007/978-3-319-23117-4_18

Earlier works in tracking adopted a deterministic approach for data association, where the correspondences depend only on the preceding and current video frame observations – thus termed f2f tracking. These methods generally define a cost function for associating each object at time $t - 1$ to observations at time t, based on some motion constraints (e.g. proximity) and/or similarity measures (e.g., appearance or shape) [10]. Minimisation of the cost function is then formulated as a combinatorial optimisation problem, which can be restricted to 1-to-1 associations only, thus allowing for the use of optimal linear assignment algorithms such as the Kuhn-Munkres Hungarian algorithm [13]. In [6] a voting algorithm is used for data association, while [12] adopts a global nearest neighbour rule-based approach. These deterministic approaches are forced to make a *hard association decision* in each video frame, and thus a single incorrect association at a particular point in time affects all of the subsequent tracking – they can't recover from object label switches, and loss of object IDs. Later works, like that of [7], extend the data association process to multi-frame association, i.e., finding object and observation correspondences over a set of consecutive frames. This allows for the application of more constraints on temporal and spatial coherency. The data association problem now becomes a graph theoretic problem, i.e., finding the best unique path for each object within the set of frames, offering a degree of robustness against occlusion events that are shorter in duration than the temporal window used for the data association.

In contrast to f2f and multi-frame methods, statistical approaches to multi-object tracking like JPDAF (joint probabilistic data association filter) [3], use *soft association decisions*, whereby the tracked object is associated with all the feasible observations that it can be matched to, and is updated via a weighted combination of these observations. The multiple hypothesis tracking (MHT) algorithm [4,9] adopts a different strategy than the single-hypothesis tracking methods discussed earlier that only keep a single hypothesis about the past. Instead, the MHT algorithm employs a deferred decision-taking mechanism for data association, by keeping multiple hypotheses about the past, and then propagating these hypotheses into the future in anticipation that subsequent data will resolve the uncertainty about which of the multiple hypotheses is the correct one. Because of the exponential increase in the number of hypotheses created by the MHT algorithm, pruning is required – this is accomplished by a sliding temporal window, as well as by discarding low-probability hypotheses. In [1], MHT is used within an ASLR context for hand tracking in the presence of skin segmentation errors. They also make use of an anatomical hand model to eliminate anatomically impossible hypotheses. Other tracking approaches include: tracklet-based tracking, where detection of tracklets is followed by the subsequent linking of the tracklets into longer tracks [5]; Bayesian network based tracking [8]; tracking based on random finite sets. A review of tracking methods is found in [10,11].

In this paper, we propose an MHT-based framework for our ASLR system, that incorporates *prior* knowledge about the constraints on hand motion as described by sign language linguistic models. We believe that the use of this knowledge yields an improvement in the tracking performance of MHT, especially when the tracker is dealing with complex hand interactions and occlusion events.

Sign language phonological models identify a number of constraints about hand motion, and the position of one hand in the signing space in relation to the other one. These constraints could be exploited by an MHT-based tracker in order to reduce the space of possible hypotheses. For example, the "symmetry" and "dominance" conditions limit the role of the non-dominant hand to serve as either a duplicate articulator (giving rise to the so-called "h2-S" signs), or as a place of articulation for the dominant hand (so-called "h2-P" signs). In "h2-S" signs, the articulation of h2 (the non-dominant hand) is symmetric to that of h1 (the dominant hand), and both must have the same handshape; while in "h2-P" signs, h2 is stationary and h1 moves using h2 as a place of reference against which the motion is performed [2]. Examples of "h2-P" and "h2-S" signs can be seen in Figures 2 & 3 respectively.

The main contribution of our work is the proposed integration of these hand motion constraints within the probabilistic framework of MHT. In particular, these constraints are incorporated within the hypothesis evaluation equation of the MHT algorithm via the use of probabilistic density maps. We demonstrate our approach by implementing one of these constraints, mainly the symmetry constraint "h2-S". Since symmetric hand motions can sometimes suffer from out-of-sync issues, our proposal takes this into account. While the MHT algorithm has been used within the context of ASLR, for example in [1], to the best of our knowledge there are no works that implement what we propose here.

Our use of the hand symmetry constraint, bears some resemblance in idea to the "common motion constraint" as described by [14,15]. In [14] the special problem of multi-target tracking is discussed, where a group of targets are highly correlated in their motion, usually exhibiting a common motion pattern with some individual variations; e.g., dancing cheerleaders.

The rest of this paper is organised as follows: Section 2 gives an overview of our ASLR system and tracking framework; Section 3 outlines the MHT algorithm which forms the basis of our tracking framework; Section 4 describes our proposed approach; Section 5 reports initial experimental results; We conclude the paper in Section 6 and highlight future work.

2   Overview of Our System

The multiple hypotheses based tracking framework proposed in our paper forms part of an ASLR system. The work described here concentrated on (1) object detection, (2) tracking, and (3) the incorporation of sign language hand motion constraints within the tracking process. The object detection stage locates the face, computes skin and motion likelihoods, which in turn serve for detecting the hands – these provide the "observations" that are fed to the second stage. The tracking stage is made up of a number of steps: track prediction, gating, hypotheses formation about the associations of observations to tracks, followed by the adjustment of hypotheses' likelihoods, and their evaluation and eventual pruning. The adjustment of the likelihoods makes use of sign language hand motion constraints, and constitutes the main contribution of this paper. Additional information can also be incorporated into this step, like kinematic hand/upper body models and contextual information, via the use of the same mechanism and principles – this is described later on as future work. Finally, the most likely hypothesis about the position and motion of the hands is fed to the sign recognition module of our system, which is still works in progress.

3   The MHT Algorithm

Reid [9] was the first to describe MHT using a strong mathematical formulation. As mentioned in the introduction, in contrast to single-hypothesis tracking methods that make a hard decision in each time step as regards to which observations are associated with which targets, the idea behind the MHT algorithm is to generate all possible association hypotheses at any one time step and then rely on future information to resolve any ambiguities and to select the most probable hypothesis amongst them. The hypothesis generation stage implicitly caters for various observation-to-track association scenarios, such as new track initiation and termination (e.g., targets entering/leaving the camera's FOV), targets which are unobserved for some time, and observations arising from noise (false alarms). As a new set of observations arrives with each new time step, newly-generated hypotheses are added to the previous ones, thus forming a tree structure.

To avoid a combinatorial explosion in the number of hypotheses generated and maintained by the algorithm, a number of pruning techniques are applied to make the tracking more tractable – these include pruning low probability hypotheses, specifying a maximum number of hypothesis, N-scan pruning, and applying clustering techniques [4].

Hypotheses clustering helps to divide the tracking problem into independent and smaller sub-problems which can be solved separately. First, observations are gated with existing tracks; any observations falling outside the validation gate of a track are considered to have a zero probability of being associated with that track, and thus can be safely ignored (assuming the statistical model used to obtain the validation gate is valid). This helps to remove those observation-to-track associations which are considered to be physically impossible. Grouping collections of tracks linked by observations then gives rise to clusters of hypotheses, which in turn results in spatially disjoint hypothesis trees [16]. In N-scan pruning, a sliding temporal window is applied to the tree of hypotheses. Within this window, multiple hypotheses are maintained and propagated in time as the window slides forward. But at the rear end of the window, a hard decision is made on the most likely hypothesis taking into consideration future observational evidence present in the window. Thus the depth of the hypotheses trees are limited to be at most equal to the window size. In [4,17] it was shown that MHT can achieve good tracking performance with quite shallow tree depths.

In [17], the efficiency of the MHT is greatly improved via the use of Murty's algorithm, which addresses the main inefficiency of the original MHT – mainly that a lot of computation is wasted on the generation and propagation of many hypotheses which in the end are discarded and never used. This is achieved by finding the m-best associations hypotheses in the current time step instead of using all possibilities. More detail on the MHT algorithm can be found in [3,4].

4 MHT and Sign Language Constraints

In this section we will describe our MHT-based system, the features we have selected for detecting the objects to be tracked (observation acquisition), and the chosen target representation. Then we will describe the proposed incorporation of sign language hand motion constraints within our tracking process.

4.1 Features for Object Detection

Choosing the right *features* to be used in a multi-object tracking system is an extremely important task – many times, the choice of features depends on the tracking domain in question. Ideally the chosen features should be unique, in order to facilitate the detection of the objects to be tracked (the observations), and should be computationally efficient to extract [10]. We use motion-based features in our ASLR tracking system. To make the extraction of these features as efficient as possible, we apply pre-filtering based on skin colour and frame differencing. We also employ a face detector, both for face localisation purposes, as well as for performing system initialisation, such as that of learning the skin colour model. A tracking by detection approach is adopted for face localisation, via the use of the Viola-Jones face detector [26]. The assumption behind our face localisation approach is that the face of the signer is frontal (or near-frontal) with respect to the camera's viewpoint. Once the face of the signer is detected, a body-centred coordinate system is defined and scaled according to the size of the face. To improve the accuracy of face localisation, a constant-velocity Kalman filter is used to smooth out the noise in global head motion.

We employ an adaptive skin colour classifier [18] for generating the skin likelihood map. The skin model used by this classifier is initialised via face detection as follows: a 24×24 mask, generated off-line using several hundred images of different persons, is applied to the face region that is found by the face detector – this mask indicates which pixels within the face region are most likely to be skin; then working within the normalised RGB colour space, a parametric skin colour model is estimated.

A motion likelihood map is generated via a weighted frame differencing algorithm. Combined together, the skin likelihood and motion likelihood maps, serve as a fast pre-processing stage by filtering out most areas of the image (moving skin-coloured regions are expected to be small in size and number). Thus we avoid having to run the costlier feature extraction process over the full image.

The motion-based features used in our ASLR system consist of clusters of KLT features (corners) exhibiting a similar affine motion model. KLT features are first located within moving skin regions (as filtered by the skin and motion likelihood maps) using the method described in [19] based on a goodness-to-track quality metric. The motion information of the chosen KLT features are then obtained via a multi-scale sparse optical flow algorithm. Similar to the work of [12], and relying on the notion of "common motion constraint", we apply an iterative method for clustering KLT features by their affine motions. The RANSAC scheme is used for robust affine motion model fitting, because of its high breakdown point (can tolerate up to 50% outliers). Finally, the clusters of KLT features and their associated affine motion models constitute the *observations* that will be fed to the MHT stage of our tracking system

$$z_i^t = \left\{ \{k_j\}_{\forall j \in C_i}, \mathbf{A}_i^t \right\} \tag{1}$$

where k_j is the jth KLT feature, C_i is the ith cluster of KLT features, and A_i^t is the affine motion model fitted to the KLT features $\{k_j\}$ of the ith cluster

$$\mathbf{A}_i^t = \begin{bmatrix} a_0 & a_1 & a_2 \\ a_3 & a_4 & a_5 \\ 0 & 0 & 1 \end{bmatrix} \tag{2}$$

4.2   Target Representation

Many different representations have been used in the object tracking literature such as: appearance-based representations (templates, active appearance models, etc.), motion-based representations, and shape-based representations (silhouettes, contours, primitive geometric shapes, articulated shape models, skeletal models, etc.) [10]. We represent objects (the hands and face) by their affine motion model $\mathbf{A}$, centroid (x, y), and their spatial extent (bounding box having width w and height h). Assuming a linear dynamic process, a constant-velocity Kalman filter is used with the following state $\mathbf{x}$ and state transition matrix $\mathbf{F}$, where $\mathbf{I}_{16 \times 16}$ is an identity sub-matrix

$$\mathbf{x} = \left[x, y, \frac{w}{2}, \frac{h}{2}, a_0, a_1, \cdots, a_5, \dot{x}, \dot{y}, \frac{\dot{w}}{2}, \frac{\dot{h}}{2}, \dot{a}_0, \dot{a}_1, \cdots, \dot{a}_5 \right]^T$$

$$\mathbf{F} = \begin{bmatrix} \mathbf{I}_{16 \times 16} & \mathbf{I}_{16 \times 16} \cdot dt \\ \mathbf{0}_{16 \times 16} & \mathbf{I}_{16 \times 16} \end{bmatrix} \tag{3}$$

This Kalman filter allows us to predict the position of the hands $\bar{x}_j^t$ at time t. The predictions of the width $w/2$ and height $h/2$ at time t given by the KF are used for occlusion prediction by checking for bounding box overlap of the 2 hands – this information is used to set the occlusion terms of the MHT. The affine motion terms a_0 to a_5 in the KF are for smoothing the target's affine motion model $\mathbf{A}$, used for KLT feature clustering and replenishment (see Section 4.1).

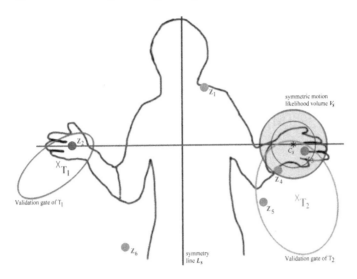

Fig. 1. Use of the symmetric motion constraint in tracking

4.3 Tracking with Sign Language Hand Motion Constraints

Our proposal in this paper is to incorporate constraints on hand motion based on sign language linguistic models. In particular, we concentrate on one such constraint from the sign language literature called the "symmetry" condition ("h2-S") [2]. This states that for the majority of 2-handed signs, the non-dominant hand serves as a duplicate articulator, i.e., its movement mirrors that of the dominant hand. Figure 1 above illustrates in a schematic way, how we integrate the symmetric motion constraint within the tracking process. Our tracking process assumes that the 2 hands are the main moving objects in the scene, and that the right and left hands start on the right and left side of the body respectively. Using the face detection results for time t, we first identify the body-centred line of symmetry L_s. Currently we ignore any sideways leaning of the signer's upper body and keep L_s oriented vertically. Then during the MHT hypothesis generation stage, given an association hypothesis ψ_i^t that associates object T_1 with observation z_2, we locate the corresponding point C_s reflected by the line of symmetry L_s, and define the symmetric motion likelihood volume V_s, depicted in Figure 1. Currently we adopt a non-parametric approach for the pdf of V_s, i.e., using a probability density map. For object T_2, the probability of associating it with the set of observations in its validation gate is then computed via a weighted combination of the standard MHT's observation-target probability ([3,4]) and the probability given by our density map:

$$\mathcal{N}'\left(z_i^t\right) \triangleq \alpha \cdot \mathcal{N}\left(z_i^t | \bar{x}_j^t, \Sigma_{ij}^t\right) + (1 - \alpha) \cdot \mathbf{M}_t^{V_s} \tag{4}$$

where $\mathbf{M}_t^{V_s}$ is the probability density map of V_s at time t, and α is a weighting factor. Continuing with the example depicted in Figure 1, the hypothesis that object T_2 is associated with observation z_3 now has a stronger bias, because of the addition of $\mathbf{M}_t^{V_s}$ term. An issue that our proposed incorporation of symmetric motion has to contend with is when the 2 hands are moving slightly out of sync – one hand lags behind the other in its mirrored trajectory position. We solve this issue by adopting a temporal window approach for the update of the probability density map $\mathbf{M}_t^{V_s}$ with a forgetting mechanism with rate γ

$$\left(\mathbf{M}_t^{V_s}\right)' = \gamma\left(\mathbf{M}_t^{V_s}\right) + (1-\gamma)\left(\mathbf{M}_{t-1}^{V_s}\right) \tag{5}$$

5   Experiments

In order to evaluate the effectiveness of our approach, video sequences from the ECHO Sign Language (NGT) Corpus [21] are used. These are colour sequences, with 352×288 resolution, running at 25 fps, and taken with a fixed camera. Although signing occurs within a simplified environment (indoors, constant illumination, plain background, signer wearing dark clothes), these sequences exhibit frequent occlusions of the hands and the face, often of medium to long duration, and with lots of complex hand interaction ('bounce backs', 'crossovers') events. Thus we believe that videos from this corpus constitute a good test bed for our proposed tracking system. As no tracking-related ground truthing is available for these video sequences, the ViPER-GT toolkit [20] was used to generate ground truth of the face and the hands for around 6000 video frames – via the visual annotation feature of ViPER-GT of the positions and the bounding boxes.

5.1   Experimental Setup

Our system was implemented in C++ and makes use of the OpenCV library. Our MHT implementation is based on the original MHT library reported in [17]; but it also includes additional modifications as suggested in [24], mainly for computational efficiency reasons, and the addition of the occlusion terms as described in [22]. Our MHT implementation can benefit from further improvements, such as more use of parallelism, especially for handling the disjoint hypothesis clusters – future work will address this.

Several algorithms used in our system have a number of configurable parameters – many of these values were set empirically. For the MHT algorithm, the temporal sliding window (used for N-scan pruning) was set to 25 frames (1 second) – this is adequate as the majority of signs last less than 1 second, thus achieving a balance between the size of the mantained hypothesis tree for sign recognition accuracy and the real-time execution speed requirement. The a priori probability values for track detection p_{det}, track termination p_{term}, and occlusion events p_{occl}, were configured as 0.7, 0.1 and 0.2 respectively (subject to the condition $p_{det} + p_{term} + p_{occl} = 1$). And the Poisson expectations for false alarms and new tracks were set to: $\lambda_{fa} = 3$, and $\lambda_{new} = 1$, respectively. Even though the number of objects being tracked in an ASLR context is fixed (2 hands and a face), the parameter values for new tracks (λ_{new}) and track termination (p_{term}) must cater for the potential loss and recovery of the targets of interest, as well as handling cases where multiple observations are returned for a single target (e.g., when apart from the hand, the arm is also visible).

Three experiments were performed. For the first experiment, we used a standard frame-to-frame (single hypothesis) tracking system and ran it on the mentioned video sequences – this system, referred to as 'baseline F2F' here, serves as a lower performance bound against which MHT-based tracking will be compared. The 'baseline F2F' system makes use of the same object detection and representation (KLT features) stage as the proposed system, but instead uses global nearest neighbour (via the Kuhn-Munkres Hungarian algorithm) for data association and a simplified rule-based track maintenance system. The second experiment made use of our MHT-based tracking system, but without the incorporation of the sign language hand motion constraints, i.e., using a regular MHT algorithm. The third and final experiment is the one making use of our contribution described in this paper – referred to as 'MHT+SL constraints' here.

The three experiments were executed on a 2.0 GHz PC with an Intel dual core CPU, and 16Gb of RAM. Tracking executed in real-time (at 20 to 23 fps).

5.2 Evaluation of Tracking Results

For evaluation purposes, we adopted the CLEAR metrics MOTP and MOTA [23]. MOTP (multiple object tracking precision) measures how well the positions of the hands are estimated by the tracker

$$MOTP = \frac{\sum_{i,t} d_{i,t}}{\sum_t c_t} \tag{6}$$

where $d_{i,t}$ is a distance score between the ground truth object $g_{i,t}$ and its corresponding tracker output; c_t is the number of successfully tracked objects at time t. In our evaluation we chose the overlap ratio between the ground truth's bounding box and that of the tracker output as the distance score $d_{i,t} = \frac{|g_{i,t} \cap o_{i,t}|}{|g_{i,t} \cup o_{i,t}|}$ MOTP score values are in range [0..1], with 0 indicating a perfect match.

MOTA (multiple object tracking accuracy) measures the number of mistakes that the tracker makes in terms of missed object detections (false negatives, FNs), false positives (FPs), and the number object mismatches (object label/identity switches, $MMEs$) that occur.

$$MOTA = 1 - \left[\frac{\sum_t \{FN_t + FP_t + MME_t\}}{\sum_t g_t} \right] \tag{7}$$

Thus MOTA gives an indication of the tracker's performance at keeping accurate trajectories, independent of the tracker's precision in estimating object positions. MOTA score values can range from negative values to 1.0 (perfect accuracy).

5.3 Discussion

The results of the quantitative evaluation using the CLEAR metrics are given in Table 1 on the next page. Also shown are the normalised FN, FP, and

Table 1. Comparative performance of MHT with SL constraints

Method	MOTP	MOTA	$FN/\sum_t g_t$	$FP/\sum_t g_t$	$MME/\sum_t g_t$
baseline F2F	0.550	0.022	0.298	0.371	0.309
MHT	0.603	0.281	0.236	0.325	0.158
MHT+SL constraints	0.601	0.313	0.225	0.328	0.134

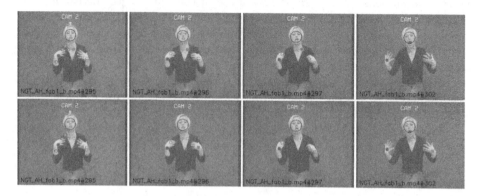

Fig. 2. Tracking results of regular MHT (top) and "MHT+SL constraints" (bottom). Correct tracks of the dominant hand (filled red circles) and non-dominant hand (filled green circles), while pruned hypotheses are shown as open circles.

mismatch rates. As can be seen, our proposed approach has an overall better performance than regular MHT. While there is only a marginal improvement in tracking precision (MOTP), tracking accuracy (MOTA) exhibits a more evident improvement. The factor that contributes most to this improvement in accuracy is the reduced number of object label mismatches ($MMEs$). In other words, the inclusion of constraints on hand motion based on sign language linguistic models increases the robustness of the tracking system to identity switches of the 2 hands. Figures 2 & 3 on the facing page illustrate this qualitatively.

The top row in Figure 2 gives the results of the regular MHT, while the bottom row shows the results of our approach. Prior to the first video frame shown, the hands were partially occluding each other near the neck area. Upon emerging from the occlusion event, the non-dominant hand in the regular MHT, is incorrectly matched to spurious observations (caused by shadows on the neck created by head motion). In our approach, the correct tracking of the dominant hand plus the rule on symmetric hand motion, help to increase the likelihood of the correct hypothesis of the non-dominant hand. Thus, with support from the dominant hand, the non-dominant hand is tracked successfully throughout all the frames – in contrast, the regular MHT only recovers successfully from the occlusion event in the last video frame of Figure 2.

In Figure 3, more results from our proposed tracking system, in the presence of complex hand interactions and cross-over events, are shown. Our approach

Fig. 3. Tracking in the presence of complex hand interactions and cross-over events.

exhibits a marginal increase in the number of FPs over regular MHT. While the reason behind this could not be ascertained, our analysis of the tracking results showed that a large number of the FP observations are caused by a too simplistic representation of hand motion, mainly the affine motion model adopted for KLT feature clustering and the constant-velocity Kalman filters. Signing exhibits abrupt hand motion with many discontinuities in hand trajectories – something which cannot be easily modelled with affine motion and constant-velocity KFs. To minimise feature cluster fragmentation and the FPs that arise from it, we could potentially use an IMM (interacting multiple model) approach, where several KFs, tuned to different hand manoeuvres, are run in parallel. In [25], an IMM is applied for tracking the hands in a natural conversation context.

6   Conclusion

We have proposed a mechanism for integrating *prior* knowledge about hand motion constraints described by sign language phonological models into our MHT-based tracking framework, in order to provide better tracking robustness especially in the presence of occlusion and hand interaction events. The constraints are integrated within the hypothesis evaluation mechanism of MHT and defined in terms of probabilistic density maps. We demonstrated this approach via the implementation of one such constraint – the hand symmetry condition. Experimental results demonstrate the effectiveness and the prospect of our approach, especially in improving tracking accuracy. And since hand tracking is central to sign recognition, it is expected that our approach will show a marked improvement in sign recognition once it is incorporated within the ASLR process.

Future work will look into: (1) adding more constraints into the tracking process from sign language phonological models (e.g. "h2-P"); (2) look into the use of handshape information both in the tracking process and the addition of phonological constraints related to the handshape; (3) integrate the hand motion constraints in a more principled and structured way, perhaps adopting a parametric or semi-parameteric probabilistic approach instead of the current non-parametric representation; (4) and employ better motion models for tracking the hands, instead of the current use of affine motion models and constant velocity Kalman filters, perhaps using IMMs to handle abrupt hand motions.

References

1. von Agris, et al.: Recent developments in visual sign language recognition. Universal Access in the Information Society **6**(4), 323–362 (2007)
2. Sandler, W., Lillo-Martin, D.: Sign Language and Linguistic Universals. Cambridge Univ. Press (2006)
3. Bar-shalom, Y., Daum, F., Huang, J.: The Probabilistic Data Association Filter. IEEE Control Syst. Mag., 82–100 (2009)
4. Blackman, S.: Multiple Hypothesis Tracking For Multiple Target Tracking. IEEE Aerosp. Electron. Syst. Mag. **19**(1), 5–18 (2004)
5. Roshtkhar, M., et al.: Multiple Object Tracking Using Local Motion Patterns. BMVC (2014)
6. Amer, A.: Voting-based simultaneous tracking of multiple video objects. IEEE Trans. Circuits Syst. Video Technol. **15**(11), 1448–1462 (2005)
7. Shafique, K., Shah, M.: A Non-Iterative Greedy Algorithm for Multi-frame Point Correspondence. IEEE Proc. Int. Conf. Comp. Vision, 110–115 (2003)
8. Klinger, A., et al.: A Dynamic Bayes Network for Visual Pedestrian Tracking. ISPRS **40**(3), 145–150 (2014)
9. Reid, D.: An algorithm for tracking multiple targets. IEEE Trans. Automat. Contr. **24**(6), 843–854 (1979)
10. Yilmaz, A.: Object Tracking: A Survey. ACM Comput. Surv. **38**(4), 1–45 (2006)
11. Ragland, K., Tharcis, P.: A Survey on Object Detection, Classification and Tracking Methods. IJERT **3**(11), 622–628 (2014)
12. Thirde, D., et al.: Robust Real-Time Tracking for Visual Surveillance. EURASIP J. Advances in Signal Proc **2007**(1), 1–23 (2007)
13. Ying, L., Xu, C., Guo, W.: Extended MHT algorithm for multiple object tracking. In: Proc. Int. Conf. Internet Multimedia Computing and Service (2012)
14. Lao, Y., Zheng, Y.: Tracking highly correlated targets through statistical multiplexing. Image and Vision Computing **29**(12), 803–817 (2011)
15. Veenman, C., Reinders, M., Backer, E.: Resolving motion correspondence for densely moving points. Trans. PAMI **23**(1), 54–72 (2001)
16. Antunes, D., et al.: A Library for Implementing the Multiple Hypothesis Tracking Algorithm. CoRR **23**(1), 54–72 (2011)
17. Cox, I.: Miller, M: On Finding Ranked Assignments With Application to Multi-Target Tracking & Motion Correspondence. Trans. Aerosp. Electron. Syst. (1996)
18. Wimmer, M.: Adaptive skin color classificator. In: Proc. GVIP, pp. 324–327 (2005)
19. Tomasi, C., Shi, J.: Good Features to Track. In: Proc. CVPR, pp. 593–600 (1994)
20. Doermann, D: Tools and Techniques for Video Performances Evaluation (2000)
21. Crasborn, O., et al.: ECHO Data Set for Sign Language of the Netherlands (NGT) (2004)
22. Arras, K., et al.: Efficient People Tracking in Laser Range Data using a Multi-Hypothesis Leg-Tracker with Adaptive Occlusion Probabilities. Int. Conf. on Robotics and Automation (2008)

23. Kasturi, R., et al.: Framework for performance evaluation of face, text, and vehicle detection and tracking in video. IEEE PAMI **31**(2), 319–336 (2009)
24. Amditis, A., et al.: Multiple Hypothesis Tracking Implementation, 199–220 (2012)
25. Wu, S., Hong, L.: Hand tracking in a natural conversational environment by the interacting multiple model and probabilistic data association (IMM-PDA) algorithm. Pattern Recognition **38**(11), 199–220 (2005)
26. Lienhart, R., Maydt, J.: An extended set of haar-like features for rapid object detection. In: Proc. Int. Conf. Image Processing (2002)

Combining Features for Texture Analysis

Anca Ignat[(✉)]

Faculty of Computer Science,
University "Alexandru Ioan Cuza", Iaşi, Romania
ancai@info.uaic.ro

Abstract. In the present paper we consider building feature vectors for texture analysis by combining information provided by two techniques. The first feature extraction method (the Discrete Wavelet Transform) is applied to the entire image. By computing the Gini index for several subimages of a given texture, we choose one that maximizes this measure. For the selected subimage we apply the second technique (a Gabor filter) for feature extraction. When we combine the two vectors, the classification results are better than the one obtained using only one set of features. The classification was performed on the Brodatz album, using a naive Bayes classifier.

Keywords: Texture · Discrete Wavelet Transform (DWT) · Gabor filters · Gini index · Naive Bayes

1 Introduction

One way to approach content-based image retrieval problems is by studying the texture content of the image [1,2]. There is no generally accepted formal definition for the notion of texture. One manner to describe texture image is as a regularity pattern which reveals some sort of spatial arrangement of the intensities. The texture issue being a intensely studied subject, there is a big variety of approaches which can be grouped as structural, spectral, statistical [3–5].

In this work we study the problem of texture analysis by combining features provided by two wavelet-based methods, the classical DWT and the Gabor filters, in order to improve the classification rate provided by DWT alone and also keep a low computational cost. The Discrete Wavelet Transform and its multiple variants were first employed for image compression but it were also used for texture feature extraction [6–9]. Much more popular for dealing with texture are the Gabor filters [10–14]. In [10] the authors present different methods for extracting features using Gabor filters. The problem of generating scale and rotation invariant using Gabor filtering was also studied [13]. Most of the approaches use the energy, mean, standard deviation of the coefficients provided by Gabor filtering.

The idea of putting together features obtained from different methods in order to improve the classification was treated in [15,16]. In [16] the authors use several combinations of features obtained by applying Fast Fourier, Cosine,

© Springer International Publishing Switzerland 2015
G. Azzopardi and N. Petkov (Eds.): CAIP 2015, Part II, LNCS 9257, pp. 220–229, 2015.
DOI: 10.1007/978-3-319-23117-4_19

Wavelet Transforms to the histogram of the coefficient provided by Local Binary Pattern analysis of the texture. For classification they use Support Vector Machine (SVM). In [15] the features are extracted using Steerable Pyramid, Gabor filters, SIFT (Scale-Invariant Feature Transform) and as classifiers they use SVM, Bayesian network, instance-based learners, naive Bayes, decision trees. They test their method on three datasets: Brodatz, UIUC, and KTH. The best results for Brodatz album was with Steerable Pyramid combined with Gabor filter extracted features and an instance based learner using k-NN as classifier.

Our approach consists of combining 'weak' features for the whole image with 'strong' features for a subimage which is selected in order to maximize a measure of information. We chose as 'weak' feature extractor the DWT and for the 'strong' features the Gabor filters. As measure of information one uses the Gini coefficient [17], a measure of income distribution usually employed in economy. We test these features on 112 textures from Brodatz database [18,19] using a naive Bayes classifier.

2 Texture Feature Extraction

The main ingredients for feature extraction that we used in the present work are the Discrete Wavelet Transform, Gabor filters and Gini index.

The Fourier transform of a signal provides frequency information about the analyzed signal but not its localization in time. Wavelets were introduced in 1981 by Morlet providing a solution for the problem by rendering both frequency and time localization. Major steps for the application of wavelet theory to signal processing were made by I. Daubechies when she found a method to compute orthogonal wavelets with compact support and also by Mallat and Meyer with the concept of multiresolution analysis. Mallat's fast algorithm for computing the wavelet transform links the wavelet domain to the sub-band coding technique for signal processing thus opening the Discrete Wavelet Transform to the wide use in digital signal processing ([20,21]).

A DWT decomposition with J levels applied to an image computes approximation coefficients denoted by C_A (the low-low subimage) and at each level three directional coefficients: vertical (low-high subimage), horizontal (result of high-low filtering) and diagonal (high-high filtering):

$$\left(C_V^j, C_H^j, C_D^j\right) \quad , \quad j = 1, ..., J. \tag{1}$$

An example of a 3-level DWT can be seen in Fig. 1.

We denote by $\mu(X)$ the mean of X and by $\sigma(X)$ the standard deviation. In order to build the feature vector, we compute the mean and the standard deviation of all coefficients provided by the DWT, i.e. we obtain the 6-dimensional vector:

$$v^j = 2^{(J-j)}\left(\mu(C_V^j), \sigma(C_V^j), \mu(C_H^j), \sigma(C_H^j), \mu(C_D^j), \sigma(C_D^j)\right) \tag{2}$$

We used the 2^{J-j} weighing factor because the size of the detail coefficients decreases as j increases and we wanted to take into account this size variation into

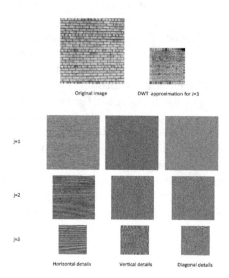

Original image   DWT approximation for j=3

j=1

j=2

j=3

Horizontal details   Vertical details   Diagonal details

Fig. 1. DWT with $J = 3$ for D95 texture image from Brodatz album

the feature vector. This type of features (without weighing) was also employed in [7]. We consider as feature vector the normalized version of the means and standard deviations for all the coefficients provided by the DWT:

$$\tilde{f} = \left(\mu(C_A), \sigma(C_A), \{v^j; j = 1, ..., J\} \right),$$

$$f = \frac{1}{\sum \tilde{f}_i} \tilde{f}. \tag{3}$$

Thus the length of a feature vector f is $6J + 2$.

The Gabor filter is a combination between a Gaussian kernel with a complex sinusoid:

$$G(x, y, \sigma, \lambda, \theta, \gamma) = g(x, y, \sigma, \gamma) \exp\left(\frac{2\pi x_t}{\lambda} i \right)$$

$$g(x, y, \sigma, \gamma) = \exp\left(-\frac{x_t^2 + \gamma^2 y_t^2}{2\sigma^2} \right) \tag{4}$$

$$x_t = x \cos\theta + y \sin\theta \quad , \quad y_t = -x \sin\theta + y \cos\theta$$

We consider the spatial aspect ratio $\gamma = 0.5$ and the link between σ and the wavelength λ is given by $\lambda = 0.5622\sigma$ [10], [22]. The result of Gabor filtering using the above kernel is complex, but we used only the amplitude of the result. In our computations we filtered the image using 6 orientations θ from $\{15°, 45°, 75°, 105°, 135°, 165°\}$ and for the wavelength λ we took J values $\{5, 10, ..., 5J\}$.

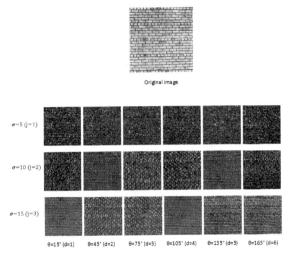

Original image

$\sigma=5$ (j=1)

$\sigma=10$ (j=2)

$\sigma=15$ (j=3)

$\theta=15°$ (d=1) $\theta=45°$ (d=2) $\theta=75°$ (d=3) $\theta=105°$ (d=4) $\theta=135°$ (d=5) $\theta=165°$ (d=6)

Fig. 2. Result of Gabor filtering applied to D95 texture with 3 wavelengths $\sigma \in \{5, 10, 15\}$ and 6 orientations $\theta \in \{15°, 45°, 75°, 105°, 135°, 165°\}$

As a result of applying the Gabor filter, we get $W_{d,j}$ filtered images, $d = 1, ...6$ (for different θ selections), $j = 1, ..., J$ (for the wavelength σ choices). These $W_{d,j}$ for texture D95 are depicted in Fig. 2. We form the feature vector as we did for the DWT, by taking the normalized vector formed with the mean and standard deviation of the $W_{d,j}$ images:

$$\tilde{f} = \left(\{\mu(W_{d,j}), \sigma(W_{d,j}); d = 1, .., 6, j = 1, ..., J\}\right) \quad , \quad f = \frac{1}{\sum \tilde{f}_i} \tilde{f}. \quad (5)$$

In [13] the authors use also the mean and standard deviation for building the feature vector. The length of this feature vector is $12J$.

The Gini index or Gini coefficient is a notion introduced in 1912 by statistician and demographer Corrado Gini in order to measure income inequality in a population [17]. The formula we used in order to compute the Gini coefficient is the following:

$$G = 1 - \frac{\sum_{i=1}^{n} f(y_i)(S_{i-1} + S_i)}{S_n} \quad , \quad (6)$$

$$S_0 = 0 \quad , \quad S_i = \sum_{j=1}^{i} f(y_j)y_j \quad i = 1, ..., n.$$

where we have a discrete probability distribution with f the probability mass function and $y_i, i = 1, ..., n$ are the distinct intensities which occur in the image, indexed in increasing order $y_i < y_{i+1}$.

The DWT and Gabor filtering features extraction methods (3), (5) are combined in the following way. First, apply the DWT to the entire texture image and compute the feature vector f_1 using (3).

We want to find a part of the texture that carries more 'importance' in texture classification than other regions from the image. For finding this region, one employs the Gini index as a measure of saliency. Starting from the upper left corner of the image we extract subimages half the size of the original one, moving with a certain step from one subimage to another (in our computations the size of this distance was 32 pixels, vertically or horizontally). For these subimages one computes the Gini index with formula (6). We choose the subimage with maximal Gini index value (if there were more than one subimage with the same maximal value, we selected one randomly). For this selected subimage one applies Gabor filtering with $(J-1)$ or $J/2$ σ wavelength choices, thus computing a second feature vector f_2 using (5).

We put together f_1 and f_2, $f = (f_1, f_2)$ and perform the classification step with each of these features.

We want to evaluate the computational complexity of these type of features for images of size $N \times N(N = 2^p)$. For computing the j-th DWT decomposition level, the following computations are done: two convolutions on $\frac{N}{2^{j-1}} \times \frac{N}{2^{j-1}}$ subimages (one with a m_H size filter and one with a m_L size filter) and four convolutions on $\frac{N}{2^j} \times \frac{N}{2^j}$ subimages (two with the m_H size filter and the other two with the m_L size filter). Summing these computations one gets $\mathcal{O}\left(\frac{3}{2}(m_H + m_L)\left(1 - \frac{1}{4^J}\right)N^2\right)$ for computing a DWT.

For each frequency-orientation pair (σ, θ) from a Gabor filter, one computes two convolution products with kernels of size m_G on $N \times N$ images. If we denote by n_f the total number of frequencies employed and by n_o the number of orientations used for computing the Gabor filter, the computational complexity for a Gabor filter applied to an $N \times N$ image is $\mathcal{O}\left(2n_f n_o m_G N^2\right)$. In our case $n_o = 6$ and $n_f = J$ so the complexity for the Gabor filter is $\mathcal{O}\left(12 J m_G N^2\right)$.

Computing the Gini coefficient for an $M \times M$ image can be performed in $\mathcal{O}\left(2M^2\right)$.

For the DWT features the components of the vectors are computed faster as the decomposition level j increases because the size of the DWT coefficients decrease as the level of decomposition increases. In the case of Gabor features, all the components of the vector require the same computational complexity.

3   Results

The numerical tests were done using MATLAB. For the DWT we used the *wavedec2* function from MATLAB's Wavelet Toolbox which employs *conv2* for the convolution product. For Gabor filtering we implemented a function which is using the same *conv2* for computing the filtered images. In the case of DWT we employed biorthogonal filters of size $m_L = m_H = 9$ ('bior4.4' MATLAB implemented wavelet filters) and for Gabor filtering the size of the kernel was $m_G = 19 \times 19 = 361$.

For testing the proposed feature extraction method we employed 112 texture images of size 512×512 from the Brodatz album [18,19] (see Fig. 3). In order to form classes representing each texture, 25 subimages of size 256×256 were randomly selected from the 512×512 original ones. We chose these subimages such that their centers are at a certain distance. We used the Euclidean distance and the threshold value was 32. After selecting these 25 images we computed the features as described above. The lengths of the feature vectors with respect to the number of decomposition levels J are in Table 1.

Table 1. Length of feature vectors

J	DWT	Gabor
2	14	24
3	20	36
4	26	48

We considered 6 situations:

DWT-Gabor The features consist of the DWT-features (3) for the whole image and the Gabor-features (5) for the subimage selected using the Gini coefficient

DWT-DWT The features for the image and the Gini index selected subimage are both computed using DWT

DWT/Gabor (256) Only the DWT/Gabor-features for the texture were computed

DWT/Gabor (128) Only the DWT/Gabor-features for the 128×128 subimage that maximizes the Gini index are considered.

The training set was build by randomly selecting 13 images from each class, the other 12 were used for testing the classification process. We tested three classification methods: nearest neighbor, naive Bayes, and SVM [23]. The naive Bayes provided better results than the other two classifiers so we present classification result using this pattern matching technique. We deliberately chose such simple classification methods, in order to test the efficacy of combining the features computed using the DWT and Gabor filtering.

Because we randomly selected the images representing the classes, we performed 20 tests, each test having different classes content. In Table 2 are the average classification rate for these 20 tests, the tests with the the best result (max) and the test with the worst result (min). The Gabor features for the Gini selected subimage were computed with $J/2$ values for σ.

In Table 3. are the total number of misidentified textures from all the 20 performed tests.

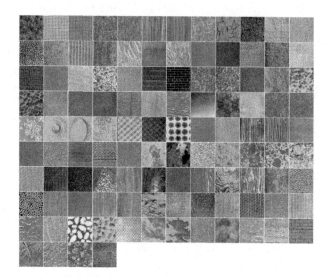

Fig. 3. The 112 textures of the Brodatz database

Table 2. Classification results using naive Bayes (no noise) on 20 tests

Features	Average	Max	Min
DWT-Gabor	98.67%	97.92%	99.26%
DWT-DWT	97.42%	96.28%	98.14%
DWT (256)	96.34%	95.24%	97.17%
Gabor (256)	99.36%	99.11%	99.78%
DWT (128)	90.12%	88.62%	91.74%
Gabor (128)	90.53%	89.06%	91.67%

Table 3. Total number of textures misclassified (no noise)

Features	No. of errors
DWT-Gabor	358
DWT-DWT	693
DWT (256)	984
Gabor (256)	154
DWT (128)	2657
Gabor (128)	2546

Table 4. Average classification results with $(J-1)$ decomposition levels (20 tests)

Features	Classification	Total no. of errors
DWT-Gabor	98.88%	300
DWT-DWT	98.37%	439
DWT (256)	98.08%	516
Gabor (256)	99.46%	145
DWT (128)	91.57%	2265
Gabor (128)	94.57%	1205

Table 5. Average classification results with noise

Features	Classification	No. of errors
DWT-Gabor	98.26%	936
DWT-DWT	96.67%	1790
DWT (256)	96.29%	1997
Gabor (256)	99.19%	438
DWT (128)	86.8%	7099
Gabor (128)	93.25%	3628

Table 6. Average time in seconds for feature extraction (with noise)

Features	Time (s)
DWT-DWT	281
DWT-Gabor	590
Gabor (256)	1654

If instead of computing Gabor filters with $J/2 = 2$, we used $J - 1 = 3$ the classification results improve, as can be seen from Table 4.

We consider also the effect of noise. We applied a 5×5 Gaussian filter to all the images. In the training set we placed 13 clean images and 13 noisy images selected randomly. We repeated the classification process, the results are reported in Table 5. In this case we used $(J-1)$ levels of decompositions for the 128×128 selected subimage.

As one can observe from Table 2, Table 3, and Table 5 that the process of combining the DWT-features for the texture image with Gabor or DWT features for a selected subimage yields better results that only DWT applied to the image. Nevertheless, one can notice that the best classification results are obtained with the Gabor-features applied to the whole image. We also measured the average time for computing the features in the cases DWT-Gabor, DWT-DWT and Gabor (256). The results are in Table 6. Mark that it is 3 times faster to compute combined features DWT-Gabor than to compute only Gabor-features for the texture images. This is a consequence of the difference of computational complexity between DWT ($\mathcal{O}(30N^2)$) and Gabor filtering ($\mathcal{O}(24 \cdot 19^2 N^2)$). When time is important, the method proposed in this work can be an option because the classification results are good. If we compare our results with those obtained Barley and Town in [15], the best rate for Brodatz image dataset is 91.5% with a combination of steerable pyramid and Gabor features and using a modified kNN classifier. In order to reduce the computational time, we considered also Gabor (256) filtering only with four orientations ($30°, 75°, 120°, 165°$), the average computational time reduces to 1150 seconds and the identification rate was 99.16%. If we combine DWT and Gabor features with only four orientations the classification result was 98.5% and the computational time 450.

We tested the contribution to the classification process introduced by using the Gini coefficient. Instead of using this measure to select the subimage, we made computation using the Shannon entropy and also by simply cropping the 128×128 subimage from the center of the texture. We used only the DWT-Gabor features for texture both clean and with noise. The Shannon entropy yields a 97,73% classification rate with 1222 errors and the middle subimage selection has 97,78% success with a total of 1193 misidentified textures. If the Gini selected subimage is of size 64×64 instead of 128×128 the classification using DWT-Gabor features gets 97.47% with 1362 errors over all the tests (with noise).

We also considered combining DWT features and Gabor features, both extracted from the 256×256 images, in the presence of noise. The average identification result was 99.31% with a total of 370 errors and 1870 seconds average computation time. This is the best identification result with the worst computational time.

4   Conclusions

We presented a method of combining two feature extracting techniques in order to improve the results obtained with the one which has lower classification rate. The first method is applied two the whole texture image and the better one is applied on a subimage selected such that it has maximal Gini coefficient. This combination of features gets better results than the 'weak' method, but still the classification rate is lower than that provided by the 'strong' method. The two techniques we used to extract features are DWT (the 'weak' one) and Gabor filters ('strong' method). Although the presented method does not yield better results than Gabor filters, the classification rates are very good and it computes the features faster.

In order to further validate the presented approach, we need to test it on other feature extraction methods, and also on other texture databases.

References

1. Datta, R., Joshi, D., Li, J., Wang, J.Z.: Image retrieval: Ideas, influences, and trends of the new age. ACM Computing Surveys **40**(2), article 5 (2008)
2. Dhale, V., Mahajan, A.R., Thakur, U.: A Survey of Feature Extraction Methods for Image Retrieval. IJARCSSE **2**(10), 1–8 (2012)

3. Nixon, M.S., Aguado, A.S.: Feature Extraction and Image Processing for Computer Vision, 3rd edn. Academic Press (2012)

4. Tian, D.P.: A Review on Image Feature Extraction and Representation Techniques. International Journal of Multimedia and Ubiquitous Engineering **8**(4), 385–396 (2013)

5. Baaziz, N., Abahmane, O., Missaoui, R.: Texture feature extraction in the spatial-frequency domain for content-based image retrieval. eprint arXiv:1012.5208

6. Sebe, N., Lew, M.S.: Wavelet based texture classification. In: Proc. of Int. Conf. on Pattern Recognition, vol. 3, pp. 959–962 (2000)

7. Arivazhagan, S., Ganesan, L.: Texture classification using wavelet transform. Pattern Recognition Letters **24**(9–10), 1513–1521 (2003)

8. Kociołek, M., Materka, A., Strzelecki, M., Szczypiński, P.: Discrete wavelet transform derived features for digital image texture analysis. In: Proc. of International Conference on Signals and Electronic Systems, Lodz, Poland, pp. 163–168 (2001)

9. Rajpoot, K.M., Rajpoot, N.M.: Wavelets and support vector machines for texture classification. In: Proceedings of 8th IEEE International Multitopic Conference, pp. 328–333 (2004)

10. Grigorescu, S.E., Petkov, N., Kruizinga, P.: Comparison of texture features based on Gabor filters. IEEE Trans. on Image Processing **11**(10), 1160–1167 (2002)

11. Zhang, D.S., Wong, A., Indrawan, M., Lu, G.: Content based image retrieval using Gabor texture features. In: Proc. of 1st IEEE Pacific Rim Conference on Multimedia (PCM 2000), Sydney, Australia, pp. 392–395 (2000)

12. Andrysiak, T., Choras, M.: Image retrieval based on hierarchical Gabor filters. Int. Journal of Mathematics and Computer Science **15**(4), 471–480 (2005)

13. Riaz, F., Hassan, A., Rehman, S., Qamar, U.: Texture classification using rotation- and scale-invariant Gabor texture features. IEEE Signal Processing Letters **20**(6), 607–610 (2013)

14. Idrissa, M., Acheroy, M.: Texture classification using Gabor filters. Pattern Recognition Letters **23**, 1095–1102 (2002)

15. Barley, A., Town, C.: Combinations of Feature Descriptors for Texture Image Classification. Journal of Data Analysis and Information Processing **2**, 67–76 (2014)

16. Nanni, L., Brahnam, S., Lumini, A.: Combining different local binary pattern variants to boost performance. Expert Systems with Applications **38**(5), 6209–6216 (2011)

17. Gini, C.:Variabilitá e mutabilita (1912); Reprinted in Memorie di metodologia statistica (Eds. Pizetti, E., Salvemini, T.). Libreria Eredi Virgilio Veschi, Rome (1955)

18. Brodatz, P.: Textures: A Photographic Album for Artists and Designers. Dover, New York (1966)

19. Brodatz: http://multibandtexture.recherche.usherbrooke.ca/index.html

20. Vetterli, M., Kovačević, J.: Wavelets and Subband Coding. Prentice Hall, Englewood Cliffs (1995)

21. Mallat, S.: A Wavelet Tour of Signal Processing, 2nd edn. Academic Press, San Diego (1998)

22. Chen, L., Lu, G., Zhang, D.: Effects of different Gabor filter parameters on image retrieval by texture. In: Proc. 10th Int. Multimedia Model. Conf., pp. 273–278 (2004)

23. Dougherty, G.: Pattern Recognition and Classification: an Introduction. Springer Science & Business Media (2012)

A Novel Canonical Form for the Registration of Non Rigid 3D Shapes

Majdi Jribi$^{(\boxtimes)}$ and Faouzi Ghorbel

CRISTAL Laboratory, GRIFT Research Group, Ecole Nationale des Sciences de l'Informatique (ENSI), La Manouba University, 2010 La Manouba, Tunisia
{majdi.jribi,faouzi.ghorbel}@ensi.rnu.tn

Abstract. In this paper, we address the problem of non rigid 3D shapes registration. We propose to construct a canonical form for the 3D objects corresponding to the same shape with different non rigid inelastic deformations. It consists on replacing the geodesic distances computed from three reference points of the original surface by the Euclidean ones calculated from three points of the novel canonical form. Therefore, the problem of non rigid registration is transformed to a rigid matching between canonical forms. The effectiveness of such method for the recognition and the retrieval processes is evaluated by the experimentation on the TOSCA database objects in the mean of the Hausdorff Shape distance.

Keywords: Registration · Non rigid · Inelastic · 3D · Surface · Canonical form · Matching · Geodesic · Euclidean · Reference points · Hausdorff shape distance

1 Introduction

3D surfaces registration has become a central issue in the field of pattern recognition. This topic has been more and more challenging especially with the growing development of the 3D data acquisition tools. The registration can be rigid or non rigid. The non rigid registration is more difficult and more complex since the transformations to estimate are not known unlike the rigid registration that consists on the determination of a rotation and a translation.

Many past works have been performed in order to cross the problem of non rigid deformations. Schwartz et al. [1] were among the first to address this challenging field. They proposed a multidimensional scaling (MDS) framework to flatten a surface onto a plane. Since limiting the study of curved surfaces to a plane leads to big errors, Elad and Kimmel [2] proposed to extend the work of Schwartz et al. [1] to a higher dimensional Euclidean space. They considered a shape as a metric structure defined by the geodesic distances between pairs of points of the surface. In fact, the geodesic distances between the points of a surface are preserved in the case of non rigid inelastic deformations. A canonical invariant form under this kind of deformations is, therefore, obtained by the application of the multidimensional scaling (MDS) framework on higher dimensions. In this new form, the Euclidean distances between pairs of points are equal

© Springer International Publishing Switzerland 2015
G. Azzopardi and N. Petkov (Eds.): CAIP 2015, Part II, LNCS 9257, pp. 230–241, 2015.
DOI: 10.1007/978-3-319-23117-4_20

to the geodesic ones between their corresponding points on the original surface. Therefore, the problem of non rigid shape matching is transformed to a rigid matching between canonical forms.

Memoli et al. [3] used the Gromov-Hausdorff distance to define a metric framework for non rigid shape matching. The comparison of two shapes can be therefore considered as a comparison between pairwise geodesic distances on these shapes using the Gromov-Hausdorff distance.

Bronstein et al. [4,5] proposed to generalize the multidimensional scaling framework (GMDS) for computing embedded one metric to another by defining the connection between the formulation of the Gromov-Hausdorff distance and the MDS framework.

Bronstein et al. [6,7] used both the Euclidean distance and the geodesic one by resembling the GMDS framework and the Iterative Closest Point (ICP) algorithm [8,9]. They obtained a shape similarity method which is more robust to topological changes than the one using only the geodesic distance. The reasons of using such two distances (geodesic and Euclidean) come from the fact that the Euclidean distance is robust to topological changes and that the geodesic one is invariant under non rigid inelastic deformations.

In [10], Bronstein et al. proposed to use the diffusion distance with the Gromov-Hausdorff distance framework for non rigid shape matching. We recall that the diffusion distance between two points of a surface is the average of all paths between these points. This method has shown its effectiveness for the recognition of 3D shapes with non rigid inelastic deformations and with topological variations than the classical method based only on the geodesic distance between points.

Others works use the graphs matching to establish a comparison between non rigid shapes. The works of Duchenne et al. [11], Torresani et al. [12] and Zeng et al. [13] based on this approach, have shown that the graphs matching is a powerful tool for non rigid 3D surfaces registration.

Another kind of methods for non rigid 3D shape registration is the spectral approaches. The works of Jain et al. [14] and Rustamov et al. [15] have proved the performance of such methods to cross the non rigid deformations.

In this paper, we propose to present a novel method for the registration of 3D shapes with non rigid inelastic deformations. It is based on the construction of a new canonical form of the objects corresponding to the same shape with non rigid inelastic deformations. The principle consists on replacing the geodesic distances computed from three reference points of the original surface by the Euclidean distances obtained from the three points (the corresponding to the three reference points on the original surface) of the canonical form. Therefore, the problem of non rigid matching between surfaces is transformed to a rigid registration between canonical forms. This novel method is applied to the surfaces of the TOSCA database. The comparison between different shpaes is established in the mean of the Hausdorff Shape distance.

Thus, this paper will be structured as follows: In the second section, we will present the construction process of the canonical form. The used algorithm for the extraction of the three reference points from the original surfaces will be described in the third section. The fourth section will give a mathematical formulation of the used similarity metric to compare between canonical forms. It corresponds to the Hausdorff Shape distance. We will expose the used database for the experimentation and the obtained results for both the recognition and the retrieval processes in the fifth section.

2   Construction of the Novel Canonical Form

Let us consider here a two dimensional differential manifold S, and let denote by U_r the geodesic potential generated from a reference point r of S. U_r is the function that computes for each point p of S the length of the geodesic curve joining p to r.

For a surface S without a perfect symmetry, every point p of S can be defined in a unique way by the lengths of the geodesic curves joining it to three points of the surface S. Let consider r_1, r_2 and r_3 three points of the surface. Thus, p can be defined as $p(d_1, d_2, d_3)$ with:

$$\begin{cases} d_1 = \tilde{\gamma}(r_1, p) \\ d_2 = \tilde{\gamma}(r_2, p) \\ d_3 = \tilde{\gamma}(r_3, p) \end{cases} \tag{1}$$

where $\gamma(p_i, p_j)$ is the geodesic curve between two points p_i and p_j of the surface S and $\tilde{\gamma}(p_i, p_j)$ is the length of this curve.

The present work consists on the extraction of a canonical form of the shapes with non rigid inelastic deformations. Therefore, the 3D objects corresponding to the same shape with different non rigid inelastic deformations will have the same canonical form. The key idea is to replace for each point p of S, the lengths of the geodesic curves joining it respectively to r_1, r_2 and r_3 by the Euclidean distances with the same values computed from three novel points. Thus, let denote by $\tilde{S}$ the canonical form corresponding to S and let denote by $\tilde{r}_1$, $\tilde{r}_2$ and $\tilde{r}_3$ the corresponding reference points on $\tilde{S}$ of r_1, r_2 and r_3. Let p be a point of S and $\tilde{p}$ be its corresponding point on $\tilde{S}$. The Euclidean distances between $\tilde{p}$ and each reference point $\{\tilde{r}_i, i = 1..3\}$ will be equal to the geodesic distances between p and the reference points $\{r_i, i = 1..3\}$. Therefore,

$$d(\tilde{r}_i, \tilde{p}) = \tilde{\gamma}(r_i, p), \forall i \in [1..3] \tag{2}$$

where $d(q_i, q_j)$ is the Euclidean distance between two points q_i and q_j.

The construction process of the canonical form can be formulated, for a given 2-differential manifold S and r_1, r_2 and r_3 three reference points chosen from the surface, as follows:

1. Computation of the three geodesic potentials U_{r_1}, U_{r_2} and U_{r_3}.
2. Determination of the coordinates of $\tilde{r}_1(x_{\tilde{r}_1}, y_{\tilde{r}_1}, z_{\tilde{r}_1})$, $\tilde{r}_2(x_{\tilde{r}_2}, y_{\tilde{r}_2}, z_{\tilde{r}_2})$ and $\tilde{r}_3(x_{\tilde{r}_3}, y_{\tilde{r}_3}, z_{\tilde{r}_3})$ the corresponding reference points of r_1, r_2 and r_3 on the canonical form:

Let denote by:

$$\begin{cases} d_{12} = U_{r_1}(r_2) \\ d_{13} = U_{r_1}(r_3) \\ d_{23} = U_{r_2}(r_3) \end{cases} \tag{3}$$

We choose by default, the coordinate of $\tilde{r}_1$ to be $\tilde{r}_1(0,0,0)$. Since $d_{12} = U_{r_1}(r_2)$, the coordinates of $\tilde{r}_2$ are chosen to be $\tilde{r}_2(d_{12},0,0)$ to preserve the length of the geodesic curve between r_1 and r_2 on the original surface.
$\tilde{r}_3$ is the intersection between the circle of a radius value equal to d_{13} around the point $\tilde{r}_1$ and the circle centered on the point $\tilde{r}_2$ and with a radius value equal to d_{23}.
It is known that the intersection between two circles (when the intersection exists) corresponds to one or two points. We make here the choice of $y_{\tilde{r}_3} \geq 0$ to have only one intersection point.
Then:

$$\begin{cases} \tilde{r}_3(x_{\tilde{r}_3}, y_{\tilde{r}_3}, z_{\tilde{r}_3}) = S^1(\tilde{r}_1, d_{13}) \bigcap S^1(\tilde{r}_2, d_{23}) \\ y_{\tilde{r}_3} \geq 0 \end{cases} \tag{4}$$

where $S^1(r,d)$ is the circle centered on the point r with a radius value equal to d.
Figure 1 illustrates the positions of the three reference points in the canonical form.

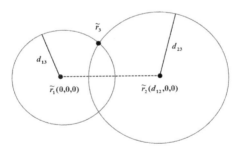

Fig. 1. The positions of the three reference points in the canonical form

3. Determination of the canonical form points:
   To ensure the fact that for each point of the canonical form, the Euclidean distances according to the obtained three reference points of $\tilde{S}$ will be equal to the geodesic ones on the 3D object S, a point $\tilde{p}_i(\tilde{x}_i, \tilde{y}_i, \tilde{z}_i)$ on the canonical form that corresponds to a point p_i of S will be defined by the intersection between the three spheres $S_{1\tilde{p}_i}$, $S_{2\tilde{p}_i}$ and $S_{3\tilde{p}_i}$ centered respectively on $\tilde{r}_1$, $\tilde{r}_2$ and $\tilde{r}_3$ and with radius values equal respectively to the geodesic distances between r_1 and p_i, r_2 and p_i and r_3 and p_i .
   Thus $S_{1\tilde{p}_i}$, $S_{2\tilde{p}_i}$ and $S_{3\tilde{p}_i}$ are defined as follows:

$$\begin{cases} S_{1\tilde{p}_i} = S^2(\tilde{r}_1, \tilde{\gamma}(r_1, p_i)) \\ S_{2\tilde{p}_i} = S^2(\tilde{r}_2, \tilde{\gamma}(r_2, p_i)) \\ S_{3\tilde{p}_i} = S^2(\tilde{r}_3, \tilde{\gamma}(r_3, p_i)) \end{cases} \tag{5}$$

Where $S^2(r, d)$ is the sphere with a center that corresponds to the point r and with a radius value equal to d.
Then

$$\begin{cases} \tilde{p}_i(\tilde{x}_i, \tilde{y}_i, \tilde{z}_i) = S_{1\tilde{p}_i} \bigcap S_{2\tilde{p}_i} \bigcap S_{3\tilde{p}_i} \\ \tilde{z}_i \geq 0 \end{cases} \tag{6}$$

We make here a choice of $\tilde{z}_i \geq 0$ since the intersection between three spheres (when the intersection exists) corresponds to two points in the most of cases.

In summary, in the canonical form, the Euclidean distances between each point $\tilde{p}_i$ and the three reference points $\tilde{r}_1$, $\tilde{r}_2$ and $\tilde{r}_3$ correspond respectively to the geodesic distances between the point p_i of S (to which $\tilde{p}_i$ corresponds) and the reference points r_1, r_2 and r_3 of the original surface.

3   Selection of the Three Reference Points

The three reference points must correspond to the same locations for the surfaces with the same shape and with non rigid inelastic deformations. They must be, therefore, selected from well detected feature points on the surface.

Since the non rigid inelastic transformations preserve the geodesic distances on the surface, we use the algorithm proposed by Tierny et al. [16] for the extraction of the feature points. It is based on a geodesic distances evaluation to detect extremal points. It is stable and invariant under geometrical transformations. The extraction process of these feature points can be described as follows:

Let v_1 and v_2 be the most geodesic distant vertices of a surface S. U_{v_1} and U_{v_2} are their corresponding geodesic potentials. We denote by E_{v_1} and E_{v_2} the sets of extremal vertices. They correspond to the sets of minima and maxima vertices and they are obtained according to their neighborhoods. The set of feature points corresponds to the intersection between E_{v_1} and E_{v_2}. In practice, the local extrema corresponding to each geodesic potential are not located on the same vertices, but in the same neighborhood.

The three reference points are chosen from the set of these feature points. Since the construction process of the canonical form consists on the intersection between three spheres. The two first reference points P_{ref_1} and P_{ref_2} are chosen to be the two farthest points from the selected feature points in the sense of the geodesic distance. The third point is the one from the feature points that has the minimal geodesic distance to P_{ref_1} or P_{ref_2}.

Figure 2 shows the feature points and the used three reference points for an object that corresponds to a man (called David) in different positions with non rigid inelastic deformations. We can observe from the obtained results the effectiveness of the used algorithm for the feature points extraction in this object. The same figure shows the used three reference points.

Fig. 2. Row 1: The feature points in the object corresponding to a man with differents non rigid inelastic deformations. Row 2: The three reference points on the same surfaces (P_{ref_1} with the red color, P_{ref_2} with the green color, P_{ref_3} with the blue color)

Figure 3 illustrates the feature points and the used three reference points from different objects with non rigid inelastic deformations.

	Dog	David	Centaur
The feature points			
The three reference points			

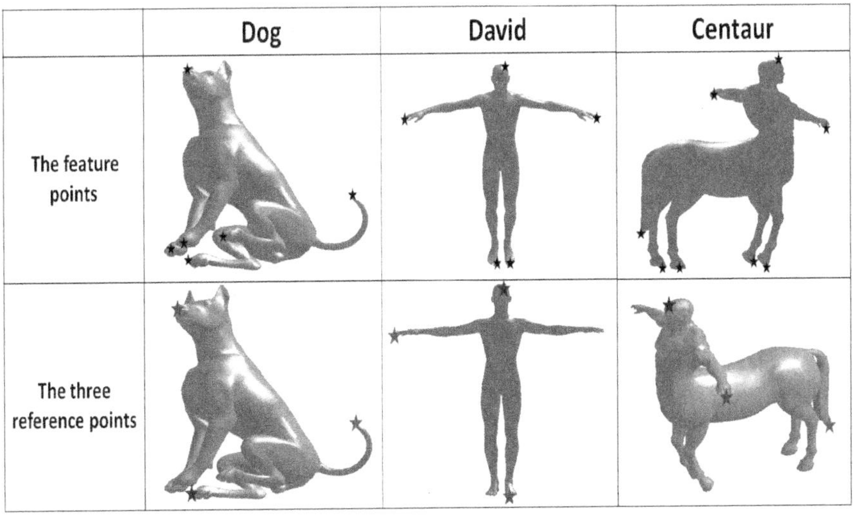

Fig. 3. The feature points and the used three reference points on different 3D objects

4 Similarity Metric

In order to compare between different canonical forms, we use the well known Hausdorff Shape distance [17,18]. Let G be the group of surfaces parametrisations. It can be either the real plane R^2 for the open surfaces or the unit sphere S^2 for the closed surfaces. The space of all surface pieces is considered as the set of all 3D objects diffeomorphic to G. This space can be defined as a subspace of $L^2_{R^3}(G)$ formed by all square integrated maps from G to R^3. The direct product of the Euler rotations group $SO(3)$ by the group G , acts on $L^2_{R^3}(G)$ in the following sense:

$$SO(3) \times G \times L^2_{R^3}(G) \rightarrow L^2_{R^3}(G) \tag{7}$$

$$\{A, (u_0, v_0), S(u, v)\} \rightarrow AS(u + u_0, v + v_0)$$

The 3D Hausdorff Shape distance Δ is defined for every S_1 and S_2 belonging to $L^2_{R^3}(G)$ and g_1 and g_2 to $SO(3)$ as follows:

$$\Delta(S_1, S_2) = max(\rho(S_1, S_2), \rho(S_2, S_1)) \tag{8}$$

Where:

$$\rho(S_1, S_2) = \sup_{g_1 \in SO(3)} \inf_{g_2 \in SO(3)} \| g_1 S_1 - g_2 S_2 \|_{L^2} \tag{9}$$

$\| S \|_{L^2}$ denotes the norm of the functional banach space $L^2_{R^3}(G)$.

A normalized version of Δ is computed so that its variations are confined to the interval [0,1]. This distance is approximated by the well known Itertive Closest Point (ICP) algorithm [8,9].

5 Experimentation

In this section, we present the used 3D objects database for the experimentation and the obtained results.

5.1 The TOSCA Database

The TOSCA database is proposed by Bronstein et al. [4]. This database contains 148 models grouped in 12 classes. Each class is composed by a 3D object with different non rigid inelastic deformations. We used in our experimentation thirty objects corresponding to six classes of 3D shapes. Each class contains five variety of a 3D shape with different poses and non rigid inelastic deformations. The six classes correspond to the following objects: The lioness, the dog, the horse, the man David, the centaur and the gorilla.

5.2   The Obtained Results

We present here the obtained results. Figure 4 illustrates some 3D objects of the database TOSCA with different poses and non rigid inelastic deformations and their corresponding canonical forms. We can observe that the canonical forms are practically similar for the same object and are invariant under non rigid inelastic deformations.

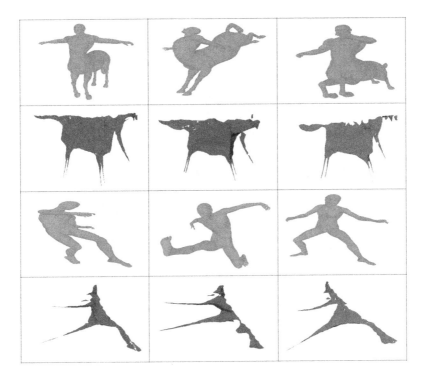

Fig. 4. Row 1: The object Centaur with different poses and non rigid inelastic deformations. Row 2: The canonical form corresponding to each centaur. Row 3: The object David with different poses and non rigid inelastic deformations. Row 4: The canonical form corresponding to each variety of the object David.

In order to show the effectiveness of the novel canonical form for non rigid 3D shapes matching, the matrix of pairwise normalized Hausdorff shape distance is computed between the canonical forms of the thirty objects of the TOSCA database. Figure 5 represents this matrix.

Table 1 summarizes the organization of the data in the same matrix.

The colors of the elements of the matrix are proportional to the distance values between the 3D objects. The elements with darker color represent the lower distances which correspond to the best matching. From the observation

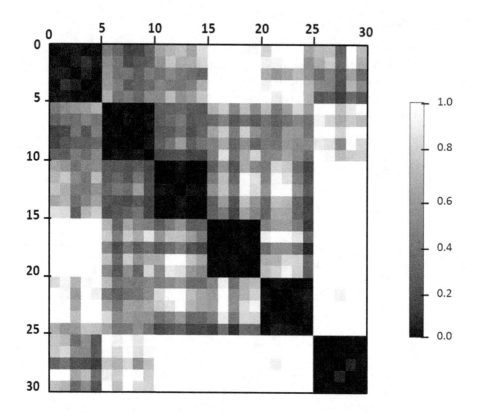

Fig. 5. Matrix of pairwise normalized Hausdorff shape distance between the thirty objects of the TOSCA database.

Table 1. Organization of the data in the matrix

Rows 1..5 Columns 1..5	Rows 6..10 Columns 6..10	Rows 11..15 Columns 11..15	Rows 16..20 Columns 16..20	Rows 21..25 Columns 21..25	Rows 26..30 Columns 26..30
Five models of the object Lioness	Five models of the object Dog	Five models of the object Horse	Five models of the object David	Five models of the object Gorilla	Five models of the object Centaur

of this matrix, we can note that, by using the canonical form, we are able to cross the problem of non rigid inelastic transformations. In fact, the distances between the objects corresponding to the same shape are lower than the other distances. This observation is available for all the objects (Six blocs of 5x5 along the matrix diagonal).

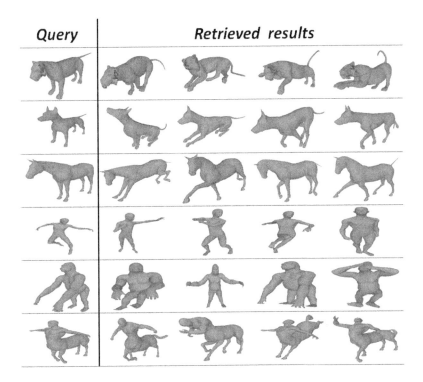

Fig. 6. Some retrieved results obtained on the TOSCA database

We test also the performance of the novel canonical form for the retrieval process. Figure 6 illustrates the obtained results. The first column contains the query and the rest contains the retrieved objects. The obtained results show that for each query object, all the retrieved 3D surfaces correspond to this query object.

This observation proves the accuracy of the canonical form for well describing objects when non rigid inelastic deformations exist.

6   Conclusion

Known as a difficult task, we have presented in this first work a solution for the registration of non rigid inelastic 3D shapes. It consists on the construction of a canonical form for the objects of the same shape with this kind of deformations. The construction process is to replace the geodesic distances computed from three reference points of the original surface by the Euclidean ones obtained from the corresponding three reference points of the canonical form. The comparison between non rigid shapes is reduced, therefore, to a rigid matching between canonical forms. The obtained results, on some 3D objects of the TOSCA database, with the Hausdorff shape distance as a similarity metric have shown the performance of such method for the registration and the retrieval processes.

The perspectives of this work are multiple. We propose to establish the experimentations on a big number of objects of the TOSCA database and to extend the experimentation to other databases. We intend also to make a finer analysis of the reference points choice. We suggest finally to study the stability of this novel method under the errors on the reference points positions and its robustness to the noise.

References

1. Schwartz, E.L., Shaw, A., Wolfson, E.: A numerical solution to the generalized map- maker's problem: flattening nonconvex polyhedral surfaces. J. IEEE Trans. Pattern Analysis and Machine Intelligence (PAMI) **11**, 1005–1008 (1989)
2. Elad, A., Kimmel, R.: On bending invariant signatures for surfaces. J. IEEE Trans. Pattern Analysis and Machine Intelligence (PAMI) **25**, 1285–1295 (2003)
3. Memoli, F., Sapiro, G.: A theoretical and computational framework for isometry invariant recognition of point cloud data. J. Foundations of Computational Mathematics **5**, 313–346 (2005)
4. Bronstein, A.M., Bronstein, M.M., Kimmel, R.: Effcient computation of isometry-invariant distances between surfaces. J. SIAM Scientific Computing **28**, 1812–1836 (2006)
5. Bronstein, A.M., Bronstein, M.M., Kimmel, R.: Generalized multidimensional scaling: a framework for isometry-invariant partial surface matching. In: National Academy of Science (PNAS), pp. 1168–1172 (2006)
6. Bronstein, A.M., Bronstein, M.M., Kimmel, R.: Rock, paper, and scissors: extrinsic vs. intrinsic similarity of non-rigid shapes. In: Int. Conf. Computer Vision (ICCV), Rio de Janeiro, pp. 1–6 (2007)
7. Bronstein, A.M., Bronstein, M.M., Kimmel, R.: Topology-invariant similarity of nonrigid shapes. J. Int'l J. Computer Vision (IJCV) **81**, 281–301 (2008)
8. Besl, P.J., McKay, N.D.: A method for registration of 3D shapes. J. IEEE Trans. Pattern Analysis and Machine Intelligence (PAMI) **14**, 239–256 (1992)
9. Chen, Y., Medioni, G.: Rock, paper, and scissors: object modeling by registration of multiple range images. In: Conf. Robotics and Automation (2007)
10. Bronstein, A.M., Bronstein, M.M., Kimmel, R., Mahmoudi, M., Sapiro, G.: A Gromov-Hausdorff Framework with Diffusion Geometry for Topologically-Robust Non-rigid Shape Matching. J. Int'l J. Computer Vision (IJCV) **89**, 266–286 (2010)
11. Duchenne, O., Bach, F., Kweon, I., Ponce, J.: A tensor-based algorithm for high-order graph matching. J. IEEE Trans. Pattern Analysis and Machine Intelligence (PAMI) **33**, 2383–2395 (2011)
12. Torresani, L., Kolmogorov, V., Rother, C.: Feature correspondence via graph matching: models and global optimization. In: Forsyth, D., Torr, P., Zisserman, A. (eds.) ECCV 2008, Part II. LNCS, vol. 5303, pp. 596–609. Springer, Heidelberg (2008)
13. Zeng, Y., Wang, C., Wang, Y., Gu, X., Samaras, D., Paragios, N.: Dense non-rigid surface registration using high-order graph matching. In: IEEE Conference on Computer Vision and Pattern Recognition (CVPR), San Francisco, pp. 13–18 (2010)
14. Jain, V., Zhang, H.: A spectral approach to shape-based retrieval of articulated 3D models. J. Computer-Aided Design **39**, 398–407 (2007)

15. Rustamov, R.M.: Laplace-beltrami eigenfunctions for deformation invariant shape representation. In: Eurographics Symposium on Geometry (2007)
16. Tierny, J., Vandeborre, J.P., Daoudi, M.: Partial 3D Shape Retrieval by Reeb Pattern Unfolding. J. Computer Graphics Forum **28**, 41–55 (2009)
17. Ghorbel, F.: A unitary formulation for invariant image description: application to image coding. J. Annals of Telecommunication **53**, 242–260 (1998)
18. Ghorbel, F.: Invariants for shapes and movement. Eleven cases from 1D to 4D and from euclidean to projectives (French version), Arts-pi edn., Tunisia (2012)

A New One Class Classifier Based on Ensemble of Binary Classifiers

Hamed Habibi Aghdam$^{(\boxtimes)}$, Elnaz Jahani Heravi, and Domenec Puig

Computer Engineering and Mathematics Department,
University Rovira i Virgili, Tarragona, Spain
{hamed.habibi,elnaz.jahani,domenec.puig}@urv.cat

Abstract. Modeling the observation domain of the vectors in a dataset is crucial in most practical applications. This is more important in the case of multivariate regression problems since the vectors which are not drawn from the same distribution as the training data can turn an interpolation problem into an extrapolation problem where the uncertainty of the results increases dramatically. The aim of one-class classification methods is to model the observation domain of target vectors when there is no novel data or there are very few novel data. In this paper, we propose a new one-class classification method that can be trained with or without novel data and it can model the observation domain using any binary classification method. Experiments on visual, non-visual and synthetic data show that the proposed method produces more accurate results compared with state-of-art methods. In addition, we show that by adding only 10% of novel data into our training data, the accuracy of the proposed method increases considerably.

Keywords: One-class classifier · Novelty detection · Random forest

1 Introduction

Traditionally, classification problems are tackled by collecting a set of input-output pairs $D = \{(\mathcal{X}_i, y_i) \mid \mathcal{X}_i \in \mathbb{R}^D, y_i \in \mathbb{Z}\}$ and training a model to predict the output value y_q given the query vector $\mathcal{X}_q$. For example, in the binary classification problem, we collect some positive and some negative data and train a binary classifier. This approach has two important problems. First, collecting an appropriate number of the negative data that can cover the whole possible negative situations is not trivial. Second, it is probable that the query vector $\mathcal{X}_q$ deviates from the probability density function of the dataset D. Regardless, the model will always classify the query vector into one of possible classes. In some applications this may produce serious problems. For instance, assume a traffic sign recognition system where the inputs are provided by a traffic sign detection module. Clearly, training a traffic sign detector with *false-positive rate* equal to zero is not trivial. Consequently, some false-positive (*i.e.* non-traffic sign) images might be fetched into the recognition module by the detection module. If the

© Springer International Publishing Switzerland 2015
G. Azzopardi and N. Petkov (Eds.): CAIP 2015, Part II, LNCS 9257, pp. 242–253, 2015.
DOI: 10.1007/978-3-319-23117-4_21

recognition model is not equipped with a novelty detection module, it will classify the non-traffic sign image into one of traffic sign classes. This might produce some fatal mistakes in the case of driver-less cars.

In the regression problem (*i.e.* $y_i \in \mathbb{R}$), we usually train a model to interpolate the output value. Concretely, the regression model has an observation domain that is determined by dataset D. If the query vector is out of this domain, the interpolation problem changes to an extrapolation problem and, consequently, the uncertainty of the estimation dramatically increases. The common point in both classification and regression problems is that when the query vector deviates from the observation domain it has a higher risk to produce meaningless results.

The remedy to this problem is to find a way for modeling the observation domain. More specifically, the aim of *one-class classification* (OCC)[1] methods is to find the boundaries of the observation domain. It should be noted that *outlier detection* is different from OCC in the sense that outlier detection problem tries to identify outliers from a *contaminated* set of data. In contrast, the basic assumption in OCC is that the data is not noisy. In general, the data representing the class of interest is called *target* class and the rest is called *non-target* or *novel* class.

Although the amount of novel data is usually much fewer than target data, but, they can be used for refining the one-class classifier. However, most state-of-art methods ignore the novel data and they only build the model using the target data. In this paper, we propose an OCC method that can be trained in two ways. First, we can build a classifier using only the target data. Second, we can build a more accurate classifier by exploiting the novel data even if their number is much less than the target data.

To this end, we first partition the target data into K disjoint groups. Then, we heuristically built a $M \times K$ table whose rows are a binary string and its number is defined manually. Next, we train a binary classifier for each row of this table. Finally, the given query vector $\mathcal{X}_q$ is classified using each of M binary classifiers and the vector is labeled as target or novel according to a truth table.

Contribution: First, our proposed method takes into account the density of the data in different regions of the feature space and it finds a more accurate boundary around the target data. Second, it works with any binary classification model. Third, it can be trained with or without negative data. This is a very important property since we may have a few novel data (even if they are much less than target data) that can be utilized to adjust the model parameters more accurately.

The rest of this paper is organized as follows: Section 2 reviews the related work and discusses their problems on a synthetic data. Section 3 describes the proposed method and Section 4 mentions the relation between visual attributes and our proposed method. Next, Section 5 shows the experimental results on visual, non-visual and synthetic data and compare the results with the state-of-art methods. Finally, Section 6 concludes the paper.

---

[1] We use the terms *novelty detection* and *one-class classification* interchangeably.

2 Related Work

Recently, Pimentel *et al.*[1] categorized the novelty detection methods into four groups including *probabilistic, distance-based, reconstruction-based* and *domain-based*. In general, the basic assumption in developing a novelty detection method is that the novel data is far from the target data. Based on this assumption, a novelty score is assigned for every input vector. Vectors with high novelty scores are more probable to be novel.

Probabilistic methods model the distribution of target data by fitting a probability distribution function. One of the probabilistic models is Gaussian mixture model where the data is partitioned into a K clusters and their distribution is modeled by a mixture of K Gaussian density functions [9]. However, Gaussian mixture model has many parameters to adjust, its objective function space is non-linear and it highly depends on the number of clusters.

Distance-based approaches compute the novelty score by analyzing the target data and computing a few prototype vectors. The novelty score of the query vector is determined by computing the minimum distance between the query vector and the prototype vectors. If the distance is less than a threshold, it is classified as target. Otherwise, it is classified as a novel vector. *K-means* method finds the prototype vectors by clustering the target data into K clusters. Also, *k-nearest neighbor* and *Fuzzy k-nearest neighbor* [8] are special cases where every target vector is selected as a prototype vector.

Selecting the prototype vectors and the threshold are very important in these methods since they determine the boundary of target data. Pitor *et al.* [2] identifies the boundary by computing the minimum spanning tree of target data and adjusting the boundary based on the structure of the tree. Bodesheim *et al.* [4] assumes that the novel data might not be far in the feature space but it is far in the null space of the target data where they have zero variance in their null space. Based on this assumption, they find the novelty score by projecting the query vector onto the null space.

Reconstruction based method are generally based on neural networks. In particular, auto-encoder networks have been used for detecting the novel inputs by calculating the reconstruction error. Interested reader can refer to [3] for detailed information. Domain-based approaches find the minimum closing boundary of the target data. Tax and Dui [5] find the minimum enclosing circle of target data. In order to deal with non-circular boundaries, the target data is projected onto a higher dimensional space through kernel trick where their boundary have a circular shape. This method is called *support vector data description*.

Kimmel *et al.*[6] proposed a one-class Guassian process and applied it on a visual dataset. Chesner *et al.*[7] proposed a one-class random forests by generating artificial outliers and training a conventional random forest classifier.

Discussion: We generated a synthetic data and applied some of the above methods on this dataset. Fig.1 shows the decision boundary of each method superimposed by target data (white points). We observe that the k-nearest neighbor and the minimum spanning tree (MST) methods has high variance and they are prone to over-fit and for this reason they might have high false-negative rate. Although increasing the threshold value could enlarge the decision boundary but it has a uniform effect on the boundary and it does not take into account the density of data in a specific region. In contrast, the k-means method has high bias and it could have a high false-positive rate. One reason is that the number of clusters is not enough to model a highly non-linear structure of the target data. The problem could be addressed by increasing the number of clusters but if the number of clusters is too high the algorithm suffers from high variance. In addition, determining the optimal number of clusters is not a trivial task.

In the second row of Fig.1 three different Gaussian mixture models have been trained on the target data. The right plot in the second row illustrates a 5-component Gaussian mixture model. Notwithstanding, we only see 4 Gaussian functions on the data. The reason is that two Gaussian functions have been mixed since the optimization function has been sucked in a local minimum. A similar situation happens with 10-component and 20-component Gaussian mixture models. However, we observe that by increasing the number of Gaussian components we are able to model more accurate boundaries. While Gaussian mixture model can accurately model the low-dimensional data but its accuracy decreases dramatically as the number of dimensions increases. Moreover, finding the optimal number of the Gaussian components is not a trivial task.

The third row shows the output of the kernel null space (KNFST), support vector data descriptor (SVDD) and one-class support vector machine (OCSVM) methods. In all the cases, they have found the minimum enclosing circle around the data. Nevertheless, they ignore the fact that there are some empty spaces inside their enclosing region where there is not any target data in those regions. This implies that they may have high bias on the target data.

Another important aspect in the all above methods except support vector data descriptor is that they neglect the negative data. However, in practice, one-class classification refers to modeling the target data when *there is no novel data or there are a few number of novel data in our dataset*. Therefore, any once-class classification algorithm must take into account the effect of novel data even if they are much less than target data. Our proposed method addresses this problem by considering the novel data (whenever they are available) to adjust its decision boundary.

3   Proposed Method

Given a dataset of target vectors $D = \{\mathcal{X}_i \in \mathbb{R}^D\}$, the aim of one-class classifier is to learn the domain or the distribution of these vectors. To this end, a function $f(\mathcal{X}) : \mathbb{R}^D \to [0..1]$ is trained such that it returns small values if the input vector $\mathcal{X}$ is in the domain of D and it returns high values, otherwise. The function $f(\mathcal{X})$ is usually called *novelty score* function.

In the k-means method, the input space is partitioned into a few clusters and the novelty score of the query vector $\mathcal{X}_q$ is computed by finding the closest

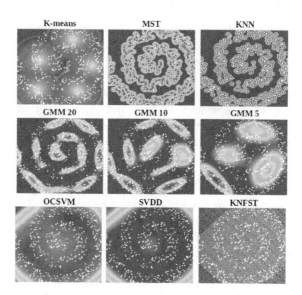

Fig. 1. Decision boundary produced by different methods on a synthetic dataset.

cluster to $\mathcal{X}_q$ and calculating its Mahalanobis or Euclidean[2] distance from the cluster. This approach has two important problems. First, it highly depends on the number of clusters. Second, it is not guaranteed that the data inside a cluster has been drawn from a Gaussian distribution. Notwithstanding, k-means method follows an effective idea which is dividing the input space into smaller groups and learning the novelty score function of each group individually. Similarly, we utilize the same idea in this paper. Our proposed one-class classification method is shown in Fig.2.

The first step in the training stage is partitioning the dataset D into K disjoint clusters. Then, M super-clusters are formed such that each super-cluster contains two or more clusters. In the figure, the points inside each super-cluster have been shown using white color while the other points have been marked as gray points. In fact, super-clusters divide the input dataset into two different groups. From classification perspective, this is a binary classification problem and we can train any classification model to categorize the data in each super-cluster. By this way, we will have M binary classifiers. In the test stage, these classifiers are used along with the information from the super-clusters to compute the novelty score of the query vector $\mathcal{X}_q$.

3.1 Partitioning

The aim of partitioning is to divide the dataset D into smaller clusters. Our method does not need an accurate clustering. In theory, semi-random partitioning also works with our method. In fact, we only need to partition the data into

---

[2] For example, when the number of data inside the cluster is less than their dimension.

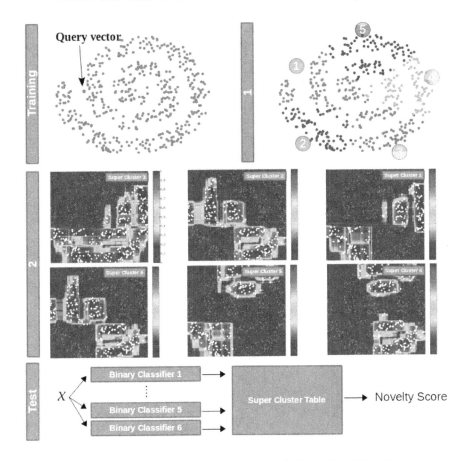

Fig. 2. Overview of the proposed method. Best viewed in color.

some clusters so we can use them to form the super-clusters. In this paper, we use the k-means clustering algorithm for this purpose.

3.2   Super-Cluster Generation

We define a super-cluster as a composition of two or more clusters. For example, super-cluster 1 in Fig.2 is composed of cluster 2 and cluster 4. We consider the data inside a super-cluster as the positive data and the data outside the super-cluster (clusters not included in the super-cluster) as the negative data. Then, we train a binary classifier to separate the negative data from the positive data. We generate several super-clusters and train a binary classifier for each of them. For example, we have defined 6 super-clusters in Fig.2. Moreover, the decision boundary of the trained classifiers have been shown using the heat-map plot. As we will discuss shortly, the binary classifiers together learn the domain of target class and build a one-class classifier.

To generate the super-clusters, we consider three constraints. First, the amount of the positive and the negative data must be balanced. In this paper, the ratio of the positive data to the negative data inside a super-cluster must be in range $[0.5..1]$ (*i.e.* $\frac{number\ of\ positive\ data}{number\ of\ negative\ data} \in [0.5\ldots 1]$). Second, all clusters should have the same contribution in forming the set of super-clusters. Assume we have 5 clusters and our aim is to generate 6 super-clusters. There are $\binom{5}{4} + \binom{5}{3} + \binom{5}{2} = 25$ possible combinations of clusters to form the super-clusters. Supposing that cluster 1 has been used in forming two super-clusters, the other clusters also should participate two times in forming the set of super-clusters. Using this constraint, we prevent from using the same cluster in every super-cluster. The third constraint is that the clusters of a super-cluster must have a large distance between each other. This makes it possible to build more complex decision boundaries and consequently, we can model a highly non-linear domains.

Taking these constraints into account, we generate the super-clusters using a local search algorithm (*e.g.* hill climbing). Given the number of clusters K and the number of super-clusters M, we represent the super-clusters using a binary matrix $A \in \{0,1\}^{M \times K}$ where $A(m,k) = 1$ if the kth clusters is used in the mth super-cluster. Then, the objective function of the algorithm is defined as:

$$cost(sc_m) = \alpha \frac{|\{c_k | \forall k\ A(m,k) = 1\}|}{|\{c_k | \forall k\ A(m,k) = 0\}|} + \gamma \sum_{\{k_1,k_2 | A(m,:)==1\}} \|c_i - c_j\| \qquad (1)$$

$$cost(A) = \sum_{m=1}^{M} cost(sc_m) + \beta \sum_{i=1}^{K-1} \sum_{j=i+1}^{K} |freq(c_i) - freq(c_j)| \qquad (2)$$

where α, β and γ are user-defined parameters to control the importance of each constraint. The first term in (1) calculates the ratio of positive data to negative data for every super-cluster (the first constraint) and the second term computes the pairwise distance of the clusters that are included in a super-cluster (third constraint). Finally, the total cost is computed by (2) where we also compute the pairwise absolute difference of the frequency of cluster (the second constraint). Table 1 shows the hill climbing algorithm for generating the binary matrix A.

Having generated the super-clusters, we train individual binary classifiers for each of them. During the test phase, the query vector X_q is classified using

Table 1. Pseudopod for generating super-clusters

```
Inputs: The number of super-clusters M, The number of clusters K
Output: The MxK binary matrix A
Solution = Generate a random MxK binary marix
While terminationCondition
      SolutionPrime = Randomly invert 10% of elements in Solution
      If cost(ObjSolutionPrime) is better than cost(ObjSolution) // (2)
            ObjSolution = ObjSolutionPrime
      End
End
```

each of the binary classifiers and their classification score is stored. Then, the scores are fetched into the decision making module where the information from super-clusters are utilized to classify the query vector as target or novel.

3.3   One-class Classification

In the first stage, we partitioned the dataset D into K disjoint clusters. We assume that the query vector $\mathcal{X}_q$ is classified as a target vector if it belongs to one of the K clusters. In other words, a vector is novel if it does not belong to any of the K clusters. It should be noted that the data inside a cluster can be drawn from any distribution. Consider the query vector illustrated in Fig.2. In order to determine if this vector belongs to one the 5 clusters, we first classify it using the trained classifiers on the super-clusters. Considering that we have 6 super-clusters in this example, we obtain a 6-dimensional binary vector whose i^{th} element indicates if the vector is classified as positive or negative by the classifier trained on i^{th} super-cluster. For example, cluster 1 has been used in super-clusters 2 and 6. Consequently, the query vector must be classified as positive by the 2nd and 6th classifiers and it must be classified as negative by the other classifiers.

Now, we can formulate the proposed one-class classification as follows. We are given a binary matrix $A \in \{0,1\}^{M \times K}$ whose element (m,k) is 1 iif the kth clusters is used in the mth super-cluster. Furthermore, we have obtained a binary vector $\mathbf{v}_q \in \{0,1\}^M$ whose m^{th} element corresponds to the classification result of the query vector $\mathcal{X}_q$ by the mth classifier. The vector $\mathcal{X}_q$ is classified as target or novel using function:

$$occ(\mathcal{X}_q) = \begin{cases} target & d(\mathbf{v}_q, A) = 0 \\ novel & otherwise \end{cases} \tag{3}$$

$$d(\mathbf{v}_q, A) = \min_{m=1...M} hamming(\mathbf{v}_q, \mathbf{a}_m). \tag{4}$$

where $\mathbf{a}_m$ is the mth column of matrix A. If the query vector $\mathcal{X}_q$ belongs to one of the clusters, the hamming distance between the vector $\mathbf{v}_q$ and one of the columns of matrix A must be zero. The function $d(\mathbf{v}_q, A)$ calculates the hamming distance between the vector $\mathbf{v}_q$ and each column of matrix A and returns the minimum value. If the minimum value is zeros this means the query vector belongs to one of the clusters and, consequently, it must be classified as target.

4   Connection with Visual Attributes

There is a strong connection between visual attributes and our proposed method. Conventionally, visual attributes are set of classifiers trained on the same feature space [10]. Assume the traffic sign recognition problem where our goal is to recognize the traffic signs included in the German traffic sign benchmark [11] using visual attributes. To this end, we might extract color and appearance

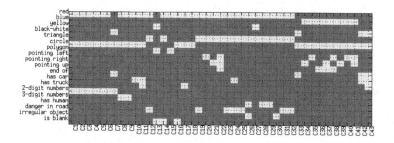

Fig. 3. Attribute table designed for the traffic sign recognition problem.

features and integrate them into a single feature vector. Similar to [12], we define a set of color, shape and appearance attributes. Fig.3 shows the attribute table for the recognizing 43 classes in the German traffic sign benchmark. For example, according to this figure, the input image is classified as C_1 if the output of the attribute classifiers *2-digit numbers*, *circle* and *red* is 1 and the output of the other classifiers is zero.

Consider a situation in which a false-positive image is fetched into the attribute classifiers and the attributes *has truck*, *red* and *pointing right* are classified positive on the image. Looking at the attribute table in Fig.3 we observe that there is no class which is described using these three attributes. Thus, the recognition module might return a value indicating that it is not able to classify the input image. In other words, it recognizes the input image as novel.

We can see the rows of the attribute table shown in Fig.3 as the super-clusters and the columns as the clusters in our proposed method. The only difference is in generating the super-clusters and clusters. In the mentioned traffic signs recognition problem, we know the classes in advance and we build some semantic attributes using our own knowledge. However, in a more general case, we are only given a dataset without any information about classes or their attributes. In the proposed method, we define the classes by clustering the dataset into K classes and design the attribute table by using super-clusters.

5   Experiments

We applied the proposed method on three different types of datasets including an object recognition dataset, eight non-visual datasets and one synthetic dataset. More specifically, the object recognition dataset was obtained from the German traffic sign benchmark where we formed the super-clusters using the semantic visual attributes mentioned in Fig.3. We selected all the signs as the target class and added some non-traffic sign image into the dataset as the novel data. For the non-visual datasets, we selected the classification datasets from the UCI machine learning repository with various feature dimensions. Table 2 shows the statistic of the datasets we have used in our experiments. In all cases we divided the dataset into *training* and *validation* parts. The training part includes only 75%

Table 2. Dataset statistic used in our experiments.

Dataset	Features	Target	Novel
German Traffic Sign (GTSR)	1100	8000	4100
Gas Sensor Array	128	2565	11345
Ionosphere	32	126	225
Pima Indians Diabetes	8	500	268
Sonar, Mines vs. Rocks	60	97	111
Spambase	57	2788	1813
Blood Transfusion	4	570	178
Internet Advertisements	1558	2820	459
Sythetic	2	476	364

of the target data and the validation part includes the remaining 25% of target data aggregated with whole negative data. We trained our one-class classifiers using the training data and tested using the validation data.

In order to compare our results with the state-of-art methods, we used PRTools[3], data description toolbox [13] and LibSVM. Moreover, in the case of kernel null space method, we utilized the codes provided by the authors [4]. Finally, the evaluation was done by computing the *area under curve*(AUC) value using the validation set. Table 3 shows the results.

Table 3. Result of applying the proposed method on the benchmark datasets using the proposed method and state-or-art methods.

Dataset		Our	GMM	K-means	SVM	SVDD	KNFST	MST	KNN
GTSR	AUC	**0.68**	0.502	0.49	0.55	0.58	NA	NA	0.51
	TPR	0.96	0.64	0.22	0.32	0.90	NA	NA	0.37
	FPR	0.61	0.63	0.24	0.21	0.73	NA	NA	0.35
Gas Sensor Array	AUC	**0.95**	0.93	0.75	0.73	0.72	0.64	0.89	0.94
	TPR	0.93	0.94	0.95	0.76	0.90	0.93	0.94	0.93
	FPR	0.02	0.05	0.43	0.30	0.45	.0.65	0.15	0.05
Ionosphere	AUC	**0.67**	0.40	0.46	0.50	0.32	0.35		0.50
	TPR	0.68	0.31	0.92	0.00	0.46	0.69		1.00
	FPR	0.30	0.51	0.99	0.00	0.82	0.98		1.00
Pima Indians Diabetes	AUC	0.62	0.60	0.56	**0.65**	0.63	0.54	0.54	0.56
	TPR	0.60	0.80	0.94	0.78	0.82	0.90	0.98	0.98
	FPR	0.36	0.59	0.89	0.47	0.56	0.81	0.88	0.85
Sonar, Mines vs. Rocks	AUC	**0.67**	0.50	0.61	0.63	0.64	0.61	0.60	0.62
	TPR	0.45	0.00	0.90	0.67	0.67	0.89	1.00	1.00
	FPR	0.12	0.00	0.67	0.40	0.39	0.67	0.79	0.75
Spambase	AUC	0.64	**0.73**	0.53	0.58	0.55	0.49	0.53	0.55
	TPR	0.65	0.85	0.93	0.50	0.92	0.99	0.97	0.97
	FPR	0.36	0.39	0.85	0.33	0.82	1.00	0.89	0.86
Blood Transfusion	AUC	**0.60**	0.53	0.53	0.54	0.52	0.50	0.53	0.53
	TPR	0.71	0.93	0.91	0.54	0.96	1.00	0.98	0.95
	FPR	0.52	0.87	0.85	0.46	0.91	1.00	0.92	0.89
Internet Ads.	AUC	0.61	0.50	0.62	0.65	0.66	0.50	0.75	**0.79**
	TPR	0.84	1.00	0.96	0.91	0.93	0.96	0.99	0.96
	FPR	0.62	1.00	0.70	0.61	0.61	0.96	0.47	0.38
Synthetic	AUC	**0.82**	0.80	0.78	0.78	0.78	0.76	0.79	0.80
	TPR	0.76	0.96	0.89	0.98	0.98	0.94	0.92	0.94
	FPR	0.12	0.36	0.32	0.41	0.41	0.41	0.33	0.33

We observe that the proposed method has produced the best results compared with the other methods applied on traffic sign recognition problem. In addition, training time and memory usage of KNFST and MST methods are

---

[3] http://prtools.org/

not tractable on GTSR dataset since it includes approximately many high-dimensional vectors so it was not practical to apply these two methods on the traffic sign recognition problem. The feature vectors extracted from GTSR dataset are sparse vectors. Consequently, the minimum enclosing ball found by SVM and SVDD methods will include a large area of novel vectors. Therefore, the false-positive rate of these methods is high on this dataset compared with their true-positive rate. Further, GMM method is not able to model the distribution of the vectors accurately. This is due to the fact that the number of data compared with the dimensions of feature vectors is not enough to partition the dataset into many clusters and find their covariance matrix. Hence, GMM partitions the dataset into very small number of groups (3 clusters in this experiment). In addiction, because the vectors inside each cluster are sparse, they cannot be modeled using a Gaussian density function accurately. As the results, the overall accuracy of GMM drops. Similarly, KNN and K-means methods suffer from the fact that the feature vectors are sparse and they do not select a proper threshold values in their novelty score function. Moreover, the AUC of KNN and MST methods is considerable higher than other methods on the Internet Ads dataset. This is due to the fact that the number of data is very low compared with the dimensions of feature vectors on this dataset. For this reason, the proposed method is not able to model the domain of the target data accurately. The same reason applies on the other methods.

In the second experiment, we utilized 10% of the novel data to refine our model. As it is shown in Table 4, using a few amount of novel data we are able to model the observation domain of the target data more accurately.

Table 4. Result of using 10% of novel data to refine our model.

Dataset	AUC	TPR	FPR	Dataset	AUC	TPR	FPR
Sythetic	0.88	0.85	0.08	Gas Sensor Array	0.98	0.96	0.003
Ionosphere	0.89	0.85	0.07	Pima Indians Diabetes	0.66	0.50	0.16
Spambase	0.85	0.81	0.10	Sonar, Mines vs. Rocks	0.71	0.50	0.08
Internet Ads.	0.88	0.80	0.05	Blood Transfusion	0.63	0.81	0.55

6   Conclusion

In this paper, we proposed a new one-class classification method by partitioning the target data into K clusters and forming M super-clusters using them. Super-clusters are composition of two or more clusters. Although the composition can be random, however, we considered three constraints in order to be able to model more complex observation domains. Using these constraints we run a local search algorithm (*e.g.* hill climbing) to generate M super-clusters. In fact, each super-cluster can be seen as a binary classification problem where the clusters included in the super-cluster are the positive data and the clusters not included in the super-cluster are the negative data. The solution to the local search algorithm is indicated by binary matrix $A \in \{0,1\}^{M \times K}$ where $A(m,k)$ indicates if the kth cluster has been used in forming the mth super-cluster. Using this formalism, we train a separate binary classifier for each of M super-clusters. In order to determine the novelty score of the query vector $\mathcal{X}_q$, we first classify it using the M binary classifiers and obtain the M-dimensional binary vector $\mathbf{v} \in \{0,1\}^M$. Then, the novelty score of the query vector is computed by calculating the hamming distance between $\mathbf{v}$ and each column of A. One advantage of the proposed method is that it can be trained with or without novel data. Our experiments on visual and non-visual datasets indicate that the proposed method improves the results compared with the state-of-art methods when it only utilizes the target data. Moreover, the results are considerably improved when we refine the models using 10% of the novel data.

References

1. Pimentel, M.A.F., Clifton, D.A., Clifton, L., Tarassenko, L.: A review of novelty detection. Signal Processing **99**, 215–249 (2014). Elsevier
2. Juszczak, P., Tax, D.M.J., Pekalska, E., Duin, R.P.W.: Minimum spanning tree based one-class classifier. Neurocomputing **72**, 1859–1869 (2009). Elsevier
3. Markou, M., Singh, S.: Novelty detection: a reviewpart 2: neural network based approaches. Signal Processing **83**, 2499–2521 (2003). Elsevier
4. Bodesheim, P., Freytag, A., Rodner, E., Kemmler, M., Denzler, J.: Kernel null space methods for novelty detection. In: IEEE Conference on Computer Vision and Pattern Recognition (CVPR), pp. 3374–3381. IEEE Press (2013)
5. Tax, D.M.J., Duin, R.P.W.: Support Vector Data Description. Machine Learning **54**, 45–66 (2004). Kluwer Academic Publishers
6. Kemmler, M., Rodner, E., Denzler, J.: One-class classification with gaussian processes. In: Kimmel, R., Klette, R., Sugimoto, A. (eds.) ACCV 2010, Part II. LNCS, vol. 6493, pp. 489–500. Springer, Heidelberg (2011). ISBN:978-3-642-19308-8
7. Désir, C., Bernard, S., Petitjean, C., Heutte, L.: One class random forests. Pattern Recognition **42**, 3490–3506 (2013). Eslevier
8. Derrac, J., García, S., Herrera, F.: Fuzzy nearest neighbor algorithms: Taxonomy, experimental analysis and prospects. Information Sciences **260**, 98–119 (2014). Eslevier
9. Ding, X., Li, Y., Belatreche, A., Maguire, L.P.: An experimental evaluation of novelty detection methods. Neurocomputing **135**, 313–327 (2014). Elsevier
10. Farhadi, A., Endres, I., Hoiem, D., Forsyth, D.: Describing objects by their attributes. In: IEEE Conference on Computer Vision and Pattern Recognition (CVPR), pp. 1778–1785. IEEE (2009)
11. Stallkamp, J., Schlipsing, M., Salmen, J., Igel, C.: Man vs. computer: Benchmarking machine learning algorithms for traffic sign recognition. Neural Networks **32**, 323–332 (2012). Eslevier
12. Aghdam, H.H., Heravi, E.J., Puig, D.: A unified framework for coarse-to-fine recognition of traffic signs using bayesian network and visual attributes. In: 10th International Joint Conference on Computer Vision, Imaging and Computer Graphics Theory and Applications (VISAPP), Berlin (2015)
13. Tax, D.M.J.: DDtools, the Data Description Toolbox for Matlab, April 2007. http://prlab.tudelft.nl/david-tax/dd_tools.html

Real-Time Head Pose Estimation Using Multi-variate RVM on Faces in the Wild

Mohamed Selim$^{(\boxtimes)}$, Alain Pagani, and Didier Stricker

Augmented Vision Research Group, German Research Center for Artificial
Intelligence (DFKI), Technical University of Kaiserslautern,
Tripstaddterstr. 122, 67663 Kaiserslautern, Germany
{mohamed.selim,alain.pagani,didier.stricker}@dfki.de
http://www.av.dfki.de

Abstract. Various computer vision problems and applications rely on
an accurate, fast head pose estimator. We model head pose estimation as
a regression problem. We show that it is possible to use the appearance
of the facial image as a feature which depicts the pose variations. We
use a parametrized Multi-Variate Relevance Vector Machine (MVRVM)
to learn the three rotation angles of the face (yaw, pitch, and roll). The
input of the MVRVM is normalized mean pixel intensities of the face
patches, and the output is the three head rotation angles. We evaluated
our approach on the challenging YouTube faces dataset. We achieved
a head pose estimation with an average error tolerance of $\pm 6.5°$ in the
yaw rotation angle, and less than $\pm 2.5°$ in both the pitch and roll angles.
The time taken in one prediction is 2-3 milliseconds, hence suitable for
real-time applications.

Keywords: Head pose estimation · Real-time · MVRVM · YouTube
faces

1 Introduction

Head pose estimation is an important computer vision problem. It can be looked
at as an individual problem, or as an important module in other problems. It
can be the goal of a system, like in detecting user's gaze in Human-Computer
Interaction systems (for example, digital signage displays). Thus, head pose estimation has a variety of uses in real world applications.

Moreover, head pose estimation is an important pre-processing step in solving various computer vision problems. Many computer vision tasks and image
understanding techniques rely on a reliable, fast, and accurate head pose estimator. Examples of such computer vision problems are: gaze direction estimation,
pose-invariant gender or age classification. In [17], the authors combined head
pose with eye localization for solving the problem of gaze estimation.

The problem depicted in literature [12] as the head pose is an important factor
when solving problems that deal with faces, or with facial analysis. For example,

© Springer International Publishing Switzerland 2015
G. Azzopardi and N. Petkov (Eds.): CAIP 2015, Part II, LNCS 9257, pp. 254–265, 2015.
DOI: 10.1007/978-3-319-23117-4_22

Fig. 1. Sample detections from the YouTube faces dataset. The red rectangle depicts the detected face, and the estimated *yaw* angle is indicated inside the green circle at the top-left corner. The circle represents a top view of the face, and the green line inside it shows the detected *yaw* angle. A detected angle of of 0 °is indicated by a line pointing downward. Despite the images having different backgrounds, presence of eye glasses or not, or some occlusion on the face, our method can predict the head pose correctly

pose estimation can be an important pre-processing step in implementing a pose-invariant age or gender classifier. One can have different classifiers for gender that are trained on different poses of the face. Another example of using the pose estimation is facial expression recognition.

Due to the importance of the head pose estimation problem, either as a goal by itself or as part of other more complex systems, considerable attraction appeared in literature [12], and considerable effort has been put in solving the head pose estimation problem. Another important aspect is that in some situations, a fast algorithm is required to allow the integration of the head pose estimator module in other systems without adding overhead.

Solving the problem of the head pose estimation can be carried out in one of several ways. When using a classifier, a rough head rotation estimation can be carried out, and the output of such system is either, the head has a frontal pose, right profile or left profile. However, the problem can be viewed a multi-class classification problem, where the data can be classified according to the main head rotation angles. For example, the classes can be according to the yaw rotation angle $+90, +45, 0, -45, -90$. The problem can be solved by for example using a sufficient amount of training dataset, and a SVM. One of the datasets that provide different poses is the FERET dataset[14].

In case we need to allow the detection of more rotation angles, modeling the problem as a classification one would result in many classes that might not be suitable for separation in prediction. Thus, we model the problem as a regression problem, where the output of the trained regressor is a value in a probabilistic range of values that are detected by the range of motion of the head. Moreover, we detect the three rotation angles of the head in prediction on a Multi Variate Relevance Vector Machine.

The paper is organized as follows, the idea behind Relevance Vector Machines and their differences from SVMs are discussed in the next section. In section 3 the theory of our approach is discussed in details. In section 4 we present the results and the evaluations carried on the challenging YouTube faces dataset[18] and also on a sample images that we collected. Finally, we conclude and summarize the paper in section 5, and present some future work ideas.

2   Related Work

This section discusses in details the Relevance Vector Machine. Later, various pose estimation techniques are presented.

2.1   Relevance Vector Machine

The RVM, short for Relevance Vector Machine, proposed by Tipping [16], adapts the main ideas of Support Vector Machines (SVM) to a Bayesian context. Results appeared to be as precise and sparse as the SVMs, moreover, yielded a full probability distribution as output of the prediction unlike the SVM which yields non probabilistic predictions [16]. The RVMs fit in our approach as the required output is the three angles of the head, which are floating point values in a probabilistic range. RVMs learn a mapping between input vector $\mathbf{y}$ and output vector $\mathbf{x}$ of the form:

$$x = W\phi(y) + \xi \tag{1}$$

where ξ is a Gaussian noise vector with 0 mean and diagonal covariance matrix. ϕ is a vector of basis function of the form:

$$\phi(y) = (1, k(y, y_1), k(y, y_2), ..., k(y, y_n))^T \tag{2}$$

where k is the kernel function. and y_1 to y_n are the input vectors from the training dataset. The weights of the basis functions are written in the matrix W. In the RVM framework, the weights of each input example are governed by a set of hyperparameters, which describe the posterior distribution of the weights.

During training, a set of input-output pairs (x_i, y_i) are used to learn the optimal function from equation 1. To achieve this, the hyperparameters are estimated iteratively. Most hyperparameters go to infinity, causing the posterior distributions to effectively set the corresponding weights to zero. This means that the matrix W only has few non-zero columns. The remaining examples with non-zero weights are called *relevance vectors*.

Tipping's original formulation only allows regression from multivariate input to univariate output. In our approach, the input vector is generated from the 2D image of the face. However, the output learnt vector is the three rotation angles of the head. Therefor, we use an extension of the RVM, called MVRVM, short for Multi Variate Relevance Vector Machine proposed by Thayananthan *et al* [15].

2.2   Pose Estimation

Head pose estimation had much interest during the recent years in literature [12]. We can look at the existing approaches according to the input data they use. Some approaches used 2D images and some uses 3D depth data. Looking into the 2D approaches, we can differentiate between them as some rely on appearances, and some rely on features that are detected on the face.

Most methods use 2D view-based models [6,10,13] or 3D models [5,8]. Regarding the approaches that need facial features detection, they rely on the visibility of the features in the different poses they need to estimate. Many work was done that use Active Appearance Models (AAMs)[6]. They rely on feature detection, tracking, and model fitting, which can lose the tracking or be error prone if the detection of the points or landmarks was not correct.

The work done by [7] uses 3D data that can be captured from depth cameras. This approach cannot be easily applied on video streams, because they use depth data which require special hardware.

In comparison to our approach, we do not rely on depth data, but our approach uses the 2D facial image as input, therefore, can be easily applied in various applications without the need to having 3D cameras. The problem of head pose estimation can be solved in different resulting spaces. Either discrete angles, or a continuous range of motion. Work done by [19], accepts results with error tolerance of $\pm 15°$. The work done by [2] estimates the head pose by detecting and tracking facial landmarks. Relying on the tracking facial landmarks limits the head pose estimation to the visibility of the landmarks. Based on this limitation, the detected head pose in the yaw angle is limited to roughly angles between -60 and +60 degrees. Our approach does not rely on landmark localization tracking, the pose is estimated using the facial image.

3   Approach

The problem considered in this paper is head pose estimation in real-time. One of the advantages of our method is the low computational complexity. Instead of using a hand crafted descriptor, simply normalized mean pixel values are being used as features in our approach, which is proven to achieve high accuracy as discussed later in section 4 in the paper. We use the Multi-Variate Relevance Vector Machines (MVRVM) as it treats the estimation of the head rotation angles as a regression problem. The approach does not rely on high quality images, but it is supposed to work on facial images taken "in the wild", where no

Fig. 2. Input images (for clarification only) are divided into patches. Feature vectors are generated for each image. The RVM is trained with the input feature vectors. The results of the training are the relevance vectors that can be used later in prediction

conditions apply while capturing the facial image. An overview of the system is shown in figure 2. The input image is partitioned into patches, followed by feature extraction. The training images are passed to the Relevance Vector Machine. In iterative learning, the relevance vectors are learnt by the RVM. The following subsections describe the approach in more details.

3.1 Features

The face image is divided into patches by a grid of size $a \times b$ blocks, where a is the number of columns in the X direction and b is the number of rows in the Y direction. For each patch, the mean value of the pixel intensity is calculated. All the mean values are concatenated together, resulting in the feature vector for the input image. The feature vector of the image is normalized as shown in the next subsection.

3.2 Normalization

In order to prepare the data from regression training by the RVM. The feature vector is normalized such that the vector has a zero mean and unit standard deviation. The normalization step adds robustness to light changes that might occur among different input images. First, σ is calculated for the feature vector.

$$\sigma = \sqrt{\frac{1}{N-1} \sum_{i=1}^{N} (x_i - \overline{x})^2}, \tag{3}$$

where N is the number of elements in the vector, and $\overline{x}$ is the mean value of the feature vector. Later, for each element in the feature vector, a normalized value is calculated as in equation 4. The simple features that are used in the training of the Relevance Vector Machine do not require any facial landmark localizations [19], or any complex tracking algorithms. This makes the computation of the pose extremely fast.

$$\forall x_i \in X, \quad v_i = \frac{x_i - \mu}{\sigma} \tag{4}$$

3.3 Parameters Optimization

In order to optimize the Relevance Vector Machine for head pose estimation problem, the parameters included in the process need to be optimized. One of the parameters is the kernel width of the relevance vector machine. It controls the sparsity of the RVM. Varying the kernel width, affects the number of relevance vectors, hence, it has be to optimized so that we avoid the over-fitting problem.

Also, the size of the grid used in feature generation has to be investigated. The partitioning of the face incorporates the pose varying information based on the face appearance. We would like to find the optimal grid size in both horizontal and vertical directions, such that we get the least error possible by the RVM.

In the next section, the datasets used in our evaluation of the approach are discussed and we show parameter optimization results. We show the result of cross validation training and prediction on the dataset used in our study.

4 Evaluation and Results

4.1 Training Dataset

In order to evaluate our approach on real data, we need a dataset that has a set of images with continuous degrees varying in the head pose. The standard datasets like FERET [14] has discrete specific values for head pose. We want to evaluate our approach on a dataset that was not captured in a controlled environment, in other words, captured in the wild. Most importantly, we need to evaluate our approach on a dataset that has continuous angles.

The Labeled faces in the wild [9] is a challenging dataset in terms of occlusion, image quality, varying poses, different illumination, etc. However, it does not provide sufficient samples for each subject in different poses. The best candidate to the best of our knowledge is the YouTube faces dataset [18]. The dataset consists of videos of different subjects, and such meets the main requirement of having faces with head rotation angles for different subjects. Also, the range of rotation of most of the subjects in the dataset is wide, for example some videos have yaw rotation from -88 degress up to 80 degrees. Moreover, it is a challenging dataset that was not captured in a controlled environment, nor was it captured using high quality cameras.

First, we tuned the parameters in our approach on the YouTube faces dataset to find the parameters that will yield results with the least error in the rotation angles. Followed by that, we ran 4-fold cross validation on the dataset and reported the results. Following in the section are more details about the datasets and the carried evaluations and optimization.

Youtube Faces Dataset. In order to have a regressor that can estimate the pose in high accuracy, a training dataset of faces is required to have different samples at different angles. The FERET dataset [14] is one of the standard datasets for face analysis. However, it only has an image for a specific pose. Each subject of the FERET dataset has a frontal image(yaw=0) and two profile images(yaw=90,-90), and some other specific angles(45,-45,-67.5,67.5). The dataset was taken with discrete angles, thus, not suitable for our application.

One important property of the dataset is to have continuous angles of the head, this can be found in videos where the subject's head is moving freely. One very challenging dataset is the YouTube faces dataset [18]. It is a dataset of face videos that was designed for studying the problem of unconstrained face recognition in videos. The dataset contains 3425 videos of 1595 different people. All videos were downloaded from YouTube [1]. Each subject in the dataset has an average of 2.15 videos. The shortest video sequence contains 48 frames, the longest one contains 6070 frames, and the average number of frames for the videos is nearly 181 frames. The authors of the dataset followed the example of the Labeled Faces in the Wild image collection [9], which resulted in a large collection of videos.

The dataset was used by [3] in video to video comparisons. Also, it was used by [11] in face verification in the wild from videos. To the best of our knowledge, it was not used for head pose estimation in the wild.

An important feature of the YouTube faces dataset that made us use it in our work is that the three rotation angles (our main interest) of the head are available for each frame in the dataset. The authors of the dataset report that they used the state of the art methods to obtain the rotation angles values. They used the face.com API. This allowed us to perform various evaluations where we can train on one subject only, or train on many subjects.

Parameters Optimization Results. The parameter σ_k controls the kernel width, and the sparsity of the RVM, and as mentioned before, it has to be taken care of in order to avoid over-fitting. As we increase the kernel width, the number of relevance vectors decreases and the RVM can predict for new input image in a probabilistic manner. If the kernel parameter is small, the RVM will use all the input feature vectors as relevance vectors, and that means it is not learning anything from the data and cannot differentiate between them.

Figure 3 shows the average error in the three head rotation angles while varying the kernel width σ_k from 1 to 55 with a different value of increments in the iterations. In each iteration we train with 75% of the data and test with the remaining 25%, assuring that the test set is not included in the training set. This is to give us an estimate of the optimal value for the kernel parameter.

We can notice that the average error is decreasing as we increase the kernel width. Also, the number of relevance vectors is decreasing too. The error roughly stayed nearly constant starting from the kernel width 7.5. We did not want to minimize the number of relevance vectors while maintaining the error as low as possible. As shown in the figure, the error starts increasing again at high kernel parameter values. We decided to proceed with kernel width of size 13 as it yields low error in the rotation angles and also not too small number of relevance vectors.

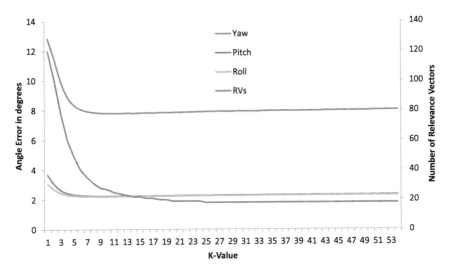

Fig. 3. The effect of varying the kernel width σ_k on the average mean error in the three head rotation angles (yaw, pitch, and roll). On the secondary axis, the number of relevance vector is shown.

We now discuss the optimization of grid size that is used in feature generation as described before. The grid size controls the number of patches on the input image. Using small number of patches (divisions) on the image of the face, reduces the size of the feature vector, which increases the prediction speed. Nevertheless, using small feature vector size reduces the regressor's precision, because the input feature vector doesn't enclose enough information for the head pose among different samples.

In order, to detect precisely, the number of divisions that yields the minimum error, we evaluated the YouTube faces dataset on using different grid sizes. We varied the size of the grid, from 5×5, up to 20×20. We maintained the kernel width σ_k at the optimized value 13. The results of that evaluation are shown in figure 4. We can notice that the size of the grid that yielded the least error in the three rotation angles was 15×15. After this value, the number of relevance vectors kept increasing.

We optimized both the kernel width that controls the sparsity of the RVM and the grid divisions that controls the feature vector size used in the training process. By the experimental evaluation shown above, the optimal value of the kernel width is 13, and the optimal value for the grid size is 15.

After performing the optimization on the YouTube faces dataset, we evaluated the whole dataset using the tuned parameters. We ran a 4-fold cross validation tests on all the subjects in the datasets using all the videos provided for each subject.

The results as shown in figure 5, show that for more than 75% of the dataset the mean error was less than 10° in the main rotation angle of the head, the yaw angle. Also, for about 20% of the dataset, the error is below 6° in the same angle.

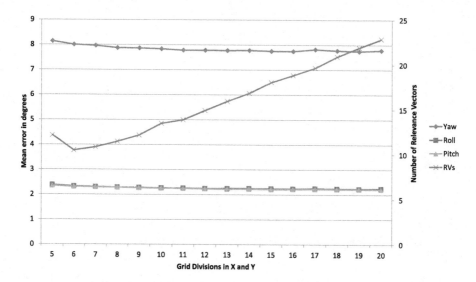

Fig. 4. The effect of varying the grid size used in feature generation, on the average mean error in the three head rotation angles (yaw, pitch, and roll). The grid of size 15×15 yields the best results.

So, our approach can achieve good performance on a very challenging dataset, by correctly detecting the head pose for more than 75% of the dataset with error tolerance of $\pm 3 - 4°$ using simple features that doesn't require complex features detection on the face of the subject.

Finally, we tested the proposed approach on unseen videos of the same subject. We used the subjects in the dataset that had more than 2 videos. We trained with two videos, and tested on an unseen video of the subject. The results of that approach as expected showed less accuracy. The number of subjects included in that test were 533 subjects. The average mean error in the rotation angles were 21, 6, and 5 degrees in the yaw, pitch, and roll rotation respectively. Keeping into consideration we didn't limit the range of the yaw angles in the training, we used the full range provided by the videos, from left profile to right profile appearances. Results are promising for an error of 20 degrees in that challenging test.

The architecture of the machine used in the evaluations is a 6-core Intel Xeon CPU with hyper-threading technology, and 64 GB of RAM. Our evaluation application runs in parallel using the 12 threads provided by the CPU.

Finally, our methods is suitable for real-time applications as the time taken by the computation of one single prediction of the three head rotation angles is only 2-3 milliseconds, with no need of complex landmark detection or model fitting or tracking.

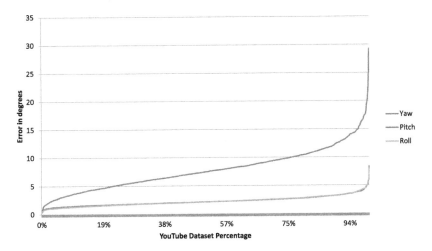

Fig. 5. Results on the YouTube faces dataset. The $\sigma_k = 13$, and the grid size for feature generation is 15×15. The X-axis represents a percentage of the dataset which consists of 1595 subjects. The Y-axis represents the mean error of the 4-fold cross validation evaluation.

5   Conclusion and Future Work

5.1   Conclusions

We present a regression scheme for head pose estimation using the appearance of the facial image. The output of our approach is an estimation of the three rotation angles in the full range of the angles, with floating point values. Our approach neither relies on complex features generation, nor does it rely on special landmark localization, but rather relies on the appearance of the facial image. The facial image is divided into patches using a grid of size 15×15.

We optimized the division parameters in the features generation. Also, we optimized the kernel parameter σ_k that controls the sparsity of the RVM and the number of relevance vectors learnt during the training. The online prediction of the three head rotation angles is very fast, it takes around 2-3 milliseconds, hence it is suitable for real-time use. This allows the use of the proposed method as a pre-processing step in other applications that rely on the head pose.

We evaluated our approach on a challenging dataset, the YouTube faces dataset. It has images from videos that were taken in uncontrolled environments, with varying face sizes, illumination, some occlusions, etc. We showed that our approach can learn the three head rotation angles using simple features. This approach doesn't rely on depth images, nor 3D information beside the 2D image. Our approach doesn't need landmark detections on the face and can predict full range of motion of the face. We showed that it can learn faces with extreme rotation angles.

The results of our evaluation on the YouTube faces dataset show that we achieve an estimation with error tolerance of $\pm 6.5°$ in the yaw rotation angle, and less than ±2.5° on the pitch and roll angles on the whole dataset. For more than 80% of the dataset, our approach estimates the angles with tolerance error of ±10°. Our final evaluation on the YouTube faces dataset was run in 4-fold cross validation. We also presented promising results on unseen videos of the subjects, taken into different conditions from the training videos.

5.2 Future Work

In order to improve the results and get more fine head pose estimations, a cascade of RVMs can be built in a way that the first RVM can give a rough estimate on the head rotation angles. Following the first regressor, a set of RVMs are to be trained on a smaller range of angles. The Set of RVMs can be one level after the main one, or different number of levels of RVMs can be trained on data with smaller range of angles. The number of levels in the cascade tree and the number of RVMs in each level must be investigated.

We also would like to compare the results of the single RVM and the cascade with more complex pose estimators which rely on facial landmarks.

Moreover, we would like to investigate the user of other light normalization techniques as a pre-processing step in the preparation of the training dataset.

Regarding the evaluations on the YouTube faces datasets, we would like to improve our results on the very challenging 20% of the dataset by running more evaluations in a scheme where the training faces and the testing faces are completely different. We also plan to test the approach on other challenging datasets like the PaSC dataset [4].

Acknowledgments. This work has been partially funded by the European project Eyes of Things under contract number GA643924, and the German Federal Ministry of Education and Research BMBF project HYSOCIATEA under contract number 01IW14001.

References

1. Youtube
2. Asthana, A., Zafeiriou, S., Cheng, S., Pantic, M.: Incremental face alignment in the wild. In: 2014 IEEE Conference on Computer Vision and Pattern Recognition (CVPR), pp. 1859–1866. IEEE (2014)
3. Best-Rowden, L., Klare, B., Klontz, J., Jain, A.K.: Video-to-video face matching: establishing a baseline for unconstrained face recognition. In: 2013 IEEE Sixth International Conference on Biometrics: Theory, Applications and Systems (BTAS), pp. 1–8. IEEE (2013)
4. Beveridge, J.R., Phillips, P.J., Bolme, D.S., Draper, B.A., Givens, G.H., Lui, Y.M., Teli, M.N., Zhang, H., Scruggs, W.T., Bowyer, K.W., Flynn, P.J., Cheng, S.: The challenge of face recognition from digital point-and-shoot cameras. In: 2013 IEEE Sixth International Conference on Biometrics: Theory, Applications and Systems (BTAS), pp. 1–8, September 2013

5. Blanz, V., Vetter, T.: Face recognition based on fitting a 3d morphable model. IEEE Transactions on Pattern Analysis and Machine Intelligence **25**(9), 1063–1074 (2003)

6. Cootes, T.F., Wheeler, G.V., Walker, K.N., Taylor, C.J.: View-based active appearance models. Image and Vision Computing **20**(9), 657–664 (2002)

7. Fanelli, G., Gall, J., Van Gool, L.: Real time head pose estimation with random regression forests. In: 2011 IEEE Conference on Computer Vision and Pattern Recognition (CVPR), pp. 617–624. IEEE (2011)

8. Gu, L., Kanade, T.: 3d alignment of face in a single image. In: 2006 IEEE Computer Society Conference on Computer Vision and Pattern Recognition, vol. 1, pp. 1305–1312. IEEE (2006)

9. Huang, G.B., Ramesh, M., Berg, T., Learned-Miller, E.: Labeled faces in the wild: A database for studying face recognition in unconstrained environments. Technical Report 07–49, University of Massachusetts, Amherst, October 2007

10. Jones, M., Viola, P.: Fast multi-view face detection. Mitsubishi Electric Research Lab TR-20003-96, 3:14 (2003)

11. Kan, M., Xu, D., Shan, S., Li, W., Chen, X.: Learning prototype hyperplanes for face verification in the wild. IEEE Transactions on Image Processing **22**(8), 3310–3316 (2013)

12. Murphy-Chutorian, E., Trivedi, M.M.: Head pose estimation in computer vision: A survey. IEEE Transactions on Pattern Analysis and Machine Intelligence **31**(4), 607–626 (2009)

13. Pentland, A., Moghaddam, B., Starner, T.: View-based and modular eigenspaces for face recognition. In: 1994 IEEE Computer Society Conference on Computer Vision and Pattern Recognition, Proceedings CVPR 1994, pp. 84–91. IEEE (1994)

14. Phillips, P.J., Moon, H., Rizvi, S.A., Rauss, P.J.: The feret evaluation methodology for face-recognition algorithms. IEEE Trans. Pattern Anal. Mach. Intell. **22**(10), 1090–1104 (2000)

15. Thayananthan, A., Navaratnam, R., Stenger, B., Torr, P.H.S., Cipolla, R.: Multivariate relevance vector machines for tracking. In: Leonardis, A., Bischof, H., Pinz, A. (eds.) ECCV 2006. LNCS, vol. 3953, pp. 124–138. Springer, Heidelberg (2006)

16. Tipping, M.E.: Sparse bayesian learning and the relevance vector machine. The Journal of Machine Learning Research **1**, 211–244 (2001)

17. Valenti, R., Sebe, N., Gevers, T.: Combining head pose and eye location information for gaze estimation. IEEE Transactions on Image Processing **21**(2), 802–815 (2012)

18. Wolf, L., Hassner, T., Maoz, I.: Face recognition in unconstrained videos with matched background similarity. In: 2011 IEEE Conference on Computer Vision and Pattern Recognition (CVPR), pp. 529–534. IEEE (2011)

19. Zhu, X., Ramanan, D.: Face detection, pose estimation, and landmark localization in the wild. In: 2012 IEEE Conference on Computer Vision and Pattern Recognition (CVPR), pp. 2879–2886. IEEE (2012)

A Verification-Based Multithreshold Probing Approach to HEp-2 Cell Segmentation

Xiaoyi Jiang[1,2]([✉]), Gennaro Percannella[3], and Mario Vento[3]

[1] Department of Mathematics and Computer Science, University of Münster,
Münster, Germany
xjiang@uni-muenster.de
[2] Cluster of Excellence EXC 1003, Cells in Motion, CiM, Münster, Germany
[3] Department of Information Engineering, Electrical Engineering and Applied
Mathematics, University of Salerno, Salerno, Italy

Abstract. In this paper we propose a novel approach to HEp-2 cell segmentation based on the framework of verification-based multithreshold probing. Cell hypotheses are generated by binarization using hypothetic thresholds and accepted/rejected by a verification procedure. The proposed method has the nice property of combining both adaptive local thresholding and involvement of high-level knowledge. We have realized a prototype implementation using a simple rule-based verification procedure. Experimental evaluation has been performed on two public databases. It is shown that our approach outperforms a number of existing methods.

1 Introduction

The Indirect Immunofluorescence (IIF) technique is becoming increasingly important for the diagnosis of several autoimmune diseases, i.e, diseases which arise from an abnormal immune response of the body against substances and tissues normally present in the body. In IIF, two antibodies are used: the first (primary) antibody specifically binds the target molecule and the secondary antibody, which carries the fluorophore, recognizes the primary antibody and binds to it. This process produces a fluorescence image observable through a microscope that represents the distribution of the target antibodies inside the tissue. The staining patterns observable in this distribution are the main information used for the diagnosis. In particular, antinuclear autoantibodies (ANAs) play a pivotal role in the serological diagnosis of autoimmune diseases. In this context, IIF with the human larynx carcinoma (HEp-2) substrate is considered as the gold standard for ANA testing. The most frequent and clinically useful ANA patterns are shown in Figure 1. Besides ANA patterns, HEp-2 slides may also reveal the cytoplasmic staining pattern, which is relevant to diagnostic purposes as well. In most cases, all the cells in the image are of the same type of staining pattern; thus the image is labeled with the common pattern.

Recently, substantial efforts have been made to automatic HEp-2 cell classification, as documented by the related contests at ICPR2012, ICIP2013, and

© Springer International Publishing Switzerland 2015
G. Azzopardi and N. Petkov (Eds.): CAIP 2015, Part II, LNCS 9257, pp. 266–276, 2015.
DOI: 10.1007/978-3-319-23117-4_23

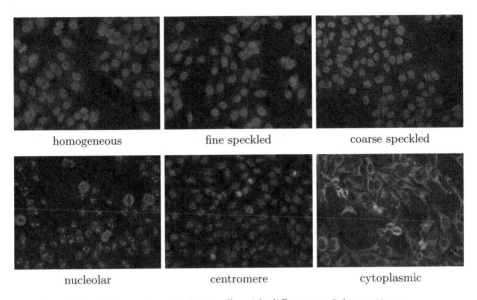

homogeneous   fine speckled   coarse speckled

nucleolar   centromere   cytoplasmic

Fig. 1. Examples of HEp-2 cells with different staining patterns.

ICPR2014. A report on the ICPR2012 contest can be found in [4], technical details of the participating classification methods are included in the Special Issue on the analysis and recognition of indirect immuno-fluorescence images [5]. Such works on single cell classification crucially depend on some cell segmentation procedure. Despite of the importance, however, only relatively few works have reported on the cell segmentation task in HEp-2 images.

In this work we propose to solve this problem in the framework of adaptive local thresholding by verification-based multithreshold probing [8]. We begin with a discussion of related work in the next section. Then, our approach is motivated and described in Section 3. Section 4 reports its experimental evaluation and comparison based on two public datasets to demonstrate superior performance over several existing methods. Finally, some discussions conclude this paper.

2   Related Work

Perhaps the first work for cell segmentation in HEp-2 images was reported by Perner *et al.* [11]. This simple method applies the popular Otsu thresholding algorithm to reveal the cells, followed by morphological filters like dilation and erosion. It has been adopted with few modifications also in [12]. This approach will fail when dealing with cells whose staining pattern is characterized by a large intensity variation inside the cell body (e.g. speckled and nucleolar patterns, see Figure 1).

To overcome this problem the authors of [7] coarsely classify the image into two classes based on the number of connected regions obtained by means of the Otsu thresholding algorithm. If it is smaller than a threshold, the cell patterns are expected to have small intensity variations inside the cell body and an edge detection (Canny operator) is applied to detect the cells, otherwise the Otsu thresholding result is used. In both cases morphological smoothing is applied for postprocessing.

In the literature there are several watershed segmentation methods. The method from [6] works in two steps. In the first step, the watershed algorithm is applied first, followed by region merging and region elimination on the green channel of the original RGB image. Then, if the numbers of detected cells is greater than a threshold, the image goes through a second step, otherwise the segmentation process ends. In the second step, a similar procedure is performed on the cyan channel (CMY transformed from RGB), where the Otsu thresholding is used to generate markers for the watershed algorithm. Other variants of watershed-based segmentation methods can be found in [1,2].

The approach from [10] substantially differs from those discussed above. It is based on the observation that the pixel intensity histogram can be divided in three bands: two bands related to the lowest and the highest intensity values can be surely attributed to the background and the foreground, respectively. They can be determined by a so-called image reconstruction algorithm on the original input image. For the remaining, unlabeled pixels in the third band the intensity information alone is not sufficient for their definitive attribution to the background or the foreground. Instead, a classification approach is adopted that uses statistical features learned from the first two bands to perform a classifier-controlled dilation of the foreground.

In general, the visual evidence that the cells are characterized by a higher intensity with respect to the background is fundamental to most existing cell segmentation methods for HEp-2 images. However, classical thresholding can only provide suboptimal results due to the high variability of both fluorescence intensity and staining patterns. In [10] this problem is bypassed by a machine learning approach. In [8] a general framework of adaptive local thresholding based on a verification-based multithreshold probing scheme has been proposed. It has been applied to segmentation in retinal images [8] and X-ray coronary angiogram images [9]. In this work we adapt this framework to solve the cell segmentation problem for HEp-2 images.

3   Verification-Based Multithreshold Probing Approach

HEp-2 images are a good example for situations, in which global thresholds do not work well. This is partly caused by an irregular intensity distribution, see Figure 2 for a typical example. With a threshold 60 we only manage to detect the cells in the upper area, but fail in the bottom area. A lower threshold 35 effects exactly inversely. This example clearly shows that a global threshold (of whatever value) generally cannot be the solution. Instead, some kind of adaptive local thresholding is required.

In addition, working with intensity values alone is on the level of processing low-level features only. On the other hand, cells are semantic units with far more information than intensity values. Indeed, it is the rich features which describe

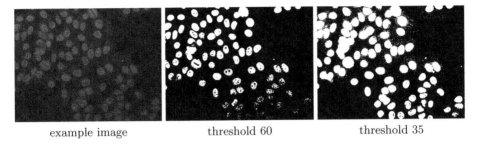

| example image | threshold 60 | threshold 35 |

Fig. 2. HEp-images with irregular intensity distribution. Thresholding is applied to a grayscale image converted from the original color image. Optimal threshold varies locally.

the full nature of cells and provide the foundation of cell classification [4,5]. Therefore, it can be expected that involving high-level semantic knowledge will further benefit cell segmentation.

3.1 Framework of Verification-Based Multithreshold Probing

A general framework has been proposed in [8], which exactly combines these two aspects (adaptive local thresholding, involvement of high-level knowledge). Object hypotheses are generated by binarization using hypothetic thresholds and accepted/rejected by a verification procedure. The application-dependent verification procedure can be designed to fully utilize all relevant informations about the objects of interest.

It is assumed that the images contain dark background and bright objects. Thresholding at a particular threshold T leads to a binary image B_T, in which pixels with intensity larger than or equal to T are marked as object pixels and all other pixels as background. Given a binary image B_T resulting from some threshold T, we are able to decide if any region in B_T can be accepted as an object by means of a decision (classification) procedure. In a more sophisticated manner, it is even possible to allow the decision procedure to accept part of a region. The operation is performed on a series of different thresholds and the final segmentation is obtained by combining the results from the individual thresholds. Overall, this framework adopts the paradigm of hypotheses generation and verification. Object hypotheses are generated by binarization using some hypothetic thresholds and accepted/rejected by the decision (classification) procedure.

More formally, the verification-based multithreshold probing framework for adaptive local thresholding is specified in Figure 3. The classification procedure is the core part of this framework that depends on the particular application. Here, one is able to incorporate any relevant information about objects, including shape, color/intensity, contrast, etc. Therefore, this approach can be regarded as knowledge-guided adaptive thresholding, in contrast to the vast majority of known thresholding algorithms based on statistical methods. Besides the verification test, the set T_S of probe thresholds must be specified. In the simplest

---

Input: intensity image I, set T_S of probe thresholds
Output: binary image B of object and background pixels

for each $T \in T_S$ **do** {
    obtain binary image B_T by thresholding I at T;
    apply verification procedure to the regions in B_T, resulting in
       binary image B_T^* consisting of surviving regions;
}
$B = \cup_{T \in T_S} B_T^*$;

Fig. 3. Adaptive local thresholding framework.

form, T_S takes values ranging from the minimum intensity $I_{\min}$ to the maximum intensity $I_{\max}$ of an image at some constant step. It is also possible to work with a non-uniform sampling.

3.2   Prototype Implementation

The framework of verification-based multithreshold probing can be easily adapted to segmenting HEp-2 cell images. As a proof of principle we have realized a prototype implementation. Its details are presented in the following.

The framework can be applied to a grayscale image converted from the original color image. Alternatively, one may also use the luminance channel in a color space (e.g. YCbCr). Our current implementation is based on the variant of grayscale images.

Smoothing is performed in two different contexts. First, we use a 3×3 kernel based smoothing as preprocessing to reduce the noise in the grayscale image converted from the original color image. The binary image B_T for a particular threshold T is generally noisy (gaps within cells and on the contours of cells). Therefore, we make use of morphological operations (closing and opening) on B_T to remove noise and small objects and to obtain improved contours and cell regions.

An essential detail that must be concretized when applying the framework of verification-based multithreshold probing is the highly application-specific verification procedure. We need to decide to either accept and reject each connected region R in B_T. In the former case R survives and is taken over for B_T^*. Currently, this is done by means of three simple filters.

- *Area filter.* Because cells have a limited range of size, R only survives if its size falls into an interval [Area_min, Area_max].
- *Shape filter.* Expecting the cells usually of an elliptic shape we compute the deviation between the area of R and the area of an ideal ellipse built upon R. The connected region R is only accepted if this deviation is smaller than a threshold thr_s. Naturally, the deviation is normalized in the interval [0,1] to cope with different region sizes.

– *Position filter.* For each connected region R it checks if there is another region that surrounds it. This is done by building a bounding box around each region. In the case of overlapping bounding boxes, the smaller related region is removed.

Area_min, Area_max, and thr_s are parameters of the algorithm. In our experimental evaluation they are learned from training data.

It is obvious that cells are usually detected several times using different thresholds, but for each cell we like to select only the best one. After the verification step in Figure 3 we thus include an additional step, where a comparison between the accepted cells (i.e. regions in B_T^*) and the cells accepted so far is made. In this comparison the same criteria are used: area, shape, and position. In this case the position constraint is more important. All regions detected in the current iteration that do not surround other cells accepted so far are always accepted. If a region R is however surrounded by some R' from the previous iterations, then we substitute R' with the new one R only if:

– R has greater area than R',
– the elliptical deviation of R is lower than that of R' multiplied by a constant factor.

In other words, if R is larger than R' we reject R only if its elliptical error is much larger than that of R'. The rationale behind this strategy is that between two reasonable cell candidates the larger one should probably be favored even if its elliptical deviation is slightly worse. It may namely happen that a cell is only partially visible in R. Therefore only in rare cases, where the elliptical deviation of R is much larger, we select the smaller region R'.

The behavior of the prototype implementation is illustrated in Figure 4 for one particular threshold. After applying the three filters the result from this iteration (threshold) is shown in B_T^*. The final segmentation after going through all thresholds is also presented. Finally, a comparison with the segmentation ground truth (GT) is also shown there. The color green represents correctly segmented cell pixels (true positive), black correctly detected background pixels (true negative). On the other hand, the red pixels are wrongly detected as cell pixel (false positive) and the blue pixels are cell pixel not detected by the algorithm (false negative).

Note that the current simple rule-based verification procedure is still rather primitive. It can be certainly replaced by more sophisticated and powerful decision (classification) method. However, as will be demonstrated later, even this first prototype implementation achieves results superior to several previous methods.

4   Experimental Evaluation

We have performed experiments on two common datasets (MIVIA dataset and ICPR2014 contest database) and performance comparison with several existing algorithms.

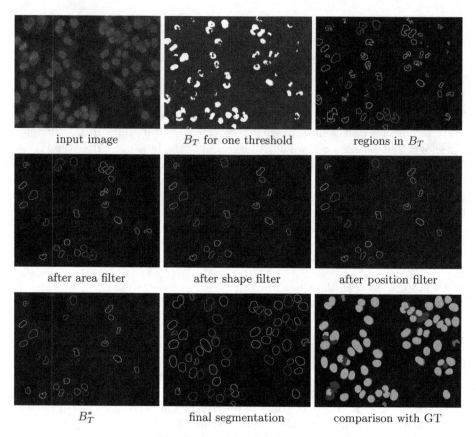

input image	B_T for one threshold	regions in B_T
after area filter	after shape filter	after position filter
B_T^*	final segmentation	comparison with GT

Fig. 4. Algorithm illustration.

4.1 Performance Measure

For performance evaluation the popular measures precision, recall, and f-index are defined by:

$$Prec = \frac{TP}{TP + FP}, \quad Recall = \frac{TP}{TP + FN}, \quad f = \frac{2 \cdot Prec \cdot Recall}{Prec + Recall}$$

where TP is the number of true positives, FP the number of false positives, and FN the number of false negatives. Note that these pixel-level measures are generally more suitable for situations, in which both the foreground and background are interpreted as a single inseparable semantic unit. But in our case the foreground consists of individual cells that should be considered separately. For a cell-level comparison we use instead the extended definition of TP, FP, and FN as proposed in [3]. Formally, given a set D of detected cells and a set G of ground-truth cells, these terms are defined by:

$$TP = \sum_{g \in G} \sum_{d \in D} \frac{|g \cap d|}{|g \cup d|}$$

$$FP = \sum_{d \in D} \frac{|d| - \max_{g \in G} |d \cap g|}{|d|}$$

$$FN = \sum_{g \in G} \frac{|g| - \max_{d \in D} |d \cap g|}{|g|}$$

where $|\cdot|$ denotes the cardinality of a set. These definitions reduce to the usual counts of TP, FP, and FN when the cells should be considered altogether as a whole (foreground). Given the extended definition, we compute again the performance measures precision, recall, and f-index.

4.2   Results on MIVIA Dataset

We used the public MIVIA dataset of HEp-2 images (available at: http://mivia.-unisa.it/datasets/biomedical-image-datasets/hep2-image-dataset/). It consists of 28 annotated IIF images with a resolution of 1388×1038 pixels and a color depth of 24 bits where specialists manually segmented and annotated each cell. The images belong to two classes of fluorescence intensity levels (borderline and positive) and exhibit one of the six main staining patterns shown in Figure 1. The use of images with different fluorescence intensity levels and the low contrast of borderline samples as well as the staining pattern variability make the segmentation task more complex.

A 4-fold cross validation was performed. The parameter values were learned from the training data based on the f-index. The performance measure reported by the 4 experiments is then averaged for performance evaluation and comparison. The achieved performance is presented in Table 1.

For performance comparison the following existing methods are used: Otsu [11], Multistage [7], Watershed [6], Auto learning [10]. There are three versions in [10]: a Multi-Layer Perceptron (MLP) and a Nearest Neighbor (NN) as statistical classifiers, and the so-called image reconstruction. Since the MLP version has shown the best performance, we only included the performance measures of this version. Other existing methods like [1,2] were not considered because these works were based on private datasets.

We focus our discussion on the f-index. Table 1 reveals that our method consistently outperforms the existing methods. For instance, the global average is raised from 55.8% (auto learning) to 72.5%. An outlier among the six staining patterns is obviously the cytoplasmic pattern. It is not an ANA pattern, but relevant for diagnostic purposes. Cytoplasmic cells appear different from the standard ANA cells, they are for instance not elliptic. The difficulty in dealing with this class of staining pattern is illustrated in Figure 5. Since the verification procedure, in particular the shape filter, is clearly dedicated to the ANA patterns, the low performance measure in this case is not surprising. But our approach still substantially improves the other methods.

Table 1. Performance measures (in %) on MIVIA dataset. Staining patterns: 1 (homogenous), 2 (fine speckled), 3 (coarse speckled), 4 (centromere), 5 (nucleolar), 6 (cytoplasmic).

	Otsu			Multistage			Watershed			Auto learning			ours		
	Prec	Rec	f	Prec	Rec	f	Prec	Rec	f	Prec	Rec	f	Prec	Rec	f
average	42.4	46.2	39.8	64.2	46.2	51.5	33.5	79.4	45.7	85.2	43.3	55.8	76.9	71.0	**72.5**
1	89.3	67.2	75.0	86.2	55.4	66.8	37.1	76.0	48.0	97.1	47.3	63.4	81.4	77.4	**78.0**
2	58.2	53.7	53.8	81.0	49.9	61.5	32.6	82.5	46.7	94.1	51.7	66.5	78.5	69.2	**69.8**
3	35.2	45.6	30.5	66.4	55.0	57.9	30.9	84.7	43.3	92.8	54.2	68.3	83.3	81.3	**82.0**
4	43.0	58.3	46.1	62.8	39.5	48.2	41.6	88.7	56.2	84.6	35.6	49.0	74.6	69.0	**70.3**
5	12.2	23.8	14.8	66.7	38.9	48.6	35.2	76.0	46.6	82.8	44.0	57.3	78.7	68.3	**72.8**
6	6.2	17.2	9.0	16.6	37.4	22.5	19.1	63.6	28.3	55.3	26.9	35.9	54.2	47.8	**50.0**

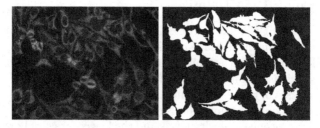

Fig. 5. Image with staining pattern cytoplasmic and GT (right).

4.3   Results on ICPR2014 Contest Dataset

As stated before, from 2012 on a special contest is organized to evaluate HEp-2 cell classification algorithms. For the ICPR 2014 Contest, a big dataset was collected. Even though the contest is focused on the classification problem, the dataset can also be used for segmentation evaluation. It is composed of 1008 HEp-2 images with seven staining patterns: homogeneous, speckled, nucleolar, centromere, golgi, nuclear membrane, and mitotic spindle. The first four patterns are the same as in the MIVIA dataset while the cells of the last three patterns are not elliptic. Thus, we only used images of the first four patterns.

The main problem with this dataset is that all ground truth images have been generated automatically and not manually so that many cells are grouped in clusters. To avoid this problem we made a hard work of perfecting the ground truth images by a manual postprocessing. Currently, this has been done for 56 selected images. For our testing, 28 were then chosen as the training set and the other 28 for the test set. 2. Also for this dataset our method produces good results, see Table 2. Indeed, it looks like this dataset is a bit easier to work with the MIVIA database. Note that because of lacking experimental results demonstrated before on this dataset no performance comparison is done in this case.

Table 2. Performance measures (in %) on ICPR2014 dataset.

	Prec	Rec	f
homogeneous	84.0	87.1	85.4
speckled	83.7	85.1	84.1
nucleolar	88.0	80.1	83.7
centromere	86.5	80.5	82.0

4.4 Computational Time

Currently, the computational time per image is about 7 seconds, measured on an Intel i5 Processor (1,6 GHz × 4 , 4 GB RAM; only one core used). There are several options of speed-up. In the prototype implementation, for instance, the hypothetic thresholds start from 11 and end with 190 with step size of one, thus resulting in a total of 180 iterations of hypotheses generation and verification. Generally, a (slightly) higher value of step size will not dramatically change the segmentation result, but substantially reduce the computational time.

5 Conclusion

Based on the nature of HEp-2 images thresholding has potential to be used for cell segmentation. However, global thresholding cannot be an option and instead adaptive local thresholding must be considered. In this work we have proposed to apply the framework of verification-based multithreshold probing for this task. The proposed method has the nice property of combining both adaptive local thresholding and involvement of high-level knowledge. It is the latter feature that makes our approach very flexible. Our current prototype implementation using a simple rule-based verification procedure already produced good performance that is superior to a number of existing methods.

In future we will concentrate on developing more sophisticated verification procedure. In particular, the vast experiences made from the recent substantial efforts in HEp-2 cell classification [4,5] should benefit our work towards powerful classification-based verification.

Acknowledgments. We thank Gennaro Finizio for his contribution to the software implementation of the segmentation algorithm and his support to the experimental phase.

References

1. Chan, Y.K., Huang, D.C., Liu, K.C., Chen, R.T., Jiang, X.: An automatic indirect immunofluorescence cell segmentation system. Mathematical Problems in Engineering **2014**, Article ID 501206 (2014)

2. Cheng, C.C., Hsieh, T.Y., Taur, J.S., Chen, Y.F.: An automatic segmentation and classification framework for anti-nuclear antibody images. BioMedical Engineering Online **12**(SUPPL 1) (2013)
3. Foggia, P., Percannella, G., Sansone, C., Vento, M.: A graph-based algorithm for cluster detection. IJPRAI **22**(5), 843–860 (2008)
4. Foggia, P., Percannella, G., Soda, P., Vento, M.: Benchmarking HEp-2 cells classification methods. IEEE Trans. Medical Imaging **32**(10), 1878–1889 (2013)
5. Foggia, P., Percannella, G., Soda, P., Vento, M.: Special issue on the analysis and recognition of indirect immuno-fluorescence images. Pattern Recognition **47**(7) (2014)
6. Huang, Y., Chung, C., Hsieh, T., Jao, Y.: Outline detection for the HEp-2 cells in indirect immunofluorescence images using watershed segmentation. In: IEEE Int. Conf. on Sensor Networks, Ubiquitous, and Trustworthy Computing, pp. 423–427 (2008)
7. Huang, Y., Jao, Y., Hsieh, T., Chung, C.: Adaptive automatic segmentation of HEp-2 cells in indirect immunofluorescence images. In: IEEE Int. Conf. on Sensor Networks, Ubiquitous, and Trustworthy Computing, pp. 418–422 (2008)
8. Jiang, X., Mojon, D.: Adaptive local thresholding by verification-based multithreshold probing with application to vessel detection in retinal images. IEEE Trans. Pattern Analysis and Machine Intelligence **25**(1), 131–137 (2003)
9. Nirmaladevi, S., Lavanya, P., Kumaravel, N.: A novel segmentation method using multiresolution analysis with 3D visualization for X-ray coronary angiogram images. Journal of Medical Engineering & Technology **32**(3), 235–244 (2008)
10. Percannella, G., Soda, P., Vento, M.: A classification-based approach to segment HEp-2 cells. In: Proc. of IEEE Int. Symposium on Computer-Based Medical Systems, pp. 1–5 (2012)
11. Perner, P., Perner, H., Müller, B.: Mining knowledge for HEp-2 cell image classification. Artificial Intelligence in Medicine **26**(1–2), 161–173 (2002)
12. Soda, P., Iannello, G.: Aggregation of classifiers for staining pattern recognition in antinuclear autoantibodies analysis. IEEE Trans. Information Technology in Biomedicine **13**(3), 322–329 (2009)

Precise Cross-Section Estimation
on Tubular Organs

Florent Grélard[1,2], Fabien Baldacci[1,2], Anne Vialard[1,2(✉)],
and Jacques-Olivier Lachaud[3]

[1] University of Bordeaux, LaBRI, UMR 5800, 33400 Talence, France
anne.vialard@labri.fr
[2] CNRS, LaBRI, UMR 5800, 33400 Talence, France
[3] Université Savoie Mont Blanc, LAMA, UMR 5127, 73376 Chambéry, France

Abstract. In this article we present a new method to estimate precisely
the cross-section of tubular organs. Obtaining a precise cross-section is
the critical step to perform quantitative analysis of those organs, for
which diameter or area are often correlated to pathologies. Our estimation method, based on a covariance measure from the Voronoi cells of
the set of studied points, can be computed either from the skeleton representation, or from the whole set of voxels of the segmented tubular
organ. This estimator can give a cross-section estimation from any point
of the organ, and is both more accurate and more robust to segmentation
errors than state-of-the-art methods.

1 Introduction

The diameter/area estimation of tubular organs such as vessels, airways or colons
is of interest since these measurements are often correlated with pathologies.
A reliable tool providing, with reproductive results, such geometric characteristics and allowing to study their variations may lead to further progress in health
research. One domain which particularly requires such tools is the research on
pulmonary diseases. The airway wall thickness is a pertinent indicator correlated
with the severity of lung diseases such as asthma [9]. It can be obtained directly
on one slice of a CT image [8,12]: an experienced radiologist selects bronchi which
appear round on a CT slice and measures them generally by using a dedicated
software. This approach is obviously limited as it can only take into account
airways which long axes are perpendicular to the image slices. A more advanced
approach is based on a segmentation of the airway tree. The segmented volume
can be skeletonized so as to obtain its central line. Given a point of the central
line and its local direction, it is possible to reconstruct a cross-section of the
3D image which is orthogonal to the airway. Measurements of the airway wall
can then be performed in the computed cross-section. A comprehensive airway
analysis process following these 4 steps from segmentation to measurements of
the airway wall is described in [11].

In this paper, we focus on one step of the analysis process of tubular organs:
the computation of accurate cross-sections. This step is hardly described in the

© Springer International Publishing Switzerland 2015
G. Azzopardi and N. Petkov (Eds.): CAIP 2015, Part II, LNCS 9257, pp. 277–288, 2015.
DOI: 10.1007/978-3-319-23117-4_24

existing works although the quality of the final measurements depends on it. It is generally based on the analysis of the skeleton which is supposed to be a curve skeleton i.e. a 3D digital curve. The main difficulty of computing an orthogonal plane, or equivalently a tangent, to a curve skeleton comes from the irregularities of the curve. A first approach is to smooth the skeleton before computing its tangents as in [11]. The drawback of this approach is that smoothing may not preserve the original object shape. A second approach is to use a 3D digital tangent estimator which captures the exact shape of the 3D curve [10]. It is thus sensitive to the skeleton defects.

We propose a new method to compute accurate orthogonal planes along an unsmoothed skeleton, based on Voronoi Covariance Measure. The covariance measure describes the shape of the Voronoi cells generated by the skeleton points, from which we can deduce the local shape of the object. Furthermore, this measure being defined on any compact, we can apply it either on the set of skeleton points, similarly to existing methods, or on the whole set of points of the segmented object, so it can take into account the full shape of the organ.

In section 2 we present the related works about the estimation of cross-section from a segmented tubular organ, i.e. the skeleton extraction and the 3D tangent estimation. In section 3 we detail the proposed method. Finally we present the results obtained on both synthetic and real data in section 4, with quantitative comparison with other methods.

2   Related Works

As was said in the introductory part, the objective of this article is to estimate precisely the cross-sections along a tubular organ. As input data, we suppose to be given a segmentation of the processed organ, i.e. a connected set of points of the 3D digital grid. The usual way to extract cross-sections consists in two steps: (1) skeletonization of the object, (2) estimation of the tangential direction at each point of the skeleton to obtain the normal vectors of the cross-section planes.

There are different definitions of the skeleton of a digital object, depending on the wanted properties. In the case of a tubular organ, a natural representation is a curve-skeleton, i.e. a thin curve of digital points following the centerline of the organ. An efficient way to obtain such a curve-skeleton is to use a thinning algorithm that will "peel" the object until its is reduced to its centerline. However the obtained skeleton always presents defects irrespective of the thinning method used. Small irregularities of the segmented object lead to unwanted small branches and deformations of the skeleton (see figure 1). Small branches can be deleted by a pruning algorithm but the skeleton deformations that are not consistent with the object shape can distort the cross-section computation. In this paper, we use the thinning algorithm presented in [6], because it is robust to noise, produces a connected skeleton and is parameter-free. Some more recent methods providing the same properties have been tested such as filtered euclidean skeletons [2], but they do not provide better results on our specific tubular case (see figure 1).

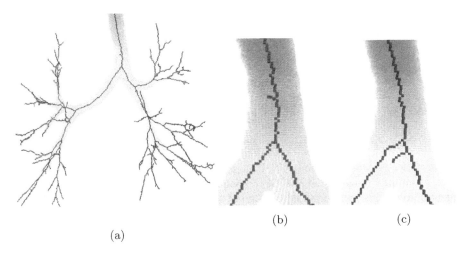

(b)   (c)

(a)

Fig. 1. (a) Part of a segmented airway-tree and its skeleton. Small irregularities of the segmented object lead to deformations of the curve-skeleton resulting of (b) the method [6] used thoughout the remainder of the article and (c) euclidean skeleton [2].

One can define the tangent vector at a point of a 3D digital curve as the vector linking this point and one of its two neighbors on the curve. However, this naive tangent estimation is obviously very sensitive to noise and can not yield accurate results in our context. Other algorithms were designed to better integrate the neighborhood around a point for tangent computation.

Among them the 3D tangent estimator λ-MST recently presented in [10] relies on the recognition of digital straight segments (DSS) along a 3D digital curve. A maximal DSS is a connected subset of the curve corresponding to the digitization of a straight line and which cannot be extended forward or backward. As one point of the curve can belong to several maximal DSS, the main idea is to average the orientations of all the DSS passing through a point in order to compute its tangent (see figure 2).

More precisely, the tangent vector at a given point x is computed as:

$$t(x) = \frac{\sum_{M \in P(x)} \lambda(e_M(x)) t_M}{\sum_{M \in P(x)} \lambda(e_M(x))} \tag{1}$$

where $P(x)$ is the set of maximal DSS passing through x and t_M is the unit direction vector of M. The weights depend on the eccentricity of the point x relatively to the segment M which is defined as $e_M(x) = \frac{i_x - m_M}{n_M - m_M}$ where $i_x - m_M$ is the distance as the difference in indices between point x and the last point of M, and $n_M - m_M$ is the DSS length. The function λ is designed to give more weight to the orientation of a DSS if x is close to its center. In our experiments, λ is the triangle function with $\lambda(0) = 0$, $\lambda(1) = 0$ and a peak at 0.5.

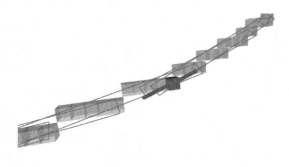

Fig. 2. Computed tangent (red line) at red point on a 3D digital curve. The computed tangent corresponds to a weighted average of the orientations of the digital straight segments (in green) passing through the point.

3   Proposed Method

In this article we propose to define a new method to compute precise cross-section for tubular organs, based on the Voronoi Covariance Measure (VCM).

The VCM was first introduced in [7] to estimate normals and curvatures on point clouds sampling a surface. This tensorial measure was shown to be resilient to Hausdorff noise. More recent results proved that it is even robust to outliers [3]. A digital variant of the VCM was defined to analyze digital sets and surfaces [4]. This digital measure was shown to be close to its continuous counterpart and to be efficiently computable. Furthermore its first eigenvector was shown to be multigrid convergent toward the surface normal. It is thus a reliable tool to estimate normals of digital shapes. We propose to develop a cross-section estimator, based on the VCM, that analyses the skeleton of an object. Furthermore we will show that this new tool can also take into account the whole segmented object. Thus the estimator does not only rely on the shape of the skeleton, but can analyze the local shape of the object.

By construction, the VCM computes a covariance matrix of vectors that are aligned with the gradient of the distance to the shape function. Hence, its first eigenvector points toward the normal to the shape (it is the direction that maximizes the distance to the shape when moving along it). Voronoi cells defined by input points tend to align themselves with this gradient. The VCM computes the covariance matrix of all vectors within neighboring cells, hence most of the vectors point in the direction of the shape normal. This is why the VCM robustly estimates the normal direction to the shape.

The VCM was designed to analyse surface sampling, but it can in fact also serve our purpose of finding cross-sections of curve-like shapes. Note that the normal cone of the curve is exactly its cross-section plane. The two first eigendirections of the VCM are not predictable, but they will both try to span the normal cone. Since they are forced to be orthogonal, they will both lie in the cross-section plane.

The digital approximation of the VCM is defined [4] on any point p of a digital set, by considering a neighborhood of p defined by a ball, and summing the covariance measure of the Voronoi cells for which the generator is inside this neighborhood.

Definition of (digital) Voronoi Covariance Measure. Let X be a set of points of the 3D digital grid $\mathbb{Z}^3$. $\Omega_X(R)$ is defined as the set of digital points contained in the R-offset of X, i.e. $\Omega_X(R) = \{x \in \mathbb{Z}^3 | \min_{y \in X} \|y - x\| \leq R\}$ (see figure 3). The Voronoi diagram of X partitions the space into cells. Each cell of this Voronoi diagram contains exactly one point of X, called the *generator* of this cell. We define the *projection* $p_X(z)$ of an arbitrary point $z \in \mathbb{R}^3$, as the generator of the cell which contains z. It follows that any point x of $\Omega_X(R)$ is projected in X through p_X. The point $p_X(x)$ is also the point of X minimizing its distance with x.

Given a point y for which we want to compute the VCM value, we center on y a ball of radius r (denoted by $\mathcal{B}_r(y)$). Then the subset of points considered for the computation consists in all the points at distance no greater than R to X (i.e. $\Omega_X(R)$) the projection of which lies in this ball. Therefore, let $DI_X(y) := \Omega_X(R) \cap p_X^{-1}(X \cap \mathcal{B}_r(y))$ be the domain of integration for point y (orange subset on figure 3, right). The *digital VCM* is then defined as a summation of tensorial products:

$$\mathcal{V}_X(y) = \sum_{x \in DI_X(y)} (x - p_X(x))(x - p_X(x))^t$$

It is also easily seen that we can split the computation per Voronoi cell, as a first pass. Then the VCM for point y is the sum of the VCM of every Voronoi cell which generator lies in the ball of radius r around y. The digital VCM can thus be computed efficiently.

In our context, the Voronoi diagram of the digital skeleton defines a partition of the space into Voronoi cells. Globally, the domain of integration is limited by parameter R, which sets the maximum distance to input data. Points further away are not taken into account. Then, for each point of the skeleton, we sum the covariance measure of neighboring Voronoi cells, which gives a smoothed geometric information of the local shape. The two first eigenvectors of $\mathcal{V}_X(y)$ then give a precise estimation of a basis of the plane that is at most orthogonal to data, hence the cross section for this point.

Parameter Setting. Our method has the same two parameters r and R than the original method, which was used to study the geometry of surfaces. In our context, we analyze tubular digital objects coming from medical images. Those parameters are set using *a priori*-knowledge about the studied organ. Parameter r corresponds to how many points must be considered to resemble the local shape of the organ. It is dependent on the resolution of the acquisition and the expected curvature of organs. Parameter R bounds the global domain of integration within Voronoi cells. In our case, since the digital sampling has a regular density, Voronoi cells are thin with almost parallel boundaries. Hence it

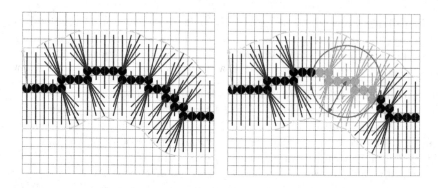

Fig. 3. Left: the limits of the R-offset of a set of digital points are drawn as a cyan contour, while vectors connecting points within the R-offset (i.e. $\Omega_X(R)$) to their projection are drawn in deep blue. Right: Voronoi cells defining the VCM Domain of integration for a kernel of radius r (i.e. $\Omega_X(R) \cap p_X^{-1}(X \cap \mathcal{B}_r(y))$) are drawn in dark orange (both germs and projection vectors). The kernel itself is drawn in red.

is not necessary to have a large value of R to get a correct estimation of normal directions, and we can expect that a wide range of value for R will give similar results.

Cross-section Estimators. In fact, the VCM is generic enough to be applied on an arbitrary set of points. Hence, it can be applied not only to the skeleton of tubular organs, but to the whole tubular organs. We will see in next section that this volumetric approach is even more precise and robust for cross-section estimation along the organs. For any non singular matrix M, we write $\pi(M)$ the plane spanned by its first two eigenvectors (in decreasing order). For a digital set V representing a tubular organ and letting X being the skeleton of V, we thus define our two cross-section estimators as:

1. The *VCM cross-section estimator* is defined for any point $x \in X$ as $\pi(\mathcal{V}_X(x))$.
2. The *Volume VCM cross-section estimator* is defined for any point $x \in X$ as $\pi(\mathcal{V}_V(x))$.

Note that this volumetric approach also approximate cross-section directions because

- the VCM is null on points located inside V, since Voronoi cells are reduced to the point itself,
- and the VCM approaches the normal direction on points located on the boundary of V.

The drawback of the second approach is that we need to know approximately the radius of the studied tubular organs in order to set parameter r consistently. It must be indeed big enough to reach the boundary of V from any point of X. This is not a problem in our context since we know the organ under study.

4   Results

In this section, the VCM efficiency for computing orthogonal planes is compared to the λ-MST method. These methods have been implemented using the DGtal library [1]. We will compare the methods both on synthetic and real data.

4.1   Noisy Synthetic Data

The goal of this section is to compare our method to the λ-MST estimator on known volumes with altered surfaces. We have generated two different synthetic data sets: a slightly curved cylinder with constant diameter (Figure 4a), and a straight elliptic cylinder with varying minor and major axes values (Figure 7a).

Tubular-like organs are obviously not perfect cylinders, and furthermore the discretization and the segmentation processes will lead to many irregularities on surfaces. These irregularities are the source of skeleton distortions. In order to generate similar irregularities on the synthetic data we have added some noise on the surfaces of the two objects. Noisy versions of the volumes are produced using a simplified version of Kanungo's algorithm [5], implemented in the DGtal library. This method adds noise on binary images by switching the value of each voxel, according to its distance d to the object boundary, with a probability α^d. Cavities and unconnected noisy voxels are then removed using morphological operators.

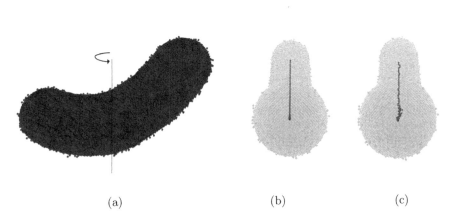

(a)   (b)   (c)

Fig. 4. (a) Noisy tubular volume generated using a ball with constant radius, disturbed by a Kanungo noise. (b) Volume with the digitized initial centerline used to generate it in red. (c) Computed skeleton showing small distortion compared to the original one.

The first test to assess our method's robustness consists in extracting geometric characteristics on the computed 2D orthogonal planes, and in comparing them to known values. At each point, we used the different methods to compute an orthogonal plane.

The intersection between each orthogonal plane and the unaltered digital curved cylinder should be a disk. In order to quantify how close to a disk the results are, two parameters are computed on the 2D shape resulting from the intersection:

- the area in number of pixels
- the roundness, given by $r = \dfrac{4A}{\pi * a^2}$ where a is the length of the major axis, and A the area. This value ranges from 0 (line) to 1 (perfect circle).

The corresponding expected values can be computed with the known radius of the cylinder (20 pixels).

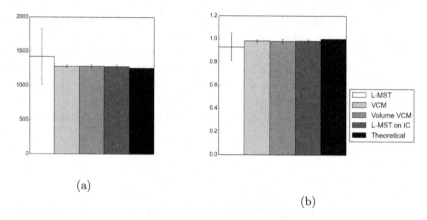

(a)

(b)

Fig. 5. (a) Area in pixels and (b) roundness mean values for all the orthogonal planes found in a generated noisy tube volume. The λ-MST on the computed skeleton (white) yields results with high-variability, whereas the λ-MST method applied on the initial centerline and the two VCM methods applied on the computerized skeleton and the volume respectively are consistent with the theoretical values.

The results are obtained on 93 cross-sections. The mean values obtained with the two variants of the VCM method (see figures 5a and 5b), are closer to the theoretical value than those obtained with λ-MST method on the computed skeleton. Furthermore the difference in standard-deviation between the two methods is significant here. The coefficient of variation, defined as the ratio of the standard deviation to the mean, is 29% and 12% for the λ-MST, against 1.5% and 1.1% for the VCM, for the area and roundness respectively. This reflects the high-variability of the λ-MST method, as it finds a substantial number of incorrect orthogonal planes, whereas the results of the proposed method are consistent.

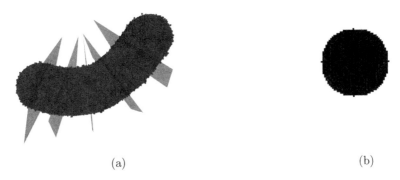

(a)   (b)

Fig. 6. (a) Examples of orthogonal planes obtained on a noisy tube-like volume with the volumetric VCM method and (b) typical associated 2D plane.

The second test on synthetic data consists in evaluating the difference between the normal direction of the estimated plane, and the known value. This test has been performed on the straight elliptic cylinder for which the normal direction at each point of its central line is constant. For each point of the skeleton, the angle defect between the computed normal and the expected normal is determined for all methods. Figure 7b shows the results we obtain.

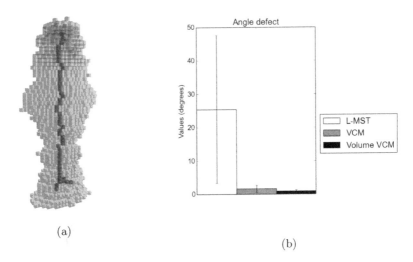

(a)

(b)

Fig. 7. (a) Noisy elliptic cynlinder with varying minor and major axes, generated along a centerline with constant normal direction. The computed skeleton is shown in red. (b) The angle defect (in degrees) between the computed normal and the expected normal shows our method outperforms the λ-MST tangent estimator.

The results are obtained on 50 slices. Using VCM on both the skeleton curve and the volume yields an angle defect close to zero, with a low standard deviation. The mean value of the angle defect are greater for the λ-MST, and again suffers from high-variability (standard deviation of 22 degrees against 1.1 and 0.46 degrees for the VCM on the curve and on the volume respectively). The λ-MST estimator does not perform well because DSS recognition is sensitive to slight pixel deviation in a curve: in some cases, short DSS are found which means the computed orientation is not representative of the actual tangent (see figure 8).

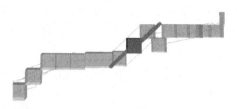

Fig. 8. Altered skeleton leading to short DSS computation and to deviated tangent (red line) at red point.

4.2   Real Data

In this section, we present results obtained on a bronchial tree acquired from a CT-scan. The bronchi have been segmented manually, and the skeleton was computed on the resulting volume with the method [6]. Parts of the skeleton are impacted by irregularities of the surface. This leads to some incorrect orthogonal planes estimation with the λ-MST method (see figure 9a) in these parts. On the contrary, similarly as what was observed on synthetic data, the VCM method gives consistent results which are not affected by slight distortions on the skeleton.

(a)   (b)

Fig. 9. Orthogonal planes computed on the skeleton of an airway-tree with (a) λ-MST and (b) VCM. The λ-MST method gives many wrong cross-section directions while the VCM method is consistent all along the path.

We would like to point out that the user must take care on branching parts, since many branches of the skeleton may influence the local computation (see figure 10). However, in practical cases, the orthogonal planes estimation is done branch by branch and thus this influence is low. Furthermore the first planes estimated after a branching part are not of interest since they will not only contain a section from a tubular part, but also a large part of the second beginning branch.

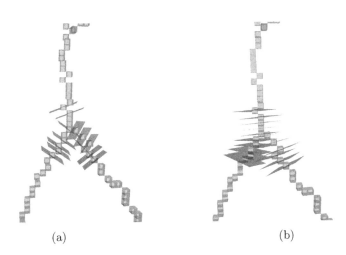

(a)   (b)

Fig. 10. Orthogonal planes computed on a branching part of an airway-tree with λ-MST method (a) and our method (b). Without branch separation, it can lead to some misplaced cross-section.

5   Conclusion and Perspectives

We have presented in this article a new reliable method to perform cross-section estimation on tubular organs. We have shown this method performs better than existing ones on the skeleton of the object, and furthermore can be defined to rely on the full shape of the object and thus not be influenced by the irregularities of the skeleton.

This is a method of choice to produce automatic and reproducible quantification of geometrical features from tubular organs, and thus can lead to new advances in health research. Our first application focus on human airways analysis, but it can also be used to study other tubular organs.

Even if the two parameters of our method can easily be set in practice thanks to the *a priori*-knowledge about studied organs, we are currently working to develop a fully automated method. Our automatic settings of those parameters will rely on local geometrical information such as curvature and distance transform (in the volumetric estimation case) to automatically set appropriate radius.

Furthermore we plan to develop a new skeletonization algorithm based on our method. Since it produces orthogonal planes directly from the volume, their centers of gravity can define the skeleton points.

References

1. DGtal: Digital geometry tools and algorithms library. http://dgtal.org
2. Couprie, M., Coeurjolly, D., Zrour, R.: Discrete bisector function and Euclidean skeleton in 2D and 3D. Image and Vision Computing **25**(10), October 2007
3. Cuel, L., Lachaud, J.O., Mérigot, Q., Thibert, B.: Robust geometry estimation using the generalized voronoi covariance measure. arXiv preprint arXiv:1408.6210 (2014)
4. Cuel, L., Lachaud, J.-O., Thibert, B.: Voronoi-based geometry estimator for 3d digital surfaces. In: Barcucci, E., Frosini, A., Rinaldi, S. (eds.) DGCI 2014. LNCS, vol. 8668, pp. 134–149. Springer, Heidelberg (2014)
5. Kanungo, T., Haralick, R., Baird, H., et al.: A statistical, nonparametric methodology for document degradation model validation. IEEE Trans. Pattern Anal. Mach. Intell. **22**(11), 1209–1223 (2000)
6. Lee, T.C., Kashyap, R.L., Chu, C.N.: Building skeleton models via 3-d medial surface/axis thinning algorithms. CVGIP: Graph. Models Image Process. **56**(6), 462–478 (1994)
7. Mérigot, Q., Ovsjanikov, M., Guibas, L.: Voronoi-based curvature and feature estimation from point clouds. IEEE Transactions on Visualization and Computer Graphics **17**(6), 743–756 (2011)
8. Orlandi, I., Moroni, C., Camiciottoli, G., et al.: Chronic obstructive pulmonary disease: Thin-section ct measurement of airway wall thickness and lung attenuation 1. Radiology **234**(2), 604–610 (2005)
9. Pare, P., Nagano, T., Coxson, H.: Airway imaging in disease: Gimmick or useful tool? Journal of Applied Physiology **113**(4), 636–646 (2012)
10. Postolski, M., Janaszewski, M., Kenmochi, Y., Lachaud, J.O.: Tangent estimation along 3d digital curves. In: ICPR, pp. 2079–2082 (2012)
11. Tschirren, J., Hoffman, E.A., McLennan, G., Sonka, M.: Intrathoracic airway trees: segmentation and airway morphology analysis from low-dose ct scans. IEEE Transactions on Medical Imaging **24**(12), 1529–1539 (2005)
12. Yamashiro, T., Matsuoka, S., Estépar, R.S.J.: Quantitative assessment of bronchial wall attenuation with thin-section ct: an indicator of airflow limitation in chronic obstructive pulmonary disease. American Journal of Roentgenology **195**(2), 363–369 (2010)

Materials Classification Using Sparse Gray-Scale Bidirectional Reflectance Measurements

Jiří Filip[1](✉) and Petr Somol[1,2]

[1] Institute of Information Theory and Automation of the CAS,
Prague, Czech Republic
filipj@utia.cas.cz

[2] Faculty of Management, Prague University of Economics, Prague, Czech Republic

Abstract. Material recognition applications use typically color texture-based features; however, the underlying measurements are in several application fields unavailable or too expensive (e.g., due to a limited resolution in remote sensing). Therefore, bidirectional reflectance measurements are used, i.e., dependent on both illumination and viewing directions. But even measurement of such BRDF data is very time- and resources-demanding. In this paper we use dependency-aware feature selection method to identify very sparse set of the most discriminative bidirectional reflectance samples that can reliably distinguish between three types of materials from BRDF database – fabric, wood, and leather. We conclude that ten gray-scale samples primarily at high illumination and viewing elevations are sufficient to identify type of material with accuracy over 96%. We analyze estimated placement of the bidirectional samples for discrimination between different types of materials. The stability of such directional samples is very high as was verified by an additional leave-one-out classification experiment. We consider this work a step towards automatic method of material classification based on several reflectance measurements only.

Keywords: BRDF · Material · Classification · Feature selection

1 Introduction

The real-world is made of countless varieties of materials having a wide range of appearance. Their automatic segmentation and classification is vital in applications where the task is quick identification of material type, based purely on its directional reflectance, i.e., without considering its surface texture and color. An automatic material type detection based purely on several reflectance measurements is relevant research task in many research fields ranging from remote sensing to paint industry, food inspection, or recycling. Especially in remote sensing a constrained set of illumination and viewing directions plays important role in significant increase of recognition accuracy [9].

Although it might seem that using reflectance only, instead of texture, might solve a data dimensionality problem, we still face a vast number of possible

© Springer International Publishing Switzerland 2015
G. Azzopardi and N. Petkov (Eds.): CAIP 2015, Part II, LNCS 9257, pp. 289–299, 2015.
DOI: 10.1007/978-3-319-23117-4_25

combinations of illumination and viewing directions. Therefore, identification those of them that have the best performance in distinguishing between different material categories is a challenging research task.

Such a bidirectional reflectance behavior can be formalized by means of Bidirectional Reflectance Distribution Function (BRDF) [7] comprising differential reflected radiance dL for incident irradiance dE

$$B(\theta_i, \varphi_i, \theta_v, \varphi_v) = \frac{dL(\theta_v, \varphi_v)}{dE(\theta_i, \varphi_i)} = \frac{dL(\theta_v, \varphi_v)}{L(\theta_i, \varphi_i) \cos \theta_i d\omega_i}. \tag{1}$$

BRDF is a four dimensional function of incoming $[\theta_i, \varphi_i]$ and outgoing $[\theta_v, \varphi_v]$ spherical angles as shown in Fig. 1-left. Helmholtz reciprocity states that illumination and viewing directions can be swapped without any effect on the BRDF value.

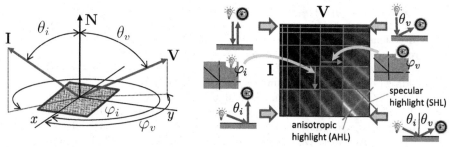

Fig. 1. A four-dimensional BRDF angular parameterization (left) and its unfolding into 2D image (right), depicting locations of specular (SHL) and anisotropic (AHL) highlights. The unfolded 2D image belongs to mean gray-scale BRDF of all tested materials. Each block (shown in red frame) depicts azimuthally-dependent (φ_i/φ_v) reflectance behavior for fixed elevation angles θ_i/θ_v.

BRDF measurements are typically fitted by analytical models achieving a compact parametric representation, missing directional data interpolation / extrapolation, as well as removal of outliers resulting from the measurement process [4]. However, reliable fitting of BRDF models to the measured reflectance values require sufficient coverage of illumination and viewing directions over the measured material. Such measurement is both time- and space-demanding and requires specialized and often expensive measurement gantry [4].

In this paper we attempt to analyze properties of three material categories using linear factorization and feature selection. Our goal is to identify an extremely compact and discriminative set of illumination/view directions combinations, that can be rapidly and inexpensively measured, and finally used for material type classification purposes. Therefore, identification of such compact set of bidirectional features reduces not only data measurement time and costs, but also computational requirements of training and classification steps of discriminative model. Therefore, the main contribution of this paper is employing feature selection (FS) technique to identify sparse directional reflectance samples appropriate for reliable material classification. Our method relies on a typical unique behavior of different types of materials, therefore, we run the FS on extensive BRDF database specifically focusing on distinguishing between three types of materials: fabric, leather, and wood.

The paper is structured as follows. Section 2 relates our research to prior work in the field. Section 3 introduces BRDF data used and analyses data within individual material categories. Section 4 proposes the method of detection of the most discriminative directional samples. Section 5 outlines the achieved results while Section 6 concludes the paper.

2 Prior Work

An automatic material type classification based on its reflectance, i.e., without need of surface texture analysis, is vital in fields of remote sensing, paint industry, food inspection, material science, recycling etc.

Prior material segmentation/classification approaches in general rely also on a very limited set of directional measurements constrained by an intended application. Known approaches use often spectral illumination, which is distributed into variable illumination pattern over hemisphere. Common application scenario is also pixel-wise segmentation of real-world object to different materials [14], [12]. Gu et al. [3] introduced spectral coded illumination by discriminative patterns, and constructed an color LED-based measurement dome for material classification. Method of material classification based on illumination using variable illumination patterns combined with random forest classifier to identify optimal illumination is presented in [5]. A recent material classification approach [15] was based on using extended full bidirectional texture measurements as a training dataset. The classification task was to recognize a correct material given a single image of its surface in arbitrary illumination/viewing conditions.

We propose a feature selection method determining an extremely sparse set of discriminative directional measurement that allows very accurate discrimination of different types of materials. Contrary to the works above and for the sake of computational simplicity we do not take into consideration any textural or spectral information.

Remote sensing applications rely on a constrained set of viewing directions (airborne or satellite imagery) and illumination directions (directional illumination of the Sun combined with diffuse atmospheric illumination). The resulted sparse measurements are typically compensated for atmospheric radiative transfer and fitted by an analytical BRDF model. A typical goal of remote sensing application is detection of presence or classification of vegetation types [9] or urban areas [6] based on its spectral and directional reflectance. Qi et al.[8] fitted leaf and vegetation directional measurements using BRDF models. Schaaf et al. [10] process data from NASAs Terra satellite and the MODerate Resolution Imaging Spectroradiometer to provide BRDF and albedo of Earth surface. Several case studies of bidirectional reflectance measurements in remote sensing applications are reviewed in [11].

Our results can be extended to application areas where the directional measurements are expensive or constrained as for instance in the case of remote sensing. Therefore, we use the same BRDF representation and test our method on a BRDF dataset containing considerable information on the illumination- and view-dependent behavior of substantial collection of various materials. By analyzing this entire collection of bidirectional samples using feature selection techniques, we aim to obtain the most discriminative set of bidirectional samples.

3   Test Data Analysis

3.1   Test Dataset

We used UTIA BRDF Database[1] [2] containing 150 anisotropic BRDF measurements. To enlarge its descriptive abilities we added another 67 BRDF anisotropic measurements obtained by averaging of BTFs with rough surface structure. We use the original resolution of BRDF measurements 81×81 illumination and viewing directions resulting in 6561 combination of incoming and outgoing directions. This number can be due to BRDF reciprocity reduced to 3321 directions. Finally, we grouped the measured BRDFs into three main categories: *fabric* (146 materials), *leather* (16 materials), and *wood* (19 materials). The remaining types of materials were not represented by a sufficient number of instances to capture their typical behavior reliably (carpet 6, plastic 6, tile 4, paper 3, wallpaper 3, plaster 2, paint 2, etc.). Due to the fact, that some of the materials have many different color variants with similar luminance behavior, individual BRDFs were converted to the luminance only, neglecting the spectral information. Moreover, as anisotropic behavior in measured BRDF depends on initial positioning of the measured sample, all BRDFs were aligned according a location of their the most intensive anisotropic highlight in azimuthal space [2]. Any reasonable computational comparison of different anisotropic BRDFs would be impossible without this step as the anisotropic highlight would be located in the azimuthal space arbitrarily.

3.2   Linear Factorization

First, we analyzed the main visual features of individual types of materials using principal component analysis (PCA). The BRDFs of each category were reshaped into column vectors and used to form a matrix that was after normalization decomposed by means of PCA. As a result we obtained principal components of the same size as original BRDF image, and principal values denoting contribution of individual principal components. Fig. 3 shows mean and standard deviation images as well as the first three principal components (PC) for the tested categories of materials. Mean standard deviation values as well as energies of individual components suggests that the highest variability is within categories *fabric* and *leather*. While *leather* retains the most energy in its first component, the energy distribution within *fabric* is more uniform. This is due to a higher

---

[1] http://btf.utia.cas.cz

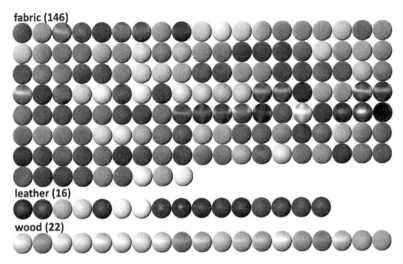

Fig. 2. BRDFs of three material categories used in our analysis.

variance within this category given by much higher number of recorded materials, and also due to different types of anisotropy presented (as shown in principal images). Although *wood* category also exhibits strong anisotropy, the energy is shifted towards first components. This is caused by a more accurate anisotropic highlights alignment and similarly shaped highlights across materials in this category.

4 Dependency-Aware Feature Selection

The above statistical differences between the three material categories inspired us as to the possibility there might be certain sparse angular features bearing all information needed for their discrimination. To this end, we employed a combination of ranking and randomization feature selection method called Dependency-Aware Feature (DAF) ranking [13],[1]. It evaluates features' contributions in a sequence of randomly generated feature subsets. The method has shown promise of selecting features reliably, even in settings where standard feature techniques fail due to problem's complexity or over-fitting issues, and where individual feature ranking results are unsatisfactory.

Denoting F the set of all features $F = \{f_1, f_2, \ldots, f_N\}$ we assume that for each subset of features $S \subset F$ a feature selection criterion $J(\cdot)$ can be used as a measure of quality of S. We assume the criterion $J(\cdot)$ to be bounded by $[0,1]$. In our case we will use estimates of classification accuracy which fulfills this property.

The starting point of dependency-aware feature ranking is a randomly generated sequence of feature subsets to be denoted *probe* subsets $\mathbf{S} = \{S_1, S_2, \ldots, S_K\}$, $S_j \subset F$, $j = 1, 2, \ldots, K$, where each subset is evaluated by the criterion function $J(\cdot)$.

mean img *fabric*	std. img. 83.9	PC1 36%	PC2 10 %	PC3 5 %
leather	92.0	61%	9 %	8 %
wood	45.7	51%	13 %	6 %

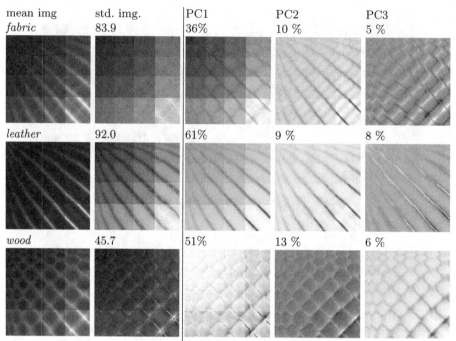

Fig. 3. PCA of three tested material categories BRDFs unfolded to 2D images (see Fig. 1-right). Each row contains mean image, standard deviation image (with mean std. value), and the first three principal components with their energy contributions.

Given a sufficiently large sequence of feature subsets $\mathbf{S}$, we can utilize the information contained in the criterion values $J(S_1), J(S_2), \ldots, J(S_K)$ to assess how each feature adds to the criterion value. Therefore, we compare the quality of probe subsets containing f with the quality of probe subsets not including f.

We compute the mean quality μ_f of subsets $S \in \mathbf{S}$ containing the considered feature

$$\mu_f = \frac{1}{|\mathbf{S}_f|} \sum_{S \in \mathbf{S}_f} J(S), \quad \mathbf{S}_f = \{S \in \mathbf{S} : f \in S\} \tag{2}$$

and the mean quality $\bar{\mu}_f$ of subsets $S \in \mathbf{S}$ *not* containing the considered feature f:

$$\bar{\mu}_f = \frac{1}{|\bar{\mathbf{S}}_f|} \sum_{S \in \bar{\mathbf{S}}_f} J(S), \quad \bar{\mathbf{S}}_f = \{S \in \mathbf{S} : f \notin S\} \tag{3}$$

with the aim to use the difference of both values as a criterion for ranking the features:

$$DAF(f) = \mu_f - \bar{\mu}_f, \quad f \in F. \tag{4}$$

The DAF evaluates a contribution of each feature to a given discrimination task by a single weight value. The higher is its value the more important it is. More details can be found in [13].

4.1 DAF Configuration Within the Experiment

We used DAF method implemented in the FST3 library[2] to compute ranking of measured directions according to their contribution to material categories separability. Due to the illumination and viewing directions reciprocity we used 3321 directions instead of the originally measured 6561. Thus our dataset has 3321 features × 146 (*fabric*), 16 (*leather*), 19 (*wood*) samples respectively. The number of classes was two or three, depending whether we computed features discriminating between two or all three tested categories. As a criterion function $J()$ identifying promising bidirectional features we used results of materials classification using linear SVM with one-level cross-validation. The SVM's penalty parameter c was optimized on a validation dataset.

We typically evaluated about 300 000 probes and the computational time was about 20 hours. Although this analysis is time-demanding it is performed once during off-line analysis of training data. Any further classification using the selected sparse features is very fast.

5   Results and Discussion

As a result of feature selection analysis we found out that only around ten bidirectional features (i.e., illumination/view directions) were enough to discriminate between all combination of classes with accuracy between 96% and 100%. By the classification accuracy we denote ratio of correctly classified materials to all materials within the classified classes. Fig. 4 shows weights of the first ten DAF features illustrating the steepest decline for pairs *wood-leather* and *wood-fabric* that have also slightly better classification accuracy (shown in the graph legend). Therefore, even less features would be sufficient to accurately distinguish between our material categories.

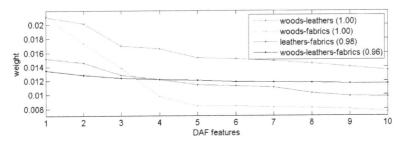

Fig. 4. Weights of the first ten DAF features (each representing a different combination of illumination and view directions) obtained for discrimination between individual categories of materials. The legend includes classification accuracy achieved using these ten features.

---

[2] http://fst.utia.cas.cz/

wood – leather categories   *wood – fabric* categories

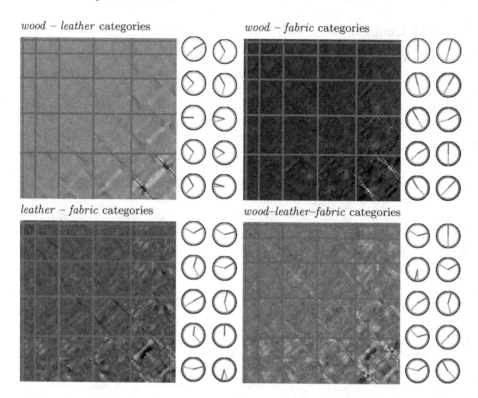

leather – fabric categories   *wood–leather–fabric* categories

Fig. 5. Importance of individual directions for separability of several material groups. Each map represents 4D BRDF space unfolded into 2D image (Fig.1-right). Each pixel represents an unique combination of illumination and viewing directions and corresponding DAF features values are shown with brightness denoting their relative importance for recognition between the material groups. The ten most important directions are shown as color dots with color coding of DAF weights values from the highest (yellow) to the lowest (red). Right side of the images illustrates relation of corresponding 10 selected illumination (green) and view (blue) directions within hemisphere over a material. The remaining less important features are shown in gray.

Fig. 5 illustrates placement of DAF features in original 4D angular BRDF space unfolded to 2D image (see Fig.1-right). Majority of the important features are located in subspace of highest elevations (i.e., 75°), where typical BRDFs exhibit the highest contrast. The ten best features are shown in color coding from the most important (yellow) to less important (red). The right-hand side of the images show mutual positions of illumination (green) and view (blue) directions of the selected bidirectional features in the hemisphere viewed from the top. Color of the hemispheres border correspond to feature importance.

One can observe that classification between *woods-fabrics* categories relies on directions that lie directly on a specular highlight, i.e. view always opposite to illumination $|\varphi_i - \varphi_v| \approx \pi$. Note that the directions located near intersection of specular (SHL) and anisotropic (AHL) highlights (shown in Fig.6) have higher

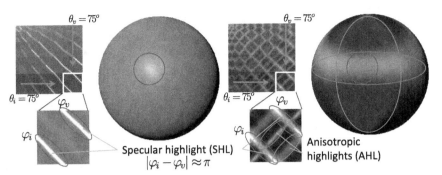

Fig. 6. Locations of specular and anisotropic highlights in the BRDF space and their appearance on a 3D object.

importance. This is due to a different typical behavior between these groups of materials.

In contrast, for *wood-leather* categories the selected features correspond to directions lying on location of main anisotropic highlight. This is intuitive as leather, in contrast to wood, does not exhibit any significant anisotropic highlight (including retro-reflection $\varphi_i \approx \varphi_v$). Again directions near intersections of SHL and AHL are deemed as more important.

For recognition between *leather-fabric* and *wood-leather-fabric* categories are the most important directions located near SHL and their primary function is detection of highlight's width. Therefore, the selected features lie on SHL and in its surrounding, as well as in retro reflective directions.

5.1   Selected Features Stability Analysis

Finally, we tested stability of the selected best features with regard to train dataset. We performed a two-level leave-one-out classification using linear SVM classifier between 17 *wood* and subset of 19 *fabric* having the most similar anisotropic properties as shown in Fig. 7 (BRDF subsets for fixed elevation angles $\theta_i/\theta_v = 75°/75°$). In each step, one material was removed from the test set the DAF features were computed on the remaining materials only.

Surprisingly, the DAF features obtained in each step were always identical. We have found that even with such a complex dataset, 12 directions (i.e., selected features) were enough to achieve an accurate classification of 97%. When we performed the same experiment for *wood*, *leather*, and the subset of *fabric* (19) with 50 directions we achieved classification accuracy 92% and stability over 98%, i.e., it suggests that about only 2% of directions changed over the cross validation.

5.2   Limitations and Future Work

Although our test BRDF dataset provides a limited number of materials for each tested category, our cross validation classification experiment showed a promising

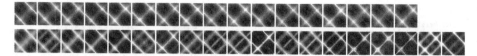

Fig. 7. Subspaces $\theta_i/\theta_v = 75°/75°$ of 17 *wood* (first row) and 19 selected *fabric* (second row) used in the stability experiment.

performance of our method. We assume that using more materials within each category would further improve classification accuracy albeit possibly at the cost of a slightly increased number of selected features describing additional variability within a class of materials.

Another challenging issue is a computational time needed for the subset identification. Depending on the compared categories dimensionality, it took between two and six hours to find optimal discriminative directions using 24 cores (3.3GHz) of Intel Xeon E5-2643. However, once this subset is learned the speed of material classification using 10 features and linear SVM is negligible and the main bottleneck becomes acquisition of these ten directional samples for the unknown material to be classified. Performing FS off-line thus enables faster on-line performance, depending mainly on a speed of the reflectance measurements (e.g. photos) and their processing. Furthermore, our experiments revealed that majority of the selected features belong to the highest illumination and view elevation angles. Therefore, by neglecting low elevation angles we could potentially limit total number of features and thus effectively decrease computational time.

6 Conclusions

The objective of this paper was identification of very compact set of bidirectional gray-scale reflectance measurements that are capable of reliable classification between three different material categories (fabric, leather, wood). The point is to enable radical reduction of the cost of bidirectional features measurement and subsequent classification. We used dependency-aware feature selection technique for selection of sparse bidirectional features using BRDF database. We conclude that ten such gray-scale reflectance features are enough to keep classification accuracy > 95% on a BRDF database with moderate number of samples (evaluated by cross-validation). Furthermore, we have found that the stability of the selected bidirectional samples is very high, i.e., does not depend significantly on any particular material in the test dataset. Finally, we identified and discussed a proper locations of bidirectional samples for discrimination between our three material categories. Our initial results sufficiently demonstrate that feature selection helps to improve material classification methods relying on a very limited set of bidirectional samples.

Acknowledgments. This research has been supported by the Czech Science Foundation grants 14-02652S and 14-10911S.

References

1. Athanasakis, D., Shawe-Taylor, J., Fernandez-Reyes, D.: Learning non-linear feature maps. CoRR abs/1311.5636 (2013)
2. Filip, J., Vavra, R.: Template-based sampling of anisotropic BRDFs. Computer Graphics Forum **33**(7), 91–99 (2014). http://staff.utia.cas.cz/filip/projects/14PG
3. Gu, J., Liu, C.: Discriminative illumination: Per-pixel classification of raw materials based on optimal projections of spectral BRDF. In: CVPR, pp. 797–804, June 2012
4. Haindl, M., Filip, J.: Visual Texture. Advances in Computer Vision and Pattern Recognition. Springer-Verlag, London (2013)
5. Jehle, M., Sommer, C., Jähne, B.: Learning of optimal illumination for material classification. In: Goesele, M., Roth, S., Kuijper, A., Schiele, B., Schindler, K. (eds.) Pattern Recognition. LNCS, vol. 6376, pp. 563–572. Springer, Heidelberg (2010)
6. Meister, G., Lucht, W., Rothkirch, A., Spitzer, H.: Large scale multispectral BRDF of an urban area. In: Proceedings of the IEEE 1999 International Geoscience and Remote Sensing Symposium, IGARSS 1999, vol. 2, pp. 821–823. IEEE (1999)
7. Nicodemus, F., Richmond, J., Hsia, J., Ginsburg, I., Limperis, T.: Geometrical considerations and nomenclature for reflectance. NBS Monograph **160**, 1–52 (1977)
8. Qi, J., Kerr, Y., Moran, M., Weltz, M., Huete, A., Sorooshian, S., Bryant, R.: Leaf area index estimates using remotely sensed data and BRDF models in a semiarid region. Remote sensing of environment **73**(1), 18–30 (2000)
9. Sandmeier, S., Deering, D.: Structure analysis and classification of boreal forests using airborne hyperspectral BRDF data from ASAS. Remote Sensing of Environment **69**(3), 281–295 (1999)
10. Schaaf, C.B., Gao, F., Strahler, A.H., Lucht, W., Li, X., Tsang, T., Strugnell, N.C., Zhang, X., Jin, Y., Muller, J.P., et al.: First operational BRDF, albedo nadir reflectance products from MODIS. Remote sensing of Environment **83**(1), 135–148 (2002)
11. Schaepman-Strub, G., Schaepman, M., Painter, T., Dangel, S., Martonchik, J.: Reflectance quantities in optical remote sensing–definitions and case studies. Remote sensing of environment **103**(1), 27–42 (2006)
12. Schick, E., Herbort, S., Grumpe, A., Wöhler, C.: Single view single light multispectral object segmentation. In: WSCG, pp. 171–178 (2013)
13. Somol, P., Grim, J., Pudil, P.: Fast dependency-aware feature selection in very-high-dimensional pattern recognition. In: Proceedings of the IEEE SCM, pp. 502–509 (2011)
14. Wang, O., Gunawardane, P., Scher, S., Davis, J.: Material classification using BRDF slices. In: CVPR 2009, pp. 2805–2811. IEEE (2009)
15. Weinmann, M., Gall, J., Klein, R.: Material classification based on training data synthesized using a BTF database. In: Fleet, D., Pajdla, T., Schiele, B., Tuytelaars, T. (eds.) ECCV 2014, Part III. LNCS, vol. 8691, pp. 156–171. Springer, Heidelberg (2014)

Multiscale Blood Vessel Delineation Using B-COSFIRE Filters

Nicola Strisciuglio[1,2]([⊠]), George Azzopardi[1,3], Mario Vento[2],
and Nicolai Petkov[1]

[1] Johann Bernoulli Institute for Mathematics and Computer Science,
University of Groningen, Groningen, The Netherlands
{n.strisciuglio,g.azzopardi,n.petkov}@rug.nl
[2] Department of Computer Engineering and Electrical Engineering
and Applied Mathematics,University of Salerno, Salerno, Italy
mvento@unisa.it
[3] Intelligent Computer Systems, University of Malta, Msida, Malta

Abstract. We propose a delineation algorithm that deals with bar-like
structures of different thickness. Detection of linear structures is applicable to several fields ranging from medical images for segmentation of
vessels to aerial images for delineation of roads or rivers. The proposed
method is suited for any delineation problem and employs a set of B-
COSFIRE filters selective for lines and line-endings of different thickness.
We determine the most effective filters for the application at hand by
Generalized Matrix Learning Vector Quantization (GMLVQ) algorithm.
We demonstrate the effectiveness of the proposed method by applying it
to the task of vessel segmentation in retinal images. We perform experiments on two benchmark data sets, namely DRIVE and STARE. The
experimental results show that the proposed delineation algorithm is
highly effective and efficient. It can be considered as a general framework for a delineation task in various applications.

1 Introduction

The automatic delineation of linear structures in images has gained interest in
the image processing community, due to its applicability to several problems
in different fields. In medical image analysis, for instance, the automatic segmentation of blood vessels from retinal fundus images, x-ray fluoroscopy images
or angiography images, among others, is a basic step before proceeding with
further processing for the diagnosis of several pathologies. Other applications
involve the quantification of length and width of cracks in walls (Fig. 1c) [17]
for earthquake damage estimation or for monitoring the flow of rivers in order
to prevent flooding disasters (Fig. 1d) [25].

In this paper we focus on the delineation of blood vessels in retinal fundus
images (Fig.1a), which is a fundamental step for further analysis for the formulation of a diagnostic hypothesis. The manual inspection of such images is a
time-consuming and expensive process. Therefore, mass screening is only possible if it is assisted by computer aided systems. The effective segmentation of the

© Springer International Publishing Switzerland 2015
G. Azzopardi and N. Petkov (Eds.): CAIP 2015, Part II, LNCS 9257, pp. 300–312, 2015.
DOI: 10.1007/978-3-319-23117-4_26

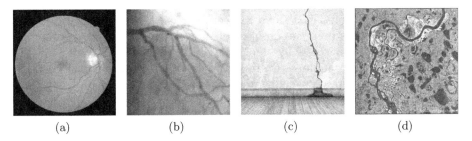

Fig. 1. Few examples where delineation algorithms are applicable: (a) blood vessels in a retinal fundus image, (b) x-ray fluoroscopy image, (c) cracks in walls and (d) a river in an aerial image.

vascular tree and the background is very important because the tree contains significant information about the geometrical structure of the vessels; furthermore, any lesions in the background can be analysed better after the vessels are segmented.

Several methods have been proposed to automatically delineate the blood vessel tree. They can be divided into two categories: (i) non-supervised, based on filtering or template matching, and (ii) supervised, based on machine learning techniques.

Among the non-supervised methods, matched filtering techniques model the profile of a vessel by a 2D-Gaussian kernel [1,6,9]. Vessel tracking methods, instead, start from an initial set of points chosen either automatically or manually, to segment the vessels by following their center-line [7,13,26]. Other methods use mathematical morphology and *a-priori* knowledge on the vessel tree structure [16,24]. In [15], a vessel growing procedure based on multiscale information about vessels' width, size and orientation is proposed. A multiconcavity modeling approach with differentiable concavity measure was proposed in [12].

Supervised methods share a common methodology: they treat the matter as a two-class problem, form pixel-wise feature vectors by some feature extraction methods and learn a classification model based on vessel and non-vessel training feature vectors. The responses of multiscale Gaussian filter and ridge detectors have been used as pixel-wise features together with a k-NN classifier in [18] and [23], respectively. In [22], a Bayesian classifier is combined with features obtained through multiscale analysis of Gabor wavelets. A rotation-invariant line operator in combination with a support vector machine (SVM) is proposed in [20], while in [14] a multilayer neural network has been applied to classify pixels based on moment-invariant features. An ensemble of bagged and boosted decision trees is employed in [8].

Supervised methods usually employ high-dimensional pixel-wise feature vectors and the choice of the features is usually influenced by domain knowledge. They are designed to overcome specific problems of retinal fundus images. In [8], for instance, morphological transformations and multiscale Gabor filters are used to eliminate bright and dark lesions, respectively.

We propose to address the problem of delineating bar-like structures (i.e. vessels) of different thickness by employing a set of B-COSFIRE filters of the type proposed in [5], configured to be selective for vessels of different thickness. In [5], a bar detector and a bar-ending detector have been combined by summing up their responses. The configuration parameters of the line-ending detector have been determined to complement the performance of a line detector. This implies a chain of dependency in the construction of the filters whose complexity increases with increasing number of filters. In this work, instead, we determine a subset of B-COSFIRE filters by means of a learning process. In particular, we use the Generalized Matrix Learning Vector Quantization (GMLVQ) method that determines a weight called relevance for each filter and we select the ones with the highest relevances.

The rest of the paper is organized as follows: in Section 2 we explain the proposed approach for filter selection. In Section 3 we present the experimental results. After a discussion of the results and comparison with the state of the art methods in Section 4, we draw conclusions in Section 5.

2   Method

The proposed delineation algorithm is based on automatic selection of the B-COSFIRE filters with the highest relevances. We configure a set of B-COSFIRE filters selective for lines of different thickness (i.e. scale). Instead of manually setting the scale of the filters, we determine them by means of a learning process. Such procedure allows to select those filters that give highest contribution to the delineation task.

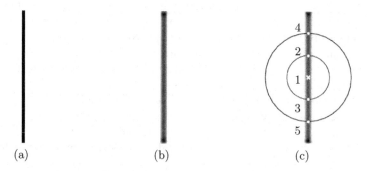

(a)   (b)   (c)

Fig. 2. Configuration of a B-COSFIRE filter. (a) A vertical line is processed by (b) a DoG filter. Then, (c) the positions of strong DoG responses along a set of concentric circles around the interest point (labeled with '1') are determined.

2.1 B-COSFIRE Filter

A B-COSFIRE filter, originally proposed in [5], takes as input the responses of a group of Difference-of-Gaussians (DoG) filters at certain positions with respect to the center of its area of support. Such positions are determined in an automatic configuration process performed on a prototype pattern, Fig. 2. We use a synthetic line as prototype pattern (Fig. 2a) and process it with a DoG filter (Fig. 2b). We consider the DoG filter responses along a number of concentric circles around the center point (labeled with '1' in Fig. 2c). The result of the configuration is a set of 3–tuples: $S = \{(\sigma_i, \rho_i, \phi_i) \mid i = 1, \ldots, n\}$, where σ_i represents the standard deviation of the outer DoG function[1], while (ρ_i, ϕ_i) are the polar coordinates of the i-th DoG response with respect to the support center of the filter.

We compute the output of a B-COSFIRE filter as the geometric mean of the responses of the concerned DoG filters at the positions determined in the configuration step:

$$r_S(x, y) \overset{\text{def}}{=} \left(\prod_{i=1}^{|S|} \left(s_{\sigma_i, \rho_i, \phi_i}(x, y) \right) \right)^{1/|S|} \tag{1}$$

where $s_{\sigma_i, \rho_i, \phi_i}(x, y)$ is the blurred DoG filter response with scale σ_i. We blur the i-th DoG response by taking the maximum response in a local neighborhood weighted by a Gaussian function centered in (ρ_i, ϕ_i). The standard deviation of such Gaussian function is a linear function of the distance ρ_i: $\sigma' = \sigma'_0 + \alpha \rho_i$.

In order to achieve rotation-tolerance, we first manipulate the parameter ϕ_i, obtaining a new set $R_\psi(S) = \{(\sigma_i, \rho_i, \phi_i + \psi) \mid i = 1, \ldots, n\}$ with orientation preference ψ. Then, we take the maximum across the responses of B-COSFIRE filters selective for different orientation preferences:

$$\hat{r}_S(x, y) \overset{\text{def}}{=} \max_{\psi \in \Psi} \left\{ r_{R_\psi(S)}(x, y) \right\} \tag{2}$$

where $\Psi = \{ \frac{\pi i}{12} \mid i = 0 \ldots 11 \}$. In this work, we use the publicly available Matlab implementation of a B-COSFIRE filter[2].

2.2 A Bank of B-COSFIRE Filters

To overcome the intrinsic delineation error at bar-endings due to the multiplicative character of B-COSFIRE filters, we employ two kinds of filter: line and line-ending detector. In order to also account for the different thickness of vessels in a given image we design a bank of 21 line ($\{S_1, \ldots S_{21}\}$) and 21 line-ending ($\{S_{22}, \ldots S_{42}\}$) B-COSFIRE filters of varying scale σ.

As an example, in Fig. 3 we show the responses of line and line-ending B-COSFIRE filters selective for thin (second column), medium (third column) and

---

[1] The standard deviation of the inner Gaussian function is $0.5\sigma_i$.
[2] http://www.mathworks.com/matlabcentral/fileexchange/49172

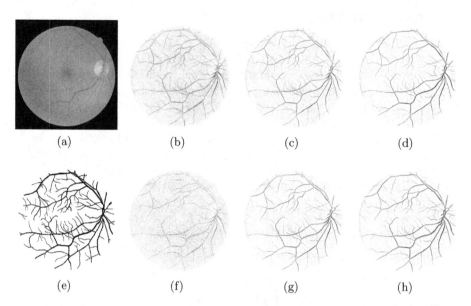

Fig. 3. (a) A retinal fundus image from the DRIVE data set and (e) its segmented vessel tree (used as a ground truth). In the second column the responses of small-scale (b) line and (f) line-ending filters are depicted. In the third and forth columns, the responses of (c,g) medium-scale and (d,h) large-scale filters are shown, respectively.

thick (forth column) vessels. It is evident how the small-scale filters respond better along thin vessels (Fig. 3b and Fig. 3f) but are more sensitive to background noise. Large-scale filters, instead, show higher responses along thicker vessels (Fig. 3d and Fig. 3h) and are more robust to noise.

In this way, we characterize a pixel at location (x, y) by the 42 responses of B-COSFIRE filters plus the intensity value of the green channel of the RGB image (further details about this choice are given in Section 3.2), which results in a 43-element feature vector denoted by $v(x, y)$:

$$v(x, y) = \left[G(x, y), \hat{r}_{S_1}(x, y), \ldots, \hat{r}_{S_{42}}(x, y) \right]^T \tag{3}$$

where $G(x, y)$ is the intensity value of the green channel and $\hat{r}_{S_i}(x, y)$ is the response of a B-COSFIRE filter S_i.

2.3   Filters Selection

We use the Generalized Matrix LVQ algorithm (GMLVQ) [21] in order to select filters. The GMLVQ is a supervised prototype-based learning algorithm that, given a feature space, determines the most representative prototypes for each class in the data set. Besides learning the prototypes, it computes the individual and pair-wise relevances of all involved features in the distance metric.

We form feature vectors composed by the responses of a bank of B-COSFIRE filters together with the classes of the corresponding pixels (vessel or background) as input to the GMLVQ algorithm. Next, GMLVQ computes a full matrix (43×43) of the relevances of all pairs of filters. The values on the diagonal of the resulting matrix, depicted in Fig 4, give an indication of the most relevant filters for the classification problem at hand. The higher the coefficient the more relevant that filter is in comparison to the others. In this work, we consider the relevances of the single B-COSFIRE filters, and select only the ones that achieve local relevance maximum along the space dimension, Fig 4. The dimensionality of the initial feature vectors is thus reduced and the overall processing time is substantially improved.

2.4   Classification

Finally, we use the training feature vectors composed of the responses of the selected filters to train a SVM classifier with a linear kernel, which is particularly suited for binary classification problems and has high generalization capabilities [10].

3   Experimental Results

3.1   Data Sets

We evaluate the proposed method on the benchmark data sets DRIVE [23] and STARE [9], that come with manually segmented images to be used as ground truth.

The DRIVE data set contains 40 images (of size 565×584 pixels), equally divided into a training and a test set. The images in the training set are manually segmented by one human observer, while the images in the test set are segmented by two other observers. The second observer segmentation is normally used to compute the human performance results. All the images come with a binary mask that indicate the field of view (FOV). The STARE data set consists of 20 color retinal fundus images (of size 700×605 pixels), 10 of which contain signs of pathologies. Each image is manually segmented by two different observers.

We measure the performance of our method by comparing the automatically generated binary images with the ground truth provided by the first observer.

3.2   Preprocessing

We only consider the green channel of the color retinal images because it shows the highest contrast between vessels and background [16,23]. In order to smoothen the high contrast along the border of the field of view (FOV) of the retina we employ the preprocessing algorithm proposed in [22]. It consists in a procedure that iteratively enlarges the region of interest delimited by the FOV. Finally, we enhance the image by using the contrast-limited adaptive histogram equalization (CLAHE) algorithm [19].

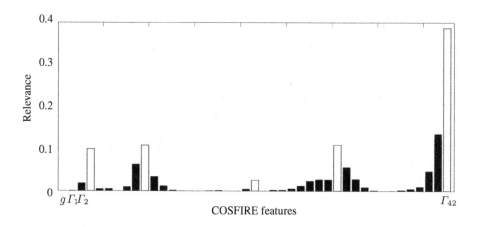

Fig. 4. The relevances of the features as obtained by the GMLVQ algorithm for the training images of the DRIVE data set. The local maxima of the relevances (white bars) represent the filters selected for classification.

3.3   Training

For the DRIVE data set we randomly select 20000 vessel pixels (1000 from each image) and 20000 non-vessel pixels (1000 from each image) from the images in the training set. The STARE data set does not have separate training and test sets. Thus, we construct the training set by randomly choosing 40000 pixels from all the 20 images in the data set (1000 vessel pixels and 1000 non-vessel pixels from each image). As suggested in [8,20], since the size of the selected training set is very small ($< 0.5\%$ of the entire data set), we evaluate the performance on the whole set of images.

For each pixel we generate a 43-element feature vector as described in Section 2.2. We configure the line-selective B-COSFIRE filters with the following σ values: $\{1.4 + 0.1j \mid 0 \leq j \leq 20\}$ for DRIVE and $\{1.7 + 0.1j \mid 0 \leq j \leq 20\}$ for STARE. For the line-ending-selective B-COSFIRE filters we use the following σ values: $\{0.9 + 0.1j \mid 0 \leq j \leq 20\}$ for DRIVE and $\{1.4 + 0.1j \mid 0 \leq j \leq 20\}$ for STARE.

In order to reduce the skewness in the data, for each element v_i in a feature vector we apply the inverse hyperbolic sine transformation function [11], defined as:

$$f(v_i, \theta) = \sinh^{-1}(\theta v_i)/\theta \tag{4}$$

For large values of v_i and $\theta > 0$ it behaves like a log transformation[3]. As $\theta \to 0$, $f(v_i, \theta) \to v_i$.

We then use the resulting feature vectors and their class labels as input to the GMLVQ algorithm, which determines the relevance of each filter. The bar plot

---

[3] The value of θ has been experimentally determined on some training images and set to 1000 for both the DRIVE and STARE data sets.

in Fig. 4 shows the relevances Γ_i of every B-COSFIRE filter used for the training images in the DRIVE data set. We select the filters whose responses correspond to local maxima in the relevance landscape to form the feature vectors. For the DRIVE data set, we select three line (at scales $\sigma_1 = 1.6, \sigma_2 = 2.2$ and $\sigma_3 = 3.4$) and two line-ending (at scales $\sigma_4 = 1.7$ and $\sigma_5 = 2.9$) B-COSFIRE filters. For the STARE data set, instead, we select two line ($\sigma_1 = 3$ and $\sigma_2 = 3.7$) and three line-ending ($\sigma_3 = 2, \sigma_4 = 2.7$ and $\sigma_5 = 3.4$) B-COSFIRE filters. For both data sets, we discard the pixel value of the green channel, since it has very low relevance. In this way the final representation results in a 5-element vector, for both data sets. It is worth noting that the different values of σ automatically selected for the two data sets depend on the different resolution and thickness of the vessels in the images of such data sets.

3.4   Evaluation and Results

The output of the SVM classifier is a probability score that indicates the vesselness of each pixel: 1 and 0 represent a vessel pixel and a background pixel with absolute certainty, respectively. We threshold the output of the SVM classifier to obtain the final binary vessel map. The threshold divides the pixels into two classes: *vessel* and *non-vessel* pixels. We compare the resulting binary map with the corresponding ground truth and compute the following measures: true positives (TP), false positives (FP), true negatives (TN) and false negatives (FN). We consider only the pixels inside the FOV for the evaluation. In order to compare the performance of the proposed method with other state of the art algorithms, we calculate the accuracy (Acc), sensitivity (Se), specificity (Sp) and Matthews correlation coefficient (MCC). These metrics are defined as follows:

$$Acc = \frac{TP + TN}{N}, \ Se = \frac{TP}{TP + FN}, \ Sp = \frac{TN}{TN + FP},$$

$$MCC = \frac{TP/N - S \times P}{\sqrt{P \times S \times (1 - S) \times (1 - P)}},$$

where $N = TN + TP + FN + FP$, $S = (TP + FN)/N$ and $P = (TP + FP)/N$.

The MCC measures the quality of a binary classification, taking into account the unbalanced cardinality of the two classes. The MCC value varies from -1 for a completely wrong prediction to 1 for a perfect classification system. A value of 0 corresponds to random prediction. ·

We compare the performance of the proposed method with others by also computing the receiving operator characteristics (ROC) curve and its underlying area (AUC). It allows the evaluation of the performance of the algorithms by considering the trade-off between sensitivity and specificity. The closer the ROC curve to the top-left corner, the better the classification is. For a perfect system the ROC curve has a point $(0, 1)$.

We compute the sensitivity, specificity and accuracy for each data set for a specific value of threshold t, the one that contributes to the maximum average MCC value on the corresponding data set. In Table 1 we report the results

Table 1. Results achieved by the proposed supervised method on the DRIVE and STARE data sets in comparison to the ones achieved in [5] by using unsupervised B-COSFIRE filters.

	DRIVE		STARE	
	[5]	Proposed method	[5]	Proposed method
Accuracy	0.9442	0.9467	0.9497	0.9537
AUC	0.9616	0.9588	0.9563	0.9629
Specificity	0.9704	0.9724	0.9701	0.9717
Sensitivity	0.7655	0.7731	0.7716	0.8011
MCC	0.7475	0.7566	0.7335	0.7452
Processing time	10 s	60 s	10 s	60 s

achieved by the proposed supervised method on the DRIVE and STARE data sets, compared with the ones obtained by the original unsupervised approach that used B-COSFIRE filters [5]. The performance improvement is attributable to the learning ability of combining the responses of B-COSFIRE filters that are selective for tiny and large vessels, as well as for vessel-endings.

4   Discussion

The performance results that we achieve on the DRIVE and STARE data sets are better than many of other methods and confirm the effectiveness of the proposed method (Table 2). For comparison purposes, we move along the ROC curve and compare the performance of the proposed method with the ones of other supervised methods. For the STARE data set and for the same specificity values reported in [22], [14] and [8] ($Sp = 0.9747$, $Sp = 0.9819$ and $Sp = 0.9763$) we achieve better sensitivity: 0.7806, 0.7316 and 07697, respectively. Similarly, for the DRIVE data set and for the same specificity reported in [22] ($Sp = 0.9782$) and in [14] ($Sp = 0.9801$) we achieve better sensitivity: 0.7425 and 0.7183, respectively. For the same specificity reported in [8] ($Sp = 9807$) we achieve a lower value of the sensitivity ($Se = 0.7181$).

The main contribution of the proposed method concerns the features extraction and selection procedure. Indeed, the employed filters are domain-independent. The proposed algorithm can be considered as a general framework for the delineation of any bar-like structures. Moreover, the filter selection process by GMLVQ is very effective to choose a small subset of filters that give a significant contribution. This generalization ability is attributable to the trainable character of B-COSFIRE filters, in that they are automatically configured by some vessel-like prototype patterns. In contrast, other methods use hand-crafted features which require domain knowledge. For instance, the features proposed in [8] are specifically designed to deal with particular issues of the retinal

Table 2. Performance results of the proposed supervised method on DRIVE and STARE data sets compared to other methods.

	Method	DRIVE data set				STARE data set			
		Se	Sp	AUC	Acc	Se	Sp	AUC	Acc
Unsupervised	*B*-COSFIRE [5]	0.7655	0.9704	0.9614	0.9442	0.7716	0.9701	0.9563	0.9497
	Hoover et al. [9]	-	-	-	-	0.6747	0.9565	0.7590	0.9275
	Mendonca and Campilho. [16]	0.7344	0.9764	-	0.9463	0.6996	0.9730	-	0.9479
	Martinez-Perez et al. [15]	0.7246	0.9655	-	0.9344	0.7506	0.6569	-	0.9410
	Al-Rawi et al. [1]	-	-	0.9435	0.9535	-	-	0.9467	0.9090
	Ricci and Perfetti [20]	-	-	0.9558	0.9563	-	-	0.9602	0.9584
	Lam et al. [12]	-	-	0.9614	0.9472	-	-	0.9739	0.9567
Supervised	Staal et al. [23]	-	-	0.9520	0.9441	-	-	0.9614	0.9516
	Soares et al. [22]	0.7332	0.9782	0.9614	0.9466	0.7207	0.9747	0.9671	0.9480
	Ricci and Perfetti [20]	-	-	0.9633	**0.9595**	-	-	0.9680	**0.9646**
	Marin et al. [14]	0.7067	0.9801	0.9588	0.9452	0.6944	**0.9819**	**0.9769**	0.9526
	Fraz et al. [8]	0.7406	**0.9807**	**0.9747**	0.9480	0.7548	0.9763	0.9768	0.9534
	Proposed method	**0.7731**	0.9724	0.9588	0.9467	**0.8011**	0.9717	0.9629	0.9537

fundus images, such as bright and dark lesions or non-uniform illumination of the FOV. The feature set may also be expanded by adding the responses of filters selective for other kinds of patterns such as bifurcations and crossovers [2,3]. In future we aim to investigate the addition of the inhibition mechanism proposed in [4], which significantly improves signal-to-noise ratio in contour detection.

Besides achieving high effectiveness, the proposed methodology is also very efficient. In practice, an image from the DRIVE (565×584 pixels) or the STARE (700×605 pixels) data set is processed (preprocessing and feature extraction followed by classification and thresholding) in less than 60 seconds, which is faster than all the other supervised approaches (15 minutes [23], 3 minutes [22], 1.5 minutes [14], 2 minutes [8]). We measured this duration by running a sequential Matlab implementation on a notebook with a 1.8 GHz processor. Since the B-COSFIRE feature extraction method relies on independent computations, the proposed methodology can become even faster by a parallel implementation.

5   Conclusion

The delineation method that we propose is highly effective and efficient for the segmentation of vessel trees in retinal fundus images. In particular, this method is very effective in the detection of tiny vessels. The results that we achieve on two publicly available benchmark data sets, DRIVE (Se = 0.7731, Sp = 0.9724) and STARE (Se = 0.8011, Sp = 0.9717) are comparable with many of the existing methods, while showing higher time efficiency.

The proposed methodology can be considered as a general delineation framework and could be used in other applications that require the segmentation of vessel-like structures. This is mainly attributable to the trainable B-COSFIRE filters coupled with the automatic feature selection performed by GMLVQ.

References

1. Al-Rawi, M., Qutaishat, M., Arrar, M.: An improved matched filter for blood vessel detection of digital retinal images. Computer in Biology and Medicine **37**(2), 262–267 (2007)
2. Azzopardi, G., Petkov, N.: Automatic detection of vascular bifurcations in segmented retinal images using trainable COSFIRE filters. Pattern Recognition Letters **34**, 922–933 (2013)
3. Azzopardi, G., Petkov, N.: Trainable COSFIRE filters for keypoint detection and pattern recognition. IEEE Transactions on Pattern Analysis and Machine Intelligence **35**, 490–503 (2013)
4. Azzopardi, G., Rodríguez-Sánchez, A., Piater, J., Petkov, N.: A push-pull CORF model of a simple cell with antiphase inhibition improves SNR and contour detection. PLoS ONE **9**(7), e98424 (2014)
5. Azzopardi, G., Strisciuglio, N., Vento, M., Petkov, N.: Trainable COSFIRE filters for vessel delineation with application to retinal images. Medical Image Analysis **19**(1), 46–57 (2015)

6. Chauduri, S., Chatterjee, S., Katz, N., Nelson, M., Goldbaum, M.: Detection of blood-vessels in retinal images using two-dimensional matched-filters. IEEE Transactions on Medical Imaging **8**(3), 263–269 (1989)

7. Chutatape, O., Liu Zheng, Krishnan, S.: Retinal blood vessel detection and tracking by matched gaussian and kalman filters. In: Chang, H., Zhang, Y. (eds.) Proc. 20th Annu. Int. Conf. IEEE Eng. Med. Biol. Soc. (EMBS 1998), vol. 17, pp. 3144–9 (1998)

8. Fraz, M., Remagnino, P., Hoppe, A., Uyyanonvara, B., Rudnicka, A., Owen, C., Barman, S.: An ensemble classification-based approach applied to retinal blood vessel segmentation. IEEE Transactions on Biomedical Engineering **59**(9), 2538–2548 (2012)

9. Hoover, A., Kouznetsova, V., Goldbaum, M.: Locating blood vessels in retinal images by piecewise threshold probing of a matched filter response. IEEE Transactions on Medical Imaging **19**(3), 203–210 (2000)

10. Joachims, T.: Estimating the generalization performance of an svm efficiently. In: Proceedings of the Seventeenth International Conference on Machine Learning, ICML 2000, pp. 431–438. Morgan Kaufmann Publishers Inc., San Francisco (2000)

11. Johnson, N.L.: Systems of frequency curves generated by methods of translation. Biometrika **36**(1–2), 149–176 (1949)

12. Lam, B., Gao, Y., Liew, A.C.: General retinal vessel segmentation using regularization-based multiconcavity modeling. IEEE Transactions on Medical Imaging **29**(7), 1369–1381 (2010)

13. Liu, I., Sun, Y.: Recursive tracking of vascular networks in angiograms based on the detection deletion scheme. IEEE Transactions on Medical Imaging **12**(2), 334–341 (1993)

14. Marin, D., Aquino, A., Emilio Gegundez-Arias, M., Manuel Bravo, J.: A New Supervised Method for Blood Vessel Segmentation in Retinal Images by Using Gray-Level and Moment Invariants-Based Features. IEEE Transactions on Medical Imaging **30**(1), 146–158 (2011)

15. Martinez-Pérez, M.E., Hughes, A.D., Thom, S.A., Bharath, A.A., Parker, K.H.: Segmentation of blood vessels from red-free and fluorescein retinal images. Medical Image Analysis **11**(1), 47–61 (2007)

16. Mendonca, A.M., Campilho, A.: Segmentation of retinal blood vessels by combining the detection of centerlines and morphological reconstruction. IEEE Transactions on Medical Imaging **25**(9), 1200–1213 (2006)

17. Muduli, P., Pati, U.: A novel technique for wall crack detection using image fusion. In: 2013 International Conference on Computer Communication and Informatics (ICCCI), pp. 1–6, January 2013

18. Niemeijer, M., Staal, J., van Ginneken, B., Loog, M., Abramoff, M.: Comparative study of retinal vessel segmentation methods on a new publicly available database. In: Proc. of the SPIE - The International Society for Optical Engineering, Medical Imaging 2004, Image Processing, San Diego. CA, USA, February 16–19, 2004, pp. 648–56. (2004)

19. Pizer, S., Amburn, E., Austin, J., Cromartie, R., Geselowitz, A., Greer, T., Ter Haar Romeny, B., Zimmerman, J., Zuiderveld, K.: Adaptive Histogram Equalization and its Varations. Computer Vision Graphics and Image Processing **39**(3), 355–368 (1987)

20. Ricci, E., Perfetti, R.: Retinal blood vessel segmentation using line operators and support vector classification. IEEE Transactions on Medical Imaging **26**(10), 1357–1365 (2007)

21. Schneider, P., Biehl, M., Hammer, B.: Adaptive relevance matrices in learning vector quantization. Neural Comput. **21**(12), 3532–3561 (2009)
22. Soares, J.V.B., Leandro, J.J.G., Cesar Jr, R.M., Jelinek, H.F., Cree, M.J.: Retinal vessel segmentation using the 2-D Gabor wavelet and supervised classification. IEEE Transactions on Medical Imaging **25**(9), 1214–1222 (2006)
23. Staal, J., Abramoff, M., Niemeijer, M., Viergever, M., van Ginneken, B.: Ridge-based vessel segmentation in color images of the retina. IEEE Transactions on Medical Imaging **23**(4), 501–509 (2004)
24. Zana, F., Klein, J.: Segmentation of vessel-like patterns using mathematical morphology and curvature evaluation. IEEE Transactions on Medical Imaging **10**(7), 1010–1019 (2001)
25. Zhang, L., Zhang, Y., Wang, M., Li, Y.: Adaptive river segmentation in sar images. Journal of Electronics (China) **26**(4), 438–442 (2009)
26. Zhou, L., Rzeszotarski, M., Singerman, L., Chokreff, J.: The detection and quantification of retinopathy using digital angiograms. IEEE Transactions on Medical Imaging **13**(4), 619–626 (1994)

Progressive Blind Deconvolution

Rana Hanocka$^{(\boxtimes)}$ and Nahum Kiryati

School of Electrical Engineering, Tel Aviv University, Tel Aviv, Israel
hanocka@mail.tau.ac.il

Abstract. We present a novel progressive framework for blind image restoration. Common blind restoration schemes first estimate the blur kernel, then employ non-blind deblurring. However, despite recent progress, the accuracy of PSF estimation is limited. Furthermore, the outcome of non-blind deblurring is highly sensitive to errors in the assumed PSF. Therefore, high quality blind deblurring has remained a major challenge. In this work, we combine state of the art regularizers for the image and the PSF, namely the Mumford & Shah piecewise-smooth image model and the sparse PSF prior. Previous works that used Mumford & Shah image regularization were either limited to non-blind deblurring or semi-blind deblurring assuming a parametric kernel known up to an unknown parameter. We suggest an iterative progressive restoration scheme, in which the imperfectly deblurred output of the current iteration is fed back as input to the next iteration. The kernel representing the residual blur is then estimated, and used to drive the non-blind restoration component, leading to finer deblurring. Experimental results demonstrate rapid convergence, and excellent performance on a wide variety of blurred images.

Keywords: Progressive blind restoration · Residual blur removal · Image deblurring · Piecewise-smooth image model · Mumford & Shah regularization · Sparse PSF prior

1 Introduction

Image deblurring algorithms can be classified as non-blind or blind, depending on whether the blur kernel is assumed to be known or unknown. Even the milder non-blind image deblurring problem is notoriously hard, as it is essentially ill-posed. Classic approaches for non-blind deblurring, notably the Wiener filter [16], implicitly regularize the problem by imposing an image-smoothness prior. In the last decade or so, substantial progress has been achieved by incorporating more realistic image priors, requiring sophisticated algorithms and numerical techniques to solve the resulting optimization problems. Notably, the Mumford & Shah image prior (originally introduced for image segmentation [15]) favors piecewise-smooth image structure, preserving edges rather than smoothing them. Bar *et al* [4] developed a non-blind deblurring algorithm using the Mumford & Shah image prior. Their method relies on the Γ-convergence approach [3] and

© Springer International Publishing Switzerland 2015
G. Azzopardi and N. Petkov (Eds.): CAIP 2015, Part II, LNCS 9257, pp. 313–325, 2015.
DOI: 10.1007/978-3-319-23117-4_27

on advanced numerical techniques to minimize the non-trivial free-discontinuity objective functional. As long as the blur kernel is known, the non-blind deblurring algorithm of Bar *et al* yields state of the art results, and can be computed in real time using a PC-type GPU [19].

In blind deblurring, the unknown blur kernel adds another layer of ambiguity to the already difficult non-blind problem. For decades, the blind deblurring problem was considered quite hopeless. Bar *et al* [7], followed by [5], settled for *semi-blind* deblurring, limited to estimating an unknown parameter of an otherwise specified family of blur kernels (*e.g.*, variance in the case of Gaussian blur). However, practical applications of semi-blind deblurring are limited, since physical blur kernels seldom conform with common theoretical blur models, and deblurring algorithms are sensitive to deviations from the assumed blur kernel.

Recently, there has been a new wave of blind deconvolution methods, employing powerful PSF priors [1,2,6,12,18]. While there have been significant advances in the field, the blind deconvolution problem is far from solved. Due to the sensitivity to blur-kernel estimation errors, non-blind methods usually outperform blind methods when the correct blur kernel is known. Various real-world applications still rely on manual tuning of the assumed blur kernel within a non-blind framework, e.g. [10].

We present a blind image deblurring algorithm employing the powerful Mumford & Shah image prior and a sparse PSF prior. The problem is cast in a coarse-to-fine progressive framework which inherits the elegance and sophistication of the Mumford & Shah image model, and addresses the residual image blur associated with blur-kernel estimation errors. Iterative reduction of the residual blur relaxes the accuracy requirements from the blur estimation component, reduces the need for parameter tuning, and leads the residual blur kernel to approach an impulse function. Experimental results demonstrate the applicability of the suggested approach to a wide range of deblurring challenges.

2 Variational Elements

2.1 Fundamentals

The standard blurred image formation model is

$$g = u * h + n \tag{1}$$

where g, u, h, and n denote the blurred image, latent image, blur kernel, and random additive noise, respectively. Image deblurring is the recovery of the latent image u given the blurred image g. Depending on whether the blur kernel h is known or unknown, deblurring methods are classified as either non-blind or blind. In practice, when using non-blind methods, the blur kernel must usually be estimated using side information regarding the imaging process, or by a manual trial-and-error procedure. Even in the non-blind scenario, image deblurring is an ill-posed problem, requiring regularization using a-priori assumptions regarding image structure. The deblurring problem is often formulated as a functional minimization problem, which in the non-blind case takes the form

$$F_{nb} = S(u, h, g) + Q(u) \tag{2}$$

where F_{nb} is the (non-blind) objective functional, $S(u, h, g)$ is a fidelity term that reflects the assumed noise distribution, and $Q(u)$ is the regularization term, *i.e.*, the image prior.

In blind methods, the blur kernel is unknown; thus, both the latent image *and* the blur kernel need to be recovered from the given blurred image. With an unknown blur kernel, blind image restoration is an extremely difficult, highly ill-posed problem. There have been several attempts, e.g. [19,20], to incorporate a PSF prior in the form of an additional kernel regularization term:

$$F_b = S(u, h, g) + Q(u) + R(h) \tag{3}$$

where F_b is the (blind) objective functional and $R(h)$ is the blur-kernel prior. In principle, this functional leads to Euler-Lagrange equations that can be solved by alternate minimization. In practice, success has been rather limited. It has been argued [18] that independent PSF estimation should precede a non-blind deblurring phase. The progressive deblurring strategy suggested in this paper diverges from both previous approaches. The deblurred outcome of the current two-stage (PSF estimation + non-blind deblurring) iteration is fed back as input to the next iteration, rapidly eliminating the residual blur. We proceed to specify the fidelity and regularization terms used in the PSF estimation and deblurring components of this work.

2.2   Image Terms

The fidelity term used in this work is the standard $\mathcal{L}_2$-norm

$$S(u, h, g) = \frac{1}{2} \int_{\Omega} (h * u - g)^2 dA \tag{4}$$

that reflects the ubiquitous Gaussian noise assumption.

The image prior is adapted from the Mumford & Shah segmentation functional (5), favoring piecewise-smooth image structure. This model holds for most natural images, with the exception of extremely textured images (where the piecewise-smooth model can be applied to texture feature maps). The Mumford & Shah segmentation functional (F_{MS}) is given by

$$F_{MS}(u, K) = \frac{1}{2} \int_{\Omega} (u - g)^2 dA + \beta \int_{\Omega/K} |\nabla u|^2 dA + \alpha \int_K d\sigma \tag{5}$$

where Ω is the image domain, K is the edge set, and α, β are positive regularization constants. Minimizing this functional is challenging, and had been an open problem for many years, especially since the unknown edge set K appears not only in the integrand but also in the integration domain.

Ambrosio and Tororelli [3] addressed this problem via the Γ-convergence framework. The irregular functional $F_{MS}(u, K)$ is approximated by a sequence of regular functionals $F_\epsilon(u)$ such that $F_{MS}(u, K) = \lim_{\epsilon \to 0} F_\epsilon(u)$. The edge set K is represented by a characteristic function $(1 - x_K)$ which is approximated by a smooth auxiliary function $v(x)$, i.e., $v(x) \approx 0$ if $x \in K$, and $v(x) \approx 1$ otherwise (not on the edges). Therefore, the functional becomes

$$F_\epsilon(u, v) = \frac{1}{2} \int_\Omega (u - g)^2 dA + \beta \int_\Omega v^2 |\nabla u|^2 dA + \alpha \int_\Omega \left(\epsilon |\nabla v|^2 + \frac{(v - 1)^2}{4\epsilon} \right) dA \tag{6}$$

which can be solved using sophisticated numerical methods.

Bar et al [4,7] demonstrated that image restoration and segmentation are tightly coupled tasks, and used the Mumford & Shah piecewise-smoothness terms in their Γ-convergence formulation to regularize the image deblurring problem. In the non-blind case, Bar et al minimized the functional

$$F(u, v) = \frac{1}{2} \int_\Omega (h * u - g)^2 dA + \beta \int_\Omega v^2 |\nabla u|^2 dA + \alpha \int_\Omega \left(\epsilon |\nabla v|^2 + \frac{(v - 1)^2}{4\epsilon} \right) dA \tag{7}$$

where

$$Q_\epsilon(u, v) \equiv \beta \int v^2 |\nabla u|^2 dA + \alpha \int_\Omega \left(\epsilon |\nabla v|^2 + \frac{(v - 1)^2}{4\epsilon} \right) dA \tag{8}$$

are the image regularization terms. Gildenblat [19] has shown that this elaborate functional can be efficiently minimized using GPU architecture, approaching real-time computation on low-cost hardware.

2.3   Sparse PSF Prior

The design of PSF priors for blur identification and blind restoration has attracted substantial attention in recent years [1,2,6,12,17,18], leading to performance breakthroughs. Following Kotera et al [1], we model the blur with a Laplace distribution on the positive PSF values, leading to the sparse prior

$$R(h) = \int_\Omega \Psi(h(x, y)) dA, \quad \Psi(h(x, y)) = \begin{cases} h(x, y), & \text{if } h(x, y) \geq 0 \\ \infty, & \text{otherwise} \end{cases} \tag{9}$$

3   Algorithm

3.1   Strategy

The proposed algorithm is an iterative process alternating between two steps. The first step consists of estimating the blur kernel h as suggested by Kotera et al, also disregarding the u solution. In the second step, given the current estimate of h, the latent image u and edge-map v are estimated by minimizing the non-blind functional (7).

Due to kernel estimation errors, residual blur is present after the non-blind deconvolution step. We progressively remove this residual blur, by iteratively feeding the residually-blurred image back into the system. Convergence is quick (after 1-3 iterations), and the estimated residual blur kernel approaches an impulse function, indicating that recovery of the latent image u has been finalized.

3.2 Solving for h

Estimating h within a MAP framework approaches the true blur kernel solution (given enough measurements in g and u) [18]. Therefore, we adopt a MAP approach to exploit the asymmetry between the dimensionality of the latent image u and the small (relative to u) blur kernel h. Refer to the functional minimized by Kotera et al [1]

$$L(u,h) = \frac{1}{2}\int_\Omega (h*u-g)^2 dA + Q(u) + \int_\Omega \Psi(h(x,y)) dA \qquad (10)$$

where $Q(u)$ corresponds to their gradient-based image prior. When minimizing with respect to h, the image prior $Q(u)$ vanishes, resulting in the functional

$$\min_h \frac{1}{2}||hu-g||^2 + R(h). \qquad (11)$$

Kotera et al minimized this functional using the augmented Lagrangian method. A new function $\tilde{h} = h$ is introduced to separate the minimization of the data term and the PSF regularizer, leading to

$$\min_{h,\tilde{h}} \frac{\gamma}{2}||hU-g||^2 + R(\tilde{h}) \quad \text{s.t.} \quad h = \tilde{h} \qquad (12)$$

where γ is a positive constant and U is a (fixed) convolutional operator constructed from u. The augmented Lagrangian method adds to the Lagrangian a quadratic penalty term for each constraint, such that the new functional we wish to minimize (after rearranging) becomes

$$\min_{h,\tilde{h}} \frac{\gamma}{2}||hU-g||^2 + R(\tilde{h}) + \frac{\zeta}{2}||h-\tilde{h}-a_h||^2 \qquad (13)$$

where a_h is proportional to the estimate of the Lagrange multiplier of the above constraint in (12). This function can be minimized using coordinate descent (for additional details see Kotera et al [1]).

3.3 Solving for u and v

The objective functional (7) is strictly convex and lower-bounded with respect to either u or v when the other is held constant along with the PSF (h) from the previous step. Note that this convexity property holds for general blur kernels (not necessarily limited to a parametric model). The Euler-Lagrange equations for v and u are

$$F_v = 2\beta v|\nabla u|^2 + \alpha \cdot \frac{v-1}{2\epsilon} - 2\epsilon\alpha\nabla^2 v = 0 \tag{14}$$

$$F_u = (h * f - g) * h(-x, -y) - 2\beta\mathrm{Div}\,(v^2\nabla u) = 0. \tag{15}$$

The objective functional is iteratively minimized by solving these equations with the Neumann boundary conditions [7].

Fig. 1. Top left: blurred image. Top right: blind deconvolution using Kotera *et al* [1]. Bottom left: blind deconvolution using Shan *et al* [6]. Bottom Right: our blind restoration result.

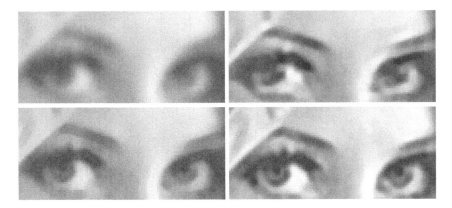

Fig. 2. Zoom in of Figure 1. Top left: blurred image. Top right: blind deconvolution using Kotera *et al* [1]. Bottom left: blind deconvolution using Shan *et al* [6]. Bottom Right: our blind restoration result. Notice the differences in the right pupil.

Fig. 3. First row: average of a video sequence following non-rigid registration [10]. Second row: manually-optimized non-blind deconvolution result [10] (non-blind). Third row: deconvolution using the proposed blind deconvolution method. Left column: video sequence courtesy of Mahpod and Yitzhaky [13]. Right column: video sequence courtesy of Oreifej [14].

Fig. 4. Top row: blurred image. Second row: proposed blind deconvolution method. Third row: enlarged blurred patches. Fourth row: recovered sharp patches.

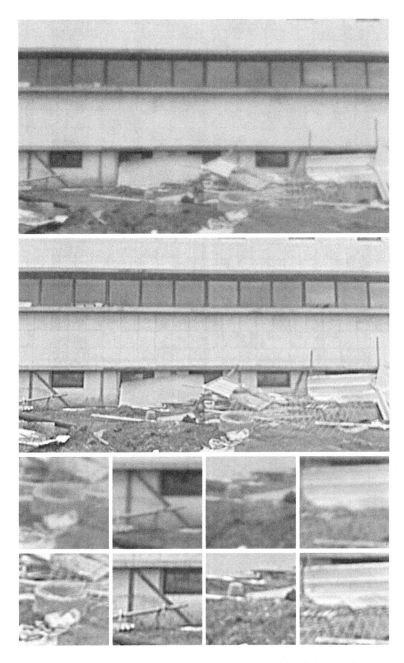

Fig. 5. Top row: blurred image. Second row: proposed blind deconvolution method. Third row: enlarged blurred patches. Fourth row: recovered sharp patches.

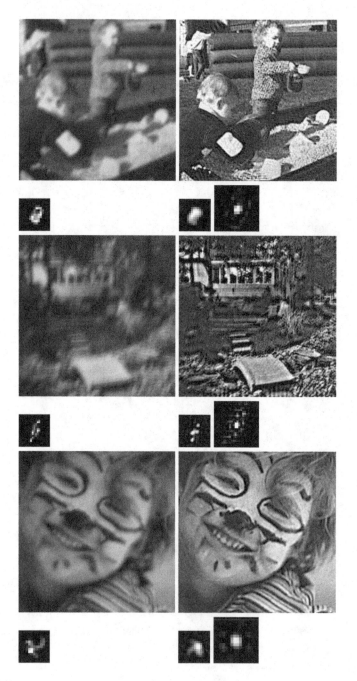

Fig. 6. Left column: blurred images. The true blur kernel is shown below each image. Right column: Our blind deconvolution result. The blur kernel estimated in the first iteration and the residual blur estimated in the second iteration are shown below each image. Dataset courtesy of [18].

4   Experiments

The top left image in Figure 1 is Lena, synthetically blurred with a Gaussian kernel. The blind deblurring results obtained using the algorithms of Kotera *et al* [1] and Shan *et al* [6] are respectively shown in the top right and the bottom left. Our result is shown in the bottom right. While all three results are adequate, our result appears to be the best, as can be seen in Figure 2, for example near the right pupil.

The recovery of a high-quality still image from a video sequence of a static scene imaged through atmospheric turbulence is a notoriously difficult problem. Certain methods apply non-rigid registration to each frame and average the results. The outcome is a blurred average image that is commonly modeled as a latent image blurred by a space-invariant Gaussian kernel. The average image is restored using a deblurring algorithm, see *e.g.*, [10]. The top row in Figure 3 shows three such average images. The middle row is the result of non-blind deconvolution using manually optimized Gaussian blur kernels [10]. The bottom row presents our blind deconvolution result. It can be seen that the blind results are on par with the manual, painstakingly optimized non-blind reconstructions.

Figures 4 and 5 show blind deblurring of pictures taken using a smartphone with incorrect focus settings and motion blur.

The left column in Figure 6 shows three heavily blurred images, with the true blur kernel shown below each image. The right column is the outcome of the suggested progressive blind restoration algorithm. Below each of the recovered images, we show the estiamted blur in the first iteration and the residual blur estimated in the second iteration.

Running time for a $255{\times}255$ image on a $3.40\,Ghz$ Intel quadcore machine using unoptimized MATLAB is approximately 20 seconds. The algorithm converges in one to three iterations, depending on the accuracy of the initial blur kernel estimation.

5   Conclusions

Iterative algorithms for concurrent blur estimation and image restoration, *e.g.*, [19,20] are mathematically elegant but lead to questionable results. Following the observations of [18], sequential blind restoration is often preferred, meaning that the blur kernel is estimated first, then non-blind deblurring is applied. This approach is followed, for example, in the state of the art algorithm of Kotera *at* [1]. However, PSF estimation errors are inevitable, and image restoration is sensitive to these errors, limiting performance. We suggest an iterative blind deblurring approach, where PSF estimation and image deblurring are decoupled within each iteration, but the deblurred outcome of each iteration is fed back as the input image to the next iteration. This leads to progressive elimination of the residual blur.

The proposed blind image restoration method incorporates the Mumford & Shah piecewise-smooth image model with a sparse PSF prior. We have thus reached a goal that Bar *et al* [7] and others [5] have not been able to accomplish. Successful results on a variety of challenging test cases demonstrate the robustness and visual quality of the suggested approach.

References

1. Kotera, J., Šroubek, F., Milanfar, P.: Blind deconvolution using alternating maximum a posteriori estimation with heavy-tailed priors. In: Wilson, R., Hancock, E., Bors, A., Smith, W. (eds.) CAIP 2013, Part II. LNCS, vol. 8048, pp. 59–66. Springer, Heidelberg (2013)
2. Fergus, R., Singh, B., Hertzmann, A., Roweis, S.T., Freeman, W.T.: Removing camera shake from a single photograph. SIGGRAPH **25**, 787–794 (2006)
3. Ambrosio, L., Tortorelli, V.M.: Approximation of functionals depending on jumps by elliptic functionals via Γ-convergence. Communications on Pure and Applied Mathematics **43**, 999–1036 (1990)
4. Bar, L., Sochen, N.A., Kiryati, N.: Variational pairing of image segmentation and blind restoration. In: Pajdla, T., Matas, J.G. (eds.) ECCV 2004. LNCS, vol. 3022, pp. 166–177. Springer, Heidelberg (2004)
5. Zheng, H., Hellwich, O.: Extended mumford-shah regularization in bayesian estimation for blind image deconvolution and segmentation. In: Reulke, R., Eckardt, U., Flach, B., Knauer, U., Polthier, K. (eds.) IWCIA 2006. LNCS, vol. 4040, pp. 144–158. Springer, Heidelberg (2006)
6. Shan, Q., Jia, J., Agarwala, A.: High-quality motion deblurring from a single image. In: SIGGRAPH (2008)
7. Bar, L., Sochen, N., Kiryati, N.: Semi-blind image restoration via Mumford-Shah regularization. IEEE Transactions on Image Processing **15**, 483–493 (2006)
8. Zhu, X., Milanfar, P.: Stabilizing and deblurring atmospheric turbulence. In: ICCP (2011)
9. Gal, R., Kiryati, N., Sochen, N.: Progress in the restoration of image sequences degraded by atmospheric turbulence. Pattern Recognition Letters **48**, 8–14 (2014)
10. Vogel, C.R., Oman, M.E.: Fast, robust total variation-based reconstruction of noisy, blurred images. IEEE Trans. Image Process **7**, 813–824 (1998)
11. Zhou, Y., Komodakis, N.: A MAP-estimation framework for blind deblurring using high-level edge priors. In: Fleet, D., Pajdla, T., Schiele, B., Tuytelaars, T. (eds.) ECCV 2014, Part II. LNCS, vol. 8690, pp. 142–157. Springer, Heidelberg (2014)
12. Mahpod, S., Yitzhaky, Y.: Compression of turbulence-affected video signals SPIE, 7444 (2009)
13. Oreifej, O., Li, X., Shah, M.: Simultaneous video stabilization and moving object detection in turbulence. IEEE Trans. PAMI. **35**, 450–462 (2013)
14. Mumford, D., Shah, S.: Optimal approximations by piecewise smooth functions and associated variational problems. Commun. Pure and Appl. Math. **42**, 577–682 (1989)
15. Wiener, N.: Extrapolation, interpolation, and smoothing of stationary time series. MIT Press (1964)

16. Michaeli, T., Irani, M.: Blind deblurring using internal patch recurrence. In: Fleet, D., Pajdla, T., Schiele, B., Tuytelaars, T. (eds.) ECCV 2014, Part III. LNCS, vol. 8691, pp. 783–798. Springer, Heidelberg (2014)
17. Levin, A., Weiss, Y., Durand, F., Freeman, W.T.: Understanding and evaluating blind deconvolution algorithms. In: CVPR (2009)
18. Gildenblat, J.: Fast GPU implementation of Mumford-Shah regularization Semi-blind image restoration. Unpublished M.Sc. project report, School of Electrical Engineering. Tel Aviv University (2012)
19. You, Y., Kaveh, M.: A Regularization Approach to Joint Blur Identification and Image Restoration. IEEE Trans. Image Processing **5**, 416–428 (1996)
20. Chan, T., Wong, C.: Total Variation Blind Deconvolution. IEEE Trans. Image Processing **7**, 370–375 (1998)

Leaf-Based Plant Identification Through Morphological Characterization in Digital Images

Arturo Oncevay-Marcos[(✉)], Ronald Juarez-Chambi, Sofía Khlebnikov-Núñez, and César Beltráon-Castañn

Department of Engineering, Research Group on Pattern Recognition and Applied Artificial Intelligence, Pontificia Universidad Católica Del Perú, Lima, Perú
{foncevay,ronald.juarez,cbeltran}@pucp.pe, sjlebn@pucp.edu.pe

Abstract. The plant species identification is a manual process performed mainly by botanical scientists based on their experience. In order to improve this task, several plant classification processes has been proposed applying pattern recognition. In this work, we propose a method combining three visual attributes of leaves: boundary shape, texture and color. Complex networks and multi-scale fractal dimension techniques were used to characterize the leaf boundary shape, the Haralick's descriptors for texture were extracted, and color moments were calculated. Experiments were performed on the ImageCLEF 2012 train dataset, scan pictures only. We reached up to 90.41% of accuracy regarding the leaf-based plant identification problem for 115 species.

Keywords: Leaf-based plant identification · Complex networks · Multi-scale fractal dimension · Haralick's descriptors · Color moments

1 Introduction

Taxonomic classification of plants is a difficult challenge to botanists due to the great biodiversity of plant species and the variety of different biological attributes to analyze. Botanists have the duty of preserve and increase the content of herbariums and plant catalogs from species collection and identification tasks. Now the identification challenge is moved to a computational approach, applying pattern recognition techniques to automatize the plant identification task using digital images of leaves.

In pattern recognition, a set of visual morphological traits are gathered to design or apply mathematical models which allow species discrimination and identification. There are many techniques in the literature related to leaf-based identification by using digital images because is the part of the plant with most visual attributes and properties: shape, boundary, color, texture, venation and so forth [1]. Some of this approaches are described below.

Leaf boundary features often were extracted taking into account the region they cover [2] or the contour analysis [3]. Another approach is carried out on the

© Springer International Publishing Switzerland 2015
G. Azzopardi and N. Petkov (Eds.): CAIP 2015, Part II, LNCS 9257, pp. 326–335, 2015.
DOI: 10.1007/978-3-319-23117-4_28

basis of leaf skeletonization [4] that can be extended to the leaf venation composition. A variety of techniques are applied over skeleton leaf such as complex networks [5–7] and fractal dimension [1,5,6,8].

Another potential features are the color and texture of the leaf. Color is usually analyzed in image retrieval problems based on visual contents [9]. In addition, four color moments are extracted from leaf-based plant identification process [10,11]. On the other hand, the texture characteristics are used for leaf classification, and although texture features can not discriminate plants on their own, they could be merged with other descriptors [12]. In this approach, some of the most tested features are based on Gabor filters [13,14], Local Binary Patterns (LBP) [6,14] and Gray Level Co-ocurrence Matrix (GLCM) [15,16].

In this paper, a leaf feature vector is obtained by processing boundary shape, color and texture properties. Complex networks and Multi-scale fractal dimension were used to extract boundary features. The Haralick's descriptors were extracted from the texture leaf area by using GLCM, and three color moments were computed (standard deviation, asymmetry and kurtosis). Then, we trained a multilayer perceptron classifier with these features. The experimentation was performed on the ImageCLEF 2012 leaf image dataset [17]. Also, a 10-fold cross validation proves high acceptance rate for the implemented framework.

The rest of the paper is organized as follows, in Section 2 we describe briefly the procedure proposed for the image processing and classification; Section 3 explains the conceptual framework of the features extracted. Furthermore, experimentation and results were detailed in Section 4. Finally, Section 5 presents the conclusion about our results and future works.

2   Procedure

The proposed procedure for this study is shown in Fig. 1. The digital images of scanned leaves go through a pre-processing phase for the leaf area segmentation using Otsu approach [18]. Also, the leaf contour and venation (known as leaf skeleton) has been extracted. Figure 2 shows the desired result. For this work, we only consider the leaf boundary for shape features extraction. The complete extraction process is explained in the next section. At the end, we applied the multilayer perceptron (MLP) [19] with the features extracted as input.

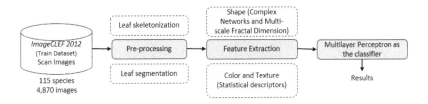

Fig. 1. Proposed procedure for the study

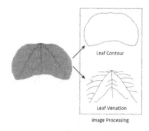

Fig. 2. Image leaf pre-processing (skeletonization)

3   Feature Extraction

3.1   Complex Networks for Boundary Shape Approach

In general, a graph or network is a set of elements called nodes and connections known as edges. However, a complex network refers to a graph with no trivial properties compared with simple graphs, as well as it has considerable number of nodes and edges [20] .

There are many theoretical models of complex networks such as Erdös-Rényi, scale-free, random models, etc. In this paper we used Watts-Strogatz network model which owns a small-world property [21]. The study of the dynamic properties of this model —measurements were obtained from the evolution based on number of connected components— will produce a set of descriptors or a feature vector which will be used for the classification task [22].

Degree Descriptors Using Complex Networks Signature. In this section, we describe the process of signature characterization focused on complex network [20]. Let S the boundary leaf trace represented as a set of points $S = [s_1, s_2, \ldots, s_N]$, whose components $s_i = [x_i, y_i]$ represent each vertex i of the boundary contour. Then, in order to apply complex networks theory to this problem, we have created the equivalence of S as a representation of graph $G = \langle V, E \rangle$. Each pixel of the skeleton is represented as a node of the network, i.e. $S = V$. A set of edges E connect each pair of vertices establishing, in this way, the network. E is calculated using Euclidean distance d. Therefore, the matrix is represented by the adjacency matrix with weight W and dimension $N \times N$:

$$w_{ij} = W([w_i, w_j]) = d(s_i, s_j) \tag{1}$$

Dynamic Evolution on Complex Networks. Initially, the set of edges E connect all vertex in the network, as a network with regular behavior. However, a regular network does not have any particular property. Therefore, it is necessary to convert this initial regular network in a complex network, in order to use relevant properties that can be applied later. In this sense, a threshold transformation is used. This approach allows a characterization that describes a list of transient features of the dynamic evolution of the network. Also, a degree normalization is required. For this reason, after consider the network transformation, the feature vector denoted by φ is calculated as the concatenation of the average (k_μ) and maximum degree (k_κ) for each stage of the network evolution and thus we get the characterization proposed for a signature by using complex networks [5].

$$\varphi = [k_\mu(T_0), k_\kappa(T_0), k_\mu(T_1), ..., k_\mu(T_Q), k_\kappa(T_Q)] \qquad (2)$$

3.2   Multi-scale Fractal Dimension for Boundary Shape Extraction

The fractal dimension is a characteristic to measure leaf's shape complexity. In this work we will use the Bouligand-Minkowski method. According to this method, fractal dimension is defined as $FD \sim 2 - \frac{log\,A(d)}{log(d)}$, where $A(d)$ is the area of the leaf dilated by a distance d. The method is based on the correlation between an object boundary and the space it occupies [1,8].

In summary, the method applies dilatation process to the object (leaf), obtaining the ratio between the area and the radius of the dilatation. The object dilatation is obtained by using a set of distances:
$D = \{1, \sqrt{2}, 2, \sqrt{5}, \sqrt{8}, 3, \sqrt{10}, ..., d\}$, where D is the Euclidean distance between pixel's position which is calculated using Euclidean Distance Transform (EDT) (as seen in Fig. 3). For each distance, the object area is calculated. In this case, the area is the sum of all pixels between original object and the dilatation with the distance d.

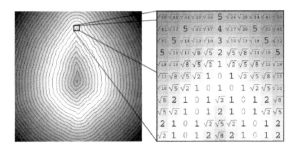

Fig. 3. Image of a leaf boundary after dilatation (left). Zoom in to a sample of distances (right).

The Fractal dimension (FD) is estimated by the $log\,A(d)$-$log(d)$ curve (as seen in Fig. 4), and the gradient of this curve is the fractal dimension.

Sometimes, the FD numeric value cannot describe the complexity of an object or does not have enough useful information, because two objects may have a similar value but belong to different classes. Another disadvantage is the dependence on the used scale [23]. Then, in order to improve the characterization of an object, the Multi-scale Fractal Dimension (MFD) was used. This is defined as:

$$MFD = 2 - \frac{du(t)}{dt} \qquad (3)$$

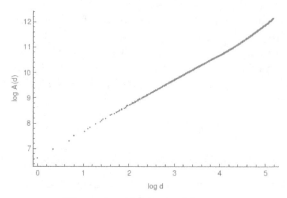

Fig. 4. $log A(d)$ by $log(d)$ curve

where $du(t)/dt$ represents the derivative of the *log-log* curve.

In this way, to obtain the MFD, we need to calculate the derivative of the *log-log* curve. In order to get this derivative, we need to smooth the *log-log* curve to clean high frequency noise. To do this, we applied at regular steps of δ size a Gaussian smoothing filter with $\sigma = \delta/2\pi$. After testing different values of δ, we found that a value of 0.05 gave us the best success rate in the identification task. A sample for the mentioned curves is shown in Fig. 5.

3.3   Color and Texture Features

Color Moments. Color moments are measures that allow similarity analysis between images through its colors. The moments are used because the different values in a color channel (from an image) could represent a probabilistic distribution. In this way, the central moments that describes a probability distribution function are used in the characterization of image colors [24].

Due to the statistical descriptive nature of the moments, this features are scalable and invariant to image rotation. The three main color moments applied by Stricker and Orengo [25] are: Mean, Standard Deviation and Asymmetry. The last one provides information about the form of the color distribution (how much symmetric or assymetric). Besides, it had been considered another color moment called Kurtosis [11], that also analyzes the distribution form by processing the proportion of the variance regarding the concentration of the near and far values to the Mean. In this work, the Mean was not considered in the analysis due to the variation of the leaf color tone through different seasons (reflected in the image dataset). Finally, the three remaining moments were calculated due to the valuable information regarding the form of the distribution of values in each RGB color space channel.

Haralick's Descriptors. The texture features proposed by Haralick [26] are statistical descriptors, and they are extracted from matrices known as GLCM (Gray Level Co-ocurrence Matrix). These matrices represent the distribution of

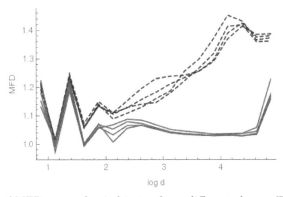

Fig. 5. Sample of MFD curves for 4 objects of two different classes. The curves of one class are shown using dashed lines, while the other ones have a solid style.

the different gray levels in pixels of an image and they have a widespread use in the image processing area due to its ability to obtain valuable information about neighboring pixels in different positions on an image [27].

Because of the amount of values embedded in the GLCM, Haralick proposes a reduction to fourteen statistical descriptors: f_H^1 a f_H^{14}. These descriptors preserve the relevance of the content in the matrix. For this research, the GLCM was calculated using four directions $(0°, 90°, 180°, 270°)$, which is usually applied in biological textures [28], and a distance $d = 1$ in order to take advantage of the analysis at the pixel adjacency level. The fourteen descriptors are calculated for each of the four directions in the neighborhood, and this also helps to reduce the dependence on the GLCM with image rotation caused by the properties of spatial relationships of the pixels.

4   Results and Discussion

For the experimentation, the selected digital images correspond to the scan leaves from the training dataset of the ImageCLEF 2012 [17]. The whole dataset is composed by images (scanned, scan-like and photograph) from 126 plant species, but only 115 plant species have scan digital images of their leaves, with a total of 4,870 instances.

For this image dataset, features described in Section 3 were extracted, and a MLP classification algorithm was trained through a 10-fold cross validation. The number of attributes for each kind of features are shown in Table 1.

The results from the classification process with different combinations of the features are displayed in Table 2. It is shown that each group of features contributes to the improvement of the classification result. For instance, the boundary approach from complex networks and multi-scale fractal dimension features perform well individually and in combination. On the other hand, the color and texture features overcome expectations working in pair, and they show satisfying results as complements from the other attributes too.

Table 1. Features extracted

Abv.	Groups of Features	#features
CND	Complex Network Degree descriptors	26
MFD	Multi-scale Fractal Dimension with $d = 0.05$	68
Har	14 Haralick's descriptors in 4 directions	56
Col	3 Color moments in each RGB's channels	9
	Total	**159**

Table 2. Results from classification

Features included	#features	Accuracy (%)
CND	26	45.83
MFD	68	64.78
(Har + Col)	65	79.85
CND + MFD	94	72.03
CND + (Har + Col)	91	86.61
MFD + (Har + Col)	94	88.31
CND + MFD + (Har + Col)	159	**90.41**

Regarding the best general result, it is obtained from the combination of all features with a 90.41% of accuracy. This score value moderately exceeds a study in the same image dataset with a similar process [29], where a maximum accuracy of 87.5% was achieved, with 218 features and even fewer species (only 54 plant species were analyzed due to the unbalanced number of samples for each class).

In order to analyze how many of the correctly classified samples are relevant, we make a detailed review of the precision score, which in our best result reached up to 90.3% (almost equal to the accuracy). Figure 6 shows a scatterplot of the individual precision obtained by each plant species versus the different number of images found in the dataset, and the analysis for this classification result is described below.

First at all, it is observed that the rightmost points (meaning a bigger number of images for each plant species) have obtained a high precision value. Also, there are eight plant species that achieved a 100% score in this metric, and their number of images is between 10 and 181, which is the maximum value. This fact supports a good overall score of the classification process.

On the other hand, it is noted that there is a very little number of plant species that obtained a precision value below to 50%. In detail, there are eleven plant species in this range, and eight of them have zero precision. However, these plant species contain the fewest number of images in the dataset (less than 10, and even several species with less than 5 images). That is the reason why those plant species got a low (even zero) score, but it did not affect the overall outcome significantly.

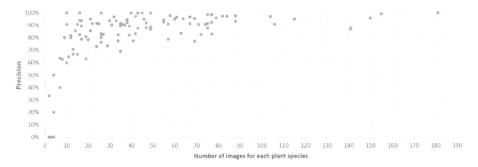

Fig. 6. From the best classification result: individual precision versus the number of images per each plant species

Fig. 7. An image sample of each plant species that achieved 100% precision on the best classification result

Fig. 8. An image sample of each plant species with zero precision on the best classification result

An image sample for the best (100% precision) and worst (zero precision) classified species from our best classification model are shown in Fig. 7 and Fig. 8, respectively. As can be seen, there are visual properties with significant differences between the image samples from both sides. Therefore, with a balanced number of images for each plant species, the overall outcome could be improved. However, the obtained results are promising, because only eight plant species (out of 115 in total) were negated by the classifier, and only three other species couldn't surpass a 50% precision margin.

5   Conclusion and Future Work

In this study, we propose a procedure for leaf-based plant identification through visual attributes extracted from digital images. We have analyzed the boundary shape (by using complex networks and multi-scale fractal dimension), texture (by extracting Haralick's descriptors) and color (with three moments: standard deviation, assymetry and kurtosis). The best classification result with the MLP achieved 90.41% of accuracy, and this is an auspicious value in the task of automatic plant specie classification from leaf digital images. Besides, there were only few species that could not obtain a relevant individual score (11 of 115 classes below a 50% precision margin).

As future work, venation features will be extracted applying complex networks and multi-scale fractal dimension from the leaf skeleton. In addition, the proposed process will be tested on other leaves image dataset, including a plant catalog (under development) collected from Amazon in Perú. Finally, the performance and time processing will be analyzed in order to scale the procedure to a bigger dataset.

Acknowledgments. For this study, the authors acknowledge the support of CONCYTEC-Perú with STIC-AmSud 2013 under the FERMI project, and the Programa Nacional de Innovación para la Competitividad y Productividad, Perú, under the contract 183-FINCyT-IA-2013. This paper is part of a bigger research project funded by grants from the aforementioned Peruvian government programs.

References

1. Bruno, O.M., de Oliveira Plotze, R., Falvo, M., de Castro, M.: Fractal dimension applied to plant identification. Inf. Sci. **178**(12), 2722–2733 (2008)
2. Lee, C.L., Chen, S.Y.: Classification of leaf images. Int. J. Imaging Syst. Technol. **16**(1), 15–23 (2006)
3. Pauwels, E.J., de Zeeuw, P.M., Ranguelova, E.B.: Computer-assisted tree taxonomy by automated image recognition. Eng. Appl. Artif. Intell. **22**(1), 26–31 (2009)
4. Gu, X., Du, J.-X., Wang, X.-F.: Leaf recognition based on the combination of wavelet transform and gaussian interpolation. In: Huang, D.-S., Zhang, X.-P., Huang, G.-B. (eds.) ICIC 2005. LNCS, vol. 3644, pp. 253–262. Springer, Heidelberg (2005)
5. Backes, A.R., Bruno, O.M.: Shape classification using complex network and multi-scale fractal dimension. Pattern Recogn. Lett. **31**(1), 44–51 (2010)
6. Casanova, D., Florindo, J.B., Gonçalves, W.N., Bruno, O.M.: Ifsc/usp at imageclef 2012: plant identification task. In: Proceeding of CLEF 2012 Labs and Workshop, Notebook Papers (2012)
7. Arora, A., Gupta, A., Bagmar, N., Mishra, S., Bhattacharya, A.: A plant identification system using shape and morphological features on segmented leaflets: team iitk, clef 2012. In: Proceeding of CLEF 2012 Labs and Workshop, Notebook Papers (2012)
8. de Oliveira Plotze, R., Falvo, M., Pádua, J.G., Bernacci, L.C., Vieira, M.L.C., Oliveira, G.C.X., Bruno, O.M.: Leaf shape analysis using the multiscale minkowski fractal dimension, a new morphometric method: a study with passiflora (passifloraceae). Can. J. Bot. **83**(3), 287–301 (2005)

9. Zhang, X., Zhang, F.: Images features extraction of tobacco leaves. In: Congress on Image and Signal Processing, CISP 2008, vol. 2, 773–776. IEEE (2008)

10. Man, Q.K., Zheng, C.H., Wang, X.F., Lin, F.Y.: Recognition of plant leaves using support vector machine. In: Huang, D.-S., Wunsch II, D.C., Levine, D.S., Jo, F.-Y. (eds.) ICIC 2008. CCIS, vol. 15, pp. 192–199. Springer, Heidelberg (2008)

11. Kadir, A., Nugroho, L.E., Susanto, A., Santosa, P.I.: Leaf classification using shape, color, and texture features. arXiv preprint arXiv:1401.4447 (2013)

12. Choras, R.S.: Image feature extraction techniques and their applications for cbir and biometrics systems. International Journal of Biology and Biomedical Engineering 1(1), 6–16 (2007)

13. Kebapci, H., Yanikoglu, B., Unal, G.: Plant image retrieval using color, shape and texture features. The Computer Journal (2010) bxq037

14. Lin, F.Y., Zheng, C.H., Wang, X.F., Man, Q.K.: Multiple classification of plant leaves based on gabor transform and lBP operator. In: Huang, D.-S., Wunsch II, D.C., Levine, D.S., Jo, K.-H. (eds.) ICIC 2008. CCIS, vol. 15, pp. 432–439. Springer, Heildelberg (2008)

15. Ehsanirad, A.: Plant classification based on leaf recognition. International Journal of Computer Science and Information Security 8(4), 78–81 (2010)

16. Kadir, A., Nugroho, L.E., Susanto, A., Santosa, P.I.: Neural network application on foliage plant identification. arXiv preprint arXiv:1311.5829 (2013)

17. Goëau, H., Bonnet, P., Joly, A., Barthelemy, D., Boujemaa, N., Molino, J.: The imageclef 2012 plant image identification task. In: ImageCLEF 2012 Working Notes (2012)

18. Otsu, N.: A threshold selection method from gray-level histograms. Automatica 11(285–296), 23–27 (1975)

19. Werbos, P.: Beyond regression: New tools for prediction and analysis in the behavioral sciences. (1974)

20. Backes, A.R., Casanova, D., Martinez, O.B.: A complex network-based approach for boundary shape analysis. Pattern Recogn. 42, 54–67 (2009)

21. Barabási, A.L.: Linked: The new science of networks. (2002)

22. Castañón, C.A.B., Chambi, R.J.: Using complex networks for offline handwritten signature characterization. In: Bayro-Corrochano, E., Hancock, E. (eds.) CIARP 2014. LNCS, vol. 8827, pp. 580–587. Springer, Heidelberg (2014)

23. Backes, A.R., Martinez, O.: Fractal and multi-scale fractal dimension analysis: a comparative study of bouligand-minkowski method. CoRR abs/1201.3153 (2012)

24. Shih, J.-L., Chen, L.-H.: Color image retrieval based on primitives of color moments. In: Chang, S.-K., Chen, Z., Lee, S.-Y. (eds.) VISUAL 2002. LNCS, vol. 2314, p. 88. Springer, Heidelberg (2002)

25. Stricker, M.A., Orengo, M.: Similarity of color images. In: IS&T/SPIE's Symposium on Electronic Imaging: Science & Technology, International Society for Optics and Photonics, pp. 381–392 (1995)

26. Haralick, R.M., Shanmugam, K., Dinstein, I.H.: Textural features for image classification. IEEE Transactions on Systems, Man and Cybernetics 6, 610–621 (1973)

27. Gonzalez, R.C., Woods, R.E.: Digital image processing (2002)

28. Porebski, A., Vandenbroucke, N., Macaire, L.: Neighborhood and haralick feature extraction for color texture analysis. In: Conference on Colour in Graphics, Imaging, and Vision, Society for Imaging Science and Technology, vol. 2008, pp. 316–321 (2008)

29. Brilhador, A., Colonhezi, T.P., Bugatti, P.H., Lopes, F.M.: Combining texture and shape descriptors for bioimages classification: a case of study in imageCLEF dataset. In: Ruiz-Shulcloper, J., Sanniti di Baja, G. (eds.) CIARP 2013, Part I. LNCS, vol. 8258, pp. 431–438. Springer, Heidelberg (2013)

Cutting Edge Localisation in an Edge Profile Milling Head

Laura Fernández-Robles[1,2]([⊠]), George Azzopardi[1,3], Enrique Alegre[2], and Nicolai Petkov[1]

[1] Johann Bernoulli Institute for Mathematics and Computer Science, University of Groningen, Groningen, The Netherlands
l.fernandez@unileon.es, {g.azzopardi,n.petkov}@rug.nl
[2] Industrial and Informatics Engineering School, University of León, León, Spain
enrique.alegre@unileon.es
[3] Intelligent Computer Systems, University of Malta, Msida, Malta

Abstract. Wear evaluation of cutting tools is a key issue for prolonging their lifetime and ensuring high quality of products. In this paper, we present a method for the effective localisation of cutting edges of inserts in digital images of an edge profile milling head. We introduce a new image data set of 144 images of an edge milling head that contains 30 inserts. We use a circular Hough transform to detect the screws that fasten the inserts. In a cropped area around a detected screw, we use Canny's edge detection algorithm and Standard Hough Transform to localise line segments that characterise insert edges. We use this information and the geometry of the insert to identify which of these line segments is the cutting edge. The output of our algorithm is a set of quadrilateral regions around the identified cutting edges. These regions can then be used as input to other algorithms for the quality assessment of the cutting edges. Our results show that the proposed method is very effective for the localisation of the cutting edges of inserts in an edge profile milling machine.

Keywords: Edge milling · Tool wear · Cutting edge localisation · Hough transform

1 Introduction

Figure 1 shows a milling head composed of replaceable cutting tools, also called inserts, that are shown surrounded by white rectangles. In this example, each insert has four edges, but only the nearly vertical left one is a cutting edge. Machining operations cause the cutting edge to get worn or even broken and it should be eventually replaced.

The development of tool wearing monitoring (TWM) systems for the evaluation of the wear level of tool inserts in milling processes is neccesary for obtaining a high quality of the final product. According to Tite [18] cutting tool failures due to wear and breakage represent about 3-12% of the total production costs.

© Springer International Publishing Switzerland 2015
G. Azzopardi and N. Petkov (Eds.): CAIP 2015, Part II, LNCS 9257, pp. 336–347, 2015.
DOI: 10.1007/978-3-319-23117-4_29

Fig. 1. Image of an edge profile milling machine. White rectangles mark the inserts. Red line segments mark the cutting edges. All markers are provided manually.

Furthermore, 20% of non-productive time is due to tool failure, and tool wear is found to have a direct impact on the quality of surface finish and precision of the finished product [23].

There are two approaches to TWM: indirect and direct methods. Indirect techniques measure machining conditions by variables (e.g. cutting forces, vibrations, etc.) that do not require the machining process to stop. Direct methods measure tool wear at the cutting edge of the worn tool [14] when the machine is in a resting position. Indirect methods are less effective than direct ones [23] because they are affected by noisy signals [9].

Recently, image processing techniques have been used for the measurement of flank and crater wear [23]. Many works evaluate isolated inserts [5,9,11,21] and skip the challenging step of first localising the inserts and their cutting edges on the milling head. In this paper we propose a method for the effective localisation of the inserts and their cutting edges in an edge profile milling machine. For the same purpose, but for a different kind of milling tool, Zhang et al. [23] apply an edge detector using a kernel similar to that of a Sobel operator followed by a noise removal step. Then, wear edge points are extracted with sub-pixel accuracy using Gauss curve approximation. In their work, however, they study ball-end milling cutters that have only two flutes and therefore two wear edges. The application at hand consists of an edge profile milling head with 8 to 10 visible rhomboid inserts, such as the one shown in Fig. 1. Localisation of inserts varies and geometry of the milling head is more complex than in [23]. Su et al. [16], Kim et al. [10] and Pfeifer et al. [14] also localise just two cutting edges for microdrills. Other works [15,19,20] deal with face milling cutting heads, where one can set the acquisition system to easily capture images containing a single insert. After locating the inserts, some of these methods could be used to localise the cutting edge and evaluate tool wear. To the best of our knowledge there is no work that evaluates tool wear in edge milling cutting heads. Neither did we find methods that locate inserts placed on a milling head with a relatively high number of inserts per image; 8 to 10 as in the application treated below.

We consider the localisation of inserts as an object detection problem. Sun et al. [17] used an edge-based geometric template-matching process to localise a clip in assembly pieces. Widely-known invariant local features such as SIFT [12],

SURF [3], HoG [6] or CCS [8] have been used for template matching and object detection. These methods rely on a number of feature points which are extracted from the template and also from the images. Therefore, their effectiveness is affected by the matching capabilities of the extracted features [1]. Due to the fact that milling heads of the type we use in our application do not have many corners or blobs, methods based on invariant local features are not suitable.

In this paper, we use the Circular Hough Transform (CHT) method in order to detect the screws that fasten the inserts. We use the screws as reference points to delineate the inserts. Then, we localize the cutting edge by using the Standard Hough Transform (SHT) algorithm [13].

The rest of the paper is organized as follows: Section 2 describes the method. In Section 3 we present a new data set of images of an edge profile shoulder milling head containing multiple inserts and we describe the experiments that we use to demonstrate the effectiveness of our approach. Finally, we provide a discussion in Section 4 and draw conclusions in Section 5.

2 Method

We propose a methodology for the automatic detection of a region of interest (ROI) around the cutting edges of inserts that can be used to evaluate their wear state at a later stage. This post-processing step is, however, beyond the scope of our work. The localisation that we propose is done in two steps. First, we detect the screws of the inserts and use them as reference points, and then we localise the cutting edges. In order to improve the quality of the images and facilitate the detection of edges, we apply the contrast-limited adaptive histogram equalization (CLAHE) method [24]. Figure 2 shows a schema with all the steps in the proposed methodology. Below we elaborate each one of them

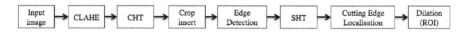

Fig. 2. Outline of the proposed methodology.

2.1 Detection of Inserts

The screw that fastens each insert has a distinctive circular shape. We use a circular Hough transform (CHT) to detect circles with radii between 20 and 40 pixels, because this is the size in which a screw appears on the images of size 1280×960 pixels. For the CHT, we use a two-stage algorithm to compute the accumulator array [2] [22]. In the bottom row of Fig. 3 we show the CHT accumulator arrays for the images in the top row. By means of experiments, we set the sensitivity parameter of the CHT accumulator array to 0.85. The range of the sensitivity parameter is [0, 1], as you increase the sensitivity factor, more

HeadTool0033.bmp   HeadTool0013.bmp   HeadTool0140.bmp

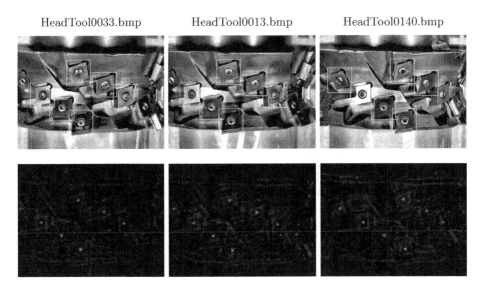

Fig. 3. Firs row: In blue, detected circles by CHT. The circles are drawn with the detected radii and positioned around coordinates that have local maximum values. In yellow, cropped areas around the centre of the detected circles that contain a whole insert. Second row: Accumulator arrays obtained with CHT on the three images in top row.

circular objects are detected. Figure 3 shows examples in which the detected circles are marked in blue. Screws that appear in the left and right peripheries of the image are usually missed due to their elliptical shape. This does not pose a problem because the same insert is seen in different positions in the previous or next images. We elaborate further on this aspect in Section 4.

We crop a rectangular area of size 210×210 pixels centred on a detected screw, the chosen dimensions are just enough to contain the whole insert. We then use this cropped area to identify the cutting edge. Figure 3 shows examples of cropped areas marked with yellow squares.

2.2 Localisation of Cutting Edges

Inserts have a rhomboid shape formed by two nearly vertical ($\pm$ 30°) and two nearly horizontal ($\pm$ 20°) line segments (Fig. 4a).

First we use Canny's method [4] to detect edges in a cropped area (Fig. 5(a-b)). Then, we apply a standard Hough transform (SHT) [7] to the edge image in order to detect lines (Fig. 4(b-d)).

We look for the strongest vertical line segment which is represented as the highest value of peaks in the Hough transform matrix. Then, we look for line segments with peak values greater than a fraction 0.75 of the maximum peak value and with slopes in a range of $\pm$ 5° with respect to the slope of the strongest nearly vertical line. In Fig. 4b we show the Hough transform of the cropped area

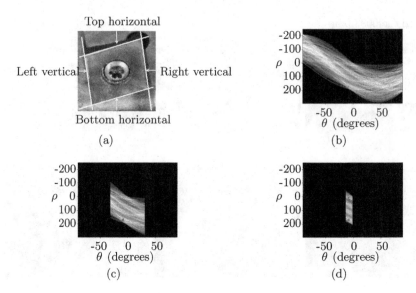

Top horizontal

Left vertical — Right vertical

Bottom horizontal

(a)

(b)

(c)

(d)

Fig. 4. (a) Automatically detected lines that form the rhomboid shape of an insert. (b) Hough transform of the image in (a). (c) Hough transform for nearly vertical lines ($\pm\ 30^o$). The black rectangle indicates the position of the largest peak ($\theta = -8^{\circ}$ and $\rho = 168$). (d) Hough transform for vertical lines with slope $(-8\pm\ 5)^o$. Black rectangles superimposed to the hough transform indicate two peaks that are greater than a fraction 0.75 of the maximum: ($\rho_1 = 7, \theta_1 = -9^{\circ}$) and ($\rho_2 = 168, \theta_2 = -8^{\circ}$).

shown in Fig. 4a. We consider the strongest nearly vertical line segment which is at least 47 pixels to the left of the center as the left edge of the insert. This detected line segment is considered as a full line and it is drawn in magenta in Fig. 5d. In this way, we avoid possible detection of lines around the screw area.

Similarly, we look for two horizontal line segments above and below the screw. In this case, the minimum distance from the line to the centre is set to 54 pixels and the range of possible slopes is $\pm\ 15^o$ with respect to the slope of the strongest horizontal line. The top and bottom detected lines are shown in yellow and cyan respectively in Fig. 5d. The points where the horizontal lines intersect with the left vertical line define the two ends of the cutting edge segment. These points are marked as dark blue dots in Fig. 5d. The localised cutting edges in these examples are shown in Fig. 5e.

If the left line segment or any of the horizontal segments are not detected, we use symmetry to determine the missing lines. For instance, if the vertical line on the left of the screw is not detected but the one on the right is detected, we reconstruct the left line by rotating by 180 degrees the left line around the center of the concerned area. The bottom three examples in Fig. 5 show this situation.

Finally, we define a ROI by dilating the detected cutting edge segment with a square structuring element of 10 pixels radius. In Fig. 6, we show the cutting edge segments and ROIs localised by the proposed method for images containing

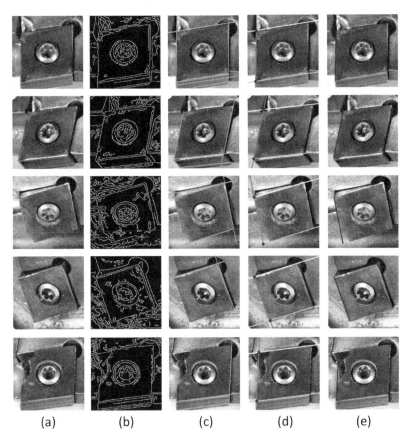

Fig. 5. (a) Cropped areas containing inserts. (b) Canny edge maps. (c) Detection of (nearly) vertical and (nearly) horizontal lines. (d) Blue spots indicate the intersections between the two horizontal lines and the left vertical line. Lines obtained by symmetry are the following. Second row: top horizontal line; third row: left vertical line; forth row: left vertical line and bottom horizontal line; fifth row: left vertical line and top horizontal line. (e) Detected cutting edges.

inserts with different wear state. Notably is the fact that the proposed method can generalise the localisation of the cutting edge even in cases of worn or broken inserts.

3   Evaluation

3.1   Data Set

To our knowledge, there are no publicly available image benchmark data sets of milling cutting heads. We created a data set that comprises 144 images of an edge profile cutting head of a milling machine which contains a total of 30

(a) HeadTool0033.bmp   (b) HeadTool0013.bmp   (c) HeadTool0140.bmp

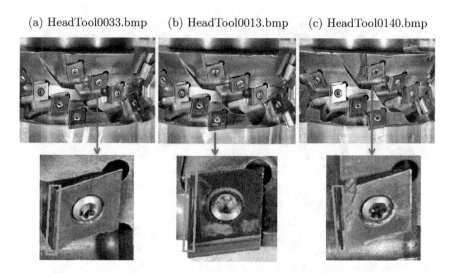

Fig. 6. The blue segments define the localized cutting edges. The green frames mark the ROI that is achieved by means of a morphological dilation. (a) Image in which cutting edges are intact. (b) Image with some worn cutting edges. (c) Image with some broken inserts.

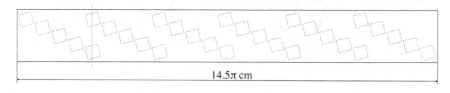

14.5π cm

Fig. 7. A diagram that represents a schema of the arrangement of inserts on a cylindrical milling head depicted developed as a rectangle. Squares represent the inserts. The vertical dashed line shows the alignment between adjacent groups of inserts.

cutting inserts. Fig. 7 illustrates the arrangement of the inserts on the surface of the cutting head. They are organized in six groups of five inserts each, with the bottom insert of one group vertically aligned with the top insert of the next group. A group of five inserts are linearly aligned at an orientation of 15°. For each group of five inserts, we systematically rotate the head in intervals of 15° while keeping the camera in a fixed position and take one picture at a time. This procedure is repeated for six sets of inserts and results in $(6 \times 24 =)$ 144 images.

The images were taken with a monochrome camera Genie M1280 1/3″ with active resolution of 1280×960 pixels. We used AZURE-2514MM fixed lens with 25 mm focal length and resolution of 2 mega-pixel. We also used two compact bar shape structures with high intensity LED arrays BDBL-R(IR)82/16H in order to intensify the lighting on the cutting edges.

| HeadTool0033.bmp | HeadTool0013.bmp | HeadTool0140.bmp |

Fig. 8. The red lines indicate the manually marked ground truth of cutting edges.

| HeadTool0001.bmp | HeadTool0002.bmp | HeadTool0003.bmp |

Fig. 9. The numbers indicate the ground truth labels of each cutting edge along three consecutive images of the data set. Consecutive images are taken by rotating the milling head by 15°. A cutting edge present in different images is labelled with the same number.

The data set of 144 images that we introduce is accompanied by the ground truth masks of all cutting edges, and is available online[1]. Figure 8 shows examples of ground truth cutting edges for the same images as in other examples.

The same insert is seen in different poses along several images of the data set because each image is taken after rotating the head tool 15^{0}. We are interested in localisating all the cutting edges of the data set at least once. For this purpose, we labelled the cutting edges with a number that is the same for the same cutting edges seen in different images. An example of this labelling along three images is shown in Fig. 9.

3.2   Experiments and Results

For each of the input images, we determine a set of ROIs around the identified cutting edges using the method described in Section 2. If the ground truth of a cutting edge lies completely in a ROI, we count that ROI as a hit and when it does not lie within any of the determined ROIs, the hit score is 0. If the ground

---

[1] http://pitia.unileon.es/varp/node/395

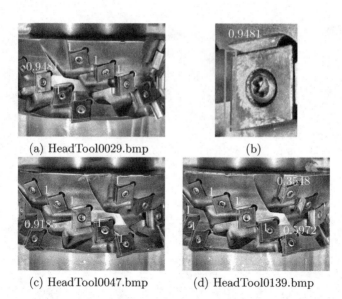

(a) HeadTool0029.bmp   (b)

(c) HeadTool0047.bmp   (d) HeadTool0139.bmp

Fig. 10. The green quadrilaterals are the ROIs detected by the proposed method and the red lines represent the ground truth for the cutting edges. The accuracy scores of the inserts are indicated in white font. (b) Example of a cutting edge that is not completely contained within the detected ROI. The accuracy of 0.9481 is the fraction of pixels of the cutting edge that lie within the detected ROI.

truth overlaps a ROI, the hit score is equal to the fraction of the ground truth segment that lies inside a ROI. Some examples can be observed in Fig. 10.

Every insert is detected in at least one of the 144 images. Moreover, whenever an insert is detected, the corresponding cutting edge on the left side is also always determined. We measure the accuracy of the method as an average of the partial scores for the individual cutting edges. Using this protocol, we obtain an accuracy measure of 98.84%.

Results can be improved by increasing the width of the structuring element in the final dilation stage. With a square structuring element of radius 34 pixels we achieve 100% accuracy. Figure 11 shows examples of the resulting ROIs.

4   Discussion

The contributions of this work are two-fold. First, we introduce a new data set of 144 images of a rotating edge milling cutting head that contains 30 inserts. It contains the ground truth information about the locations of the cutting edges. The data set is publicly available. Second, to the best of our knowledge the proposed approach is the first one automatically localises multiple inserts and cutting edges in an edge profile milling head.

Parameters have been computed in order that they can generalise for every insert at any position in the milling head tool given the geometry and features

HeadTool0029.bmp   HeadTool0047.bmp   HeadTool0139.bmp

Fig. 11. Red line segments define the ground truth and green quadrilaterals define the detected ROIs with a morphological dilation operation of 34 pixel radius square structuring element.

of the system. For a specific head tool, parameters can be easily estimated and then no further need of adjustment is needed if the system is not modified.

The milling process evaluated does not use oils or lubricants. The inserts on the data set are directly taken from real milling processes with the same type of milling head tool. So no extra dirtiness is found under existing conditions and defects of the inserts are a fair representation of the on-line situation.

We achieve an accuracy of 98.84% for the detection of cutting edges. This is achieved by dilating the automatically detected line using a square structuring elements of 20 pixel side. When the quadrilateral is 68 pixels wide, the accuracy reaches 100%.

In future works, the ROIs defined around the detected cutting edges can be used for further evaluation of the wear state of the cutting edges.

Furthermore, the proposed method can be used for different milling heads containing polygonal inserts fastened by screws, a design which is typical in edge milling machines. We implemented the proposed approach in Matlab and ran all experiments on a personal computer with a 2 GHz processor and 8 GB RAM. It takes less than 1.5 seconds to process all the steps on one image it takes about 1 minute to capture and process the 24 images taken to the head tool. This milling head tools are resting between 5 to 30 minutes, so the implementation reaches real time performing.

5   Conclusions

The approach that we propose for the localization of cutting edges in milling machines is highly effective and efficient. Its output is a set of regions surrounding cutting edges, which can be used as input to other methods that perform quality assessment of the edges.

Acknowledgments. This work has been supported by DPI2012-36166 grant from the Spanish Government.

References

1. Amiri, M., Rabiee, H.: A novel rotation/scale invariant template matching algorithm using weighted adaptive lifting scheme transform. Pattern Recognition 43(7), 2485–2496 (2010)
2. Atherton, T., Kerbyson, D.: Size invariant circle detection. Image and Vision Computing 17(11), 795–803 (1999)
3. Bay, H., Ess, A., Tuytelaars, T., Gool, L.V.: Speeded-up robust features (surf). Computer Vision and Image Understanding 110(3), 346–359 (2008). Similarity Matching in Computer Vision and Multimedia
4. Canny, J.: A computational approach to edge detection. IEEE Transactions on Pattern Analysis and Machine Intelligence(PAMI) 8(6), 679–698 (1986)
5. Castejón, M., Alegre, E., Barreiro, J., Hernández, L.: On-line tool wear monitoring using geometric descriptors from digital images. International Journal of Machine Tools and Manufacture 47(12–13), 1847–1853 (2007)
6. Dalal, N., Triggs, B.: Histograms of oriented gradients for human detection. In: IEEE Computer Society Conference on Computer Vision and Pattern Recognition, CVPR 2005, vol. 1, pp. 886–893, June 2005
7. Hough, P.: Method and Means for Recognizing Complex Patterns. U.S. Patent 3.069.654, December 1962
8. Jacobson, N., Nguyen, T., Crosby, R.: Curvature scale space application to distorted object recognition and classification. In: Conference Record of the Forty-First Asilomar Conference on Signals, Systems and Computers, ACSSC 2007, pp. 2110–2114, November 2007)
9. Jurkovic, J., Korosec, M., Kopac, J.: New approach in tool wear measuring technique using ccd vision system. International Journal of Machine Tools and Manufacture 45(9), 1023–1030 (2005)
10. Kim, J.H., Moon, D.K., Lee, D.W., Kim, J.S., Kang, M.C., Kim, K.H.: Tool wear measuring technique on the machine using ccd and exclusive jig. Journal of Materials Processing Technology 130–131, 668–674 (2002)
11. Lim, T., Ratnam, M.: Edge detection and measurement of nose radii of cutting tool inserts from scanned 2-d images. Optics and Lasers in Engineering 50(11), 1628–1642 (2012)
12. Lowe, D.: Distinctive image features from scale-invariant keypoints. International Journal of Computer Vision 60(2), 91–110 (2004)
13. Mukhopadhyay, P., Chaudhuri, B.B.: A survey of hough transform. Pattern Recognition 48(3), 993–1010 (2015)
14. Pfeifer, T., Wiegers, L.: Reliable tool wear monitoring by optimized image and illumination control in machine vision. Measurement 28(3), 209–218 (2000)
15. Sortino, M.: Application of statistical filtering for optical detection of tool wear. International Journal of Machine Tools and Manufacture 43(5), 493–497 (2003)
16. Su, J., Huang, C., Tarng, Y.: An automated flank wear measurement of microdrills using machine vision. Journal of Materials Processing Technology 180(1–3), 328–335 (2006)
17. Sun, J., Sun, Q., Surgenor, B.: An adaptable automated visual inspection scheme through online learning. The International Journal of Advanced Manufacturing Technology 59(5–8), 655–667 (2012)
18. Teti, R.: Machining of composite materials. CIRP Annals - Manufacturing Technology 51(2), 611–634 (2002)

19. Wang, W., Hong, G., Wong, Y.: Flank wear measurement by a threshold independent method with sub-pixel accuracy. International Journal of Machine Tools and Manufacture **46**(2), 199–207 (2006)
20. Weis, W.: Tool wear measurement on basis of optical sensors, vision systems and neuronal networks (application milling). In: Conference Record WESCON 1993, pp. 134–138, September 1993
21. Xiong, G., Liu, J., Avila, A.: Cutting tool wear measurement by using active contour model based image processing. In: 2011 International Conference on Mechatronics and Automation (ICMA), pp. 670–675, Auguest 2011
22. Yuen, H.K., Princen, J., Illingworth, J., Kittler, J.: A comparative study of hough transform methods for circle finding. In: Proc. 5th Alvey Vision Conf., Reading, pp. 169–174, August 1989
23. Zhang, C., Zhang, J.: On-line tool wear measurement for ball-end milling cutter based on machine vision. Computers in Industry **64**(6), 708–719 (2013)
24. Zuiderveld, K.: Graphics gems chap. iv. Contrast Limited Adaptive Histogram Equalization, pp. 474–485. Academic Press Professional Inc, San Diego, CA, USA (1994)

Recognition of Architectural and Electrical Symbols by COSFIRE Filters with Inhibition

Jiapan Guo[1], Chenyu Shi[1(✉)], George Azzopardi[1,2], and Nicolai Petkov[1]

[1] Johann Bernoulli Institute for Mathematics and Computer Science, University of Groningen, Groningen, The Netherlands
{j.guo,c.shi,g.azzopardi,n.petkov}@rug.nl
[2] Intelligent Computer Systems, University of Malta, Msida, Malta

Abstract. The automatic recognition of symbols can be used to automatically convert scanned drawings into digital representations compatible with computer aided design software. We propose a novel approach to automatically recognize architectural and electrical symbols. The proposed method extends the existing trainable COSFIRE approach by adding an inhibition mechanism that is inspired by shape-selective TEO neurons in visual cortex. A COSFIRE filter with inhibition takes as input excitatory and inhibitory responses from line and edge detectors. The type (excitatory or inhibitory) and the spatial arrangement of low level features are determined in an automatic configuration step that analyzes two types of prototype pattern called positive and negative. Excitatory features are extracted from a positive pattern and inhibitory features are extracted from one or more negative patterns. In our experiments we use four subsets of images with different noise levels from the Graphics Recognition data set (GREC 2011) and demonstrate that the inhibition mechanism that we introduce improves the effectiveness of recognition substantially.

Keywords: COSFIRE · Trainable filters · Architectural and electrical symbols · Shape · Inhibition · Brain-inspired · Visual cortex

1 Introduction

The recognition of symbols in sketches or scanned documents facilitates the automatic conversion to digital representations that can be processed by computer aided design software. Examples of applications are the recognition of architectural and electrical symbols, optical music notes, document analysis, logo and mathematical expressions [13–15,18]. In such applications, it is common to find that a symbol is contained within another symbol that has a different meaning. Fig. 1 shows four patterns presented in the top images that are contained in the corresponding bottom images. The addition of extra strokes can radically change the meaning of a symbol.

Existing symbol recognition algorithms can be categorized into statistical and structural-based approaches. The former methods extract hand-crafted features from symbols and use them to form feature vectors and train classification

© Springer International Publishing Switzerland 2015
G. Azzopardi and N. Petkov (Eds.): CAIP 2015, Part II, LNCS 9257, pp. 348–358, 2015.
DOI: 10.1007/978-3-319-23117-4_30

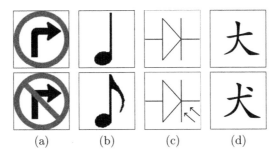

Fig. 1. Examples of pairs of symbols with different meanings. (a) Two traffic signs which give opposite instructions: permission and prohibition of turning right. (b) Two music notes: quarter and eighth. (c) Two electrical symbols: a normal and a light-emitting diode. (d) Two Chinese characters that are translated as "big" and "dog".

models [19]. While such methods may be effective, they require large numbers of training examples. Moreover, the selection of features is specific to the application at hand and typically requires domain knowledge. The structural-based approaches, which usually describe symbols by the geometrical relation between their constituent parts [9], are not suitable to distinguish symbols with similar shapes [17].

In this paper, we use inspiration from the function of shape-selective neurons in area TEO in visual cortex to develop an inhibitory mechanism that we add to the COSFIRE filters introduced in [3]. By means of single cell recordings on macaque monkeys, Connor et al. [4] discovered that such a neuron responds strongly for a certain arrangement of curvatures (Fig. 2a), but its response is suppressed by the presence of a specific curvature element (Fig. 2b). The effectiveness of COSFIRE filters have already been shown in various applications including detection of vascular bifurcations in retinal images [2], classification of handwritten digits [1] and localization and recognition of traffic signs [3]. A COSFIRE filter, as published in [3], can be configured to be selective for one of the symbols in the top row of Fig. 1. It will, however, also respond to the symbol underneath it, and thus it is not suitable to distinguish between such patterns.

The response of a COSFIRE filter with inhibition that we propose is computed by subtracting a fraction of the combined responses of inhibitory part detectors from the combined responses of excitatory part detectors. The excitatory and inhibitory parts together with their spatial arrangement are determined in an automatic configuration procedure. A strong response by a COSFIRE filter indicates that the input pattern is similar to the positive prototype used to configure that filter.

The rest of the paper is organized as follows. In Section 2 we explain how a COSFIRE with inhibition is configured and applied. In Section 3 we describe our experiments on four subsets of images from the Graphics Recognition (GREC 2011) data set [16]. We provide a discussion in Section 4 and draw conclusions in Section 5.

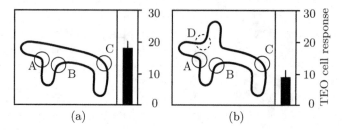

Fig. 2. Selectivity of a shape-selective neuron in posterior inferotemporal cortex [4]. (a) The contour segments marked with solid circles indicate curvatures that evoke excitation of the concerned cell, while (b) the segment marked with a dashed circle indicates a curvature that inhibits the activation of the cell. The bars specify the strength of the response.

2   Method

Let us consider the two symbols shown in Fig. 3a and Fig. 3b, which we refer to as a positive and a negative prototype, respectively. The configuration procedure, that we explain below, automatically determines the excitatory and inhibitory parts, and results in a filter which is able to respond selectively only to patterns similar to Fig. 3a and not to Fig. 3b.

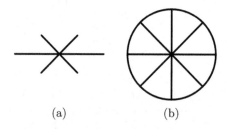

(a)   (b)

Fig. 3. Example of (a) a symbol that is contained within (b) another one. We use the former pattern as a positive example and the latter one as a negative example.

2.1   Configuration of a COSFIRE Filter with Inhibition

First, we use the publicly available implementation[1] to configure two COSFIRE filters of the type proposed in [3], one to be selective for the positive pattern in Fig. 3a and the other for the negative pattern in Fig. 3b. Such a filter uses a representation of the line segments and their mutual geometrical arrangement. A line segment i is described by the preferred scale λ_i and preferred orientation θ_i of a symmetric Gabor filter together with the polar coordinates (ρ_i, ϕ_i) of the position of the segment with respect to the center of the concerned COSFIRE filter. We denote by $P_f = \{(\lambda_i, \theta_i, \rho_i, \phi_i) \mid i \in 1 \ldots n_1\}$ and

---

[1] Matlab scripts: http://mathworks.com/matlabcentral/fileexchange/37395

$N_f = \{(\lambda_j, \theta_j, \rho_j, \phi_j) \mid j \in 1 \ldots n_2\}$ the configured COSFIRE filters for the positive and negative prototypes, respectively. The parameters n_1 and n_2 denote the number of tuples in the corresponding sets. Fig. 4a and Fig. 4b show the structures of the resulting two COSFIRE filters. For more technical details about the Gabor filters and the COSFIRE configuration method, we refer the reader to [3,5–8,10–12] and to an online implementation[2]. We only mention that the configuration of a COSFIRE filter takes as input three parameters, a set of wavelengths λ and a set of orientations θ that characterize a bank of Gabor filters, together with a set of radius values ρ that represent a number of concentric circles around the center of the filter along which the Gabor filter responses are considered. Fig. 4 illustrates the structure of the COSFIRE filter with inhibition that is configured by the positive and negative images in Fig. 3. The configuration uses $\lambda \in \{18, 36\}$, $\theta \in \{\frac{\pi i}{8} \mid i = 0\ldots7\}$ and $\rho \in \{0, 40, \ldots, 200\}$.

Second, we form a new set S_f by taking tuples from the two sets P_f and N_f and marking them with tags that represent the type of contribution (i.e. excitatory or inhibitory). We include all the tuples in P_f into the set S_f and mark them with a tag $\delta = +1$ to indicate that the involved Gabor responses provide excitatory input to the resulting filter. Then we compute the minimum distance $d(N_f^j, P_f)$ between the spatial coordinates of one tuple from N_f and the spatial coordinates of all the tuples from P_f:

$$d(N_f^j, P_f) = \min_{i \in \{1, \ldots, |P_f|\}} \left\{ \sqrt{(\rho_i \cos \phi_i - \rho_j \cos \phi_j)^2 + (\rho_i \sin \phi_i - \rho_j \sin \phi_j)^2} \right\}$$

If this distance $d(N_f^j, P_f)$ is larger than a threshold ζ, we conclude that the tuple N_f^j is sufficiently different from the tuples in P_f and we include the tuple N_f^j into the new set S_f and mark it with a tag $\delta = -1$ indicating that the corresponding Gabor response provides inhibitory input. We repeat this procedure for each tuple in set N_f. In this way we obtain a new set $S_f = \{(\lambda_k, \theta_k, \rho_k, \phi_k, \delta_k) \mid k \in 1 \ldots n_3\}$ of labeled excitatory and inhibitory tuples. The parameter n_3 denotes the number of tuples in set S_f. In Section 3, we provide the value of the parameter ζ that we use in our experiments. With this procedure we ensure that a line segment that is present in both the positive and negative prototypes in roughly the same positions is considered to give excitatory input. On the other hand, a line segment that is only present in the negative prototype is considered to give inhibitory input.

Fig. 4c shows the structure of the resulting COSFIRE filter with inhibition. The white ellipses indicate the line segments that provide excitatory input and the black ellipses indicate the ones that provide inhibitory input.

In order to extract as much detail as possible from a given prototype symbol, in our experiments we use a large set of radii values ($\rho = \{i \mid i = 0, 1, \ldots, 362\})^3$. Subsequently, we remove any redundant tuples from the resulting filter by computing the distances between the spatial coordinates of all pairs of tuples. For

---

[2] http://matlabserver.cs.rug.nl
[3] The maximum ρ value 362 is the largest diagonal distance with respect to the center of the image.

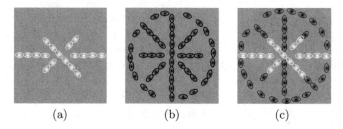

(a)   (b)   (c)

Fig. 4. (a-b) The structures of COSFIRE filters configured with the positive and negative prototype in Fig. 3a and Fig. 3b, respectively. (c) The structure of the resulting filter with inhibition. The ellipses illustrate the wavelengths and orientations of the selected Gabor filters and their positions indicate the locations at which their responses are used as input to the concerned COSFIRE filter. The blobs within the ellipses represent blurring functions that are used to provide some tolerance regarding the preferred positions. White and black ellipses and blobs indicate Gabor responses that provide respectively positive and negative inputs to the COSFIRE filter with inhibition.

any pair that has a distance lower than 12 pixels we delete one of the tuples randomly.

This configuration procedure is also applicable when multiple negative examples are used. In that case we have one COSFIRE filter P_f selective for the positive prototype and a number of COSFIRE filters $(N_{f_1}, N_{f_2}, \dots)$ selective for the negative prototypes. Then we apply the above procedure to determine the inhibitory tuples from each of the N_{f_i} sets. Each set of inhibitory tuples has a unique tag. For instance, the inhibitory tuples determined from the set N_{f_1} are assigned a tag $\delta = -1$, the inhibitory tuples determined from the set N_{f_2} are assigned the tag $\delta = -2$, and so forth.

2.2   Response of a COSFIRE Filter with Inhibition

The response of a COSFIRE filter with inhibition is computed as follows. First we compute the weighted geometric mean as defined in [3] for each group of tuples that share the same tag value. The intermediate representation defined by a tuple $(\lambda_i, \theta_i, \rho_i, \phi_i, \delta_i)$ is computed by blurring the response map obtained by a Gabor filter (with parameter values λ_i and θ_i) with a Gaussian function[4]. The blurred response is then shifted by ρ_i pixels in the direction opposite to ϕ_i. In this way, all the Gabor responses described by different tuples meet at the same location. We denote by $r_{S_f^+}(x, y)$ the output of the group of excitatory tuples with tag $\delta = +1$. Similarly, we denote by $r_{S_f^{-1}}(x, y)$ the output of the group of inhibitory tuples with tag $\delta = -1$.

Finally, we denote by $r_{S_f}(x, y)$ the filter response, which we compute by subtracting a factor of the maximum response of all groups of inhibitory tuples

---

[4] For the blurring function we use a fixed standard deviation of 4, which we found empirically.

from the response of the group of excitatory tuples:

$$r_{S_f}(x, y) \stackrel{\text{def}}{=} |r_{S_f^+}(x, y) - \eta \max_{j=1}^{n}\{r_{S_f^{-j}}(x, y)\}|_{t_3} \qquad (1)$$

where $S_f^+ = \{(\lambda_i, \theta_i, \rho_i, \phi_i) \mid \forall \ (\lambda_i, \theta_i, \rho_i, \phi_i, \delta_i) \in S_f, \delta_i = +1\}$,
$S_f^{-j} = \{(\lambda_i, \theta_i, \rho_i, \phi_i) \mid \forall \ (\lambda_i, \theta_i, \rho_i, \phi_i, \delta_i) \in S_f, \delta_i = -j\}$, $n = \max |\delta_i|$, η is a coefficient that we call inhibition factor and $|.|_{t_3}$ represents the thresholding operation of the response at a fraction t_3 of its maximum across all image coordinates (x, y).

2.3   Tolerance to Geometric Transformations

The proposed COSFIRE filters with inhibition can achieve tolerance to scale, rotation and reflection by similar manipulation of parameters as proposed for the original COSFIRE filters [3]. We do not elaborate on these aspects here as we do not use them in our experiments. We refer the reader to [3] for a thorough explanation.

3   Experiments

3.1   Data Sets

We use the GREC 2011 data set [16] that contains 150 model architectural and electrical symbols, and three data sets (called NoiseA, NoiseB and NoiseE) of images with different levels of degradation. In each of the three noisy data sets, there are 25 degraded images for every symbol class.

   We configure 150 COSFIRE filters to be selective for the 150 models. Subsequently, we apply each resulting filter to the remaining 149 symbols that have different meaning than the symbol used for its configuration. It turns out that 26 COSFIRE filters give strong responses also to non-preferred symbols. In our experiments we only use test images that come from the 26 problematic symbol classes, Fig. 5. In practice, we form three subsets of test images, namely sub-NoiseA, sub-NoiseB and sub-NoiseE of $(25 \times 26 =)$ 650 images each. The model symbol images are of size 512×512 pixels, while the noisy images in the subsets are of size 256×256 pixels. The lines in the ideal models have a thickness of 9 or 18 pixels.

   Fig. 6a shows a model symbol and Fig. 6(c-d) show three symbols of the same class from the subsets sub-NoiseA, sub-NoiseB and sub-NoiseE, respectively.

3.2   Pre-processing

We resize by a factor of 2 the degraded images in the sets sub-NoiseA, sub-NoiseB and sub-NoiseE in order to bring them to the same size of the model images. For the images in sub-NoiseA and sub-NoiseB we apply some morphological operations, which we explain below, so that the thickness of their lines becomes

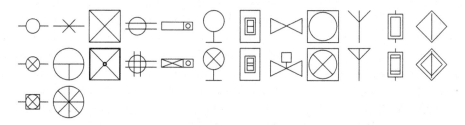

Fig. 5. A set of 26 symbols from the GREC 2011 data set. [16]. The symbol in the top left corner is contained within the symbol below it, which in turn is contained within the symbol in the bottom left corner. The top two symbols in the second column are both contained within the symbol in the third row of same column. The symbols in the first row of the remaining columns are contained within the corresponding symbols of the second row.

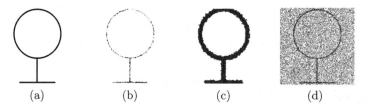

(a)   (b)   (c)   (d)

Fig. 6. Examples from the GREC 2011 data set [16]. (a) A model symbol image. (b-d) Degraded symbols of the same class from the data sets of noisy images; (a) sub-NoiseA, (b) sub-NoiseB and (c) sub-NoiseE.

similar to those of the model symbols. Since the images in sub-NoiseE have roughly the preferred line thicknesses, we do not apply any pre-processing.

For the images in sub-NoiseA, we first dilate them by six line-shaped structuring elements of 6 pixel length with different orientations ($\{0, \frac{\pi}{6}, \frac{\pi}{3}, \ldots, \frac{5\pi}{6}\}$). After that, we take the maximum value in every location across these six dilation maps. Then we perform a thinning operation followed by six dilations using line-shaped structuring elements of 4 pixel length with equidistant orientations. The final preprocessed image is obtained by taking the maximum value in every pixel location among the resulting dilation maps.

For the images in sub-NoiseB, we perform opening and thinning followed by a dilation operation using a series of line-shaped structuring elements of 4 pixels length in six orientations. Finally, we superimpose these six dilation maps by taking the maximum value in each location.

Fig. 7a and Fig. 7b show the preprocessed images corresponding to the noisy images in Fig. 6b and Fig. 6c.

3.3   Implementation

We configure 26 COSFIRE filters with inhibition to be exclusively selective for the 26 model symbols. For the configuration we apply the following approach. We configure a COSFIRE filter without inhibition for a given model symbol,

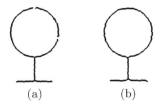

Fig. 7. Examples of the preprocessed images. (a) The improved image of Fig. 6b in sub-NoiseA and (b) the preprocessed image of Fig. 6c in sub-NoiseB.

apply the resulting filter to the remaining 25 model symbols and threshold the maximum values of each response map at a given threshold ε. The value of the threshold parameter ε is a fraction of the maximum response that the filter achieves when it is applied to its preferred model symbol. The symbol images that evoke responses greater than $(\varepsilon =) 0.3$ are considered as negative prototype patterns. Then we use these automatically selected negative patterns to determine the inhibitory line segments and configure a COSFIRE filter with inhibition ($\zeta = 12$ pixels) that is exclusively selective for patterns similar to the positive prototype symbol (of size 512×512 pixels). We perform this procedure for each of the 26 symbols.

Next, we apply the 26 filters with inhibition to each model symbol by using the method in Section 2.3. We investigate the inhibition factor by systematically varying the value of parameter η between 0 and 3 in intervals of 0.2. For $\eta = 1.4$ the filters give responses only to the preferred positive prototype patterns.

Then we apply these 26 inhibition-based COSFIRE filters with $\eta = 1.4$ to the preprocessed images in sets sub-NoiseA and sub-NoiseB and to the non preprocessed images of sub-NoiseE.

3.4 Evaluation and Results

In the first experiment we only use the 26 model images. Fig. 8 shows a comparison between the results obtained by the COSFIRE filters in their basic form and COSFIRE filters with the proposed inhibition mechanism. The results are shown in the form of a confusion matrix where the value at location (i, j) is the maximum response of the filter S_{f_i} (that was configured by model i) to a model image j. Fig. 8a shows the results of the COSFIRE filters without inhibition, the matrix of which is less sparse than that in Fig. 8b that is achieved by COSFIRE filters with inhibition. The off-diagonal non-zero elements in the left panel indicate that the corresponding COSFIRE filters without inhibition respond to more than one symbol. The absence of such elements in the right pannel means that each of the COSFIRE filters with inhibition responds only to one symbol, the positive pattern with which it was configured.

A given image is classified to the class of the positive prototype symbol by which the inhibition-based COSFIRE filter that achieves the maximum response

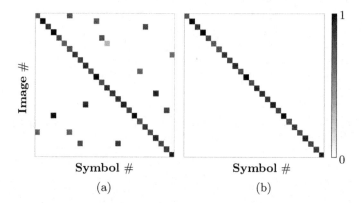

Fig. 8. Results of COSFIRE filters (a) without and (b) with inhibition. The matrices are of size 26×26; the columns represent model images and the rows represent configured COSFIRE filters. The elements of the matrices are the maximum responses of the filters to the 26 images.

was configured. The proposed inhibition-based approach achieves 100% accuracy while the one without inhibition achieves 97.78% accuracy.

In Table. 1 we report the results that we achieve for the three noisy subsets of test images.

Table 1. Accuracy (%) on three sub sets of ($26 \times 25 =$) 650 noisy images each taken from the GREC data set [16]

	sub-NoiseA	sub-NoiseB	sub-NoiseE	Average
Inhibition-based COSFIRE	99.85	99.35	99.92	99.71
Original COSFIRE	97.83	97.46	91.51	95.60

4   Discussion

We propose an inhibition mechanism to the COSFIRE filters in order to increase their discrimination ability. The inhibition mechanism involves the determination of line segments from training examples whose presence is used to suppress the response of the filter. This was inspired by the functionality of shape-selective TEO neurons in visual cortex. The firing rate of such a neuron can be suppressed by certain contour parts in specific positions within its receptive field [4].

The way we perform classification follows what is known as the grandmother cell hypothesis in neuroscience, in that the label of an input image is determined from one filter, the one that gives the strongest response. As already shown in [3], COSFIRE filters can be used in what is known as population coding in neuroscience, whereby a feature vector is formed by their maximum responses to an input image. In this technique COSFIRE filters are configured with small parts of patterns of interest and it is suitable for applications where the involved patterns are more deformable, such as handwritten digits [1]. In future work we aim to investigate the effectiveness of feature vectors formed by the responses of the proposed COSFIRE filters with inhibition in classification tasks. Our speculation is that the resulting sparser vectors will improve the discriminating power. In principle, sparseness is a desirable feature as it increases storage capacity and allows the discrimination of more patterns.

Besides the recognition of architectural and electrical symbols the proposed methodology can be considered as a general framework for the classification of any sketched symbols. It first configures a number of COSFIRE filters, then it learns inhibitory input for each filter. At application stage it applies them simultaneously to a test image and classifies the image with the label of the filter that achieves the maximum response.

5   Conclusions

The proposed COSFIRE filters with inhibition mechanism are highly effective. In our experiments on architectural and electrical symbols we demonstrated that COSFIRE filters with inhibition improve the classification performance significantly on symbol classes that are contained within other classes. We achieve a recognition rate of 100% for the subset of 26 models and an average rate of 99.71% for the three subsets of noisy images.

References

1. Azzopardi, G., Petkov, N.: A shape descriptor based on trainable COSFIRE filters for the recognition of handwritten digits. In: Wilson, R., Hancock, E., Bors, A., Smith, W. (eds.) CAIP 2013, Part II. LNCS, vol. 8048, pp. 9–16. Springer, Heidelberg (2013)
2. Azzopardi, G., Petkov, N.: Automatic detection of vascular bifurcations in segmented retinal images using trainable COSFIRE filters. Pattern Recognition Letters **34**, 922–933 (2013)
3. Azzopardi, G., Petkov, N.: Trainable COSFIRE Filters for Keypoint Detection and Pattern Recognition. IEEE Transactions on Pattern Analysis and Machine Intelligence **35**(2), 490–503 (2013)
4. Brincat, S., Connor, C.: Underlying principles of visual shape selectivity in posterior inferotemporal cortex. Nature Neuroscience **7**(8), 880–886 (2004)
5. Grigorescu, C., Petkov, N., Westenberg, M.: Contour detection based on non-classical receptive field inhibition. IEEE Transactions on Image Processing **12**(7), 729–739 (2003)
6. Grigorescu, C., Petkov, N., Westenberg, M.: The Role of Non-CRF Inhibition in Contour Detection. Journal of Computer Graphics, Visualization, and Computer Vision (WSCG) **11**(2), 197–204 (2003)
7. Grigorescu, S., Petkov, N., Kruizinga, P.: Comparison of texture features based on Gabor filters. IEEE Transactions on Image Processing **11**(10), 1160–1167 (2002)

8. Kruizinga, P., Petkov, N.: Non-linear operator for oriented texture. IEEE Transactions on Image Processing **8**(10), 1395–1407 (1999)
9. Lin, Y., Wenyin, L., Jiang, C.: A structural approach to recognizing incomplete graphic objects. In: Proceedings of the 17th International Conference on Pattern Recognition, ICPR 2004, vol. 1, pp. 371–375, August 2004
10. Petkov, N.: Biologically motivated computationally intensive approaches to image pattern-recognition. Future Generation Computer Systems **11**(4–5), 451–465 (1995). 1994 Europe Conference on High Performance Computing and Networking (HPCN Europe 94), Munich, Germany, 1994
11. Petkov, N., Kruizinga, P.: Computational models of visual neurons specialised in the detection of periodic and aperiodic oriented visual stimuli: Bar and grating cells. Biological Cybernetics **76**(2), 83–96 (1997)
12. Petkov, N., Westenberg, M.: Suppression of contour perception by band-limited noise and its relation to non-classical receptive field inhibition. Biological Cybernetics **88**(10), 236–246 (2003)
13. Rebelo, A., Fujinaga, I., Paszkiewicz, F., Maral, A.R.S., Guedes, C., Cardoso, J.S.: Optical music recognition: state-of-the-art and open issues. IJMIR **1**(3), 173–190 (2012)
14. Tang, P., Hui, S.C., Fu, C.W.: Online chemical symbol recognition for handwritten chemical expression recognition. In: ICIS, pp. 535–540. IEEE (2013)
15. Valveny, E., Dosch, P., Winstanley, A., Zhou, Y., Yang, S., Yan, L., Wenyin, L., Elliman, D., Delalandre, M., Trupin, E., Adam, S., Ogier, J.M.: A General Framework for the Evaluation of Symbol Recognition Methods. Int. J. Doc. Anal. Recognit. **9**(1), 59–74 (2007)
16. Valveny, E., Delalandre, M., Raveaux, R., Lamiroy, B.: Report on the symbol recognition and spotting contest. In: Kwon, Y.-B., Ogier, J.-M. (eds.) GREC 2011. LNCS, vol. 7423, pp. 198–207. Springer, Heidelberg (2013)
17. Yajie, Y., Zhang, W., Wenyin, L.: A new syntactic approach to graphic symbol recognition. In: Ninth International Conference on Document Analysis and Recognition, ICDAR 2007, vol. 1, pp. 516–520, September 2007
18. Zanibbi, R., Blostein, D., Cordy, J.R.: Recognizing Mathematical Expressions Using Tree Transformation. IEEE Transactions on Pattern Analysis and Machine Intelligence **24**(11), 1455–1467 (2002)
19. Zhang, W., Wenyin, L., Zhang, K.: Symbol Recognition with Kernel Density Matching. IEEE Transactions on Pattern Analysis and Machine Intelligence **28**(12), 2020–2024 (2006)

Improving Cross-Domain Concept Detection via Object-Based Features

Markus Mühling[1]($\boxtimes$), Ralph Ewerth[2], and Bernd Freisleben[1]

[1] Department of Mathematics and Computer Science, University of Marburg,
Hans-Meerwein-Str. 6, 35032 Marburg, Germany
{muehling,freisleb}@informatik.uni-marburg.de
[2] Department of Electrical Engineering and Information Technology,
Jena University of Applied Sciences, Carl-Zeiss-Promenade 2, 07745 Jena, Germany
ralph.ewerth@fh-jena.de

Abstract. Learned visual concept models often do not work well for other domains not considered during training, because a concept's visual appearance strongly depends on the domain of the corresponding image or video source. In this paper, a novel approach to improve cross-domain concept detection is presented. The proposed approach uses features based on object detection results in addition to Bag-of-Visual-Words features as inputs to concept classifiers. Experiments conducted on TRECVid videos using a high-performance computing cluster show that the additional use of object-based features significantly improves the generalization properties of the learned concept models in cross-domain settings, for example, from broadcast news videos to documentary films and vice versa.

1 Introduction

Content-based search in multimedia databases becomes more and more important due to the rapidly increasing proliferation of digital images and videos. The fundamental problem of content-based search is to overcome the discrepancy between the extracted features and the human interpretation of the (audio-)visual data. In the literature, this discrepancy is known as the "semantic gap" [14]. State-of-the-art approaches in the field of image and video retrieval focus on semantic concepts serving as an intermediate description to bridge the "semantic gap" between data representation and human interpretation. Given a semantic index, search queries on large-scale multimedia databases can be processed very efficiently. Hauptmann et al. [5] stated that approximately 5,000 concepts, detected with a minimum accuracy of 10% mean average precision, are sufficient to provide search results comparable to text retrieval in the World Wide Web.

The detection of arbitrary concepts is a challenging task due to the large complexity and high variability in the appearance of visual concepts. In particular, the generalization properties of learned visual concept models applied to foreign target domains are often poor, because in some cases the visual appearance of semantic concepts strongly depends on the domain of the corresponding

© Springer International Publishing Switzerland 2015
G. Azzopardi and N. Petkov (Eds.): CAIP 2015, Part II, LNCS 9257, pp. 359–370, 2015.
DOI: 10.1007/978-3-319-23117-4_31

image or video source. This can be easily observed, for example, in the difference of television news and user-generated YouTube videos. Even within the news domain, the appearance of several concepts depends on the broadcast channel due to different editing styles or studio layouts. The appearance of the concepts "anchor", "maps", or "weather forecast" in news videos, for example, are typically related to a TV broadcaster or program. The spatial composition of these shots is specific for a TV cast, such as the moderator's position, the camera distance in an anchor shot, or the used colors for displaying a map. Thus, a major problem in the field of concept detection is to find robust features for successful cross-domain concept detection systems.

In this paper, a novel approach to improve cross-domain concept detection is presented. The proposed approach uses features based on object detection results and combines them with state-of-the art Bag-of-Visual-Words (BoVW) features using multiple kernel learning (MKL). The generalization properties of the proposed approach are investigated in a channel cross-domain and in a genre cross-domain setting, using the MARC2 high-performance computing cluster at the University of Marburg, Germany. In these experiments, object-based features significantly improve cross-domain concept detection performance, both for different channels and different genres.

The paper is organized as follows. Section 2 discusses related work. Section 3 presents the proposed approach to improve cross-domain concept detection. In Section 4, experimental results are described. Section 5 concludes the paper and outlines areas for future work.

2   Related Work

The main progress in recent years in the field of concept detection is due to improvements in the feature extraction stage. These improvements are inspired by text retrieval and rely on the extraction of region-based image descriptors where SIFT [9] is the most successful descriptor. Similar to the representation of documents in the field of text retrieval, an image or a video shot can be represented by BoVW features. Using BoVW approaches, continuous progress has been reported in recent years. The top runs at the semantic indexing task of the TRECVid Challenge heavily rely on BoVW representations [11].

Recently, convolutional neural networks experience a renaissance in computer vision. Similar to the BoVW approach, "features" are locally extracted and combined in different network layers using a max-pooling strategy. The features are automatically learned during training instead of using predefined features. Superior results have been obtained in object detection and single-label image classification[1]. The top results at the TRECVid Challenge 2013 and 2014 rely on a combination of BoVW and convolutional neural network approaches [15]. However, the evidence that convolutional neural networks outperform BoVW approaches in visual concept detection is still missing.

---

[1] http://www.image-net.org

Undoubtedly, significant improvements of concept detection approaches are required to satisfy the needs of various use cases. This is especially true for concept detection across different domains. Yang and Hauptmann [22] have shown that concept detection approaches based on Support Vector Machines (SVM) learn little beyond memorizing most of the positive training data and thus generalize poorly to domains other than the training domain. There are two main strategies to improve cross-domain concept detection performance: robust feature representations and model adaptation. The first strategy is to design more stable feature representations leading to more robust concept detection systems within and across different domains. Second, concept models can be adapted based on training examples from the target domain. This strategy is also called domain transfer learning. There are only a few approaches that propose model adaptation for video indexing and retrieval purposes [1,7,17,21,23]. Yang et al. [23], for example, have investigated methods for adapting existing concept classifiers to domains other than the training domain. The authors have proposed adaptive SVMs to adapt one or more existing classifiers to a new sparsely-labeled data set. An objective function similar to SVMs is used to learn a "delta function" between the original and adapted classifier. To select the best existing classifier for adaptation, the performance is estimated by analyzing the score distribution on a few labeled instances of the new data. Wu et al. [21] have addressed the problem of concept drifting, i.e., the appearance of concepts changes over time, in videos. The authors have used Generalized Markov Models (GMM) to model a concept and have proposed an incremental online learning framework to cope with concept drifting.

Domain transfer learning is similar to transductive learning [3,12,18,20]. Compared to inductive learning, transductive learning is not aimed at obtaining a general classification model for all possible test data items, but at obtaining an optimal classification model for the given test data only.

3   Concept Detection Using Object-Based Features

In this section, the proposed approach for improving cross-domain concept detection is presented. Similar to other state-of-the-art approaches, the concept detection problem is considered as a supervised learning task. SVM-based concept classifiers are used for the classification of each concept. As an appropriate fusion scheme, MKL is used to combine BoVW and object-based feature representations. The used BoVW features, the proposed object-based features and the developed fusion scheme are described below.

3.1   Bag-of-Visual-Words Features

A dense sampling strategy is used to extract SIFT [9] descriptors, because a sparse representation using keypoint detectors such as Harris-Laplace [10] or Difference of Gaussians (DoG) [9] is often insufficient to describe natural images.

To extract dense sampled SIFT features, the Vision Lab Features Library[2] is used with a step size of 5 pixels. Color information is integrated using RGB-SIFT [13]. For this purpose, the SIFT descriptors are computed independently for the three channels of the RGB color model. The final keypoint descriptor is the concatenation of the individual descriptors. Due to the normalizations during SIFT feature extraction, RGB-SIFT is equal to the transformed color SIFT descriptor, and thus invariant against light intensity and color changes [13].

A 4000-dimensional codebook is generated using a K-means algorithm, and an image is then described as a histogram indicating the frequency of each visual word. Instead of mapping a SIFT descriptor only to its nearest neighbor or to all visual words, the codebook candidates are locally constrained to the l-nearest visual words. This locality constraint has been shown to be superior for BoVW approaches [8]. Using a visual vocabulary of N visual words, the importance of a visual word v_t in an image is represented by the weights of the resulting histogram bins $w = [w_1, \ldots, w_t, \ldots, w_N]$ with

$$w_t = \sum_{i=1}^{K} \begin{cases} sim(d_i, v_t) & \text{if } v_t \in N_i^l \\ 0 & \text{otherwise} \end{cases} \tag{1}$$

where K is the number of local descriptors, N_i^l are the l-nearest neighbors of the local descriptor d_i in the visual vocabulary and $sim(d_i, v_t)$ is a similarity function based on the Euclidean distance d:

$$sim(d_i, v_t) = exp(-\gamma \cdot d(d_i, v_t)). \tag{2}$$

The γ-value is chosen as the maximum Euclidean distance between two codebook candidates.

3.2 Object-Based Features

State-of-the-art object detectors [4][19] are utilized to find object appearances for the following 21 object classes: "face", "aeroplane", "bicycle", "bird", "boat", "bottle", "bus", "car", "cat", "chair", "cow", "dining table", "dog", "horse", "motorbike", "person", "potted plant", "sheep", "sofa", "train", "tv-monitor". The object detectors, trained on separate public data sets, are applied to the keyframe images of the shots. Frontal faces are detected using the Adaboost-based approach provided by the OpenCV library,[3] which is an implementation of the approach suggested by Viola and Jones [19]. The face detector is used to derive the number of faces, the maximum and average probability as well as the maximum and average size of the facial areas. The remaining 20 object classes of the VOC Challenge [2] are detected by an approach based on deformable part

---

[2] http://www.vlfeat.org
[3] http://opencv.org

models [4]. The object detectors are applied using low thresholds to also obtain detection results with low confidence scores. The confidence scores of the object detectors based on deformable part models are transformed to probabilities by normalizing the values to the interval $[0, 1]$ using the following logistic function:

$$prob(x) = \frac{1}{1 + \exp(-Ax)} \quad \text{with} \quad A \in \mathbb{R}^+. \tag{3}$$

In the case of "faces", the features are normalized to the interval $[0, 1]$ by using a linear function of the form

$$prob(x) = \max(A \cdot x, 1) \quad \text{with} \quad A \in \mathbb{R}^+. \tag{4}$$

The proposed object-based feature representations are inspired by BoVW approaches. Let M be the number of object classes and D_m the number of object detection results in an image I for the object class m. The object detection results are given by $d_i^m = (x, y, w, h, s)$ with $m \in \{1, \ldots, M\}$ and $i \in \{1, \ldots, D_m\}$. The parameters x, y, w and h are the spatial coordinates of the bounding box and s is the probability.

Using a max-pooling strategy, an image is represented as a M-dimensional feature vector $[v_1, \ldots, v_M]$ with

$$v_m = \begin{cases} \max_{i \in 1, \ldots, D_m} s_i^m & \text{if } D_m > 0 \\ 0 & \text{otherwise} \end{cases} \tag{5}$$

where v_m intuitively measures the probability of object class m being present in an image or video shot.

Furthermore, the component information of the deformable part models is taken into account. Treating the mixture components as separate object classes, the feature vector dimension results in $M \cdot L$ where L is the number of mixture components. Altogether, the proposed object-based feature representation yields a 125-dimensional feature vector per shot.

3.3 Multiple Kernel Learning

Object-based features and BoVW features are combined using MKL. This fusion strategy tries to find an optimal kernel weighting

$$k_{combined} = \alpha \cdot k_{bovw} + \beta \cdot k_{obj} \quad \text{with } \alpha \geq 0, \ \beta \geq 0 \tag{6}$$

where the kernel functions k_{bovw} and k_{obj} take into account both feature modalities. For both representations, the χ^2-kernel is used. It is based on the corresponding histogram distance:

$$k_{\chi^2}(x, y) = e^{-\gamma \chi^2(x, y)} \tag{7}$$

with

$$\chi^2(x, y) = \sum_i \frac{(x_i - y_i)^2}{x_i + y_i}. \tag{8}$$

The l_1-norm is used to control the sparsity of the kernel weights in the MKL framework. To implement the proposed approach, the MKL framework provided by the Shogun library [16] in combination with the SVM implementation of Joachims [6], called SVM^{light}, is used.

4   Experimental Results

In this section, the generalization properties of the developed concept models are investigated in a channel cross-domain and in a genre cross-domain setting. The experiments are based on two different data sets[4]: news videos of the *TRECVid Challenge* 2005 and documentary films of the *TRECVid Challenge* 2007. The common concept set consists of the LSCOM-lite concepts except "entertainment", "government leader", and "corporate leader", since these three concepts have been dropped at the *TRECVid Challenge* 2007.

To build the newly proposed concept models, the MARC2 computing cluster at the University of Marburg, Germany, has been used. The MARC2 cluster has 96 compute nodes, each consisting of 4 AMD Opteron 6276 or 6376 with 16 cores@2.3 GHz each, i.e., 6144 cores. In addition, there are two head nodes with the same specification. In total, MARC2 has 24 TB RAM and 192 TB of disk storage space. The operating system is Red Hat Enterprise Linux for the headnodes, and CentOS for the compute nodes. The Sun Grid Engine 6.2u5 is used as the job scheduler.

In our experiments, we submitted jobs for codebook generation, feature extraction, model training and classification. For about 61 hours of training data and 25 hours of test data in the channel cross-domain experiments and about 50 hours of training data and 50 hours of test data in the genre cross-domain experiments, the generation of the object-based features using a single CPU core requires a total amount of approximately 2930 hours of computation time and the extraction of the BoVW features using a single CPU core takes 279 CPU hours. 432 concept models for the channel cross-domain experiments and 144 models for the genre cross-domain experiments have been built. This training phase takes about 219 hours of computation time on a single CPU core. The classification of the test instances requires about 123 CPU hours on a single core. In total, our experiments require about 3551 hours (= 148 days) of computation time on a single CPU core.

To reduce the time required for performing our experiments, the feature extraction phase has been parallelized by dividing the video shots (key frames) into chunks. To speed up the execution time of the training phase, a multi-threaded job has been submitted for each concept using 16 cores per node.

---

[4] http://trecvid.nist.gov/trecvid.data.html

Table 1. Number of training and test images for the different news channels.

Channel	Train	Test
CCTV4	8,147	2,749
CNN	8,036	2,992
LBC	11,875	3,398
MSNBC	6,407	2,498
NBC	4,784	4,538
NTDTV	4,766	1,715
Total	**44,015**	**17,890**

The classification of the test instances again uses data parallelism to reduce computation time.

Altogether, using the MARC2 computing cluster and the data parallel approach described above, we could reduce the execution time of the experiments to about 3 days (instead of the 148 days required for sequential execution on a single CPU core). Since we could not use the MARC2 computing cluster exclusively for our computations, the total computation time depends on the current load on MARC2 and the maximum number of jobs (= 500 jobs) allowed on MARC2. The concept models required 471.6 GB of hard disk capacity, and 4917 jobs have been submitted to the Sun Grid Engine.

4.1 Channel Cross-Domain

The channel cross-domain experiments were conducted using the TRECVid 2005 development set that has been divided by the Mediamill Challenge[5] into a training and a test set. It consists of 86 hours of news videos from different news channels including English (CNN, NBC, and MSNBC), Chinese (CCTV and NTDTV), and Arabic (LBC) channels. While the Mediamill Challenge merges subsequent (sub)shots that are shorter than two seconds to "master shots", the LSCOM-lite annotations are based on the subshots. Thus, the dataset consists of 44,015 training shots and 17,890 test shots. The number of training and test shots of the channel subsets is presented in Table 1.

To evaluate the overall performance for multiple concepts, the *mean average precision (mean AP)* score is calculated by taking the mean value of the *average precision (AP)* scores from the individual concepts. The AP score is calculated from a list of ranked images or video shots as follows:

$$AP(\rho) = \frac{1}{|R|} \sum_{k=1}^{N} \frac{|R \cap \rho^k|}{k} \psi(i_k) \tag{9}$$

$$\text{with} \quad \psi(i_k) = \begin{cases} 1 & \text{if } i_k \in R \\ 0 & \text{otherwise} \end{cases}$$

[5] https://ivi.fnwi.uva.nl/isis/mediamill/challenge/

Table 2. Confusion matrix: channel cross-domain, BoVW features.

AP [%]	CNN	CCTV4	LBC	MSNBC	NBC	NTDTV
CNN	38.8	27.7	23.1	28.0	24.1	22.7
CCTV4	24.0	38.1	26.4	21.1	22.7	22.6
LBC	23.7	28.3	46.0	23.1	22.8	25.2
MSNBC	28.0	24.6	23.0	32.2	25.1	20.8
NBC	23.8	23.7	24.0	24.0	37.0	21.4
NTDTV	19.7	21.5	22.3	18.8	19.3	34.6

Table 3. Confusion matrix: channel cross-domain, BoVW plus object-based features.

AP [%]	CNN	CCTV4	LBC	MSNBC	NBC	NTDTV
CNN	39.1	28.6	23.4	29.2	25.5	22.5
CCTV4	25.4	38.1	22.8	23.0	24.7	23.1
LBC	24.5	28.9	44.6	24.1	24.8	26.2
MSNBC	28.6	25.6	23.0	32.6	27.0	21.9
NBC	24.4	24.6	22.4	24.3	36.6	22.7
NTDTV	21.2	22.7	23.5	20.4	21.2	35.9

Table 4. Confusion matrix: significance tests, showing runs using object-based features that performed significantly better than the reference system (significance level of 5%).

	CNN	CCTV4	LBC	MSNBC	NBC	NTDTV
CNN		>		>	>	
CCTV4	>			>	>	>
LBC	>	>		>	>	>
MSNBC	>	>		>	>	>
NBC						>
NTDTV	>	>	>	>	>	>

where N is the length of the ranked document list, $\rho^k = \{i_1, i_2, \ldots, i_k\}$ is the ranked document list up to rank k, R is the set of relevant documents, $\left| R \cap \rho^k \right|$ is the number of relevant documents in the top-k of ρ and $\psi(i_k)$ is the relevance function. In our experiments, N is equal to the corresponding number of test shots.

While the average within channel performance using BoVW representations achieves 37.77% mean AP, the average channel cross-domain performance achieves only 23.51% mean AP. This result shows the poor generalization capabilities of the concept models across different news channels. Additionally using object-based features achieves an average within channel performance of 37.82% mean AP and an average channel cross-domain performance of 24.35% mean AP. The individual results are presented in the confusion matrices of Table 2 and Table 3. In most cross-channel combinations, the additional use of object-based features yields a significantly better result than using BoVW features alone. Table 4 shows the confusion matrix of the significance test results. The significance tests were conducted using the official partial randomization test of the TRECVid Challenge with a significance level of 5%.

Table 5. Genre cross-domain experiments from news videos to documentary films using the 36 LSCOM-lite concepts from *TRECVid* 2007.

Source Domain	Target Domain	DSIFT	DSIFT +OBJ	Performance Measure	Rel. Perf. Improvement
News	News	41.7%	42.1%	mean AP	0.9%
News	Documentaries	22.9%	24.4%	mean AP	6.62%
News	News	35.6%	36.0%	mean deltaAP	1.1%
News	Documentaries	16.1%	18.0%	mean deltaAP	9.44%

4.2 Genre Cross-Domain

Further experiments have been conducted in a genre cross-domain setting for news videos and documentary films. The documentary films of the TRECVid Challenge 2007 consist of 50 hours of development data and 50 hours of test data. Shot segmentation yielded 21,532 training and 22,084 test shots. The ground truth labels for the *TRECVid* 2007 development set are the result of a collaborative annotation effort of the participating teams. While the development set is completely annotated by the 36 LSCOM-lite concepts, ground truth data for the test videos exist only for a subset of 20 concept classes. The runs on the TRECVid 2007 test set have been evaluated by the infAP measure [24]. The infAP is a statistical method for evaluating large-scale retrieval results using incomplete judgements. This measure is calculated using the `trec_eval` tool, which is publicly available at the TRECVid website.

In a first experiment, the generalization properties of "news models" to documentary films are investigated. Models for the 36 LSCOM-lite concepts have been built based on the training set of the news videos. These models are applied to the news videos of the test set and to the documentary films of the *TRECVid* 2007 development set. Both runs have been evaluated in terms of AP as well as deltaAP [22]. DeltaAP has been calculated to consider the different occurrence frequencies of concept classes in the different domains. It is the difference between AP and randomAP, where randomAP corresponds to the concept frequency in a given test set. The results of the experiments from news videos to documentary films for the 36 LSCOM-lite concepts are shown in Table 5. For BoVW features, the application of concept models built on news videos and applied to documentary films leads to a relative performance loss of 45.1% in terms of mean AP and of even 54.8% in terms of mean deltaAP in comparison to the performance within the same domain. These results show the poor generalization properties of the learned news models. By additionally using object-based features, the cross-domain concept detection performance has been improved significantly, at a significance level of 1%. While the relative performance improvement amounts to 0.9% in terms of mean AP and 1.1% in terms of mean deltaAP for BoVW features, the relative performance improvements are 6.62% and 9.44%, respectively, using object-based features.

In a second experiment, the subset of 20 concepts judged by the *TRECVid* team on the documentary films of the TRECVid 2007 test set is evulted using

Table 6. Genre cross-domain experiments based on the subset of 20 concept classes of the *TRECVid Challenge* 2007.

Source Domain	Target Domain	DSIFT	DSIFT +OBJ	Performance Measure	Rel. Perf. Improvement
Documen.	Documen.	9.74%	9.84%	mean infAP	1.0%
News	Documen.	5.96%	6.97%	mean infAP	16.9%
Documen.	News	8.94%	9.83%	mean AP	10.0%
News	News	35.66%	35.89%	mean AP	0.6%

the infAP measure. Table 6 shows the results of applying the news and the documentary models to the documentary films of the *TRECVid* 2007 test set. In the domain of documentary films, the news models achieve a performance of 5.96% mean infAP with BoVW features and 6.97% mean infAP using additional object-based features. This is a relative cross-domain performance improvement of 16.9%, which is significantly better at a significance level of 1%. While the relative performance loss compared to documentary models amounts to 38.8% using BoVW features, it has an average value of only 29.2% using additional object-based features.

Furthermore, news and documentary models for the 20 concept classes have been applied to the test set of the news videos. In the news domain, the documentary models achieved only 8.94% mean AP without object-based features and 9.83% mean AP with object-based features compared to the news models with 35.66% and 35.89% mean AP, respectively. The documentary films seem to be more difficult than the news. Nevertheless, this is relative cross-domain improvement of 9.96%, which is significantly better at a significance level of 1%.

The models built on news videos have also been applied to the development set of documentary films. These models yielded 11.35% mean AP using BoVW features and 13.22% mean AP using additional object-based features, compared to 5.96% and 6.97% mean infAP on the test set. This shows that although infAP is an estimation of AP, the measurements are not directly comparable. Nevertheless, the relative performance improvements are almost the same.

5   Conclusion

In this paper, a novel approach to improve cross-domain concept detection has been presented. The proposed approach uses features based on object detection results and combines them with state-of-the-art BoVW features using multiple kernel learning. The generalization properties of the approach have been investigated in a channel cross-domain and in a genre cross-domain setting, using the MARC2 computing cluster at the University of Marburg, Germany. The experiments have shown that object-based features significantly improve cross-domain concept detection performance, both for different channels and genres.

There are several areas for future work. First, since it is infeasible to incorporate detection results for all possible objects, the next step is to determine a minimum set of reliable object detectors to achieve a maximum improvement in concept detection. Our experimental results suggest that it is reasonable to use object detectors for frequent object classes. Second, besides their benefits as context features, object sequences can be exploited for further temporal analysis. For example, person sequences can be used to improve the recognition of events, like person sitting down or cycling. Furthermore, in the field of object detection, the application of multi-class detectors for different subsets of object classes should be investigated.

Acknowledgments. This work is financially supported by the German Research Foundation (DFG, Project VideoSearch@DRA) and the German Ministry for Economic Affairs and Energy (BMWi, ZIM Project GoVideo).

References

1. Duan, L., Tsang, I.W., Xu, D., Maybank, S.J.: Domain transfer SVM for video concept detection. In: Proceedings of the IEEE Conference on Computer Vision and Pattern Recognition (CVPR 2009), pp. 1375–1381, June 2009
2. Everingham, M., Van Gool, L., Williams, C.K.I., Winn, J., Zisserman, A.: The Pascal Visual Object Classes (VOC) Challenge. International Journal of Computer Vision **88**(2), 303–338 (2010)
3. Ewerth, R., Mühling, M., Freisleben, B.: Robust Video Content Analysis via Transductive Learning. ACM Transactions on Intelligent Systems and Technology (TIST) **3**(3), 1–26 (2011)
4. Felzenszwalb, P.F., Girshick, R.B., McAllester, D.: Cascade object detection with deformable part models. In: Proceedings of the 23rd IEEE Conference on Computer Vision and Pattern Recognition (CVPR 2010), pp. 2241–2248. IEEE, San Francisco (2010)
5. Hauptmann, A., Yan, R., Lin, W.-H.: How many high-level concepts will fill the semantic gap in news video retrieval? In: Proceedings of the 6th ACM International Conference on Image and Video Retrieval (CIVR 2007), pp. 627–634. ACM, Amsterdam (2007)
6. Joachims, T.: Text categorization with support vector machines: learning with many relevant features. In: Nédellec, Claire, Rouveirol, Céline (eds.) ECML 1998. LNCS, vol. 1398, pp. 137–142. Springer, Heidelberg (1998)
7. Li, H., Shi, Y., Liu, Y., Hauptmann, A.G., Xiong, Z.: Cross-domain video concept detection: A joint discriminative and generative active learning approach. Expert Systems with Applications **39**(15), 12220–12228 (2012)
8. Liu, L., Wang, L., Liu, X.: In defense of soft-assignment coding. In: Proceedings of the 13th International Conference on Computer Vision (ICCV 2011), pp. 2486–2493. IEEE, Barcelona, November 2011
9. Lowe, D.G.: Distinctive Image Features from Scale-Invariant Keypoints. International Journal of Computer Vision **60**(2), 91–110 (2004)
10. Mikolajczyk, K., Schmid, C.: Indexing based on scale invariant interest points. In: Proceedings of the 8th IEEE International Conference on Computer Vision (ICCV 2001), pp. 525–531, IEEE, Vancouver (2001)

11. Over, P., Fiscus, J., Sanders, G., Shaw, B., Awad, G., Michel, M., Smeaton, A., Kraaij, W., Quéenot, G.: TRECVID 2013 - An overview of the goals, tasks, data, evaluation mechanisms, and metrics. In: Proceedings of the TREC Video Retrieval Evaluation Workshop (TRECVid 2013), pp. 1–45. National Institute of Standards and Technology (NIST), Gaithersburg (2014)

12. Qi, G.-J., Hua, X.-S., Song, Y., Zhang, H.-J.: Transductive inference with hierarchical clustering for video annotation. In: Proceedings of the 8th IEEE International Conference on Multimedia and Expo (ICME 2007), pp. 643–646. IEEE, Beijing (2007)

13. van de Sande, K.E.A., Gevers, T., Snoek, C.G.M.: A comparison of color features for visual concept classification. In: Proceedings of the 7th ACM International Conference on Content-Based Image and Video Retrieval (CIVR 2008), pages 141–150. ACM, Niagara Falls (2008)

14. Smeulders, A.W.M., Worring, M., Santini, S., Gupta, A., Jain, R.: Content-Based Image Retrieval at the End of the Early Years. IEEE Transactions on Pattern Analysis and Machine Intelligence (PAMI) **22**(12), 1349–1380 (2000)

15. Snoek, C., Fonjne, D., Li, Z., van de Sande, K., Smeulders, A.: Deep nets for detecting, combining, and localizing concepts in video. In: Proceedings of the TREC Video Retrieval Evaluation Workshop (TRECVid 2013), Gaithersburg, Maryland, USA (2014)

16. Sonnenburg, S., Rätsch, G., Henschel, S., Widmer, C., Behr, J., Zien, A., Bona, F., Binder, A., Gehl, C., Franc, V.: The SHOGUN Machine Learning Toolbox. Journal of Machine Learning Research **11**(1), 1799–1802 (2010)

17. Sun, Y., Sudo, K., Taniguchi, Y.: Cross-domain concept detection with dictionary coherence by leveraging web images. In: He, X., Luo, S., Tao, D., Xu, C., Yang, J., Hasan, M.A. (eds.) MMM 2015, Part II. LNCS, vol. 8936, pp. 415–426. Springer, Heidelberg (2015)

18. Tian, X., Yang, L., Wang, J.: Transductive video annotation via local learnable kernel classifier. In: Proceedings of the IEEE International Conference on Multimedia and Expo (ICME 2008), pp. 1509–1512. IEEE, Hannover (2008)

19. Viola, P., Jones, M.J.: Robust Real-Time Face Detection. International Journal of Computer Vision **57**(2), 137–154 (2004)

20. Wang, J., Zhao, Y., Wu, X., Hua, X-S.: Transductive multi-label learning for video concept detection. In: Proceedings of the 1st ACM International Conference on Multimedia Information Retrieval (MIR 2008), pp. 298–304. ACM, Vancouver (2008)

21. Wu, J., Ding, D., Hua, X.-S., Zhang, B.: Tracking concept drifting with an online-optimized incremental learning framework. In: Proceedings of the 7th ACM SIGMM International Workshop on Multimedia Information Retrieval (MIR 2005), pp. 33–40. ACM, Singapore (2005)

22. Yang, J., Hauptmann, A.G.: (Un)Reliability of video concept detection. In: Proceedings of the 7th ACM International Conference on Image and Video Retrieval (CIVR 2008), pp. 85–94. ACM, Niagara Falls (2008)

23. Yang, J., Yan, R., Hauptmann, A.G.: Cross-domain video concept detection using adaptive SVMs. In: Proceedings of the 15th International Conference on Multimedia (MM 2007), pp. 188–197. ACM, Augsburg (2007)

24. Yilmaz, E., Aslam, J.A.: Estimating average precision with incomplete and imperfect judgments. In: Proceedings of the 15th ACM International Conference on Information and Knowledge Management (CIKM 2006), pp. 102–111. ACM, Arlington (2006)

Deep Learning for Feature Extraction of Arabic Handwritten Script

Mohamed Elleuch[1,2(✉)], Najiba Tagougui[3], and Monji Kherallah[2]

[1] National School of Computer Science (ENSI), University of Manouba, Manouba, Tunisia
{mohamed.elleuch.2015, monji.kherallah2014}@ieee.org
[2] Advanced Technologies for Medicine and Signals (ATMS), University of Sfax, Sfax, Tunisia
[3] The Higher Institute of Management of Gabes, University of Gabes, Gabès, Tunisia
najiba.tagougui@isggb.rnu.tn

Abstract. In recent years, systems based on deep learning have gained great popularity in the pattern recognition filed. This is basically to benefit from the hierarchical representations used to unlabeled data which is becoming the focus of many researchers since it represents the easiest way to deal with a huge amount of data. Most of the architecture in deep learning is constructed by a stack of feature extractors, such as Restricted Boltzmann Machine and Auto-Encoder. In this paper, we highlight how these deep learning techniques can be effectively applied for recognizing Arabic Handwritten Script (AHS) and this by investigating two deep architectures: Deep Belief Networks (DBN) and Convolutional Deep Belief Networks (CDBN) which are applied respectively on low-level dimension and high-level dimension in textual images. The experimental study has proved promising results which are comparable to the state-of-the-art Arabic OCR.

Keywords: Deep learning · Feature extractors · CDBN · Arabic Handwritten Script

1 Introduction

During the five last decades, handwritten Arabic script recognition has been the subject of intense research owing to their potential application in various engineering technological fields [1]. Many investigations are being conducted to classify handwritten Arabic characters using hand-crafted features and unsupervised feature learning [2].

Building good features from the image represents hard and complex work. It requires expertise on the field of feature extraction methods (Segmentation, HoG / SIFT / GIST features in computer vision, MFCC features in speech domains, etc.). The choice of these hand-crafted features determines the performance of systems applied for classification and recognition (MLP, SVM, HMM, K-means, etc.). Using unlabeled data or raw data in training developed handwriting systems is becoming the focus of many researchers since

© Springer International Publishing Switzerland 2015
G. Azzopardi and N. Petkov (Eds.): CAIP 2015, Part II, LNCS 9257, pp. 371–382, 2015.
DOI: 10.1007/978-3-319-23117-4_32

it represents the easiest way to deal with a huge amount of data. Fig. 1 presented a deep learning approach using deep belief network (DBN) or convolutional DBN for extraction features phase.

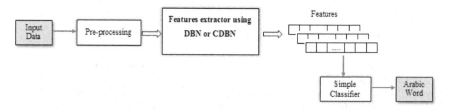

Fig. 1. System based in deep architecture (DBN, Convolutional DBN)

2   Related Works

Recently, deep learning architectures have been used for unsupervised feature learning [3, 4], such as Convolutional Neural Network (CNN), Deep Belief Network (DBN) and Convolutional DBN:

Convolutional Neural Network developed by LeCun et al. [5], is a specialized type of neural network which learns the good features at each layer of the visual hierarchy via backpropagation (BP). Ranzato et al. [6] achieves improvements in performance when they applied an unsupervised pre-training to a CNN. These networks have been successful in various vision problems such as digit and character recognition. The problem using neural network approaches is that the objective function is non-convex, and their learning algorithms may get stuck in local minima during gradient descent [7]. To overcome these limitations, many studies have proposed replacing these approaches successfully by a classifier, namely the deep networks [8]. The new concept behind it the use of hidden variables as observed variables to train each layer of the deep structure independently and greedily.

Deep Belief Network is a multilayer generative model [9] which learns higher-level feature representations from unlabeled data using an unsupervised learning algorithms, such as RBMs [9], auto-encoders [3] and sparse coding [10, 11]. These algorithms have only succeeded in learning low-level features such as "edge" or "stroke" detectors with simple invariances. Hinton et al. [9, 12] proposed a greedy layer-wise algorithm for training a multilayer belief network (stack of RBMs) with a layer of observable variables v and a number of hidden layers h. This model has been applied to MNIST digits [9] [13], phone [14] [15] and handwritten Arabic text [16] recognition.

In DBN, the units between two layers are fully connected. Thus, it is difficult to apply DBN to large images (e.g. 300 x 100). To deal with this problem Lee et al. [17] proposed a Convolutional architecture which alternate between detection and pooling layers called Convolutional DBN.

CDBN, which is composed of convolutional restricted Boltzmann machines (CRBMs), has been applied in several fields such as vision recognition task [17] [18], automatic speech recognition (ASR) [19] and EEG signal [20] classification.

Lee et al. [21] demonstrated that CDBN had good performance. The principal idea is to scale up the algorithm to deal with high-dimensional data.

In our work we compared the performance of two Deep architectures: DBN and CDBN to recognize in the first attempt single Arabic characters using HACDB Database and to recognize in the second attempt Arabic words using the IFN/ENIT Database and thus to discuss or to deal with the low and high-level dimension in the handwritten textual images.

The rest of the paper is organized as follows: In section 3, we describe the basic concepts behind Deep leaning and convolutional architecture. Section 4 shows the adopted architecture of DBN and CDBN classifier. Our experimental study using DBN and CDBN is next presented in the section 5. And finally, discussion and some concluding remarks are presented in Section 6.

3   Deep Architectures

We first review the Deep Belief Networks (DBN) which is based on Restricted Boltzmann Machine (RBM), and then we present Convolutional Deep Belief Network (CDBN).

3.1   Deep Belief Networks (DBN)

A Deep Belief Network (DBN) is a generative graphical model [9] composed by a stack of Restricted Boltzmann Machines (RBMs) [22], which consist of one layer of visible units (input data) and several layers of hidden units. The connection between the top two layers of the DBN is undirected while the rest of the connections are directed but there is no connection for nodes in the same layer (see fig. 2-b).

An RBM is a two layer undirected graphical model composed of one layer of visible unit's "v", and one layer of hidden units "h", with a full set of connections between them (see fig. 2-a). The energy function and the probabilistic semantics for an RBM are defined as:

$$E(v, h) = -\sum_{i,j} v_i W_{ij} h_j - \sum_j b_j h_j - \sum_i c_i v_i \tag{1}$$

$$P(v, h) = \frac{1}{Z} \exp(-E(v, h)) \tag{2}$$

Where

- w_{ij} represents the weights between visible units v_i and hidden units h_j,
- b_j are hidden unit biases,
- c_i are visible unit biases,
- Z is the partition function.

If the visible units are real valued, we can write the energy function as:

$$E(v, h) = \frac{1}{2}\sum_i v_i^2 - \sum_{i,j} v_i W_{ij} h_j - \sum_j b_j h_j - \sum_i c_i v_i \tag{3}$$

RBMs can be trained to learn a generative model in a unsupervised manner. One efficient learning algorithm for RBMs is contrastive divergence "CD" [23], which is a form of contrastive optimization that approximates the gradient of the log-likelihood of the learning data. For more details you can refer to work in [24].

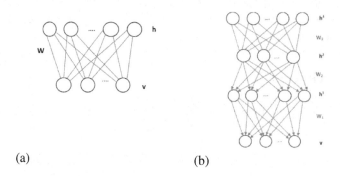

(a)   (b)

Fig. 2. Illustration of a RBM (a) and a DBN with three hidden layers (b).

3.2   Convolutional Deep Belief Networks (CDBN)

Building hierarchical structures of features is a challenge and CDBN is among the famous features extractor which was frequently used in last decade in the area of pattern recognition.

Convolutional DBN is a hierarchical generative model: supports efficient bottom-up and top-down probabilistic inference. Like to the standard DBN, this architecture consists of several layers of max-pooling CRBMs stacked on top of one another, and training is accomplished by the greedy layer-wise procedure [3, 9]. Building convolutional deep belief network, the algorithm learns high-level features, such as groups of the strokes and object-part. In our experiments, we trained CDBN with two layers of CRBM, and for inference we use feed-forward approximation.

The CRBM is the foundation of CDBN. We train the CDBN model by learning a stack of CRBMs where the output of one CRBM is the input of the next CRBM in the stack. Fig. 3 shows the structure of CRBM which consists of two layers: a visible layer V and a hidden layer H that are connected by sets of local and shared parameters. The visible units are binary-valued or real-valued, and the hidden units are binary-valued.

Suppose the visible input layer consists of L images (with arbitrary aspect ratios), and each image consists of $N_v \times N_v$ real units (intensity pixel image). The hidden units H are divided into K groups (also called maps), where each group is an $N_H \times N_H$ array of binary units and is associated with a $N_w \times N_w$ convolutional filter (where $N_w \triangleq N_v - N_H + 1$).

The filter weights are shared among all locations in the hidden units within the same map. There is also a shared bias b_k for each group and a shared bias c for the visible units.

Lee et al. [17] developed a novel operation for CDBN architecture called "probabilistic max-pooling", which shrink the representation of the detection layers in a probabilistically sound way. Shrinking the representation with max-pooling allows higher layer representations to be invariant to local translations of the input data, reduces the computational burden [21] and it has been shown to be useful in visual recognition problems [25]. The energy function of the probabilistic max-pooling CRBM with real-valued visible units can then be defined as:

$$E(v,h) = \frac{1}{2}\sum_{i,j=1}^{N_V} v_{i,j}^2 - \sum_{k=1}^{K}\sum_{i,j=1}^{N_H}\sum_{r,s=1}^{N_W} h_{i,j}^k W_{r,s}^k v_{i+r-1,j+s-1} - \sum_{k=1}^{K} b_k \sum_{i,j=1}^{N_H} h_{i,j}^k - c\sum_{i,j=1}^{N_V} v_{i,j} \qquad (4)$$

The joint and conditional probability distributions of the CRBM can be written as follows:

$$P(v,h) = \frac{1}{Z}\exp\big(-E(v,h)\big) \qquad (5)$$

$$P\big(v_{i,j} = 1\big|h\big) = N\big((\textstyle\sum_k W^k *_f h^k)_{i,j} + c, 1\big) \qquad (6)$$

$$P\big(h_{i,j}^k = 1\big|v\big) = \frac{\exp\big(I\big(h_{i,j}^k\big)\big)}{1 + \sum_{(i',j')\in B_\alpha}\exp\big(I\big(h_{i',j'}^k\big)\big)} \qquad (7)$$

where $I\big(h_{i,j}^k\big) \triangleq b_k + (\widetilde{W}^k *_v v)_{i,j}$ is the data hidden units in group k obtained from visible layer V, $\widetilde{W}$ defined as the matrix filter W flipped in both up-down side and left-right directions, $*_v$ is a valid convolution, $*_f$ is a full convolution and $\mathcal{N}(.)$ is a normal distribution. B_α refers to a $C \times C$ block denoted α where is connected (pooled) to one binary node P_α^k in the pooling layer. The pooling node P_α^k is defined as $P_\alpha^k \triangleq \sum_{(i,j)\in B_\alpha} h_{i,j}^k$ and the conditional probability is given by:

$$P(p_\alpha^k = 1|v) = \frac{\sum_{(i',j')\in B_\alpha}\exp\big(I\big(h_{i',j'}^k\big)\big)}{1 + \sum_{(i',j')\in B_\alpha}\exp\big(I\big(h_{i',j'}^k\big)\big)} \qquad (8)$$

Using the operators defined previously (4),

$$E(v,h) = \frac{1}{2}\sum_{i,j=1}^{N_V} v_{i,j}^2 - c\sum_{i,j=1}^{N_V} v_{i,j} - \sum_{k=1}^{K}\sum_{i,j} (h_{i,j}^k ((\widetilde{W}^k *_v v)_{i,j} + b_k)) \qquad (9)$$

In the same manner as RBM, training CRBM is performed by using contrastive divergence (CD) algorithm [9] which is an approximation of maximum-likelihood estimation. Moreover, CD allows us to estimate an approximate gradient effectively [26]. Inference and learning algorithms are based on block Gibbs sampling method. After training a max-pooling CRBM, we can use it to compute the posterior of the hidden (pooling) units given the input data. These hidden unit "activations" can be used as input to further train the next layer CRBM.

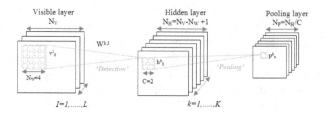

Fig. 3. Illustration of a probabilistic max-pooling CRBM. N_V and N_H refer to the size of visible and hidden layer, and N_W to the size of convolution filter. $W^{k,l}$ is the convolutional filter and C is the max-pooling ratio.

4   The Adopted DBN Versus CDBN Architecture

In this section, we identify the parameters setting of the adopted DBN and CDBN architectures.

4.1   DBN Architecture

Regarding DBN, Our choice of parameters (N_{hl}, N_n) is based on the criterion of the error rate on the validation set. To calculate this criterion, a soft-max layer with 66 output units is first added to the top of each unsupervised trained DBN and later learned with BP. The output of each unit is just the probability of assigning the corresponding label. The optimal architecture of DBN was 2500-1000-1000- 66, i.e., it consisted of two RBMs each one with 1000 hidden neurons and the number of epoch is fixed at 200 for DBN train (See fig. 4). Each RBM of the DBN was trained using greedy layer-wise unsupervised learning algorithm [3] with contrastive divergence [27]. The obtained error rate was 2.1 %. Technical implementation details of the adopted system can be more explained when by referring to our previous work [28].

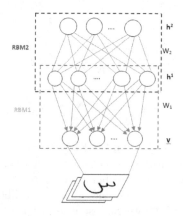

Fig. 4. Illustration of the proposed DBN architecture

4.2   Convolutional DBN Architecture

As already mentioned above in the paper, our CDBN architecture is composed of two layers of CRBM (See fig. 5). We evaluated the performance of this architecture, first on the HACDB and then on IFN/ENIT handwritten characters/words classification task.

The description of the CDBN architecture used in experiments applied to HACDB dataset is given in the following way: 1x50x50-11W40G-MP2-11W40G-MP2 represents a net with input images of size 50x50, the first and second layer consisted of 40 maps ("groups of hidden and pooling layers") of 11×11 pixel filters and the pooling ratio C for each layer was 2. Every group in the hidden layer is connected to one pooling unit. We used 0.05 as the target sparsity for the first and second layer to fix the number of activation weight at a time. The first layer bases learned strokes that contain the characters, and the second layer bases learned parts of characters by groupings of the strokes. Combining the first and second layer activations we construct feature vectors, an SVM (Support Vector Machine) classifier is used for classifying these features. Our result obtained using CDBN/SVM architecture is 1.82% error rate classification.

For the IFN/ENIT datasets we train following CDBN, 1x300x100-12W24G-MP2-10W40G-MP2. This architecture represents a net with input images of size 300x100, the first layer consisted of 24 groups of 12×12 pixel filters and the pooling ratio C for each layer was 2. The second layer consisted of 40 maps, each 10x10. We fixed a sparsity parameter of 0.03.With such architecture, we achieve 16.3% error rate.

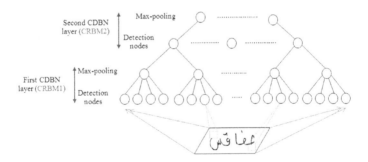

Fig. 5. Illustration of the proposed CDBN architecture

5   Experiment Study and Results

In order to evaluate the effectiveness of convolutional deep belief network, we tested on two handwritten characters/words recognition datasets: HACDB [29], and IFN/ENIT [30]. In our experiment, each image in IFN/ENIT resized to the same input size (300 x 100 pixels) for the visible layer, whereas in HACDB database the images are normalized to 50 by 50 pixels. These images are in the gray scale and the resizing is not necessarily square. For the setting architecture, we must determine the number of filters, size of the filters, max-pooling region size, and sparsity of the hidden units in each layer of CDBN. According to the size of the images used (low-high dimensional data) we define two settings of hyper-parameters for CRBM architecture.

A second experimental study was established using Deep Belief Network classifier on the HACDB database to fix the number of hidden layers (N_{hl}) and the number of neurons (N_n) by each hidden layer.

5.1   Recognizing Single Arabic Characters

Compared to Latin character recognition, isolated Arabic character recognition is a much harder problem, mainly because of the much larger category set, but also because of wide variability of writing styles, and the confusion between similar characters. We used Handwritten Arabic Characters Database (HACDB), which contains 6.600 shapes of handwritten characters written by 50 persons. Each writer has generated two forms for 66 shapes: 58 shapes of characters and 8 shapes of overlapping characters (see Table 1). The dataset is divided into a training set of 5.280 images and a test set of 1.320 images.

Table 1. Samples from the HACDB database written by 10 different writers

Arabic Characters	
سـ seen	سـ سـ سـ سـ سـ سـ سـ سـ سـ سـ
لا laa	لا لا لا لا لا لا لا لا لا لا
الحـ alha	الحـ الحـ الحـ الحـ الحـ الحـ الحـ الحـ الحـ الحـ
ع ain	ع ع ع ع ع ع ع ع ع ع

Table 2 shows the results obtained with the two proposed approaches on single Arabic characters using HACDB database. The Character Error Rate (CER) achieved by CDBN outperforms the one achieved by the DBN system. This confirms the results reported in [9] [17].

Table 2. Our proposed systems applied on Arabic characters

Approach	Database	CER
Convolutionl DBN	HACDB	1.82 %
Deep Belief Network	HACDB	2.1 %

In the following table, the presented results confirm that our proposed CDBN structure achieved very good performance in comparison with state-of-the-art recognition systems which are using extracted features. Our proposed approach present considerable efficiency over the others reported in the literature since it deals with unlabeled raw data.

Table 3. Character error rate comparison

Authors	Approach	Feature extraction	Databases	CER
Present work	CDBN	No (Automatic)	HACDB	**1.82 %**
Albakoor et al., [31]	NN	Yes (Manual)	---	1.3 %
Hamdi et al., [32]	SVM	Yes	---	4 %
Boubaker et al., [33]	MLP	Yes	LMCA	5.86 %

5.2   Recognizing Single Arabic Words

For evaluating the performance of two systems, the IFN/ENIT database is used. In fact, the IFN/ENIT database consists of 26459 Arabic words handwritten by more than 411 different writers. The handwritten words represent 946 Tunisian town/village names. Table 4 shows different samples of words in the used database.

Table 4. Samples from the IFN/ENIT database written by 10 different writers

Arabic Words
صفاقس sfax
قفصة gafsa
المهدية almahdia

The achieved Word Error Rate (WER) with the CDBN approach is reported in the following table. It equals to 16.3% using the IFN/ENIT database. Furthermore, the obtained rate is compared to the other ones reported in leading previous works. Although, our present work is not better than the reported previous ones [34], it can be considered very competitive comparable with the state of the art using AMA Arabic PAW dataset [16] (WER equals to 19.58 %) and IFN/ENIT database [35] (see table 5) applying Deep Belief Network and Dynamic Time Warping (DTW) approaches respectively. It is a hard task and getting such WER values is a promising result.

Table 5. Word error rate comparison using the IFN/ENIT database

Authors	Approach	Feature extraction	WER
Present work	CDBN	No (Automatic)	**16.3 %**
AlKhateeb et al., 2011 [34]	HMM	Yes (Manual)	13.27 %
Saabni and El-Sana [35]	DTW	Yes	21.79 %

6 Conclusion

In this work, we presented two deep learning approaches for handwritten Arabic script recognition namely DBN and CDBN. The purpose was to take advantages of the power of these deep networks that are able to manage large dimensions input, which allows the use of unlabeled raw data inputs rather than to extract a feature vector and learn complex decision border between classes. In an experimental section we showed that the results were promising with an ECR of 2.1% using DBN and 1.82 % with the CDBN classifier when applied to the HACDB database. Further, have we reconfigured our proposed CDBN network architecture to be able to deal with high-dimension data like words and evaluated on the IFN/ENIT database. The achieved WER was 16.3%. Although, our present work yields a satisfactory performance compared with the previous reported WER in the literature, it can be considered very competitive since we work on raw data and not on extracted data. Hence, our work shows that it is possible to train neurons (nodes detectors) to be selective for high-level concepts using entirely unlabeled data to construct an efficient feature vectors.

As perspective, we have to combine hierarchical representations building from unlabeled data using CDBN with hand-crafted features to improve further the accuracy rate.

References

1. Mota, R., Scott, D.: Education and Innovation. Chapter in Education for Innovation and Independent Learning, pp. 55–71 (2014)
2. Porwal, U., Shi, Z., Setlur, S.: Machine learning in handwritten arabic text recognition. In: Chapter in Handbook of Statistics, vol. 31, pp. 443–46 (2013)
3. Bengio, Y., Lamblin, P., Popovici, D., Larochelle, H., Greedy layer-wise training of deep networks. In: Proceedings of Annual Conference on Neural Information Processing Systems (NIPS), pp. 153–160 (2006)
4. Ranzato, M., Boureau, Y., LeCun, Y.: Sparse feature learning for deep belief networks. In: Proceedings of Annual Conference on Neural Information Processing Systems (NIPS) (2007)
5. LeCun, Y., Bottou, L., Bengio, Y., Haffner, P.: Gradient-based learning applied to document recognition. Proceedings of the IEEE **86**(11), 2278–2324 (1998)

6. Ranzato, M., Huang, F., Boureau, Y., LeCun, Y.: Unsupervised learning of invariant feature hierarchies with applications to object recognition. In: Proc. Computer Vision and Pattern Recognition Conference (CVPR). IEEE Press (2007)

7. Rumelhart, D., Hinton, G., Williams, R.: Learning representations by back-propagating errors. Nature **323**, 533–536 (1986)

8. Larochelle, H., Bengio, Y., Louradour, J., Lamblin, P.: Exploring strategies for training deep neural networks. The Journal of Machine Learning Research **10**, 1–40 (2009)

9. Hinton, G.E., Osindero, S., The, Y.W.: A fast learning algorithm for deep belief nets. Neural Computing **18**(7), 1527–1554 (2006)

10. Olshausen, B.A., Field, D.J.: Emergence of simple-cell receptive field properties by learning a sparse code for natural images. Nature **381**, 607–609 (1996)

11. Lee, H., Battle, A., Raina, R., Ng, A.Y.: Efficient sparse coding algorithms. In: Proceedings of Annual Conference on Neural Information Processing Systems (NIPS) (2007)

12. Hinton, G., Salakhutdinov, R.: Reducing the dimensionality of data with neural networks. Science **313**(5786), 504–507 (2006)

13. Vincent, P., Larochelle, H., Lajoie, I., Bengio, Y., Manzagol, P.A.: Stacked Denoising Autoencoders: Learning Useful Representations in a Deep Network with a Local Denoising Criterion. Journal of Machine Learning Research **11**, 3371–3408 (2010)

14. Mohamed, A., Dahl, G., Hinton, G.: Acoustic modeling using deep belief networks. IEEE Transactions on Audio, Speech, and Language Processing **20**(1), 14–22 (2011)

15. Dahl, G.E., Ranzato, M., Mohamed, A., Hinton, G.E.: Phone recognition with the mean-covariance restricted Boltzmann machine. Advances in Neural Information Processing Systems **23**, 469–477 (2010)

16. Porwal, U., Zhou, Y., Govindaraju, V.: Handwritten arabic text recognition using deep belief networks. In: 21st International Conference on Pattern Recognition (ICPR) (2012)

17. Lee, H., Grosse, R., Ranganath, R., Ng, A.Y.: Unsupervised learning of hierarchical representations with convolutional deep belief networks. Communications of the ACM **54**(10), 95–103 (2011)

18. Huang, G.-B., Zhou, H., Ding, X., Zhang, R.: Extreme Learning Machine for Regression and Multiclass Classification. IEEE Transactions on Systems, Man, and Cybernetics - Part B: Cybernetics **42**(2), 513–529 (2012)

19. Lee, H., Pham, P.T., Largman, Y., Ng, A.Y.: Unsupervised feature learning for audio classification using convolutional deep belief networks. In: Advances in Neural Information Processing Systems (NIPS), pp. 1096–1104 (2009)

20. Ren, Y., Wu, Y.: Convolutional deep belief networks for feature extraction of EEG signal. In: International Joint Conference on Neural Networks (IJCNN), pp. 2850–2853 (2014)

21. Lee, H., Grosse, R., Ranganath, R., Ng, A.Y.: Convolutional deep belief networks for scalable unsupervised learning of hierarchical representations. In: ICML (2009)

22. Mohamed, A., Sainath, T.N., Dahl, G., Ramabhadran, B., Hinton, G.E., Picheny, M.A.: Deep belief networks using discriminative features for phone recognition. In: Proceedings of the IEEE International Conference on Acoustics, Speech and Signal Processing, pp. 5060–5063, May 2011

23. Hinton, G.E.: Training products of experts by minimizing contrastive divergence. Neural Computation **14**(8), 1771–1800 (2002)

24. Hinton, G.E.: A practical guide to training restricted boltzmann machines. In: Montavon, G., Orr, G.B., Müller, K.-R. (eds.) Neural Networks: Tricks of the Trade. LNCS, vol. 7700, pp. 599–619. Springer, Heidelberg (2012)

25. Jarrett, K., Kavukcuoglu, K., Ranzato, M., LeCun, Y.: What is the best multistage architecture for object recognition? In: ICCV (2009)

26. Hinton, G.E.: Training products of experts by minimizing contrastive divergence. Neural Computation **14**(8), 1771–1800 (2002)
27. Carreira-Perpinan, M.A., Hinton, G.E.: On contrastive divergence learning. In: Proceedings of the tenth International Workshop on Artificial Intelligence and Statistics, pp. 33–40, January 2005
28. Elleuch, M., Tagougui, N., Kherallah, M.: Arabic handwritten characters recognition using deep belief neural networks. In: 12th International Multi-Conference on Systems, Signals and Devices - Conference on Communication & Signal Processing (2015) (in press)
29. Lawgali, A., Angelova, M., Bouridane, A.: HACDB: handwritten arabic characters database for automatic character recognition. In: EUropean Workshop on Visual Information Processing (EUVIP), pp. 255–259 (2013)
30. Pechwitz, M., Maddouri, S.S., Märgner, V., Ellouze, N., Amiri, H.: IFN/ENIT database of handwritten Arabic words. In: Colloque International Francophone sur l'Ecrit et le Document (CIFED), pp. 127–136 (2002)
31. Albakoor, M., Saeed, K., Sukkar, F.: Intelligent system for arabic character recognition. In: World Congress on Nature & Biologically Inspired Computing (NaBIC), pp. 982–987 (2009)
32. Hamdi, R., Bouchareb, F., Bedda, M.: Handwritten arabic character recognition based on SVM classifier. In: 3rd International Conference on Information and Communication Technologies: From Theory to Applications (ICTTA) (2008)
33. Boubaker, H., Tagougui, N., Elbaati, A., Kherallah, M., Elabed, H., Alimi, A.M.: Online arabic databases and applications. In: Märgner, V., El Abed, H. (eds.) Guide to OCR for Arabic Scripts Chp. Part IV: Applications. Springer (2012)
34. AlKhateeb, H., Ren, J., Jiang, J., Al-Muhtaseb, H.: Offline handwritten Arabic cursive text recognition using Hidden Markov Models and re-ranking. Pattern Recognition Letters **32**(8), 1081–1088 (2011)
35. Saabni, R.M., El-Sana, J.A.: Comprehensive synthetic Arabic database for on/off-line script recognition research. Int. J. Doc. Anal. Recognition (IJDAR) **16**(3), 285–294 (2013)

Automatic Summary Creation by Applying Natural Language Processing on Unstructured Medical Records

Daniela Giordano, Isaak Kavasidis[(✉)], and Concetto Spampinato

Department of Electrical, Electronics and Informatics Engineering,
University of Catania, Viale Andrea Doria, 6, 95125 Catania, Italy
{dgiordan,ikavasidis,cspampin}@dieei.unict.it

Abstract. In this paper we present a system for automatic generation of summaries of patients' unstructured medical reports. The system employs Natural Language Processing techniques in order to determine the most interesting points and uses the MetaMap module for recognizing the medical concepts in a medical report. Afterwards the sentences that do not contain interesting concepts are removed and a summary is generated which contains URL links to the Linked Life Data pages of the identified medical concepts, enabling both medical doctors and patients to further explore what is reported in. Such integration also allows the tool to interface with other semantic web-based applications. The performance of the tool were also evaluated, achieving remarkable results in sentence identification, polarity detection and concept recognition. Moreover, the accuracy of the generated summaries was evaluated by five medical doctors, proving that the summaries keep the same relevant information as the medical reports, despite being much more concise.

1 Introduction

Every day a large amount of medical reports, in the form of free text (i.e. not structured according to a logical scheme) is generated. Not possessing any structural information hampers the ability of automatic document digitization and analysis and subsequently all the applications that could be built upon these. The information included in the text can be deductible only through reading. The adoption of free text documents is done mainly due to the doctors' lack of time, who have to write reports quickly, or due to hospitals' internal procedures or traditions. Moreover, the readability of these documents could become a problem as it may not be easy for the reader to pinpoint the most important parts.

The medical domain suffers particularly by an overload of information and rapid access to key information is of crucial importance to health professionals for decision making. For instance, a concise and synthetic representation of medical reports (i.e. a summary), could serve to create a precise list of what was performed by the health organization and derive an automatic method for

© Springer International Publishing Switzerland 2015
G. Azzopardi and N. Petkov (Eds.): CAIP 2015, Part II, LNCS 9257, pp. 383–393, 2015.
DOI: 10.1007/978-3-319-23117-4_33

calculating hospitalization costs. Given the plethora in number and diversity of sources of medical documents, the purpose of summarization is to make users able to assimilate and easily determine the contents of a document, and then quickly determine the key points of it. In particular, as reported in [1]: *"A summary can be loosely defined as a text that is produced from one or more texts, that conveys important information in the original text(s), and that is no longer than half of the original text(s) and usually significantly less than that"*, but also denotes its most important challenge: *"Identifying the information segments at the expense of the rest is the main challenge in summarization"*. Generating summaries, however, is not trivial as it implies a deep understanding of the underlying semantics. This is even more challenging in the medical domain since medical reports include a highly specialized vocabulary, words in upper and lowercase letters and numbers that require ad-hoc tokenization. These problems urged the development of domain-specific resources such as PubMed/MEDLINE and PubMedCentral[1], ontologies and other semantic lexical resources, such as Gene Ontology[2] and Unified Medical Language System *(UMLS)*[3], and annotated databases, such as Entrez Gene[4] which are used heavily by a variety of text mining applications.

The objectives of the work presented herein is 1) to create automatically a summary that conveys the key points of medical reports and 2) to provide a tool for annotating the medical concepts found in the text with Linked Life Data *(LLD)*[5], so that the doctors or the patients can explore further what is being reported and also enable interoperability with other semantic web-enabled applications.

The remainder of the paper is as follows: the next section briefly presents related works, while Section 3 describes the method in detail and in Section 4 a performance evaluation of the system is carried out. Finally, in the last section conclusions are drawn and future works are given.

2   Related Work

Text summarization of medical documents was brought to the attention of the scientific community due to the tremendous growth of information that are available to physicians and researchers: the growing number of published journals, conference proceedings, medical sites and portals on the World Wide Web, electronic medical records, etc.

In particular, in the clinical context, there has been an increase of interest in the use of Electronic Medical Records *(EMR)* systems which may contain large amounts of text data, to improve the quality of healthcare [14]. To make full use of the information contained in the EMR and to support clinical decision,

---

[1] http://www.ncbi.nlm.nih.gov/pubmed

[2] http://www.geneontology.org/

[3] http://www.nlm.nih.gov/research/umls/

[4] http://www.ncbi.nlm.nih.gov/gene/

[5] http://linkedlifedata.com/

text mining techniques based on Natural Language Processing *(NLP)* have been especially proposed for information retrieval purposes or for extracting clinical summaries.

In [16], an information extraction system that extracts three types of information (numeric values, medical terms and categories) from semi-structured patient records, is presented. An extension to this system is presented in [15]: The MEDical Information Extraction (MedIE) system extracts a variety of information from free-text clinical records of patients with breast related diseases. MedIE uses GATE [5], WordNet [11] and UMLS, and employs a graph-based approach for numeric attribute extraction capable of performing the majority of information extraction tasks achieving remarkable results. In [10], the Keyphrase Identification Program *(KIP)* is proposed, for identifying medical concepts in medical documents. KIP combines two functions: noun phrase extraction and keyphrase identification. It automatically extracts phrases containing nouns using a part-of-speech tagger achieving fair results (0.26 in precision and 0.60 in recall, best case scenario). KIP ranks all the noun phrases in terms of their relevance to the main subject of the document, and selects only the most relevant ones by creating a glossary database from the Medical Subject Headings (MeSH) site. In [12] is presented a pipeline-based system for automated annotation of surgical pathology reports with UMLS terms built on GATE. The system implements a simple method for detecting and annotating UMLS concepts as well as annotating negations based on the NegEx algorithm [4], achieving very good results in terms of precision (0.84) and recall (0.80). In [13] another example of application that mines textual information by employing NLP methods is presented, but this time such information is being integrated with other types of biological data found on-line.

While all of these tools offer great insight on how concept identification and annotation can be done they do not offer any functionalities for single-document text summarization. Such feature can be found in more complex works, as in [9,2] where summarization of single documents is done by applying robust NLP techniques combined with conceptual mapping based on ad-hoc ontologies or lexicons. The main problem with these approaches is that the accuracy of the concept extraction, and subsequently the accuracy of the summarization, depends on the underlying lexicon, and in this particular case, the ontology. Not using well established ontologies carries the drawback of limiting the available identifiable concepts and also, their interoperability with other semantic web-based complementary systems. In [8], *UMLS* is used for concept mapping but the system does not deal with negative expressions leading to misinterpretations in the final summary.

In the next section the description of a system aiming at creating summaries out of medical records written in free text form by implementing a GATE pipeline, and also for assigning UMLS codes to the medical entities found inside them, is proposed.

3   Method

In order to produce a reliable summary, the corpus of medical documents must undergo through several processing steps. In this section, the tools used during this process are introduced and described. The basis of the developed system is GATE, which is the most used tool for implementing NLP-based applications. GATE uses regular expressions to configure all of its components (Tokenization, Sentence Splitter, POS tagging, Named Entity Recognition (NER) etc...).

The general architecture of the proposed system is shown in Fig. 1.

3.1   Text Processing and Annotation

ANNIE [6] is the information extraction component of the GATE platform and it substantially encapsulates the main NLP functions. In our case, an ANNIE pipeline was defined that employs the following components:

- **English Tokenizer:** The text in the corpus is divided into very simple tokens such as numbers, punctuation symbols or simple words. The main objective of this module is to maximize the efficiency and flexibility of the whole process by reducing the complexity introduced by the grammar rules.
- **Gazetteer:** Its role is to identify the names of entities based on lists, fed into the system in the form of plain text files. Each list is a collection of names, such as names of cities, organizations, days of the week, etc...
- **Sentence Splitter:** As its name suggests, it splits the text in simple sentences by using a list of abbreviations to distinguish sentence markers.
- **Part-of-speech Tagger:** Marks a word as corresponding to a particular part of speech based on both its definition and context. This is useful for the identification of words as nouns, verbs, adjectives, adverbs, etc. The results of this plug-in are the tokens used for the implementation of regular expressions.
- **Named Entity Transducer:** ANNIE's semantic tagger contains rules that work on the annotations of the previous phases to produce new annotations. It is used to create annotations regarding the terms related on negations, sections and phrases.
- **MetaMap Annotator:** This module serves the role of identifying medical terms found in text and map them to UMLS concepts by using NLP methods combined with computational linguistics [3].
- **Words Correction:** Given that the vast majority of the medical reports that we are dealing with were produced in a completely manual manner, misspellings do occur, making the medical term identification process less accurate. For this reason, each unannotated term (i.e. a word that does not exist) in the text is used as a query term against a dataset containing medical terms and the term with the smallest Levenshtein distance is retrieved. The result is used in place of the misspelled word in the original document.
- **Negated Expressions:** In order to achieve a correct interpretation of the text found in medical documents, it is very important be able to identify

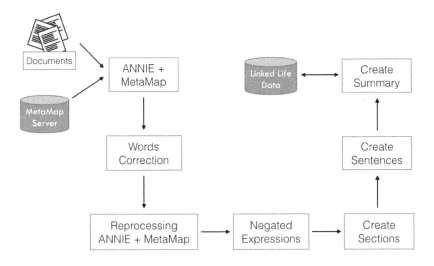

Fig. 1. General architecture of the proposed system.

negated expressions, which indicate the absence of a particular symptom or condition. MetaMap helps to identify negated concepts by providing a pair of features, namely "NegExType" and "NegExTrigger"; the former one identifies the negation, while the latter one specifies the term that expresses it. In this phase there are two problems that must be dealt with: a) the negated medical concept must be correlated to the term that triggers the negation effect and b) there are words that imply negation but MetaMap cannot identify them as such (e.g. the word inexistence). To overcome these problems, the Gazetteer is used again, by creating a new class of annotations relating exclusively to terms of negation.

- **Section Parsing:** For this phase, the Gazetteer plug-in is used by defining tags that could be possibly represent section labels. For our experiments the following tags were defined: admitting diagnosis, discharge diagnosis, symptoms, past medical history, family history, social history, hospital course, medications, diagnostic studies, discharge instructions.

3.2   Summary Generation

Not all of the annotations generated by the MetaMap Annotator are needed in the final summary. Each MetaMap annotation contains also the semantic type of the corresponding term (e.g. "Body Part" for the word "leg", "Manufactured Object" for the word "scalpel" etc...). Inevitably, terms belonging to certain semantic types are excluded from the summary because their importance might be negligible.

An issue that needs to be dealt with during summary generation is that many annotated phrases should be merged to one sentence. For example, the sentence "x-rays including left foot, right knee, left shoulder and cervical spine" would normally be divided in the tokens "x-rays", "left foot", "right knee", "cervical spine" and "left shoulder" even though all of them belong to the same sentence.

Regular expressions were employed to face this problem. In our case, the following regular expression was used:

$$(PRE)?(NEG)?((METAMAP)(NEG)?)+(POSTCONCEPT)?(POST)?,$$

where $METAMAP$ denotes the main medical concept identified by MetaMap (e.g. "amoxicillin", PRE denotes attributes that can precede the main concept (e.g. "significant", "treated with", "diagnosis of", "presence of" etc...), $POSTCONCEPT$ indicates a word directly correlated to the main concept (e.g. "1 g" for expressing dosage etc...) and $POST$ denotes eventual tokens that may represent a continuation of the sentence (e.g. commas, conjunctions etc...). Finally, the NEG term indicates whether a token expresses negativity or not.

The "+" and "?" operators describe the cardinality of each term with the "+" operator meaning "at least one or more" and the "?" operator meaning "zero or more".

For each identified section, the annotations relative to affirmative and negative expressions are created and for each sentence, the annotations produced by MetaMap are used. The same annotations are also used as query terms on the LLD site and the URLs pointing to the corresponding medical concepts are embedded to the final summary and exported in an HTML file.

An example of how the system works is shown below. Given the following discharge summary (the underlined words represent typographical errors):

ADMITTING DIAGNOSES: Intrauterine pregnancy at 36 weeks. Twin gestation. Breech presentation of twin A.

DISCHARGE DIAGNOSES: Intrauterine prengancy at 36 weeks. Twin gestation. Breech presentation of twin A. Status post primary low transverse cesarean section for malpresentation of twins.

CHIEF COMPLAINT: At the time of admission, contractions.

HISTORY: The patient is a 32-year-old pregnant at 36 weeks with known twins with contractions and good fetal movement, no bleeding, no loss of fluids.

OB HISTORY: Present pregnancy with previous receipt of a steroid window.

GYN HISTORY: Significant for chamydia, which was treated.

MEDICATIONS: Prenatal vitamins.

SOCIAL HISTORY: No drinking, smoking or drug use. No domestic violence. The father of the baby is currently involved, and the patient is living with a friend.

PHYSICAL EXAMINATION: Temperature is 36.2, pulse 88, respirations 18 and blood pressure 121/58. HEART: Regular rate and rhythm. LUNGS: Clear. ABDOMEN: Soft and gravid.

HOSPITAL COURSE: Postoperatively, the patient did well. She was eating, ambulating and voiding, passing gas by postoperative day 2, and on postoperative day 3, she continued to do well. She had been seen by Social Work and

options made aware to the patient. She was ready for discharge. She remained afebrile throughout her hospital course.
DISCHARGE INSTRUCTIONS: She will be discharged to home to follow up in two weeks for a wound check.
MEDICATIONS AT THE TIME OF DISCHARGE: Percocet, Motrin and Colace.

The result is a more compact form of the input document, with both the wrong words corrected and also contains the Linked Life Data links identified by MetaMap:

ADMITTING DIAGNOSIS: Intrauterine pregnancy. Breech presentation of twin.
SYMPTOMS: contractions.
DISCHARGE DIAGNOSIS: Intrauterine pregnancy. Breech presentation of twin. Malpresentation of twins.
DIAGNOSTIC STUDIES: Temperature 36.2, pulse 88, respirations 18 and blood pressure 121/58. HEART. LUNGS. ABDOMEN.VAGINAL
PAST MEDICAL HISTORY : Significant for chlamydia. known twins with contractions and good fetal movement ,. pregnancy. Receipt of a steroid window.
PAST MEDICAL HISTORY NEGATIVE: no bleeding, no loss of fluids.
SOCIAL HISTORY NEGATIVE : No drinking, smoking or drug use. No domestic violence.
MEDICATIONS : Prenatal vitamins. Percocet, Motrin and Colace.

By clicking on the underlined terms, the system redirects the reader to its *LLD* page (Fig. 2).

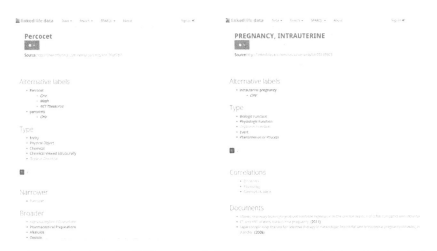

Fig. 2. Image showing the *LLD* pages of the terms *Percocet* (left) and *Intrauterine pregnancy* (right)

4 Performance Evaluation

As stated in [1], evaluating the performance of a summarization system is not a trivial task. To be more precise, while the quantitative evaluation can be based on clear and objective metrics, the qualitative one is not that straightforward because summarization efficiency is most often expressed as a subjective opinion of the individual rater (i.e. Inter-rater reliability). Nevertheless, because of the two-fold nature of these kind of systems, their performance evaluation should cover both these aspects. So, in order to assess exhaustively the performance of the proposed system we tested it under three different perspectives and compared the results to a hand-crafted ground-truth (described in Subsection 4.1). For all the evaluations we employed Precision-Recall and F_1 measure values defined as follows:

$$Precision = \frac{TP}{TP + FP},$$

$$Recall = \frac{TP}{TP + FN}$$

and

$$F_1 = \frac{Precision \times Recall}{Precision + Recall}$$

The FP, TP and FN values are defined separately for each of the aspects tested. The obtained results were compared against a manually created dataset by five medical doctors that contained both positive and negative sentences. The dataset was comprised by 125 medical reports containing 3611 annotated sentences (2824 positive and 787 negative) and 15641 annotated medical concepts.

- **Medical concept recognition**: The first aspect of the system that was tested was its ability to identify correctly the medical concepts found inside the medical reports.
  - A True Positive *(TP)* results when an identified medical concept is the same with the manual annotation.
  - A False Negative *(FN)* results when a medical concept was not identified correctly or was not identified at all.
  - A False Positive *(FP)* results when a medical concept was assigned a different label or when a non medical term was identified as such.

Table 1. Performance of the system in recognizing correctly the medical concepts.

N	TP	FP	FN	P	R	F_1
15641	12499	2419	3142	0.84	0.8	0.82

– **Sentence identification and polarity detection**: The second aspect of the system that was tested was its ability to extract correctly the single sentences in the medical report and also to assign correctly the negation attribute to the medical concepts detected by the previous test, using regular expressions.
  - A True Positive *(TP)* results when an identified sentence is found also in the ground truth and was assigned the correct polarity.
  - A False Negative *(FN)* results when a sentence found in the ground truth was not identified as such or when an annotated sentence was divided erroneously between two other sentences or when the negation property was not assigned to a negative sentence .
  - A False Positive *(FP)* when a sentence is erroneously identified as such, but instead, in the ground truth, its terms do not belong in the same one or when the negation property was assigned to a positive sentence.

Table 2. Performance of the system on sentence detection and polarity detection.

N	TP	FP	FN	P	R	F_1
3611	2808	531	803	0.84	0.78	0.81

– **Summary relevance**: Additionally, the quality of the produced summary was evaluated. To achieve this, the same five medical doctors were presented with both the original reports and the final results and then asked to assess qualitatively the relevance of the summaries (i.e. express their personal opinions on what medical concepts should be included in the final summary versus what should be excluded). After that, the following parameters were defined:
  - A True Positive *(TP)*: A concept that the medical doctors felt that should be included in the final summary and it was.
  - A False Negative *(FN)*: A concept that the medical doctors felt that should be included in the final summary but it was not.
  - A False Positive *(FP)*: A concept that the medical doctors felt that should not be included in the final summary but it was.

Table 3. Performance of the system on summary accuracy. The final result was calculated based on the sum of the votes of the medical doctors.

N	TP	FP	FN	P	R	F_1
15641	11499	3514	4142	0.77	0.74	0.75

5 Discussion

Sentence identification and polarity detection performance was very good. Indeed, an $F_1 score$ value of 0.81 means that the algorithms employed to do this task performed very well. More detailed inspection of the failing sentences were due to misplaced punctuation marks and missing negative keywords from the employed dictionary that could provoke ambiguity problems if they were ultimately included (e.g. the word *"will"* in the sentence *"...will develop cancer..."* does not imply that the patient has cancer). The results in medical concept recognition are almost equal as high. An $F_1 score$ value of 0.82 means that the MetaMap module is very accurate in identifying the medical concepts found in the reports. Especially important are the results in the summary accuracy test where the subjective opinion of the intended end users of the system (the medical doctors) determine its utility. An $F_1 score$ value of 0.75 implies that the generated summaries are valid and also demonstrates that the proposed system can be a robust solution for other applications that will make use of its functionalities, such as [7].

In this paper a system that automatically generates summaries taking as input the corpus of unstructured medical reports, was presented. Such summaries, are also annotated with links which the reader can follow in order to get a short description of the corresponding medical concepts. The same system could be configured to use the International Classification of Diseases (ICD) dictionary, instead of or in addition to UMLS, to assign codes to diseases making the system more compatible with existing systems.

References

1. Afantenos, S., Karkaletsis, V., Stamatopoulos, P.: Summarization from medical documents: a survey. Artificial Intelligence in Medicine **33**(2), 157–177 (2005)
2. Aramaki, E., Miura, Y., Tonoike, M., Ohkuma, T., Mashuichi, H., Ohe, K.: Text2table: medical text summarization system based on named entity recognition and modality identification. In: Proceedings of the Workshop on Current Trends in Biomedical Natural Language Processing, pp. 185–192. Association for Computational Linguistics (2009)
3. Aronson, A.R.: Effective mapping of biomedical text to the umls metathesaurus: the metamap program. In: Proceedings of the AMIA Symposium, p. 17. American Medical Informatics Association (2001)
4. Chapman, W.W., Bridewell, W., Hanbury, P., Cooper, G.F., Buchanan, B.G.: A simple algorithm for identifying negated findings and diseases in discharge summaries. Journal of biomedical informatics **34**(5), 301–310 (2001)
5. Cunningham, H.: Gate, a general architecture for text engineering. Computers and the Humanities **36**(2), 223–254 (2002)
6. Cunningham, H., Maynard, D., Bontcheva, K., Tablan, V.: GATE: a framework and graphical development environment for robust NLP tools and applications. In: Proceedings of the 40th Anniversary Meeting of the Association for Computational Linguistics (ACL 2002) (2002)

7. Giordano, D., Kavasidis, I., Spampinato, C., Bella, R., Pennisi, G., Pennisi, M.: An integrated computer-controlled system for assisting researchers in cortical excitability studies by using transcranial magnetic stimulation. Computer methods and programs in biomedicine **107**(1), 4–15 (2012)
8. Johnson, D.B., Zou, Q., Dionisio, J.D., Liu, V.Z., Chu, W.W.: Modeling medical content for automated summarization. Annals of the New York Academy of Sciences **980**(1), 247–258 (2002)
9. Lenci, A., Bartolini, R., Calzolari, N., Agua, A., Busemann, S., Cartier, E., Chevreau, K., Coch, J.: Multilingual summarization by integrating linguistic resources in the mlis-musi project. LREC **2**, 1464–1471 (2002)
10. Li, Q., Wu, Y.F.B.: Identifying important concepts from medical documents. Journal of biomedical informatics **39**(6), 668–679 (2006)
11. Miller, G.A.: Wordnet: a lexical database for english. Communications of the ACM **38**(11), 39–41 (1995)
12. Mitchell, K.J., Becich, M.J., Berman, J.J., Chapman, W.W., Gilbertson, J., Gupta, D., Harrison, J., Legowski, E., Crowley, R.S.: Implementation and evaluation of a negation tagger in a pipeline-based system for information extraction from pathology reports. Medinfo **2004**, 663–667 (2004)
13. Spampinato, C., Kavasidis, I., Aldinucci, M., Pino, C., Giordano, D., Faro, A.: Discovering biological knowledge by integrating high-throughput data and scientific literature on the cloud. Concurrency and Computation: Practice and Experience (2013)
14. Wang, S.J., Middleton, B., Prosser, L.A., Bardon, C.G., Spurr, C.D., Carchidi, P.J., Kittler, A.F., Goldszer, R.C., Fairchild, D.G., Sussman, A.J., et al.: A cost-benefit analysis of electronic medical records in primary care. The American journal of medicine **114**(5), 397–403 (2003)
15. Zhou, X., Han, H., Chankai, I., Prestrud, A., Brooks, A.: Approaches to text mining for clinical medical records. In: Proceedings of the 2006 ACM symposium on Applied computing, pp. 235–239. ACM (2006)
16. Zhou, X., Han, H., Chankai, I., Prestrud, A.A., Brooks, A.D.: Converting semi-structured clinical medical records into information and knowledge. In: 21st International Conference on Data Engineering Workshops, 2005, pp. 1162–1162. IEEE (2005)

Bilateral Filtering of 3D Point Clouds
for Refined 3D Roadside Reconstructions

Bradley Moorfield[1]([✉]), Ralf Haeusler[1], and Reinhard Klette[2]

[1] Department of Computer Science, The University of Auckland,
Auckland, New Zealand
bmoo063@aucklanduni.ac.nz

[2] School of Engineering, Auckland University of Technology,
Auckland, New Zealand

Abstract. Stereo vision systems mounted on mobile platforms such as a road vehicles facilitate quick and inexpensive 3D reconstructions. However, reconstructed point clouds are noisy and appear unappealing in visualizations if not using shape priors or other specific ways of improvement. This paper describes a generic method to enhance the appearance of reconstructed meshes using bilateral filtering to smooth point clouds while preserving edge features and other small details. We demonstrate on synthetic and measured data that the proposed filtering process is beneficial for visualizations of noisy 3D data, and also for the preservation of the basic geometry of a real-world scene.

1   Introduction

Applications of high-fidelity 3D reconstructions of urban areas include the understanding of, and reacting to the physical environment of driver assistance systems, and the ability to interact with the reconstruction. This develops into a basis for technologies such as virtual reality or high-accuracy 3D city maps.

Building a 3D reconstruction on a large scale in an efficient manner is still a challenging task. There is a large trade-off in time spent manually adjusting reconstruction parameters and quality of the reconstruction. An automated system which produces acceptable results would permit rapid large scale reconstructions. Most commonly laser scanners or camera systems are used for 3D reconstruction. Laser scanners produce very accurate depth information, but are still slow if used for high-resolution scans, expensive, and do not capture colour. Camera systems are inexpensive, can be used in real time, and do capture colour information. Calculating accurate depth information, however, is still a challenging problem for camera systems. Results are frequently not as accurate as those of laser scanners.

There are commercial products providing 3D reconstructions of satisfactory quality, such as 3D Reality Maps [1], which is based on aerial camera systems, the automated analysis of stereo data, but also on extensive manual intervention, the use of shape priors and replacement of standard objects (e.g. of trees) by

G. Azzopardi and N. Petkov (Eds.): CAIP 2015, Part II, LNCS 9257, pp. 394–402, 2015.
DOI: 10.1007/978-3-319-23117-4_34

templates. Incorporation of data from automatically generated detailed reconstructions at street level may enhance this process.

Ground-based techniques for automatically generating 3D roadside visualisations have been presented by Xiao et al. [17] or Geiger et al. [7]. Using shape priors, results from a single 3D stereo pair can be mapped into a realistically looking 3D model. These methods do not support generation of 3D models from stereo video streams.

Huang and Klette [10] presented a method to combine ground level and aerial images to improve accuracy and detail in large scale reconstructions. Recently, Zeng and Klette [18] proposed a framework for merging multiple roadside reconstructions based on stereo vision with data captured from a moving vehicle. Klette [11] also discussed a multi-run roadside reconstruction framework used to generate point cloud and surface reconstructions from stereo image sequences, where data of the same location is captured repeatedly and unified into a single consistent 3D model. Zeng and Klette [18] identified open problems in the field, such as automated refinement of reconstructed surfaces for ensuring consistency with actual scene geometry. This paper contributes a solution to address the issue of large amounts of noise present in reconstructed point clouds which may impact robust meshing.

We propose a point cloud filtering method which smoothes noise while retaining sharp corners and detail and demonstrate results of the method applied to large-scale data.

The paper is structured as follows. Section 2 introduces a method for smoothing noise in point clouds. Sections 3.1 and 3.2 present experiments and an evaluation on synthetic and real-world data. Section 4 concludes.

2   Bilateral Filtering of Point Clouds

The bilateral filter, introduced as a 2D image filter by Tomasi and Manduchi [16], is an edge preserving smoothing filter based on Gaussian blur which has been used for denoising 3D meshes [5,12] with excellent results. The method in [12] uses face normals, which can only be obtained after the mesh has been reconstructed. Our method is applied on point clouds before any mesh has been reconstructed. This gives the advantage that meshing is performed on a smoothed point cloud. There have been experiments with alternative techniques such as anisotropic diffusion [14] and robust estimation [4]. However, these are strongly related to bilateral filtering [2,4]. In this work we give preference to bilateral filtering [12] for denoising as it is non-iterative and simple to implement.

The bilateral filter for an image $I(\mathbf{u})$, at coordinate $\mathbf{u} = (x,y)$, was defined by Tomasi and Manduchi [16] as follows:

$$\hat{I}(\mathbf{u}) = \frac{\sum_{\mathbf{p} \in N(\mathbf{u})} W_c(\|\mathbf{p} - \mathbf{u}\|) W_s(|I(\mathbf{u}) - I(\mathbf{p})|) I(\mathbf{p})}{\sum_{\mathbf{p} \in N(\mathbf{u})} W_c(\|\mathbf{p} - \mathbf{u}\|) W_s(|I(\mathbf{u}) - I(\mathbf{p})|)} , \tag{1}$$

where $N(\mathbf{u})$ is the neighbourhood of $\mathbf{u}$, defined as the set of points

$$\{\mathbf{q}_i : \|\mathbf{u} - \mathbf{q}_i\| < \rho = 2\sigma_c\} . \tag{2}$$

The spatial smoothing function W_c is a standard Gaussian filter $W_c(x) = e^{-x^2/2\sigma_c^2}$ with standard deviation σ_c. The intensity smoothing function is also chosen to be a standard Gaussian filter $W_s(x) = e^{-x^2/2\sigma_s^2}$, with standard deviation σ_s.

We adapt existing definitions of bilateral filtering on 3D triangular meshes [12] for point clouds, such that vertex normals instead of face normals are modified. For a mesh vertex i with unit vertex normal $\hat{\mathbf{n}}_i$ and location $\mathbf{c}_i$, the bilateral filtered normal $\bar{\mathbf{n}}_i$ at the vertex i is defined as follows:

$$\bar{\mathbf{n}}_i = \frac{\sum_{j \in N(i)} W_c(\|\mathbf{c}_j - \mathbf{c}_i\|) W_s(d_{ij}) \hat{\mathbf{n}}_j}{\sum_{j \in N(i)} W_c(\|\mathbf{c}_j - \mathbf{c}_i\|) W_s(d_{ij})} , \qquad (3)$$

where $N(i) = \{j : \|\mathbf{c}_j - \mathbf{c}_i\| < \rho = \lceil 2\sigma_c \rceil\}$ is the set of neighbourhood vertices j of vertex i, with unit vertex normal $\hat{\mathbf{n}}_j$, and d_{ij} is the *intensity difference* between the two vertex normals $\hat{\mathbf{n}}_i$ and $\hat{\mathbf{n}}_j$. The intensity difference is defined to be the projection of the normal difference vector $\hat{\mathbf{n}}_i - \hat{\mathbf{n}}_j$ on the vertex normal $\hat{\mathbf{n}}_i$:

$$d_{ij} = \hat{\mathbf{n}}_i \cdot (\hat{\mathbf{n}}_i - \hat{\mathbf{n}}_j) . \qquad (4)$$

For each vertex i, we use the bilateral filter as in Equation (3) to compute the smoothed normal $\bar{\mathbf{n}}_i$. The bilateral filter is then run to smooth the position of the vertices using the smoothed normals; see [6].

For each vertex i, the prediction from a neighbour point $\hat{\mathbf{c}}_j$ is the projection of $\mathbf{c}_i$ onto the plane through $\mathbf{c}_j$ with normal $\mathbf{n}_j$. The resulting displacement is projected on the line through $\mathbf{c}_i$ with direction $\mathbf{n}_i$, which constrains the movement of the vertex along its smoothed normal. The displacement of point c_i is then given by

$$\hat{\mathbf{x}}_i = \frac{\sum_{j \in N(i)} W_c(\|\mathbf{c}_j - \mathbf{c}_i\|) W_s(d_{ij}) \mathbf{x}_j}{\sum_{j \in N(i)} W_c(\|\mathbf{c}_j - \mathbf{c}_i\|) W_s(d_{ij})} , \qquad (5)$$

Algorithm 1. Bilateral point cloud filtering

1: **procedure** POINTCLOUDBILATERAL(C)   ▷ Input: Point cloud C
2:     Intialise empty cloud of normal vectors D
3:     **for all** $i \in C$ **do**   ▷ Compute normal based on neighbourhood N
4:         $\mathbf{n}_i \leftarrow$ normal estimated from covariance matrix of $N(i)$
5:         Add $\mathbf{n}_i$ to D
6:     Intialise empty cloud of normal vectors E
7:     **for all** $i \in D$ **do**
8:         $\mathbf{n}_i \leftarrow$ Update normal vector as in Equation (3)
9:         Add updated normal vector $\mathbf{n}_i$ to E
10:     Intialise empty point cloud F
11:     **for all** $i \in E$ **do**
12:         $\hat{\mathbf{x}}_i \leftarrow$ result of bilateral filter at current point location as in Equation (5)
13:         $\hat{\mathbf{p}}_i \leftarrow$ corresponding $\mathbf{c}_i$ in C displaced by $\hat{\mathbf{x}}_i$
14:         Add $\hat{\mathbf{p}}_i$ to F
15:     Output F

Table 1. Comparison of distance measures of deformed and smoothed point clouds with the base mesh. In most cases, the proposed bilateral filter produces more accurate reconstructions than Laplacian filtering. Values are shown as mean distance with standard deviation in brackets.

Mesh	Deformed	Laplacian smooth	Bilateral smooth
Cube	0.16 (0.12)	0.27 (1.1)	0.07 (0.05)
Cone	0.29 (0.02)	0.30 (0.15)	0.012 (0.009)
Tophat	28.9 (17.7)	14.2 (19.8)	14.3 (11.2)
Fandisk	0.019 (0.01)	0.010 (0.01)	0.010 (0.01)
House	4.78 (2.9)	1.82 (2.8)	1.19 (1.1)

where the displacement from c_i to the predicted position $\hat{c}_j$ is

$$x_j = (((n_i \cdot n_j)n_j) \cdot n_i)n_i .\tag{6}$$

Algorithm 1 outlines the procedure.

3   Results and Discussion

This section first presents results of bilateral filtering applied to synthetic meshes followed by a quantitative comparison with conventional filtering methods. The second part of this section illustrates applications of the proposed bilateral filter to 3D data obtained by a stereo-matching process from real-world scenes. These are discussed qualitatively.

3.1   Synthetic Data

As a "proof of concept" we illustrate the effect of Algorithm 1, which is designed to process large-scale data, on three point clouds with vertices synthetically

Fig. 1. Visual comparison of methods on the tophat mesh. From left to right: the base mesh, base mesh with vertices displaced by 0.3% of bounding box diagonal, deformed mesh after three iterations of Laplacian smoothing, and mesh after smoothing with the bilateral filter.

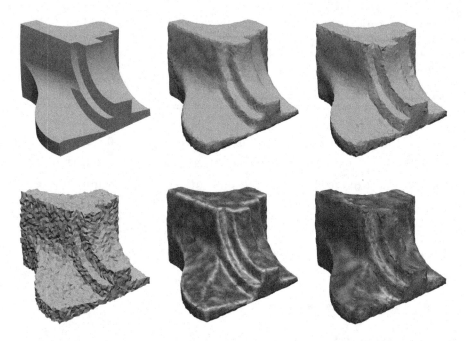

Fig. 2. Visual comparison of methods on the fandisk mesh. The first column shows original *(top)* and deformed (5%) *(bottom)* meshes. The middle column shows the deformed mesh after smoothing with three iterations of Laplacian smoothing, and the last column shows the deformed mesh after smoothing with the bilateral filter.

displaced by normally distributed noise. Laplacian smoothing and Bilateral filtering both update each vertex position based on locations of neighbouring vertices; see Figs. 1, 2, and 3.

Figure 1 compares methods on a tophat mesh. It shows the base mesh, the base mesh with vertices displaced by 0.3% of bounding box diagonal, a deformed mesh after three iterations of Laplacian smoothing, and a mesh after smoothing with the bilateral filter. Figure 2 compares methods on the geometrically more complex fandisk mesh, showing the original and a deformed (5%) mesh; the deformed mesh then again after smoothing with three iterations of Laplacian smoothing. The surface is shown coloured according to distance from the original mesh. The last column shows the deformed mesh after smoothing with the bilateral filter, using the same colour scale to indicate geometric distances. Figure 3 illustrates methods for the geometrically even more complex house mesh, starting with showing the original and a deformed (0.1% displacement) mesh in the top row.

Visual inspection of the resulting meshes indicates that both algorithms smooth out the noise well, but the bilateral filter better preserves the edges present in base meshes. Laplacian smoothing has the undesirable effect of reducing volume in regions of high curvature, as the neighbouring vertices draw the

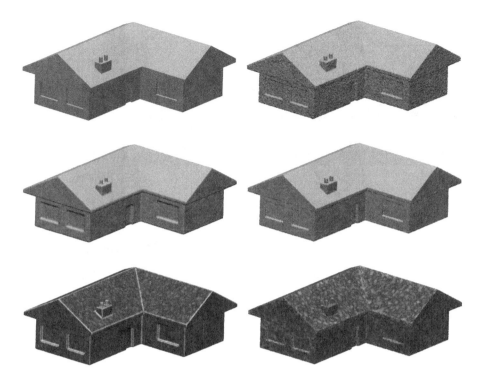

Fig. 3. Visual comparison of methods on the house mesh. The first row shows the original and deformed (0.1% displacement) meshes. The middle row shows the deformed mesh after smoothing with three iterations of Laplacian smoothing *(left)* and smoothing using the bilateral filter *(right)*. The bottom row shows the smoothed meshes coloured by the distance from the original mesh.

vertex towards the inside of the curve. This is visible in the meshes when coloured by distance from the original mesh. Laplacian smoothing has regions of high distance around all edges in the Fandisk and House models, whereas bilateral filtering preserves edges. The distance between smoothed and original meshes is much smaller in high curvature regions. To quantify algorithm performance, we measure distances between the base point cloud and the smoothed point cloud; see Tab. 1. Here, the distance of a vertex in the smoothed point cloud is defined as the smallest distance to the nearest face on the base mesh.

3.2   Reconstructed Data

We apply the proposed bilateral filter to 3D data generated from stereo recordings of real-world scenes. These stereo pairs were captured at 30 Hz from a moving vehicle, using a trinocular camera set-up, with 16 bit per pixel and at resolution of 2046 × 1080. Ten minutes of recording generate about 126 GB of data. Correspondingly, the number of generated 3D points is fairly large.

Fig. 4. Data delivered by stereo cameras installed in test vehicle HAKA1. *top left*: Left camera image. *top right*: Raw point cloud rendered with image intensities. *bottom left*: Meshed point cloud after Laplacian smoothing. *bottom right*: Meshed point cloud after bilateral filtering.

Fig. 5. A scene reconstructed from data of the KITTI benchmark. Top left shows the unfiltered reconstruction. Top right shows the reconstruction when the point cloud is filtered using Laplacian smoothing. Bottom left shows the reconstruction when the point cloud is filtered using the bilateral filter. Bottom right shows the reconstruction coloured according to the distances between the Laplacian and bilateral filtered reconstructions.

For stereo matching we use a variant of semi-global matching [8] as available currently in OpenCV.

Fig 4 illustrates resulting data. The input stereo video data have been recorded in the test vehicle of the *enpeda..* project. Recorded images (see top left in the figure for an example) are of 2046 by 1080 pixel resolution, but the shown and used raw point cloud has been reduced in resolution using a voxel grid filter, reducing the size of the point cloud by approximately six times. The filtered meshes have smoothed flat regions, however the Laplacian smoothing has reduced the volume of shapes in the reconstruction. Note that there is no vertical curb in this road

We illustrate the performance of the designed filter also on data from the KITTI benchmark, using the same stereo matcher as above.

Fig. 5 illustrates 3D geometry generated from KITTI data. Top left shows the unfiltered reconstruction, top right shows the reconstruction when the point cloud is filtered using Laplacian smoothing, bottom left shows the reconstruction when the point cloud is filtered using the bilateral filter, and bottom right shows the reconstruction coloured according to the distances between the Laplacian and bilateral filtered reconstructions.

4   Conclusions

Bilateral filtering is known in general as being an effective method for smoothing noise in 2D images and 3D meshes. In this paper we have described a simple, non-iterative method for smoothing point clouds while preserving sharp edges and corners, based on a method for applying the bilateral filter on a 3D mesh. The paper provided a particular adaptation of a bilateral filter on 3D data designed for dealing with very large-scale, incrementally generated roadside data.

The presented generic method of bilateral filtering of 3D point clouds leads to visual improvements of 3D meshes reconstructed from noisy 3D data without using any shape prior. The method can be recommended for a general processing pipeline for creating 3D roadside models from streams of stereo video data.

References

1. 3D Reality Maps, April 2013. www.realitymaps.de/en/ (accessed)
2. Barash, D.: A fundamental relationship between bilateral filtering, adaptive smoothing and the nonlinear diffusion equation. IEEE Trans. Pattern Analysis Machine Intelligence **24**, 121–131 (2002)
3. Bay, H., Tuytelaars, T., Van Gool, L.: SURF: speeded up robust features. In: Leonardis, A., Bischof, H., Pinz, A. (eds.) ECCV 2006, Part I. LNCS, vol. 3951, pp. 404–417. Springer, Heidelberg (2006)
4. Black, M., Sapiro, G., Marimont, D., Heeger, D.: Robust anisotropic diffusion. IEEE Trans. Image Processing **7**, 421–432 (1998)
5. Fleishman, S., Drori, I., Cohen-Or, D.: Bilateral mesh denoising. ACM Trans. Graphics **22**, 950–953 (2003)

6. Gao, Z., Neumann, U.: Feature enhancing aerial LiDAR point cloud refinement. In: Proc. SPIE 9013 (2014)
7. Geiger, A., Ziegler, J., Stiller, C.: StereoScan: dense 3d reconstruction in real-time. In: Proc. IEEE IV, 963–968 (2011)
8. Hirschmüller, H.: Accurate and efficient stereo processing by semi global matching and mutual information. In: Proc. CVPR (2005)
9. Hermann, S., Klette, R.: Iterative semi-global matching for robust driver assistance systems. In: Lee, K.M., Matsushita, Y., Rehg, J.M., Hu, Z. (eds.) ACCV 2012, Part III. LNCS, vol. 7726, pp. 465–478. Springer, Heidelberg (2013)
10. Huang, F., Klette, R.: City-scale modeling towards street navigation applications. J. Information Convergence Communication Engineering 10 (2012)
11. Klette, R.: Concise Computer Vision: An Introduction into Theory and Algorithms. Springer, London (2014)
12. Lee, K., Wang, W.: Feature-preserving mesh denoising via bilateral normal filtering. In: CADCG (2005)
13. Nister, D., Naroditsky, O., Bergen, J.: Visual odometry. Proc. CVPR 1, 652–659 (2004)
14. Persona, P., Malik, J.: Scale-space and edge detection using anisotropic diffusion. IEEE Trans. Pattern Analysis Machine Intelligence 12, 629–639 (1990)
15. Sünderhauf, N., Konolige, K., Lacroix, S., Protzel, P.: Visual odometry using sparse bundle adjustment on an autonomous outdoor vehicle. In: Proc. Autonome Mobile Systems, pp. 157–163 (2005)
16. Tomasi, C., Manduchi, R.: Bilateral filtering for gray and color images. In: Proc. ICCV, pp. 839–846 (1998)
17. Xiao, J., Fang, T., Zhao, P., Lhuilier, M., Quan, L.: Image-based street-side city modeling. In: Proc. SIGGRAPH, pp. 114:1–114:12 (2009)
18. Zeng, Y., Klette, R.: Incremental 3D streetside reconstruction from a vehicle. In: Proc. CAIP, pp. 580–588 (2013)

Can Computer Vision Problems Benefit from Structured Hierarchical Classification?

Thomas Hoyoux[1]([⊠]), Antonio J. Rodríguez-Sánchez[2], Justus H. Piater[2], and Sandor Szedmak[2]

[1] INTELSIG, Montefiore Institute, University of Liège, Liège, Belgium
thomas.hoyoux@ulg.ac.be
[2] Intelligent and Interactive Systems, Institute of Computer Science,
University of Innsbruck, Innsbruck, Austria

Abstract. While most current research in the classification domain still focuses on standard "flat" classification, there is an increasing interest in a particular type of structured classification called hierarchical classification. Incorporating knowledge about class hierarchy should be beneficial to computer vision systems as suggested by the fact that humans seem to organize objects into hierarchical structures based on visual geometrical similarities. In this paper, we analyze whether hierarchical classification provides better performance than flat classification by comparing three structured classification methods – Structured K-Nearest Neighbors, Structured Support Vector Machines and Maximum Margin Regression – with their flat counterparts on two very different computer vision tasks: facial expression recognition, for which we emphasize the underlying hierarchical structure, and 3D shape classification. The obtained results show no or only marginal improvement, which questions the way the data should be exploited for hierarchical classification in computer vision.

Keywords: Hierarchical classification · Flat classification · Structured K-Nearest Neighbors · Structured Support Vector Machines · Maximum Margin Regression · 3D shape classification · Expression recognition

1 Introduction

Most current efforts in the classification domain involve multiclass or binary classification, also known as flat classification [14]. In these types of classification a bee, an ant and a hammer are considered to be different to the same degree; they belong to different classes in a flat sense because all classes are defined at the same semantic level. However ants and bees are in the same superclass of insects, while hammers belong to another superclass about tools. In the context of classification based on visual features, exploiting geometrical and part similarities in a hierarchical fashion seems to reflect the natural way in which humans recognize the objects they see.

© Springer International Publishing Switzerland 2015
G. Azzopardi and N. Petkov (Eds.): CAIP 2015, Part II, LNCS 9257, pp. 403–414, 2015.
DOI: 10.1007/978-3-319-23117-4_35

Accordingly, it is only logical to believe that current computer vision systems can benefit from classifiers that are able to exploit geometrical similarities using a pre-established taxonomy in a similar way the human visual system does. A recent survey paper [14] reports that – after analyzing dozens of articles published over the past decade – the hierarchical approach to classification outperforms the flat approach for various tasks, although most tasks studied were not visual.

In this paper, we further examine the potential of hierarchical classification in computer vision by applying it to two inherently hierarchical vision problems. The first problem of interest is the recognition of facial expressions, seen as a combination of Action Units (AUs) as defined in the Facial Action Coding System (FACS) [4]. The second problem of interest is that of 3D shape classification, for which we take five popular 3D shape descriptors into consideration. In practice there are various ways of implementing the concept of hierarchical classification. In this work, we are interested in global hierarchical classification methods as opposed to local methods. Global exploration means that one single classifier is trained and used by considering the entire class hierarchy at once. For both problems of interest, results obtained with Maximum Margin Regression [1] (MMR), Structured Support Vector Machines [16] (SSVM) and a structured output version of the standard K-Nearest Neighbor algorithm (which we call SkNN) are compared. All three methods implement the global approach to hierarchical classification which makes them especially suited to such a comparison. We compare as well with their flat counterparts, which are MMR not using structured information, a multiclass kernel-based SVM, and the standard kNN. In order to get a meaningful evaluation of the hierarchical approach potentiality, we take care of using appropriately designed evaluation measures.

Our starting hypothesis is that hierarchical classification can improve performance over flat classification in computer vision, independently of the classifier used and the task to which it is applied. We would like to stress here that our aim is not to outperform previous facial expression recognition methods in our first set of experiments, or to show which descriptor among those used here is better in our second set of experiments.

The remainder of this paper is organized as follows. Section 2 describes the framework and terminology we adopt for defining our hierarchical classification problems and methods, and provides the details of the hierarchical methods used in this work. Section 3 presents our experimental results for the computer vision problems we take into consideration. Those results are further discussed in section 4, and conclusions are drawn in section 5.

2   Materials and Methods

2.1   Framework and Terminology

Recently a necessary effort to unify the hierarchical classification framework has been made [14]. We follow on their terminology which is summarized next.

A class taxonomy $\mathcal{C}$ is a finite set of nodes $\{c_i \mid i = 1 \ldots n\}$ enumerating all classes and superclasses, which can be organized as a tree or as a Directed Acyclic Graph (DAG). A *hierarchical classification problem* and its corresponding *hierarchical classification algorithm* deals with either multiple or single labeled path(s), i.e. whether or not a single data instance can be labeled with more than one path, and either full or partial depth labeling, i.e. whether or not any labeled path must cover all hierarchy levels. In all our applications, we use tree taxonomies with full depth labeling. For facial expression recognition, we have multiple labeled paths per instance (see section 3.1), and for 3D shape classification we have a single labeled path for each instance (see section 3.2). In the context of hierarchical classification, we assume a vectorial representation for a label $\mathbf{y} \in \mathcal{Y}$, more specifically a Boolean category vector – or indicator vector – representation, i.e. $\mathcal{Y} := \{0,1\}^n$, where the ith component of $\mathbf{y}$ takes value 1 if the sample belongs to the (super)class – i.e. hierarchy node – $c_i \in \mathcal{C}$, and 0 otherwise.

Evaluation measures used in classical flat classification may not be appropriate when comparing hierarchical algorithms to each other, or flat algorithms to hierarchical algorithms. Those measures do not penalize structural errors and do not consider that misclassification at different levels of the class hierarchy should be treated in different ways. We will adopt the following metrics [6], also recommended by [14]: hierarchical precision (hP), hierarchical recall (hR) and hierarchical F-measure (hF). These metrics are extensions of the classical precision, recall and F-score measures and reduce to them as special cases if applied to a flat classification problem:

$$ hP = \frac{\sum_i |\hat{P}_i \cap \hat{T}_i|}{\sum_i |\hat{P}_i|}, \qquad hR = \frac{\sum_i |\hat{P}_i \cap \hat{T}_i|}{\sum_i |\hat{T}_i|}, \qquad hF = \frac{2\,hP\,hR}{hP + hR}, \qquad (1) $$

where $\hat{P}_i$ is the set of the most specific class(es) predicted for a test example i and all its (their) ancestor classes, and $\hat{T}_i$ is the set of the true most specific class(es) of a test example i and all its (their) ancestor classes.

2.2   Structured Hierarchical Classifiers

We modified the classical kNN classification method to make it able to cope with a structured vectorial output, that is, vectorial outputs which are guaranteed to respect a predefined class taxonomy. We call the resulting classification method Structured output K-Nearest Neighbors (SkNN). We train the SkNN classifier in the same way as the standard kNN classifier, i.e. projecting the training data instances into the feature space. The choice of the feature map ϕ is left to the user, as well as the metric ρ used for finding the neighbors and the number k of neighbors to consider. Let $\mathcal{D} \subset \mathcal{X} \times \mathcal{Y}$ be the training set of a hierarchical classification problem. Given the k nearest neighbors $\mathcal{N} = \{(\mathbf{x}_i, \mathbf{y}_i) \mid i \in \{1 \ldots k\}\} \subset \mathcal{D}$ to a test data instance $\mathbf{x} \in \mathcal{X}$, the classification rule for SkNN is

$$ \hat{\mathbf{y}}(\mathbf{x}; \mathcal{N}) = \underset{\mathbf{y} \in \mathcal{Y}}{\operatorname{argmax}} \left\langle \sum_{i=1}^{k} w_i \frac{\mathbf{y}_i}{\|\mathbf{y}_i\|}, \frac{\mathbf{y}}{\|\mathbf{y}\|} \right\rangle, \qquad (2) $$

where w_i are the weights attributed to the neighbors. Weights may be determined using various strategies; they can for example reflect the distances of the neighbors to the test instance, i.e. $w_i = \rho(\phi(\mathbf{x}_i), \phi(\mathbf{x}))^{-1}$, or they can be the same for all neighbors, i.e. $w_i = 1/k$, or any other weighting strategy the user would find suitable.

Our second hierarchical classification method is the Structured output Support Vector Machine (SSVM) [16], which extends classical SVM to arbitrary output spaces with non-trivial structure. SSVM defines the relation between an input data point $\mathbf{x} \in \mathcal{X}$ and its prediction $\hat{\mathbf{y}} \in \mathcal{Y}$ on the basis of a joint score maximization,

$$\hat{\mathbf{y}}(\mathbf{x}; \mathbf{w}) = \underset{y \in \mathcal{Y}}{\operatorname{argmax}} \langle \mathbf{w}, \ \psi(\mathbf{x}, \mathbf{y}) \rangle, \tag{3}$$

where ψ is a user-defined joint feature map $\psi : \mathcal{X} \times \mathcal{Y} \to \mathbb{R}^d$ which projects any pair $(\mathbf{x}, \mathbf{y})$ to its real-valued vectorial representation in a joint feature space. We define the joint feature map for our custom SSVM framework as

$$\psi : \quad \mathcal{X} \times \mathcal{Y} \to \mathbb{R}^d, \quad (\mathbf{x}, \mathbf{y}) \mapsto \phi(\mathbf{x}) \otimes \frac{\mathbf{y}}{||\mathbf{y}||}. \tag{4}$$

For our third structured output classification method, we apply a Maximum Margin based Regression (MMR) technique, see for example in [1], which is also an extension of the classical SVM but has several differences with the SSVM method that makes it much faster to train. MMR relies on the fact that the normal vector of the separating hyperplane in the SVM can be interpreted as a linear operator mapping the feature vectors of input items into the space of the feature vectors of the outputs. Inference with MMR is done in the same way as with SSVM (Eq. (3)) with the same joint feature map definition (Eq. (4)).

For each proposed method, the inference argmax problem can be done by exhaustively searching the set $\mathcal{Y}$, which is efficient enough in most applications. In any case, the optimum must belong to the set of valid structured labels, which guarantees that the class taxonomy is respected at all times.

3   Experimental Evaluation

3.1   Facial Expression Recognition

The Problem. We define an expression using the Facial Action Coding System (FACS) [4] which gives a very detailed description of the human facial movements in terms of Action Units (AUs). AUs represent atomic facial actions which can be performed independently (though not always spontaneously) by a person. They are associated with the action of a muscle or a group of muscles. The FACS describes more than a hundred AUs; a valid code in this system can be for instance 1+2+5+26, where we have the presence of AU1 (inner eyebrow raiser), AU2 (outer eyebrow raiser), AU5 (upper lid raiser) and AU26 (jaw drop). AUs can be taxonomized according to the region of the face where the action occurs and the type of local deformation the action applies on the face.

We therefore propose the tree taxonomy in Figure 1 for the face expression, inspired by how AUs are usually grouped when presented in the literature [4]. As their names suggest, up-down actions, horizontal actions and oblique actions gather AUs for which the deformation movement in the frontal face is mostly vertical (e.g. AU26: jaw drop), horizontal (e.g. AU20: lip stretcher) or oblique (e.g. AU12 lip corner puller) respectively. Orbital actions group AUs for which the deformation seems to be radial with respect to a fixed point (e.g. AU24: lip pressor, which closes the mouth and puckers the lips, seemingly bringing them closer to the centroid point of the mouth region).

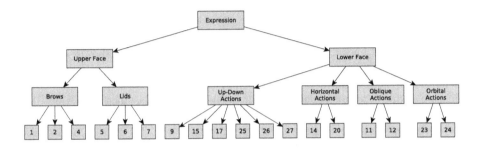

Fig. 1. Facial expression taxonomy. Leaves correspond to Action Units.

The Extended Cohn-Kanade Dataset (CK+). The CK+ dataset [8] consists of 123 subjects between the age of 18 to 50 years, of which 69% are female, 81% Euro-American, 13% Afro-American, and 6% other groups. Subjects were instructed to perform a series of 23 facial displays. In total, 593 sequences of 10 to 60 frames were recorded and annotated with an expression label in the form of a FACS code. All sequences start with an onset neutral expression and end with the peak of the expression that the subject was asked to display. Additionally, landmark annotations are provided for all frames of all sequences: 68 fiducial points have been marked on the face, sketching the most salient parts of the face shape.

Face Features. We use face features very similar to the similarity-normalized shape (SPTS) and canonical normalized appearance (CAPP) features used in [8]. On the CK+ dataset, they consist of a 636-dimensional real-valued vector for each video sequence. 136 elements are encoding information about the face shape, while 500 elements encode information about the face appearance. We chose to subtract the onset frame data from the peak frame data, like it was done [8], in order to avoid mixing our expression recognition problem with an unwanted identity component embodying static morphological differences. For that reason, the face features we use can be called "identity-normalized".

Results. The three hierarchical classification methods of interest – SkNN, SSVM and MMR – are compared to their flat counterparts – kNN, Multiclass Kernel based Vector Machines (MKSVM [3]) and "flat setup" MMR, i.e. MMR not exploiting the hierarchical information. For each tested method, there exists a main parameter the tuning of which can have a large influence on the results. For SkNN and kNN, this parameter is the number of neighbors to consider during the test phase. For SSVM and MKSVM, the core parameter is the training "C" parameter, which – in the soft-margin approach – tells the SSVM optimization training process the allowed misclassification rate on each training sample. For MMR, the core parameter is the degree of the polynomial kernel used in the method. Fig. 2 shows the hierarchical F-measure (hF) curves obtained for the facial expression recognition task. We can observe that, globally, hierarchical classification does not outperform flat classification with either method on the proposed range of parameter values, and that it even performs less well than flat classification in the case of MMR. Having a closer look at the best – i.e. highest - hF points on each of those performance curves, one can see that the best classification results are not always in favor of hierarchical classification (Table 1). Surprisingly, they suggest that there is no improvement in the recognition rate when bringing high-level hierarchical information within the classification task of the face features. It can even be said that this additional information seems to bring confusion in the case of MMR.

3.2   3D Shape Classification

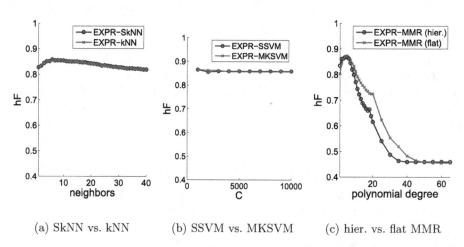

(a) SkNN vs. kNN   (b) SSVM vs. MKSVM   (c) hier. vs. flat MMR

Fig. 2. Facial expression recognition results. Blue and red curves show hF for hierarchical and flat classification respectively, against (a) the number of neighbors for SkNN vs. kNN (b) the "C" parameter for SSVM vs. MKSVM (c) the degree of the polynomial kernel for MMR (hierarchical vs. flat setup).

Table 1. Best hF performances from Fig. 2 along with corresponding hP and hR performances obtained for the facial expression recognition task.

Measure	SkNN	kNN	SSVM	MKSVM	MMR hier	MMR flat
hP	83.63%	83.12%	85.22%	85.68%	85.84%	86.46%
hR	88.00%	87.98%	87.87%	87.54%	87.76%	88.07%
hF	85.76%	85.48%	86.52%	86.60%	86.79%	87.26%

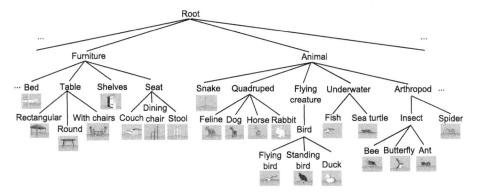

Fig. 3. Princeton Shape Benchmark dataset. Two superclasses are presented (Furniture, Animal), which show how they are hierarchically organized as well as some examples of each of the leaf classes.

The Problem. Given a tree taxonomy of 3D objects such as that in Fig. 3, the task is to determine to which class (and ancestor classes) a new object instance belongs based on its 3D shape information.

The Princeton Shape Benchmark (PSB). The PSB dataset (Fig. 3) [13] is one of the largest and most heterogeneous datasets of 3D objects: 1814 3D models corresponding to a wide variety of natural and man-made objects are grouped into 161 classes. These models encode the polygonal geometry of the object they describe. The grouping was done hierarchically and corresponds to how humans *see* the similarities between objects (e.g., an ant and a bee belong to the same superclass of insects).

3D Shape Descriptors. Each object instance is encoded into a point cloud which is sampled from its original mesh file: 5000 points from the triangulated surface, where the probability of a point being selected from a triangle is related to the area of the triangle that contains it. From this sampling, we calculate five 3D descriptors for each object: Ensemble of Shape Functions (ESF) [19], Viewpoint Feature Histogram (VFH) [11], Intrinsic Spin Images (SI) [17], Signature of Histograms of Orientations (SHOT) [15] and Unique Shape Contexts (USC) [2]). The reason for choosing those are (1) uniqueness (preference to heterogeneity of algorithms) and (2) accessibility (the methods used are available from the Point Cloud Library [10]). Our aim here is not to show which descriptor is the best, since some will work better under some conditions than others, but to show that using any of those descriptors there is a benefit in performing a hierarchical classification over a flat classification.

Results. 3D shape classification using five different descriptors – ESF, VFH, SI, SHOT and USC – is performed using each one of the three hierarchical classification methods of interest – SkNN, SSVM and MMR – as well as their flat counterparts – kNN, MKSVM [3] and "flat setup" MMR, i.e. MMR not exploiting the hierarchical information. Again, we vary the most influencial parameter for each method in our tests; those are the number of neighbors for SkNN and kNN, the "C" parameter for SSVM and MKSVM (controlling the misclassification rate during training) and the degree of the polynomial kernel for MMR. All other parameters of the methods we hold fixed.

Figure 4 shows the hierarchical F-measure (hF) curves obtained for all test cases. There seems to be, for some of the five descriptors, a consistent yet very slight trend showing some performance improvement when using hierarchical classification. Indeed, the VFH and ESF descriptors seem to benefit a little from hierarchical information in all three methods, as it is further illustrated in Table 2 which gives details about the best hF values obtained. For SI, SHOT and USC descriptors, results are mixed: either hierarchical or flat classification performs slightly better, depending on the method. Again, hierarchical classification does not clearly appear to give better results than flat classification but for a few cases. We discuss and comment further on these results in the next section.

4   Discussion

Object recognition and face analysis are very challenging problems for a computer, as indicated by the fact that for fifty years thousands of scientists have been working towards improved solutions. Some of those scientists have resorted to trying to model the human visual system, and many models have appeared, [9,12,18] to name a few. We think it is not enough to model neurons through mathematical approximations, we must also follow human strategies in order to improve our computer vision systems. One such strategy can be information transfer, which is currently being explored in the machine learning literature [5,7].

Can a computer vision system benefit from classifying objects in a hierarchical fashion? This was the starting point of this study. We have selected two very different tasks; the first one was about recognizing facial expressions seen as complex hierarchical combinations of Action Units which, as atomical components of the expression, define not only a multiclass but also a leaf-level multilabel hierarchical classification problem. The expression taxonomy we proposed and the face features we used in this work were inspired and supported by the expert literature. The second task involved the classification of a very large number of classes and objects. We have chosen one of the most heterogeneous datasets

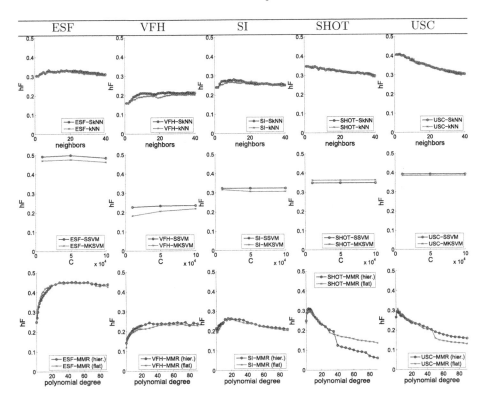

Fig. 4. 3D shape classification results. Blue and red curves show hF for hierarchical and flat classification respectively, against the number of neighbors for SkNN vs. kNN in the first row, the "C" parameter for SSVM vs. MKSVM in the second row and the degree of the polynomial kernel for MMR (hierarchical vs. flat setup) in the third row. Each column corresponds to the use of a particular descriptor: ESF, VFH, SI, SHOT and USC.

where there are objects as different in shape and meaning as a house, an ant, a tree or a plane. However the main reason for selecting this dataset was its similarity to how humans classify objects, which is related to our main hypothesis. Additionally we have used five different descriptors for this second task, and three different classifiers were compared for both tasks.

While we expected an improvement when using hierarchical classification this has not been the case for any of the two tasks. Even though a small number of combinations of a descriptor and a classifier benefited from it in the second task, the improvement was marginal, and in most cases the performances were similar for flat and for hierarchical classification. We would like to mention that we also tested many variations of the presented experiments. Those included PCA feature reduction, face features focusing more or only on the shape component, different ways to normalize the features, different weighting strategies during training and inference, different loss functions including one based on the

Table 2. Best hF performances from Fig. 4 along with corresponding hP and hR performances obtained for the 3D shape classification task using the shape descriptors ESF, VFH, SI, SHOT and USC.

	Measure	ESF	VFH	SI	SHOT	USC
	hP	32.23%	20.38%	27.24%	34.36%	40.26%
SkNN	hR	34.40%	23.07%	29.07%	34.95%	41.08%
	hF	33.28%	21.64%	28.12%	34.65%	40.67%
	hP	32.00%	19.60%	26.42%	33.99%	40.78%
kNN	hR	34.22%	21.42%	27.79%	35.48%	41.18%
	hF	33.07%	20.47%	27.09%	34.72%	40.98%
	hP	49.72%	23.47%	31.15%	33.43%	37.58%
SSVM	hR	49.92%	23.62%	33.58%	36.35%	40.88%
	hF	49.82%	23.55%	32.32%	34.83%	39.16%
	hP	47.78%	21.84%	31.01%	35.79%	37.56%
MKSVM	hR	47.45%	21.84%	32.23%	36.67%	39.41%
	hF	47.61%	21.84%	31.61%	36.22%	38.46%
MMR	hP	45.56%	24.70%	26.07%	30.35%	28.40%
(hier.	hR	44.93%	24.44%	26.57%	31.86%	30.53%
setup)	hF	45.24%	24.57%	26.32%	31.09%	29.43%
MMR	hP	44.72%	23.63%	26.05%	28.98%	29.96%
(flat	hR	45.02%	23.62%	26.62%	30.03%	31.70%
setup)	hF	44.87%	23.62%	26.33%	29.50%	30.81%

Hamming distance and another based on the hierarchical F-measure, etc. In all test cases the results obtained were very similar to the ones reported here.

At this point we may ask ourselves why this is the case, since in many other fields hierarchical classification boosts results over flat classification (protein function prediction, music genre classification, text categorization, etc.), even in some areas of computer vision – where it has been much less explored, though. Our hypothesis is that these computer vision methods based on structured classifiers fail to exploit the structure of the hierarchy because the features and descriptors commonly used carry no information about parts. Humans classify objects in terms of their geometric and part similarities: a dog and a rabbit are quadruped animals, but there is no real representation for a *quadruped* animal when using current descriptors and geometric similarities are exploited to a very small extent due to the way these descriptors are created (section 3.2). In this sense, it is worth mentioning that under some classification strategies, some descriptors seem to take advantage – even if minimal – of this geometric similarity thanks to the inclusion of some local shape information. Our experiments also show that SSVM seems to be the best at this specific task although at the expense of much more computationally intensive training (training the SSVM classifier on half of the PSB dataset typically took between 30 and 50 hours, depending on which descriptor was used).

We strongly believe that computer vision systems have to follow strategies of representation by parts. As we have commented before, we mean not to criticize face descriptors or 3D shape descriptors which are very well suited for the environments for which they were developed. On the other hand we believe that there is still much room for improvement at the representation level in computer vision systems. Our study shows that structured classifiers cannot exploit hierarchical information for better, more efficient classification considering the current status of 3D shape representation and expression analysis. We propose that richer and more abstract representations are needed in order to advantageously emulate human strategies for better computer vision systems. How exactly can the representations be improved in that sense is a quite open topic; the process may need more human intervention and validation through feedback than the almost always fully automatic extraction and selection of features commonly used in flat classification. This also echoes one of the conclusions from [14] stating that even though most researchers think that classes at different hierarchy levels are better discriminated by features of a different nature, not much attention has been given to how efficient feature selection for hierarchical classification should be performed, in particular in the global approach.

5   Conclusions

The starting hypothesis that led us to design this work is that computer vision systems – similarly to the human visual system – may benefit from structured class hierarchies by using classifiers that can exploit those structures and thus provide better classification results. We failed to prove this hypothesis through our experiments, even though state-of-the-art hierarchical methods and feature descriptors were used. The succes of the hierarchical approach in other fields such as text categorization or protein function prediction [14] suggests that there is still work to do in computer vision systems at the representation level before structured machine learning methods can take full advantage of the information present in the hierarchical organization of visual content, in particular taxonomies of 3D objects and facial expressions.

Acknowledgments. The research leading to these results has received funding from the European Community's Seventh Framework Programme FP7-ICT/ 2011-2015 (Challenge 2, Cognitive Systems and Robotics) under grant agreement no. 270273, "Xperience". This work has also been supported by the grant no. 600914 "PaCMan" (Probabilistic and Compositional Representations of Object for Robotic Manipulation) within the FP7-ICT-2011-9 program (Cognitive Systems).

References

1. Astikainen, K., Holm, L., Pitkänen, E., Szedmak, S., Rousu, J.: Towards structured output prediction of enzyme function. BioMed. Central (2008)
2. Belongie, S., Malik, J., Puzicha, J.: Shape matching and object recognition using shape contexts. IEEE PAMI **24**(24), 509–522 (2002)

3. Crammer, K., Singer, Y.: On the algorithmic implementation of multiclass kernel-based vector machines. JMLR **2**, 265–292 (2001)
4. Ekman, P., Rosenberg, E.L.: What the face reveals: Basic and applied studies of spontaneous expression using the Facial Action Coding System (FACS). Oxford University Press (1997)
5. Fei-Fei, L., Fergus, R., Perona, P.: One-shot learning of object categories. IEEE PAMI **28**(4), 594–611 (2006)
6. Kiritchenko, S., Matwin, S., Famili, A.F.: Functional annotation of genes using hierarchical text categorization. In: BioLINK SIG: LLIKB (2005)
7. Lampert, C., Nickisch, H., Harmeling, S.: Attribute-based classification for zero-shot learning of object categories. IEEE PAMI (2013)
8. Lucey, P., Cohn, J.F., Kanade, T., Saragih, J., Ambadar, Z., Matthews, I.: The extended cohn-kanade dataset (ck+): A complete dataset for action unit and emotion-specified expression. In: CVPRW, pp. 94–101 (2010)
9. Rodríguez-Sánchez, A., Tsotsos, J.: The roles of endstopped and curvature tuned computations in a hierarchical representation of 2D shape. PLOS ONE **7**(8), 1–13 (2012)
10. Rusu, R.B., Cousins, S.: 3D is here: Point cloud library (PCL). In: IEEE ICRA, pp. 1–4 (2011)
11. Rusu, R., Bradski, G., Thibaux, R., Hsu, J.: Fast 3D recognition and pose using the viewpoint feature histogram. In: IROS, pp. 2155–2162 (2010)
12. Serre, T., Wolf, L., Bileschi, S., Riesenhuber, M.: Robust object recognition with cortex-like mechanisms. IEEE PAMI **29**(3), 411–426 (2007)
13. Shilane, P., Min, P., Kazhdan, M., Funkhouser, T.: The princeton shape benchmark. In: Shape Modeling Applications, pp. 167–178 (2004)
14. Silla Jr., C.N., Freitas, A.A.: A survey of hierarchical classification across different application domains. DMKD **22**(1–2), 31–72 (2011)
15. Tombari, F., Salti, S., Di Stefano, L.: Unique shape context for 3D data description. In: Workshop on 3D Object Retrieval, pp. 57–62. ACM (2010)
16. Tsochantaridis, I., Hofmann, T., Joachims, T., Altun, Y.: Support vector machine learning for interdependent and structured output spaces. In: ICML, p. 104. ACM (2004)
17. Wang, X., Liu, Y., Zha, H.: Intrinsic spin images: A subspace decomposition approach to understanding 3D deformable shapes. In: 3DPVT, vol. 10, pp. 17–20 (2010)
18. Weidenbacher, U., Neumann, H.: Extraction of surface-related features in a recurrent model of V1–V2 interactions. PLOS ONE **4**(6), e5909 (2009)
19. Wohlkinger, W., Vincze, M.: Ensemble of shape functions for 3D object classification. In: IEEE ROBIO, pp. 2987–2992 (2011)

A Multiple Classifier Learning by Sampling System for White Blood Cells Segmentation

Cecilia Di Ruberto, Andrea Loddo, and Lorenzo Putzu[✉]

Department of Mathematics and Computer Science, University of Cagliari,
via Ospedale 72, 09124 Cagliari, Italy
{dirubert,lorenzo.putzu}@unica.it

Abstract. The visual analysis and the counting of white blood cells in microscopic peripheral blood smears is a very important procedure in the medical field. It can provide useful information concerning the health of the patients, e.g., the diagnosis of Acute Lymphatic Leukaemia or other important diseases. Blood experts in clinical centres traditionally use these methods in order to perform a manual analysis. The main issues of the traditional human analysis are certainly related to the difficulties encountered during this type of procedure: generally, the process is not rapid and it is strongly influenced by the operator's capabilities and tiredness. The main purpose of this work is to realize a reliable automated multiple classifier system based on Nearest Neighbour and Support Vector Machine in order to manage all the regions of immediate interests inside a blood smear: white blood cells nucleus and cytoplasm, erythrocytes and background. The experimental results demonstrate that the proposed method is very accurate and robust being able to reach an accuracy in segmentation of 99%, indicating the possibility to tune this approach to each couple of microscope and camera.

Keywords: Automatic detection · Biomedical image processing · Segmentation · Machine learning · White blood cell analysis

1 Introduction

The main purpose of this work was to develop an automatic system able to extract appropriate information from blood cell images taken by microscopes in order to easily perform a useful activity on them, e.g., white blood cells count. Ideally, there are several useful operations for what this method can be used for: essentially, identify, analyse, classify or count the white blood cells held in one or more microscopic images. Nevertheless we can say that the most important and key step of the entire automatic process is, certainly, the image segmentation, which differentiates meaningful objects from the background. It is a crucial step because its accuracy greatly affects both the computational speed and the overall accuracy of the whole system. However, it is also a very difficult problem to manage because of the complex nature of the cells, low resolution of microscopic images and complex scenes, e.g. cells can overlap each other or cells can have

© Springer International Publishing Switzerland 2015
G. Azzopardi and N. Petkov (Eds.): CAIP 2015, Part II, LNCS 9257, pp. 415–425, 2015.
DOI: 10.1007/978-3-319-23117-4_36

different sizes or shapes. On the other hand, the colour and contrast between the cells and the background can vary so often according to the frequent, inconsistent staining technique, thickness of smear and illumination. Although standardization is useful to avoid superfluous differences in the features of similar images, a robust segmentation approach can cope with the described issues. One natural way for colour image segmentation is to perform pixels clustering or classification in colour space. Unsupervised and supervised schemes [1], such as k-means, neural network et al., have been widely used for this purpose even if there are many disadvantages to deal with. Generally, the biggest problem of an unsupervised clustering scheme is how to determine the number of clusters, which is known as cluster validity. And as for a colour image, the selection of colour space is quite critical. The supervised scheme needs training. The training set and initialization may affect the results, and overtraining should be avoided. So a supervised clustering/classification algorithm with good generalization property is most appealing. Our method aims to solve the segmentation problem in a non-linear feature space obtained by kernel methods in order to overcome the non-linearity of data distribution and the shift/offset of colour representing the different regions of interest inside a blood sample: mature erythrocytes, nuclei and cytoplasm of white blood cells. We wanted to develop an automatic machine learning to perform image segmentation of blood and bone marrow cells images. SVM (Support Vector Machines) and ANN (Artificial Neural Network) are machine learning models with excellent performances in classification, but their main drawbacks are that a training phase is absolutely necessary to make them work and the training phase could be computationally hard with large datasets.Our solution has been developed following the suggestions of [2–4]. We used the ALL-IDB dataset [5], a public and free dataset that contains microscopic images of blood samples, specifically designed for the evaluation and the comparison of algorithms for segmentation and image classification. Our idea is to use a part of this dataset as a training set for our learning by sampling algorithm. The first step of the algorithm is to apply a classic segmentation method to obtain pure samples related to the regions of white blood cells nucleus and cytoplasm, mature erythrocytes and background. The pixels obtained from this region have been reduced in number through a Nearest Neighbour Search (NNS) by removing any duplicates or elements with distance next to zero. Then we prepared the training samples by adapting sampling from the regions obtained from the classic segmentation phase so as to perform the training process of a multiclass SVM in order to correctly classify all the pixels of a given image. Finally, the SVM is used to segment the image for extracting whole white cells, using a classification phase by means of a classification model. Since the size of training set could be controlled and reduced in sampling, SVM training is really fast. Section 2 introduces some background concepts about peripheral blood analysis and the dataset for our purposes. Section 3 illustrates a brief summary about the classic segmentation methods, known in literature. Section 4 presents SVM basis theory and how it can be used for our purposes. Section 5 shows the proposed solution and some experimental results. Section 6 describes how to tune the proposed approach to each dataset. Discussions, conclusions and future aspects are given in Section 7.

2 Background

A typical blood image usually consists of three components: red blood cells (RBCs) or erythrocytes, leukocytes, and platelets. Leukocytes are easily identifiable, as their nucleus appears darker than the background. However, the analysis and the processing of data related to the WBCs are complicated due to wide variations in cell shape, dimensions and edges. The generic term leukocyte refers to a set of cells that are quite different from each other (Fig. 1). Leukocyte cells containing granules are called granulocytes, and they include neutrophils, basophils and eosinophils. Cells without granules are called mononuclear, and they include lymphocytes and monocytes. Furthermore, lymphocytes suffering from ALL, called lymphoblasts, have additional morphological changes that increment with increasing severity of the disease. In particular, lymphocytes are regularly shaped and have a compact nucleus with regular and continuous edges, whereas lymphoblasts are irregularly shaped and contain small cavities in the cytoplasm, termed vacuoles, and spherical particles within the nucleus, termed nucleoli [5]. In Fig. 1 some images examples of healthy and sick WBCs. As we previously said our idea is to use a part of ALL-IDB dataset as a training set for our learning by sampling algorithm, while the other part of this dataset will be used to test the method. The ALL-IDB is a public image dataset of peripheral blood samples from normal individuals and leukaemia patients. These samples were collected by the experts at the M. Tettamanti Research Centre for childhood leukaemia and haematological diseases, Monza, Italy. The ALL-IDB database has two distinct version (ALL-IDB1 and ALL-IDB2). The ALL-IDB1 can be used both for testing segmentation capability of algorithms, as well as the classification systems and image pre processing methods. This dataset is composed

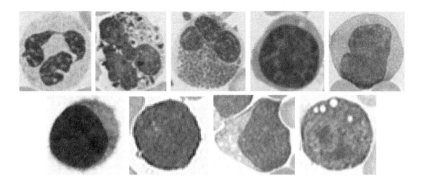

Fig. 1. (Top) The different types of WBCs: neutrophils, basophils, eosinophils, lymphocytes and monocytes. (Bottom) A comparison between a healthy lymphocyte (left) and lymphocytes suffering from ALL of class L1, L2 and L3, respectively [6]

of 108 images captured with an optical laboratory microscope coupled with an Olympus Optical C2500L camera or a Canon PowerShot G5 camera. All images are in JPG format with 24-bit colour depth. The first 33 have 1712×1368 resolution, the remaining have 2592×1944 resolution. The images are taken with different magnifications of the microscope ranging from 300 to 500 which brings the colour differences that we managed grouping the images with same brightness characteristics together. The ALL-IDB2 is a collection of cropped area of interest of normal and blast cells that have been extracted from the ALL-IDB1 dataset. It contains 260 images and the 50% of these represent lymphoblasts. Some images example belonging to the ALL-IDB are showed in Fig. 2.

3   Related Works

According to the literature, few examples of automated systems are able to analyse and classify WBCs from microscopic images, and the existing systems are only partially automated. In particular, a considerable amount of work has been performed to achieve leukocytes segmentation. For example, Madhloom [7] developed an automated system to localise and segment WBC nuclei based on image arithmetical operations and threshold operations. Sinha [8] and Kovalev [9] attempted to differentiate the five types of leukocytes in cell images. Sinha used k-means clustering on the HSV colour space for WBCs segmentation and different classification models for cell differentiation. Kovalev first identified the nuclei and then detected the entire membrane by region growing techniques. Few papers sought to achieve robust segmentation performance under uneven lighting conditions. However, a study by Scotti [10], used a low-pass filter to remove background, different threshold operations and image clustering to segment WBCs. Moreover, other authors proposed methods for automated disease classification. In particular, Piuri [11] proposed an approach based on edge detection for WBC

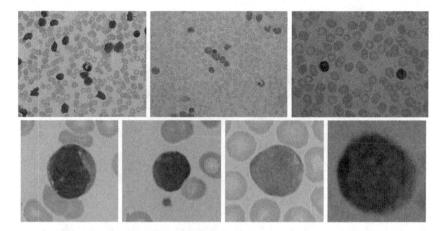

Fig. 2. Original images from the ALL-IDB1 and original images from the ALL-IDB2

segmentation, and they used morphological features to train a neural network to recognise lymphoblasts. Halim [12] proposed an automated blast counting method to detect acute leukaemia in blood microscopic images that identifies WBCs through a thresholding operation performed on the S component of the HSV colour space, followed by morphological erosion for image segmentation. Although the results of this study seem very encouraging, there is no method to determine the optimum threshold for segmentation, and no feature or classifiers were presented. Mohapatra [13] investigated the use of an ensemble classifier system for the early diagnosis of ALL in blood microscopic images. The identification and segmentation of WBCs is realised through image clustering followed by the extraction of different types of features, such as shape, contour, fractal, texture, colour and Fourier descriptors, from the sub-image. Finally an ensemble of classifiers is trained to recognise ALL. The results of this method were good, but they were obtained by using a proprietary dataset, so the reproducibility of the experiment and comparisons with other methods are not possible.

4   SVM for Segmentation

Remembering that our starting objective was to segment blood cells images, now we explain how this classification method can be used to reach our segmentation purposes and targets. SVM has been chosen in order to perform a classification of every single pixel belonging to the images we have to segment, following the method proposed in [1]. Once the manually segmented images have been obtained on a certain training set, we used a set of these produced images to train the different SVM we realized. The **first strategy** works as a normal binary SVM classifier, hence we have exactly two classes in which the pixels will be classified: the positive class groups together the white blood cell nuclei and cytoplasm pixels, instead the negative class represents pixels belonging to erythrocytes or background. Fig. 3 shows the segmentation result using this solution, in which the WBC is exactly recognized and segmented, but the lighter region of erythrocytes are misclassified as WBC region. The **second strategy** substantially works like the first one, with the main difference that we exclude from the training samples all the pixels belonging to the cytoplasm, in order to avoid misclassification due to similarities with the lighter region of erythrocytes. Fig. 3 shows the segmentation result using this solution. Again the nucleus is well detected but for determined classes of WBCs the cytoplasm is not well detected. The **third strategy** is based on the results obtained with the two previous version. In fact the classifier needs more valid training samples for cytoplasm only. So, in this version we performed a three-class SVM, using both the pixels belonging from WBCs nuclei (class 1) and both pixels belonging to the WBCs cytoplasm (class 2). Thus, pixels belonging to erythrocytes or background are labelled with class 3. Fig. 3 shows the segmentation result using this solution in which both nucleus and cytoplasm is well detected.

5   System Implementation

For each strategy present, the training set is formed by sampling pixels from the images belonging to the ALL-IDB2 presenting healthy WBCs chosen to make part of the available training images. On the other hand, the test set is formed of the first 33 images of ALL-IDB1, acquired in the same lighting conditions and with the same camera. In order to provide to the SVM the most accurate pixels related to white blood cell nuclei and cytoplasm all the images belonging to the ALL-IDB2 have been manually segmented by skilled operators, creating two ground-truth images for each sample. The first one contains the white blood cells segmented in their entirety while the second one contains only the white blood cells nuclei. From these images, the segmented cytoplasm region could be easily obtained performing a difference operation between the first image and the second one and remembering that the cytoplasm region is always placed around the white blood cell nucleus. The obtained cytoplasm and nucleus images are used as masks to extract the pixels from the original images.

5.1   Classifiers Setting

Now our interest became to perform a properly training phase over the given pixels just obtained, as we already proposed in [17]. But, since the chosen pixels must be the most various possible all over the regions, this time we used the kNN with Euclidean distance in order to provide to the SVM a smaller but more effective set of pixels. In this way the SVM should realize a more robust classification model during the training phase. In particular we performed a NNS all over the pixels belonging from the same region, in order to remove duplicates (pixels with distance = 0) or too close values (pixels with distance close to 0). Also pixels that presents a distance higher than the others have been removed, in fact they can be considered as outliers. The distances computed with the NNS

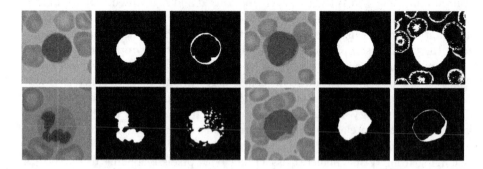

Fig. 3. (Top) From left to right: training original image from ALL-IDB2, manually segmented nucleus and cytoplasm; test original image, segmentation result for nucleus an cytoplasm with the first strategy. (Bottom) From left to right: test original image, segmentation result for nucleus an cytoplasm with the second strategy; test original image, segmentation result for nucleus an cytoplasm with the third strategy

have also been used to select pixels that compose our training set. In fact not all the pixels will be used, but only a small portion that permits to obtain a fast but accurate segmentation. Pixel selection uses distances so as to consider all the possible variations in colour inside a region. So, a uniform sampling have been made. Once obtained our training set we performed two main experiments. The first one have been realised to verify our implementation performances over single WBCs and in order to identify the most suitable parameters for the SVM. Thus, through a 10 fold cross-validation each time we divided the original training set in two subsets, the first was used to train the SVM and the second one was used to test the obtained model. The parameters that permitted to obtain an ideal average accuracy value was c parameter equal to $1e3$ and γ equal to $1e1$. The second and final experiment have been realised to verify the segmentation performances of the proposed method. Thus the whole original training set was used to create the SVM model. The first 33 native resolution images belonging to ALL-IDB1 were used as test set and to check the method applied to a natural image composed of several white blood cells of many different classes.

5.2 Experimentation

Once the first (visual) results have been obtained we started experimenting with various features that can be used to train the classifier. In fact, even though we are talking of a segmentation technique, pixels are used as features for the SVM classifier. Until now the only one descriptors that we used a the colour values. Although in many cases these features are enough to reach a good segmentation result, in other cases a poor feature set like this is not able to discriminate pixels belonging to regions with wide variations in colours. Thus the first intuition was to add the average colour values of each pixel neighbourhood. These average values have been tested for neighbourhood of size 3×3, 5×5 and 7×7. For the same neighbourhood we have also computed other statistical features that are often used for segmentation purposes: standard deviation, uniformity and entropy. While the segmentation accuracy highly benefits from the use of these new features, the overall system became to slow, both in training and segmentation phase. Furthermore, the step of samples selection, used to train the classifier, became too complex, due to a higher number of samples with different values. For all these reasons the features previously mentioned have been extracted only for neighbourhood of size 3×3, showing excellent performances as showed in fig. 4, outperforming previous results. After the segmentation, all the images have been automatically cleaned, as we have already proposed in [18,19], in order to remove small artefacts from the background and to give to the reader an idea about the goodness of the results. In order to evaluate the segmentation performances of the proposed method, also a subset of images (10 random samples) belonging to the ALL-IDB1 have been manually segmented by skilled operators, creating two ground-truth images for each sample. These images display respectively the WBCs and the WBCs nuclei present in the image. Fig. 4 shows an image belonging to the ALL-IDB1, its relative ground-truth images and our segmentation result. Using the manually segmented images we have also computed the segmentation accuracy of the proposed method comparing pixel-wise our segmentation results that often reaches the 99%.

6   System Extension

Since, getting manually segmented images is not so simple and cheap, we propose an extension of our system to be applied to each dataset of peripheral blood images, acquired in each illumination condition and with different combinations of cameras and microscopes. Our propose is based on ROI (Region of Interest) selection. Thus, making use of few original images the object of interest (WBCs) could be selected and used as positive example for our multiple classifier. Considering that we are talking of a segmentation method based on classifiers also negative instances are needed, so the background region, that comprises red blood cells and plasma, must be selected. An example of ROI selection for positive and negative example is showed in Fig. 5.

Obviously for the negative example the selected regions mustn't present WBCs. In fact in this case the NNS is performed also over pixels belonging from different region, in order to avoid errors committed during the ROI selection and in order to remove pixels with close values. In this way the obtained training set should present again uniform pixel values. Note that with this approach the WBC cytoplasm and nucleus are managed as a unique region, both because the ROI selection is not so suitable for adjacent region and both because they can be easily separated in a further step by using a simple threshold. Differently with this approach we are able to take into account also RBCs, considering them as a

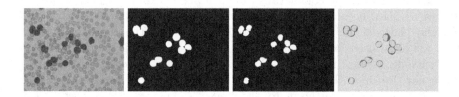

Fig. 4. Original images from the ALL-IDB1 database, ground-truth for whole leukocyte, ground-truth for leukocyte nuclei and final segmentation result.

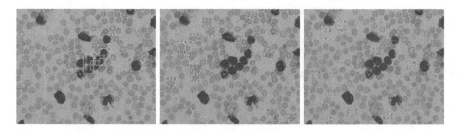

Fig. 5. Examples of ROI selection for WBCs, RBCs and plasma.

different class. Thus it is possible to perform a binary segmentation or a multiple segmentation as showed in Fig. 6.

As it can be seen also in this case the segmentation is really accurate, being able to properly segment WBCs and also RBCs. Using the manually segmented images we have computed the segmentation accuracy of this version that again reaches the 99%.

7 Conclusions

This work proposed and investigated a new automated white blood cell recognition method that can be applied to support some existing medical methods, like the WBCC, White Blood Cells Counting. It is realized using lots of notions already known in literature but combining them to build an essentially brand new method in which the major innovation is brought by the use of a multiple classifier approach that makes use of the Nearest Neighbour and Support Vector Machine. Whereas the aim of a fully automated cell analysis and diagnosis of with blood cell has not yet reached, many important steps in the image segmentation using Learning by Sampling method have been realized. We proposed a segmentation approach using several variations in the schemes. The experimental results demonstrate that the new approach is very accurate and robust in relation to some traditional methods. The performances achieved with the ALL-IDB often reaches the 99% of accuracy, but in particular we want to highlight the possibility to tune this approach to each couple of microscope and camera using only few image samples. Despite the good results, we do not consider the development of our project totally concluded. Our purposes and hopes are certainly to continue the work in order to experiment several new investigations that could potentially bring to better results. Among the future works we can indicate the extension to different colour spaces in which segmentation process could be easily and more effective. A further step will include analysis and recognition of the different types of healthy and blasted white blood cells. Finally, our idea is to export the whole procedure to bone marrow images, in which the first segmentation phase is, usually, more difficult than in the peripheral blood images, since the brightness conditions could be very different and large clusters of cells can exist.

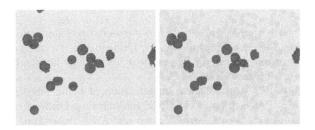

Fig. 6. Segmentation results after ROI selection for two and three classes.

Acknowledgments. This work has been funded by Regione Autonoma della Sardegna (R.A.S.) Project CRP-17615 DENIS: Dataspace Enhancing Next Internet in Sardinia. Lorenzo Putzu gratefully acknowledges Sardinia Regional Government for the financial support of his PhD scholarship (P.O.R. Sardegna F.S.E. Operational Programme of the Autonomous Region of Sardinia, European Social Fund 2007-2013 - Axis IV Human Resources, Objective 1.3, Line of Activity 1.3.1.).

References

1. Pan, C., Lu, H., Cao, F.: Segmentation of blood and bone marrow cell images via learning by sampling. In: Huang, D.-S., Jo, K.-H., Lee, H.-H., Kang, H.-J., Bevilacqua, V. (eds.) ICIC 2009. LNCS, vol. 5754, pp. 336–345. Springer, Heidelberg (2009)
2. Fukunaga, K., Hostetler, L.: The estimation of the gradient of a density function, with applications in pattern recognition. IEEE Transactions on Information Theory **21**(1), 32–40 (1975)
3. Shapiro, L.G., Stockman, G.C.: Computer Vision, chap. 12, pp. 279–325. Prentice Hall, New Jersey (2001)
4. Gonzalez, R.C., Woods, R.E.: Digital Image Processing, 3rd edn. Prentice Hall Pearson Education, Inc., New Jersey (2008)
5. Donida Labati, R., Piuri, V., Scotti, F.: ALL-IDB: the acute lymphoblastic leukemia image database for image processing. In: Macq, B., Schelkens, P. (eds.) Proceedings of the 18th IEEE ICIP International Conference on Image Processing, pp. 2045–2048. IEEE Publisher, Brussels (2011)
6. Bennett, J.M., Catovsky, D., Daniel, M.T., Flandrin, G., Galton, D.A., Gralnick, H.R., Sultan, C.: Proposals for the classification of the acute leukemias. French-American-British (FAB) co-operative group. British Journal of Hematology **33**(4), 451–458 (1976)
7. Madhloom, H.T., Kareem, S.A., Ariffin, H., Zaidan, A.A., Alanazi, H.O., Zaidan, B.B.: An Automated White Blood Cell Nucleus Localization and Segmentation using Image Arithmetic and Automated Threshold. Journal of Applied Sciences **10**(11), 959–966 (2010)
8. Sinha, N., Ramakrishnan, A.G.: Automation of differential blood count. In: Chockalingam, A. (ed.) Proceedings of the Conference on Convergent Technologies for the Asia-Pacific Region, vol. 2, pp. 547–551. IEEE Publisher, Taj Residency (2003)
9. Kovalev, V.A., Grigoriev, A.Y., Ahn, H.: Robust recognition of white blood cell images. In: Kavanaugh, M.E., Werner, B. (eds.) Proceedings of the 13th International Conference on Pattern Recognition, pp. 371–375. IEEE Publisher, Vienna (1996)
10. Scotti, F.: Robust segmentation and measurements techniques of white cells in blood microscope images. In: Daponte, P., Linnenbrink, T. (eds.) Proceedings of the IEEE Instrumentation and Measurement Technology Conference, pp. 43–48. IEEE Publisher. Sorrento (2006)
11. Piuri, V., Scotti, F.: Morphological classification of blood leucocytes by microscope images. In: Proceedings of the IEEE International Conference on Computational Intelligence for Measurement Systems and Applications, pp. 103–108. IEEE Publisher, Boston (2004)

12. Halim, N.H.A., Mashor, M.Y., Hassan, R.: Automatic Blasts Counting for Acute Leukemia Based on Blood Samples. International Journal of Research and Reviews in Computer Science **2**(4), August 2011

13. Mohapatra, S., Patra, D., Satpathy, S.: An Ensemble Classifier System for Early Diagnosis of Acute Lymphoblastic Leukemia in Blood Microscopic Images. Journal of Neural Computing and Applications, Article in Press (2013)

14. David, J.F., Comaniciu, D., Meer, P.: Computer-assisted discrimination among malignant lymphomas and leukemia using immunophenotyping, intelligent image repositories, and telemicroscopy. IEEE Transaction on Information Technology in Biomedicine **4**(4), 12–22 (2000)

15. Lezoray, O., Elmoataz, A., Cardot, H., Gougeon, G., Lecluse, M., Elie, H., Revenu, H.M.: Segmentation of Color Images from Serous Cytology for Automated Cell Classification. Journal of Analytical and Quantitative Cytology and Histology/the International Academy of Cytology [and] American Society of Cytology **22**(4), 311–322 (2000)

16. Vapnik, V.N., Vapnik, V.: Statistical learning theory, vol. 1, Wiley New York (1998)

17. Di Ruberto, C., Loddo, A., Putzu, L.: Learning by sampling for white blood cells segmentation. In: LNCS of the International Conference on Image Analysis and Processing (ICIAP) (2015) (in press)

18. Putzu, L., Di Ruberto, C.: Investigation of different classification models to determine the presence of leukemia in peripheral blood image. In: Petrosino, A. (ed.) ICIAP 2013, Part I. LNCS, vol. 8156, pp. 612–621. Springer, Heidelberg (2013)

19. Putzu, L., Caocci, G., Di Ruberto, C.: Leucocyte Classification for Leukaemia Detection using Image Processing Technique. Artificial Intelligence in Medicine **62**(3), 179–191 (2014)

TECA: Petascale Pattern Recognition for Climate Science

Prabhat[1]([✉]), Surendra Byna[1], Venkatram Vishwanath[2], Eli Dart[1], Michael Wehner[1], and William D. Collins[1]

[1] Lawrence Berkeley National Laboratory, Berkeley, CA, USA
prabhat@lbl.gov
[2] Argonne National Laboratory, Argonne, IL, USA

Abstract. Climate Change is one of the most pressing challenges facing humanity in the 21st century. Climate simulations provide us with a unique opportunity to examine effects of anthropogenic emissions. High-resolution climate simulations produce "Big Data": contemporary climate archives are $\approx 5PB$ in size and we expect future archives to measure on the order of Exa-Bytes. In this work, we present the successful application of TECA (Toolkit for Extreme Climate Analysis) framework, for extracting extreme weather patterns such as Tropical Cyclones, Atmospheric Rivers and Extra-Tropical Cyclones from TB-sized simulation datasets. TECA has been run at full-scale on Cray XE6 and IBM BG/Q systems, and has reduced the runtime for pattern detection tasks from years to hours. TECA has been utilized to evaluate the performance of various computational models in reproducing the statistics of extreme weather events, and for characterizing the change in frequency of storm systems in the future.

Keywords: Pattern detection · Climate science · High performance computing · Parallel I/O · Data mining · Petascale

1 Introduction

Climate simulations provide us with an unprecedented view of the state of earth's present, and potential future climate under global warming. State of the art climate codes, such as the Community Atmosphere Model (CAM v5) [2], when run in 25-km spatial resolution with 6-hour data dumps, produce over 100TB from a single 25-year integration period. The current CMIP-5 archive [3], consisting of international contributions from a number of climate modeling groups consists of over 5PB of data; this dataset was mined extensively for the IPCC AR5 report [5]. It is anticipated that CMIP-6 dataset [8] will cross the exabyte threshold with 25-km model runs being the norm. Faced with this massive deluge of multi-variate, spatio-temporal data, sophisticated and scalable "pattern detection" tools are critical for extracting meaningful scientific insights.

© Springer International Publishing Switzerland 2015
G. Azzopardi and N. Petkov (Eds.): CAIP 2015, Part II, LNCS 9257, pp. 426–436, 2015.
DOI: 10.1007/978-3-319-23117-4_37

Fig. 1. Examples of extreme weather phenomena observed through satellite and radar. Clockwise from bottom-left: Extra-Tropical Cyclone, Atmospheric River, Derecho and Tropical Cyclone events.

One example of the types of climate data analytics of societal relevance is the identification and tracking of extreme weather. Figure 1 illustrates the types of extreme weather observed in the natural climate system. Phenomena such as cyclones and atmospheric rivers can have widespread and long-lasting impact on national economies. Understanding how extreme weather events will change in the future climate is an important open question.

In order to address this important challenge, we have developed the Toolkit for Extreme Climate Analysis (TECA)[12] to identify storms in high-frequency climate model output (CAM5 in our case). To date, we have applied our technique to identify three different classes of storms: tropical cyclones, atmospheric rivers and extra-tropical cyclones. Due to the high-frequency nature of the data required to identify and track individual storms in a climate model simulation, the raw input datasets that we have analyzed range from 0.5TB to 13TB. As the entire climate modeling community starts to upgrade their infrastructure to run at comparably high resolutions (25 km or better), we expect the publicly available datasets necessary for this type of analysis to exceed 10PB. Manual labeling and extraction of patterns at such scales is simply impossible, thereby requiring the development and application of "Big Data" analytics methods. The techniques that we have developed are amenable to parallel execution, and are demonstrated to scale up to full size of the largest machines available to us, including a 150,00 core Cray XE6 and 750,000 core IBM BG/Q platform.

2   Methods

2.1   TECA : Toolkit for Extreme Climate Analytics

TECA [12] is a climate-specific, high-performance pattern detection toolkit that is designed for efficient execution on HPC systems. We have developed the code in

C/C++, and utilize MPI for inter-process communication. We utilize NetCDF-4 for parallel reads, and MPI-IO for storing results.

The design and implementation of TECA is based on our first hand experience with pattern detection problems in climate science. After analyzing the climate pattern detection literature for a number of event types, we discovered the following "design pattern". The detection process can be typically broken down into two steps:

1. Detection of candidate points that satisfy multi-variate constraints
2. Stitching of candidate points into a trajectory that satisfies spatio-temporal constraints

Step 1 tends to be data-intensive, involving loading anywhere between 10GB-10TB of data. The algorithm has to scan through all of the relevant fields to select candidate points. However, this step can be executed in parallel across timesteps. The degree of parallelism can be as high as the number of timesteps in the processed dataset (typically 10^2-10^5); hence a dramatic speedup in overall runtime is feasible. Step 2 involves pairwise analysis on potential storm matches across consecutive time slices in order to stitch trajectories. However, a small amount of data (typically 10MB-1GB) is required for this analysis, and this can be easily loaded on memory on a single node and executed in serial.

Conceptually, Steps 1 and 2 can be directly translated to the MapReduce computational paradigm powering much of the commercial Big Data Analytics workloads. TECA implements a custom framework for processing scientific datasets, with an eye towards high performance. We utilize the Message Passing Interface (MPI) for optimizing job launch; communication and synchronization traffic. In the instance of multi-model archives, sub-communicators corresponding to individual models and ensemble members are created and initialized; thereby minimizing synchronization with other tasks. NetCDF files are striped across multiple low-level storage targets to optimize read performance. Writing (relatively small) partial results in Step 2 can create metadata bottlenecks, especially at concurrencies in excess of 50,000 cores. We implement a 2-phase collective I/O mechanism to aggregate writes on a smaller ($O(1000)$) number of nodes and perform file-per-node writes using MPI-IO. The cumulative effect of these best practices in HPC and Parallel I/O, is that we are able to successfully run TECA jobs at full concurrency on petascale platforms.

2.2   TECA for Detecting Tropical Cyclones

We have implemented the Tropical Cyclone (TC) detection procedure outlined in [11]. The detection step consists of finding co-located vorticity maxima, pressure minima (within a radius of 5°) and temperature warm-core centers. Splines are fitted to relevant fields, which are defined on latitude-longitude grids. Local maxima and minima of functions are computed by performing a line search on the splines within the prescribed spatial window. Once potential storm center candidates have been identified, the next step is to impose spatial and temporal

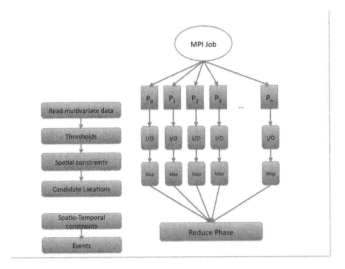

Fig. 2. TECA utilizes the Map Reduce computational paradigm for exploiting parallel computing resources.

constraints to connect the storm centers into a trajectory. In the case of TCs, the stitching step involves linking storms across subsequent 6-hr time windows. Candidate storms are prescribed to travel less than 400km in 6-hrs, persist for at least 2 days, and have a wind velocity (greater than 17m/s) during at least 2 days within their lifetime.

2.3   TECA for Detecting Atmospheric Rivers

Atmospheric Rivers (AR) are large, spatially coherent weather systems with high concentrations of elevated water vapor. These systems often cause severe downpours and flooding over the western coastal United States and western Europe. We have implemented an algorithm to detect ARs in the TECA framework [9]. We first compute a 2D Integrated Water Vapor (IWV) by performing a vertical integral on the specific humidity field. Following the definition of physical features of an AR [13]; we perform a thresholding operation for identifying all grid points with IWV greater than 2cm. We then use a connected component labeling algorithm to find all the connected regions of grid points. We test if a candidate originates in the tropics, and makes landfall on the US coast. For all the polygons satisfying the origin and the landfall conditions, we compute a medial axis, and check if the length of the AR greater than 2000km and if the width of the AR less than 1000km. If a polygon satisfies all of these geometric constraints, we declare it to be an atmospheric river.

2.4   TECA for Detecting Extra-Tropical Cyclones

We implement the Extra-Tropical Cyclone (ETC) detection and tracking procedure documented in [14]. We detect a local minima in the pressure field within a 100x100 km radius. Ties between adjacent low-pressure storm centers are resolved based on strength of the local laplacian (i.e. storm centers with largest laplacian are declared to be storm center candidates). Potential candidates are stitched into trajectories by performing a nearest neighbor analysis with distance constraints: storms are restricted to travel less than 1000km in a 6-hr window, and less than 700 km in a 6-hr window in the North, South, and Westward directions. We only retain storms that persist for more than 24 hours, and travel greater 500km over their lifetime. Storms over high elevation areas (greater than 1500km) are excluded.

All of these detection and stitching criteria can be easily accommodated within the design of TECA; thereby utilizing parallel job launch, execution and parallel I/O capabilities. Apart from returning summary statistics on storm counts and location, we are also able to pull out valuable detailed information on precipitation patterns and velocity profiles of storms during the course of their lifetime.

3   Experimental Setup

3.1   Data

We utilized multi-model output from the community produced CMIP-5 archive [3], and a high-resolution version of the Community Atmospheric Model (CAM5)[2] simulations conducted by our group at NERSC. The CMIP-5 datasets are freely and publicly accessible via a number of international Earth System Grid Federation web portals and are the basis of most climate model results presented in the IPCC AR5 WG1 report [4]. The observational SSM/I datasets are available via a web portal [7]. In all cases, the datasets are available as multiple netcdf files. Each file typically contains all relevant 2D variables and spans one year's worth of data.

3.2   Platforms

We utilized the Hopper system at NERSC, and the Mira system at ALCF for all results reported in this paper. Hopper is a 1.28 PF, Cray XE6 system featuring 153,216 compute cores, 212TB of memory and 2PB of disk available via a 35 GB/s Lustre filesystem. Mira is a 10PF, IBM BG/Q system featuring 786,432 cores, 768 TB of memory with 384 I/O nodes accessible via GPFS.

4   Results

We now report on both the scaling performance obtained by TECA on various HPC platforms, as well as the scientific results facilitated by these runs.

4.1   Scaling Performance

Table 1 summarizes the performance of TECA on a range of pattern detection problems. We analyzed CAM5 model output (0.5-13 TB), CMIP-5 multi-model output (6 TB), and the SSMI (35 GB) satellite data product. We ran TECA at full scale on Hopper and Mira platforms, facilitating pattern detection on these massive datasets. Needless to say, such pattern detection problems cannot be tackled on individual workstations in a reasonable amount of time.

Table 1. Scaling results obtained with TECA on various HPC platforms

Climate Pattern	Dataset	Dataset Size	Serial runtime (Estimated)	Parallel runtime	Concurrency	Platform
Tropical Cyclones	CAM5 1°	0.5 TB	≈ 8 years	31 min	149,680 cores	Hopper
Tropical Cyclones	CAM5 0.25°	13 TB	≈ 9 years	58 min	80,000 cores	Hopper
Atmospheric Rivers	SSM/I	35 GB	≈ 11 hours	5 sec	10,000 cores	Hopper
Extra-Tropical Cyclones	CMIP-5	6 TB	≈ 10 years	95 min	755,200 cores	Mira

4.2   Science Results

Tropical Cyclones. One of the primary scientific utilities of the TECA software is to evaluate how well models perform in reproducing extreme event statistics, compared to observational records. If we assess models to perform well for the historical period, we can have greater confidence in the trends projected by the same models for future runs. We have applied TECA to the CAM5 0.25-degree output, over a simulated time period spanning 1979-2005 [15]. For this time period, the hand-labelled IBTrACS dataset [6] reports 87 (+/- 8) storms every year. TECA reports 84 (+/-9) storms, which is rather accurate. Figures 3 and 4 highlight the spatial distribution of the storms, as well as the seasonal distribution. In terms of model evaluation, we note that CAM5 does a good job of reproducing the spatial pattern, with perhaps too many storms in the central pacific. The model also does a good job of reproducing the seasonal pattern in various ocean basins (North Atlantic, Indian Ocean, Northwest Pacific), but the storms counts are off in the Pacific.

After validating the TECA output for the historical period, we decided to apply the TC detection capabilities for climate change experiments conducted by various US and international efforts. We processed a climate change experiment specified by the CliVAR Working Group [1]. We used the CAM5 model to simulated the earth's climate under a baseline (climo), a scenario consisting of 2xCO2, SSTs increased uniformly by 2°C, and the conjunction of both CO2 and SST conditions. Figure 5 shows the average number of tropical storms, tropical cyclones and intense tropical cyclones per year simulated by the high-resolution version (0.23°x0.31°) of CAM5.1 for the four idealized configurations. Error bars represent 5%-95% confidence intervals based on inter-annual variability. The baseline (1990) climatology is in blue. A two degree warmer simulation with elevated atmospheric carbon dioxide levels (660ppm) is shown in red. While

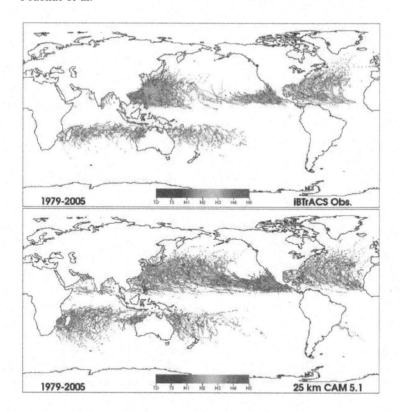

Fig. 3. Application of TECA to CAM5 0.25-degree output. Tropical Cyclones (Category 1 through 5) are illustrated in the bottom figure. TC tracks from the IBTrACS observational product are plotted for an identical time period.

the total number of tropical storms over all intensities is reduced in a warmer world, the number of intense tropical cyclones (Category 4 and 5) is increased.

Atmospheric Rivers. We applied the TECA AR detection capability to the SSM/I satellite product. Figure 6 shows a range of diverse AR features returned by our implementation. We note that the implementation is robust to various shapes and sizes of AR events. In order to validate the procedure, we compared the events returned by TECA to a hand-curated database of known AR events maintained by [10]. We note that TECA was able to detect 93% of all events reported in the database. We furthermore applied the TECA toolkit to various CMIP-3 and CMIP-5 models over the historical period. Figure 7 shows that several models match reasonably well with the observed record, however, some models do exhibit hyperactivity with regards to generation of ARs. Similar to the Tropical Cyclone work, we are currently investigating the application of TECA to climate change scenarios.

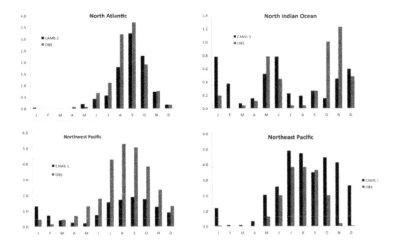

Fig. 4. TECA can produce detailed diagnostics for storm tracks. In this case, monthly TC activity is plotted by major oceanic basins. CAM5 output is plotted in black, and observational products are plotted in red.

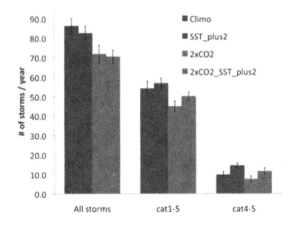

Fig. 5. Number of annual Tropical Cyclones under the CliVAR scenarios. There is a significant decrease in the overall number of storms, and an increase in number of annual Category 4 and 5 storms under the SST warming scenarios.

Extra-Tropical Cyclones. We have successfully applied TECA to detect Extra-Tropical Cyclones in climate data. In perhaps the leading example of Scientific Big Data analytics, we scaled TECA to process the entire CMIP-5 archive (historical and RCP8.5 runs, all ensemble members, 6-hourly data) in one shot on 755,200 cores of the Mira IBM BG/Q system. Preliminary results in Figure 8 indicate that the extra-tropical cyclone count will decrease in a warming world,

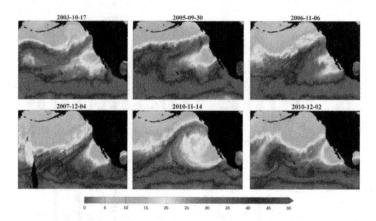

Fig. 6. Sample Atmospheric River events detected by the TECA implementation on the SSM/I dataset. Note the distinct appearance of various AR patterns detected by our algorithm.

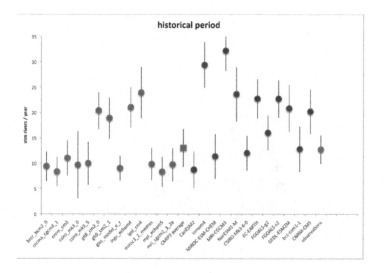

Fig. 7. Number of Atmospheric River events in the CMIP-3 (red) and CMIP-5 (blue) archives compared to observations (green). It appears that there are two modes in the CMIP-3 and CMIP5-archive: models that are generally consistent with the observed record, and models that are hyperactive in reproducing atmospheric rivers.

and that this trend is consistent across the entire CMIP-5 multi-model archive. We are currently designing custom aquaplanet simulations that will test specific hypothesis behind the decreasing trend in ETC activity.

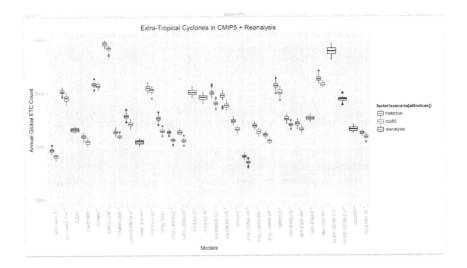

Fig. 8. Summary of Annual Extra-Tropical Cyclone activity in all of CMIP-5. A clear decrease is observed is observed from the blue (historical) to the future rcp8.5 (red) periods

5   Limitations and Future Work

This work is one of the leading example of the use of high performance computing for solving pattern "detection" problems. The definition of a pattern is assumed to be conveniently prescribed by various experts in the climate science community. While this is true for the three events that we examined, a much broader class of events exist (e.g. weather fronts, mesoscale convective systems, derechos, blocking events), for which there does not exist an algorithmic definition that could be implemented in TECA. Such problems are more amenable to the classic machine learning paradigm, wherein a modest number of training examples would be provided by human experts, and a learning algorithm could determine the relevant features and inter-relationships that "define" the extreme weather pattern. We are currently examining the use of Deep Learning methods, as a complementary approach to TECA for targeting a much broader class of weather patterns.

6   Conclusions

Pattern recognition problems are increasingly common in the scientific world. As a leading example, climate science requires sophisticated pattern recognition on TB-PB sized datasets. We have developed and successfully applied TECA to the problem of finding extreme weather phenomena (such as tropical cyclones, atmospheric rivers and extra-tropical cyclones) across most contemporary climate models (CAM5), data archives (CMIP-5) and observational products (SSMI).

We have scaled TECA on DOE's leading HPC platforms at NERSC and ALCF, and obtained important scientific insights on the potential change in extreme weather phenomena in future climate regimes.

References

1. Clivar hurricane working group. http://www.usclivar.org/working-groups/hurricane
2. Community earth system model. http://www.cesm.ucar.edu/working-groups/Atmosphere/development
3. Coupled model intercomparison project phase 5. http://cmip-pcmdi.llnl.gov/cmip5/
4. Earth system grid federation. http://pcmdi9.llnl.gov/esgf-web-fe/
5. Intergovernmental panel on climate change, fifth assessment report. http://www.ipcc.ch/report/ar5
6. Noaa ncdc ibtracs dataset. http://www.ncdc.noaa.gov/ibtracs/
7. Remote sensing systems special sensor microwave imager instrument. http://www.remss.com/missions/ssmi
8. Wcrp coupled model intercomparison project phase 6. http://www.wcrp-climate.org/wgcm-cmip/wgcm-cmip6
9. Byna, S., Prabhat, Wehner, M.F., Wu, K.J.: Detecting atmospheric rivers in large climate datasets. In: Proceedings of the 2nd International Workshop on Petascal Data Analytics: Challenges and Opportunities, PDAC 2011, pp. 7–14. ACM, New York (2011)
10. Dettinger, M.D., Ralph, F.M., Das, T., Neiman, P.J., Cayan, D.R.: Atmospheric rivers, floods and the water resources of california. Water 3(2), 445–478 (2011)
11. Knutson, T.R., Sirutis, J.J., Garner, S.T., Held, I.M., Tuleya, R.E.: Simulation of the recent multidecadal increase of atlantic hurricane activity using an 18-km-grid regional model. Bulletin of the American Meteorological Society 88(10), 1549–1565 (2007)
12. Prabhat, Rbel, O., Byna, S., Wu, K., Li, F., Wehner, M., Bethel, W.: Teca: A parallel toolkit for extreme climate analysis. Procedia Computer Science 9, 866–876 (2012); Proceedings of the International Conference on Computational Science (2012)
13. Ralph, F.M., Neiman, P.J., Rotunno, R.: Dropsonde observations in low-level jets over the northeastern pacific ocean from caljet-1998 and pacjet-2001: Mean vertical-profile and atmospheric-river characteristics. Monthly Weather Review 133(4), 889–910 (2005)
14. Wang, X.L., Feng, Y.: Inter-comparison of extra-tropical cyclone activity in eight reanalysis datasets. EGU General Assembly Research Abstract (2014)
15. Wehner, M.F., Reed, K.A., Li, F., Prabhat, Bacmeister, J., Chen, C.-T., Paciorek, C., Gleckler, P.J., Sperber, K.R., Collins, W.D., Gettelman, A., Jablonowski, C.: The effect of horizontal resolution on simulation quality in the community atmospheric model, cam5. 1. Journal of Advances in Modeling Earth Systems (2014)

Visualization of Regression Models Using Discriminative Dimensionality Reduction

Alexander Schulz[(✉)] and Barbara Hammer

CITEC Centre of Excellence, Bielefeld University, Bielefeld, Germany
{aschulz,bhammer}@techfak.uni-bielefeld.de

Abstract. Although regression models offer a standard tool in machine learning, there exist barely possibilities to inspect a trained model which go beyond plotting the prediction against single features. In this contribution, we propose a general framework to visualize a trained regression model together with the training data in two dimensions. For this purpose, we rely on modern nonlinear dimensionality reduction (DR) techniques. In addition, we argue that discriminative DR techniques are particularly useful for the visualization of regression models since they can guide the projection to be more sensitive for those aspects in the data which are important for prediction. Given a data set, our framework can be utilized to visually inspect any trained regression model.

Keywords: Model interpretation · Nonlinear dimensionality reduction · Fisher information

1 Introduction

The increasing complexity of data as concerns their dimensionality, size and form constitutes a major challenge on the task of automated data analyses. In many scenarios, it is not possible to formalize an analysis task in advance and, hence, interactive data analysis is required. In this scenario, humans interactively specify learning goals and the appropriate tools [9,12,15,20] in order to interpret heterogeneous and high-dimensional data sets. In this context, data visualization and model interpretability become increasingly important. A trained regression model is not judged by its prediction error only, rather, other questions come into focus, such as: what are particularly difficult regions in the data space for the model, which instances seem to be noisy to the model or which regions of the data space are too sparsely represented by data?

Data visualization is a particular useful tool, since it presents relations among many data points in a well comprehensible way for humans. This field constitutes a well-investigated research topic with many different proposed visualization techniques in the machine learning context. Besides classical methods such as linear mappings computed by principal component analysis or linear discriminant analysis and nonlinear extensions such as the self-organizing map (SOM) or generative topographic mapping (GTM), a variety of (often nonparametric) dimensionality reduction (DR) techniques has been proposed in the last decade, such

© Springer International Publishing Switzerland 2015
G. Azzopardi and N. Petkov (Eds.): CAIP 2015, Part II, LNCS 9257, pp. 437–449, 2015.
DOI: 10.1007/978-3-319-23117-4_38

as t-distributed stochastic neighbor embedding (t-SNE), neighborhood retrieval visualizer (NeRV), or maximum variance unfolding (MVU), see e.g. the articles [7,10,16,17,19] for overviews on DR techniques. These approaches are often utilized to visualize data in two dimensions. However, they cannot be directly applied to additionally project the prediction function of a trained regression model. Such a visualization could provide further insights into the regression problem: is the model particularly complex in certain regions of the data space, is it too simplistic in others, how are noisy regions and outliers treated, how does the model extrapolate, and so on.

Besides approaches to judge the quality of trained regression models with quantitative estimates [4], there exists only little work which aims to visualize the regression function itself. For the special case of Decision Trees, a direct inspection is possible through the special tree structure of the model. However, these models can get unclear with increasing size and data complexity. More general approaches such as Breheny and Burchett [2] try to analyze the relationship between the target and a single explanatory variable by visualizing the predictions of the model for different values of this variable while keeping the others fix. However, this approach treats the explenatory variables independently (or a small subset simultaneously) and thus cannot find information that is present in many dependent features.

Our proposed approach, conversely, aims to visualize the whole data set together with the model in one plot, such treating all features simultaneously. Our contribution is based on ideas from a similar approach which was designed recently in our group to visualize classification methods [13]. We adapt these ideas such that they are applicable to the visualization of regression models.

Given a trained regression model, we identify typical user tasks which can be addressed with our framework. These include the questions:

1. How complex is the learned function? Does it overfit/underfit some regions?
2. Is the data multi-modal, i.e. are clusters present in the data and how does the regression model deal with those? What is the prediction for the regions in-between the clusters?
3. Are specific aspects of the selected model visible (such as local linear functions) and are these suited for the data at hand.
4. Are there potential outliers in the data and how does the model treat these?

We will exemplarily show how these questions can be addressed in the experiments section.

The remaining of the paper is structured as follows: First, we discuss popular dimensionality reduction techniques with certain properties which are important for our proposed framework. Section 3 presents our main contribution, the general framework to visualize regression models. Subsequently, we present the experiments where we exemplarily address the user tasks and argue that discriminative DR is particularly suited for this purpose. Finally, section 5 gives a short discussion.

2   Dimensionality Reduction

Dimensionality reduction (DR) mappings try to find low-dimensional embeddings $\pi(\mathbf{x}) = \boldsymbol{\xi} \in \Xi = \mathbb{R}^2$ for given high-dimensional data points $\mathbf{x} \in X = \mathbb{R}^d$ while preserving as much information as possible. The formalization of the latter goal, however, yields many different approaches [7,10,16,17,19].

Having such a dimensionality reduction mapping π, some approaches also provide an inverse mapping $\pi^{-1} : \mathbb{R}^2 \mapsto \mathbb{R}^d$. This is in particular the case for parametric DR techniques. Since we will need such a mapping, we will discuss how to compute it if it is not provided by the DR method in subsection 2.2.

First, we give a short description of popular DR approaches which we utilize.

- The goal of *Multidimensional scaling (MDS)* is to embed the data such that the distances in X and in Ξ agree. If these distances are Euclidean, MDS is equivalent to PCA. However, other metrics can be integrated directly.
- One popular nonlinear alternative is the parametric *generative topographic mapping (GTM)* [1]. Essentially, GTM relies on data being generated by a constraint mixture of Gaussians. The centers of the Gaussians are generated by a smooth mapping from regular lattice positions in a two-dimensional latent space which can be used for data visualization. GTM is optimized by a maximization of the data log likelihood function. The GTM provides a smooth mapping of the data to its low-dimensional projection $\pi(\mathbf{x})$ and vice versa $\pi^{-1}(\boldsymbol{\xi})$. Different metrics can be integrated [8].
- *T-distributed stochastic neighbor embedding (t-SNE)* [16] is a nonparametric approach and defines local neighborhoods in a probabilistic sense by using Gaussians based on pairwise distances in the feature space and student-t distributions induced by euclidean distances in the projection space. Training takes place by a minimization of the error in between these distributions as measured by the Kullback Leibler divergence.

2.1   Discriminative Dimensionality Reduction with the Fisher Metric

Dimensionality reduction in general is an ill-defined problem. This is particularly critical if the data is intrinsically high-dimensional and hence not embeddable in two dimensions. Then, the DR methods have to make compromises and omit information. This choice which information to omit is often arbitrary or even depends on random aspects.

Hence, the class of discriminative DR approaches has been proposed[1]. These methods suggest to use auxiliary information to guide the DR method. These can be data labels or the values of the target variable, y in our case.

A particular successful and general approach is to use the Fisher information metric as a basis for the DR techniques. The general idea is to define a Riemannian manifold which takes the auxiliary information of the data into account. This modified metric can then be plugged into any DR technique which relies

---

[1] We use the terms *discriminative* and *supervised* as synonyms, in the following.

on distances only. This idea has been applied for classification problems very successfully [11,13], and very recently for the case of regression problems [14].

The distance from a point $\mathbf{x}$ to $\mathbf{x}'$ on the Riemannian manifold can be computed by finding the shortest path

$$d_M(\mathbf{x}, \mathbf{x}') = \inf_P \int_0^1 \sqrt{P'(t)^\top \mathbf{J}(P(t)) P'(t)} dt \tag{1}$$

where the infimum is over all differentiable paths $P : [0,1] \to X$ with $P(0) = \mathbf{x}$ and $P(1) = \mathbf{x}'$. Here, local distances are defined using the Fisher information matrix

$$\mathbf{J}(\mathbf{x}) = \mathbb{E}_{p(y|\mathbf{x})} \left\{ \left(\frac{\partial}{\partial \mathbf{x}} \log p(y|\mathbf{x}) \right) \left(\frac{\partial}{\partial \mathbf{x}} \log p(y|\mathbf{x}) \right)^\top \right\} \tag{2}$$

at the position $\mathbf{x}$.

In [14], a Gaussian Process is used to estimate $p(y|\mathbf{x})$. Further, approximations for the path integrals are investigated in [11]. A good compromise between performance and quality is to restrict arbitrary paths on the Riemannian manifold to a straight line and to approximate the integral (1) by T piecewise constant terms. More formally, assume $\mathbf{x}_t = \mathbf{x} + (t-1)/T \cdot (\mathbf{x}' - \mathbf{x})$. Then the distance on the manifold d_M can be approximated by

$$d_T(\mathbf{x}, \mathbf{x}') = \sum_{t=1}^T \sqrt{(\mathbf{x}_t - \mathbf{x}_{t+1})^\top J(\mathbf{x}_t)(\mathbf{x}_t - \mathbf{x}_{t+1})}. \tag{3}$$

2.2   Inverse Dimensionality Reduction

We have seen in a previous part of this section, that parametric DR methods often provide an approximate inverse DR mapping π^{-1}, which is not the case for nonparametric methods.

In this subsection, we repeat the ideas from [13] to define such a mapping for an arbitrary DR approach.

We assume that points $\mathbf{x}_i \in X$ and projections $\pi(\mathbf{x}_i) = \boldsymbol{\xi}_i \in \Xi$ are available. For an inverse projection, we assume the following functional form

$$\pi^{-1} : \Xi \to X, \boldsymbol{\xi} \mapsto \frac{\sum_j \beta_j k_j(\boldsymbol{\xi}, \boldsymbol{\xi}_j)}{\sum_l k_l(\boldsymbol{\xi}, \boldsymbol{\xi}_l)} \tag{4}$$

where $\beta_j \in X$ are parameters of the mapping and $k_j(\boldsymbol{\xi}, \boldsymbol{\xi}_j) = \exp(-0.5\|\boldsymbol{\xi} - \boldsymbol{\xi}_j\|^2/(\sigma_j^{\boldsymbol{\xi}})^2)$ constitutes a Gaussian kernel with bandwidth determined by $\sigma_j^{\boldsymbol{\xi}}$. Summation is over a random subset Ξ' of the given data projections $\boldsymbol{\xi}_i = \pi(\mathbf{x}_i)$, or over codebooks resulting from a previously run vector quantization on the $\boldsymbol{\xi}_i$.

Formalizing a valid cost function to optimize the parameters of π^{-1} constitutes a challenge, if the intrinsic data dimensionality is larger then 2. In this case, the inverse position of a given projection $\boldsymbol{\xi}$ can be ambiguous. In order to emphasize those directions in the data space that are relevant for the target variable we utilize the distance as measured with the Fisher metric in the cost function:

$$E = \sum_i \left(d_1 \left(\mathbf{x}_i, \pi^{-1}(\boldsymbol{\xi}_i) \right)^2 \right) = \sum_i \left(\mathbf{x}_i - \pi^{-1}(\boldsymbol{\xi}_i) \right)^\top \mathbf{J}(\mathbf{x}_i) \left(\mathbf{x}_i - \pi^{-1}(\boldsymbol{\xi}_i) \right) \quad (5)$$

We utilize the distance d_T with $T = 1$ in order to save computational time. This local approximation works usually well since in the course of optimization the points $\mathbf{x}_i$ and $\pi^{-1}(\boldsymbol{\xi}_i)$ will get close to each other. Minimization of these costs with respect to the parameters $\boldsymbol{\beta}_j$ takes place by gradient descent.

3   General Framework for Visualizing Regression Models

In this section, we are in the position to put the pieces together towards a general framework for the visualization of regression models. We assume the following scenario: a data set including points $\mathbf{x}_i \in X$ is given. Every data point is accompanied with a target value $y_i \in \mathbb{R}$. In addition, a regression model $f : X \to \mathbb{R}$ has been trained on the given training set, such as a support vector machine for regression (SVR). A visualization of the given data set and the regression model would offer the possibility to visually inspect the prediction result and to address user tasks as formulated in section 1. We propose a general framework how to visualize a regression model and a given data set.

3.1   Naive Approach

Assuming a nonlinear dimensionality reduction method is given, a naive approach to visualize a regression model could be like follows:

- Sample the full data space X by points $\mathbf{z}_i$.
- Project these points nonlinearly to two-dimensional points $\pi(\mathbf{z}_i)$ using some nonlinear dimensionality reduction technique.
- Display the data points $\pi(\mathbf{x}_i)$ and the contours induced by the sampled function $(\pi(\mathbf{z}_i), f(\mathbf{z}_i))$, the latter approximating the prediction of the model.

This simple method, however, fails unless X is low-dimensional because of two reasons:

- Sampling X sufficiently requires an exponential number of points, hence it is infeasible for high-dimensional X.
- It is impossible to map a full high-dimensional data set faithfully to low dimensions, hence topological distortions are unavoidable when projecting the prediction function.

The problem is that this procedure tries to visualize the function in the full data space X. It would be sufficient to visualize only those parts of the function which are relevant for the given training data and the given prediction function.

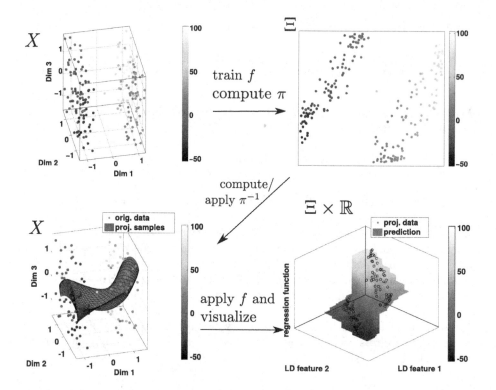

Fig. 1. Illustration of our proposed approach to visualize a regression model (in this case a Decision Tree).

3.2   Our Proposed Approach

Hence, we propose to sample in the projection plane instead of the original data manifold, and we propose to use a discriminative DR technique to make the problem of data projection well-posed in the sense that discriminative methods define clearly what structure preservation means (see [14] for a discussion on this). Together with the techniques presented in the last section, this leads to the following feasible procedure for the visualization of regression models:

- Project the data $\mathbf{x}_i$ using a nonlinear discriminative DR technique leading to points $\pi(\mathbf{x}_i) \in \Xi$.
- If not provided by the selected DR technique, compute an inverse mapping π^{-1} by optimization of equation (5).
- Utilize the mapping $f \circ \pi^{-1}(\mathbf{z})$ to visualize the regression function on any position $\mathbf{z} \in \Xi$ in the low-dimensional space.

In order to execute the last step, we sample the projection space Ξ in a regular grid leading to points $\{\mathbf{z}_i\}_{i=1}^n$. Finally, we visualize the pairs $(\mathbf{z}_i, f \circ \pi^{-1}(\mathbf{z}_i))$ as contours of a two-dimensional plot, or plotting $f \circ \pi^{-1}(\mathbf{z}_i)$ over the third axis as done in Fig. 1. An illustration of this approach is depicted in Fig. 1 with a three-dimensional data set, where dimension 3 is irrelevant for prediction (see section 4 for further details of this data set). The Fisher GTM has been utilized to obtain π and π^{-1} in this example.

Unlike the naive approach, sampling takes place in $\mathbb{R}^2$ only and, thus, is feasible. Further, only those parts of the space X are considered along which the regression function changes. Such, directions irrelevant for the target mapping are neglected.

3.3   Evaluation Measure

In order to evaluate the quality of the obtained visualization of the regression model, we propose to utilize the Pearson correlation of $f(\mathbf{x})$ and $f \circ \pi^{-1} \circ \pi(\mathbf{x})$:

$$\frac{\mathbb{E}\left\{(f(\mathbf{x}) - \mathbb{E}(f(\mathbf{x}))) \cdot \left(f \circ \pi^{-1} \circ \pi(\mathbf{x}) - \mathbb{E}\left(f \circ \pi^{-1} \circ \pi(\mathbf{x})\right)\right)\right\}}{\sqrt{\mathbb{E}\left\{(f(\mathbf{x}) - \mathbb{E}(f(\mathbf{x})))^2\right\}} \cdot \sqrt{\mathbb{E}\left\{\left(f \circ \pi^{-1} \circ \pi(\mathbf{x}) - \mathbb{E}\left(f \circ \pi^{-1} \circ \pi(\mathbf{x})\right)\right)^2\right\}}} \tag{6}$$

This criterion does not measure in how far π^{-1} is the exact inverse of π. Obtaining such an inverse mapping would be impossible for the most data sets. Instead, equation 6 evaluates the precision of π^{-1} with respect to f, i.e. errors along directions where f doesn't chage are not accounted as such. This way, only directions in the data space are considered which are relevant for the prediction.

This procedure estimates the quality of the visualization of the regression model at the positions of the data points. Other regions are not evaluated with this approach. We prefer the Pearson correlation over the normalized MSE, because the former is always normalized between -1 and 1.

For the computation, we utilize only those points $\mathbf{x}$ which were not utilized to train the mapping π^{-1}. Further, we approximate $f \circ \pi^{-1} \circ \pi(\mathbf{x})$ by the prediction value of the closest sampled point $\mathbf{z}'$ of $\pi(\mathbf{x})$, simply because we have already computed $f \circ \pi^{-1}$ for these points.

4   Experiments

In this section we demonstrate our proposed approach with artificial and real life data sets. We employ the popular Support Vector Machine for regression and the Decision Tree scheme as the models that we interpret. Furthermore, since we do not assume any particular property of the regression model, any regression scheme could be visualized in the same way. A description of the models follows.

- The Support Vector Machine for regression (SVR) [18] employs a linear function $f(\mathbf{x}) = \phi(\mathbf{x})^\top \mathbf{w}$ in the feature space for prediction. Errors are penalized linearly, where small errors, i.e. predictions lying in an ϵ-tube around the target, are not penalized. Since the whole approach can be formulated using scalar products of the data only, kernels can be employed. In the experiments, we utilize the Gaussian kernel $k(\mathbf{x}_i, \mathbf{x}_j) = \exp\left(-\beta \|\mathbf{x}_i - \mathbf{x}_i\|^2\right)$. We use the implementation provided by the libsvm [5].

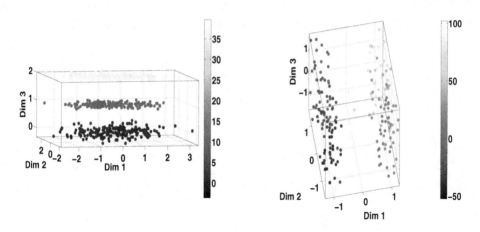

Fig. 2. Two toy data sets: data set1 (left) and data set2 (right).

- Decision Trees (DecTree) [3] for regression partition the data space X, where the prediction value in each partition is the mean of the points lying in the according partition. Splits are optimized such that the mean squared error is minimized. We utilize the Matlab implementation here.

In the following, we demonstrate how the user tasks described in section 1 can be tackled with of our proposed approach, what effects the choice of the employed dimensionality reduction can have and we apply our presented approach to a real world data set. In the following, we briefly characterize the utilized data sets.

- *Data set1* is depicted in Fig. 2 (left) and consist of three two-dimensional clusters positioned above each other. One of these clusters (the bottom one) has additional noise in the third dimension. The prediction function is again encoded in the color and is a squared function of dimension three.
- *Data set2* consists of two three-dimensional clusters with an outlier in-between these two clusters. Fig. 2 (right) depicts this set, where the color indicates the target variable of the regression task which is a linear function for the left cluster and a squared function for the right one. In both cases, the target function depends only on the first two dimensions.
- The *diabetes* [6] data set describes 442 patients by the 10 features age, sex, body mass index, blood pressure and 6 blood serum measurements. The target variable is a measure of the progression of the diabetes disease one year after feature acquisition.

4.1   Effect of the Selected Dimensionality Reduction Technique

One key ingredient in our proposed approach is the DR. However, since any DR technique can be applied, we discuss in this section effects of the selected methods. For this purpose, we train a SVR model on data set1 and visualize it with different techniques.

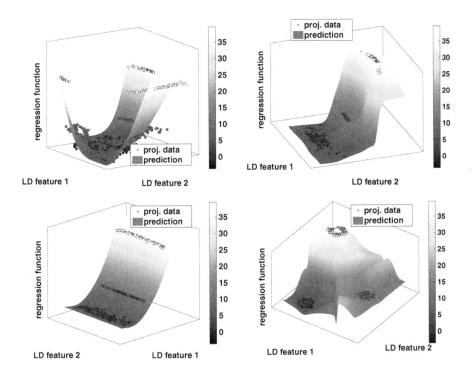

Fig. 3. Four different visualizations of the same regression model. These are based on (from top left to bottom right): GTM, Fisher MDS, Fisher GTM, Fisher t-SNE.

The most common visualization approach is PCA. However, the latter is driven only by the variance of the data and neglects other structure. Hence, using PCA for data set1 yields to overlapping clusters and hence to a bad visualization of the underlying regression model: the accordance as evaluated by (6) is 0.21, i.e. the visualized model has only a small correlation to the original one.

In a scenario where the structure of the data is not known, more powerful nonlinear DR methods can be necessary. We investigate here the two methods GTM as a generative model and t-SNE as a neighborhood embedding.

Applying our regression model visualization approach to the trained SVR using the GTM yields a visualization with a quality of 0.95 (as summed up in Table 1). The visualized model is depicted in the top left corner of Fig. 3. Although, the accordance of the visualized prediction model with the original one is high, the visualization tears the cluster structure apart. So, more powerful methods for DR can increase the visualization quality. However, there still might be undesired effects, especially if the approaches act in an unsupervised way. An other option, besides choosing more powerful methods, is to utilize supervised ones. This can be done, as discussed earlier with the use of a supervised metric.

To demonstrate the effect of such a supervised visualization, we apply our regression model visualization approach using Fisher MDS, Fisher GTM and Fisher t-SNE. Applying these techniques, we obtain three different visualizations

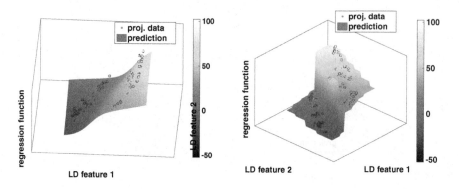

Fig. 4. A Fisher GTM induced visualization of the SVR (left) and Decision Tree (right) with data set1. The continuous surfaces depict the prediction of the regression models.

of the same regression model. We evaluate them and obtain a quality of 0.99 for each visualization (summed up in Table 1). The visualizations (in Fig. 3) of Fisher MDS (top right) and Fisher GTM (bottom left) agree largely, while the Fisher GTM based visualization shows the shape of the squared polynomial target function without any distortions. In the Fisher t-SNE projection, the squared prediction for the single clusters can be observed, but it is not so clear as in the Fisher GTM mapping. One reason for this is that t-SNE often tears clusters apart since it has a high focus on local neighborhood preservation.

4.2   Illustration of Potential User Tasks

We utilize data set2 to illustrate the identified user tasks. For this purpose, we train a SVR and a Decision Tree using this data set. For the DR, we employ the supervised technique Fisher GTM - an unsupervised approach would try to embed this intrinsically three-dimensional data set in two dimensions and, hence, might result in an embedding not well suited to visualize the target function.

Using these ingredients, we can visualize the two regression models with our proposed approach. Employing the numerical evaluation scheme in 3 implies a quality of 0.99 for both visualizations, as measured by the Pearson correlation. I.e. the regression model is shown accurately at least at the positions of the data. The evaluation results for all experiments are summed up in Table 1.

Table 1. Visualization qualities for the regression models, as measured by the Pearson correlation.

	PCA	GTM	Fisher MDS	Fisher GTM	Fisher t-SNE
data set1,	0.21	0.95	0.99	0.99	0.99
data set2, SVR	–	–	0.99	0.99	0.99
data set2, DecTree	–	–	0.99	0.99	0.99
diabetes	–	–	–	0.94	0.92

The resulting visualized models are shown in Fig. 4. The left plot depicts the SVR and the right one the Decision Tree. In both cases, the first two coordinate axes encode the two-dimensional embedding space of the data. The target variable is encoded both by the third axis and by the coloring. The surface depicts the prediction of the respective regression model.

We exemplarily address the user tasks for these visualizations. Considering user task 1, the complexity of the prediction functions can be observed directly in the visualizations: the SVR instance shows a smooth predictive function while the Decision Tree instance is very complex. This is particularly the case for the cluster with the squared function: the trained SVR might be considered underfitted, here. Dealing with user task 2, the user can observe that the complexities of the target functions are quite different in the two present clusters. The user could prefer to train two independent local models on these clusters, for instance. The extrapolation between these clusters is smooth in the left image but very steep in the right one, which might lead to bad predictions if future data are expected to lie also between the clusters. In the right visualization, the piecewise constant regions are good visible which is typical for Decision Tree models (user task 3). Considering user task 4, the visualizations directly imply how both models treat the outlier point: the SVR ignores it and the Decision Tree overfits it. Having this insight, the user can judge which model handles the data point of interest better, depending on his estimation of the regularity of this point.

4.3   Applying the Proposed Framework to Real World Data

For the diabetes data set, we train the SVR model by splitting the data set multiple times randomly in a training and a test set in order to estimate a good parameter value for the kernel of the SVR.

In the previous subsections we have argued that discriminative nonlinear DR methods are best suited for the visualization of regression models. Hence, we apply two such methods, i.e. Fisher GTM and Fisher t-SNE to the SVR model trained on the diabetes data set.

The evaluation based on (6) yields a quality value of 0.94 for the visualization based on Fisher GTM and a value of 0.92 for the Fisher t-SNE induced visualization. Both are shown in Fig. 5.

Interestingly, both visualizations agree in that sense that they show an almost linear prediction function. We have validated this by training a linear model and have obtained a similar error on the test data.

5   Discussion

We have proposed a general framework to visualize a given trained regression model together with the training data. This allows the user to inspect various properties of the trained model.

While the approach is in that sense general, that it allows to use any DR and any regression technique, only the Support Vector Regression and Decision Tree approaches have been utilized so far. Further work will demonstrate this framework on other regression models as well as on more real life data sets.

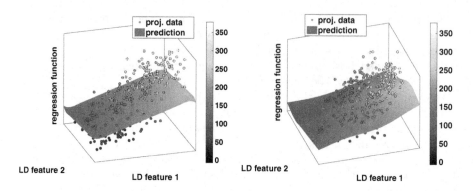

Fig. 5. A Fisher GTM (left) and a Fisher t-SNE (right) visualization of a SVR model trained on the diabetes data set.

References

1. Bishop, C.M., Svensén, M., Williams, C.K.: Gtm: The generative topographic mapping. Neural computation **10**(1), 215–234 (1998)
2. Breheny, P., Burchett, W.: Visualization of regression models using visreg (2013)
3. Breiman, L., Friedman, J.H., Olshen, R.A., Stone, C.J.: Classification and Regression Trees. Statistics/Probability Series. Wadsworth Publishing Company, Belmont (1984)
4. Cameron, A.C., Windmeijer, F.A.G.: An r-squared measure of goodness of fit for some common nonlinear regression models. Journal of Econometrics **77**(2), 329–342 (1997)
5. Chang, C.-C., Lin, C.-J.: LIBSVM: A library for support vector machines. ACM Transactions on Intelligent Systems and Technology **2**, 27:1–27:27 (2011). http://www.csie.ntu.edu.tw/ cjlin/libsvm
6. Efron, B., Hastie, T., Johnstone, I., Tibshirani, R.: Least angle regression. Annals of Statistics **32**, 407–499 (2004)
7. Gisbrecht, A., Hammer, B.: Data visualization by nonlinear dimensionality reduction. WIREs Data Mining and Knowledge Discovery (2014)
8. Gisbrecht, A., Mokbel, B., Hammer, B.: Relational generative topographic mapping. Neurocomputing **74**(9), 1359–1371 (2011)
9. House, T.W.: Big data research and development initiative (2012)
10. Lee, J.A., Verleysen, M.: Nonlinear dimensionality reduction. Springer (2007)
11. Peltonen, J., Klami, A., Kaski, S.: Improved learning of riemannian metrics for exploratory analysis. Neural Networks **17**, 1087–1100 (2004)
12. Rauber, P.E., Silva, R.R.O.D., Feringa, S., Celebi, M.E., FalÃo, A.X., Telea, A.C.: Interactive image feature selection aided by dimensionality reduction. In: Bertini, E., Roberts, J.C. (eds.) EuroVis Workshop on Visual Analytics (EuroVA). The Eurographics Association (2015)
13. Schulz, A., Gisbrecht, A., Hammer, B.: Using discriminative dimensionality reduction to visualize classifiers. Neural Processing Letters, 1–28 (2014)
14. Schulz, A., Hammer, B.: Discriminative dimensionality reduction for regression problems using the fisher metric. In: Accepted in IJCNN 2015 (2015)
15. Simoff, S.J., Böhlen, M.H., Mazeika, A. (eds.): Visual Data Mining - Theory, Techniques and Tools for Visual Analytics. LNCS, vol. 4404. Springer, Heildelberg (2008)

16. van der Maaten, L., Hinton, G.: Visualizing data using t-sne. The Journal of Machine Learning Research **9**(2579–2605), 85 (2008)
17. van der Maaten, L., Postma, E., van den Herik, H.: Dimensionality reduction: A comparative review. Technical report, Tilburg University Technical Report, TiCC-TR 2009–005 (2009)
18. Vapnik, V.N.: The Nature of Statistical Learning Theory. Springer, New York (1995)
19. Venna, J., Peltonen, J., Nybo, K., Aidos, H., Kaski, S.: Information retrieval perspective to nonlinear dimensionality reduction for data visualization. JMLR-10 **11**, 451–490 (2010)
20. Ward, M., Grinstein, G., Keim, D.A.: Interactive Data Visualization: Foundations, Techniques and Application. A.K. Peters Ltd. (2010)

Evaluation of Multi-view 3D Reconstruction Software

Julius Schöning$^{(\boxtimes)}$ and Gunther Heidemann

Institute of Cognitive Science, University of Osnabrück, Osnabrück, Germany
{juschoening,gheidema}@uos.de

Abstract. A number of software solutions for reconstructing 3D models from multi-view image sets have been released in recent years. Based on an unordered collection of photographs, most of these solutions extract 3D models using structure-from-motion (SFM) algorithms. In this work, we compare the resulting 3D models qualitatively and quantitatively. To achieve these objectives, we have developed different methods of comparison for all software solutions. We discuss the perfomance and existing drawbacks. Particular attention is paid to the ability to create printable 3D models or 3D models usable for other applications.

Keywords: Multi-view 3D reconstruction · Benchmark · Structure from Motion (SFM) · Software comparison · Photogrammetry

1 Introduction

In the last decade, a huge number of reconstruction software solutions for multi-view images has been released. This trend was boosted by the development of 3D printers. While current software solutions like *Autodesk 123D Catch* [3] and *Agisoft PhotoScan* [2] promised, e.g., to create printable models out of image collections. However, the number of printed replicas is still fairly low. In this paper we provide an overview of existing 3D reconstruction software solutions and benchmark them against each other.

The main aim of this research is to rank the four most common 3D reconstruction software solutions in a benchmark. We propose a method to objectively quantify the quality of the 3D models produced by these software solutions. Based on two different multi-view image data sets [25,29], we evaluate the solutions with respect to practical applicability in one real scenario and one planned shooting scenario. We provide objective evaluation indicators regarding both the qualitative and quantitative results of each image-based 3D reconstruction software.

The paper is structured as follows: First we give a brief overview of related work with respect to existing benchmarks and evaluations. Then, we describe the used multi-view software solutions and give the reasons for our selection of data sets. After describing the model generation and our benchmark methodology, we rank the software solutions.

© Springer International Publishing Switzerland 2015
G. Azzopardi and N. Petkov (Eds.): CAIP 2015, Part II, LNCS 9257, pp. 450–461, 2015.
DOI: 10.1007/978-3-319-23117-4_39

2   Related Work

For 3D reconstruction, various approaches such as *123D Catch* [3], *PhotoScan* [2], Photo tourism [23], VideoTrace [11], Kinect fusion [17], ProFORMA [18] etc. with various inputs like image collections, single images and video footage are in use. Each approach has its own drawbacks, for instance if stereo vision is used, depth information only up to a limited distance of typically less than $5m$ [12,20] is available for the reconstruction process. Furthermore 3D reconstructions have issues with e.g., shiny, textureless, or occluded surfaces, currently [19].

In archeology, traditional 3D recording technologies like terrestrial laser scanners or fringe projection systems, are still expensive, inflexible and often require expert knowledge for operation. Hence, most benchmarks, evaluation and taxonomies of 3D reconstruction software is published in the archeology context. Kersten and Lindstaedt [13] demonstrated and discussed the application of image based reconstruction of archaeological findings. Additionally, the accuracy of data produced by multi-image 3D reconstruction software is compared to the traditional terrestrial 3D laser scanners and light detection and ranging (LIDAR) systems [9,14].

3   Multi-view 3D Reconstruction

In this chapter we describe our benchmark as well as the chosen software solutions and data sets.

3.1   Multi-view Software Solutions

While there is a large body of academic and commercial software solutions for 3D reconstruction out of multi-view data sets, we chose four most well-known ones for our evaluation: *Agisoft PhotoScan Standard Edition* [2], *Autodesk 123D Catch* [3], *VisualSFM* [30–32] with *CMVS* [10] and *ARC 3D* [28]. With respect to other software solutions [1,15], these four tools are, in our opinion, the most widely used. Moreover these four tools are constantly present in many articles [9, 13,14,22].

PhotoScan Standard Edition [2] is introduced as first software. It is the only fee-based software solution in this benchmark, but provides quite a lot of features like photogrammetric triangulation, dense point cloud generation and editing, 3D model generation and texturing, and spherical panorama stitching. *PhotoScan* is available for *Windows*, *Mac OS* and *Linux* distribution and supports GPU acceleration during 3D reconstruction.

123D Catch by *Autodesk* [3] creates 3D models from a collection of up to 70 images. Currently this software is a free solution and is available for *Windows*, *Mac OS* and *Android*. To increase speed during the overall process, the reconstruction process is outsourced to cloud computing, thus an internet connection for uploading the images is needed. Since it is a software for users without expert knowledge, only a few parameters can be set. As a result, the reconstruction process is quite intuitive.

Wu's *VisualSFM* is an academic software solution, which bundles his SFM-approaches [30–32] with Furukawa et al.'s multi-view-stereo techniques [10] into a powerful tool. As an academic software it is freely available for *Windows*, *Mac OS* and *Linux*. Like *PhotoScan* , it uses GPU acceleration, and especially for *nVidia* graphic cards CUDA is supported.

ARC 3D is an academic web-based 3D reconstruction service primarily designed for the needs of the cultural heritage field. Due to its web-based design the automatic reconstruction process including preprocessing steps like feature point detection, set of image pairs computation, camera calibration and full scale reconstruction is running on a cluster of computers at the Departement of Electrical Engineering of the K.U.Leuven. With the *ARC 3D* upload tool the user uploads a photo sequence over the Internet to the cluster. When the cluster has finished the reconstruction process, the user is notified by email and can download the results. A closer look into *ARC 3D* is given by Vergauwen and Van Gool [28].

3.2   Data Sets

During the planning stage of this benchmark, very soon it became obvious that a benchmark should include real scene photographs as well as photographs taken in a controlled indoor environment. Another essential requirement to the multi-view data sets is the availability of a ground truth. Based on these two criteria, several multi-view data sets were examined [6,21,24,25,29] and the below mentioned ones are chosen.

Since ground truth is required, the data sets *fountain-P11* and *Herz-Jesu-P8* [25] as a real scene and the *Oxford Dinosaur* [29] as planned photographs are chosen. The data set *dino* and *temple* [21] as planned photographs are also considered, but due to scaling problems our first submission to the evaluation platform did not succeed. These results will be integrated into future work. Data sets for special issues as, e.g., repeated structures [6] are not taken into account, because they can cause anomalies in the reconstruction pipelines of the software solutions.

We now describe the used data sets — the *fountain-P11*, *Herz-Jesu-P8* and *Oxford Dinosaur* — and the necessary adaptations made in this paper in detail. The first two pictures of Figure 1 show examples of the multi-view data set of outdoor architectural heritage by Strecha et al. [25], initially designed for benchmarking automatic reconstruction from multiple view imagery as a replacement for LIDAR systems. The scenes of the fountain and the Herz-Jesu church have been captured with a Canon D60 with a resolution of 3072×2028 pixels. The data set comprises eleven images of the fountain and eight of the Herz-Jesu church. The corresponding ground truth has been taken by a LIDAR system. A more detailed description of these data sets including the estimation procedures can be found in [25].

As a data set for a controlled indoor environment, the quite old *Oxford Dinosaur* [29] data is used. This is because such toy models, as seen in the third picture of Figure 1, are quite interesting for 3D printing. This data set includes 36 images of 720×576 pixels of a toy dinosaur captured on a turntable. As there is no ground truth available, the meshed model of Fitzgibbon et al. [8] results is taken as ground truth.

In order to provide the same conditions for all reconstruction solutions, the data sets must be adapted to a data format that all reconstruction tools can handle. Thus, all images have been converted to JPEG. As JPEG is a lossy compression algorithm, some details of the native data sets get lost. In the preparation phase, the data set *Oxford Dinosaur* causes some problems like incomplete reconstruction. To improve this behavior, we decided to also provide this data set with removed black background as seen in the last picture of Figure 1.

3.3 3D Model Generation

For 3D model generation, the converted images are put into the processing pipeline of each above mentioned solution.[1] Other additional a priori information, e.g., on internal camera calibration parameters was not provided for the reconstruction process. On a stand alone computer system dense point clouds for the data sets were computed and exported sequentially with all software solutions. The system was equipped with a 4-Core *Intel i7-3770* at 3.4Ghz, 16GB of RAM and a *nVidia Quadro K600* graphics card running *Windows 7 64bit* as operating system. Using different parameter configurations in the solutions, the user has a limited influence on the resulting dense point cloud. To simplify the benchmark, the initial default parameters of each software tool are taken if the model creation succeeded. For the reproduction of this benchmark, the parameters used are attached in Table 2. As output format the polygon file format (ply) is selected. As *123D Catch* cannot export the model as ply, the model was converted from obj to ply by Meshlab [16]. The resulting reconstructed 3D models of all software tools are shown in the center of Figure 1. Unfortunately, *ARC 3D* was not able to deliver results for the *Oxford Dinosaur*, neither with the original set nor with the background-removed set.

4 Comparison and Evaluation

The trickiest part is to define an evaluation scheme to compare the reconstructed models of Section 3.3. Each model comprises a particular number of points, and some of the reconstructed models have points beyond the boundaries of the ground truth. Hence, a simple point to ground truth comparison can generate poor results.

---

[1] For the benchmark *PhotoScan* Version 1.1.0.2004, *123D Catch* Build 3.0.0.54, *VisualSFM* Version 0.5.26 and *ARC 3D* uploader Version 2.2 was used.

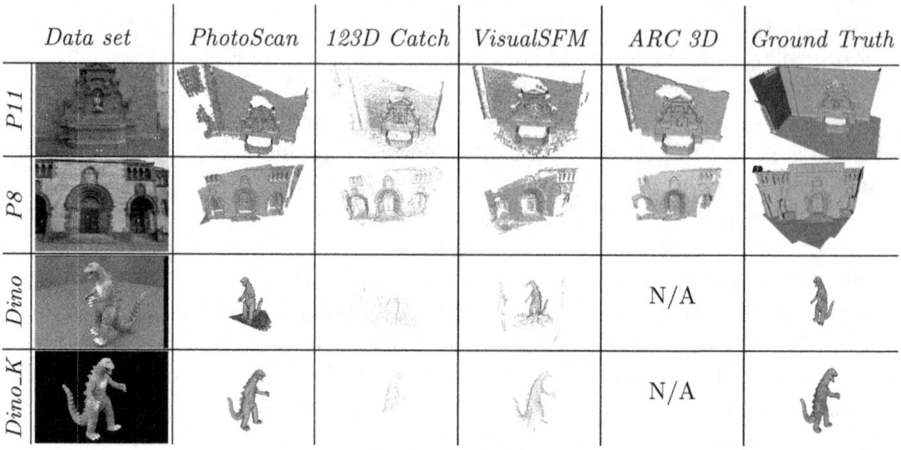

Data set	PhotoScan	123D Catch	VisualSFM	ARC 3D	Ground Truth
P11					
P8					
Dino				N/A	
Dino_K				N/A	

Fig. 1. Created 3D models of *PhotoScan* [2], *123D Catch* [3], *VisualSFM* [30–32] and *ARC 3D* [28] on four data sets: *fountain-P11* (11 images), *Herz-Jesu-P8* (8 images), *Oxford Dinosaur* (36 images) and *Oxford Dinosaur* with removed background (36 images). One sample image of each data set is shown on the left, reconstruction results of each tool are shown in the center and the corresponding ground truths are shown on the right.

4.1 Methodology

For this benchmark we mainly focus on the accuracy of the reconstructed models. The least common denominator of all the software involved is a dense point cloud of the model, which is used as starting point for our comparison, if no sufficient triangular mesh is provided by the software. We also documented the computing time required by each tool. But due to the web-based architecture of *123D Catch* and *ARC 3D*, the runtime does not give considerable evidence about the computational effort.

The following 3D model comparison pipeline includes the open source software *Meshlab* [16] and *CloudCompare* [7] for all 3D operation as well as *Matlab* for provision of statistics.[2] Based on the dense point clouds of each model, a rough direction and size alignment with the ground truth date is performed manually. Thereby, the global coordinate system is scaled on meters. If no mesh is provided, the aligned point clouds are meshed with the ball-pivoting algorithm by Bernardini et al. [4]. As pivoting ball radius the auto-guess setting of *Meshlab* is used. At this stage, the ground truth data alongside with each model is loaded into *CloudCompare*. In order to finely register the model with the ground truth, the iterative closest point algorithm (IPC) by Besl and McKay [5] with a target error difference of $1 \cdot 10^{-8}$ is used. For the registered models the minimal distance between every point to any triangular face of the meshed model is computed. Using the normal of the closest face the sign of each distance value is set. Note, that the comparison is made between each created, meshed model to the point

---

[2] Used 64*bit* version: *Meshlab* 1.3.3, *CloudCompare* 2.6.0, *Matlab* R2014.

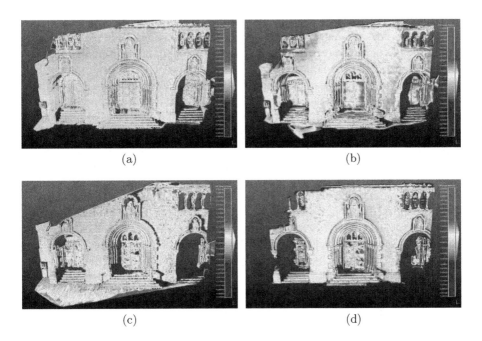

(a)   (b)

(c)   (d)

Fig. 2. Heat map of the minimal distance between the ground truth point cloud and the triangular mesh of the created model as reference on the *Herz-Jesu-P8* data set. Points with distance differences more than ±0.1 are not visualized; distance differences between -0.05 and 0.05 are colorized in the scheme blue–green–red. On the right next to the legend, the distance distribution is shown. Models are created by (a) *PhotoScan*, (b) *123D Catch*, (c) *VisualSFM* and (d) *ARC 3D*.

cloud of the ground truth, so the created model is set as the reference. For qualitative results, all distances of more than ±0.1 are not visualized, an example is shown in Figure 2. Distances between -0.1 to -0.05 are colorized blue, red is used for 0.05 to 0.1. Between -0.05 and 0.05 the color scheme blue–green–red is applied.[3] The scaling values for the *Oxford Dinosaur* data sets differ due to smaller model sizes. For quantitative results, all computed distances of a model are exported. On these exported data the mean value (μ) and standard deviation (σ) of the distance distribution as seen as in Table 1 are calculated. Further, Figure 3 shows the histograms of each model from each tool to represent the distance distribution. For a direct comparison, an empirical cumulative distribution function (CDF) is calculated and plotted in Figure 4. The computation time of each solution is simply measured in seconds and can be found in Table 1.

4.2 Reasoning of Our Methodology

In contrast to common practice [26,27], we made the comparison between each reconstructed model as the reference to the ground truth, and not vice versa.

---

[3] For more results cf. https://ikw.uos.de/~cv/publications/caip15/

Why? Each software solution yields a different number of dense points, partially depending on parameter settings, which can not be influenced by the user. To get comparable histograms and statistic figures, the same number of points for each model is needed. Since it is not possible to parameterize all solutions such that all reconstructed models have the same number of points, random sampling from the points appears to be a good idea at first glance. However, a random sample of points may cause misleading results in our setup, because some reconstructed models protrude beyond the ground truth. For that reason we do not use random sampling. Our method to compare the ground truth to the created models (as reference) is much simpler, by this means, we always have the same numbers of points.

A second particularity of our methodology could be the comparison against the meshed model and not against the point cloud. The fact that the different software solutions provide a different number of points leads in most cases to substantial distances, if only a small number of points is available. Thus, the distance is calculated to the mesh to not adversely affect tools which creates a small number of points.

5   Result and Discussion

Three of the four tools were able to compute models out of the four data sets as seen in Figure 1. Further, this figure shows that all tested software tools yield useful results for data sets *fountain-P11* and *Herz-Jesu-P8*. However, for the two *Oxford Dinosaur* data sets, only *PhotoScan* and *VisualSFM* come up with useful results, the result of *123D Catch* is seriously deformed or incomplete and *ARC 3D* returns a *ARC3D reconstruction failed* email with no model. We made a qualitative ranking based on the heat maps of distances, see Figure 2 as examples. The heat maps make clear that *PhotoScan* exhibits exceedingly few deviations to the ground truth, followed by *VisualSFM*, *ARC 3D* and *123D Catch*. However, the ranking of *ARC 3D* is done bearing in mind it has failed on two data sets. A printable model of the toy dinosaur from the *Oxford Dinosaur* has only been created by *PhotoScan* and *VisualSFM*.

For the quantitative analysis we excluded *ARC 3D* for the reason of the missing models. As seen in Figure 3 we assume a statistical normal distribution of the distance deviation. The quantitative ranking is done by a scoring system. On each data value the best value gets one and the worst gets three scoring points. The mean value (μ), the standard deviation (σ) and the time are scored separately. For example, the model created by *VisualSFM* provides the lowest mean value deviation, which is indicated in Table 1 by the lowest average of points for mean value. Finally, the quantitative ranking based on the mean value (μ) and standard deviation (σ) is headed by *VisualSFM* (12 points) followed by *PhotoScan* (17 points) and *123D Catch* (19 points). To confirm the previous ranking and to rank *ARC 3D* we also analyse the CDF. As seen in all plots of Figure 4, the probabilities are mainly close to zero. The probability distribution in the CDF reflects the results of Table 1. Neglecting the data set of the *Oxford Dinosaur*, *ARC 3D* can be inserted between *PhotoScan* and *123D Catch*.

Table 1. Mean value (μ), standard deviation (σ) and computation time of each software tool with the scoring in points on each attribute.

	PhotoScan [2]			123D Catch [3]			VisualSFM [30–32]			ARC 3D [28]		
	μ[m]	σ[m]	time[s]	μ[m]	σ[m]	time[s]	μ[m]	σ[m]	time[s]	μ[m]	σ[m]	time[s]
fountain-P11	$-1.90\cdot10^{-2}$	1.01	9136	$1.87\cdot10^{-1}$	$83.73\cdot10^{-1}$	600	$9.14\cdot10^{-3}$	1.14	221	$-2.14\cdot10^{-2}$	1.47	1620
Herz-Jesu-P8	$-8.59\cdot10^{-2}$	1.37	1634	$9.95\cdot10^{-2}$	1.36	900	$-4.58\cdot10^{-3}$	1.31	170	$-2.56\cdot10^{-1}$	2.05	1380
Dinosaur	$6.09\cdot10^{-4}$	$2.65\cdot10^{-3}$	139	$8.44\cdot10^{-3}$	$2.01\cdot10^{-2}$	420	$5.43\cdot10^{-4}$	$4.37\cdot10^{-4}$	30	—	—	—
Dinosaur_K	$4.52\cdot10^{-4}$	$2.48\cdot10^{-3}$	106	$3.86\cdot10^{-5}$	$2.06\cdot10^{-2}$	720	$-1.55\cdot10^{-4}$	$3.62\cdot10^{-3}$	28	—	—	—
Scoring		9	8		10	10	5	7	4		—	—

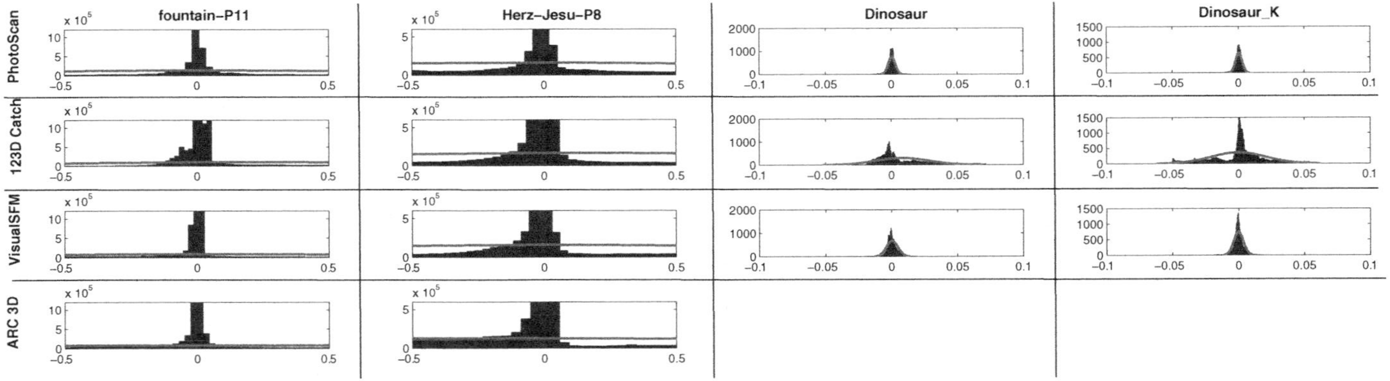

Fig. 3. Histogram plots of the distances between the created models and the ground truth data. *fountain-P11* contains $12,991,849$, *Herz-Jesu-P8* contains $18,101,559$ and *Oxford Dinosaur* with our without background contains $67,448$ elements. The normal distribution fit is represented by the red line.

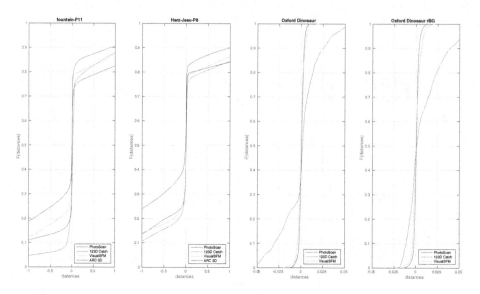

Fig. 4. Empirical cumulative distribution function per data sets. It describes the probability of the distance between the created model and the ground truth normalized on a scale from 0 to 1 over the distance. $F(distance) = P(-a < distance < a)$ with $a = 1$ for *fountain-P11* and *Herz-Jesu-P8* or with $a = 0.05$ for both *Oxford Dinosaur* sets

Based on this benchmark data, we deduce our own ranking, which also considers soft facts like runtime, license and execution by command line. As a result, *VisualSFM* is our selection of choice because of its quality, academic licensing and runtime. In our ranking, *VisualSFM* is followed by *PhotoScan*, *ARC 3D* and *123D Catch*.

In consideration of our benchmark, several issues can be questioned. First, we have noticed the used ground truth model of the *Oxford Dinosaur* does not seem to represent the real proportions, it could be stretched in height. Furthermore, problematic reconstruction scenes with repeated, shiny or textureless structures have been purposely neglected.

6   Conclusion

This paper presents a benchmark which compares the performance of multi-view 3D reconstruction software qualitatively and quantitatively on four different data sets. The data sets are two outdoor architectural scenes and planned shots of a toy dinosaur. Four different software solutions — *PhotoScan*, *123D Catch*, *VisualSFM* and *ARC 3D*— were tested and ranked. Summarizing, the quality of the tested tools is remarkably good but focused on specific fields. The available software solutions for multi-view 3D reconstruction can be ranked in terms of reconstruction quality, runtime etc. but due to the broad application field it is not possible to provide a general ranking.

Acknowledgments. This work was funded by German Research Foundation (DFG) as part of the Priority Program "Scalable Visual Analytics" (SPP 1335).

All *ARC 3D* marked 3D models are created by the *ARC 3D* webservice, developed by the VISICS research group of the KULeuven in Belgium.

References

1. Acute3D: Smart3DCapture - Acute3D — capturing reality with automatic 3D photogrammetry software, January 2015. http://www.acute3d.com/
2. Agisoft: Agisoft PhotoScan, January 2015. http://www.agisoft.ru/
3. Autodesk Inc: Autodesk 123D Catch — 3D model from photos, January 2015. http://www.123dapp.com/catch
4. Bernardini, F., Mittleman, J., Rushmeier, H., Silva, C., Taubin, G.: The ball-pivoting algorithm for surface reconstruction. IEEE Trans. Vis. Comput. Graphics **5**(4), 349–359 (1999)
5. Besl, P., McKay, H.: A method for registration of 3-D shapes. IEEE Trans. Pattern Anal. Mach. Intell. **14**(2), 239–256 (1992)
6. Ceylan, D., Mitra, N.J., Zheng, Y., Pauly, M.: Coupled structure-from-motion and 3D symmetry detection for urban facades. ACM Trans. Graphics **33**(1), 1–15 (2014)
7. CloudCompare : Cloudcompare, January 2015. http://www.danielgm.net/cc/
8. Fitzgibbon, A.W., Cross, G., Zisserman, A.: Automatic 3D model construction for turn-table sequences. In: Koch, R., Van Gool, L. (eds.) SMILE 1998. LNCS, vol. 1506, pp. 155–170. Springer, Heidelberg (1998)
9. Fonstad, M.A., Dietrich, J.T., Courville, B.C., Jensen, J.L., Carbonneau, P.E.: Topographic structure from motion: a new development in photogrammetric measurement. Earth Surface Processes and Landforms **38**(4), 421–430 (2013)
10. Furukawa, Y., Curless, B., Seitz, S.M., Szeliski, R.: Towards internet-scale multi-view stereo. In: IEEE Computer Vision and Pattern Recognition (CVPR), pp. 1434–1441 (2010)
11. van den Hengel, A., Dick, A., Thormählen, T., Ward, B., Torr, P.H.S.: VideoTrace. ACM Trans. Graphics **26**(3), 86 (2007)
12. Henry, P., Krainin, M., Herbst, E., Ren, X., Fox, D.: RGB-D mapping: using depth cameras for dense 3D modeling of indoor environments. In: Khatib, O., Kumar, V., Sukhatme, G. (eds.) Experimental Robotics. STAR, vol. 79, pp. 477–491. Springer, Heidelberg (2012)
13. Kersten, T.P., Lindstaedt, M.: Image-based low-cost systems for automatic 3D recording and modelling of archaeological finds and objects. In: Ioannides, M., Fritsch, D., Leissner, J., Davies, R., Remondino, F., Caffo, R. (eds.) EuroMed 2012. LNCS, vol. 7616, pp. 1–10. Springer, Heidelberg (2012)
14. Koutsoudis, A., Vidmar, B., Ioannakis, G., Arnaoutoglou, F., Pavlidis, G., Chamzas, C.: Multi-image 3D reconstruction data evaluation. Journal of Cultural Heritage **15**(1), 73–79 (2014)
15. Lukas Mach: insight3d - opensource image based 3D modeling software, January 2015. http://insight3d.sourceforge.net/
16. MeshLab: Meshlab, January 2015. http://meshlab.sourceforge.net/

17. Newcombe, R.A., Izadi, S., Hilliges, O., Molyneaux, D., Kim, D., Davison, A.J., Kohi, P., Shotton, J., Hodges, S., Fitzgibbon, A.: Kinectfusion: real-time dense surface mapping and tracking. In: IEEE International Symposium on Mixed and Augmented Reality (ISMAR), pp. 127–136 (2011)

18. Pan, Q., Reitmayr, G., Drummond, T.: Proforma: probabilistic feature-based online rapid model acquisition. In: Proceedings of the British Machine Vision Conference (BMVC) (2009)

19. Schöning, J., Heidemann, G.: Interactive 3D modeling - a survey-based perspective on interactive 3D reconstruction. In: Proceedings of the International Conference on Pattern Recognition Applications and Methods (ICPRAM), vol. 2, pp. 289–294 (2015)

20. Schöning, J., Pardowitz, M., Heidemann, G.: Taxonomy of 3D sensors: A survey of state-of-the-art low cost 3D-reconstruction sensors and their field of application. Low Cost 3D (2014)

21. Seitz, S., Curless, B., Diebel, J., Scharstein, D., Szeliski, R.: A comparison and evaluation of multi-view stereo reconstruction algorithms, vol. 1, pp. 519–528 (2006)

22. Singh, S.P., Jain, K., Mandla, V.R.: 3D scene reconstruction from video camera for virtual 3d city modeling. American Journal of Engineering Research 3(1), 140–148 (2014)

23. Snavely, N., Seitz, S.M., Szeliski, R.: Photo tourism: Exploring photo collections in 3d. ACM Trans. Graphics 25(3), 835 (2006)

24. Société Internationale de Photogrammétrie et de Télédétection (ISPRS): The isprs data set collection, January 2015. http://www.isprs.org/data/default.aspx

25. Strecha, C., von Hansen, W., Van Gool, L., Fua, P., Thoennessen, U.: On benchmarking camera calibration and multi-view stereo for high resolution imagery. In: IEEE Computer Vision and Pattern Recognition (CVPR), pp. 1–8 (2008)

26. Thoeni, K., Giacomini, A., Murtagh, R., Kniest, E.: A comparison of multi-view 3D reconstruction of a rock wall using several cameras and a laser scanner. Int. Arch. Photogramm. Remote Sens. Spatial Inf. Sci. XL-5, 573–580 (2014)

27. Uh, Y., Matsushita, Y., Byun, H.: Efficient multiview stereo by random-search and propagation. In: International Conference on 3D Vision (2014)

28. Vergauwen, M., Van Gool, L.: Web-based 3D reconstruction service. Machine Vision and Applications 17(6), 411–426 (2006)

29. Visual Geometry Group, University of Oxford: Multi-view and oxford colleges building reconstruction - dinosaur, August 2014

30. Wu, C.: Towards linear-time incremental structure from motion. In: International Conference on 3D Vision (2013)

31. Wu, C.: SiftGPU: A GPU implementation of scale invariant feature transform (SIFT), January 2015. http://cs.unc.edu/ccwu/siftgpu

32. Wu, C., Agarwal, S., Curless, B., Seitz, S.M.: Multicore bundle adjustment. In: IEEE Computer Vision and Pattern Recognition (CVPR) (2011)

Appendix

Table 2. Software parameters used for the reconstruction process

	Parameters

PhotoScan	*Align Photos*
	    Accuracy: High, Pair preselection: Disable,
	    Key point limit:40000, Tie point limit:1000
	Build Dense Cloud
	    Quality: Ultra high, Depth filtering: Aggressive

123D Catch	*Mesh Quality* Maximum
VisualSFM	Default settings
ARC 3D	*Subsample images* Subsample to (%): 100

Sample Size for Maximum Likelihood Estimates of Gaussian Model

Josef V. Psutka[1,2] and Josef Psutka[1,2]($\boxtimes$)

[1] New Technologies for the Information Society, Plzen, Czech Republic
{psutka_j,psutka}@kky.zcu.cz
[2] Department of Cybernetics, University of West Bohemia, Pilsen, Czech Republic

Abstract. Significant properties of maximum likelihood (ML) estimate are consistency, normality and efficiency. However, it has been proven that these properties are valid when the sample size approaches infinity. Many researches warn that a behavior of ML estimator working with the small sample size is largely unknown. But, in real tasks we usually do not have enough data to completely fulfill the conditions of optimal ML estimate. The question, which we discuss in the article is, how much data we need to be able to estimate the Gaussian model that provides sufficiently accurate likelihood estimates. This issue is addressed with respect to the dimension of space and it is taken into account possible property of ill conditioned data.

Keywords: Maximum likelihood estimate · Log-likelihood · Sample size

1 Introduction

The maximum likelihood (ML) method is widely used in many applications for estimating parameters of statistical models. The accuracy of the estimation directly corresponds to the amount of data utilized in the estimation process. Theory of probability and mathematical statistics indicates that the desired properties of the ML estimation, namely consistency, normality and efficiency, can be achieved only if the number N of data grows to infinity. This is of course in practical tasks, where we usually have available only limited number of data, an unsolvable assumption. So the question is how it is with precision of the ML estimate in relation to the number of available data. It is very difficult to answer this question exactly. Many rigorous statisticians argue that this question cannot be good answered because the number of required data for the ML estimate is heavily influenced by possible ill conditionality of data, by correlation of features in multidimensional samples etc.

Most of the studies dealing with the impact of data for maximum likelihood estimation is focused on the accuracy of the estimate model parameters.

This paper was supported by the project no. P103/12/G084 of the Grant Agency of the Czech Republic.

G. Azzopardi and N. Petkov (Eds.): CAIP 2015, Part II, LNCS 9257, pp. 462–469, 2015.
DOI: 10.1007/978-3-319-23117-4_40

In [1], [2] and in various forums on the web many recommendations are presented, according to which the number of data (e.g. for models with covariance structure) should be at least 5 (better 10) per feature. Furthermore, it is also reported that in the case of small space dimension the number of data for estimation should be significantly increased. For instance, at least 100 samples for estimating Gaussian model in dimension $n = 1$ (only 2 parameters are estimated) should be suitable. Similar studies can be found even in tasks of structural equation modeling [3], [4] etc.

The question we want to answer in the present article is: how much data we indicatively need in order to estimate the parameters of the Gaussian model, which would then provide the likelihood values with a defined accuracy. We do not therefore deal with the accuracy of estimation of each model parameter, but the precision of the likelihood function.

For such a defined task, which would be also tied to the various dimensions of space, we can find only a minimum of publications. It is however a very important and the current job, which is directly applicable in areas such as pattern recognition, where just a log-likelihood often play a key role for classification. For example, we should mention a task of automatic speech recognition, where the log-likelihood values are typically calculated every 10ms and they are the inputs of a decoder. Although we often work with Gaussian Mixture Models it is always a question of how much data is needed for "correct" assessment of individual Gaussian components and creating high-quality statistical model. Similar issues are address also in other areas, for example computer vision, medical and technical diagnostics etc. The present article would like to contribute to solving these problems.

2   Determining the Accuracy of the Likelihood Estimate

Our goal is to determine statistical dependency of accuracy of likelihood function values on the number of data from which parameters of this function are estimated. Our effort will be concentrated on the family of Gaussian functions. For this purpose we construct in a space of dimension n a generator G of random numbers (vectors), which will be directed by a Gaussian model with randomly determined mean $\boldsymbol{\mu}^G$ and covariance matrix $\boldsymbol{C}^G$, i.e. $\boldsymbol{\Theta}^G = (\boldsymbol{\mu}^G, \boldsymbol{C}^G)$.

For Gaussian source with parameters $\boldsymbol{\Theta}^G$ we now determine the mean value of log-likelihood function $\mathrm{E}\{\ln L(\boldsymbol{\Theta}^G|X)\}$, i.e.

$$\mathrm{E}\left\{\ln L(\boldsymbol{\Theta}^G|X)\right\} = \lim_{N \to \infty} \left\{ \frac{1}{N} \sum_{i=1}^{N} \ln p\left(\boldsymbol{x}_i|\boldsymbol{\Theta}^G\right)\right\}, \tag{1}$$

where $X = \{\boldsymbol{x}_1, ..., \boldsymbol{x}_N\}$.

Lemma 1. *Let* $\boldsymbol{\Theta} = (\boldsymbol{\mu}, \boldsymbol{C})$, *where* $\boldsymbol{\mu}$ *and* $\boldsymbol{C}$ *are mean* $\boldsymbol{\mu}^T = [\mu_1, ..., \mu_n]$ *and covariance matrix* $\boldsymbol{C} = \{c_{ij}\}_{n \times n}$, *respectively, describing Gaussian distribution in the space* n *with the density function* $p(\boldsymbol{x}|\boldsymbol{\mu}, \boldsymbol{C})$. *Let* $X = \{\boldsymbol{x}_1, ..., \boldsymbol{x}_N\}$ *are* *independent observations (in the space n), which are randomly generated by the Gaussian distribution model with parameters $\{\boldsymbol{\mu}, \boldsymbol{C}\}$. Then the mean of log-likelihood values is*

$$E\{\ln L(\boldsymbol{\Theta}|X)\} = -\frac{n}{2}\ln 2\pi - \frac{1}{2}\ln \det \boldsymbol{C} - \frac{1}{2}n. \qquad (2)$$

Proof. The mean of the independent observations generated by the Gaussian distribution with parameters $\boldsymbol{\Theta} = (\boldsymbol{\mu}, \boldsymbol{C})$ in the space n may be using (1) and after simple mathematical modification rewritten as

$$\mathrm{E}\{\ln L(\boldsymbol{\Theta}|X)\} = -\tfrac{n}{2}\ln 2\pi - \tfrac{1}{2}\ln \det \boldsymbol{C} - \lim_{N\to\infty}\tfrac{1}{2N}\sum_{i=1}^{N}(\boldsymbol{x}_i - \boldsymbol{\mu})^T \boldsymbol{C}^{-1}(\boldsymbol{x}_i - \boldsymbol{\mu}).$$

$$(3)$$

Now we can only deal with the last expression in (3), i.e. with the term containing the limit. After multiplication of vectors $(\boldsymbol{x}_i - \boldsymbol{\mu})^T = [x_{i1}-\mu_1;\ x_{i2}-\mu_2;\ \ldots\ ;\ x_{in}-\mu_n]$ and inverse matrix $\boldsymbol{C}^{-1} = \{c_{ij}^{-1}\}$ we get

$$\lim_{N\to\infty}\frac{1}{2N}\sum_{i=1}^{N}[(x_{i1}-\mu_1)(x_{i1}-\mu_1)c_{11}^{-1} + (x_{i1}-\mu_1)(x_{i2}-\mu_2)c_{12}^{-1} + \ldots +$$

$$+ (x_{in}-\mu_n)(x_{in}-\mu_n)c_{nn}^{-1}]. \quad (4)$$

If X satisfies the above described distribution, then for a sufficient large number of samples $\boldsymbol{x}$ (ideally $N \to \infty$) we get

$$\lim_{N\to\infty}\frac{1}{N}\sum_{i=1}^{N}[(x_{ij}-\mu_j)(x_{ik}-\mu_k)] = \lim_{N\to\infty}\{\hat{c}_{jk}\} = c_{jk}, \qquad (5)$$

where c_{jk} are the elements of the covariance matrix $\boldsymbol{C}$. For further derivations we utilize two relationships, which are known from the theory of linear algebra and the theory of matrices [5], [6], see the footnote[1]. It holds that

$$c_{k1}c_{1k}^{-1} + c_{k2}c_{2k}^{-1} + \ldots + c_{kn}c_{nk}^{-1} = c_{k1}\frac{(-1)^{k+1}\det \boldsymbol{M}_{k1}}{\det \boldsymbol{C}} +$$

$$+ c_{k2}\frac{(-1)^{k+2}\det \boldsymbol{M}_{k2}}{\det \boldsymbol{C}} + \ldots + c_{kn}\frac{(-1)^{k+n}\det \boldsymbol{M}_{kn}}{\det \boldsymbol{C}} = \frac{\det \boldsymbol{C}}{\det \boldsymbol{C}} = 1 \quad (8)$$

---

[1] Let $\boldsymbol{A} = \{a_{ij}\}_{n\times n}$ is a square non-singular matrix for which there is an inverse matrix $\boldsymbol{A}^{-1}$. For elements a_{ij}^{-1} of this inverse matrix is then valid

$$a_{ij}^{-1} = \frac{(-1)^{i+j}\det(\boldsymbol{M}_{ji})}{\det \boldsymbol{A}}, \qquad (6)$$

where $\det(\boldsymbol{M}_{ji})$ is a subdeterminant obtained from the matrix $\boldsymbol{A}$ by skipping the j-th line and the i-th column. For matrix $\boldsymbol{A}$ is also true, that

$$\det \boldsymbol{A} = a_{i1}(-1)^{i+1}\det(\boldsymbol{M}_{i1}) + a_{i2}(-1)^{i+2}\det(\boldsymbol{M}_{i2}) + \ldots + a_{in}(-1)^{i+n}\det(\boldsymbol{M}_{in}), \quad (7)$$

where $i \in \{1, 2, ..., n\}$ is an arbitrary index.

where we used (6) in appointing c_{ij}^{-1}. To modify (4) we now utilize (8) and (7):

$$\lim_{N\to\infty} \frac{1}{2N} \sum_{i=1}^{N} (\boldsymbol{x}_i - \boldsymbol{\mu})^T \boldsymbol{C}^{-1} (\boldsymbol{x}_i - \boldsymbol{\mu}) = \frac{1}{2}\left[\left(c_{11}c_{11}^{-1} + c_{12}c_{21}^{-1} + \ldots + c_{1n}c_{n1}^{-1}\right) + \right.$$

$$\left. + \left(c_{21}c_{12}^{-1} + \ldots + c_{2n}c_{n2}^{-1}\right) + \ldots + \left(c_{n1}c_{1n}^{-1} + \ldots + c_{nn}c_{nn}^{-1}\right)\right] = \frac{1}{2}n \qquad (9)$$

So, the Lemma is proved.

□

To simplify writing the mean of the log-likelihood function we will further use notation in the form $L_{\mathrm{E-ln}}(G)$, for which we can using (1) and (2) write

$$L_{\mathrm{E-ln}}(G) = \mathrm{E}\left\{\ln L(\boldsymbol{\Theta}^G|X)\right\} = 1.4189\,n - 0.5\ln\det\boldsymbol{C}^G , \qquad (10)$$

where n is dimension of the space, $\boldsymbol{C}^G$ is the covariance matrix of the source model.

By this source G we generate a set of training data $Y = \{\boldsymbol{y}_1, ..., \boldsymbol{y}_I\}$ and a set of test data $Z = \{\boldsymbol{z}_1, ..., \boldsymbol{z}_J\}$. Generally, a set of samples Y does not contain samples from the set Z and vice versa. Now we use the set Y of training data and for increasing number of samples we will gradually estimate (using ML approach) the parameters of the Gaussian model. If the set of training data $Y_i = \{\boldsymbol{y}_1, ..., \boldsymbol{y}_i\}$ has been used for estimating parameters, we denote the estimated parameters as $\boldsymbol{\Theta}_i = (\boldsymbol{\mu}_i, \boldsymbol{C}_i)$ (note: it must hold that $i \geq n+1$). Now we define the average value $L_{\mathrm{Av-ln}}(\boldsymbol{\Theta}_i|Z)$ of log-likelihoods on the Gaussian model with parameters $\boldsymbol{\Theta}_i$ and a set of test data $Z = \{\boldsymbol{z}_1, ..., \boldsymbol{z}_J\}$ as

$$L_{\mathrm{Av-ln}}(\boldsymbol{\Theta}_i|Z) = \frac{1}{J}\sum_{j=1}^{J} \ln p(\boldsymbol{z}_j|\boldsymbol{\Theta}_i). \qquad (11)$$

We will look for the minimum number i^* of training data $Y_{i^*} = \{\boldsymbol{y}_1, ..., \boldsymbol{y}_{i^*}\}$, for which the difference between the mean value of log-likelihood of the generator $L_{\mathrm{E-ln}}(G)$ and the $L_{\mathrm{Av-ln}}(\boldsymbol{\Theta}_i|Z)$ is smaller than established error Δ

$$i^* = \min_{i}\ \{\,[\,L_{\mathrm{E-ln}}(G) - L_{\mathrm{Av-ln}}(\boldsymbol{\Theta}_i|Z)\,]\leq\Delta\}. \qquad (12)$$

The question now is: "How to set up reasonably the error Δ?" Due to the fact that we are working in the equation (12) with log-likelihoods, it can be found good arguments for the derivation of Δ on a percentage basis of the log-likelihood characteristics. But, the lower border of the difference of both log-likelihood characteristics in (12) may (for models estimated from small amount of training data and in the space with the high dimension) approach minus infinity. So, it is therefore difficult to obtain a basis for calculating the percentage. Instead of deriving the error Δ based on the log-likelihood characteristics $L_{\mathrm{Av-ln}}(\boldsymbol{\Theta}_i|Z)$

and $L_{\text{E}-\ln}(G)$, we infer the error by using the likelihood (not log-likelihood) characteristic. For this purpose we rewrite the equation (10) in the form

$$L_{\text{E}-\ln}(G) = \text{E}\left\{\ln L(\boldsymbol{\Theta}^G|X)\right\} = \ln\left\{\lim_{N\to\infty}\left[\prod_{i=1}^{N}p(\boldsymbol{x}_i|\boldsymbol{\Theta}^G)\right]^{\frac{1}{N}}\right\} = \ln\{L_{\text{E}}(G))\}$$

(13)

where $L_E(G)$ is "mean value"', more precisely the geometric mean of the likelihood function of the generator G. Similarly, it is possible to adjust the equation (11)

$$L_{\text{Av}-\ln}(\boldsymbol{\Theta}_i|Z) = \ln\left\{\left[\prod_{j=1}^{N}p(z_j|\boldsymbol{\Theta}_i)\right]^{\frac{1}{J}}\right\} = \ln\{L_{\text{Av}}(\boldsymbol{\Theta}_i|Z)\} ,$$

(14)

where $L_{\text{Av}}(\boldsymbol{\Theta}_i|Z)$ is again the geometric average of likelihood values computed on the Gaussian model with parameters $\boldsymbol{\Theta}_i$ and a set of test data Z.

We will now consider the ratio $L_{\text{Av}}(\boldsymbol{\Theta}_i|Z)/L_{\text{E}}(G)$. Its property is, that with increasing number i of data for estimation of model $\boldsymbol{\Theta}_i$, the ratio changes from 0 to 1, where the value 1 should be achieved for i approaching infinity. For increasing i we will now look for a model $\boldsymbol{\Theta}_i$, in order the ratio $L_{\text{Av}}(\boldsymbol{\Theta}_i|Z)$ and $L_{\text{E}}(G)$ just crossed the predetermined value β, i.e. $L_{\text{Av}}(\boldsymbol{\Theta}_i|Z)/L_{\text{E}}(G) \geq \beta$, where β can be set in terms of estimation accuracy, which varies from 0 to 1 (alternatively, from 0% to 100%). To the given inequality we now apply the logarithm and after adjustment we get

$$\ln L_{\text{E}}(G) - \ln L_{\text{Av}}(\boldsymbol{\Theta}_i|Z) = L_{\text{E}-\ln}(G) - L_{\text{Av}-\ln}(\boldsymbol{\Theta}_i|Z) \leq -\ln\beta \quad (15)$$

This inequality can now be used to adjust the relationship (12)

$$i_\beta^* = \min_i\{[L_{\text{E}-\ln}(G) - L_{\text{Av}-\ln}(\boldsymbol{\Theta}_i|Z)] \leq -\ln\beta = \Delta_\beta\} . \quad (16)$$

The interpretation of this inequality is therefore such, that we are looking for the least number of training data i_β^* with which we are able to estimate model parameters $\boldsymbol{\Theta}_i$, that will provide (geometric) mean of likelihood values for test data set Z with accuracy higher than $\beta L_E(G)$, where $L_E(G)$ is (geometric) mean of likelihood function of generator G. At the same time we always assume a sufficiently large number of test data J.

If we now perform in a space of dimension n a sufficient number of experiments (this number K should be at least 100) with randomly generated model parameters $\boldsymbol{\Theta}^G$ and randomly generated sets of training and test data, we can for selected β obtain the resulting set $i_\beta^*(k)(k=1, \dots , K)$ and calculate the values of some interesting statistics.

3   Results of Analytical Studies and Experiments

To verify the proposed method for estimating the number of training data to determine the Gaussian model, which will provide likelihood values with above

Table 1.

β	0.5	0.8	0.9	0.95	0.98	0.99
$\Delta_\beta = -\ln\beta$	0.693	0.223	0.105	0.051	0.020	0.010

defined properties, we carried out a number of experiments in the spaces of dimension n=1, 2, 3, 4, 5, and 10 and for likelihood accuracy β =0.5, 0.8, 0.9, 0.95, 0.98, and 0.99. For selected values of β we have determined the corresponding values of Δ_β , see Table 1.

For each combination of n and β we carried out at least 100 experiments (for n=1, 2, and 3 several hundred), each with randomly generated parameters and randomly generated training Y and test Z data sets.

In addition to the mean value $i^*_\beta(k)$ calculated for each n and β we wanted to define a suitable interval or rather a kind of upper limit for the number of required samples, for which it is possible to achieve desired accuracy of likelihood values. The analysis of procedure of obtaining values $i^*_\beta(k)$ (i.e. procedures of randomly generated parameters μ^G and C^G, randomly generated training Y and test Z data, averaging operations etc.) brings us to the assumption (and the reality confirms it) that $i^*_\beta(k)$ will follow a normal distribution. In this case the confidence interval can be defined for $i^*_\beta(k)$. In our case we are interested in upper endpoint $i^*_{\beta-\text{upper}}$ of this interval, for which holds [8]

$$i^*_{\beta-\text{upper}} = i^*_{\beta-\text{mean}} + 1.64\frac{\sigma^*_i}{\sqrt{K}}, \tag{17}$$

where $i^*_{\beta-\text{mean}} = \frac{1}{K}\sum_{k=1}^{K} i^*_\beta(k)$, σ^*_i is the standard deviation computed from $i^*_\beta(k)$ and K is the number of samples in experiment. It should be noted that the expression (17) is valid for confidence level 95%. Results of experiments are shown in Table 2 and illustrated in Figure 1.

Finally, let's mention the influence of ill-conditionality of the task on the results. Mention that for all experiments with randomly generated Gaussian distribution parameters we always determined the condition number of matrix $\kappa(C^G)$, specially the Frobenius norm condition number defined as [9]

$$\kappa(C^G) = \left\| (C^G)^{-1} \right\|_F \left\| C^G \right\|_F . \tag{18}$$

Matrix with condition number near 1 is said to be well-conditioned, whereas when the condition number $\kappa(.)$ becomes large, the problem is regarded as being ill-conditioned. But, how large does $\kappa(.)$ must be before a problem is classified as ill-conditioned? There is no clear answer on this question. Analytical studies indicate, that for a system with condition number $\kappa(.)$ we can expect a loss of roughly $\log_{10} \kappa(.)$ decimal places in the accuracy of the solution. Standard double precision number of computing works with about 16 decimal digits of accuracy. So, these are limits for computing of ill-conditioned covariance matrices. In our case in all experiments, most of the values $\kappa(C^G)$ were in the interval $< 1; 10^6)$. However, even for several tens of values, for which $\kappa(C^G) > 10^6$,

Table 2. Results of experiments for β=0.5, 0.8, 0.9, 0.95, 0.98, and 0.99.

β		Space dimension					
		$n=1$	$n=2$	$n=3$	$n=4$	$n=5$	$n=10$
0.5	mean $i^*_{0.5}$	4.4	8.4	12.5	18.2	23.5	66.2
	upper $i^*_{0.5}$	4.6	8.8	13.1	19.1	24.5	68.2
0.8	mean $i^*_{0.8}$	7.5	15.4	26.1	38.5	53.3	163.0
	upper $i^*_{0.8}$	7.9	16.2	27.4	40.3	55.9	167.3
0.9	mean $i^*_{0.9}$	12.0	27.1	50.6	72.7	103.3	349.8
	upper $i^*_{0.9}$	12.6	38.6	53.3	77.2	109.1	359.0
0.95	mean $i^*_{0.95}$	19.5	47.0	92.3	134.7	188.0	675.6
	upper $i^*_{0.95}$	20.6	49.6	97.6	142.0	199.2	696.1
0.98	mean $i^*_{0.98}$	36.9	101.9	205.8	330.6	446.3	1 623.2
	upper $i^*_{0.98}$	39.0	108.5	217.3	354.7	473.0	1 674.4
0.99	mean $i^*_{0.99}$	62.8	195.1	390.4	698.7	923.2	3 306.5
	upper $i^*_{0.99}$	67.1	208.9	413.7	750.6	977.7	3 458.9

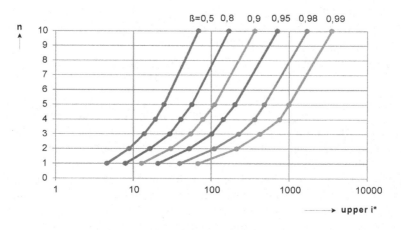

Fig. 1. Illustration of experimental results for β =0.5, 0.8, 0.9, 0.95, 0.98, and 0.99.

was not observed any excess or problems in computing and the values i^*_β were within the standard specified limits.

4   Conclusion

The present paper would like to contribute to solving problems that frequently appear in practical tasks, where statistical modeling with Gaussian model is applied. A frequent issue that is solved is the number of data needed for maximum likelihood estimates of this Gaussian model. Referred results provide useful recommendations for the authors of application tasks where it is necessary to create statistical models from experimental data with a given accuracy. It must be said that the results presented in the paper should be seen rather as recommendation for estimation of accuracy of the model or the need to seek additional training data for increasing model robustness. We assume that they could help in the statistical pattern recognition, speech recognition etc. Future work will be focused on statistical models in spaces with higher dimensions.

References

1. Long, J.S.: Regression Models for Categorical and Limited Dependent Variables, 282p. SAGA Publications, Thousand Oaks (1997)
2. Long, J.S., Freese, J.: Regression Models for Categorical Dependent Variables Using Stata, p. 589. Stata Press, College Station (2014)
3. Jackson, D.L.: Revising Sample Size and Number of Parameter Estimates: Some Support for the N: q Hypothesis. Structural Equation Modeling: A Multidisciplinary journal 10(1), 128–141 (2003)
4. Bartlett, J.E., Kotrlik, J.W., Higgins, C.C.: Organizational Research: Determining Appropriate Sample Size in Survey Research. Information Technology, Learning, and Performance Journal 19(1). Spring (2001)
5. Shafarevich, I.R., Remizov, A.O.: Linear Algebra and Geometry, 530p. Springer-Verlag, Berlin 2013)
6. Strang, G.: Linear Algebra and Its Applications, 495p. Hardcover (2005)
7. Leon, S.L.: Linear Algebra with Applications, 523p. Prentice Hall (2005)
8. Smithson, M.: Confidence Intervals, 128p. SEGE Publications Inc. (2003)
9. Golub, G.H., Van Loan, C.F.: Matrix Computations. Johns Hopkins, Baltimore (1996)

Projective Label Propagation by Label Embedding

Zhao Zhang[1(✉)], Weiming Jiang[1], Fanzhang Li[1], Li Zhang[1],
Mingbo Zhao[2], and Lei Jia[1]

[1] School of Computer Science and Technology, Soochow University, Suzhou 215006, China
cszzhang@gmail.com, {zhangliml,lfzh}@suda.edu.cn
[2] Department of Electronic Engineering, City University of Hong Kong,
Tat Chee Avenue, Kowloon, Hong Kong
mbzhao4@cityu.edu.hk

Abstract. In this paper, we propose a projective label propagation (ProjLP) framework by label embedding that can gain the more discriminating "deep" labels of points in an transductive fashion to enhance representation. To show the deep property of the embedded "deep" labels over the "shallow" ones that usually have unfavorable mixed signs delivered by existing transductive models, the auxiliary multilayer network architecture of our ProjLP is illustrated. The deep architecture has three layers (i.e., input layer, hidden layer, and output layer). For semi-supervised classification, ProjLP delivers the deep labels of data via two-layer label propagation (i.e., hidden and output layer) on the network at each iteration. In hidden layer, ProjLP delivers the "shallow" soft labels F of points in the original input space. Then, ProjLP embeds F onto a subspace spanned by a robust projection to obtain the deep soft labels in output layer. Finally, the most discriminating deep labels are obtained for enhancing performance. The method of achieving the deep labels of outside points is also elaborated. Simulations on several artificial and UCI datasets demonstrate the validity of our model, compared with other state-of-the-arts.

1 Introduction

Graph based semi-supervised learning (GSSL) [1-9] is a popular method in the fields of computer vision and pattern recognition. In more recent years, label propagation (LP) settings for GSSL have attracted considerable attention due to its efficiency and effectiveness [19-24]. LP aims at propagating the label information of labeled data to unlabeled data according to their distributions. Popular LP methods are the *Gaussian Fields and Harmonic Function* (GFHF) [20], *Learning with Local and Global Consistency* (LLGC) [19], *Linear Neighborhood Propagation* (LNP) [21][22], and *Special Label Propagation* (SLP) [23]. Compared with GFHF and LLGC, both LNP and SLP can not only detect outliers in data effectively, but also output the estimated soft labels of samples as probabilistic values [24].

Note that virtually all existing LP settings make efforts to improve the performance mainly from two aspects. The first one is to investigate how to define an informative weighted graph based on the clustering or manifold assumptions [11][19] for measuring pairwise similarities of labeled and unlabeled data. There are three widely

© Springer International Publishing Switzerland 2015
G. Azzopardi and N. Petkov (Eds.): CAIP 2015, Part II, LNCS 9257, pp. 470–481, 2015.
DOI: 10.1007/978-3-319-23117-4_41

used weight assignments: Gaussian function [19-20][23], Locally Linear Embedding (LLE)-style reconstruction weights [21-22], and the adaptive weights by sparse codes [9][12-14]. The other one is to address the out-of-sample extensions of LP for including outside points. The authors of [21-22] suggested to reconstruct the label of each new data from the soft labels of its neighbors in training set. But it is worth noticing that almost all above LP criteria directly estimate the "shallow" soft labels of points in the original input space, which usually results in noisy labels that include unfavorable entries and mixed signs, as can be seen from our simulations. So, the inclusion process for the outside data may be greatly affected by the "shallow" results. That is, investigating the way of improving the transductive results by gaining more discriminating labels is undoubtedly very important. Besides, not all existing transducitve models can ensure the prediction results are probabilistic values [9]. To overcome the above shortcoming of existing models, we propose a deep label prediction framework that can obtain the more discriminating "deep" labels to enhance representation and classification. The main contributions of this paper include:

(1) A projective label propagation (ProjLP) framework through label embedding is technically proposed to estimate the more discriminating "deep" labels of samples. ProjLP is originally proposed to boost the transductive results by simultaneously learning a robust projection to remove the unfavorable mixed signs and convert the shallow labels into discriminating deep ones. Note that $l_{2,1}$-norm that has been proved to be robust to outliers and noise [10][16-18] is regularized on the projection to make it sparse in rows so that discriminative features can be obtained in the latent subspace for predicting soft labels. We also elaborate the approach for ProjLP to compute the deep labels of outside samples, i.e., reconstructing the deep label of new data from the deep soft labels of its neighbors.

(2) To show the deep property of embedded deep labels over "shallow" ones, the auxiliary multilayer network architecture of ProjLP is illustrated. The deep architecture has three layers, i.e., input layer, hidden layer (or first-layer LP) and output layer (or second-layer LP). For classification, ProjLP delivers the deep labels by the two-layer label propagation on the network. In hidden layer, ProjLP outputs the "shallow" soft labels F of points in the original space. Hereafter, ProjLP embeds F onto a deep embedding matrix to gain the deep soft labels in output layer.

2   Linear Neighborhood Propagation

For a given collection of N data points in the training set $X = [X_L, X_U] \in \mathbb{R}^{n \times (l+u)}$, where n is the dimensionality of original data, $l + u = N$ is number of training data, $X_L = [x_1, x_2, ..., x_l] \in \mathbb{R}^{n \times l}$ is labeled set, $X_U = [x_{l+1}, x_{l+2}, ..., x_{l+u}] \in \mathbb{R}^{n \times u}$ is an unlabeled set and each column vector $x_i \in \mathbb{R}^n$ is a sample. We assume each sample in X_L has a unique label belonging to $\{1, 2, ..., c\}$, where c is class number. As a typical SSL setting, a test set $X_T = [x_1, x_2, ..., x_{N_T}] \in \mathbb{R}^{n \times N_T}$ with all unlabeled data is often available for evaluation, where N_T is the total number of test points. Based on X, the weights $\tilde{w}_{i,j}$ for reconstructing each point $x_i \in X$ can be obtained from:

$$\underset{\tilde{w}_i}{Min} \sum_i \left\| x_i - \sum_{j: x_j \in \mathbb{N}(x_i)} \tilde{w}_{i,j} x_j \right\|_2^2, \text{Subj} \sum_{j: x_j \in \mathbb{N}(x_i)} \tilde{w}_{i,j} = 1, \tilde{w}_{i,j} \geq 0, \tag{1}$$

where $\mathbb{N}(x_i)$ is the K-neighbor set of point $x_i \in X$, $\|\cdot\|_2$ is l_2-norm, and $\tilde{w}_{i,j}$ can measure the contribution of points x_j for reconstructing x_i. By repeating the above steps for each point, a weight matrix $\widetilde{W} = \left[\widetilde{w}_{i,j} \right] \in \mathbb{R}^{N \times N}$ can be formed. Obviously, the more similar x_i and x_j, the larger $\widetilde{w}_{i,j}$ will be. Thus, the weights $\widetilde{w}_{i,j}$ can characterize how similar x_j to x_i [21][22]. Let $Y = \left[y_1, y_2, ..., y_{l+u} \right] \in \mathbb{R}^{c \times (l+u)}$ denote the initial labels of all points, where $y_{i,j} = 1$ if $x_j \in X$ labeled as i ($1 \le i \le c$) and $y_{i,j} = 0$ otherwise. For each unlabeled data $x_u \in X$, all $y_{i,u} = 0$, $1 \le i \le c$. Then, the prediction result of LNP can approximate the solution of the following problem [21][22]:

$$F = \arg \min_{F} tr\left(F\left(I^N - \widetilde{W} \right) F^{\mathrm{T}} \right) + \mu \sum_{i=1}^{l+u} \| f_i - y_i \|_2^2 , \tag{2}$$

where I^N denotes an identity matrix in $\mathbb{R}^N$, $tr(\bullet)$ denotes the matrix trace operator, $F = [f_1, f_2, ..., f_{l+u}] \in \mathbb{R}^{(c+1) \times (l+u)}$ is a soft label matrix, $\mu > 0$ is a parameter. To solve the out-of-sample issue, LNP [21][22] reconstructs the soft label of each new data $x_{new} \in X_T$ from the soft labels of its neighbors in training set X:

$$f\left(x_{new} \right) = \sum_{j: x_j \in X, \, x_j \in \mathrm{N}(x_{new})} W\left(x_{new}, x_j \right) f_j , \tag{3}$$

where $f\left(x_{new} \right)$ denotes the soft label of $x_{new} \in X_T$ to estimate. $W\left(x_{new}, x_j \right)$ denotes the coefficient vector for measuring the similarity between x_{new} and its neighbors $x_j \in X$ based on nearest neighbor search on $x_{new} \cup X$. Note that this kind of extension may suffer from the drawback that a relatively "bad" label prediction result of training may greatly decrease the test accuracy, since the classification of test points is mainly determined by the predicted "shallow" soft labels of training samples and the "shallow" soft labels obtained from the original input space usually include unfavorable entries and mixed signs. To this end, we shall propose a projective LP framework to gain the deep soft labels for improving the transductive label prediction result of training phase directly so that the above shortcoming can be addressed.

3   Projective Label Propagation (ProjLP)

3.1   Proposed Formulation

We present ProjLP to deliver the "deep" labels of points for enhancing the prediction performance. To enable ProjLP to deliver more discriminating results, we learn a $l_{2,1}$-norm regularized robust projection $P = [p_1, p_2, ..., p_d] \in \mathbb{R}^{(c+1) \times d}$ to transform the "shallow" labels into deep ones by label embedding, where d is dimensionality of learned subspace and $d = c+1$ in this work. The discriminating property of the prediction results means less number of unfavorable mixed signs that may decrease the performance is included in the estimated results. Let $Y = \left[y_1, y_2, ..., y_{l+u} \right] \in \mathbb{R}^{(c+1) \times (l+u)}$ be the initial labels of all points, where $y_{i,j}$ denotes the i-th entry of column vector y_j in Y. For the labeled point x_j, $y_{i,j} = 1$ if x_j belongs to class i, and else $y_{i,j} = 0$, where $1 \le i \le c$. For each unlabeled x_j, $y_{i,j} = 1$ if $i = c+1$ and $y_{i,j} = 0$ otherwise. That is, we add an additional class $c+1$ to detect outliers and to ensure that the sum of each column of Y is 1, similarly as SLP [23]. Let $F = [f_1, f_2, ..., f_{l+u}] \in \mathbb{R}^{(c+1) \times (l+u)}$ denote the soft label matrix, by trading-off the manifold smoothness, label fitness and $l_{2,1}$-norm regularization, the criterion of our ProjLP is defined as

$$\underset{F, P}{Min} \; J = \sum_{i=1}^{l+u} \left\| P^{\mathrm{T}} f_i - P^{\mathrm{T}} \sum_{j: x_j \in \mathrm{N}(x_i)} W_{i,j} f_j \right\|_2^2 + \sum_{i=1}^{l+u} \mu_i V_{ii} \left\| P^{\mathrm{T}} f_i - y_i \right\|_2^2 + \alpha \sum_{i=1}^{c+1} \left\| p^i \right\|_2 , \tag{4}$$

where p^i is the i-th row vector of P, $P^{\mathrm{T}} f_i$ is the projected "deep" label, W is a similarity matrix with entries $W_{i,j}$ being the reconstruction coefficients, V is a diagonal matrix with $V_{ii} = \sum_j W_{i,j}$. For efficiency, we use the inexpensive LLE-reconstruction weights $w_{i,j}$ [30] to measure pairwise similarities between points. After obtaining $\widetilde{W} = \left[\widetilde{w}_{i,j} \right] \in \mathbb{R}^{N \times N}$, we symmetrize it as $\widetilde{W} \leftarrow \left(\widetilde{W} + \widetilde{W}^{\mathrm{T}} \right)\big/2$ and then normalize $\widetilde{W}$ as

$$W = \widetilde{D}^{-1/2} \widetilde{W} \widetilde{D}^{-1/2}, \widetilde{D}_{ii} = \sum_j \widetilde{W}_{i,j}, \tag{5}$$

where $\widetilde{D}$ is a diagonal matrix with entries being $\widetilde{D}_{ii}$. Note that this normalization can strengthen or weaken the weights in different density regions, which is useful in handling the cases that the density of dataset varies dramatically [19][23].

In Eq.4, the first term measures the smoothness of resulted projected "deep" label, letting each object absorb a fraction of label information from its neighbors by believing that the embedded deep soft labels share the same neighborhood relationships as the "shallow" soft labels from the original space. The second term is a fitting constraint that measures the difference between the resulted deep soft labels and the initial label assignments so that data objects can retain some label information of its initial label Y. The third term, i.e., $\sum_{i=1}^{c+1} \left\| p^i \right\|_2 = \left\| P \right\|_{2,1}$, is included to reduce the unfavorable mixed signs and make the results more discriminating. The main motivations of regularizing the $l_{2,1}$-norm on P are as follows. $l_{2,1}$-norm has been proved to be robust to outliers and noise [10][16-18][31][34][45], so the regularization term $\left\| P \right\|_{2,1}$ ensures that P is sparse in rows so that discriminative features can be chosen in the latent subspace for predicting the soft labels [17]. Note that the positive effects of the $l_{2,1}$-norm regularization on P and the projected deep labels on the performance will be verified by simulations. The trade-offs of terms are controlled by μ_i and α.

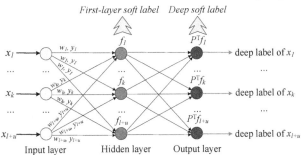

Fig. 1. The *learning* network architecture of our ProjLP method.

It should be noted that the concept of "deep" labels in this present work is mainly corresponded to estimated "shallow" labels of existing LP methods from the original space, and is essentially different from the deep concept in traditional deep learning and neural networks [15][26]. To demonstrate the "deep" property of projected labels by label embedding over the "shallow" labels well, we borrow the idea of network architecture in the deep learning and neural networks, and illustrate the multilayer network architecture of our ProjLP in Figure 1, including one input layer and two LP layers (hidden layer and output layer). ProjLP firstly outputs the "shallow" soft labels F of points of the original input space in the first LP layer. Then the "shallow" soft labels are treated as inputs for the second LP layer, and in this layer the deep soft labels are obtained by embedding F onto the projection P.

3.2   Optimization for Solution

From the problem in Eq.4, one can easily convert it using the matrix form into

$$\underset{F,P}{Min}\ \widehat{\Omega} = \left\| P^T F - P^T F W^T \right\|_F^2 + tr\left(\left(P^T F - Y \right) UV \left(P^T F - Y \right)^T \right) + \alpha \| P \|_{2,1},\tag{5}$$

where $\|A\|_F$ is the Frobenius norm of matrix A, U is a diagonal matrix with the i-th entry being μ_i, and V is a diagonal matrix with the elements being $V_{ii} = \sum_j W_{i,j}$. The regularization parameter μ_i is set to $\mu_i = 10^{10}$ for the labeled data x_i, and is set to $\alpha_u = 10^{-10}$ for unlabeled data x_i in our simulations. It is worth noting that the problem of ProjLP involves two main variables (i.e., P and F) that are depends on each other and so cannot be solved directly, thus we propose to solve ProjLP by updating the variables alternately. Specifically, each variable is computed by fixing the others.

We first compute F in the first LP layer by fixing variable P to minimize $\widehat{\Omega}(F)$:

$$\widehat{\Omega}(F) = tr\left(P^T F Q F^T P \right) + tr\left(\left(P^T F - Y \right) UV \left(P^T F - Y \right)^T \right),\tag{6}$$

where $Q = \left(I^N - W \right)^T \left(I^N - W \right)$ denotes an auxiliary matrix. By setting the derivative of $\widehat{\Omega}(F)/\partial F$ to zero, the solution F to the above problem can be obtained from

$$\widehat{\Omega}(F)/\partial F = PP^T F Q + P\left(P^T F - Y \right) UV = 0.\tag{7}$$

Then, the "shallow" soft labels of points in the original input space is derived as

$$F = \left(PP^T \right)^\dagger PYUV \left(Q + UV \right)^\dagger,\tag{8}$$

where † is pseudo inverse. After F is gained, we compute the feature subspace P for embedding F to deliver the deep soft labels by minimizing the problem $\widehat{\Omega}(P)$:

$$\widehat{\Omega}(P) = tr\left(P^T F Q F^T P \right) + tr\left(\left(P^T F - Y \right) UV \left(P^T F - Y \right)^T \right) + \alpha \| P \|_{2,1}.\tag{9}$$

According to [16][18], although term $\|P\|_{2,1}$ is convex, but the derivative of $\|P\|_{2,1}$ does not exist for each $p^i = 0$ ($i = 1, 2, ..., n$). So, when $p^i \neq 0$ for $i = 1, 2, ..., c+1$, by taking the derivative of $\widehat{\Omega}(P)$ w.r.t the variable P and by setting the derivative $\partial\widehat{\Omega}(P)/\partial P = FQF^T P + FUVF^T P + \alpha\Theta P - FUVY^T = 0$ to zero, one can easily check that

$$P = \left(FQF^T + FUVF^T + \alpha\Theta \right)^\dagger FUVY^T.\tag{10}$$

Let p^i be the i-th row vector of P, the entries of $\Theta \in \mathbb{R}^{(c+1)\times(c+1)}$ are defined as

$$\Theta_{ii} = 1/2\|p^i\|_2,\ i = 1, 2, ..., c+1,\tag{11}$$

Let $F_Y = P^T F - Y$, the derivative $\partial\widehat{\Omega}(P)/\partial P$ can be treated as the derivative of the following criterion [16][18]:

$$\Im(P) = tr\left(P^T F Q F^T P \right) + tr\left(F_Y UV F_Y^T \right) + tr\left(\alpha P^T \Theta P \right).\tag{12}$$

Hence, we can solve the following approximate problem instead for computing the projection P to achieve the deep soft labels by involving two variables (i.e. P and Θ):

$$(P, \Theta) = \arg\min_{P, \Theta} \left\{ \left\| P^{\mathrm{T}} F - P^{\mathrm{T}} F W^{\mathrm{T}} \right\|_F^2 + tr\left(F_y U V F_y^{\mathrm{T}} + \alpha P^{\mathrm{T}} \Theta P \right) \right\}, \tag{13}$$

from which one can easily obtain $tr\left(P^{\mathrm{T}} \Theta P \right) = \left\| P \right\|_{2,1} / 2$ for $p^i \neq 0$. So, minimizing $tr\left(P^{\mathrm{T}} \Theta P \right)$ will add explicit sparsity constraint on P [16][18], i.e., the extracted deep soft labels ($\widehat{F} = P^{\mathrm{T}} F$ or $\widehat{f}_i = P^{\mathrm{T}} f_i$) by P will hold the sparsity property and thus can enhance the discriminating power. Note that deep soft label matrix $P^{\mathrm{T}} F$ is the final deep soft label to pursue, the convergence condition can be set as

$$F_p^{diff} = \left\| \left(P^{\mathrm{T}} F \right)^{t+1} - \left(P^{\mathrm{T}} F \right)^t \right\|_F = \sqrt{\sum_{j=1}^{l+u} \sum_{i=1}^{c+1} \left| \left(P^{\mathrm{T}} F \right)_{i,j}^{t+1} - \left(P^{\mathrm{T}} F \right)_{i,j}^t \right|^2} \leq \varepsilon, \tag{14}$$

which measures the divergence between two sequential deep soft label matrix and can ensure the deep soft labels will not change drastically that will be verified by simulations, where ε is set to 10^{-6}, and $\left(P^{\mathrm{T}} F \right)^t$ denotes the delivered deep soft labels of points at the t-th iteration. We first initialize the projection P as an identity matrix. Similar to [16] [18], we initialize matrices G and M to be identity matrices so that $\left(p^i \right)^{k+1} \neq 0$, $i = 1,...,c+1$, and $\left(A^i \right)^{k+1} \neq 0, i = 1,...,n$ are satisfied during iterative optimizations. It is also worth noting that the nonnegative constraint $\forall_i, P^{\mathrm{T}} f_i > 0$ and sum-to-one constraint $e^{\mathrm{T}} \left(P^{\mathrm{T}} f_i \right) = 1$ are imposed at each iteration to make the results always satisfy the definition of probability. Since the ProjLP model is non-convex, the theoretical convergence proof is not easy, but we experimentally observe our ProjLP can usually converge with the iteration number less than 10. For complete presentation of the method, we summarize ProjLP in Table 1.

Input: Training data $X = [X_L, X_U] \in \mathbb{R}^{n \times (l+u)}$; Neighbor number K, parameters μ_i and α.
Initialization: $t=0$, $P^0 = I^{c+1}$, $F^0 = Y$, $\Theta^0 = I$.
While not converged do
1. Construct the neighborhood graph and define the normalized weights;
2. Fix P and update the "shallow" soft labels F^{t+1} by $F^{t+1} = \left(P^t P^{t\mathrm{T}} \right)^{-1} P^t Y U V \left(Q + U V \right)^{-1}$;
3. Fix F and Θ, and update P^{t+1} by $P^{t+1} = \left(F^{t+1} Q F^{t+1\mathrm{T}} + F^{t+1} U V F^{t+1\mathrm{T}} + \alpha \Theta^t \right)^{-1} F^{t+1} U V Y^{\mathrm{T}}$;
4. Fix P and update the auxiliary matrix Θ^{t+1} by $\Theta_{ii}^{t+1} = 1/2 \left\| p_i^{t+1} \right\|_2$, $i = 1, 2, ..., c+1$;

5. Check for convergence: if $F_p^{diff} = \left\| \left(P^{t+1} \right)^{\mathrm{T}} F^{t+1} - \left(P^t \right)^{\mathrm{T}} F^t \right\|_F \leq \varepsilon$, stop; else $t = t+1$; ***End while***

6. Output the deep soft labels $\widehat{F}^* = \left(P^{t+1} \right)^{\mathrm{T}} F^{t+1}$ in output layer.

3.3   Inclusion of Outside Samples by Label Reconstruction for DeepLP

In this part, we discuss our ProjLP to handle outside samples by deep label reconstruction, called Inductive ProjLP (reconstruction). Note that the label reconstruction approach is similar to LNP, but differently we aim at reconstructing the deep soft label of each new test data x_{new} from the deep soft labels of its neighbors, that is,

$$\widehat{f}(x_{new}) = \sum_{j:x_j \in X, x_j \in \mathbb{N}(x_{new})} W\left(x_{new}, x_j \right) \left(P^{\mathrm{T}} F \right)_j, \tag{15}$$

where $\left(P^{\mathrm{T}} F \right)_j$ denotes the j-th column vector of the deep soft label matrix, and the coefficient weight vector $W\left(x_{new}, x_j \right)$ is similarly defined as LNP does.

4   Simulation Results and Analysis

4.1   Settings and Data Preparation

We mainly test our ProjLP for transductive learning, along with illustrating the comparison results with GFHF, LLGC, SLP and LNP, which are all closely related to our work. For fair comparison, we compute the LLE-reconstruction weights [27] for GFHF, LLGC, SLP and LNP as well. Since the LLE-reconstruction matrix W is asymmetric, we preprocess it by symmetrizing W as $W = (W + W^{\mathrm{T}})/2$ for each approach. The diagonal entries of the weight matrix are also set as zeros for LLGC. The neighborhood size K is fixed to 7 for each model. For our ProjLP, model parameters ψ_i and α are selected empirically by using grid search from $\{10^{-8}, 10^{-6}, \ldots, 10^6, 10^8\}$, similarly as [18]. We perform all simulations on a PC with Intel (R) Core (TM) i7-3770 CPU @ 3.4 GHz 3.4GHz 4G.

In this study, one toy and 8 UCI datasets from the ML Repository (http://archive. ics.uci.edu/ml/) are evaluated. For transductive classification, we randomly split each set into labeled and unlabeled. Then, we estimate the labels of points by GFHF, LLGC, LNP, SLP and our ProjLP. Finally, the accuracy is obtained by comparing the predicted labels with the ground-truth labels provided by the original data corpus. Before label prediction, *Principal Component Analysis* (PCA) [25] operator is employed as a preprocessing step to preserve 96% energy of each dataset.

4.2   Visualization of Soft Labels

We first use a visualization experiment to visually compare our ProjLP algorithm with GFHF, LLGC, LNP and SLP for transductive learning. This experiment is mainly addressed to compare the estimated deep soft labels of our ProjLP with the "shallow" soft labels of other algorithms by visualization. In this experiment, a "three-arm spirals" dataset is used for the evaluation. This data set includes 600 data points belonging to three classes denoted by using different colors, that is, each class has 200 data points and follows a spiral distribution or manifold. Due the complex structure of dataset, we select 8 data points from each spiral distribution as labeled, and treat the remaining as unlabeled whose labels are to be estimated by using each method. We show the original distribution and partition of the "three-arm spirals" dataset in Figure 2, where Figure 2(a) reports the original distribution of the dataset, and in Figure 2(b) we exhibit the original partition of labeled (highlighted by three different symbols, i.e., '+', '×' and '*'), and unlabeled points denoted by black color.

Figure 3 shows the transductive result of points and the visualization of the soft labels by each algorithm. Note that we still highlight the labeled data points in the transductive result of each method for clear observation. It can be clearly seen from the transductive results in Figure 3 that due to the complex structure of dataset more points are misclassified to other classes by other compared approaches than our ProjLP, although generally speaking each criterion delivers somewhat satisfactory results on this toy set for label prediction. Note that Figures 3(b1-b5) show the visualization result of soft labels of each criterion in a three-dimensional (3D) space. It is known that the biggest entries of the estimated soft labels determine the hard label of points, thus ideally those biggest entries in soft labels are all ones and other elements are all zeros [19][20][21][22][23]. That is, satisfactory or "good" soft labels of points should be close to the vertices of the 3D cube as much as possible. By comparing the transductive results in the Figures 3(a1-a5), and the visualization results of the soft labels in Figures 3(b1-b5), we can find the soft labels of other exiting methods (i.e., GFHF, LLGC, LNP and SLP) are more noisy (more mixed signs are included) than the deep soft labels of our ProjLP. That is, the prediction results of our ProjLP are more promising, since its outputted deep soft labels are closer to the vertices of the cube than the "shallow" soft labels of other methods. It must be pointed out that this toy can provide a visual direct comparison between the other state-of-the-arts and our ProjLP, since the transductive results of points and inclusion of outside points can benefit greatly from the estimated deep labels of our ProjLP

4.3   Data Classification

We mainly test our ProjLP for transductive classification on several UCI datasets. The transductive result is compared with those of GFHF, LLGC, LNP and SLP. The widely used simple and effective one-nearest-neighbor (1NN) classifier with Euclidean metric is also added as the baseline, and the 1NN classifies the unlabeled points based on the labeled points directly. The eight used UCI datasets include Monks-1, Monks-2, Diagnostic Wisconsin Breast Cancer (Diagnostic WBC), Hepatitis, Soybean, Sonar, Hayes-Roth and Auto-Mpg. In our simulations, we merge the original-training set and test set provided by the UCI ML Repository into a whole one and all points in each dataset are used as inputs for the propagable learning of labels. Detailed information of the datasets is given in Table 2, where "Labeled Ratio" represents the ratio of randomly labeled number of data to the total number of data in each class. We mainly evaluate the transductive performance by varying the labeled ratios.

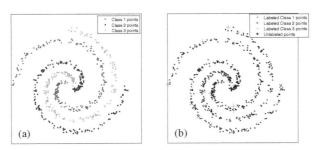

Fig. 2. Original distribution and partition of the "*three-arm spirals*" dataset.

Convergence Analysis. We first conduct simulations to show the convergence behaviors of our ProjLP. In this study, six datasets, i.e., Monks-1, Diagnostic WBC, Hepatitis, Soybean, Sonar, and Hayes-Roth, are evaluated. For each dataset, all data points are used as inputs and the labeled ratio is fixed as 0.3 to show the convergence of two consecutive deep soft matrices by our proposed method. We illustrate the averaged results over 20 times iterations in Figure 4. In each figure, the horizontal-axis is the number of iterations and the vertical-axis represents the divergence between two consecutive deep soft matrices produced using our formulations in the iterative process.

We can easily observe the divergence between two consecutive deep soft matrices can converge to zero, i.e., the final soft labels of points will not be changed drastically. It is also worth noting that the convergence speed of our ProjLP is fast and the numbers of iteration (t) are usually less than 10. Thus, the computational burden of the proposed ProjLP will be comparable with the other models, as can be seen from the actual running time performance in the simulations.

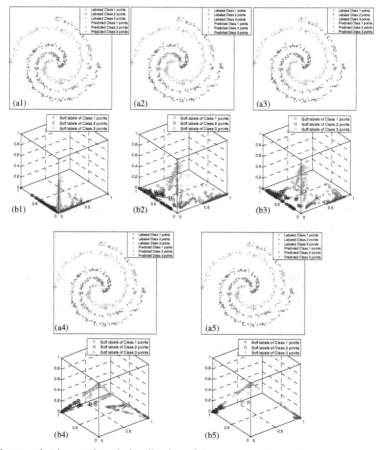

Fig. 3. The transductive result and visualization of the corresponding soft labels by each model on "three-arm spirals", where a_i, $i=1, 2,..., 5$ is the transductive result of GFHF, LLGC, LNP, SLP and our ProjLP respectively, b_i, $i=1, 2,..., 5$ shows the visualization of outputted soft labels by the corresponding method.

Table 1. List of used UCI datasets and dataset descriptions.

Dataset	#Dim	#Point	#Class (c)	Labeled Ratios
Monks-1	7	556	2	0.1, 0.2, ..., 0.9
Monks-2	7	601	2	0.1, 0.2, ..., 0.9
Diagnostic WBC	31	569	2	0.1, 0.2, ..., 0.9
Hepatitis	19	155	2	0.1, 0.2, ..., 0.9
Soybean	35	47	4	0.05, 0.05, ..., 0.5
Sonar	60	208	2	0.1, 0.2, ..., 0.9
Hayes-Roth	5	132	3	0.1, 0.2, ..., 0.9

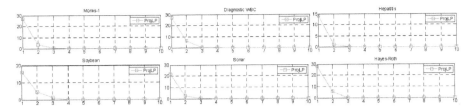

Fig. 4. Convergence behavior of our ProjLP approach.

Table 2. Mean classification results on UCI (results in bold show the highest accuracies).

Method Dataset	1NN Mean±STD Best Time (s) p-value	GFHF Mean±STD Best Time (s) p-value	LLGC Mean±STD Best Time (s) p-value	LNP Mean±STD Best Time (s) p-value	SLP Mean±STD Best Time (s) p-value	ProjLP Mean±STD Best Time (s) p-value
Monks-1	70.53±1.88 95.45 0.0188 2.5872e-005	78.95±14.04 97.27 0.2221 2.7828e-004	79.53±13.70 97.33 0.6917 0.0010	79.57±13.73 97.30 0.4803 4.9083e-004	79.61±13.69 97.31 0.6749 7.8132e-004	**83.70±15.13** **99.82** 1.4581 /
Monks-2	71.13±16.05 96.39 0.0233 2.7844e-004	82.34±14.34 98.42 0.2743 3.4525e-004	83.27±13.70 98.45 0.7942 0.0075	83.30±13.77 98.52 0.5730 0.0063	83.35±13.76 98.53 0.7962 0.0066	**85.45±15.01** **99.89** 1.9119 /
Hepatitis	64.33±6.75 73.12 0.0094 5.4634e-005	80.59±13.45 96.77 0.0250 0.0574	81.66±11.73 96.88 0.0476 0.8411	81.68±11.70 96.88 0.0310 0.8139	81.53±11.76 96.88 0.0468 0.9844	**82.54±13.30** **97.96** 0.0831 /
Sonar	77.00±5.89 82.33 0.0142 5.7022e-005	87.22±10.96 98.08 0.0417 0.0736	88.01±9.85 **98.16** 0.0786 0.0065	88.00±9.57 **98.16** 0.0562 0.0071	87.91±9.76 **98.16** 0.0689 0.0063	**88.82±9.13** 98.16 0.1947 /
Soybean	93.30±4.33 97.83 0.0018 0.0027	92.43±8.55 99.29 0.0082 0.0499	96.10±2.98 99.29 0.0130 0.0135	95.89±3.10 99.29 0.0108 0.0197	95.58±3.66 99.29 0.0114 0.0157	**97.77±1.31** **99.65** 0.0232 /
Hayes-Roth	71.01±17.47 97.44 0.0115 1.5050e-004	79.29±16.30 97.22 0.0238 0.0048	79.67±16.49 97.73 0.0432 0.0128	79.62±16.56 97.73 0.0315 0.0059	79.73±16.38 97.73 0.0426 0.0227	**80.71±17.28** **99.62** 0.0647 /
Auto-Mpg	84.90±9.93 98.75 0.0159 8.2250e-005	87.29±14.30 99.41 0.1301 0.1479	89.99±8.95 99.46 0.3210 0.2834	89.98±8.97 99.46 0.2686 0.2756	89.97±8.92 99.46 0.3456 0.2765	**90.27±9.63** **99.91** 0.7226 /
Diagnostic WBC	86.64±10.67 97.66 0.0221 4.5271e-005	89.16±10.87 98.80 0.2438 6.2034e-006	89.95±9.88 98.89 0.7251 0.0818	89.97±9.67 98.89 0.4945 0.0988	89.75±10.03 98.90 0.7235 0.0052	**90.68±10.47** **99.36** 1.7386 /

Classification Results. We report the transductive results on the eight UCI datasets. We always average the results over 20 random splits of training/test points and report the averaged transductive classification results. We describe the mean and best accuracy (%) according in Table 3, where STD denotes the standard deviation (%), and the highest accuracies are highlighted in bold. The mean time, including both training and test phases are also described. In addition to reporting the accuracies, we also perform paired t-test [10] that compares existing methods to our ProjLP. The p-value for each test is the probability of the observed or a greater difference between two classification accuracies, under the assumption of the null hypothesis that there is no difference between the classification accuracy distributions. That is, the smaller the p-value, the less likely that the observed difference resulted from identical classification accuracy distributions. In Table 3, the p-value denotes the outputs of paired t-tests comparing 1NN, GFHF, LLGC, LNP and SLP with our ProjLP. We can have the following observations. First, the performance of our ProjLP is superior to other criteria by delivering higher accuracies in most cases. We experimentally observe that the LP methods can outperform the baseline for classification in almost all cases. Second, for runtime performance, we find 1NN is the fastest one, since it does not train a real classification model and just stores the training data for similarity measure. Since we use the LLE-weights for LNP, the running time of GFHF, LLGC, LNP and SLP are comparable in most cases. Although our ProjLP delivers the projected "deep" labels by an iterative process, the needed time is also acceptable and even highly competitive with other methods over some datasets, since our model can converge with small number of iterations in most cases, as can be observed from simulations. Third, for the t-tests, a typical threshold for p-values is 0.05. If the p-value is smaller than 0.05, we can conclude that the paired methods have different accuracies on this set. We can find the performance difference between our ProjLP and other models is statistically significant, since most p-values are less than 0.05.

5   Concluding Remarks

We have mainly discussed the deep label prediction problem and proposed projective label propagation (ProjLP) via label embedding for enhancing semi-supervised representation and classification. ProjLP improves the performance by enhancing the transductive prediction process of training phase directly to deliver more discriminating "deep" labels of training data points with less inaccurate predictions and unfavorable mixed signs. The objective is realized by jointly calculating a robust sparse projection from one objective function to remove the unfavorable mixed signs and embed the "shallow" labels into the discriminating "deep" ones.

We have mainly examined the effectiveness of our ProjLP by visualizing the soft labels on toy set and classifying several UCI datasets. The visualizations on two toys illustrate that the "shallow" soft labels from the original space in deed contain many unfavorable mixed signs. Classification on UCI datasets demonstrated the superiority of the computed "deep" labels by our method over the "shallow" ones by the existing criteria. We will explore to extend the proposed method to the out-of-sample scenario for dealing with the outside samples by robust embedding in our future work.

Acknowledgements. This work is partially supported by the National Natural Science Foundation of China (61402310 and 61373093), and the Major Program of Natural Science Foundation of Jiangsu Higher Education Institutions of China (15KJA520002).

References

1. Chapelle, O., Scholkopf, B., Zien, A.: Semi-Supervised Learning. MIT Press, Cambridge (2006)
2. Zhu, X.: Semi-supervised learning literature survey. Technical Report 1530, Univ. Wisconsin-Madison (2005)
3. Culp, M., Michailidis, G.: Graph-based semi-supervised learning. IEEE Tran. on Pattern Analysis and Machine Intelligence **30**(1), 174–179 (2008)
4. Nie, F.P., Xu, D., Li, X.L., Xiang, S.M.: Semi-Supervised Dimensionality Reduction and Classification through Virtual Label Regression. IEEE Transactions on Systems, Man and Cybernetics Part B: Cybernetics **41**(3), 675–685 (2011)

5. Cai, D., He, X.F., Han, J.W.: Semi-supervised discriminant analysis. In: Proceedings of IEEE International Conference on Computer Vision, Rio de Janeiro, Brazil, pp. 1–7 (2007)
6. Song, Y.Q., Nie, F.P., Zhang, C.S., Xiang, S.: A unified framework for semi-supervised dimensionality reduction. Pattern Recognition 41(9), 2789–2799 (2008)
7. Zhang, Z., Chow, T., Zhao, M.B.: Trace Ratio Optimization based Semi-Supervised Nonlinear Dimensionality Reduction for Marginal Manifold Visualization. IEEE Trans. on Knowledge and Data Engineering 25(5), 1148–1161 (2013)
8. Nie, F.P., Xiang, S.M., Jia, Y.Q., Zhang, C.S.: Semi-supervised orthogonal discriminant analysis via label propagation. Pattern Recognition 42(1), 2615–2627 (2009)
9. Zhang, Z., Zhao, M.B., Chow, T.: Graph based Constrained Semi-Supervised Learning Framework via Label Propagation over Adaptive Neighborhood. IEEE Trans. on Knowledge and Data Engineering (December 2013). doi:10.1109/TKDE.2013.182
10. Mangasarian, O., Wild, E.W.: Multisurface Proximal Support Vector Machine Classification via Generalized Eigenvalues. IEEE Trans. on Pattern Analysis and Machine Intelligence 28(1), 69–74 (2006)
11. Belkin, M., Niyogi, P.: Laplacian Eigenmaps for Dimensionality Reduction and Data Representation. Neural Computation 15(6), 1373–1396 (2003)
12. Zang, F., Zhang, J.S.: Label propagation through sparse neighborhood and its applications. Neurocomputing 97, 267–277 (2012)
13. Yang, N., Sang, Y., He, R., Wang, X.: Label propagation algorithm based on non-negative sparse representation. In: Li, K., Jia, L., Sun, X., Fei, M., Irwin, G.W. (eds.) LSMS 2010 and ICSEE 2010. LNCS, vol. 6330, pp. 348–357. Springer, Heidelberg (2010)
14. Cheng, H., Liu, Z., Yang, J.: Sparsity induced similarity measure for label propagation. In: Proceedings of the IEEE International Conference on Computer Vision (2009)
15. Bengio, Y.: Learning Deep Architectures for AI. Foundations and Trends in Machine Learning 2(1), 1–127 (2009)
16. Hou, C.P., Nie, F.P., Li, X.L., Yi, D.Y., Wu, Y.: Joint Embedding Learning and Sparse Regression: A Framework for Unsupervised Feature Selection. IEEE Transactions on Cybernetics 44(6), 793–804 (2014)
17. Li, Z.C., Liu, J., Tang, J.H., Lu, H.Q.: Robust Structured Subspace Learning for Data Representation. IEEE Trans. on Pattern Analysis and Machine Intelligence (2015). doi:10.1109/TPAMI.2015.2400461
18. Yang, Y., Shen, H.T., Ma, Z.G., Huang, Z., Zhou, X.F.: $L_{2,1}$-norm regularized discriminative feature selection for unsupervised learning. In: Proceeding of the International Joint Conferences on Artificial Intelligence (2011)
19. Zhou, D., Bousquet, O., Lal, T.N., Weston, J., Cholkopf, B.S.: Learning with local and global consistency. In: Proc. Advances in Neural Information Processing Systems (2004)
20. Zhu, X., Ghahramani, Z., Lafferty, J.D.: Semi-supervised learning using Gaussian fields and harmonic functions. In: Proceedings of the International Conference on Machine Learning (2003)
21. Wang, F., Zhang, C.S.: Label propagation through linear Neighborhoods. IEEE Trans. on Knowledge and Data. Engineering 20(11), 55–67 (2008)
22. Wang, F., Zhang, C.S.: Label propagation through linear neighborhoods. In: Proceedings of International Conference on Machine Learning, Pittsburgh, Pennsylvania (2006)
23. Nie, F.P., Xiang, S.M., Liu, Y., Zhang, C.S.: A general graph-based semi-supervised learning with novel class discovery. Neural Computing Applications 19(4), 549–555 (2010)
24. Liu, Y., Nie, F.P., Wu, J.G., Chen, L.H.: Semi-supervised feature selection based on label propagation and subset selection. In: Proceedings of the International Conference on Computer and Information Application (2010)
25. Turk, M., Pentland, A.: Face recognition using eigenfaces. In: Proceedings of the IEEE International Conference on Computer Vision and Pattern Recognition (1991)
26. Lee, H.: Tutorial on deep learning and applications. In: NIPS Workshop on Deep Learning and Unsupervised Feature Learning (2010)
27. Roweis, S., Saul, L.: Nonlinear dimensionality reduction by locally linear embedding. Science 290(5500), 2323–2326 (2000)

Simplifying Indoor Scenes for Real-Time Manipulation on Mobile Devices

Michael Hödlmoser[1,3]([⊠]), Patrick Wolf[2,3], and Martin Kampel[2,3]

[1] Imaging and Computer Vision, Siemens Corporate Technology, München, Germany
michael.hoedlmoser@siemons.com
[2] Visualization and Data Analysis Group, University of Vienna, Vienna, Austria
patrick_wolf@unive.ac.it, martin.kampel@tuwien.ac.at
[3] Computer Vision Lab, Vienna University of Technology, Vienna, Austria

Abstract. Having precise measurements of an indoor scene is important for several applications - e.g.augmented reality furniture placement - whereas geometric details are only needed up to a certain scale. Depth sensors provide a highly detailed reconstruction but mobile phones are not able to display and manipulate these models in real-time due to the massive amount of data and the lack of computational power. This paper therefore aims to close this gap and provides a simplification of indoor scenes. RGB-D input sequences are exploited to extract wall segments and object candidates. For each input frame, walls, ground plane and ceiling are estimated by plane segments, object candidates are detected using a state-of-the-art object detector. The objects' correct poses and semantic types are gathered by exploiting a 3D CAD dataset and by introducing a Markov Random Field over time. A vast variety of experiments outline the practicability and low memory consumption of the resulting models on mobile phones and demonstrate the ability of preserving precise 3D measurements based on a variety of real indoor scenes.

1 Introduction

Detailed reconstruction of an indoor scene is important for many applications, e.gindoor navigation, room organization, or virtual furniture placement. Nevertheless, *detailed* in this context does not mean to have as many measurements per unit as possible but it is even more important to provide precise 3D measurements. To answer shopping questions like "Does this bed fit into this spot?", or "What are the maximum dimensions the shelf may have when placed in this room?", it is inevitable to have the dimensions of the room layout and the objects populating the room. Apart from that, it is also important for 3D modeling and manipulation to have semantic information attached to the scene in order to remove and exchange certain objects. Additionally, it needs to be feasible to store and share these 3D models between mobile devices within a blink of an eye and without the need of large memory capacities or bandwidth. As can be seen from human capabilities, obtaining a 3D layout, detecting occluded objects and even gathering 3D relationships among objects is something which is obviously

G. Azzopardi and N. Petkov (Eds.): CAIP 2015, Part II, LNCS 9257, pp. 482–493, 2015.
DOI: 10.1007/978-3-319-23117-4_42

Fig. 1. Simplification of an indoor scene while preserving precise 3D measurements and providing semantic enrichment. From left to right: Input point cloud, wire-frame and rendered model, real-time manipulation on a mobile device.

beyond the visible 2D scene. This paper therefore goes beyond the visible scene and presents a simple but efficient workflow which preserves precise 3D measurements of the scene, removes noise and holes in the dataset and obtains semantic labels for all meaningful parts the scene consists of. Consider an indoor scene as the one shown on the top left image of Fig. 1. To describe the scene and provide the aforementioned information needed for several applications, it is necessary to precisely determine wall segments as well as all the objects of the configuration in combination with their correct poses. With recent efforts on the development of inexpensive RGB-D sensors like Microsoft Kinect, Asus Xtion, the *Structure* sensor or Google's project Tango, it is possible to obtain depth information from indoor scenes without noticeable efforts. To capture whole rooms and other configurations in indoor scenes, multiple frames must be obtained which leads to large memory consumptions and high computing performance requirements. Mobile devices recently provide substantial computational power (e.g graphics processor and multi-core processing unit), nevertheless their power is still far less compared to desktop computers. The presented pipeline therefore brings us one step towards closing this gap by simplifying the input scene.

We present an approach to meaningfully describe an indoor scene while keeping memory consumption and computational power on a minimum, which allows real-time manipulation on mobile devices. We first extract several planes from the input cloud for each frame, serving as wall, ceiling, or ground plane. These plane segments are merged over time by finding corresponding feature matches in the RGB images and by applying sequential plane fitting. Potential objects are detected by using a state-of-the-art 2D object detector. A set of defined, synthetic objects (sofa, chair, table, potted plant) is used to find the most similar one and the poses of potential objects. A Markov Random Field (MRF) is exploited over time in order to increase robustness.

2   Related Work

Transferring human image interpretation ability to computers is one of the main challenges in computer vision. When only RGB images and no corresponding depth information is available, there are several methods which make use of predefined information on how to combine geometric with semantic data and choose a label for each pixel from a set of geometrically meaningful classes. By finding a corresponding geometric label for each pixel, the ill-posed problem of 3D reconstruction from a single image is solved [12].

Fig. 2. Proposed workflow. (a) Fused input point cloud. (b) Merged planes (*wall*, *ground plane, ceiling*). (c) Projection on the floor and triangulation of 3D points located within *ground plane* segments. (d) Extrusion of wall segments. (e) Object detection, pose estimation and optimization. (f) Final result. See text for details.

Going beyond labeling-based 3D reconstruction leads to reconstructing and understanding the scene from higher-level representations, which can be a simplified room layout estimation [9,16], or reasoning about the scene using the configuration between objects [3,8,14], or a semantic point cloud densification [2,11]. Aubry et al[1] solve the 2D-3D alignment problem and extract view-dependent patches from synthetic objects. Object detection in RGB-D data using sliding shapes was introduced in [17].

Introducing inexpensive RGB-D sensors allows easy reconstruction without having the ill-posed problem of 3D reconstruction from a single image. This can be done by fusing point clouds coming from multiple views [13], where an extension towards semantic reasoning is presented in [19], or by introducing plane primitives in order to increase the the pose alignment robustness [18]. An extension of the layout estimation method of Schwing et al[16] towards depth source integration is presented by Zhang et al. [20].

Contributions. Gathering a rough pixel orientation of a scene [9,12,16] helps in understanding the room layout, detecting existing 3D models in 2D images in their correct pose helps classifying a scene [1,3], and adding depth information to RGB images helps reconstructing the scene in a more detailed way [10,18]. The contribution of this paper is three-fold. First, it combines the strengths coming from these three areas of research, refines reconstruction and object detection results over time while keeping the complexity and the memory consumption of the reconstructed model on a minimum in order to allow real-time manipulation on mobile phones. Second, we model walls, ceilings and ground planes by using multiple plane segments which results in simplifying the camera pose estimation problem between subsequent frames. Third and different to [9,20], we do not use simple box models or labeling-based inference for object localization and representation, but use a dataset of defined synthetic 3D models to represent the pose and type of the objects.

3   RGB-D Indoor Scene Simplification

In the following we describe the workflow of the layout estimation as well as the object detection and pose estimation framework as shown in Fig. 2.

3.1   Layout Estimation

Having a scene composed of N input frames, in a first step, we want to extract the ground plane. As the images are assumed to be taken in an indoor scenario where man-made structures are available, dominant rectilinear directions can be found in the image. Each color input image is segmented into patches using the superpixel segmentation method described in [6]. For each patch, planes are fitted on the corresponding 3D points using RANSAC and co-planar planes are then merged. The vertical vanishing point is estimated in the corresponding color image in order to obtain the gravity vector $\mathbf{g}_i$ of the camera for frame i. Merged ground plane segments are aligned with the gravity vector. Ceiling segments are determined in the same manner, since the ceiling is located above the camera center. Following the idea of [18], a dynamic programming approach enforcing depth continuity is used to obtain an initial ground plane.

The coordinate system is transformed according to the determined ground plane. As we now have the same ground plane for each image, overlapping images can be aligned using both color and depth information. Corresponding SIFT features are extracted from the RGB images in order to find overlapping images. These matches are then used to align the individual 3D point clouds and to obtain a rigid transformation between the two 3D camera poses in a global coordinate system. The alignment is done by exploiting multiple feature matches in combination with RANSAC. Note that only SIFT features, where first a depth value is available and second corresponding features are located on the same 3D plane, are taken into account for this calculation (i.etwo pairs of points located on the same 3D plane have the same Euclidean distance when projected on their assigned 3D plane in each image individually). When having a vector of at least three matching point pairs $(\mathbf{f}, \mathbf{f}')$ between two consecutive point clouds, a rotation $\mathbf{R}$ and a translation $\mathbf{t}$ (which aligns the adjacent clouds) can be estimated by minimizing the error $E = \sum_{k=1}^{M} |\mathbf{f}'_k - \mathbf{R}\mathbf{f}_k + \mathbf{t}|^2$, where M is the number of matches. The point clouds are fused incrementally by finding rigid transformations between overlapping frames.

In a next step, the ground plane boundary as well as wall segments must be found. The 3D points labeled as ground plane are downsampled using a grid filter. Next, we need to generate a mesh from these points. In order to be able to model both convex and concave ground plane layouts, alpha shapes and Delaunay triangulation [4] are used instead of a convex hull. All triangles are then filled and holes are closed using morphological operations. In a next step, the ground plane is trimmed depending on the wall segments. Wall segments are assumed to be perpendicular to the ground. Using a perpendicular vector to $\mathbf{g}_i$ in each image allows finding the wall segments. All 3D points belonging to a wall segment are projected onto the ground plane and a line is then fitted through these points. By using these lines, we obtain the boundary of the corresponding ground plane. There are two main goals of the workflow, namely first obtaining a watertight model and second obtaining a simplified model. As we now have a watertight ground plane, its boundary points are traced and triangulated. The boundary points are simplified by exploiting mesh simplification [7].

The remaining vertices are then used for extruding the wall parts until they intersect with the ceiling, or - when no ceiling is detected in the scene - up to a defined height (we use a height of 2.5 meters in our experiments). The extruded segments are triangulated in order to obtain watertight 3D wall segments.

3.2 Object Detection

We define different object classes, which we want to detect, namely *couch, chair, table,* and *potted plant.* The main goal of this step is to extract only 3D points belonging to an object and search for the most similar object type at the most similar pose within a predefined dataset. This search is optimized by combining object detection and pose estimation results coming from subsequent frames. A trained 2D object detector [5] is applied on the RGB image to obtain initial hypotheses of object positions in 2D space. We do not use [17] as missing depth values and occlusions lead to problems, as can be seen in their experiments.

For each object, the corresponding 3D point cloud of its bounding box is extracted. We then filter out all points belonging to the ground plane. Related to the four object classes, it can safely be assumed that all objects are located on the ground plane. If the object's point cloud is found above a certain height in 3D space (a threshold of 50 centimeters is determined empirically) or does not consist of a meaningful amount of 3D points (500 in our experiments), we exclude the detection candidate from further calculations. We then apply a voxelgrid filter on the remaining points and perform Euclidean clustering, the largest cluster is then taken as the one representing the object in question.

The goal of the next step is to find a temporal consistent result for the object's pose and type. The solution to this problem corresponds to finding the maximum posterior (MAP) configuration of a chain-structured MRF. Let $\mathcal{G} = (\mathcal{V}, \mathcal{E})$ be a graph described by vertices $\mathcal{V}$ which in this case are represented by the N frames within the image sequence and edges $\mathcal{E}$ which in this case are the transitions between subsequent frames. When having a set of random variables $\mathbf{X} = \{X_1, X_2, \ldots X_N\}$ and a label configuration $\mathbf{x} = \{x_1, x_2, \ldots x_N\}$ which can take values from the discrete set of labels $\mathcal{L}$, the energy term E of the pairwise chain-structured MRF is defined by

$$E(\mathbf{x}) = \sum_{i \in \mathcal{V}} \psi_i(x_i) + \sum_{i=2}^{N} \psi_{i,i-1}(x_i, x_{i-1}), \tag{1}$$

where ψ_i is the unary potential in the graph and $\psi_{i,i-1}$ is the pairwise potential, or smoothness term, between subsequent poses. The MAP configuration $\hat{\mathbf{x}}$ is then found by $\hat{\mathbf{x}} = \mathrm{argmin}_{\mathbf{x}} E(\mathbf{x})$.

Unary Potentials. In order to rank poses for each object for each frame, it is first needed to specify which poses are relevant. We generate an icosahedron and place each of the 3D models from the dataset at the origin of it. Each face of the icosahedron is then split up into 4 triangles and virtual cameras are placed at the barycenters of these triangles. The model is rendered from each viewpoint using a depth buffer in order to obtain a partial point cloud. As we assume that objects are sitting on the ground plane, the clouds are aligned with that plane. Unfeasible poses, i.ethe camera is facing the chair from below, are filtered out. Fig. 3 shows a sample 3D model and rendered views.

Fig. 3. Generation of partial views of a CAD model using virtual cameras placed on the surface of an icosahedron.

As we do not know the scaling of the objects in advance, we need to describe the point cloud using scale-invariant features. Having a partial point cloud of the 3D model, a Darboux coordinate system $(\mathbf{u}_j, \mathbf{v}_j, \mathbf{w}_j)$ [15] can be directly formed by using a single point $\mathbf{p}_j$ and the centroid $\mathbf{c}$ of a point cloud. For each point $\mathbf{p}_j$ in the cloud, the relative pan (α_1), tilt (α_2) and yaw angle (α_3) between its normal $\mathbf{n}_j$ and the centroid's normal, as well as an angle α_4, depending on the viewpoint $\mathbf{V}$, is determined by[15]

$$\alpha_1 = \arccos\left(\mathbf{v}_j \cdot \mathbf{n}_j\right), \alpha_2 = \arccos\left(\mathbf{u}_j \cdot \frac{\mathbf{p}_j - \mathbf{c}}{\|\mathbf{p}_j - \mathbf{c}\|}\right) \quad (2)$$

$$\alpha_3 = \arctan\left(\mathbf{w}_j \cdot \mathbf{n}_j, \mathbf{u}_j \cdot \mathbf{n}_j\right), \alpha_4 = \arccos\left(\mathbf{n}_j \cdot \frac{\mathbf{V} - \mathbf{c}}{\|\mathbf{V} - \mathbf{c}\|}\right).$$

VFH then bins the angular differences between all points in the cloud and the centroid in order to obtain a valid histogram, where each partial point cloud is described by a single histogram. The whole rendering and VFH calculation for each model is done in an offline stage.

For each frame, we now have a single 3D point cluster coming from the depth sensor. For each of these clusters, a single VFH is calculated in the same fashion as for the 3D models. The resulting histogram is then compared to the histograms of the partial models generated from the training stage using the chi-squared distance. This distance gives us a first ranking how well the different types and poses of the training set fit the corresponding 3D point clouds.

As one of the main drawbacks of the VFH is the high sensibility to occlusions [15], we propose to combine VFH with another descriptor, namely Principle Component Analysis (PCA). The main advantage of PCA is its discriminativeness, even in scenarios, where parts of the object are occluded (please see our experiments section for validation). For each model type, we therefore obtain a number of best matching poses (in our experiments, this threshold is empirically set to 10) using the VFH. On these best matching partial views, a PCA is exploited in addition to calculating the VFH. We can safely assume that the 3D model is sitting on the ground plane. Having a partial 3D model m, we therefore project the point cloud onto the ground plane. We perform PCA on these projected points to obtain its main orientation vector $\mathbf{e}_m$. In the same manner, PCA is also performed on the input point cloud to gather a corresponding orientation vector $\mathbf{e}_p$. For frame i and a partial model m, the unary potential is therefore defined by $\psi_i = \frac{\arccos(\mathbf{e}_{p,i} \cdot \mathbf{e}_m)}{\pi}$.

Binary Potentials and Model Type Estimation. To achieve a globally correct result, we can safely assume that the object's pose must not change between subsequent frames. As camera poses between overlapping frames do only change slightly and an object's pose behaves inverse to the camera pose, we aim for a solution where the object's pose variation between frames is minimized, which in other words means that the energy E of the configuration is minimized. When assuming a constant model type over time, the binary potential between subsequent frames is therefore modeled by $\psi_{i,i-1} = \frac{\arccos(\mathbf{e}_{m,i} \cdot \mathbf{e}_{m,i-1})}{\pi}$.

We then obtain an optimized energy $\hat{E}$ for each model type s by $\hat{E}_s = \min_{\mathbf{x}_s} E(\mathbf{x}_s)$. The MAP configuration $\tilde{\mathbf{x}}$, describing the best matching model type sequence, is then found by $\tilde{\mathbf{x}} = \operatorname{argmin}_s \hat{E}_s$. Both VFH and PCA are scale-invariant. In order to obtain a correct scaling between the 3D point cloud and the 3D model, we calculate a scaling factor between the resulting layout model and the object's CAD model using the 3D bounding boxes. For plants the scaling factor is estimated using their lengths, for chairs and couches the height is used, for tables the distance between the table surface and the floor is obtained.

4   Experiments

Our pipeline describes an indoor scene simply by semantically meaningful objects as well as wall, ceiling and ground plane segments. As the object detection in combination with the pose estimation and the 3D layout estimation are performed individually, these two steps are also evaluated individually. For object detection, we define four different classes, namely *couch* (12 different models), *chair* (8), *table* (8), and *potted plant* (5). For each class we train the framework with a variety of different CAD models from 3D Warehouse[1]. Note that the number between the brackets denotes the number of instances obtained for each model where more instances are used for classes with a higher intra-class variability. Fig. 4a shows some sample models from the dataset.

Layout Estimation. In a first experiment, we compare our scene understanding results with results coming from methods which only use color but no depth information, namely the algorithms of Hedau et al[9] and Choi et al[3]. We therefore captured 21 different indoor scenes with a Microsoft Kinect having a resolution of 640×480 pixels. Fig. 4b shows sample input images and corresponding qualitative results. Having a manually ground truth labeled image $\mathcal{G}$ and a resulting image $\mathcal{R}$, the accuracy for label l is determined by $\frac{|\mathcal{G}_l \cap \mathcal{R}_l|}{|\mathcal{G}_l \cup \mathcal{R}_l|}$, where $|\cdot|$ refers to the number of pixels of label l in an image. The percentage of correctly classified pixels for each label can be seen in Fig. 5a. We provide two different metrics. First, we compare the labeling only for layouts and exclude regions labeled as objects and second, we also take regions labeled as objects into account, represented by column 1 and 2 of each method, respectively. Note that the method of Choi et al[3] does not provide precise object boundaries but

---

[1] https://3dwarehouse.sketchup.com

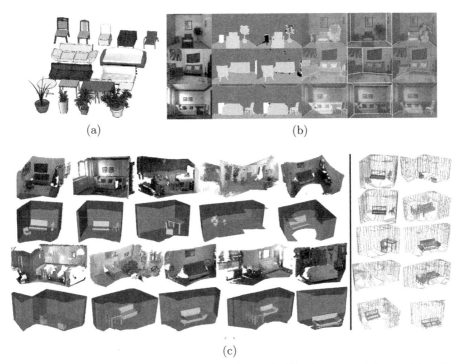

Fig. 4. (a) Sample CAD models obtained from 3D Warehouse used for training the framework.(b) Qualitative labeling results for layouts with a single input frame. From left to right: Input image, ground truth, raw depth, [9], [3], ours.(c) Qualitative results. Left: input clouds (rows 1/3), rendered models (rows 2/4) for sequences 1-10. Right: wireframe models (top to bottom,left to right).

only bounding boxes, therefore we only compare the layout and exclude objects in the evaluation. We additionally compare our results to the raw 3D point cloud coming from the depth sensor (denoted as *Raw depth*, note that regions which do not provide any depth information are labeled black in Fig. 4b). As can be seen, the classification results when excluding objects are better than the ones for populated scenes. The proposed method achieves a mean classification result of 95% for all pixels and empty scenes, which means that we outperform the noisy input data by roughly 5%. This occurs as the proposed method fills depth information holes.

As our pipeline is able to handle multiple input frames, we captured 10 different scenes each of them consisting of up to 20 frames using a Microsoft Kinect. Fig. 4c shows qualitative results from our pipeline. As can be seen, the estimated layout clearly represents the structure of the 3D point cloud. To compare the performance of the layout estimation using a single shot and the estimation consisting of multiple input shows, we perform the layout estimation for each frame separately and once for the whole sequence. We therefore manually segment each input 3D point cloud into plane segments, fit a plane on the filtered points and calculate the distance of the output model plane to the corresponding

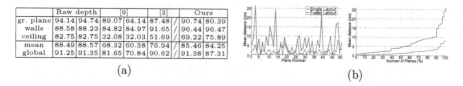

	Raw depth		[9]		Ours			
gr. plane	94.14	94.74	89.07	64.14	87.48	/	90.74	80.39
walls	88.58	88.23	84.82	84.97	91.65	/	96.44	96.47
ceiling	82.75	82.75	32.08	32.03	51.69	/	69.22	75.89
mean	88.49	88.57	68.32	60.38	76.94	/	85.46	84.25
global	91.25	91.35	81.65	70.84	90.62	/	91.38	87.31

(a)   (b)

Fig. 5. (a) Percentage of correctly classified pixels for each label. First column of each method represents layout without considering objects, second column represents results where object labels are considered.(b) Quantitative results for 10 different scenes when estimating the layout using each frame separately and when fusing the point cloud and estimating the layout afterwards.

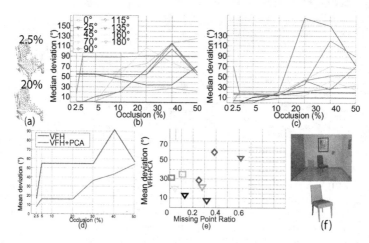

Fig. 6. (a) Occlusion Simulation. Median estimation errors using (b) VFH, (c) VFH + PCA. (d) Mean error for VFH/VFH + PCA. (e) Pose error when considering point cloud size. (f) Input image and used 3D model.

plane. Fig. 5b shows (a) the mean distance in centimeters for each plane and all its corresponding points and (b) the mean distance of RANSAC inlier points for the corresponding percentage of planes for both using a single and using multiple input frames. As can be seen, the mean distance for 92% of all planes have a mean distance to all inlier points of less than 5 centimeters when using 6 input frames, whereas the same percentage of planes show a mean distance of more than 17 centimeters when only using one single frame. This means that the more input information is available, the better the layout will be estimated.

Object Detection. As we want to determine the performance between different pose estimation features, Fig. 7 shows a comparison between the pose estimation error using VFH, VFH+PCA and optimizing the VFH+PCA results using an MRF. The graph shows the results using all input sequences shown in Fig. 4c. As can be seen, when using an MRF, for 80% of the poses we obtain an error less than 20°, whereas VFH+PCA or VFH without MRF deliver an error of 30° or even more than 50°, respectively.

It takes 30 seconds to perform both layout estimation as well as object detection and classification using a non-optimized Matlab implementation on a Macbook Pro 2.5GHz/4GB RAM. As the task can be parallelized, the runtime can dramatically be reduced when executing the code on the GPU.

Fig. 7. Comparison of pose estimation error using VFH, VFH+PCA and an MRF. Arrow denotes camera viewing direction.

How robust is the proposed feature descriptor when noise occurs? The following experiment analyzes the performance of VFH and the proposed combination of VFH + PCA when the input point cloud is incomplete or noisy. We therefore place a chair with different orientations $(0-180°)$ in a room and perform the pose estimation using only the most similar object from the dataset (see Fig. 6(f)). We then simulate the occlusions and missing parts by randomly removing a defined percentage of connected 3D points from the input cloud, as can be seen in Fig. 6(a). In order to be robust against variations coming from removing different parts of the point clouds, the experiment is performed 30 times for each orientation and the median is calculated. Fig. 6(b-d) show the pose estimation difference between the calculated pose and the manually labeled one for VFH, VFH + PCA and a mean error for VFH and VFH + PCA, respectively. As can be seen, the mean deviation over all orientation estimations is less when using VFH+PCA compared to using VFH only. The estimation accuracy decreases when the occlusion increases. As different input clouds consist of different numbers of 3D points, we also show the pose estimation error for VFH+PCA when considering the completeness of the input point cloud, i.ethe ratio of missing points from the synthetic model when aligned and compared with the input cloud (see Fig. 6(e)). As can be seen, positions 90° and 180° provide less points compared to the other scenes which results in a higher pose estimation error.

3D Models on Mobile Devices. As can be seen in Fig. 8a, both the storage consumption and the number of 3D points are reduced by more than 99.9% when applying the proposed pipeline. The computational power of mobile phones is less compared to desktop computers and the bandwidth is limited when connected via cellular networks. Nevertheless, our pipeline allows displaying and manipulating the 3D models in real-time on mobile devices by this massive data reduction while still preserving the semantic information and precise geometric properties. Additionally, the low memory consumption enables storing and sharing files between mobile devices within a blink of an eye and without the need of high storage capacities or a large bandwidth (e.gin social networks).

Scene	Size		Number of Points			
	Input[MB]	Ours [KB]	Input	Ours [Layout/Obj./Tot.]		
1	137.98	465	3 379 200	260	7 412	7 672
2	113.46	59	2 764 800	270	756	1 026
3	75.14	100	1 843 200	205	1 337	1 542
4	228.89	331	5 529 600	520	4 776	5 296
5	174.78	29	4 300 800	380	220	600
6	88.18	104	2 150 400	320	1 355	1 675
7	164.34	58	3 993 600	295	732	1 017
8	62.74	171	1 536 000	260	253	2 513
9	163.50	196	3 543 200	360	2 565	2 925
10	74.85	41	1 843 200	265	440	705

(a)   (b)

Fig. 8. (a) Memory consumption / number of points for input cloud and the proposed results (number of points split up in layout, objects, total).(b) Screenshots of sequences 1, 7 when manipulating the 3D model on a Samsung Galaxy S3.

5   Conclusion

Using a depth sensor results in massive amounts of data, where displaying and manipulating the point cloud in real-time can not be handled on mobile devices. This paper therefore presents a pipeline for automatic simplification of an indoor scene, obtained from an RGB-D sequence, using semantic meaningful attributes. These attributes are described by the scene layout and the objects present in the scene. The layout, consisting of ground plane, wall and ceiling segments, is estimated using a combination of plane fitting and merging. Objects are detected in 2D and extracted in the 3D point cloud. This cloud is then replaced by a CAD model coming from a defined dataset. Calculating a similarity score between 3D point cloud and CAD model is obtained by using a combination of VFH, PCA and a temporal optimization of all results using an MRF. The data can be reduced by more than 99.9% in terms of both number of points and memory consumption, which allows manipulation and interaction in real-time on mobile devices. Please see our supplemental video for additional results.

In future, the whole framework can be implemented highly parallelized on a GPU. For future research we plan to implement a cloud computing service which enables processing via mobile devices. Since detected objects are scaled along one direction only, our experimental results show limitations concerning the scene configuration (e.gobjects intersect with wall segment). Thus, the method should be further developed in order to optimize both the layout and the object configuration together in a single step.

References

1. Aubry, M., Maturana, D., Efros, A., Russell, B., Sivic, J.: Seeing 3d chairs: exemplar part-based 2d–3d alignment using a large dataset of CAD models. In: Proc. of CVPR, pp. 3762–3769 (2014)
2. Bódis-Szomorú, A., Riemenschneider, H., Gool, L.V.: Fast, approximate piecewise-planar modeling based on sparse structure-from-motion and superpixels. In: Proc. of CVPR, pp. 469–476 (2014)
3. Choi, W., Chao, Y., Pantofaru, C., Savarese, S.: Understanding indoor scenes using 3d geometric phrases. In: Proc. of CVPR, pp. 33–40 (2013)
4. Edelsbrunner, H., Kirkpatrick, D., Seidel, R.: On the shape of a set of points in the plane. Trans. on Information Theory 29(4), 551–558 (1983)
5. Felzenszwalb, P., Girshick, R., McAllester, D., Ramanan, D.: Object detection with discriminatively trained part-based models. TPAMI 32(9), 1627–1645 (2010)
6. Felzenszwalb, P., Huttenlocher, D.: Efficient graph-based image segmentation. IJCV 59(2), 167–181 (2004)
7. Garland, M., Heckbert, P.: Surface simplification using quadric error metrics. In: SIGGRAPH, pp. 209–216 (1997)
8. Gupta, A., Efros, A.A., Hebert, M.: Blocks world revisited: image understanding using qualitative geometry and mechanics. In: Daniilidis, K., Maragos, P., Paragios, N. (eds.) ECCV 2010, Part IV. LNCS, vol. 6314, pp. 482–496. Springer, Heidelberg (2010)
9. Hedau, V., Hoiem, D., Forsyth, D.: Recovering the spatial layout of cluttered rooms. In: Proc. of ICCV (2009)
10. Hermans, A., Floros, G., Leibe, B.: Dense 3d semantic mapping of indoor scenes from RGB-D images. In: Proc. of ICRA, pp. 2631–2638 (2014)
11. Hödlmoser, M., Mičušík, B., Kampel, M.: Sparse point cloud densification by combining multiple segmentation methods. In: Proc. of 3DV (2013)
12. Hoiem, D., Efros, A., Hebert, M.: Recovering surface layout from an image. IJCV 75(1) (2007)
13. Newcombe, R., Izadi, S., Hilliges, O., Molyneaux, D., Kim, D., Davison, A., Kohli, P., Shotton, J., Hodges, S., Fitzgibbon, A.: Kinectfusion: real-time dense surface mapping and tracking. In: Proc. of ISMAR, pp. 127–136 (2011)
14. Pero, L.D., Bowdish, J., Fried, D., Kermgard, B., Hartley, E., Barnard, K.: Bayesian geometric modeling of indoor scenes. In: Proc. of CVPR (2012)
15. Rusu, R.B., Bradski, G., Thibaux, R., Hsu, J.: Fast 3d recognition and pose using the viewpoint feature histogram. In: Proc. of IROS, October 2010
16. Schwing, A., Hazan, T., Pollefeys, M., Urtasun, R.: Efficient structured prediction for 3d indoor scene understanding. In: Proc. of CVPR, pp. 2815–2822 (2012)
17. Song, S., Xiao, J.: Sliding shapes for 3D object detection in depth images. In: Fleet, D., Pajdla, T., Schiele, B., Tuytelaars, T. (eds.) ECCV 2014, Part VI. LNCS, vol. 8694, pp. 634–651. Springer, Heidelberg (2014)
18. Taylor, C., Cowley, A.: Parsing indoor scenes using RGB-D imagery. In: Robotics: Science and Systems (2012)
19. Valentin, J., Sengupta, S., Warrell, J., Shahrokni, A., Torr, P.: Mesh based semantic modelling for indoor and outdoor scenes. In: CVPR, pp. 2067–2074 (2013)
20. Zhang, J., Kan, C., Schwing, A., Urtasun, R.: Estimating the 3d layout of indoor scenes and its clutter from depth sensors. In: Proc. of ICCV, pp. 1273–1280 (2013)

Image Contrast Enhancement by Distances Among Points in Fuzzy Hyper-Cubes

Mario Versaci[✉], Salvatore Calcagno, and Francesco Carlo Morabito

Dipartimento di Ingegneria Civile, Energia, Ambiente e Materiali (DICEAM),
Universitá Mediterranea Degli Studi di Reggio Calabria,
Cittadella Universitaria - Feo di Vito, 89122 Reggio Calabria, Italy
mario.versaci@unric.it

Abstract. A new geometrical fuzzy approach for image contrast enhancement is here presented. Synergy among ascending order statistics and entropy evaluations are exploited to get contrast enhancement by evaluation of distances among points inside fuzzy unit hyper-cube. The obtained results can be considered interesting, especially compared with consolidated techniques which encourages further studies in this direction.

1 Introduction

Contrast enhancement techniques, representing the first treatment to enhance image quality, are subdivided in two main trends. The first, direct type one, formulates a criterion of contrast measurement and enhances the image quality by improving of such measure. The second one, of indirect type (such as histogram equalization), acts on the image histogram modifying the intensity of the gray levels of pixels has a gray levels transformation in which dark pixels appear darker and light ones appear brighter. Both techniques produce a stretching of the global distribution of the intensity of the gray levels requiring the elaboration of adaptive procedures of features extraction directly and automatically from the image. Owing to the uncertainty and vagueness of the sampling techniques, the construction of an image is not free from uncertaintess and noise (loss of informative content during the transformation of objects from three-dimensional to bi-dimensional images, ambiguity of the definition of edges, regions and boundaries). So, it follows the necessity to implement an adaptive procedure of contrast enhancement which manipulates data uncertainty. For the reasons given above, scientific research has produced important results through fuzzy techniques both with direct and indirect approaches [1], [2], [3]. In addition, a lot of efforts have been done about adaptive formulation of contrast indicators enhancing the image quality by evaluations of differences of gray levels in local neighborhoods [2]. By adaptive extraction of features, meaningful contributions have been proposed where the main fuzzy entropy plays a determining role for the gray levels fuzzification [3]. Good results have been also obtained by wavelet-fuzzy techniques in which approximation/detail coefficients and transformation/saturation operators are exploited to get contrast enhancement [4], [5].

© Springer International Publishing Switzerland 2015
G. Azzopardi and N. Petkov (Eds.): CAIP 2015, Part II, LNCS 9257, pp. 494–505, 2015.
DOI: 10.1007/978-3-319-23117-4_43

In addition, a lot of papers deal with got contrast enhancement by fuzzy generation of histogram equalization [6], [12], [13], [14] and specific statistical applications [7], [9], [10] can be considered particularly meaningful. However, scientific
literature is poor in papers in which histogram stretching is carried out by fuzzy
geometrical approaches where intelligible contrast enhancement procedures have
been adjusted (particularly helpful for not technical experts). So, in this work,
the authors present a new approach based on a particular fuzzy formulation in
which the features extraction characterizes the fuzzification of the gray levels
ranges. Moreover, some statistical-entropic considerations calibrate the procedure adaptively. Finally, synergy among ascending order statistics and fuzzy
geometries yields contrast enhancement steps automatically. The proposed procedure, characterized by a low computational load shows very useful for real-time
applications, when applied to a lot of images with different features, being in
addition the obtained results wholly qualitatively and quantitatively comparable
with those obtained by consolidated techniques. The paper is organized as follows. Starting from gray levels images, the steps of the proposed procedure will
be illustrated giving a reason for each operational choice. Then, the obtained
results on images with different features are presented, making qualitative and
quantitative comparisons with the same images treated by using already consolidated techniques. Finally, some conclusions are drawn.

2   Material and Methods

Generally, an $M \times N$ image I with L levels can be defined by means of a matrix
of pixels on which, for each pixel position (i, j), $i = 0, 1, 2, ..., M - 1$ and $j =
0, 1, 2, ..., N - 1$, we associate its gray level x_{ij}. In a fuzzy domain, it is imperative
to fix the membership value to each pixel to I by means a function $\mu_I(x_{ij}) : I \rightarrow
[0, 1]$ defining the membership degree of x_{ij} to I. In particular, if $\mu_I(x_{ij}) = 1$
the corresponding pixel is totally belonging to I; if $\mu_I(x_{ij}) = 0$ x_{ij} does not
belong to I totally. Intermediate values of μ show a partial membership of x_{ij}
to I. If $\mu_I(x_{ij})$ is the informative content of x_{ij} in I, we can represent I by
$\sum_{i=0}^{M-1} \sum_{j=0}^{N-1} [x_{ij}, \mu_I(x_{ij}) = g_{ij}], \forall x \in I, i = 0, 1, 2, ..., M-1, j = 0, 1, 2, ..., N-1$
where $\mu_I(x_{ij}) = g_{ij}$ is the gray level of x_{ij} [8], [11]. So, contrast enhancement
process can be defined thinking that if x_{ij} is *dark* it has to be made darker; if
x_{ij} is *light* it has to be made lighter; if x_{ij} is *gray* it has to remain gray. Stating
that *dark*, *light* and *gray* are fuzzy terms, it is necessary to express them by a
suitable function regulating the mapping of I in the fuzzy domain by means of
the image features themself. In this way, image contrast enhancement is designed
as the transformation of this function making darker the gray levels considered
dark, and clearer the ones thought as clear.

2.1   Choice of the Typology of Mapping in the Fuzzy Domain

Scientific literature suggests us different typologies of mapping functions:
linear piecewise (triangular, trapezoidal, sigma-functions) and smoother ones

(S-functions, bell-shaped, broken gaussian) to guarantee a better transaction among gray levels. Here, let here choose, define and exploit an S-function as follows

$$g_{ij} = \mu_I(x_{ij}) = \begin{cases} 0 & 0 \leq x_{ij} \leq a \\ \frac{(x_{ij}-a)^2}{(b-a)\cdot(c-a)} & a \leq x_{ij} \leq b \\ 1 - \frac{(x_{ij}-c)^2}{(c-b)\cdot(c-a)} & b \leq x_{ij} \leq c \\ 1 & x_{ij} \geq c \end{cases} \tag{1}$$

in which a, b, c (b not necessarily equal to $(a+c)/2$) have to be adaptively determined.

2.2   Adaptive Setting of S-Function Parameters

S-function construction has to perform principles of noise reduction and loss information minimization. So, to determine a and c, it has been elaborated an algoritm acting directly on the image histogram to reduce the noise, starting from the approach developed in [3]. Regarding b, a consolidated approach based on maximum fuzzy entropy principle has been exploited because high value of entropy is a measure of a better fuzzy information in the image.

How Determine Parameters a and c. Let g_{max}, g_{min} and $H_{ist}(g)$ be the maximum and minimum values of gray levels in I and the relative histogram respectively. $H_{ist}(g)$ will present z maximum locals (peaks) labeled by $H_{ist}(g_1)$, $H_{ist}(g_2)$,..., $H_{ist}(g_z)$ and their mean value, $\overline{X_{ist_{max}}}(g)$, will gets the form [3] $\overline{X_{ist_{max}}}(g) = \frac{1}{z}\sum_{i=1}^{z}\overline{X_{ist_{max}}}(g_i)$. From the set of peaks we select k of them ($k \leq z$) which exceed $\overline{X_{ist_{max}}}(g)$ excluding the other ones because they can be considered less meaningful. From the selected k peaks, let consider only the first one $(\overline{X_{ist_{max}}}(g_1))$ and the last one $(\overline{X_{ist_{max}}}(g_k))$. The gray levels lower than $(\overline{X_{ist_{max}}}(g_1))$ can be considered as background, and the upper to $(\overline{X_{ist_{max}}}(g_k))$ can be considered as noise: this way we preserve the informative content of the image and, at the same time, we reduce the noise. Two particular gray levels, L_A and L_B will be determined, so that the loss of information in the ranges $[g_{min}, L_A]$ and $[L_B, g_{max}]$ is equal to a particular value f_1, with $0 < f_1 < 1$ (tipically $f_1 = 0.01$):

$$\sum_{i=g_{min}}^{L_A} H_{ist}(i) = \sum_{i=L_B}^{g_{max}} H_{ist}(i) = f_1 \tag{2}$$

However, the selection of the peaks occurs by thresholding on a mean value evaluated by Eq.(2) [3] which does not consider the mutual positions of the peaks. Here, the authors propose a weighted mean computed as

$$\overline{X_{ist_{max}}}(g) = \frac{\sum_{i=1}^{z} H_{ist_{max}}(g_i) \cdot g_i}{\sum_{i}^{z} g_i} \tag{3}$$

so that $X_{ist_{max}}(g)$ is the height of the centre of gravity of the histogram taking into account the mutual positions above mentioned. Finally, a and c parameters can be determined by $a = \frac{g_{max}-g_{min}}{2} + g_{min}$ if $(a > L_A) \rightarrow a = B_1$ and $c = \frac{g_{max}-g_k}{2} + g_k$ if $(a > L_A) \rightarrow a = B_1$.

How Determine Parameter b. Being fuzzy entropy a reliable measure of uncertainty of a system and high entropy values keeping anhigh informative content, the evaluation of b occurs by fuzzy entropy maximisation: $b \in [a+1, c-1]$, so its optimal evaluation, b_{opt}, can be determined by $H_{max}(I, a, b_{opt}, c) = \{H(I, a, b, c) \in' g_{min} \le a < b < c \le g_{max}\}$. If H is Shannon's entropy (or other entropic formulations depending on the application under study), the ambiguity of an image I, $H(I)$, can be expressed as

$$\frac{1}{MN} \sum_{m=1}^{M} \sum_{n=1}^{N} S(g_{mn}) = -g_{mn} \cdot log_2 g_{mn} - (1 - g_{mn}) \cdot log_2 (1 - g_{mn}), \quad 0 < H(I) < 1$$

$$(4)$$

with Shannon's function S increasing monotonically on $[0, 0.5]$ and decreasing monotonically on $[0.5, 1]$ with a maximum falling on $g_{mn} = 0.5$.

2.3   S-Function Transformation

S-Function Partition in Partially Superimposed Portions. We subdivide the range $[g_{min}, g_{max}]$ in three sub-intervals partially superimposed, generating fuzzy rectangular patches labelled by A, B and C respectively. Specifically, A is set around 0.5 value of fuzzy membership (gray area of image); B and C are sets around dark and bright areas of the image respectively (Fig. 1). Moreover, each patch is supported on its sub-interval: $Support_A = \frac{b+c}{2} - \frac{a+b}{2}$, $Support_B = b-a$, $Support_C = c - b$ in which $Support_j$ (j=A, B, C), represents the basis of each fuzzy rectangular patch characterized by particular values of ascending order statistics which represent a set of features dirtectly extracted from the image. Contrast enhancement will be done by transformation of the S-function starting from the statistics above obtained (Table I and Fig. 1). Next section highlights the details of such idea.

Extraction and Fuzzification of Statistical Features. From $Support_j$, we evaluate mean, variance, skewness and kurtosis, labelled by $MN(\cdot)$, $VAR(\cdot)$, $SK(\cdot)$, $KU(\cdot)$, constituting the following patterns $[MN(Support_j), VAR(Support_j), SK(Support_j), KU(Support_j)], j = A, B, C$ which, inside $\mathbb{R}^4$, represents three points

$$P_j = [MN(Support_j), VAR(Support_j), SK(Support_j)KU(Support_j)] \in \mathbb{R}^4.$$

$$(5)$$

To underline the fuzzy nature of the approach, it is advisable to fuzzify P_j by a sigmoidal function (anyway other types of function can be taken into account)

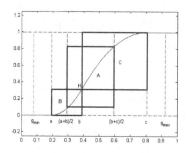
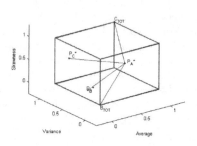

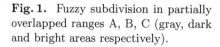

Fig. 1. Fuzzy subdivision in partially overlapped ranges A, B, C (gray, dark and bright areas respectively).

Fig. 2. Gray, dark and bright areas as points inside a Fuzzy Unit Hyper-Cube ($FUHC^4$).

as $P_j^* = \frac{1}{1+e^{-m(P_j-n)}}$ (tipically $m = 11$ and $n = 0.5$): in this way P_j^* fall inside a four-dimensional Fuzzy Unit Hyper-Cube, $FUHC^4$ (Fig. 2) [15]:

$$P_j^* = [\frac{1}{1 + e^{-m(MN(Support_j)-n)}},$$

$$\frac{1}{1 + e^{-m(VAR(Support_j)-n)}}, \frac{1}{1 + e^{-m(SK(Support_j)-n)}},$$

$$\frac{1}{1 + e^{-m(KU(Support_j)-n)}}] \in FUHC^4 \tag{6}$$

So, S-function transformation occurs by evaluation of mutual distances of the points P_j^* and two crucial fuzzy points (B_{TOT} and C_{TOT}) inside $FUHC^4$ as detailed in the following subsection.

Construction of the Transformed S-Function. Having obtained P_A^*, P_B^* and P_C^* points as above described, their mutual distances are evaluated as

$$d(P_i^*, P_j^*) = ||P_i^* - P_j^*||_2, \quad i,j = A, B, C. \tag{7}$$

So, the following cases can occur:
a) $d(P_A^*, P_B^*) = ||P_A^* - P_B^*||_2 > d(P_A^*, P_C^*) = ||P_A^* - P_C^*||_2$ where patch A represents brighter areas with respect to the other ones;
b) $d(P_A^*, P_B^*) = ||P_A^* - P_B^*||_2 < d(P_A^*, P_C^*) = ||P_A^* - P_C^*||_2$ in which patch A has to be considered as darker with respect to the other ones. In both cases, S-function transformation is made by an anticlockwise rotation of the tangent line to S-function (t-line in short) in a crucial point H (where brightness and darkness are concomitant) (Fig. 1) representing the superimposition among S-function and patches A, B and C: $H = (S-function) \cap Patch(A) \cap Patch(B) \cap Patch(C)$. If A is brighter than dark, in $FUHC^4$, P_A^* is closer to the point of maximum brightness, i.e. C_{TOT} (membership value equals to unity), and farther from to point

of maximum darkness darkness, i.e. B_{TOT} (membership values equals to zero), so the t-line slope will be increased by the factor $\frac{d(P_A^*,C_{TOT})}{d(P_A^*,B_{TOT})} = \frac{||P_A^* - C_{TOT}||_2}{||P_A^* - B_{TOT}||_2}$. Dually, if patch A is darker instead of brighter, t-line slope will be decreased by the factor $\frac{d(P_A^*,B_{TOT})}{d(P_A^*,C_{TOT})} = \frac{||P_A^* - B_{TOT}||_2}{||P_A^* - C_{TOT}||_2}$.

S-function transformation for patch A (brighter than dark)
Being $H = (b, (b-a)/(c-a))$, t-line can be written as:

$$\mu(g_{mn}) = \frac{b-a}{c-a} + \frac{2}{c-a}(g_{mn} - b) \tag{8}$$

Considering that $d(P_A^*, P_B^*) > d(P_A^*, P_C^*)$, the new slope $(\mu_t')_{new}$ becomes:

$$(\mu_t')_{new} = (\mu_t')_{old} + (\mu_t')_{old}\frac{d(P_A^*,C_{TOT})}{d(P_A^*,B_{TOT})} = \tag{9}$$

$$\frac{2}{c-a}(1 + d(P_A^*,C_{TOT})/d(P_A^*,B_{TOT}))$$

So, the new tangent line (r-line), written as

$$\mu(g_{mn}) = \frac{b-a}{c-a} + \frac{2}{c-a}(1 + d(P_A^*,C_{TOT})/d(P_A^*,B_{TOT}))(g_{mn} - b) \tag{10}$$

intersects $\mu(g_{mn}) = 0$ and $\mu(g_{mn}) = 1$ in

$$K = \left(b + \frac{a-b}{2 \cdot \left(1 + \frac{d(P_A^*,C_{TOT})}{d(P_A^*,B_{TOT})}\right)}, 0\right)$$

and

$$Z = \left(\left(1 - \frac{b-a}{c-a}\right) \cdot \frac{a-b}{\frac{2}{c-a} \cdot \left(1 + \frac{d(P_A^*,C_{TOT})}{d(P_A^*,B_{TOT})}\right)}, 1\right)$$

respectively where

$$g_K = b + \frac{a-b}{2 \cdot \left(1 + \frac{d(P_A^*,C_{TOT})}{d(P_A^*,B_{TOT})}\right)}$$

and

$$g_Z = \left(1 - \frac{b-a}{c-a}\right) \cdot \frac{a-b}{\frac{2}{c-a} \cdot \left(1 + \frac{d(P_A^*,C_{TOT})}{d(P_A^*,B_{TOT})}\right)}$$

are the gray levels of K and Z. So, the new S-function $\mu(g_{mn})_{new}$ becomes (Fig. 3):

$$\begin{cases} 0 & g_{mn} \leq g_K \\ \frac{b-a}{c-a} + \\ + \frac{2}{c-a} \cdot \left(1 + \frac{d(P_A^*,C_{TOT})}{d(P_A^*,B_{TOT})}\right) \cdot (g_{mn} - g) & g_K \leq g_{mn} \leq g_Z \\ 1 & g_{mn} \leq g_Z \end{cases} \tag{11}$$

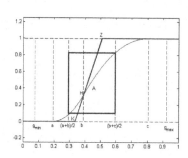

Fig. 3. Modification of the S-function.

Fig. 4. Low contrast image of a religious building with a lot of architectural details.

Defuzzification procedure to obtain the enhanced image
Finally, we need to apply an inverse transformation μ^{-1} to extract the new values of fuzzy membership $(\mu'_t)_{new}$ to come back in the space domain with the enhanced gray levels (g'_{mn}). Specifically, the procedure can be expressed as $\mu^{-1}((\mu'_t)_{new})$.

Defuzzification for Patch A Darker Instead of Brighter. Dually, if $d(P_A^*, P_B^*) < d(P_A^*, P_C^*)$, t-line slope is reduced to the value:

$$(\mu'_t)_{new} = (\mu'_t)_{old} - (\mu'_t)_{old} \cdot \frac{d(P_A^*, B_{TOT})}{d(P_A^*, C_{TOT})} = \qquad (12)$$
$$= \frac{2}{c-a} \cdot \left(1 + \frac{d(P_A^*, B_{TOT})}{d(P_A^*, C_{TOT})}\right)$$

So, S-function transformation and defuzzification are analogous to the above detailed ones as for $d(P_A^*, P_B^*) > d(P_A^*, P_C^*)$.

Table 1. Features of localization of each patch covering S-function

Fuzzy Patches	Localizzation	Support Range
A	around membership value=0.5	$\frac{b+c}{2} - \frac{a+b}{2}$
B	around dark areas	$b - a$
C	around bright areas	$c - b$

3   Results and Discussion

The proposed algorithm have been applied to a wide set of images with different features. In particular, qualitative/quantitative comparisons with histogram equalization and the approach elaborated in [3] have been carried out to evaluate the goodness of the procedure. From Fig. 4 to Fig.19 the most meaningful examples of the elaborations are shown. In particular, Fig.4 refers to a very low contrast image of a religious building with many architectural details; Fig. 8 visualizes a monument showing extended shadowy zones; Fig. 12 concerns a human face poorly lighted and Fig. 16 displays a low contrast seascape. In Table 2, for each image under study, sizes and adaptive setting of S-function parameters are reported. Figs. 5-9-13 and 17 refer to the image obtained by the proposed algorithm, while Figs. 6-10-14 and 18 refer to the treatment by [3]. Finally, Figs. 7-11-15 and 19 show the contrast enhancement by histogram equalization. After treatments, owing to the excessive brightness, the religious building preserves its architectural details but with a loss of sharpness (Fig. 6) and, owing to the low increase of contrast, loss of architectural shadings (Fig. 7). Fig. 8, after the treatment, was subjected to an increase of the contrast with a slight darkening of the shadowy areas and a meaningful increase of the shading details (Fig. 9), while the following elaborations enhance a bit the quality of the image (Fig. 10) and in a remarkable way the contrast (Fig. 11) respectively. Fig. 12 is a quite dark image with a low contrast; after the treatment with the algorithm proposed (Fig. 13), the contrast is sensibly enhanced, even if original obscurity remains. The outlines are well defined with a good presence of luminosity in the top of the hat. Elaborations reported in Figs. 14 and 15 enhance sensibly luminosity and contrast, but there is no trace of such peculiarities in Fig. 13. Finally, the proposed algorithm on the seascape image (Fig. 16) gets good results in terms of contrast enhancement and levels of details in the sea areas, but the perception of fog (Fig. 17) remains ans persists even applying other elaborations (Figs. 18 and 19). Such qualitative analysis is confirmed by qualitative

Fig. 5. Contrast enhancement carried out by the proposed algorithm: good highlighting of dark areas, architectural and chiaroscuro details.

Fig. 6. Contrast enhancement by [3] where an excessive increase of bright with loss of details and chiaroscuro effects are shown.

Fig. 7. Contrast enhancement by histogram equalization where a good preservation of details takes place. Nevertheless, the contrast increase is reduced.

Fig. 8. Particular of a sculpture with a good presence of details.

Fig. 9. The proposed algorithm shows a good differentiation of details both in bright and shadowy areas with shaded effects (poorly highlighted in the original image).

Fig. 10. Contrast enhancemen by [3], which increases the brightness of a lot of details.

Fig. 11. Contrast enhanement by histogram equalization. It comes out a further increase in brightness together with a better contrast in shadowy zones.

Fig. 12. Low contrast human face with high presence of shadowy areas.

Fig. 13. The proposed algorithm brings about a good increase of the contrast keeping the shadiness of the image.

Fig. 14. Contrast enhancement by [3] where details, hardly recognizable in the starting-image, are here in the limelight.

Fig. 15. Contrast enhancement by histogram equalization: light increase of the performance with respect to the proposed algorithm.

Fig. 16. Low contrast seascape with presence of details and background line extremely darkened.

Fig. 17. Contrast enhancement by the proposed procedure. Good global image enhancement, with clearness of the details of the rocks and a remarkable reduction of the fog.

Fig. 18. Contrast enhancement by [3]. Image enhancement acceptable even if the foggy effect remains.

Fig. 19. Good contrast quality obtained by histogram equalization.

evaluations of $MSE/PSNR$ as reported in Table 2. If $N \times M$ is the number of pixel contaned in the image, and referring to the i-th pixel in the original image (g_{mn}) and in the image to evaluate (g'_{mn}), MSE can be computed as $MSE = \frac{1}{N \times M} \sum_{m=1}^{N} \sum_{n=1}^{M} (g_{mn} - g'_{mn})^2$. Moreover, if L is the dinamic range of the pixel values (tipically equal to $2^n - 1, n = bits/pixel$), PSNR gets the form $PSNR = 10 \cdot log_{10} \frac{L^2}{MSE}$.

Table 2. Adaptive setting of S-function parameters for each approach and quantitative evaluations of the contrat enhancement quality

Image	Size	a	b	c	MSE/PSNR proposed algorithm	MSE/PSNR approach [3]	MSE/PSNR histogram equalization
Church	480 × 320	39	85	136	1229/17.26	1421/16.638	343/22.81
Statue	480 × 320	19	55	145	924/18.508	739/19.478	895/18.645
Male Face	480 × 320	37	128	177	1153/17.546	922/18.517	883/18.705
Seascape	480 × 320	4	17	122	1224/17.657	1261/17.157	1039/17.998

4   Conclusions

The proposed approach may find wide applications in image processing, pattern recognition and computer vision. In particular, contrast enhancement of the image quality represents the first step in image processing. To face this topic, Scientific Community has consolidated two main categories of approach: direct and indirect ones, both producing noteworthy results in several application fields. Starting form the assumption that gray levels structure of an image can be formalized by fuzzy algoritms for contrast enhancement, the presence of fuzziness in the informative content of an image needs *ad-hoc* procedures for elaborating suitable protocols for getting satisfactory performance. In addition, the increasing requirement from non technical experts to hand simple contrast enhancement protocols (for example, medical and paramedical staff in biomedical ambit) it is imperative to tune intelligible algorithms characterized by a low computational complexity (useful for real-time applications). For the reasons mentioned above, the authors have proposed a new geometrical adaptive approach to get the purpose. In particular, has been here presented an indirect fuzzy approach to enhance the contrast, based on statistical-geometrical considerations and entropic formulations, to modify the histogram distribution of the original gray levels of an image: an adaptive setting of the parameters of a properly defined S-function has been done, which reduces the possibility over and/or under enhancement. The experimental results can be considered, both qualitatively and qualitatively, particularly encouraging in sight of further studies in this direction.

References

1. Rajal, J.S.: An Approach for Image Enhancement Using Fuzzy Inference System for Noisy Image. Journal of Engineering Computers & Applied Sciences **2**(5), 5–11 (2013)
2. Hasikin, K.: Adaptive Fuzzy Contrast Factor Enhancement Technique for Low Contrast and Nonuniform Illumination Images. Springer, London (2012)
3. Cheng, H.D., Xu, H.: A Novel Fuzzy Logic Approach to Contrast Enhancement. Pattern Recognition **33**(5), 809–819 (2000)
4. Khera, B.S., Pharwaha, A.P.S.: Integration of Fuzzy Wavelet Approaches Towards Mammogram Contrast Enhancement. Journal of the Institution of Engineers (INDIA). Springer, Series B, London (2012)
5. Hasikin, K, Isa, N.A.B.: Enhancement of the low contrast image fuzzy set theory. In: Proc. International Conference on Computer Modelling and Simulation, Cambridge, UK (2012)
6. Magudeeswaran, V., Ravichandran, C.G.: Fuzzy-Logic Based Histogram Equalization for Image Contrast Enhancement. American Journal of Intelligent Systems **2**(6), 141–147 (2012)
7. Kannan, P., Deepa, S., Ramakrishnam, R.: Contrast Enhancement of Sports Images Using Two Comparative Approaches. Mathematical Problems in Engineering, Hindawi Corporation **4**, 1–10 (2013)
8. Chaira, T., Ray, A.K.: Fuzzy Image Processing and Applications with MatLab. CRC Press, Taylor and Francis Group, London (2010)
9. Jahne, B., Hne, B.: Digital Image Processing. Springer, London (2012)
10. Gopsh, S.K.: Digital Image Processing. Alpha Science International Ltd, London (2012)
11. Gonzales, R.C., Woods, R.E.: Digital Image Processing. Prentice Hall, New York (2002)
12. Zenga, B.M., et al.: Improving Histogram-Based Image Contrast Enhancement Using Gray-level Information Histogram with Application to X-Ray Images. Optik **123**, 511–520 (2012)
13. Balasubramaniam, S., Govindaswarmy, U.: Novel Processing Technique in the Computer Aided Detection of Breast Cancer. Journal of Computer Science **8**, 1957–1960 (2012)
14. Celik, T., Tjahjadi, T.: Automatic Image Equalization and Contrast Enhancement Using Gaussian Mixture Modeling. IEEE Transaction on Image Processing **21**(1), 145–156 (2012)
15. Kosko, B.: Fuzzy Engineering. Prentice Hall, New York (1997)

Iris Recognition Using Discrete Cosine Transform and Relational Measures

Aditya Nigam[1,2]($\boxtimes$), Balender Kumar[1], Jyoti Triyar[1], and Phalguni Gupta[1,3]

[1] Department of Computer Science and Engineering,
Indian Institute of Technology Kanpur, Kanpur 208016, UP, India
`aditya@iitmandi.ac.in`, `{naditya,balendk,jyotit,pg}@cse.iitk.ac.in`
[2] School of Computing and Electrical Engineering,
Indian Institute of Technology Mandi, Mandi 175001, HP, India
[3] National Institute of Technical Teacher's & Research,
Salt Lake, Kolkata 700106, India

Abstract. Iris is one of the most discriminative biometric trait because it has random discriminating texture which does not change much, over a long time period. They are unique for all individuals, even for twins and the left and right eyes of the same individuals. In this paper an iris recognition system is presented that does iris segmentation, normalization, segregating of unwanted parts like occlusion, specular reflection and noise. Later iris images are enhanced and feature extraction and matching is performed. Iris features are extracted using Discrete Cosine Transform (DCT) and Relational Measure (RM). Later fusion of the dissimilarity scores of two feature extraction techniques has been proposed to get better performance. The results have been shown on large publicly available databases like CASIA-4.0 Interval, Lamp and self-collected IITK. The proposed fusion have achieved encouraging results.

Keywords: DCT · Sobel operator · Score-level fusion

1 Introduction

Personal authentication is a prime social requirement. Biometric based solutions are found to be much better than the traditional system of using passwords or identity card for authentication because they are easier to use and harder to circumvent. Most commonly used biometric traits in such systems are finger-print, facial features, iris, gait, hand-writing, retina, palm-prints, ear etc. The human iris is an annular part lying between pupil and sclera, and has good amount of irregular characteristics like freckles, furrows, ridges, stripes, etc. These characteristics are unique to each individual, even to different eyes of the same person. Also these textures of iris remain stable during lifetime of an individual. Moreover, it is an internal organ and externally visible so non-invasive acquisition can be done. Also they are much safely protected from damage as compared to fingerprint and palmprint.

© Springer International Publishing Switzerland 2015
G. Azzopardi and N. Petkov (Eds.): CAIP 2015, Part II, LNCS 9257, pp. 506–517, 2015.
DOI: 10.1007/978-3-319-23117-4_44

However, there are some challenges while using iris as biometric trait, like occlusion(hiding of data) due to eyelashes, eyelids and specular reflection and noise, which makes iris recognition inaccurate. In the proposed recognition system, first the image is acquired which is then segmented, normalized, denoised and enhanced. The features are extracted using Discrete Cosine Transform (DCT) and Relational Measures (RM). The matching scores of both the approaches are fused using weighted average. Figure 1 shows the flow-chart of the entire proposed iris recognition system. This paper is organized as follows. Section 2 gives an overview of some of the previous approaches used in iris recognition. Section 3 describes the proposed approach for the recognition system. Experimental results on standard databases are shown in Section 4. Conclusions are given in the last section.

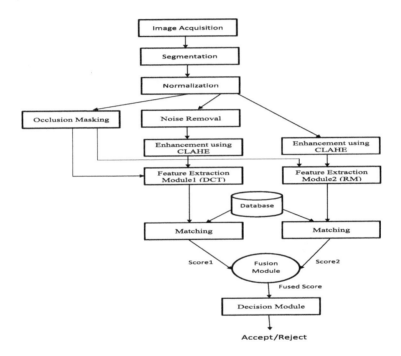

Fig. 1. Overview of the Proposed Iris Recognition System

2   Literature Review

Iris is one of the most efficient and accurate biometric trait. It can provides high accuracy and less error rate than other biometric traits like fingerprint, palmprint, ear and face. Possibly, Flom and Safir [6] are the first one to propose the concept of iris recognition system. Daugman has used the concept of multi-scale Gabor filters to extract iris features [4], [3]. Despite of many advantages of iris, the system should also work over noisy iris images. In [2], [5], Noisy

Iris Recognition Integrated Scheme(N-IRIS) has been proposed. Two local feature extraction techniques, i.e., Linear Binary Pattern (LBP) and Binary Large Objects(BLOBs) have been combined to design the scheme. Blobs are extracted from iris image using different LoG (Laplacian of Gaussian) filter banks which removes noise from the image as well as helps in better detection of blob. This feature extraction approach is invariant to rotation, translation as well as scale.

In [7], [12], the Gabor filter alongwith its response to the image has been discussed. Depending on different spatial frequencies and orientations, Gabor filter can be used effectively for extracting features. Also as the number of Gabor filters for extracting features increases, the more effective discriminative feature vector is extracted. In [9], a new approach of extracting iris features using local frequency variations between adjacent patches of enhanced normalized iris image has been proposed. Overlapping rectangular blocks with some orientation are considered as patches. In this, the patches are averaged widthwise to reduce the noise that gives 1-D signal on which window is applied to reduce spectral leakage and then Fast Fourier Transform (FFT) is applied to obtain spectral coefficients. The differences between the frequency magnitudes of adjacent patches are binarized using zero crossings. This approach gives better performance parameters than other existing state-of-the-art approaches of [3] and [8].

3   Proposed Technique

The iris segmentation is done using the technique proposed in [1]. Iris region is normalized to a fixed size strip in order to deal with iris dilations. One of the major hurdles in iris recognition is occlusion (hiding of iris) due to eyelids, eyelashes, specular reflection and shadows. It hides most of the useful iris texture and introduces irrelevant parts like eyelids and eyelashes which are not even an integral part of every iris image.

3.1   Occlusion Mask Creation

Occlusion detection is done in three steps: eyelid detection followed by eyelash and reflection detection.

[A] **Eyelid Detection:** Statistically, upper eyelid can be found at the center of left half while lower eyelid at the center of the right half of the normalized image. Eyelids have almost uniform texture and a boundary flooded with eyelashes and shadows. These challenges have motivated us to use region-growing approach to determine the eyelids. It uses only the texture information to separate eyelid region from the rest. Region growing is a morphological flooding operation which helps to find objects of uniform texture. A set S of seed points is selected from the image lying in the region S_d, that is required to be detected. All pixels in 8-neighborhood of any pixel in the set S are checked for their intensity difference with the mean intensity of the set S. Pixels which are having this difference less than a certain threshold are added to S. This process is iterated until no pixel

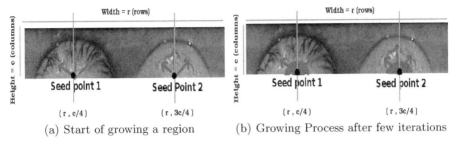

(a) Start of growing a region   (b) Growing Process after few iterations

Fig. 2. Application of Region-Growing

can be added further. Finally, S covers the desired region S_d. Figure 2 shows the results of the region-growing algorithm on an image after a few iterations.

Eyelid detection from the normalized iris strip of size $r \times c$ requires two seed points for region-growing, one for each lower and upper eyelid. They are selected as $(r, \frac{c}{4})$ and $(r, \frac{3c}{4})$ for upper and lower eyelid respectively as shown in Fig. 2. These two seed points are chosen because after normalization, upper and lower eyelids are centered mostly at $\left(\frac{\pi}{2}\right)^{\circ}$ and $\left(\frac{3\pi}{2}\right)^{\circ}$ angles $w.r.t.$ x-axis. Region-growing begins with these seeds using a low threshold and expands the region until a dissimilar region is encountered. This gives the expected lower and upper eyelid regions. Detected eyelids are shown in Figure 3. If region grows beyond a limit, it indicates that there is no eyelid. Finally, a binary mask is generated in which all eyelid pixels are set to 1, as shown in Figure 3.

(a) Normalized Image   (b) Eyelid Mask

Fig. 3. Eyelid Regions: Arrows Denote the Direction for Region-Growing

[B] Eyelash Detection: There are two types of eyelashes: separable and multiple. Separable eyelashes are like thin threads whereas multiple eyelashes constitute a shadow like region. Eyelashes have high contrast with their surrounding pixels, but having low intensity. As a result, standard deviation of gray values within a small region around separable eyelashes is high. The standard deviation for every pixel in a normalized image is computed using its 8-neighborhood. It is high in areas where there are separable eyelashes. Multiple eyelashes may have high standard deviation, but they also have dark intensity value. Hence, the low gray value intensity is also given some weight. The computed standard deviation for each pixel is normalized using $max - min$ normalization method and is saved in a $2D$-array SD. If SD is used alone for segregating eyelash regions, then multiple eyelashes may not be detected and iris texture which has large standard deviation at some points gets wrongly classified as eyelashes. Hence for each pixel, a fused value $F(i,j)$ is computed which considers both the computed standard deviation as well as the gray value intensity of that pixel defined as :

$$F(i,j) = 0.5 \times SD(i,j) + 0.5 \times (1 - N(i,j)) \tag{1}$$

where $N(i,j)$ is the normalized gray intensity values $(0-1)$ and $SD(i,j)$ is the standard deviation computed using 8 neighborhood pixel intensities for the pixel (i,j). This fused value $F(i,j)$ boosts up the gap between eyelash and non-eyelash part. The image histogram F_H of F has two distinct clusters: a cluster of low values of F consisting of the iris pixels and the second cluster with high values of F representing eyelash pixels. To identify the two clusters, Otsu thresholding is applied on the histogram F_H of F to obtain binary eyelash mask. It determines two clusters in a histogram by considering all possible pairs of clusters and chooses that clustering threshold that minimizes the intra-cluster variance. It thus separates the eyelash portion from the iris portion. The detected eyelash of an iris image is shown in Figure 4(c).

[C] **Reflection Detection:** Pixels which exceed a threshold value in gray-scale image are declared as reflections because reflections are very bright in every acquisition setting. Also, since occlusion due to reflection is not a major component, it is chosen not to do complex computation to remove reflection. Detected reflection from a sample image is shown in Figure 4(d). A binary mask $Mask_{reflection}$ (reflection mask) is generated in which pixels affected by reflection are set to 1. Final occlusion mask is generated by addition (logical OR) of the binary masks of eyelid, eyelash and reflection. Detected occlusion of a sample image is shown in Figure 4.

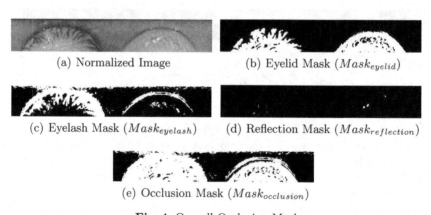

(a) Normalized Image   (b) Eyelid Mask ($Mask_{eyelid}$)

(c) Eyelash Mask ($Mask_{eyelash}$)   (d) Reflection Mask ($Mask_{reflection}$)

(e) Occlusion Mask ($Mask_{occlusion}$)

Fig. 4. Overall Occlusion Mask

3.2   Iris Enhancement

The iris texture is enhanced in such a way that it increases its richness as well as its discriminative power. The iris ROI is divided into blocks and the mean

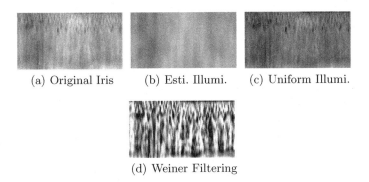

(a) Original Iris   (b) Esti. Illumi.   (c) Uniform Illumi.

(d) Weiner Filtering

Fig. 5. Iris Texture Enhancement

of each block is considered as the coarse illumination of that block. This mean is expanded to the original block size as shown in Fig. 5(b). Selection of block size plays an important role. It should be such that the mean of the block truly represents the illumination effect of the block. So, larger block may produce improper estimate. We have seen that a block size of 8×8 is the best choice for our experiment. The estimated illumination of each block is subtracted from the corresponding block of the original image to obtain the uniformly illuminated *ROI* as shown in Fig. 5(c). The contrast of the resultant *ROI* is enhanced using Contrast Limited Adaptive Histogram Equalization (*CLAHE*). It removes the artificially induced blocking effect using bilinear interpolation and enhances the contrast of image without introducing much external noise. Finally, Wiener filter is applied to reduce constant power additive noise and the enhanced iris texture is obtained shown in Figure 5(d).

3.3 Feature Extraction

The main aim of iris recognition system is to minimize intra-class differences and to maximize the inter-class differences. In this paper, two different types of feature extraction techniques *viz.* DCT and RM are discussed. The matching scores of both the techniques are fused by taking weighted average of their scores.

[A] Feature Extraction Using DCT: This paper proposes the feature extraction using DCT with some parameters optimized for best performance. A non-conventional technique of applying 1-D DCT on overlapping blocks of particular size for extracting feature variations has been proposed. It is observed that DCT coefficients are robust when applied over values lying between -128 to 127, so 128 is subtracted from each pixel value of the enhanced normalized image. This results in a matrix levelled off by 128 from each pixel entry such that all entries in the matrix lie between -128 to 127.

[A.1] Segmentation Into Rectangular Blocks: The levelled-off matrix is divided into rectangular blocks of size $M \times N$ with overlapping of half the width between vertically adjacent blocks and overlapping of half the length between horizontally adjacent blocks as shown in Figure 6(a). These rectangular blocks form the basis of extracting features in our proposed approach. Parameters like length and width of rectangular blocks are tuned to achieve optimum performance.

[A.2] Coding of Rectangular Blocks: The rectangular block is first averaged across its width. This gives a one-dimensional intensity signal of size $1 \times N$. Formally, a rectangular block of width M and length N, averaged across width gives a 1-D intensity signal R' of size $1 \times N$ which can be represented by

$$R'_j = \sum_{k=1}^{M} R_{j,k} \quad where \ j = 1, 2, ..., N \tag{2}$$

Averaging smoothens the image and reduces the effect of noise and other image artifacts. The obtained intensity signal R' is windowed using Hanning window of size N to reduce spectral leakage during the transformation. Application of averaging and windowing also results in reduction of resolution of the image in the horizontal direction. Also image registration becomes easier for broad patches, thereby making iris recognition rotation invariant [10]. The generated 1-D DCT coefficient matrix CM of each rectangular block is binarized using zero crossing to give a binary sub-feature vector B as given below :

$$B_j = \begin{cases} 1 & \text{if } CM_j > 0 \quad \text{where } j=1, 2, ..., N \\ 0 & \text{otherwise} \end{cases} \tag{3}$$

A second level occlusion mask based on the feature vector calculation is generated as follows: The corresponding occlusion mask *occmask* is also divided into blocks in the same way as the levelled-off matrix. The summation across its width gives a block or patch of size $1 \times N$. If the summation along its width is more than 80% of the width of the block (M), then the bit is masked (set to 1) in the second level occlusion mask; otherwise it is left unmasked. The next bit is then added to the next row and so on. It gives a block of size $N \times 1$. This is done for each overlapping $M \times N$ block in the occlusion mask. Second level mask is required as the feature vector is block-based and not pixel-based. Figure 6(b) illustrates the steps involved in generating feature vector of enhanced normalized iris image. The steps to calculate the feature vector and second level occlusion mask is summarized in Algorithm 1.

[B] Feature Extraction Using Relational Measures. The relational measures approach has been used as second feature extraction technique. Relational Measures are features which are based on relational operators like $<$, $>$ and $=$. Unlike giving the exact difference between any two quantities, the concept of relational measures is based on finding the relative difference between the two. This encoding into bits is fast and also takes less memory. Also the iris texture has lot of variations in texture; so relational measures concept can be used to encode iris. Vertically and horizontally overlapping regions are chosen from the enhanced normalized image. A central region of size $b \times b$ is chosen. Its four

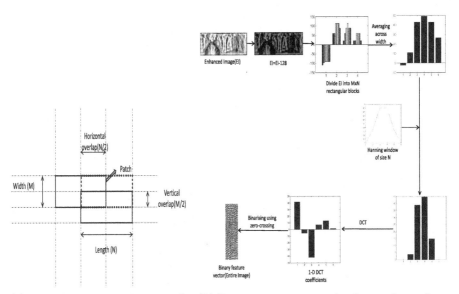

(a)   Overlapping   Rectangular (b) Feature vector generation from enhanced nor-
Blocks and parameters   malized iris image (width M=4, length N=6)

Fig. 6. Feature Extraction using DCT

neighboring regions of same size is taken but at a particular distance d, where d is large as compared to b. A symmetric 2-D Gaussian filter centrally clipped to size $b \times b$ is put and convoluted over each of these five regions. The response of central region is compared to each of its neighboring regions. If the response of central region is greater than its neighbor, then the bit is encoded as 1, otherwise it is set to 0. In this way, four bits of code are obtained for each central region named as RM bits. This is then iterated for other vertical and horizontal overlapping regions over the entire image. All such RM bits concatenated together gives the 2-D binary template. Second level mask is also generated from the raw occlusion mask of iris based on the feature vector calculation. If the central block has more than 80% of the occluded pixels, then the RM bits for that block are encoded as [1 1 1 1], i.e., masked; otherwise it is encoded as [0 0 0 0], i.e., unmasked. This is repeated for overlapping central blocks according to parameters chosen. This second-level mask is required because the feature vector is block-based and not pixel-based.

3.4   Feature Matching

The feature vector templates and corresponding second level occlusion masks are used in matching. Matching between two iris images using their respective feature vector templates and second level occlusion masks can be done by computing a dissimilarity score between them. The dissimilarity score is calculated using hamming distance metric. Consider two templates t_1 and t_2 of same size, say

---

Algorithm 1 $FeatExtract(I, occmask)$

Require: Enhanced Normalized image I of size $Rows \times Cols$, Occlusion Mask $occmask$ of same size as I, M is the width of the rectangular block, N is the length of the rectangular block

Ensure: Feature vector template $Feat$ and Second level occlusion mask $Mask$

1: $I_{new} \leftarrow$ Level off image by subtracting 128 from each pixel value
2: Initialize a variable $HannFil$ to a Hanning window of size N
3: $Feat \leftarrow AllocateZero$
4: $Mask \leftarrow AllocateZero$
5: Divide I_{new} and $occmask$ into rectangular blocks $B_{i,j}$ and $occBlk_{i,j}$ of size $M \times N$ with overlapping of $M/2$ between vertically adjacent blocks and overlapping of $N/2$ between horizontally adjacent blocks
6: **for** each rectangular block $B_{i,j}$ and $occBlk_{i,j}$ **do**
7:     $MeanBlk_i \leftarrow$ Compute the mean of $B_{i,j}$ across width
8:     $HannBlk_i \leftarrow$ ElementWiseMultiplication $(HannFil, \text{Transpose of } MeanBlk_i)$
9:     $dctBlk_i \leftarrow DCT(HannBlk)$ //Extract the 1-D DCT coefficients
10:    Binarize the 1-D DCT coefficients using zero-crossing to give sub-feature vector f_i
11:    //Calculating Second level occlusion mask
12:    $sumarr_i \leftarrow$ Compute the sum of $occBlk_{i,j}$ across width
13:    **for** each sum in $sumarr_i$ **do**
14:      **if** $sum > 0.8 * M$ **then**
15:        $resMask \leftarrow 1$ //bit masked
16:      **else**
17:        $resMask \leftarrow 0$ //bit unmasked
18:      **end if**
19:      Concatenate the bits resMask vertically to give a sub-mask $maskBlk_i$
20:    **end for**
21:    Concatenate the sub-features $\{f_i\}$ to give the final feature vector $Feat$
22:    Concatenate the sub-masks $\{maskBlk_i\}$ to give the final second-level occlusion mask $Mask$
23: **end for**
24: Return $(Feat, Mask)$

$X \times Y$ and their second level occlusion masks o_1 and o_2 of same size as that of their feature vector templates, then Hamming distance hd between the templates is calculated using the formula

$$hd(t_1, t_2, o_1, o_2) = \frac{\Sigma_{i=1}^{X} \Sigma_{j=1}^{Y} [t_1(i,j) \oplus t_2(i,j)] \mid [o_1(i,j) + o_2(i,j)]}{X \times Y - \Sigma_{i=1}^{X} \Sigma_{j=1}^{Y} [o_1(i,j) + o_2(i,j)]} \tag{4}$$

where the operators $\oplus$, $\mid$ and $+$ represent binary XOR, NAND and OR operations respectively. Second level occlusion masks are considered while calculating the dissimilarity score between the two iris images. It enables us to perform matching only in valid bits and ignore the occluded parts of iris image. The value of hd is zero if both feature templates are similar, i.e., have all bits of same value. Hence for genuine matching hd should be low.

[3.4.1] Robustness Against Rotation: While acquiring image, there can be some amount of rotation in the image. Rotation of the eye in Cartesian coordinate-space corresponds to horizontal translation in the normalized image. When a probe template is matched with a gallery template, the gallery template is circularly shifted in horizontal direction to get the minimum hamming distance which is taken as the final dissimilarity score. When gallery template is rotated, its corresponding second level mask is also rotated.

4   Experimental Results

The proposed iris recognition system has been tested on two publicly available CASIA-4.0 Interval and CASIA-4.0 Lamp databases and also over our own IITK database. The iris database is divided into two sets - **gallery set** and **probe set**. All images of the probe set are matched against the images of the gallery set. System performance is tested in terms of CRR and EER [11].

[A] Databases: CASIA-4.0 Interval consists of 2639 images of 249 subjects of size 320×280 pixels taken in two sessions. First three images are taken in the gallery set and rest in the probe set. So total there are 1047 gallery images and 1508 probe images in this database. CASIA-4.0 Lamp Database consists of 16,212 images of 411 people of size 640×480 pixels collected in one session with variable illumination conditions with lamp being switched on/off. Each subject has 20 images. First 10 images per subject have been taken in the gallery set and rest 10 images in the probe set. So total there are 7830 images in both the gallery and the probe sets in this database. The IITK Database consists of 20,420 images of 1021 subjects of size 640×480 pixels collected in two sessions. In each session, 10 images per subject have been collected, with 5 images for each eye. Images in first session are taken in the gallery set and images of second session are considered in the probe set. So finally there are 10,210 images in both the gallery and the probe sets in this database.

[B] Performance Analysis of the Proposed System: The fusion of matching scores of DCT approach and RM approach is done on the basis of weights determined empirically which gives the best system performance. All parametric evaluation is done over a small validation set consisting of only first 1000 images of that dataset optimized $w.r.t$ performance. Higher weight is given to matching scores of DCT approach as compared RM because the DCT approach performance is better than RM. Table 1 shows the individual performance parameters of the both approaches as well as fusion performance parameters.

In both DCT and RM approaches, some matchings have been discarded in which the individual mask or the combined mask is more than 85% of the image size. This has been done to avoid inaccuracies caused due to heavy occlusion. So in all, around 1.5% of the overall matchings are discarded. The $Rank - 10$ accuracy of the proposed system over all databases got saturated to 100%.

[C] Comparative Performance Analysis: The proposed approach has been compared with that of Daugman's recognition system [3]. All the pre-processing

Table 1. Fused Result with weightage given to matching scores of DCT and RM

Database	Proposed DCT		RM		Weightage		Fused	
	CRR(%)	EER(%)	CRR(%)	EER(%)	DCT	RM	CRR(%)	EER(%)
Interval	99.40	1.81	99.07	2.26	0.75	0.25	99.40	1.52
Lamp	98.69	3.89	98.69	4.21	0.72	0.28	98.91	2.91
IITK	98.46	2.07	98.66	2.12	0.60	0.40	98.92	1.52

Table 2. Comparison of Results on various Databases with different approaches

Database	CRR(%)				EER(%)			
	Gabor	RM	DCT	Fused	Gabor	RM	DCT	Fused
Interval	99.47	99.07	99.40	99.40	1.88	2.26	1.81	1.52
Lamp	98.90	98.69	98.69	98.91	5.59	4.21	3.89	2.91
IITK	98.85	98.66	98.46	98.92	2.49	2.12	2.07	1.52

stages including segmentation, normalization and occlusion masking have been
kept common. They differ only in their feature extraction phase. The matching
scores of both DCT and RM approaches have been fused using weighted average
to get better performance results. All these approaches have been tested on all
three databases. Table 2 shows the performance metrics of the four approaches
(Gabor, DCT, RM and Fusion approaches). The ROC graphs of the system on
all three databases comparing the four approaches are shown in Figure 7(a),
Figure 7(b) and Figure 7(c) respectively. From these figures, it can be seen
that DCT approach performers better than Gabor-filtering and RM approaches.
The fusion approach of DCT and RM has the best performance because weak
classifier fusion works better than individuals.

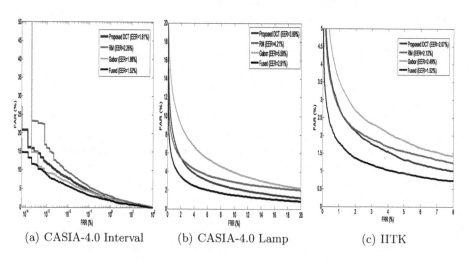

(a) CASIA-4.0 Interval   (b) CASIA-4.0 Lamp   (c) IITK

Fig. 7. ROC Graph based Performance Comparison of all the four approaches

5   Conclusions

This paper presents an iris recognition system which has been tested on three databases to claim its superior performance. It has presented the segmentation, normalization, occlusion mask detection, denoising and enhancement as preprocessing steps. A non-conventional technique based on 1-D DCT has been used to extract robust iris features. Another feature extraction technique of Relational Measures (RM) is used that is based on calculating intensity relationships between local regions and encoding them on the basis of relative difference of intensities. Matching of images is done by using Hamming distance metric which gives a dissimilarity score. Score-level fusion technique is used to compensate for some images which have been rejected by one classifier while accepted by other. Such a fusion has shown much improved accuracy with less error rates.

References

1. Bendale, A., Nigam, A., Prakash, S., Gupta, P.: Iris segmentation using improved hough transform. In: Huang, D.-S., Gupta, P., Zhang, X., Premaratne, P. (eds.) ICIC 2012. CCIS, vol. 304, pp. 408–415. Springer, Heidelberg (2012)
2. Chenhong, L., Zhaoyang, L.: Efficient iris recognition by computing discriminable textons, vol. 2, pp. 1164–1167 (2005)
3. Daugman, J.: High confidence visual recognition of persons by a test of statistical independence. IEEE Transactions on Pattern Analysis and Machine Intelligence 15(11), 1148–1161 (1993)
4. Daugman, J.: Statistical richness of visual phase information: update on recognizing persons by iris patterns. International Journal of Computer Vision 45(1), 25–38 (2001)
5. De Marsico, M., Nappi, M., Riccio, D.: Noisy iris recognition integrated scheme. Pattern Recogn. Lett. 33(8), 1006–1011 (2012)
6. Flom, L., Safir, A.: Iris recognition system, February 3, 1987. US Patent 4,641,349
7. Grigorescu, S.E., Petkov, N., Kruizinga, P.: Comparison of texture features based on gabor filters. IEEE Transactions on Image Processing 11(10), 1160–1167 (2002)
8. Ma, L., Tan, T., Wang, Y., Zhang, D.: Efficient iris recognition by characterizing key local variations. IEEE Transactions on Image Processing 13(6), 739–750 (2004)
9. Monro, D., Zhang, Z.: An effective human iris code with low complexity, vol. 3, p. III-277 (2005)
10. Monro, D., Zhang, Z.: An effective human iris code with low complexity. In: IEEE International Conference on Image Processing, ICIP 2005, vol. 3, p. III-277. IEEE (2005)
11. Nigam, A., Gupta, P.: Iris recognition using consistent corner optical flow. In: Lee, K.M., Matsushita, Y., Rehg, J.M., Hu, Z. (eds.) ACCV 2012, Part I. LNCS, vol. 7724, pp. 358–369. Springer, Heidelberg (2013)
12. Prasad, V.S.N., Domke, J.: Gabor filter visualization (2005)

3D Texture Recognition for RGB-D Images

Guoqiang Zhong, Xin Mao, Yaxin Shi, and Junyu Dong$^{(\boxtimes)}$

Department of Computer Science and Technology, Ocean University of China,
238 Songling Road, Qingdao 266100, China
{gqzhong,dongjunyu}@ouc.edu.cn, helloxinxiang@gmail.com,
Yaxin.Shi@hotmail.com

Abstract. In this paper, we present a novel 3D object recognition system. In this system, we capture both the color and depth information of 3D objects using *Kinect*, and represent them in RGB-D images. To alleviate the deformations and partial defects of the obtained 3D surface textures, 3D texture reconstruction techniques are applied. In order to improve the recognition accuracy, we exploit metric learning methods for the K-nearest neighbor (KNN) classifier. Promising results are obtained on a real-world 3D object recognition application.

Keywords: 3D object recognition · RGB-D images · 3D texture recognition · 3D texture reconstruction · Metric learning

1 Introduction

Three-dimensional (3D) object recognition is a long standing and challenging problem in computer vision. Nowadays, 3D object recognition techniques have been closely related to various smart products, such as intelligent robots and video surveillance systems. In the process of recognition, however, the obtained 3D surface textures always suffer from deformations and partial defects, due to improper camera angle or illumination. This greatly reduces the effectiveness of the captured information of 3D objects, and directly affects the recognition rate. Therefore, developing methods that can correctly recognize 3D surface textures remains an active research area in computer vision, which is also our focus in this paper.

In recent years, with the emergence of cheap equipments that can simultaneously capture both color and depth information of the scenes, more and more RGB-D images have been collected to exploit the 3D object recognition problems. In this work, we use *Kinect*, to obtain the color and depth information of 3D objects. Kinect is a line of motion sensing input devices by Microsoft. It is a horizontal bar connected to a small base with a motorized pivot. Fig. 1 shows the captured color image and depth image of a 3D object by Kinect.

To alleviate the deformations and partial defects of the 3D surface textures obtained by Kinect, 3D texture reconstruction techniques, such as background modelling using Gaussian mixture model [13] and texture extraction using the

© Springer International Publishing Switzerland 2015
G. Azzopardi and N. Petkov (Eds.): CAIP 2015, Part II, LNCS 9257, pp. 518–528, 2015.
DOI: 10.1007/978-3-319-23117-4_45

(a) Color image.   (b) Depth image.

Fig. 1. Color image and depth image captured by Kinect. For sub-figure (b), it's better to be viewed by zooming in.

region growing algorithm [1], are applied. The local binary patterns (LBP) approach [11] is used to extract features from the reconstructed 3D texture images. In order to improve the recognition accuracy, we exploit metric learning methods for the K-nearest neighbor (KNN) classifier. To evaluate the effectiveness of the proposed system, we test it on a real-world 3D object recognition application.

The rest of this paper is organized as follows: In Section 2, we introduce some related work on 3D object recognition and metric learning. In Section 3, we present the proposed 3D texture recognition system in detail. The experimental results on a real-world 3D object recognition application are reported in section 4, while Section 5 concludes this paper with remarks and future work.

2   Related Work

In this section, we review some related work on 3D object recognition and metric learning.

2.1   3D Object Recognition

Recent developments in techniques for modeling, digitizing and visualizing 3D objects has led to an explosion in the number of available 3D models in the computer vision area. Pontil and Verri [12] first used linear SVMs for 3D object recognition. The proposed system does not require feature extraction and performs recognition on high dimensional representations of images. To recognize 3D face images, Xu et al. proposed to use 3D eigenfaces with K-nearest neighbor classifiers [20]. Their approach reached a recognition rate around 70% when tested on a dataset of 120 subjects. Hetzel et al. [5] explored a view-based approach to recognize free-form objects in range images. A set of local features were used.

By combining those features in a multidimensional histogram, highly discriminant classifiers could be obtained without the need for segmentation. In recent year, Nair and Hinton [9] proposed a new type of deep belief nets (DBNs) [6] for 3D object recognition. The proposed model was a third-order Boltzmann machine, trained using a hybrid algorithm that combines both generative and discriminative gradients. Although these methods have been successfully applied to 3D object recognition tasks, they have a common shortage that the depth information of the 3D objects have been ignored. Depth information carries important features of 3D objects, to some extent, which is helpful for object recognition problems. Many recent papers are based on this idea and have got promising results in their experiments. For example, in [3], a robot system exploits to use a Kinect to improve the object recognition capability thanks to depth-map, while in [4], depth-map are employed for face detection problems. In our work, we use Kinect to capture both the color information and depth information of 3D objects, and combine them for the 3D texture recognition tasks.

To combine depth images with intensity images for 3D face recognition, Tsalakanidou et al. made two attempts. In their first attempt, they used eigenfaces and got a recognition rate of 99% on a database of 40 subjects [16]. In a second attempt, embedded hidden markov models were used to the combined depth images and intensity images [15]. This approach had an error rate between 7% and 9%. Recently, Lai et al. [8] introduced a large-scale, hierarchical multiview object data set collected using an RGB-D camera. The data set contains 300 objects organized into 51 categories. In this paper, we mainly focus on 3D object recognition based on surface textures, and metric learning techniques are used to improve recognition accuracy.

2.2 Metric Learning

Distance metric is an important component in many learning algorithms, such as K-nearest neighbor classification and K-means clustering. Since about a decade ago, many research papers [2,18,19,21] have shown the improvement of well-designed distance metric over the standard Euclidean distance. In this work, to leverage the recognition accuracy, we adopt metric learning techniques before the K-nearest neighbor classifier is applied. However, in order to guarantee the learned matrix is positive semi-definite (PSD), the computational complexity of most of the existing metric learning approaches is very high. Hence, we choose the information-theoretic metric learning (ITML) method [2], which updates the learned matrix based on pairwise data.

The objective function of ITML is

$$\min_{\mathbf{A} \succeq 0} \ D_{ld}(\mathbf{A}, \mathbf{A}_0)$$
$$s.t. \ \ \text{tr}(\mathbf{A}(\mathbf{x}_i - \mathbf{x}_j)(\mathbf{x}_i - \mathbf{x}_j)^T) \leq u, \quad (i,j) \in \mathfrak{S},$$
$$\text{tr}(\mathbf{A}(\mathbf{x}_i - \mathbf{x}_j)(\mathbf{x}_i - \mathbf{x}_j)^T) \geq l, \quad (i,j) \in \mathfrak{D}, \quad (1)$$

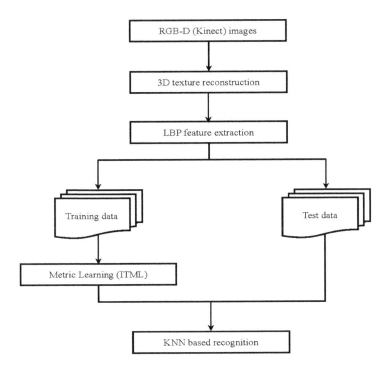

Fig. 2. Flowchart of the proposed 3D texture recognition system.

where $\mathbf{A} \succeq 0$ means that $\mathbf{A}$ is a PSD matrix, $D_{ld}(\mathbf{A}, \mathbf{A}_0)$ denotes the LogDet divergence with respect to $\mathbf{A}$ and $\mathbf{A}_0$, $\mathbf{A}_0$ is a PSD matrix used to initialize $\mathbf{A}$, l and u are the lower and upper bound of the Mahalanobis distance between two data points, while $\mathfrak{S}$ and $\mathfrak{D}$ are two sets indicating pairs of similar and dissimilar data, respectively. Problem (1) can be iteratively solved using Bregman projections [7].

3   3D Texture Recognition for RGB-D Images

Based on several image processing and metric learning techniques, in this paper, we propose a novel 3D texture recognition system for RGB-D images. The flowchart of this system is shown in Fig. 2. Firstly, the color and depth information of 3D objects are captured using Kinect, and represented in RGB-D images. Secondly, to alleviate the deformations and partial defects of the obtained 3D surface textures, we implement 3D texture reconstruction techniques on both the color images and depth images. Thirdly, LBP features are extracted from the reconstructed images. Finally, in order to improve the recognition accuracy, we exploit metric learning methods for the K-nearest neighbor (KNN) classifier. In the following, we introduce each step of the proposed system in detail.

Fig. 3. Example color images of two objects.

3.1   RGB-D Images

As mentioned above, we used Kinect to capture the color and depth information of 3D objects. Concretely, for each object, we took images from different angles. Fig. 1 shows both the color image and depth image of an object, and Fig. 3 shows the color images of two objects taken from different angles. We considered images of a same object as samples of a class.

3.2   3D Texture Reconstruction

In order to alleviate the deformations and partial defects of the captured 3D surface textures, we implement 3D texture reconstruction techniques on both the color images and depth images. Concretely, the operations include denoising the depth images, background modelling for the color images and texture images extraction. In the following, we introduce these operations in detail.

Denoising the Depth Images Due to the low resolution of Kinect, there in general exist plenty of noises in the depth images. In our work, we use the bilateral filtering approach [14] for denoising.

Bilateral filtering is a non-linear, edge-preserving denoising approach, which updates the value of each pixel with a weighted average of the values of nearby pixels (For more details about bilateral filtering, please refer to https://en.wikipedia.org/wiki/Bilateral_filter). Suppose that a pixel at (i, j) is to be denoised in image using its neighbouring pixels, and one of its neighbouring pixels is located at (k, l). Then, the weight assigned for pixel (k, l) to denoise the pixel (i, j) can be written as

$$\omega(i, j, k, l) = e^{\left(-\frac{(i-k)^2 + (j-l)^2}{2\sigma_d^2} - \frac{\|I(i,j) - I(k,l)\|^2}{2\sigma_r^2}\right)}, \tag{2}$$

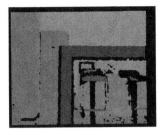 

Fig. 4. Original depth image (left) and the denoised image (right) by using the bilateral filtering approach.

where σ_d and σ_r are smoothing parameters, and $I(i,j)$ and $I(k,l)$ are the values of pixels (i,j) and (k,l), respectively. After calculating the weights, we can obtain the denoised value of pixel (i,j) as

$$I_D(i,j) = \frac{\sum_{k,l} I(k,l) \times \omega(i,j,k,l)}{\sum_{k,l} \omega(i,j,k,l)}. \tag{3}$$

Fig. 4 shows an original depth image, and the denoised one by using the bilateral filtering approach. We can see that, noises are properly reduced.

Background Modelling for the Color Images In order to alleviate the effect of complex background on the recognition accuracy, and improve the recognition efficiency, we use the Gaussian mixture models (GMM) for background modelling on the color images [13]. With the obtained background information, we can further extract the foreground objects in both the color images and depth images.

At the t-th iteration, we assume the probability of observing the current pixel value, $\mathbf{x}_t$, is

$$P(\mathbf{x}_t) = \sum_{i=1}^{K} w_{i,t} \mathcal{G}(\mathbf{x}_t, \mu_{i,t}, \Sigma_{i,t}), \tag{4}$$

where K is the number of Gaussian distributions, $w_{i,t}$ is an estimate of the weight of the i-th Gaussian component in the mixture ($0 \leq w_{i,t} \leq 1$ and $\sum_{i=1}^{K} w_{i,t} = 1$), $\mu_{i,t}$ is the mean value of the i-th Gaussian in the mixture, $\Sigma_{i,t}$ is the covariance matrix of the i-th Gaussian in the mixture, and $\mathcal{G}(\mathbf{x}, \mu, \Sigma)$ is a Gaussian probability density function

$$\mathcal{G}(\mathbf{x}, \mu, \Sigma) = \frac{1}{(2\pi)^{\frac{1}{2}} |\Sigma|^{\frac{1}{2}}} e^{-\frac{1}{2}(\mathbf{x}-\mu)^T \Sigma^{-1} (\mathbf{x}-\mu)}. \tag{5}$$

To facilitate the computation, we assume covariance matrix is of the form

$$\Sigma = \sigma_k^2 \mathbf{I}. \tag{6}$$

We sort the Gaussian components with a descent order according to the value of $\rho = \frac{w_{i,t}}{\sigma_i}$, as this value increases both as a Gaussian distribution gains more evidence and as its variance decreases. And then, we check each pixel value, $\mathbf{x}_j$, against the existing K Gaussian distributions, until a match is found, where the condition of a match is $|\mathbf{x}_j - \mu_i| < 2.5\sigma_i$. For the matched pixels, we update the parameters, $w_{i,t}$, $\mu_{i,t}$ and $\sigma_{i,t}$, as follows:

$$w_{i,t} = (1 - \alpha)w_{i,t-1} + \alpha, \tag{7}$$
$$\mu_{i,t} = (1 - \beta)\mu_{i,t-1} + \beta\mathbf{x}_j, \tag{8}$$
$$\sigma_{i,t}^2 = (1 - \beta)\sigma_{i,t-1}^2 + \beta(\mathbf{x}_j - \mu_{i,t})^T(\mathbf{x}_j - \mu_{i,t}), \tag{9}$$

where α is the learning rate and $\beta = \alpha\mathcal{G}(\mathbf{x}_j|\mu_{i,t}, \sigma_{i,t})$. For the unmatched pixels, we update $w_{i,t}$ as

$$w_{i,t} = (1 - \alpha)w_{i,t-1}, \tag{10}$$

and keep $\mu_{i,t}$ and $\sigma_{i,t}$ unchanged. After updating the parameters, we re-order the Gaussian distributions according to the values of $\rho = \frac{w_{i,t}}{\sigma_i}$. Finally, the first B distributions are chosen as the background model, where

$$B = \operatorname*{argmin}_b(\sum_{k=1}^b w_k > T), \tag{11}$$

where T is a threshold. In our experiments, $T = 9$ was used.

Texture Images Extraction To facilitate the object recognition task, for the 3D surface texture of each object, we extract the maximum plane area, and only use this plane area for object recognition. We use the region growing algorithm [1] on the depth image to extract the maximum plane area of each surface texture. The region growing algorithm is initialized with a seed region, and iteratively combines nearby pixels to discover a plane area.

Based on the relationship between the coordinates of the depth image and the world coordinates, we can define an affine transformation matrix and use this affine transformation matrix to unify the angle of the texture images. Accordingly, this transformation step can reduce the deformations of the captured images and improve the object recognition accuracy.

Fig. 5 shows one original texture image and the transformed image. We can see that, the affine transformation reduces deformations of the original image.

3.3   LBP Feature Extraction

To recognize the 3D objects, we extract LBP features [11] from the reconstructed images.

LBP labels the pixels of an image by thresholding the neighborhood of each pixel and considers the result as a binary number [10]. Due to its discriminative

Fig. 5. Original texture image (left) and the transformed image (right).

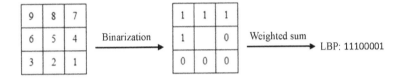

Fig. 6. LBP feature extraction on a 3 × 3 neighborhood.

power and computational simplicity, LBP texture operator has become a popular approach in various applications. The most important property of LBP is its robustness to monotonic gray-scale changes, for example, that caused by illumination variations. Another important property of LBP is its computational simplicity, which makes it possible to analyze images in challenging real-time tasks.

Fig. 6 shows an example for computing the LBP features on a 3 × 3 neighborhood. The LBP feature can be calculated as

$$LBP = \sum_{p=0}^{7} s(g_p - g_c)2^p, \quad s(x) = \begin{cases} 1, x \geq 0; \\ 0, x > 0, \end{cases} \tag{12}$$

where g_c is the gray value of the center pixel and g_p is the gray value of the neighborhood pixel. As there are 8 neighbors of the center pixel, $2^8 = 256$ possible binary numbers can then be used as LBP feature for such a 3 × 3 neighborhood.

The LBP operator was extended to use neighborhoods of different sizes [11]. Using a circular neighborhood and bilinearly interpolating values at non-integer pixel coordinates allow any radius and number of pixels in the neighborhood. Another extension to the original operator is the definition of the so called uniform patterns, which can be used to reduce the length of the feature vector and to implement a simple rotation-invariant descriptor through further extension. A local binary pattern is called uniform if the binary pattern contains at most

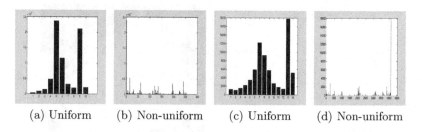

(a) Uniform   (b) Non-uniform   (c) Uniform   (d) Non-uniform

Fig. 7. Histograms of the LBP feature extracted from the texture images. Here, (a) and (b) are for 8-neighbors, and (c) and (d) are for circular-neighborhood.

two bitwise transitions from 0 to 1 or vice versa when the bit pattern is traversed circularly.

In our work, we used four settings of the LBP features. Fig. 7 shows the histograms of the LBP feature extracted from the texture images.

4   Results

As mentioned in Section 2, we use ITML for metric learning on the training data and use KNN classifier for 3D object recognition. Since the quality of the RGB-D images is low, we extract LBP features on the whole image. For the uniform 8-neighborhood setting, the dimensionality of the extracted LBP features is 14; for the 8-neighbors setting, that is 4096; for the uniform circular-neighborhood setting, that is 10; and for the circular-neighborhood setting, that is 256.

We collected 7 classes of 3D objects for a real-world recognition application. Fig. 1 shows the color image and depth image of a 3D object, whilst Fig. 3 shows the color images of two objects captured from different angles. 630 samples are randomly selected for model training, and 140 for testing. Table 1 shows the recognition accuracy without using the 3D texture reconstruction techniques, while Table 1 shows the recognition accuracy with the 3D texture reconstruction techniques. In both tables, the results obtained with different numbers of the nearest neighbors in the KNN classifiers are reported. It is easy to see that, on the one hand, the proposed system is effective for the 3D object recognition tasks, and on the other hand, the 3D texture reconstruction techniques greatly improve the 3D texture recognition results.

Table 1. Accuracy (%) of 3D texture recognition without 3D texture reconstruction. Here, '8' denotes 8-neighbors, 'C' denotes circular-neighborhood, 'R' denotes rotation-invariant, 'U' denotes uniform, and 2.5 and 12 are radius and number of neighbors for the corresponding circular-neighborhood.

KNN	LBP(8,RU)	LBP(8,R)	LBP(C,2.5,12,RU)	LBP(C,2.5,12,R)
K = 1	85.00	86.43	86.43	87.14
K = 3	80.00	82.86	84.29	85.71
K = 5	86.43	87.86	88.57	89.29

Table 2. Accuracy (%) of 3D texture recognition with 3D texture reconstruction.

KNN	LBP(8,RU)	LBP(8,R)	LBP(C,2.5,12,RU)	LBP(C,2.5,12,R)
K = 1	96.43	97.14	97.86	98.57
K = 3	93.57	96.43	97.14	97.86
K = 5	97.14	98.57	98.57	99.29

5 Conclusion

In this paper, we present a novel 3D object recognition system. In this system, the color and depth information of 3D objects are represented in RGB-D images. To improve the recognition accuracy, 3D texture reconstruction techniques and metric learning methods are adopted. Promising results are obtained on a real-world 3D object recognition application. In future work, we plan to test more metric learning methods, such as large margin nearest neighbor (LMNN) [18], and test other classifiers, such as support vector machines (SVMs) [17].

Acknowledgments. This research was supported by the National Natural Science Foundation of China (NSFC) under Grant no. 61403353 and no. 61271405, Ph.D. Program Foundation of Ministry of Education of China no. 20120132110018 and the Fundamental Research Funds for the Central Universities of China.

References

1. Adams, R., Bischof, L.: Seeded region growing. IEEE Transactions on Pattern Analysis and Machine Intelligence **16**(6), 641–647 (1994)
2. Davis, J., Kulis, B., Jain, P., Sra, S., Dhillon, I.: Information-theoretic metric learning. In: ICML, pp. 209–216 (2007)
3. Filliat, D., E.Battesti, Bazeille, S., Duceux, G., Gepperth, A., Harrath, L., Jebari, I., Pereira, R., Tapus, A., Meyer, C.: RGBD object recognition and visual texture classification for indoor semantic mapping. In: TePRA, pp. 127–132. IEEE (2012)
4. Goswami, G., Vatsa, M., Singh, R.: RGB-D face recognition with texture and attribute features. IEEE Transactions on Information Forensics and Security **9**(10), 1629–1640 (2014)
5. Hetzel, G., Leibe, B., Levi, P., Schiele, B.: 3D object recognition from range images using local feature histograms. In: CVPR, vol. 2, pp. 394–399. IEEE (2001)
6. Hinton, G., Osindero, S., Teh, Y.W.: A fast learning algorithm for deep belief nets. Neural Computation **18**(7), 1527–1554 (2006)
7. Kulis, B., Sustik, M., Dhillon, I.: Low-rank kernel learning with bregman matrix divergences. Journal of Machine Learning Research **10**, 341–376 (2009)
8. Lai, K., Bo, L., Ren, X., Fox, D.: A large-scale hierarchical multi-view RGB-D object dataset. In: ICRA, pp. 1817–1824 (2011)
9. Nair, V., Hinton, G.: 3D object recognition with deep belief nets. In: NIPS, pp. 1339–1347 (2009)

10. Ojala, T., Pietikäinen, M., Harwood, D.: A comparative study of texture measures with classification based on featured distributions. Pattern recognition **29**(1), 51–59 (1996)
11. Ojala, T., Pietikäinen, M., Maenpaa, T.: Multiresolution gray-scale and rotation invariant texture classification with local binary patterns. IEEE Transactions on Pattern Analysis and Machine Intelligence **24**(7), 971–987 (2002)
12. Pontil, M., Verri, A.: Support vector machines for 3D object recognition. IEEE Transactions on Pattern Analysis and Machine Intelligence **20**(6), 637–646 (1998)
13. Stauer, C., Grimson, W.: Adaptive background mixture models for real-time tracking. In: CVPR, vol. 2, pp. 246–252. IEEE (1999)
14. Tomasi, C., Manduchi, R.: Bilateral filtering for gray and color images. In: ICCV, pp. 839–846. IEEE (1998)
15. Tsalakanidou, F., Malassiotis, S., Strintzis, M.G.: Integration of 2d and 3d images for enhanced face authentication. In: FGR, pp. 266–271 (2004)
16. Tsalakanidou, F., Tzovaras, D., Strintzis, M.: Use of depth and colour eigenfaces for face recognition. Pattern Recognition Letters **24**(9–10), 1427–1435 (2003)
17. Vapnik, V.: Statistical learning theory (1998)
18. Weinberger, K., Blitzer, J., Saul, L.: Distance metric learning for large margin nearest neighbor classification. In: NIPS, pp. 1473–1480 (2005)
19. Xing, E.P., Ng, A.Y., Jordan, M.I., Russell, S.J.: Distance metric learning, with application to clustering with side-information. In: NIPS, pp. 505–512 (2002)
20. Xu, C., Wang, Y., Tan, T., Quan, L.: A new attempt to face recognition using 3D eigenfaces. In: ACCV, vol. 2, pp. 884–889. Citeseer (2004)
21. Zhong, G., Huang, K., Liu, C.L.: Low rank metric learning with manifold regularization. In: ICDM, pp. 1266–1271 (2011)

Detection and Classification of Interesting Parts in Scanned Documents by Means of AdaBoost Classification and Low-Level Features Verification

Andrzej Markiewicz and Paweł Forczmański[✉]

Faculty of Computer Science and Information Technology,
West Pomeranian University of Technology, Żołnierska Str. 52,
71–210 Szczecin, Poland
{amarkiewicz,pforczmanski}@wi.zut.edu.pl

Abstract. This paper presents a novel approach to detection and identification of selected document's parts (stamps, logos, printed text blocks, signatures and tables) on digital images obtained through paper document scanning. This task is realized in two main steps. The first one includes element detection, which is done by means of AdaBoost cascade of weak classifiers. Resulting image blocks are, in the second step, subjected to verification process. Eight feature vectors based on recently proposed descriptors were selected and combined with six different classifiers that represent numerous approaches to the task of data classification. Experiments performed on large set of paper document images gathered from Internet gave encouraging results.

1 Introduction

Paper documents are one of the basic means of human communication. Each of them contains much information in different languages, structures, forms and carries information of different value. Regardless of those features there are common elements such as stamps, signatures, tables, logos, blocks of text and background. In order to prevent the process of document accumulation most of valuable pieces are digitally scanned and kept as digital copies on computers. Storing data this way makes process of document organizing, accessing and exchange easier but, even then without a managing system it is difficult to keep things in order. As stated in [1] a system that is able to recognize digital image of paper document can be used to transform a document into its digital, hierarchical representation in terms of structure and content, which would allow to exchange, edit, browse, index, fill and retrieve much easier.

Developed algorithm can be a part of document managing system, whose main purpose is to determine parts of the document that should be processed further (text [2]), be subjected to enhancement and denoising process (graphics, pictures, charts etc.) [3]. It could be integral part of any content-based image retrieval system, or simply a filter that would select only documents containing

© Springer International Publishing Switzerland 2015
G. Azzopardi and N. Petkov (Eds.): CAIP 2015, Part II, LNCS 9257, pp. 529–540, 2015.
DOI: 10.1007/978-3-319-23117-4_46

specific elements [4], segregate them in terms of importance (colored documents containing stamps and signatures are more valuable than monochromatic ones, which suggest a copy [5]) etc. Our approach is document type independent, hence can be applied to formal documents, newspapers, envelopes, bank checks etc.

The rest of the paper is organized as follows: first we provide a review of related works and point out their characteristic features, then we present an algorithm consisting of two stages and present the experimental results. We conclude the paper with a discussion on the results.

2   Previous Works

Document segmentation can be performed using global (multi-class detection and classification) and individual (class-specific detection and classification) methods. Global approaches can be divided in three categories of methods [6]: top-up, bottom-up and heuristic-based. Top-down methods could be useful when it comes to documents of previously known structure. Bottom-up strategy starts with pixel-level analysis, and then pixels of common properties are grouped into bigger structures. Heuristic-based procedures attempt to combine robustness of top-down approach and accuracy of bottom-up methods.

Bottom-up strategy is used in [7], where documents are segmented into 3 classes (background, graphics and text). A sliding window technique is used to segment input image into blocks. Each block is subjected to feature extraction stage and, based on a number of rules, is classified. Reported accuracy of text detection is 99%. Result for other classes were not provided. Very similar approach is presented in [8], but it uses different set of features, that are calculated from GLCM (Gray-Level Coocurrence Matrix), as well as k-means algorithm for grouping. Mean accuracy equals to 94%.

Top-down strategies rely on run-length analysis performed on binarized, skew-corrected documents [6]. Vertical and horizontal profiles are examined in terms of valley occurrence, which represent white space between blocks. Other solutions include usage of Gaussian pyramid in combination with low-level features or Gabor-filtered pixel clustering. Heuristic methods combine bottom-up and top-down strategies are especially useful while processing documents of high complexity [1]. Zone classification issue as a multi-class discrimination problem was investigated i.e. in [3]. It provides a comparative analysis of commonly used features for 8 classes. Tamura's histogram achieved highest accuracy, but due to it's computation complexity was discarded in favor of more simple features vector. Reported error rate is equal to 2.1%, but 72.7% of logos and 31.4% tables were misclassified. Wang et al. [1] proposed a 69-element feature vector, which was reduced to 25 elements in feature selection stage, which allowed to achieve mean accuracy of 98.45%, however 84.64% logos and 72.73% 'other' elements were misclassified.

The problem of class-specific detection and classification is widely represented in literature. In our previous works [5,9–11] a problem of stamp detection and recognition was addressed. Our observation is that logo detection is very similar problem and can be solved with little tweak to our previously presented solution. Others use keypoint analyzing algorithms i.e. SIFT, SURF and FAST or ART.

Text block detection can be realized by means of statistical analysis [12], edge information [13], texture analysis [13,14], stroke filters [15–17], cosinus transform [18] and LBP algorithm [19].

Tabular objects are hard to detect and classify, since they feature high intra-class variance. A simplification of this problem includes the assumption about one column of text with easily separable, non-overlapping lines [20].

The same high intra-class variance influences the accuracy of signature detection. That is why keypoint-based algorithms are widely-applicable. In [21] Zhu et al. proposed algorithm consisting of extensive pre-processing, multi-scale signature saliency measure calculation for each connected component and component connecting based on proximity and curvilinear constraints. High accuracy (92.8%) was achived on popular *Tobacco-800* database. In [22] SUFR algorithm was used to determine keypoint location on images containing results of connected component analysis. Again, connected component analysis is crucial part of [23]. The paper provides a comparative analysis of HOG, SIFT, gradient, TBP and low-level features. Classification is performed by SVM classifier. Experiments performed on *Tobacco-800* database proved that for the set containing gradient and low-level features the accuracy reached 95%.

The analysis of the literature shows, that most of algorithms use some pre-processing (e.g. document rectification), restrict forms of analysed documents (e.g. to cheques) and employ sophisticated features and multi-tier approaches.

In the proposed solution, we do not pre-process images of scanned documents and employ very efficient AdaBoost cascade which is implemented using integral image, hence giving very high processing speed. It is worth noticing, that we analyse probably all possible object types that can be found in documents, which is, surprisingly, not so popular in other works.

3 Algorithm Description

Presented algorithm consists of two subsequent elements. The first one is devoted to rough detection, while the second one is applied for verification of found candidates. The assumption is that the cascade results in rather high number of false positives, so they are subject to verification using additional set of more complex features.

3.1 Cascade Training and Detection

Detection process is performed by a set of AdaBoosted cascades of weak classifiers [24,25]. It means, that we trained 5 separate cascades for specific type of objects, namely: stamps, logos/ornaments, texts and signatures. Example objects selected from all classes are presented in Tab. 1. Background blocks, being an additional class, are taken further as negative examples for training other cascades. The detection was performed using 24×24 block on a pyramid

Table 1. Exemplary training images

Class	Images
stamps	
logos	
text	
signatures	
tables	
backgrounds	

of scales where in each iteration we downscale an input image by 10%. The training procedure was performed in two iterations. The first, preliminary training, was to initialize the classifier. For this stage we used 150 positive and 740 negative samples for each class, taken from Internet and from SigComp2009 [26].

In order to increase the detection accuracy we performed a second iteration, in which we extended training database with objects resulted from the first iteration. The positive results were added to the positive samples while the negative, to negative ones, respectively.

3.2 Verification Stage

Detected objects are verified using a set of eight following low-level features. The classification is performed using several popular classifiers. The initial training set, upon which reference features were calculated, consist of 219 logos, 452 text blocks, 251 signatures, 1590 stamps, 140 tables, and 719 background areas. As in case of detection, background block were used as negative examples and we do not evaluate background detection accuracy. After the fist iteration, we identified problems and solved them by extending the training database.

First Order Statistics (FOS) - a vector of six, direct, low-level features calculated from histogram of pixel intensities. The features are: mean pixel intensity, second (variance), third (skewness), fourth (kurtosis) central moment and entropy. They provide information about global characteristic of input image.

Gray-Level Run Length Statistics (GLRLS) - a vector of eleven features calculated from run-length matrix: short run emphasis, long run emphasis, gray-level nonuniformity, run length nonuniformity, run length nonuniformity, run percentage, low gray-level run emphasis, high gray-level run emphasis, short run low gray-level emphasis, short run high gray-level emphasis, long run low gray-level emphasis, long run high gray-level emphasis. Those features provide information about texture coarseness and/or fineness. Algorithm for GLRLM matrix calculation along with respective equations are in [27–29].

Haralick's Statistics (HS) is a set of 22 features calculated from Gray-Level Co-occurence matrix. Appropriate algorithms are available in [30–32]. List of features used consist of: autocorrelation, contrast, correlation, cluster shade, cluster prominence, dissimilarity, energy, entropy, homogeneity, maximum probability, sum of squares: variance, sum average, sum variance, sum entropy, difference variance, difference entropy, information measures of correlation, inverse difference, inverse difference normalized, inverse difference moment normalized.

Neighboring Gray-Level Dependence Statistics (NGLDS) is a 5-element vector of features (small number emphasis, large number emphasis, number nonuniformity, second moment, entropy) derived from NGLDM matrix. Element and their value distribution inside NGLDM matrix provides information about the level of texture coarseness. Algorithm for matrix calculations and respective equations are in [33].

Low-Level Features (LLF) is a vector of eleven features developed for our previous research on stamp recognition [5,11]. This approach shares common features with measures proposed by Haralic et al. Contrast, correlation, energy and homogenity are calculated in the same way with use of GLCM matrix. Other features include: average pixel intensity, standard deviation of intensity, median intensity, contrast, mean intensity to contrast ratio, intensity of edges, mean intensity to edges intensity ratio.

Histograms of Oriented Gradients (HOG) is a method proposed by Dalal and Triggs in [34] and proved to be an effective method for human detection in digital images and later on in video sequences, but as mentioned in the paper algorithm is also capable of determining between objects of different type. Feature vector of HOG descriptor is 256-elements long.

Local Binary Patterns LBP were introduced in [35] as universal, fine-scale texture descriptor [36]. Similarly to HOG the output vector consist of 256 elements. In our case, Local Binary Patterns come in two, different variants. The first one is calculated on monochromatic image, for the second binarized image was supplied (LBPB).

4   Experiments

In the experimental evaluation the detection stage is performed first. In next step all generated examples were divided into two categories: positive and negative detections. This allowed us to calculate confusion matrices for each combination of classifier and feature set. The details of document images database we used in experiments are provided in [5]. Exemplary documents are shown in Fig. 1.

Fig. 1. Exemplary documents used in the experimental part

4.1   Detection Stage

The decision whether the result should be considered positive or negative was made based on its bounding box area. Objects that are covered by approximately 75% of resulting bounding box were classified positively. The results for both iterations are provided in Tab. 2. The mean accuracy after first iteration of detection was equal to 54% (with highest 80% for text and lowest 14% for signatures). Observed low accuracy is caused by high resemblance between classes, e.g. many logos were classified as stamps, large number of tables (which according to [6] should be considered as graphics) as printed text. The low accuracy for signatures comes from the lack of signatures in input documents, hence we included the samples from SigComp2009, which are quite different in character. Examples of difficult to detect objects are presented in Fig. 4.1.

Fig. 2. Ambiguous objects: overlapped signatures and tables containing text

Lowest accuracy of signature detector results from different characteristics of examples used to train cascade (high resolution, light and noise-free background, clear strokes, contrast ink) and the ones that are actually located on scanned documents (varying background and ink colour, often overlapping with other elements). Those observations were taken into account when preparing data for the second learning iteration.

Analysing the results in Tab. 2 one can see a significant increase in detection accuracy after second iteration of training procedure. After this iteration, there is a significantly lower number of false detections, yet also slightly lower number of positive detections. A clearly visible significant increase in signatures detection rate is still far from ideal. It is caused by the fact, that in most cases signatures are overlapped with other elements, such as stamps, text and signature lines.

Table 2. Detection results

Class	1st iteration			2nd iteration		
	TP	FP	Acc. [%]	TP	FP	Acc. [%]
Stamps	174	281	42.54	235	187	60.04
Logos	444	394	65.29	236	75	84.01
Texts	557	919	80.38	136	84	91.63
Signatures	75	38	13.99	461	92	29.23
Tables	1133	1209	67.48	546	67	94.75

4.2   Verification Stage

Experiments described below were aimed at determining a combination of classifier and feature set (presented above) that gives the highest verification rate. The set of classifiers we investigated consist of: 1-Nearest Neighbour (1NN), Naïve Bayes (NBayes), Binary Decision Tree (CTree), Support Vector Machine (SVM), General Linear Model Regression (GLM) and Classification and Regression Trees (CART). There were two iterations of processing. The first one was performed on an initial features calculated for manually selected samples (see Sec. 3.2). The second iteration of training was performed on a set with certain extra samples, derived from the first iteration output.

In Tables 3 - 7 verification accuracy for each class is presented (there are two columns of results for each classifier, each for subsequent iterations, respectively). The highest accuracy in the first iteration is underlined, while the highest accuracy in the second iteration is double underlined, respectively. Sometimes, more that one accuracy is the highest, hence more results are underlined.

Table 3. Stamps verification accuracy [%]

	1NN		NBayes		CTree		SVM		GLM		CART	
FOS	52.57	53.42	48.66	41.24	61.86	64.96	41.56	39.96	39.85	52.99	64.30	55.77
GLRLS	45.48	48.93	44.01	35.26	52.57	60.04	48.66	40.81	52.32	40.81	58.68	38.89
HS	58.19	60.68	55.75	50.21	74.57	63.25	79.46	71.37	81.17	71.79	73.35	35.47
HOG	73.84	79.06	73.84	69.44	60.39	63.46	65.53	51.07	69.44	66.45	69.19	41.45
LBP	55.01	61.54	48.17	36.97	55.99	56.84	73.84	43.38	73.35	38.46	54.77	39.53
LBPB	56.97	63.46	69.93	39.96	69.44	64.74	76.77	62.39	78.24	65.17	64.30	42.52
LLF	63.81	60.47	62.35	63.89	71.15	67.95	57.46	39.96	64.30	63.46	75.55	68.80
NGLDS	46.94	53.63	52.57	37.82	45.97	53.63	40.10	57.05	37.90	44.02	47.92	39.32

Table 4. Logos verification accuracy [%]

	1NN		NBayes		CTree		SVM		GLM		CART	
FOS	40.44	23.03	42.35	19.19	49.12	23.03	34.71	15.99	38.68	16.63	45.88	20.26
GLRLS	42.79	26.44	54.12	39.45	53.97	37.10	67.94	51.60	42.35	19.40	45.88	26.65
HS	42.35	18.98	59.12	32.41	54.12	33.48	61.18	39.23	49.12	23.67	44.26	20.26
HOG	53.82	30.28	55.88	39.23	51.32	35.61	60.74	43.07	58.53	49.12	47.21	31.34
LBP	40.00	18.76	47.65	17.70	37.50	21.54	46.76	22.17	43.24	21.32	38.53	18.76
LBPB	41.47	40.51	61.91	20.04	43.68	32.62	62.06	50.75	48.53	32.84	42.65	30.92
LLF	50.44	25.16	58.82	37.10	61.62	43.07	34.71	15.99	61.18	38.38	40.44	48.83
NGLDS	39.12	18.98	32.21	25.59	51.62	25.37	58.38	34.12	34.71	15.99	59.85	21.96

Table 5. Texts verification accuracy [%]

	1NN		NBayes		CTree		SVM		GLM		CART	
FOS	38.67	33.30	39.11	49.25	43.97	44.27	19.62	08.37	26.84	28.71	31.17	31.70
GLRLS	48.92	38.19	85.71	83.55	66.67	61.02	84.42	08.37	47.76	33.80	49.35	45.26
HS	39.83	36.39	69.70	74.88	67.82	55.83	59.31	86.64	64.79	67.80	38.67	45.36
HOG	71.28	79.56	84.70	87.64	54.69	66.00	55.41	87.04	77.63	85.34	61.76	58.23
LBP	62.91	60.42	77.34	69.69	67.53	68.79	80.52	83.25	72.87	79.36	46.75	47.16
LBPB	49.35	40.68	64.36	72.88	55.56	55.03	73.74	08.37	74.17	77.87	54.40	52.14
LLF	53.82	50.05	59.60	56.33	61.18	62.91	19.62	08.37	43.43	40.28	61.04	57.13
NGLDS	39.39	33.80	42.86	59.82	44.16	42.47	77.20	81.26	30.74	19.44	24.39	19.34

Table 6. Signatures verification accuracy [%]

	1NN		NBayes		CTree		SVM		GLM		CART	
FOS	84.51	69.23	85.45	52.31	85.63	64.62	77.43	70.77	80.97	67.69	84.33	65.38
GLRLS	85.45	71.54	85.82	70.77	86.01	70.77	85.82	57.69	79.85	66.15	85.63	66.92
HS	84.70	70.00	86.01	56.92	85.82	71.54	85.82	71.54	84.70	70.77	81.34	70.00
HOG	80.41	80.00	78.92	73.08	71.08	67.69	79.85	71.54	83.77	64.62	82.84	64.62
LBP	86.01	72.31	86.01	70.77	86.01	70.77	86.01	71.54	86.01	76.15	85.63	69.23
LBPB	86.01	72.31	80.22	63.85	86.01	69.23	86.01	75.38	86.01	75.38	85.82	72.31
LLF	83.96	70.00	85.63	63.08	85.63	70.00	86.01	70.77	82.46	56.92	76.31	66.15
NGLDS	86.01	71.54	86.01	70.77	86.01	70.77	86.01	70.77	86.01	70.77	85.07	72.31

Table 7. Tables verification accuracy [%]

	1NN		NBayes		CTree		SVM		GLM		CART	
FOS	32.70	05.02	31.98	05.09	32.28	05.17	31.63	05.09	32.28	05.25	32.76	05.64
GLRLS	23.47	06.27	31.51	05.02	32.34	05.09	32.04	04.86	32.28	05.09	33.53	05.09
HS	32.46	05.17	32.10	05.25	32.22	05.02	31.21	05.17	32.58	05.17	32.34	06.50
HOG	27.99	05.02	32.28	05.02	29.30	04.78	22.45	04.70	20.49	05.49	29.18	07.68
LBP	24.54	21.87	32.94	06.90	32.88	07.21	29.60	04.86	28.23	08.54	31.80	13.40
LBPB	47.41	33.07	41.16	11.29	32.58	12.77	27.34	04.62	32.04	05.49	41.27	19.91
LLF	58.13	54.78	69.62	57.60	60.21	54.39	32.52	05.25	55.39	50.63	51.58	40.20
NGLDS	27.04	21.94	18.76	12.07	25.25	08.86	23.05	12.07	22.57	05.72	27.34	06.82

4.3 Discussion

As shown in Tab. 4 verification accuracy of logo-detecting cascade had decreased. Large number of detected samples were misclassified as negative instead of positive. This is due quite rigorous character of classifiers used. Taking into account the accuracy of detection process (which is done through classification) a cascade could be assigned a higher decision weight than the best pair of feature set and classifier used in verification to compensate for low precision in verification stage. Similar situation occurs in case of tables - again high detection accuracy is combined with low verification result. This is caused mostly by fuzzy line separating tables containing text and text class.

Average accuracies achieved at both stages of stamps and texts processing mean that equal decision weight could be assigned to both cascade and best combination of feature set and classifier. In both cases high precision of detection is coupled with high verification result. It is important to note that tables filled with text were classified as text. Otherwise, the results would be much lower.

As it was noted, signatures class causes most of the problems. Higher detection accuracy is only a result of much lower FP rate. This is caused by extension of learning set (both in training of cascade and at verification stage). Further increase, especially in case of positive samples number, would be beneficial.

The analysis of presented verification results shows that all of discussed object classes should be considered separately. It is impossible to point out a single pair classifier/features set that wins in all cases. There seems to be no one rule that is behind above results.

In case of stamp class the most accurate pair consist of GLM classifier and HC features set and pair of 1NN classifier and HOG descriptor comes at second. Those pairs alternate between iterations. Analogous observations were made in case of the worst pair. In the first iteration, GLM classifier and NGLDS features were worst and NBayes+GLRS were second worst. Reverse relationship occurred in the second iteration. The average accuracy across all sets is equal to 60.17% and 53.37% in first and second iteration respectively. HS is the most accurate descriptor (average accuracy of 70.42%) in the first iteration and HOG (with 61.82% average accuaracy) in the second. An accuracy of 63.51% places CART classifier as the best in the first iteration and 61.86% places CTree classier at the top in the second iteration. Results for remaining classes were described in similar manner - first percentage value always corresponds to the result achieved in the first iteration and so on.

In both the first and the second iteration of logo verification SVM classifier and GLRLS features set proved to be the best. There were no recurrence in case of the worst pair. Average accuracy is equal to 48.6% and 29.04%. The highest average score was achieved by SVM classifier (53.31%, 34.12%) and HOG descriptor (54.58%, 38.11%).

Bayes-based classifiers, namely NBayes+GLRLS and NBayes+HOG achieved the highest accuracies in the first and the second iteration of text verification process, respectively. Analogous switch in terms of the best and the second best as in case of stamp occurred. Overall accuracy stands at 55.52% and 52.99%. The LBP and HOG descriptors proved to be the most accurate (67.99%, 77.3%). In both cases NBayes was selected as the best (65.42%, 69.26%).

The analysis of signature verification results shown that GLM+LBP achieved high scores in both stages, only to be defeated by 1NN+HOG pair in the second iteration. Overall accuracy equals to 84.02% and 68.94%. In both iterations the same feature set and classifier produced the highest scores: LBP (85.95%, 71.8%) and 1NN (84.63%, 72.12%).

Only in case of tables verification there is significant domination of one classifier and feature set pair (NBayes+LLF) over all other combinations. Although, the average accuracy is low (33.47% and 12.66%), the accuracy achieved by the best pair is satisfactory. NBayes classier paired with LLF feature set reached 69.62% and 54.17% accuracy. Mean result of classification with use of NBayes classifier is equal to 36.29% and 19.14%, and mean accuracy of LLF feature set stands at 54.58%, 43.81% in the first and the second iteration, respectively.

5   Summary

Based on results we obtained, it is justified to say that the idea of using boosted cascade of weak classifiers to solve the task of graphical element detection in digital images of scanned paper documents proved to be valid. High accuracies achieved in extensive analysis performed on large, real document set prove this fact further. Results from the second iteration (see Tab. 2) are particularly encouraging. Although, there is a high similarity between some classes and numerous challenging examples throughout image database (see Fig. 4.1), the detection is successful. The signatures class is an exception and can be put down to the poor representation across databases. Increasing the size of learning set for signatures detection with high degree of probability would boost results as shown in case of the first and the second iteration.

High accuracies for certain classes in particular could lead to dropping the verification stage as it is redundant if cascade looks as like what it really is - a classifier itself. However, as long as there is more than a few of misclassified samples the use of this stage is justified. If we decide to use the verification stage, it is important to examine each class separately, as shown in previous section. It is well illustrated in Tab. 7. While overall accuracy is really low, accuracy for LLF feature set is several times higher than in case of any other feature set.

References

1. Wang, Y., Phillips, T.I., Haralick, M.R.: Document zone content classification and its performance evaluation. Pattern Recognition **39**(1), 57–73 (2006)
2. Lech, P., Okarma, K.: Fast histogram based image binarization using the monte carlo threshold estimation. In: Chmielewski, L.J., Kozera, R., Shin, B.-S., Wojciechowski, K. (eds.) ICCVG 2014. LNCS, vol. 8671, pp. 382–390. Springer, Heidelberg (2014)
3. Keysers, D., Shafait, F., Breuel, M.T.: Document image zone classification - a simple high-performance approach. In: 2nd Int. Conf. on Computer Vision Theory and Applications, pp. 44–51 (2007)
4. Marchewka, A., Pasela, R.: Extraction of Data from Limnigraf Chart Images. In: S. Choras, R. (ed.) Image Processing and Communications Challenges 5. AISC, vol. 233, pp. 263–269. Springer, Heidelberg (2014)

5. Forczmański, P., Markiewicz, A.: Stamps Detection and Classification Using Simple Features Ensemble. Mathematical Problems in Engineering. Article ID 367879 (2014) (in press)
6. Okun, O., Doermann, D., Pietikäinen, M.: Page Segmentation and Zone Classification: The State of the Art. Technical Report: LAMP-TR-036/CAR-TR-927/CS-TR-4079, University of Maryland, College Park (1999)
7. Sauvola, J., Pietikäinen, M.: Page Segmentation and classification using fast feature extraction and connectivity analysis. In: Proceedings of 3rd International Conference on Document Analysis and Recognition, ICDAR 1995, pp. 1127–1131 (1995)
8. Lin, M.-W., Tapamo, J.-R., Ndovie, B.: A texture-based method for document segmentation and classification. South African Computer Journal 36, 49–56 (2006)
9. Frejlichowski, D., Forczmański, P.: General shape analysis applied to stamps retrieval from scanned documents. In: Dicheva, D., Dochev, D. (eds.) AIMSA 2010. LNCS, vol. 6304, pp. 251–260. Springer, Heidelberg (2010)
10. Forczmański, P., Frejlichowski, D.: Robust stamps detection and classification by means of general shape analysis. In: Bolc, L., Tadeusiewicz, R., Chmielewski, L.J., Wojciechowski, K. (eds.) ICCVG 2010, Part I. LNCS, vol. 6374, pp. 360–367. Springer, Heidelberg (2010)
11. Forczmański, P., Markiewicz, A.: Low-level image features for stamps detection and classification. In: Burduk, R., Jackowski, K., Kurzynski, M., Wozniak, M., Zolnierek, A. (eds.) CORES 2013. AISC, vol. 226, pp. 383–392. Springer, Heidelberg (2013)
12. Su, C., Haralick, M.R., Ihsin, T.P.: Extraction of text lines and text blocks on document images based on statistical modeling. International Journal of Imaging Systems and Technology 7(4), 343–356 (1996)
13. Pietikäinen, M., Okun, O.: Edge-based method for text detection from complex document images. In: Proceedings. Sixth International Conference on Document Analysis and Recognition, pp. 286–291 (2001)
14. Jain, A.K., Zhong, Y.: Page segmentation using texture analysis. Pattern Recognition 29(5), 743–770 (1996)
15. Jung, C., Liu, Q., Kim, J.: A stroke filter and its application to text localization. Pattern Recognition Letters 30(2), 114–122 (2009)
16. Liu, Q., Jung, C., Kim, S., Moon, Y., Kim, J.: Stroke filter for text localization in video images. In: IEEE Internat. Conf. on Image Processing, pp. 1473–1476 (2006)
17. Li, X., Wang, W., Jiang, S., Huang, Q., Gao, W.: Fast and effective text detection. In: 15th IEEE International Conference on Image Processing, pp. 969–972 (2008)
18. Zhong, Y., Zhang, H., Jain, A.K.: Automatic caption localization in compressed video. IEEE TPAMI 22(4), 385–392 (2000)
19. Ojala, T., Pietikäinen, M., Mäenpää, T.: Gray scale and rotation invariant texture classification with local binary patterns. In: Proc. of the 6th European Conference on Computer Vision, pp. 404–420 (2000)
20. Hu, J., Kashi, R., Lopresti, D., Wilfong, G.: Evaluating the performance of table processing algorithms. International Journal on Document Analysis and Recognition 4(3), 140–153 (2002)
21. Zhu, G., Zheng, Y., Doermann, D., Jaeger, S.: Signature Detection and Matching for Document Image Retrieval. IEEE TPAMI 31(11), 2015–2031 (2009)
22. Ahmed, S., Malik, M.I., Liwicki, M., Dengel, A.: Signature segmentation from document images. In: International Conference on Frontiers in Handwriting Recognition (ICFHR), pp. 425–429 (2012)
23. Cüceloğlu, I., Oğul, H.: Detecting handwritten signatures in scanned documents. In: Proceedings of the 19th Computer Vision Winter Workshop, pp. 89–94 (2014)

24. Viola, P., Jones, M.: Rapid object detection using a boosted cascade of simple features. In: Proc. IEEE Computer Society Conference on Computer Vision and Pattern Recognition CVPR 2001, pp. 511–518 (2001)
25. Burduk, R.: The AdaBoost algorithm with the imprecision determine the weights of the observations. In: Nguyen, N.T., Attachoo, B., Trawiński, B., Somboonviwat, K. (eds.) ACIIDS 2014, Part II. LNCS, vol. 8398, pp. 110–116. Springer, Heidelberg (2014)
26. Liwicki, M.: ICDAR 2009 Signature Verification Competition (2009). http:// www.iapr-tc11.org/mediawiki/index.php/ICDAR_2009_Signature_Verification_ Competition_(SigComp2009) (accessed: February 24, 2015)
27. Galloway, M.M.: Texture analysis using gray level run lengths. Computer Graphics and Image Processing 4(2), 172–179 (1975)
28. Tang, X.: Texture information in run-length matrices. IEEE Trans. on Image Processing 7(11), 1602–1609 (1998)
29. Dasarathy, R.B., Holder, B.E.: Image characterizations based on joint gray-level run-length distributions. Pattern Recognition Letters 12, 497–502 (1991)
30. Haralick, M.R., Shanmugam, K., Dinstein, I.: Textural Features of Image Classification. IEEE Trans. on Systems, Man and Cybernetics SMC–3(6), 610–621 (1973)
31. L, S., Tsatsoulis, C.: Texture Analysis of SAR Sea Ice Imagery Using Gray Level Co-Occurrence Matrices. IEEE Trans. on Geoscience and Remote Sensing 37(2), 780–795 (1999)
32. Clausi, A.D.: An analysis of co-occurrence texture statistics as a function of grey level quantization. Can. J. Remote Sensing 28(1), 45–62 (2002)
33. Siew, L.H., Hodgson, R.M., Wood, E.J.: Texture measures for carpet wear assessment. IEEE TPAMI 10(1), 92–105 (1988)
34. Dalal, N., Triggs, B.: Histograms of oriented gradients for human detection. In: Internat. Conf. on Computer Vision & Pattern Recognition, vol. 2, pp. 886–893 (2005)
35. Ojala, T., Pietikäinen, M., Mäenpää, T.: Multiresolution gray-scale and rotation invariant texture classification with local binary patterns. IEEE TPAMI 24(7), 971–987 (2002)
36. Maturana, D., Mery, D., Soto, Á.: Face recognition with local binary patterns, spatial pyramid histograms and naive bayes nearest neighbor classification. In: Proceedings of the 2009 International Conference of the Chilean Computer Science Society, pp. 125–132 (2009)

Speed Parameters in the Level-Set Segmentation

Luigi Cinque[1] and Rossella Cossu[2]($\boxtimes$)

[1] Dipartimento Informatica, Sapienza Universitá di Roma,
Via Salaria 113, 00185 Rome, Italy
[2] Istituto per le Applicazioni del Calcolo-CNR, Via dei Taurini 19, 00185 Rome, Italy
r.cossu@iac.cnr.it

Abstract. In image segmentation, based on the level set method, the evolution of the curve is determined by the speed function. In this paper we apply the level set segmentation to speckled images, in particular SAR (Synthetic Aperture Radar) images. Moreover we propose a parameters tuning of the speed function, obtained from the linear combination of the speed function of average intensities and of the image gradient. To show the validity of the proposed approach, we compare the segmentation results obtained from both synthetic and real images. Since there are not benchmark SAR images, computer images are been synthesized using speckle noise. Thus we show that the proposed speed function produces the best results, tuning the parameters in opportune way. The SAR images are PRecision Images (PRI), acquired during European Remote Sensing (ERS2) mission and CosmoSkyMed (CSM) image.

1 Introduction

Segmentation is the process of dividing an image into disjoint regions which are homogeneous according to some characteristics. It is used to locate the objects and contours in the image. Image segmentation, based on the level set method, starts from an initial curve (zero level set) that evolves until it stops at the contour of the interest object. The evolution of the initial curve is determined by a speed function. In this paper we propose a parameters tuning of the speed function, obtained from the linear combination of the speed function based on average intensities of the image and a speed function based on the image gradient. The speckled images, as SAR images, are characterized by a granular aspect, small contrast between foreground and background and also strong inhomogeneities [1][2].

Variational approaches and Partial Differential Equation (PDE) models have been important tools for solving image segmentation problems.

These methods, compared with traditional ones, like threshold, edge detection and region based segmentation, present better properties as the pixels accuracy and the generation of closed curves [3].

In the case of variational approach, a functional is defined by using various image features. The segmentation of images is obtained by computing the minimum of this functional [4][5]. Traditional level set methods were introduced for capturing moving fronts and used for segmenting objects using curves. The basic

© Springer International Publishing Switzerland 2015
G. Azzopardi and N. Petkov (Eds.): CAIP 2015, Part II, LNCS 9257, pp. 541–553, 2015.
DOI: 10.1007/978-3-319-23117-4_47

idea is to represent a curve as a level set or an equal-height contour of a given function. The intersection between this function and a plane parallel to the coordinate plane produces the curve. This function, which is implicitly defined and usually referred as the level set function, evolves according to a partial differential equation (PDE) until to reach the region contour to be segmented [6][7]. In variational segmentation formulations, the minimization of a functional by curve evolution, can be obtained through the associated Euler-Lagrange descent equations implemented via level sets. This type of methods are known as variational level set methods [8][9][10] [11].

In this work we present the level set segmentation process that operates a tuning of the speed parameters. The speed is obtained by the linear combination of two speed functions. In the former [12], the regions of the SAR images are modeled by the GAMMA-distribution. For this reason the starting curve evolves until to coincide with the GAMMA-homogeneous regions boundaries. In this case the speed of the level set equation is based on average intensities of the regions. We will refer to this formulation by using average-based speed.

In the latter [6], the curve evolves with a propagation speed, based on the image gradient. Since speckled images are corrupted by strong noise, the computation of gradient could detect false edges. Thus we have pre-processed these images by means of the SRAD algorithm (Speckle Reducing Anisotropic Diffusion) which is an extension of Perona-Malik one [13][14]. In this case we will refer to this formulation using gradient-based speed.

We will describe and compare the segmentation results applied to both speckled synthetic and real images and we will show that the better results are obtained by setting parameters in opportune way.

The real SAR images are PRecision Images (PRI), acquired during European Remote Sensing ERS2 (2000) mission and CosmoSkyMed CSM image (2007) related to coast regions. The paper is organized as follows. In Section 2, the level set method is described. In Section 3, speed computation related to level set method and noise reducing are presented. In section 4 experimental results are reported and SAR images application is presented. Conclusions are drawn in Section 5.

2   Mathematical Approach: Level Set Model

In image segmentation the main advantage of using the level set approach is that complex shaped regions can be detected and handled implicitly, allowing numerically stable topological changes.

Let $I\colon \Omega \to \Re^2$ be the intensity image function where $\Omega \subset \Re^2$.

Let a family of parametrized closed contours $\gamma(\mathbf{x(t)}) : [0, \infty) \to \Re^2$ be, where $\mathbf{x(t)} = (x(t), y(t))$, is the position vector of the curve and t is the evolution time. Initial contour is $\gamma_0(\mathbf{x(0)})$.

Let $\gamma(\mathbf{x(t)})$ be a dynamic front in the image and be the zero level of a smooth continuous scalar 3D function $\phi(\mathbf{x(t)})$, known as the level set function, the implicit contour at any time t is given by

$$\gamma(\mathbf{x}(t)) \equiv \{(\mathbf{x}(t))/\phi(\mathbf{x}(t)) = 0\}$$

By differentiating with respect to t the expression $\phi(\mathbf{x}(t)) = 0$, the level set equation is

$$\frac{\partial \phi(\mathbf{x}(t))}{\partial t} + \frac{dx(t)}{dt}\frac{\partial \phi(\mathbf{x}(t))}{\partial x} + \frac{dy(t)}{dt}\frac{\partial \phi(\mathbf{x}(t))}{\partial y} = 0 \tag{1}$$

The level set function has to satisfy the condition $|\nabla\phi(\mathbf{x}(t))| \neq 0$ for all $(\mathbf{x}(t)) \in \gamma(\mathbf{x}(t))$; this is possible because $\gamma(\mathbf{x}(t))$ is a regular curve.

Let $\mathbf{n} \equiv (n_1, n_2)$ be the unit normal vector to the curve $\gamma(\mathbf{x}(t))$

$$n_1 = \frac{\frac{\partial \phi(\mathbf{x}(t))}{\partial x}}{|\nabla\phi(\mathbf{x}(t))|}, \qquad n_2 = \frac{\frac{\partial \phi(\mathbf{x}(t))}{\partial y}}{|\nabla\phi(\mathbf{x}(t))|}, \qquad \mathbf{n} = -\frac{\nabla\phi}{|\nabla\phi|}$$

that is

$$\frac{\partial \phi(\mathbf{x}(t))}{\partial x} = |\nabla\phi(\mathbf{x}(t))|n_1,$$

$$\frac{\partial \phi(\mathbf{x}(t))}{\partial y} = |\nabla\phi(\mathbf{x}(t))|n_2.$$

substituting them in (1), we obtain

$$\frac{\partial \phi(\mathbf{x}(t))}{\partial t} + (n_1\frac{dx(t)}{dt} + n_2\frac{dy(t)}{dt})|\nabla\phi(\mathbf{x}(t))| = 0, \tag{2}$$

where $(n_1\frac{dx(t)}{dt} + n_2\frac{dy(t)}{dt})$ describes the curve evolution in the normal direction, so that we have

$$(n_1\frac{dx(t)}{dt} + n_2\frac{dy(t)}{dt}) = \frac{d\gamma(\mathbf{x}(t))}{dt}.$$

Then, (2) becomes

$$\frac{\partial \phi(\mathbf{x}(t))}{\partial t} + \frac{d\gamma(\mathbf{x}(t))}{dt}|\nabla\phi(\mathbf{x}(t))| = 0, \tag{3}$$

or also

$$\frac{d\gamma(\mathbf{x}(t))}{dt} = -\frac{\partial \phi(\mathbf{x}(t))/\partial t}{|\nabla\phi\mathbf{x}(t))|}. \tag{4}$$

In the following, we make use of another important intrinsic geometric property, that is the curvature of each level set, given by

$$k(\mathbf{x}(t)) = -\nabla \cdot \left(\frac{\nabla\phi(\mathbf{x}(t))}{|\phi(\mathbf{x}(t))|}\right). \tag{5}$$

We now introduce a function $v(\mathbf{x}(t))$, named speed function, which is defined as

$$\frac{d\gamma(\mathbf{x}(t))}{dt} = v(\mathbf{x}(t))\mathbf{n}. \tag{6}$$

Moreover, for the sake of simplicity, we can write $\mathbf{x} \equiv (x(t), y(t))$, $\gamma \equiv \gamma(\mathbf{x}(t))$ and $k \equiv k(\mathbf{x}(t))$.

2.1   Level Set Implementation

For the numerical approximation in a domain $\Omega \subset \Re^2$, we introduce the computational domain Ω^* obtained by considering a uniform partition of Ω in $(N-1) \times (M-1)$ disjoint rectangles Ω_{ij} with edges $\Delta x = \Delta y = 1$

Let $P_{i,j} \equiv P(x_i, y_j)(i = 1, ..., N; j = 1, ..., M)$ be a point in Ω^* and $\phi_{i,j}^n$ the value of the function $\phi(\mathbf{x}, t)$ at $P_{i,j}$ at time t^n.

The $\phi(\mathbf{x}, t)$ function is initialized as a signed distance function

$$\phi(\mathbf{x}, t = 0) = \pm d \quad \textbf{where} \quad d(\mathbf{x}) = \min_{\mathbf{x}_\gamma \in \gamma} |\mathbf{x} - \mathbf{x}_\gamma|$$

Now, known the value of $\phi_{i,j}^n$, the value $\phi_{i,j}^{n+1}$ is computed by a 2-order ENO scheme with the TVD (Total Variation Diminishing) Runge Kutta scheme for the time integration. The distance calculation is performed in the process of re-initialization [15].

3   Methodology

In the level set equation, the evolution of the initial curve is determined by the speed function. The combined speed, proposed in this paper, is obtained by the contributions of the two speed functions:

- average-based speed, based on variational level set formulation. In this case the speckled image intensity is described by the Gamma distribution [12]. The speed function depends on mean intensity of each region Gamma-distributed. The minimization of the functional is to seek in the Euler-Lagrange descent equations, implemented via curves evolution and level sets.
- gradient-based speed, based on level set method [6]. In this case the speed function depends on gradient image.

The main steps of the proposed segmentation process, shown in Figure 1, are

- the re-initialization, where the distance calculation is performed in order to transform the function ϕ in a signed distance function,
- the speed computation obtained by the combination between the average-based speed and gradient-based speed,
- the level set function ϕ computation that, at the convergence, determines the contour to be extracted.

3.1   Average-Based Speed

The goal of the segmentation process in this work is to extract different types of regions, foreground and background R_i, $i \in \{1, ..., n\}$ [12]. In this section n will be $n = 2$: object and background.

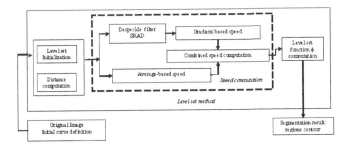

Fig. 1. Segmentation process

Let $I(\mathbf{x})$ be the SAR image intensity which we model by a Gamma distribution [12]:

$$P_{\mu_{Ri},L}(I(\mathbf{x})) = \frac{L^L}{\mu_{R_i}\Gamma(L)}\left(\frac{I(\mathbf{x})}{\mu_{R_i}}\right)^{L-1} e^{-\frac{L\,I(\mathbf{x})}{\mu_{R_i}}}, \tag{7}$$

where L is the number of *looks*, that we assume to be the same in each region R_i and μ_{R_i} is the mean intensity of R_i. After some probabilistic considerations and algebraic manipulations we obtain the average-based speed given

$$v(\mathbf{x}(t)) = \frac{d\gamma}{dt} = -\left(\log\mu_{R_1} + \frac{I(\mathbf{x}(t))}{\mu_{R_1}} - \log\mu_{R_2} - \frac{I(\mathbf{x}(t))}{\mu_{R_2}} + \lambda k\right) \tag{8}$$

where a λk is a regularization term, with λ a positive real constant and k the mean curvature function defined in (5), μ_{R_1} and μ_{R_2} are the mean intensities of the foreground and background regions. From (3) we obtain the following level set equation

$$\frac{\partial\phi(\mathbf{x}(t))}{\partial t} + v(\mathbf{x}(t))|\nabla\phi(\mathbf{x}(t))| = 0 \tag{9}$$

At any time during the evolution of the curve the speed values are different, as the two regions change and consequently the means and the areas have to be re-computed.

3.2 Gradient-Based Speed

In this section the image gradient is used to identify the edges. Indeed, if in a zone the value of the gradient is high then the related pixels correspond to an edge [6] . The gradient-based speed function, in this case, is given

$$v(\mathbf{x},t) = -\frac{1}{1+|\nabla I(\mathbf{x})|^2} - \lambda k. \tag{10}$$

Substituting this expression in (9) we obtain the corresponding level set equation.

So, the speed term is defined in such a way that the curve proceeds rather fast in low gradient zones, while it wades through to high gradient ones. This strategy allows the curve to propagate until it achieves the limits of the regions contours in the image and then goes slowly close to those limits.

It is well known that in images corrupted by strong noise, the computation of gradient could detect false edges.

Because the SAR images are affected by speckle noise, they are pre-processed by means of the SRAD (Speckle Reducing Anisotropic Diffusion) algorithm which is an extension of Perona-Malik algorithm [13] for the speckled images. Thus a partial differential equation (PDE) approach to speckle removal is applied. It is solved numerically by an iterative method.

Let n_{SRAD} be the iteration number which performs the anisotropic diffusion on the image. After a certain number of executions, experimentally the more appropriate number was $n_{SRAD} = 20$.

3.3   Combined Speed

In this section we propose the new speed function. This function is constituted by the linear combination of the two functions corresponding to the average-based speed and gradient based speed and it is given by the following expression:

$$v(\mathbf{x}, t) = -\alpha \left(\log \frac{\mu_{R_2}}{\mu_{R_1}} + I(\mathbf{x}) \frac{\mu_{R_1} - \mu_{R_2}}{\mu_{R_1}\mu_{R_2}} \right) +$$
$$- (1 - \alpha) \left(\frac{1}{1 + |\nabla I'(\mathbf{x})|^2} \right) - \lambda k. \tag{11}$$

where parameter $\alpha \in (0, 1)$. As it is possible to see in the (11) the second term is computed on the image filtered by SRAD I', while the first term is computed on the original image I.

The first term is related to the smoothness of the contour, while the second term is related to boundary of the object.

In order to compare the segmentation results obtained changing the α parameter, we use a synthetic image (150 × 150), the leaf, which is a not easy image, since it is constituted by many indentations. The Figure 2 (a) shows a leaf image, speckled by *variance* 0.2 and the starting curve containing the object to be segmented respectively.

We underline the importance of the choice of the values of λ and n_{SRAD}, changing α. The Figure 2 (b) shows the resulting image obtained applying (9) and the average-based speed mainly, setting $\lambda = 0.3$, $n_{SRAD} = 20$ and $\alpha = 0.9$. In this case the speed based on the average intensities does not allow to discriminate the small indentations of the leaf outline. So the final curve stops outside the contour of the object. The Figure 2 (c) shows the resulting image obtained applying (9) and gradient-based speed mainly, setting $\lambda = 0.3$, $n_{SRAD} = 20$ and $\alpha = 0.3$. In this type of image, setting the value $\alpha = 0.1, 0.2$ leads the evolution curve passes through the boundary, even if we applied the SRAD filter to preserve and enhance the edges. In this case, the filtered image and the speed

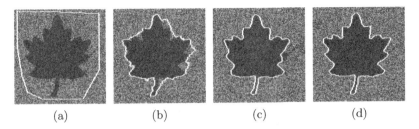

Fig. 2. Leaf speckled image of *variance* 0.2: (a) Starting contour, (b) result of average-based speed, (c) result of gradient-based speed, (d) result of combined speed

based on the image gradient stops the final curve internally to the contour of the object.

In Figure 2 (d), the combined speed, increasing the parameter $\alpha = 0.5$ and therefore balancing the contribute of the two speeds, improves significantly the result.

4   Tuning of Speed Parameters to Test Images

To demonstrate the efficiency of the proposed approach, the results obtained changing the α value are shown and compared. We used test images to have an exact reference of the contours to detect, since the real location of the edges is not known *a priori* in the images. Moreover there are not benchmark for the SAR images. The tests used were synthesized by corrupting the original images with the multiplicative noise speckle. The proposed procedure is applied to the test image (150×150), constituted by a single region and background. The Figure 3 shows an image of a single object: (a) clean image without noise; (b), (c) and (d) images with speckle noise of *variance* 0.1, 0. 2 and 0.3 respectively; (e) and (f) with noise obtained by patterns of SAR image.

To evaluate results obtained, accuracy indicators are calculated:

- Maximum distance (Max dist) and Mean distance (Mean dist), calculated as Euclidean distances between pixels of the real curve and the computed one,
- Regions Error (RE), percentage of error in the resulting regions identified by the procedure, given by the following expression:

$$RE = \frac{c}{m \times n} \times 100$$

where $m \times n$ is the number of total pixels of the image and e is the number of wrong pixels in the regions computed.

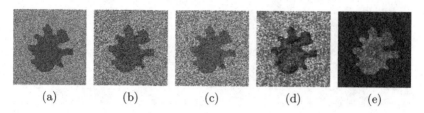

(a)   (b)   (c)   (d)   (e)

Fig. 3. Test images (150×150): (a) speckled image of *variance* 0.1, (b) speckled image of *variance* 0.2, (c) speckled image of *variance* 0.3, (d) and (e) speckled images by SAR patterns

Results of Single Region. In this section we present the contours obtained by setting the parameters $\lambda = 0.3$, $n_{SRAD} = 10$ and varying $\alpha \in (0.1, 0.9)$.

Moreover we calculated the corresponding error indicators, reported in the Tables.

In Figure 4 the resulting contours of the Figure 3 (a) are reported. In Table 1 the accuracy indicators related to the resulting contours of Figure 4 are synthesized.

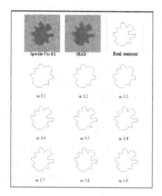

Fig. 4. Resulting contours for the image of Figure 3(a)

Table 1. Accuracy parameters of Figure 4

α	Max dist	Mean dist	RE
0.1	19	2.7	3.0%
0.2	19	2.3	2.2%
0.3	19	2.2	1.9%
0.4	7.2	0.7	0.5%
0.5	7.3	0.6	0.2%
0.6	7.3	0.5	0.4%
0.7	7.3	0.5	0.4%
0.8	7.3	0.4	0.4%
0.9	7.6	0.5	0.5%

In this image, *variance* $= 0.1$, we can note the best result is obtained by $\alpha = 0.5$.

In Figure 5 the resulting contours of Figure 3 (b) are reported. In Table 2 the error indicators related to the results of Figure 5 are synthesized.

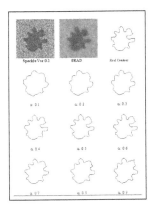

Table 2. Accuracy parameters of Figure 5

α	Max dist	Mean dist	RE
0.1	23	5	5.9%
0.2	19	3.4	3.9%
0.3	15	2.2	2.5%
0.4	3	0.5	0.5%
0.5	3	0.5	0.3%
0.6	3	0.5	0.4%
0.7	12	1.3	1.3%
0.8	14.8	1.6	1.8%
0.9	14.8	1.7	2.2%

Fig. 5. Resulting contours for the image of Figure 3(b)

In this image, *variance* = 0.2, the best result is given by α = 0.5.

In Figure 6 the resulting contours of Figure 3 (c) are reported. In Table 3 the error indicators related to the Figure 6 are synthesized.

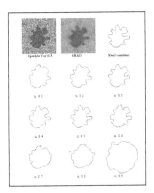

Table 3. Accuracy parameters of Figure 6

α	Max dist	Mean dist	RE
0.1	17	3.1	3.5%
0.2	17	2.3	2.3%
0.3	8.8	1.2	1.3%
0.4	7.6	1.1	1.3%
0.5	7.6	1.1	0.6%
0.6	9.1	1.4	2.2%
0.7	27.3	5	5.9%
0.8	29	6.4	7.9%
0.9	51.3	23.9	38.2%

Fig. 6. Resulting contours for the image of Figure 3(c)

In this image, *variance* = 0.3 the best result is given by α = 0.5. We can point out that the increasing of the *variance*, that is of the noise, implies the increasing of the error, in particular the Region Error increases.

In Figure 7 the resulting contours are reported. In Table 4 the error indicators related to the Figure 7 are synthesized.

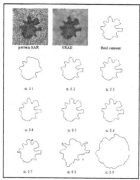

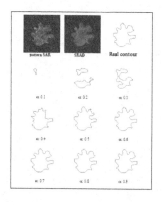

Fig. 7. Resulting contours for the
image of Figure 3(d)

Table 4. Accuracy parameters of
Figure 7

α	Max dist	Mean dist	RE
0.1	22	3.6	3.5%
0.2	7	0.6	0.5%
0.3	6.3	0.5	0.3%
0.4	5.8	0.5	0.3%
0.5	6.7	0.5	0.6%
0.6	6.7	0.5	0.8%
0.7	6.7	0.6	1.2%
0.8	25.6	4.6	9.6%
0.9	52.2	25	41.9%

In this image, in which the speckle noise is obtained by SAR image pattern, the best result is given by $\alpha = 0.4$.

Table 5. Accuracy parameters of
Figure 8

α	Max dist	Mean dist	RE
0.1	70.1	37.6	21.4%
0.2	26.1	6.7	12.7%
0.3	25.5	6.7	11.3%
0.4	21	3	3.3%
0.5	8.6	0.6	0.7%
0.6	2.8	0.3	0.1%
0.7	2.8	0.3	0.4%
0.8	2.8	0.3	0.4%
0.9	2.8	0.2	0.2%

Fig. 8. Resulting contours for the
image of Figure 3(e)

In Figure 8 the resulting contours of the Figure 3 (e) are shown. In Table 5 the error indicators related to the Figure 8 are synthesized.

In this image, in which the speckle noise is obtained by SAR pattern, the best result is given by $\alpha = 0.6$. In the graph of the Figure 9 (a) the values of the Tables 1, 2 and 3 of RE versus α are represented. In particular the solid line is related to the image of Figure 3 (a) with *variance* $= 0.1$, the dashed line to the Figure 3 (b) with *variance* $= 0.2$ and finally the dotted line to the Figure 3 (c) with *variance* $= 0.3$. We can note that the best result is given for $\alpha \cong 0.5$. In the Figure 9 (b) the graph shows the values of the Tables 4 and 5 of RE versus α. The solid line and dashed line are related to the results of the images of Figure 3 (d) and (e) respectively. Also in this case we can say that the best result is given for values with $\alpha \cong 0.5$.

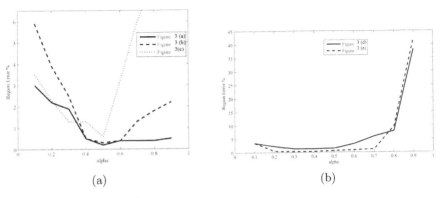

(a)   (b)

Fig. 9. Plots of error indicators RE: (a) RE of images of Figures 3 (a), (b) and (c), (b) RE of images of Figures 6 (d) and (e)

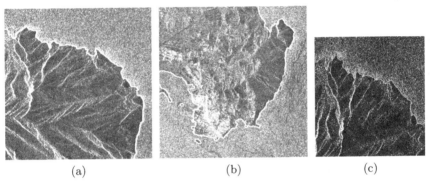

(a)   (b)   (c)

Fig. 10. ERS2 images: (a) resulting contour from Elba Island image, $\alpha = 0.5$, (b) resulting contour from the Toscana coast image, $\alpha = 0.4$, (c) CSM image -portion of Elba Island: resulting contour, $\alpha = 0.5$

In synthesis, as it is possible to see from the tests carried out, the α value, which determines the best segmentation, is given by $\alpha \cong 0.5$ with $\lambda = 0.3$ and $n_{SRAD} = 10$.

4.1 Application to SAR Images

We evaluate the performance of the level set segmentation applied to real images of coast regions given by systems ERS2 (2000) and CSM (2008), by using the combined speed by parameters tuning. It is important to underline that there are not benchmark SAR images. For this reason we compared the results obtained on synthetic images. We set the parameters $n_{srad} = 10$ and $\lambda = 0.3$. An example of indented contour is in Figure 10 (a), that shows the result obtained on a SAR image of 600×600 pixels representing part of the coast of Elba Island. The parameter $\alpha = 0.5$ is set.

In Figure 10 (b) the result, obtained on a SAR image of 750×750 pixels, representing part of the coast of the Toscana, is shown. The parameter $\alpha = 0.4$ is set. The image of Figure 10 (c) is an example of resulting contour from a low contrast image of (500×500) pixels.

We applied the proposed approach to images characterized by regions with different types of contours, regular and indented, and by low contrast between foreground and background. A important result has been obtained by the images of the Figures 10 (a) and 10 (c). These images represent the same portion of Elba Island acquired by the different satellites, ERS2 and CSM. We can underline that the proposed speed works in both images, locating the boundary of the coast which appears in the images. Both results were obtained, setting $\alpha = 0.5$. In the opinion of the experts, the results obtained are considered very good.

5   Conclusions

In this paper, we presented a fine tuning of the speed parameters in the level set equation in order to segment speckled images. This speed function is constituted by a linear combination of two distinct functions. The former, based on the average intensities of the regions, does not need to reduce speckle noise; the latter, based on the image gradient, takes into account filtering speckle noise using the SRAD technique. We have computed the solutions for synthetic images. The best results were obtained by combining of the parameters α, λ and n_{SRAD} in opportune way. We have obtained very good results also for real images constituted by regions characterized by different types of contours indented and by low contrast, by using the value of $\alpha \cong 0.5$. Moreover we have applied the method to the same portion of the Elba Island acquired by ERS2 SAR and CSM SAR satellites. In both images the resulting contours are very similar.

References

1. Maitre, H.: Processing of synthetic aperture radar images. John Wiley & Sons, Great Britain (2008)
2. Franceschetti, G., Lanari, R.: Synthetic aperture radar processing. CRC Press, Boca Raton (2000)
3. Germain, O., Refregier, P.: Edge location in SAR images: performance of the likehood ratio filter and accuracy improvement with an active contour approach. IEEE Trans. Image Processing 10, 72–77 (2001)
4. Mumford, D., Shah, J.: Optimal approximations by piecewise smooth functions and associated variational problems. Comm. Pure Appl. Math. 42, 577–685 (1989)
5. Chesnaud, C., Refregier, P., Boulet, V.: Statistical region snake-based segmentation adapted to different physical noise models. IEEE Trans. Pattern Analysis and Machine Intelligence 21, 1145–1157 (1999)
6. Sethian, J.A.: Evolution, implementation and application of level set and fast marching methods for advancing front. Journal of Computational Physics 169, 503–555 (2001)

7. Osher, S., Fedkiw, R.: Level Set Methods and Dynamic Implicit Surfaces. Springer, New York (2002)
8. Ben Salah, M., Ben Ayed, I., Mitiche, A.: Active curve recovery of region boundary patterns. IEEE Trans. Pattern Analysis and Machine Intelligence **34**, 834–849 (2012)
9. Liu, L., Zeng, L., Shen, K., Luan, X.: Exploiting local intensity information in Chan-Vese model for noisy image segmentation. Signal Processing **93**(9), 2709–2721 (2013)
10. Chan, T.F., Vese, L.A.: Active Contours Without. IEEE Trans. on Image Processing **10**, 266–276 (2001)
11. Mitiche, A., Ben Ayed, I.: Variational and level set methods in image segmentation. Springer (2011)
12. Ben Ayed, I., Mitiche, A., Belhadj, Z.: Multiregion level-set partitioning of synthetic aperture radar images. IEEE Trans. Pattern Analysis and Machine Intelligence 27, 793–800 (2005)
13. Yu, Y., Acton, S.T.: Speckle reducing anisotropic diffusion. IEEE Trans. on Image Processing **11**, 1260–1270 (2002)
14. Perona, P., Malik, J.: Scale space and edge detection using anisotropic diffusion. IEEE Trans. Pattern Analysis and Machine Intelligence **12**, 629–639 (1990)
15. Li, C., Xu, C., Gui, C., Fox, D.: Distance regularized level set evolution and its application to image segmentation. IEEE Transactions on Image Processing **19**(20), 3243–3254 (2010)

Bayesian Networks-Based Defects Classes Discrimination in Weld Radiographic Images

Aicha Baya Goumeidane[1](✉), Abdessalem Bouzaieni[2], Nafaa Nacereddine[1], and Salvatore Tabbone[2]

[1] Welding and NDT Research Center (CSC), BP 64, Cheraga, Algiers, Algeria
a.goumeidane@csc.dz
[2] Université de Lorraine-LORIA, UMR 7503 BP 239, 54506 Vandoeuvre-lés-Nancy, France

Abstract. Bayesian (also called Belief) Networks (BN) is a powerful knowledge representation and reasoning mechanism. Based on probability theory involving a graphical structure and random variables, BN is widely used for classification tasks and in this paper, BN is used as a class discrimination tool for a set of weld defects radiographic images using suitable attributes based on invariant geometric descriptors. Tests are performed on a database of few hundred elements where the results are outstanding and very promising, since they outperform those given by powerful SVM classifiers.

Keywords: Bayesian networks · Weld defects · Geometric descriptors · Radiography

1 Introduction

Welding is one of the major joining processes which are of an utmost importance in almost modern industries such aeronautic, oil and gas, nuclear, etc. The quality of the resulting welded joints determines whether they are suitable for subsequent manufacturing operation, or not. Radiographic Testing is still one of the most effective used Non Destructive Testing (NDT) methods. It describes the internal structure of the piece under investigation by the transmission of X-rays or Gamma-rays through it. Penetrated rays show variations in intensity on the receiving films depending upon the absorption characteristics of the object [1]. These characteristics rely upon the thickness, density, and material properties of the object exposed at a selected energy level. These films are examined by skilled operators called inspectors, to identify, after analysis, most types of defects in films [2]. Some of the most common weld defects that can be identified in the radiographic images are the porosities (due to entrapped gas), the solid inclusions (foreign matter entrapped during welding), the lack of fusion (lack of union between weld and parent metal), the crack (discontinuity by fracture in the metal) and the lack of penetration (the weld metal fails to penetrate the joint). Nevertheless, such analysis make the decisions based on the own experience and the visual acuity of the inspectors which could be inaccurate and subjective.

© Springer International Publishing Switzerland 2015
G. Azzopardi and N. Petkov (Eds.): CAIP 2015, Part II, LNCS 9257, pp. 554–565, 2015.
DOI: 10.1007/978-3-319-23117-4_48

Great efforts have been made towards the design of a computer-based inspection system with the purpose of improving robustness, accuracy, and speed of the inspection process [3]. These efforts dedicated to the development of such a system, should have three major functions: detecting defective regions from the background, extracting flaws from these regions and classifying them. These developments rely on image processing and pattern recognition. Therefore, this paper is concerned with the last step of the inspection system i.e., classifying the weld defects from the image background. Many works have been devoted to the classification of flaws in radiographic images in which artificial neural networks (ANN) are extensively exploited. Used alone [4][5][6][7] or combined to techniques like support vector machine (SVM)[8] , fuzzy reasoning [9][10], both of them [11] or with other technics like principal components analysis (PCA) [7], the results have enhanced the classification efficiency. Also other studies have been done in the scope of weld defect classification using, among others, SVM [12][13], Fuzzy logic [14] alone, minimum distance classifier [15], with different degrees of success. It is well known that classification is the basic task in data analysis and pattern recognition to identify the class labels for instances based on a set of attributes; that is, a function that assigns a class label to instances described by a set of attributes [16]. A Bayesian network consists of a combination of a structure and a set of conditional probabilities. The structure is a directed acyclic graph in which nodes represent random variables and arcs represent variable dependencies. These dependencies are quantified by conditional probabilities for each node given its parents. Bayesian networks are often used as classifiers. As reported by [17], Bayesian network classifiers have many advantages over other classification techniques by offering, among others, an explicit, graphical, and interpretable representation of uncertain knowledge in a probabilistic framework. As they have as output a probabilistic model, decision theory is applicable for dealing, for example, with cost-sensitive problems. Its representation obtained by mixing expert knowledge and data, permits the expression of conditional dependencies and independencies, handles incomplete data in both learning and inference stages, and fits more complex classification problems in discrete, continuous, and mixed data domains. And last but not least, numerous successful real-world applications, dealing with BN, have been reported in the literature, with competitive performance results against state-of-the-art classifiers [17] [18]. The remainder of the paper is organized as follows. Section 2 is devoted to the features extraction. Section 3 is dedicated to the BN-based the proposed classification method. In section 4 we will present the experiments and discuss the results. Conclusion will be drawn in the section 5.

2   Radiographic Images Segmentation and Features Extraction

2.1   Image Segmentation

One of the essential processes in computer vision consists of reducing the huge quantity of information, contained in an image, by preserving only the most important points for further image analysis. This is done by image segmentation which is a very significant issue because the result, obtained at the end of it, strongly governs the image analysis and pattern recognition stage [19]. Image segmentation can be achieved by different segmentation techniques reported in the literature. Since there is no general solution with the problem of image segmentation, these techniques must often take into consideration the specificities of the image to treat, the type of visual indices to extract, the nature of the problem to be solved downstream of the segmentation and the exploiting constraints such as algorithmic complexity, real time processing, material constraints related to acquisition system and storage capacity [19]. Because of the bad contrast, the non-uniform illumination and the noise that characterize the radiographic films, we have used the defect extraction technique described in [20] to recover defect shapes as illustrated by Fig.1.

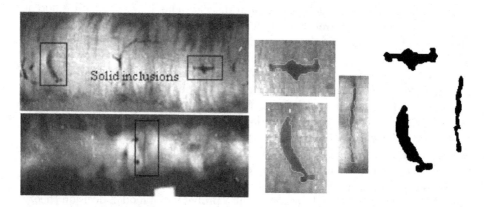

Fig. 1. Some defects and binarized versions after the segmentation step using the method in [20].

2.2 Features Extraction

The proposed weld defect classification consists of two steps. The first one relies on the feature computation on the defects indicators. The second one deals with the classifier design. The purpose of this first step is to discriminate between all the classes of the defects that can occur in the weld bead. The used features must combine all available information sources to solve the class defect classification problem. Unfortunately, many different factors come into play when creating the radiographic films which make the use, for example, of intensity to our sense, not recommended as long as the illumination can change drastically from a film to another. For this reason, we find that there is no real common measurement between the intensities and even textures of defects when changing source of radiation and condition of films creation. However, we can take advantage from the defects shape characteristics, and therefore, select features with discrimination capacities. This fact is fortunate since the defect shape is one of the most important aspects that make the radiographic inspectors able to distinguish between weld defect classes. A review work, among many others, on the shape description techniques can be found in [21]. Generally, the shape description is done via a representation of the shape by highlighting properties such as fidelity, discrimination, adaptability with the operations of pattern recognition, compactness, and invariance to the geometric transformations of translation, rotation and scaling. In fact, this last property is justified by the fact that the defect can be viewed from different angles depending on the orientation and the position of the investigated piece involving variations of dimensions, position and orientation in the radiographic film. Geometric shape descriptors reveal to be effective for weld defect description because they are directly linked to weld defect types or classes [3]. The following invariant geometric features are retained:

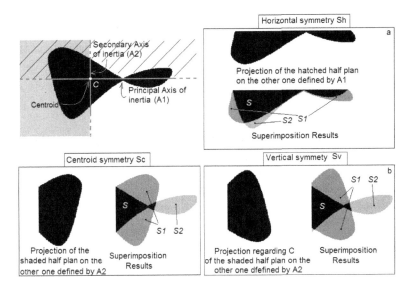

Fig. 2. Symmetry computation over the half-plan projections along the inertia axis and the centroid. S is the matching pixels after projection, S_1 and S_2 are the difference pixels

Compactness (Rp): It is the measure of how closely the shape of a defect approaches a disk. It equals $4\pi A/p^2$ where p and A are the perimeter and the area of defect, respectively. This shape attribute assumes values that belong to $[0\ 1]$. Close to 1 for a disk shaped defect (porosity) and close to 0 for something infinitely non-circular (as cracks).

Elongation index (Ei): It is the ratio of the width and the length of the oriented minimum bounding box of the defect. It takes a value between 0 and 1. This index gives little values for elongated defects (cracks and lack of penetration) and quite big values for porosity and solid inclusion.

Rectangularity (Rc): It is the ratio of the defect area to its minimum oriented bounding box one. This is the feature that fits the lack of penetration defects that are nearly rectangular. This feature exhibits values close to 1 for them.

Solidity (Sl): It is the ratio of the defect area to the one of the convex hull defined on the defect. It equals 1 for convex defects (close to 1 for lack of penetrations and porosities).

Symmetry (Sm): Computed as $Sup\left(\frac{S_h+S_v}{2}, S_c\right)$ where S_h, S_v and S_c are the symmetries along the principal axis of inertia, the secondary axis of inertia and the centroid respectively (see Fig.2). They are equal to the ratios of the number of the matched pixels (S) in the semi-plan projection cases (depicted in Fig.2a-c) on the superimposition of the total number of pixels, which is the sum of S and the differences pixels S_1 and S_2. The highest values of this index go to porosities and lack of penetration (nearby 1) and the lowest ones to inclusions and twisted cracks.

Deviation index to the largest inscribed circle (Di): It is the ratio of the defect maximum inscribed circle area to the defect one, and it approaches 1 for porosities.

Euclidian lengthening (El): It is the ratio of the maximum inscribed disk radius of the defect to the minimum circumscribed disk radius. The lowest El are evidences of cracks. The biggest ones go to the porosities.

To summarize, Fig.3 shows some geometric parameters used in the features computation.

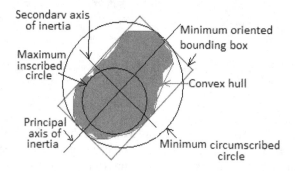

Fig. 3. Geometric parameters used in the features computation

3   Bayesian Networks-Based Weld Defect Classification

A Bayesian network (BN) is an annotated directed acyclic graph (DAG) that encodes a joint probability distribution over a set of random variables $\{X_1, \ldots, X_n\}$. Formally, a Bayesian network is a pair $B =< G, \Theta >$, where G, is a DAG whose vertices correspond to random variables $X_1, \ldots, X_n$, and whose edges represent direct dependencies between them [22]. G encodes independence assumptions: each variable X_i is independent of its non-descendants given its parents in G. Θ represents the set of parameters that quantifies the graph. It contains a parameter $\Theta_{x_i/\pi_{x_i}}$ for each possible value x_i of X_i, and π_{x_i} of π_{X_i} denotes the set of parents of X_i in G. That is, a BN B defines a unique joint probability distribution over the random variables set given by

$$P_B(X_1, X_2, ..., X_n) = \prod_{i=1}^{n} P_B(X_i/\pi_{X_i}) = \prod_{i=1}^{n} \Theta_{X_i}/\pi_{x_i} \qquad (1)$$

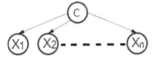

Fig. 4. An example of Naïve Bayes Network.

The Naïve Bayes Network (NBN) is the simplest Bayesian network in terms of graphical structure and parameter learning. The graph representing NBN is restricted to a tree where the root can be considered as a class variable C and the directed edges lead from the root (the class) to the remaining variables (attributes) [23]. Hence, the class node is the parent of all attribute nodes in NBN as depicted in Fig.4. Derived from BN by assuming the conditional independence of its attributes, the NBN is fully defined by the conditional probabilities of each attribute given the class. According to the hypothesis of conditional independence between child nodes and the special case of $\pi_C = \{\}$, the joint probability of all nodes can be written as follows

$$P_B(C, X_1, ..., X_n) = P_B(C) \prod_{i=1}^{n} P_B(X_i/C) \qquad (2)$$

in which $X_1, X_2, \ldots, X_n$ denote the n features (attributes) and C denotes the class variable. The conditional independence property simplifies, therefore, the process of model learning from data and the calculation of posterior probabilities. Despite its simplicity, the NBN is known to be a robust method that exhibits good performance in terms of classification accuracy, including cases in which the independence hypothesis is violated. Because of its fast induction, the NBN is often considered as a reference method in classification studies [24]. Let c be the value of C, the corresponding NBN classification is the function that assigns a class label $\hat{c}$ as follows

$$\hat{c} = \arg \max_{c \in C} P_B(C) \prod_{i=1}^{n} P_B(X_i/C) \tag{3}$$

3.1   Naïve Bayes Network Learning

The goal of learning a Bayesian network is to find $B =< G, \Theta >$ that accurately models the distribution of the data. The selection of G is known as the structure learning and the selection of Θ is known as parameters learning. A NBN is easy to construct as the structure is given a priori (no structure learning procedure is required). Moreover, it is easy to learn the parameters for a given structure as the a priori probabilities are estimated from the training examples by counting the observed frequencies.

3.2   Automatic Space Feature Partitioning

In the BN, discrete variables should have a finite number of states, although all the chosen attributes take their values in [0 1], which represents a huge number of possibilities. To this end, a meaningful automatic partitioning of each feature space must be done during the training stage, based on the observed feature values distribution for all the classes. The states mentioned above cover then, all the feature values interval. Fig.5 illustrates this interval for the compactness for all the defects classes. It is worth to note that such a partitioning used on the training data, which is just a subset of the whole database, should take into account the spread of the feature values for the remaining data. Statistics on mean and standard deviation, μ and σ respectively, are then used. We assume as that, in real-time applications, we have no access to the test data. Since the interval division is made taking into account the feature interval values explained above, the space allocated to the variation of the feature for one class is equal to $[\mu - \sigma \ \mu + \sigma]$. If two successive intervals of the classes k and m overlap, the upper limit of the class k and the lower limit of the class m denoted respectively, U_k and L_m, are removed and replaced by one at the new location $Lc_{k,m}$ depending on the number of feature values lying in $[L_m \ U_k]$. If these values are V_m and V_k for the classes m and k, respectively, then

$$Lc_{k,m} = \frac{V_k}{V_k + V_m} U_k + \frac{V_m}{V_k + V_m} L_m \tag{4}$$

If these successive intervals are completely disjoint, then the two limits evoked before are moved in the middle of $[U_k \ L_m]$.

4   Experiments

With the aim to carry out the experiments, 344 weld defect regions extracted from weld radiographic films provided by the International Institute of Welding,

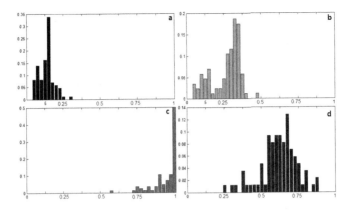

Fig. 5. Distribution of the compactness feature in the whole database for (a) cracks, (b) lack of penetration (c) porosities and (d) solid inclusions

are used. These defects represent four weld defect classes: crack (CR), lack of penetration (LP), porosity (PO) and solid inclusion (SI). After the segmentation step, the weld defect region is represented by its binary version as shown in Fig. 6. Hence, the database is indexed by the selected shape descriptors, Rp, El, Rc, Sl, Sm, Di and El. The database so created, consists then of a set of 344 feature vectors containing eight components. These components are the seven features components preceded by their belonging class which is kept in the training step and hidden in test one. For experiments purpose, the database is divided in two sets, one for the training and the other for the test. To ensure statistical validity of the results, for a given proportion of Data Training/Data Test, the experiments are carried out N times, $N = 40$, where the training set is selected randomly, and the results are averaged. Three proportions are used to achieve this first test. 25%, 50% and 75% for the training data against 75% ,50% and 25% for the test data. Results of the classification accuracy expressed in terms of confusion matrix are shown in Tables 1-3. We can remark from these confusion matrices that the accuracy increases when the number of training data increases to reach a global score of 96,25 % of good classification when the training data proportion is 75% of the whole data. In return the error classification rate is 3,75% which can be considered as a good performance.

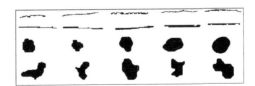

Fig. 6. Samples from the binarized images data, from top to down: cracks, lack of penetrations, porosities and Solid inclusions.

We have, then, compared theses results to two SVM multiclass-based classifiers applied on the same database [13] using the same features exploited by the proposed classifier. The classification score for the training set proportion of 75% for these classifiers are given in Tables 4 and 5. In Table 6, to compare our method to the SVM-based ones, the recognition rates for the whole weld defect image database are summarized. Even if this improvement is around 1.4% which could be considered as not very significant, but it remains very crucial for a domain such as the weld inspection because the NDT inspectors try at any price to prevent the incidence of false diagnostics. It is obvious that the latter is prejudicial for the examined component, and consequently for the overall industrial plan in question. That said, it is ascertained clearly that the proposed classifier outperforms the SVM-based ones.

Table 1. Confusion matrix for Training set percentage equals to 25%

Real \ Classified	CR	LP	PO	SI
CR	0.9500	0.0500	0	0
LP	0.0891	0.9063	0	0.0047
PO	0.0102	0	0.9531	0.0367
SI	0.0512	0.0004	0.0496	0.8988

Table 2. Confusion matrix for Training set percentage equals to 50%

Real \ Classified	CR	LP	PO	SI
CR	0.9651	0.0349	0	0
LP	0.0901	0.9064	0	0.0035
PO	0	0	0.9634	0.0367
SI	0.0157	0.0006	0.0552	0.9285

Table 3. Confusion matrix for Training set percentage equals to 75%

Real \ Classified	CR	LP	PO	SI
CR	0.9786	0.0214	0	0
LP	0.0512	0.9476	0	0
PO	0.0012	0	0.9679	0.0310
SI	0.0024	0	0.417	0.9560

Table 4. Confusion matrix for Training set percentage equals to 75% obtained by Multiclass-SVM classifier one against all

Classified Real	CR	LP	PO	SI
CR	0.9988	0.0012	0	0
LP	0.0930	0.9023	0	0.0047
PO	0	0	0.9832	0.0168
SI	0.0227	0.0004	0.0797	0.8973

Table 5. Confusion matrix for Training set percentage equals to 75% obtained by Multiclass-SVM classifier one against one

Classified Real	CR	LP	PO	SI
CR	0.9844	0.0156	0	0
LP	0.0832	0.9168	0	0
PO	0	0	0.9648	0.0352
SI	0.0023	0	0.0680	0.9297

Table 6. Total accuracy for Naïve Bayes classifier and Multiclass-SVM classifiers for a training percentage equal to 75%

Classification method	Accuracy
Proposed NBN	0.9625
SVM one against one	0.9454
SVM one against all	0.9489

Table 7. Confusion matrix for LOO

Classified Real	CR	LP	PO	SI
CR	0.9767	0.0233	0	0
LP	0.0349	0.9651	0	0
PO	0	0	0.9651	0.0349
SI	0	0	0.0465	0.9535

Furthermore, to assess more deeply the overall performance of the proposed classifier, we have carried out the leave one-out cross-validation process (LOO). LOO is a special case of k folds cross-validation where k equals the number of instances in the data. The learning algorithm is applied one time for each instance, using all the others as a training set, while the selected instance is used as a single-item test. This assessment permits, among others, to see which defects were misclassified when compared to all the defects. The results were not surprising since the mismatch occurs for cases where the defects in question have shapes that are closely related to the shapes of the class they were affected to. The mismatch appears inside the volumetric defect classes (solid inclusions/porosities) and also inside planar defect classes (cracks/ lack on penetrations). One can notice that few cracks were classified incorrectly as lack of penetrations and reciprocally. The same thing happens with porosities and solid inclusions. This fact remains reasonable because of their shapes similarities. Indeed, when a porosity looks like a solid inclusion, for example, even a human eye will be get into confusion and may classify this porosity as a solid inclusion, this is true for the other classes.

5   Conclusion

In this work we have investigated the use of Naïve Bayesian Network in the scope of weld defects classification in radiographic images by using discrete nodes and invariant geometric shape descriptors. The results are very promising for such a sensitive application despite of the structure simplicity of the used classifier. It is opportune then to go further in our investigations to use more complex descriptors in 2D and improve the Bayes network structure.

References

1. Halmshaw, R.: The Grid: Introduction to the Non-Destructive Testing in Welded Joints. Woodhead Publishing, Cambridge (1996)
2. Schwartz, C.: Automatic Evaluation of Welded Joints using Image Processing. Conference Proceeding of American Institute of Physics **657**(1), 689–694 (2003)
3. Nacereddine, N., Ziou, D., Hamami, L.: Fusion-based shape descriptor for weld defect radiographic image retrieval. Int. J. Adv. Manuf. Technol. **68**(9–12), 2815–2832 (2013)
4. Zapata, J., Vilar, R., Ruiz, R.: Automatic Inspection System of welding Radiographic Images Based on ANN Under a Regularisation Process. J. Nondestruct. Eval. **31**, 34–45 (2012)
5. Senthil Kumar, G., Natarajan, U., Ananthan, S.S.: Vision nspection system for the identification and classification of defects in MIG welding joints. Int. J. Adv. Manuf. Technol. **61**, 923–933 (2012)
6. Zahran, O., Kasban, H., El-Kordy, M., AbdEl-Samie, F.E.: Automatic weld defect identification from radiographic images. NDT&E International **57**, 26–35 (2013)

7. Nacereddine, N., Tridi, M.: Computer-aided shape analysis and classification of weld defects in industrial radiography based invariant attributes and neural network. In: Proceedings of the 4th International Symposium on Image and Signal Processing and Analysis ISPA, pp. 88–93 (2005)
8. Valavanis, I., Kosmopoulos, D.: Multiclass defect detection and classification in weld radiographic images using geometric and texture features. Expert Systems with Applications 37(12), 7606–7614 (2010)
9. Kim, T.-H., Cho, T.-H., Moon, Y.S., Park, S.H.: Visual inspection ystem for the classification of solder joints. Pattern Recognition 32, 565–575 (1999)
10. Sikora, R., Baniukiewicz, P., Chady T., Lopato, P.: Detection and Classification of Weld Defects in Industrial Radiography with Use of Advanced AI Methods (FENDT), 12–17 (2013)
11. Zhang, X.-G., Ren, S., Zhang, X., Zhao, F.: Fuzzy neural network classification design using support vector machine in welding defect. In: Liu, D., Fei, S., Hou, Z., Zhang, H., Sun, C. (eds.) ISNN 2007, Part II. LNCS, vol. 4492, pp. 216–223. Springer, Heidelberg (2007)
12. Zhang, X.-W., Ding, Y.-Q., Lv, Y., Shi, A., Liang, R.: A vision nspection system for the surface defects of strongly reflected metal based on multi-class SVM. Expert Systems with Applications 38(5), 5930–5939 (2011)
13. Mekhalfa, F., Nacereddine, N.: Multiclass Classification of Weld Defects in Radiographic Images Based on Support Vector Machines. In: Proceedings of the 10th International Conference on Signal-Image Technology & Internet-Based Systems, pp. 1–6 (2014)
14. Zapata, J., Vilar, R., Ruiz, R.: An adaptive network-based fuzzy inference system for classification of welding defects. NDT & E International 43(3), 191–199 (2010)
15. Liao, T.W.: Classification of weld flaws with imbalanced class data. Expert Systems with Applications 35(3), 1041–1052 (2008)
16. Friedman, N., Geiger, D., Goldszmidt, M.: Bayesian network classifiers. Mach. Learn. 29, 131–163 (1997)
17. Bielza, C., Plarrannaãga, P.: Discrete Bayesian Network Classifiers: A Survey. ACM Computing Surveys 47,1 (5) (2014)
18. Goldszmidt, M.: Bayesian network classifiers. In Wiley Encyclopedia of Operations Research and Management Science. John Wiley & Sons, pp. 1–10 (2010)
19. Soler, L., Malandrin, G., Delingette, H.: Segmentation automatique: Application aux angioscanners 3D. Revue de Traitement de Signal 15(5), 411–431 (1998)
20. Nacereddine, N., Hamami, L., Ziou, D., Goumeidane, A.B.: Adaptive B-spline model based probabilistic active contour for weld defect detection in radiographic imaging. Image Processing & Communications Challenges 2, AISC, vol. 84, pp. 189–197 (2010)
21. Zhang, D., Lu, G.: Review of shape representation and description techniques. Pattern Recognition 37(1), 1–19 (2004) (resumé sur les description)
22. Barrat, S., Tabbone, S.: A Bayesian network for combining descriptors: application to symbol recognition. IJDAR 13(1), 65–75 (2010)
23. Soria, D., Garibaldi, J.M., Ambrogi, F., Biganzoli, E.M., Ellis, I.O.: A 'nonparametric' version of the naive Bayes classifier. Knowledge-Based Systems 24(6), 775–784 (2011)
24. Tao, J., Li, Q., Zhu, C., Li, J.: A hierarchical naive Bayesian network classifier embedded GMM for textural Image. International Journal of Applied Earth Observation and Geo Information 14, 139–148 (2012)

Feature Selection in Gait Classification Using Geometric PSO Assisted by SVM

Tze Wei Yeoh, Saúl Zapotecas-Martínez, Youhei Akimoto, Hernán E. Aguirre, and Kiyoshi Tanaka$^{(\boxtimes)}$

Faculty of Engineering, Shinshu University, 4-17-1 Wakasato, Nagano 380-8553, Japan
yeohtzewei@gmail.com,
{zapotecas,y_akimoto,ahernan,ktanaka}@shinshu-u.ac.jp

Abstract. Gait recognition is used to identify individuals by the way they walk. Recent research in automated human gait recognition has mainly focused on developing robust features representations and matching algorithms. To our best knowledge, feature selection is rarely addressed in gait classification problems. In this paper, we evaluate the performance of a *particle swarm optimization* (PSO) algorithm assisted by a *support vector machine* (SVM) for feature selection in gait classification. In this way, while PSO generates trial feature subsets, SVM estimates their fitness value during the search process. The resulting subset is evaluated by means of a SVM classifier to obtain the fitness value (correct classification rate) of such particle. The performance of the proposed approach is evaluated by using the well-known *Southampton covariate database* (SOTON). Our experimental results indicate that our proposed approach is able to achieve highly competitive results with respect to state-of-the-art approaches adopted in our comparative study.

Keywords: Particle swarm optimization · Gait classification · Feature selection · Support vector machines

1 Introduction

Robust and reliable human identification for surveillance and access control has became highly sought these days. Biometric-based human identification using physiological or behavioral characteristics is particulary interesting due to their universality and uniqueness [18]. Many biometric-based authentication methods have been proposed by using a wide variety of cues, such as fingerprint, face, iris, hand and gait. Among them, human gait identification (i.e., identifying individuals by the way they walk), has gained considerable attention due to its ability to recognize person's identity at a distance while being unobtrusive and non-perceivable [22]. Besides, gait can be observed and measured at low resolution, which could be extremely useful when the high-resolution face or the iris information are not available. There is much evidence from psychophysical, medical and biomechanical experiments indicating that gait patterns are unique to each individual [9]. In comparison to other biometric modalities, gait is also less likely to be obscured [22].

© Springer International Publishing Switzerland 2015
G. Azzopardi and N. Petkov (Eds.): CAIP 2015, Part II, LNCS 9257, pp. 566–578, 2015.
DOI: 10.1007/978-3-319-23117-4_49

In the specialized literature, a wide variety of gait recognition systems have been proposed (for a recent review see [18]). Some of these approaches [8,24] have mainly considered conventional dimensionality reduction or statistical tools, such as: Principal Component Analysis (PCA) and Analysis of Variance (ANOVA). In [6], Guo and Nixon used Mutual Information (MI) to measure the utility of selected features in recognition. Bashir et al. [1] developed a cross validation-based approach and an effective measurement of the relevance of Gait Energy Image (GEI) features in their approach. However, these approaches in gait analysis, have mostly been evaluated without explicitly considering the most relevant gait features, which might have compromised the classification performance. Since gait features extracted from segmented video sequences are frequently interspersed with background noise or covariate factors, the classification could be misguided. Without employing gait feature selection, however, many of the gait features being extracted could be redundant or irrelevant to the gait recognition task. In general, feature selection could provide valuable clues in terms of understanding the underlying distinctness among human gait patterns.

In the features subset selection, there exist two main approaches that have been commonly adopted [10,17]: the wrapper and filter approaches. For feature subset, the wrapper approach uses machine learning algorithms in the search process, while the filter approach filters undesirable features of data before the classification process. Wrapper approaches commonly utilize machine learning techniques to search the best features subset, i.e., they need to train a data set for selecting the best features. In contrast, filter selection methods become efficient (in terms of computational complexity) because they use heuristic searches on general characteristics of the data instead of training a large data set as wrapper methods.

Swarm intelligence is a branch of artificial intelligence (more precisely computational intelligence) that involves optimization problems [14]. Among these bio-inspired techniques, *Particle Swarm Optimization* (PSO) [12] algorithms have gained popularity for their capacity to solve, in an effective way, continuous [11,12] and combinatorial [13,15,19] optimization problems. The idea of using an evolutionary computational approach for feature selection in gait recognition was firstly explored in our previous work [23]. To our best knowledge, we introduce in this paper, the first gait classification algorithm based on PSO. The proposed approach adopts a novel version of PSO, called Geometric PSO (GPSO) [19] by using binary representation of solutions in the Hamming space. During the search, our PSO algorithm generates trial feature subsets while SVM estimates their fitness value. We test and evaluate the performance of our bio-inspired algorithm by using the *Southampton covariate database* (SOTON) [21] and comparing its performance with respect to GA-SVM and various conventional approaches found in the specialized literature. As we will see later on, our proposed approach was found to be highly competitive against the gait classification methods adopted in our comparative study.

The remainder of this paper is organized as follows: Section 2 presents the basic concepts to understand our proposed approach. Section 3 describes the methodology of our proposed approach. The discussion and analysis of experimental results are presented in Section 4. Finally, Section 5 draws the conclusion and offers some directions for future research.

2 Background

2.1 Particle Swarm Optimization

Particle swarm optimization (PSO) is a metaheuristic originally proposed by Kennedy and Eberhart [12] for dealing with continuous and unconstrained optimization problems. PSO simulates the movements of a flock of birds which aim to find food. In PSO, a population of particles, commonly called *swarm*, is a set of candidate solutions encoded in a search space. PSO starts with the random initialization of a population of particles. The whole swarm moves in the search space to find the best solution by updating the position of each particle based on experience of its own and its neighboring particles. The current position of particle i is represented by a vector $\boldsymbol{x}_i = (x_{i1}, x_{i2}, ..., x_{iD})$, where D is the dimensionality of decision space. The velocity of particle i is represented as $\boldsymbol{v}_i = (v_{i1}, v_{i2}, ..., v_{iD})$. The best previous position of a particle is recorded as the personal best and the best position found in whole population is called global best. Each particle has a current position vector and a velocity vector for directing its movement. At each iteration, all the particles move in the search space to find the global optimum by updating the velocity and the position of each particle according to the following inertia equations [12]:

$$v_{id}^{t+1} = wv_{id}^t + c_1 r_1 (\boldsymbol{x}_{pb,i} - \boldsymbol{x}_{id}^t) + c_2 r_2 (\boldsymbol{x}_{gb,i} - \boldsymbol{x}_{id}^t) \tag{1}$$

$$\boldsymbol{x}_{id}^{t+1} = \boldsymbol{x}_{id}^t + \boldsymbol{v}_{id}^{t+1} \tag{2}$$

where t denotes the tth iteration, $d \in D$ denotes the dth dimension in the search space, $w \geq 0$ represents the inertia factor, $c1, c2 \geq 0$ are the constraints on the velocity, r_1, r_2 are two random variables having a uniform distribution in the range $[0, 1]$, $\boldsymbol{x}_{pb,i}$ and $\boldsymbol{x}_{gb,i}$ represent the personal best and the global best position for the dth dimension, respectively.

2.2 Support Vector Machine

Support vector machine (SVM) [5] is a powerful supervised learning tool for several pattern recognition problems. This learning technique is based on structural risk minimization principle which optimizes the training data to create machine learning model. Given a training set of instance-label pairs: $(\boldsymbol{x}_i, y_i)$, $i = 1, ..., l$ where $\boldsymbol{x}_i \in \mathbb{R}^n$ and $y_i \in \{1, -1\}$ (n and l denote the space dimensions and size of training set). In this particular case, if $\boldsymbol{x}$ belongs to positive category then $y_i = 1$; if $\boldsymbol{x}$ belongs to negative category then $y_i = -1$. SVM tries to find the optimal hyperplane to separate different classes by solving the following quadratic optimization problem:

$$\min_{\boldsymbol{w},b,\xi} : \frac{1}{2}\|\boldsymbol{w}\|^2 + C\sum_{i=1}^{l}\xi_i \qquad (3)$$
$$\text{subject to}: y_i(\boldsymbol{w}\cdot\phi(\boldsymbol{x}_i)) + b \geq 1 - \xi_i \ ,$$
$$\xi_i \geq 0, i = 1,...,l \ ,$$

where $\boldsymbol{w}$, b and ξ_i denote the weight vector for the learned decision hyperplane, the model bias, and the slack variable respectively. Parameter C is a penalty factor which keeps the balance of classification accuracy. In this work, C is fixed as $C = 1$. SVM classifies the test instance $\boldsymbol{x}$ based on the following decision function:

$$f(\boldsymbol{x}) = sgn\left(\sum_{i=1}^{l}\alpha_i y_i K(\boldsymbol{x}_i, \boldsymbol{x}) + b\right) \qquad (4)$$

where i, α_i and $K(\boldsymbol{x}_i, \boldsymbol{x}) \equiv \phi(\boldsymbol{x}_i)^T\phi(\boldsymbol{x})$ represent the support vectors, the Lagrange multipliers and kernel function, respectively.

3   Gait Feature Selection and Classification by GPSO-SVM

In this section, we describe our proposed approach for gait features selection and classification process. The proposed approach is designed to find the best gait feature subset in order to reduce the features for the classification process. Fig. 1 shows the general operational idea of our proposed approach, we can observe a simple framework of how gait features are extracted from the SOTON dataset and how the resulted subset is evaluated.

3.1   Gait Features Extraction

The original human silhouette images are obtained from the *Southampton covariate database* (SOTON) covariate database [21]. This database was used to evaluate the recognition rate of the walking subjects with different covariate factors. In most of the human silhouette images, shadow is chronically found near to the feet. This will hinder the gait feature extraction as it interferes with the body joint identification. Morphological opening is initially applied in order to reduce the background noise on the extracted human silhouette images. Each human silhouette is then measured for its width and height. Next, each of the enhanced human silhouettes is segmented into eight body segments based on anatomical knowledge. The lower body joints that define the pivot points in human gait are automatically identified and the joint trajectories are computed. After that, step size and crotch height are measured. In total, five joint angular trajectories have been extracted. There are various properties of gait that might serve as recognition features. For instance, the angular trajectories for walking sequence from right to left are hip angular trajectory (θ_1), left knee angular trajectory (θ_2), right knee angular trajectory (θ_3), left ankle angular trajectory (θ_4) and right ankle angular trajectory (θ_5). Fig. 2 shows nine gait features extracted from a human silhouette.

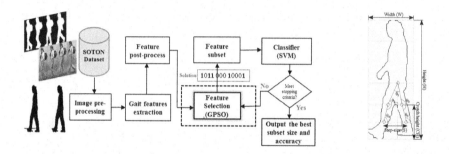

Fig. 1. The general process for gait features subset selection and classification using GPSO-SVM approach.

Fig. 2. All the extracted gait features.

3.2 Feature Post-Process

Feature Vector Construction To construct the feature vector, maximum hip trajectory (θ_1^{max}) is determined during a walking sequence from right to left. When θ_1^{max} is identified, the corresponding left knee angular trajectory (θ_2), right knee angular trajectory (θ_3), left ankle trajectory (θ_4), right ankle trajectory (θ_5), step size (S), width (W), height (H) and crotch height (CH) are also determined. For obtaining optimal performance, nine additional features are used. These features are the average of the local maxima detected for hip trajectory (A^{θ_1}), left knee angular trajectory (A^{θ_2}), right knee angular trajectory (A^{θ_3}), left ankle angular trajectory (A^{θ_4}), right ankle angular trajectory (A^{θ_5}), step-size (A^S), width (A^W), height (A^H) and crotch-height (A^{CH}). Thus, eighteen gait features are used to construct the feature vector as it is shown below:

$$
\begin{aligned}
F = \{ &\theta_1^{max}, \theta_2, \theta_3, \theta_4, \theta_5, W, H, S, CH, A^{\theta_1}, \\
&A^{\theta_2}, A^{\theta_3}, A^{\theta_4}, A^{\theta_5}, A^W, A^H, A^S, A^{CH} \}
\end{aligned}
\tag{5}
$$

Data Preprocess. Feature normalization is an important process, which needs to take place before using the gait features in the classification process. We normalize each extracted gait feature in different dimensions, thus, such features can be independent and standardized. In this way, the problem of biasing towards a particular feature can be avoided.

3.3 Feature Subset Selection by Using GPSO-SVM

Particle swarm optimization algorithms were introduced for dealing with continuous optimization problems. However, in real-world applications, there exist several problems which are formulated as combinatorial optimization problems. Since our gait feature selection problem can be represented in a binary way, we are interested in optimization problems which can be encoded in a binary representation. In the specialized literature, several binary versions of PSO can be found, see for example those introduced in [13,15]. In order to deal with the features selection problem for gait classification, we introduce an approach based on the geometric PSO framework [19]. This enables to us to generalize PSO to virtually any solution representation in a natural and straightforward way. This property was demonstrated for the cases of Euclidean, Manhattan and Hamming spaces in the referenced literature. In this work, we use a binary representation in Hamming space version of the *Geometric Particle Swarm Optimization* (GPSO) [19].

In the geometric PSO, the ith particle is represented by the vector $\boldsymbol{x}_i = \langle x_{i,1}, \ldots, x_{i,n} \rangle$ where each component $x_{i,j}$ takes binary values, i.e., $x_{i,j} \in \{0,1\}$ for each $j \in \{1, \ldots, n\}$ and $i = 1, \ldots, N$ (N denotes the number of particles in the swarm). In contrast with the original version of PSO [12], geometric PSO uses a *three-parent mask-based crossover* (CX) operator instead of the notion of velocity in order to compute the new position of the particle. Such operator is defined as follows [19]:

Three-Parent Mask-Based Crossover (CX): Given three parents $\boldsymbol{a}, \boldsymbol{b}$ and $\boldsymbol{c}$ in $\{0,1\}^n$, generate randomly a crossover mask of length n with symbols from the alphabet $\{\boldsymbol{a}, \boldsymbol{b}, \boldsymbol{c}\}$. Build the offspring $\boldsymbol{o}$ filling each position with the bit from the parent appearing in the crossover mask at the position.

To be more precise, for a particle i, the global best position $\hat{\boldsymbol{g}}$, the personal best position $\hat{\boldsymbol{x}}_i$ and the current position $\boldsymbol{x}_i$ take part in the CX operator. In this way, the position $\boldsymbol{x}_i$ is updated by the following equation.

$$\boldsymbol{x}_i = CX((\boldsymbol{x}_i, w_1), (\hat{\boldsymbol{g}}, w_2), (\hat{\boldsymbol{x}}_i, w_3)) \tag{6}$$

where weights w_1, w_2 and w_3 are convex combination of real values indicating, for each position, the crossover probability of having values from $\boldsymbol{x}_i$, $\hat{\boldsymbol{g}}$ or $\hat{\boldsymbol{x}}_i$. The weight values $w_1.w_2$ and w_3 associated to each parent represent the inertia value of the current position, the social influence of the global/local best position and the individual influence of the personal best position, respectively [19]. A constriction of the geometric crossover forces w_1, w_2 and w_3 to be non-negative and add up to one. Finally, the resulting particle is mutated by using uniform mutation with a probability P_m. For a more detailed description of GPSO, the interested readers are referred to [19].

In the proposed approach, a feature subset from F (see equation (5)) is represented by a particle in the swarm. Since a gait features subset is represented by the position of $\boldsymbol{x}_i$, the SVM classifier will evaluate each particle to assess the quality of the represented gait feature subset. The classification accuracy derived from the SVM classifier is directly used to as the fitness function. The evolutionary process is repeated until a termination condition is satisfied. In our proposed approach, the stopping criterion is based on the maximum number of generations parameter, predefined by the user.

4 Experimental Results and Comparisons

4.1 Experimental Setup

In this study, the experiments were carried out by using a SVM with a *radial basis function* (RBF) kernel. For the SVM, we refer to the description given by Burges [3] which implements the one-against-one approach [16] for multi-class classification. The experiment was carried out on SVM classification technique with various optimization parameters which were obtained during the training. Kernel's parameters such as penalty parameter (C) and gamma (γ) were trained and set as 45 and 2, respectively. For the SVM configuration, the same parameters were used in GPSO-SVM and SINGLE-SVM algorithms. The SVM classifier implementation in both approaches is based on the LIBSVM package [4]. The performance evaluation was in terms of Correct Classification Rate (CCR), True Positive Rate (TPR) and False Positive Rate (FPR).

The gait features extraction algorithms was implemented in C++ using the IDL workbench student version 7.1.1 64-bit (win64). For our GPSO-SVM approach, the PSO was implemented in JAVA referring to the Weka Package Library [7] in order to explore the feature space to identify the best subset of gait features for classification. The fitness function used in GPSO-SVM is the same one (described in Section 3.3) as in SINGLE-SVM. The empirical evaluation was performed using a PC with Intel® Core™ i5-2320 CPU running at 3.00GHz and 4.0 Gb RAM. GPSO-SVM and SINGLE-SVM algorithms on SOTON dataset were independent executed 10 times.

Dataset. The experiment was carried out for eleven subjects walking in parallel towards a static camera with fifteen covariate factors provided by the SOTON covariate database [21]. Each subject was captured wearing a variety of clothes (rain coat, trench coat and normal), footwear (flip flops, bare feet, socks, boots, trainers and own shoes) and carrying various bags (barrel bag slung over the shoulder or carried by hand on shoulder, hand bag held in hand, and rucksack). They were also recorded walking at different speed (slow, fast, and normal speed). For each subject, there are approximately twenty sets of walking sequences from right to left and vice-versa way on a normal track. The dataset consists of 3178 walking sequences from 11 subjects spanning 15 covariates. In total, there are 3,178 walking sequences that are used for training and testing process. We used normal walking sequences for training and other covariate factors walking sequences for testing. Individuals are unique in the gallery and each probe set, and there are no common sequence among the gallery set and all probe sets. Some examples of subjects with different apparels and the identified body joints are shown in Fig. 3.

Parameter Settings. The parameters used in our GPSO-SVM are shown in Table 1. These parameters were chosen based on several test evaluations of our proposed approach and should not be considered the optimal configurations. Table 2 summarizes the problem complexity of the dataset.

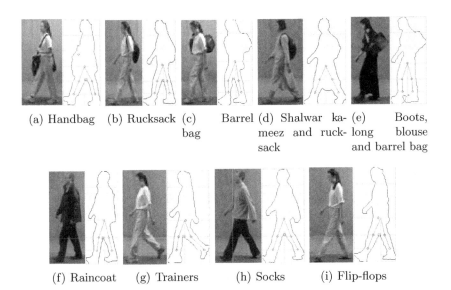

(a) Handbag   (b) Rucksack   (c)   Barrel   (d) Shalwar ka-   (e)   Boots,
                          bag   meez and ruck-   long   blouse
                                          sack   and barrel bag

(f) Raincoat   (g) Trainers   (h) Socks   (i) Flip-flops

Fig. 3. Body joint identification on human silhouettes with different apparels.

4.2   Discussion and Analysis

In this section, we aim to show the effectiveness of GPSO-SVM in Feature Selection for gait classification. We first utilize GPSO-SVM into the feature selection in a gait classification problem to test whether the feature subset can improve the accuracy of classification. Then, we compare the performance of the proposed approach with respect to other approaches on the gait classification problems. In this work, fair comparisons were done by employing (in the experiments) the same implementation conditions and the same database. In general, the evolution process of our proposed approach towards an optimal subset of gait features for the SOTON dataset is illustrated in Table 3. It is noticeable that in the iterative search process, the algorithm achieved the maximum fitness value at five iterations and then, it maintained the same value in the rest of iterations until the termination condition was satisfied. At the end of the search process, only sixteen features were selected as optimal set of features as it is shown below:

$$F^\star = \{\theta_1^{max}, \theta_2, \theta_4, W, H, S, CH, A^{\theta_1}, A^{\theta_2}, \atop A^{\theta_3}, A^{\theta_4}, A^{\theta_5}, A^W, A^H, A^S, A^{CH}\} \tag{7}$$

On the Effects of Covariate Factors. Robust human identification based on gait is challenging because of the presence of various types of covariate factors such as clothing, load carrying condition, footwear and walking speed. Variations in covariate factors have a strong impact on the recognition of gait. In order to assess the performance of our proposed approach on different covariate factors in

Table 1. Parameters for gait subset selection and classification.

Default parameters	Value
Swarm size	20
Number of generations (*Iter.*)	10
Neighborhood size	20
Probability of mutation (P_m)	0.1
(w_1, w_2, w_3)	(0.32, 0.33, 0.34)

Table 2. Problem complexity of the dataset.

Parameters	Value
Number of features	18
Number of classes	11
Number of instances	3178
Nominal features	Yes
Numeric features	Yes
Missing values	No

Table 3. Illustration of a typical searching process on the SOTON dataset.

Iter.	Best Solution	Fitness Value (%)	BFSL[1]
1	$\theta_1^{max}, \theta_2, \theta_3, \theta_4, \theta_5, W, H, S, CH, A^{\theta_1}, A^{\theta_2}, A^{\theta_3}, A^{\theta_4}, A^{\theta_5}, A^W, A^H, A^S, A^{CH}$	94.37	18
2	$\theta_1^{max}, \theta_2, \theta_3, \theta_4, \theta_5, W, S, CH, A^{\theta_1}, A^{\theta_2}, A^{\theta_3}, A^{\theta_4}, A^{\theta_5}, A^W, A^H, A^S, A^{CH}$	96.06	17
3	$\theta_1^{max}, \theta_2, \theta_3, \theta_4, \theta_5, H, S, CH, A^{\theta_1}, A^{\theta_2}, A^{\theta_3}, A^{\theta_4}, A^{\theta_5}, A^W, A^H, A^S, A^{CH}$	96.25	17
4	$\theta_1^{max}, \theta_2, \theta_4, \theta_5, W, H, S, CH, A^{\theta_1}, A^{\theta_2}, A^{\theta_3}, A^{\theta_4}, A^{\theta_5}, A^W, A^H, A^S, A^{CH}$	96.62	17
5-10	$\theta_1^{max}, \theta_2, \theta_4, W, H, S, CH, A^{\theta_1}, A^{\theta_2}, A^{\theta_3}, A^{\theta_4}, A^{\theta_5}, A^W, A^H, A^S, A^{CH}$	97.98	16

the SOTON database, five experiments were performed: Experiment 1 (Exp. 1) consists of walking sequences with various types of clothing; Experiment 2 (Exp. 2) consists of walking sequences with various load carrying; Experiment (Exp. 3) consists of walking sequences at different speeds; Experiment 4 (Exp. 4) consists of walking sequences with a variety of shoes; Experiment 5 (Exp. 5) consists of walking sequences from normal walking condition. Each experiment was carried out on the complete dataset, i.e., contemplating the eleven different subjects. The overall results are summarized in Table 4. From this table, we can observe that all solutions after applying our proposed feature selection technique reached a classification rate higher than 94% (see column "After FS (%)"). On the other hand, the feature subset length was reduced at least 22.22% while maintained high classification rate. These experiments revealed that the proposed approach is able to provide high classification accuracy even when the gait features selected to classify are reduced.

Comparing GPSO-SVM with GA-SVM and SINGLE-SVM. We have compared the results obtained by our proposed approach with respect to those achieved by the other classification methods, in order to have a better overview of the effect of GPSO-SVM in the search of an optimal features subset. From the point of view of average accuracy (in all independent runs), the proposed GPSO-SVM obtained a better performance even when the difference with regard to other approaches, as it is shown in Fig. 4, became insignificant.

---

[1] It denotes the Best Feature Subset Length. The resulting reduction of the original features length is evaluated by means of a SVM classifier to obtain the fitness value (CCR) of such particle.

Table 4. Feature selection on the effects of different covariate factors.

Experiment (Exp.)	Covariate Factors	No. Walking Sequences	Fitness Value Before FS (%)	After FS (%)		BFSL Reduction (%)
1	Clothes	448	94.34	95.36	13	27.78
2	Carrying conditions	886	93.70	94.68	14	22.22
3	Walking speeds	680	97.18	97.18	13	27.78
4	Footwear	923	97.51	97.77	14	22.22
5	Normal condition	241	98.34	98.34	11	38.89

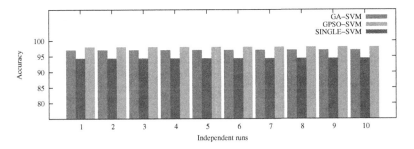

Fig. 4. Accuracy obtained for each independent run.

From Table 5, the best recognition rate, i.e. 98%, was achieved using the GPSO-SVM-based feature selection algorithm. In this instance, the selection algorithm reduced the size of the original feature vector by nearly 11%. In general, our proposed approach and the GA-SVM selection algorithms had comparable performance in terms of classification rates, but in all test cases, the number of selected features was less when using the GA-SVM-based selection algorithm. On the other hand, in terms of computational time, GA-SVM-based selection algorithm takes less computational time than GPSO-SVM-based selection algorithm in all tested instances. However, GPSO-SVM was computationally expensive than GA-SVM but the effectiveness of GPSO-SVM in finding the optimal feature subset in comparison to GA-SVM compensated its computational inefficiency. In Table 5, we can observe that SINGLE-SVM (all gait features have been exploited in classification) leads to worst performance amongst all. Therefore, we hypothesized that our approach could be, perhaps, performed well in complex datasets which may include a high number of gait features. In this sense, we show the feasibility of utilizing our proposed approach to select good feature subset for gait classification problems when deal with a large number of gait features.

Comparing GPSO-SVM with Conventional Approaches. Table 6 summarizes the comparison of results with respect to other conventional approaches (those without using features reduction, i.e. SVM-based methods) on the

---

[3] It refers to the fact that no feature selection was done on the dataset and all features have been exploited in classification.

Table 5. Comparison of GPSO-SVM with respect to GA-SVM and SINGLE-SVM.[3]

	GPSO-SVM	GA-SVM [23]	SINGLE-SVM
CCR (%)	97.98	96.99	94.37
TPR (%)	98.00	97.00	94.40
FPR (%)	0.20	0.30	0.60
Time (s)	210	190	20
Best Feature Subset Length (BFSL)	16	15	None
Total no. of attributes	18	18	18
Percentage reduction (%)	11.1	17	0

Table 6. Comparison of GPSO-SVM with respect to conventional approaches.

	GPSO-SVM	Bouchrika et al. [2]	Pratheepan et al. [20]	Bashir et al. [1]
CCR (%)	98.0	73.4	86	97.1
No. of subjects	11	10	10	11
No. of covariate factors	15	11	4	Unspecified
No. of walking sequences	3178	440	180	373
Feature extraction technique	Human silhouette joint identification	Elliptic Fourier descriptor	Dynamic static silhouette template	Gait representation using flow fields

SOTON covariate database. Our approach outperformed the results obtained by Bouchrika et al. [2], Pratheepan et al. [20] and Bashir et al. [1] after comparing the number of subjects, the number of covariate factors and the number of walking sequences which were used for the SVM training. The poor result obtained by Bouchrika et al. [2] is attributed to the requirement to manually label the model template to describe the motion of joints. Conversely, the results obtained by our proposed approach outperformed those achieved by the approach presented by Pratheepan et al. [20]. The main reason of such performance is because we do not incorporate the selection or estimation of the gait cycle. Although Bashir et al. [1] achieved better results, it is inappropriate to compare our results with them since they have only tested 10% of the total walking sequences on SOTON covariate database. Moreover, the total numbers of the covariate factors being evaluated is unclear.

5   Conclusion and Future Work

In this paper, a GPSO-SVM algorithm for feature selection in gait classification was introduced. Our proposed approach was based on the geometric version of PSO and it was assisted by SVM in order to identify the best features for gait classification. Experimental results showed GPSO-SVM feature selection algorithm in achieving excellent Correct Classification Rate (CCR) with the minimal set of selected features. We showed the effectiveness of geometric PSO when solving the feature selection problem in gait classification. Thus, our approach has shown the applicability of geometric PSO for gait feature selection problem.

As part of our future work, we are interested to explore the performance of the proposed PSO when dealing with larger gait dataset. Meanwhile, we will also focus to study the effect of variations in the parameters and their influence on the results. We will intend to further investigate whether the proposed approach can be used as a general Framework for different machine learning algorithms. Finally, it is also desirable to model the feature selection problem in a multi-objective optimization context, in this way, we can analysis human gait patterns from other perspective.

References

1. Bashir, K., Xiang, T., Gong, S., Mary, Q.: Gait representation using flow fields. In: BMVC, pp. 1–11 (2009)
2. Bouchrika, I., Nixon, M.S.: Exploratory factor analysis of gait recognition. In: 8th IEEE International Conference on Automatic Face & Gesture Recognition, FG 2008, pp. 1–6. IEEE (2008)
3. Burges, C.J.: A tutorial on support vector machines for pattern recognition. Data Mining and Knowledge Discovery $2(2)$, 121–167 (1998)
4. Chang, C.C., Lin, C.J.: Libsvm: A library for support vector machines. ACM Transactions on Intelligent Systems and Technology (TIST) $2(3)$, 27 (2011)
5. Cortes, C., Vapnik, V.: Support-vector networks. Machine learning $20(3)$, 273–297 (1995)
6. Guo, B., Nixon, M.S.: Gait feature subset selection by mutual information. IEEE Transactions on Systems, Man and Cybernetics, Part A: Systems and Humans $39(1)$, 36–46 (2009)
7. Hall, M., Frank, E., Holmes, G., Pfahringer, B., Reutemann, P., Witten, I.H.: The weka data mining software: an update. ACM SIGKDD Explorations Newsletter $11(1)$, 10–18 (2009)
8. Han, J., Bhanu, B.: Individual recognition using gait energy image. IEEE Transactions on Pattern Analysis and Machine Intelligence $28(2)$, 316–322 (2006)
9. Johansson, G.: Visual perception of biological motion and a model for its analysis. Attention, Perception, & Psychophysics $14(2)$, 201–211 (1973)
10. John, G.H., Kohavi, R., Pfleger, K., et al.: Irrelevant features and the subset selection problem. In: Machine Learning: Proceedings of the Eleventh International Conference, pp. 121–129 (1994)
11. Kennedy, J.: Bare bones particle swarms. In: Proceedings of the 2003 IEEE Swarm Intelligence Symposium, SIS 2003, pp. 80–87. IEEE (2003)
12. Kennedy, J., Eberhart, R.C.: Particle swarm optimization. In: Proceedings of the IEEE International Conference on Neural Networks, pp. 1942–1948 (1995)
13. Kennedy, J., Eberhart, R.C.: A discrete binary version of the particle swarm algorithm. In: 1997 IEEE International Conference on Systems, Man, and Cybernetics, 1997. Computational Cybernetics and Simulation, vol. 5, pp. 4104–4108. IEEE (1997)

14. Kennedy, J., Kennedy, J.F., Eberhart, R.C., Shi, Y.: Swarm intelligence. Morgan Kaufmann (2001)
15. Khanesar, M.A., Teshnehlab, M., Shoorehdeli, M.A.: A novel binary particle swarm optimization. In: Mediterranean Conference on Control & Automation, MED 2007, pp. 1–6. IEEE (2007)
16. Knerr, S., Personnaz, L., Dreyfus, G.: Single-layer learning revisited: a stepwise procedure for building and training a neural network. In: Neurocomputing, pp. 41–50. Springer (1990)
17. Kohavi, R., John, G.H.: Wrappers for feature subset selection. Artificial Intelligence 97(1), 273–324 (1997)
18. Lee, T.K., Belkhatir, M., Sanei, S.: A comprehensive review of past and present vision-based techniques for gait recognition. Multimedia Tools and Applications 72(3), 2833–2869 (2014)
19. Moraglio, A., Di Chio, C., Poli, R.: Geometric Particle Swarm Optimisation. In: Ebner, M., O'Neill, M., Ekárt, A., Vanneschi, L., Esparcia-Alcázar, A.I. (eds.) EuroGP 2007. LNCS, vol. 4445, pp. 125–136. Springer, Heidelberg (2007)
20. Pratheepan, Y., Condell, J.V., Prasad, G.: Individual Identification Using Gait Sequences under Different Covariate Factors. In: Fritz, M., Schiele, B., Piater, J.H. (eds.) ICVS 2009. LNCS, vol. 5815, pp. 84–93. Springer, Heidelberg (2009)
21. Shutler, J.D., Grant, M.G., Nixon, M.S., Carter, J.N.: On a large sequence-based human gait database. In: Lotfi, A., Garibaldi, J.M. (eds.) Applications and Science in Soft Computing. AISC, vol. 24, pp. 339–346. Springer, Heidelberg (2004)
22. Yeoh, T.-W., Tan, W.-H., Ng, H., Tong, H.-L., Ooi, C.-P.: Improved Gait Recognition with Automatic Body Joint Identification. In: Badioze Zaman, H., Robinson, P., Petrou, M., Olivier, P., Shih, T.K., Velastin, S., Nyström, I. (eds.) IVIC 2011, Part I. LNCS, vol. 7066, pp. 245–256. Springer, Heidelberg (2011)
23. Yeoh, T., Zapotecas-Martinez, S., Akimoto, Y., Aguirre, H., Tanaka, K.: Genetic algorithm assisted by a svm for feature selection in gait classification. In: 2014 International Symposium on Intelligent Signal Processing and Communication Systems (ISPACS), pp. 191–195. IEEE (2014)
24. Yoo, J.H., Nixon, M.S.: Automated markerless analysis of human gait motion for recognition and classification. Etri Journal 33(2), 259–266 (2011)

Automatic Images Annotation Extension Using a Probabilistic Graphical Model

Abdessalem Bouzaieni[1]([⊠]), Salvatore Tabbone[2], and Sabine Barrat[3]

[1] LORIA-Université de Lorraine, XILOPIX, Nancy, France
abdessalem.bouzaieni@loria.fr
[2] LORIA-Université de Lorraine, Nancy, France
tabbone@loria.fr
[3] Laboratory of Computer Science, François Rabelais University, Tours, France
sabine.barrat@univ-tours.fr

Abstract. With the fast development of digital cameras and social media image sharing, automatic image annotation has become a research area of great interest. It enables indexing, extracting and searching in large collections of images in an easier and faster way. In this paper, we propose a model for the annotation extension of images using a probabilistic graphical model. This model is based on a mixture of multinomial distributions and mixtures of Gaussians. The results of the proposed model are promising on three standard datasets: Corel-5k, ESP-Game and IAPRTC-12.

Keywords: Image annotation · Annotation extension · Probabilistic graphical models · Gaussian mixtures · Visual characteristics · Textual characteristics

1 Introduction

The fast growth of available visual contents, such as websites for sharing photos or videos, has led a need for indexing and search of multimedia information technology, especially in indexing and retrieval of images. The image annotation is one of the image semantic indexing techniques. We distinguish three types of image annotation: manual annotation, automatic annotation and semi-automatic annotation. The manual annotation consists on manually assigning a set of keywords to an image by a user. It is efficient but very expensive and time consuming for a human. The automatic annotation is intended to generate new semantic metadata for images via a computer system. Such metadata can be used by a search query of images. When the automatic image annotation process requires user intervention, we are talking about a semi-automatic annotation.

Automatic image annotation [1–4] has become an effective research topic since many years with the appearance of annotated image datasets as benchmarks. Machine learning techniques have been used increasingly in the area of images annotation. These techniques used a supervised learning process on a dataset of

© Springer International Publishing Switzerland 2015
G. Azzopardi and N. Petkov (Eds.): CAIP 2015, Part II, LNCS 9257, pp. 579–590, 2015.
DOI: 10.1007/978-3-319-23117-4_50

manually annotated images. The major drawback of these methods is that they require a large number of annotated examples to perform the learning. Another disadvantage is that the annotation is done all at once and can not be refined.

In this paper, we present a model of automatic annotation extension of images using a probabilistic graphical model. This latter allows combining the characteristics of low and high levels in order to extend the annotation to partially annotated images. This model does not require all the images in the learning dataset to be annotated. Quite the opposite, it can treat the problem of missing data. The model can also be used for image classification tasks.

The paper is organized as follows. In Section 2, an overview of existing works is given. Then, in Section 3, we present our annotation extension model using a probabilistic graphical model. Section 4 is devoted to experimental results and performance measurements on three datasets. Finally, our conclusion and future research lines are given in Section 5.

2   Related Work

The problem of image annotation has been widely studied in the last years, and several approaches have been proposed to solve this problem. These approaches can be classified into generative and discriminative models.

Generative models build a joint distribution between visual and textual characteristics of an image in order to find correspondences between image descriptors and annotation keywords. In the Duygulu et al.[18] model, images are segmented into regions. These latter are classified using a variety of descriptors. Learning correspondences between regions and keywords provided with images is performed to predict keywords for a new image. Liu et al. [19] have proposed the DCMRM model (dual cross-media relevance model) which estimates the joint probability by the expectation of the words in a predefined lexicon such as WordNet [15]. This model involves two types of relations in the image annotations: the word-to-image relations and the word-to-word relations. Both relations can be estimated using either research techniques of web data or from available training data. In [13], the authors used two types of graphs: graph based on images where the nodes are the images and the arcs are the relations between images, and graph based on words where nodes are words and arcs are relations between words. The first graph is used for learning relations between images and words, that is to say for getting candidate annotation for each image. The second graph is used to refine relationships between images and words for obtaining the final annotation for each image. SKL-CRM model is presented in [21]. This model is an improvement of the continuous relevance model (CRM)[17]. The latter is a static model which allows to assign keywords to an image using a training set. This is done by computing $P(w|f)$, where W is a set of keywords and f is a vector of characteristics of the annotated image. In [6], Barrat et al. proposed GM-Mult model for image annotation extension. In this model, the sample of visual characteristics (continuous variables) follows a law whose density function is a Gaussian mixture density and discrete variables (keywords) follow a multinomial distribution. In [5], a probabilistic graphical model was presented for images classification and annotation.

This model introduces a latent random variable to make the link between visual characteristics and keywords. This model has the disadvantage of requiring a preliminary segmentation of the images without textually annotating the image regions.

Discriminative models enable converting the problem of annotation into classification problem. Several classifiers were used for annotation such as SVM [20,28], KNN [11,24] and decision trees [27,29]. Lu et al. [23] propose a heuristic called the HSVM MIL of the SVM algorithm in order to learn the correspondences between image regions and keywords. Fu et al. [27] present a method for annotating images using random forests. They use the annotations contained in the learning images as control information to guide the generation of random trees, allowing collecting the closest neighbors, not only visually but also semantically related. This method considers the random forest as a whole and introduces two new concepts: semantic nearest neighbors (SSN) and the semantic similarity measure (SSM). In [24], the goal is to automatically annotate images using the method 2PKNN, a variant of the classical KNN method, and to propose a metric learning of weights and distances. For a non annotated image, its closest semantic neighbors corresponding to all labels are identified. Then, labels corresponding to this image are found from the selected samples. Guillaumin et al. [26] proposed the TagProp algorithm based on the KNN method and have achieved a very competitive performance annotation.

Other approaches [20,22] are a combination of a generative model and a discriminative model. In [20], the authors presented a hybrid model for the image annotation. More precisely, this model is based on a SVM used as discriminant model to solve the problem of poor annotations (the images are not annotated with all the relevant keywords). A DMBRM model is used as a generative model to solve the problem of unbalanced data (large variations in number of training samples by keyword).

From a learning set of annotated images, many automatic annotation methods [6,13,18,19] aim to learn the relationship between the visual characteristics and semantic concepts (keywords). These relationships are used to predict keywords for new images. The problem with these methods is that they require a large number of examples to perform the learning. However, in the real world, it is not always true that the available annotated images are sufficient. Several other methods of automatic annotation are based on the KNN [11,24,26,27]. These methods suffer from the problem of the semantic gap [4,27]. Indeed, the nearest neighbors according to the similarities of visual characteristics do not always have the same semantic meaning. A solution to this problem could be to take a set of partially annotated images and to extend the annotation to other images. In this perspective, we propose in this paper an automatic extension of images annotation.

The spirit of our works is the same as published in [6]. However, in our model of automatic annotation extension of images, the extracted visual features and the model structure are different. Our model has the advantage of using more relevant visual features and adding conditional dependencies in the structure to represent semantic relations between keywords. In addition, one advantage of the probabilistic graphical models is to treat the problem of missing data and to offer the possibility of combining multiple sources of information.

3 Image Annotation Extension

In this section, we detail our method of image annotation extension using a probabilistic graphical model.

This model is a mixture of multinomial distribution and Gaussian mixture. The proposed model is presented in Fig. 1. We assume that the visual characteristics are considered as continuous variables. They follow a law whose density function is a Gaussian mixture density. The semantic characteristics (keywords) are considered as discrete variables. They follow a multinomial distribution. The visual characteristics of an image are represented by two nodes:

- The *Gaussian* node is modeled by a continuous random variable which is used to represent the computed descriptors on the image.
- The *Component* node is modeled by a hidden random variable which is used to represent the weights of used Gaussians. It may take g values corresponding to the number of Gaussians used in the mixture.

The textual characteristics (keywords) are modeled by N discrete nodes, where N is the maximum number of keywords used to annotate an image. Arcs are added between the N nodes to represent conditional dependencies between the keywords. A *Class* root node is used to represent the class of image. It may take k values corresponding to the predefined classes $C_1, ..., C_k$.

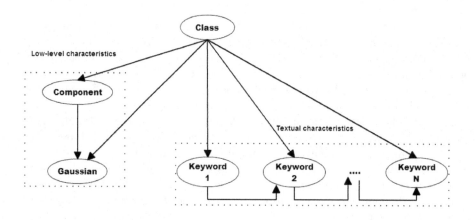

Fig. 1. Mixture model of multinomial distributions and Gaussian mixtures

Using such a network, we can write the joint probability:

$$P(C, TC, LLC) = P(C) \prod_{i=1}^{n} P(LLC_i|C) \prod_{i=1}^{N} P(TC_i|C) \qquad (1)$$

where TC represent textual characteristics (keywords $Kw_1, ..., Kw_N$) and LLC represent low-level characteristics (visual characteristics).

Let $Kw_1, ..., Kw_N$ be the set of keywords in an image. Each variable $Kw_j, \forall j \in \{1, ..., N\}$ may be represented by a Boolean vector space of the vocabulary words: $Kw_j = \{m_1, ..., m_n\}$, where $m_i = 0$ or $1, \forall i \in \{1, ..., n\}$ and $\sum_{i=1}^{n} m_i = k$.

Each variable $Kw_j, \forall j \in \{1, ..., N\}$ follows a multinomial distribution with parameters $\Phi_{TC} = (k, p_1, ..., p_n)$, where p_i is the probability associated with each value m.

$$p(m_1 = p_1, ..., m_n = p_n) = \frac{k!}{m_1! m_2! ... m_n!} p_1^{m_1} p_2^{m_2} ... p_n^{m_n} \qquad (2)$$

Let I be a set of m images $(im_1, ..., im_m)$ and $G_1, ..., G_g$ be g groups. Each group has a Gaussian density with a mean $\mu_l, \forall l \in \{1, ..., g\}$ and a covariance matrix $\sum_l$.

Let $\pi_1, ..., \pi_g$ be the proportions of the various groups, we denote by $\theta_k = (\mu_k, \sum_k)$ the parameter of each Gaussian, and $\Phi_{LLC} = (\pi_1, ..., \pi_g, \theta_1, ..., \theta_g)$ the global parameter of the mixture. Then the probability density of I conditionally to the class $c_i, \forall i \in \{1, ..., k\}$ is defined by:

$$P(im, \Phi_{LLC}) = \sum_{l=1}^{g} \pi_l p(im, \theta_l) \qquad (3)$$

where $p(im, \theta_l)$ is the multivariate Gaussian defined by the parameter θ_l. We denote by Φ the global parameter of this model:

$$\Phi = (\Phi_{LLC}, \Phi_{TC}) = (\pi_1, ..., \pi_g, \theta_1, ..., \theta_g, k, p_1, ..., p_n) \qquad (4)$$

Eq. (1) can be rewritten:

$$P(C, TC, LLC) = P(C) f(\pi_1, ..., \pi_g, \theta_1, ..., \theta_g, k, p_1, ..., p_n) \qquad (5)$$

The model parameters must be learned from a training set of images in order to estimate the joint probability of every image and every class. We must maximize the log-likelihood L_I of I:

$$L_I = log(P(C, TC, LLC)$$
$$= \sum log P(C) + \sum log f(\pi_1, ..., \pi_g, \theta_1, ..., \theta_g) + \sum log f(k, p_1, ..., p_n)$$
$$(6)$$

Since, the training set of images is incomplete, we use the EM algorithm [7] to learn the parameters of our model. This algorithm is the most used in the case of missing data. For a partially annotated image, represented by its visual characteristics $im_1, im_2, ..., im_m$ and its existing keywords $Kw_1, Kw_2, ..., Kw_n$, we use the bayesian inference to extend the annotation of this image with other keywords. We calculate the posterior probability:

$$P(Kw_i|im_1, im_2, ..., im_m, Kw_1, Kw_2, ..., Kw_n) \quad \forall\ i \in \{1, ..., N\} \qquad (7)$$

where N is the size of the used vocabulary. The keyword maximising the probability will be retained as a new image annotation. We can also calculate the posterior probability:

$$P(C_i|im_1, im_2, ..., im_m, Kw_1, Kw_2, ..., Kw_n) \quad \forall\ i \in \{1, ..., k\} \qquad (8)$$

with the aim to identify the class of image. The query image is assigned to the class C_i maximizing this probability.

4 Experimentations

In this section, we first present the image datasets used in our experiments, and the different performance evaluation criteria for the annotation. Then, we present experimental results obtained with our image annotation model.

4.1 Dataset and Evaluation Metrics

We performed our experiments on the three popular image annotation datasets Corel-5K, ESP-Game and IAPRTC-12.

- **Corel-5K:** This dataset is the most used for image annotation and retrieval. It is divided into 4500 images for learning and 500 images for testing with a vocabulary of 260 keywords. The images are grouped into 50 categories, each one containing 100 images. Each image is manually annotated with 1-5 keywords with an average of 3.4 keywords per image.
- **ESP-Game:** This dataset is obtained from an online game. We use the subset of 20770 images used in [20,24,26]. This subset is divided into 18689 images for learning and 2081 images for testing with a vocabulary of 268 keywords. Each image is annotated with an average of 4.7 keywords per image.
- **IAPRTC-12:** This dataset is a collection of about 20000 natural images. It is divided into 17665 images for learning and 1962 images for testing with a vocabulary of 291 keywords. Each image is annotated with an average of 5.7 keywords per image.

To compare our work with state of the art, we evaluate our approach with standard evaluation measurements. We annotate each image in the test dataset by 5 labels and calculate recall, precision, $F1$ and $N+$. Suppose a keyword

Kw_i is present in m_1 images in the ground truth, and it is expected to m_2 images during the test from which m_3 predictions are correct. The precision (P_{Kw_i}) is the proportion of images correctly annotated by Kw_i relative to all the images annotated by this keyword by the method: $P_{Kw_i} = m_3/m_2$. The recall (R_{Kw_i}) is the percentage of images correctly annotated with a keyword Kw_i relative to all the images annotated by this keyword in the ground truth: $R_{Kw_i} = m_3/m_1$. P and R are respectively the average of P_{Kw_i} and R_{Kw_i} on all labels. $Recall = \sum_{i=1}^n \frac{R_{Kw_i}}{n}$; $Precision = \sum_{i=1}^n \frac{P_{Kw_i}}{n}$

$N+$ is the number of words that are correctly assigned to at least one test image (number of words with strictly positive recall). The F_1 measure is the harmonic average between recall and precision: $F_1 = 2(P \times R)/(P + R)$.

Table 1. Details of the three datasets (Corel-5k, ESP-Game and IAPRTC-12)

Dataset	Number of Images	Vocabulary Size	Training Images	Test Images	Words Per Image	Images Per Word
Corel-5K	5 000	260	4 500	500	3.4	58.6
ESP-Game	20 770	268	18 689	2 081	4.7	362.7
IAPRTC-12	19 627	291	17 665	1 962	5.7	347.7

4.2   Features

We used global and local descriptors. The GIST descriptor has been proposed by Oliva and Torralba [30]. It captures precisely the global shape of an image by characterizing the orientation of the different contours that appear. The SIFT detector [31] can detect and identify similar elements between different pictures (landscapes, objects, person, ..). SIFT descriptors are numerical informations derived from local analysis of an image, and which characterizes the visual contents of this image independently from the scale, the observation angle and the brightness. They are generally calculated around interest points. SURF descriptor [32] is inspired from the SIFT descriptor. It is faster and more robust for different image transformations. It is based on the determination of the rotation angle of the analysis zone with the construction of a directed gradient histogram. The LBP [33] texture descriptor compares the luminance level of a pixel with the levels of its neighbors. Thanks to its discriminating power and the simplicity of computation, LBP became a popular approach in diverse applications.

4.3   Results

Fig. 2 illustrates the annotation of some images of the dataset Corel-5k where the labels of the ground truth are given. The bold keywords are found automatically by our annotation model. The bold and underlined keywords are added automatically by our annotation extension. For example, the fourth image is annotated manually by three keywords, two new keywords "arch" and "pyramid" are automatically added after the automatic extension.

sky, sun, clouds, tree	sky, jet, plane	bear, polar, snow, tundra
sky, sun, clouds, tree, <u>palm</u>	**sky, jet, plane, <u>f-16</u>, <u>kit</u>**	**bear, polar, snow, <u>ice</u>, slope**
water, boats, bridge	tree, horses, mare, foals	sky, buildings, flag
water, boats, bridge, <u>arch</u>, <u>pyramid</u>	**tree, horses, mare, foals, <u>field</u>**	**sky, buildings, <u>skyline</u>, <u>street</u>, <u>outside</u>**
flowers, house, garden	plants	mountain, sky, water, tree
flowers, house, garden, <u>lawn</u>, <u>reptile</u>	**plants, <u>leaf</u>, <u>stems</u>, <u>interior</u>, <u>zebra</u>**	**mountain, sky, <u>clouds</u>, tree, <u>whales</u>**

Fig. 2. Examples of image annotation dataset Corel-5k

Table 2 shows the performance of proposed model with different descriptors on dataset Corel-5k. The results are almost similar at both recall and precision criteria, but superiority is achieved at the $N+$ criterion for both LBP and SIFT descriptors. Therefore, in the following experiments we use the LBP descriptor thanks to its simplicity of computation.

The results of our model compared with other approaches on three datasets Corel-5k, ESP-Game and IAPRTC-12 are presented in Table 3. In this table, P represents the average precision, R the average recall, $F1$ the harmonic average between recall and precision, and $N+$ the number of different keywords which were correctly assigned to the test images.

The proposed method gives competitive results in terms of two criteria R and $N+$ compared to others methods. Moreover, our approach does not penalize the few labels that are present in few learning images. It provides the best R on ESP-Game.

Table 2. Results of the annotation dataset Corel-5k with different descriptors

descriptors	LBP	GIST	SIFT	SURF
Precision	25	25	27	25
Recall	43	42	42	41
$F1$	31	32	33	31
$N+$	165	162	165	160

Table 3. Performance of our model against other models annotation of the state of the art on three datasets (Corel-5k, ESP-Game and IAPRTC-12)

Method	Corel-5K				ESP-Game				IAPRTC-12			
	P	R	$F1$	$N+$	P	R	$F1$	$N+$	P	R	$F1$	$N+$
CRM [17]	16	19	17	107	–	–	–	–	–	–	–	–
MBRM [16]	24	25	25	122	18	19	18	209	24	23	23	223
SML [10]	23	29	26	137	–	–	–	–	–	–	–	–
JEC [25]	27	32	29	139	22	25	23	224	28	29	28	250
GS [9]	30	33	31	146	–	–	–	–	32	29	30	252
RF [27]	29	40	34	157	41	26	32	235	44	31	36	253
TagProp [26]	33	42	37	160	39	27	32	239	46	35	40	266
GMM-Mult [6]	19	31	24	104	29	26	27	224	28	22	25	227
Corr-LDA [5]	22	33	26	138	21	19	20	201	24	21	22	207
NMF-KNN [11]	38	**56**	**45**	150	33	26	29	238	–	–	–	–
SVM-DMBRM [20]	36	48	41	**197**	55	25	34	259	**56**	29	38	**283**
SKL-CRM [21]	39	46	42	184	41	26	32	248	47	32	38	274
2PKNN [24]	**44**	46	**45**	191	53	27	**36**	252	54	**37**	**44**	278
Our method	27	42	33	165	30	**35**	32	248	32	35	33	256

Table 4. Performance of our model with cross validations on three datasets (Corel-5k, ESP-Game and IAPRTC-12)

Test (%)	Learning (%)	Corel-5K				ESP-Game				IAPRTC-12			
		P	R	$F1$	$N+$	P	R	$F1$	$N+$	P	R	$F1$	$N+$
20	80	22	39	28	175	29	35	32	257	29	32	30	269
30	70	21	37	27	185	28	34	31	263	28	31	29	278
40	60	19	35	25	187	27	33	30	261	27	31	29	281
50	50	19	34	24	194	26	33	29	264	25	30	27	283

We can remark in Table 3 that method [24] presents better results on the three datasets than ours. However, this method has the disadvantage of a larger annotation time. Indeed, every image to be annotated must be compared with all images of the dataset. While for our method, the learning is done once and for all, and to annotate an image, we calculate only the probability presented in Eq.7. Furthermore, as all methods based on KNN, this method encounters the problem of the choices of neighbors number and the distance to be used between the visual characteristics. The method [20] presents good results on the three datasets. However, this method is a combination of a discriminative model and a generative model, it is a highly complex model. In addition, as all methods based on SVM, this method is badly adapted to problems with missing data and is disrupted with a large number of classes. We used the Corr-LDA model [5] without segmentation of images. In addition, we considered that the latent random variable corresponds to our variable *Class*. Besides its lower complexity, our model presents better results on the three datasets compared to Corr-LDA model [5]. With regard to the methods listed in Table 3, the proposed method has the advantage of being used for both annotation and classification tasks. This method can also be used for the annotation extension by combining visual and textual features of both. Compared to the GMM-mult model [6], the results show a significant improvement in all evaluation criteria and for the three datasets. This means that the addition of semantic relations between keywords improves the results of the annotation.

To make the results more stable, we evaluated our method by performing four cross validations (Table 4), each proportion of the training sample is fixed at 80%, 70%, 60% and 50% of the dataset. The 20%, 30%, 40% and 50% remaining respectively are selected for the test sample. In each case, the tests were repeated five times. The final result is an average of these repetitions. We can remark in Table 4 that results remain acceptable if the learning samples decrease. This shows that our approach is effective even in the presence of few learning samples.

Table 5. Annotation precision with different thresholds on three datasets (Corel-5k, ESP-Game and IAPRTC-12)

Dataset	Corel-5K			ESP-Game			IAPRTC-12		
Threshold (λ)	0.1	0.2	0.3	0.1	0.2	0.3	0.1	0.2	0.3
P	37	37	37	38	41	50	36	40	44
Words Per Image	3.43	3.28	3.0	4.07	3.67	3.21	4.43	3.87	2.75

To improve the precision level of the proposed method we can define a threshold λ on the probability of a keyword. An image will be annotated by a keyword KW only if

$$P(KW|im_1, im_2, ..., im_m, Kw_1, Kw_2, ..., Kw_n) > \lambda \tag{9}$$

Table 5 shows the precision of our model with different thresholds on the three datasets. We note clearly that the use of a threshold improves significantly the precision of our model. The use of the threshold penalizes the annotations which have a lower probability than λ. For example, for ESP-Game, a threshold of 0.1 removes on average one keyword per image.

5   Conclusion and Future Works

We have proposed a probabilistic graphical model for the annotation extension of images. This model is based on a mixture of multinomial distributions and mixtures of Gaussian where we have combined visual and textual characteristics. The experimental results on Corel-5k, ESP-Game and IAPRTC-12 demonstrated that the consideration of semantic relations between keywords improves significantly the annotation performances. Our future work will be dedicated to the integration of the user through a relevance feedback process.

References

1. Wang, F.: A survey on automatic image annotation and trends of the new age. Procedia Engineering **23**, 434–438 (2011)
2. Hanbury, A.: A survey of methods for image annotation. Journal of Visual Languages & Computing **19**(5), 617–627 (2008)
3. Zhang, D., Islam, M.M., Lu, G.: A review on automatic image annotation techniques. Pattern Recognition **45**(1), 346–362 (2012)
4. Tousch, A.M., Herbin, S., Audibert, J.Y.: Semantic hierarchies for image annotation: A survey. Pattern Recognition **45**(1), 333–345 (2012)
5. Wang, C., Blei, D., Li, F.F.: Simultaneous image classification and annotation. Computer Vision and Pattern Recognition, 1903–1910 (2009)
6. Barrat, S., Tabbone, S.: Classification and Automatic Annotation Extension of Images Using Bayesian Network. SSPR/SPR, 937–946 (2008)
7. Dempster, A.P., Laird, N.M., Rubin, D.B.: Maximum likelihood from incomplete data via the em algorithm. Journal of the Royal Statistical Society **39**, 1–38 (1977)
8. Wang, C., Yan, S., Zhang, L., Zhang, H.J.: Multi-label sparse coding for automatic image annotation. In: CVPR (2009)
9. Zhang, S., Huang, J., Huang, Y., Yu, Y., Li, H., Metaxas, D.: Automatic Image Annotation Using Group Sparsity. In: CVPR (2010)
10. Carneiro, G., Chan, A., Moreno, P., Vasconcelos, N.: Supervised learning of semantic classes for image annotation and retrieval. PAMI **29**(3), 394–410 (2007)
11. Kalayeh, M., Idrees, H., Shah, M.: NMF-KNN: Image Annotation using Weighted Multi-view Non-Negative Matrix Factorization. In: CVPR (2014)
12. Barrat, S., Tabbone, S.: Modeling, classifying and annotating weakly annotated images using Bayesian network. International Journal of Visual Communication and Image Representation 21 (2010)
13. Liu, J., Li, M., Liu, Q., Lu, H., Ma, S.: Image annotation via graph learning. Pattern Recognition **42**(2), 218–228 (2009)
14. Zhang, S., Tian, Q., Hua, G., Huang, Q., Gao, W.: ObjectPatchNet: Towards scalable and semantic image annotation and retrieval. Computer Vision and Image Understanding **118**, 16–29 (2014)
15. Miller, G.: WordNet: A Lexical Database for English. Communications of the ACM (1995)
16. Feng, S., Manmatha, R., Lavrenko, V.: Multiple bernoulli relevance models for image and video annotation. In: Conference on Computer Vision and Pattern Recognition, pp. 1002–1009 (2004)
17. Lavrenko, V., Manmatha, R., Jeon, J.: A model for learning the semantics of pictures. In: NIPS, pp. 553–560 (2004)

18. Duygulu, P., Barnard, K., de Freitas, J.F.G., Forsyth, D.: Object Recognition as Machine Translation: Learning a Lexicon for a Fixed Image Vocabulary. In: Heyden, A., Sparr, G., Nielsen, M., Johansen, P. (eds.) ECCV 2002, Part IV. LNCS, vol. 2353, pp. 97–112. Springer, Heidelberg (2002)

19. Liu, J., Wang, B., Li, M., Li, Z., Ma, W., Lu, H., Ma, S.: Dual cross-media relevance model for image annotation. In: Proceedings of the 15th International Conference on Multimedia, pp. 605–614 (2007)

20. Murthy, V.N., Can, E.F., Manmatha, R.: A Hybrid Model for Automatic Image Annotation. In: International Conference on Multimedia Retrieval, pp. 369–376 (2014)

21. Moran, S., Lavrenko, V.: Sparse kernel learning for image annotation. In: International Conference on Multimedia Retrieval, pp. 113–120 (2014)

22. Wang, M., Xia, X., Le, J., Zhou, X.: Effective automatic image annotation via integrated discriminative and generative models. Inf. Sci. **262**, 159–171 (2014)

23. Jing, L., Shaoping, M.: Region-Based Image Annotation Using Heuristic Support Vector Machine in Multiple-Instance Learning. Journal of Computer Research and Development **46**(5), 864–871 (2009)

24. Verma, Y., Jawahar, C.V.: Image Annotation Using Metric Learning in Semantic Neighbourhoods. In: Fitzgibbon, A., Lazebnik, S., Perona, P., Sato, Y., Schmid, C. (eds.) ECCV 2012, Part III. LNCS, vol. 7574, pp. 836–849. Springer, Heidelberg (2012)

25. Makadia, A., Pavlovic, V., Kumar, S.: Baselines for Image Annotation. ECCV 90 (2008)

26. Guillaumin, M., Mensink, T., Verbeek, J., Schmid, C.: TagProp: Discriminative metric learning in nearest neighbor models for image auto-annotation. In: ICCV (2009)

27. Fu, H., Zhang, Q., Qiu, G.: Random Forest for Image Annotation. In: Fitzgibbon, A., Lazebnik, S., Perona, P., Sato, Y., Schmid, C. (eds.) ECCV 2012, Part VI. LNCS, vol. 7577, pp. 86–99. Springer, Heidelberg (2012)

28. Alham, N.K., Li, M., Liu, Y., Qi, M.: A MapReduce based distributed SVM ensemble for scalable image classification and annotation. Computers & Mathematics with Applications **66**(10), 1920–1934 (2013)

29. Fakhari, A., Moghadam, A.: Combination of classification and regression in decision tree for multi-labeling image annotation and retrieval. Appl. Soft Comput. **13**(2), 1292–1302 (2013)

30. Oliva, A., Torralba, A.: Modeling the shape of the scene: A holistic representation of the spatial envelope. IJCV 42(3) (2001)

31. Lowe, G.D.: Object recognition from local scale-invariant features. Proceedings of the International Conference of Computer Vision **2**, 1150–1157 (1999)

32. Bay, H., Tuytelaars, T., Gool, L.V.: Surf : speeded up robust features. Computer Vision and Image Understanding **110**(3), 346–359 (2008)

33. Ojala, T., Pietikinen, M., Harwood, D.: A comparative study of texture measures a with classification based on feature distributions. Pattern Recognition **29**, 51–59 (1996)

An Improved ANOVA Algorithm for Crop Mark Extraction from Large Aerial Images Using Semantics

R. Marani$^{(\boxtimes)}$, V. Renò, E. Stella, and T. D'Orazio

ISSIA CNR, via Amendola 122/D-I, 70126 Bari, Italy
marani@ba.issia.cnr.it

Abstract. In this paper, an approach based on the analysis of variance (ANOVA) for the extraction of crop marks from aerial images is improved by means of preliminary analyses and semantic processing of the extracted objects. The paper falls in the field of digitalization of images for archaeology, assisting expert users in the detection of unexcavated sites. The methodology is improved by a preliminary analysis of local curvatures, able to determine the most suitable direction for the ANOVA formulation. Then, a semantic processing, based on the knowledge of the shape of the target wide line, is performed to delete false positive detections. Sample analyses are always performed on actual images and prove the capability of the method to discriminate the most significant marks, aiding archaeologists in the analysis of huge amount of data.

Keywords: Crop mark extraction · Archaeology · Image processing · Aerial images · Analysis of variance

1 Introduction

The problem of archaeological trace extraction, such as crop and soil marks, is receiving a large amount of attention from the scientific community since these marks can bring evidence to the presence of ancient human settlements. Crop marks are due to differences in plant height, color and surface density. Depending on the type of feature, crop vigor may be enhanced or reduced by buried archaeological features. The analysis of aerial images requires the processing of large amount of data, therefore automation and computer vision can help users to concentrate their attention only on selected areas where candidate marks are already found. In the literature, much work has been done to develop automatic algorithms to support the digitalization of man-made structures such as buildings and roads, namely identifiable portions of an image that can be interpreted as a single and well defined shape. In [1] a shape analysis for the extraction of agricultural field boundaries has been applied in high resolution panchromatic satellite imagery. Rectangle features are extracted in [2] from an initial edge detection step and further optimized to detect buildings. Roads and

© Springer International Publishing Switzerland 2015
G. Azzopardi and N. Petkov (Eds.): CAIP 2015, Part II, LNCS 9257, pp. 591–603, 2015.
DOI: 10.1007/978-3-319-23117-4_51

junctions are extracted in [3] by a low level feature detection process which uses an improved ridge detector. A review of statistical pattern recognition methods in remote sensing has been presented in [4].

However image processing algorithms for edge or wide line detection cannot be immediately applied for the detection of archaeological marks as their poor boundary information and their similarity with many other recurrent lines, typical of farmlands, make this task very difficult. For these reasons, the analysis of aerial data has been essentially based on the efforts of expert users. In order to provide a support to this time consuming task of manual selection and digitalization, image processing algorithms have to be properly set to develop automatic extraction methods of archaeological traces. In this way, a small selection of regions from large aerial images can be fast validated by expert archaeologists.

In the recent years, many papers have faced the problem of mark detection. In [5] a semi-automatic approach for archaeological trace identification is based on an active contour approach, modified by the introduction of a directional energy model. An automatic method for the extraction of archaeological tops of Qanat shafts from VHR Imagery is presented in [6] which uses the circular Hough transform (CHT) followed by mathematical morphological processing (MMP) and the Canny edge detector (CED). A method based on the analysis of pixel variances (ANOVA) over regions is proposed in [7] to decide whether a point belongs to an archaeological mark, by comparing their neighbor with the expected line shape. This recent approach produces satisfying results, but it does not prevent the extraction of many other artifacts especially in regions where the ploughing direction or the presence of particular kinds of intensive crops give rise to background periodic textures, comparable to the target lines. For this reason, starting from the methodology presented in [7], in this paper we propose a modified ANOVA approach for the extraction of crop marks from aerial images improved by means of a preliminary analyses and a semantic processing of the extracted objects. The method aims to the reduction of false positives due to the erroneous labelling of farmland as archaeological marks. For this reason images have been analyzed preliminary by expert users in order to understand which are the distinctive traits of actual archaeological marks against those of agricultural areas. The paper is organized as follows: Section 2 describes the modified ANOVA algorithm and introduces the method for the choice of the best direction of computation. Section 2.2 reports the pipeline for the semantic postprocessing, whereas Section 4 discusses on experiments performed on actual aerial images. Final conclusions and remarks are in Section 5.

2   Methodology

2.1   Modified ANOVA Algorithm

As stated previously, the modified ANOVA algorithm solves the problem of extraction of archaeological marks on crops due to possible un-excavated human settlements. In this context, large aerial images with high resolution on the ground are scanned to search for wide line with weak boundaries, among an

Fig. 1. Example of large aerial image (14240 × 11360 pixels) to be processed for crop mark extraction. The sample picture is taken from the area of the *Apulian Tavoliere* (Italy).

additive noise. A sample large image ($7.4 \times 6.6\ km$) is reported in Figure 1. This is taken from a dataset of the *Apulian Tavoliere* (Italy) and is acquired using the digital aerial pushbroom scanner ADS40 by Leica Geosystems [8].

These crop marks take the characteristic profile of a smooth parabola within a slightly uniform background [7]. Given this preliminary observation, the basic idea is that actual crop marks can be detected by defining three adjacent rectangular regions, $w \times h$ each, where the pixel intensities can be fitted on well-defined analytical models. It is important to notice that the choice of a rectangular shaped region will not alter the capability of the method to extract also circular marks as long as their curvature radii are great enough to ensure that the mark is completely included within the central region. Then, following the principles of the ANOVA formulation, variances within the populations of the three groups and among them can be compared to determine whether the central region, or equivalently its center, belongs to a wide line.

With higher formalism, we can assume that the pixel intensities $p(u, v)$ are defined for any point of a discrete grid defined on the local axes (u, v) of the $n - th$ region ($n = 1, 2, 3$) as the summation of an analytical function in two dimensions $f_n(u, v)$ and a white noise contribution $\sigma_{u,v}$. The local discrete grid is displayed in Figure 2. In particular, the u-axis is rotated by an angle α with respect to the i-axis of the image plane.

Then, it is possible to assume that a *line pixel* occurs when side regions can be modelled by first-order functions f_1 and f_3, whereas the profile of the pixel intensities can be represented by a second-order model f_2. This choice is driven by the observation of the profile of archaeological traces annotated by expert users, which follow parabolic profiles on an almost flat background. Moreover, given that the pixel intensities evolve uniformly along the v-axis, the f_n models can be expressed in one dimension without any loss in the fitting accuracy [7]:

$$\begin{cases} f_1(u) = a_{l,1}u + a_{l,2}, & l = 1,3 \\ f_2(u) = a_{2,1}u^2 + a_{2,2}u + a_{2,3}, \end{cases} \tag{1}$$

where $a_{l,1}, a_{l,2}, a_{2,1}, a_{2,2}$ and $a_{2,3}$ are the seven parameters of the three models. Once the parameters are determined in the least square sense, the modified ANOVA formulation can be easily invoked. Specifically, the total sum of squared deviations (SS_T) is:

$$SS_T = \sum_{\substack{n=1,2,3 \\ u}} (p_n(u) - \mu_T)^2 = \sum_{\substack{n=1,2,3 \\ u}} (f_n(u) - \mu_T)^2 + \sum_{\substack{n=1,2,3 \\ u}} (p_n(u) - f_n(u))^2 \tag{2}$$

where μ_T is the average value of all the pixel observations. The resulting term is the sum of SS_B and SS_W, which are the sum of squared deviations between groups of populations and within the groups, respectively.

The first test to verify if the population of the central group belongs to a wide line consists of the estimation of the parameter t, which is defined as:

$$t = \frac{(P-3) \displaystyle\sum_{n=1,2,3} c_n \mu_n}{SS_W \displaystyle\sum_{n=1,2,3} \frac{c_n}{P_n}} \tag{3}$$

being P the total number of pixel observations, equal to the sum of the numbers of pixels P_n belonging to the $n-th$ group, and $C = (c_1, c_2, c_3)^T$ a constant vector. If $C = (1, -2, 1)^T$ and the target lines are darker than the background level, a one-tailed test on the parameter t ensure that the pixels of the regions belong to different populations. Then, a second test can be performed to give more statistical evidence. Here a novel parameter η^2, defined as the ratio between SS_B and SS_T, measures how populations differ because of the presence of a textured background, having spatial properties comparable with the extension of a single region. Also in this case, if the resulting parameter η^2 is higher than a threshold value, the central pixel is labelled as a line element.

2.2   Strategies for the ANOVA Formulation

The previous description of the modified ANOVA algorithm is based on a fundamental assumption: the size and the orientation of the three regions are univocally determined.

The problem of designing the regions, i.e. finding the most appropriate values of w and h, has been already solved in [7] by means of an iterative process. The ANOVA algorithm is looped changing the entity of w and h within discrete allowed values, determined by the widths and curvature radii of the target lines. As an example, running the ANOVA in two steps with $w = 3, 5$, but keeping $h = 5$, is enough to ensure the best results in the extraction of crop marks, as

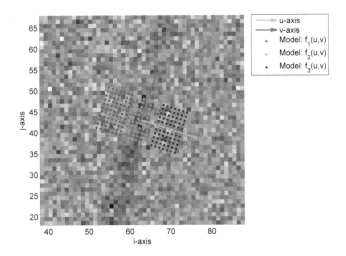

Fig. 2. Mask for ANOVA computation with $w = 7$ and $h = 11$. Red and blue dots are referred to side regions, whereas green dots belongs to the central region where a line is expected. Cyan and magenta arrows are the local axes of the mask.

the ground resolution of the aerial images used in our experiments leads to a target line with a maximum width of 5 pixels.

On the other hand, the choice of the orientation angle α is still an open problem. As a first step, the mask can be rotated n_A times by equally-spaced discrete steps around 180 degrees in order to cover all the possible directions that a line can follow. In principle, the more the angular sampling is dense, the more the results are accurate. However the increasing sensitivity of the line detector can induce a huge number of false positives. At the same time, the ANOVA algorithm has to be run n_A times with a significant growth in the total time required to perform the numerical experiments.

A novel way to select the most suitable α, exploiting again the knowledge of the expected profile of the target line, is presented within these lines. Referring to Figure 3, for each pixel $p(i,j)$ of the image, a circular region of given radius centered in (i,j) is picked out of the source image (see the red dots in Figure 3). Since the target lines have an expected profile of the second order, the extracted pixel samples can be modelled by a paraboloid. Knowing the six parameters (k_1, k_6) of the fitting paraboloid (see the blue mesh in Figure 3), the principal curvatures can be determined straightforwardly as the eigenvalues of the matrix:

$$M = \begin{bmatrix} 2k_1 & k_3 \\ k_3 & 2k_2 \end{bmatrix} \tag{4}$$

and the corresponding eigenvectors are the direction of the principle curvatures. As a consequence, the maximum curvature (the green arrow in Figure 3) can be used to identify the most probable direction orthogonal to the possible line under

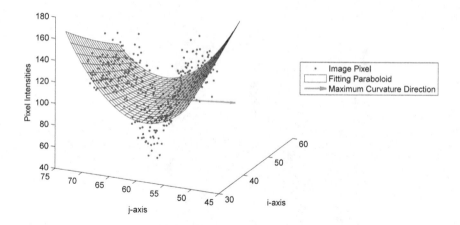

Fig. 3. Direction of the principal curvature (green arrow) extracted by fitting the pixel intensities (red dots) on a second-order model (blue patches)

investigation. Accordingly, the local u-axis of the mask can be aligned on this direction. Finally, it is important to notice that the direction of the maximum curvature can span continuously between 0 and 180 degrees. Consequently, the mask discretization, defined by the values of (u, v), would likely not match the starting grid defined by the indices (i, j) of the image. The corresponding pixel intensities $p(u, v)$ are obtained by performing a bilinear interpolation on the starting intensity values $p(i, j)$ in order to preserve the validity and the strength of the algorithm. Hence, pixel intensities $p(u, v)$ are arranged in a $\mathbb{R}^{h \times 3w}$ matrix, whose entries are still bounded in the range $[0, 255]$.

3   Semantic Postprocessing

The proposed algorithm is developed for the specific field of crop mark extraction in aerial images for archaeological applications. In this case the solution of the problem is driven by the knowledge of the objectives, which can be exploited for the reduction of false positive detections. As an example, aerial images show a deeply textured background which is often made of parallel lines, typical of farmlands. Such lines can be properly detected by the ANOVA approach, but their recognition would not increase the result accuracy. For this reason, the binary image determined by the sequential application of the t and η^2 tests is input for a semantic processing described by the flowchart in Figure 4. The image processing is divided in three main boxes: the local gradient analysis, the investigation global orientations and the morphological treating.

As a first step of the local gradient analysis, the starting image is processed by two isotropic Sobel operators [9], having a 3×3 kernel, in order to obtain two discrete derivatives along the i- and j-axis. Consequently, for each pixel of the aerial image, a local gradient direction can be easily obtained. Then, each connected component of the binary image found by the ANOVA approach

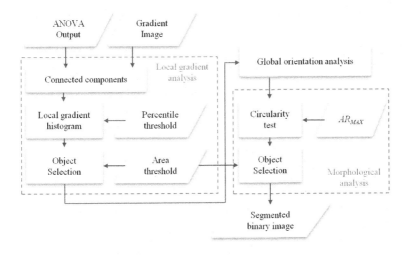

Fig. 4. Flowchart of the semantic processing following the variance analysis.

is processed to find a circular area able to include the whole object. This area constitutes a mask for the gradient direction image. Resulting values are collected in an angular histogram of 20 bins. Finally a percentile threshold on the number of observations in the histogram bins is defined to delete those pixels of the binary image having recurrent gradient orientations. At the end of the local analysis, meaningless objects in the binary image, i.e. connected regions with small areas, are set to zero.

The second step in the semantic processing of the ANOVA results is related to the investigation of the global orientation of the remaining objects. Each connected component is studied to find an ellipse with the same second-moments as the object and, then the orientation angle between the i-axis and its major axis. Also in this case, results are collected in bins producing an angular histogram which enables the easy detection of the most recurrent line direction among the whole image. This contribution can be deleted from the results, thus decreasing the detection of false positives.

Finally, a morphological analysis is required to further remove those segments with a circular-like shape. In this case a circularity test is performed following the definition of the object Aspect Ratio (AR), equal to the ratio between $(4\pi Area)$ and the squared perimeter of the connected region. Here the area is computed as the number of pixels of the connected region, whereas the perimeter is the sum of the distances between each adjoining pair of pixels around the region border. Circular areas are removed from the binary image if their AR values are greater than a threshold (AR_{MAX}). Small objects are than erased to clean the final segmented image.

4 Experiments and Discussion

The proposed methodology has been validated by means of several experiments performed on an aerial image database related to the area of Foggia, Italy (see the example in Figure 1). The next subsections report a detailed discussion on the comparison of the mask rotation strategies and the application of the semantic analysis of the ANOVA outputs.

4.1 Comparison of Mask Rotation Strategies

As reported in Section 2.2, the first improvement of our previous implementation of the modified ANOVA is due to the use of a second-order model of the pixel intensities for the computation of the direction of the maximum surface curvature, which presumably is orthogonal to the target wide lines. Figure 5 shows a comparison of results of the modified ANOVA obtained using fixed mask orientations (left column) and exploiting the curvature analysis (right column). In this regard, the colored regions represent the areas where the two approaches return different results. The deep insight of Figure 5 reveals that the curvature-based strategy produces results qualitatively comparable with the case of $n_A = 4$. Accordingly with the feedback brought by an expert user, all significant marks are properly extracted. This remark is further proved by the inspection of Figure 5(c), obtained with $n_A = 12$. In this case it is possible to observe the increase

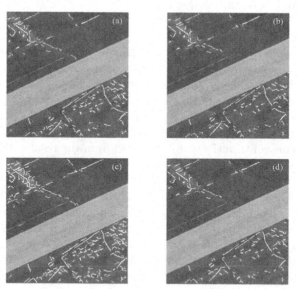

Fig. 5. (a), (c) Line extraction results obtained with fixed orientations of the mask: (a) $n_A = 4$ and (c) $n_A = 12$. (b), (d) Results obtained exploiting the direction of the maximum curvature. Looking at the plots along the rows, yellow lines are found with fixed mask orientations, but are not detected by the curvature approach. Cyan lines (if any) are found in the opposite case.

of detected regions, which does not improve the task of mark extraction. As expected, almost all the additional detected regions are not useful for the digitalization of the images; on the contrary, they produce false positives which can lower the algorithm precision.

4.2   Results of the Semantic Processing

As effect of the characteristic texture of the crop, the modified ANOVA can label wrong pixels as a line, although both the t and η^2 tests have been successfully passed. Semantics can help the method in the exact discrimination of actual lines.

Since farmlands often generate periodic one-dimensional lattices of the pixel intensities, parallel lines can be extracted. The semantic approach first aims to understand whether a line is actually significant studying the local gradient orientation. As already explained, for each object of the ANOVA output, a circular mask around the region bounding box is defined (see the example in Figure 6). The corresponding angular histogram derived by the collection of local gradient directions of the pixels in the circular mask is reported in Figure 7. Here, the one-dimensional lattice of gray levels induces a sharp peak in the angular histogram, i.e. a range of angles, which can be set to 0 by using a proper threshold on the pixels repetition (e.g. 0.8-percentile). It is important to observe that the range selection is performed by finding the continuous interval of bins over the threshold that holds the one with the highest number of observations. In this way, when homogeneous regions are investigated, the number of repetitions of the local gradient is almost constant across the bins, and bin levels fluctuate around the percentile threshold. Consequently, only few pixels are removed from the binary images, till the limit of the actual deletion of the ones in the highest bin. This prevents actual lines over flat backgrounds to be

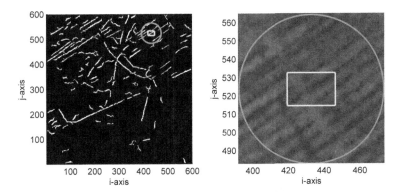

Fig. 6. Selection of a circular area (green circle) around a generic connected region bounded by the yellow rectangle. (a) is the binary image out of the ANOVA analysis and (b) is a magnified view of the starting image.

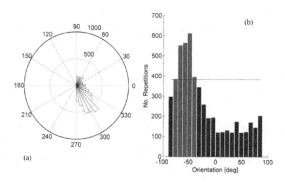

Fig. 7. (a) Angle histogram plot and (b) bin selection for the specific connected region highlighted in Figure 6. In (b), red bins belong to the continuous interval over the percentile threshold (0.8-percentile) defined by the horizontal line.

Fig. 8. Results of the local gradient analysis. Yellow regions have not passed the test.

erroneously kept out of the binary image. The results of the local gradient analysis are reported in Figure 8. As effect of the processing, parallel lines, oriented accordingly with the most recurrent ones, are removed from the binary image.

Then the algorithm goes through the analysis of the global orientation of the connected regions of the binary image producing the results in Figure 9, where yellow pixels are the ones removed by this processing step. Here the filter is responsible for the removal of false positives still due to plantations that do not produce a prevalent direction of the local gradient. This is the case of the arrangement of trees in Figure 9 which are correctly detected as small line segments, but evidently are not relevant for the image digitalization of possible archaeological sites.

Finally, the morphological analysis of the last mark candidates produces the results in Figure 10, which reports the comparison between the input and the output of the morphological processing. The insight of Figure 10(a) demonstrates the need of a morphological study of the residual objects, which can correspond to dark areas not carrying information for the reconstruction of interesting crop marks.

Fig. 9. Global orientation analysis: yellow regions are deleted from the binary image.

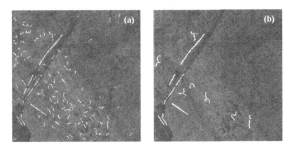

Fig. 10. Morphological analysis with $AR = 0.3$: (a) starting binary image resulting from the global orientation analysis and (b) corresponding results.

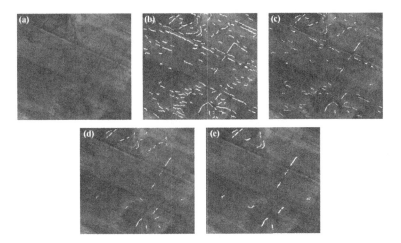

Fig. 11. Example of the sequential application of the proposed processing. (a) Starting image, (b) application of the ANOVA algorithm, (c) local and (d) global gradient analysis and (e) final result after the morphological filters.

As an example, Figure 11 summaries the processing steps performed on a specific image, starting from the application of the ANOVA algorithm, through the semantic analyses of the obtained results. In this case the modified ANOVA creates a set of line candidates which includes several erroneous detections, as well as true positives. The local gradient analysis almost halves the number of detected candidates (from 185 to 95 connected regions) which are further reduced as effects of the study of global orientations, till reaching the number of 32 objects. At the end of the processing, the morphological treatment carries to the final result made of 17 line objects, which are the set of most reliable candidates. This inspection proves how the proposed processing can help archaeologists in the task of image digitalization, limiting their assignment to the validation of a much lighter set of trace candidates.

5   Discussion and Conclusions

In this paper, the modified ANOVA approach has been improved for the detection of crop marks of archaeological significance. Here, the knowledge of the target line profile has been used to estimate the best direction of the rectangular masks used to select the three groups investigated by the ANOVA approach. Curvature analysis has enabled the fast processing of the method with comparable results with those of our previous implementation. At the same time, the specific problem of trace extraction within farmlands has driven a semantic treatment of the binary images produced by the modified ANOVA algorithm. The pipeline flows through the local and then global analysis of the directions of the image gradient in order to delete lines with recurrent orientations. Finally, a morphological inspection is performed to cut small line segments, having circular-like shapes, which do not add significant information to image digitalization. Results have demonstrated the clear reduction of false positives, i.e. ambiguous regions labelled as archaeological marks, but actually due to the presence of farmlands. In this way archaeologists are asked to process a lighter set of more reliable candidate regions corresponding to possible un-excavated archaeological sites.

Acknowledgments. This work was developed under grant "Progetto Strategico Regione Puglia Archaeoscapes" PS061. The Authors would like to thank Dr. P. Da Pelo and Mr. A. Argentieri for their contributions.

References

1. Mueller, M., Segl, K., Kaufmann, H.: Edge- and region-based segmentation technique for the extraction of large man-made objects in high-resolution satellite imagery. Pattern Recognition **37**(8), 1619–1628 (2004)
2. Wang, Y., Tupin, F., Han, C.: Building detection from high resolution PolSAR data at the rectangle level by combining region and edge information. Pattern Recognition Letters **31**, 1077–1088 (2010)

3. Gautama, S., Goeman, W., Haeyer, J.D., Philips, W.: Characterizing the performance of automatic road detection using error propagation. Image and Vision Computing **24**, 1001–1009 (2006)
4. Chen, C.H., Peter Hoi, P.G.: Statistical pattern recognition in remote sensing. Pattern Recognition **41**(9), 2731–2741 (2008)
5. D'Orazio, T., Palumbo, F., Guaragnella, C.: Archaeological Trace extraction by a local directional active contour approach. Pattern Recognition **45**, 3427–3438 (2012)
6. Luo, L., Wang, X., Guo, H., Liu, C., Liu, J., Li, L., Du, X., Qian, G.: Automated extraction of the archaeological tops of qanat shafts from VHR imagery in google earth. Remote Sensing **6**, 11956–11976 (2014)
7. D'Orazio, T., Da Pelo, P., Marani, R., Guaragnella, C.: Automated extraction of archaeological traces by a modified variance analysis. Remote Sensing **7**, 3565–3587 (2015)
8. Sandau, R., Braunecker, B., Driescher, H., Eckardt, A., Hilbert, S., Hutton, J., Kirchhofer, W., Lithopoulos, E., Reulke, R., Wicki, S.: Design principles of the LH Systems ADS40 air-borne digital sensor. Int. Arch. Photogramm. Remote Sens. **33**, 258–265 (2000)
9. Gonzalez, R.C., Woods, R.E.: Digital Image Processing. Prentice-Hall, Upper Saddle River (2001)

An Electronic Travel Aid to Assist Blind and Visually Impaired People to Avoid Obstacles

Filippo L.M. Milotta$^{(\boxtimes)}$, Dario Allegra, Filippo Stanco,
and Giovanni M. Farinella

Image Processing Laboratory, Department of Mathematics and Computer Science,
University of Catania, Catania, Italy
{milotta,allegra,fstanco,gfarinella}@dmi.unict.it

Abstract. When devices and applications provide assistance to people they become part of *assistive technology*. If the assistance is given to impaired people, then it is possible to refer those technologies as *adaptive technologies*. The main aims of these systems are substitution of physical assistants and the improvement of typical tools already available for impaired people. In this paper some benefits and examples of adaptive technology applications will be discussed. Moreover we present an adaptive technology framework to avoid obstacles to be exploited by visually impaired and blind people. The proposed assistive technology has been designed to perform vision substitution; specifically it provides *Electronic Travel Aid (ETA)* capabilities through the processing of information acquired with a depth sensor such that the user can avoid obstacles during the environment exploration. In the proposed system we require to know just the height of the sensor with respect to the ground floor to calibrate the ETA system. Experiments are performed to asses the proposed system.

Keywords: Electronic travel aid · Assistive technology · Obstacle avoidance

1 Introduction and Motivations

In the last years many devices and applications to assist people, such as fall detectors and Braille translator and others quality of life technologies, have been developed [1–3]. These innovations can be categorized as assistive technology systems. The main aim of these systems is to enhance or improve skills of people. The benefits of these technologies become clearer looking at the potential of an application specifically developed to assist people with some kind of impairment. In this particular case, where assistance is given specifically to impaired people, the assistive technology system can be defined also as an adaptive technology system.

There is a growing interest in assistive and adaptive applications. Indeed, these applications, which usually do simple tasks (e.g., recognize the color of

© Springer International Publishing Switzerland 2015
G. Azzopardi and N. Petkov (Eds.): CAIP 2015, Part II, LNCS 9257, pp. 604–615, 2015.
DOI: 10.1007/978-3-319-23117-4_52

a dress for a visually impaired person), can assist impaired people substituting sometimes the physical assistant person in some specific cases.

Among others assistive technologies, the one in the context of visual impairment are relevant. In August 2014 the World Health Organization reports that 285 million people were estimated to be visually impaired worldwide (39 million are blind and 246 have low vision) [4]. For these people the most affordable devices are white cane and trained dog. The former is the most diffused because about 90% of the world's visually impaired live in low-income settings [4] and because in many cases the cost of a trained dog cannot be afforded. Although the cane became reliable for these people after the right time for practice, it will never give information about speed, size or distance of moving object in the environment: it allows to acquire information on only the closest range space around the user. Moreover, cane presents problems in detecting overhanging objects, such as tables, chairs or shelves.

For all the above reasons, we consider electronic travel aid (*ETA*) devices for visually impaired able to give information on obstacles in the scene and hence help to avoid them. We develop a framework which exploits the depth-maps given by a Kinect sensor to estimate the ground plane. This estimation is only sensor height dependent. The algorithm is supported by a predictor-corrector for plane estimation error. After ground plane estimation the objects in a region of interest are detected and the framework gives feedback to the user through the audio channel which play a sound when possible obstacles are detected in the environment.

The paper is organized as following: Section 2 discusses the state of the art in the context of this paper. The proposed ETA system will be described in Section 3. Experiments are reported in Section 4. Finally, Section 5 concludes the paper.

2   Related Works

In recent years different assistive and adaptive technologies for visually impaired domain have been developed by exploiting computer vision algorithms. They can be categorized as following [5]:

- *Vision Enhancement*: those systems which acquire views of the environment and display them on monitors that can be wearable. The output video is usually enhanced through some image processing or augmented reality technique [5].
- *Vision Replacement*: those systems implanted inside the eye retinas to acquire views of the environment which are transmitted directly to the optic nerve or the cerebral cortex [5,6].
- *Vision Substitution*: those systems which acquire views of the environment and transform them in audio or tactile information [5].

The mostly considered category in this paper is the *Vision Substitution* one. It is possible to define three subcategories of vision substitution systems [5]:

– *Electronic Travel Aids (**ETAs**)*: devices that use sensors to understand the environment and through sensory modality (different from the visual one) assist the user to explore the environment.
– *Electronic Orientation Aids (**EOAs**)*: devices that assist the user in the choice of the best direction for continue the travel into the environment. They could be part or not of an ETA system.
– *Position Locator Devices (**PLDs**)*: devices that assist the user to locate his own position in the environment (like the GPS system).

Several ETAs devices for impaired and blind people exist [5, 7]. Hence, it is important to distinguish devices according to output modality. Typically, audio and tactile feedback are employed.

In 1992, Meijer [8] developed a system called vOICe which consists of a wearable camera on a pair of glasses. The acquired video data are processed and an image-to-sound mapping is performed by transforming the image in to time-multiplexed auditory representation [8]. This approach is motivated by the idea that the brain is able to process information contained in the alternation of complex sounds. Another audio-feedback strategy employs ultrasonic sensors (pointed in to 6 different directions) and an algorithm based on *Head-Related Transfer Function (HRTF)* [9]. Briefly, headphones play a sound with different frequencies and loudness, so a mental map of the environment can be represented thanks to holophonic technique. Since ultrasonic sensors are expensive, in [10] a low cost system is proposed. It uses two color cameras to estimate a *depth-map* through the stereoscopic vision algorithms. The depth-map is converted in an audio signal that is played according to distance from the objects.

On the other hand, tactile-feedback systems typically work sending a specific vibration to the user body. For example *Virtual White Cane* [11] simulates a white cane through a laser pointer. Then, a mobile device performs a $3D$ triangulation to estimate the distance of possible obstacles. User hand receives different vibrations according to the estimated distance [11]. A similar strategy can be used on a Vibratory Belt [7], where a Kinect Sensor (for depth-map acquisition) and a gyroscope (for plane orientation detection), are placed on the user waist. The depth-map is divided in 3 vertical regions with 3 different orientations and a vibrator device is associated to each of them. Vibration intensity depends on the closer obstacle detected for each region. Touch can be stimulate also through an electrode system on a pair of gloves. Electron-Neural Vision System [7] uses this approach, sending an electrical impulse to the final user. A specific finger is stimulated for a specific direction.

Furthermore, we also taken into account related works in the robotic field, in which the capability of obstacle avoidance is a primary requirement for autonomous robot environment exploration. To this aim several techniques can be exploited, like monocular 2D raster vision system [12], linear structured light projected in front of robot camera [13], as well as Kinect infrared dots structured pattern [14]. In particular, in [14] Yue et al. define a slop analysis function to distinguish staircases from ramps.

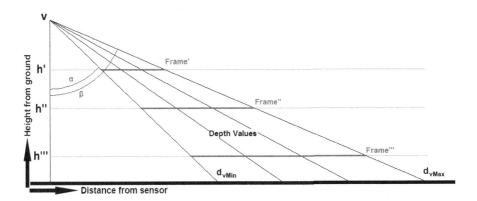

Fig. 1. System calibration: let be v the sensor position; h be the sensor height from ground; α and β be respectively the minimum and maximum view frustum vertical angles; Frame refers to image resolution acquired by the device with respect to h; d represents detectable depth values inside view frustum.

3   Proposed Model

The main aim of this work is the development of an *Electronic Travel Aid (ETA)* system for visually impaired which is able to detect obstacles and help the user to avoid them. Our framework consists of a Kinect (*v1.0*) device [15] to acquire the depth of the scene and a control unit to process the acquired data, that also sends feedback to user about obstacle detected. The output modality used is the audio channel, with different levels of sound intensity corresponding to different distances of detected obstacles. The scene acquired with the Kinect is divided in a 3×3 cells, and for each cell a risk index R is estimated. This index measures the risk degree of clashing with an obstacle and is directly proportional on the average distance of detected obstacles in each cell. The system works by analyzing the *depth-maps* acquired by Kinect where each voxel in the 3D space represents the distance from sensor. The idea is to have a wearable Kinect system attached to belt. This is useful to have less angular vibrations due to movement with respect to the ones which can be observed mounting the Kinect on top of an helmet.

The first step required to use the proposed system is the calibration. In this step the height h from ground of the Kinect sensor and its inclination with respect to the ground are fixed. The inclination can assume values from an angle α (lower vertical part of sensor field of view) to an angle β (upper vertical part) (Figure 1). These three parameters, together with measurements derivated from them, are called *"environmental measures"*. Actually, the only one required environmental measure is height h, as the other parameters, like tilt angle, can be usually obtained by sensor device itself (Figure 2). Using Kinect it is possible to acquire depth stream at different resolutions [15]: from 80×60 to 640×480. However, using smaller resolution the obstacle detector is less reliable despite more efficient.

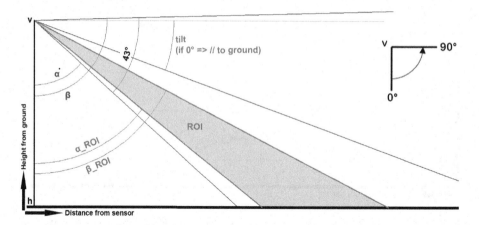

Fig. 2. Data acquisition through infrared sensor: let be v the sensor position; h be the sensor height from ground; α and β be respectively the minimum and maximum view frustum vertical angles (note that $43°$ is Kinect vertical field of view); ROI be the region of interest (if used).

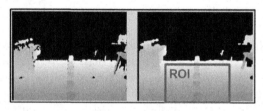

Fig. 3. Noise Reduction: on the left side, the depth-map as it is acquired by Kinect device. Environmental setting is the floor of our laboratory, with some books vertically placed on it at different distances from sensor. Books are almost 30 cm height. On the right side, the same depth-map after noise reduction phase using morphological operators. Moreover, the region of interest (ROI) considered for obstacle detection is highlighted in the processed depth-map.

We choose to take into account a reduced portion of the scene, defined as the region of interest (ROI) (Figures 2 and 3). In this way, we can reduce the number of pixels with "undefined depth" values (i.e., the ones with depth greater than 4 meters) and decrease the computational complexity. Moreover, it can be noticed that height h of the device linearly affects detectable distances range: indeed, higher height corresponds to larger detectable distances, and viceversa (Figure 1).

Acquired frames are processed and the measurements of the environment are performed after a preprocessing and a subsampling of depth frames. Firstly, morphological operators based on region and hole filling are applied to depth-map to reduce noise (Figure 3) and then it is subsampled to a fixed resolution. The obtained depth-map is used for obstacle detection.

Once we have defined environmental measures and the region of interest (ROI) the angles α and β have to be properly tuned (Figure 2). To this aim

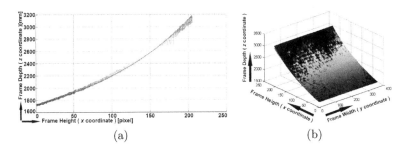

(a)   (b)

Fig. 4. Acquired plane is in color (depth values raise from blue to red), while ideal plane is depicted with black. This is an example of ideal plane estimation in an environment without any obstacle: (a) lateral section, (b) 3D view.

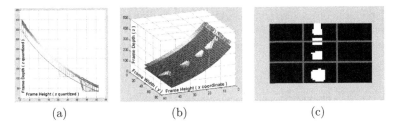

(a)   (b)   (c)

Fig. 5. Acquired scene is in color (depth values raise from blue to red), while threshold plane is depicted with black. This is an example of detection in an environment with several obstacles (5 books placed on ground). (a) Lateral section, lower side is closer to user. (b) 3D view of obstacle regions with depth values exceeding the threshold plane. (c) A boolean map related to the ROI partitioned in a 3 × 3 left to right and far to near monitored areas. White blobs are the detected obstacle.

we consider the following statements: standard vertical field of view in Kinect is set to 43°; Kinect can rotate of ±27° around horizontal axis (tilt rotation T_{rot}); Kinect can be considered to have an orientation error ϵ_{rot}. Therefore, making these assumptions and considering a reference system starting at −90°, the α and β vertical view angles can be computed as following (Figure 2):

$$\alpha = 90° + T_{rot} - \frac{43°}{2} + \epsilon_{rot} \;\; ; \qquad \beta = 90° + T_{rot} + \frac{43°}{2} + \epsilon_{rot} \qquad (1)$$

Since angles α and β can be derived from Kinect applying Equation 1, the only remaining parameter to calibrate the proposed system is the height h.

Furthermore, the correctness of environmental measures is critical because using them an ideal plane depth-map without obstacles can be estimated, considering an offset error $\epsilon_{IdealPlane}$ (Figure 4). Setting a threshold value t_{Obs} a threshold plane for obstacles detection can be estimated too. The threshold plane represents the minimum height from the ideal plane that objects should have to be considered as obstacles. This plane is used in the detection step (Figure 5).

The ideal plane is estimated using the following equation, derived from trigonometric rules:

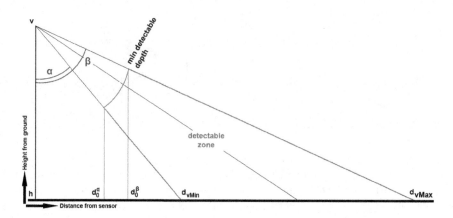

Fig. 6. Detectable obstacles range height h_D, depending on estimated distance d. Let be v sensor position; h be the sensor height from ground; α and β be view frustum vertical angles. Highlighted red polygon shows detectable zone.

$$IdealPlane(i,:) = \frac{h - t_{Obs}}{\cos\left(\alpha + \left[(\beta - \alpha) * \frac{i}{rows}\right]\right)} \tag{2}$$

Where $i = 1, \ldots, rows$ iterates on plane rows; ':' means that result of the first column of each row is copied to other columns of the same row. t_{Obs} is the threshold value (or *offset*) used in threshold plane estimation. In Equation 2, in each iteration an angle between α and β is interpolated and its related depth (hypotenuse) is computed using trigonometry.

We have formalized range of detectable obstacles height h_D, depending on estimated distance d, where d can be derived from detected obstacle average depth. The obstacle height h_D can be defined as follows (Figure 6):

$$h_D \in \begin{cases} [(d_{vMin} - d) * \cot\alpha \ ; \ (d^\gamma - d) * \cot\gamma] & \text{if } d_0^\alpha < d \le d_0^\beta \\ [(d_{vMin} - d) * \cot\alpha \ ; \ (d_{vMax} - d) * \cot\beta] & \text{if } d_0^\beta < d \le d_{vMin} \\ [0 \ ; \ (d_{vMax} - d) * \cot\beta] & \text{if } d_{vMin} < d \le d_{vMax} \end{cases} \tag{3}$$

Where d^γ is the distance proportional to d in range $[d_{vMin} \ ; \ d_{vMax}]$ and γ is the angle related on d^γ computed proportionally with respect to range $[\alpha \ ; \ \beta]$ as follows

$$d^\gamma = \frac{d - d_0^\alpha}{d_0^\beta - d_0^\alpha}(d_{vMax} - d_{vMin}) + d_{vMin} \ ; \qquad \gamma = \frac{d - d_0^\alpha}{d_0^\beta - d_0^\alpha}(\beta - \alpha) + \alpha \tag{4}$$

Let d_{vMin} and d_{vMax} be respectively the minimum and maximum obstacles distances detectable inside view frustum; d_0^α and d_0^β are minimum detectable obstacle distances related to α and β respectively, once sensor minimum detectable depth is set. Note that in this case we have $d_0^\beta \le d_{vMin}$.

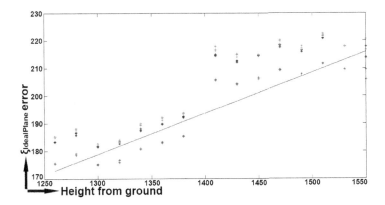

Fig. 7. $\epsilon_{IdealPlane}$ predictor-corrector, depending on height h. Horizontal axis is related to height h, while vertical axis represents the correction value. Three metrics have been taken in to account: average (blue), median (red) of global differences and median of average of rows-wise differences (green). In this case function of fitting is computed with a linear regression. All reported data are to be considered in millimeters.

Other cases will not be treated, as sensor should be too close to ground, resulting in an unusable system.

We realized a predictor for the plane estimation error $\epsilon_{IdealPlane}$, depending just on environmental measure height h. The predictor has been implemented acquiring an environment without obstacles at 15 different heights (3 times for each considered height) and known environmental measures. For each acquired ideal plane, the measured plane and the punctual differences with the ideal one have been computed, in order to gain 3 statistical measures: average and median computed on global differences and median of averages computed on rows-wise differences. In this way we obtained 135 statistical indices, which are used to derive a predictor for the error $\epsilon_{IdealPlane}$ depending on height h through linear regression (Figure 7).

Making use of the threshold plane, a boolean map D_m is trivially generated from quantized depth-map D_q checking if each pixel of D_q exceeds the threshold plane. Then, each connected component in D_m is considered an "obstacle region" (Figures 5).

Therefore, D_m is used for *masking* D_q, and for each corresponding obstacle region an average depth d_a is computed. Starting from d_a, the estimated obstacle distance is derivable using trigonometric rules or similarity between triangles. In our implementation we exploited the similarity between triangles:

$$IdealDistance = \sqrt{IdealDepth^2 - h^2}$$

$$ObsDist_{est} = IdealDistance * \frac{d_a}{IdealDepth}$$

$$(5)$$

Where $IdealDistance$ is distance between ground projection of sensor position and point d on ideal plane related to d_a, representing measurable distance in

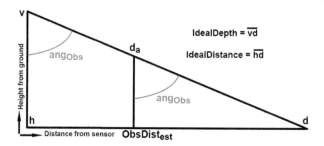

Fig. 8. Distance estimation. Let be v sensor position; h be the sensor height; d_a be the average depth of an obstacle region; ang_{obs} be the angle between normal to ground v and the centroid of obstacle region; $ObsDist_{est}$ be the estimated obstacle distance.

absence of obstacle. $IdealDepth$ is the measurable depth in absence of obstacle. $ObstDist_{est}$ is estimated obstacle distance (Figure 8).

Once $ObstDist_{est}$ is computed, we define a total of 4 possible indexes related to each area and representing the risk of clashing with an obstacle: 0-none, 1-very near, 2-near or 3-almost far away detected obstacle. In order to obtain these indexes the depth-map D_q is partitioned in a 3×3 areas (Figure 5(c)), and for each area the minimum value of $ObsDist_{est}$ computed is further quantized with 2 thresholds t_{R1} and t_{R2}. The values of these two thresholds depends on distance, and then on height h, since distance is closely related to it (Figure 1). They have been defined through the following equation (Figure 6):

$$t_{R1} = \left[(d_{vMax} - d_0^\alpha) * \tfrac{1}{3} \right] + d_0^\alpha$$

$$t_{R2} = \left[(d_{vMax} - d_0^\alpha) * \tfrac{2}{3} \right] + d_0^\alpha \tag{6}$$

Finally, using these risk indexes it is possible to compute a more general index R for the entire scene or several indexes for each area (for instance, left, central and right), representing the final degree of danger and having 4 possible risk values computed in the same way of single risk indexes. Therefore, when there are several obstacles, the closer one determines the risk of the global scene. In our framework the feedback is given to the user with a sound whose loud is proportional to the risk R of the entire scene. Moreover, sound is differenciated in tone taking into account left, central and right areas so the user can understand the position of the obstacle.

4   Experimental Settings and Results

We set the threshold t_{Obs} defined in Section 3 to $100mm$ in order to detect obstacles of the environment higher than $100mm$. The remaining thresholds used by our system can be derived as defined in Equation 6 after fixing the height h of the Kinect sensor.

We tested the proposed system on a set of scenes where obstacles have been placed and their distance from the sensor have been manually measured.

Table 1. Results of the proposed system on the 27 depth-maps with a single obstacle acquired in different areas of the ROI (Figure 3). In this table we compare absolute differences between real and estimated distances of the 27 different detected obstacles. The Root Mean Square Error is also reported. ROI is divided in 9 areas as shown in Figure 5(c)), and table is divided in 9 groups of cells, respectively; so, for each group in the table we have 3 measurements. Each group is color-coded (blue to red) with relation on its average computed difference. All reported data are to be considered in millimeters. In the table the ground truth distance (GT), the distance measured by the proposed system (M) and the absolute difference (D) between GT and M are reported. Moreover it is reported the average (AVG) of the absolute distances and the Root Mean Squared Error ($RMSE$).

GT	M	D	GT	M	D	GT	M	D		
1660	1563	97	1485	1489	4	1560	1509	51	104,9	Avg. (1st row)
1675	1443	232	1645	1551	94	1690	1564	126	70,1	RMSE (1st row)
1740	1532	208	1660	1613	47	1790	1705	85		
1240	1230	10	1265	1273	8	1290	1325	35	28,0	Avg. (2nd row)
1260	1180	80	1300	1310	10	1340	1323	17	24,4	RMSE (2nd row)
1310	1258	52	1365	1366	1	1355	1394	39		
950	962	12	970	1007	37	950	978	28	34,0	Avg. (3rd row)
1000	1020	20	1010	1052	42	1010	1058	48	14,2	RMSE (3rd row)
1050	1031	19	1020	1063	43	1030	1087	57		
Avg. (1st col.)		81,1	Avg. (2nd col.)		31,8	Avg. (3rd col.)		54,0	55,6	Avg. (tot)
RMSE (1st col.)		79,9	RMSE (2nd col.)		28,1	RMSE (3rd col.)		31,3	55,9	RMSE (tot)

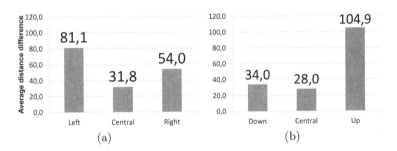

Fig. 9. Bar plots related to the average differences between ground truth and measured distances with respect to left, central and right areas (a) and near to far (b) of the areas of the ROI. All reported data are to be considered in millimeters.

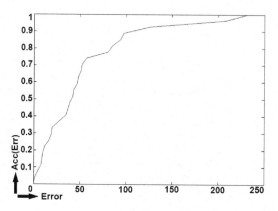

Fig. 10. REC curve.

These ground truth measures have been compared with respect to the measures obtained by our system. We acquired a total of 27 depth-maps with a single obstacle. We divided the ROI in 9 areas (Figures 3 and 5(c)) and for each area we acquired 3 depth-maps corresponding to the positioning of three different obstacles. The results, shown in Table 1, report a total average error in obstacle distance estimation of almost $5cm$, that is definitively acceptable. Average differences between ground truth and measured distances with respect to left to right and near to far of ROI areas are bar plotted in Figure 9.

To better highlight the results we have used the REC curve [16]. It is essentially the cumulative distribution function of the error. The area over the curve is a biased estimation of the expected error of an employed regression model [16]. The REC curve related to our experiments is reported in Figure 10.

5   Conclusion

In this paper we presented an ETA system for obstacle detection and the related calibration settings. Obstacle avoidance is performed by binarizing the measured depth with a thresholding plane. In order to reduce error in plane estimation we developed an $\epsilon_{IdealPlane}$ predictor-corrector. We also formalized the range of the height of the detectable obstacles, depending on their estimated distance. Indexes representing the degree of risk in the environment have been defined. Finally, the risk indexes are converted into sound for the final user.

References

1. Stanco, F., Buffa, M., Farinella, G.M.: Automatic Braille to Black Conversion. In: Baldoni, M., Baroglio, C., Boella, G., Micalizio, R. (eds.) AI*IA 2013. LNCS, vol. 8249, pp. 517–526. Springer, Heidelberg (2013)
2. Website of OrCam wearable adaptive technology device for visually impaired people. (last visited on April 1, 2015). http://www.orcam.com/

3. Kanade, T.: Quality of life technology [scanning the issue]. Proceedings of the IEEE **100**(8), 2394–2396 (2012)
4. Website of the World Health Organization. (Updated august 2014, last visited on June 11, 2015). http://www.who.int/mediacentre/factsheets/fs282/en/
5. Dakopoulos, D., Bourbakis, N.G.: Wearable obstacle avoidance electronic travel aids for blind: A survey. IEEE Transaction on Systems, Man, and Cybernetics-Part C: Applications and Reviews 40(1) (January 2010)
6. Italian website of International Agency for the Prevention of Blindness (Published April 2009, last updated August 2014, last visited on June 11, 2015). http://www.iapb.it/news2.php?ozim=54
7. Terven, J.R., Salas, J., Raducanu, B.: New opportunities for computer vision-based assistive technology systems for the visually impaired. Computer **47**(4), 52–58 (2014)
8. Meijer, P.B.L.: An experimental system for auditory image representations. IEEE Transactions on Biomedical Engineering **39** (February 1992)
9. Aguerrevere, D., Choudhury, M., Barreto, A.: Portable 3d sound / sonar navigation system for blind individuals. In: Second LACCEI International Latin American and Caribbean Conference for Engineering and Technology (June 2004)
10. Spanish website of Espacio Acstico Virtual (Virtual Acoustic Space) (last visited on April 1, 2015). http://www.iac.es/proyecto/eavi/
11. Vera, P., Zenteno, D., Salas, J.: A smartphone-based virtual white cane. Pattern Analysis and Applications 17 (August 2014)
12. Aggarwal, A., Kukreja, A., Chopra, P.: Vision based collision avoidance by plotting a virtual obstacle on depth map. In: IEEE International Conference on Information and Automation (ICIA), pp. 532–536 (2010)
13. Boyu, W., Junyao, G., Li, K., Fan, Y., Xueshan, G., Gao, B.: Indoor mobile robot obstacle detection based on linear structured light vision system. In: IEEE International Conference on Robotics and Biomimetics, pp. 834–839 (2009)
14. Yue, H., Chen, W., Wu, X., Zhang, J.: Kinect based real time obstacle detection for legged robots in complex environments. In: 8th IEEE Conference onIndustrial Electronics and Applications (ICIEA), pp. 205–210 (2013)
15. Website of Microsoft Kinect (Components and Specifications). (last visited on April 1, 2015). http://msdn.microsoft.com/en-us/library/jj131033.aspx
16. Bi, J., Bennett, K.P.: Regression error characteristic curves. In: International Conference on Machine Learning, pp. 43–50 (2003)

Cellular Skeletons: A New Approach to Topological Skeletons with Geometric Features

Aldo Gonzalez-Lorenzo[1,2]([✉]), Alexandra Bac[1], Jean-Luc Mari[1], and Pedro Real[2]

[1] CNRS, LSIS UMR 7296, Aix Marseille Université, 13397 Marseille, France
[2] Institute of Mathematics IMUS, University of Seville, Seville, Spain
aldo.gonzalez-lorenzo.@univ-amu.fr

Abstract. This paper introduces a new kind of skeleton for binary volumes called the *cellular skeleton*. This skeleton is not a subset of voxels of a volume nor a subcomplex of a cubical complex: it is a chain complex together with a reduction from the original complex.

Starting from the binary volume we build a cubical complex which represents it regarding 6 or 26-connectivity. Then the complex is thinned using the proposed method based on elementary collapses, which preserves significant geometric features. The final step reduces the number of cells using Discrete Morse Theory. The resulting skeleton is a reduction which preserves the homology of the original complex and the geometrical information of the output of the previous step.

The result of this method, besides its skeletonization content, can be used for computing the homology of the original complex, which usually provides *well shaped* homology generators.

1 Introduction

The notion of skeleton (or *medial axis*) was introduced by H. Blum in 1967 [Blu67]. Given a subset $S \subset \mathbb{R}^n$, its medial axis is the set of all the points in S that are centres of maximal balls included in S. It is a good descriptor of shape, it is thin, it has the same type of homotopy as S (one can be *continuously deformed* into the other) and it is reversible (we can reconstruct S by using the distance of each point to the boundary).

Skeletons are widely used for various applications such as video tracking [GSdA09], shape recognition [YWZ08], surface sketching [Mar09] and in many other scientific domains.

In the discrete context there is no unique equivalent to the continuous definition. A *discrete medial axis* gives a skeleton which is not homotopically equivalent to the discrete object. Discrete skeletons are usually based on the *thinning* of the object, using mathematical morphology or parallel approaches: simple points [KR89], simple P-points [LB07], critical kernels [CB14]. The given skeleton is a subset of voxels, much smaller, which is homotopically equivalent and should preserve in an uncertain way the geometrical features of the object. There is another class of skeletons which first computes a cubical complex associated to an object

G. Azzopardi and N. Petkov (Eds.): CAIP 2015, Part II, LNCS 9257, pp. 616–627, 2015.
DOI: 10.1007/978-3-319-23117-4_53

and then selects a subcomplex (see [CC09, LCLJ10, Cou11, Cou13, DS14]). We must note that geometrical preservation is more intuitive or heuristic in the context of discrete skeletons than in the continuous one. Hence, all previous approaches exist, with their respective strengths and weaknesses.

This paper presents a three-step method:

1. Starting from a binary volume (a set of voxels in a regular grid), we define its associated cubical complex. We propose two different constructions which encode 6 and 26-connectivity. These associated cubical complexes were separately defined in [CC09, LCLJ10]
2. We compute a skeleton of this cubical complex. We propose a method strongly based on [LCLJ10] which performs elementary collapses which are encoded in a *discrete gradient vector field* (DGVF). It is a simple algorithm producing satisfying results. This step can also be addressed with the algorithms found in [LCLJ10, DS14] or in [CC09, Cou11, Cou13] given a fixed parameter. As a result, the shape of the skeleton is defined
3. This step is completely new. Given the reduced cubical complex, we extend the previous DGVF in order to obtain a *reduction* (see [Ser92]) between the chain complex of the original cubical complex and a reduced one, with the property of maintaining the shape of the skeleton computed in the second step.

Our approach presents several advantages: the topology preservation throughout the thinning is guaranteed by the Discrete Morse Theory; our method dissociates connectivity and skeleton extraction, thus the thinning algorithm becomes independent of the connectivity relation; the obtained reduction accelerates the computation of its homology since the reduced complex contains fewer cells. Moreover, starting the homology computation from this cellular skeleton should produce *well shaped* homology generators, as they are included in the skeleton. This reveals an advantage of computing homology using Discrete Morse Theory: we can control the shape of the homology generators.

In Sect. 2, we introduce all the necessary definitions for understanding our method. In Sect. 3, we describe our approach. Section 4 shows some results of our framework on some binary volumes. We finish this paper by presenting our conclusion and our future perspectives.

2 Preliminaries

2.1 Binary Volumes and Cubical Complexes

A *3D binary volume* is a set of voxels centred on integer coordinates. We will describe it by the set of the coordinates of its elements.

The rest of this section is derived from [KMM04]. For a deeper understanding of these concepts, the reader can refer to it. An *elementary interval* is an interval of the form $[k, k+1]$ (nondegenerate) or a set $\{k\}$ (degenerate), also denoted as $[k, k]$, where $k \in \mathbb{Z}$. An *elementary cube* in $\mathbb{R}^n$ is the Cartesian product of n

elementary intervals, and the number of nondegenerate intervals in this product is its *dimension*. An elementary cube of dimension q will be called q-cube for short, or even q-cell, since cubical complexes are a special kind of cell complexes.

Given two elementary cubes P and Q, we say that P is a *face* of Q if $P \subset Q$ and we note it $P < Q$. It is a *primary face* if the difference of their dimensions is 1. The definitions of the dual concepts *coface* and *primary coface* are immediate.

A *cubical complex* is a set of elementary cubes with all of their faces. The *boundary* of an elementary cube is the collection of its primary faces.

A cubical complex can be completely described by its *Hasse diagram*. It is a directed graph whose vertices are all the elementary cubes, and whose arrows go from each cube to its primary faces. In this paper we will usually not make the distinction between the vertices and the elementary cubes they represent, so we will mix the terms vertex, cube and cell.

2.2 Chain Complexes

A *chain complex* (C_*, d_*) is a sequence of $\mathfrak{R}$-modules $C_0, C_1, \dots$ (called *chain groups*) and homomorphisms $d_1 : C_1 \to C_0, d_2 : C_2 \to C_1, \dots$ (called *differential* or *boundary operators*) such that $d_{q-1}d_q = 0, \forall q > 0$, where $\mathfrak{R}$ is some ring, called the *ground ring* or *ring of coefficients*.

Given a cubical complex, we define its chain complex (with coefficients in $\mathbb{Z}_2$) as follows:

- C_q is the free group generated by the q-cubes of the complex. Their elements are called q-*chains*.
- d_q gives the "algebraic" boundary, which is the sum of the primary faces of the q-cubes.

2.3 Discrete Morse Theory

Discrete Morse Theory was introduced by Robin Forman as a discretization of the Morse Theory [For02]. The main idea is to obtain some homological information by means of a function defined on the complex. This function is equivalent to a discrete gradient vector field and we will rather use this notion.

A *discrete vector field* on a cubical complex is a matching on its Hasse diagram, that is a collection of edges such that no two of them have a vertex in common. From a Hasse diagram and a discrete vector field we can define a *Morse graph*: it is a graph similar to the Hasse diagram except for the arrows contained in the matching, which are reverted. These arrows will be called *integral arrows*, and the others, *differential arrows*.

A $\mathcal{V}$-*path* is a path on the Morse graph which alternates between integral and differential arrows. A *discrete gradient vector field* is a discrete vector field which does not contain any closed $\mathcal{V}$-path. A *critical vertex* (or critical cell) is a vertex which is not paired by the matching. Figure 1 shows a cubical complex with a DGVF.

Fig. 1. A DGVF over a cubical complex. Red segments represent integral arrows going from one cell to some of its primary cofaces. The critical cells are represented in blue.

A DGVF can be given by a set of elementary collapses. An *elementary collapse* [Whi50] consist of removing a *free pair* from a cell complex, that is a cell with a primary face which does not have any other coface. A *collapse* is a sequence of elementary collapses. The homotopy type of a complex is invariant under collapses. The free pairs of a collapse define a DGVF.

2.4 Reduction

The Effective Homology theory [Ser92] provides a tool that establishes a strong relation between two chain complexes, called *reduction*. Formally, a reduction between two chain complexes (C_*, d_*) and (C'_*, d'_*) is a triple of homomorphisms (h_*, f_*, g_*) such that:

- $h_q : C_q \to C_{q+1}$ for every $q \geq 0$
- $f_q : C_q \to C'_q$ is a chain map $(fd = d'f)$
- $g_q : C'_q \to C_q$ is also a chain map $(gd' = dg)$
- $gf = 1 - dh - hd$
- $fg = 1_{C'}$
- $hh = hf = hg = 0$

This notion is a special case of *chain contraction* [EL53] or *strong deformation retraction data* [LS87]. It is a usual tool for reducing chain complexes in order to compute their homology. We will use it to define the *Morse complex* of a cubical complex endowed with a DGVF. The exact definition is given in [GBMR14]. Roughly speaking, the Morse complex is a cell complex composed of the critical cells, which is homotopically equivalent to the original cubical complex.

3 Our Framework

3.1 Overview

In this section we present the structure of our framework. It should be noted that, although the algorithms are designed for 3D volumes, they can be generalized to any dimension: one only needs to replace parameter 3 by n.

Let us briefly recall the structure of our approach, previously described in the introduction. We start with a binary 3D volume. Depending of the connectivity relation which we want to use (6 or 26), we build its associated cubical complex with one of the methods explained in Sect. 3.2. Next, we make a *homotopic thinning* of the cubical complex based on elementary collapses encoded in a DGVF. Finally we minimize the number of cells in the Morse complex by preserving its shape in Algorithm 4.

The final result is a *cellular skeleton*: a reduction from the original complex to a reduced one. Then we give a representation of this skeleton by showing the cells of the chain $f(\sigma)$ (see Sect. 2.4) for every critical cell.

3.2   Construction of the Cubical Complex: Choosing the Connectivity

As explained earlier, the first step of our approach consists in building the cubical complex associated to the digital volume and the connectivity relation chosen. Hence, there are two encodings: one for 6-connectivity (that is $2n$-connectivity in dimension n) and other for 26-connectivity (($3^n - 1$)-connectivity). Figure 2 illustrates these two cubical complexes associated to the same binary volume.

Fig. 2. Left: a binary volume. Center: its primal associated cubical complex. Right: its dual cubical complex

The Primal Associated Cubical Complex. We encode a binary volume equipped with 26-connectivity into a cubical complex (called *primal associated cubical complex*). In this case, the construction is quite elementary as every voxel $x = (x_1, x_2, x_3)$ generates the 3-cube $[x_1, x_1 + 1] \times [x_2, x_2 + 1] \times [x_3, x_3 + 1]$ and all its faces. This method was already presented in [CC09].

The Dual Associated Cubical Complex. Another approach consists in encoding a binary volume equipped with 6-connectivity into a cubical complex (called *dual associated cubical complex*). Let us first adapt the notion of *clique* to our context: a *d-clique* is a maximal (in the sense of inclusion) set of voxels such that their intersection is a d-cube. First, for every voxel (in fact 3-clique) $x = (x_1, x_2, x_3)$ of the volume, we add the 0-cube $\sigma = [x_1] \times [x_2] \times [x_3]$. Then, for every d-clique ($d < 3$) in the volume, we add to the cubical complex a $(3 - d)$-cube such that its vertices are the voxels of the d-clique. This approach was used in [LCLJ10].

3.3 Homotopic Thinning Algorithm

This step performs a homotopic thinning of the cubical complex. This is done by establishing a DGVF, which can be seen as a set of elementary collapses (deletion of free pairs). Actually, this DGVF describes the relation between the original complex and the thinned one (the Morse complex) in terms of a reduction. Let us point out that our approach does not have to deal with simple points, critical kernels, etc.

A simple thinning algorithm with satisfying results was given in [LCLJ10]. The algorithm is described in three steps:

Step 1: Thinning. Perform an iterative thinning: at each iteration, all free pairs are identified and then collapsed while it is possible. For every cell σ, $I(\sigma)$ is the first iteration after which σ has no cofaces and $R(\sigma)$ is the iteration in which σ is removed. If $I(\sigma)$ is defined,

$$M_{abs}(\sigma) = R(\sigma) - I(\sigma) \text{ and } M_{rel}(\sigma) = 1 - \frac{I(\sigma)}{R(\sigma)}$$

Step 2: Clustering. Given some thresholds ε_{abs}^q, ε_{rel}^q and τ^q ($k = 1, 2$), consider the set B of the cells scoring higher than ε_{abs}^q and ε_{rel}^q. Remove from this set those cells whose connected component size is fewer than τ^q.

Step 3: Thinning. Repeat the first step while maintaining the cells in B.

Note that when we identify all the free pairs, we can find several pairs ($\tau > \sigma_1$), ($\tau > \sigma_2$), ... and we must choose one of them. This choice was defined as arbitrary in [LCLJ10] and it was pointed out that this should be studied. Our contribution in this step is an alternative to the simple iterative collapse which makes some of these collapses order-independent. It is described in detail in Algorithm 2, which calls Algorithm 1.

Indeed, for each elementary collapse between a maximal cell τ and one of its primary faces $\sigma_1, \ldots, \sigma_n$, we must choose one of them. We partially solve this problem by performing multiple elementary collapses (see Algorithm 1) in the same iteration in order to remove some of these cells. Sometimes the choice of the cell σ_1 is irrelevant, as shown in Fig. 3. This seems to be related to the notion of *simple cell* [DS14, Def. 3.3].

Algorithm 1. AdvancedCollapse

Require: K a cubical complex; $[\tau, \sigma_1, \ldots, \sigma_n]$ cells such that $(\tau > \sigma_i)$ are free pairs; *it* the iteration; R, I two maps over K; V a DGVF over K.
Ensure: R', I', V' extensions of R, I, V.
1: $V' \leftarrow V$, $R' \leftarrow R$, $I' \leftarrow I$, Q an empty queue
2: $V' \leftarrow (\sigma_1, \tau)$; $R'(\sigma_1), R'(\tau) \leftarrow it$
3: **for all** σ_i, $i = 2, \ldots, n$ **do**
4:      $I'(\sigma_i) \leftarrow it$
5: **for all** $\rho < \sigma$ critical primary face **do**
6:      $Q \leftarrow \rho$
7: **while** Q not empty **do**
8:      $\rho \leftarrow Q$, $C \leftarrow$ set of its critical primary cofaces
9:      **if** C is empty **then**
10:         Make an elementary collapse if there exists $\pi < \rho$ critical primary face with only one critical coface; update V', R' and I'
11:      **if** $C = \{\sigma_i\}$ **then**
12:         $V' \leftarrow (\rho, \sigma_i)$; $R'(\rho), R'(\sigma_i) \leftarrow it$
13:         **for all** $\rho' < \sigma_i$ critical primary face **do**
14:            $Q \leftarrow \rho'$
      return (R', I', V')

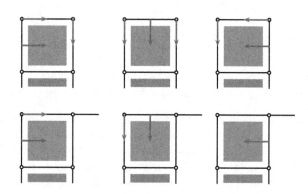

Fig. 3. Up: the choice of the first elementary collapse does not affect the collapse. Down: only the two first (left and center) collapses are independent of the first elementary collapse. In such a situation, a choice is necessary.

3.4   Cell Clustering: Minimizing the Number of Cells

After the previous step, the shape of the skeleton is already defined and we have reduced the number of cubes. Nevertheless, this can be improved. Algorithm 4, which calls Algorithm 3, describes this step.

This step, which is the main novelty of this article, has the following property. Let V be the DGVF computed at step 2 and V' its extension returned at the end of the step 3: for each critical cell σ of V, there exists one and only one critical cell σ' of V' such that σ appears in the chain $f(\sigma)$.

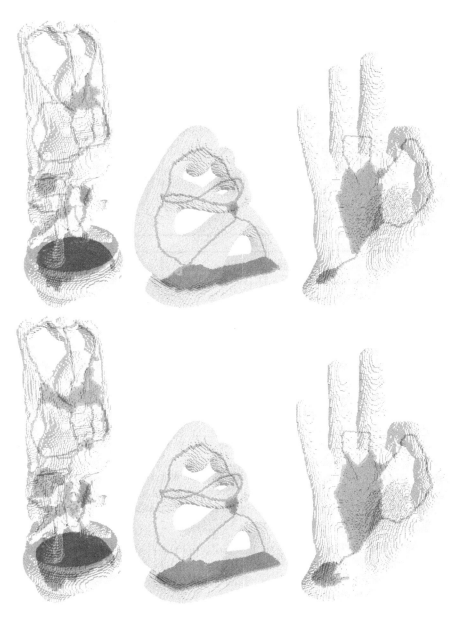

Fig. 4. Top: cellular skeletons computed using the proposed method. Bottom: cellular skeletons computed with the algorithm in [LCLJ10].

Algorithm 2. Alternative to Step 1: Thinning

Require: K a cubical complex.
Ensure: R, I two maps K; $\mathcal{V}$ a DGVF over K.
1: $it \leftarrow 0$
2: $M \leftarrow$ set of the maximal critical cells (without critical cofaces)
3: **for all** $\sigma \in M$ **do**
4:     $I(\sigma) \leftarrow it$, if it is not defined
5: **repeat**
6:     $it \leftarrow it + 1$
7:     **for all** $\tau \in M$ of dimension > 0 **do**
8:         $(\tau, \sigma_1), \ldots, (\tau, \sigma_n) \leftarrow$ the free pairs containing τ
9:         $(R, I, \mathcal{V}) \leftarrow$ AdvancedCollapse$(K, [\tau, \sigma_1, \ldots, \sigma_n], it, R, I, \mathcal{V})$
10:     $M \leftarrow$ set of the maximal critical cells
11:     **for all** $\sigma \in M$ **do**
12:         $I(\sigma) \leftarrow it$, if it is not defined
13: **until** idempotency
14: **return** $(R, I, \mathcal{V})$

Algorithm 3. BlockedCollapse

Require: K a cubical complex, $\mathcal{V}$ a DGVF over K, B a set of (blocked) cells
Ensure: $\mathcal{V}'$ an extension of $\mathcal{V}$
1: $\mathcal{V}' \leftarrow \mathcal{V}$
2: FreePairs $\leftarrow \emptyset$
3: **for all** critical cell $\sigma \in K$ not in B **do**
4:     **if** σ has only one critical primary coface τ not in B **then**
5:         FreePairs $\leftarrow (\sigma, \tau)$
6: **for all** (σ, τ) in FreePairs **do**
7:     **if** τ is critical **then**
8:         $\mathcal{V}' \leftarrow (\sigma, \tau)$
    return $\mathcal{V}'$

A direct consequence of this property is that when we visualize the chains $f(Cr)$ (Cr the set of critical cells in $\mathcal{V}'$), we obtain the skeleton computed at step 2. Hence, this DGVF *preserves* the geometric structure of $\mathcal{V}'$.

Algorithm 4 has two motivations:

- Following the previous property, by displaying the chains $f(Cr)$ we obtain a cell complex homotopically equivalent to the initial cubical complex, in which the q-cells are unions of q-cubes. This can be considered as a classification of the skeleton in terms of manifolds.
- This step accelerates a later homology computation based on the reduction induced by the resulting DGVF. Moreover, as homology generators are contained in the skeleton, they are supposed to be well shaped, according to the geometric properties of the skeleton.

Algorithm 4. CellClustering

Require: K a cubical complex endowed with a DGVF $\mathcal{V}$
Ensure: $\mathcal{V}'$ an extension of $\mathcal{V}$.
1: $\mathcal{V}' \leftarrow \mathcal{V}$
2: FinalCells $\leftarrow \emptyset$
3: **for** q = 2, 1 **do**
4:      BlockedCells $\leftarrow \emptyset$
5:      **for all** critical $(q-1)$-cell $\sigma \in K$ **do**
6:          **if** σ has $\neq 2$ critical primary cofaces **then**
7:              BlockedCells $\leftarrow \sigma$
8:      **repeat**
9:          Take any critical q-cell γ not in FinalCells
10:         FinalCells $\leftarrow \gamma$
11:         **repeat**
12:             $\mathcal{V}' \leftarrow$ BlockedCollapse$(K, \mathcal{V}',$ BlockedCells $\cup$ FinalCells$)$
13:         **until** idempotency
14:     **until** idempotency
        return $\mathcal{V}'$

---

4 Validation and Discussion

Our algorithms have been implemented in C++ using the library DGtal [DGt].

In the following we only consider the dual associated cubical complex. Also, as in [LCLJ10] we will consider the thresholds $\varepsilon_{abs}^q = 0.05 \cdot L$, $\varepsilon_{rel}^q = 0.05$ and $\tau^q = (0.05 \cdot L)^k$, where L is the width of the bounding box.

Seeing points or edges belonging to big cellular skeletons can be difficult. Hence, we propose a *voxelized* version of the cellular skeleton. Its construction is quite simple: every cubical cell $[a_1, a_2] \times [b_1, b_2] \times [c_1, c_2]$ produces all the possible voxels $(a_1, b_1, c_1), (a_2, b_1, c_1), (a_1, b_2, c_1), (a_2, b_2, c_1), (a_1, b_1, c_2), \ldots \ldots$. These voxels are coloured following the dimension of the cubical cell which created them: red for 2-cubes, green for 1-cubes and blue for 0-cubes.

Figure 4 compares some cellular skeletons obtained with our algorithm and [LCLJ10] over some voxels sets. Let us remark that both give similar results, even on the third example, which does not keep all the fingers. There is the need to study further how different fixed orders in the elementary collapses affect both algorithms. Also, we observe that upper skeletons are thinner. Hence, we intend to study whether we can obtain even more similar skeletons by adjusting the thresholds.

5 Conclusion and Future Perspectives

The present paper introduces a new kind of skeleton for binary volumes which is a chain complex together with a reduction, which is obtained by a three-step method. It works for different connectivity relations and it does not make use of look-up tables. Our main contribution is the third step, which is completely new and provides an alternative skeleton representation, synthesizing further homology computations and geometric representation (each cell in the cellular skeleton actually stands for a piece of manifold in the geometric skeleton).

Our future goals are:

- to better understand the difference between choosing the primal or the dual associated cubical complex. The primal associated cubical complex contains more cells, and this can affect the complexity of our algorithms;
- to study different thresholds for the second step. Since it differs from [LCLJ10], we need to study further appropriate thresholds;
- to estimate the complexity of our method.

Acknowledgement. The hand and the statue datasets are courtesy of Michel Couprie, and the Happy Buddha is courtesy of the Stanford University Computer Graphics Laboratory.

References

Blu67. Blum, H.: A transformation for extracting new descriptors of shape. In: Wathen-Dunn, W. (ed.) Models for the Perception of Speech and Visual Form, pp. 362–380. MIT Press, Cambridge (1967)

CB14. Couprie, M., Bertrand, G.: Isthmus-based parallel and asymmetric 3D thinning algorithms. In: Barcucci, E., Frosini, A., Rinaldi, S. (eds.) DGCI 2014. LNCS, vol. 8668, pp. 51–62. Springer, Heidelberg (2014)

CC09. Chaussard, J., Couprie, M.: Surface thinning in 3D cubical complexes. In: Wiederhold, P., Barneva, R.P. (eds.) IWCIA 2009. LNCS, vol. 5852, pp. 135–148. Springer, Heidelberg (2009)

Cou11. Couprie, M.: Hierarchic euclidean skeletons in cubical complexes. In: Debled-Rennesson, I., Domenjoud, E., Kerautret, B., Even, P. (eds.) DGCI 2011. LNCS, vol. 6607, pp. 141–152. Springer, Heidelberg (2011)

Cou13. Couprie, M.: Topological maps and robust hierarchical euclidean skeletons in cubical complexes. Computer Vision and Image Understanding **117**(4), 355–369 (2013). Special issue on Discrete Geometry for Computer Imagery

DGt. DGtal: Digital geometry tools and algorithms library. http://dgtal.org

DS14. Dlotko, P., Specogna, R.: Topology preserving thinning of cell complexes. IEEE Transactions on Image Processing **23**(10), 4486–4495 (2014)

EL53. Eilenberg, S., Mac Lane, S.: On the groups h(, n), i. Annals of Mathematics **58**(1), 55–106 (1953)

For02. Forman, R.: A user's guide to discrete morse theory. Seminaire Lotharingin de Combinatoire **48**, (2002)

GBMR14. Gonzalez-Lorenzo, A., Bac, A., Mari, J.-L., Real, P.: Computing homological information based on directed graphs within discrete objects. In: 16th International Symposium on Symbolic and Numeric Algorithms for Scientific Computing, SYNASC 2014, Timisoara, Romania, September 22–25, pp. 571–578 (2014)

GSdA09. Gall, J., Stoll, C., de Aguiar, E., Theobalt, C., Rosenhahn, B., Seidel, H.-P.: Motion capture using joint skeleton tracking and surface estimation. In 2009 IEEE Conference on Computer Vision and Pattern Recognition: CVPR 2009, pp. 1746–1753. IEEE, Miami (2009)

KMM04. Kaczynski, T., Mischaikow, K., Mrozek, M.: Computational Homology, vol. 157, chapter 2, 7, pp. 255–258. Springer (2004)

KR89. Kong, T.Y., Rosenfeld, A.: Digital topology: Introduction and survey. Computer Vision, Graphics, and Image Processing **48**(3), 357–393 (1989)

LB07. Lohou, C., Bertrand, G.: Two symmetrical thinning algorithms for 3D binary images, based on p-simple points. Pattern Recognition **40**(8), 2301–2314 (2007)

LCLJ10. Liu, L., Chambers, E.W., Letscher, D., Ju, T.: A simple and robust thinning algorithm on cell complexes. Computer Graphics Forum **29**(7), 2253–2260 (2010)

LS87. Lambe, L., Stasheff, J.: Applications of perturbation theory to iterated fibrations. Manuscripta Mathematica **58**(3), 363–376 (1987)

Mar09. Mari, J.-L.: Surface sketching with a voxel-based skeleton. In: Brlek, S., Reutenauer, C., Provençal, X. (eds.) DGCI 2009. LNCS, vol. 5810, pp. 325–336. Springer, Heidelberg (2009)

Ser92. Sergeraert, F.: Effective homology, a survey (1992). http://www-fourier.ujf-grenoble.fr/sergerar/Papers/Survey.pdf (accessed June 11, 2014)

Whi50. Whitehead, J.H.C.: Simple homotopy types. American Journal of Mathematics **72**(1), 1–57 (1950)

YWZ08. Yu, K., Wu, J., Zhuang, Y.: Skeleton-based recognition of chinese calligraphic character image. In: Huang, Y.-M.R., Xu, C., Cheng, K.-S., Yang, J.-F.K., Swamy, M.N.S., Li, S., Ding, J.-W. (eds.) PCM 2008. LNCS, vol. 5353, pp. 228–237. Springer, Heidelberg (2008)

Model-Free Head Pose Estimation Based on Shape Factorisation and Particle Filtering

Stefania Cristina$^{(\boxtimes)}$ and Kenneth P. Camilleri

Department of Systems and Control Engineering, University of Malta,
Msida MSD2080, Malta
{stefania.cristina,kenneth.camilleri}@um.edu.mt

Abstract. Head pose estimation is essential for several applications and is particularly required for head pose-free eye-gaze tracking where estimation of head rotation permits free head movement during tracking. While the literature is broad, the accuracy of recent vision-based head pose estimation methods is contingent upon the availability of training data or accurate initialisation and tracking of specific facial landmarks. In this paper, we propose a method to estimate the head pose in real-time from the trajectories of a set of feature points spread randomly over the face region, without requiring a training phase or model-fitting of specific facial features. Conversely, without seeking specific facial landmarks, our method exploits the sparse 3-dimensional shape of the surface of interest, recovered via shape and motion factorisation, in combination with particle filtering to correct mistracked feature points and improve upon an initial estimation of the 3-dimensional shape during tracking. In comparison with two additional methods, quantitative results obtained through our model- and landmark-free method yield a reduction in the head pose estimation error for a wide range of head rotation angles.

1 Introduction

Head pose estimation plays an important role in the process of estimating the eye-gaze [8], providing an initial coarse indication of the gaze direction which may then be refined according to the eyeball rotation to define the gaze at a finer level. Information relating to the head pose is relevant to a host of applications, such as in human-computer interaction (HCI) where, in conjunction with eye tracking, the estimation of head rotation permits the calculation of a point-of-regard on a monitor screen at different eye and head configurations. This is especially desirable in unconstrained eye-gaze tracking scenarios where the estimation of head pose permits free head movement during tracking, hence eliminating the need for a chin-rest which would otherwise be required to maintain the head stationary.

The problem of head pose estimation has been receiving increasing interest over the years, leading to the development of various methods that seek to estimate the head pose reliably [13]. Existing methods may be broadly classified into two major categories based on their approach in exploiting either the holistic appearance [3,9,12,14] or distinct features [4,10,11,15,21] of the face

© Springer International Publishing Switzerland 2015
G. Azzopardi and N. Petkov (Eds.): CAIP 2015, Part II, LNCS 9257, pp. 628–639, 2015.
DOI: 10.1007/978-3-319-23117-4_54

for head pose estimation. Appearance-based methods generally exploit the face image information entirely to estimate the head orientation. Typical variants of appearance-based methods search for the best matching head pose from a collection of pose-annotated templates [3], register a flexible model of the facial shape to target colour [14] or texture maps [12], or seek low-dimensional manifolds which model the variations in head pose robustly [9]. Feature-based methods, on the other hand, rely on a sparse set of feature points sampled at specific feature positions within the face region. The chosen features often serve as landmarks for non-rigid [4, 10, 11, 21] or geometrical face models that infer the head orientation from the relative configuration of the facial features [15]. In general, the main challenges associated with existing appearance and feature-based methods relate to the necessity for training data prior to head pose estimation and the capability to estimate the head pose accurately especially in the presence of large head rotation angles. In this regard, the achievable estimation accuracy of methods that rely on a training stage is often contingent upon the size of the training set and the conditions under which the training data was captured [3, 9, 12, 21]. Furthermore, the estimation accuracy of methods that rely on model-fitting generally depends upon accurate initialisation and tracking of specific facial features. Face feature detection is, however, an open problem in itself [21], prompting several model-based methods to resort to manual initialisation of the facial features [4, 11], while the accuracy of feature tracking is typically susceptible to distortion and self-occlusions which may hamper the range of achievable head rotations [15].

In light of these challenges, we propose a method to estimate the head pose in real-time based on the trajectories of salient feature points spread randomly over the face region, in order to allow larger head rotation angles without requiring prior training or accurate initialisation of specific facial features. In the absence of specific facial landmarks that fit the face models typically proposed in the literature [10, 11, 21], we propose to apply shape and motion factorisation to the problem of head pose estimation to recover a sparse 3-dimensional representation of the surface of interest [18]. Factorisation theory is well-known in the domain of structure from motion (SfM), for the purpose of recovering the 3-dimensional shape from the trajectories of a sparse set of feature points, however, to the best of our knowledge, it has never been considered within the context of head pose estimation. Nonetheless, despite its effectiveness, the factorisation method is susceptible to the presence of noise and outliers in the feature trajectories due to drifting feature trackers, which in turn reduce the accuracy of the recovered shape and motion information [20]. Hence, we propose to combine factorisation with particle filtering in order to correct mistracked feature points in real-time, preventing the feature trackers from drifting off the features of interest due to distortion or self-occlusion, while permitting correctly tracked feature points to contribute to the factorisation result and improve upon an initial estimation of the sparse 3-dimensional shape. In comparison with other methods which employ particle filtering to estimate the head rotation [3, 4, 11], we base our estimation upon the 3-dimensional shape of the face rather than the photometric properties, hence reducing the susceptibility of the method to intensity variations and repetitive skin texture. Furthermore, we exploit the 3-dimensional information of the surface of interest without necessitating the use of depth sensors [5] or stereo-vision [7], which may reduce the portability of the setup especially in unconstrained scenarios.

This paper is organised as follows. Section 2 describes the details of the proposed method for head pose estimation. Section 3 presents and discusses the experimental results, while Section 4 draws the final remarks and concludes the paper.

2   Method

The following sections describe the stages of the proposed method, by first outlining the overarching idea of the proposed algorithm in Section 2.1 and subsequently presenting the implementation details in Section 2.2.

2.1   Outline of the Algorithm

Our method estimates the head pose angles in real-time by exploiting the sparse 3-dimensional shape of salient feature points randomly distributed over the surface of interest, in combination with particle filtering to generate hypotheses and estimate the head pose at every image frame. In the absence of a specific face model, we employ shape and motion factorisation theory to recover the sparse 3-dimensional surface from feature trajectories initially collected over a sequence of image frames [18]. At every time step, the image frame is first rotated according to the roll angle recovered via factorisation at the previous time step, in order to compensate for the head roll by aligning the horizontal and vertical head axes with the corresponding image axes. Subsequently, the 3-dimensional shape is rotated according to a set of N particles, where each particle defines a hypothesis of the head yaw and pitch angles, and re-projected to the image space such that the image space distance between the x and y-coordinates of the re-projected and the tracked feature positions is calculated separately. This distance permits the particles to be weighted accordingly such that the head yaw and pitch angles are then defined by a weighted average of the particle set. In order to improve the initially estimated 3-dimensional shape and correct the x and y-coordinates of mistracked feature points during tracking, a weighted average between the image coordinates of the tracked features and the feature positions corresponding to the re-projected 3-dimensional shape defined by the particle filter is also computed at every image frame. An updated 3-dimensional shape is finally recovered from this information via factorisation to be used at the next time step.

Specifically, therefore, the proposed algorithm initially tracks P salient feature points through K time steps, where each time step corresponds with the acquisition of a new image frame. The coordinates, $(u_{k,p}, v_{k,p}) \mid k = 1, \ldots, K$

and $p = 1, \ldots, P$, of the feature trajectories are subsequently collected inside a measurement matrix W of size $2K \times P$ as follows,

$$\mathbf{W} = \begin{bmatrix} U \\ \hline V \end{bmatrix} \tag{1}$$

According to the factorisation theory [18], in the absence of noise, matrix $\mathbf{W}$ is at most of rank three and may be decomposed into motion and shape, denoted by matrices $\mathbf{M}$ and $\mathbf{S}$ respectively, as follows,

$$\mathbf{W} = \mathbf{MS} \tag{2}$$

In the presence of noise matrix $\mathbf{W}$ is not of rank three and this decomposition may instead be approximated by singular value decomposition (SVD), which results in unitary matrices $\mathbf{U}$ and $\mathbf{V}$, and a diagonal matrix Σ,

$$\mathbf{W} = \mathbf{U}\Sigma\mathbf{V}^T \tag{3}$$

hence allowing the estimation of the motion and shape matrices,

$$\mathbf{M} = \mathbf{U}\Sigma^{\frac{1}{2}} \quad \mathbf{S} = \Sigma^{\frac{1}{2}}\mathbf{V}^T \tag{4}$$

Following the computation of the 3-dimensional shape $\mathbf{S}$, a set of N particles $\mathbf{x}_k^{(n)} \sim p(\mathbf{x}_k), n = 1, \ldots, N$ is generated at time step $k = (K+1)$, where each particle denotes a hypothesis of state $\mathbf{x}_k = (\alpha_k, \beta_k)$ with known probability density function $p(\mathbf{x}_k)$. The feature coordinates $(u_{k,p}, v_{k,p})$ are also updated at time step $k = (K+1)$ by tracking the feature positions inside a newly acquired image frame following image rotation to compensate for the head roll angle recovered in matrix, $\mathbf{M}$. The 3-dimensional shape is then transformed by a rotation matrix $\mathbf{R}_k^{(n)}$ according to every particle,

$$\mathbf{S}_k^{(n)} = \mathbf{R}_k^{(n)}\mathbf{S} \tag{5}$$

and re-projected back inside the image space such that each feature of interest p is assigned a set of candidate coordinates, $C_k(p) = \{(c_{k,p}^{(n)}, d_{k,p}^{(n)})\} \mid n = 1, \ldots, N$. We define distance measurements, $D_k^{(n)}(\alpha)$ and $D_k^{(n)}(\beta)$, for the yaw and pitch angles respectively as follows,

$$D_k^{(n)}(\alpha) = \sum_{p=1}^{P} \left| u_{k,p} - c_{k,p}^{(n)} \right| \qquad D_k^{(n)}(\beta) = \sum_{p=1}^{P} \left| v_{k,p} - d_{k,p}^{(n)} \right| \tag{6}$$

which permit the calculation of the horizontal and vertical distances between the coordinates of the tracked feature positions, $\mathbf{u}_{k,p}$, and the candidate coordinates of the re-projected shape inside the image space, $\mathbf{c}_{k,p}^{(n)}$, according to each particle n. Based on these distances, we define the likelihood model of the particle filter corresponding to the head yaw by a normal distribution having mean, $\mu = 0$, and standard deviation, σ, as follows,

$$p(u_{k,p|1,...,P} \mid \mathbf{x}_k^{(n)}) = \frac{1}{\sigma\sqrt{2\pi}} e^{-\frac{D_k^{(n)}(\alpha)^2}{2\sigma^2}} \tag{7}$$

and similarly for the head pitch angles. The likelihood model allows each particle to be assigned a weight, $w_k^{(n)}(\alpha)$, according to the likelihood $p(u_{k,p|1,...,P} \mid \mathbf{x}_k^{(n)})$ of representing the actual measurement $u_{k,p|1,...,P}$ [1],

$$w_k^{(n)}(\alpha) = w_{k-1}^{(n)}(\alpha) \frac{p(u_{k,p|1,...,P} \mid \mathbf{x}_k^{(n)}) p(\mathbf{x}_k^{(n)} \mid \mathbf{x}_{k-1}^{(n)})}{q(\mathbf{x}_k^{(n)} \mid \mathbf{x}_{k-1}^{(n)}, u_{k,p|1,...,P})} \tag{8}$$

where, $p(\mathbf{x}_k^{(n)} \mid \mathbf{x}_{k-1}^{(n)})$ and $q(\mathbf{x}_k^{(n)} \mid \mathbf{x}_{k-1}^{(n)}, u_{k,p|1,...,P})$, denote the prior probability distribution and importance function respectively. Since the distance measurements in Equation 6 consider the horizontal and vertical components of the feature positions separately, each particle is assigned weights $w_k^{(n)}(\alpha)$ and $w_k^{(n)}(\beta)$ denoting the likelihood of representing the true head yaw and pitch angles respectively. These weights are subsequently normalised such that the state, $\mathbf{x}_k = (\alpha_k, \beta_k)$, is estimated as a weighted average of the particle set for the yaw and pitch angles respectively. It is worth noting that we base the process of weighting the particles upon the shape information of the object of interest rather than its photometric properties, in order to reduce the susceptibility of the method to intensity variations and repetitive skin texture.

Following the estimation of the state, $\mathbf{x}_k = (\alpha_k, \beta_k)$, the re-projection of shape $\mathbf{S}$ inside the image space corresponding to the estimated head rotation angles permits correction of mistracked feature points, hence preventing the feature trackers from drifting off the features of interest during tracking. In turn, the correctly tracked feature points permit the estimated 3-dimensional shape to be updated at every time step via factorisation, in order to improve upon the initial estimation of the shape information. To this end, a weighted average between the re-projected shape coordinates, $\hat{c}_{k,p}$, according to the state estimate, $\mathbf{x}_k = (\alpha_k, \beta_k)$, and the tracked feature positions at time step k is calculated as follows,

$$\hat{\mathbf{u}}_{k,p} = a_{k,p}\mathbf{u}_{k,p} + (1 - a_{k,p})\hat{c}_{k,p} \quad p = 1, \ldots, P \tag{9}$$

The value of the weighting parameter, $a_{k,p}$, corresponds to a measure of tracking confidence for every feature point and assumes a value between 0 and 1, with 1 denoting the highest tracking confidence. If a feature point is lost during tracking, denoted by a tracking confidence of 0, the corrected feature coordinates $\hat{\mathbf{u}}_{k,p}$ are defined entirely by the corresponding re-projected shape coordinates for that particular feature. This addresses one of the issues that is commonly associated with factorisation relating to the occurrence of missing entries inside the measurement matrix $\mathbf{W}$, hence ensuring reliable factorisation results by correcting the measurement information in real-time. The averaged coordinates, $\hat{\mathbf{u}}_{k,p}$, are finally included in the measurement matrix such that the shape information of the surface of interest is updated at every image frame by factorisation.

2.2   Implementation Details

Following an overview of the proposed algorithm in Section 2.1, the next sections describe the implementation details to extract the required information from the image frames.

Face Region Detection. The first stage in the implementation of the method detects the bounding box enclosing the face region such that this constrains the initialisation of the salient features to track, as explained in the next section. We chose the Viola-Jones algorithm for rapid detection of the face region given the real-time requirements of our application. The Viola-Jones framework combines several weak classifiers of increasing complexity into a cascade structure, where each classifier is trained by a technique called boosting to search for specific image features by classifying between positive and negative candidate image samples [19]. In our work, we employed the trained cascade classifier available in MATLAB since its detection capabilities were found to generalise well across different subjects.

Initialisation and Tracking of Feature Points. In order to track the object of interest and hence generate the feature trajectories to populate the measurement matrix $\mathbf{W}$, several feature trackers were latched upon salient facial features within the boundaries of the face region detected earlier. The chosen feature points were randomly distributed over the surface of interest and selected according to the method proposed by Shi and Tomasi [16], who define the good features to track as points characterised by a steep brightness gradient along at least two directions. The initialised salient features are subsequently tracked between successive image frames via the Kanade-Lucas-Tomasi (KLT) feature tracker, which matches search windows between consecutive image frames to identify correspondences based on a measure of similarity [17].

Particle Filter. Following the estimation of the 3-dimensional shape of the surface of interest by factorising the trajectories of salient feature points, the implemented particle filter algorithm generates hypotheses of state $\mathbf{x}_k = (\alpha_k, \beta_k)$ at every time step. To this end, we chose to implement the Bootstrap filter [1] due to its simplicity in applying the prior probability distribution, $p(\mathbf{x}_k^{(n)} \mid \mathbf{x}_{k-1}^{(n)})$, as the importance function, $q(\mathbf{x}_k^{(n)} \mid \mathbf{x}_{k-1}^{(n)}, u_{k,p|1,...,P})$, hence simplifying the definition of the particle weights to,

$$w_k^{(n)}(\alpha) = w_{k-1}^{(n)}(\alpha) \frac{p(u_{k,p|1,...,P} \mid \mathbf{x}_k^{(n)}) p(\mathbf{x}_k^{(n)} \mid \mathbf{x}_{k-1}^{(n)})}{q(\mathbf{x}_k^{(n)} \mid \mathbf{x}_{k-1}^{(n)}, u_{k,p|1,...,P})} \tag{10}$$

for the head yaw and similarly for the head pitch angles. In order to avoid degeneration of the particle set, where all but one of the particle weights are equal to zero, a bootstrap re-sampling algorithm was implemented to re-sample the particle set with replacement and hence preserve the particles having the highest weights at every time instance [1]. Furthermore, we approximate the state evolution of the implemented particle filter by a Gaussian random walk model that serves to propagate the particles to the next time step. Hence, the state evolution model may be defined by,

$$p(x_k \mid x_{k-1}) = \mathcal{N}(\mu_k, \sigma) \tag{11}$$

where $\mathcal{N}(.)$ denotes a Gaussian distribution having mean, $\mu_k = x_{k-1}$, and constant standard deviation, σ.

3 Experimental Results and Discussion

To evaluate the proposed head pose estimation method, we selected several video clips from the Head Pose and Eye Gaze (HPEG) Dataset owing to the availability of various head yaw and pitch rotations, and corresponding ground truth information [2]. The HPEG dataset aggregates webcam recordings of 10 different participants into two separate sets, the first of which was recorded while the participants performed various head rotations in different directions, while the second set of recordings was more focused on changes in gaze direction. Hence, we opted to evaluate our method on webcam videos selected from the first set of recordings given their relevance to our work. Each video in the set has been captured at 30 frames per second and spatial resolution of 640×480 pixels, and lasts for 10 seconds. The ground truth information has been extracted from the relative positioning of three green light emitting diodes mounted on the head and tracked across all image frames.

We compare our results to those obtained through the implementation of two additional methods. The first method estimates the yaw and pitch angles by factorising the feature trajectories generated via a standard KLT feature tracker alone, in order to evaluate the error in head pose attributed to the occurrence of outliers and missing entries in the measurement matrix from drifting or lost feature trackers respectively. The KLT algorithm is used extensively in the factorisation literature due to its ease of implementation and low computational cost, nonetheless the feature trackers tend to drift slowly off the feature of interest especially across long image sequences, or tracking is lost entirely if the feature of interest is occluded [20]. The second method is a model-based approach which adapts the geometric face model proposed by Gee et al. in [6], originally proposed to infer the gaze direction by estimating the orientation of near-frontal head poses in static paintings, to a real-time gaming application which operates by estimating the head pose in a stream of webcam image frames [15]. In their approach, Sapienza and Camilleri [15] fit a generic face model to previously detected facial features, specifically the eyes, nose and mouth regions, and subsequently estimate the head pose from the relative tracked positions of these facial features. The resulting mean absolute error (MAE) and standard deviation (SD) of the head yaw and pitch angles estimated by the proposed method

Table 1. Mean absolute error (MAE) and standard deviation (SD) of the head yaw and pitch angles estimated by the proposed method and a KLT-based method alone to generate the feature trajectories, for different subjects in the HPEG dataset.

Subject Number	Proposed Method		KLT-based Method	
	Yaw (MAE(°), SD(°))	Pitch (MAE(°), SD(°))	Yaw (MAE(°), SD(°))	Pitch (MAE(°), SD(°))
1	(3.29, 3.13)	(2.63, 1.75)	(8.32, 8.73)	(4.45, 4.03)
4	(3.04, 2.39)	(4.52, 4.04)	(12.53, 9.45)	(3.90, 2.19)
5	(7.33, 3.87)	(4.85, 4.06)	(8.76, 5.69)	(6.00, 6.14)
6	(6.05, 3.70)	(3.61, 1.95)	(4.03, 3.30)	(8.29, 4.58)
7	(4.64, 3.80)	(3.87, 1.76)	(31.20, 14.75)	(18.85, 21.29)
8	(2.86, 3.23)	(6.33, 4.83)	(20.51, 11.89)	(40.00, 45.00)
9	(2.51, 1.13)	(0.99, 0.65)	(8.61, 6.23)	(0.01, 0.01)
Mean	(4.25, 3.04)	(3.83, 2.72)	(13.42, 8.58)	(11.64, 11.89)

Table 2. Mean absolute error (MAE) and standard deviation (SD) of the head yaw and pitch angles estimated by a model-based method, for different subjects in the HPEG Dataset.

Subject Number	Yaw (MAE(°), SD(°))	Pitch (MAE(°), SD(°))
1	(5.68, 4.00)	(3.41, 3.14)
4	(5.51, 4.03)	(6.30, 2.15)
5	(10.02, 8.89)	(11.97, 9.19)
6	(4.47, 2.65)	(12.74, 5.64)
7	(5.79, 4.14)	(15.77, 7.81)
8	(11.24, 10.61)	(7.98, 5.19)
9	(5.63, 3.51)	(6.01, 0.82)
Mean	(6.90, 5.40)	(9.17, 4.85)

in Section 2 in comparison to the results obtained by the KLT-based method and the model-based method are presented in Tables 1 and 2 respectively.

The results presented in Table 1 indicate a significant reduction in the calculated MAE and SD values when the head yaw and pitch angles were estimated by the method proposed in Section 2, in comparison to the results obtained by generating the feature trajectories prior to factorisation via the KLT-based method alone. It may be noted that several of the highest MAE and SD values for the KLT-based method, such as the results for subjects 7 and 8, correspond to the widest ranges of head yaw or pitch rotations as tabulated in Table 3. The increased error corresponding to larger head rotation angles is caused by an increase in the occurrence of outliers inside the measurement matrix $\mathbf{W}$, and in the absence of a suitable mechanism that detects and corrects the outlying information, the factorisation method produces incorrect head yaw and pitch estimates. Indeed, as shown in Figure 1(d), during larger head rotations several feature points become self-occluded causing the corresponding feature trackers to gradually drift off and collect outlying information, and eventually lose the fea-

Fig. 1. Head pose estimation results obtained through our method (a-c), factorisation of the feature trajectories generated via a standard KLT feature tracker alone (d-f) and the geometric model-based method in [15] (g-i), for subject 8 in the HPEG Dataset.

ture of interest as indicated by the lost feature trackers marked in red, in Figures 1(e) and 1(f). In comparison, our method addresses this problem by exploiting the 3-dimensional shape of the surface of interest in order to correct drifting feature trackers, while permitting the trajectories of correctly tracked features to contribute towards the improvement of the 3-dimensional shape. Hence, the occurrence of outliers in the measurement matrix is reduced in real-time, which allows for increased robustness in estimating larger head rotation angles as shown in Figures 1(a-c), where the relative configuration of the feature trackers is preserved by preventing the trackers from drifting off the object of interest during head rotations. Furthermore, Figure 2 compares the head yaw and pitch angles estimated through our method to the motion information recovered by factorisation in real-time during tracking, for subject 8 in the HPEG dataset. This figure indicates a reduction in jitter for the results obtained by our method,

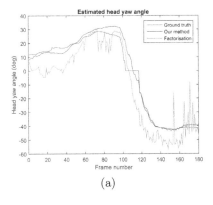
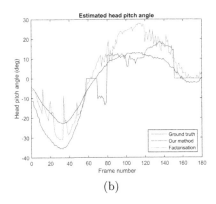

(a)   (b)

Fig. 2. Head pose estimation results obtained through our method (red) and via factorisation during tracking (green), in comparison to ground truth data (blue) for subject 8 in the HPEG Dataset.

while higher MAE and SD values were obtained for the head yaw, (9.74, 6.53), and pitch, (7.55, 6.33), angles estimated by the factorisation algorithm in comparison to our method, hence indicating the validity of combining factorisation with particle filtering.

Furthermore, the results in Table 2 also indicate a reduction in the calculated MAE and SD values for the head yaw and pitch estimates obtained by our method, in comparison to those obtained through an implementation of the model-based method in [15]. In evaluating the results for the model-based method, it has been noted that distortion and partial occlusion of the tracked facial features of interest contribute significantly to the error in the estimated head yaw and pitch angles. Indeed, as shown in Figures 1(g-i), a leftward and rightward rotation of the head produces a displacement of the feature bounding boxes to the opposite direction from their true image positions as the appearance of these features distorts, resulting in reduced head pose estimation accuracy. As expected and similar to the KLT-based results discussed earlier, several of the highest MAE and SD values for the model-based method also correspond to large head yaw or pitch angles as tabulated in Table 3, due to increased distortion of the facial features during extensive out-of-plane head rotation. The effectiveness of our method, on the other hand, is not contingent on a specific head-model and hence a larger set of salient features to track may be better distributed over the surface of interest without being constrained to specific model landmarks. As discussed earlier, this permits the feature trackers latched onto visible feature points to collectively compensate for partially or fully occluded trackers without compromising the estimation accuracy.

Table 3. Ranges of head rotation yaw and pitch angles for different subjects in the HPEG Dataset.

Subject Number	Yaw [Min (°), Max (°)]	Pitch [Min (°), Max (°)]
1	[-27.44, 14.72]	[-21.53, 0.00]
4	[-27.57, 29.85]	[-4.63, 2.98]
5	[-33.41, 26.00]	[-36.70, 0.00]
6	[-17.21, 16.81]	[0.00, 22.30]
7	[-30.87, 39.13]	[-4.20, 30.56]
8	[-42.53, 28.42]	[18.59, -35.61]
9	[-18.17, 11.40]	[0.00, 0.00]

4   Conclusion

In this paper, we proposed a method to estimate the head pose based on the trajectories of salient feature points distributed randomly over the face region rather than specific facial features that fit the landmarks of typical face models, hence allowing larger head rotations without requiring prior training or accurate initialisation of specific feature points. In the absence of specific facial landmarks, we proposed the application of factorisation theory to the problem of head pose estimation in combination with particle filtering. This allowed us to exploit the recovered sparse 3-dimensional shape information in order to prevent the feature trackers from drifting off the features of interest, while at the same time permitting correctly tracked feature points to improve upon the initial estimation of the sparse 3-dimensional shape during tracking. The experimental results revealed a reduction in the head yaw and pitch estimation error when compared to the results obtained by a KLT-based method and a model-based method, hence indicating increased robustness especially in the presence of feature distortion and self-occlusion typically associated with larger head rotation angles.

Future work aims to focus upon increasing the estimated degrees-of-freedom of the head movement, such as translational movement which has not been considered in this work.

Acknowledgement. This work forms part of the project *Eye-Communicate* funded by the Malta Council for Science and Technology through the National Research & Innovation Programme (2012) under Research Grant No. R&I-2012-057.

References

1. Arulampalam, M., Maskell, S., Gordon, N., Clapp, T.: A tutorial on particle filters for online nonlinear/non-gaussian bayesian tracking. IEEE Transactions on Signal Processing **50**(2), 174–188 (2002)
2. Asteriadis, S., Soufleros, D., Karpouzis, K., Kollias, S.: A natural head pose and eye gaze dataset. In: Proceedings of the International Workshop on Affective-Aware Virtual Agents and Social Robots (AFFINE 2009) (2009)

3. Ba, S., Odobez, J.: A probabilistic framework for joint head tracking and pose estimation. In: Proceedings of the 7th International Conference on Pattern Recognition, vol. 4, pp. 264–267 (2004)
4. Chen, C., Schonfeld, D.: A particle filtering framework for joint video tracking and pose estimation. IEEE Transactions on Image Processing 19(6), 1625–1634 (2010)
5. Fanelli, G., Gall, J., Van Gool, L.: Real time head pose estimation with random regression forests. In: IEEE Conference on Computer Vision and Pattern Recognition. pp. 617–624 (2011)
6. Gee, A., Cipolla, R.: Determining the gaze of faces in images. Image and Vision Computing 12(10), 639–647 (1994)
7. Gurbuz, S., Oztop, E., Inoue, N.: Model free head pose estimation using stereovision. Pattern Recognition, 33–42 (2012)
8. Hansen, D.W., Ji, Q.: In the eye of the beholder: A survey of models for eyes and gaze. IEEE Transactions on Pattern Analysis and Machine Intelligence 32(3), 478–500 (2010)
9. Ho, H., Chellappa, R.: Automatic head pose estimation using randomly projected dense sift descriptors. In: Proceedings of the 19th IEEE International Conference on Image Processing, pp. 153–156 (2012)
10. Kim, J., Kim, H., Park, R.: Head pose estimation using a coplanar face model for human computer interaction. In: Proceedings of the IEEE Conference on Consumer Electronics, pp. 560–561 (2014)
11. Kwolek, B.: Model based facial pose tracking using a particle filtering. In: Proceedings of the Geometric Modeling and Imaging - New Trends, pp. 203–208 (2006)
12. La Cascia, M., Sclaroff, S., Athitsos, V.: Fast, reliable head tracking under varying illumination: an approach based on registration of texture-mapped 3d models. IEEE Transactions on Pattern Analysis and Machine Intelligence 22(4), 322–336 (2000)
13. Murphy-Chutorian, E., Trivedi, M.: Head pose estimation in computer vision: A survey. IEEE Transactions on Pattern Analysis and Machine Intelligence 31(4), 607–626 (2009)
14. Rougier, C., Meunier, J., St-Arnaud, A., Rousseau, J.: 3d head tracking for fall detection using a single-calibrated camera. Image and Vision Computing 31, 246–254 (2013)
15. Sapienza, M., Camilleri, K.: Fasthpe: A recipe for quick head pose estimation. Tech. Rep. TR-SCE-2011-01, University of Malta. https://www.um.edu.mt/library/oar/handle/123456789/859 (2011)
16. Shi, J., Tomasi, C.: Good features to track. In: Proceedings of the 1994 IEEE Computer Society Conference on Computer Vision and Pattern Recognition, pp. 593–600 (1994)
17. Tomasi, C., Kanade, T.: Detection and tracking of point features. Tech. Rep. CMU-CS-91-132, Carnegie Mellon University (1991)
18. Tomasi, C., Kanade, T.: Shape and motion from image streams under orthography: a factorization method. International Journal of Computer Vision 9(2), 137–154 (1992)
19. Viola, P., Jones, M.: Robust real-time object detection. International Journal of Computer Vision (2001)
20. Wang, G., Wu, Q.M.J.: Introduction to structure and motion factorization. Advances in Pattern Recognition, pp. 63–86 (2011)
21. Zhu, X., Ramanan, D.: Face detection, pose estimation, and landmark localization in the wild. In: Proceedings of the IEEE Conference on Computer Vision and Pattern Recognition, IEEE Biometrics Compendium, pp. 2879–2886 (2012)

Plane-Fitting Robust Registration for Complex 3D Models

Yuan Cheng$^{(\boxtimes)}$, Shudong Xie, Wee Kheng Leow, and Kun Zhang

Department of Computer Science, National University of Singapore,
Singapore, Singapore
{cyuan,xshudong,leowwk,zhangkun}@comp.nus.edu.sg

Abstract. In surgery planning, forensic and archeology, there is a need to perform analysis and synthesis of complex 3D models. One common first step of 3D model analysis and synthesis is to register a reference model to a target model using similarity transformation. In practice, the models usually contain noise and outliers, and are sometimes incomplete. These facts make the 3D similarity registration challenging. Existing similarity registration methods such as Iterative Closest Point algorithm (ICP) [1] and Fractional Iterative Closest Point algorithm (FICP) [2] are misled by the outliers and are not able to register these models properly. This paper presents a plane-fitting registration algorithm that is more robust than existing registration algorithms. It achieves its robustness by ensuring that the symmetric plane of the reference model is registered to the planar landmarks of the target model. Experiments on patients' skull models show that the proposed algorithm is robust, accurate and efficient in registering complex models.

Keywords: Robust registration · Symmetric plane · Defected skull

1 Introduction

In surgery planning, forensic and archeology, there is a need to perform 3D model analysis and synthesis such as skull and face reconstruction, pose estimation by registration, etc. [3–5]. 3D model analysis and synthesis are challenging tasks because the models' shapes can be very complex and can vary from case to case. For example, human skull contain 22 complex 3D bones that are fused together (Fig. 1). It is much more complex than other 3D models such as face model which contains only a single surface.

One common first step of 3D model analysis and synthesis is to register a reference model to a target model using similarity transformation. In practice, due to noise and outliers caused by deformities and incompleteness of models, it is difficult to perform 3D similarity registration. For example, in craniomaxillofacial surgery planning, patients' skull models are usually incomplete, because only the region to be operated on are scanned so as to reduce radiology exposure. In addition, patients' skull models are either deformed congenitally or fractured due

© Springer International Publishing Switzerland 2015
G. Azzopardi and N. Petkov (Eds.): CAIP 2015, Part II, LNCS 9257, pp. 640–651, 2015.
DOI: 10.1007/978-3-319-23117-4_55

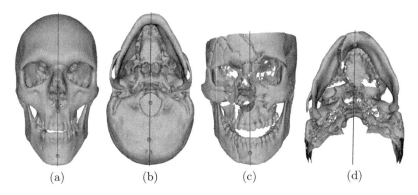

Fig. 1. Skull Models. (a, b) normal skull model. (c, d) fractured skull model. Green landmarks are planar landmarks that should lie on the symmetric plane (grey lines).

to injuries. The skull shown in Fig. 1(c) is fractured into several pieces, which are separated from each other and displaced away from their normal positions. Consequently, existing similarity registration methods such as Iterative Closest Point (ICP) [1], and Fractional Iterative Closest Point (FICP) [2] are misled and not able to register these models properly.

Fortunately, in complex 3D models like skulls, there is an approximate lateral symmetry with respect to a symmetric plane (Fig. 1). This symmetric plane is identified by a set of landmarks on the models [6], and these planar landmarks (Fig. 1) should approximately lie on the symmetric plane.

This paper presents a plane-fitting registration algorithm that is more robust than existing registration algorithms such as ICP and FICP. It achieves robustness by ensuring that the symmetric plane of the reference model is registered to the planar landmarks of the target model. Experiments on patients' skull models show that the proposed algorithm is robust, accurate and efficient in registering complex models.

2   Related Work

ICP algorithm [1] is popular in solving similarity registration problems. It formulates the problem as minimizing the mean-square distance from the points of the reference model to their closest points on the target model. ICP then solves the problem by iteratively finding optimal closest points and computing the optimal transformation. It converges to a local minimum and provides a standard solution to similarity registration problem.

Variances of ICP algorithm have been proposed to improve robustness [2,7–10] and efficiency [11–13]. Robustness improvement is necessary for real applications, because the original ICP algorithm is not robust against noise and outliers [9].

One kind of robust ICP methods uses statistical methods. Gruen and Akca [10] proposed a method based on a generalized Gauss-Markov model to model noise statistically and reduce its effect on the registration result. This kind of methods is able to overcome noise, but it is still sensitive to outliers.

Another kind of robust ICP methods explicitly identifies outliers and excludes them from transformation computation. Zhang's method [7] rejects pairs of points that are too far from each other. Pajdla and Gool's method [8] rejects pairs of points by reciprocal correspondence distance. The idea is that inlier pairs computed from reference to target or from target to reference should be relatively the same. Therefore, pairs that do not satisfy this property can be identified and excluded. Chetverikov et al.'s method [9] trims the correspondence set to a fixed fraction of it. This method requires prior knowledge about the fraction of inliers, which is not available in most applications. Phillips et al. proposed an algorithm called Fractional Iterative Closest Point (FICP) [2]. FICP extends the objective function in ICP algorithm to fractional mean-square distance. By minimizing the extended objective function, FICP algorithm tends to find a large set of inlier pairs separated by small distances to compute transformation.

This paper presents a robust registration algorithm that ensures the matching of reference symmetric plane to target model's planar landmarks that are not affected by outliers. Ensuring planar constraints on symmetric plane and planar landmarks helps the algorithm to explicitly differentiate outliers and inliers and thus improves robustness.

3   Fractional Iterative Closet Point Method

Fractional Iterative Closest Point (FICP) algorithm is a variant of ICP that is more robust than ICP. Like ICP, FICP iteratively computes the best similarity transformation that registers the reference model to the target model. The difference is that in each iteration, FICP computes the transformation using only a subset of mesh points on the reference model whose distances to the target model are the smallest. This set of mesh points is called the inlier set.

Given two point sets , the reference model F and the target model D with unknown correspondence, FICP minimizes the fractional mean-square distance

$$E_1 = \left(\frac{|F|}{|G|}\right)^\lambda \frac{1}{|G|} \sum_{p \in G} \|T(p) - c(p)\|^2 \tag{1}$$

where G is a subset of F containing only the inliers, $c()$ is the correspondence mapping function of p that finds p's closest point on the target model, λ is a constant positive parameter, and T is the similarity transformation to be optimized. By minimizing E_1, FICP finds a large inlier set G with small errors and outputs the transformation computed only on G.

4   Plane-Fitting Registration

Reference model F and target model D can differ in size and shape details due to deformation caused by injury, normal variation among individuals, and possible incomplete scanning of the target skull. The registration algorithm should be robust to these variations, and find the common parts between the two models to align them. In addition, the plane P_F of the reference model should match the planar landmarks $v \in L$ of the target model.

The proposed plane-fitting registration algorithm enforces the matching of the reference plane to the planar landmarks of target model. In addition to the fractional mean-square distance (Eq. 1), a plane-fitting error E_2 is added to the objective function:

$$E_2 = \frac{1}{|L|} \sum_{v \in L} d_\pi^2(v) \qquad (2)$$

where L is the set of planar landmarks on the target model, and $d_\pi(v)$ is the distance from target landmark v to the plane of the transformed reference model F. The overall objective function to be minimized becomes

$$E_r = E_1 + E_2. \qquad (3)$$

The transformation T that minimizes E_r is the optimal transformation that registers F to D. Optimizing E_r is a difficult problem to solve. The proposed algorithm extends FICP algorithm to iteratively minimize E_r (Eq. 3) instead of E_1.

FICP finds the similarity transformation T that minimizes E_1 in Eq. 1 by iteratively performing four steps until convergence:

1. Finds correspondence between F and D.
2. Finds inlier subset G of F.
3. Computes similarity transformation T using correspondence of points in G.
4. Applies T on all points of F.

Phillips et al. [2] proved that the objective function E_1 decreases in each step of the iteration and the algorithm converges to a local minimum.

Out proposed algorithm has the same structure as FICP, but differs in algorithm details. In the first step, FICP finds the closest point as corresponding points only for the set F of mesh points. In the proposed algorithm, for a mesh vertex $p \in F$, its corresponding point $q \in D$ is the closest point of p. On the other hand, for a landmark $q \in L$, its corresponding point p of the reference model is the orthogonal projection of q on the plane P_F of the reference model. Let us denote the set of points p as P, and the set of corresponding points q as Q.

In the third step, FICP applies Horn et al.'s algorithm [14] to solve for the optimal similarity transformation T between P and Q that minimizes:

$$E = \sum_{p \in P} \|sRp + t - q\|^2 \qquad (4)$$

where s, R and t are the scale factor, rotation matrix and translation vector of the similarity transformation T.

To minimize E_1 and E_2 in Eq. 3 at the same time, we introduce weights to Eq. 4 and reformulate Eq. 3 as:

$$E = \sum_{p \in P} w_p^2 \|sRp + t - q\|^2 \tag{5}$$

where

$$w_p^2 = \begin{cases} \left(\dfrac{|F|}{|G|}\right)^\lambda \dfrac{1}{|G|}, & \text{for } p \in G, \\[2ex] \dfrac{1}{|L|}, & \text{for other } p. \end{cases}$$

This minimization can be achieved by adding the weights w_p into Horn et al.'s algorithm [14] where the rotation R and translation t are computed [15,16]. After computing s, R and t, the points p are transformed by the similarity transformation:

$$q = sRp + t. \tag{6}$$

The proposed algorithm converges to a local minimum because registration error E_r decreases in each step of the iteration. In the first step, finding closest points for mesh vertices would reduce E_1 because the new closest points for vertices in F are closer than the closest points in the previous iteration. Finding new corresponding points for planar landmarks also reduces registration error because the orthogonal projection p on the symmetric plane of reference model is closer to q than the previous corresponding point on the same plane. In the second step, E_r decreases because E_1 decreases as proved in [2] and E_2 is unchanged in this step. Finally, in the third and forth steps, the optimal transformation that minimizes E_r (in the form of Eq. 5) is applied to the reference model. E_r is also reduced in these two steps. Therefore, same as ICP and FICP, the proposed plane-fitting registration algorithm also converges to a local minimum.

5   Experiments and Discussion

Experiments on complex skull models were conducted to evaluate the proposed plane-fitting registration algorithm by comparing it against existing algorithms. In this section, we first evaluate the registration accuracy of the proposed algorithm. Then, we study the robustness of the algorithm, and finally show its application in skull reconstruction.

5.1   Registration Quality

The first experiment evaluated the accuracy and efficiency of the proposed registration method. In this experiment, 124 full normal skull models were used. One of them was used as the reference (Fig. 1(a)). In practice, target skull models are usually patients skulls with deformities. For this reason, 5 skulls were manually

Table 1. Comparison of registration methods. E_S denotes surface error (mm), and E_P denotes plane-fitting error (mm). The proposed plane-fitting registration algorithm attained the overall best performance with the lowest plane-fitting error and satisfactory surface error E_S.

Skull	ICP		FICP		Proposed	
Model	E_S	E_P	E_S	E_P	E_S	E_P
Normal	**3.69**	3.54	4.16	3.49	6.55	**1.42**
Synthetic fractured	**3.83**	3.82	4.10	3.27	3.92	**1.10**
Patient	**6.25**	9.05	15.38	2.07	14.21	**0.86**

cut and displaced in a manner similar to real fractures in patients to synthesize 5 fractured skull models. One of the manually cut skulls is presented in Fig. 2(2). Moreover, 5 skull models of real patients from a local hospital were also used for testing. Fig. 2(3-5) shows three of them. In addition to deformities caused by fracture, real patients' skulls were also incomplete because on the parts of the skulls under treatment were scanned.

The resolution of the CT images used to generate mesh models ranged from 0.31 to 3 mm/pixel. The CT images were segmented and 3D mesh models were reconstructed from them.

The proposed plane-fitting registration algorithm was applied to register the reference model to all the test target models. For comparison, two popular similarity registration algorithms, ICP [1] and FICP [2], were also tested.

To quantitatively assess the registration results produced by the algorithms, three errors were measured. First, surface error E_S measured the root-mean-square distance from the reference surface to the target surface. Second, plane-fitting error E_P measured the root-mean-square distance from target models' planar landmarks to the reference model's symmetric plane. Finally, to examine the convergence of the algorithms, registration errors of one severely fractured skull (Fig. 2(3)) were measured for the intermediate results after each iteration according to the algorithms' objective functions. For ICP, FICP and the proposed plane-fitting registration algorithm, the registration errors are mean-square error, fractional mean-square error, and the error E_r shown in Eq. 3, respectively. Execution time was measured on a PC with a 3.4GHz CPU.

Fig. 2 shows the skull registration results. ICP algorithm was able to find reasonable results for normal skulls (Fig. 2(1)). However, ICP registration results were greatly affected by outliers caused by incompleteness and fractures of fractured models. Synthetic fractured skulls and real fractured skulls were not properly aligned by ICP algorithm (Fig. 2(2-5)). For the case in Fig. 2(3), ICP shrunk the reference model to a small region, and failed to find reasonable alignment between the reference and the patient's model. Due to inaccurate alignment, the symmetric plane of the reference model were not accurately aligned with the planar landmarks of the patients' models. In all the three categories of skull models, ICP had the lowest surface error E_S because it minimized points distance without the symmetric plane, resulting in large plane-fitting error E_P (Table 1).

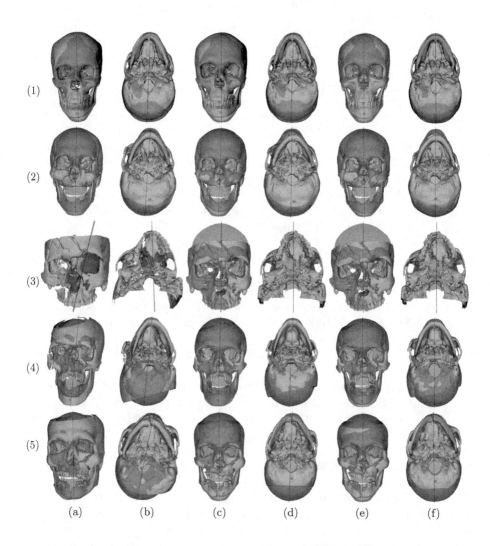

Fig. 2. Skull registration results. (1) normal skull. (2) synthetic fractured skull. (3-5) patients' fractured skulls. (a, b) ICP. (c, d) FICP. (e, f) proposed algorithm. The proposed plane-fitting registration algorithm attained the best overall performance compared to ICP and FICP. It aligned the reference skull models' symmetric planes (grey lines) accurately to the target skull models' planar landmarks (green balls). Surfaces of the reference models are colored red and the target models are colored grey.

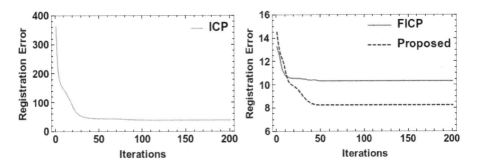

Fig. 3. Convergence curves. Same as ICP and FICP, the proposed algorithm converges to a stable value quickly.

FICP was robust to outliers and aligned the reference model relatively well to synthetic and patients' models (Fig. 2). FICP had larger surface error E_S (Table 1) than ICP algorithm, because it identified a portion of outliers, which were discarded. Therefore, errors of the outliers may be arbitrarily large and result in large E_S, even though the overall shape and the inliers are properly registered. This contradiction shows that surface error E_S is not a reliable assessment of registration quality. Fig. 2(c-d) shows that the alignment between the reference model's symmetric plane and the target models' planar landmarks were not accurate. Some landmarks were obviously off from the planes. Table 1 also shows that FICP had large plane-fitting error E_P because FICP did not consider plane-fitting in the registration process.

The proposed plane-fitting registration algorithm inherited its robustness from FICP. In addition to robustly registering the reference models to the target model, it also matched the symmetric plane of the reference model to the patients' planar landmarks accurately (Fig. 2). It was more robust to outliers than FICP due to the fitting of symmetric plane. The outliers that violated the fitting of plane were also identified and excluded from the computation of similarity transformation. Therefore, the symmetric plane of the reference model was aligned accurately to the patients' planar landmarks, and the inlier surface points were robustly registered, resulting in the lowest plane-fitting error and similar surface error compared to FICP (Table 1).

Fig. 3 shows the convergence curves of the three algorithms on a patient's skull (Fig. 2(3)). The convergence curves validate that ICP (green) and FICP (red) converge quickly to local minimum. The convergence curve of the proposed algorithm (blue) shows that the proposed algorithm also converged quickly to a local minimum after a few iterations. As discussed in the previous paragraphs, ICP had the smallest E_S but the registration result may not be reliable, and the proposed algorithm was the most reliable one among the three methods.

In all the experiments, the convergence condition is to terminate when the reduction of registration error in an iteration was smaller than 1   . For the model in Fig. 2(3), ICP converged in 52 iterations and 0.48 second, FICP converged in 27 iterations and 0.60 second, and the proposed plane-fitting registration algorithm converged in 45 iterations and 1.01 second. The proposed algorithm is about 0.5 second slower than the other two algorithms, which is worthy considering the significant improvement in robustness and registration quality. In intensive applications where there are a large number of models to be registered, computational efficiency would become the main limitation of the proposed algorithm. Future research should be performed to improve the efficiency of the algorithm.

5.2   Robustness

To study the robustness of the proposed method, 124 normals skulls were manually cut off by different proportions f to synthesize 620 incomplete skull models with different levels of incompleteness. Together with the 124 original normal skulls, the experiment dataset contains skull models with 0% to 50% missing data. Due to the missing data in the target models, the reference model would have similar proportions of points that do not have corresponding parts in the target model.

We registered the reference model to the target models using three registration algorithms, ICP, FICP and plane-fitting registration. Plane-fitting error E_P was measured on the registration results. However, surface error E_S was not computed because of the incomplete target models. Instead, target surface error E_T measured the root-mean-square distance from the target surface to the reference surface. It reflected the registration quality because it only used the surfaces of the target models that had correspondence in the reference model. They should have small errors in ideal registration.

Fig. 4 shows the errors measured for different proportions f of incompleteness. ICP is not robust to incompleteness because E_T and E_P increased as the proportion f of missing parts increased. FICP is more robust than ICP. Its E_T was quite stable when f increased, while there is a noticeable increase of E_P when f increased from 20% to 30%. The proposed method was the most

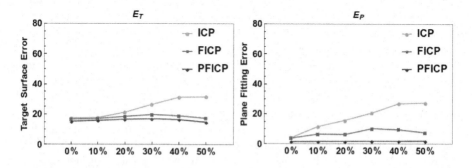

Fig. 4. Robustness. The proposed plane-fitting registration algorithm is more robust to incompleteness that ICP and FICP.

robust. Its errors E_T and E_P were the smallest among all methods in all levels of incompleteness, and they did not increase when proportion f of incompleteness increased.

5.3 Application to Skull Reconstruction

This experiment compared the proposed method against FICP method in skull reconstruction that reconstructs normal complete skull models from fractured skull models. The experiment used the 5 synthetic fractured skull models described in Section 5.1. It also used the original models without fractures as ground truth to access the reconstruction accuracy.

We followed the statistical skull reconstruction framework described in [17] to reconstruct the fractured models. First, we registered the reference skull model to the fractured skull model. After registration, we built dense correspondences between the reference model and the target model using the Thin-Plate Spline (TPS) method developed in [18]. Then, we applied statistical shape model fitting method [17] to estimate complete normal model by fitting a statistical model to healthy parts of the fractured model.

Reconstruction error E_R measured the root-mean-square surface distance between ground truth and the reconstructed mesh. It was computed to quantitatively evaluate the reconstructed skull models generated.

Table 2 shows the results. Although the proposed plane-fitting registration method had larger surface error, it produced smaller plane-fitting error E_P and smaller reconstruction error E_R than did FICP. The robust plane-fitting registration algorithm helped to improve the skull reconstruction accuracy.

Table 2. Comparison of registration methods in application of skull reconstruction. E_S denotes surface error (mm), E_P denotes plane-fitting error (mm), and E_R denotes restoration error (mm).

Registration method	E_S	E_P	E_R
FICP	33.57	2.36	7.47
Proposed	36.38	1.64	6.26

6 Conclusion

Similarity registration is a common first step in complex 3D model analysis and synthesis. In many applications, 3D models to be registered contain large amount of noise and outliers, and are sometimes incomplete. Existing similarity registration methods are not able to register these models properly. This paper presents a plane-fitting registration algorithm that is more robust than existing registration algorithms. It achieves its robustness by ensuring that the symmetric plane of the reference model is registered to the planar landmarks of the target model. Quantitative and qualitative experimental results on real patients' skull models showed that the proposed algorithm is efficient and can robustly align the overall structures of the models while matching the symmetric plane of the reference model to the planar landmarks of target model accurately. Experimental results also showed that the proposed robust registration algorithm can benefit applications such as skull reconstruction.

References

1. Besl, P.J., McKay, N.D.: A method for registration of 3d shapes. IEEE Transactions on Pattern Analysis and Machine Intellinegce **14**(2), 239–256 (1992)
2. Phillips, J.M., Liu, R., Tomasi, C.: Outlier robust icp for minimizing fractional rmsd. In: Proc. of International Conference on 3D Digital Imaging and Modeling (2007)
3. Jayaratne, Y.S., Zwahlen, R.A., Lo, J., Tam, S.C., Cheung, L.K.: Compute-aided maxillofacial surgery: An update. Surgical Innovation (2010)
4. Claes, P., Vandermeulen, D., De Greef, S., Willems, G., Clement, J.G., Suetens, P.: Computerized craniofacial reconstruction: conceptual framework and review. Forensic Science International **201**(1), 138–145 (2010)
5. Benazzi, S., Stansfield, E., Milani, C., Gruppioni, G.: Geometric morphometric methods for three-dimensional virtual reconstruction of a fragmented cranium: the case of angelo poliziano. International Journal of Legal Medicine **123**(4), 333–344 (2009)
6. Taylor, K.T.: Forensic Art and Illustration. CRC Press (2010)
7. Zhang, Z.: Iterative point matching for registration of free-form curves and surfaces. International Journal of Computer Vision **13**(2), 119–152 (1994)
8. Pajdla, T., Gool, L.V.: Matching of 3-d curves using semi-differential invariants. In: Proc. of International Conference on Computer Vision (1995)
9. Chetverikov, D., Stepanov, D., Krsek, P.: Robust euclidean alignment of 3d point sets: the trimmed iterative closest point algorithm. Image and Vision Computing **23**(3), 299–309 (2005)
10. Gruen, A., Akca, D.: Least squares 3d surface and curve matching. ISPRS Journal of Photogrammetry and Remote Sensing **59**(3), 151–174 (2005)
11. Chen, Y., Medioni, G.: Object modelling by registration of multiple range images. Image and Vision Computing **10**(3), 145–155 (1992)
12. Fitzgibbon, A.W.: Robust registration of 2d and 3d point sets. Image and Vision Computing **21**(13), 1145–1153 (2003)
13. Pottmann, H., Huang, Q., Yang, Y., Hu, S.: Geometry and convergence analysis of algorithms for registration of 3d shapes. International Journal of Computer Vision **67**(3), 277–296 (2006)
14. Horn, B.: Closed-form solution of absolute orientation using unit quaternions. JOSA A **4**(4), 629–642 (1987)
15. Kabsch, W.: A solution for the best rotation to relate two sets of vectors. Acta Crystallographica Section A: Crystal Physics, Diffraction, Theoretical and General Crystallography **32**(5), 922–923 (1976)

16. Damm, K.L., Carlson, H.A.: Gaussian-weighted rmsd superposition of proteins: a structural comparison for flexible proteins and predicted protein structures. Biophysical Journal **90**(12), 4558–4573 (2006)
17. Zhang, K., Leow, W.K., Cheng, Y.: Performance analysis of active shape reconstruction of fractured, incomplete skulls. In: Submitted to International Conference on Computer Analysis of Images and Patterns (2015)
18. Zhang, K., Cheng, Y., Leow, W.K.: Dense correspondence of skull models by automatic detection of anatomical landmarks. In: Wilson, R., Hancock, E., Bors, A., Smith, W. (eds.) CAIP 2013, Part I. LNCS, vol. 8047, pp. 229–236. Springer, Heidelberg (2013)

Incremental Fixed-Rank Robust PCA for Video Background Recovery

Jian Lai$^{(\boxtimes)}$, Wee Kheng Leow, and Terence Sim

Department of Computer Science,
National University of Singapore, Singapore, Singapore
{laij,leowwk,tsim}@comp.nus.edu.sg

Abstract. Video background recovery is a very important task in computer vision applications. Recent research offers robust principal component analysis (RPCA) as a promising approach for solving video background recovery. RPCA works by decomposing a data matrix into a low-rank matrix and a sparse matrix. Our previous work shows that when the desired rank of the low-rank matrix is known, fixing the rank in the algorithm called FrALM (fixed-rank ALM) yields more robust and accurate results than existing RPCA algorithms. However, application of RPCA to video background recovery requires that each frame in the video is encoded as a column in the data matrix. This is impractical in real applications because the videos can be easily larger than the amount of memory in a computer. This paper presents an algorithm called iFrALM (incremental fixed-rank ALM) that computes fixed-rank RPCA incrementally by splitting the video frames into an initial batch and an incremental batch. Comprehensive tests show that iFrALM uses less memory and time compared to FrALM. Moreover, the initial batch size and batch quality can be carefully selected to ensure that iFrALM reduces memory and time complexity without sacrificing accuracy.

Keywords: Background recovery · Incremental SVD · Fixed-rank robust PCA

1 Introduction

Video background recovery is a very important task in applications such as video surveillance, traffic monitoring, etc. Traditionally, various approaches have been developed for this task. Background recovery is closely related to moving object detection and some works [10,12–14] attempt to simultaneously solve these two problems within one framework. Recent research offers robust principal component analysis (RPCA) as a promising alternative approach for solving a wide range of problems including video background recovery [2,16]. RPCA utilizes the fact that the image frames in a video contain consistent information about the common background. It constructs a *data matrix* from multiple video frames and decomposes it into a *low-rank matrix* and a *sparse matrix*, such that the low-rank matrix corresponds to the background in the images and the sparse

© Springer International Publishing Switzerland 2015
G. Azzopardi and N. Petkov (Eds.): CAIP 2015, Part II, LNCS 9257, pp. 652–663, 2015.
DOI: 10.1007/978-3-319-23117-4_56

matrix captures the non-background components. It has been proved that exact solution of RPCA is available if the data matrix is composed of a sufficiently low-rank matrix and a sufficiently sparse matrix [2,3,8,15,19]. Various algorithms have been proposed for solving RPCA problems [6,8,9,15,16]. In [6], we show that when the desired rank of the low-rank matrix is known, fixing the rank in the algorithm yields more robust and accurate results than the method based on *augmented Lagrange multiplier* (ALM), which is among the most efficient and accurate methods [8]. In particular, our fixed-rank algorithm called FrALM is less sensitive than ALM to the choice of the weighting parameter λ.

Application of RPCA to video background recovery requires that each frame in the video is encoded as a column in the data matrix. This is impractical in real applications because the videos can be easily larger than the amount of memory in a computer. For online application where the video frames are received continuously over long duration, this limitation is especially severe.

This paper presents an algorithm called iFrALM (incremental fixed-rank ALM) that computes fixed-rank RPCA incrementally by splitting the video frames into an *initial batch* and an *incremental batch*. Instead of reserving memory for all the video frames, iFrALM requires only enough memory to keep the incremental batch of video frames and the fixed-rank components of the initial batch. As new video frames arrive, iFrALM accumulates them into a fixed-size batch and uses them to update the results, thus overcoming memory limitation. Moreover, with prudent choices of batch size and content, iFrALM can execute more efficiently than our previous FrALM without sacrificing accuracy.

2   Related Work

2.1   Incremental PCA and RPCA

Singular value decomposition (SVD) is a powerful tool that is used in PCA and RPCA. Its computational cost on a $m \times n$ $(m > n)$ matrix is $O(mn^2)$, which limits its application to small data set. To overcome this limitation, incremental SVD (iSVD) has been studied and many methods [1,5,17] are proposed. With iSVD, both computation time and memory are greatly saved.

One successful application of iSVD is incremental PCA, which gives rise to the eigenspace update algorithm [4] and Sequential Karhunen-Loeve method [7]. However, approximation errors of these methods cannot be estimated. To tackle this problem, Zhao et al. [18] proposed a SVD updating based approach for incremental PCA, which has a mathematically proven error bound.

Incremental SVD has also been used for RPCA. Rodriguez et al. [11] used iSVD in their incremental principal component pursuit (iPCP) algorithm but implementation details are not discussed. As iPCP updates the low-rank and sparse components by appending only a single column to the existed data, its accuracy cannot be guaranteed. To our best knowledge, no incremental method for fixed-rank RPCA has been proposed. In this paper, we show that proper application of iSVD can increase efficiency without sacrificing accuracy.

3   Incremental Fixed-Rank RPCA

Our original fixed-rank RPCA algorithm FrALM [6] solves the problem

$$\min_{\mathbf{A},\mathbf{E}} \|\mathbf{E}\|_F, \text{ subject to } \text{rank}(\mathbf{A}) = \text{known } r, \ \mathbf{D} = \mathbf{A} + \mathbf{E}, \tag{1}$$

where $\| \cdot \|_F$ is the Frobenius norm, and $\mathbf{D}, \mathbf{A}$ and $\mathbf{E} \in \Re^{m \times n}$ are data matrix, rank-r matrix and noise matrix, respectively. It uses SVD to minimize Eq. 1. SVD factorizes a matrix $\mathbf{A} \in \Re^{m \times n}$ as $\mathbf{USV}^\top$, where $\mathbf{S} \in \Re^{n \times n}$ is a diagonal matrix whose diagonal elements are singular values, and $\mathbf{U} \in \Re^{m \times n}$ and $\mathbf{V} \in \Re^{n \times n}$ are the left and right singular matrix, respectively. In applications such as video background recovery, the number of pixels m is much greater than the number of frames n, and essential information lies in a significantly low-dimensional space defined by the first r (i.e., $r \ll n$) dominant singular vectors and values. Thus, $\mathbf{A}$ can be well approximated by the rank-r SVD

$$\mathbf{A}^r = \mathbf{U}^r \mathbf{S}^r \mathbf{V}^{r\top}, \tag{2}$$

where the diagonal elements of $\mathbf{S}^r \in \Re^{r \times r}$ are the largest r singular values, and $\mathbf{U}^r \in \Re^{m \times r}$ and $\mathbf{V}^r \in \Re^{n \times r}$ are the matrices consisting of the corresponding r left and right singular vectors, respectively.

Given an incremental batch of data encoded in the matrix $\mathbf{D}_i \in \Re^{m \times l}$, the rank-$r$ SVD of the combined matrix $[\mathbf{A}^r \ \mathbf{D}_i]$ can be computed using incremental SVD (iSVD) [17], which works on $\mathbf{U}^r$, $\mathbf{S}^r$, and $\mathbf{V}^r$ instead of $\mathbf{A}^r$. Consequently, the computation cost of iSVD is $O(ml^2)$, which is much smaller than that of applying normal SVD on the combined matrix, which is $O(m(n+l)^2)$.

Our incremental fixed-rank RPCA algorithm works on the data matrix that is split into an initial batch $\mathbf{D}_0$ and an incremental batch $\mathbf{D}_1$. It applies the non-incremental FrALM on the initial batch $\mathbf{D}_0$ to recover rank-r matrices $\mathbf{U}_0$, $\mathbf{S}_0$, and $\mathbf{V}_0$. Then, it applies incremental fixed-rank ALM algorithm (iFrALM, Algorithm 1) to compute the rank-r solutions of the combined matrix $[\mathbf{A}_0 \ \mathbf{D}_1]$, where $\mathbf{A}_0 = \mathbf{U}_0 \mathbf{S}_0 \mathbf{V}_0^\top$, and produces rank-$r$ matrices $\mathbf{U}_1$, $\mathbf{S}_1$, and $\mathbf{V}_1$. Consequently, the rank-r component of $[\mathbf{A}_0 \ \mathbf{D}_1]$ can be recovered as $\mathbf{A}_1 = \mathbf{U}_1 \mathbf{S}_1 \mathbf{V}_1^\top$. This incremental process can be repeated for additional incremental batches $\mathbf{D}_i, i > 1$. In general, iFrALM takes $\mathbf{U}_{i-1}$, $\mathbf{S}_{i-1}$, $\mathbf{V}_{i-1}$ and $\mathbf{D}_i$ as inputs and produces $\mathbf{U}_i$, $\mathbf{S}_i$ and $\mathbf{V}_i$ as outputs, which can be used in the next incremental step.

The iFrALM algorithm has a similar structure as the non-incremental FrALM. In line 2, $\text{sgn}(\cdot)$ is the sign function which computes the sign of each matrix element, and $J(\cdot)$ computes a scaling factor

$$J(\mathbf{X}) = \max(\|\mathbf{X}\|_2, \ \lambda^{-1}\|\mathbf{X}\|_\infty) \tag{3}$$

as recommended in [8]. T_ϵ in line 7 denotes the soft-thresholding function

$$T_\epsilon(x) = \begin{cases} x - \epsilon, & \text{if } x > \epsilon, \\ x + \epsilon, & \text{if } x < -\epsilon, \\ 0, & \text{otherwise.} \end{cases} \tag{4}$$

Algorithm 1. iFrALM

Input: $\mathbf{U}_{i-1}, \mathbf{S}_{i-1}, \mathbf{V}_{i-1}, \mathbf{D}_i, r$, and λ.

1 $\mathbf{A} = 0, \mathbf{E} = 0$.

2 $\mathbf{Y} = sgn(\mathbf{D}_i)/J(sgn(\mathbf{D}_i)), \mu > 0, \rho > 1$.

3 **repeat**

4   **repeat**

5     $\mathbf{U}_i, \mathbf{S}_i, \mathbf{V}_i^\top = \text{iSVD}_r([\mathbf{A}_{i-1} \ \ \mathbf{D}_i - \mathbf{E} + \mathbf{Y}/\mu])$.

6     $\mathbf{A} = \mathbf{U}_i \mathbf{S}_i \mathbf{V}_i(n+1:n+l,:)^\top$.

7     $\mathbf{E} = T_{\lambda/\mu}(\mathbf{D}_i - \mathbf{A} + \mathbf{Y}/\mu)$.

8   **until** *convergence*;

9    $\mathbf{U}', \mathbf{S}', \mathbf{V}' = \text{SVD}(\mathbf{S}_i \mathbf{V}_i(1:n,:)^\top)$.

10   $\mathbf{U}_{i-1} = \mathbf{U}_i \mathbf{U}', \mathbf{S}_{i-1} = \mathbf{S}', \mathbf{V}_{i-1} = \mathbf{V}'$.

11   $\mathbf{Y} = \mathbf{Y} + \mu(\mathbf{D}_i - \mathbf{A} - \mathbf{E}), \mu = \rho\mu$.

12 **until** *convergence*;

Output: $\mathbf{U}_i, \mathbf{S}_i, \mathbf{V}_i$.

In line 5, a rank-r iSVD (iSVD$_r$) [17] is used to compute the SVD of the combined matrix $[\mathbf{A}_{i-1} \ \ \mathbf{D}_i - \mathbf{E} + \mathbf{Y}/\mu]$. It computes the rank-$r$ matrices $\mathbf{U}_i$, $\mathbf{S}_i$, and $\mathbf{V}_i$ from $\mathbf{U}_{i-1}$, $\mathbf{S}_{i-1}$, and $\mathbf{V}_{i-1}$ instead of directly from $\mathbf{A}_{i-1} = \mathbf{U}_{i-1}\mathbf{S}_{i-1}\mathbf{V}_{i-1}^\top$. Next, lines 6 and 7 compute the low-rank matrix $\mathbf{A}$ and error matrix $\mathbf{E}$ of $\mathbf{D}_i$, which are represented by the last l rows of $\mathbf{V}_i$. It is not necessary to compute the error matrix of $\mathbf{A}_{i-1}$ because $\mathbf{A}_{i-1}$ is already a low-rank matrix.

Lines 9 and 10 are used to update $\mathbf{U}_{i-1}$, $\mathbf{S}_{i-1}$, and $\mathbf{V}_{i-1}$. Without them, the subspaces spanned by $\mathbf{U}_i$ will be identical to that of $\mathbf{U}_{i-1}$, which defeats the incremental algorithm. These matrices can be updated either in the inner loop or the outer loop. Updating in the inner loop before it converges may cause instability and incur additional computation cost. Therefore, we choose to update them in the outer loop. Note that $\mathbf{U}_i \mathbf{S}_i \mathbf{V}_i(1:n,:)^\top$ is an $m \times n$ matrix, which is much larger than the $r \times n$ matrix $\mathbf{S}_i \mathbf{V}_i(1:n,:)^\top$. Therefore, line 9 performs SVD on the smaller matrix $\mathbf{S}_i \mathbf{V}_i(1:n,:)^\top$, whose results are used to update $\mathbf{U}_{i-1}$, $\mathbf{S}_{i-1}$, and $\mathbf{V}_{i-1}$ as shown in line 10. Finally, line 11 is the standard technique for applying augmented Lagrange multiplier (ALM) method.

The time complexity of iFrALM is dominated by the incremental SVD, which is $O(ml^2)$. Its memory complexity is $O(ml)$, the amount required for storing $\mathbf{D}_i$, $\mathbf{A}$, $\mathbf{E}$, and $\mathbf{Y}$. Thus, it uses less time and memory compared to FrALM on the whole combined matrix $[\mathbf{A}_{i-1} \ \mathbf{D}_i]$, which has time and memory complexity of $O(m(n+l)^2)$ and $O(m(n+l))$, respectively.

4 Experiments and Discussions

4.1 Data Preparation

The performance of the proposed iFrALM was tested on recovering the stationary backgrounds of three videos: Kungfu [6], Traffic [6] and Shopping Center (available from http://perception.i2r.a-star.edu.sg/bk_model/bk_index.html).

These color videos were converted to gray images. For Shopping Center video, the gray images were downsampled to 128×160. The other videos had image size of 150×200. Test programs were implemented in Matlab and ran in a 64-bit Windows 7 PC with Intel Core i7-2600 CPU and 16GB RAM.

Four test scenarios were set by varying the following properties:

1. initial batch size (Section 4.2),
2. incremental batch size (Section 4.3),
3. batch quality (Section 4.4), and
4. multiple incremental batches (Section 4.5).

Both iFrALM and FrALM were executed under these four conditions. In addition, the average image of each video was computed to indicate the complexity of a video. Compared to the ground truth, average image with small error corresponds to a simple problem.

Once the background is recovered, the moving objects can be easily detected by thresholding the differences between the input image and the recovered background $\mathbf{A}$. Therefore, we also compare iFrALM with some baselines of moving object detection in Section 4.6.

As all videos were captured with stationary cameras, the fixed rank r was 1 for both FrALM and iFrALM. The parameters λ, ρ and initial μ were fixed to $1/\sqrt{m}$, 1.5 and $0.5/\|\mathbf{Y}\|_2$. The algorithms' accuracy was measured in terms of the mean squared error (MSE) between the ground truth $\mathbf{G}$ and the algorithm outputs $\mathbf{U}_i$, $\mathbf{S}_i$, and $\mathbf{V}_i$:

$$E_g = \frac{1}{mn}\|\mathbf{G} - \mathbf{U}_i\mathbf{S}_i\mathbf{V}_i^{\top}\|_F^2. \tag{5}$$

For Kungfu video, the background only image was available and it served as the ground truth. For Shopping Center and Traffic videos, their ground truths were not available. In this case, FrALM was applied to the whole video and the recovered rank-1 matrix was regarded as the ground truth. In addition, execution time of FrALM and iFrALM were recorded.

4.2   Initial Batch Size

In this experiment, 70 frames each of Shopping Center and Kungfu videos were used. Their initial batch size varied from 5 to 50 consecutive frames in increments of 5, and their incremental batch size was fixed at 20 consecutive frames. The Traffic video had 250 frames. So, its initial batch size was set to 10, 20, 50, 100, 150, and 200, and its incremental batch size was fixed at 50 frames.

Figure 1(a) shows the results of running FrALM on all video frames in the initial and incremental batches, FrALM on the initial batch, iFrALM on the incremental batch, and average of all video frames. Given enough video frames, the fixed-rank methods are much more accurate than the average frame. Moreover, the error (MSE) curves of iFrALM and FrALM on initial batch have the same trend. As the initial batch size increases, iFrALM's error decreases and approaches that of FrALM on all video frames.

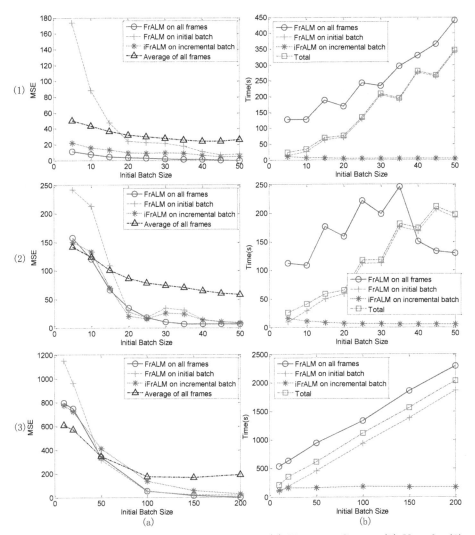

Fig. 1. The results of varying initial batch size. (1) Shopping Center. (2) Kungfu. (3) Traffic. (a) MSE. (b) Running time.

Figure 1(b) shows the algorithms' running time of the algorithms. Note that the results of FrALM on initial batch serve as inputs of iFrALM. So, the total execution time is sum of the execution times of FrALM on initial batch and iFrALM on the incremental batch. FrALM's running time increases with increasing initial batch size. On the other, iFrALM's running time is not significantly affected by the initial batch size. Moreover, it is much smaller than FrALM's running time on the initial batch. As a result, the total execution time is significantly smaller than FrALM's running time (in most cases) on all video frames.

4.3   Incremental Batch Size

This experiment used the same data as that in Section 4.2. For both Shopping Center and Kungfu videos, their initial batch size was fixed at 20 consecutive frames and their incremental batch size varied from 5 to 50 consecutive frames in increments of 5. For the Traffic video, its initial batch size was fixed at 50 and its incremental batch size was set to 10, 20, 50, 100, 150, and 200.

Figure 2 shows that algorithms' performance is consistent with that in Section 4.2. In particular, iFrALM's error approaches that of FrALM on all frames as incremental batch size increases. The errors of both iFrALM and FrALM on all frames are small compared to that of average frame. FrALM's error on initial batch is constant because there is no change in initial batch size. iFrALM's running time is small compared to that of FrALM on the initial batch, and it increases more gradually with increasing incremental batch size compared to that of FrALM on all video frames. Therefore, the total execution time is smaller and increases more gradually than that of FrALM on all frames.

Figure 3 shows some sample results for the case where all incremental frames are processed. For the Shopping Center video, image averaging produces an acceptable result, indicating that this video is relatively easy to process. On the other hand, for the Kungfu and Traffic videos, image averaging produces visible "ghost" defects in the recovered background images, whereas FrALM and iFrALM produce cleaner background images, which is confirmed by the quantitative results shown in Fig. 2(a).

4.4   Batch Quality

The quality of the initial batch can affect the accuracy of iFrALM. Its quality is bad if it contains slowly moving or temporary stationary objects, which can be confused with the actual stationary background. On the other hand, its quality is good if it contains only stationary background or fast moving objects. For this test scenario, 50 frames of the Shopping Center videos and Kungfu videos were selected for both the initial and incremental batches. Four test cases were performed: (1) FrALM on a bad initial batch, whose results were fed to (2) iFrALM on a good incremental batch, (3) FrALM on a good initial batch, whose results were fed to (4) iFrALM on a bad incremental batch.

Table 1 shows that initial batch quality significantly affects result of iFrALM. With a bad initial batch, initial results fed to iFrALM is inaccurate. Although iFrALM can reduce error with good incremental batch, error is still large compared to the $4th$ case. On the other hand, with good initial results from FrALM, iFrALM working a bad incremental batch still produces a lower error compared to the $2nd$ case. This result is expected because iFrALM uses iSVD to obtain approximate solutions. So, good quality initial batch is crucial for iFrALM.

4.5   Multiple Incremental Batches

In online application, incoming video frames are accumulated into a batch and sent to the incremental algorithm. As time progresses, more video frames are

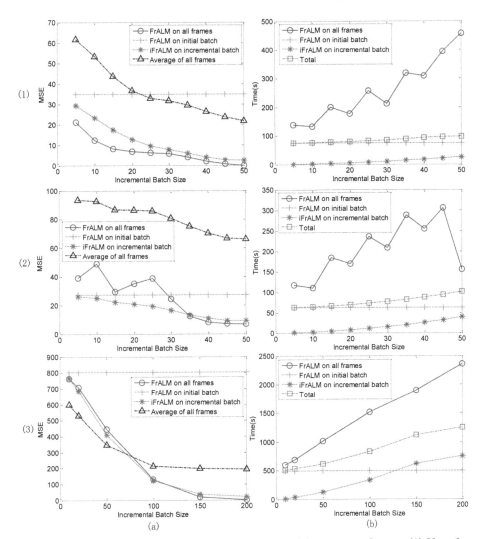

Fig. 2. The results of varying incremental batch size. (1) Shopping Center. (2) Kungfu. (3) Traffic. (a) MSE. (b) Running time.

accumulated and multiple batches are sent to the algorithm iteratively. This subsection describes a test performed under the same scenario using 1000 consecutive frames of the Shopping Center video. The first 50 frames formed the initial batch and was processed by FrALM to obtain the initial results for iFrALM. Subsequently, incremental batches of video frames were processed by iFrALM iteratively for the remaining 950 frames. The incremental batch size b varied for various test cases, namely 10, 20, 30, 40, 50, 100, and 200, and the number of iterations $k = \lceil 950/b \rceil$. Two incremental batch selection schemes were tested: (1) consecutive selection, (2) regular sampling at regular frame intervals. In comparison, regular sampling requires a large buffer for storing the incoming frames

Fig. 3. Results of processing all image frames. (1) Shopping Center. (2) Kungfu. (3) Traffic. (a) Sample video frame. (b) Average frame. (c) FrALM. (d) iFrALM.

Table 1. Effect of batch quality of iFrALM's error (MSE).

Dataset	Shopping Center	Kungfu
FrALM with bad initial batch	101.8	139.3
iFrALM with bad initial and good incremental batch	35.1	48.5
FrALM with good initial batch	10.3	8.2
iFrALM with good initial and bad incremental batch	17.8	18.3

for selection at regular intervals, whereas consecutive selection requires a small buffer to store just the b consecutive frames.

Figure 4 plots MSE vs. execution time for each test case under the two selection schemes. Test result shows that smaller batch size b leads to lower total running time but higher MSE. This is because the computational cost of iFrALM is $O(km(l/k)^2) = O(ml^2/k) = O(mlb)$, which is proportional to b. With smaller sample size b, less information is available at each iteration, which leads to higher error.

Compared to consecutive selection, regular sampling captures more global information over the video. Therefore, it achieves a higher accuracy than consecutive selection at the same batch size b. Regular sampling takes more time than consecutive selection because its iFrALM takes more iterations to converge. For all 1000 frames, FrALM takes 2640 seconds. Our iFrALM, though much faster than

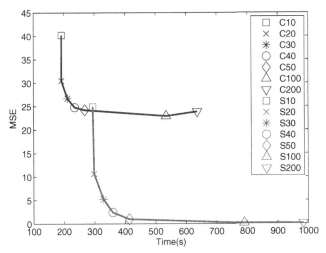

Fig. 4. Plot of MSE vs. execution time. 'C' denotes consecutive selection and 'S' denotes regular sampling. The number denotes incremental batch size b.

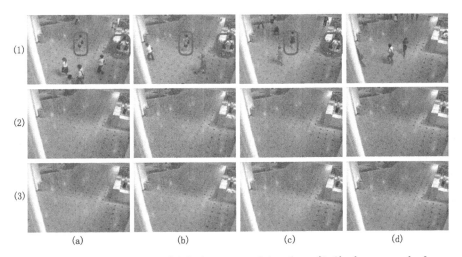

Fig. 5. Results processing multiple incremental batches. (1–3) show sample frames of Shopping Center video, iFrALM's results with consecutive selection and regular sampling, respectively. (a) Ground truth background. (b–d) show iFrALM's results with $b = 1, 50$ and 200, respectively.

FrALM, is still not capable of handling background recovery problem in realtime, e.g., 30 frames per second at 1920×1080 pixels.

Figure 5 shows some recovered background images of this test. When the people, highlighted by the red rectangle in Fig. 5(1), remain at the same location for extended periods, consecutive selection scheme cannot remove them completely from the recovered background image (Fig. 5(2b–2d)). In contrast, regular sampling scheme can recover the stationary background well when b is at least 50 (Fig. 5(3c, 3d)).

4.6 Moving Object Detection

In this experiment, the first 100 frames of Kungfu video were used. The proposed iFrALM was compared with average, PCA [10], mixture of Gaussian (MoG) [12] and FrALM. For iFrALM, we split the 100 frames into 5 subsets by regular sampling. The first subset was used as initial batch and the other were used as multiple incremental batches. The results are shown in Figure 6. Thanks to multimodal modeling of background, MoG outperforms average and PCA. However, MoG cannot detect some interior pixels of the object. iFrALM and FrALM achieve similar results, which are much better than those of the others.

Fig. 6. The detected moving objects of various methods on the 60th frame. The input frame is in Column 1. The results of average, PCA, MoG, FrALM and iFrALM are presented from Column 2 to 6, respectively.

5   Conclusion

This paper presented an incremental method for computing fixed-rank robust PCA. The method works on the data matrix that is split into an initial batch and an incremental batch. It applies the non-incremental FrALM on the initial batch to recover a rank-r solution, which is used as the input for the incremental iFrALM to compute the rank-r solution of the incremental batch. iFrALM can be repeated for additional incremental batches iteratively. iFrALM uses incremental SVD to reduce computation time and SVD on a small matrix to reduce memory cost. Comprehensive tests were performed on three videos of varying lengths. Test results show that both iFrALM and FrALM produce more accurate results compared to video frame averaging, which is not robust. iFrALM uses less memory and time compared to FrALM. Test results also show that the initial batch size and batch quality can be carefully selected to ensure that iFrALM reduces memory and time complexity without sacrificing accuracy. These promising results thus pave the way for the application of incremental fixed-rank RPCA for online video background recovery.

Acknowledgments. This research is supported by MOE grant MOE2014-T2-1-062.

References

1. Brand, M.: Incremental singular value decomposition of uncertain data with missing values. In: Heyden, A., Sparr, G., Nielsen, M., Johansen, P. (eds.) ECCV 2002, Part I. LNCS, vol. 2350, pp. 707–720. Springer, Heidelberg (2002)
2. Candès, E.J., Li, X.D., Ma, Y., Wright, J.: Robust principal component analysis? Journal of ACM **58**(3), 11 (2011)
3. Candès, E.J., Plan, Y.: Matrix completion with noise. In: Proceedings of the IEEE, pp. 925–936 (2010)
4. Chandrasekaran, S., Manjunath, B.S., Wang, Y.F., Winkeler, J., Zhang, H.: An eigenspace update algorithm for image analysis. Graphical Models and Image Processing **59**(5), 321–332 (1997)
5. Gu, M., Eisenstat, S.C.: A stable and fast algorithm for updating the singular value decomposition. Technical Report YALEU/DCS/RR-966, Yale Univ. (1994)
6. Leow, W.K., Cheng, Y., Zhang, L., Sim, T., Foo, L.: Background recovery by fixed-rank robust principal component analysis. In: Wilson, R., Hancock, E., Bors, A., Smith, W. (eds.) CAIP 2013, Part I. LNCS, vol. 8047, pp. 54–61. Springer, Heidelberg (2013)
7. Levey, A., Lindenbaum, M.: Sequential karhunen-loeve basis extraction and its application to images. IEEE Trans. on Image Processing **9**(8), 1371–1374 (2000)
8. Lin, Z.C., Chen, M.M., Wu, L.Q., Ma, Y.: The augmented Lagrange multiplier method for exact recovery of corrupted low-rank matrices. Technical Report UILU-ENG-09-2215, UIUC (2009)
9. Lin, Z.C., Ganesh, A., Wright, J., Wu, L.Q., Chen, M.M., Ma, Y.: Fast convex optimization algorithms for exact recovery of a corrupted low-rank matrix. In: Proc. CAMSAP (2009)
10. Oliver, N.M., Rosario, B., Pentland, A.P.: A bayesian computer vision system for modeling human interactions. IEEE Trans. on PAMI **22**(8), 831–843 (2000)
11. Rodriguez, P., Wohlberg, B.: A matlab implementation of a fast incremental principal component pursuit algorithm for video background modeling. In: Proc. ICIP (2014)
12. Stauffer, C., Grimson, W.E.L.: Adaptive background mixture models for real-time tracking. In: Proc. CVPR (1999)
13. Toyama, K., Krumm, J., Brumitt, B., Meyers, B.: Wallflower: principles and practice of background maintenance. In: Proc. ICCV (1999)
14. Varadarajan, S., Karam, L.J., Florencio, D.: Background recovery from video sequences using motion parameters. In: Proc. ICASSP (2009)
15. Wright, J., Ganesh, A., Rao, S., Ma, Y.: Robust principal component analysis: Exact recovery of corrupted low-rank matrices via convex optimization. Journal of ACM (2009)
16. Wright, J., Peng, Y.G., Ma, Y., Ganesh, A., Rao, S.: Robust principal component analysis: exact recovery of corrupted low-rank matrices by convex optimization. In: Proc. NIPS (2009)
17. Zha, H.Y., Simon, H.D.: On updating problems in latent semantic indexing. SIAM Journal on Scientific Computing **21**(2), 782–791 (1999)
18. Zhao, H.T., Yuen, P.C., Kwok, J.T.: A novel incremental principal component analysis and its application for face recognition. IEEE Trans. on SMC, Part B: Cybernetics **36**(4), 873–886 (2006)
19. Zhou, Z.H., Li, X.D., Wright, J., Candès, E.J., Ma, Y.: Stable principal component pursuit. In: Proc. ISIT (2010)

Sperm Cells Segmentation in Micrographic Images Through Lambertian Reflectance Model

Rosario Medina-Rodríguez[1]($\boxtimes$), Luis Guzmán-Masías[2],
Hugo Alatrista-Salas[1], and Cesar Beltrán-Castañón[1]

[1] Department of Engineering, Research Group on Pattern Recognition and Applied
Artificial Intelligence, Pontificia Universidad Católica Del Perú, Lima, Perú
r.medinar@pucp.pe
[2] Group of Assisted Reproduction, Pranor S.R.L., Lima, Perú

Abstract. Nowadays, male infertility has increased worldwide. Therefore, a rigorous analysis of sperm cells is required to diagnose this problem. Currently, this analysis is performed based on the expert opinion. In order to support the experts in fertility diagnosis, several image processing techniques have been proposed. In this paper, we present an approach that combines the Lambertian model based on surface reflectance with mathematical morphology for sperm cells segmentation in micrographic images. We have applied our approach to a set of 73 images. The results of our approach have been evaluated based on ground truth segmentations and similarity indices, finding a high correlation between our results and manual segmentation.

1 Introduction

The World Health Organization (WHO) defines infertility as *"a disease of the reproductive system associated with the failure to achieve a clinical pregnancy after 12 months or more of regular unprotected sexual intercourse"*. This problem affects about 15-20% couples around the world. Particularly, male infertility is often associated with low sperm production, abnormal sperm function and/or low rate of sperm cells with an appropriate structure and motility. Furthermore, illnesses, injuries, chronic health problems, lifestyle choices, environmental elements, medical treatments and other factors can also cause this problem.

Reproductive health specialists, point out that semen analysis (measurement of the amount and quality of a man's semen and sperm) is the best way to evaluate the male fertility. This analysis is focused on the concentration, motility, morphology and sperm vitality. Indeed, among these features, the sperm morphology is widely considered one of the most important male sperm characteristics [13], to determine sperm cells abnormalities and therefore male fertility.

Although, infertility is a well-known problem, the causes of a decrease in male reproductive health remains unclear [14]. To better understand the male infertility problem, CASA (Computer Assisted Semen Analysis) systems have been available for more than 25 years. Most commercial CASA products study recorded video sequences of sperm cells through a powerful microscope. The

© Springer International Publishing Switzerland 2015
G. Azzopardi and N. Petkov (Eds.): CAIP 2015, Part II, LNCS 9257, pp. 664–674, 2015.
DOI: 10.1007/978-3-319-23117-4_57

captured frames are digitalized and analyzed to provide objective and precise information on the morphological (and others) characteristics of semen samples. A lot of methods to analyse sperm morphology performed by CASA systems are focused on staining[1], which may frustrate our understanding of the current sperm morphology [10]. Despite the effectiveness of CASA systems, most of the specialists continue to rely on manual methods.

In literature, there are different methods and tools to improve the study of sperm cells through image processing techniques. However, techniques based on background subtraction, usually applied in video sequences, have not been explored yet for sperm morphology assessment. In order to deal with this need, we propose a method to segment complete sperm cells (head, mid-piece and tail) using a combination of two techniques: (i) background subtraction based on Lambertian reflectance model, and; (ii) morphological operations. Our results showed that, this method achieves high similarity indices extracting complete sperm cells when compared with manual image segmentation. It is important to notice that, the process presented in this article is part of an ambitious project composed by several steps. The goal is to perform a complete framework oriented to the study of male infertility problem.

The rest of this paper is organized as follows: in Section 2, we review the existing methods of sperm cell segmentation. The set of micrographic images used in our experimentations is described in Section 3. Later, Section 4, details our approach, while the results and discussion are presented in Section 5. The paper ends with our conclusions and future perspectives.

2 Related Work

Image processing techniques for sperm cells segmentation is a dynamic research field [1,7,13]. Most of these techniques are used for the assessment of sperm concentration and motility characteristics. In this related work section, we will focus on literature associated to the study of sperm cells segmentation to analyze their morphology.

One of the first methods that apply image processing techniques to sperm cells segmentation was proposed by Park et. al. [9]. To segment each sperm head present in the image, a region of interest is selected by calculating the density difference between the sperm cell head and the background. Then, the edge of the head is approximated to an ellipse represented by five parameters obtained after applying the Hough transform.

Later, Carrillo et. al. [3] propose a pre-processing task to transform a RGB image into a grayscale color space and apply the Otsu thresholding algorithm. The resulting objects are classified according to their area in order to remove small objects which represent noise. Finally, the remaining objects are classified again through a histogram analysis. Thus, only objects with a specific number of dark pixels are finally segmented. This analysis is necessary due to the staining

---

[1] Staining is a technique used in microscopy to magnify contrast in the image and change the color of sperm cells observed under the microscope.

method used, which provides a clear differentiation between the background and the sperm head.

In other work, the sperm identification task was performed using thresholding and morphological operations to remove small regions which represent noise. Finally, regions that are significantly bigger or smaller than an average sperm are removed. This method have been performed by Tomlinson et. al. in [11]

Afterwards, Bijar [2] evaluates the components of RGB color space. First, the author select the R (red) on RGB image. Then, noise and small objects are removed. Finally, a bounding box is defined around each sperm head to highlight it. In addition, to segment the components of each sperm cell, the author uses a Bayesian classifier based on the expectation maximization algorithm (EM) and a random Markov model.

Recently, Chang et. al. [4] propose the segmentation of the head, acrosome and nucleus of sperm cells evaluating three different color spaces (L*a*b, YCbCr and RGB+YCbCr+L*a*b). Their results proved to be better than the present methods on the literature.

Based on the above cases, we may conclude that, literature approaches adopt different techniques and color spaces to analyze the morphology of sperm cells using image processing. However, to our knowledge, no works have explored techniques for video sequences (background subtraction) in sperm cells segmentation task. In fact, we are taking advantage of the background similarity in our micrographic images set. As can be seen in Figure 1, our approach follows a multi-step process to perform the segmentation composed by two main stages: (*i*) micrographic images acquisition, and; (*ii*) sperm cell segmentation. These two tasks will be described in the following sections.

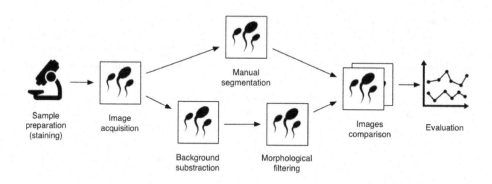

Fig. 1. General process of our approach for sperm cell segmentation

3   Micrographic Images Dataset

This section details the materials and the process performed once a set of semen samples is received and stored, i.e., the protocol conducted for micrographic image acquisition by observing the samples under a microscope with an adapted camera.

3.1   Sample Preparation

- **Materials:** (i) glass slide, (ii) oil immersion, (iii) distilled water, (iv) Coplin jars and (v) staining media.
- **Reagents:** (i) Reagent A: red stain 50ml or 250ml; (ii) Reagent B: pale green 50ml or 250ml; (iii) Reagent C: dark green 50ml or 250ml.
- **Staining kit:** Spermac Stain®FertiPro. The purpose of this diagnostic kit is to be able to differentiate morphologically normal from abnormal sperm cells.
- **Method:**
  1. Fix the smear by immersing the glass slide for a minimum of 5 minutes in a Coplin jar containing the fixative.
  2. Wash in distilled water.
  3. Dry and stain 2 minutes in reagent A.
  4. Wash 7 times in distilled water (two replicates).
  5. Repeat the staining process with the Reagents B and C.
  6. Finally, observe staining under a light microscope (1000x) using immersion oil: (i) acrosome = dark green, (ii) nucleus = stained red, (iii) equatorial region = pale green and (iv) mid piece and tail = green.

3.2   Image Acquisition

Every stained smear were observed under an AXIO Carl Zeiss light microscope using 10x eye-pieces and 100x objective (total magnification of 1000x). Then, we acquire a set of 73 images with a 0.63x zoom AxioCam ICc5 camera in JPG format. Each image has a total resolution of 2452×2056 pixels, equivalent to 5 Mp (see Figure 2). The dataset consists of 111 sperm cells, including normal and abnormal cells.

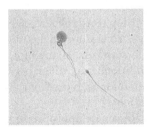

Fig. 2. Example of one micrographic image obtained after the staining process using Spermac Stain®FertiPro

4   Sperm Cells Segmentation Process

Image segmentation is an important topic in image processing. The main goal of segmentation process is to subdivide an image into several meaningful regions. There are numerous methods to perform image segmentation based on different image properties like color intensity, contrast, among others. In the following subsections, a briefly description of the techniques used in our proposal is presented, as well as, the proposed segmentation process.

4.1   General Aspects

Frequently, segmentation algorithms are susceptible to illumination changes, shadows or highlights. As it was previously described in Section 3, our method for image acquisition includes the manipulation of a light microscope by specialists at laboratory. This lead us to get an image dataset with several light changes, due to the microscope parameters fixed by the specialists (i.e. for each image the specialists fixed different parameters). Therefore, we need an algorithm that deals with the illumination problems and that also takes advantage of their similar background.

Our proposal is based on the combination of two methods: (i) a background subtraction task based on a Lambertian reflectance model, and; (ii) a refinement process using morphological operations. These methods will be further described below:

Segmentation Based on Lambertian Reflectance Model: This segmentation method is based on two techniques. First, the Lambertian model, which perceive the color as the product of illumination and surface spectral reflectance. In other words, it separates the brightness from the chromaticity component. Second, background subtraction technique that separates the image on evaluation from a reference image that models the background scene. Then, differences between the background image and the current image are evaluated. Typically, this method is used for object detection on video sequences.

In this context, Horprasert et al. [6] propose a background subtraction algorithm based on Lambertian reflectance model. The general process performed by this algorithm is:

1. The background modelling step constructs a reference image representing the background using N images to train a background model. The images have the same size and resolution without changing the zoom or the orientation. However, illumination conditions may differ between them.
2. A statistic model is computed for each pixel of the training dataset evaluating its brightness and chromaticity.
3. The threshold selection determines appropriate threshold values for brightness and chromaticity, to be used in the subtraction operation to obtain a desired detection rate, as it was proposed by Horprasert.
4. The subtraction operation or pixel classification classifies the type of a given pixel belongs by comparing the brightness and chromaticity with the precalculated thresholds. For instance, the pixel is the part of background (including ordinary background and shaded background).

Mathematical Morphological Operations: On image processing, mathematical morphology is a set-theoretic method of image analysis providing a quantitative description of geometrical structures. The two basic morphological operations are erosion and dilation. These operations involve the interaction between an image A (the object of interest) and a structuring set B, called the structuring element (SE). The structuring element is a shape, used to interact with a given image. It is positioned at all possible locations in the image and it is compared with the corresponding neighboring pixels. Depending on the operation, it is evaluated how this shape fits or misses the shapes in the image. The choice of a certain structuring element (including its shape and size) for a particular morphological operation influences the information that we can obtain.

Simplify image data, preserve essential shape characteristics and eliminate noise are the main goals of morphological operations [5]. In this paper, we have used these operations to remove imperfections introduced during segmentation.

4.2   Segmentation of Sperm Cells in Micrographic Images

At our knowledge, does not exist a generic algorithm for segmentation that works perfectly on every image. In this case, for our micrographic image dataset we have used the segmentation process based on background subtraction and removed small areas which may represent seminal cells or stain spots using morphological operations. Our approach consists on the following steps:

- First, we build a training dataset for background modelling using a set of images (see Figure 3). These images have been acquired by observing under the microscope the glass slide regions without sperm cells or using a slide with only immersion oil.

Fig. 3. Examples of background pattern obtained by images without sperm cells or using only immersion oil

- Once the background model is computed, we apply it into our micrographic image dataset. Figure 4(a) is an example of the image dataset at our disposal. The results obtained after segmentation can be seen on Figure 4(b). Each pixel of the image is colored depending on the class it belongs to, after classification. Each pixel could be: blue for the foreground; green for the background; red for the background shadow, and; black for the background highlight.
- Finally, we perform a refinement process in order to remove small areas (i.e. seminal cells or stain spots) using morphological operations. This is an automatic process and it is applied on each image in the dataset.

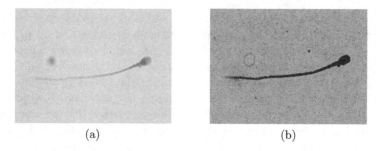

(a)   (b)

Fig. 4. Example extracted from our image dataset: (a) before background subtraction, and; (b) after background subtraction

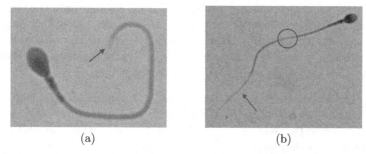

(a)   (b)

Fig. 5. Problems of the refinement process: (a) misses a part of the sperm tail, and; (b) misses two parts of the sperm cell tail (middle and end)

- It transforms the segmented image into a binary image by applying an Otsu threshold on the red channel of the RGB color space. Then, we apply a closing operation followed by an opening operation using a disk shaped structuring element with empirically-chosen sizes. Thus, the SE for closing operations is a 3×3 matrix and, for opening operations is a 4×4 matrix.
- As can be seen in Figure 5, the refinement process produces some problems such as: (i) the last tail's pixels could not be completely segmented, and; (ii) some areas of interest (parts of the sperm cell) were removed by the morphological operations. Both problems were highlighted with arrows and a circle, respectively.

5   Experimental Results and Discussion

To evaluate the proposed approach, we have performed experiments on our set of 73 images. This set has a similar background, which suggest that the background subtraction technique should have a good performance. Figure 6 shows each step of our proposal applied on two representative examples, the worst case and an interesting but not the best case. The later shows the weakness of our proposal in contrast with the best cases (images 2-4, cf. Figure 7).

As can be seen, from top to bottom, Figure 6(a) contains images number 15 and 25 from the image dataset at our disposal. In the first row, we can see the presence of artifacts generated by the staining process performed at laboratory. Then, Figure 6(b) shows the manual image segmentation. It is worth mentioning that, these images were segmented by hand using an image manipulation program, thus, we considered this images as our ground-truth.

Images obtained after the background subtraction are shown in Figure 6(c). In these figures, the background is represented by the green color and the object of interest (sperm cell) in blue. Now, we refine these results applying combinations of morphological operations (closing and opening). The result of this procedure is shown in Figure 6(d).

Finally, a new image was created overlapping two images (manual segmentation and our result) to visually highlight differences between them. These results can be seen in Figure 6(e), where the colors represent: (i) red, manual segmentation; (ii) green, our result, and; (iii) yellow, similar areas between both images.

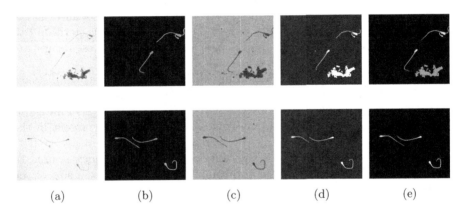

(a)   (b)   (c)   (d)   (e)

Fig. 6. Segmentation results: (a) original image; (b) manual segmentation; (c) segmentation using background subtraction; (d) image after applying the refinement process, and; (e) difference between images (b) and (d)

Discussion:

The evaluation of our approach could be easily made by a visually comparison between the manual segmentation and our results. However this is a very subjective assessment.

Unnikrishnan [12], refers that the evaluation of segmentation algorithms can judge the effectiveness of a technique based on intuition and usually results in the form of a few examples of segmented images. In addition, the author describes a set of measures to be used in order to validate the effectiveness of a segmentation algorithm in a better way, using quantitative measures like PR-Index, NPR-Index, among others. To validate our segmentation results we use some measures based on image registration (transforming different sets of data

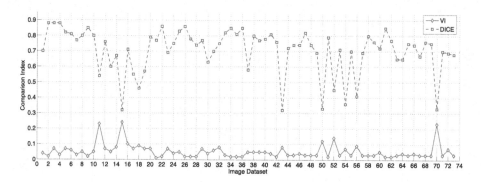

Fig. 7. Dice coefficient values with the variation of information obtained for the set of images

into one coordinate system), information theory, nonparametric statistics tests and distances between points:

- Root Mean Square Difference (RMSDIFF): this measure is defined as the degree of similarity between two images. For each pixel, the algorithm calculates the difference in color intensity for both images. If these images are identical, the measure value is zero.
- Variation of Information (VI): according Meila [8], VI represents the distance between two segmentations and it is defined as the average of the conditional entropy segmentation A given a segmentation A'. In summary, VI measures the amount of randomness in our segmentation that is not present in the original image.
- Dice coefficient: also known as the Sørensen index. This index is used to compare the similarity between two samples by measuring the size of the union of these two sets divided by the average size of them. This measure is bounded between 0 and 1.
- Normalized Manhattan: given two images, this measure calculates the sum of the absolute differences of both images, to quantitatively measure how much the image has changed.

Figures 7 and 8 plot the measures mentioned above, computed by comparing our results with the manual segmentations (Figure 6(d) and Figure 6(b), respectively). As can be seen in Figure 8, the results of our approach are similar to the manual segmentations. We quantify the similarity or difference between them using distances (see Manhattan curve). For instance, image 15 (first row of Figure 6) has a minimum distance between its manual segmentation and our result. Moreover, in the same figure (Figure 8), the RMSDIFF curve presents a low value for image 25, when compared with the values obtained for the image 15. As can be seen on the Dice curve, most of the values are high, which indicates a high correlation between our results and the manual segmentation.

Furthermore, 82.2% of our image dataset, has a Dice coefficient value over 0.6, i.e. the segmentation approach has good results. In contrast, there is a 6.8%

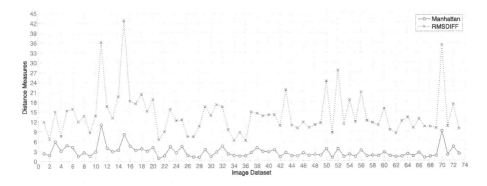

Fig. 8. Distance values Manhattan and Quadratic Mean Difference obtained for our set of images

of images, where this coefficient is not acceptable (< 0.4, see the valleys in Dice curve, on Figure 7). These low values are mainly caused by some artifacts in the image produced after the staining process. For instance, in image 15 (first row of Figure 6), we can see that the variation of information has a high value and a low Dice coefficient. This shows that the difference between the manual segmentation and our result is significant, due to some artifacts that could not be completely removed.

To confirm our results, in Figure 7, the VI measure curve proves the efficiency of this index to verify the loss of information between two images. As we can see in this figure, VI curve shows a constant behavior with some variations in three images (11, 15 and 70), i.e. manual segmentation and image segmented using our proposal share meaningful information.

6   Conclusions and Future Works

Analysis of human sperm cells is mostly carried out manually in fertility labs with poorly results. To overcome this problem, new techniques based on image processing have been developed. Along this line, we present an approach for sperm cells segmentation in micrographic images based on the combination of two well-known methods: background subtraction based on Lambertian reflectance model and morphological operations.

Our results show a good performance on 73 images, due to the presence of similar background. In addition, we have used four quantitative measures to evaluate our approach. However, they highlighted some problems in our segmentation results due to image complexity.

Further studies will be perform with respect to the refinement process in order to completely remove or differentiate the stain spots from sperm cells in our micrographic images. For this purpose, additional morphological analysis should be explored taking into account different structuring elements. Also, another techniques and equipment will be used to obtain a new background model. It is important to notice that, this paper describes the first part of an ambitious project which main goal is to analyse human sperm cells in order to diagnose male infertility.

Acknowledgments. This work was funded by the Fondos para la Innovación, Ciencia y Tecnología (FINCyT-Perú) under contract 208-FINCYT-IA-2013 and CONCYTEC-Perú with STIC-AmSud 2013 under the FERMI project.

References

1. Alegre, E., Biehl, M., Petkov, N., Sánchez, L.: Automatic classification of the acrosome status of boar spermatozoa using digital image processing and {LVQ}. Computers in Biology and Medicine **38**(4), 461–468 (2008)
2. Bijar, A., Benavent, A.P., Mikaeili, M., Khayati, R.: Fully automatic identification and discrimination of sperm's parts in microscopic images of stained human semen smear. Journal of Biomedical Science & Engineering (2012)
3. Carrillo, H., Villarreal, J., Sotaquira, M., Goelkel, M., Gutierrez, R.: A computer aided tool for the assessment of human sperm morphology. In: Proceedings of the 7th IEEE International Conference on Bioinformatics and Bioengineering, BIBE 2007, pp. 1152–1157. IEEE (2007)
4. Chang, V., Saavedra, J.M., Castañeda, V., Sarabia, L., Hitschfeld, N., Härtel, S.: Gold-standard and improved framework for sperm head segmentation. Computer Methods and Programs in Biomedicine **117**(2), 225–237 (2014)
5. Dai Qingyun, Y.Y.: The advanced of mathematieal morphology in image processing. Control Theory and Applications **18**(04), 479–481 (2001)
6. Horprasert, T., Harwood, D., Davis, L.S.: A robust background subtraction and shadow detection. In: Proc. ACCV, pP. 983–988 (2000)
7. Mack, S.O., Wolf, D.P., Tash, J.S.: Quantitation of specific parameters of motility in large numbers of human sperm by digital image processing. Biology of Reproduction **38**(2), 270–281 (1988)
8. Meilă, M.: Comparing clusterings–an information based distance. Journal of Multivariate Analysis **98**(5), 873–895 (2007)
9. Park, K.S., Yi, W.J., Paick, J.S.: Segmentation of sperms using the strategic hough transform. Annals of Biomedical Engineering **25**(2), 294–302 (1997)
10. Soler, C., García-Molina, A., Sancho, M., Contell, J., Núñez, M., Cooper, T.G.: A new technique for analysis of human sperm morphology in unstained cells from raw semen. Reproduction, Fertility and Development (2014)
11. Tomlinson, M.J., Pooley, K., Simpson, T., Newton, T., Hopkisson, J., Jayaprakasan, K., Jayaprakasan, R., Naeem, A., Pridmore, T.: Validation of a novel computer-assisted sperm analysis (casa) system using multitarget-tracking algorithms. Fertility and Sterility **3**(6), 1911–1920 (2010)
12. Unnikrishnan R., Hebert, M.: Measures of similarity. In: Seventh IEEE Workshops on Application of Computer Vision, WACV/MOTIONS 2005, vol. 1 (2005)
13. Wang, Y., Jia, Y., Yuchi, M., Ding, M.: The computer-assisted sperm analysis (casa) technique for sperm morphology evaluation. In: 2011 International Conference on Intelligent Computation and Bio-Medical Instrumentation (ICBMI), pp. 279–282, December 2011
14. Winters, B.R., Walsh, T.J.: The epidemiology of male infertility. Urologic Clinics of North America **41**(1), 195–204 (2014)

Interactive Image Colorization Using Laplacian Coordinates

Wallace Casaca[1,2]([✉]), Marilaine Colnago[1], and Luis Gustavo Nonato[1]

[1] Institute of Mathematics and Computer Sciences, University of São Paulo (USP),
São Carlos, SP 13566-590, Brazil
wallace.coc@gmail.com

[2] School of Engineering, Brown University, 182 Hope St., Providence, RI 02912, USA

Abstract. Image colorization is a modern topic in computer vision which aims at manually adding colors to grayscale images. Techniques devoted to colorize images differ in many fundamental aspects as they often require an excessive number of image scribbles to reach pleasant colorizations. In fact, spreading lots of scribbles in the whole image consists of a laborious task that demands great efforts from users to accurately set appropriate colors to the image. In this work we present a new framework that only requires a small amount of image annotations to perform the colorization. The proposed framework combines the high-adherence on image contours of the Laplacian Coordinates segmentation approach with a fast color matching scheme to propagate colors to image partitions. User can locally manipulate colored regions so as to further improve the segmentation and thus the colorization result. We attest the effectiveness of our approach through a set of practical applications and comparisons against existing colorization techniques.

1 Introduction

Colorization is a computer-supervised process by which colors are imparted to grayscale images or to black-and-white films. It has been successfully used in photo editing and scientific illustration, to modernize old motion pictures and to enhance the visual appear of an image. Traditionally, colorization is tedious, time consuming and it requires artistic skills to precisely set suitable colors to an off-color image.

Aiming at making the colorization task simpler and less laborious, several computational systems have been proposed in the last two decades, which can be roughly divided into two major groups: *example-based* [1–6], and *scribble-based* [6–11]. Example-based methods accomplish the colorization process by matching the luminance of the monochromatic image with the luminance of a reference color image used to drive the color propagation. In scribble-based methods, the user guides the colorization by manually defining colored strokes onto the grayscale image.

Considering the flexibility to operate arbitrary colorizations and the non-requirement for an additional reference image, scribble-based strategy has performed better than the example-based one in recent years [12]. This trend has

© Springer International Publishing Switzerland 2015
G. Azzopardi and N. Petkov (Eds.): CAIP 2015, Part II, LNCS 9257, pp. 675–686, 2015.
DOI: 10.1007/978-3-319-23117-4_58

been observed especially due to the simplicity of scribble-based methods which basically relies on an interactive interface in order to operate.

The classical work by Levin et al. [7] is a good representative of scribble-based approach. Levin's method aims at optimizing the color of all image pixels using the scribbles as constraints. Although it presents satisfactory results for various types of images, Levin's approach tends to convey colors beyond the texture boundaries, thus resulting in unpleasant colorizations. The technique proposed by Yi-Chin Huang et al. [8] employs adaptive edge detection so as to prevent colors from going beyond region boundaries. Further improvements of this technique have been proposed by Yatziv and Sapiro [9], who present a faster scribble-based color optimization method that relies on chrominance blending to perform the colorization. In [10] and [11], the authors employ texture continuity to colorize manga-cartoons and natural images, respectively. In a more recent work, Casaca et al. [6] has introduced an innovative user-based interface namely *ProjColor* that relies on a simple drag-and-drop manipulation of badly colorized pixels using multidimensional data projection as an recursive tool.

Despite good results, most existing scribble-based methods require intensive user involvement, especially when the image contains complex structures or has different texture patterns, which can demand lots of scribbles until acceptable outcomes are reached.

In this work we propose a new framework for colorizing grayscale images that makes use of a scribble-driven interface to replace the excessive provision of user strokes typically employed by existing colorization methods. Moreover, the proposed approach holds the good segmentation properties derived from the *Laplacian Coordinates (LC)* methodology [13,14]. Since Laplacian Coordinates is used to precompute a prior segmentation of the monochromatic image, our framework leads to pleasant results and requires just a few user interventions to fully colorize the image. As we shall show, by one-shot stroking the grayscale image, the user can colorize complex textured areas quite easily, preserving region boundaries and preventing the addition of new scribbles.

1.1   Contribution

In summary, the main contributions of this work are:

- A novel interactive colorization technique that combines the accuracy of the Laplacian Coordinates approach with a fast color propagation scheme to colorize images.
- An easy-to-implement and efficient framework that allows for recursively colorizing the image by reintroducing new seeds in an intuitive and non-laborious manner.
- A comprehensive set of practical applications typically performed by professional photo editors which shows the effectiveness of the proposed approach.

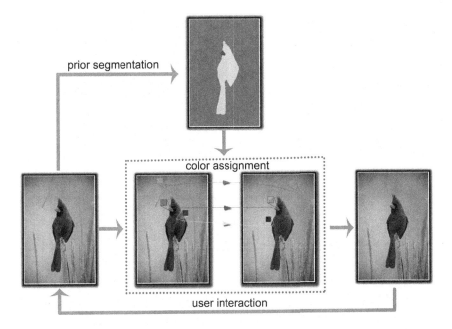

Fig. 1. Pipeline of our colorization framework.

2 Laplacian Coordinates-Based Colorization

As illustrated in Figure 1, the proposed colorization pipeline comprises three main steps, namely, *prior segmentation, color assignment* and *progressive colorization*. First, color scribbles given by the user are taken as constraints to the Laplacian Coordinates approach aiming at producing a prior segmentation. The partitioning obtained is then used to promote color data transfer between input scribbles and image segments. Badly colored regions can be modified by interacting with the Laplacian Coordinates segmentation interface and our colorization apparatus in order to produce better outcomes. Details of each stage of the pipeline are presented bellow.

2.1 Prior Segmentation

In our approach, we use the Laplacian Coordinates methodology [13] to assist the colorization process by fragmenting the image into disjoint regions. Color labels are manually chosen by the user and freely spread inside representative image regions, as illustrated in Figure 2(b). Those labels are then designed to condition the linear system of equations obtained from the Laplacian Coordinates energy function:

$$\mathcal{F}(\mathbf{x}) = \sum_{i \in B} \|x_i\|_2^2 + \sum_{i \in F} \|x_i - 1\|_2^2 + \frac{1}{2} \sum_{i \sim j} \|w_{ij}(x_i - x_j)\|_2^2, \tag{1}$$

Fig. 2. Illustration of the segmentation procedure. (a) Grayscale image, (b) marked image with color scribbles, (c) prior segmentation, and (d) the resulting colorization after applying color transfer.

where $\mathbf{x} = (x_1, x_2, ..., x_n)$ is the sought solution, that is, a saliency map which assigns a scalar to each pixel i of the image, w_{ij} denotes the weight of pixel pair (i, j) locally determined by a regular 9-point stencil, and B and F represent the sets of labeled pixels (we assume a binary segmentation to simplify the notation).

In less mathematical terms, the unitary components in $\mathcal{F}$ enforce fidelity of brushed pixels to scalars 0 (*background*) and 1 (*foreground*), and the pairwise term imposes spatial smoothness within image regions while promoting sharp jumps across image boundaries.

Energy (1) is efficiently computed by solving a sparse linear system of equations as detailed in [13,14]. Weights w_{ij} are calculated from an image gradient-based function such as [13,15]. Finally, the segmentation can be achieved by specifying an image cutting criterium. For instance, one can obtain partitions by trivially assigning foreground and background labels as follows:

$$\mathcal{S}_i = \begin{cases} 1, \text{if} \quad x_i \geq \frac{1}{2} \\ 0, \text{otherwise} \end{cases}. \tag{2}$$

The partitions generated (see Figure 2(c)) are then used to support the next step of our pipeline, *color assignment*, which is described below.

2.2   Color Assignment

This stage is responsible for propagating the colors initially chosen by the user to the partitions generated by the LC segmentation.

The propagation mechanism is accomplished as follows: given the set of color labels provided during the segmentation stage, we first convert those labels to $L\alpha\beta$ coloring system by employing basic matrix transformations as outlined in [16]. The L channel in $L\alpha\beta$ space determines the luminance of the labels and it does not carry any color information as the remaining components. Moreover, no correlation is established between L, α and β. As a result, if a grayscale pixel p is labeled as "background", that is, $S_p = 0$ in Equation (2), its color coordinates α and β are obtained by taking the corresponding components in the specified color label. Similar procedure is performed until colorizing the remaining partitions (see the middle step in Figure 1).

2.3   Progressive Colorization

One of the main contributions of the proposed framework is to exploit the flexibility provided by the Laplacian Coordinates methodology to interactively promote progressive colorization. Similar to [17], Laplacian Coordinates enables an interactive tool that allows for repartitioning data by inserting new seeded pixels. In fact, if the result is not satisfactory, the user can select badly colored pixels, turning them into a different color label that can be reintroduced into the Laplacian Coordinates system of equations to partition the image and, thereby, improve the resulting colorization.

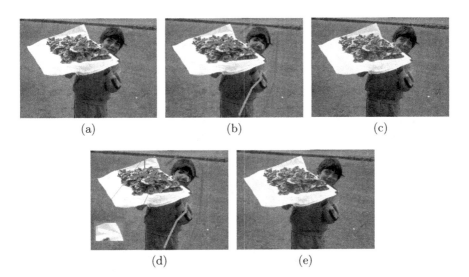

(a)   (b)   (c)

(d)   (e)

Fig. 3. The use of our colorization framework when allowing for user recolorization. (a) Input image, (b) initial scribbles, (c) 1st colorization, (d) improvement performed by the user, and (e) colorization after user interaction.

Figure 3 illustrates the need for user intervention. Notice that the group of pixels located on the upper right corner of the boy's tray was not colored suitably (see Fig. 3(c)). User can then provide an additional color scribble to the region with badly colorized pixels as highlighted in Fig. 3(d), creating new constraints for the Laplacian Coordinates and, thus generating a better result as shown in Fig. 3(e).

3   Experimental Results

In this section we illustrate the use of the proposed approach in practical scenarios such as multiple colorization and portraiture. We also provide experimental comparisons against traditional scribble-based methods [6,7,9,12].

3.1   Multiple Color Substitution and Portraiture

Our first experiment shows the capability of the proposed framework in producing different visual effects by just keeping the initial strokes (Fig. 4(a)) and modifying user-selected colors. Changing the colors that guide the colorization gives rise to multiple representations of the image, as shown in Fig. 4(b)-(d). Selective colorization problem (portraiture) is investigated in Fig. 4(e)-(k). This application aims at accentuating certain features on a photography so that the vintage aspect of the image is preserved. Notice from Fig. 4(e)-(f) that no excessive image annotations were required to reach a pleasant result. Another example of portraiture is presented in Fig. 4(g)-(k), where the eyes and lips were successfully elucidated.

3.2   Qualitative Comparisons

Figure 5 compares the proposed approach against Levin's and Projcolor methods. In contrast to Fig. 5(b), Projcolor and our technique have produced similar results, however, our approach does not make use of any data exploratory interface as the one used by Projcolor algorithm.

Figure 6 brings another comparison between Levin's and our framework, but now taking into account the effectiveness of both colorization scribble interfaces. The seeding mechanism provided by Laplacian Coordinates is simpler than the traditional scribble-based employed in [7], as the user does not need to spread an excessive number of scribbles in the image to reach a reasonable result.

The experiment presented in Figure 7 establishes comparisons between the proposed approach and the popular scribble-based methods [7,9,12]. Colorizations produced from [7] and [9] smoothed the images considerably almost all cases while the outcomes obtained from [12] and our technique have produced more refined results. By reintroducing just a small amount of seeds in the marked images in Fig. 7(g),(o) and Fig. 7(w), one can see that our approach is quite flexible in capturing intrinsic details of the image such as pieces surrounded by image segments, a characteristic not present in the technique [12].

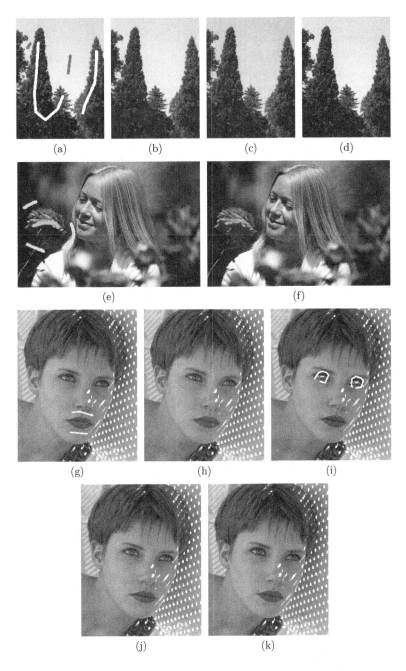

Fig. 4. Practical applications supported by the proposed framework. (a) Input scribbles used by our method, (b)-(d) the resulting colorizations taking as input the scribbles provided in (a) and varying multiple colors, (e)-(f) the scribbled image and its selective colorization, (g)-(k) portraiture example performed by our framework.

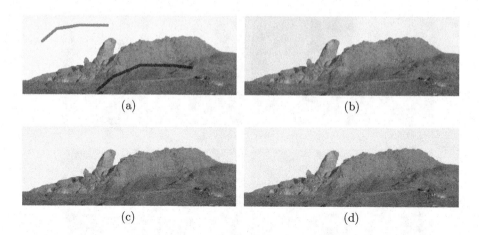

Fig. 5. Comparison between Levin's technique [7], Projcolor [6], and our approach. (a) Initial scribbles, (b) Levin's colorization, (c) Projcolor colorization after some user involvement, and (d) result obtained by our framework in a one-shot colorization.

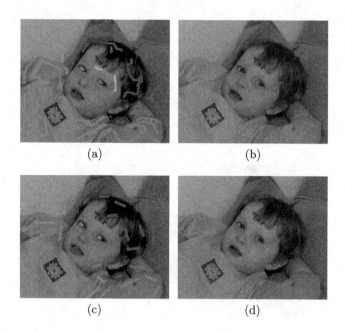

Fig. 6. Comparison between [7] and our technique. (a) Scribbles used by Levin's method, (b) Levin's colorization, (c) scribbles used by our method, and (d) our result.

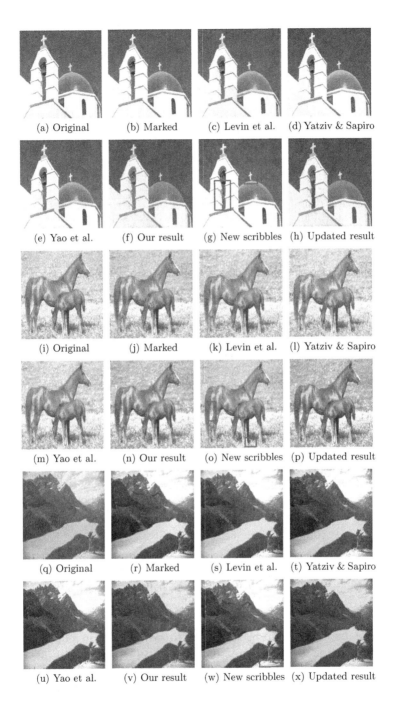

(a) Original   (b) Marked   (c) Levin et al.   (d) Yatziv & Sapiro

(e) Yao et al.   (f) Our result   (g) New scribbles   (h) Updated result

(i) Original   (j) Marked   (k) Levin et al.   (l) Yatziv & Sapiro

(m) Yao et al.   (n) Our result   (o) New scribbles   (p) Updated result

(q) Original   (r) Marked   (s) Levin et al.   (t) Yatziv & Sapiro

(u) Yao et al.   (v) Our result   (w) New scribbles   (x) Updated result

Fig. 7. Comparison between colorization techniques [7,9,12] and our approach.

Table 1. Quantitative comparison against [7], [9] and [12] when computing MAE (↓) and PSNR (↑) measures for images from Fig. 7. Bold values indicate the best score.

Image	Levin et al.		Yatziv-Sapiro		Yao et al.		Proposed		Updated	
	MAE	PSNR	MAE	PSNR	MAE	PSNR	MAE	PSNR	MAE	PSNR
Church	20.24	35.06	23.70	34.38	18.13	35.54	12.95	37.00	**11.73**	**37.43**
Horse	99.75	28.14	89.28	28.62	57.58	30.53	42.39	31.85	**42.27**	**31.87**
River	74.16	29.42	72.02	29.55	72.94	29.50	18.26	35.51	**18.19**	**35.53**
Average	64.71	30.87	61.66	30.85	49.55	31.85	24.53	34.78	**24.06**	**34.94**

Table 2. Quantitative comparison against [7], [9] and [12] when computing SSIM (↑) and UIQI (↑) measures for images from Fig. 7. Bold values indicate the best score.

Image	Levin et al.		Yatziv-Sapiro		Yao et al.		Proposed		Updated	
	SSIM	UIQI	SSIM	UIQI	SSIM	UIQI	SSIM	UIQI	SSIM	UIQI
Church	0.8373	0.9065	**0.8566**	0.9153	0.8404	0.9097	0.8440	0.9379	0.8443	**0.9392**
Horse	0.2042	0.7828	0.7243	0.9878	0.8228	**0.9925**	**0.8259**	0.9920	0.8258	0.9916
River	0.8461	0.9392	0.8601	0.9438	0.8500	0.9421	0.8555	0.9407	**0.8640**	**0.9551**
Average	0.6292	0.8762	0.8137	0.9490	0.8377	0.9481	0.8418	0.9569	**0.8447**	**0.9620**

3.3 Quantitative Comparisons

Finally, in this section we make use of multiple image quality metrics traditionally employed by the computer vision community to quantitatively evaluate the effectiveness of the proposed approach against the well-established colorization techniques [7,9,12].

Tables 1 and 2 summarize the quantitative measurements of *Mean Absolute Error* (MAE), *Peak-to-Noise-Ratio* (PSNR), *Structural Similarity Index* (SSIM) [18], and *Universal Image Quality Index* (UIQI) [19] between ground-truth color images and the colorizations produced by the algorithms from Fig.7. One notices that our method outperforms others (in average) for all evaluated metrics, being also superior for most of the measurements (bold values indicate better results).

4 Conclusion

In this work we address the fundamental problem of image colorization as an interactive framework that unifies scribble-based image partition and recursive colorization. Besides enabling a local modification of badly colored regions, the combination of Laplacian Coordinates approach, fragment-based colorization and scribble-driven mechanism turns out to be effective in popular practical applications such as progressive retouching, multiple colorization and portraiture. The experimental results we provided shows that the proposed framework outperforms existing representative techniques in terms of accuracy, flexibility and quantitative measurement, rendering it a very attractive interactive tool in the context of image colorization.

Acknowledgments. The authors would like to thank the anonymous reviewers for their constructive comments. This research has been funded by FAPESP (the State of São Paulo Research Funding Agency, grants #2014/16857-0 and #2011/22749-8), and CNPq (the Brazilian Federal Research Funding Agency).

References

1. Hertzmann, A., Jacobs, C.E., Oliver, N., Curless, B., Salesin, D.: Image analogies. In: ACM Transactions on Graphics (TOG), pp. 327–340 (2001)
2. Reinhard, E., Ashikhmin, M., Gooch, B., Shirley, P.: Color transfer between images. IEEE Computer Graphics and Applications **21**(5), 34–41 (2001)
3. Welsh, T., Ashikhmin, M., Mueller, K.: Transferring color to greyscale images. ACM Transactions on Graphics (TOG) **21**(3), 277–280 (2002)
4. Irony, R., Cohen-Or, D., Lischinski, D.: Colorization by example. In: Proc. of the Eurographics Symposium on Rendering, pp. 201–210 (2005)
5. Liu, X., Wan, L., Yingge, Q., Wong, T.-T., Lin, S., Leung, C.-S., Heng, P.-A.: Intrinsic colorization. ACM Transactions on Graphics (TOG) **27**(5), 152:1–152:9 (2008)
6. Casaca, W., Gomez-Nieto, E., de O.L. Ferreira, C., Tavares, G., Pagliosa, P., Paulovich, F., Nonato, L.G., Paiva, A.: Colorization by multidimensional projection. In: 25th Conference on Graphics, Patterns and Images (SIBGRAPI), pp. 32–38. IEEE Computer Society (2012)
7. Levin, A., Lischinski, D., Weiss, Y.: Colorization using optimization. ACM Transactions on Graphics (TOG) **23**(3), 689–694 (2004)
8. Huang, Y.-C., Tung, Y.-S., Chen, J.-C., Wang, S.-W., Wu, J.-L.: An adaptive edge detection based colorization algorithm and its applications. In: Proc. of the 13th ACM International Conference on Multimedia, pp. 351–354 (2005)
9. Yatziv, L., Sapiro, G.: Fast image and video colorization using chrominance blending. IEEE Transactions on Image Processing **15**(5), 1120–1129 (2006)
10. Yingge, Q., Wong, T.-T., Heng, P.-A.: Manga colorization. ACM Transactions on Graphics (TOG) **25**(3), 1214–1220 (2006)
11. Luan, Q., Wen, F., Cohen-Or, D., Liang, L., Xu, Y.-Q., Shum, H.-Y.: Natural image colorization. In: Proc. of the Eurographics Symposium on Rendering, pp. 309–320 (2007)
12. Yao, C., Yang, X., Chan, L., Yi, X.: Image colorization using bayesian nonlocal inference. Journal of Electronic Imaing **20**(2), 023008-1–023008-6 (2011)
13. Casaca, W., Nonato, L.G., Taubin, G.: Laplacian coordinates for seeded image segmentation. In: IEEE Conference on Computer Vision and Pattern Recognition (CVPR), pp. 384–391. IEEE Computer Society (2014)
14. Casaca, W.: Graph Laplacian for Spectral Clustering and Seeded Image Segmentation. Ph.d. thesis, University of São Paulo (ICMC-USP), Brazil (2014)
15. Casaca, W., Paiva, A., Gomez-Nieto, E., Joia, P., Nonato, L.G.: Spectral image segmentation using image decomposition and inner product-based metric. Journal of Mathematical Imaging and Vision **45**(3), 227–238 (2013)

16. Torres Mendez, L.A., Ramirez-Bejarano, C.A., Ortiz-Alvarado, G., de Alba-Padilla, C.A.: A fast color synthesis algorithm using the l-alpha-beta color space and a non-parametric mrf model. In: 8th Mexican International Conference on Artificial Intelligence (MICAI), pp. 53–58 (2009)

17. Casaca, W., Motta, D., Taubin, G., Nonato, L.G.: A user-friendly interactive image inpainting framework using laplacian coordinates. In: IEEE International Conference on Image Processing (ICIP), pp. 1–5 (2015)

18. Wang, Z., Bovik, A.C., Sheikh, H.R., Simoncelli, E.P.: Image quality assessment: From error visibility to structural similarity. IEEE Transactions on Image Processing **13**(4), 600–612 (2004)

19. Bovik, A.C.: A universal image quality index. IEEE Signal Processing Letters **9**(3), 81–84 (2002)

LBP and Irregular Graph Pyramids

Martin Cerman[1], Rocio Gonzalez-Diaz[2], and Walter Kropatsch[1]($^{(\boxtimes)}$)

[1] PRIP Group, Vienna University of Technology, 1040 Wien, Austria
mcerman@prip.tuwien.ac.at, rogodi@us.es
[2] Applied Mathematics Department, School of Computer Engineering,
University of Seville, Seville, Spain
krw@prip.tuwien.ac.at

Abstract. In this paper, a new codification of Local Binary Patterns (LBP) is given using graph pyramids. The LBP code characterizes the topological category (local max, min, slope, saddle) of the gray level landscape around the center region. Given a 2D grayscale image I, our goal is to obtain a simplified image which can be seen as "minimal" representation in terms of topological characterization of I. For this, a method is developed based on merging regions and Minimum Contrast Algorithm.

Keywords: Local binary patterns · Irregular graph pyramid · Primal and dual graph · Topological characterization · Minimum contrast algorithm

1 Introduction

Given a grayscale digital image I, the Local Binary Pattern $LBP(I)$ [12,13] is a grayscale digital image used to represent the texture element at each pixel in I. This is currently the most frequently used texture descriptor [18] with outstanding results in applications ranging from segmentation and classification [15], object detection [11] to gender classification [16]. Typically the LBP operator is applied to all 3×3 image windows of the considered texture (region). Then the histogram provides the characteristic features of the texture. After training the feature space with the textures of interest new textures can be classified with very good discrimination.

While the LBP code of a 3×3 window needs 8 bits for a single code, larger windows need more bits or even a varying number of bits if a multiresolution approach is chosen. The new encoding overcomes this drawback by transferring the code from the pixels to the neighbor relations (edges of the neighborhood

M. Cerman—Acknowledges the support of the PRIP Club, the organization of friends and promoters of Pattern Recognition and Image Processing activities, Vienna, Austria.

R. Gonzalez-Diaz—Author partially supported by IMUS, Spanish Ministry under grant MTM2012-32706 and ESF ACAT program.

G. Azzopardi and N. Petkov (Eds.): CAIP 2015, Part II, LNCS 9257, pp. 687–699, 2015.
DOI: 10.1007/978-3-319-23117-4_59

graph). We propose a new equivalent encoding using one bit per edge of the graph.

It is known that the LBP encodes the basic topological categories of a digital image's landscape, e.g. extrema, saddle points, plateaus and slopes. After the contraction of all plateaus, these categories can be identified by simple local detectors except for the saddle points. In a discrete image a saddle can be either an identified pixel or a 2×2 non-well composed configuration. As the first major novelty introduced in this paper, we show a way to handle also such situations. We further propose a repetitive contraction process leading to hierarchy of successively smaller graphs, a graph pyramid, preserving the basic topological categories in a substantially smaller graph structure.

The second novelty in this paper is the definition of a minimum contrast representative (MCR) image. It stands for the large class of all possible images that produce the same LBP codes and, consequently, also the same LBP histograms. This may allow to understand the trained classifiers since it defines the equivalence class of images of the trained class.

The paper is organized as follows: In Section 2, the topological category of the gray level landscape around a pixel c characterized by its LBP code, is defined. Section 3 recalls irregular graph pyramids. In Section 4, we introduce the notion of well-composed images and explain how any image can be made well-composed by inserting a few dummy regions. The goal of the rest of the sections is to obtain a "minimal" representation of a given image in terms of topological characterization. Our idea is to merge pixels (or regions, in general) that provide redundant information, to create the pyramid. The first step in the process is to remove the asymmetry caused by the sign function (see Eq. (1)). For this, in Section 5, we merge regions with same gray value (plateaus). After merging all plateaus, we define the notion of structurally redundant edges that should be removed to reach our goal. In Section 6, we define the topological category of a region. Section 7 is devoted to a particular topological category named singular slope that can be merged without changing the topological category of the rest of the regions. Finally, in Section 8, we adapt Minimum Contrast Algorithm given in [17] to be applied to our pyramid in order to obtain a "minimal" representation of the image. Section 9 is devoted to conclusions, experiments and future works.

2   Local Binary Patterns (LBP)

The intensity of a pixel $p = (x, y)$, denoted by $g(p)$, is expressed within a given range between a minimum and a maximum, inclusive. Without loss of generality we will work with 8 bits, i.e., we will suppose that the range is $[0, 255]$.

The standard LBP code [12] is computed for a (center) pixel as in Eq. (1) where P is the number of neighbors, R is the distance between the center pixel and the neighbors (we assume 1 here), c is the center pixel of the operator and p is the local neighbor indexed by p. The basic operator uses the sign function $s(x) = 1$ if $x \geq 0$ and $s(x) = 0$ otherwise.

$$LBP_{P,R} = \sum_{p=0}^{P-1} s(g(p) - g(c))2^p . \qquad (1)$$

In this paper, the 4 neighbors (on its top, bottom, right, left) of each pixel are considered for comparison. That is, follow the 4 pixels along a circle (for example, clockwise). Where the center pixel's gray value is greater than the neighbor's gray value, write 0. Otherwise, write 1. Example:

113	240	23
20	25	12
15	30	40

$\Rightarrow$ $\begin{matrix} & 1 & \\ 0 & 25 & \mathbf{0} \\ & 1 & \end{matrix}$ $\Rightarrow$ $\mathbf{0101}$ $\Rightarrow$ 9

The 4-neighbor LBP codification has been used in the past for solving problems in Image Processing and Analysis such as, for example, face detection and recognition [6], or iris extraction [5].

The LBP code characterizes the *topological category* of the gray level landscape around the center pixel. A pixel is a *local maximum* if the LBP code is composed just by 0s. A *local minimum* produces an LBP code only with 1s. Notice however that a local minimum can also be created by a *plateau* (a region composed by neighboring pixels sharing the same gray value) due to the asymmetry of the sign function s. It is a *slope* if there is exactly one transition from 0s to 1s or 1s to 0s in its LBP code. Otherwise, it is a *saddle*.

3   LBP Codes and Irregular Graph Pyramids

A *region adjacency graph* (RAG) encodes the adjacency of regions in a partition. A vertex v is associated to each region r. Vertices of neighboring regions are connected by edges. Classical RAGs do not contain any self-loops or parallel edges. An *extended region adjacency graph* (eRAG) is a RAG that contains the so-called *pseudo edges*, which are self-loops and parallel edges used to encode neighborhood relations to a region completely enclosed by one or more other regions [7].

The *dual* graph of an eRAG G is denoted by $\bar{G}$ (G is said to be the *primal* graph of $\bar{G}$). The edges of $\bar{G}$ represent the boundaries (borders) of the regions encoded by G, and the vertices of $\bar{G}$ represent points where boundary segments meet. G and $\bar{G}$ are planar graphs if they represent a 2D decomposition into regions. There is a one-to-one correspondence between the edges of G and the edges of $\bar{G}$, which induces a one-to-one correspondence between the vertices of G and the 2D cells (regions) of $\bar{G}$. The dual of $\bar{G}$ is again G. The following operations are equivalent: edge contraction in G with edge removal in $\bar{G}$, and edge removal in G with edge contraction in $\bar{G}$. Edge removal preserves the topology (i.e., regions are always homeomorphic to disks) [3].

A (dual) irregular graph pyramid [7,8] is a stack of successively reduced planar graphs $P = \{(G_0, \bar{G}_0), \ldots, (G_n, \bar{G}_n)\}$. Each level $(G_k, \bar{G}_k), 0 < k \le n$ is

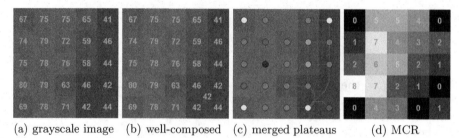

(a) grayscale image   (b) well-composed   (c) merged plateaus   (d) MCR

Fig. 1. An 8-bit grayscale image (highlighted grayscale values) is (b) made well-composed. (c) Plateaus are merged (for color legend see Fig. 3(c)) and (d) Minimum Contrast Algorithm produces the minimum contrast representative (MCR in Section 8).

obtained by first contracting edges in G_{k-1} (removal in $\bar{G}_{k-1}$), if the corresponding regions should be merged, and then removing edges in G_{k-1} (contraction in $\bar{G}_{k-1}$) to simplify the structure.

In this paper, pixels are considered unit-square regions, 4-neighborhood is used for constructing the RAG and each vertex v of the RAG associated to each region r is labeled with the gray value of the region, i.e., $g(v) := g(r)$.

4   Creating Well-Composed Images

A 2D image is *well-composed* [9] if it does not contain the following *non-well composed configuration* (modulo reflection and 90-degree rotation):

$$\begin{array}{|c|c|} \hline a & b \\ \hline c & d \\ \hline \end{array} \quad \text{where } g(a) < g(b),\ g(a) < g(c),\ g(d) < g(b) \text{ and } g(d) < g(c). \quad (2)$$

Lemma 1. *If the image is well-composed, then the topological category provided by $LBP_{4,1}$ is the same as $LBP_{8,1}$.*

Proof. Consider the following 3×3 block $\begin{array}{|c|c|c|} \hline a & d & x \\ \hline b & e & h \\ \hline c & f & i \\ \hline \end{array}$. The topological class of e using $LBP_{4,1}$ is given by b, d, f, and h. $LBP_{8,1}$ is additionally given by a, c, x, and i. The topological category of $LBP_{8,1}$ is the same as $LBP_{4,1}$, if by adding the diagonal 8-neighbors to $LBP_{4,1}$ the number of transitions from 0s to 1s or 1s to 0s does not change. In the following we show that any addition of a diagonal element, which would change the topological class, causes the image to become non-well composed (modulo reflection and 90-degree rotation):

- *Local minimum* (resp. *maximum*) is defined by $g(e) < g(p)$ (resp. $g(e) > g(p)$) for $p = b, d, f, h$. If $g(e) > g(q)$ (resp. $g(e) < g(q)$) for $q = a, c, x$ or i, the image becomes non-well composed.
- *Slope* is defined by either:

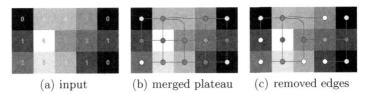

(a) input   (b) merged plateau   (c) removed edges

Fig. 2. The plateaus of an image with highlighted values are first merged and then structurally redundant edges are removed.

- $g(e) > g(b), g(f), g(h)$ and $g(e) < g(d)$ (resp. $g(e) < g(b), g(f), g(h)$ and $g(e) > g(d)$). If $g(e) < g(c)$ or $g(e) < g(i)$ (resp. $g(e) > g(c)$ or $g(e) > g(i)$) the image becomes not well-composed. Here, $g(a)$ and $g(x)$ are irrelevant.
- $g(e) < g(b), g(d)$ and $g(e) > g(f), g(h)$. If $g(e) > g(a)$ or $g(e) < g(i)$ the image becomes not well-composed. Here, $g(c)$ and $g(x)$ are irrelevant.
- *Saddle* (resp. *plateaus*) is defined by $g(e) > g(b), g(h)$ and $g(e) < g(d), g(f)$ (resp. $g(e) = g(b) = g(d) = g(h)$). Here $g(a)$, $g(c)$, $g(x)$, and $g(i)$ are irrelevant. □

The main problem in a non-well composed configuration like Eq. (2), is that the relation between a and d (resp. b and c) cannot be deduced from the relation of 4-adjacent regions. To solve this, we insert a new "dummy" region r in the center of the non-well composed configuration: $\begin{array}{|c|c|} \hline a & b \\ \hline \multicolumn{2}{|c|}{r} \\ \hline c & d \\ \hline \end{array}$.

The new region r with a new gray value $g(r)$ reflects the relations between a, b, c, d and in a way that the 8-connectivity LBP code can be deduced from the LBP code of the modified configuration. Without loss of generality, suppose that $g(a) \leq g(d) < g(b) \leq g(c)$. Following cases can occur:

1. $g(a) = g(d) < g(b) = g(c)$ (resp. $g(a) < g(d) < g(b) < g(c)$). In this case, the vertex v represents a saddle. Set $g(r) = \frac{g(d)+g(b)}{2}$. We have that $g(a) = g(d) < \frac{g(b)+g(d)}{2} < g(b) = g(c)$ (resp. $g(a) < g(d) < \frac{g(b)+g(d)}{2} < g(b) < g(c)$). Therefore, the LBP code of r is 0101 which is a saddle and all three new vertices have degree 3 and, hence, are well-composed.
2. $g(a) = g(d) < g(b) < g(c)$ (resp. $g(a) < g(d) < g(b) = g(c)$). Set $g(r) = g(d)$ (resp. $g(r) = g(b)$). In our process, regions a, r, d (resp. b, r, c) form a plateau. See Fig. 1(a) and 1(b).

5 Merging Plateaus and Removing Edges

The first step in our process to obtain a simplified image with the same topological information as the original, is to merge plateaus. This way, by contracting adjacent vertices with same value in the primal graph (i.e., merging neighboring

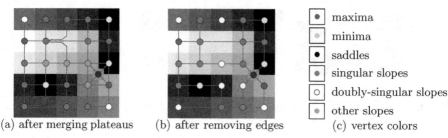

(a) after merging plateaus   (b) after removing edges   (c) vertex colors

Fig. 3. Removing structurally redundant edges from the primal graph.

regions with same value in the dual), we remove the asymmetry caused by the sign function. See Fig. 2(b).

After merging all plateaus, a direction can be associated to each non-self-loop edge between different vertices of the primal graph G:

$$(u,v) \in E \text{ has direction } u \to v \text{ iff } g(u) > g(v).$$

Proposition 1. *After merging plateaus, $G \setminus \{self\text{-}loops\}$ is a directed graph such that: (a) G does not contain directed cycles. (b) Vertices in $\bar{G}$ do not increase degrees.*

Proof. (a) Suppose that G has a directed cycle $u_0 \to u_1 \to \cdots \to u_n = u_0$. Then $u_0 > u_1 > \cdots > u_n = u_0$, which is a contradiction. (b) Merging plateaus in G consists of removing edges and merging vertices of degree ≤ 2 in $\bar{G}$. Therefore, vertices in $\bar{G}$ have degree 3 or 4.   □

An oriented edge $(u,v) \in E$ is considered *"structurally redundant"* if there exists a dual vertex $\bar{w} \in \bar{V}$ bounded by (u,v) and a directed path $p(u,v)$ from u to v. Structurally redundant edges can be removed in G (see Fig.2(c) and 3(b)).

Finally, the notion of well-composed configurations can be extended to regions in $\bar{G}$ due to Prop. 1(b).

6   Topological Category of Regions

After merging plateaus, in the same way as for pixels, we can define the *topological category* of a vertex v of G by considering the edges incident to v. See Fig. 1(c) and 3(a). Following the edges incident to v:

- v is a *local minimum* if it is the head of all the edges incident to it.
- v is a *local maximum* if it is the tail of all the edges incident to it.
- v is a *doubly-singular slope* if it has degree two and it is the tail of one of the edges incident to it and the head of the other.
- v is a *singular slope* if it has degree greater than two and it is the tail (resp. head) of exactly one edge incident to it and the head (resp. tail) of the others.
- v is a *slope* if v is the tail of the first edges incident to it and the head of the others, clockwise or counter-clockwise.
- v is a *saddle* otherwise.

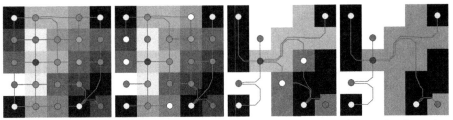

(a) graph -plateaus   (b) -redundant edges   (c) -singular slopes   (d) minimal graph

Fig. 4. The primal graph G is successively reduced by merging plateaus and (doubly)-singular slopes. Merge operations and removal of structurally redundant edges are applied in an alternating fashion. The last image is considered "minimal".

Proposition 2. *After removing redundant edges, the topological category of the vertices of G may be simplified: singular slopes may change to doubly-singular slopes, and slopes to singular slopes (see Fig. 2(c), 3(b) and 4(b)). Nevertheless, local maxima, minima and saddles are always preserved in the primal graph.*

Proof. For each structurally redundant edge $e = (u, v) \in E$ there exists a monotonic path connecting u to v. Therefore the removal would not disconnect an extremum. And since it is monotonic, the extremum remains extremum.

Assume the endpoint v of a structurally redundant edge $e = (u, v)$ is a saddle. The last directed edge $q = (v_k, v)$ of the alternative path $p(u, v) = (u, x_0, \ldots, q)$ must have the same orientation as (u, v) due to the monotonicity of the path. Since the bounded dual cell $\overline{w}$ does not contain any hole both e and q succeed each other at the saddle v. Since they both are either below or above the saddle the removal of e would not change the property of the saddle. $\qquad \square$

7 Merging Singular Slopes

After merging plateaus, a direction is associated to the edges of the primal graph and a topological category to its vertices. Structurally redundant edges are then removed and the topological category of the vertices is updated.

Further steps in our process to obtain a simplified image with same topological information as the original, should remove topologically redundant information by merging regions. In general, a region obtained after merging slopes around a local maximum (resp. minimum) is not a local maximum (resp. minimum). *Singular slopes* make an exception. Merging singular slopes propagates well around local extrema since a local extremum in the surrounding regions often is or becomes a singular slope. However non-well composed configurations (corresponding to saddles in the dual graph) can block propagation. This is why we insert dummy regions in non-well composed configurations.

Prop. 3 asserts that contracting a singular slope p to a vertex q in the primal graph, does not change the topological category of q.

Proposition 3. *Consider a vertex p which is a singular slope in the primal graph. Let E be the set of edges incident to p. Let p be the head (resp. tail) of exactly one edge e ∈ E and it is the tail of the rest. Let q be the tail (resp. head) of e. Then the vertex obtained after contracting p to q (i.e., after merging the two associated regions in the dual graph) inherits the topological category of the region q, i.e. local max, min, saddle or slope.*

Proof. After contracting p to q, the edge e is replaced by the set of edges $E \setminus e$ in such a way that q is the tail (resp. head) of all these edges. Since q was the tail (resp. head) of e, then, the topological category of q does not change. There is no inconsistency in the new graph: Let w be the head (resp. tail) of one edge in $E \setminus e$. Then $g(w) < g(p) < g(q)$ (resp. $g(w) > g(p) > g(q)$), therefore $g(w) < g(q)$ (resp. $g(w) > g(q)$), e.g. no new oriented cycle has been generated.   □

Conjecture 1. The result of merging all singular slopes does not depend on the order we merge.

Observe that no new singular slopes can appear after merging singular slopes, since the topological category of the rest of the vertices remains invariant. But, new structurally redundant edges can appear. Therefore, the removal of structurally redundant edges and merging singular slopes can be repeated until no more reductions are possible. Finally, surviving slopes are merged to saddles. This way, we obtain an irregular graph pyramid. On the top of the pyramid, only local maxima, minima and saddles can appear. Besides, the number of local maxima, minima and saddles of the original and reduced image coincide (see Fig. 4).

Note that after merging a singular slope p, no "corner" adjacent regions with same gray values could become adjacent later since it would mean that p would have at least two 0s in its LBP code. Besides, as a result after contracting plateaus, the reconstructed LBP code is defined for regions thus having as many bits as adjacent regions. Moreover, after merging all plateaus, the LBP codes are symmetric, and, the operations "image complement" and "LBP code" for regions are commutative. Finally, observe that after merging all singular slopes, each slope has at least two 1s and two 0s in its LBP code.

8   Reconstruction - Representative Image

In [17] and much earlier in [10], the authors leverage an inverse problem approach to show that it is possible to directly reconstruct the image content from Local Binary Patterns. For this aim, ascending and descending monotonic paths are considered. Their algorithm, MCA[1] assumes a minimum contrast of one between two successive pixels; and reconstructs some of the contrast lost in the LBP process. Fig. 5(b) illustrates MCA: after initializing the result with 0, neighbors which should be higher (red >) are repeatedly incremented until all inequalities

---

[1] Minimum Contrast Algorithm.

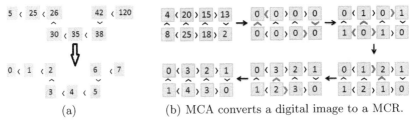

(a)   (b) MCA converts a digital image to a MCR.

Fig. 5. (a) A monotonic ascending path with same inequalities than a minimum contrast path. (b) A naive illustration of MCA.

are satisfied. This problem of reconstructing images from features is also dealt in [1] in which the image is encoded using LBD (Local Binary Descriptors) codes which are related but different to LBP codes.

After merging plateaus and singular slopes and removing structurally redundant edges, our image is decomposed in not-necessarily squared regions. In this section we show that the method explained in [17] can be translated in terms of primal and dual graphs. The key is that LBP categories of the MCR^2 must be equal to those of original image. For this, longest monotonically increasing (decreasing) paths from local minima (maxima) are computed.

Definition 1. *Given an image I, a monotonic ascending path is a sequence $p_1, p_2, \ldots, p_n$ of regions such that: (1) p_i is adjacent[3] to p_{i-1} and (2) $g(p_{i-1}) < g(p_i)$, for $1 < i \leq n$. Whenever $g(p_{i-1}) > g(p_i)$, for $1 < i \leq n$, the path is called monotonic descending (see Fig. 5(a)).*

To simulate MCA on our graph after contracting plateaus we initialize all vertices with 0. We then repeat following update operation for every oriented edge (u, v): replace $g(v)$ by the maximum of $g(v)$ and $g(u) + 1$ until no further change occurs. When starting with maxima we initialize with 255 and repeatedly replace $g(u)$ by the minimum of $g(u)$ and $g(v) - 1$. In Fig. 1(d) a naive example of the application of MCA is given.

This process opens a door to what we call *representative image*. Let I be an image and $LBP(I)$ its associated image of LBP codes. There is a whole set of images $\rho(I)$ for which the LBP codification is identical. Let $LBP_{min}^{-1}(I)$ be the image obtained after applying MCA on all monotonic ascending paths, and $LBP_{max}^{-1}(I)$ be the image obtained from all monotonic descending paths. Then both $LBP_{min}^{-1}(I)$ and $LBP_{max}^{-1}(I)$ can be used to represent $\rho(I)$. In particular $LBP_{min}^{-1}(I) \in \rho(I)$ and it is the smallest $LBP_{min}^{-1}(I) \leq J$ for all $J \in \rho(I)$. Analogously, $LBP_{max}^{-1}(I) \in \rho(I)$ and it is the largest $LBP_{max}^{-1}(I) \geq J$ for all $J \in \rho(I)$. Fig. 6 shows the original image I and the two representative images. Notice, how visually different these images from the same LBP class may look.

Proposition 4. *For any two images $I, J \in \rho(I)$, $I \neq J$ the property $LBP_{min}^{-1}(I) = LBP_{min}^{-1}(J)$ and $LBP_{max}^{-1}(I) = LBP_{max}^{-1}(J)$ holds.*

---

[2] Minimal Contrast Representative.

[3] In the image we assume 4-adjacency while edges encode adjacency in the graph.

Fig. 6. From left to right: The original image; Reconstructed image by MCA on monotonic ascending paths; Reconstructed image by MCA on monotonic descending paths.

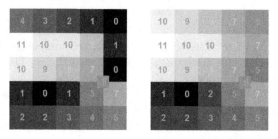

Fig. 7. Image A on the left is an output of the current MCA. Image B on the right has the property $LBP(B) = LBP(A)$, and also has a lower total contrast than A.

Proof. The direction of each edge (u, v) remains the same during the computation process of the representative images. Starting points for generating $LBP_{min}^{-1}(I)$ and $LBP_{max}^{-1}(I)$ are well defined, namely all local minima and all local maxima. The minimum contrast value of each region is defined by the longest distance from any reachable starting point, from which follows that the order of propagation of the minimum contrast values does not matter.   □

9   Conclusion, Experiments and Future Works

In this paper, a new codification of Local Binary Pattern is given using graph pyramids. For well-composed images, we demonstrate that from 4 neighbors' topological information, we can obtain 8 neighbors topological information what makes classical 8-neighbor LBP topologically redundant. By inserting a few dummy regions every image can be made well-composed! A sequence of merging regions and removal of edges obtains a "minimal" image I with the same topological information as the original. MCA is adapted[4] to obtain a minimum contrast image from I.

In Fig. 8, the whole process on two grayscale images is shown. After merging plateaus and removing redundant edges, (doubly-)singular slopes are merged successively. After each merging, redundant edges are removed. Finally, if slopes survive, they are merged with saddles. Therefore, only local maxima, minima and saddles survive on the top of the pyramid.

---

[4] A preliminary version of Section 8 was presented in [4].

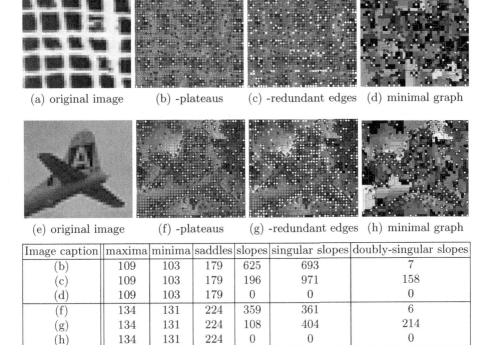

(a) original image   (b) -plateaus   (c) -redundant edges   (d) minimal graph

(e) original image   (f) -plateaus   (g) -redundant edges   (h) minimal graph

Image caption	maxima	minima	saddles	slopes	singular slopes	doubly-singular slopes
(b)	109	103	179	625	693	7
(c)	109	103	179	196	971	158
(d)	109	103	179	0	0	0
(f)	134	131	224	359	361	6
(g)	134	131	224	108	404	214
(h)	134	131	224	0	0	0

Fig. 8. The original images are reduced first by merging plateaus and second by removing structurally redundant edges. After removing all (doubly-)singular slopes, regular slopes are merged with saddles. Finally, only local maxima, minima and saddles survive.

"Truly" Minimum Contrast Image. The MCA can be improved to minimize the total contrast $\sum_{(u,v) \in E} g(u) - g(v)$. See, for example, Fig. 7. This approach may start by initializing the absolute minimum to 0 or an arbitrary vertex to an arbitrary value, and subsequently use the sign of the contrast associated at the edges to compute the minimal contrast representative.

Image Segmentation. Modifications made to the proposed approach in form of attributed vertices and weighted edges allow the definition of texture aware image segmentation algorithms. A first attempt made in this direction was presented in [19].

Towards 3D. Several researchers have been trying to extend the LBP codification from 2D plane to 3D volume (see, for example, [2,14]); however, it is not so straightforward as it appears at first glance. In our case the notion of well-composed images and irregular graph pyramids also works for 3D images. Characterizations of pixels using LBP codes not only depend on the number of connected components but also on the number of holes (1-dimensional homology classes).

Shape LBP. Textures have particular shapes. The idea is to label the darts as 0 or 1 in the dual graph depending on concavity-convexity of the boundary of a region. Computing LBP codification using concavity-convexity rule could help to recognize shapes.

References

1. D'Angelo, E., Jacques, L., Alahi, A., Vandergheynst, P.: From Bits to Images: Inversion of Local Binary Descriptors. IEEE Transactions on Pattern Analysis and Machine Intelligence **36**(5), 874–887 (2014)
2. Fehr, J., Burkhardt, H.: 3D rotation invariant local binary patterns. In: Proc. of 19th Int. Conf. on Pattern Recognition (ICPR 2008), pp. 1–4 (2008)
3. Gonzalez-Diaz, R., Ion, A., Iglesias-Ham, M., Kropatsch, W.G.: Invariant representative cocycles of cohomology generators using irregular graph pyramids. Computer Vision and Image Understanding **115**(7), 1011–1022 (2011)
4. Gonzalez-Diaz, R., Kropatsch, W.G., Cerman, M., Lamar, J.: Characterizing configurations of critical points through LBP. In: Int. Conf. on Computational Topology in Image Context (CTIC 2014). Extended Abstract. http://www.prip.tuwien.ac.at/people/krw/more/papers/2014/CTIC/Gonzalez2014b.pdf
5. Guo, G., Jones, M.J.: Iris extraction based on intensity gradient and texture difference. In: Proc. of the 2008 IEEE Workshop on Applications of Computer Vision (WACV 2008), pp. 1–6. IEEE Computer Society, Washington, DC (2008)
6. Hadid, A., Pietikäinen, M., Ahonen, T.: A discriminative feature space for detecting and recognizing faces. In: Proc. of the 2004 IEEE Computer Society Conf. on Computer Vision and Pattern Recognition (CVPR 2004), pp. 797–804. IEEE Computer Society, Washington, DC (2004)
7. Kropatsch, W.G.: Building irregular pyramids by dual-graph contraction. IEEE Proc. on Vision Image and Signal Processing **142**(6), 366–374 (1995)
8. Kropatsch, W.G., Haxhimusa, Y., Pizlo, Z., Langs, G.: Vision pyramids that do not grow too high. Pattern Recognition Letters **26**(3), 319–337 (2005)
9. Latecki, L., Eckhardt, U., Rosenfeld, A.: Well-composed sets. Computer Vision and Image Understanding **61**, 70–83 (1995)
10. Lindahl, T.: Study of Local Binary Patterns. Master's thesis, Linköpings Tekniska Högskola (2007)
11. Nguyen, D.T., Ogunbona, P.O., Li, W.: A Novel Shape-based Non-redundant Local Binary Pattern Descriptor for Object Detection. Pattern Recognition **46**(5), 1485–1500 (2013)
12. Ojala, T., Pietikainen, M., Harwood, D.: A comparative study of texture measures with classification based on featured distributions. Pattern Recognition **29**(1), 51–59 (1996)
13. Ojala, T., Pietikainen, M., Maenaa, T.: Multiresolution Gray-scale and Rotation Invariant Texture Classification with Local Binary Patterns. IEEE TPAMI **24**(7), 971–987 (2002)
14. Paulhac, L., Makris, P., Ramel, J.-Y.: Comparison between 2D and 3D local binary pattern methods for characterisation of three-dimensional textures. In: Campilho, A., Kamel, M.S. (eds.) ICIAR 2008. LNCS, vol. 5112, pp. 670–679. Springer, Heidelberg (2008)
15. Pietikäinen, M., Hadid, A., Zhao, G., Ahonen, T.: Computer Vision Using Local Binary Patterns, vol. 40. Springer Verlag (2011)

16. Shan, C.: Learning Local Binary Patterns for Gender Classification on Real-world Face Images. Pattern Recognition Letters **33**(4), 431–437 (2012)
17. Waller, B.M., Nixon, M.S., Carter, J.N.: Image reconstruction from local binary patterns. In: IEEE proc. of the 2013 Int. Conf. on Signal-Image Technology & Internet-Based Systems (SITIS), pp. 118–123 (2013)
18. LBP 2014 Workshop on Computer Vision With Local Binary Pattern Variants. https://sites.google.com/site/lbp2014ws/
19. Cerman, M.: Structurally Correct Image Segmentation using Local Binary Patterns and the Combinatorial Pyramid. Technical Report 133, Vienna University of Technology, Pattern Recognition and Image Processing (PRIP) Group (2015). ftp://ftp.prip.tuwien.ac.at/pub/publications/trs/tr

Fusion of Intra- and Inter-modality Algorithms for Face-Sketch Recognition

Christian Galea[(✉)] and Reuben A. Farrugia

Department of Communications and Computer Engineering, Faculty of ICT,
University of Malta, Msida, Malta
{christian.galea.09,reuben.farrugia}@um.edu.mt

Abstract. Identifying and apprehending suspects by matching sketches created from eyewitness and victim descriptions to mugshot photos is a slow process since law enforcement agencies lack automated methods to perform this task. This paper attempts to tackle this problem by combining Eigentransformation, a global intra-modality approach, with the Eigenpatches local intra-modality technique. These algorithms are then fused with an inter-modality method called Histogram of Averaged Orientation Gradients (HAOG). Simulation results reveal that the intra- and inter- modality algorithms considered in this work provide complementary information since not only does fusion of the global and local intra-modality methods yield better performance than either of the algorithms individually, but fusion with the inter-modality approach yields further improvement to achieve retrieval rates of 94.05% at Rank-100 on 420 photo-sketch pairs. This performance is achieved at Rank-25 when filtering of the gallery using demographic information is carried out.

Keywords: Face recognition · Synthesis · Intra-modality · Inter-modality · Hand-drawn sketches

1 Introduction

Recollections of eye-witnesses and victims are important to assist law enforcement agencies in identifying and apprehending suspects, especially when there is lack of evidence at the crime scene [5,10]. Facial composite sketches created using witness descriptions are then disseminated to the public so that any persons recognising the suspect in the sketch may come forward with information that will hopefully lead to an arrest. However, this process is time-consuming, not guaranteed to be successful and inefficient since resources such as mugshot photo galleries available at law enforcement agencies cannot be utilised [10]. Hence, automated methods are required to match sketches with photos.

Several algorithms have been proposed in the literature for this task, which can be categorised as either intra-modality or inter-modality approaches [2]. Algorithms belonging in the first category attempt to reduce the modality gap by transforming a photo to a sketch (or vice versa) so that all images to be compared

© Springer International Publishing Switzerland 2015
G. Azzopardi and N. Petkov (Eds.): CAIP 2015, Part II, LNCS 9257, pp. 700–711, 2015.
DOI: 10.1007/978-3-319-23117-4_60

lie within the same modality. Any kind of face recogniser can then be applied to match the synthesised pseudo-sketches (photos) with original sketches (photos). However, these algorithms have been criticised for being potentially more complex than the task of face recognition itself [2,4]. On the other hand, inter-modality approaches perform face sketch recognition by extracting modality-invariant features to compare sketches with photos directly.

To the best of the authors' knowledge, even though numerous algorithms have been proposed for both types of approaches, neither the fusion of intra-modality methods nor the fusion of both intra- and inter-modality algorithms has been considered for photo-sketch recognition. In this paper, the combination of a global intra-modality method with a local intra-modality method is performed along with the fusion of these methods with a reportedly robust inter-modality technique. It is shown that these approaches provide complementary information to each other and provide superior performance when combined, across almost all ranks especially at lower ones.

The rest of this paper is organised as follows: the related work in the area of matching sketches with photos is presented in Section 2 followed by a description of the proposed method in Section 3. An overview of the experimental protocol used and the evaluation of the proposed method are given in Section 4. Conclusions and ideas for future work are finally outlined in Section 5.

2   Related Work

Several algorithms have been proposed for matching sketches with photos, although most can be categorised as being intra-modality techniques. One of the first such methods was the Eigentransformation algorithm [14], a global method based on Eigenfaces [15] which synthesises whole faces. A local-based intra-modality method was later proposed by the authors of [11], based on the Locally Linear Embedding (LLE) manifold learning technique such that patches are reconstructed using a linear combination of neighbouring patches. Kernel-based non-linear discriminant analysis (KNDA) is then used to match a probe sketch with the pseudo-sketches. This approach was improved in [16] by modelling spatial relationships among patches by a multi-scale Markov Random Fields (MRF) model. Patches were extended to encompass entire facial components in the Embedded Hidden Markov Model (E-HMM) method proposed in [3], where non-linear mapping between photo/sketch pairs is learned using HMMs for each component. Multiple models are obtained and fused using selective ensemble to improve the system's generalisation ability and thus enable the synthesis of more accurate pseudo-sketches. Recognition between probe sketches and pseudo-sketches is performed using the Principal Component Analysis (PCA) classifier.

Although most approaches have focused on reducing the modality gap, inter-modality methods are being given more attention lately especially by the Biometrics Research Group at Michigan State University [4,7,9,10]. These approaches are based on the extraction of Multi-scale Local Binary Pattern (MLBP) and

Scale-Invariant Feature Transform (SIFT) descriptors from patches to directly match sketches and photos in terms of their feature representations. The recently proposed FaceSketchID system [10] combines the component-based approach proposed in [4], in which MLBP codes were extracted for each facial component, with the holistic-based heterogeneous face recognition algorithm in [9] to obtain a system with performance that was shown to exceed that of either of the two techniques individually. In other words, the fusion of local and global inter-modality algorithms yielded improvements in performance. The authors of [8] also attained performance gains with the fusion of two inter-modality approaches, namely using 'common' and 'direct' matching of multi-scale SIFT descriptors. Fusion with a commercial face recogniser yielded further improvement.

The work presented in this paper differs from the related work since (i) a local intra-modality algorithm based on the computation of a global intra-modality approach on a local level is implemented, (ii) the fusion of two intra-modality methods is investigated, and (iii) the fusion of intra- and inter-modality approaches is also analysed. To the best of the authors' knowledge, these contributions have never been investigated in previous works.

3   Proposed Approach

The proposed approach combines the scores output by three algorithms, namely the Eigentransformation [14] and Eigenpatches intra-modality techniques and the Histogram of Averaged Orientation Gradients (HAOG) [2] inter-modality descriptor. The system flow diagram is shown in Figure 1. Both Eigentransformation and Eigenpatches use a set of training photo/sketch pairs to synthesise a pseudo-sketch or pseudo-photo, while the HAOG method extracts the inter-modality features for each image in the test set to be compared. The synthesised pseudo-sketches (pseudo-photos) derived from gallery photos (probe sketches) are compared to probe sketches (gallery photos) using the PCA face recogniser while the Chi-Square (χ^2) histogram matching method is used to evaluate the distance between the HAOG descriptors of probe sketches and those of the gallery photos. The resulting scores are then normalized using the *Normalisation module* which are finally fused with the *Fusion module*. A summary of each of these algorithms will now be given.

3.1   Intra-modality Approaches

In the traditional Eigenfaces approach [15], face photos are reconstructed by using a weighted summation of a set of eigenvectors $\mathbf{U}_p$ representing faces, consequently called Eigenfaces, as follows:

$$\boldsymbol{P}_r = \mathbf{U}_p \boldsymbol{b}_p \tag{1}$$

where $\boldsymbol{P}_r$ is a column vector representing the reconstructed face photo and $\boldsymbol{b}_p$ is a vector containing the projection coefficients in the eigenvector space. As demonstrated in [14], (1) may be rewritten as follows:

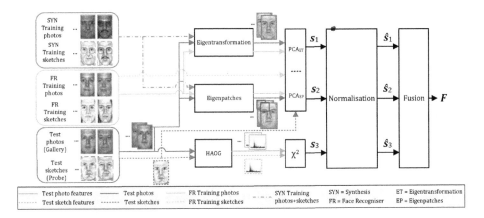

Fig. 1. System flow diagram of the proposed approach, for photo-to-sketch synthesis. Photos and sketches simply switch roles for sketch-to-photo synthesis.

$$P_r = \bar{P} + \sum_{i=1}^{M} c_p^{\{i\}} \Phi^{\{i\}} \qquad (2)$$

where $\bar{P}$ is the mean face computed over M training face images, $\Phi^{\{i\}} = P^{\{i\}} - \bar{P}$ and $c_p^{\{i\}}$ is a column vector of dimension M representing the contribution of the ith training image $P^{\{i\}}$ in the reconstruction of a test face image computed according to [14]. Hence, (2) shows that a reconstructed photo can be approximated to the original image using a weighted linear addition of the training images [14]. Since a photo and corresponding sketch should also be similar in terms of structure, (2) may be modified such that the training photos $P^{\{i\}}$ are replaced by the corresponding training sketches $S^{\{i\}}$, as follows:

$$S_r = \bar{S} + \sum_{i=1}^{M} c_p^{\{i\}} \Psi^{\{i\}} \qquad (3)$$

where S_r is the reconstructed sketch, $\bar{S}$ is the mean sketch, $\Psi^{\{i\}} = S^{\{i\}} - \bar{S}$ and $S^{\{i\}}$ is a column vector representing the ith sketch. This is based on the hypothesis that if a photo contributes more weight to a reconstructed face photo, then the corresponding sketch will also contribute more weight to the reconstructed sketch [14].

The Eigentransformation approach has recently been extended to operate on local patches by the authors of [1] for the area of face super-resolution. This approach may be applied for sketch (or photo) synthesis by synthesising each patch in an image (rather than the whole image) and can be achieved by learning the optimal linear combination of patches found in the same local area of images in the training set. Formally, for each of the n patches in an image, (3) can be rewritten as follows:

$$S_r^{\{j\}} = \bar{S}^{\{j\}} + \sum_{i=1}^{M} c_p^{\{i,j\}} \Psi^{\{i,j\}} \quad \text{for } j = 1, 2, \dots, n \ . \qquad (4)$$

where $\mathbf{S}_r^{\{j\}}$ is the jth patch of the synthesised sketch, $\mathbf{\Psi}^{\{i,j\}} = \mathbf{S}^{\{i,j\}} - \bar{\mathbf{S}}^{\{j\}}$, $\mathbf{S}^{\{i,j\}}$ is the ith training sketch of patch j, $\bar{\mathbf{S}}^{\{j\}}$ is the jth mean patch and $\mathbf{c}_p^{\{i,j\}}$ are the reconstruction weights for the jth patch derived using the ith training face image. To the best of the authors' knowledge, this is the first use of Eigenpatches for face-sketch synthesis. Similar to other approaches involving patch-based operations, the overlap of patches with their neighbours is arbitrarily fixed at half the patch size and a simple averaging operation is done on overlapping areas to combine patches together.

For both methods, the role of sketches and photos is simply interchanged for pseudo-photo synthesis. Although any face recogniser can then be used to match the pseudo-sketches (photos) with the original sketches (photos), PCA (Eigenfaces method) [15] is implemented due to its widespread use in the literature for intra-modality methods. Hence, photo and sketch subspaces are learned and the face images to be compared are projected into these subspaces, similar to the approach in [14].

3.2   Inter-modality Approach

The authors of [2] observed that effective inter-modality matching of sketches with photos may be obtained by extracting features only from those regions exhibiting the smallest amount of modality gap, namely those corresponding to coarse texture which represent boundaries of facial components critical in representing face images. Using a histogram whose bins represent orientation gradients for each patch, coarse textures are emphasised by accumulating squared magnitudes in those bins corresponding to the orientations of the patch being considered. In other words, more weighting is applied to those regions having high magnitudes when constructing a histogram of orientation gradients. The histograms of each patch are concatenated to yield the final HAOG descriptor and comparison of histograms is performed by finding the χ^2 distance, which is also the match score between two face images. More information on the HAOG descriptor is provided in [2].

3.3   Fusion

Fusion of the two intra-modality algorithms together and with the HAOG algorithm is performed at the matching score level, by first normalising the scores output from face recogniser using min-max normalisation. If a gallery contains a total of T subjects, then there will be T scores for each probe sketch representing the distance between the probe and all the photos in the gallery. The normalisation of these scores is achieved using min-max normalisation:

$$\hat{s} = \frac{(s - min)}{(max - min)} \tag{5}$$

where s is a vector of dimension T containing the scores output by a face-sketch recognition algorithm for matching a probe with the T gallery images, $\hat{s}$ contains the corresponding normalised scores, and min and max represent the minimum and maximum values of s, respectively [13].

The sum-of-scores method is then used to fuse the normalised scores together:

$$F = \sum_{k=1}^{N} \hat{s}_k \qquad (6)$$

where $\hat{s}_k$ is the score of kth face recognition method, N represents the number of intra- and inter- modality methods considered, and F is the final similarity score between a sketch (pseudo-photo) and the T pseudo-sketches (photos) [13]. Sum-of-scores fusion and min-max normalisation were chosen since they have been shown to provide some of the best results for fusion of multi-biometric systems in [6] and [13].

4 Results

The algorithms described in Section 3 are evaluated on the Chinese University of Hong Kong Face Sketch FERET (CUFSF) database [17] [1]. This database contains pairs of photos and viewed hand-drawn sketches of subjects in the Color FERET database [12]. In this paper, 842 subjects are considered.

For the intra-modality approaches, training is required for the transformation and face recognition stages. An approach similar to that used in [16] is adopted, namely $M = 211$ subjects are first used to train the transformation algorithm being considered (Eigentransformation or Eigenpatches). Another 211 subjects are then selected to train the PCA face recogniser, where their photos (sketches) are used along with the corresponding synthesised pseudo-photos (sketches) derived from the sketches (photos) for sketch-to-photo synthesis (photo-to-sketch synthesis). The remaining 420 subjects are then used for testing, i.e. $T = 420$. In addition, the performance of Eigenpatches for varying patch sizes is evaluated to determine the optimal patch size. Patch overlap is set to be half the patch size in all cases. For the HAOG algorithm, the parameters are set to those reported in [2].

Photos and sketches in the testing set form the gallery and probe sets, respectively. For photo-to-sketch synthesis, photos in the gallery are transformed into pseudo-sketches and matched with each sketch in the probe set. For sketch-to-photo synthesis, probe sketches are transformed to pseudo-photos and then matched with photos in the gallery.

Since PCA is used as a face recogniser in the intra-modality approaches, recognition using PCA only (without performing synthesis) is also carried out as a baseline performance measure, where each sketch in the probe set is directly matched with photos in the gallery. For all face recognition experiments carried out with PCA, the distance between the resultant vectors of the images to be compared represents the match score between face images and is found using $L2$-norms (i.e. Euclidean distance). In addition, each image was converted to

---

[1] Available at: http://mmlab.ie.cuhk.edu.hk/archive/cufsf/

grayscale, aligned using eye and mouth coordinates such that they are at fixed locations in all images considered and cropped to the same size of 300×190 pixels.

The subjects in the Color FERET dataset were pre-labelled with gender and race information, enabling filtering of the gallery based on the characteristics of the probe sketch. For example, if the sketch depicts a female subject, then all male subjects can be eliminated from the gallery. Statistics of the demographic distribution for the subjects considered in this study are shown in Table 1.

While face recognisers are typically measured at Rank-1 matching accuracy, the best match is often not the required suspect due to inaccuracies provided by a witness in describing facial details [4,5]. As a result, the top 100 matches are typically examined with equal importance in forensic investigations and therefore the performance of an automatic system is recommended to be measured at around Rank-100 [4]. Graphs depicting the cumulative rank retrieval rates are thus shown to evaluate the ability of the algorithms in identifying persons.

For brevity, 'photo-to-sketch' synthesis will be denoted as 'P2S' and 'sketch-to-photo' synthesis will be denoted as 'S2P' in the remainder of this paper.

Table 1. Demographic statistics. Labels used are the same as those given in the Color FERET dataset.

Gender		Race	
Male	57.14%	White	63.33%
Female	42.86%	Asian	15.00%
		Black-or-African-American	9.29%
		Hispanic	6.19%
		Asian-Middle-Eastern	4.52%
		Pacific-Islander	0.95%
		Asian-Southern	0.24%
		Other	0.48%

4.1 Eigenpatches Patch Size

The rank retrieval rates using different values of the patch size are given in Figure 2. Patch sizes were set to be equal to $2^p \times 2^p$ for $p = 3, 4, \ldots, 7$. Firstly, it can be observed that P2S synthesis is superior to S2P synthesis for all patch sizes at all ranks. This is likely due to the fact that in transforming photos to sketches, a large amount of information is being compressed into a smaller representation since photos tend to be more complex and therefore contain more information. This is a more stable operation than attempting to expand a small representation into a larger one, as in the case of S2P synthesis [14]. As can also be observed from Figure 3, it is evident that S2P synthesis is unable to recover a face photo adequately. It should also be noted that the performance tends to improve with increasing patch size. From empirical observations, low patch sizes resulted in high amounts of noise which decreased with larger patch sizes. In addition, at

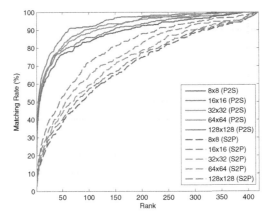

Fig. 2. Recognition rate for varying patch sizes of the Eigenpatches algorithm, using the Color FERET/CUFSF datasets

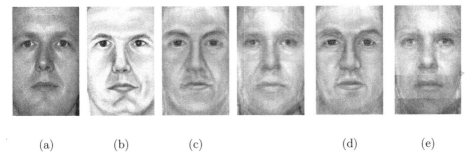

(a)   (b)   (c)   (d)   (e)

Fig. 3. Synthesised images of one subject in the Color FERET/CUFSF datasets: (a) Original photo, (b) Original sketch, (c) Eigentransformation P2S, (d) Eigentransformation S2P, (e) Eigenpatches P2S, (f) Eigenpatches S2P

the largest patch size of 128×128 pixels, the patches roughly overlap with the individual facial components. Hence, synthesis is virtually being done for each component and is therefore a contributor to increased quality of the synthesised images. Based on these observations, Eigenpatches with a patch size of 128×128 pixels is used for the remainder of the experiments.

4.2   Matching Rate

This section investigates the performance of the independent intra- and inter-modality methods mentioned in this paper and a combination of these methods. The direct use of PCA (without performing synthesis) is used as a baseline. The Rank retrieval rates are shown in Figure 4 and Table 2. It should be noted that all algorithms outperform the baseline face recogniser at all ranks. This clearly indicates the need of using approaches designed specifically for person identification via matching of sketches with photos. In particular, the fact that PCA is better

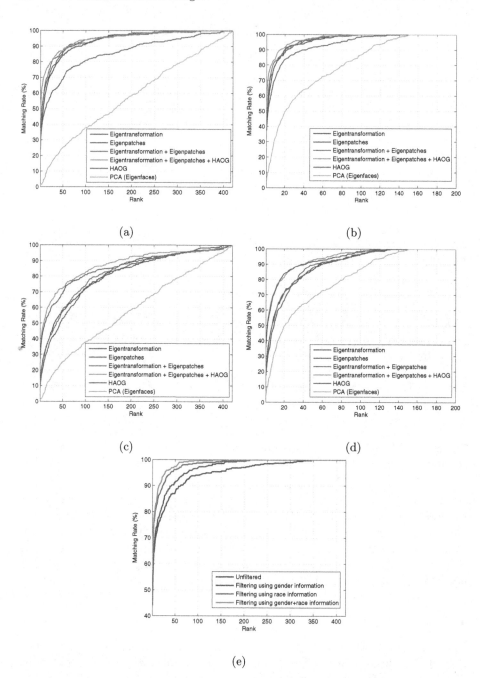

Fig. 4. Matching performance for: (a) P2S synthesis, (b) P2S synthesis with filtering, (c) S2P synthesis, (d) S2P synthesis with filtering, (e) Filtering the gallery using different types of demographic information for P2S synthesis of the proposed method (using the fusion of Eigentransformation, Eigenpatches and HAOG).

Table 2. Rank retrieval rates for the algorithms considered when evaluated on the CUFSF dataset, without demographic filtering; ET = Eigentransformation, EP = Eigenpatches. The best result for each rank is highlighted in boldface.

Metric	Matching Rate (%) at Rank-N					
	Rank-1	Rank-10	Rank-50	Rank-100	Rank-150	Rank-200
PCA	0.71	5.48	25.00	37.62	46.43	58.57
HAOG	27.14	48.10	68.81	80.95	84.76	89.05
ET (P2S)	24.05	56.90	84.29	91.43	96.19	97.38
ET (S2P)	9.29	30.48	57.62	72.38	82.14	85.71
EP (P2S)	29.05	62.86	86.19	91.90	**96.90**	97.62
EP (S2P)	8.57	26.19	52.86	72.14	81.19	87.86
ET + EP (P2S)	26.90	64.52	**87.38**	94.04	95.71	**98.57**
ET + EP (S2P)	8.81	29.05	58.33	73.81	83.10	89.29
ET + EP + HAOG (P2S)	**44.05**	**71.90**	**87.38**	**94.05**	95.48	97.14
ET + EP + HAOG (S2P)	24.52	51.43	72.14	82.38	88.10	92.62

able to match synthesised images indicates that the intra-modality approaches are successfully reducing the modality gap between photos and sketches.

The Eigentransformation and Eigenpatches intra-modality approaches yield superior performance to the HAOG inter-modality approach for P2S synthesis, across almost all ranks. For S2P synthesis, the intra-modality approaches are inferior to HAOG especially for Ranks below 150. It can also be noticed that Eigenpatches typically achieves higher matching rates at lower ranks (until roughly Rank-50) for P2S synthesis. This indicates that Eigenpatches is able to construct images which are able to discriminate between persons more reliably due to the utilisation of local features, while Eigentransformation also encodes spatial information which enables it to perform better at higher ranks when faces are being compared at a more global level.

Fusion of the two intra-modality algorithms yields noticeable improvements at most ranks. Even in cases where the performance is less than the best performance of either of the intra-modality algorithms, generally the difference is only marginal and is better than one of the intra-modality algorithms. This holds for both S2P and P2S synthesis and indicates that the two approaches contain complementary information which can improve performance. Given that the Eigentransformation algorithm can be considered as a holistic algorithm whereas the Eigenpatches algorithm can be viewed as a local descriptor, this result is in line with the observations reported in [10] where the fusion of holistic- and component-based inter-modality algorithms yielded the best performance.

Further improvements in matching rates can be achieved with the fusion of the HAOG algorithm. In fact, this yields the best performance of all algorithms considered at almost all ranks, especially at lower ranks (roughly below Rank-100). The gain is more substantial when the intra-modality algorithms using P2S synthesis are fused, likely due to the better performance of these algorithms with respect to when they are used for S2P synthesis. These results not only demonstrate that Eigentransformation, Eigenpatches and HAOG contain complementary information which can be exploited for increased matching rates, but they are also indicative that the combination of both intra- and inter-modality algorithms may be the ideal approach for matching sketches with photographs rather than using *either* intra-modality algorithms *or* inter-modality algorithms.

Filtering using demographic information yields substantial improvements for all algorithms considered. In addition, as demonstrated in Figure 4e, filtering with race information provides better performance than with gender information. For example, the Rank-1 retrieval rate of the proposed approach improves from 44.05% to 46.43% using gender information and to 55.71% using race information. This is likely due to the fact that subjects are distributed more evenly in terms of gender. This observation was also reported in other works in the literature, e.g. in [7].

5   Conclusion

This work presented the use of Eigenpatches for intra-modality sketch-to-photo and photo-to-sketch applications. It was demonstrated that Eigenpatches performs similarly to Eigentransformation except at lower ranks for photo-to-sketch synthesis, where it is superior. This indicates that Eigenpatches is able to synthesise images having more accurate local structures which are better able to discriminate between persons. It was also observed that photo-to-sketch synthesis generally provides superior results over both sketch-to-photo synthesis and the HAOG inter-modality approach.

Furthermore, it was shown that the fusion of intra- and inter-modality algorithms yields the best performance across virtually all ranks. This indicates that not only do the local and global intra-modality methods and the inter-modality method considered in this paper provide complementary information, but their combination provides the best performance for matching sketches with photos.

Use of demographic information to filter the gallery yielded substantial improvements to result in a Rank-25 retrieval rate of 94.05%. Future work includes the suppression of blocking artefacts created due to patch averaging for images synthesised with Eigenpatches and the use of software-generated composites which are widely used in forensics.

Acknowledgments. The research work disclosed in this publication is partly funded by the Malta Government Scholarship Scheme. The authors would like to thank the Malta Police Force for their assistance in this research.

References

1. Chen, H.Y., Chien, S.Y.: Eigen-patch: position-patch based face hallucination using eigen transformation. In: IEEE International Conference on Multimedia and Expo, pp. 1–6 (2014)
2. Galoogahi, H.K., Sim, T.: Inter-modality face sketch recognition. In: IEEE International Conference on Multimedia and Expo, pp. 224–229 (2012)

3. Gao, X., Zhong, J., Li, J., Tian, C.: Face Sketch Synthesis Algorithm Based on E-HMM and Selective Ensemble. IEEE Transactions on Circuits and Systems for Video Technology **18**(4), 487–496 (2008)
4. Han, H., Klare, B.F., Bonnen, K., Jain, A.K.: Matching composite sketches to face photos: A component-based approach. IEEE Transactions on Information Forensics and Security **8**(1), 191–204 (2013)
5. Jain, A.K., Klare, B., Park, U.: Face matching and retrieval in forensics applications. IEEE MultiMedia **19**(1), 20–28 (2012)
6. Jain, A.K., Nandakumar, K., Ross, A.: Score normalization in multimodal biometric systems. Pattern Recognition **38**(12), 2270–2285 (2005)
7. Klare, B., Li, Z., Jain, A.K.: Matching forensic sketches to mug shot photos. IEEE Transactions on Pattern Analysis and Machine Intelligence **33**(3), 639–646 (2011)
8. Klare, B., Jain, A.K.: Sketch-to-photo matching: a feature-based approach. In: Proceedings of the SPIE Conference on Biometric Technology for Human Identification VII, vol. 7667, pp. 766702–766702-10 (2010)
9. Klare, B.F., Jain, A.K.: Heterogeneous face recognition using kernel prototype similarities. IEEE Transactions on Pattern Analysis and Machine Intelligence **35**(6), 1410–1422 (2013)
10. Klum, S.J., Han, H., Klare, B., Jain, A.K.: The FaceSketchID System: Matching Facial Composites to Mugshots. Tech. Rep. MSU-CSE-14-6, Michigan State University (2014)
11. Liu, Q., Tang, X., Jin, H., Lu, H., Ma, S.: A nonlinear approach for face sketch synthesis and recognition. In: IEEE Computer Society Conference on Computer Vision and Pattern Recognition, vol. 1, pp. 1005–1010 (2005)
12. National Institute of Standards and Technology (NIST): The Color FERET Database version 2. http://www.nist.gov/itl/iad/ig/colorferet.cfm
13. Snelick, R., Indovina, M., Yen, J., Mink, A.: Multimodal biometrics: issues in design and testing. In: Proceedings of the 5th International Conference on Multimodal Interfaces, ICMI 2003, pp. 68–72 (2003)
14. Tang, X., Wang, X.: Face sketch recognition. IEEE Transactions on Circuits and Systems for Video Technology **14**(1), 50–57 (2004)
15. Turk, M., Pentland, A.: Eigenfaces for recognition. Journal of Cognitive Neuroscience **3**(1), 71–86 (1991)
16. Wang, X., Tang, X.: Face photo-sketch synthesis and recognition. IEEE Transactions on Pattern Analysis and Machine Intelligence **31**(11), 1955–1967 (2009)
17. Zhang, W., Wang, X., Tang, X.: Coupled information-theoretic encoding for face photo-sketch recognition. In: 2011 IEEE Conference on Computer Vision and Pattern Recognition (CVPR), pp. 513–520 (2011)

View-Independent Enhanced 3D Reconstruction of Non-rigidly Deforming Objects

Hassan Afzal[1]([⊠]), Djamila Aouada[1], François Destelle[2],
Bruno Mirbach[3], and Björn Ottersten[1]

[1] Interdisciplinary Centre for Security, Reliability and Trust, University of
Luxembourg, 4, rue Alphonse Weicker, L-2721 Luxembourg, Luxembourg
{hassan.afzal,djamila.aouada,bjorn.ottersten}@uni.lu
[2] Insight: Centre for Data Analytics, Dublin City University, Dublin, Ireland
francois.destelle@dcu.ie
[3] Advanced Engineering, IEE S.A., Contern, Luxembourg
bruno.mirbach@iee.lu

Abstract. In this paper, we target enhanced 3D reconstruction of
non-rigidly deforming objects based on a view-independent surface representation with an automated recursive filtering scheme. This work
improves upon the *KinectDeform* algorithm which we recently proposed.
KinectDeform uses an implicit view-dependent volumetric *truncated
signed distance function (TSDF)* based surface representation. The
view-dependence makes its pipeline complex by requiring surface prediction and extraction steps based on camera's field of view. This paper
proposes to use an explicit projection-based *Moving Least Squares (MLS)*
surface representation from point-sets. Moreover, the empirical weighted
filtering scheme in *KinectDeform* is replaced by an automated fusion
scheme based on a *Kalman filter*. We analyze the performance of the
proposed algorithm both qualitatively and quantitatively and show that
it is able to produce enhanced and feature preserving 3D reconstructions.

1 Introduction

Data acquired by commodity 3D sensing technologies is noisy and of limited
resolution. This limits its direct use in applications ranging from environment
mapping for mobile autonomous systems and preservation of historical sites,
to human activity and gesture recognition for virtual communications, assistive
robotics, security and surveillance.

Research has been carried out to build techniques around commodity 3D
sensing technologies to accurately reconstruct captured 3D objects or scenes by
relying on training data or use of templates such as in the case of [13] and [25] or
by fusing a specified number of captured frames to produce a single high quality
3D reconstruction [19]. *KinectFusion* and similar techniques provide an effective
and efficient mechanism to recursively fuse and filter the incoming information to
produce enhanced 3D reconstructions of the environment [15], [17]. The downside
of these techniques is that they lack the ability to tackle the non-rigid behavior

G. Azzopardi and N. Petkov (Eds.): CAIP 2015, Part II, LNCS 9257, pp. 712–724, 2015.
DOI: 10.1007/978-3-319-23117-4_61

of deforming objects [5], [16], [20]. Some of these techniques. e.g., for human face modeling and full-body 3D reconstruction, are restricted to very limited non-rigid behavior and require subjects to remain as rigid as possible [14], [7], [21]. To tackle these issues researchers have proposed other methods such as [27], [26] and [12], which use high quality pre-built templates or construct them as a first step and use them to track the non-rigidities and provide accurate and complete 3D recontructions.

Recently, researchers have focused on tracking highly non-rigid behaviors of deforming objects without the knowledge of any prior shape or reference [18], [8], for the purposes of, for example, depth video enhancement [3]. In our previous work, known as *KinectDeform*, we showed that a non-rigid registration method can be used in a recursive pipeline similar to *KinectFusion* to produce enhanced 3D reconstructions of deforming objects [2]. The non-rigid registration step in the pipeline is followed by surface filtering or fusion using volumetric *truncated signed distance function* (TSDF) based implicit surface representation. This surface representation scheme is view-dependent and requires organized point clouds as input. Since non-rigid registration deforms and hence destroys the organization of input point clouds, an expensive data-reorganization step in the form of meshing and ray-casting is required before surface fusion. Moreover, for fusion, a weighted average scheme is used for which parameters are chosen empirically for each iteration. Ray-casting is used again to extract the resulting point-based surface from fused *TSDF* volumes after every iteration.

In this paper, we propose a method called *View-Independent KinectDeform (VI-Kinect-Deform)* which improves upon the *KinectDeform* algorithm by replacing the volumetric *TSDF* based view-dependent surface representation with an octree-based view-independent and explicit surface representation using *Point Set Surfaces* based on the method of *Moving Least Squares* [4]. This results in a simplified version of *KinectDeform* with the removal of an expensive data reorganization step. Moreover, we also improve upon the fusion mechanism by proposing an automated recursive filtering scheme using a simple *Kalman filter* [10]. Due to our explicit surface representation, surface prediction step at the end of each iteration is also not required resulting in a simpler algorithm. We compare the results of *VI-KinectDeform* with those of *KinectDeform* using non-rigidly deforming objects and show that for the same number of iterations *VI-KinectDeform* produces stable and more accurate 3D reconstructions.

The remainder of this paper is organized as follows: Section 2 describes the problem at hand and gives a background on the surface representation and recursive filtering method proposed in *KinectDeform*. This is followed by an introduction to the *Point Set Surfaces* based on *MLS*. Section 3 details the proposed approach. Section 4 presents qualitative and quantitative evaluation of results of the proposed method and compares them with the results of *KinectDeform* and other methods. This is followed by a conclusion in Sect. 5.

2   Background

2.1   Problem Formulation and KinectDeform

At each discrete time-step $i \in \mathbb{N}$, a static or moving camera acquires a point cloud $\mathcal{V}_i$ containing a number of points $U \in \mathbb{N}$. Note that $\mathcal{V}_i$ may be organized or unorganized. The point-set $\{\mathbf{p}_j\}$ in $\mathcal{V}_i$, where $\mathbf{p}_j \in \mathbb{R}^3$ and $j \in \{1, \ldots, U\}$, approximates the underlying surface of deformable objects in camera's field of view. Considering a sequence of N such acquired point clouds $\{\mathcal{V}_0, \mathcal{V}_1, \ldots, \mathcal{V}_{N-1}\}$, each acquisition $\mathcal{V}_i$ is associated with the previous acquisition $\mathcal{V}_{i-1}$ via [2]:

$$\mathcal{V}_i = h_i(\mathcal{V}_{i-1}) + \mathcal{E}_i, \tag{1}$$

where $h_i(\cdot)$ is the non-rigid deformation which deforms $\mathcal{V}_{i-1}$ to $\mathcal{V}_i$, and $\mathcal{E}_i$ represents the sensor noise and sampling errors. The problem at hand is therefore to reduce $\mathcal{E}_i$ for $i > 0$, to recover an enhanced sequence $\{\mathcal{V}_0^{f'}, \mathcal{V}_1^{f'}, \ldots, \mathcal{V}_{N-1}^{f'}\}$ starting from the input sequence $\{\mathcal{V}_0, \mathcal{V}_1, \ldots, \mathcal{V}_{N-1}\}$ [2]. In *KinectDeform*, we defined a recursive filtering function $f(\cdot, \cdot)$ to solve this problem which sequentially fuses the current measurement $\mathcal{V}_i$ with the result of the previous iteration $\mathcal{V}_{i-1}^{f'}$ by tracking the non-rigid deformations between them such that:

$$\mathcal{V}_i^{f'} = \begin{cases} \mathcal{V}_i & \text{for } i = 0, \\ f(\mathcal{V}_{i-1}^{f'}, \mathcal{V}_i) & i > 0. \end{cases} \tag{2}$$

As mentioned before a major shortcoming of the *KinectDeform* scheme lies in the 3D surface representation based on the view-dependent *truncated signed distance function (TSDF)* volume for data fusion and filtering [2]. Construction of a *TSDF* volume for a point cloud $\mathcal{V}_i$ requires computing a scalar *TSDF* value for each voxel represented by its centroid $\mathbf{c} \in \mathbb{R}^3$. The *TSDF* function $S_{\mathcal{V}_i}$ may be defined as follows:

$$S_{\mathcal{V}_i}(\mathbf{c}) = \Psi(\|\mathbf{c}\|_2 - \|\mathbf{p}_j\|_2), \tag{3}$$

where $j = \pi(\mathbf{K}\mathbf{c})$, $j \in \{1, \ldots, U\}$, is projection of the centroid $\mathbf{c}$ to camera's image plane using camera's intrinsic matrix $\mathbf{K}$. This, in turn, requires the points in $\mathcal{V}_i$ to be organized with respect to the image plane, moreover:

$$\Psi(\eta) = \begin{cases} min\{1, \frac{\eta}{\mu}\} \cdot sgn(\eta) & \text{iff } \eta \geq -\mu, \\ 0 & \text{otherwise,} \end{cases} \tag{4}$$

where μ is the truncation distance and *sgn* is the sign function. Therefore, after non-rigid registration which destroys the data organization of our input point cloud $\mathcal{V}_i^{f'}$, an expensive data reorganization step based on meshing and ray-casting is required for computation of a *TSDF*. After that, the *TSDF* volumes created using $\mathcal{V}_i^r$ and $\mathcal{V}_i$ are fused together using an empirical weighting scheme whereby the weighting parameters are chosen manually. This is followed by another surface prediction step via ray-casting to extract the final filtered surface from the fused volume.

2.2   Point Set Surfaces

Keeping in view the *KinectDeform* method explained in Sect. 2.1, a simpler approach would be to replace the view-dependent *TSDF* volume-based surface representation for fusion and filtering with a view-independent surface representation. This would result in avoiding data reorganization and surface prediction steps. As mentioned before the input points $\{\mathbf{p}_j\}$ approximate the underlying surface of objects in the scene. In [4], Alexa et al. built upon Levin's work [11], and proposed a view-independent ·point-based surface reconstruction method based on *Moving Least Squares (MLS)*. This method projects a point $\mathbf{q}$ lying near $\{\mathbf{p}_j\}$ on the underlying surface approximated by the local neighborhood of $\mathbf{q}$. Apart from facilitating the computation of the differential geometric properties of the surface such as normals and curvatures, this method is able to handle noisy data and provides smooth reconstructions. Moreover, the local nature of projection procedure improves the efficiency of the algorithm [6].

The projection procedure as proposed by Alexa et al. is divided into two steps [4]. In the first step a local reference domain, i.e., a plane $H_{\mathbf{q}} = \{\mathbf{p} \in \mathbb{R}^3 : \mathbf{n}^T\mathbf{p} = \mathbf{n}^T\mathbf{v}\}$, $\mathbf{v}, \mathbf{n} \in \mathbb{R}^3$ and $\|\mathbf{n}\| = 1$, is computed by minimizing the following non-linear energy function [6]:

$$e_{MLS}(\mathbf{v}, \mathbf{n}) = \sum_{s_{\mathbf{q}}=1}^{U_{\mathbf{q}}} w(\|\mathbf{p}_{s_{\mathbf{q}}} - \mathbf{v}\|)\langle \mathbf{n}, \mathbf{p}_{s_{\mathbf{q}}} - \mathbf{v}\rangle^2, \tag{5}$$

where $\{\mathbf{p}_{s_{\mathbf{q}}}\} \subset \{\mathbf{p}_j\}$, $s_{\mathbf{q}} \in \{1, \ldots, U_{\mathbf{q}}\}$ and $U_{\mathbf{q}}$ is the total number of neighboring points within a fixed radius around $\mathbf{q}$. Also $\mathbf{n} = (\mathbf{q} - \mathbf{v})/\|\mathbf{q} - \mathbf{v}\|$, $\langle ., . \rangle$ is the dot product and $w(e) = \exp^{(-\frac{e^2}{d^2})}$ is the Gaussian weight function where d represents the anticipated spacing between neighboring points [4]. The surface features of size less than d are smoothed out due to the *MLS* projection. Replacing $\mathbf{v}$ by $\mathbf{q} + t\mathbf{n}$ where $t \in \mathbb{R}$ in (5) we have:

$$e_{MLS}(\mathbf{q}, \mathbf{n}) = \sum_{s_{\mathbf{q}}=1}^{U_{\mathbf{q}}} w(\|\mathbf{p}_{s_{\mathbf{q}}} - \mathbf{q} - t\mathbf{n}\|)\langle \mathbf{n}, \mathbf{p}_{s_{\mathbf{q}}} - \mathbf{q} - t\mathbf{n}\rangle^2. \tag{6}$$

The minimum of (6) is found with the smallest t and the local tangent plane $H_{\mathbf{q}}$ near $\mathbf{q}$ [4]. The local reference domain is then defined by an orthonormal coordinate system in $H_{\mathbf{q}}$ with $\mathbf{v}$ as its origin [6]. In the next step, we find the orthogonal projections of points in $\{\mathbf{p}_{s_{\mathbf{v}}}\} \subset \{\mathbf{p}_j\}$, where $s_{\mathbf{v}} \in \{1, \ldots, U_{\mathbf{v}}\}$, lying in the local neighborhood of $\mathbf{v}$ to get their corresponding 2D representations $(x_{s_{\mathbf{v}}}, y_{s_{\mathbf{v}}})$ in the local coordinate system in $H_{\mathbf{q}}$. The height of $\mathbf{p}_{s_{\mathbf{v}}}$ over $H_{\mathbf{q}}$ is found via:

$$h_{s_{\mathbf{v}}} = \langle \mathbf{n}, \mathbf{p}_{s_{\mathbf{v}}} - \mathbf{q} - t\mathbf{n}\rangle. \tag{7}$$

Using the local 2D projections and the height map, a local bivariate polynomial approximation $g : \mathbb{R}^2 \to \mathbb{R}$ is computed by minimizing the weighted least squares error:

$$\sum_{s_\mathbf{v}=1}^{U_\mathbf{v}} w(\|\mathbf{p}_{s_\mathbf{v}} - \mathbf{q} - t\mathbf{n}\|)(g(x_{s_\mathbf{v}}, y_{s_\mathbf{v}}) - h_{s_\mathbf{v}})^2. \tag{8}$$

The degree of the polynomial to be computed is fixed beforehand. At the end, projection P of $\mathbf{q}$ onto the underlying surface is defined by the polynomial value at the origin, i.e.:

$$P(\mathbf{q}) = \mathbf{v} + g(0,0)\mathbf{n} = \mathbf{q} + (t + g(0,0))\mathbf{n}. \tag{9}$$

The projected point is considered to be the resulting filtered point lying on the approximated surface. These two steps are repeated for all points which need to be sampled to sufficiently represent the surfaces of objects in camera's field of view to get enhanced 3D reconstructions.

3   Proposed Technique

Figure 1 shows the pipeline of *VI-KinectDeform* which is an improved/simplified version of *KinectDeform*. After the non-rigid registration step which deforms $\mathcal{V}_{i-1}^{f'}$ to produce $\mathcal{V}_{i-1}^{r}$ which is mapped to $\mathcal{V}_i$, the data reorganization step is removed. Instead, a view-independent surface representation and filtering based on the *MLS* method is proposed. Since the *MLS* method works on the local neighborhoods of sampled points, voxelizing/sub-dividing the space of input 3D point clouds not only provides us with sampling information but also helps in accelerating the search for local neighborhoods of the sampled points. After that, the sampled points are projected onto the underlying surfaces of both point clouds based on the *MLS* method. The resulting projections are then fused together via an automatic *Kalman filtering* based scheme to give enhanced 3D reconstructions. These steps are explained as follows:

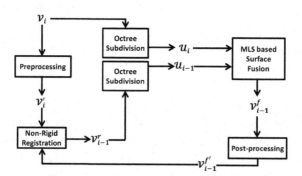

Fig. 1. Detailed pipeline of *VI-KinectDeform*. $\mathcal{V}_i$: input point cloud at time-step i. $\mathcal{V}_i'$: result of pre-processing on $\mathcal{V}_i$. $\mathcal{V}_i^r$: result of non-rigid registration of $\mathcal{V}_{i-1}^{f'}$ to $\mathcal{V}_i'$. $\mathcal{U}_i$ and $\mathcal{U}_{i-1}$: resulting voxel sets based on octree sub-division corresponding to $\mathcal{V}_i$ and $\mathcal{V}_{i-1}$ respectively. $\mathcal{V}_{i-1}^f$: the result of projection-based *MLS* surface computation and *Kalman filtering-based* fusion. $\mathcal{V}_{i-1}^f$: the final result after post-processing. For more details please read Sects. 2 and 3.

3.1 Sampling and *MLS* Based Projection

We use octree data structure to sample the space occupied by $\mathcal{V}_i$ and $\mathcal{V}_{i-1}^r$ resulting in two voxel sets $\mathcal{U}_i$ and $\mathcal{U}_{i-1}$ with a pre-defined depth $l \in \mathbb{N}$. At depth level l, $\mathcal{U}_i$ and $\mathcal{U}_{i-1}$ contain m_i^l and m_{i-1}^l non-empty voxels, respectively. It is to be noted that since $\mathcal{V}_i$ and $\mathcal{V}_{i-1}^r$ are mapped, the corresponding voxels in $\mathcal{U}_i$ and $\mathcal{U}_{i-1}$ occupy the same space. Each voxel $u_{i,a}^l \in \mathcal{U}_i$ where $a \in \{1, \ldots, m_i^l\}$ (or similarly each voxel $u_{i-1,b}^l \in \mathcal{U}_{i-1}$) is represented by its geometric center $\mathbf{c}_{i,a}^l$ (or $\mathbf{c}_{i-1,b}^l$), the points contained in the voxel and information about its immediate neighbors. These centroids lying near input points provide us with suitable sampling points to be projected onto the underlying surface based on the procedure explained in Sect. 2.2. Therefore, in the next step the centroid of each non-empty leaf voxel in $\mathcal{U}_i \cup \mathcal{U}_{i-1}$ lying in the vicinity of points from both $\mathcal{V}_i$ and $\mathcal{V}_{i-1}^r$ is projected on the approximated underlying surfaces using its corresponding neighborhood points in $\mathcal{V}_i$ and $\mathcal{V}_{i-1}^r$ respectively via the *MLS* method to get:

$$\mathbf{p}_{i,k} = P_i(\mathbf{c}_{i,a}^l), \mathbf{p}_{i-1,k} = P_{i-1}(\mathbf{c}_{i,a}^l), or$$
$$\mathbf{p}_{i,k} = P_i(\mathbf{c}_{i-1,b}^l), \mathbf{p}_{i-1,k} = P_{i-1}(\mathbf{c}_{i-1,b}^l). \tag{10}$$

The degree of the bivariate polynomial approximating the underlying surface computed for each centroid is kept variable (max. 3 for our experiments) depending on the number of points found in the neighborhood. Hence as a result of the *MLS*-based projection procedure, two sets of corresponding filtered points, $\{\mathbf{p}_{i,k}\}$ and $\{\mathbf{p}_{i-1,k}\}$, are generated.

3.2 Fusion

It is clear that under ideal conditions, i.e., sensor noise free and with perfectly registered inputs $\mathcal{V}_i$ and $\mathcal{V}_{i-1}^r$, $\{\mathbf{p}_{i,k}\}$ and $\{\mathbf{p}_{i-1,k}\}$ should be same. Therefore in this step we propose a methodology to fuse the corresponding projected points $\{\mathbf{p}_{i,k}\}$ and $\{\mathbf{p}_{i-1,k}\}$, taking into account noise factors affecting them to produce a filtered 3D reconstruction $\mathcal{V}_i^f$. In *KinectDeform* we performed a surface fusion/filtering using a weighted average of *TSDF* values of corresponding voxels [2]. The weights are chosen empirically based on an analysis of noise factors affecting the two input voxel sets per iteration. The main noise factor affecting the current measurement $\mathcal{V}_i$, and hence $\{\mathbf{p}_{i,k}\}$, is the sensor noise while on the other hand for $\mathcal{V}_{i-1}^r$ it is assumed that, due to pre-processing, some amount of this sensor noise is mitigated with some loss of details and hence the main noise factor is error due to non-rigid registration [2]. This should be coupled with iterative effects of filtering as $\mathcal{V}_{i-1}^r$ is indeed a deformed state of the filtered $\mathcal{V}_{i-1}^{f'}$.

To tackle these factors, we propose an automatic filtering approach by point tracking with a *Kalman filter* [10]. The observation model is based on the current measurements i.e. $\{\mathbf{p}_{i,k}\}$, and the associated sensor noise n_i^s is assumed to follow a Gaussian distribution $n_i^s \sim \mathcal{N}(0, \sigma_{s,i}^2)$. Similarly the process/motion model is based on $\{\mathbf{p}_{i-1,k}\}$, and the associated process noise n_{i-1}^r is assumed to follow a Gaussian distribution $n_{i-1}^r \sim \mathcal{N}(0, \sigma_{r,i-1}^2)$. Therefore the prediction step is:

$$\begin{cases} \mathbf{P}_{i|i-1,k} = \mathbf{P}_{i-1,k}, \\ \sigma_{i|i-1}^2 = \sigma_{i-1|i-1}^2 + \sigma_{r,i-1}^2, \end{cases} \tag{11}$$

and measurement update is given as:

$$\begin{cases} \mathbf{P}_{i|i,k} = \mathbf{P}_{i|i-1,k} + k_i(\mathbf{p}_{i,k} - \mathbf{p}_{i|i-1,k}), \\ \sigma_{i|i}^2 = \sigma_{i|i-1}^2 - k_i\sigma_{i|i-1}^2, \end{cases} \tag{12}$$

where:

$$k_i = \frac{\sigma_{i|i-1}^2}{\sigma_{i|i-1}^2 + \sigma_{s,i}^2}. \tag{13}$$

This results in the filtered set of points $\{\mathbf{p}_{i|i,k}\}$ which constitutes $\mathcal{V}_i^f$.

4   Experiments and Results

The quality of *VI-KinectDeform* is analyzed both quantitatively and qualitatively. We use the "Facecap" dataset which captures a person's face deforming non-rigidly due to changing expressions in different scenes [23]. The selected scene includes 40 frames. We simulate a depth camera in *V-Rep* [1], placed approximately at 0.5 m away from the object and add *Gaussian* noise with zero mean and standard deviations of 0.01 m, 0.03 m and 0.05 m, respectively. Experiments are carried out using these datasets for both *VI-KinectDeform* and *KinectDeform*. A bilateral filter is used in the pre-processing step to obtain improved registration for both methods [22]. We use the algorithm proposed by Destelle et al. [8] for non-rigid registration in both methods. We use the proposed automated fusion scheme in both *VI-KinectDeform* and *KinectDeform* by replacing the empirical fusion scheme used previously. Post-processing is based on the bilateral mesh de-noising with very small parameters for the neighborhood size and the projection distance for both *VI-KinectDeform* and *KinectDeform* [9].

The quantitative evaluation of *VI-KinectDeform* as compared to *KinectDeform* is reported in Fig. 2. It shows the root mean square error (RMSE) of the data enhanced with *VI-KinectDeform*, and the data enhanced with *KinectDeform* with respect to the ground truth data for different noise levels. These results show superior performance of *VI-KinectDeform* in terms of overall accuracy of 3D reconstructions as compared to *KinectDeform*. It is noted that the accuracy of the proposed technique is restricted by the accuracy of the considered non-rigid registration algorithm. We have tested our proposed *VI-KinectDeform* by using non-rigid registration parameters obtained from noise free data. Post-processing step is skipped in this case. The resulting curve in Fig. 2(a) shows a significant decrease in error when using *VI-KinectDeform* as compared to its

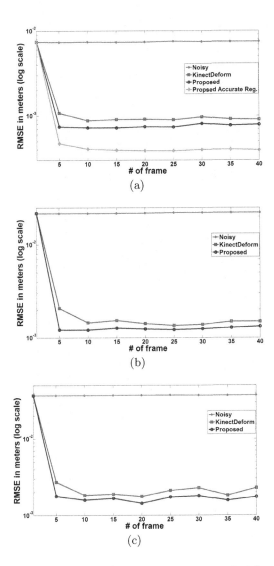

Fig. 2. "Facecap" dataset. Quantitative analysis on data with different levels of *Gaussian* noise. Each figure contains RMSE in log scale of: noisy data, result of *Kinect-Deform* and result of *VI-KinectDeform*. (a) Results for *Gaussian* noise with standard deviation of 0.01 *m*. It also contains RMSE in log scale of *VI-KinectDeform* with registration based on noise free data. (b) Results for *Gaussian* noise with standard deviation of 0.03 *m*. (c) Results for *Gaussian* noise with standard deviation of 0.05 *m*.

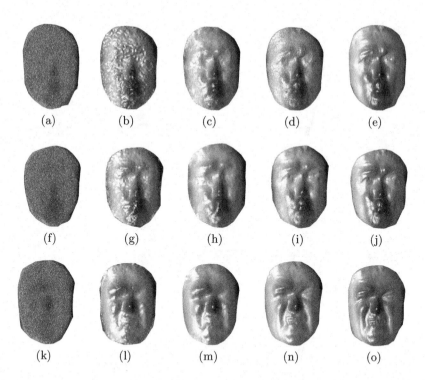

Fig. 3. "Facecap" dataset. **First row:** Frame #5, **Second row:** Frame #15, **Third row:** Frame #35. Each row contains noisy data with *Gaussian* noise of standard deviation 0.01 *m*, result of *KinectDeform*, result of *VI-KinectDeform*, result of *VI-KinectDeform* with registration based on noise free data and ground truth respectively.

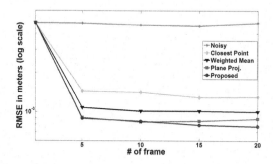

Fig. 4. "Swing" dataset. RMSE in log scale of: noisy data with *Gaussian* noise of standard deviation 0.0075 *m*, result of closest point-based surface representation, result of weighted-mean based surface representation, result of local plane projection-based surface representation and result of the proposed projection-based *MLS* surface representation. Please read Sect. 4 for more details.

earlier version. This is observed through all frames. The qualitative analysis presented in Fig. 3, corresponding to the noise level and results in Fig. 2(a), shows

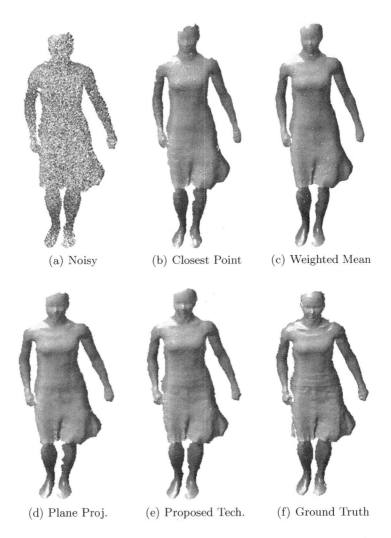

(a) Noisy   (b) Closest Point   (c) Weighted Mean

(d) Plane Proj.   (e) Proposed Tech.   (f) Ground Truth

Fig. 5. "Swing" dataset. **First row:** *Left:* noisy data with *Gaussian* noise of standard deviation 0.0075 m, *Center:* result of closest point-based surface representation, *Right:* result of weighted mean-based surface representation. **Second row:** *Left:* result of local plane projection-based surface representation, *Center:* result of the proposed projection-based *MLS* surface representation, *Right:* ground truth.

superior quality of 3D reconstructions obtained via *VI-KinectDeform* in terms of feature preservation and smoothness when compared to the results obtained via *KinectDeform*.

For further analysis of performance of the proposed technique, we use the "Swing" dataset [24]. We, again, simulate a depth camera in *V-Rep* placed approximately at 1.5 m away from the object and add *Gaussian* noise with zero mean and standard deviation of 0.0075 m. We use 20 frames for this experiment. We analyze the performance of the proposed *VI-KinectDeform* with 3 other view-independent surface representation schemes. These representation schemes are based on finding the surface approximation with respect to each centroid belonging to the leaf nodes of $\mathcal{U}_i$ and $\mathcal{U}_{i-1}$ lying close to $\mathcal{V}_i$ and $\mathcal{V}_{i-1}^r$.

The first scheme is based on finding the closest points in local neighborhoods of the centroids. The second scheme is based on finding the weighted mean of all points lying in local neighborhoods of each centroid using the weighting scheme similar to the one used in (5). The third scheme fits tangent planes to points in local neighborhoods and finds the projections of the centroid on them. It is similar to the proposed scheme wherein the degree of the polynomial is fixed to one.

Quantitative and qualitative results are shown in Fig. 4 and Fig. 5, respectively. As expected, Fig. 4 shows that the closest point-based method is least accurate followed by the weighted mean-based method, the plane projection-based method, and the proposed projection-based *MLS* method in terms of overall accuracy. Similar results are obtained via quantitative analysis as shown in Fig. 5 wherein the proposed method produces the most accurate and feature preserving reconstruction. Plane projection-based method also gives good results but small features such as nose and curves on clothing are not well preserved. This experiment also shows that the proposed pipeline is generic enough such that any view-independent point-based surface representation scheme using local neighborhoods can replace the proposed *MLS*-based scheme.

5   Conclusion and Future Work

In this work we have proposed *VI-KinectDeform*, an automated recursive filtering scheme for producing enhanced 3D reconstructions of non-rigidly deforming objects. It improves upon our previous work, i.e., *KinectDeform* [2], by replacing the implicit view-dependent *TSDF* based surface representation scheme with an explicit *MLS*-based view-independent surface representation scheme [4]. This simplifies the pipeline by removing surface prediction and extraction steps. Moreover we improve upon the data fusion scheme by proposing an automated point tracking with a *Kalman filter* [10], The quantitative and qualitative evaluation of our method shows that it is able to produce smooth and feature preserving 3D reconstructions with an improved accuracy when compared to *Kinect-Deform*. We also show that the proposed pipeline is generic, and can use any view-independent point-based surface representation scheme. The generic and view-independent nature of this algorithm allows for the extension to a multi-view system to produce complete 360° enhanced 3D reconstructions of scenes containing non-rigid objects. This constitutes our future work.

Acknowledgments. The "Facecap" dataset was provided courtesy of the *Graphics, Vision & Video Research Group of the Max Planck Institute for Informatics* [23]. This work was supported by the National Research Fund (FNR), Luxembourg, under the CORE project C11/BM/1204105/FAVE/Ottersten.

References

1. V-REP. http://www.coppeliarobotics.com/
2. Afzal, H., Al Ismaeil, K., Aouada, D., Destelle, F., Mirbach, B., Ottersten, B.: KinectDeform: enhanced 3D reconstruction of non-rigidly deforming objects. In: 3DV Workshop on Dynamic Shape Measurement and Analysis. Tokyo, Japan (2014)
3. Al Ismaeil, K., Aouada, D., Solignac, T., Mirbach, B., Ottersten, B.: Real-time non-rigid multi-frame depth video super-resolution. In: CVPR Workshop on Multi-Sensor Fusion for Dynamic Scene Understanding. Boston, MA, USA (2015)
4. Alexa, M., Behr, J., Cohen-Or, D., Fleishman, S., Levin, D., Silva, C.T.: Computing and rendering point set surfaces. IEEE Transactions on Visualization and Computer Graphics **9**(1), 3–15 (2003)
5. Bylow, E., Sturm, J., Kerl, C., Kahl, F., Cremers, D.: Real-time camera tracking and 3D reconstruction using signed distance functions. In: Robotics: Science and Systems Conference (RSS), June 2013
6. Cheng, Z.Q., Wang, Y.Z., Li, B., Xu, K., Dang, G., Jin, S.Y.: A survey of methods for moving least squares surfaces. In: Proceedings of the Fifth Eurographics / IEEE VGTC Conference on Point-Based Graphics, SPBG 2008, pp. 9–23. Eurographics Association, Aire-la-Ville (2008)
7. Cui, Y., Chang, W., Nöll, T., Stricker, D.: KinectAvatar: fully automatic body capture using a single kinect. In: Park, J.-I., Kim, J. (eds.) ACCV Workshops 2012, Part II. LNCS, vol. 7729, pp. 133–147. Springer, Heidelberg (2013)
8. Destelle, F., Roudet, C., Neveu, M., Dipanda, A.: Towards a real-time tracking of dense point-sampled geometry. In: International Conference on Image Processing, pp. 381–384 (2012)
9. Fleishman, S., Drori, I., Cohen-Or, D.: Bilateral mesh denoising. In: ACM SIGGRAPH 2003 Papers, SIGGRAPH 2003, pp. 950–953. ACM, New York (2003)
10. Kalman, R.E.: A new approach to linear filtering and prediction problems. Transactions of the ASME-Journal of Basic Engineering **82**(Series D), 35–45 (1960)
11. Levin, D.: Mesh-independent surface interpolation. In: Brunnett, H., Mueller (eds.) Geometric Modeling for Scientific Visualization, pp. 37–49. Springer-Verlag (2003)
12. Li, H., Adams, B., Guibas, L.J., Pauly, M.: Robust single-view geometry and motion reconstruction. In: ACM SIGGRAPH Asia 2009 Papers, SIGGRAPH Asia 2009, pp. 175:1–175:10. ACM, New York (2009). http://doi.acm.org/10.1145/1661412.1618521
13. Mac Aodha, O., Campbell, N.D.F., Nair, A., Brostow, G.J.: Patch based synthesis for single depth image super-resolution. In: Fitzgibbon, A., Lazebnik, S., Perona, P., Sato, Y., Schmid, C. (eds.) ECCV 2012, Part III. LNCS, vol. 7574, pp. 71–84. Springer, Heidelberg (2012)
14. Mrcio, C., Apolinario Jr, A.L., Souza, A.C.S.: KinectFusion for faces: real-time 3D face tracking and modeling using a kinect camera for a markerless AR system. SBC Journal on 3D Interactive Systems **4**, 2–7 (2013)
15. Newcombe, R.A., Izadi, S., Hilliges, O., Molyneaux, D., Kim, D., Davison, A.J., Kohli, P., Shotton, J., Hodges, S., Fitzgibbon, A.: KinectFusion: real-time dense surface mapping and tracking. In: Proceedings of the 2011 10th IEEE International Symposium on Mixed and Augmented Reality, ISMAR 2011, pp. 127–136. IEEE Computer Society, Washington (2011). http://dx.doi.org/10.1109/ISMAR.2011.6092378

16. Nießner, M., Zollhöfer, M., Izadi, S., Stamminger, M.: Real-time 3D Reconstruction at Scale using Voxel Hashing. ACM Transactions on Graphics (TOG) (2013)
17. Roth, H., Vona, M.: Moving volume KinectFusion. In: Proceedings of the British Machine Vision Conference, pp. 112.1–112.11. BMVA Press (2012)
18. Rouhani, M., Sappa, A.D.: Non-rigid shape registration: a single linear least squares framework. In: Fitzgibbon, A., Lazebnik, S., Perona, P., Sato, Y., Schmid, C. (eds.) ECCV 2012, Part VII. LNCS, vol. 7578, pp. 264–277. Springer, Heidelberg (2012)
19. Schuon, S., Theobalt, C., Davis, J., Thrun, S.: LidarBoost: depth superresolution for ToF 3D shape scanning. In: Proc. of IEEE CVPR 2009 (2009)
20. Steinbrcker, F., Kerl, C., Cremers, D.: Large-scale multi-resolution surface reconstruction from RGB-D sequences. In: Proceedings of the 2013 IEEE International Conference on Computer Vision, ICCV 2013, pp. 3264–3271. IEEE Computer Society, Washington (2013). http://dx.doi.org/10.1109/ICCV.2013.405
21. Sturm, J., Bylow, E., Kahl, F., Cremers, D.: CopyMe3D: scanning and printing persons in 3D. In: Weickert, J., Hein, M., Schiele, B. (eds.) GCPR 2013. LNCS, vol. 8142, pp. 405–414. Springer, Heidelberg (2013)
22. Tomasi, C., Manduchi, R.: Bilateral filtering for gray and color images. In: Proceedings of the Sixth International Conference on Computer Vision, ICCV 1998, p. 839. IEEE Computer Society, Washington (1998)
23. Valgaerts, L., Wu, C., Bruhn, A., Seidel, H.P., Theobalt, C.: Lightweight Binocular Facial Performance Capture Under Uncontrolled Lighting. ACM Trans. Graph
24. Vlasic, D., Baran, I., Matusik, W., Popović, J.: Articulated mesh animation from multi-view silhouettes. In: ACM SIGGRAPH 2008 Papers, SIGGRAPH 2008, pp. 97:1–97:9. ACM, New York (2008)
25. Wang, K., Wang, X., Pan, Z., Liu, K.: A two-stage framework for 3d facereconstruction from RGBD images. IEEE Transactions on Pattern Analysis and Machine Intelligence 36(8), 1493–1504 (2014)
26. Zeng, M., Zheng, J., Cheng, X., Jiang, B., Liu, X.: Dynamic human surface reconstruction using a single kinect. In: 2013 International Conference on Computer-Aided Design and Computer Graphics (CAD/Graphics), pp. 188–195 (2013)
27. Zollhöfer, M., Nießner, M., Izadi, S., Rehmann, C., Zach, C., Fisher, M., Wu, C., Fitzgibbon, A., Loop, C., Theobalt, C., Stamminger, M.: Real-time Non-rigid Reconstruction using an RGB-D Camera. ACM Transactions on Graphics (TOG) (2014)

Automated Fast Marching Method for Segmentation and Tracking of Region of Interest in Scintigraphic Images Sequences

Yassine Aribi[✉], Ali Wali, and Adel M. Alimi

REGIM: REsearch Groups on Intelligent Machines, University of Sfax,
National School of Engineers (ENIS), BP 1173, Sfax 3038, Tunisia
{yassine.aribi.tn,ali.wali,adel.alimi}@ieee.org

Abstract. This article introduces an efficient method that combines the advantages of Fast Marching Method (FMM) in conjunction with Harris corner descriptor. An application of Dynamic Renal Scintigraphy imaging has been chosen and a new approach has been applied to see its ability to have a high accuracy of Region Of Interest (ROI) segmentation and tracking in scintigraphic images sequences. The introduced system starts with an image processing algorithm to enhance the contrast of the input images.

This is followed by the segmentation phase which consists of an automated algorithm. Finally, the ROI tracking phase was described.

To evaluate the performance of the presented approach, we present tests on synthetic and real images are presented.

The experimental results obtained show that the effectiveness and performance of the proposed system is satisfactory.

Keywords: Automated Fast Marching Method · ROI · Segmentation · Tracking

1 Introduction

Recent advances in the imaging systems design of nuclear medicine have resulted in significant improvements in the areas of anatomical, functional, and dynamic imaging procedures. With these developments, computer-aided diagnosis is becoming a reality; computer-based tools allow physicians to understand and diagnose human disease through computer-aided interaction. However, the imaging techniques which are isolated form automatic image analysis are only helpful for qualified physicians to derive the diagnosis. In many cases the computer-based automated analysis could save a lot of time that can be otherwise devoted by doctors to clinical treatment or making decisions instead of analyzing large number of images at the same time. Scintigraphy is a medical imaging technique that uses radioactive isotopes to study the functioning of organs. Scintigraphy is employed in medical diagnostics in the form of specific tests such as myocardial scintigraphy (physiological study of the heart and myocardial perfusion) lung scan (allows the diagnosis of pulmonary embolism), bone scintigraphy (allows to diagnose

© Springer International Publishing Switzerland 2015
G. Azzopardi and N. Petkov (Eds.): CAIP 2015, Part II, LNCS 9257, pp. 725–736, 2015.
DOI: 10.1007/978-3-319-23117-4_62

fractures, sports pathologies, inflammatory diseases of the skeleton, bone tumors or infections) or renal scintigraphy (investigation of kidneys' functions). The last one is the main focus of this paper since the proposed methodology of scintigraphy measurement data processing is applied to study the dynamic renal functions. Dynamical renal scintigraphy is a nuclear imaging medical diagnostic technique that allows the exploration of kidneys functions by monitoring an activity of radioactive product injected to a patient. Monitoring is realized by measuring the movement and radiation of the product over time. The measurements are presented in the form of a video image sequence with consecutive frames captured usually each several tens of seconds. The computer processing of the scintigraphic image provides a more reliable image for much better diagnostic orientation and a clear understanding of the pathological phenomenon. The scintigraphic images are difficult to process automatically since they have low signal to noise ratio [1]. Though the low quality, the images still convey sufficient information useful to the physician. Renal radionuclide study can be essential in different clinical applications to renal diseases such as renovascular hypertension, hydronephrosis, vesicoureteric reflux, renal failure or renal transplant cases [2]. One of the main targets of such study is usually the appropriate assessment of renal functions or in other words the quantification of possible renal disfunctions [3] The automated computer tool can be beneficial for the treatment and the analysis of scintigraphic images, particularly regarding the quantification. The quantification in nuclear medicine is mostly based on the identification of regions of interest (ROI) in order to further analyze the parameter values associated with the pixels. The crucial factor for the calculation of the renal function is determining the ROI of each kidney. The extraction of ROI requires a segmentation phase. This is the most critical phase for automated analysis in medical imaging [4]. Segmentation in image processing aims to aggregate neighboring pixels according to predefined criteria. Those pixels are grouped into regions in order to have a partition the image for easier analysis. Dynamic renal scintigraphy consists in the acquisition of series of images taken in distinct time intervals after injection of radioactive tracer, also called radiopharmaceuticals or radio-tracers, which are substances marked by a radioactive element that loses its activity within a few hours. After the identification of ROI in all images, the time-activity curves registered at each kidney are plot and the renal differential function can be determined from these curves. In order to enable the calculation of renal functions' parameters, we propose in this paper an Intelligent System for the ROI Segmentation and tracking in Dynamic Renal Scintigraphy sequences.

The main contribution of this work is (a) the development of a robust method to define renal ROI without any intervention of the user, (b) to track automatically the ROI in scintigraphic image sequence in order to generate the relative renal function.

This paper is organized as follows. In Section 2, the related work is introduced. Then, the system architecture for ROI segmentation and tracking are described in Section 3. Section 4 is devoted for the results of segmentation and tracking. The concluding remarks are presented in section 5.

2   Related Works

Scintigraphic image is often accompanied with noise that makes it difficult to collect its regions of interest. Furthermore, it suffers from a low contrast [21].

Several methods such as EM clustering algorithm have certain limitations to segment the scintigraphic image. Indeed, statistical methods have much high performance when the population is large (which is reflected in the case of the image by the high spatial resolution, which is not the case for the scintigraphic image).

To detect the left ventricle in cardiac scintigraphy images, a system of image segmentation using a method based on a priori knowledge has been presented in [5]. Houston et al [6] described the use of image registration to generate automatic ROI for cardiac studies using an affine transform.

The region growing segmentation technique is conceptually simple and fast. But it is sensitive to noise. This method has been used by [7] for the detection of renal ROI on scintigraphic images.

In 2014, Rahmatpour et al. [8] presented a study which aims at obtaining an automatic method to determine ROI of the kidney based on the threshold method in order to reduce the operator's manual method errors.

The active contour is a segmentation technique used frequently, it consists in initializing a curve (closed or not, in fixed extremities or not) in the circle of acquaintances of the border of an object to be detected. This noted curve C moves and deform as snakes from a position of initialization situated near the object of interest according to an iterative process of deformation controlled by a test of convergence.

The active contour was used by [9] for the segmentation of thyroid scintigraphy images. The same technique was employed by [10] for the detection of the left ventricle in scintigraphic images.

In literature, very few works presented a system of automatic segmentation of ROI in the dynamic scintigraphy, in [11] the authors have developed an automated system to define the ROI in dynamic scintigraphy. Their algorithm is based on cluster analysis. Other authors have also proposed an automatic analysis of dynamic renal scintigraphy in [12].

In [13] a relatively new method for automatic detection of the renals ROI is presented using RBF neural networks. Another segmentation method specific to renal scintigraphy is proposed in [14]. An automatic thresholding algorithm is used to segment each kidney. To avoid the under-segmentation, pixels in an area around the initial boundary are classified as kidney pixels or in the background. This method does, however, not consider the fact that diseased kidneys may show lower uptake in wedge-shaped areas around its boundary. A semi-automatic system for the segmentation of regions of interest kidney based on the fast marching method was developed in [15].

3   Overview of the Proposed System

Segmentation methods based on active contours have proved their effectiveness and robustness to avoid noise. However, the major drawbacks of these methods are that they are very time consuming and exclude any wide propagation. The Fast Marching Method algorithm "FMM", introduced by Sethian [16] can support these facts. Indeed, the major advantage of this method is that it provides a solution in a single iteration.

In this paper, we propose to use the FMM in an attempt to solve the problem of segmentation taking into account the speed of the approach.

Figure 1. illustrates the architecture of the image processing system for the analysis of scintigraphic renal dynamic studies. It contains three main stages: (1) Pre-processing phase; (2) Segmentation phase and (3) Analysis phase.

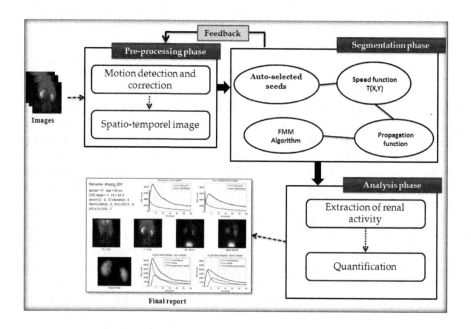

Fig. 1. Global Overview of the System

3.1   Proposed Segmentation Algorithm

The FMM algorithm proceeds as follows:

1. All points in the initial conditions are tagged as Accepted.
2. All points in the neighbourhood of the accepted points are tagged as Trial.
3. The remaining grid points are tagged as Far.
4. The begin loop: find a Trial point with the smallest T value.
5. The chosen Trial point is added to the accepted ones and removed from the Trial list.

6. All the neighbours of the point chosen in Step 4 that are not Accepted are tagged as Trial.

7. The values of all the new Trial points are recomputed.

8. Return to Step 4.

In Figure 2, the Fast Marching algorithm is graphically illustrated. In order to have a better understanding of the algorithm, we consider the case of an isolated accepted node in the domain and we replace the network grid representation with the table format. The algorithm steps are:

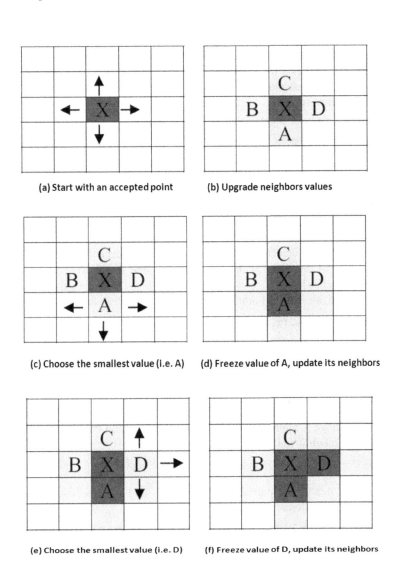

(a) Start with an accepted point   (b) Upgrade neighbors values

(c) Choose the smallest value (i.e. A)   (d) Freeze value of A, update its neighbors

(e) Choose the smallest value (i.e. D)   (f) Freeze value of D, update its neighbors

Fig. 2. Update procedure for Fast Marching Method

The proposed method is based on the segmentation algorithm FMM. Indeed this algorithm has three basic steps. Once we have defined a set of starting points, we can move on to the definition of a speed function to ensure the propagation and to the step by step construction of the region of interest. Our contribution lies in improving the manual selection of the starting points by automating the selection of these points. To automate this initialization point of departure, we proceed as follows.

3.2   Seeds Selected Based on Harris Corner Detector

The selection of a seed is based on the nature of the problem. The edge based method is used by some researchers to select seeds because the conventional seed selection method is not automatic. If the selected seed is from the center of the region, the segmentation becomes much more effective and efficient. The three criteria for an automatic seed selection are:

1. A seed pixel must have high similarity to its neighbour.

2. For an expected region, at least one seed must be generated in order to produce this region.

3. Seeds for different regions must be disconnected.

Automated seed selection is the efficient time consuming criteria achieved through the use of Harris corner detect theory. The strong invariance to rotation, scale, illumination variation and image noise makes Harris corner detector a very popular detecting method.

In the Harris corner detector method, the local autocorrelation function measures the local changes of the signal with shifted patches and the discreteness refers to the shifting of the patches [17].

Given a shift (dx, dy) and a point (x, y), the auto correlation function is defined as

$$S(x,y) = \sum_{x_i y_i} W(x_i, y_i)[I(x_i + \delta x, y_i + \delta y) - I(x_i, y_i)]^2 \qquad (1)$$

Where $I(x,y)$ denotes the image function and (x_i, y_i) are the points in the Gaussian window w centered on (x,y). The window function W centered on (x, y) is given in Eq. (2)

$$W(x,y) = \frac{1}{2\pi\sigma^2} e^{-(x^2+y^2)/2\sigma^2} \qquad (2)$$

The shifted image is approximated by a Taylor expansion truncated to the first order terms is given below in (3),

$$I(x_i + \delta x, y_i + \delta y) = I(x_i, y_i) + [I_x \, I_y] \begin{bmatrix} \delta x \\ \delta y \end{bmatrix} \qquad (3)$$

where Ix and Iy denote the partial derivatives in x and y, respectively. Substituting Eq. 3 into Eq. 1, we will get

$$S(x,y) = (\delta x, \delta y)S(x,y) \begin{bmatrix} \delta x \\ \delta y \end{bmatrix} \qquad (4)$$

where the matrix s(x, y) captures the intensity structure of the local neighborhood. In this process, the Gaussian window size is 5*5, s= 0.7, and to get the most flat point and not too many points be detected we used a non-minimum inhibition window.

The non-minimum inhibition window size is used with much lesser seeds selected. The threshold of λ1 and λ2 also influenced the number of selected seeds. The lower threshold will generate much lesser seeds and bigger region of interest. Here, the threshold is 0.02.

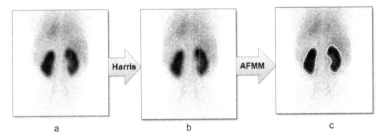

Fig. 3. (a) Original image (b)Auto-selected seeds based on Harris in all image part (c) Segmented image

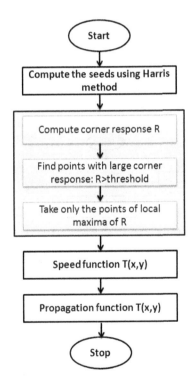

Fig. 4. Flowchart of the proposed AFMM

3.3   Tracking ROI Using the Proposed AFMM

The tracking of moving objects in an image sequence is an important task in many applications (e.g. medical imaging, robotics). However, this task is usually difficult due to inherent problems that could happen in sequences (i.e. possible occlusion of the object, large interframe motion).

The goal in these images is to segment the right and the left kidneys. The difficulties of this task are the high inter and intra-patient kidney shape, the similarities in terms of gray levels between the kidneys and the nearby tissues and the irregularities and the low contrast of the contour. We have already seen that the scintigraphic images have both low resolution and quality. Thus, there is a need, to integrate our approach to improve these features to reach the finest possible segmentation.

As a front propagation speed, we choose the edge detector of the equation:

$$F|x| = \left(\frac{1}{\epsilon + |\nabla(x)|} \right) \left(\frac{1}{m} \right)$$

Where ϵ and m are parameters to be determined.

For the standard FMM, we can extract several parameters that influence the segmentation:

- the parameters of the algorithm.
- the shape and position of the initial contour.
- the different methods of image preprocessing.

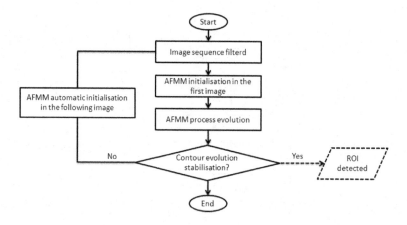

Fig. 5. Tracking process based on AFMM

4   Experimental Results

4.1   Validation on Synthetic Data

Before moving on to the validation of results on a real database, we chose to test the performance of our method on synthetic sequences in order to deduce its effectiveness in an ideal case.

Figure 5 shows an example of the result of the proposed AFMM segmentation obtained on a synthetic test sequence.

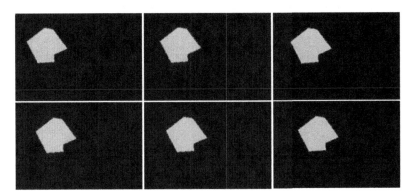

Fig. 6. Result of AFMM segmentation obtained on a synthetic sequence

Not surprisingly, we note that the AFMM method arrived to locate the target shape in all images of the sequence correctly.

4.2   Validation on Real Data

The AFMM segmentation method was applied to 1200 images from 10 patients with various renal diseases. We also applied to these images the Level Set Methods (LSM), which are a conceptual framework for using the level sets as a tool for numerical analysis of surfaces and shapes [18]. The advantage of the level set model is that one can perform numerical computations involving curves and surfaces on a fixed Cartesian grid without having to parameterize these objects (this is called the Eulerian approach). Also, the level set method makes it very easy to follow the shapes that change topology (Contour of ROI in our case), for example when a shape splits in two, develops holes, or the reverse of these operations.

In order to estimate quantitatively the obtained segmentation results, three indices are calculated to compare two contours A and B. The Dice coefficient D(A;B) measures the overlap between A and B and is defined by [19]:

$$D(A, B) = \frac{2|A \cap B|}{|A| + |B|}$$

D (A, B) is 1 in case of perfect correspondence between the two edges, and 0 if recovery is zero. Complementing two indices measuring the average and maximum distance (Hausdorff distance [20]) between the contours is calculated according to:

$$d_m (A,B) = \frac{1}{A} \sum_{a \in A} min_{b \in B} d(a,b)$$

$$d_H (A,B) = max_{a \in A} \{min_{b \in B} d(a,b)\}$$

Where | A | denotes the number of contour points A. Note that these two indices are given in mm, taking account the spatial resolution of the image. The results of the mean averages   are summarized in Table1.

Table 1. Mean results and standard deviations of the proposed AFMM method and Level Set method.

Distances	AFMM	LSM
Dice	0.83 +/- 0.05	0.72 +/-0.04
$d_m(mm)$	1.62 +/-1.13	3.48 +/-4.17
$d_H(mm)$	5.51+/-4.:47	10.52 +/-10.69

The evaluation of our segmentation method yielded good statistical results. Indeed the average DSC is 0.82 with a 0.82 median. Hausdorf distance, and visual inspection of the results also show good agreement segmentation of kidneys for our method (AFMM). Typical results of the segmentation are shown in Figure 7.

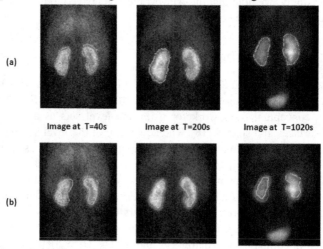

(a)   Image at T=40s   Image at T=200s   Image at T=1020s

(b)

Fig. 7. Segmentation results of (a) AFMM (green contour) (b) LSM (green contour) and manual segmentation in both a and b(red contour).

5   Conclusions and Future Works

In this paper, we proposed a new system to segment and track automatically the renal ROI from renal scintigraphy images based on an automated Fast Marching Method. Results of the comparison with classical methods showed good compliance with referential images and advantage of the proposed method in terms of accuracy and execution time over the other methods. The paper describes the environment of our system including image processing procedure.

Results are discussed in the context of both significant set of patients data and carefully chosen cases which are difficult to be assessed.

The proposed method and approach remains open to other areas of applications including different dynamical medical diagnostic imaging techniques and other applications.

Acknowledgment. The authors would like to acknowledge the financial support of this work consisting in grants from General Direction of Scientific Research (DGRST), Tunisia, under the ARUB program.

References

1. Pretorius, P.H., Fung, L.C.T., Schell, C.P., Nishinaka, K., Groiselle, C.J., Glick, S.J., Narayanan, M.V., King, M.A.: Dynamic and static tomographic renal coincidence imaging with a gamma camera using Rb-82: a feasibility study. IEEE Transactions on Nuclear Science **49**, 5 (2002)
2. Caglar, M., Gedik, G.K., Karabulut, E.: Differential renal function estimation by dynamic renal scintigraphy: influence of background definition and radiopharmaceutical. Nuclear Medicine Communications, 1002–5 (November 2008)
3. Prigent, A., Cosgriff, P., Piepsz, A., Rehling, M., Rutland, M., Taylor, A.: Consensus report on quality control of quantitative measurements of renal function obtained from the renogram: International Consensus Committee from the Scientific Committee of Radionuclides in Nephrourology. Seminars in Nuclear Medicine, 146–159 (April 1999)
4. Hu, Grossberg and Mageras,Survey of Recent Volumetric Medical Image Segmentation Techniques, 2009
5. Khalifa, N., Ettaeib, S., Wahabi, Y., Hamrouni, K.: Left Ventricle Tracking in Isotopic Ventriculography Using Statistical Deformable Models. Int. Arab J. Inf. Technol, 213–222 (2010)
6. White, D.R.R., Sampson, W.F.D., Macleod, M.A., Pilkington, J.B.: An assessment of two methods for generating automatic regions of interest. Nuclear Medicine Communications, 1005 (1998)
7. Aribi, Y., Wali, A., Hamza, F., Alimi, A.M., Guermazi, F.: Analysis of scintigraphic renal dynamic studies: an image processing tool for the clinician and researcher. In: Hassanien, A.E., Salem, A.-B.M., Ramadan, R., Kim, T.-h. (eds.) AMLTA 2012. CCIS, vol. 322, pp. 267–275. Springer, Heidelberg (2012)
8. Rahmatpour, M., Rajabi, H., Sardari, D., Babapour, F., Ahmadi, S.: Semi-Automation of renal region of interest in renography images by thresholding and edge detection. Romanian Reports in Physics, 127–132 (2014)

9. Kaur, J., Jindal, A.: Segmentation Algorithms for Thyroid Scintigraphy Images. IJCST, **3** (2012)

10. Hraiech, N., Weinland, D., Hamrouni, K.: An active contour model based on splines and separating forces to detect the left ventricle in scintigraphic images. In: 2nd International Conference on Machine Intelligence, ACIDCA-ICMI 2005, November 2005

11. Kaur, J., Hannequin, P., Liehn, J.C., Valeyre, J.: Cluster analysis for automatic image segmentation in dynamic scintigraphies. Nucl. Med. Commun., 383–393 (1990)

12. Ståhl, D., Åström, K., Overgaard, N.C., Landgren, M., Sjöstrand, K., Edenbrandt, L.: Automatic compartment modelling and segmentation for dynamical renal scintigraphies. In: Heyden, A., Kahl, F. (eds.) SCIA 2011. LNCS, vol. 6688, pp. 557–568. Springer, Heidelberg (2011)

13. Siogkas, G.K., Dermatas, E.S.: Automating Medical Diagnosis in Renal Scintigrams using RBF Networks. First International Conference From Scientific Computing to Computational Engineering (2004)

14. Marcuzzo, M., Masiero, P.R., Scharcanski, J.: Quantitative parameters for the assessment of renal scintigraphic images. In: 29th Annual International Conference of the IEEE. EMBS 2007, pp. 3438–3441. Engineering in Medicine and Biology Society (2007)

15. Aribi, Y., Wali, A., Alimi, A.M.: An intelligent system for renal segmentation. In: IEEE 15th International Conference on e-Health Networking, Applications Services (Healthcom), pp. 11–15 (2013)

16. Sethian, J.A.: A fast marching level set method for monotonically advancing fronts. In: Proceedings of the National Academy of Science, pp. 1591–1595 (1996)

17. Moravec, H.P.: Obstacle avoidance and navigation in the real world by a seeing robot rover. Ph.D. thesis, Stanford, CA, USA (1980)

18. Sethian, J., Adalsteinsson, D.: An overview of level set methods for etching, deposition, and lithography development. IEEE Transactions on Semiconductors Manufacturing **10**(1), 167–184 (1997)

19. Dice, L.R.: Measures of the Amount of Ecologic Association Between Species. Ecology **26**(3), 297–302 (1945)

20. Huttenlocher, D.P., Klanderman, G.A., Rucklidge, W.J.: Comparing images using the Hausdorff distance. IEEE Transactions on Pattern Analysis and Machine Intelligence **15**(9), 850–863 (1993)

21. Aribi, Y., Hamza, F., Wali, A., Alimi, M.A., Guermazi, F.: An Automated System for the Segmentation of Dynamic Scintigraphic Images. Applied Medical Informatics **34**(2), 1–12 (2014)

Adaptive Saliency-Weighted 2D-to-3D Video Conversion

Hamed Taher, Muhammad Rushdi$^{(\boxtimes)}$, Muhammad Islam, and Ahmed Badawi

Department of Biomedical and Systems Engineering, Cairo University,
Giza 12613, Egypt
hamedtaher181@gmail.com, {mrushdi,mislam,ambadawi}@eng.cu.edu.eg
http://www.bmes.cufe.edu.eg

Abstract. Creating 3D video content from existing 2D video has been stimulated by recent growth in 3DTV technologies. Depth cues from motion, focus, gradient, or texture shading are typically computed to create 3D world perception. More selective attention might be introduced using manual or automated methods for entertainment or educational purposes. In this paper, we propose an adaptive conversion framework that combines depth and visual saliency cues. A user study was designed and subjective quality scores on test videos were obtained using a tailored single stimulus continuous quality scale (SSCQS) method. The resulting mean opinion scores show that our method is favored by human observers in comparison to other state-of-the-art conversion methods.

Keywords: 3D video · Saliency · Depth cues · Subjective quality evaluation

1 Introduction

Stereoscopic video technologies have been well recognized as the next major milestone in digital video industry nowadays. In recent years, 3D videos have become increasingly widespread and more popular. For generating 3D images and video content, three different approaches can be distinguished [6]. First, 3D content can be captured by two or more synchronized cameras in a multi-view arrangement and augmented by depth information captured with a depth sensor. Second, techniques from computer graphics can be used to generate 3D content from a 3D model of the scene. Finally, existing 2D content can be converted into 3D content using manual or automatic video processing techniques [10,21]. Indeed, some classic 2D movies or TV programs can be revived through the conversion. It is desirable to have techniques that can convert legacy 2D movies to 3D in an efficient and inexpensive way. Currently, the movie industry uses expensive solutions that tend to be highly manual. The visual quality and comfort must at least be comparable to conventional standards to guarantee a strain-free viewing experience. Depth cues are the key for generating 3D videos from 2D ones. Binocular and monocular depth cues generate depth information through the use

ⓒ Springer International Publishing Switzerland 2015
G. Azzopardi and N. Petkov (Eds.): CAIP 2015, Part II, LNCS 9257, pp. 737–748, 2015.
DOI: 10.1007/978-3-319-23117-4_63

of both eyes and one eye, respectively. Several methods have been proposed for depth extraction from depth cues for 2D-to-3D conversion [10,20]. In particular, monocular depth cues can be grouped into pictorial and motion cues. Pictorial cues include focus/defocus cues, geometric cues, and color and intensity cues. Focus cues for object depth come from the amount of blur which increases as the object's surface moves away from the camera's focusing distance. Geometry-related pictorial depth cues include information such as relative size, distance to horizon, occlusion, shadows, interposition, linear perspective, height on a plane and texture gradient [20]. Color and intensity variations could give information on the depth of objects. Depth cues based on these variations include atmospheric scattering, light and shadow distribution, figure-ground perception, and local contrast. Motion cues in video come from motion parallax which refers to the relative motion of objects at different distances. Objects close to the observer appear to move faster than objects that are further away. Structure-from-stereo (SfS) and structure-from-motion (SfM) [16] can be applied to estimate motion parallax and convert it into depth cues. Moreover, the 2D-to-3D conversion outcomes can be further suited to human observers by exploiting the theory of selective visual attention. Visual attention is an important feature of the human visual system. The human eye can detect visually distinctive scene regions in a pre-attentive, effortless, and rapid manner. These filtered regions are then attentively perceived and processed in finer details for extraction of richer high-level information [1]. The important regions for visual attention are also termed as salient regions or Regions of Interest (ROIs) in natural images and videos [14]. Many computer vision techniques have been proposed to detect saliency in images and videos [1,2,4]. In this work, we compare three different approaches to investigate the role of selective visual attention during the 2D-to-3D video conversion process. For the first approach, we used depth cues obtained from a 2D video by nonparametric sampling for creating a corresponding 3D video [10]. For the second approach, selective attention is given to scene objects by adjusting the depth map obtained in the first approach. The adjusted depth cues are then used for converting the 2D video to a 3D one. Selective attention can be given to specific objects manually or automatically. We chose to follow an automated approach in which more attention is given to moving objects that are automatically detected from motion fields using image features, such as color, shape, texture, contours [9,11,18,19]. For the third approach that we propose here, we adapted the depth field obtained from the first approach using visual saliency cues to create novel saliency-weighted 3D videos from their 2D counterparts. Indeed, there have been several attempts to study the effect of depth on saliency and attention [3,12]. Moreover, several methods have been proposed to detect saliency for stereoscopic (3D) images [5,17]. However, for saliency computation in our proposed approach, we are given a 2D video and our goal is to compute saliency for this video as a step towards converting the 2D video into a 3D one. Consequently, we used the approach of Ruksana and Kumar [15] of obtaining the saliency map from 2D video by a bottom-up computational model of visual attention based on wavelet transforms. The rest of the paper is as follows. In Section 2, the three different conversion approaches are explained. In Section 3, we give the details of the subjective quality assessment methodology to compare the outcomes of the three conversion approaches. Analysis and promising results of our approach are outlined in Section 4. Conclusions and suggestions for future work are given in Section 5.

2   2D-to-3D Conversion Methods

2.1   Video Conversion Using Monocular Depth Cues

Karsch *et al.* [10] proposed a nonparametric depth sampling approach to generate depth maps from 2D videos. These 2D videos can be then converted into 3D videos. We adopt this approach as the-state-of-art baseline method since the method is automatic; it exhibits visually pleasing results; and it is applicable in cases where other methods fail, such as those based on motion parallax and structure from motion; and also works for single images and dynamic scenes. Given an input image, this method makes three steps. First, given a database of RGBD images, matching candidate images in the database that are similar to the input image in RGB space are found. Second, the SIFT Flow [13] warping procedure is applied to the candidate images and depths to align them with the input image. Third, a global optimization procedure incorporating temporal information (motion estimation and optical flow) is used to interpolate and smooth the warped candidate depth values; this results in the inferred depth. In particular, the global optimization objective for handling video is formulated by adding two terms to the single-frame objective [10]:

$$E_{vid}(D) = E(D) + \sum_{i:pixel} \nu E_c(D_i) + \mu E_m(D_i) \qquad (1)$$

where E_c encourages temporal coherence while E_m uses motion cues to improve the depth of moving objects. The weights ν and μ balance the relative influence of each term. Then, the inferred depth is used for the 2D-to-3D video conversion.

2.2   Video Conversion Using Motion-Weighted Monocular Depth

In this approach, selective attention is given to some scene objects by adjusting the depth map obtained in the first approach. The selection can be done either manually through user interaction or automatically. We choose here the automatic option where moving objects are selected in two steps. First, we detect motion in the 2D video using an optical-flow based approach [9]. The moving objects are then separated from the background in each frame by applying a threshold to the motion vector magnitudes [11]. Hence, the depth values (computed using the baseline method of Subsection 2.1) for the pixels of foreground moving objects P_{FG} are scaled down to get the objects *closer* to the observer:

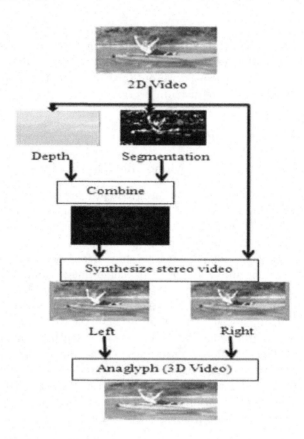

Fig. 1. A flowchart of the 2D-to-3D conversion process using depth weighted with motion cues. The estimated motion field is used to segment the foreground moving object. Depth is then adapted by the motion cues to get the moving object closer to the viewer.

$$D(P_{FG}) = \lambda D(P_{FG}) \tag{2}$$

where the user-specified scale-down parameter $0 \leqslant \lambda \leqslant 1$ is set here to 0.1. Figure 1 summarizes this approach.

2.3   2D-to-3D Conversion Using Saliency-Weighted Monocular Depth

In this approach, we propose to adapt the depth map (computed using the baseline method of Subsection 2.1) using visual saliency cues to create novel saliency weighted depth map for video conversion (See Figure 2). For saliency computation, we followed the recent approach of Ruksana and Kumar [15] of obtaining the saliency map from 2D video by a bottom-up computational model of visual

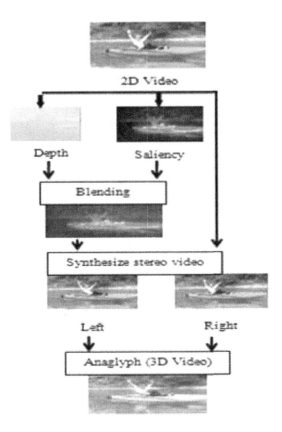

Fig. 2. 2D-to-3D conversion using depth weighted with the 2D video saliency map. Depth is adapted by the saliency cues to get the salient objects closer to the viewer.

attention based on wavelet transforms. In this model, an input image is first preprocessed and analyzed in the wavelet domain. Second, the resulting wavelet coefficients that represent the details of the image at various scales are used to create several feature maps with increasing frequency bandwidths. Third, local and global features such as color, contrast, luminance, orientation, texture, and motion are used to produce corresponding saliency maps. Fourth, a final saliency map is obtained by combining the local and global saliency maps. Integration is performed to modulate the local saliency map with its corresponding global saliency map [15]:

$$S(x,y) = M(S_l(x,y)C^{S_G(x,y)})I_{k \times k} \qquad (3)$$

where $S(x,y)$ is the final saliency map, $S_l(x,y)$, $S_G(x,y)$ are the local and global saliency maps, $M(.)$ is a non-linear normalization function to diminish the effect of amplification on the map, and $I_{k \times k}$ is a $k \times k$ 2D Gaussian low-pass filter with $k = 5$. The depth values are then blended with the saliency values:

$$D_S(x,y) = \alpha D_S(x,y) + (1 - \alpha)S(x,y) \qquad (4)$$

where $0 \leqslant \alpha \leqslant 1$ is the blending weight which is chosen to be 0.5. Hence, the saliency-weighted depth values $D_S(x,y)$ are used for the 2D-to-3D conversion process.

3 Subjective Quality Assessment

3.1 Equipment

A 15.4-inch display (Sony Vaio VGN-NS21S), with a resolution of 1280 × 800 pixels has been used to display the test stimuli with the subject putting on 3D glasses (resin glass) to view the 3D videos. The subject was seated in line with the center of the monitor.

3.2 Observers

Twenty subjects (2 females, 18 males) participated in the test. Half of the subjects are non-expert viewers with a marginal experience of 3D image and video viewing. The age distribution ranged from 20 to 42 years with an average of 27. The stereo vision was tested according to the ITU recommendation BT.1438 [7].

3.3 Stimuli

Three test video sequences were used in the experiments: Rhino (Figure3), Boat (Figure 4), and Bicycle (Figure 5). For each video sequence, 3D video stimuli were generated from the 2D video using the baseline depth estimation method (Subsection 2.1), the motion-weighted depth estimation method (Subsection 2.2), and our saliency-weighted depth estimation method (Subsection 2.3).

3.4 Procedure

Several recommendations for the subjective evaluation of 2D visual quality according to standardized methods have been issued by the International Telecommunication Union (ITU) including the ITU-R BT.500 recommendation [8] which describes methods for the subjective quality assessment of Standard Definition Television (SDTV) pictures. The most prominent methods are the Double Stimulus Continuous Quality Scale (DSCQS), the Double Stimulus Impairment Scale (DSIS) and the Single Stimulus Continuous-Quality Evaluation (SSCQE). A Single Stimulus (SS) method has been adopted for the subjective quality evaluation. In order to determine the influence of the different methods on the 3D quality, a continuous quality scale with 5 levels (excellent, good, fair, poor, bad), as described in ITU-R BT.500 [8], has been used. During the testing the subjects evaluated the quality of the 9 test stimuli, which are displayed in random order. The 9 stimuli correspond to the 3D videos that were generated with the three approaches outlined in Section 2. For each subject, each stimulus is shown and a short break between stimuli is given, during which human subjects provide their opinion scores.

4   Analysis and Results

4.1   Outlier Detection

The screening of subjects was performed according to the guidelines described in Section 2.3.1 of Annex 2 of ITU-R BT.500-11 recommendation [6,8]. First, for each stimulus, the distribution of scores across subjects is tested for normality. This is done by evaluating the kurtosis of the distribution. If the kurtosis coefficient is between 2 and 4, the distribution is assumed to be normal. Then, the score of each observer is compared with an upper and a lower threshold computed as the mean value ± the standard deviation associated to that stimulus (times two, if normal, or times 20, if non-normal).

For each subject, every time his or her score exceeds the upper threshold, a counter, P_i, is incremented. Similarly, every time his or her score is found to be below the lower threshold, a counter Q_i is incremented. Finally, the following two ratios are calculated: $P_i + Q_i$ divided by the total number of scores from each subject for the whole session, and $P_i - Q_i$ divided by $P_i + Q_i$ as an absolute value. If the first ratio is greater than 5% and the second ratio is less than 30%, then subject i is considered to be an outlier and all his or her scores are discarded.

Using the outlier detection described above, 2 of the 20 subjects have been discarded as outliers. Thus the statistical analysis is based on the scores from 18 subjects only.

4.2   Score Computation

After the outlier removal, the mean opinion score is computed for each test condition j as:

$$MOS_j = \frac{\sum_{i=1}^{N} s_{ij}}{N} \tag{5}$$

where N is the number of valid subjects and s_{ij} is the score by subject i for the test condition j [6]. The relationship between the estimated mean opinion scores based on a sample of the population (namely, the subjects who took part in the experiments) and the true mean values of the entire population is given by the confidence interval of the estimated mean. Due to the small number of subjects (18 persons), the $100 \times (1 - \alpha)\%$ confidence intervals (CI) for mean opinion scores are computed using the Student's t-distribution, as follows:

$$CI_j = t(1 - \frac{\alpha}{2}, N)\frac{\sigma_i}{\sqrt{N}} \tag{6}$$

where $t(1 - \frac{\alpha}{2}, N)$ is the t-value corresponding to a two tailed t-Student distribution with $N - 1$ degrees of freedom and a desired significance level (equal to 1-degree of confidence), N corresponds to the number of subjects after outlier detection (18 in our experiments), and σ_i is the standard deviation of a single test condition across the subjects. The interpretation of a confidence interval is that if the same test is repeated for a large number of times, using each time a

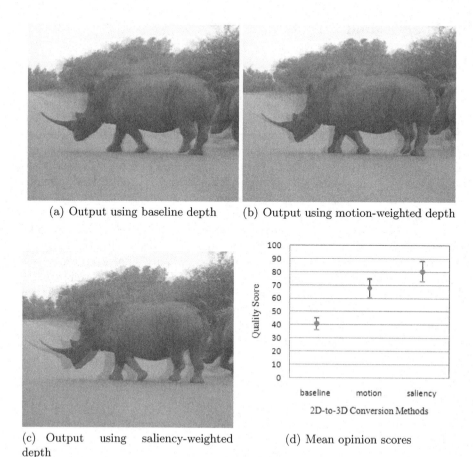

(a) Output using baseline depth   (b) Output using motion-weighted depth

(c) Output   using   saliency-weighted   (d) Mean opinion scores
depth

Fig. 3. 3D conversion results for the Rhino sequence. Sample 3D video frames generated using different depth weighting methods: (a) the baseline method, (b) the motion-weighted method and (c) our saliency-weighted method. Images are best viewed with 3D glasses on the screen. (d) Mean opinion scores show clear preference for our saliency-based method. The rhino has clear saliency and motion features that can be exploited to improve the human visual experience.

random sample of the population, and a confidence interval is constructed every time, then $100(1 - \alpha)\%$ of these intervals will contain the true value [6]. We computed our confidence intervals for an α, equal to 0.05, which corresponds to a significance level of 95%. The mean opinion scores and confidence intervals versus the methods are plotted for the Rhino (Figure 3(d)), Boat (Figure 4(d)), and Bicycle (Figure 5(d)). Several remarks can be made. First, in general, the small width of the confidence intervals shows that the subjective evaluation has appropriate and representative complexity of the population opinion scores. Second, the individual ratings (not shown) are very similar and consistent across

(a) Output using baseline depth

(b) Output using motion-weighted depth

(c) Output using saliency-weighted depth

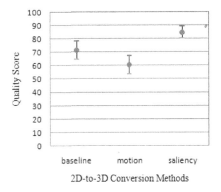

(d) Mean opinion scores

Fig. 4. 3D conversion results for the Boat sequence. Sample 3D video frames generated using different depth weighting methods: (a) the baseline method, (b) the motion-weighted method and (c) our saliency-weighted method. Images are best viewed with 3D glasses on the screen. (d) Mean opinion scores show clear preference for our saliency-based method. The scores of different methods are close since the boat has slow motion and relatively low saliency features.

the subjects. Third, our saliency-weighted conversion method achieves the best mean opinion scores across all video examples. Fourth, the influence of different methods on the 3D video quality depends on the motion and saliency characteristics of the input scene. On one hand, the 3D quality for the Rhino and Bicycle scenes changes sharply with different methods. This is probably because of the fast motion and relatively high saliency of the foreground objects. On the other hand, for the Boat scene, the quality changes relatively slowly. This can be ascribed to the slow motion of the boat and its relatively low saliency. A closer look at the individual curves reveals that the quality of the 3D video for the Rhino is between fair and excellent, the quality of the 3D videos for the Boat is mostly above good and the Bicycle video covers the quality range between poor and good. In summary, our saliency-weighted depth estimation method

(a) Output using baseline depth   (b) Output using motion-weighted depth

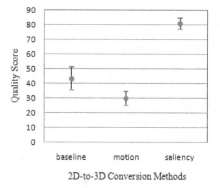

(c) Output using saliency-weighted depth   (d) Mean opinion scores

Fig. 5. 3D conversion results for the Bicycle sequence. Sample 3D video frames generated using different depth weighting methods: (a) the baseline method, (b) the motion-weighted method and (c) our saliency-weighted method. Images are best viewed with 3D glasses on the screen. (d) Mean opinion scores show clear preference for our saliency-based method. The sharp difference between the motion and saliency-based outputs shows the importance of saliency for improving the human visual experience.

has a better 3D subjective quality over the range of the test videos. Hence, the proposed method can serve to enhance the 3D human visual experience.

5   Conclusions and Future Work

We investigated in this work several approaches for incorporating selective visual attention cues in the depth estimation process for the 2D-to-3D conversion process. In particular, our novel saliency-weighted approach was shown through subjective quality assessment to be the most favorable by human observers. Of course, testing with more subjects on a larger set of natural videos is needed to strengthen our conclusions. The results suggest research directions on the interaction between visual saliency and depth to create better 3D visual experience for human observers.

Moreover, this work may be applied for making more appealing 3D video content for the cinema and TV industries.

References

1. Borji, A., Cheng, M., Jiang, H., Li, J.: Salient object detection: A survey (2014). CoRR abs/1411.5878. http://arxiv.org/abs/1411.5878
2. Borji, A., Cheng, M., Jiang, H., Li, J.: Salient object detection: A benchmark. CoRR abs/1501.02741 (2015). http://arxiv.org/abs/1501.02741
3. Ciptadi, A., Hermans, T., Rehg, J.M.: An in depth view of saliency. In: British Machine Vision Conference (BMVC), September 2013
4. Duncan, K., Sarkar, S.: Saliency in images and video: a brief survey. Computer Vision **IET 6**(6), 514–523 (2012)
5. Fang, Y., Wang, J., Narwaria, M., Le Callet, P., Lin, W.: Saliency detection for stereoscopic images. IEEE Transactions on Image Processing **23**(6), 2625–2636 (2014)
6. Goldmann, L., De Simone, F., Ebrahimi, T.: A comprehensive database and subjective evaluation methodology for quality of experience in stereoscopic video (2010). http://dx.doi.org/10.1117/12.839438
7. ITU-R: Bt.1438 subjective assessment of stereoscopic television pictures
8. ITU-R: Bt.500- 11 methodology for the subjective assessment of the quality of television pictures
9. Karasulu, B., Korukoglu, S.: Performance Evaluation Software - Moving Object Detection and Tracking in Videos. Springer Briefs in Computer Science. Springer (2013). http://dx.doi.org/10.1007/978-1-4614-6534-8
10. Karsch, K., Liu, C., Kang, S.B.: Depth extraction from video using non-parametric sampling. In: Fitzgibbon, A., Lazebnik, S., Perona, P., Sato, Y., Schmid, C. (eds.) ECCV 2012, Part V. LNCS, vol. 7576, pp. 775–788. Springer, Heidelberg (2012)
11. Krishna, M., Ravishankar, M., Babu, D.: Automatic detection and tracking of moving objects in complex environments for video surveillance applications. In: 2011 3rd International Conference on Electronics Computer Technology (ICECT), vol. 1, pp. 234–238, April 2011
12. Lang, C., Nguyen, T.V., Katti, H., Yadati, K., Kankanhalli, M., Yan, S.: Depth matters: influence of depth cues on visual saliency. In: Fitzgibbon, A., Lazebnik, S., Perona, P., Sato, Y., Schmid, C. (eds.) ECCV 2012, Part II. LNCS, vol. 7573, pp. 101–115. Springer, Heidelberg (2012). http://dx.doi.org/10.1007/978-3-642-33709-3_8
13. Liu, C., Yuen, J., Torralba, A.: SIFT flow: Dense correspondence across scenes and its applications. IEEE Transactions on Pattern Analysis and Machine Intelligence **33**(5), 978–994 (2011)
14. Ramenahalli, S., Niebur, E.: Computing 3D saliency from a 2D image. In: 2013 47th Annual Conference on Information Sciences and Systems (CISS), pp. 1–5, March 2013
15. Ruksana, S., Kumar, V.: A novel saliency detection framework using low level multi scale image features based on wavelet transformation technique. International Journal of Soft Computing and Engineering (IJSCE) **III**(1), 8–18 (2014)
16. Szeliski, R.: Computer Vision: Algorithms and Applications, 1st edn. Springer-Verlag New York Inc., New York (2010)

17. Wang, J., Fang, Y., Narwaria, M., Lin, W., Le Callet, P.: Stereoscopic image retargeting based on 3D saliency detection. In: 2014 IEEE International Conference on Acoustics, Speech and Signal Processing (ICASSP), pp. 669–673, May 2014
18. Wu, Y., Lim, J., Yang, M.H.: Online object tracking: a benchmark. In: 2013 IEEE Conference on Computer Vision and Pattern Recognition (CVPR), pp. 2411–2418, June 2013
19. Zhang, D., Javed, O., Shah, M.: Video object segmentation through spatially accurate and temporally dense extraction of primary object regions. In: 2013 IEEE Conference on Computer Vision and Pattern Recognition (CVPR), pp. 628–635, June 2013
20. Zhang, L., Vazquez, C., Knorr, S.: 3D-TV content creation: Automatic 2D-to-3D video conversion. IEEE Transactions on Broadcasting **57**(2), 372–383 (2011)
21. Zhang, Z., Wang, R., Zhou, C., Wang, Y., Gao, W.: A compact stereoscopic video representation for 3D video generation and coding. Data Compression Conference (DCC) **2012**, 189–198 (2012)

Variational Multiple Warping for Cardiac Image Analysis

Shun Inagaki[1], Hayato Itoh[1], and Atsushi Imiya[2]([envelope])

[1] School of Advanced Integration Science, Chiba University, Chiba, Japan
[2] Institute of Management and Information Technologies, Chiba University,
Yayoi-cho 1-33, Inage-ku, Chiba 263-8522, Japan
`imiya@faculty.chiba-u.jp`

Abstract. This paper focuses on multiple image warping that is used to compute deformation fields between an image and a collection of images as an extension of variational registration. First, we develop a variational method for the computation of the average of volumetric beating-heart images. Second, we also develop a variational method for the frame-rate up-conversion of optical-flow fields, in which we combine motion coherence in an image sequence and the smoothness of the temporal flow field.

1 Introduction

In this paper, we develop a method to compute deformation fields between an image and a collection of images. Image warping between an image and a collection of images provides the average image and shape of a collection of volumetric images and objects. We apply this method to the computation of the average of volumetric beating-heart images and for the frame rate up-conversion of beating-heart images. We deal with a mathematical theory for the computation of anatomical averages of organs from view point of shape analysis [1,2]. Furthermore, we prove several mathematical properties of the computation of temporal 3D organs. These properties clarify that we are required to select an average computation method which is suitable to clinical and research purposes.

Various methods of computing the average of geometrical shapes are proposed [4–7], based on the mathematical definition that shapes are the boundary contours of physical objects [5,6]. In medical image diagnosis and retrieval [3], the average images of individual organs provide anatomical and geometrical properties for the general expression of organs. In the comparative reading of medical images, image registration, which has attracted the attention of researchers for decades, is used to classify the differences among images by establishing local deformation fields among elements of a collection of given shapes [4–6]. For spatiotemporal volumetric data, we can compute (1) the temporal average, which is the average of a heart during a cycle, (2) the frame average, which is the average of hearts at a given frame in a sequence and (3) the temporal average of frame averages. The first, second and third averages derive the standard shape

© Springer International Publishing Switzerland 2015
G. Azzopardi and N. Petkov (Eds.): CAIP 2015, Part II, LNCS 9257, pp. 749–759, 2015.
DOI: 10.1007/978-3-319-23117-4_64

of the organ of a human, the standard shape of a frame of beating hearts and the standard shape of a collection of beating hearts, respectively. The second average detects abnormalities of a heart from a collection of hearts.

Furthermore, for applications of image analysis algorithms developed in computer vision to low-frame-rate image sequences, which are common in biomedical imaging and image video analysis, the up-conversion of the frame rate of image sequences is a fundamental preprocessing [8]. Therefore, we develop a method for simultaneous up-conversion of both an image sequence and their deformation motion fields. Several methods of frame-rate up-conversion for an image sequence using the optical-flow field have been proposed [9]. Superresolution recovers high-resolution images and/or image sequences from low-resolution images and/or image sequences [10]. There are some methods based on temporal coherence [10–12], which is based on the idea that successive frames have similar contents and small transformations.

2   Variational Average Computation

Multiple Variational Warping. We define a variational average image g of volumetric images $\{f_i\}_{i=1}^m$ in the three-dimensional Euclidean space $\mathbf{R}^3$ as the minimiser of the variational problem

$$J(\{u_k\}_{k=1}^m) = \sum_{k=1}^m \int_{\mathbf{R}^3} (g(x - u_k) - f_k(x))^2 dx + \lambda \int_{\mathbf{R}^3} |\nabla g|^2 dx$$

$$+ \mu \sum_{k=1}^m \int_{\mathbf{R}^3} |\nabla u_k|^2 dx + \sigma \int_{\mathbf{R}^3} \left(\sum_{k=1}^m u_k\right)^2 dx. \tag{1}$$

For regularisers,

$$\Gamma = \int_{\mathbf{R}^3} |\nabla g|^2 dx, \ U_k = \int_{\mathbf{R}^3} |\nabla u_k|^2 dx, \ S = \sum_{k=1}^m u_k \tag{2}$$

imply that the average g and the deformation fields are smooth and that the average image exists at the median point of the deformation fields.

Variational Average Computation. We set the solution of the variational problem of eq. (1) as

$$g = \mathrm{VA}_k(\{f_k\}_{k=1}^m). \tag{3}$$

For a collection of spatiotemporal functions $\{h_i(x, t)\}_{i=1}^m$ defined in the interval $0 \le t \le T$, we define a collection of temporally sampled data as

$$h_{ij}(x) = h_i(x, (j - 1)\Delta), i = 1, 2, \cdots, m, j = 1, \cdots, n \tag{4}$$

for $(n - 1)\Delta = T$. For $\{h_{ij}\}_{i=1 \ j=1}^{m \ n}$, we define a pair of collections of averages as

$$\{g_i(x)\}_{i=1}^m = \mathrm{VA}_j(\{h_{ij}\}_{i=1 \ j=1}^{m \ n}), \ \{g(x, j)\}_{j=1}^n = \mathrm{VA}_i(\{h_{ij}\}_{i=1 \ j=1}^{m \ n}). \tag{5}$$

Here, $g_i(\boldsymbol{x})$ and $g(\boldsymbol{x}, j_0)$ are the temporal average of the sequence $h_i(\boldsymbol{x}, t)$ and the frame average of $h_i(\boldsymbol{x}, j_0\Delta)$ for a fixed j_0 such that $1 \leq j \leq n$, respectively. Moreover, these two averages derive

$$\overline{g}(\boldsymbol{x}) = \text{VA}_i(\{g_i\}_{i=1}^m), \ \underline{g}(\boldsymbol{x}) = \text{VA}_j(\{g(\boldsymbol{x}, j)\}_{j=1}^n). \tag{6}$$

Here, $\overline{g}$ and $\underline{g}$ are the spatial average of the temporal averages and the temporal average of the spatial averages, respectively. Figure 1 shows the relations among these averages for temporal volumetric image data. For two averages $\overline{g}$ and $\underline{g}$, we have the following property.

Property 1. The spatial average of the temporal average $\overline{g}$ and the temporal average of the spatial averages $\underline{g}$ generally satisfy the inequality $\overline{g}(\boldsymbol{x}) \neq \underline{g}(\boldsymbol{x})$.

This property implies that the order of operations for average computation affects the results.

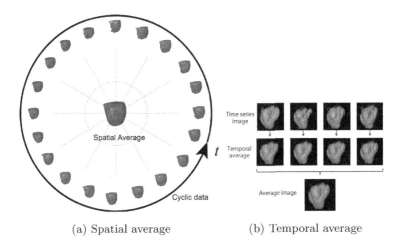

(a) Spatial average   (b) Temporal average

Fig. 1. Average image. (a) The average shape of organs is computed by the uni-step method. (b) The average shape of temporal organs, such as beating hearts, is computed by the bi-step method. First, we compute the temporal average of an organ. Then, the spatial average is computed from individual temporal averages.

Variational Frame Rate Up-conversion. Setting $f(\boldsymbol{x}, t)$ to be a spatiotemporal image, we develop an algorithm to compute the optical-flow field $\boldsymbol{u}_{\frac{1}{2}}(\boldsymbol{x}, t)$ of $f(\boldsymbol{x}, t + \frac{1}{2})$.

For the convenience of analysis, we set

$$f^+(\boldsymbol{x}) = f(\boldsymbol{x}, t + 1), \ f^-(\boldsymbol{x}, t) = f(\boldsymbol{x}, t), \tag{7}$$

$$g(\boldsymbol{x}) = f(\boldsymbol{x}, t + \frac{1}{2}), \tag{8}$$

$$\boldsymbol{v} = \boldsymbol{u}_{\frac{1}{2}}(\boldsymbol{x}, t), \ \boldsymbol{w} = \boldsymbol{u}_{\frac{1}{2}}(\boldsymbol{x}, t + \frac{1}{2}). \tag{9}$$

Furthermore, stting

$$g(\boldsymbol{x}) = f^+(\boldsymbol{x} - \boldsymbol{w}), \; g(\boldsymbol{x}) = f^-(\boldsymbol{x} + \boldsymbol{v}), \; \boldsymbol{u} = \boldsymbol{v} + \boldsymbol{w}, \qquad (10)$$

we can have the interframe image g and the up-converted optical flow fields, $\boldsymbol{v}$ and $\boldsymbol{w}$ using variational method.

Figure 2(a) shows the relationships of eq. (10).

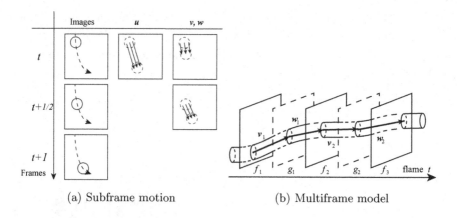

(a) Subframe motion   (b) Multiframe model

Fig. 2. Interframe motion and subframe image. (a) Geometric relations of g, f^-, f^+, $\boldsymbol{u}$, $\boldsymbol{v}$ and $\boldsymbol{w}$. (b) Input images f_1, f_2 and f_3, output images g_k and g_{k+1}, and output optical flow $\boldsymbol{v}_k$, $\boldsymbol{w}_k$, $\boldsymbol{v}_{k+1}$ and $\boldsymbol{w}_{k+1}$.

Let the interframe image g_k be the image between two given frames

$$f_k := f(x, y, k), \; f_{k+1} := f(x, y, k+1). \qquad (11)$$

Setting the vectors $\boldsymbol{v}_k$ and $\boldsymbol{w}_k$ to be the flow vector fields between f_k and g_k and between g_k and f_{k+1}, respectively, we assume that each $\boldsymbol{v}_k$ and $\boldsymbol{w}_k$ satisfy the optical flow constraint. Figure 2(b) shows the relationships of multiframe up-conversion. Then, we have the energy functional

$$J(\{g_k, \boldsymbol{v}_k, \boldsymbol{w}_k\}_{k=1}^{n-1}) = \int_\Omega (J_d + \alpha J_g + \beta J_s + \gamma J_t)\mathrm{d}\boldsymbol{x}, \qquad (12)$$

where

$$J_d = \sum_{k=1}^{n-1}((g_k(\boldsymbol{x}) - f_k(\boldsymbol{x} + \boldsymbol{v}_k))^2 + (f_{k+1}(\boldsymbol{x} - \boldsymbol{w}_k) - g_k(\boldsymbol{x}))^2), \qquad (13)$$

$$J_g = \sum_{k=1}^{n-1}|\nabla g_k|^2 d\boldsymbol{x}, \; J_s = \sum_{k=1}^{n-1}(|\nabla \boldsymbol{v}_k|^2 + |\nabla \boldsymbol{w}_k|^2), \qquad (14)$$

$$J_t = \sum_{k=1}^{n-1}(|\boldsymbol{w}_k - \boldsymbol{v}_k|^2) + \sum_{k=1}^{n-2}(|\boldsymbol{v}_{k+1} - \boldsymbol{w}_k|^2)$$

$$+ \sum_{k=1}^{n-2}(|\boldsymbol{v}_{k+1} - 2\boldsymbol{w}_k + \boldsymbol{v}_k|^2 + |\boldsymbol{w}_{k+1} - 2\boldsymbol{v}_k + \boldsymbol{w}_k|^2). \tag{15}$$

Here, J_d is the data term for image registration. J_s, J_t and J_g are regularisation terms for the computation of smooth flow fields. The constraints J_t^{1st} and J_t^{2nd} require that the flow field is temporally piecewise smooth and temporally piecewise linear, respectively. As the minimisers of the variational problem, we obtain vector fields $\boldsymbol{v}_k$ and $\boldsymbol{w}_k$ and generate g_k simultaneously for the estimation of high-frame-rate optical-flow fields and images.

3   Fast Numerical Computation

We derive a numerical method for solving eq. (1). From eq. (1), for the variational average image g and the deformation fields $\boldsymbol{u}_k$, we derive the Euler-Lagrange equations

$$\alpha \Delta g(\boldsymbol{x}) - G = 0, \quad \beta \Delta \boldsymbol{u}_k(\boldsymbol{x}) - U_k = 0, \tag{16}$$

where

$$G = \sum_{k=1}^{m}(g(\boldsymbol{x}) - f_k(\boldsymbol{x} - \boldsymbol{u}_k)), \tag{17}$$

$$U_k = \gamma(\sum_{k=1}^{m} \boldsymbol{u}_k + (g(\boldsymbol{x}) - f_k(\boldsymbol{x} - \boldsymbol{u}_k))\nabla(g(\boldsymbol{x}) - f_k(\boldsymbol{x} - \boldsymbol{u}_k))). \tag{18}$$

Next, we convert the elliptic partial differential equations in eq. (16) to the diffusion equations

$$\frac{\partial g}{\partial t} = \Delta g(\boldsymbol{x}) - \frac{1}{\alpha}G, \quad \frac{\partial \boldsymbol{u}_k}{\partial t} = \Delta \boldsymbol{u}_k(\boldsymbol{x}) - \frac{1}{\beta}U_k, \tag{19}$$

and discretise them as

$$\frac{g^{(n+1)} - g^{(n)}}{\tau} = \boldsymbol{L}g^{(n+1)} - \frac{1}{\alpha}G^{(n)}, \tag{20}$$

$$\frac{\boldsymbol{u}_k^{(n+1)} - \boldsymbol{u}_k^{(n)}}{\tau} = \boldsymbol{L}\boldsymbol{u}_k^{(n+1)} - \frac{1}{\beta}U_k^{(n)}, \tag{21}$$

where $\boldsymbol{L}$ is the discrete Laplacian operation.

To minimise the energy functional of eq. (12), setting

$$V_k = (g_k(\boldsymbol{x}) - f_k(\boldsymbol{x} + \boldsymbol{v}_k))\nabla f_k(\boldsymbol{x} + \boldsymbol{v}_k) + \gamma_1(2\boldsymbol{v}_k - \boldsymbol{w}_k - \boldsymbol{w}_{k-1})$$
$$+ \gamma_2(\boldsymbol{v}_{k+1} - 4\boldsymbol{w}_k + 6\boldsymbol{v}_k - 4\boldsymbol{w}_{k-1} + \boldsymbol{v}_{k-1}), \tag{22}$$
$$W_k = (g_k(\boldsymbol{x}) - f_{k+1}(\boldsymbol{x} - \boldsymbol{w}_k))\nabla f_{k+1}(\boldsymbol{x} - \boldsymbol{w}_k) + \gamma_1(2\boldsymbol{w}_k - \boldsymbol{v}_k - \boldsymbol{v}_{k+1})$$
$$+ \gamma_2(\boldsymbol{w}_{k+1} - 4\boldsymbol{v}_{k+1} + 6\boldsymbol{w}_k - 4\boldsymbol{v}_k + \boldsymbol{w}_{k-1}), \tag{23}$$
$$G_k = (2g_k(\boldsymbol{x}) - (f_k(\boldsymbol{x} + \boldsymbol{v}_k) + f_{k+1}(\boldsymbol{x} - \boldsymbol{w}_k))), \tag{24}$$

the Euler-Lagrange equations of eq. (12) are

$$\Delta \boldsymbol{v}_k - \frac{V_k}{\beta} = 0, \ \Delta \boldsymbol{w}_k - \frac{W_k}{\beta} = 0, \ \Delta g_k - \frac{G_k}{\alpha} = 0. \tag{25}$$

For the associate diffusion equations of the Euler-Lagrange equations of eq. (25),

$$\frac{\partial \boldsymbol{v}_k}{\partial t} = \Delta \boldsymbol{v}_k - \frac{1}{\beta}V_k, \ \frac{\partial \boldsymbol{w}_k}{\partial t} = \Delta \boldsymbol{w}_k - \frac{1}{\beta}W_k, \ \frac{\partial g_k}{\partial t} = \Delta g_k(\boldsymbol{x}) - \frac{1}{\alpha}G_k \tag{26}$$

using semi-implicit discretisation, we obtain the iteration form

$$(\boldsymbol{I} - \tau \boldsymbol{L})\boldsymbol{v}_k^{(m+1)} = \boldsymbol{v}_k^{(m)} - \frac{\tau}{\beta}V_k^{(m)},$$
$$(\boldsymbol{I} - \tau \boldsymbol{L})\boldsymbol{w}_k^{(m+1)} = \boldsymbol{w}_k^{(m)} - \frac{\tau}{\beta}W_k^{(m)}, \tag{27}$$
$$(\boldsymbol{I} - \tau \boldsymbol{L})g_k^{(m+1)} = g_k^{(m)} - \frac{\tau}{\alpha}G_k^{(m)},$$

where $\boldsymbol{L}$ and $\boldsymbol{I}$ are the discrete Laplacian matrix and the identity matrix whose degree depends on the size of the discrete images.

Iteration forms derived in this section are described as

$$\boldsymbol{a}^{(n+1)} = (\boldsymbol{I} - \alpha \boldsymbol{L})^{-1}\boldsymbol{a}^{(n)} + f(\boldsymbol{a}^{(n)}), \tag{28}$$

For the Neumann boundary condition setting $\boldsymbol{U}$ to be the DCT-II matrix such that

$$\boldsymbol{U} = \left(\left(\epsilon \cos \frac{(2j+1)i}{2\pi}\pi M\right)\right), \ \epsilon = \begin{cases} 1 & \text{if } j = 0 \\ \frac{1}{\sqrt{2}} & \text{otherwise.} \end{cases} \tag{29}$$

and $\boldsymbol{\Sigma} = Diag(-4\sin^2 \frac{\pi k}{2M})$, we have the relation

$$\boldsymbol{I} - \alpha \boldsymbol{L} = \boldsymbol{U}^{(3)^\top}(\boldsymbol{I} - \alpha \boldsymbol{\Sigma}^{(3)})^{-1}\boldsymbol{U}^{(3)} \tag{30}$$

where

$$\boldsymbol{U}^{(3)} = \boldsymbol{U} \otimes \boldsymbol{U} \otimes \boldsymbol{U}, \ \boldsymbol{\Sigma}^{(3)} = \boldsymbol{\Sigma} \otimes \boldsymbol{\Sigma} \otimes \boldsymbol{\Sigma}. \tag{31}$$

Since

$$(\boldsymbol{I} - \alpha \boldsymbol{\Sigma}^{(3)})^{-1} = Diag\left(\frac{1}{1 - \alpha(\lambda_i + \lambda_j + \lambda_k)}\right), \tag{32}$$

where $\lambda_m = 4\sin^2 \frac{\pi m}{2M}$) the iteration forms are computed by using DCT and filtering operations. The matrix expression of this filtering operation is

In each iteration step, values which do not lie on the grids are generated from values on the grids as shown in Fig. 3(a). Therefore, as the initial values for the next step, values on the grids are generated by using the Delaunay triangulation. as shown in Fig. 3(b). The generated function f using this procedure minimises the criterion

$$J = \int_\Omega |\nabla f|^2 dx \tag{33}$$

in the region of interest $\Omega \subseteq \mathbf{R}^n$ for $n \geq 2$.

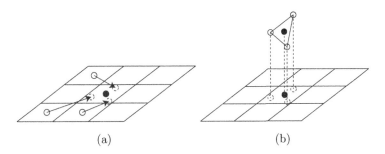

(a)   (b)

Fig. 3. Interpolation. (a) From values on the grids, values which do not lie on the grids are generated. (b) As the initial values for the next step, values on the grids are generated by using the Delaunay triangulation.

4   Numerical Examples

For numerical examples, we computed the averages of seven hearts with 20 frames. These images show rendered surfaces of volumetric grey valued images in the three-dimensional Euclidean space. The numerical results show the rendered surfaces. The resolution of each volumetric heart is Grey-value × Horizontal × Vertical × Depth $= 256 \times 128 \times 128 \times 15$. In total, the size of the data is $256 \times 128 \times 128 \times 15 \times 20 \times 7$. For the numerical computation, we adopt the regularisation parameters $\alpha = 10^{-1}$, $\beta = 10^2$ and $\gamma = 10^4$.

Figure 4(a) shows the spatial average of the temporal averages. Figure 4(b) shows the total deformation fields from the average to the individual temporal averages. In this radar chart, 20 frames of a volumetric beating-heart sequence are shown on the circle and the arrow from the origin of the circle is the deformation energy required to deform the temporal average, which is shown in the centre of the chart, to the volumetric image at each frame. The arrows show the total difference between the average and each shape on the circle.

Figures 5(a) and 5(b) show radar charts of the spatial temporal averages and the temporal spatial averages of a collection of heart sequences, respectively. Figure 5(c) shows relations among averages. In these evaluations, the volumetric

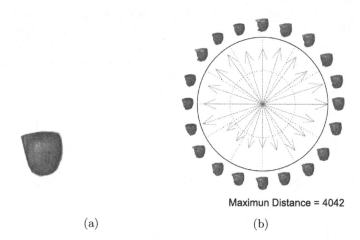

Maximun Distance = 4042

(a)   (b)

Fig. 4. The averages of a beating heart. (a) Variational average of a beating-heart sequence. (b) Radar chart of the total deformation norms for the variational temporal average of a beating heart. In the radar charts, 20 frames of a volumetric beating-heart sequence are shown on the circle and the arrow from the origin of the circle is the deformation energy required to deform the temporal average, which is shown in the centre of the chart, to the volumetric image at each frame. The arrows show the total difference between the average and each shape on the circle.

centroids of the average and each frame are aligned as the pre-processing In the radar charts, the arrows show the volumetric difference between the average at the centre and each frame of motion. Figure 5(d) shows the spatial average of the temporal averages. The boundary shape of the average heart shown in Fig. 5(d) is smoother than the boundary of the average heart shown in Fig. 4(a), since Figs. 4(a) and 5(d) are the temporal average of a beating heart and the spatial average of the temporal averages, respectively. Although temporal average of a beating heart is computed from 20 frame volumetric images, the spatial average of the temporal averages is computed from seven temporal averages. This geometrical property of average computation yields a shape with the smooth boundary.

Figure 6(a) shows the original image for the beating-heart sequence. Figure 6(b) shows, from top to bottom rows, three frames from the input image sequence, the optical flow fields computed by the large-displacement optical flow computation, the subframe image sequence and its optical flow fields computed by the two-frame method and the subframe image sequence and its optical flow fields computed by the multiple frame method using three frames and the subframe image sequence. Figure 6(b) shows that the interframe images are clearly generated. Figure 5(d) is the spatial average of the temporal averages For numerical computation, we set $(\alpha, \beta, \gamma) = (8 \times 10^{-2}, 10^3, 10^3)$,

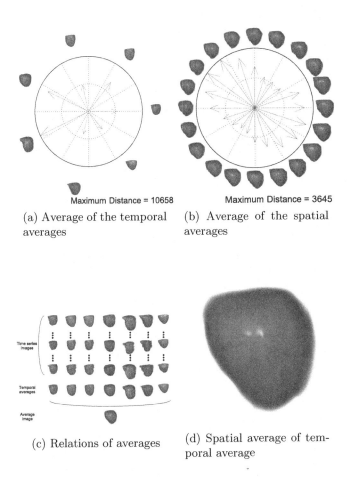

Fig. 5. Average of heart (a) Spatial temporal averages and (b) Temporal spatial averages of a collection of heart sequences (c) Relations among averages. (d) The spatial average of the temporal averages.

and $(\alpha, \beta, \gamma) = (8 \times 10^{-2}, 3 \times 10^2, 3 \times 10)$ for two- and three-frame methods, respectively.

Figure 6(b) implies that, for the beating heart sequence, the interframe optical flow fields computed using smoothness constrain produces are clear and accurate comparing the optical flow fields.

For the validation and performance evaluation procedures, we used standard pattern classification methods such as multiple scale description and linear discriminations [13]. This methodology for static organs provided theoretical evaluation measures.

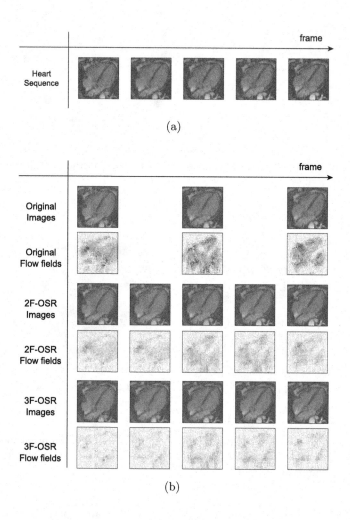

Fig. 6. Up-conversion of the optical flow fields and interframe images for the beating heart sequence. (a) is the original image sequence of the beating heart sequence. (b) From the top to the bottom row, shows three frames from the input image sequence, the optical flow fields computed by the large-displacement optical flow computation, the subframe image sequence and its optical flow fields computed by the two-frame method and the subframe image sequence and and its optical flow fields by the multi-frame method using three frames.

5   Conclusions

Using multiple image warping, which is used to compute deformation fields between an image and a collection of images, we developed a variational method for the computation of the average images and the average shapes of both static and temporal biological organs in three-dimensional Euclidean space. We combined the diffusion registration technique and optical-flow computation for the computation of the spatial deformation field between the average image and input organs. We also developed a variational method for the frame-rate up-conversion of the optical-flow field sequence in which we combine motion coherence in an image sequence and the smoothness of the temporal flow field.

This research was supported by the "Multidisciplinary Computational Anatomy and Its Application to Highly Intelligent Diagnosis and Therapy" projects funded by a Grant-in-Aid for Scientific Research on Innovative Areas from MEXT, Japan.

References

1. Younes, L.: Shapes and Diffeomorphisms. Springer (2010)
2. Bronstein, A.M., Bronstein, M.M., Kimmel, R.: Numerical Geometry of Non-Rigid Shapes. Springer (2008)
3. Fischer, B., Modersitzki, J.: Ill-posed medicine- an introduction to image registration. Inverse Prob. **24**, 1–17 (2008)
4. Rumpf, M., Wirth, B.: A nonlinear elastic shape averaging approach. SIAM J. Imaging Sci. **2**, 800–833 (2009)
5. Rumpf, M., Wirth, B.: An elasticity-based covariance analysis of shapes. IJCV **92**, 281–295 (2011)
6. Wirth, B., Bar, L., Rumpf, M., Sapiro, G.: A continuum mechanical approach to geodesics in shape space. IJCV **93**, 293–318 (2011)
7. Fonseca, G.G., et al.: The Cardiac Atlas Project?an imaging database for computational modeling and statistical atlases of the heart. Bioinformatics **27**, 2288–2295 (2011)
8. Lorenzo-Valdés, M., et al.: Segmentation of 4D cardiac MR images using a probabilistic atlas and the EM algorithm. Medical Image Analysis **8**, 255–265 (2004)
9. Werlberger, M., Pock, T., Unger, M., Bischof, H.: Optical flow guided TV-L^1 video interpolation and restoration. In: Boykov, Y., Kahl, F., Lempitsky, V., Schmidt, F.R. (eds.) EMMCVPR 2011. LNCS, vol. 6819, pp. 273–286. Springer, Heidelberg (2011)
10. Volz, S., Bruhn, A., Valgaerts, L., Zimmer, H.: Modeling temporal coherence for optical flow. In: ICCV 2011, pp. 1116–1123 (2011)
11. Zimmer, H., Bruhn, A., Weickert, J.: Optic flow in harmony. IJCV **93**, 368–388 (2011)
12. Sadek, R., Ballester, C., Garrido, L., Meinhardt, E., Caselles, V.: Frame interpolation with occlusion detection using a time coherent segmentation. In: Proc. VISAPP 2012, pp. 367–372 (2012)
13. Inagaki, S., Imiya, A., Hontani, H., Hanaoka, S., Masutani, Y.: Variational method for computing average images of biological organs. In: Pack, T. (ed.) SSVM 2013. LNCS, vol. 7893, pp. 440–451. Springer, Heidelberg (2013)

Facial Expression Recognition Using Learning Vector Quantization

Gert-Jan de Vries[1,2]([envelope]), Steffen Pauws[1], and Michael Biehl[2]

[1] Philips Research - Healthcare, High Tech Campus 34,
5656 AE Eindhoven, The Netherlands
gj.de.vries@philips.com
[2] Johann Bernoulli Institute for Mathematics and Computer Science,
University of Groningen, Groningen, The Netherlands

Abstract. Although the detection of emotions from facial video or images has been topic of intense research for several years, the set of applied classification techniques seems limited to a few popular methods. Benchmark datasets facilitate direct comparison of methods. We used one such dataset, the Cohn-Kanade database, to build classifiers for facial expression recognition based upon Local Binary Patterns (LBP) features. We are interested in the application of Learning Vector Quantization (LVQ) classifiers to this classification task. These prototype-based classifiers allow to inspect of prototypical features of the emotion classes, are conceptually intuitive and quick to train. For comparison we also consider Support Vector Machine (SVM) and observe that LVQ performances exceed those reported in literature for methods based upon LBP features and are amongst the overall top performing methods. Most prominent features were found to originate, primarily, from the mouth region and eye regions. Finally, we explored the specific LBP features that were found most influential within these regions.

1 Introduction

Many applications, especially in human-computer interaction can benefit from facial expression recognition of its users [15], ranging from affective content selection to adaptive system behavior to the affective state of the user. For many of these applications, users have restricted range of motion, enabling the recognition of affect through unobtrusive measurement using video or photo cameras. Examples of such systems range from affective music players [29] to intelligent car safety systems [10] and air traffic control [14]. Although performances of facial expression recognizers are already high, there is still room for improvement, which will optimize user satisfaction and allow for integration of such systems in daily life.

As addressed by Van den Broek et al. [2], publicly available data sets that can be used as benchmarks are scarce in affective computing. For facial emotion recognition, however, such benchmark databases are available. Kanade, Cohn and Tian published a "Comprehensive Database for Facial Expression Analysis" in 2000 [7], later known as the Cohn-Kanade database. It consists of image

G. Azzopardi and N. Petkov (Eds.): CAIP 2015, Part II, LNCS 9257, pp. 760–771, 2015.
DOI: 10.1007/978-3-319-23117-4_65

sequences displaying the faces of participants who were instructed to show a range of "facial displays" consisting of at least one Action Unit (AU) [3]. The participants were university students between 18 and 50 years of age, 69% of them female, and represented of a mix of ethnicities. The image sequences are labeled per still image with AUs that are active, which can be translated to emotion labels using a set of rules provided by Ekman, Friesen and Hager [3]. For 100 of the participants at least one of the prototypic emotions (Anger, Disgust, Fear, Joy, Sadness, and Surprise) has been recorded and can be used for the classification of emotions from facial expressions.

We observe that Support Vector Machine (SVM) is a very popular technique applied at this boundary of affective computing and computer vision. While SVMs have been applied successfully to various classification tasks, there are various reasons to investigate how alternative classification methods perform as affective classifiers. Learning Vector Quantization (LVQ) methods have been successfully applied in many settings [12], including facial expression recognition on other datasets [1], but to the best of our knowledge, not to the task of recognizing facial expressions from the Cohn-Kanade database. This type of classifier has several benefits, such as low computational complexity resulting in fast training times, conceptually intuitive nature, and possibility to inspect relevant features without performing additional analyses. In order to put our work into perspective, we performed a comprehensive literature review of methods applied to the Cohn-Kanade database which will be treated in the next section. After that, we present the methods used for our affective classifiers and results obtained. Finally, we present a discussion and conclusion.

2 Cohn-Kanade Database

The Cohn-Kanade database has been widely used to develop and validate techniques for facial emotion recognition. To obtain an overview of techniques and their performances, we have searched the literature systematically using Web of Science [21]. The search terms "Cohn AND Kanade" resulted in 153 publications. We selected 43 publications for full analysis by excluding e.g., those using temporal information (video). In these papers we identified 199 classification schemes for 6 or 7 emotion classes, which were trained using the Cohn-Kanade database [7] and for which a performance was reported.

We applied the following criteria for further filtering: accuracy of a model should be reported; and it should be validated using data from at least 50 participants, which is half of the available participants in the Cohn-Kanade database. These criteria were satisfied by 96 models, of which Table 1 shows a summary. First of all, it shows that the task of classifying unseen faces, using per person (pp)-cross-validation, is more difficult than classifying unseen instances of known faces (using cross-validation). Most studies concern the 7-class problem that considers the expressions Anger (A), Disgust (D), Fear (F), Joy (J), Sadness (Sa), Surprise (Su) and a Neutral (N) expression. On average, the cross-validation performances reach 90.75% accuracy; exceptionally high performance

Table 1. Meta analysis of 150 models from literature.

Nr. of Classes	Classes[1]	Validation method	Nr. of models	Accuracy		
				min	mean	max
7	A,D,F,J,N,Sa,Su	cross	31	78.90%	90.75%	99.40%
7	A,D,F,J,N,Sa,Su	pp-cross	26	73.40%	85.94%	94.88%
6	A,D,F,J,Sa,Su	cross	20	82.52%	89.21%	96.70%
6	A,D,F,J,Sa,Su	pp-cross	17	76.12%	86.54%	96.40%
6	A,D,F,J,Sa,Su	single split	2	83.05%	87.43%	91.81%

[1] Abbreviations used: A(nger), D(isgust), F(ear), J(oy), (N)eutral, (Sa)dness, (Su)rprise

is reported [27] when using ensembles of SVMs: 99.40% accuracy, 3% more than the second best published result.

We focus on the most difficult cross validation type (pp-cross-validation) that assesses the performance on classifying emotions from unseen faces. Table 2 shows the 26 classifiers that are published for the 7-class problem, showing that accuracy ranges from 73.40% [19] to 94.88% [28]. The most frequently used feature-type is Local Binary Patterns (LBP) followed by Gabor features. Highest performance is obtained by methods that use projections of the original images to some lower dimensional space, such as KDIsomap, Linear Discriminant Analysis (LDA) and Principal Component Analysis (PCA). Slightly inferior are the methods based upon feature extraction such as Local Directional Patterns (LDP) and LBP and less successful are methods based upon Gabor features. The most popular classification techniques are SVM and LDA.

In this work, we will explore the application of LVQ classifiers to this classification problem and will use the open box nature of these classifiers to gain more insight into the classification problem. We will use LBP-features because they have been used most often, can be obtained relatively efficiently and have been demonstrated to give good performance.

3   Methods

From the Cohn-Kanade database we selected 310 image sequences, coming from 95 subjects, that could be labeled as one of the emotions Anger, Disgust, Fear, Joy, Sadness or Surprise. For each sequence, the neutral face and three peak frames, i.e., those with highest emotional intensity, were used for emotional expression recognition. Following Shan et al. [5,19] and Tian [22], we used the distance between manually annotated location of the eyes to rotate, crop and scale the images to 108x147 pixels, which were used as input to the further pre-processing. First, the images were rotated to ensure horizontal alignment of the eyes. The distance between the eyes (d_{eyes}) was determined and then the images were cropped such that they measured $2d_{eyes}$ by $3d_{eyes}$, and finally they were resized to 108x147 pixels.

Table 2. Literature overview of studies that classify 7 emotion classes using the Cohn-Kanade database and validated using participant wise cross validation, grouped by feature type.

Reference	Features	Classifier type	Accuracy	#pp used in validation	#images used in validation
Zhao et al., 2011[28]	KDIsomap	SVM	94.88%	96	1409
Zhao et al., 2011[28]	KIsomap	SVM	75.81%	96	1409
Zhao et al., 2011[28]	KLDA	SVM	93.32%	96	1409
Zhao et al., 2011[28]	LDA	SVM	90.18%	96	1409
Zhao et al., 2011[28]	KPCA	SVM	92.59%	96	1409
Zhao et al., 2011[28]	PCA	SVM	92.43%	96	1409
Jabid et al., 2010[6]	LDP	SVM	93.40%	96	1632
Jabid et al., 2010[6]	LDP	Template matching	86.90%	96	1632
Jabid et al., 2010[6]	LBP	SVM	88.90%	96	1632
Shan et al., 2009[19]	LBP	SVM	88.90%	96	1280
Lajevardi & Hussain, 2010[9]	LBP	LDA	88.40%	100	?
Zavaschi et al., 2013[27]	LBP	SVM	84.30%	100	1281
Shan et al., 2009[19]	LBP	Linear programming	82.30%	96	1280
Jabid et al., 2010[6]	LBP	Template matching	79.10%	96	1632
Shan et al., 2009[19]	LBP	Template matching	79.10%	96	1280
Shan et al., 2009[19]	LBP	LDA	73.40%	96	1280
Shan et al., 2009[19]	LBP	LDA&ANN	73.40%	96	1280
Zavaschi et al., 2013[27]	LBP&Gabor	SVM ensemble	88.90%	100	1281
Zavaschi et al., 2013[27]	LBP&Gabor	SVM	79.20%	100	1281
Lajevardi & Hussain, 2010[9]	HLACLF	LDA	91.60%	100	?
Lajevardi & Hussain, 2010[9]	HLAC	LDA	89.90%	100	?
Lajevardi & Hussain, 2010[9]	Gabor	LDA	89.70%	100	?
Jabid et al., 2010[6]	Gabor	SVM	86.80%	96	1632
Shan et al., 2009[19]	Gabor	SVM	86.80%	96	1280
Lu et al., 2006[11]	Gabor	NKFDA	85.59%	93	≤ 651
Zavaschi et al., 2013[27]	Gabor	SVM	78.70%	100	1281

As discussed in the previous section, the most frequently used feature type is LBP, which is also our choice. We derived the LBP-features from the scaled images in the following way:

Per grey valued pixel (i_c) the LBP-value is calculated by comparing the pixel to its eight neighbors, resulting in a binary string of which the decimal value is taken, according to:

$$LBP(x_c, y_c) = \sum_{n=0}^{7} s(i_n - i_c) \, 2^n \qquad (1)$$

where s is the Heaviside step function. The $2^8 - 1$ possible outcomes are reduced to $L = 59$ by regarding only those LBP values with at most 2 bitwise transitions when considered as a circular pattern, as proposed by Ojala et al. [13]. The patterns in this subset are termed "Uniform" patterns and represent bright and dark spots, corners and edges.

The images are divided into ($6*7 = 42$) regions R_j of size 18x21 pixels, where per region a histogram $H_i = \sum_{x,y} \delta_{LBP(x,y),i}$ (with $(x, y) \in R_j, i = 0, \ldots, L-1$) is built. These histograms are placed next to each other, forming a single vector of length $N = 42 * 59 = 2478$.

Learning Vector Quantization (LVQ) comprises a family of classifiers that is of open box nature, that is, they provide direct insight into the information learned by the classifier. LVQ, initially proposed by Kohonen [8], defines prototypes in the same (mathematical) space as the data to represent the classes. These prototypes are directly interpretable as they show characteristics of classes in terms of the features chosen. During training, samples are presented sequentially, and for each sample the closest prototypes are updated by moving them towards or away from the presented sample. Several variants have been proposed, amongst which Robust Soft Learning Vector Quantization (RSLVQ) [18]. It introduces soft prototype assignments which corresponds to a soft window around the decision boundary [26]. In addition, we apply SVM [23], the most popular technique in this domain of computer vision applications. Next to the "linear SVM", i.e., the large margin perceptron classifier [24], we also applied SVM with a Radial Basis Function (RBF) kernel, which however, did not improve upon the results. For further reference, we also include a baseline classifier that always assigns the label corresponding to the class with the highest prior probability.

Validation was performed using 10x10-fold participant-wise cross validation, i.e., 10 repetitions of randomly chosen 10-fold cross validation, where participants are strictly separated in training and test data. In this way, the performances obtained reflect the generalization performances to unseen participants. We applied the classifiers to the 7 class facial expression recognition task, compared their generalization performances, and inspected the confusion matrices. Finally, we inspected the prototypes trained by RSLVQ, with specific attention for the relevances it (implicitly) assigns to the features. To this end, we considered differences between the 'Neutral' prototype and other prototypes.

4   Results

The results, given in Table 3 show that our classifiers reach over 91% accuracy. RSLVQ competes well with SVM, the latter reaching insignificantly better performance, especially when using the LBP features with overlapping regions. On the other hand, the results over the 10 times 10-folds are slightly more stable for RSLVQ.

Table 3. Generalization performances on 10x10 fold participant-wise cross validation per subtask.

	Method	Accuracy
7 class	Baseline	21.6%
	RSLVQ	91.2% ± 0.5%
	SVM	91.4% ± 0.5%

Confusion matrices of SVM and RSLVQ are available in Tables 4 and 5. Differences between the confusions made by both classifiers are small and for both we observe that most errors correspond to misclassifying various emotions as 'Neutral'. This might suggest that the classifiers have most difficulty with low-intensity instances of emotions (other than Neutral) while the emotions themselves are quite well separable. Most difficult emotions are Fear, of which 13% is misclassified as Joy, and Anger, which is often confused with Neutral and Sadness.

Table 4. Confusion matrix (averaged over 10x10-fold cross validation) for 7class classification by SVM. Entries are percentages per actual emotion.

Actual \ Predicted	A	D	F	J	N	Sa	Su
Anger	78.8	3.3	0	0.1	10.7	7.1	0
Disgust	3.6	90.3	0	0	2.3	3.7	0
Fear	0	0	78.6	12.6	6.8	1.9	0.1
Joy	0	0	0.2	99	0.9	0	0
Neutral	0.5	0	0	1	94.5	2.7	1.3
Sadness	2.6	0.3	0	0	9	85.6	2.5
Surprise	0	0	0	0	1	0	99

Table 5. Confusion matrix (averaged over 10x10-fold cross validation) for 7class classification by RSLVQ. Entries are percentages per actual emotion.

Actual \ Predicted	A	D	F	J	N	Sa	Su
Anger	81.8	5.9	0	0.6	7.9	3.7	0
Disgust	2.1	93.3	0	0	1.8	2.8	0
Fear	1.2	0.4	79.4	13.5	2.3	2.2	1
Joy	0.4	0	0.7	97.7	1.3	0	0
Neutral	1	0.2	0	1.5	93.2	2.4	1.8
Sadness	3.9	0.8	0	0.3	7.8	84	3.2
Surprise	0	0	0	0	1.4	0	98.6

In order to inspect the (implicit) relevances assigned by RSLVQ, we summed up all absolute pairwise differences between the prototype representing 'Neutral' faces and the other emotions. The difference vector of two prototypes corresponds to the direction in feature space along which the two classes are discriminated.

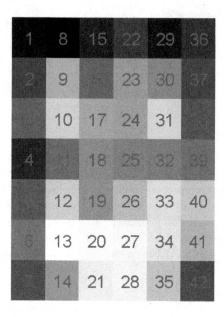

Fig. 1. Relevance of image regions in the RSLVQ classifier (white levels indicate relevance).

The absolute value of its components can be interpreted as to measure the relevance of the corresponding feature. Figure 1 shows this information aggregated per region as used in the building of the LBP histograms. It indicates that most informative to the classifier are the regions around the mouth, followed by the eyes and eye-brows.

The feature vectors we used represent the frequency of observing certain textural elements within 42 different regions of the face. Figure 2 shows the LBP-features linked to the 48 most relevant histogram entries. We see that, out of the 42 regions, the regions around the mouth are best represented. Regions 20 and 27 represent the (upper side of the) mouth and the LBP-features represented in the top 48 indicate the importance of textural components that are lighter at the top than on the bottom. Similarly, regions 21 and 28 represent the chin and lower side of the mouth, from which LBP-features that indicate lighter bottom and darker top are present. Finally, we observe that regions 13 and 34, corresponding to the left and right side of the mouth, are mostly represented by textural components that have darker right and left sides, respectively. These observations seem to indicate that opening of the mouth, which is accompanied by dark pixels in the center of the mouth-region, is the most important distinction between various emotions.

Figure 3 shows the aggregated relevances per region for each of the emotions in isolation, i.e., representing the difference to the 'Neutral' emotion. We observe that the relevances for Surprise are quite distributed, and more expressive around the central mouth regions and chin. Sadness shows even higher relevance of the

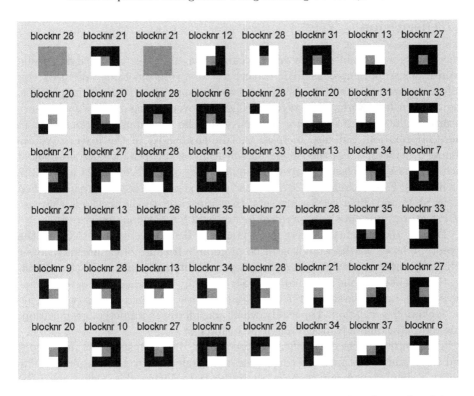

Fig. 2. Top 48 most relevant LBP-features used the RSLVQ classifier; ordered from let to right, top to bottom. The block numbers refer to the regions as numbered in Figure 1.

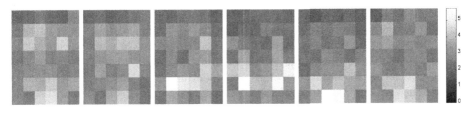

Fig. 3. Relevance of image regions in the RSLVQ classifier for Anger, Disgust, Fear, Joy, Sadness and Surprise (from left to right).

chin areas; Joy is most different from Neutral in the outer and upper mouth regions, while Fear differs in the outer and central mouth regions. Finally, the relevances of Anger and Disgust are more scattered, but in comparison to the other emotions have relatively high contributions of the features from the eyes, brows and forehead.

5 Discussion

The results we obtained show high accuracy on the tasks of classifying facial expressions, represented as LBP feature vectors, into emotions. We used two different representations, one using non-overlapping regions in the facial pictures, the other using overlapping regions. The non-overlapping regions yield more intuitively interpretable feature vectors, while the overlapping regions contain more information, but also increase the dimensionality of the feature vectors almost by a factor 4. For the 7-class classification task, which includes the neutral face as a class, our classifiers reached an accuracy of 91.4% for SVM and 91.2% for RSLVQ. Four techniques [28] from one paper show better performances when using SVM and different feature sets. In comparison to the methods that use LBP features, our classifiers perform better by 2.5 percentage points.

Despite the marginally lower performance of RSLVQ compared to SVM, the prototype based method might still be preferable because of significantly lower computational complexity due to the inherent ability to handle multi-class classification problems while SVM requires to train many more classifiers in an ensemble scheme, i.e., k classifiers in a one-vs-all or $k(k-1)/2$ in a one-vs-one scheme for k-class classification. Especially when considering parameter optimization, this computational advantage might be of interest.

The prototype based classifiers we used enabled us to inspect the prototypes and infer which features are considered most relevant by the classifiers. The mouth region turned out to be most influential. Within this region the LBP features that correspond to various mouth openings were most important. While eye-brows are known to be activated in many different emotions [4], and they are found to be the prominent facial elements to highlight prosody [20], our results suggest that for automated facial expression recognition, the mouth-region is more important. The regions representing the eye-brows and forehead, however, do help our classifier in distinguishing especially Anger and Disgust from the other emotions. Shan and colleagues [19] used AdaBoost in combination with pattern matching to determine the most influential LBP histograms from an exhaustive set of 16640 facial regions and identified most discriminant regions around the eyes and mouth. With our approach, we obtained these indications of relevance directly from the trained classifier, rather than performing additional and computationally intensive analyses.

We also observed that not only the occurrence frequencies of uniform LBP features are relevant for the classification, but also the frequency of non-uniform patterns, which were joined together in one bin in each histogram representing a photo region, were represented in the list of most influential features. Moreover, the 1st, 3rd and 29th most influential features were such non-uniform patterns. On the other hand, the use of uniform patterns rather than all LBPs reduced the feature space with more than a factor 4 and helps keeping the search space manageable.

6 Conclusion

We have performed a comprehensive literature overview of attempts to classify facial expressions from the Cohn-Kanade database and observed that generalization performances on the 7 class task average at 85.9%. Maximum reported accuracies on this task were 94.9%. While being the most popular, or at least most frequently used, type of features, LBP features reached only up to 88.9%.

To the best of our knowledge, we have applied LVQ classifiers for the first time to the task of facial expression recognition using the Cohn-Kanade database. The generalization accuracies obtained (91.2% for 7-class classification) show that RSLVQ is among the most successful classifiers overall and outperforms all reported efforts using LBP features. As a reference we used SVM, which showed even slightly better performances (91.4% for 7-class) but, in contrast to RSLVQ, does not allow for direct inspection of the knowledge learned and used by the classifiers and requires significantly more time to train and optimize. By inspecting the prototypes trained by RSLVQ we noticed that the most prominent features originate from the mouth region, followed by the eye-regions. The specific LBP features that are used most prominently by the classifier confirm that mouth opening/closing is discriminative for various emotions.

In the present work, we have used implicit relevances obtained from difference vectors of RSLVQ prototypes. Other LVQ variants can be designed that explicitly train relevance vectors along with prototypes; examples are Generalized Matrix Learning Vector Quantization (GMLVQ)[16] and Matrix Robust Soft Learning Vector Quantization (MRSLVQ)[17]. Future work includes the application of such methods to the challenge of facial expression recognition. Another interesting future extension of the current work is to observe how our methods perform on spontaneous emotions. Although being more challenging, recent developments[25] indicate that results obtained in one setting can be transferred successfully to the other. Finally, the literature review we performed indicates that performances might be further improved by considering different feature sets such as LDP or Scale-Invariant Feature Transform (SIFT).

The high performances obtained indicate that implementation in consumer products becomes more and more feasible. Natural choices of first applications include real time behavior adaptation of laptops or tablets to their users' emotions. By, for example, being able to distinguish frustration from happiness, human-computer interaction can be greatly improved because it allows for detection of suboptimal interactions and adapt at real time by offering alternative actions when frustration is detected. The flexibility of LVQ to directly handle multi-class classification (i.e., without requiring classification schemes such as 'one-vs-all' that are needed by binary classifiers), allows for quick training times and opens up the ability to train user specifics and personalize the model by learning at real time. Such personalized systems should be able to obtain even better performances for facial expression recognition.

Acknowledgments. The authors would like to thank the Affect Analysis Group of the University of Pittsburgh, and in particular Prof. Cohn and Prof. Kanade, for providing access to their database of facial expression images. Furthermore, we would like to thank Vincent Jeanne and Caifeng Shan (Philips Research) for their help in image preprocessing and feature extraction.

References

1. Bashyal, S., Venayagamoorthy, G.K.: Recognition of facial expressions using Gabor wavelets and learning vector quantization. Engineering Applications of Artificial Intelligence **21**(7), 1056–1064 (2008)
2. van den Broek, E., Janssen, J., Westerink, J., Healey, J.: Prerequisites for affective signal processing (asp). In: Encarnao, P., Veloso, A. (eds.) Biosignals 2009: Proceedings of the Second International Conference on Bio-Inspired Systems and Signal Processing, pp. 426–433. INSTICC Press, Portugal (2009)
3. Ekman, P., Friesen, W.V., Hager, J.C.: Facial Action Coding System [E-book]. Research Nexus, Salt Lake City (2002)
4. Ekman, P.: About brows: emotional and conversational signals. In: von Cranach, M., Foppa, K., Lepenies, W., Ploog, D. (eds.) Human Ethology: Claims and limits of a new discipline, pp. 169–248. Cambridge University Press (1979)
5. Gritti, T., Shan, C., Jeanne, V., Braspenning, R.: Local features based facial expression recognition with face registration errors. In: 8th IEEE International Conference on Automatic Face Gesture Recognition, FG 2008, pp. 1–8 (2008)
6. Jabid, T., Kabir, M., Chae, O.: Facial expression recognition using local directional pattern (LDP). In: 2010 17th IEEE International Conference on Image Processing (ICIP), pp. 1605–1608 (2010)
7. Kanade, T., Cohn, J., Tian, Y.: Comprehensive database for facial expression analysis. In: Proceedings of the Fourth IEEE International Conference on Automatic Face and Gesture Recognition, 2000, pp. 46–53 (2000)
8. Kohonen, T.: Improved versions of learning vector quantization. In: International Joint Conference on Neural Networks, vol. 1, pp. 545–550. IEEE (1990)
9. Lajevardi, S.M., Hussain, Z.M.: Novel higher-order local autocorrelation-like feature extraction methodology for facial expression recognition. IET Image Processing **4**(2), 114–119 (2010)
10. Lisetti, C.L., Nasoz, F.: Affective intelligent car interfaces with emotion recognition. In: Proceedings of the 11th International Conference on Human Computer Interaction, p. 41. ACM, Las Vegas (2005)
11. Lu, H., Wang, Z., Liu, X.: Facial expression recognition using NKFDA method with gabor features. In: The Sixth World Congress on Intelligent Control and Automation, WCICA 2006, vol. 2, pp. 9902–9906 (2006)
12. Neural Networks Research Centre, Helsinki: Bibliography on the self-organizing maps (SOM) and learning vector quantization (LVQ). Otaniemi: Helsinki Univ. of Technology (2002). http://liinwww.ira.uka.de/bibliography/Neural/SOM.LVQ.html
13. Ojala, T., Pietikäinen, M., Mäenpää, T.: Multiresolution gray-scale and rotation invariant texture classification with local binary patterns. IEEE Transactions on Pattern Analysis and Machine Intelligence **24**(7), 971–987 (2002)
14. Pantic, M., Sebe, N., Cohn, J.F., Huang, T.: Affective multimodal human-computer interaction. In: Proceedings of the 13th Annual ACM International Conference on Multimedia MULTIMEDIA 2005, pp. 669–676. ACM, New York (2005)

15. Peter, C., Beale, R. (eds.): Affect and Emotion in Human-Computer Interaction. LNCS, vol. 4868. Springer, Heidelberg (2008)
16. Schneider, P., Biehl, M., Hammer, B.: Adaptive relevance matrices in learning vector quantization. Neural Computation **21**(12), 3532–3561 (2009)
17. Schneider, P., Biehl, M., Hammer, B.: Distance learning in discriminative vector quantization. Neural computation **21**(10), 2942–2969 (2009)
18. Seo, S., Obermayer, K.: Soft learning vector quantization. Neural Computation **15**, 1589–1604 (2003)
19. Shan, C., Gong, S., McOwan, P.W.: Facial expression recognition based on local binary patterns: A comprehensive study. Image and Vision Computing **27**(6), 803–816 (2009)
20. Swerts, M., Krahmer, E.: Facial expression and prosodic prominence: Effects of modality and facial area. Journal of Phonetics **36**(2), 219–238 (2008)
21. Thomson Reuters: Web of science (2014). http://apps.webofknowledge.com/
22. Tian, Y.L.: Evaluation of face resolution for expression analysis. In: Conference on Computer Vision and Pattern Recognition Workshop, CVPRW 2004, pp. 82–82 (2004)
23. Vapnik, V.: Statistical learning theory. Wiley (1998)
24. Vapnik, V.N.: The Nature of Statistical Learning Theory. Springer-Verlag New York Inc., New York (1995)
25. Wan, S., Aggarwal, J.K.: Spontaneous facial expression recognition: A robust metric learning approach. Pattern Recognition **47**(5), 1859–1868 (2014)
26. Witoelar, A.W., Ghosh, A., de Vries, J.J.G., Hammer, B., Biehl, M.: Window-based example selection in learning vector quantization. Neural Computation **22**(11), 2924–2961 (2011)
27. Zavaschi, T.H., Britto Jr, A.S., Oliveira, L.E., Koerich, A.L.: Fusion of feature sets and classifiers for facial expression recognition. Expert Systems with Applications **40**(2), 646–655 (2013)
28. Zhao, X., Zhang, S.: Facial expression recognition based on local binary patterns and kernel discriminant isomap. Sensors (Basel, Switzerland) **11**(10), 9573–9588 (2011)
29. van der Zwaag, M.D., Janssen, J.H., Westerink, J.H.: Directing physiology and mood through music: Validation of an affective music player. IEEE Transactions on Affective Computing **4**(1), 57–68 (2012)

Learning Vector Quantization with Adaptive Cost-Based Outlier-Rejection

Thomas Villmann[1]([✉]), Marika Kaden[1], David Nebel[1], and Michael Biehl[2]

[1] Computational Intelligence Group, University of Applied Sciences Mittweida,
Mittweida, Germany
`thomas.villmann@hs-mittweida.de`
[2] Johann Bernoulli Institute for Mathematics and Computer Science,
University of Groningen, P.O. Box 407, 9700 AK Groningen, The Netherlands

Abstract. We consider a reject option for prototype-based Learning Vector Quantization (LVQ), which facilitates the detection of outliers in the data during the classification process. The rejection mechanism is based on a distance-based criterion and the corresponding threshold is automatically adjusted in the training phase according to pre-defined rejection costs. The adaptation of LVQ prototypes is simultaneously guided by the complementary aims of low classification error, faithful representation of the observed data, and low total rejection costs.

1 Introduction and Motivation

The adequate representation of data is one of the most important topics in machine learning. This task is inherently involved in visualization and dimensionality reduction for visual analytics. However, also for supervised learning tasks like regression and classification problems, the model performance can benefit from an adequate underlying data representation. One challenging issue in this context is *novelty detection* or the identification of outliers, i.e. data samples, which do not belong to the typical data distribution with high probability. Obviously, the detection of outliers is essential, when a previously adjusted system is in its working phase. However, the presence of outliers in the training data may corrupt the model already in the learning process leading to decreased performance.

Many established methods for outlier detection are based on probabilistic approaches. For vectorial data, the outlier likelihood probability is frequently estimated based on distance measures in feature space whereas thresholds on the likelihood for novelty detection translate to cut-off distances. Clearly, the success of these approaches depends on a sufficiently precise estimation of the true density of data. However, the determination of an appropriate probabilistic model is often difficult, in particular for very high-dimensional data. Frequently, Gaussian mixture models are applied but may suffer significantly from *curse of dimensionality*.

Another key issue is to choose an adequately precise decision criterion. In particular for unsupervised models, suitable thresholds have to be determined.

G. Azzopardi and N. Petkov (Eds.): CAIP 2015, Part II, LNCS 9257, pp. 772–782, 2015.
DOI: 10.1007/978-3-319-23117-4_66

Obviously, outlier separation is an inherently ill-defined problem comparable to, for instance, cluster validity evaluation [36,37]. For classification tasks the situation appears clearer, because outlier penalties can be related to misclassification costs [4,19]. The difficulty to determine a respective threshold value, however, persists [7,22].

So far we only discussed rejection strategies to be applied a posteriori for previously adjusted models. Corresponding approaches usually do not take into account the outlier-reject option in the training process. This seems appropriate if training data is considered to be free from outliers which are only expected in the working phase. Clearly, making use of available information about potential outliers in the training data will help to optimize the classifier with respect to working phase performance.

This contribution addresses both above-mentioned issues. We discuss outlier rejection within the example framework of prototype-based vector quantization, which provides an intuitive and adequate data representation independent from explicit assumptions on the density of data.

Rejection mechanisms for prototype-based systems have been suggested earlier by several authors [8,12,31], addressing, for instance, the rejection of feature vectors which are too close to the decision boundary for reliable classification.

We will concentrate here on classification along the lines of Learning Vector Quantization (LVQ) [17]. We employ and put forward the concept of cost-based rejection introduced by CHOW, which is derived mathematically within the framework of Bayesian classification [5]. A respective LVQ-scheme for a reject strategy regarding uncertain class decisions is recently proposed in [32]. In this contribution we want to deal with outliers. Particularly, we extend LVQ to take into account the detection of outliers already during training in order to optimize the model also with respect to the reject option. To this end, a distance-based outlier-threshold is automatically adapted during the LVQ training guided by pre-defined rejection-costs while, at the same time, prototypes are adjusted in order to achieve good classification performance.

2   Cost Function Based LVQ

One of the most popular and intuitive approaches to the classification of n-dimensional feature vectors $\mathbf{v} \in \mathbb{R}^n$ is Learning Vector Quantization (LVQ) as introduced by KOHONEN [16]. LVQ requires the availability of a set V containing training samples $\mathbf{v}$ with known class labels $c(\mathbf{v}) \in \mathcal{C} = \{1, \ldots, K\}$. Further, LVQ employs a set of prototypes $W = \{\mathbf{w}_j \in \mathbb{R}^n\}_{j=1}^M$ with labels $y(\mathbf{w}_j) \in \mathcal{C}$, such that at each class is represented by at least one prototype. Motivated by Bayesian decision theory, LVQ schemes distribute the prototypes in feature space in the learning phase according to a strategy of attracting and repulsing prototypes depending on the comparison of their labels with the class memberships of observed example data [18]. After training, novel feature vectors $\mathbf{v} \in \mathbb{R}^n$ are mapped to a particular class according to a winner–takes–all (WTA) scheme:

$$\mathbf{v} \xrightarrow{LVQ} y(\mathbf{w}_s) \quad \text{with} \quad s(\mathbf{v}) = \operatorname{argmin}_{j=1\ldots M} d(\mathbf{v}, \mathbf{w}_j) \tag{1}$$

providing the index $s(\mathbf{v})$ of the *overall best matching prototype* with respect to a given distance or dissimilarity measure $d(\mathbf{v}, \mathbf{w})$ [21]. The most frequently used measure in this context is the squared Euclidean distance $d(\mathbf{v}, \mathbf{w}) = (\mathbf{v} - \mathbf{w})^2$. We restrict the discussion to this standard measure in the following, having in mind that extensions to many other choices are possible, see e.g. [2].

The total LVQ classification error with respect to the training data can be written as

$$C_{\mathrm{LVQ}}(W) = \sum_{v \in V} H(\mu(\mathbf{v})) \tag{2}$$

where

$$\mu(\mathbf{v}) = \frac{d^+(\mathbf{v}) - d^-(\mathbf{v})}{d^+(\mathbf{v}) + d^-(\mathbf{v})} \tag{3}$$

is a distance based *classifier function* and $H(z)$ is the Heaviside function. In (3), $d^+(\mathbf{v}) = d(\mathbf{v}, \mathbf{w}^+)$ denotes the dissimilarity (distance) between the data vector $\mathbf{v}$ and the closest prototype $\mathbf{w}^+$ with the same class label $y(\mathbf{w}^+) = c(\mathbf{v})$, the so-called *correct winner*. Analogously, $d^-(\mathbf{v}) = d(\mathbf{v}, \mathbf{w}^-)$ is the dissimilarity corresponding to the *incorrect winner* $\mathbf{w}^-$, i.e. the closest prototype carrying a class label $y(\mathbf{w}^-)$ different from $c(\mathbf{v})$. Thus $\mu(\mathbf{v}) \in [-1, 1]$ with negative values corresponding to correct classification. Hence, C_{LVQ} in Eq. (2) is the overall classification error.

SATO and YAMADA introduced a smoothed cost function $C_{\mathrm{GLVQ}}(W)$ in (2) by replacing the Heaviside function by a differentiable approximation using the sigmoidal function

$$f_\vartheta(x) = \frac{1}{1 + \exp\left(-\frac{x}{\vartheta}\right)} \tag{4}$$

which depends on a parameter ϑ. Hereafter, we set $\vartheta = \theta_e$ when referring to the approximation of the classification error [23]. The emerging modification of LVQ is known as Generalized LVQ (GLVQ) and allows for prototype adjustments based on gradient information, e.g. by means of stochastic gradient descent according to

$$\Delta \mathbf{w}^\pm \propto -\frac{\partial_S C_{\mathrm{GLVQ}}(W)}{\partial \mathbf{w}^\pm} \tag{5}$$

where $\frac{\partial_S}{\partial \mathbf{w}^\pm}$ denotes the formal stochastic gradient operator and $\mathbf{w}^+$, $\mathbf{w}^-$ correspond to the correct and wrong winners, respectively, as introduced in Eq. (3).

From a vector quantization point of view, after training the prototype distribution reflect the class distribution inducing a partition of the data space into Voronoi-cells according to the WTA-rule (1). However, the aims of generalization ability and faithful representation of the data by prototypes are not necessarily aligned [11]. Representative properties of prototypes can be enforced by adding the local description error

$$g(\mathbf{v}) = d\left(\mathbf{v}, \mathbf{w}_{s(\mathbf{v})}\right) \tag{6}$$

as a generative term to the costs $C_{\text{GLVQ}}(W)$ weighted by a positive constant $\gamma > 0$ [11,19,20]. Thus, we finally obtain

$$C_{\text{GLVQ}}(W) = \sum_{v \in V} f_{\theta_e}(\mu(\mathbf{v})) + \gamma \cdot g(\mathbf{v}) \tag{7}$$

as a generative classifier model balancing classification and the representation costs. As discussed in [15,34], class border sensitivity for GLVQ can be achieved by using small smoothness parameters θ_e.

3   Integrating Outlier-Reject Options Into GLVQ

3.1   Cost Based Rejection for Classifiers

Frequently, the certainty of predictions is a crucial problem in supervised learning. Several approaches exist, which provide a level of uncertainty together with each classification [24,28,33]. An alternative concept is to reject data points which display uncertain class decisions [6,10,12,30].

We have to distinguish clearly between the rejection of samples located in the vicinity of a class decision boundary, resulting in ambiguity, and the reject option for data which is dis-similar to all previously observed samples, i.e. actual *outlier-rejection* [25,29,35].

CHOW formulated classification costs in terms of a loss function instead of the simple classification error when introducing reject options for Bayesian classifiers [4]. In this approach, one associates different costs C_e, C_c, and C_r with the classification error, the correct classification, and with a reject case, respectively. Usually, the restriction $0 \le C_c < C_r < C_e$ holds. Suppose that π_k are the class prior probabilities and $p(\mathbf{v}|k)$ is the conditional probability of observing a data vector $\mathbf{v}$ given the class k. According to this framework, a data point has to be rejected when

$$\max_k [\pi_k \cdot p(\mathbf{v}|k)] < (1 - \tau) \sum_{j=1}^K \pi_j \cdot p(\mathbf{v}|j) \tag{8}$$

with the optimal *reject threshold* $\tau = \frac{C_r - C_c}{C_e - C_c}$ as shown in [5]. However, the evaluation of the reject rule (8) requires a precise estimation of the class conditional probabilities $p(\mathbf{v}|k)$, which is known to be difficult, in particular in high-dimensional spaces. An alternative could be prototype-based classifiers like LVQ, which implicitly estimate the data distribution and are known to be robust [11,26,27]. Accordingly, misclassifications in GLVQ can also be associated with appropriate costs [13,14].

However, outlier-rejection is not considered in the original approach of CHOW. Recent approaches consider several strategies to deal with ambiguity as well as outlier-reject mechanisms as an option to be applied after the model training [8–10]. In [32], LVQ is modified to integrate the reject decisions regarding the ambiguity during learning. However, to the best of our knowledge, no attempts have been made so far to incorporate such mechanisms for outlier-reject options in LVQ.

3.2 Distance Based Outlier-Reject Options for GLVQ

To include an outlier-reject option into GLVQ we start from the cost function (7). Following the approach of CHOW we assume outlier rejection costs C_o with $C_e > C_o > C_c = 0$ and introduce

$$\varrho\left(\mathbf{v}, \beta\right) = d\left(\mathbf{v}, \mathbf{w}_{s(\mathbf{v})}\right) - \beta \tag{9}$$

as the outlier-reject function with distance-related threshold $\beta \geq 0$. The outlier-reject option relates to the local loss

$$l\left(\mathbf{v}, c\left(\mathbf{v}\right)\right) = \begin{cases} 0 & \mu\left(\mathbf{v}\right) < 0 \text{ and } \varrho\left(\mathbf{v}, \beta\right) < 0 \\ C_e & \mu\left(\mathbf{v}\right) > 0 \text{ and } \varrho\left(\mathbf{v}, \beta\right) < 0 \\ C_o & \varrho\left(\mathbf{v}, \beta\right) \geq 0 \end{cases} \tag{10}$$

which implicitly depends on the distance via the classifier function $\mu\left(\mathbf{v}\right)$ from (3) and the outlier-reject function $\varrho\left(\mathbf{v}, \beta\right)$ from (9). The resulting, modified cost function of GLVQ including the oulier-reject option (oGLVQ) is obtained as

$$C_{\text{oGLVQ}}\left(W\right) = \sum_{\mathbf{v}} C\left(\mathbf{v}\right) + \gamma \cdot g\left(\mathbf{v}\right) \cdot \left(1 - f_{\theta_0}\left(\varrho\left(\mathbf{v}, \beta\right)\right)\right) \tag{11}$$

where

$$C\left(\mathbf{v}\right) = C_o \cdot f_{\theta_o}\left(\varrho\left(\mathbf{v}, \beta\right)\right) + C_e \cdot f_{\theta_e}\left(\mu\left(\mathbf{v}\right)\right) \cdot \left(1 - f_{\theta_0}\left(\varrho\left(\mathbf{v}, \beta\right)\right)\right) \tag{12}$$

is the outlier-reject option dependent local classification costs based on the local loss (10). Note that the generative term $g\left(\mathbf{v}\right)$ is also multiplied by $\left(1 - f_{\theta_0}\right)$. Hence it is also not taken into account for rejected outliers.

Formally, we make use in (11) of the same sigmoidal soft-approximation as for the classification error in GLVQ, but with softness parameter $\theta_o > 0$. Due to this approximation, the cost function $C_{\text{oGLVQ}}\left(W\right)$ is differentiable and, therefore, stochastic gradient learning can be applied for its minimization. In particular, we obtain for the prototype adaptation of $\mathbf{w}^+$ and $\mathbf{w}^-$ in oGLVQ, in analogy to Eq. (5), the gradients

$$\frac{\partial C_{\text{oGLVQ}}}{\partial \mathbf{w}^{\pm}} = \frac{\partial C\left(\mathbf{v}\right)}{\partial \mathbf{w}^{\pm}} + \gamma \cdot \frac{\partial\left[d\left(\mathbf{v}, \mathbf{w}_{s(\mathbf{v})}\right) \cdot \left(1 - f_{\theta_0}\left(\varrho\left(\mathbf{v}, \beta\right)\right)\right)\right]}{\partial \mathbf{w}^{\pm}} \delta_{\pm}^{s} \tag{13}$$

with

$$\frac{\partial C\left(\mathbf{v}\right)}{\partial \mathbf{w}^{\pm}} = C_o \frac{\partial f_{\theta_o}\left(\varrho\left(\mathbf{v}, \beta\right)\right)}{\partial \mathbf{w}^{\pm}} + C_e \cdot \frac{\partial f_{\theta_e}\left(\mu\left(\mathbf{v}\right)\right)}{\partial \mathbf{w}^{\pm}} - C_e \cdot \frac{\partial\left[f_{\theta_e}\left(\mu\left(\mathbf{v}\right)\right) f_{\theta_0}\left(\varrho\left(\mathbf{v}, \beta\right)\right)\right]}{\partial \mathbf{w}^{\pm}}, \tag{14}$$

and

$$\frac{\partial f_{\theta_o}\left(\varrho\left(\mathbf{v}, \beta\right)\right)}{\partial \mathbf{w}^{\pm}} = \frac{\partial f_{\theta_o}\left(\varrho\left(\mathbf{v}, \beta\right)\right)}{\partial \varrho} \cdot \frac{\partial d\left(\mathbf{v}, \mathbf{w}_{s(\mathbf{v})}\right)}{\partial \mathbf{w}^{\pm}} \delta_{\pm}^{s}, \tag{15}$$

$$\frac{\partial f_{\theta_e}\left(\mu\left(\mathbf{v}\right)\right)}{\partial \mathbf{w}^{\pm}} = \frac{\partial f_{\theta_e}\left(\mu\left(\mathbf{v}\right)\right)}{\partial \mu} \cdot \frac{\pm 2 \cdot d^{\mp}\left(\mathbf{v}\right)}{\left(d^{+}\left(\mathbf{v}\right) + d^{-}\left(\mathbf{v}\right)\right)^2} \cdot \frac{\partial d^{\pm}\left(\mathbf{v}\right)}{\partial \mathbf{w}^{\pm}}. \tag{16}$$

For the latter two eqs. we used the relations $\frac{\partial \varrho(\mathbf{v}, \beta)}{\partial d} = 1$ and $\frac{\partial \mu(\mathbf{v})}{\partial d^{\pm}} = \frac{\pm 2 \cdot d^{\mp}(\mathbf{v})}{(d^{+}(\mathbf{v}) + d^{-}(\mathbf{v}))^{2}}$. The Kronecker-like symbol

$$\delta_{\pm}^{s} = \begin{cases} 1 & \mathbf{w}_{s(\mathbf{v})} = \mathbf{w}^{\pm} \\ 0 & \text{else} \end{cases}$$

is used to single out the correct and incorrect winners with respect to the considered feature vector $\mathbf{v}$. The prototype updates in oGLVQ are accompanied by the outlier-reject threshold update, which is proportional to the gradient

$$\frac{\partial_{S} C_{\text{oGLVQ}}}{\partial \beta} = C_{o} \cdot \frac{\partial f_{\theta_{o}}(\varrho(\mathbf{v}, \beta))}{\partial \beta} - C_{e} \cdot f_{\theta_{e}}(\mu(\mathbf{v})) \frac{\partial f_{\theta_{0}}(\varrho(\mathbf{v}, \beta))}{\partial \beta} \qquad (17)$$

with
$$\frac{\partial_{S} f_{\theta_{o}}(\varrho(\mathbf{v}, \beta))}{\partial \beta} = -f_{\theta_{o}}(\varrho(\mathbf{v}, \beta))(1 - f_{\theta_{o}}(\varrho(\mathbf{v}, \beta))), \qquad (18)$$

taking into account the specific properties of the sigmoidal function (4).

Both, the prototype as well as the threshold update contribute to the decrease of the overall oGLVQ cost function (9). Obviously, the system can make use of the reject option in order to reduce the number of explicit misclassifications. In turn, the positioning of prototypes is partly guided by the aim of avoiding rejection costs.

4   Numerical Examples

4.1   Illustrating Artificial Toy Data

The first data set to be used is an artificial toy dataset (ATD) of two-dimensional vectors with two overlapping classes of different variability. In particular, one of the classes comprises a small cluster of data separate from two over-lapping clusters which represent the bulk of the data, see Fig. (1).

We trained the oGLVQ with one prototype for each class. The weight of the generative term was set to $\gamma = 0.01$. Outlier reject costs varied from zero to one while the misclassification costs were set to $C_{e} = 1$ in all experiments. Results for the ATD are depicted in Fig. 2. For increasing reject costs, fewer data points are rejected (right panel) and, consequently, the observed accuracy decreases (left panel). However, the small cluster of outliers from one of the classes remains rejected also for relatively high reject costs.

This behavior is visualized in Fig. 3. We note that the number of rejected samples in the ATD does not vanish even for full rejection cost $C_{0} \to 1$, because in this limit misclassifications cause the same costs.

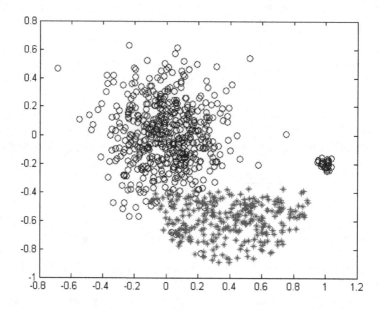

Fig. 1. Visualization of the ATD. There are two overlapping classes, one of them containing a small separated cluster.

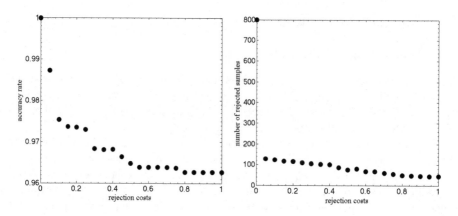

Fig. 2. Accuracy rate (*left*) and number of rejected samples (*right*) in dependence on outlier rejection costs for ATD.

4.2   Steroid Metabolomic Data for Tumor Classification

Here we illustrate our reject option approach in terms of a medical tumor data (MTD) set which was recently analyzed by use of LVQ [1,3]. Tumors of the adrenal gland are mostly found incidentally in about 1-2% of the population.

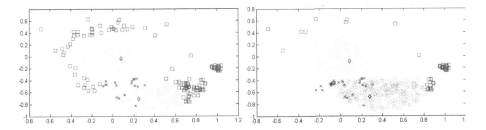

Fig. 3. Visualization of rejected samples for the ATD: *left* - low outlier reject costs $C_o = 0.05$, *right* - high outlier reject costs $C_o = 0.95$. Rejected samples are red.

The development of a diagnostic tool for the reliable, non- invasive detection of malignant Adrenocortical Carcinoma (ACC) vs. benign Adrenocortical Adenomas (ACA) was the aim of a recent retrospective study [1]. The 24h excretion of a set of 32 steroid metabolites – produced by the adrenal gland - was analyzed for a number of patients, including 102 ACA and 45 confirmed cases of malignant ACC. Preprocessing and normalization steps are explained in greater detail in [1,3]. Here, we revisit the set of 147 feature vectors comprising 32 log-transformed excretion values. For simplicity, we replaced 56 missing entries (corresponding to 3.9% of, in total, 1440 values) by the corresponding class-conditional means. Thereafter, the data was z-score transformed, yielding features v_j with mean $\langle v_j \rangle = 0$ and variance $\langle v_j^2 \rangle = 1$ for $j = 1,\ldots 32$, where $\langle \ldots \rangle$ denotes an average over the available data.

Again we applied oGLVQ with only one prototype per class and the same parameter setting as for ATD. The results in terms of the accuracy rate and number of rejected samples are displayed in Fig. 4. Also for the MTD we observe

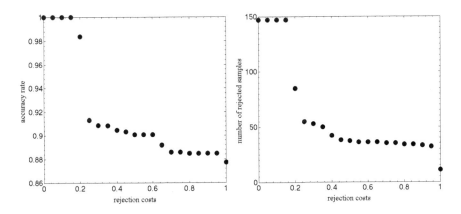

Fig. 4. Accuracy rate (*left*) and number of rejected samples (*right*) in dependence on outlier rejection costs for MTD.

the expected dependency of accuracy and number of rejected events on the reject costs C_0, demonstrating the applicability of the method in real world data sets.

5   Conclusions

In this paper we propose a variant of GLVQ allowing for the cost based identification of outliers. Both, misclassifications and the rejection of outliers, contribute to the overall cost function, which is minimized during the training process. Taking into account outlier rejection costs, the new oGLVQ adjusts automatically the distance based outlier threshold while adapting the class prototype vectors at the same time. Thus, the possibility of outlier rejection is already incorporated in the oGLVQ training process. This incorporation distinguishes oGLVQ from other classifiers with outlier-reject option, which are trained first separately without reject option and are are equipped with this option only during the recall phase. Here, however, we assume that training data may comprise outliers already and oGLVQ infers their characteristics in order to adjust the classifier accordingly. The presented oGLVQ approach can be seen as the counterpart to the GLVQ with self-adjusting classification reject options based on ambiguity evaluations recently proposed in [32].

References

1. Arlt, W., Biehl, M., Taylor, A.E., Hahner, S., Libe, R., Hughes, B.A., Schneider, P., Smith, D.J., Stiekema, H., Krone, N., Porfiri, E., Opocher, G., Bertherat, J., Mantero, F., Allolio, B., Terzolo, M., Nightingale, P., Shackleton, C.H.L., Bertagna, X., Fassnacht, M., Stewart, P.M.: Urine steroid metabolomics as a biomarker tool for detecting malignancy in adrenal tumors. J. Clinical Endocrinology and Metabolism **96**, 3775–3784 (2011)
2. Biehl, M., Hammer, B., Villmann, T.: Distance measures for prototype based classification. In: Grandinetti, L., Lippert, T., Petkov, N. (eds.) BrainComp 2013. LNCS, vol. 8603, pp. 100–116. Springer, Heidelberg (2014)
3. Biehl, M., Schneider, P., Smith, D., Stiekema, H., Taylor, A., Hughes, B., Shackleton, C., Stewart, P., Arlt, W.: Matrix relevance LVQ in steroid metabolomics based classification of adrenal tumors. In: Verleysen, M., (ed.) 20th European Symposium on Artificial Neural Networks (ESANN 2012), pp. 423–428. d-side publishing (2012)
4. Chow, C.: An optimum character recognition system using decision functions. IRE Transactions on Electronic Computers **EC–6**, 247–254 (1957)
5. Chow, C.: On optimum recognition error and reject tradeoff. IEEE Transactions in Information Theory **16**(1), 41–46 (1970)
6. de Stefano, C., Sansone, C., Vento, M.: To reject or not to reject: That is the question - an answer in case of neural classifiers. IEEE Transactions on Systems Man and Cybernetics - Part C: Applications and Reviews **30**(1), 84–94 (2000)
7. Devarakota, P., Mirbach, B., Ottersten, B.: Confidence estimation in classification decision: a method for detecting unseen patterns. In: International Conference on Advances Pattern Recognition (ICaPR), pp. 136–140 (2007)

8. Fischer, L., Hammer, B., Wersing, H.: Rejection strategies for learning vector quantization. In: Verleysen, M., (ed.) Proc. of European Symposium on Artificial Neural Networks, Computational Intelligence and Machine Learning (ESANN 2014), pp. 41–46, Louvain-La-Neuve, Belgium (2014). i6doc.com
9. Fischer, L., Hammer, B., Wersing, H.: Efficient rejection strategies for prototype-based classification. Neurocomputing, page to appear (2015)
10. Fischer, L., Nebel, D., Villmann, T., Hammer, B., Wersing, H.: Rejection strategies for learning vector quantization – a comparison of probabilistic and deterministic approaches. In: Villmann, T., Schleif, F.-M., Kaden, M., Lange, M. (eds.) Advances in Self-Organizing Maps and Learning. AISC, vol. 295, pp. 109–118. Springer, Heidelberg (2014)
11. Hammer, B., Nebel, D., Riedel, M., Villmann, T.: Generative versus discriminative prototype based classification. In: Villmann, T., Schleif, F.-M., Kaden, M., Lange, M. (eds.) Advances in Self-Organizing Maps and Learning. AISC, vol. 295, pp. 123–132. Springer, Heidelberg (2014)
12. Hellman, M.: The nearest neighbor classification rule with a reject option. IEEE Transactions on Systems Science and Cybernetics **6**, 179–185 (1970)
13. Kaden, M., Hermann, W., Villmann, T.: Attention based classification learning in GLVQ and asymmetric classification error assessment. In: Villmann, T., Schleif, F.-M., Kaden, M., Lange, M. (eds.) WSOM 2014. AISC, vol. 295, pp. 77–88. Springer, Heidelberg (2014)
14. Kaden, M., Lange, M., Nebel, D., Riedel, M., Geweniger, T., Villmann, T.: Aspects in classification learning - Review of recent developments in Learning Vector Quantization. Foundations of Computing and Decision Sciences **39**(2), 79–105 (2014)
15. Kaden, M., Riedel, M., Hermann, W., Villmann, T.: Border-sensitive learning in generalized learning vector quantization: an alternative to support vector machines. Soft Computing, page in press (2015)
16. Kohonen, T.: Learning vector quantization for pattern recognition. Report TKK-F-A601, Helsinki University of Technology, Espoo, Finland (1986)
17. Kohonen, T.: Learning Vector Quantization. Neural Networks **1**(Supplement 1), 303 (1988)
18. Kohonen, T.: Self-Organizing Maps. Springer Series in Information Sciences, vol. 30. Springer, Heidelberg (1995). (Second Extended Edition 1997)
19. Lazebnik, S., Raginsky, M.: Supervised learning of quantizer codebooks by information loss minimization. IEEE Transactions on Pattern Analysis and Machine Intelligence **31**(7), 1294–1309 (2009)
20. Oehler, K., Gray, R.: Combining image compressing and classification using vector quantization. IEEE Transactions on Pattern Analysis and Machine Intelligence **17**(5), 461–473 (1995)
21. Pekalska, E., Duin, R.: The Dissimilarity Representation for Pattern Recognition: Foundations and Applications. World Scientific (2006)
22. Pillai, I., Fumera, G., Roli, F.: Multi-label classification with a reject option. Pattern Recognition **46**, 2256–2266 (2013)
23. Sato, A., Yamada, K.: Generalized learning vector quantization. In: Touretzky, D.S., Mozer, M.C., Hasselmo, M.E. (eds.) Proceedings of the 1995 Conference on Advances in Neural Information Processing Systems 8, pp. 423–429. MIT Press, Cambridge (1996)
24. Schleif, F.-M., Zhu, X., Hammer, B.: A conformal classifier for dissimilarity data. In: Iliadis, L., Maglogiannis, I., Papadopoulos, H., Karatzas, K., Sioutas, S. (eds.) Artificial Intelligence Applications and Innovations, Part II. IFIP AICT, vol. 382, pp. 234–243. Springer, Heidelberg (2012)

25. Schölkopf, B., Williamson, R., Smola, A., Shawe-Taylor, J., Platt, J.: Support vector method for novelty detection. In: Solla, S., Leen, T., Müller, K.-R., (eds.) Advances in Neural Information Processing Systems, vol. 12, pp. 582–588. MIT Press (2000)
26. Seo, S., Bode, M., Obermayer, K.: Soft nearest prototype classification. IEEE Transaction on Neural Networks **14**, 390–398 (2003)
27. Seo, S., Obermayer, K.: Soft learning vector quantization. Neural Computation **15**, 1589–1604 (2003)
28. Shafer, G., Vovk, V.: A tutorial on conformal prediction. Journal of Machine Learning Research **9**, 371–421 (2008)
29. Tax, D.: One-class classification - Concept-learning in the absence of counter-examples. ASCI dissertation series 65, Delft University of Technology, June 2001
30. Tax, D., Duin, R.: Growing a multi-class classifier with a reject option. Pattern Recognition Letters **29**, 1565–1570 (2008)
31. Vailaya, A., Jain, A.: Reject option for VQ-based bayesian classification. In: Proceedings 15th International Conference on Pattern Recognition, ICPR 2000, vol. 2, pp. 48–51. IEEE Comput. Soc., Los Alamitos (2000)
32. Villmann, T., Kaden, M., Bohnsack, A., Villmann, J.-M., Drogies, T., Saralajew, S., Hammer, B.: Learning vector quantization with self-adjusting reject option for uncertain classification decisions. In: Merényi, E., Mendenhall, M., (eds.) Advances in Self-Organizing Maps and Learning Vector Quantization: Proceedings of 11th International Workshop WSOM 2016, LNCS, page to appear. Springer, Heidelberg (2016)
33. Vovk, V., Gammerman, A., Shafer, G.: Algorithmic learning in a random world. Springer, Berlin (2005)
34. Witoelar, A., Gosh, A., de Vries, J., Hammer, B., Biehl, M.: Window-based example selection in learning vector quantization. Neural Computation **22**(11), 2924–2961 (2010)
35. Ypma, A., Duin, R.P.W.: Novelty detection using self-organizing maps. In: Kasabov, N., Kozma, R., Ko, K., O'Shea, R., Coghill, G., Gedeon, T. (eds.) Progress in Connectionist-Based Information Systems, vol. 2, pp. 1322–1325. Springer, London (1997)
36. Zhang, J.: Advancements of outlier detection: A survey. ICST Transactions on Scalable Information Systems **13**(01–03), e2 (2013)
37. Zimek, A., Schubert, E., Kriegel, H.-P.: A survey on unsupervised outlier detection in high-dimensional numerical data. Statistical Analysis and Data Mining **5**(5), 363–387 (2012)

Tensorial Orientation Scores

Jasper J. van de Gronde[(⊠)]

Johann Bernoulli Institute for Mathematics and Computer Science,
University of Groningen, P.O. Box 407, 9700 AK Groningen, The Netherlands
j.j.van.de.gronde@rug.nl

Abstract. Orientation scores [7, 10] are representations of images built using filters that only select on orientation (and not on the magnitude of the frequency). Importantly, they allow (easy) reconstruction, making them ideal for use in a filtering pipeline. Traditionally a specific set of orientations has to be chosen, and the response is determined for those orientations. This work introduces an alternative, where a tensorial representation is built that approximates an idealized orientation score in a well-defined way. It is shown that the filter's output can be usefully interpreted in terms of tensor decompositions. Tensorial orientation scores can be considered to fit in a family of filtering schemes that includes not just traditional orientation scores, but also monomial filters [16] and curvelets [3].

Keywords: Orientation scores · Monomial filters · Curvelets · Tensors

1 Introduction

Typical wavelet transforms can be used to both analyse and synthesize signals in terms of their content in different frequency bands, but provide only very coarse-grained information on orientation. Orientation scores [7, 10] on the other hand do not concern themselves with frequency magnitude at all, but can give very detailed orientation information, all the while still allowing for both analysis *and* synthesis of signals. This means they are ideally suited as part of a filtering pipeline, as we can convert an image to an orientation score, filter that, and then turn the orientation score into an image again, such that if the filter does not do anything, one simply recovers the original image (rather than a blurred version for example).

In their original formulation, orientation scores only allowed for a discrete set of orientations. More recently, van de Gronde et al. [14] used a tensorial variant of orientation scores. Tensor decompositions were used to extract very precise orientation information, even while using tensors of relatively low degree. This was then used as part of a larger filtering pipeline to extract thin and long (but curved) structures. Unfortunately there was too little room at the time to give a good description and analysis of how these filters worked exactly. This work remedies the situation, by showing how tensorial orientation scores can be developed from first principles.

© Springer International Publishing Switzerland 2015
G. Azzopardi and N. Petkov (Eds.): CAIP 2015, Part II, LNCS 9257, pp. 783–794, 2015.
DOI: 10.1007/978-3-319-23117-4_67

Having defined idealized tensorial orientation scores it is discussed how such filters can be applied in practice, showing that any singularities present in the idealized filters naturally go away in the spatially bounded and band limited case. Next, the interpretation of the filter output in terms of tensor decompositions is discussed, laying the foundation for a scheme in the spirit of tensor voting [21]. Finally, tensorial orientation scores are compared to traditional orientation scores, monomial filters [16], and curvelets [3].

2   Definitions and Notation

Throughout this work, the following definitions for the Fourier transform and its inverse are assumed:

$$\mathcal{F}[f](\boldsymbol{\xi}) = \int_{\mathbb{R}^d} f(\mathbf{x}) \, e^{-2\pi \, i \, \mathbf{x} \cdot \boldsymbol{\xi}} \, d\mathbf{x}, \text{ and}$$

$$\mathcal{F}^{-1}[g](\mathbf{x}) = \int_{\mathbb{R}^d} g(\boldsymbol{\xi}) \, e^{2\pi \, i \, \boldsymbol{\xi} \cdot \mathbf{x}} \, d\boldsymbol{\xi}.$$

In addition $\hat{f}$ will be used to denote the Fourier transform of f.

This work makes extensive use of symmetric tensors. These can be viewed as a generalization of vectors and symmetric matrices. Symmetric tensors can be built from a vector space $\mathbb{C}^d$ using the symmetric tensor product '$\odot$' [18, ch. 4 Proposition 5.7] (which is linear in both arguments). In terms of vectors and matrices, one could say that $\mathbf{a} \odot \mathbf{b}$ $(\mathbf{a}, \mathbf{b} \in \mathbb{C}^d)$ is equivalent to the matrix $\frac{1}{2}(\mathbf{a}\,\mathbf{b}^T + \mathbf{b}\,\mathbf{a}^T)$. The result of the n-times repeated tensor multiplication of $\mathbf{a}$ by itself, a degree-n symmetric tensor, will be denoted by $\mathbf{a}^{\odot n}$. It can be shown that a general tensor of degree n is symmetric if and only if it can be written as a sum of such tensor "powers" [5, Lemma 4.2]; the number of such tensor powers needed is the (symmetric) rank of the tensor, so a rank one tensor of degree n can be written as $\mathbf{a}^{\odot n}$, for some $\mathbf{a} \in \mathbb{C}^d$. Note that lower-case letters are used for vectors, while upper-case letters are used for (higher degree) tensors.

The inner product on symmetric tensors can be defined [1, §V.3; 13, §1.25; 19, Eq. (2.1)] based on its linearity and the inner product on the underlying vector space $(\mathbf{a}, \mathbf{b} \in \mathbb{C}^d)$:

$$\mathbf{a}^{\odot n} \cdot \mathbf{b}^{\odot n} = (\mathbf{a} \cdot \mathbf{b})^n.$$

Note that this inner product is roughly equivalent to the Frobenius inner product on matrices [11, p. 332].

The symmetric degree-n identity tensor $\mathbf{I}_n$, with n even, is defined here as the unique symmetric tensor that satisfies $\mathbf{a}^{\odot n} \cdot \mathbf{I}_n = \|\mathbf{a}\|^n$ for all non-zero $\mathbf{a} \in \mathbb{R}^d$ (this characterization does not hold for non-real vectors). It can be given explicitly be either of the following equivalent constructions:

$$\mathbf{I}_n = D_{n,d} \int_{S_d} \mathbf{s}^{\odot n} \, d\mathbf{s} \qquad \text{or} \qquad \mathbf{I}_n = \mathbf{I}_2^{\odot n/2}.$$

Here S_d is the sphere of all unit length vectors in $\mathbb{R}^d$ and $D_{n,d}$ is a (positive real) constant fully determined by $\mathbf{a}^{\odot n} \cdot \mathbf{I}_n = \|\mathbf{a}\|^n$ (for any non-zero $\mathbf{a} \in \mathbb{R}^d$), while $\mathbf{I}_2$ can be seen to be $\sum_{k \in \mathcal{K}} \mathbf{e}_k^{\odot 2}$ for any orthonormal basis $\{\mathbf{e}_k\}_{k \in \mathcal{K}}$ of $\mathbb{R}^d$.

The fractional anisotropy of a degree-2 tensor on a 2D vector space is defined here as the ratio between the absolute difference of the largest and smallest eigenvalue, and the square root of the sum of the squares of the eigenvalues. This is one for a rank one tensor, and zero for the identity tensor.

3 Tensorial Orientation Scores

To find local orientations, traditional orientation scores use filters that divide the Fourier domain into several sectors, resembling the way a pie (or cake) is cut. If we increase the number of sectors and take the limit as the number of sectors goes to infinity, then instead of getting values for a discrete number of orientations per point, we would – per point – get a function whose domain is the unit sphere. So any method to represent such a function can be used for computing orientation scores, and here tensors are used instead of sampling.

The continuous orientation score can be considered to take infinitesimal slices from the spectrum. Since at each point the cross-section of such a slice is proportional to the $(d-1)$-th power of the radius, we have ($\mathbf{x} \in \mathbb{R}^d$, $\mathbf{s} \in S_d$):

$$U_f(\mathbf{x}, \mathbf{s}) = \int_0^\infty r^{d-1}\, \mathcal{F}[f](r\,\mathbf{s})\, e^{2\pi\, i\, r\, \mathbf{s} \cdot \mathbf{x}}\, \mathrm{d}r. \tag{1}$$

Note that the integral over the unit sphere of $U_f(\mathbf{x})$ recovers $f(\mathbf{x})$.

Now, instead of sampling the continuous orientation score, here it is approximated using symmetric tensors. In particular, if $U_f : \mathbb{R}^d \times S_d \to \mathbb{C}$ is the continuous orientation score, then we compute a symmetric tensor field $\mathbf{U}_{n,f} : \mathbb{R}^d \to (\mathbb{C}^d)^{\odot n}$ such that for any (symmetric) degree-n tensor $\mathbf{A}$ and position $x \in \mathbb{R}^d$

$$\int_{S_d} (\mathbf{A} \cdot \mathbf{s}^{\odot n})\, U_f(\mathbf{x}, \mathbf{s})\, \mathrm{d}s = \mathbf{A} \cdot \mathbf{U}_{n,f}(\mathbf{x}). \tag{2}$$

An explicit form for $\mathbf{U}_{n,f}$ can be found by plugging in Eq. 1 in Eq. 2:

$$\int_{S_d} (\mathbf{A} \cdot \mathbf{s}^{\odot n})\, U_f(\mathbf{x}, \mathbf{s})\, \mathrm{d}s = \mathbf{A} \cdot \int_{S_d} \mathbf{s}^{\odot n} \int_0^\infty r^{d-1}\, \mathcal{F}[f](r\,\mathbf{s})\, e^{2\pi\, i\, r\, \mathbf{s} \cdot \mathbf{x}}\, \mathrm{d}r\, \mathrm{d}s$$

$$= \mathbf{A} \cdot \int_{S_d} \int_0^\infty \frac{\mathbf{s}^{\odot n}}{r^d}\, r^{d-1}\, \mathcal{F}[f](r\,\mathbf{s})\, e^{2\pi\, i\, r\, \mathbf{s} \cdot \mathbf{x}}\, \mathrm{d}r\, \mathrm{d}s$$

$$= \mathbf{A} \cdot \int_{\mathbb{R}^d} \frac{\boldsymbol{\xi}^{\odot n}}{\|\boldsymbol{\xi}\|^n}\, \mathcal{F}[f](\boldsymbol{\xi})\, e^{2\pi\, i\, \boldsymbol{\xi} \cdot \mathbf{x}}\, \mathrm{d}\boldsymbol{\xi}.$$

The tensor-valued filter can thus be defined by

$$\hat{\mathbf{H}}_n(\boldsymbol{\xi}) = \frac{\boldsymbol{\xi}^{\odot n}}{\|\boldsymbol{\xi}\|^n}. \tag{3}$$

Here $\hat{\mathbf{H}}_n$ is the Fourier transform of $\mathbf{H}_n$.

For even n the inner product between $\mathbf{U}_{n,f}(x)$ and the identity tensor gives $f(x)$, as $\frac{\xi^{\odot n}}{\|\xi\|^n} \cdot \mathbf{I}_n = 1$, away from the origin at least. This ensures that the per-position inner product between a filtered signal and $\mathbf{I}_n$ recovers the original signal. One way to make sense of what happens at the origin is to say that $\hat{\mathbf{H}}_n(0) = \frac{\mathbf{I}_n}{\mathbf{I}_n \cdot \mathbf{I}_n}$. This is compatible with convolving (in the frequency domain) $\hat{\mathbf{H}}_n$ with a rotationally invariant Gaussian that integrates to one, and taking the limit as the standard deviation goes to zero. Similarly, for odd n the response at the origin can be considered zero. Note that it can be shown that $\mathbf{H}_n$ is homogeneous of degree $-d$: $\mathbf{H}_n(\mathbf{x}) = \|\mathbf{x}\|^{-d} \mathbf{H}_n(\mathbf{x}/\|\mathbf{x}\|)$.

It is useful to note that $\mathbf{H}_n$ has the form of the n-th (tensorial) derivative of the fundamental solution to the $n/2$-Laplace equation [2,4,12]. For example, $\mathbf{H}_n$ is the Hessian of the fundamental solution to the ordinary Laplace equation. In general, for all n and d except when $n = d + 2m$ for some $m \in \mathbb{N}$,

$$\mathbf{H}_n(\mathbf{x}) = \nabla^{\odot n} \left[\frac{\Gamma(d/2 - n/2) \|\mathbf{x}\|^{n-d}}{(2i)^n \, \pi^{d/2} \, \Gamma(n/2)} \right]. \tag{4}$$

Here $\nabla^{\odot n} f(x)$ is taken to be the symmetric tensor corresponding to the n-fold application of the gradient operator. When n does equal $d + 2m$, there unfortunately seems to be some disagreement in the literature about the correct general form. The interested reader is referred to Gel'fand and Shilov [12] and Boyling [2].

The observant reader may have deduced from Eq. 4 that for odd n, the filters are purely imaginary in the spatial domain, while for even n the filters are purely real. This stems from the fact that the odd numbered filters capture "odd" structures, while the even numbered filters capture "even" structures, and that a real-valued signal has conjugate symmetry in the Fourier domain. This also means one needs both an odd and an even filter to give a proper approximation of U_f (although this will be ignored for now). Knutsson and Westin [15] discuss how to combine even and odd filters to get phase-invariant filters.

3.1   Computation

Although the completely continuous and unbounded filters defined in Eq. 3 are useful for reasoning about the idealized form of the filters, some care is needed in applying them in real life situations. In particular: the filters have a singularity at the origin, and the integral of the filter is problematic (considering the filter in the spatial domain). That is, although above we have seen that one can in fact give meaning to the overall integral of the entire filter, this is a fairly fragile trick, and it breaks down as soon as we are interested in integrating the absolute value of the filter or in integrating over a wedge of the filter for example. Luckily, these problems go away as soon as the filters are made band-limited and spatially bounded.

Making the filters band limited is (conceptually) easy: just convolve the spatial representation with a sampling kernel k (or multiply its frequency domain

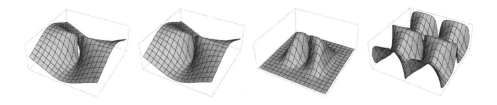

Fig. 1. The different stages in constructing a properly sampled and bounded kernel (in the Fourier domain). From left to right: the idealized filter ($\hat{\mathbf{H}}_n$, undefined at the origin), the windowed filter ($\hat{w} \star \hat{\mathbf{H}}_n$), the filter after applying the sampling kernel ($\hat{k}\,(\hat{w} \star \hat{\mathbf{H}}_n)$), and the filter after convolving with a Dirac comb to implement spatial sampling. Here, k was a third order cardinal spline, while w was a Gaussian with $\sigma = 20$. The graphs show the Fourier transforms on the domain $[-1, 1]^2$.

representation with $\hat{k}$). As a result, the inner product with the identity tensor no longer gives the Dirac delta, but rather the kernel used for limiting the bandwidth. Similarly, it can be seen that the response at the origin is now finite and well-defined, since the integral (in the Fourier domain) of the original filter multiplied by the Fourier transform of the sampling kernel will be bounded. The integral of the filter in the spatial domain is still ill-defined though.

Making the filters spatially bounded is equally easy: just multiply with the windowing function w in the spatial domain (or convolve with $\hat{w}$ in the frequency domain). Analogous to the usual requirement that the integral of a sampling kernel is one, the spatial windowing function must be one at the origin. As a result, the corresponding kernel in the frequency domain can be considered to be a smoothing kernel (effectively a sampling kernel for the frequency domain). If the kernel is rotationally symmetric, we recover the previously stated result that the integral of the spatial response of the filter is $\frac{\mathbf{I}_n}{\mathbf{I}_n \cdot \mathbf{I}_n}$ (the scaling follows from the fact that $\frac{\boldsymbol{\xi}^{\odot n}}{\|\boldsymbol{\xi}\|^n} \cdot \mathbf{I}_n = 1$ away from the origin). In general, if the signal is already band limited, and a suitable windowing function is chosen, the integral of the windowed filter (in the spatial domain) becomes perfectly well-defined.

The trick is now in combining the above two procedures. For example, $w(\mathbf{x})\,(k \star \mathbf{H}_n)(\mathbf{x}) \cdot \mathbf{I}_n = w(\mathbf{x})\,(k \star (\mathbf{H}_n \cdot \mathbf{I}_n))(\mathbf{x}) = w(\mathbf{x})\,(k \star \delta)(\mathbf{x}) = w(\mathbf{x})\,k(\mathbf{x})$, which may not be what we want (as it breaks our model of the signal). On the other hand, $k \star (w\,\mathbf{H}_n) \cdot \mathbf{I}_n = k \star (w\,\mathbf{H}_n \cdot \mathbf{I}_n) = k \star (w\,\delta) = k$, as long as $w(0) = 1$. Of course the the convolution with k now interacts with the windowing function w, but this is expected to be less objectionable. Either procedure yields a kernel that is both band limited as well as spatially bounded. Note that spatially bounded should be taken to mean that the bulk of the kernel is concentrated in a bounded region (around the origin). In this work the convention $\mathbf{H}_n^* = k \star (w\,\mathbf{H}_n)$ will be used.

Note that when convolving the filter $\mathbf{H}_n$ with a sampled signal f represented using splines, the ideal procedure would involve computing $\overset{\circ}{\varphi} \star (w\,\mathbf{H}_n) \star \varphi \star f$

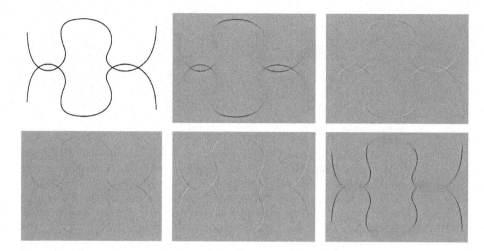

Fig. 2. Original image and images showing the corresponding tensor component images corresponding to: 1111, 1112, 1122, 1222, 2222. The tensor component images' intensities have been scaled, and subsequently adjusted so the background is grey, all images are rotated 90 degrees anti-clockwise. The inner product with the degree-four identity tensor corresponds to summing the 1111, 1122, and 2222 images, weighted by 1, 2, and 1, respectively; this recovers the original image.

and sampling the result. Here φ is a reconstruction filter, while $\overset{\circ}{\varphi}$ is the complementary prefilter, as described by Unser [22]. Because of the commutativity of convolution it is equivalent to compute $\mathbf{H}_n^* \star f = k \star (w\,\mathbf{H}_n) \star f$, where $k = \overset{\circ}{\varphi} \star \varphi$. We now just need to sample the result on the same grid as f.

It should be noted that, perhaps counter intuitively, the width of w does not affect the integral of $w\,\mathbf{H}_n$. Instead it couples scale with orientation sensitivity: the narrower w is, the worse the orientation sensitivity for large features. It can be determined[1] that for a Gaussian windowing function $w(\mathbf{x}) = e^{-\|\mathbf{x}\|^2/(2\sigma^2)}$ – in a 2D context with degree-two tensors – setting σ to the width of an infinite line (box profile) results in a fractional anisotropy (FA) of roughly 0.55, while setting it to twice the width results in an FA of roughly 0.78, and three times the width corresponds to an FA of 0.86.

The filters used here have been generated by working in the Fourier domain[1], using numerical integration to incorporate the effects of the windowing function w (a Gaussian in our case, with $\sigma = 20$), and summation to implement (approximate) the effect of sampling in the spatial domain. The end result – which can be reused over and over – is an array representing $\hat{\mathbf{H}}_n^*$. Note that there should be some spatial aliasing, due to sampling the frequency domain (and a windowing function with infinite support), but this appears to be negligible. The process is illustrated in Fig. 1, some examples of filtered results are shown in Figs. 2 and 3.

---

[1] Code available at http://bit.ly/1xc3OC3.

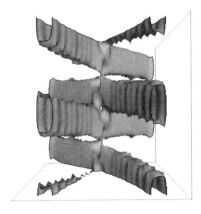

Fig. 3. Showing a contour of $\mathbf{U}_{4,f}$ for a section of the image in Fig. 2 (around the left-most crossing), with angle along the vertical axis. Note that each curve is present at two angles, corresponding to the even symmetry of a degree-four tensor. Also, the crossing can be seen to be less present at this contour, which is a result of the intensity of the curve being spread over both angles. It also interesting to note that since the curves are *curved*, their angle varies along the curve (as evidenced by the tapered sections at the top and bottom of the plot).

A faster method to compute (not apply!) an analogue of $\hat{\mathbf{H}}_n^*$ is to go back to the observation that $\mathbf{H}_n$ can be built by differentiating the fundamental solution to the Laplace operator. Both differentiation and the Laplace operator have standard discrete approximations (using finite differences) that can be used instead of their continuous counterparts. This directly gives a closed expression for a spatially discrete kernel. So far this seems to give a visibly lower quality result than directly windowing and sampling $\hat{\mathbf{H}}_n$ though, so it has not been used here. It would, however, be interesting to look at this option further in the future, in the interest of simplifying the generation of tensorial orientation score kernels.

3.2 Interpretation of Output

An examination of the (idealised) behaviour of the filters developed above can provide additional insight, as well as help in developing post-processing tools. In particular, it turns out tensor decompositions can play an important role in analysing the filter output.

First of all, if the original signal is constant, then the Fourier transform of this signal is clearly a Dirac delta at the origin, whose weight is equal to the constant. This can be easily verified by looking at the *inverse* Fourier transform of such a Dirac delta:

$$\mathcal{F}^{-1}[\boldsymbol{\xi} \mapsto c\,\delta(\boldsymbol{\xi})](\mathbf{x}) = \int_{\mathbb{R}^d} c\,\delta(\boldsymbol{\xi})\,e^{2\pi\,i\,\boldsymbol{\xi}\cdot\mathbf{x}}\,\mathrm{d}\boldsymbol{\xi} = c\,e^{2\pi\,i\,0\cdot\mathbf{x}} = c.$$

The corresponding symmetric tensor field can be seen to be $\frac{c}{\mathbf{I}_n\cdot\mathbf{I}_n}\,\mathbf{I}_n$ for even n and zero otherwise.

If the input is zero except for a single infinite line through the origin, then the Fourier transform is zero except for a hyperplane through the origin, oriented perpendicularly to the original line. From Eq. 3 it is then clear that all tensors in the resulting tensor field are orthogonal to $\mathbf{v}^{\odot n}$, where $\mathbf{v}$ is the direction of the line. Furthermore, we can see that cross-sections of the tensor field that are perpendicular to the line correspond to a lower-dimensional version of the filter.

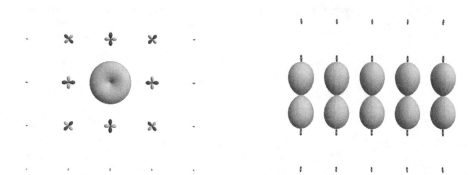

Fig. 4. Slices of two 3D orientation score tensor fields, visualizing the degree-2 tensors as spherical plots of $\mathbf{s}^{\odot 2} \cdot \mathbf{U}_2(\mathbf{x})$. The original image for the left tensor field had a single line (of finite length for this example), perpendicular to and through the middle of the slice. One can see that the middle tensor is effectively an identity tensor constrained to a 2D plane perpendicular to the line. The dark lobes of the other tensors correspond to negative responses (the inner product with the identity tensor should give the original value: zero). On the right we see the effect of a plane, resulting in rank one tensors on the plane (oriented perpendicularly to the plane).

In general, an even feature of dimension e corresponds to an even degree tensor that has a zero response along the feature itself, and has a uniform response (like an identity tensor) along the other $d - e$ dimensions. This is illustrated in Fig. 4. This makes it interesting to compute decompositions of such tensors into sums of rank one tensors, as well as components corresponding to (scaled) identity tensors on (higher dimensional) linear subspaces of the underlying vector space, as these components correspond directly to features of a certain dimension (similar in spirit to what was done by Tang and Medioni [21]). This strategy was used by van de Gronde et al. [14] to convert tensorial orientation scores into a sparse set of tangent vectors for further processing. For odd tensors it is a little harder to give a good characterization, but a similar pattern occurs (see Fig. 5).

3.3 Related Methods

The above filters were inspired by the orientation scores developed by Duits [6] Duits and Franken [7,8]. A fairly accessible discussion can be found in Franken and Duits [10], where the following kernel is proposed (in 2D):

$$\psi(\mathbf{x}) = \frac{1}{N} \mathcal{F}^{-1} \left[\omega \mapsto B^k \left(\frac{(\varphi \bmod 2\pi) - \pi/2}{s_\theta} \right) f(\rho) \right] (\mathbf{x}) \, G_s(\mathbf{x}).$$

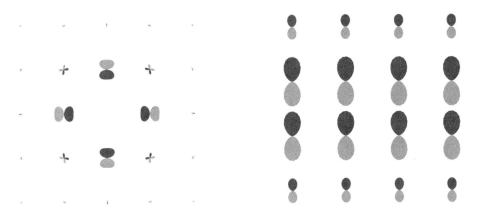

Fig. 5. Details of two 2D orientation score tensor fields, showing the degree-3 tensors as glyphs corresponding to a polar plot of $|\mathbf{s}^{\odot 2} \cdot \mathbf{U}_2(\mathbf{x})|$ (with dark lobes corresponding to negative values). The original image for the left tensor field had a single dot in the middle, while on the right the original had ones on the top half and zeroes on the bottom. Note how the "width" of the response is inversely related to the dimensionality of the feature.

Here N is a normalization constant, B^k denotes the k-th order B-spline[2], $\boldsymbol{\omega} = (\rho\cos(\varphi), \rho\sin(\varphi))$ (note that it is not entirely clear what convention was used for the Fourier transform), $s_\theta = \frac{2\pi}{n_\theta}$ (n_θ is the number of orientations), f ensures the signal is band limited (a Gaussian divided by its Taylor series up to order q), and G_s is a Gaussian with standard deviation s. Clearly, f plays the role of the Fourier transformed sampling kernel $\hat{k}$, while G_s plays the role of the windowing function w (note though that here $w\,(k \star \mathbf{H}_n)$ is used). In essence, this filter is very similar to $\mathbf{H}_n^* \cdot \mathbf{s}^{\odot n}$, but sampling specific directions rather than building a tensor-based representation. Note that in 3D it is non-trivial to find a good set of orientations, and that the tensor-based representation in principle makes it easier to finely pinpoint a particular orientation (in any dimension).

Knutsson et al. [16] introduced monomial filters consisting of a directional part and a (bandpass) radial part, for the purpose of *analysing* local orientation in images. The directional part, given by $D_n(\omega/\|\omega\|) = (\omega/\|\omega\|)^{\odot n}$ can be seen to be exactly equal to $\hat{\mathbf{H}}_n$. However, this work shows that these filters can in fact also be used without applying a bandpass filter, and that doing so gives us an invertible transformation (like with orientation scores). Also, some more insight into the filter response is given: the filter can be seen as a (higher order) derivative of the fundamental solution to the p-Laplace equation, and it is shown how the filter responds to features of various dimensionalities, suggesting the potential of tensor decompositions to aid in extracting features from the output of the filter.

---

[2] This convention does not guarantee that the different orientations sum to one. As an alternative, cardinal splines [22] could be used.

Table 1. A summary of methods related to tensorial orientation scores. All-pass means that the filters have (virtually) no radial selectivity in the frequency domain, while band-pass filters select a specific band (or bands, in the case of curvelets). Sampled filters select a specific set of orientations to filter on, while tensorial filters build a tensor-based representation that describes the response for all orientations. Note that both types of orientation scores allow local (per-position) reconstruction. Monomial filters do not allow reconstruction, while curvelets form a tight frame.

	All-pass	Band-pass
Sampled	Orientation scores	Curvelets
Tensorial	Tensorial orientation scores	Monomial filters

Finally, it is interesting to note that curvelets [3] also divide the spectrum into segments similar to an orientation score's "cake kernels", except that the segments are *also* divided radially. More precisely, given a suitable angular window ν and radial window w, for all integers j and l, such that $j \geq 0$ and $\ell = 0, 1, \ldots, 2^j - 1$, [3, Eq. 2.1]

$$\chi_{j,\ell}(\boldsymbol{\xi}) = w(2^{-2j} \|\boldsymbol{\xi}\|) \left(\nu(2^j\,\theta - \pi\,\ell) + \nu(2^j\,\theta - \pi\,(\ell - 2^j)) \right).$$

Here $\boldsymbol{\xi}$ presumably equals $(\|\boldsymbol{\xi}\| \cos(\theta), \|\boldsymbol{\xi}\| \sin(\theta))$. Note that the amplitude of the filters defined by $\chi_{j,\ell}$ in the frequency domain does not depend on j (the radial level), giving overall scale invariant behaviour similar to orientation scores. Also, [3, Eq. 2.6]

$$|\chi_0(\boldsymbol{\xi})|^2 + \sum_{j\geq 1} \sum_{\ell=0}^{2^j-1} |\chi_{j,\ell}(\boldsymbol{\xi})|^2 = 1,$$

illustrating that the entire spectrum is filled uniformly. Note that this equation does imply that curvelets have a different method of reconstruction from orientation scores: they form a tight frame rather than allowing purely local reconstruction. Also rather than selecting a single band like monomial filters, a complete representation is built from the responses in different bands. Table 1 summarizes the properties of the methods discussed here.

4   Conclusion and Future Work

A tensorial analogue of orientation scores has been presented. It is shown that the resulting filter of degree n can be interpreted in the spatial domain as a (tensorial) derivative of order n of the fundamental solution to the $n/2$-Laplace equation. Furthermore, despite this filter having a singularity at the origin and having an ill-defined integral, it is demonstrated that it can in fact be applied to real world signals, detailing the steps required in computing the discretized filter. Unfortunately this method is relatively complicated and slow (although once one has generated the filter it can of course be used many times). A different technique is suggested that is much simpler. However, it still has to be seen how far this simpler technique can come in terms of the quality of the result.

Tensorial orientation scores are compared to traditional orientation scores, monomial filters, and curvelets. It is argued that these four methods all share the same underlying idea, but with different combinations of features. Tensorial orientation scores represent a novel combination of features, in that they do not filter on frequency magnitude (like traditional orientation scores), but are based on tensors rather than sampling specific directions (like monomial filters). Compared to curvelets, the method of reconstruction is different though: curvelets form a tight frame, while orientation scores allow local reconstruction. It is not immediately obvious which option is to be preferred, but it would definitely be interesting to see if a variant of tensorial orientation scores can be built that forms a tight frame.

One question about the currently proposed method (and to some extent monomial filters as well) is whether the discretization of the filter introduces bias (so features at certain orientations are better detected than features at other orientations). Similarly, a more extensive evaluation of the effect of making the filters spatially bounded would be quite interesting as well. Also, this work only considers using the developed filters to analyse an image and then possibly reconstructing an image (after having filtered the orientation score for example), but what about using the tensor components as basis functions to represent an image? Given the nature of the functions this might have some relation to the work done by Elder [9] and Orzan et al. [20].

Knutsson et al. [17, §3] suggested a scheme based on the gradient operator that could generate a family of monomial filters that is superficially similar to the family of curvelets, in that the bandwidths follow a geometric progression, and higher bandwidths allow for better orientation selectivity. It would be interesting to see if such a scheme could be used to develop a true tensorial analogue of curvelets.

References

1. Bourbaki, N.: Topological vector spaces. Springer-Verlag, Elements of Mathematics (1987)
2. Boyling, J.B.: Green's functions for polynomials in the Laplacian. Z. angew. Math. Phys. **47**(3), 485–492 (1996)
3. Candès, E.J., Donoho, D.L.: New tight frames of curvelets and optimal representations of objects with piecewise C2 singularities. Comm. Pure Appl. Math. **57**(2), 219–266 (2004)
4. Cheng, A.H.-D., Antes, H., Ortner, N.: Fundamental solutions of products of Helmholtz and polyharmonic operators. Eng. Anal. Bound. Elem. **14**(2), 187–191 (1994)
5. Comon, P., Golub, G., Lim, L.H., Mourrain, B.: Symmetric Tensors and Symmetric Tensor Rank. SIAM J. Matrix Anal. Appl. **30**(3), 1254–1279 (2008)
6. Duits, R.: Perceptual organization in image analysis: a mathematical approach based on scale, orientation and curvature. Ph.D. thesis, Eindhoven University of Technology (2005)

7. Duits, R., Franken, E.: Left-invariant parabolic evolutions on SE(2) and contour enhancement via invertible orientation scores Part I: Linear left-invariant diffusion equations on SE(2). Quart. Appl. Math. **68**(2), 255–292 (2010)
8. Duits, R., Franken, E.: Left-invariant parabolic evolutions on SE(2) and contour enhancement via invertible orientation scores Part II: Nonlinear left-invariant diffusions on invertible orientation scores. Quart. Appl. Math. **68**(2), 293–331 (2010)
9. Elder, J.H.: Are Edges Incomplete? Int. J. Comput. Vis. **34**(2), 97–122 (1999)
10. Franken, E., Duits, R.: Crossing-Preserving Coherence-Enhancing Diffusion on Invertible Orientation Scores. Int. J. Comput. Vis. **85**(3), 253–278 (2009)
11. Friedberg, S.H., Insel, A.J., Spence, L.E.: Linear algebra. Pearson Education (2003)
12. Gel'fand, I.M., Shilov, G.E.: Generalized Functions, vol. 1. Academic Press, London (1964)
13. Greub, W.H.: Multilinear algebra. Springer-Verlag (1978)
14. van de Gronde, J.J., Lysenko, M., Roerdink, J.B.T.M.: Path-based mathematical morphology on tensor fields. In: Visualization and Processing of Higher Order Descriptors for Multi-Valued Data. Dagstuhl Follow-Ups, Schloss Dagstuhl-Leibniz-Zentrum fuer Informatik, Dagstuhl, Germany (2014) (to appear)
15. Knutsson, H., Westin, C.F.: Monomial phase: a matrix representation of local phase. In: Westin, C.F., Vilanova, A., Burgeth, B. (eds.) Visualization and Processing of Tensors and Higher Order Descriptors for Multi-Valued Data. Math. Vis., pp. 37–73. Springer, Heidelberg (2014)
16. Knutsson, H., Westin, C.-F., Andersson, M.: Representing local structure using tensors II. In: Heyden, A., Kahl, F. (eds.) SCIA 2011. LNCS, vol. 6688, pp. 545–556. Springer, Heidelberg (2011)
17. Knutsson, H., Westin, C.F., Andersson, M.: Structure tensor estimation: introducing monomial quadrature filter sets. In: Laidlaw, D.H., Vilanova, A. (eds.) New Developments in the Visualization and Processing of Tensor Fields. Math. Vis., pp. 3–28. Springer, Heidelberg (2012)
18. Kostrikin, A.I., Manin, I.I.: Linear algebra and geometry, Algebra, Logic and Applications, vol. 1. Gordon and Breach (1997)
19. Minc, H.: Permanents, Encyclopedia of mathematics and its applications, vol. 6. Addison-Wesley (1978)
20. Orzan, A., Bousseau, A., Winnemöller, H., Barla, P., Thollot, J., Salesin, D.: Diffusion Curves: A Vector Representation for Smooth-Shaded Images. ACM Transactions on Graphics **27**(3), 92:1–92:8 (2008)
21. Tang, C.K., Medioni, G.: Inference of integrated surface, curve and junction descriptions from sparse 3D data. IEEE Trans. Pattern Anal. Mach. Intell. **20**(11), 1206–1223 (1998)
22. Unser, M.: Splines: a perfect fit for signal and image processing. IEEE Signal Processing Magazine **16**(6), 22–38 (1999)

Author Index

Printed in the United States
By Bookmasters